IPv6 Advanced Protocols Implementation

The Morgan Kaufmann Series in Networking

Series Editor: David Clark, M.I.T.

For further information on these books and for a list of forthcoming titles, please visit our Web site at http://www.mkp.com.

IPv6 Advanced Protocols Implementation

Qing Li
Blue Coat Systems, Inc.

Tatuya Jinmei
Toshiba Corporation

Keiichi Shima
Internet Initiative Japan, Inc.

AMSTERDAM • BOSTON • HEIDELBERG • LONDON
NEW YORK • OXFORD • PARIS • SAN DIEGO
SAN FRANCISCO • SINGAPORE • SYDNEY • TOKYO

Morgan Kaufmann Publishers is an imprint of Elsevier

Senior Acquisitions Editor Rick Adams
Publishing Services Manager George Morrison
Senior Production Editor Dawnmarie Simpson
Acquisitions Editor Rachel Roumeliotis
Production Assistant Lianne Hong
Cover Design Eric DeCicco
Cover Image Side-by-Side Design
Cover Illustration Side-by-Side Design
Composition diacriTech
Technical Illustration diacriTech
Copyeditor JC Publishing
Proofreader Janet Cocker
Indexer Joan Green
Interior printer The Maple-Vail Book Manufacturing Group
Cover printer Phoenix Color Corporation

Morgan Kaufmann Publishers is an imprint of Elsevier.
500 Sansome Street, Suite 400, San Francisco, CA 94111

This book is printed on acid-free paper.

Library of Congress Cataloging-in-Publication Data
Li, Qing, 1971-
    IPv6 advanced protocols implementation/Qing Li, Tatuya Jinmei, Keiichi Shima.
        p. cm.
    Includes bibliographical references and index.
    ISBN-13: 978-0-12-370479-5 (hardcover: alk. paper)
    ISBN-10: 0-12-370479-0 (hardcover: alk. paper) 1. TCP/IP (Computer network protocol)
I. Jinmei, Tatuya, 1971- II. Shima, Keiichi, 1970- III. Title.
    TK5105.585.L536 2007
    004.6′2–dc22

                                                                                    2006038489

ISBN: 978-0-12-370479-5

For information on all Morgan Kaufmann publications,
visit our Web site at *www.mkp.com* or *www.books.elsevier.com*

Printed and bound by CPI Group (UK) Ltd, Croydon, CR0 4YY

Transferred to Digital Print 2011

To Huaying, Jane and Adalia
in Him
—Qing Li

To my colleagues at KAME: working with you talented geeks was an exciting experience and
has even made this derivative project possible.
—Tatuya Jinmei

To all KAME developers, all people who developed the Internet, and all people who
will develop the future Internet.
—Keiichi Shima

Contents

Preface

This book is the second installment of our series detailing IPv6 and related protocols through the KAME implementation. KAME is a widely deployed de facto reference implementation for IPv6 and IP security protocols developed on multiple variants of the BSD operating systems.

The first installment of this series is titled *IPv6 Core Protocols Implementation*, which is referred to as the *Core Protocols* book below, and it focuses on the fundamentals of IPv6 and the essential protocols that are supported by most implementations. These essential protocols operate in IPv6-capable devices, large or small. Our *Core Protocols* book also describes IPv6 implication on higher layer protocols, such as TCP and UDP, and covers IPv6 related application programming interfaces.

This second book discusses those protocols that are found in more capable IPv6 devices, are commonly deployed in more complex IPv6 network environments, or are not specific to IPv6 but are extended to support IPv6. Specifically, this book engages the readers in more advanced topics, such as routing, multicasting, DNS, mobility, and security.

The general structure and style of this book is the same as that of the *Core Protocols* book; each chapter begins with a summary of the relevant specifications followed by line-by-line code description and analysis of the actual implementation.

We hope to help the readers establish a solid and empirical understanding of IPv6 with our book series. Our two books together cover a wide spectrum of the IPv6 technology and are paralleled by none.

This book consists of the following chapters:

- Chapter 1 ("IPv6 Unicast Routing Protocols") discusses general routing concepts and the fundamentals of various types of unicast routing protocols. This chapter details RIPng, a simple routing protocol for IPv6, and summarizes IPv6-specific extensions defined for the BGP4+ and OSPFv3 routing protocols. Comparisons are made among these protocols in regards to protocol complexity, stability, and the operational issues and solutions offered by each. This chapter also provides the necessary background to implement IPv6 routing protocols on BSD variants through descriptions of the routing API for IPv6 and code narrations of KAME's RIPng implementation, the **route6d** daemon. This chapter concludes with configuration examples of **route6d** for some typical scenarios.

- Chapter 2 ("IPv6 Multicasting") discusses details about IPv6 multicasting, especially on multicast routing mechanisms. It first provides the basics of a host-to-router protocol and multicast routing protocols, specifically the Multicast Listener Discovery protocol version 1 (MLDv1) and Protocol Independent Multicast (PIM), focusing on IPv6 specific issues. The latter part of this chapter describes the KAME kernel implementation of MLDv1 and IPv6 multicast forwarding.

- Chapter 3 ("DNS for IPv6") describes IPv6 extensions to the DNS (Domain Name System) protocol specification and implementation. It begins with a general description of the DNS protocol and its extensions that support IPv6. It then describes KAME's DNS client (called a *resolver*) implementation, and highlights the support for IPv6. This section also gives a complete view of the `getaddrinfo()` library function, which was partially described in the *Core Protocols* book. The latter half of this chapter shows how to operate the BIND9 DNS server to support IPv6 with notes about common pitfalls and issues specific to IPv6-related operations.

- Chapter 4 ("DHCPv6") details DHCPv6 (Dynamic Host Configuration Protocol for IPv6) both on the protocol specification and on KAME's implementation. Although the basic concept of the protocol is largely derived from DHCP for IPv4 (DHCPv4), DHCPv6 has introduced various improvements in its design and the expected usage model differs from that of DHCPv4; this chapter clarifies such major differences. The implementation descriptions cover all protocol functionalities, that is, clients, servers, and relay agents, and will provide an in-depth understanding of how the protocol works. This chapter also provides how to operate DHCPv6 with the KAME implementation for some common usage scenarios.

- Chapter 5 ("Mobile IPv6") covers the IPv6 host mobility protocol known as Mobile IPv6. The chapter begins with a basic description of Mobile IPv6, and then details protocol specifications and data structures. The actual implementation is discussed in the middle of the chapter. The KAME Mobile IPv6 implementation supports both home agent and mobile node functions. The code description section will discuss all data structures and functions in detail. This chapter also provides a brief instruction of Mobile IPv6 operation with sample configuration files using the KAME Mobile IPv6 implementation at the end of the chapter.

- Chapter 6 ("IPv6 and IP Security") begins with an introduction of the IPsec protocols and the concept of keying in the context of the Internet Key Exchange (IKE) protocol. The remainder of this chapter then focuses on describing the popular **racoon** IKE daemon. Its configuration and operation are thoroughly explained. This chapter concludes with some practical examples of using **racoon**. Unlike other chapters, this chapter does not provide any code description because the basic mechanism of IP Security and most of its implementation are not specific to IPv6; including non-IPv6 specific code description would change the main objective of this book.

Intended Audience

In general, this book is intended for the same class of readers as was the *Core Protocols* book: developers implementing IPv6 and related protocols, and students who are going to start a project on these protocols, especially on top of or using the KAME/BSD implementation. Unlike the *Core Protocols* book, however, this book discusses more advanced topics, such as protocols that have been standardized relatively recently, so it can also be used as a reference to these protocols per se; DHCPv6 and Mobile IPv6 are two specific examples of this.

As in the *Core Protocols* book, it is assumed that readers are fluent in the C programming language. In addition, this book assumes knowledge of the basic notions of IPv6 and related protocols described in the *Core Protocols* book, though other references within this book will help those who cannot refer to the *Core Protocols* book to understand the contents. Chapters 2 and 5 also require general understanding of the BSD kernel implementation.

Unlike the *Core Protocols* book, each chapter of this book is quite independent; although there are several cross references among the chapters, readers can generally start from any chapter based on their interest.

Typographical Conventions

This book adopts the same typographical conventions as those for the *Core Protocols* book, which is summarized as follows:

Variable, function, or structure names, structure members, and programming language key-words are represented in a `constant-width` font when referred to in the code descriptions. Function names are in a `constant-width` font followed by parentheses, as in `ip6_mforward()`, and structure names are in a `constant-width` font followed by braces, as in `ip6_mh{}`.

Program names are displayed in bold fonts, as in **route6d**. The command line input and the output of a program are displayed in a `constant-width` font.

Accompanying Software found at http://www.elsevierdirect.com/companion/9780123704795

This book comes with a companion web site that includes FreeBSD4.8-RELEASE, which is the base operating system covered in Chapters 1, 2, 3, and 6.

Similarly, there is FreeBSD4.9-RELEASE, which is the base operating system covered in Chapter 5.

Note: FreeBSD 4.8 and 4.9 RELEASEs are known to have several security flaws and are no longer supported by the FreeBSD project. Therefore, these systems should only be used for reference on learning the KAME implementation as part of reading this book. It is not advisable to use these versions of FreeBSD in a production environment connected to the Internet.

The software includes the KAME source code discussed in this book. It is accessed via the `appendix` directory located at the root directory, which has two subdirectories, `kame-snap` and `rtadd6`.

The `kame-snap` subdirectory contains the following archive files:

- `kame-20030421-freebsd48-snap.tgz`
  A KAME snapshot for FreeBSD 4.8 taken on April 21, 2003.

- `kame-20040712-freebsd49-snap.tgz`
  A KAME snapshot for FreeBSD 4.9 taken on July 12, 2004. This is referred to in Chapter 5, and should be used with the FreeBSD 4.9 system contained in the second CD-ROM.

- `kame-dhcp6-20050509.tgz`
  KAME's DHCPv6 implementation included in a KAME snapshot taken on May 9, 2005, which is referred to in Chapter 4.

To install the KAME snapshot, unpack the archive, go down to the top level directory named `kame` (which is also referred to as `${KAME}` throughout this book), and see the `INSTALL` file located in the directory. For those who have the *Core Protocols* book, its Chapter 1 provides a more detailed description of the usage. Chapter 4 of this book explains how to install the DHCPv6 implementation.

The other subdirectory, `rtadd6`, contains the source code of the `rtadd6` program referred to in Chapter 1, which was newly written for this book.

Source Code Copyright

This book presents many parts of the source code developed by the KAME project and external contributors. It also refers to system header files that are part of the FreeBSD distributions. All of the source code has copyright notices.

Reporting Errors and Errata Page

The authors are happy to receive error reports on the content of this book, and plan to provide an error correction page on the Internet. It will be available at the following web page: `http://books.elsevier.com/companions/9780123704795`.

Acknowledgments

The authors, first and foremost, thank all KAME developers. As in our first book, this book is half-filled with the KAME source code, which means they are the shadow authors of this book.

We are also deeply indebted to technical reviewers who read selected chapters of this book and provided many valuable comments and suggestions, as well as error corrections: Mark Andrews, David Borman, Francis Dupont, Daniel Hartmeier, Jeffrey Hsu, Akira Kato, T. J. Kniveton, Ted Lemon, Tsuyoshi Momose, George Neville-Neil, Yasuhiro Ohara, Shawn Routhier, Shoichi Sakane, Shigeya Suzuki, Shinsuke Suzuki, Christian Vogt, and Carl Williams. As with our first book, reviewing this book required thorough knowledge of the related protocol specifications, as well as high level programming skills. We knew very few people have such talents, and we were very lucky to have the world's best reviewer team.

The book cover is based on the well-known KAME turtle image, which was designated as a project mascot, and was designed by Manabu Higashida and Chizunu Higashida.

Next, we would like to thank our editors Rick Adams, Rachel Roumeliotis, Dawnmarie Simpson, and the editorial staff at Morgan Kaufmann/Elsevier for their continuing patience and encouragement over the three and a half years of this project.

Finally, we are grateful to Gary R. Wright and W. Richard Stevens. Their work inspired us to start our own project and kept us confident about the value of this work.

LI, Qing—I would like to thank Rick Adams for his keen understanding of the importance of this book, as it fulfills a market void. His prompt acceptance of my book proposal has been an invaluable motivation. I want to thank my wife Huaying Cheng for her understanding and support of me during this book project. I would like to thank VMware Inc. for its donation of a single license for the VMware Workstation 4 software. I would also like to thank MKS Software for its donation of a single license for the MKS Toolkit for Enterprise Developers version 8.6 software.

JINMEI, Tatuya—I would like to thank my current and former managers at Toshiba for their approval and support of this work: Yukio Kamatani, Toshio Murai, Yasuhiro Katsube, and Atsushi Inoue. My thanks also go to my "supervisors" at the WIDE project, Jun Murai and Hiroshi Esaki.

SHIMA, Keiichi—I thank all of the people who worked hard to publish this book and those who supported this work, especially my manager Eiiti Wada at Internet Initiative Japan, Inc. Also my thanks go to all operators, engineers, and researchers of the Internet.

About the Authors

Li, Qing is a senior architect at Blue Coat Systems, Inc. leading the design and development efforts of the next-generation IPv6 enabled secure proxy appliances. Prior to joining Blue Coat Systems, Qing spent 8 years at Wind River Systems, Inc. as a senior architect in the Networks Business Unit, where he was the lead architect of Wind River's embedded IPv6 products since the IPv6 program inception at the beginning of 2000. Qing holds multiple U.S. patents. Qing is a contributing author of the book titled *Handbook of Networked and Embedded Control Systems* published in June of 2005 by Springer-Verlag. He is also the author of the embedded systems development book titled *Real-Time Concepts for Embedded Systems* published in April of 2003 by CMP Books. Qing participates in open source development projects and is an active FreeBSD src committer.

Jinmei, Tatuya, PhD, is a research scientist at Corporate Research & Development Center, Toshiba Corporation (Jinmei is his family name, which he prefers is presented first according to the Japanese convention). He had been a core developer of the KAME project since the launch of the project through its conclusion. In 2003, he received his PhD degree from Keio University, Japan, based on his work at KAME. He also coauthored three RFCs on IPv6 through his activity in KAME. His research interests spread over various fields of the Internet and IPv6, including routing, DNS, and multicasting.

Shima, Keiichi is a senior researcher at Internet Initiative Japan Inc. His research area is IPv6 and IPv6 mobility. He was a core developer of the KAME project from 2001 to the end of the project and developed Mobile IPv6/NEMO Basic Support protocol stack. He is now working on the new mobility stack (the SHISA stack) for BSD operating systems that is a completely restructured mobility stack.

IPv6 Unicast Routing Protocols

1.1 Introduction

Any time when communication takes place between any pair of nodes, especially when that communication involves nodes that reside on different network segments, a decision must be made about where each packet should go. This decision is often known as a packet *routing* decision, or a packet *forwarding* decision. The intermediate network devices, commonly known as *routers*, perform the routing functions that involve making the routing decision normally based on each packet's final destination.

The routing decision could be made based on manually configured routing information at each router, but such practice is obviously impractical for a complex network of middle to large scale. *Routing protocols* provide the necessary information that enable the routers to make correct routing decisions automatically. Since a packet's destination may be a unicast destination or a multicast destination (treating broadcast destination as a special case of multicast), routing protocols are designed for either *unicast routing* or *multicast routing*. We will focus on the routing protocols in this chapter.

In the IPv4 world, RIPv2 [RFC2453], the integrated IS-IS [RFC1195], and OSPFv2 [RFC2328] are commonly deployed unicast routing protocols in networks of small to middle scale such as enterprise environments, while BGP-4 [RFC4271] is the common routing protocol deployed among large organizations such as Internet Service Providers (ISPs). In general, since the routing concept is identical between IPv4 and IPv6, these routing protocols have been naturally extended to support IPv6. Even though the packet formats may have changed, the principles remain largely the same.

Yet there are IPv6 specific issues. In particular, most IPv6 routing protocols rely heavily on link-local addresses since communication using these addresses is stable in terms of routing, thanks to their limited scope. On the other hand, the ambiguity of link-local addresses discussed in Chapter 2 of *IPv6 Core Protocols Implementation*, "IPv6 Addressing Architecture", requires special care in implementing these protocols. It is therefore important to understand the details of the protocols and how they should be implemented even for those who are familiar with IPv4 routing protocols.

In this chapter we provide all the essential information to understand and implement IPv6 unicast routing protocols. We first describe the basic routing concepts followed by an introduction to IPv6 unicast routing protocols. These unicast routing protocols include RIPng [RFC2080], OSPFv3 [RFC2740] and BGP4+ [RFC2545]. We provide full coverage on the RIPng protocol. In addition, we summarize the general protocol operations of OSPFv3 and BGP4+ without diving into the protocol specifics, other than the IPv6-related protocol packets. Readers who do not require such advanced topics can safely skip these sections (1.5 and 1.6) as they are not needed in any other part of the book.

Sections that follow the protocol background focus on implementation, which will provide all of the essential information to develop IPv6 routing programs on BSD systems, covering the kernel architecture to routing application code. We first explain how to deal with IPv6 routing information on BSD systems, from the kernel internal data structures to application interfaces (APIs). We also note major pitfalls in handling link-local addresses with these APIs. We then describe the implementation of the **route6d** program, KAME's RIPng routing daemon, focusing on its RIPng protocol processing. The provenance of RIP is the **routed** program, a popular implementation that is widely available on various platforms. Its popularity is due to the simplicity in both its implementation and its operation. The **route6d** daemon is the IPv6 counterpart of **routed**.

Finally, we conclude this chapter by showing how to operate **route6d** for some typical scenarios.

1.2   Overview of Routing Concepts

Routing information enables a node to determine whether a given destination is reachable and where to send the packet en route to the destination. Routing information can be either configured statically or obtained dynamically. Routers exchange routing information with one another through one or more dynamic routing protocols. Each router builds a local database, called the *Routing Information Base* (RIB) to store the exchanged routing information. A subset of this RIB is then selected to build a *Forwarding Information Base* (FIB) for the purpose of forwarding packets.

The routing concepts are identical between IPv4 and IPv6. That is, the goal of routing is to find a loop-free path for the destination address between any pair of end systems, and the best path is chosen according to some defined criteria at the time of route selection. Many of the existing dynamic routing protocols have been updated to support IPv6. Three well-known routing protocols—RIP, OSPF and BGP—have been extended to support IPv6, resulting in RIPng, OSPFv3 (OSPF for IPv6) and BGP4+, respectively. Another deployed routing protocol, IS-IS, was also extended to support both IPv4 and IPv6 (see the note on page 4).

The choice of the routing protocol depends on many factors, such as the diameter of the routing domain, the size and complexity of the networks within the routing domain, the level of tolerance to changing network topology by applications, and the complexity and the ease of deployment of the routing protocol.

In general, routing protocols are classified as either *interior routing protocols* or *exterior routing protocols*, based on where the protocol is deployed. Interior routing protocol is also known as *interior gateway protocol* (IGP) while exterior routing protocol is also known as *exterior gateway protocol* (EGP).

An interior routing protocol is deployed within a routing domain that is controlled by a single administrative entity. In this context, a routing domain is also known as an *autonomous system* (AS). Each autonomous system should have only one governing routing policy. For example, an interior routing protocol is deployed within the intranet of an organization, which may comprise multiple sub-networks. In other words, an interior routing protocol is deployed within a single routing domain to exchange routing information about these sub-networks among routers that belong to the same routing domain. Examples of interior routing protocols are RIPng and OSPFv3.

An exterior routing protocol is deployed among routing domains that are under the management of different administrative entities. For example, an exterior routing protocol is deployed between two different *Internet Service Providers* (ISPs). In other words, an exterior routing protocol is deployed to exchange routing information among routers that belong to different autonomous systems. BGP4+ is an example of an exterior routing protocol.

Within each AS, a small subset of the routers are situated at the boundary of the AS. These boundary routers, sometimes referred to as either *border gateways* or *edge routers*, exchange route information over EGP with other edge routers that belong to different ASs. An edge router also typically participates in IGP within its AS to advertise externally reachable networks, or it simply acts as the default router for the AS to reach the rest of the Internet. Figure 1-1 illustrates this relationship. In this example each AS has one edge router that participates in the EGP.

The purpose of running a dynamic routing protocol is to provide reachability information about networks and individual nodes to routers that participate in the routing domain. The

FIGURE 1-1

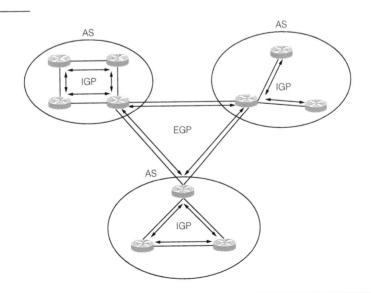

Relationship between IGP and EGP among different autonomous systems.

reachability information allows each router to compute the appropriate next hop or the paths to these networks and nodes using a specific routing algorithm. Whether the paths are loop-free depends on the routing protocol and the information distributed by the routing protocol. The way the routing algorithm works determines the type of information distributed in the routing protocol messages. Therefore routing protocols are also classified according to the routing algorithms by which the routing protocols are employed for route computation. The routing algorithms can be classified as *vector-based* algorithms or *link-state* algorithms. The vector-based algorithms can be further classified as either *distance vector* algorithms or *path-vector* algorithms. RIPng is a routing protocol representative of the distance vector algorithm; BGP4+ is a routing protocol representative of the path-vector algorithm; OSPFv3 is a routing protocol representative of the link-state algorithm.

Another link-state algorithm-based routing protocol is the *Intermediate System to Intermediate System* (IS-IS) routing protocol. IS-IS was originally designed for ISO's protocol stack known as the *Connectionless Network Protocol* (CLNP), which was meant to be the replacement of TCP/IP. The CLNP protocol stack was developed in anticipation of the greater adoption of the OSI's 7-layer communication model, but such migration has not taken place in reality. The IS-IS routing protocol is an IGP and is another link-state routing protocol. The *Integrated IS-IS* supports both CLNP and IP. In actual deployment, IS-IS is largely deployed for routing in the IP network. IS-IS is quite similar to OSPF. For this reason, we will focus on OSPF as the representative protocol for describing the link-state routing algorithm. IS-IS is defined by [ISO-10589]. The Integrated IS-IS is defined in [RFC1195]. The reader is encouraged to consult [ISIS-IPV6] for details on the IPv6 extension for IS-IS.

The routing protocols are designed to satisfy a different set of goals. A routing protocol, more precisely the algorithm used by the routing protocol, must be capable of selecting the optimal route according to predefined selection criteria. For example, a routing algorithm can select the best route according to the least number of hops traversed to reach the destination. A routing protocol must be robust to changing network topologies and network conditions. For example, the routing protocol must continue to function when an interface on the router fails, or when one or more routers fail. A routing protocol should have a good *convergence rate*. When network topologies or network conditions change, the routing protocol should have the ability to convey this information to all participating routers quickly to avoid routing problems. The convergence rate refers to the time taken for all routers in the domain to become aware of the changing condition. Routing protocols should be designed to have small operational overhead and should be relatively easy to deploy.

A predefined selection criteria determines what is considered the optimal route or the best route according to one or more metrics. The metrics can be either static or dynamic. Examples of static metrics are path length or monetary cost of using a particular path. Path length can be either simple hop counts, or the sum of the costs of all links in a given path. Typically a system administrator assigns the cost of each link. Examples of dynamic metrics are the measured network load, delay, available bandwidth, and reliability (such as error rate and drop rate).

1.3 Overview of Vector-based Algorithms and Link-State Algorithm

1.3.1 Distance-Vector Algorithm

A router running the distance-vector algorithm, as is the case with RIPng, initializes its local routing database with the addresses and costs of the directly attached networks and nodes. This information is exchanged with other directly connected routers through routing protocol messages. When a router receives routing messages from its neighboring routers, it adds the cost of the network on which the routing messages arrived to all of the destinations that are advertised in the routing messages. A destination can appear in multiple routing messages that were sent by different neighboring routers. The receiving router chooses the router that advertised the smallest metric to that destination as the preferred next hop. The smallest metric value is updated with the cost of the network. The receiving router then readvertises that destination with the updated metric.

Figure 1-2 illustrates how the distance-vector algorithm works for a very simple network topology (a more interesting example will be shown in Section 1.4). There are three routers (A, B and C) connected in series, and router A is attached to a leaf network N. For simplicity, let us just concentrate on the routing information about network N, and assume that the cost of any link is 1.

The arrows shown in Figure 1-2 are labeled with the routing information distributed among the routers, which highlights the destination information (N) and the total cost to reach the destination. The box drawn next to each router represents its routing table, whose entry is a combination of <destination, metric, next hop router>. For example, router B accepts the information advertised by router A (which by default has the smallest metric because that route is the only route about network N) and installs the route to its routing table. Router B then readvertises that route toward router C with the updated cost. Eventually all of the routers will converge to a stable state in which each router knows the path to leaf network N. Router C forwards any packet destined to network N toward router B, which then forwards the packet to router A. Router A will then deliver the packet to the final destination on N.

FIGURE 1-2

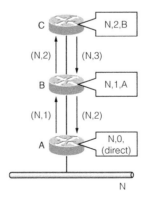

Routing with the distance-vector algorithm.

As seen in this example, the major advantage of the distance-vector algorithm is its simplicity. The algorithm is easy to understand and implement. In fact, KAME's RIPng implementation consists of only about 3500 lines of source code written in C, including all optional features.

The simplicity comes with a different cost. One major disadvantage of the distance-vector algorithm is that it is vulnerable to changes in topology.

Consider the scenario shown in Figure 1-3, where the link between router A and router B is down. Router B detects the link failure, removes the route information about network N because B knows N is now unreachable. In the pure distance-vector algorithm, router B does nothing further. Since the information is still in router C, router C advertises that stale route back to B, which is then installed in router B with a higher cost. B accepts C's advertisement because B is aware that router A is no longer reachable due to the dead link, and B has not accepted any route about network N from C previously. At this point a routing loop between routers B and C is created. Router B will subsequently advertise that same route back to router C with a higher cost. This higher cost route will override C's entry because router C knows its route about N came from B's original advertisement. This iterative process continues until the advertised cost reaches some upper limit set by the protocol, allowing these routers to finally detect the failure. This symptom is called the *counting to infinity* problem.

Although several techniques are available to mitigate this problem (see Section 1.4.3), none of them can completely eliminate the algorithm flaw. Even when such remedies do solve the problem in some types of deployment, route convergence generally takes a longer time with the distance-vector algorithm than other algorithms on a topology change, especially when the network contains slower links.

In the distance-vector algorithm, the router stores and distributes only the current best route to any known destination. Therefore, the computation of a route at each router depends largely on the previous computation results made by other routers. Additionally, since only the distance to any destination is given, it is impossible for the distance vector algorithm to identify the origin of a route and to guarantee loop-free routes.

FIGURE 1-3

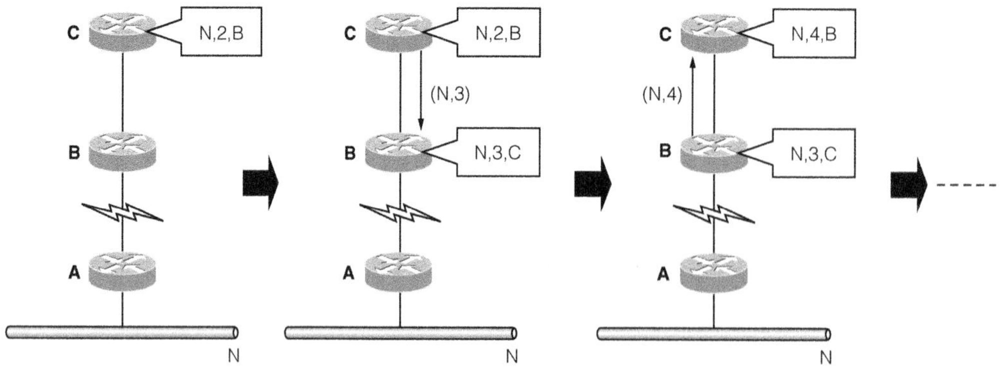

Counting to infinity problem with the distance vector algorithm.

1.3.2 Path-Vector Algorithm

With the path-vector algorithm, the reachability information does not include the distance to the destination. Instead, the reachability information includes the entire path to the destination, not just the first hop as is the case for the distance-vector algorithm. A router running the path-vector algorithm includes itself in the path when redistributing a route. The path-vector algorithm allows a router to detect routing loops. Consider the path-vector example depicted in Figure 1-4.

Each router advertises the destination network N along with the full path to reach N. Router A advertises the route about N to B. The only router on this path is A because N is a directly attached network. Router B adds itself into the path when it redistributes that route to router C. At router C the path to N contains A and B. If router C were to advertise this route back to B, B would find itself in that path and immediately detect the routing loop. In this case B will reject this route advertisement from C, thus breaking the loop.

Since the complete path information is available for each advertised route, the path-vector algorithm allows better policy control in terms of what advertised routes to accept, and allows policy to influence route computation and selection.

1.3.3 Link-State Algorithm

A router running the link-state algorithm advertises the state of each of its attached links, called its *link-state*, to its adjacent routers. A receiving router of the advertised state stores this information in its local database. This receiver then redistributes the received link-state information

FIGURE 1-4

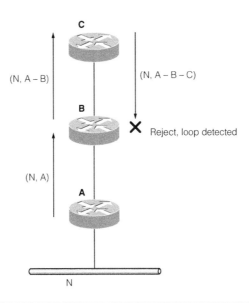

Loop detection in path-vector algorithm.

unmodified to all of its adjacent routers, resulting in every router in that AS which participates in the routing protocol to receive the same link-state information. Each router then computes the paths to all possible destinations based on this link-state information independently.

Figure 1-5 illustrates a state where routers in a routing domain have collected all link-states. For simplicity, this example assumes that a link-state is a set of neighbor routers. In actual routing protocol such as OSPFv3, a link-state contains many more parameters, such as per link cost and leaf network information. This example also assumes that some *flooding* mechanism is provided to advertise the link-states throughout the routing domain.

Once a router collects the link-states from all other routers, it can construct a tree-based map (also known as a *shortest path tree*) of the entire network that gives the shortest path to every part of the network as shown in Figure 1-6. The procedure used for the tree construction is called the *Dijkstra* algorithm, which is explained in Section 1.6.5.

Once every router computes the map, packet forwarding can be done based on the map. Figure 1-7 illustrates the forwarding path from router A to router F. Each router forwards the packet to the appropriate next hop following the path in the tree, and the result is a loop-free, shortest route to the destination.

The flooding of the link-state information which originated from all of the routers enables each router to gain a complete view of the topology of the routing domain. Each router can build a routing table independently. As can be seen from the comparisons made between distance-vector algorithm and link-state algorithm, in the distance-vector algorithm, each router sends its entire routing database to neighboring routers because vector-based algorithms deploy a distributed route computation scheme. In contrast, since only per router link-state information is distributed, the amount of information that is exchanged among routers that run the link-state algorithm is considerably smaller. In response to changing network conditions, information exchanged among routers running the distance-vector may contain stale information,

FIGURE 1-5

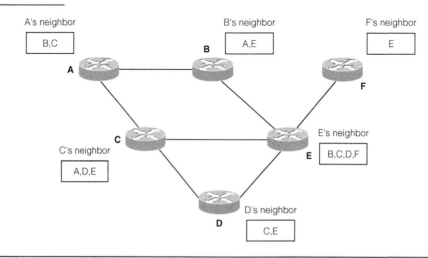

First stage of the link-state algorithm: flooding link-states (each router advertises its local state throughout the domain).

FIGURE 1-6

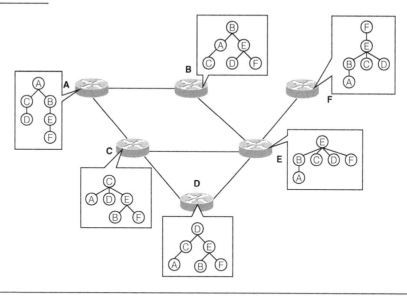

Second stage of the link-state algorithm: building the shortest path tree.

FIGURE 1-7

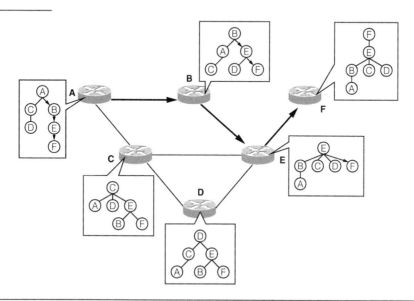

Routing based on the shortest path tree.

that is, an unreachable network may still be advertised as reachable by some routers. Such stale information will result in longer convergence time. Since the link-state algorithm exchanges information that pertains to a specific router, each router is more independent in calculating its routing database. This is one reason that the link-state algorithm has a fast convergence rate.

In conclusion, the distance-vector algorithm sends global routing information (a router's entire routing table) locally, while the link-state algorithm floods local information (attached interfaces and links) globally.

1.4   Introduction to RIPng

The RIPng protocol is based on the distance-vector algorithm commonly known as the Bellman-Ford algorithm. Consider the example in Figure 1-8. Router RT-1 advertises its directly connected network N-1 of prefix `2001:db8:0:1000::/64` with a metric of 1 on the point-to-point links to RT-2 and RT-3. The costs of the links from RT-1 to RT-2 and RT-3 are 1 and 3 respectively, which have RT-2 and RT-3 advertise the same prefix on networks N-2 and N-3 (where router RT-4 resides) but with different metrics. RT-2 advertises a metric value of 2 while RT-3 advertises a metric value of 4. After processing the routing messages from RT-2 and RT-3, RT-4

FIGURE 1-8

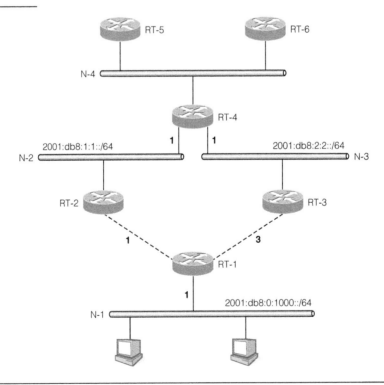

Example of RIPng route propagation.

selects the route with the smaller metric and chooses RT-2 as the next hop to reach network `2001:db8:0:1000::/64` with a metric of 2. RT-4 adds the cost of its network to the received metric and advertises that prefix with a metric of 3 on network N-4. RT-4 also advertises prefixes `2001:db8:1:1::/64` and `2001:db8:2:2::/64` for networks N-2 and N-3 on N-4. RT-5 and RT-6 receive this routing information and build their routing tables.

We can see from this example that RT-4 is able to compute the optimal route to prefix `2001:db8:0:1000::/64` from just the information exchanged with RT-2 and RT-3. The direction going toward this network is through RT-2.

1.4.1 RIPng Message Formats

Figure 1-9 depicts the RIPng protocol message format. Each decimal value in parentheses refers to the field size in bytes.

command This field specifies whether the RIPng message is a request message or a response message. A value of 1 indicates a request message, a value of 2 indicates a response message.

version This field specifies the version of the RIPng protocol in operation. [RFC2080] defines version 1 of RIPng.

The next two bytes must be set to zero by the sender.

Each Routing Table Entry (RTE) field is 20 bytes in size and specifies a reachable IPv6 destination. The format of the RTE field is shown in Figure 1-10.

IPv6 prefix The IPv6 prefix is 16 bytes in size and specifies either an IPv6 network or an IPv6 end node depending on the prefix length. The prefix is stored in network byte order.

FIGURE 1-9

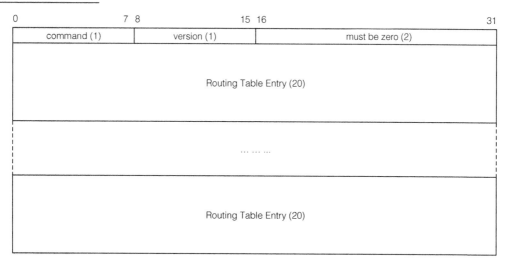

RIPng protocol message format.

FIGURE 1-10

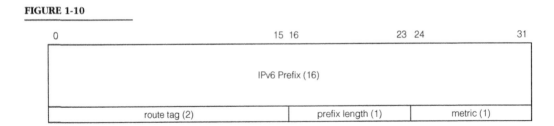

Routing table entry.

FIGURE 1-11

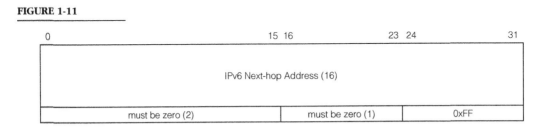

Specifying next hop address.

route tag The route tag is considered an attribute of the advertised destination. The route tag was designed for distinguishing the origin of the route, that is, whether the advertised prefix was imported from another routing protocol. In practice the route tag is used by operators to define sets of routes for custom handling in RIPng. The receiving router must preserve this field and readvertise it with the prefix.

prefix length The prefix length specifies the number of significant bits of the prefix field, counting from left to right. The valid prefix length is 0 to 128 inclusive. The prefix field is ignored if the prefix length is 0, which indicates that the advertised route is a default route. In this case it is good practice to set the prefix field to $0:0:0:0:0:0:0:0$, or $::$ in compressed form.

metric Even though the metric field is 1 byte in size, the valid values are 0 to 15, which specifies the cost of reaching the advertised destination. Value 16, known as infinity, indicates the advertised destination is not reachable. We will revisit the infinity value in Section 1.4.2.

In general the receiving router sets the advertising router as the next hop for the advertised destination. The advertising router may optionally specify a next hop router for one or more destinations by a special RTE. Figure 1-11 illustrates the special RTE that is used for specifying a next hop address.

The IPv6 next hop address field contains a link-local address of the next hop router, which belongs to the interface that shares the same network segment as the advertising router. The metric field is set to 0xFF. If the next hop address is $::$, then the originating router of the message is used as the next hop router. If the next hop address is not a link-local address, then again the originating router is used as the next hop router. All of the RTEs that follow this special RTE will use the given address as the next hop router until either another special RTE is encountered, or the end of the message is reached. For example, consider Figure 1-12.

In this example, the advertising router is treated as the next hop router for RTE 1 to N. The next hop router specified in the special RTE 1 applies to destination M, and the next hop router specified in the second special RTE applies to destination P.

FIGURE 1-12

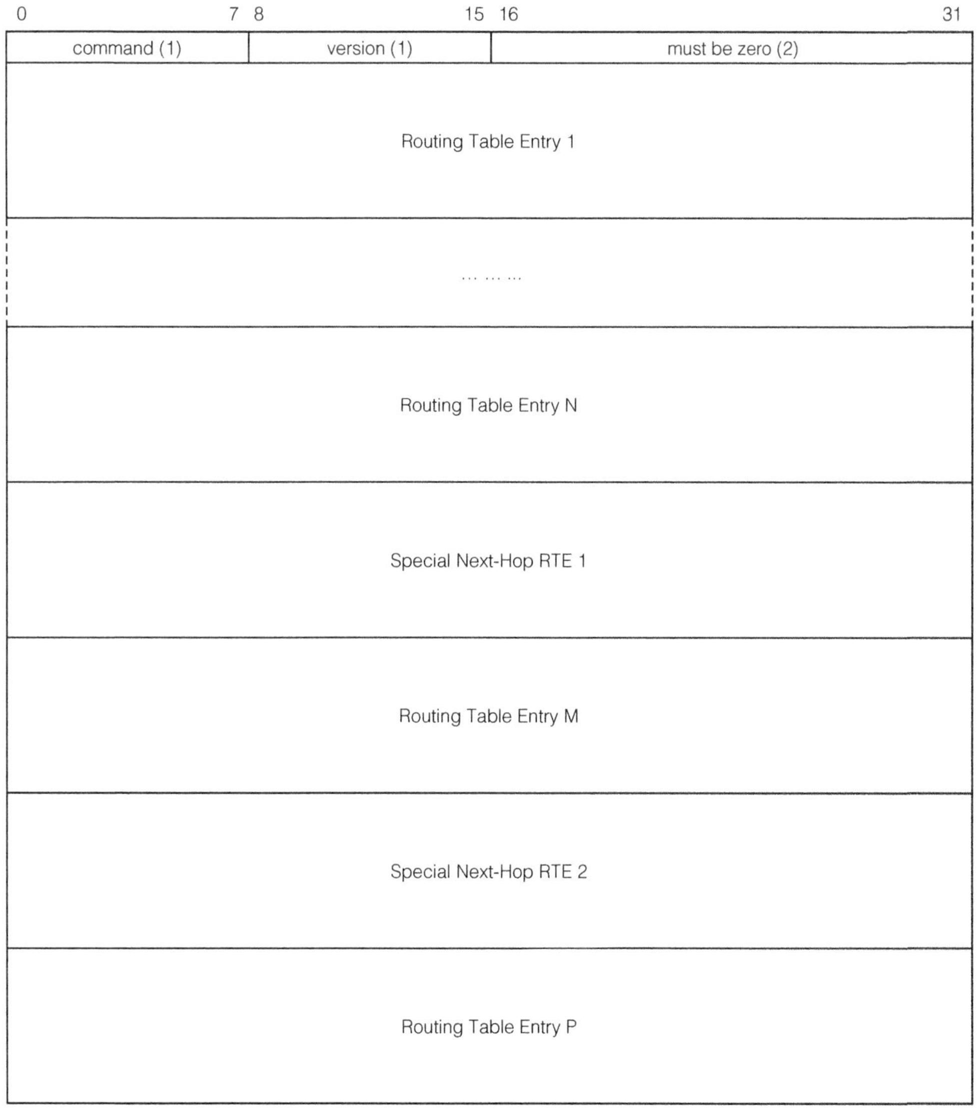

0	7	8	15	16	31
command (1)		version (1)		must be zero (2)	

Routing Table Entry 1
... ...
Routing Table Entry N
Special Next-Hop RTE 1
Routing Table Entry M
Special Next-Hop RTE 2
Routing Table Entry P

RIPng Route Advertisement containing next hop information.

The number of RTEs that can be carried in a single RIPng message is limited by the link MTU. The formula for calculating the number of RTEs is given as:

$$\text{number of RTEs} = \frac{\text{MTU} - (\text{length of IPv6 headers}) - (\text{UDP header length}) - (\text{RIPng header length})}{\text{size of RTE}} \quad (1.1)$$

1.4.2 RIPng Operation

The RIPng protocol operates over UDP. The IANA assigned port number for the RIPng process is 521.

A router sends its entire routing table to all its directly connected neighboring routers every 30 seconds—called a *regular update*. This unsolicited transmission has a UDP source port 521 and a destination port 521. The source address must be a link-local address of the transmitting interface of the originating router. The destination address is the *all-rip-routers* multicast address ff02::9.

When a router first comes up and is in the initialization phase, it may request other routers to send their routing tables in order for it to populate its routing table. This request may be sent to the all-rip-routers multicast address on each attached interface. If there exists only a single RTE in the RIPng request message, and the prefix in this RTE is ::, the prefix length is 0, and the metric value is 16, then the requesting router is asking the receiving router to send its entire routing table.

A router may send a request to a specific peer soliciting a specific list of destinations. In this case, the receiving router processes each RTE by performing a search of the given prefix in its routing table. If an entry is found, then the metric value is retrieved and is set in the RTE. If an entry is not found, then the metric value is set to 16 indicating the destination is not reachable from this router's perspective. Once all of the RTEs have been processed, the command field is changed from request to response and is sent to the requesting router.

When a router receives a message from a neighbor, if it contains a destination that is not already in its routing table, or if either the metric or the next hop address of an existing route entry is updated by the newly received RTE, then the corresponding route entry in the routing table is created or updated with new information. The next hop address of the entry is set to the source address of the received message or the next hop address specified by a next hop RTE (shown in Figure 1-11); note that in either case the address is a link-local address. The receiving router will then send an update message on all other interfaces. This process is called a *triggered update*, and is limited to one transmission per 1 to 5 seconds, depending on the timer expiration.

There are two timers associated with each route entry: the *timeout* timer and the *garbage collection* timer. The timeout timer is initialized to 180 seconds when the route entry is first created. Each time a response message which contains the destination of this route entry is received, the timeout timer is reset to 180 seconds. The route entry is considered expired if a message has not been received which covers that destination. In this case, once the route entry expires, a garbage collection timer is initialized to 120 seconds for the expired entry. The route entry is removed from the routing table when the garbage collection timer expires. The reason for setting the garbage collection timer is to aid convergence, as explained in Section 1.4.3.

The following points summarize the key characteristics of the RIPng protocol:

- The routing algorithm selects a best route for each possible destination using distance as the main selection criteria.

- Each piece of routing information consists of a destination, a gateway and the distance to the destination.

- A router exchanges routing information with only directly connected routers. Route information from a new neighboring router can be dynamically reflected, but the state of each router is not maintained.

- Distribution of routing information is unreliable because the routing information is exchanged over UDP without any application-level acknowledgments.

- Origin of a route cannot be identified.

- Route computation is distributed in that selection decision made at one router depends largely on the route selection decisions made by other routers.

- Routing loop cannot always be detected or avoided.

- The algorithm can be vulnerable to topological changes and can converge slowly.

1.4.3 Problems with RIPng

The main advantage of RIPng is that RIPng is a simple routing protocol and its implementation is fairly straightforward. This simplicity, however, causes a number of operational problems. The most visible problems are its inability to detect routing loops in more complex network topologies and that it may converge slowly in some situations. This was briefly discussed in Section 1.3.1; this section revisits and details the problem in the context of the RIPng protocol. Consider the example given in Figure 1-13.

In this figure, the horizontal axis represents time. The first vertical column lists the available routers RT-1, RT-2 and RT-3. Starting from the second column, each pair of values represents each router's perspective on the reachability of the IPv6 prefix `2001:db8:0:1000/64`, that is, the gateway to the prefix and the cost of that path. For example, at time t_1, RT-1 sees the prefix `2001:db8:0:1000::/64` as directly reachable, and the cost of that route is 1. At the same time, router RT-2 and RT-3 view the prefix as reachable through router RT-1, and the costs of the route are 2 and 4 respectively.

Router RT-1 advertises network `2001:db8:0:1000::/64` to both RT-2 and RT-3 with metric 1. At time t_2, the link between RT-1 and N-1 is broken. This link is the only one to reach N-1. Now RT-1 correctly marks `2001:db8:0:1000::/64` as unreachable. However, at time t_3 both RT-2 and RT-3 still advertise a route to `2001:db8:0:1000::/64` with metric 2 and 4 respectively. At time t_4, upon receiving these routes from RT-2 and RT-3, RT-1 incorrectly thinks that N-1 is reachable through either RT-2 or RT-3. Since RT-2 advertises a smaller metric, RT-1 treats RT-2 as the next hop router and inserts the route with the updated metric 3 into its routing table. This route entry is then advertised to RT-2 and RT-3 causing both RT-2 and RT-3 to think N-1 is now reachable via RT-1 but with a new metric value. RT-2 and RT-3 update their metric values accordingly and readvertise the route to RT-1. RT-1 again updates its metric value and then advertises the update route back to RT-2 and RT-3. This process continues until eventually

FIGURE 1-13

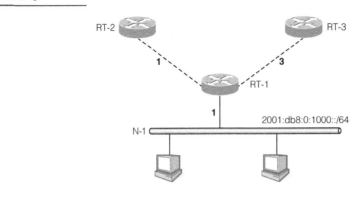

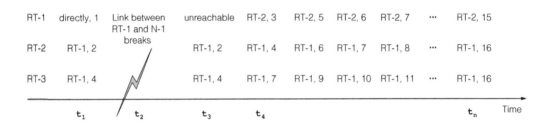

RT-1	directly, 1	Link between RT-1 and N-1 breaks	unreachable	RT-2, 3	RT-2, 5	RT-2, 6	RT-2, 7	···	RT-2, 15
RT-2	RT-1, 2		RT-1, 2	RT-1, 4	RT-1, 6	RT-1, 7	RT-1, 8	···	RT-1, 16
RT-3	RT-1, 4		RT-1, 4	RT-1, 7	RT-1, 9	RT-1, 10	RT-1, 11	···	RT-1, 16

t_1 t_2 t_3 t_4 t_n Time

Problem of counting to infinity.

all three routers have a metric value of 16 to `2001:db8:0:1000::/64`, which indicates this network is no longer reachable, that is, this is a symptom of the counting to infinity problem described in Section 1.3.1.

With the counting to infinity problem, none of the routers would know that N-1 is no longer reachable until the metric value reaches 16 at a time long passed t_2, (i.e., at time t_n). One reason that the metric for RIPng has a maximum allowed value of 16 is that the larger the allowable metric, the longer RIPng takes to reach the convergence state. The maximum value of 16 also implies that RIPng is limited to networks that have diameters of at most 15 hops, assuming the cost of each hop is 1. Note in this example, RT-3 converges faster than both RT-1 and RT-2 due to its larger metric value.

As illustrated by this example, due to the counting to infinity problem, RIPng has a large convergence time when it is deployed in more complex networks. As can be seen from this example, the source of the problem is that RT-2 is advertising to RT-1 a route which RT-2 had learned from RT-1. The problem disappears if RT-2 never advertises any route that was learned from RT-1 back to RT-1. This solution is called the *Split Horizon* algorithm. Alternatively, RT-2 may advertise the route that it learned from RT-1 back to RT-1, but RT-2 sets the metric to 16 which indicates that destination is not reachable through RT-2, which is known as *route poisoning*. The garbage collection timer mentioned in the pevious section, also known as the *hold-down* timer, is used for route poisoning. During the hold-down time, an expired route is

FIGURE 1-14

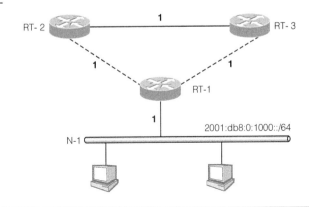

Network configuration causing RIPng routing loop.

advertised to the neighbors with a metric of 16. Split horizon combined with route poisoning is called *Split Horizon with Poisoned Reverse.*

The Split Horizon algorithm solves the problem depicted in Figure 1-13, but this algorithm still cannot detect the routing loop if the network has a configuration as shown in Figure 1-14.

In this figure, because RT-2 and RT-3 share a common link, the two routers will advertise 2001:db8:0:1000::/64 with a metric of 2 to each other. Due to Split Horizon with Poisoned Reverse, RT-2 and RT-3 both advertise to RT-1 that 2001:db8:0:1000::/64 is unreachable. When the link between RT-1 and N-1 is broken, RT-1 will mark N-1 as unreachable. At this point RT-2 considers the new route to 2001:db8:0:1000::/64 is through RT-3 with a metric of 3. RT-2 will also advertise this route to RT-1. RT-1 is led to believe that 2001:db8:0:1000::/64 is now reachable through RT-2. Again the counting to infinity problem occurs and the Split Horizon algorithm could not detect the routing loop in this configuration.

1.5 Introduction to BGP4+

The BGP-4 protocol as defined in [RFC4271] is an exterior routing protocol that is mainly deployed between different autonomous systems (ASs). Since the original BGP-4 specification assumes the routing protocol operates over the IPv4 network, the routing messages carry only IPv4 routes. [RFC2858] updates the BGP-4 specification to support additional protocols such as IPv6. The extended BGP is commonly known as BGP4+. The specific use of BGP4+ by IPv6 is documented in [RFC2545]. We will use BGP4+ to refer to BGP4+ as deployed in the IPv6 network. We will also use the terms BGP4+ and BGP interchangeably for the remainder of this chapter.

In the context of BGP4+, each AS has an *Autonomous System Number* or ASN. The ASN can be either a public ASN or a private ASN. A public ASN is a globally unique identifier and is assigned by an organization such as RIR or NIR. The IANA has reserved AS64512 to AS65535 as private ASNs. [RFC1930] discusses ASN in detail.

RIR stands for the *Regional Internet Registry*, which is responsible for the allocation and management of IP adresses and ASNs for a specific region of the world. Today there exist five RIRs: AfriNIC (Africa), APNIC (Asia Pacific), ARIN (North America), LACNIC (Central and South America), and RIPE-NCC (Europe).

NIR stands for the *National Internet Registry*, which is responsible for IP address allocation and management for a specific country.

BGP4+ uses the path-vector algorithm and solves the routing loop detection problem by including the path to the destination in the route message. When a BGP4+ router receives a route update, a router will update the path information to include its ASN before redistributing that route to other ASs. Since BGP4+ is an exterior routing protocol, routing information is exchanged among ASs, each with a different routing policy that governs what information could be made externally visible. For this reason, the path information carried in the route message is a list of ASNs instead of a list of specific routers in order to hide the internal topology of each AS on that path. Consider the example given in Figure 1-15.

As illustrated in the figure, each router records its ASN in the route message before distributing that route to another router. But first, each router must validate the received route message

FIGURE 1-15

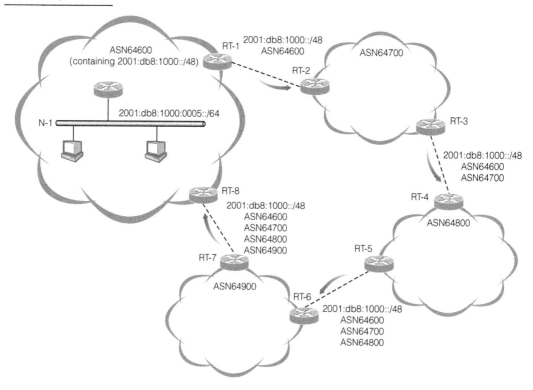

by examining the path information and verify that its ASN is not present in the path. Routers RT-2 to RT-7 accept the received route message according to this rule. RT-8 finds its ASN in the route message originated from RT-7, therefore detecting the routing loop. In this case RT-8 rejects the advertised route from RT-7, thus breaking the loop.

1.5.1   BGP4+ Operation

BGP4+ operates over TCP. A BGP4+ router establishes a *peering* relationship with another BGP4+ router by establishing a TCP connection to port 179 of that other router. The two BGP4+ routers are called *BGP peers*, also known as *BGP speakers*. Typically BGP4+ is deployed for inter-AS routing, but large organizations and enterprises that have hundreds of branch offices also deploy BGP4+ within an AS. When a BGP4+ router peers with another BGP4+ router of the same AS, these routers are called *internal BGP* (IBGP) peers. When a BGP4+ router peers with a BGP4+ router of another AS, these routers are called *external BGP* (EBGP) peers. Figure 1-16 illustrates the concept of EBGP and IBGP peers.

As shown in the figure, routers RT1, RT2 and RT3 are IBGP peers because these routers belong to the same AS(64600). RT1 and RT5 are EBGP peers. Similarly RT2 and RT4 are EBGP peers. In this figure, router RT3 acts as a *route reflector* that redistributes routing information learned from one IBGP peer to another IBGP peer. BGP route reflector is fully described in [RFC2796].

FIGURE 1-16

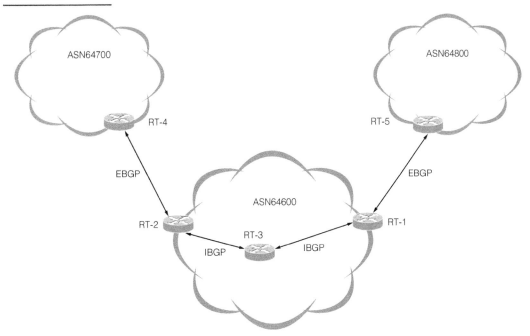

BGP4+ IBGP and EBGP peers.

The BGP4+ routers cannot exchange any routing information until the peering process completes successfully. BGP defines a *Finite State Machine* (FSM) to represent its operation. Associated with the FSM is a set of events and timers that trigger state transition. The BGP peering process is part of the FSM but we omit the discussion of the BGP FSM in detail. Instead, we will describe the peering process through one possible scenario as illustrated in Figure 1-17.

The peering process begins by first establishing a TCP connection. One BGP4+ router initiates the TCP connection to another BGP4+ router. It is possible that both routers try to initiate the TCP connection to each other at the same time. In order to avoid establishing two TCP connections, the BGP router with the smaller BGP Identifier (see Figure 1-19) will cancel its TCP connection request. The OPEN message is the first BGP message sent once the underlying TCP connection has been established successfully. A subsequent KEEPALIVE message confirms the OPEN message. Notice two BGP speakers send the OPEN and the KEEPALIVE messages. The BGP speakers then exchange their routing databases through the UPDATE message once the BGP peering session is established.

FIGURE 1-17

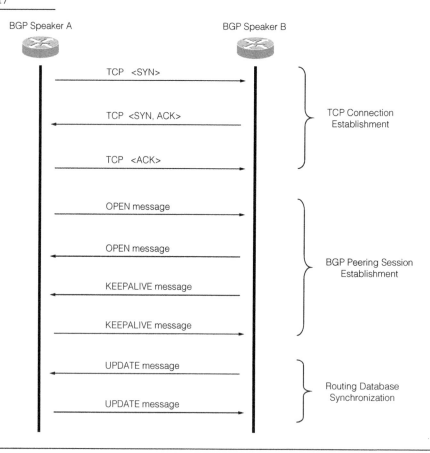

BGP4+ peering process.

For each of its peers, a BGP router maintains a database that stores the routes advertised by its peer, and a separate database that stores the routes that it advertised to the peer. By maintaining separate databases on incoming and outgoing route exchanges, each BGP router is able to determine which updated routes affect its peer, and distributes to its peer only those updates to reduce routing traffic.

Since BGP is mainly deployed between different ISPs or between different companies, routing policies and enforcement of those policies play a significant role in BGP. It is important for an ISP or a company to define what types of routes can be accepted from a peer, what types of routes can be distributed to a peer, what external routes can be redistributed internally and externally, which entry points inbound traffic should take, which exit points outbound traffic should take, and much more.

The following points summarize the key characteristics of the BGP4+ routing protocol:

- The routing algorithm selects a best route for each possible destination by examining the path information in conjunction with the locally administered routing policies.

- Routes are re-advertised to other routers that are not directly connected. There is no dynamic discovery of neighboring routers. Routes are exchanged with configured peer routers.

- Each piece of routing information consists of the destination, a gateway and the entire path to the destination.

- Distribution of routing information is reliable because route exchanges are carried over TCP.

- Origin of each route can be identified.

- Routing loops can be easily detected and avoided.

- Route computation is distributed in that selection decision made at one router depends largely on the route selection decisions made by other routers; however, decision of route selection can be made by local policy with a good degree of flexibility due to the explicit loop avoidance mechanism.

1.5.2 BGP4+ Messages

There are four message types in BGP, which are shown in Table 1-1.

Message Header

The BGP message header format is shown in Figure 1-18.

Marker This 4-byte field must be filled with all ones.

Length This 2-byte field specifies the size of the BGP message. The message header is 19 bytes, so Length can have the minimum value of 19. The maximum value that Length can have is 4096 including the header size.

Type This 1-byte field specifies the BGP message type as described in Table 1-1.

TABLE 1-1

Type	Name	Description
1	**OPEN**	The OPEN message is the first message that is sent over the TCP connection to initiate the peering exchange.
2	**UPDATE**	The UPDATE message carries routing information and is exchanged between the peers. A router also sends the UPDATE message to withdraw a previously advertised route.
3	**NOTIFICATION**	A router sends the NOTIFICATION message when it detects an error condition and closes the connection.
4	**KEEPALIVE**	Instead of relying on the TCP keep-alive mechanism, a BGP4+ router sends the KEEPALIVE message to detect the liveliness of its peer. The KEEPALIVE message is also sent in response to an OPEN message to complete the initial peering handshake.

BGP message types.

FIGURE 1-18

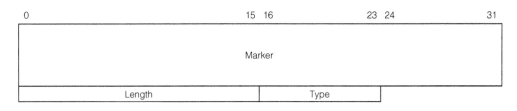

BGP4+ message header.

OPEN message

The OPEN message is the first message that is exchanged between two BGP speakers once the TCP connection is established between them. The OPEN message serves as the request to establish a peering relation. The OPEN messages also allow the BGP speakers to identify each other's capabilities. The BGP speakers may fail to establish the peering relationship if incompatibilities are found.

The OPEN message contains the message header and the additional fields that are shown in Figure 1-19.

Version This 1-byte field specifies the BGP protocol version number. The current BGP version is 4.

My Autonomous System Number This 2-byte field contains the ASN of the sender of the OPEN message.

Hold Time This 2-byte field specifies the maximum duration between successive KEEPALIVE or UPDATE messages. This value is proposed from the sender. The receiver sets its Hold

FIGURE 1-19

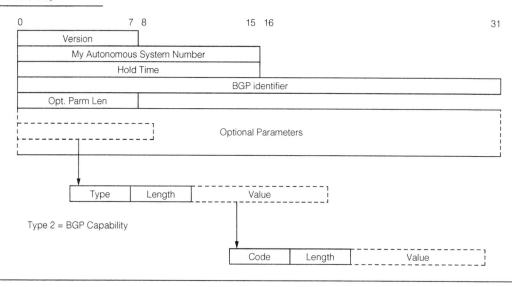

BGP4+ OPEN message.

Time to be the smaller of its configured value and the proposed Hold Time from the received OPEN message. A zero Hold Time implies the sender does not need to send any message. The Hold Time must be at least 3 seconds if its value is not zero. In this case the TCP connection is closed if the receiver does not receive a KEEPALIVE, UPDATE or NOTIFICATION message when the Hold Time expires. The value received in the Hold Time field may cause a BGP speaker to reject the peering request.

BGP Identifier The 4-byte field contains a valid IPv4 unicast address of the sender.

Optional Parameters Length This 1-byte field specifies size of the optional parameters that are present in the message. No options are present if the length is zero. Otherwise these optional parameters will be negotiated with the receiver.

Optional Parameters The variable length Optional Parameters field contains the parameters to be negotiated with the receiver. Each optional parameter has the <type, length, value> format. The Type 2 parameter represents the BGP capabilities. The value field of a Type 2 parameter is encoded as <code, length, value>. Table 1-2 lists the currently defined capability codes, their descriptions and the documents in which they are defined.

KEEPALIVE message

The KEEPALIVE message contains only the message header and is therefore 19 bytes in size. The KEEPALIVE message is sent to avoid the expiration of the Hold Time and serves the same purpose as the TCP keepalive packets, that is, to verify the connection state. The KEEPALIVE message is rate limited and more than one message per second must not be sent. The KEEPALIVE message must not be sent if the negotiated Hold Time is zero.

TABLE 1-2

Value	Description	Reference
0	Reserved	[RFC3392]
1	Multiprotocol Extensions for BGP-4	[RFC2858]
2	Route Refresh Capability for BGP-4	[RFC2918]
3	Cooperative Route Filtering Capability	[ROUTE-FILTER]
4	Multiple routes to a destination capability	[RFC3107]
5–63	Unassigned	
64	Graceful Restart Capability	[IDR-RESTART]
65	Support for 4-byte AS number capability	[AS4BYTES]
66	Deprecated (2003-03-06)	
67	Support for Dynamic Capability (capability specific)	
68–127	Unassigned	
128–255	Vendor Specific	

BGP capability codes.

FIGURE 1-20

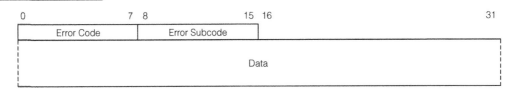

BGP4+ NOTIFICATION message.

NOTIFICATION message

The NOTIFICATION message is sent when an error condition is detected by a BGP speaker. The BGP speaker terminates the connection immediately after sending the message. The NOTIFICATION message contains the message header and the additional fields that are shown in Figure 1-20.

Error Code This 1-byte field indicates the type of error that has occurred either during the peering process or during an established BGP session.

Error Subcode The value of this 1-byte field depends on the value of the Error Code field.

Data The Data field is variable in length and its content depends on both the Error Code and the Error Subcode. At a minimum the NOTIFICATION message is 21 bytes in size if Data is not present.

The various error codes are listed in Table 1-3.

TABLE 1-3

Error Code	Description	Subcode	Description
1	Message Header Error	1	Connection Not Synchronized
		2	Bad Message Length
		3	Bad Message Type
2	OPEN Message Error	1	Unsupported Version Number
		2	Bad Peer AS
		3	Bad BGP Identifier
		4	Unsupported Optional Parameters
		5	Deprecated
		6	Unacceptable Hold Time
3	UPDATE Message Error	1	Malformed Attribute List
		2	Unrecognized Well-known Attribute
		3	Missing Well-known Attribute
		4	Attribute Flags Error
		5	Attribute Length Error
		6	Invalid ORIGIN Attribute
		7	Deprecated
		8	Invalid NEXT_HOP Attribute
		9	Optional Attribute Error
		10	Invalid Network Field
		11	Malformed AS_PATH
4	Hold Time Expired		
5	Finite State Machine Error		
6	Cease		

NOTIFICATION Error Codes.

UPDATE message

Routing information are exchanged between BGP peers through the UPDATE message. The UPDATE message may advertise a new route, update an existing route, or withdraw a route. The format of the UPDATE message is shown in Figure 1-21.

Withdrawn Routes Length This 2-byte field specifies the size of the Withdrawn Routes field in bytes. This field is an IPv4 specific field and is not used by other protocols such as IPv6.

Withdrawn Routes This is a variable sized field and contains a list of routes that are withdrawn from service, perhaps due to change in reachability. This field is an IPv4 specific field and is not used by other protocols such as IPv6. For IPv6, the MP_UNREACH_NLRI path attribute is used to withdraw IPv6 routes. The MP_UNREACH_NLRI attribute is described in detail

FIGURE 1-21

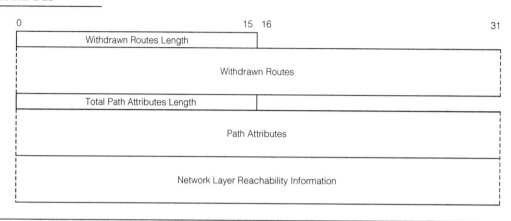

BGP4+ UPDATE message.

in Section 1.5.4. Path attributes are described in Section 1.5.3. Each entry has the <length, prefix> format.

Length This 1-byte field specifies the size of the prefix in bits that immediately follows this field. 0 is a special value indicating that the prefix matches all IP addresses, that is, the prefix has all zero values in every byte.

Prefix This field contains the prefix to be withdrawn. The Prefix field is variable in size. This field may be padded such that the prefix is aligned on the byte boundary. For example, if the Length field contains the value 19, then the Prefix field will be 3 bytes large.

Total Path Attributes Length This 2-byte field specifies the size of the Path Attributes field in bytes. The Path Attributes field and the Network Layer Reachability Information field are not present if this field has a 0 value.

Path Attributes This is a variable length field and has the <type, length, value> format. This field describes the properties of a path to a destination that is given in the Network Layer Reachability Information field. We will defer the discussion of this field to Section 1.5.3.

Network Layer Reachability Information (NLRI) This variable length field contains a list of destinations that are reachable and should be added into the local routing table. The paths to these destinations share the same set of properties that are described by the Path Attributes field. The NLRI field is an IPv4-specific field and is not used by other protocols such as IPv6. For IPv6, the NLRI is conveyed through the MP_REACH_NLRI path attribute, which is described in detail in Section 1.5.4. Each entry in the NLRI field has the <length, prefix> format.

Length This 1-byte field specifies the size of the prefix in bits that immediately follows this field. 0 is a special value indicating that the prefix matches all IP addresses, that is, the prefix has all zero values in every byte.

Prefix This field contains the reachable prefix. The Prefix field is variable in size. This field may be padded such that the prefix is aligned on the byte boundary. For example, if the Length field contains the value 19, then the Prefix field will be 3 bytes large.

1.5.3 Path Attributes

Path Attributes describe the various properties of the routes to which the attributes apply. The BGP route selection algorithm includes the path attributes in its computation for the best route as we will describe in Section 1.5.5. The Path Attributes are classified into four categories:

- Well-known mandatory
- Well-known discretionary
- Optional transitive
- Optional non-transitive

The well-known mandatory attributes must be recognized and processed by every BGP speaker. The well-known mandatory attributes must be included in all UPDATE messages that contain the NLRI. The well-known discretionary attributes must also be recognized and processed by every BGP speaker, but these discretionary attributes may be omitted in an UPDATE message. A BGP speaker that receives either types of well-known attributes and subsequently modifies the attributes must then propagate these attributes to its peers in the UPDATE messages.

A BGP speaker is not required to support the optional transitive and optional non-transitive attributes. These types of attributes may be omitted in the UPDATE messages. A BGP speaker should accept NLRI with unrecognized optional transitive attributes, in which case the unrecognized optional transitive attributes are redistributed along with the received NLRI to the peers. A BGP speaker must silently ignore unrecognized optional non-transitive attributes and these attributes are not redistributed to the peers.

The Path Attributes are encoded in the <type, length, value> format. The attribute type is a two-byte field that is divided into Attribute Flags and Attribute Type Code as shown in Figure 1-22.

FIGURE 1-22

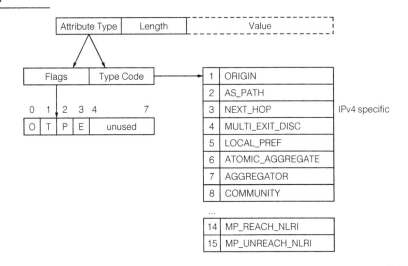

BGP4+ Path Attribute.

The O bit is the Optional bit, and if it is set to 1, the attribute is an optional attribute. The T bit is the Transitive bit, and if it is set to 1 then the attribute is an optional transitive attribute. The P bit is the Partial bit. When a BGP speaker receives an unrecognized optional non-transitive attribute and the BGP speaker decides to accept the associated NLRI, the BGP speaker sets the P bit before redistributing the unknown attributes to its peers. The P bit must not be reset to 0 once it is set to 1. The E bit is the Extended Length bit, and if it is set to 1, the third and fourth bytes are used for the attribute length field; otherwise only the third byte belongs to the length field. The remaining four bits are unused. The Type Code field contains the attribute type and each type is described in the following:

ORIGIN The ORIGIN attribute specifies the source of the prefix, which can be

> **IGP** indicates the prefix was obtained from an interior gateway protocol (IGP).
>
> **EGP** indicates the prefix was obtained from an exterior gateway protocol (EGP).
>
> **INCOMPLETE** indicates the source of the prefix is neither IGP nor EGP but by other methods, for example, through manual route injection by the system administrator.

> The ORIGIN attribute is a well-known mandatory attribute.

AS_PATH The AS_PATH attribute contains the list of AS path segments. Each path segment contains the AS that the route has traversed. The BGP speaker inserts its ASN in the AS_PATH when it redistributes a route to its external peers. The AS_PATH attribute is a well-known mandatory attribute that is used by each BGP speaker to detect routing loops. The AS_PATH attribute allows the route selection algorithm to choose the shortest path route when multiple routes have the same properties.

NEXT_HOP The NEXT_HOP attribute specifies the next hop router for reaching the prefixes that are provided in NLRI. This is a mandatory well-known attribute. This attribute is not used for IPv6.

MULTI_EXIT_DISC The MULTI_EXIT_DISC attribute is called the *Multi-Exit Discriminator* and is used by a BGP speaker to set the metric values on multiple paths that enter into the local AS, thereby informing an EBGP peer about the optimal entry point for inbound traffic. The smaller the metric value is, the more preferred the path is. Since the MULTI_EXIT_DISC attribute is an optional non-transitive attribute, a receiving BGP speaker must not propagate this attribute to other peers.

LOCAL_PREF The LOCAL_PREF attribute is called the *Local Preference* and is used by IBGP peers to convey path preference within an AS, thereby informing IBGP peers about the optimal exit point for outbound traffic. The higher the value is, the more preferred the path is. The LOCAL_PREF attribute is a well-known attribute. The LOCAL_PREF attribute is used by the administrator to specify the optimal AS exit point. A BGP speaker must not include the LOCAL_PREF attribute in UPDATE messages that are sent to EBGP peers.

> LOCAL_PREF was previously categorized as discretionary, but [RFC4271] has removed the discretionary categorization from this attribute. The reason is not clear, but we speculate perhaps the change made was because the requirement level of this attribute for IBGP is different from that for EBGP.

FIGURE 1-23

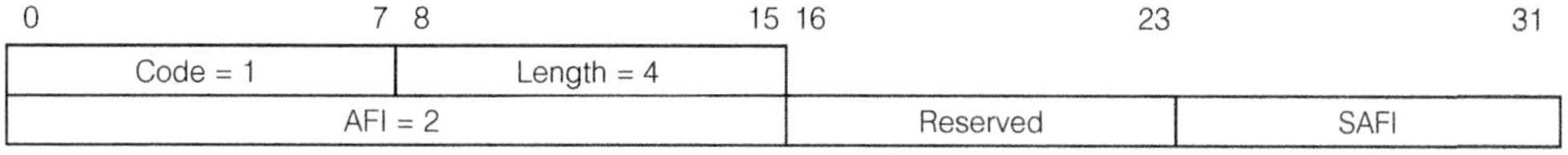

0	7	8	15	16	23	31

Code = 1	Length = 4		
AFI = 2		Reserved	SAFI

BGP4+ IPv6 capability advertisement.

ATOMIC_AGGREGATOR A BGP speaker may aggregate multiple prefixes into a single prefix and advertise that prefix to its peers. In this case the BGP speaker that performed the aggregation would include the ATOMIC_AGGREGATOR attribute to indicate to its peer that the less specific prefix is being advertised. The ATOMIC_AGGREGATOR attribute is a well-known discretionary attribute.

AGGREGATOR The AGGREGATOR attribute contains the BGP identifier and the IPv4 address of the BGP speaker that performed the route aggregation. This attribute is an optional transitive attribute.

COMMUNITY The usage of the COMMUNITY attribute is outside the scope of this book. Therefore its description is omitted here.

The MP_REACH_NLRI and the MP_UNREACH_NLRI attributes are described in the next section.

1.5.4 IPv6 Extensions for BGP4+

A BGP4+ speaker that understands IPv6 must indicate it supports the multiprotocol extensions for BGP4+ by setting the necessary capability in the OPEN message. The fields of the capability parameter are shown in Figure 1-23.

The capability code is set to 1 for multiprotocol extensions. The Address Family Identifier (AFI) field is set to 2, which is the address family number assigned by IANA for IPv6. The Subsequent Address Family Identifier (SAFI) provides additional information about the NLRI carried in the multiprotocol NLRI attributes. [RFC2858] defines the following values:

1 NLRI used for unicast forwarding. This value is used for IPv6 unicast routing.

2 NLRI used for multicast reverse path forwarding calculation.

3 NLRI used for both unicast and multicast.[1]

An UPDATE message that carries only IPv6 routes will set the Withdrawn Routes Length field to 0, and the NLRI field would not be present. Since the NEXT_HOP attribute is an IPv4-specific attribute, it is omitted in UPDATE messages that carry IPv6 NLRI.

---

1. [BGP4-MPEXT] term the definition for the SAFI value 3.

[RFC2858] indicates the NEXT_HOP attribute may be omitted, but in practice this attribute is normally set to 0.0.0.0 and is included in UPDATE messages that carry IPv6 NLRI. The main reason was due to the observation made that a specific BGP implementation rejected BGP messages due to the lack of a well-known mandatory attribute.

Advertising IPv6 Routes

BGP4+ uses the MP_REACH_NLRI path attribute to advertise IPv6 routes. The MP_REACH_NLRI attribute is an optional non-transitive attribute. Figure 1-24 shows the format of this attribute.

Address Family Identifier The two-byte AFI field is set to value 2 for IPv6.

Subsequent AFI The 1-byte SAFI field is set according to the value defined in [RFC2858].

Length of Next Hop Address This 1-byte field specifies the size of the next hop address. Typically the next hop address carries only the global IPv6 address of the next hop router. In this case the length field is set to 16. The link-local address may be included as the additional next hop address if the advertising BGP speaker shares a common link with the next hop and the peer to which the route is advertised. In this case the length field is set to 32.

Next Hop Address This field contains the global IPv6 address of the next hop router. Depending on the value of the next hop address length field, the link-local address of the router may be included in addition to the global IPv6 address.

FIGURE 1-24

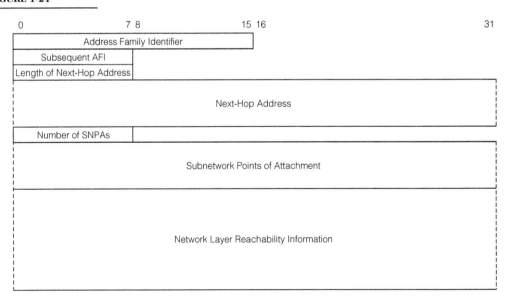

BGP4+ MP_REACH_NLRI attribute format.

Number of SNPAs This 1-byte field specifies the number of Subnetwork Points of Attachment (SNPA) that are present in the attribute. This field is set to 0 for IPv6, which means the SNPA field is omitted.

NLRI The NLRI lists the routes that are advertised by this attribute. For IPv6 the NLRI is encoded in the <length, prefix> format.

    Length This 1-byte field specifies the size of the prefix in bits that immediately follows this field. 0 is a special value that indicates the prefix matches all IP addresses, that is, the prefix has all zero values in every byte.

    Prefix This field contains the reachable prefix. The Prefix field is variable in size. This field may be padded such that the prefix is aligned on the byte boundary.

Withdraw IPv6 Routes

BGP4+ uses the MP_UNREACH_NLRI attribute to withdraw IPv6 routes. The MP_UNREACH_NLRI attribute is an optional non-transitive attribute. Figure 1-25 shows the format of this attribute.

Address Family Identifier The two-byte AFI field is set to value 2 for IPv6.

Subsequent AFI The 1-byte SAFI field is set according to the value defined in [RFC2858].

Withdrawn Routes This field contains the list of prefixes to be removed from the routing table. For IPv6 the withdrawn routes are encoded in the <length, prefix> format.

    Length This 1-byte field specifies the size of the prefix in bits that immediately follows this field. 0 is a special value indicating that the prefix matches all IP addresses, that is, the prefix has all zero values in every byte.

    Prefix This field contains the prefix to be withdrawn. The Prefix field is variable in size. This field may be padded such that the prefix is aligned on the byte boundary.

1.5.5 BGP4+ Route Selection Process

BGP path selection takes place when a BGP router receives an UPDATE message from its peer. The BGP4+ route selection process needs to take into account the path segment that is

FIGURE 1-25

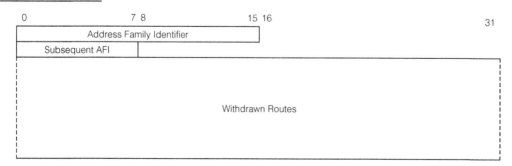

BGP4+ MP_UNREACH_NLRI attribute format.

internal within the AS, and the path segment that is external to the AS. Typically the policies that apply to route selections are different for the two path segments, which are reflected in the settings of the various attributes such as the LOCAL_PREF and the MULTI_EXIT_DISC attributes.

The BGP path selection algorithm is called the *best path selection* algorithm because route selection is based on degree of preference. The path selection algorithm is composed of two phases. In the first phase the preference of each route is determined. In the second phase, all feasible routes are considered and the route with the highest preference is chosen as the best route. Tie-breaker rules are executed to select a single entry when multiple routes have the same preference. A route is considered feasible if the NEXT_HOP attribute is resolvable and the AS_PATH attribute does not contain the receiver's ASN.

Computing Route Preference

The preference of a route is determined by the LOCAL_PREF attribute if the UPDATE message is received from an internal peer. It is also allowable to calculate the preference of a route based on locally configured policy even when an IBGP peer originated the UPDATE message. In this case, however, the preference calculated may result in the route to be selected as the best route, which may cause a routing loop subsequently.

The locally configured policy is used to calculate route preference when the UPDATE message is received from an EBGP peer. The resulting preference may be redistributed to IBGP peers in the LOCAL_PREF attribute if the received route is deemed eligible.

Route Selection

The BGP4+ route selection algorithm chooses the route with the highest degree of preference among all possible paths to the same prefix.

A route is chosen as the best path if that route is the only route to a given prefix. Since the LOCAL_PREF is used instead of the preconfigured policy when computing degree of preference, routes with the highest LOCAL_PREF value are preferred.

When multiple routes to the same prefix have the same degree of preference, the following rules serve as the tie-breakers to select a single route:

- The route with the shortest AS_PATH is preferred.

- The route with the lowest ORIGIN code is preferred. In other words, routes that are originated from IGP are preferred over routes that are originated from EGP.

- The route with the lowest value MULTI_EXIT_DISC is preferred. The comparison of the MULTI_EXIT_DISC applies to routes that are learned from the same AS. In this context, the route without the MULTI_EXIT_DISC attribute is preferred over the one with the MULTI_EXIT_DISC attribute attached.

- The route advertised by an EBGP peer is preferred over the same route that is advertised by an IBGP peer.

- The route with the smallest interior cost (or metric) to the next hop router, which is specified by the Next Hop Address field of the MP_REACH_NLRI attribute for IPv6, is preferred.

- The route that was advertised by the BGP router having the lowest identifier is preferred.

- The route that was advertised by the BGP router with the lowest address is preferred.

1.6   Introduction to OSPFv3

The OSPF protocol is a link-state routing protocol, that is, each router maintains a *link-state database* (LSDB) that comprises link-state information collected from all participating OSPF routers within an AS. Link-state information (or just link-state) refers to a router's local view of its immediate network topology, which includes the router's operational interfaces, the cost of sending traffic out on an interface and the address information of its attached networks. Each router floods its link-state throughout the AS resulting in each participating OSPF router having an identical LSDB (we will revisit this sentence in Section 1.6.2). In essence, this LSDB represents the complete network topology of the entire AS. As we will explain in Section 1.6.3, this LSDB may also contain information about networks that are outside the AS, and may include routing information that is derived from other routing protocols such as BGP or RIPng.

In RIPng, each router computes its routing table based on the computation results of other routers. Unlike RIPng, each OSPF router computes its routing table to reachable nodes and networks from its LSDB independently. Entries of this LSDB represent a directed graph. Route computation involves the construction of the shortest path tree to each destination out of this graph. This shortest path tree represents the most efficient routing paths to all reachable destinations.

OSPF can operate over various types of networks. In the following sections we will focus our discussions around broadcast-capable networks so that we can concentrate on the more important concepts.

1.6.1   Router Adjacency and LSDB Synchronization

The key to the correct link-state protocol operation is the reliable timely synchronization of the LSDB. A router newly becoming operational must acquire a large part of its LSDB from another router that has been in operation for a period of time. OSPF introduces the concept of *adjacency* that is similar to the BGP *peer* concept. Two routers may be neighbors but they may not be adjacent. An OSPF router exchanges routing information (thus LSDB synchronization) only with its adjacent routers.

When N routers are present on a subnetwork, if a router were to form adjacency with all of its neighbors and synchronize its LSDB with these neighbors, the number of LSDB exchanges is in the order of N^2 and may cause a large amount of routing traffic and overhead. OSPF introduces the concepts of *designated router* (DR) and *backup designated router* (BDR) to solve this problem. A DR and a BDR are elected dynamically on each subnetwork. Instead of forming adjacency with every other neighbor, all routers form adjacencies to just the DR and the BDR. Since each router establishes adjacency to only the DR and the BDR, LSDB synchronization would be performed with just the DR resulting in both routing traffic reduction and time reduction. Routing update from one router is propagated to all other neighbors through the DR.

An OSPF router discovers its neighbors and then subsequently forms adjacency with the DR and BDR through the OSPF *Hello* protocol. The Hello protocol also allows an OSPF router to verify bidirectional connectivity with its neighbors. In addition, the DR and BDR are elected through the Hello protocol. BDR provides protocol reliability because when the BDR detects that the DR is unavailable through the Hello protocol, the BDR becomes the DR and a new BDR is chosen.

The LSDB synchronization begins with each router sending *database description* packets to its adjacent neighbor. Each database description packet describes a list of *link state advertisements* (LSA) that exist in the LSDB of the sending router. The receiving router checks these LSAs against its own LSDB, and remembers those LSAs that are either missing from its LSDB or are more recent than those in its LSDB. Subsequently the receiving router requests those specific LSAs from its adjacent neighbor. The LSDB synchronization completes when both adjacent routers have sent the database description packets to each other and have received from each other their requested LSAs.

Two link-local scope multicast addresses are assigned to OSPFv3. The `ff02::5` multicast address is known as the *AllSPFRouters* address. All OSPFv3 routers must join this multicast group and listen to packets for this multicast group. The OSPFv3 Hello packets are sent to this address. The `ff02::6` multicast address is known as the *AllDRouters* address. The DR and BDR must join this multicast group and listen to packets for this multicast group. The use of these multicast groups depends on the protocol packet type and the router that is sending the packet. The use of the ALLSPFRouters and the AllDRouters addresses is similar to that of IPv4. The reader should consult [RFC2328] for more details.

The following points summarize the key characteristics of the OSPF protocol.

- The link-state information originated by one router is not modified by any of the receiving routers.

- The link-state information is flooded, unmodified, throughout the routing domain.

- Distribution of routing information is reliable because each LSA is explicitly acknowledged. We do not cover this topic in this chapter. The reader is encouraged to consult [RFC2328] for details.

- Dynamic neighboring router discovery can be done by the Hello protocol.

- A router sends the link-state information to its adjacent routers.

- Each router maintains an identical database that contains all of the link-state information that has been advertised by all of the participating routers.

- The routing algorithm can compute loop-free paths.

- Route computation is independently performed at each router; however, since loop avoidance relies on the synchronized shortest paths, route selection decision is not as flexible as BGP4+.

1.6.2 Area Types and Router Classification

The amount of route information exchanged over OSPF can be reduced with the concept of *areas*. An OSPF area is a collection of subnetworks. The reachability information distributed by the responsible router for the area is about the area as a whole, not about the individual subnetwork. Thus an area reduces routing traffic and the amount of routing information flooded in the AS. Besides route aggregation, an area offers routing protection because topological change taking place outside the area does not affect shortest path tree calculation in an area. An area may also restrict the flow of external routes into the area depending on the area type. OSPF areas can be *normal areas*, *stub areas*, and *not-so-stubby areas* (NSSA). Routing within an area is called *intra-area routing* while routing between areas is called *inter-area routing*.

A router can now be classified as *internal router, area border router* (ABR), or *AS boundary router* (ASBR). A router with attached networks that all belong to the same area is called an internal router. A router that is attached to multiple areas is called an area border router. An ABR maintains a separate LSDB for each attached area. In Section 1.6 we indicated that each router would have an identical LSDB. To be more precise, each router in an area would have identical LSDBs for that area. A router that exchanges routing information with routers in other ASs[2] and distributes the external routing information in the local AS is called an AS boundary router.

Figure 1-26 illustrates the area concept and the situations of the various types of routers.

As shown in the figure, routers R1, R2, R3, R4 and R6 are internal routers. Routers R5, R7, and R9 are ABRs. Routers R8 and R9 are ASBRs. Router R5 maintains one LSDB for Area-1 and one LSDB for Area-2. All of the routers in Area-1, including R5 have the same LSDB about Area-1. Similarly routers R5, R6 and R9 have the same LSDB about Area-2.

Area 0 is a special area called the *backbone area*. Routing information about other areas are distributed through the backbone area. In Figure 1-26, routers R5, R7, R8 and R9 are connected to the backbone area and share a common network. *Virtual links* are used to connect these routers if they are physically separate. In this case a virtual link is similar to an unnumbered point-to-point link. Virtual links are always part of the backbone. Although these routers may be physically separate, they must share a common area. This common area is called the *transit area* because the virtual link is connected across this area. A related concept is the *transit network*. Transit network is defined as a network on which pass-through traffic can flow across.

All link state information, including routing information that is external to an AS, is flooded into a normal area. AS external routes are not flooded into the stub areas. Virtual links cannot be configured through a stub area. Details of an NSSA are beyond the scope of this book and are omitted.

1.6.3 Link State Advertisement and LSA Types

An OSPF router sends the link-state information through a set of *Link State Advertisements* (LSAs), contained in *Link State Update* packets. OSPF deploys a reliable flooding mechanism,

---

2. Technically, these routers may be in the same AS but outside the OSPF domain.

FIGURE 1-26

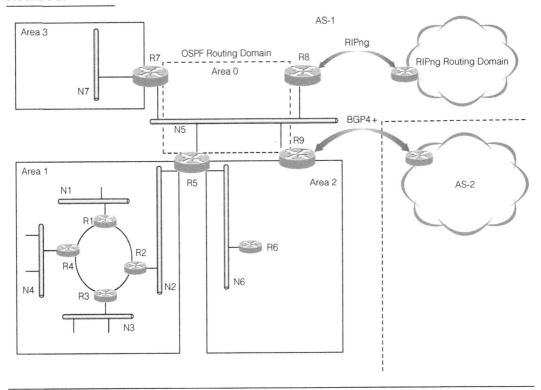

OSPF areas.

that is, each LSA is explicitly acknowledged by a *Link State Acknowledgment* packet. OSPFv3 is described in [RFC2740] and defines the following types of LSA:

Router-LSA The Router-LSA describes the advertising router's interfaces that are attached to the area. The state and cost of each interface is described by the Router-LSA. Each router originates a set of Router-LSAs for its interfaces. The Router-LSA is flooded throughout the area.

Network-LSA The Network-LSA is originated by a link's DR, which describes all of the attached routers to that link. The Network-LSA is flooded throughout the area.

Inter-Area-Prefix-LSA The Inter-Area-Prefix-LSA is originated by the ABR, which describes the reachable IPv6 prefixes that are part of other areas. The Inter-Area-Prefix-LSA is flooded throughout the area.

Inter-Area-Router-LSA The Inter-Area-Router-LSA is originated by an ABR, which describes the reachable routers of other areas. The Inter-Area-Router-LSA is flooded throughout the area.

AS-External-LSA The AS-External-LSA is originated by an ASBR, which describes the reachable prefixes that belong to other ASs. The AS-External-LSAs are flooded throughout the entire AS (except certain stub areas).

TABLE 1-4

LSA type	Flooding scope	Originator	IPv4 equivalent
Router-LSA	area	each router	Router-LSA
Network-LSA	area	DR	Network-LSA
Inter-Area-Prefix-LSA	area	ABR	Type-3 summary-LSA
Inter-Area-Router-LSA	area	ABR	Type-4 summary-LSA
AS-external-LSA	AS	ASBR	AS-external-LSA
Link-LSA	link	each router	(none)
Intra-Area-Prefix-LSA	area	each router	(none)

LSA types and flooding scope.

Link-LSA The Link-LSA is generated by each router attached to that link, which conveys the following information to other routers attached to that same link:

- the link-local address of the advertising router on that link
- the prefixes that are assigned to that link
- the options to be set in the Network-LSA to be generated by the DR of that link

The Link-LSA is flooded on that link only.

Intra-Area-Prefix-LSA The Intra-Area-Prefix-LSA is originated by each router to describe the IPv6 address prefixes that are assigned to the router. The Intra-Area-Prefix-LSA is also sent by each router to describe the IPv6 address prefixes that are associated with an attached stub network segment or a transmit network segment. The Intra-Area-Prefix-LSA is flooded throughout the area.

The flooding scope of each type of LSA is summarized in Table 1-4.

1.6.4 LSA Formats

In this section we will describe the formats of the various types of LSAs. We first explain the detail of the Options that are part of the Link-LSAs, Network-LSAs, Router-LSAs, and Inter-Area-Router-LSAs, which indicate router capabilities such as whether an advertising OSPF router is capable of forwarding IPv6 transit traffic. We then discuss the detail of the Prefix Options field that is part of the Inter-Area-Prefix-LSA, the Intra-Area-Prefix-LSA, the AS-External-LSA and the Link-LSA. The LS Type field is another field with subcomponents and its structure is explained. Then the LSA Header is described followed by the descriptions on the individual LSAs.

Options

Figure 1-27 shows the format of the Options field.

The most relevant bits for this chapter are the R-bit and the V6-bit. The R-bit indicates whether an advertising router is an active router or not. The router will participate in the routing protocol but will not forward transit traffic if the R-bit is cleared. In this case routes that transit through the non-active router node cannot be computed. Otherwise the router is an active

FIGURE 1-27

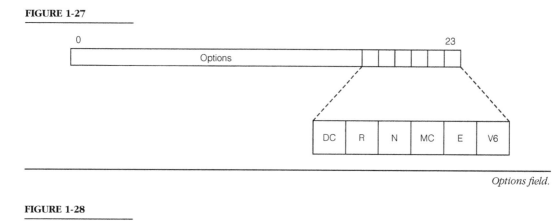

Options field.

FIGURE 1-28

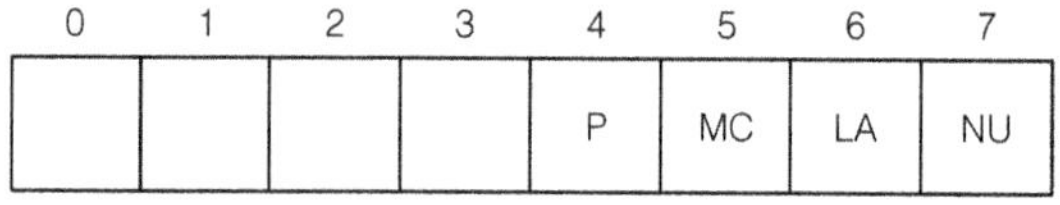

Prefix Options field.

router that both participates in the routing protocol and forwards the transit traffic. The V6-bit must be set in order for the router and its link to be included in the calculation. Both the R-bit and the V6-bit must be set in order for IPv6 transit packets to be forwarded through a particular router.

Prefix Options

Figure 1-28 shows the format of the Prefix Options field.

NU This bit is called the *no unicast* capability bit. When this bit is set, the given prefix should be excluded from IPv6 unicast calculation; otherwise the prefix should be included.

LA This bit is called the *local address* capability bit. The advertised prefix is an IPv6 address of the advertising router if this bit is set.

MC This bit is called the *multicast* capability bit. When this bit is set, the given prefix should be included in the IPv6 multicast routing calculation; otherwise the prefix should be excluded.

P This bit is called the *propagate* bit. The advertised prefix should be readvertised at the NSSA area border.

LS Type

Figure 1-29 shows the format of the LS Type field.

U This bit indicates how a router should handle LSAs with an unrecognized LSA function code. When this bit is 0, the LSAs are given link-local flooding scope. When this bit is set to 1, the LSAs are stored and flooded as if the function code is recognized.

FIGURE 1-29

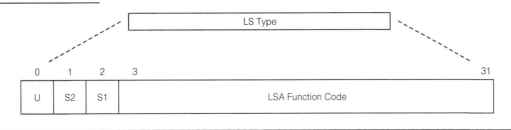

LS type field.

TABLE 1-5

Function code	LSA type	Description
1	0x2001	Router LSA
2	0x2002	Network LSA
3	0x2003	Inter-Area-Prefix LSA
4	0x2004	Inter-Area-Router LSA
5	0x4005	AS-External LSA
6	0x2006	Group-membership LSA (not discussed)
7	0x2007	Type-7 LSA (not discussed)
8	0x0008	Link LSA
9	0x2009	Intra-Area-Prefix LSA

LSA type.

<u>S2 S1</u> These two bits determine the flooding scope of the given LSA. The values of these two bits and the flood scope these bits represent are as follows:

0 0 link-local
0 1 area
1 0 AS
1 1 Reserved

The remaining bits of the LS Type field belong to the LSA function code. Table 1-5 outlines the LSA function code and the final LSA type.

LSA Header

Figure 1-30 shows the format of the LSA header.

<u>LS age</u> This 16-bit field specifies the time in seconds since the LSA was originated. The LS age field allows a router to identify an expired LSA that needs to be removed from the routing domain.

<u>LS type</u> This 16-bit field identifies the LSA type. This field is divided into the bit definition given in Figure 1-29.

FIGURE 1-30

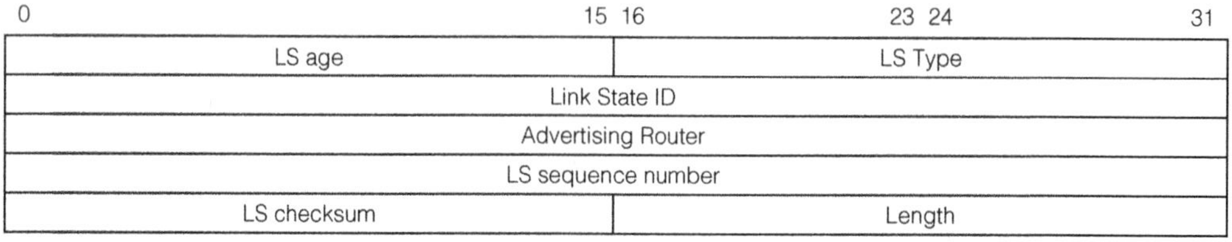

0	15 16	23 24	31
LS age		LS Type	
Link State ID			
Advertising Router			
LS sequence number			
LS checksum		Length	

LSA header.

Link State ID The combination of this field, the LS Type and the Advertising Router uniquely identifies an LSA in the LSDB.

Advertising Router This field specifies the router ID of the advertising router. The router ID is assigned to the OSPF router and uniquely identifies the router within the AS. A typical value used for router ID is an IPv4 address of an interface attached to the router.

LS sequence number This is a 32-bit signed integer that is used to detect old and duplicated instances of an LSA.

LS checksum This field holds the Fletcher checksum of the entire LSA packet, which includes the LSA header but excludes the LS age field. The Fletcher checksum is documented in [RFC905].

Length This field specifies the length of the entire LSA packet including the LSA header.

Router-LSA

Figure 1-31 shows the format of the Router-LSA.

W The W-bit is used by Multicast OSPF and is not discussed in this book.

V The V-bit identifies the advertising router as an endpoint of at least one virtual link over a transit area.

E The E-bit identifies the advertising router as an ASBR.

B The B-bit identifies the advertising router as an ABR.

Options This field describes the advertising router's capabilities. Figure 1-27 shows the structure of this field. The advertising router describes each of its active attached interfaces using the Type, Metric, Interface ID, Neighbor Interface ID, and the Neighbor Router ID fields. One set of these fields is used for each interface.

Type This field identifies the type of the interface. The values and the interface types these values represent are as follows:

    1 a point-to-point interface
    2 connection to a transit network
    3 reserved
    4 virtual link

FIGURE 1-31

0	3	4	7	8	15	16	17	18		31

```
0        3  4     7  8                    15 16 17 18                           31
┌──────────────────────────────────────┬──┬──┬──┬─────────────────────────────┐
│             LS age                    │ 0│ 0│ 1│              1              │
├──────────────────────────────────────┴──┴──┴──┴─────────────────────────────┤
│                              Link State ID                                   │
├──────────────────────────────────────────────────────────────────────────────┤
│                            Advertising Router                                │
├──────────────────────────────────────────────────────────────────────────────┤
│                           LS sequence number                                 │
├─────────────────────────────────────────┬───────────────────────────────────┤
│              LS checksum                 │              Length               │
├─────┬──┬──┬──┬──┬────────────────────────┼───────────────────────────────────┤
│  0  │ W│ V│ E│ B│                        │              Options              │
├─────┴──┴──┴──┴──┴────────────┬───────────┴───────────────────────────────────┤
│            Type              │     0          │            Metric            │
├──────────────────────────────┴────────────────┴──────────────────────────────┤
│                              Interface ID                                    │
├──────────────────────────────────────────────────────────────────────────────┤
│                          Neighbor Interface ID                               │
├──────────────────────────────────────────────────────────────────────────────┤
│                           Neighbor Router ID                                 │
├ ─ ─ ─ ─ ─ ─ ─ ─ ─ ─ ─ ─ ─ ─ ─ ─ ─ ─ ─ ─ ─ ─ ─ ─ ─ ─ ─ ─ ─ ─ ─ ─ ─ ─ ─ ─ ─ ┤
│                            ...    ...    ...                                  │
├ ─ ─ ─ ─ ─ ─ ─ ─ ─ ─ ─ ─ ─ ─ ─ ─ ─ ─ ─ ─ ─ ─ ─ ─ ─ ─ ─ ─ ─ ─ ─ ─ ─ ─ ─ ─ ─ ┤
│            Type              │     0          │            Metric            │
├──────────────────────────────┴────────────────┴──────────────────────────────┤
│                              Interface ID                                    │
├──────────────────────────────────────────────────────────────────────────────┤
│                          Neighbor Interface ID                               │
├──────────────────────────────────────────────────────────────────────────────┤
│                           Neighbor Router ID                                 │
└──────────────────────────────────────────────────────────────────────────────┘
```

Router-LSA.

Metric This field specifies the cost of using the described interface for outbound traffic.

Interface ID The interface ID is assigned by the advertising router, which uniquely identifies an interface within that router.

Neighbor Interface ID This field identifies the interface ID of the neighboring router that shares the same link as the advertising router. For a Type 2 interface the Neighbor Interface ID stores the interface ID of the DR on the transit network.

Neighbor Router ID This field contains the router ID of the neighboring router. For a Type 2 interface this router ID stores the router ID of the DR on the transit network. For Type 2 links, the combination of the Neighbor Interface ID and the Neighbor Router ID uniquely identifies the Network-LSA advertised for the attached link in the LSDB.

Network-LSA

Figure 1-32 shows the format of the Network-LSA.

The Network-LSA is advertised by a DR. All of the routers that are adjacent to the DR are included in the Network-LSA.

Options This field identifies the router capabilities described in Figure 1-27 (page 38).

Attached Router This field contains the router ID of the router that is adjacent to the DR.

FIGURE 1-32

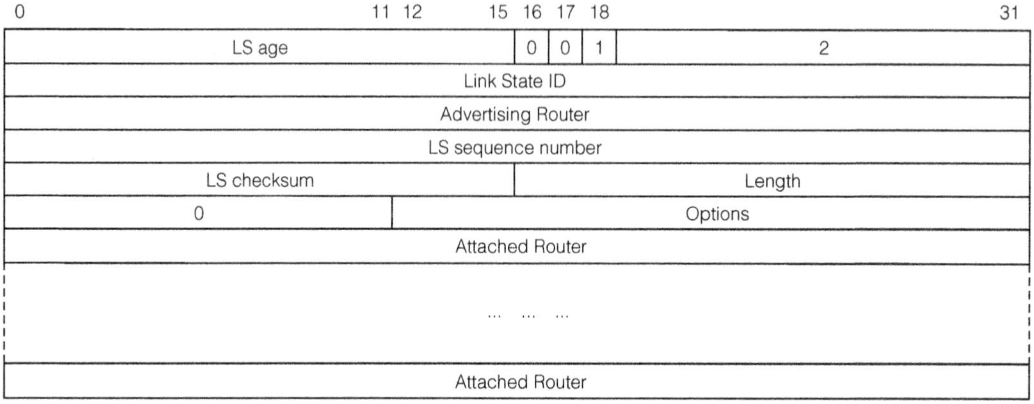

| 0 | 11 12 | 15 16 17 18 | 31 |

0	11 12	15 16 17 18			31
LS age			0	0	1	2

(table representation)

LS age		0	0	1	2
Link State ID					
Advertising Router					
LS sequence number					
LS checksum			Length		
0			Options		
Attached Router					
... ...					
Attached Router					

Network-LSA.

FIGURE 1-33

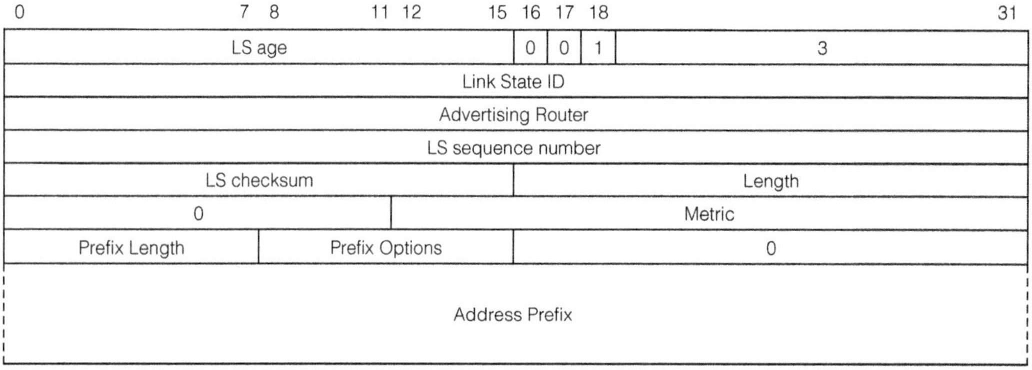

0	7 8	11 12	15 16 17 18	31
LS age			0 0 1	3
Link State ID				
Advertising Router				
LS sequence number				
LS checksum			Length	
0			Metric	
Prefix Length	Prefix Options		0	
Address Prefix				

Inter-Area-Prefix-LSA.

Inter-Area-Prefix-LSA

Figure 1-33 shows the format of the Inter-Area-Prefix-LSA.

<u>Metric</u> This field specifies the cost of the advertised route.

<u>Prefix Length</u> This field specifies the significant bits in the Address Prefix field.

<u>Prefix Options</u> This field is shown in Figure 1-28 (page 38).

<u>Address Prefix</u> This field contains the address prefix. Its size is determined by the Prefix Length rounded to the nearest 32-bit word.

FIGURE 1-34

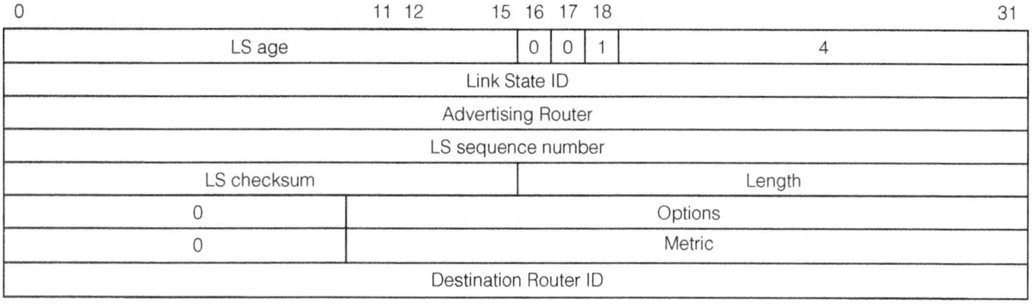

0	11 12	15 16 17 18	31

LS age	0	0	1	4
Link State ID					
Advertising Router					
LS sequence number					
LS checksum		Length		
0	Options			
0	Metric			
Destination Router ID					

Inter-Area-Router-LSA.

Inter-Area-Router-LSA

The Inter-Area-Router-LSA is generated by an ABR. Each Inter-Area-Router-LSA describes a single reachable ASBR in the external area.

Figure 1-34 shows the format of the Inter-Area-Router-LSA.

Options This field identifies the router capabilities shown in Figure 1-27 (page 38).

Metric This field specifies the cost of reaching the advertised router.

Destination Router ID This field specifies the router ID of the reachable router that is being described by the LSA.

AS-External-LSA

Figure 1-35 shows the format of the AS-External-LSA.

E The E-bit identifies the metric type. If the E-bit is not set, then the metric is a normal metric value having the same unit as the link-state metric. If the E-bit is set, then the metric is considered to be larger than the cost of any intra-AS path, which gives preference to intra-AS paths.

F If the F-bit is set, then the optional Forwarding Address field is set in the LSA.

T If the T-bit is set, then the optional External Route Tag field is set in the LSA.

Prefix Length, Prefix Options, Address Prefix These fields specify the reachable prefix that is imported from outside the AS. These fields have the same meaning as those for the Inter-Area-Prefix-LSA described in Figure 1-33.

Referenced LS Type This field, together with the Referenced Link State ID, and the Advertising Router field helps to associate another LSA that contains additional information about the external route with this LSA. If this field contains a non-zero value then the optional Referenced Link State ID is present in the LSA.

Forwarding Address This field, if present, holds the next hop address for the advertised external route. The unspecified address (::) is invalid for this field.

External Route Tag This field is typically used to help a router in identifying the origin of a route, but its full usage is outside the scope of this chapter.

FIGURE 1-35

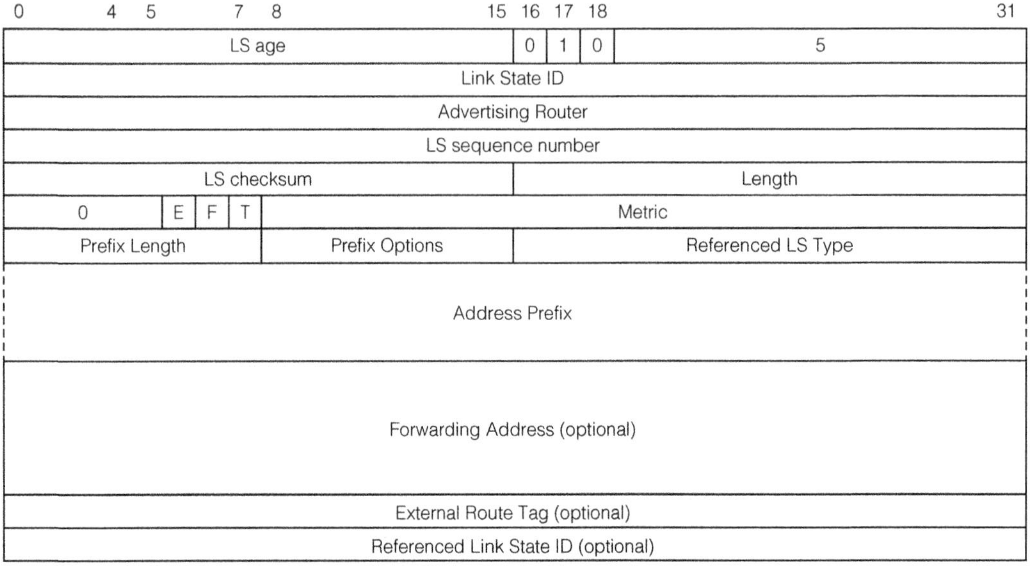

| 0 | 4 | 5 | 7 | 8 | 15 | 16 | 17 | 18 | 31 |

LS age						0	1	0	5
Link State ID									
Advertising Router									
LS sequence number									
LS checksum						Length			
0		E	F	T		Metric			
Prefix Length			Prefix Options			Referenced LS Type			
Address Prefix									
Forwarding Address (optional)									
External Route Tag (optional)									
Referenced Link State ID (optional)									

AS-External-LSA.

Referenced Link State ID This field, if present, along with other fields, helps to identify additional information concerning the advertised external route. However, this additional information is not used by OSPFv3.

Link-LSA

Figure 1-36 shows the format of the Link-LSA.

Router Priority This field specifies the router priority on the interface that is attached to the link being described by this LSA. The router priority is a configured value and it is configurable per interface.

Options This field contains the options that the advertising router would like to set in the Network-LSA to be advertised by the link's DR.

Link-local Interface Address This field contains the link-local address of the router's interface that is attached to the link being described by the LSA.

Number of Prefixes This field specifies the number of prefixes that are described by the LSA. Each prefix is described by one set of Prefix Length, Prefix Options and the Address Prefix.

Prefix Length, Prefix Options, Address Prefix These fields specify a prefix that is associated with the link that is being described by the LSA. These fields have the same meaning as those for the Inter-Area-Prefix-LSA described in Figure 1-33.

FIGURE 1-36

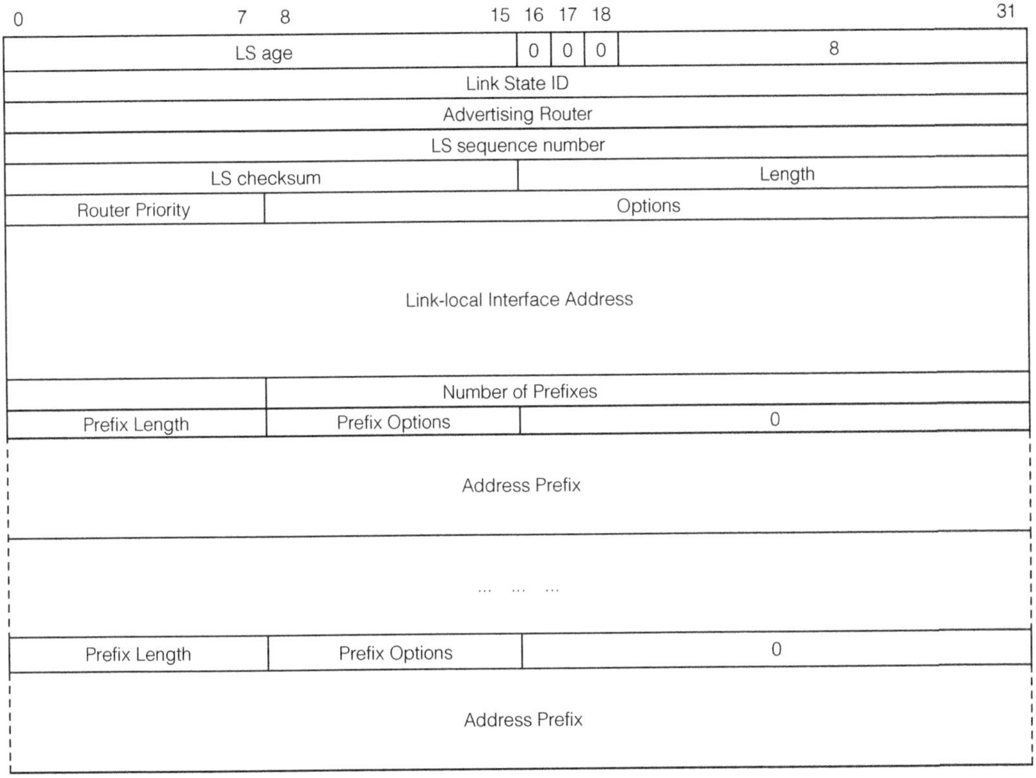

0	7	8	15 16 17 18	31

LS age	0	0	0	8

Link State ID

Advertising Router

LS sequence number

LS checksum	Length

Router Priority	Options

Link-local Interface Address

Number of Prefixes

Prefix Length	Prefix Options	0

Address Prefix

... ...

Prefix Length	Prefix Options	0

Address Prefix

Link-LSA.

Intra-Area-Prefix-LSA

Figure 1-37 shows the format of the Intra-Area-Prefix-LSA.

<u>Number of Prefixes</u> This field specifies the number of prefixes that are described by the LSA.

<u>Referenced LS Type, Referenced Link State ID, Referenced Advertising Router</u> These fields together identify the LSA (either a Router-LSA or a Network-LSA), which is associated with the advertised prefixes. The advertised prefixes are associated with a Router-LSA if the Referenced LS Type is 0x2001. In this case the Link state ID must be set to 0, and the Referenced Advertising Router field must be set to the router ID of the LSA's originating router. The advertised prefixes are associated with a Network-LSA if the Referenced LS Type is set to 0x2002. In this case the Referenced Link State ID field is set to the interface ID of the corresponding interface of the DR. The Referenced Advertising Router field is set to the DR's router ID.

<u>Prefix Length, Prefix Options, Address Prefix</u> These fields specify a prefix that is associated with the router, or one of its attached stub-network segments, or one of its attached

FIGURE 1-37

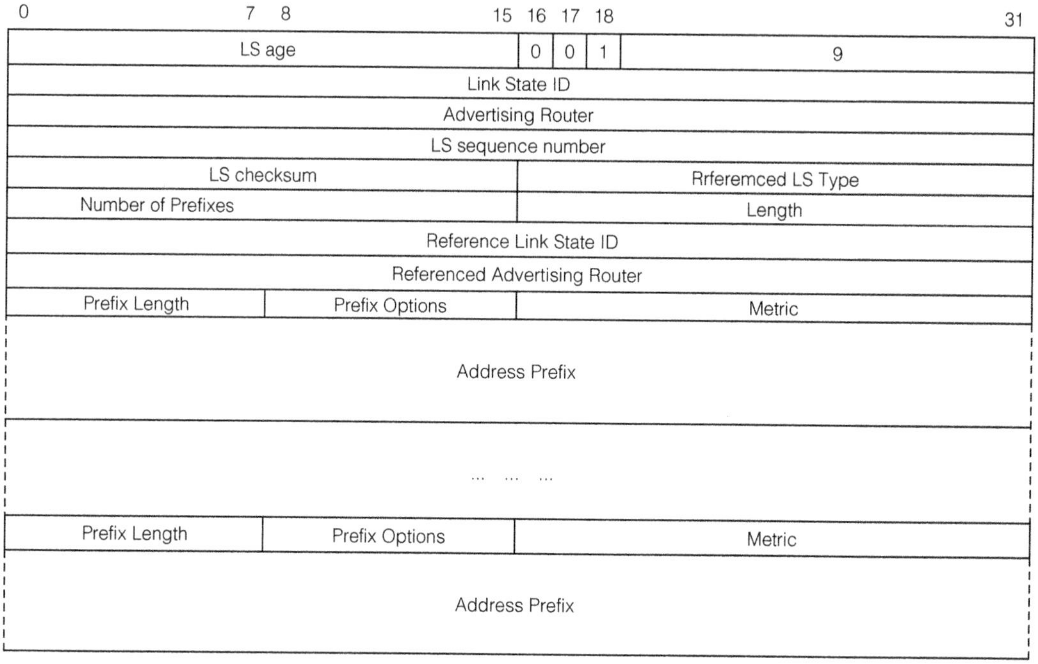

0	7	8	15	16	17	18		31
LS age				0	0	1	9	
Link State ID								
Advertising Router								
LS sequence number								
LS checksum				Rrferemced LS Type				
Number of Prefixes				Length				
Reference Link State ID								
Referenced Advertising Router								
Prefix Length		Prefix Options		Metric				
Address Prefix								
... ...								
Prefix Length		Prefix Options		Metric				
Address Prefix								

Intra-Area-Prefix-LSA.

transit network segments. These fields have the same meaning as those for the Inter-Area-Prefix-LSA described in Figure 1-33.

<u>Metric</u> This field specifies the cost of the advertised prefix.

1.6.5 OSPF Tree Construction and Route Computation

The OSPF LSAs allow each router to build a connected, directed graph that contains all of the reachable networks and nodes within the AS. Each graph node represents a network or a router. Once this graph is built, each router runs the *Dijkstra/Prim* algorithm to compute a minimum cost route to each possible destination network and node. At the completion of running the Dijkstra algorithm, the graph becomes a tree structure called a *shortest path tree* because the cost between any pair of tree nodes has the lowest cost out of all alternatives.

The Dijkstra algorithm belongs to a class of algorithms that are known as the *greedy algorithm* used to solve optimization problems. The *greedy* aspect comes from the fact that each step picks a local-optimal solution that may eventually lead to a global optimal solution. The reader is encouraged to read references such as [Baa88] for more discussion on the Dijkstra algorithm.

Figure 1-38 illustrates a network configuration that we will use to describe the creation of a shortest path tree from an LSDB. We will consider only the Router-LSA, Link-LSA, Intra-Area-Prefix-LSA, the Network-LSA, and AS-External-LSA to simplify the discussion. In the

FIGURE 1-38

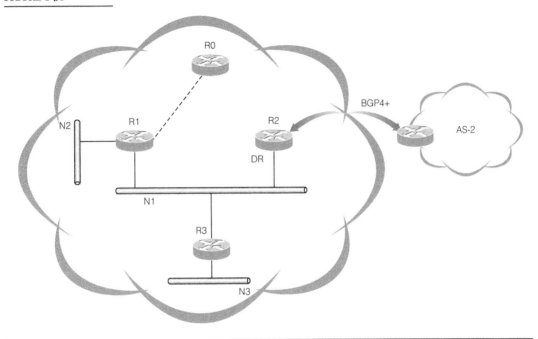

An example network configuration.

resulting tree, a reachable router and a network are represented by tree nodes, while the link between routers or the link between a router and a network is represented by an edge. These nodes and edges are described by the Router-LSAs, Intra-Area-Prefix-LSA, Link-LSAs and Network-LSAs, which are all maintained in the LSDB. We call a node that is already a part of the shortest path tree a *tree node*, while a node that is still in the LSDB and remains to be selected as a part of the tree we call a *fringe node*. The router that runs the Dijkstra algorithm begins by building the tree with itself as the first tree node. Then the algorithm runs an iterative process that:

Step 1. selects a minimum cost link between a tree node and a fringe node among all possible alternatives between this pair of nodes

Step 2. repeats the previous step until all fringe nodes have been selected and become tree nodes

Figure 1-39 illustrates router R0's view of the AS at the completion of the Dijkstra algorithm. As can be seen from this figure, once the shortest path tree is obtained, the router has the complete path to each possible destination of the AS, although the routing table contains only the first hop of each path. Also shown in the figure are some of the LSAs that generated the tree nodes.

Router R0 builds the tree by adding itself first into an empty tree. R1's Router-LSA allows R0 to add R1 into the tree. The link type and the cost of the link are identified by the Link-LSA, which is represented by the edge between the two nodes labeled R0 and R1 in the figure. Inside R1's Router-LSA, the Neighbor Interface ID and the Neighbor Router ID allow R0 to identify R2's Network-LSA from the LSDB regarding network N1. Note R2 is the DR for N1 and thus R2 generates the Network-LSA. From this Network-LSA, R0 can subsequently add routers R2 and R3 into the tree. Once R2 is inserted into the tree, R0 can identify and retrieve R2's AS-External-LSA and adds the referenced prefix (an external network) into the tree. Once R3 is inserted into the tree, R0 can identify R3's Intra-Area-Prefix-LSA and adds the referenced prefix (a subnetwork N3) into the tree as a reachable node.

Each edge in this graph has a weight or cost associated with it. For example, the cost of the edge between R1 and N2 is the metric value advertised by the Intra-Area-Prefix-LSA. The cost between R1 and network N1 is specified by the metric value of the interface advertised by R1's Router-LSA.

Figure 1-39 and its description illustrates only a simple example for the purpose of explaining the shortest path tree concept in the context of OSPFv3. In reality, for example, when R0 adds R2

FIGURE 1-39

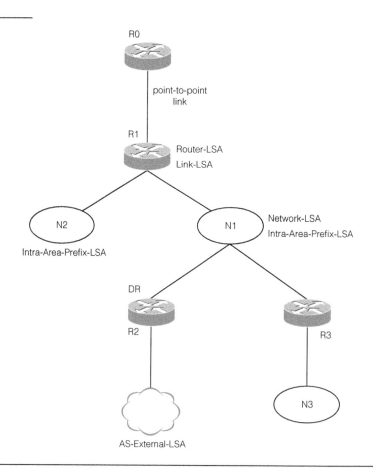

A representation of a shortest path tree.

into the tree, it must examine multiple LSAs from the LSDB and consider all of the possibilities of reaching R2. R0 then chooses the minimum cost path between itself and R2. This path, which includes nodes (routers and networks) and edges (various links), is inserted along with R2 into the shortest path tree. This minimum cost is the sum of the costs of the edges between R0 and R2.

After completing the shortest path tree, R0 will use the link-local address of R1 as advertised in its Link-LSA as the next hop to reach the networks N1 and N2, the routers R2 and R3, and the external network. R3 will use the link-local address of R2 as advertised in its Link-LSA as the next hop to reach the external network.

1.7 Code Introduction

In BSD systems the Routing Information Base (RIB) is maintained in a user process called a *routing daemon* while the Forwarding Information Base (FIB) is stored in the kernel routing table. The routing daemon builds its RIB through routing information exchanges with other routers, and communicates with the kernel via a special type of socket named a *routing socket* so that the RIB and FIB are consistent. Some routing daemons also use a supplemental `sysctl()` interface to get access to the FIB and other kernel internal information. Packet forwarding is performed in the kernel network protocol stack, referring to the FIB, as explained in Chapter 3 of *IPv6 Core Protocols Implementation* ("Internet Protocol version 6"); the routing daemon is not involved in this process. Figure 1-40 summarizes the overall implementation architecture.

The succeeding sections provide the KAME and FreeBSD implementation of some of the components shown in Figure 1-40 in more detail, focusing on IPv6-related topics. Section 1.8 describes IPv6 route entries in the kernel routing table; Section 1.9 explains how the routing socket and `sysctl()` interface can be used to deal with IPv6 routing information through

FIGURE 1-40

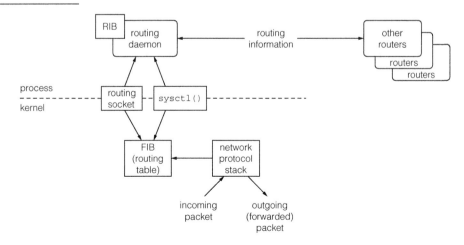

Overall implementation architecture for routing and forwarding.

TABLE 1-6

File	*Description*
`${KAME}/freebsd4/usr.bin/netstat/route.c`	The `netstat` command implementation
`${KAME}/freebsd4/sys/net/route.h`	Routing table and message structure
`${KAME}/kame/kame/route6d/route6d.c`	The **route6d** daemon implementation
`${KAME}/kame/kame/route6d/route6d.h`	Internal definitions for **route6d**
`rtadd6.c`	A sample program to install IPv6 route entry

Files discussed in this chapter.

code examples; finally, Sections 1.10 through 1.13 detail KAME's **route6d** implementation, a simple example of the RIPng routing daemon. This set of descriptions will provide a solid base for developing IPv6 routing applications. The program files listed in Table 1-6 are covered in this chapter.

1.8   IPv6 Routing Table in the BSD Kernel

Consider the simple network topology depicted in Figure 1-41. Of our particular interest is the FreeBSD IPv6 router, which connects two Ethernet links with interfaces ne0 and ne1. The other router on the link attached to interface ne0, whose link-local address is `fe80::1`, connects the

FIGURE 1-41

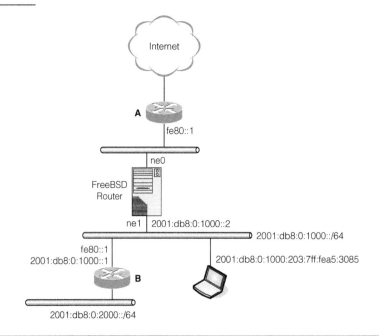

Sample network for routing example.

entire example network to the Internet, and provides the default route for the FreeBSD router. On the other hand, the link attached to ne1 has a global IPv6 prefix, `2001:db8:0:1000::/64`. There is another router on that link whose link-local address is also `fe80::1`, the gateway to a different subnet of `2001:db8:0:2000::/64`. Even though the two additional routers have the same link-local address, there is no conflict since these are in different links.

Assume the FreeBSD router has enough routes to reach all the visible networks in Figure 1-41. Then it should have IPv6 routing entries as shown in Listing 1-1.

Listing 1-1
── IPv6 routing table shown by the **netstat** program.

```
% netstat -rn -f inet6

Routing tables

Internet6:
Destination                          Gateway              Flags    Netif Expire
default                              fe80::1%ne0          UGc      ne0
2001:db8:0:1000::/64                 link#2               UC       ne1
2001:db8:0:1000::2                   00:03:47:a5:32:57    UHL      lo0
2001:db8:0:1000::1                   00:00:87:68:41:31    UHLW     ne1
2001:db8:0:1000:203:47ff:fea5:3085   00:03:47:a5:30:85    UHLW     ne1
2001:db8:0:2000::/64                 fe80::1%ne1          UGc      ne1
fe80::%ne0/64                        link#1               UC       ne0
fe80::1%ne0                          00:20:ed:20:83:3a    UHLW     ne0
fe80::%ne1/64                        link#2               UC       ne1
fe80::1%ne1                          00:00:87:68:41:31    UHLW     ne1
...
```
── IPv6 routing table shown by the **netstat** program.

The default route and the route to `2001:db8:0:2000::/64` are indirect routes, which have the *gateway flag* (G), and are likely to be learned from the other routers via some routing protocol. Notice that the gateway addresses are differentiated with the appropriate link zone index, as represented by the extended format with the percent character (e.g., `%ne0`). As can be seen in this example, the gateway address of an IPv6 indirect route is usually a link-local address, since all interior routing protocols for IPv6 use link-local addresses for exchanging routes with adjacent routers and those addresses are often used as the gateway address; refer to Section 1.4.2 for RIPng and to Section 1.6.5 for OSPFv3.

Other network routes are direct routes to an interface and have the *cloning flag* (C). Specific routes under the direct routes are cloned as necessary, and store the corresponding link-layer address as the gateway. Those routes also specify Neighbor Cache entries in terms of IPv6 (see also Chapter 5 of *IPv6 Core Protocols Implementation*, "Neighbor Discovery and Stateless Address Autoconfiguration"). An example of such routes is the one for `2001:db8:0:1000:203:47ff:fea5:3085`. The specific host route to this router's own global address, `2001:db8:0:1000::2`, is an exception in that the outgoing interface is a loopback interface (lo0) and does not have the *cloned flag* (W); it is automatically generated when the address is configured as explained in Chapter 2 of the *Core Protocols* book.

In the kernel, each routing entry is represented as an `rtentry{}` structure, which is defined in the `route.h` header file. Figure 1-42 depicts major members of this structure corresponding to some characteristic entries in Listing 1-1. The first entry is an example of an indirect route for `2001:db8:0:2000::/64`. The middle entry is a direct route for `fe80::%ne1/64`. Finally, the last entry is the route for `fe80::1%ne1`, cloned from the middle entry.

As one might notice, the link index of a link-local destination or gateway is represented differently. This will be explained in more detail in Section 1.8.1.

The set of `rt_key` and `rt_mask` (which are actually function macros taking `rtentry{}` and returning pointers to `sockaddr{}` structures) defines a single IPv6 prefix and acts as a *key* in the routing table. In the BSD's routing table, a network prefix is always defined as a set of an address and network mask. This also applies to IPv6 even though IPv6 does not support the notion of general network masks, especially non-contiguous ones, as explained in Chapter 2 of the *Core Protocols* book. For example, a prefix length of 64 bits is represented as an IPv6 address `ffff:ffff:ffff:ffff:0000:0000:0000:0000` as shown in Figure 1-42. In the actual routing table, some trailing parts of a network mask are often redundant and truncated. For instance, in order to represent prefix "/64", it suffices to have the non-zero fields of the

FIGURE 1-42

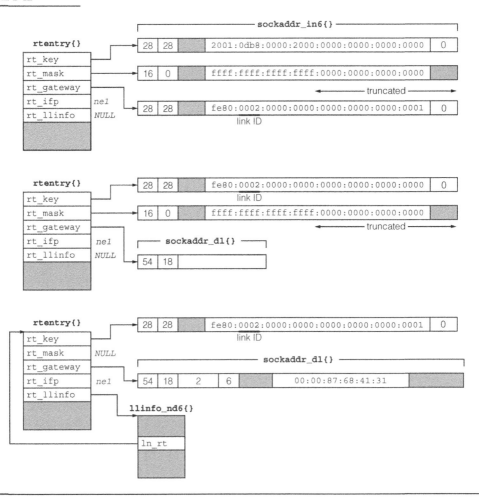

Structures of routing table entries for Listing 1-1.

`sin6_addr` member, assuming the rest of the structure is all zero. Examples in Figure 1-42 show the truncated form.

The `rt_mask` member is NULL for host routes (ones that have the "H" flag set in Listing 1-1). In Figure 1-42, the last entry is an example of this case.

The `rt_gateway` member is a pointer to a `sockaddr{}` structure, which specifies the next hop of this entry. As mentioned above, this can be a link-layer `sockaddr{}` structure, in which case this entry usually associates with a Neighbor Cache entry via the `rt_llinfo` member (see Chapter 5 of the *Core Protocols* book). Additionally, the `rt_gateway` member points to a `sockaddr_dl{}` structure which stores the Ethernet address of the destination.

The `rt_ifp` member is a pointer to an `ifnet{}` structure, specifying the outgoing interface to the next hop.

1.8.1 Scope Zone Representation in the Routing Table

Notice that the link index(*) of link-local addresses in Figure 1-42 is embedded in the 128-bit address field. For example, link-local address `fe80::1%ne1` in Listing 1-1 is represented as `fe80:2::1` in Figure 1-42. Since link-local addresses may not be unique on different links and the single routing table must contain all the possibly ambiguous addresses, it is necessary to specify the associated link of a link-local address in the routing table in some way. In theory, this could be done using the dedicated `sin6_scope_id` field because the BSD's routing table can generally handle addresses with `sockaddr{}` structures, but the KAME implementation uses this odd form because of historical and compatibility reasons as explained in Chapter 2 of the *Core Protocols* book.

(*) The KAME implementation assumes a one-to-one mapping between links and interfaces whereas links are larger in scope than interfaces from a pure architectural point of view [RFC4007]. This assumption allows link indices to be represented as interface identifiers of the outgoing interface. In the example routing table shown in Listing 1-1, the interface index is represented as in `link#1`, where 1 is the index.

The *Core Protocols* book explained that some special applications need to interpret the embedded form of addresses. Routing daemons, which generally handle addresses passed from a routing socket (see Section 1.9.1), are a common example of such applications. They also need to embed the appropriate scope zone index in an address before passing it to the kernel through a routing socket. Another class of applications that suffers from the embedded format is one that directly refers to the kernel memory in order to manage the kernel routing table or interface address structures, such as the **netstat** program.

Figure 1-43 is a copy of the figure shown in the *Core Protocols* book, highlighting the main applications discussed in this section: routing and management applications. It should be noted that a routing application usually also acts as a "normal application" when it sends or receives routing messages via an `AF_INET6` socket. In addition, it often uses the source address of an inbound routing message as a next hop to some destination and installs the corresponding routing message in the kernel via a routing socket. This means the application needs to convert the standard form of address into the embedded form by themselves.

FIGURE 1-43

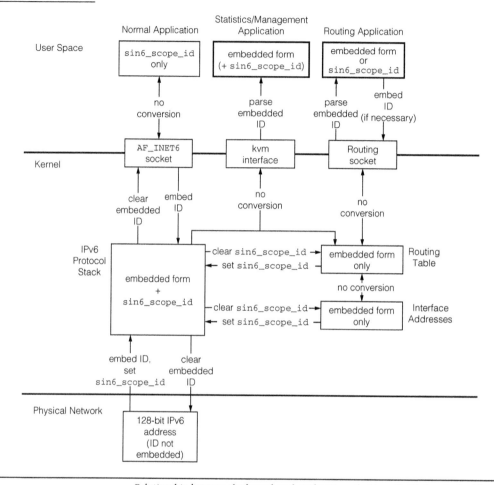

Relationship between the kernel and applications that handle IPv6 scoped addresses.

One may notice that the actual output from **netstat** hides the embedded form of link-local addresses from users as shown in Listing 1-1. This is because the program applies a special filter to IPv6 addresses of some narrower scopes before printing those addresses.

Listing 1-2 shows this filter. If the specified address has the link-local or interface-local scope(*), the 128-bit IPv6 address is in the kernel internal form, embedding the scope zone index as a 16-bit integer in its third and fourth bytes. Lines 584 and 585 extract the embedded index, copy it to the `sin6_scope_id` field, and clear the embedded value. Later, separate routines will call the `getnameinfo()` function, which converts the scoped address into a textual representation using the extended notation (see Chapter 7 of **IPv6** *Core Protocols Implementation*, "Socket API Extensions").

(*) The interface-local scope was previously called node-local, which was renamed in [RFC3513]. Unfortunately, the standard API does not catch up to this change, so portable applications need to keep using the old terminology.

Listing 1-2

route.c

```
571            case AF_INET6:
572                {
573                    struct sockaddr_in6 *sa6 = (struct sockaddr_in6 *)sa;
574                    struct in6_addr *in6 = &sa6->sin6_addr;
575
576                    /*
577                     * XXX: This is a special workaround for KAME kernels.
578                     * sin6_scope_id field of SA should be set in the future.
579                     */
580                    if (IN6_IS_ADDR_LINKLOCAL(in6) ||
581                        IN6_IS_ADDR_MC_LINKLOCAL(in6) ||
582                        IN6_IS_ADDR_MC_NODELOCAL(in6)) {
583                        /* XXX: override is ok? */
584                        sa6->sin6_scope_id = (u_int32_t)ntohs(*(u_short *)&
     in6->s6_addr[2]);
585                        *(u_short *)&in6->s6_addr[2] = 0;
586                    }
587
588                    if (flags & RTF_HOST)
589                        cp = routename6(sa6);
590                    else if (mask)
591                        cp = netname6(sa6,
592                                      &((struct sockaddr_in6 *)mask)->sin6_addr);
593                    else {
594                        cp = netname6(sa6, NULL);
595                    }
596                    break;
597                }
```

route.c

— Line 584 is broken here for layout reasons. However, it is a single line of code.

As detailed in the *Core Protocols* book, such a workaround is a bad practice; applications should not care about the kernel-specific details for many reasons. It complicates application programs and can easily be a source of bugs. Despite those defects, this is something that such special application programs must endure as a matter of fact.

1.9   Routing API

There are two major interfaces for BSD variants to get access to the kernel routing table. One is through a generic *routing socket*, and the other is via the `sysctl()` library function.

1.9.1   Routing Sockets

A routing socket is a generic socket interface to the kernel's routing table. Via a routing socket, an application can add or delete a routing table entry, modify an existing entry, or get the entry that would be used for a given destination.

An application and the kernel communicate messages over a routing socket, which begin with common header fields, followed by specific information depending on the message type. From the unicast routing perspective, the most important messages are routing messages, which consist of a fixed format header structure followed by a set of socket address structures. The header of a routing message is the `rt_msghdr{}` structure, whose definition is shown in Listing 1-3.

Listing 1-3

```
                                                                                route.h
168    struct rt_msghdr {
169            u_short    rtm_msglen;     /* to skip over non-understood messages */
170            u_char     rtm_version;    /* future binary compatibility */
171            u_char     rtm_type;       /* message type */
172            u_short    rtm_index;      /* index for associated ifp */
173            int        rtm_flags;      /* flags, incl. kern & message, e.g. DONE */
174            int        rtm_addrs;      /* bitmask identifying sockaddrs in msg */
175            pid_t      rtm_pid;        /* identify sender */
176            int        rtm_seq;        /* for sender to identify action */
177            int        rtm_errno;      /* why failed */
178            int        rtm_use;        /* from rtentry */
179            u_long     rtm_inits;      /* which metrics we are initializing */
180            struct     rt_metrics rtm_rmx; /* metrics themselves */
181    };
                                                                                route.h
```

The first three members are common to all messages communicated over a routing socket. The `rtm_type` member uniquely identifies the purpose of the message. Two message types are particularly important for unicast routing: RTM_ADD for adding a new routing entry to the kernel, and RTM_DELETE for deleting an existing routing entry from the kernel.

Another important member is `rtm_addrs`, which specifies which types of addresses are to follow the `rt_msghdr{}` structure. This is a flag bit field as commented. The flags shown in Table 1-7 are commonly used for unicast routing purposes. Among those, RTA_NETMASK and (when present) RTA_DST define a specific prefix, the key of the corresponding routing entry.

In this subsection we show a complete example application that installs an IPv6 routing entry using a routing socket. This is essentially the same as the `addroute()` function of the **route6d** program, but we use a separate program here as a complete template for any IPv6 routing application.

TABLE 1-7

Flag name	*Description*
RTA_DST	destination address
RTA_GATEWAY	gateway address
RTA_IFA	associated interface address
RTA_IFP	outgoing interface
RTA_NETMASK	network mask for the destination

Routing message flags used in this chapter.

This program, which we call **rtadd6**, takes two command-line arguments. The first one is an IPv6 address or prefix, the key of the routing entry. The second argument is the gateway IPv6 address for this entry. As indicated in Listing 1-1 (page 51), the second argument is usually a link-local IPv6 address. And, in this case, the link identifier must be uniquely specified using the extended textual format as defined in [RFC4007].

For example, the execution

```
# rtadd6 2001:db8:1234::/48 fe80::1%ne0
```

will create a new routing entry for prefix `2001:db8:1234::/48` with the gateway address of `fe80::1` on the link attached to interface ne0. Note that **rtadd6** requires super-user privilege.

Then the **netstat** output will contain the following line:

```
Destination                Gateway                  Flags    Netif
...
2001:db8:1234::/48         fe80::1%ne0              UGc      ne0
```

Main Function of rtadd6

The following listings cover the entire source code of the **rtadd6** program. We begin with the main function of **rtadd6**, which is located at the lower part of the source file, `rtadd6.c`.

Open Routing Socket

Listing 1-4

———`rtadd6.c`
```
56   int
57   main(int argc, char *argv[])
58   {
59           int s, error, len;
60           int plen = -1;
61           int rtflags = RTF_UP | RTF_GATEWAY;
62           int rtaddrs = RTA_DST | RTA_GATEWAY;
63           char *p, buf[512];
64           struct sockaddr_in6 dst, gw, mask, *sin6;
65           struct addrinfo hints, *res;
66           struct rt_msghdr *rtm;
67
68           if (argc < 2) {
69                   fprintf(stderr, "usage: rtadd6 destination gateway\n");
70                   exit(1);
71           }
72
73           s = socket(PF_ROUTE, SOCK_RAW, 0);
74           if (s < 0) {
75                   perror("socket");
76                   exit(1);
77           }
```
———`rtadd6.c`

59–66 The `rtflags` and `rtaddrs` variables are initialized with the default settings for the `rtm_flags` and `rtm_addrs` members of the `rt_msghdr{}` structure. This program always specifies the destination address and the gateway, and the corresponding flags are set by default. `RTF_UP` is specified just in case and is actually not necessary; the kernel will automatically set this flag when creating a new entry.

Buffer buf is a placeholder for the routing message. The buffer size (512 bytes) is an arbitrary choice, but is in fact more than enough for the purpose here.

73–77 A routing socket is created as a raw protocol interface.

Parse Destination and Gateway Addresses

Listing 1-5

```
                                                                                ── rtadd6.c
 79         p = strchr(argv[1], '/');
 80         if (p != NULL) {
 81                 *p++ = '\0';
 82                 plen = atoi(p);
 83                 if (plen < 0 || plen > 128) {
 84                         fprintf(stderr,
 85                                 "prefix length is out of range: %s\n", p);
 86                         exit(1);
 87                 }
 88                 plen2mask(plen, &mask);
 89                 rtaddrs |= RTA_NETMASK;
 90         } else
 91                 rtflags |= RTF_HOST;
 92
 93         memset(&hints, 0, sizeof(hints));
 94         hints.ai_family = AF_INET6;
 95         hints.ai_socktype = SOCK_DGRAM;
 96         hints.ai_flags = AI_NUMERICHOST;
 97
 98         error = getaddrinfo(argv[1], NULL, &hints, &res);
 99         if (error != 0) {
100                 fprintf(stderr, "getaddrinfo(%s): %s\n", argv[1],
101                         gai_strerror(error));
102                 exit(1);
103         }
104         dst = *(struct sockaddr_in6 *)res->ai_addr;
105         freeaddrinfo(res);
106
107         error = getaddrinfo(argv[2], NULL, &hints, &res);
108         if (error != 0) {
109                 fprintf(stderr, "getaddrinfo(%s): %s\n", argv[2],
110                         gai_strerror(error));
111                 exit(1);
112         }
113         gw = *(struct sockaddr_in6 *)res->ai_addr;
114         freeaddrinfo(res);
                                                                                ── rtadd6.c
```

79–89 If the first argument to this program contains a "slash," it should be an IPv6 prefix; otherwise it is an IPv6 address. In the former case, the plen2mask() function converts the prefix length (which should follow the slash character) into the corresponding network mask and stores it to variable mask as an IPv6 socket address structure. The RTA_NETMASK bit is set in rtaddrs.

90–91 If the first argument does not contain a "slash," this is a host route, and the RTF_HOST flag is set in rtflags.

98–114 The destination address (which might be the address part of a prefix) and the gateway address are converted to IPv6 socket address structures by the getaddrinfo() library function. If any of the addresses is a link-local address represented in the extended format, getaddrinfo() will interpret it and set the sin6_scope_id member of the resulting socket address structure to the corresponding link index (see Chapter 7 of *IPv6 Core Protocols Implementation*).

Prepare and Send Routing Message

Listing 1-6

```
                                                                      rtadd6.c
116          memset(buf, 0, sizeof(buf));
117          rtm = (struct rt_msghdr *)buf;
118          rtm->rtm_type = RTM_ADD;
119          rtm->rtm_version = RTM_VERSION;
120          rtm->rtm_seq = 0;
121          rtm->rtm_pid = getpid();
122          rtm->rtm_flags = rtflags;
123          rtm->rtm_addrs = rtaddrs;
124
125          sin6 = (struct sockaddr_in6 *)(rtm + 1);
126
127          *sin6 = dst;
128          convertscope(sin6);
129          sin6 = (struct sockaddr_in6 *)((char *)sin6 + ROUNDUP(sizeof(*sin6)));
130
131          *sin6 = gw;
132          convertscope(sin6);
133          sin6 = (struct sockaddr_in6 *)((char *)sin6 + ROUNDUP(sizeof(*sin6)));
134
135          if ((rtaddrs & RTA_NETMASK) != 0) {
136                  *sin6 = mask;
137                  sin6 = (struct sockaddr_in6 *)((char *)sin6 +
138                      ROUNDUP(sizeof(*sin6)));
139          }
140
141          len = (char *)sin6 - buf;
142          rtm->rtm_msglen = len;
143
144          if (write(s, buf, len) < 0) {
145                  perror("write");
146                  exit(1);
147          }
148
149          close(s);
150
151          exit(0);
152  }
                                                                      rtadd6.c
```

116–123 The base `rt_msghdr{}` structure is initialized. Since this program is adding a new routing entry, the message type (`rtm_type`) is RTM_ADD. The `rtm_seq` and `rtm_pid` members do not actually have any effect on this program, but are initialized appropriately just in case. The `rtm_flags` and `rtm_addrs` members are set to the values as preset above.

125–129 The `sin6` variable points to the end of the `rt_msghdr{}` structure (with appropriate padding so that the pointer is naturally aligned, when necessary). The destination address stored in variable `dst` is copied there. The `convertscope()` function is then called in case the address is a link-local address, in which case it should be converted into the kernel internal form (as shown in Figure 1-42). Finally, variable `sin6` is adjusted so that it points to the end of the socket address structure just filled in. ROUNDUP() is a macro function that adds necessary padding so that the resulting pointer is aligned at the natural boundary, defined as follows:

```
#define ROUNDUP(a) (1 + (((a) - 1) | (sizeof(long) - 1)))
```

For a 32-bit machine architecture, this is actually a no-operation, since the size of the `sockaddr_in6{}` structure (28 bytes) is a multiple of 32 bits.

131–133 Likewise, the gateway address is copied in the succeeding region of the buffer, and the `convertscope()` function makes possible adjustment for link-local addresses.

135–139 If the network mask is to be specified, `mask` is copied after the gateway address. Since there is no ambiguity about scope zones for a network mask, `convertscope()` need not be called here.

Figure 1-44 shows the buffer content after building the `rt_msghdr{}` structure and all the necessary address structures for the execution example shown above. Notice that the link-local address of the gateway embeds the link index (assuming it is 1 here) in the address field, while we specified the address in the standard format per [RFC4007]. The `convertscope()` function performed the conversion.

141–147 The `rtm_msglen` member is set to the total length of the message, and the message is written to the routing socket. The kernel will first check whether a routing entry for the specified destination exists, and will create a new one with the specified gateway if not. Otherwise, the `write()` system call will fail with the error of `EEXIST`. For example, if we execute this program with the same arguments as above two times, the second execution will fail as follows:

```
# rtadd6 2001:db8:1234::/48 fe80::1%ne0
write: File exists
```

A careful implementation may thus want to separate this particular error from other general errors (in fact, the **route6d** program does that).

FIGURE 1-44

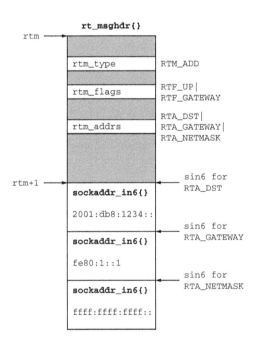

Routing message for adding a route entry via a routing socket.

`plen2mask()` Function

The `plen2mask()` function (Listing 1-7) is a subroutine called from the main part of the **rtadd6** program. This function performs the straightforward conversion from an IPv6 prefix length to the corresponding bit mask.

Listing 1-7

```
                                                                          rtadd6.c
17    static void
18    plen2mask(int plen, struct sockaddr_in6 *mask)
19    {
20            u_char *p;
21            u_char pl2m[9] = {0x00, 0x80, 0xc0, 0xe0,
22                              0xf0, 0xf8, 0xfc, 0xfe, 0xff};
23            int i;
24
25            memset(mask, 0, sizeof(*mask));
26            mask->sin6_family = AF_INET6;
27            mask->sin6_len = sizeof(*mask);
28
29            p = (u_char *)&mask->sin6_addr;
30            for (i = 0; i < 16; i++, p++, plen -= 8) {
31                    if (plen >= 8) {
32                            *p = 0xff;
33                            continue;
34                    }
35                    *p = pl2m[plen];
36                    break;
37            }
38    }
                                                                          rtadd6.c
```

`convertscope()` Function

The `convertscope()` function (Listing 1-8) is one of the most tricky parts of IPv6 routing programs on BSD variants. If the `sin6_scope_id` field of the given `sockaddr_in6{}` structure is non-zero, this function embeds this value as a 16-bit integer in network byte order into the third and fourth bytes of the `sin6_addr` field(*). The `sin6_scope_id` field is then cleared with 0. As emphasized in Section 1.8.1, and as commented in the code, this is a bad practice for many reasons. Unfortunately, this is an inevitable workaround for any applications that perform IPv6 routing via a routing socket on BSD variant systems.

> (*) Since the `sin6_scope_id` field is a 32-bit integer, this conversion may result in an overflow. The error handling is omitted for brevity, but a careful implementation should catch the case. This is another reason why this conversion is a bad practice.

Listing 1-8

```
                                                                          rtadd6.c
40    static void
41    convertscope(struct sockaddr_in6 *sin6)
42    {
43            u_int16_t id16;
44
45            if (sin6->sin6_scope_id != 0) {
46                    /*
```

```
47                      * XXX: yes, this is UGLY, but is a necessary evil for the BSD
48                      * kernel.
49                      */
50                     id16 = htons((u_int16_t)sin6->sin6_scope_id);
51                     memcpy(&sin6->sin6_addr.s6_addr[2], &id16, sizeof(id16));
52                     sin6->sin6_scope_id = 0;
53              }
54      }
```

——— rtadd6.c

1.9.2   Dumping Routing Table via `sysctl()`

The `sysctl` interface provides access to various types of system information maintained in the
kernel. For example, with `sysctl` we can dump the entire kernel routing table.

Some network applications in fact use this interface. In particular, routing daemons such as
route6d, **Quagga** (http://quagga.net/) and **xorp** (http://www.xorp.org/) are common users of
this API. They use `sysctl` to synchronize their internal state with the forwarding information
in the kernel (i.e., FIB).

Listing 1-9 is a code segment of the **route6d** program, which is a typical usage example of
dumping the kernel routing table.

Listing 1-9

——— route6d.c

```
2501    void
2502    krtread(again)
2503            int again;
2504    {
2505            int mib[6];
2506            size_t msize;
2507            char *buf, *p, *lim;
2508            struct rt_msghdr *rtm;
2509            int retry;
2510            const char *errmsg;
2511
2512            retry = 0;
2513            buf = NULL;
2514            mib[0] = CTL_NET;
2515            mib[1] = PF_ROUTE;
2516            mib[2] = 0;
2517            mib[3] = AF_INET6;          /* Address family */
2518            mib[4] = NET_RT_DUMP;       /* Dump the kernel routing table */
2519            mib[5] = 0;                 /* No flags */
2520            do {
2521                    retry++;
2522                    errmsg = NULL;
2523                    if (buf)
2524                            free(buf);
2525                    if (sysctl(mib, 6, NULL, &msize, NULL, 0) < 0) {
2526                            errmsg = "sysctl estimate";
2527                            continue;
2528                    }
2529                    if ((buf = malloc(msize)) == NULL) {
2530                            errmsg = "malloc";
2531                            continue;
2532                    }
2533                    if (sysctl(mib, 6, buf, &msize, NULL, 0) < 0) {
2534                            errmsg = "sysctl NET_RT_DUMP";
2535                            continue;
```

```
2536                         }
2537                 } while (retry < 5 && errmsg != NULL);
2538                 if (errmsg) {
2539                         fatal("%s (with %d retries, msize=%lu)", errmsg, retry,
2540                             (u_long)msize);
2541                         /*NOTREACHED*/
2542                 } else if (1 < retry)
2543                         syslog(LOG_INFO, "NET_RT_DUMP %d retires", retry);
2544
2545                 lim = buf + msize;
2546                 for (p = buf; p < lim; p += rtm->rtm_msglen) {
2547                         rtm = (struct rt_msghdr *)p;
2548                         rt_entry(rtm, again);
2549                 }
2550                 free(buf);
2551     }
```
                                                                            ——— route6d.c

2514–2519 To dump the routing table, the NET_RT_DUMP sysctl name is specified at the fifth level (mib[4]) under the CTL_NET/PF_ROUTE level (mib[0] and mib[1]). By specifying AF_INET6 for mib[3], **route6d** tells the kernel that it only needs IPv6 routing table entries.

2520–2537 The sysctl() library function must normally be called at least twice. The third argument for the first call (line 2525) is NULL, indicating the caller only wants to estimate the necessary buffer length, which is stored in variable msize. A buffer of that size is allocated, then the second call to sysctl() (line 2533) with the allocated buffer copies the routing table into the buffer. Since there can be a change to the routing table between those two calls, although atypical, the second call can fail. Unfortunately, there is no guaranteed way to make the second call successful, and the program must try the process again. The maximum number of attempts, 5 (including the first one), is just an arbitrary chosen value.

2545–2549 The buffer now consists of a set of rt_msghdr{} structures, each of which corresponds to a single routing table entry. Figure 1-45 is an example of the received buffer for the routing table shown in Listing 1-1 (page 51). There are several remarkable points in this example:

1. Network mask for the default route is a special case. This is effectively single-byte data, containing 0, which means the prefix length is 0. The 1-byte data requires the following empty field for padding.

2. The network mask for the second message is actually truncated as shown in Figure 1-42 (page 52), and the sin6_len field is decreased (e.g., to 16). The parser must prepare for such truncated addresses.

3. It contains two additional address types as specified by the RTA_IFP and RTA_IFA flags. These mean the outgoing interface for the route and an IPv6 address assigned on that interface (which is usually a link-local address), respectively.

4. IPv6 link-local addresses in the address fields (corresponding to the RTA_IFA flag) are represented in the kernel-internal form which embeds the link index into the sin6_addr field.

The rt_entry() function (not described in this book) is called for each entry, and incorporates some of the route entries into **route6d**'s internal database (RIB).

FIGURE 1-45

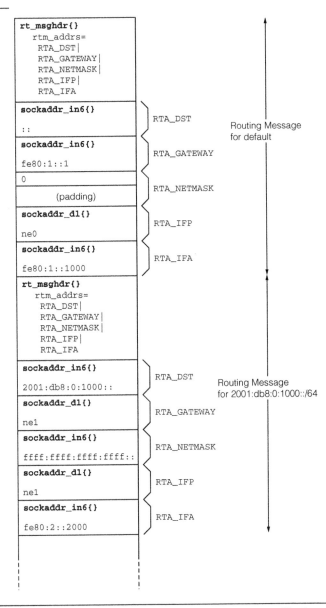

Routing messages returned by the NET_RT_DUMP sysctl.

1.10 Overview of route6d Daemon

The **route6d** program is an IPv6 routing daemon that runs on BSD variants and operates RIPng. It was developed as part of the KAME IPv6 protocol stack kit and has been incorporated into the base component of BSD systems.

This is a simple program but offers most of the basic features that would be required for a routing daemon. The features supported by **route6d** include:

- RIPng protocol operation based on [RFC2080][3]
- Inbound and outbound route filtering
- Route aggregation
- Automatic synchronization with changes of the kernel routing table, including addition and deletion of static and interface direct routes

It is simple to run **route6d**; it does not require a configuration file and normally works without any command line option. In order to support non default behavior of routing information exchange such as route filter, **route6d** has several command line options. Table 1-8 shows some of these options that are referenced in this chapter. The complete description of the option switches can be found in the manual page of the **route6d** daemon.

The −l option would require additional notes; it was introduced and set to "off" by default because site-local route information could be ambiguous and might confuse **route6d** if this router were located at a site boundary. Note, however, that the IETF has deprecated unicast site-local addresses [RFC3879] and this option is now meaningless as long as the network administrator uses valid types of addresses.

The following several sections will describe details about the **route6d** implementation. The descriptions will provide pragmatic hints of how an IPv6 routing daemon should be implemented on BSD variants.

1.11 Common Data Structures, Routines and Global Variables

This section introduces data structures that are commonly used in the **route6d** implementation and are frequently referred to in subsequent sections. The description in this section will also provide a run-time image about how a particular network configuration and command line options map to these data structures.

1.11.1 Structures for RIPng Messages

Listing 1-10 defines the `rip6{}` structure, the common leading part of RIPng messages.

Listing 1-10

──route6d.h
```
49      struct  rip6 {
50              u_char  rip6_cmd;
51              u_char  rip6_vers;
52              u_char  rip6_res1[2];
```

---

3. As explained in Section 1.13, **route6d** has some noncompliant behavior and it does not support Poisoned Reverse.

```
53          union {
54                  struct   netinfo6         ru6_nets[1];
55                  char     ru6_tracefile[1];
56          } rip6un;
57   #define rip6_nets       rip6un.ru6_nets
58   #define rip6_tracefile  rip6un.ru6_tracefile
59   };
```
———route6d.h

TABLE 1-8

Name	Description
-N if1[,if2...]	Do not listen to or advertise route information from/to interfaces specified by the parameter.
-L prefix/prefixlen,if1[,if2...]	Accept route information specified as prefix/prefixlen from interface if1 and other interfaces if any other interfaces are specified. The prefix information ::/0 is treated as a default route, that is, it means the default route, rather than any route information, is accepted.
-T if1[,if2...]	Advertise only the default route toward if1 and other interfaces if specified.
-t tag	Bind the route tag tag to originated route entries. tag can be a decimal, octal prefixed by 0 or hexadecimal value prefixed by 0x.
-A prefix/prefixlen,if1[,if2...]	Aggregate route entries covered by prefix/prefixlen and advertise the prefix when sending route information toward the specified network interfaces.
-S, -s	Advertise statically defined routes that exist in the kernel routing table before the **route6d** daemon is launched. -s is the same as -S except that the split horizon algorithm does not apply.
-h	Disable the split horizon algorithm.
-l	Exchange site-local prefixes. With this switch, **route6d** daemon exchanges site-local prefixes, assuming all of the prefixes belong to the same site.

*Option switches of **route6d** used in this chapter.*

Refer to Figure 1-9 (page 11), rip6_cmd maps to the command field; rip6_vers maps to the version field; rip6_res1 maps to the "must be zero" field. The rip6un{} union, in particular, the rip6_nets macro definition maps to the first RTE contained in the message. This makes sense because a valid RIPng message has at least one RTE. If a request message asks for specific routes, then there would be one or more RTEs corresponding to the required routes; if it asks for the entire routing table, then there will be exactly one RTE, with the destination prefix being ::/0 and the metric being 16, meaning infinity. Also, a valid response message must have at least one RTE.

The `netinfo6{}` structure used in `rip6{}` as a single RTE is shown in Listing 1-11.

Listing 1-11
                                                                        ─────route6d.h
```
42      struct netinfo6 {
43              struct  in6_addr        rip6_dest;
44              u_short rip6_tag;
45              u_char  rip6_plen;
46              u_char  rip6_metric;
47      };
```
                                                                        ─────route6d.h

This structure is a straightforward representation of the RTE format as shown in Figure 1-10 (page 12): `rip6_dest` maps to the IPv6 prefix field; `rip6_tag` maps to the route tag field; `rip6_plen` maps to the prefix length field; and `rip6_metric` maps to the metric field.

1.11.2   route6d's Routing Table

The `riprt{}` structure, as defined in Listing 1-12, is a single route entry of **route6d**'s internal routing table (i.e., RIB).

Listing 1-12
                                                                        ─────route6d.c
```
171     struct  riprt {
172             struct  riprt *rrt_next;         /* next destination */
173             struct  riprt *rrt_same;         /* same destination - future use */
174             struct  netinfo6 rrt_info;       /* network info */
175             struct  in6_addr rrt_gw;         /* gateway */
176             u_long  rrt_flags;               /* kernel routing table flags */
177             u_long  rrt_rflags;              /* route6d routing table flags */
178             time_t  rrt_t;                   /* when the route validated */
179             int     rrt_index;               /* ifindex from which this route got */
180     };
```
                                                                        ─────route6d.c

The current **route6d** implementation manages its routing table using a simple linked list(*) whose head is pointed to by a global variable `riprt`. `rrt_next` links the routing table entries. `rrt_same` is an unused member. `rrt_info` is a `netinfo6{}` structure that contains the actual route information (Listing 1-11). `rrt_gw` holds the next hop address. `rrt_flags` contains the kernel routing entry flags such as `RTF_UP` and `RTF_HOST`. `rrt_rflags` may take on one of the `RRTF_????` flags described in Listing 1-13 below. `rrt_t` stores the time when the route was created or refreshed; for a static route entry `rrt_t` is set to 0. How the route lifetime and hold-down times are manipulated based on `rrt_t` is covered in detail in Section 1.13.5. `rrt_index` has the index of the interface on which the route was obtained.

(*) This singly linked list is inefficient when performing a route search with a moderate number of route entries. The simple list also makes route aggregation difficult to accomplish. Although the overhead may be negligible for the typical scale of network where RIPng is performed, it would generally be better to use more efficient data structures such as a tree-based table.

Listing 1-13

route6d.c

```
218     #define RRTF_AGGREGATE          0x08000000
219     #define RRTF_NOADVERTISE        0x10000000
220     #define RRTF_NH_NOT_LLADDR      0x20000000
221     #define RRTF_SENDANYWAY         0x40000000
222     #define RRTF_CHANGED            0x80000000
```

route6d.c

RRTF_AGGREGATE marks a route entry as the aggregate route to be advertised. RRTF_NOADVERTISE marks a route entry not to be advertised. RRTF_NH_NOT_LLADDR notes that a route entry contains a next hop address that is not a link-local address. RRTF_SENDANYWAY is not set in the `rrt_rflags` field of the `riprt{}` structure. Instead, when necessary, this flag is specified as an argument to the `ripsend()` function (Section 1.13.4) to indicate that a response message is generated in answer to a request and the split horizon algorithm should be disabled. RRTF_CHANGED marks a route entry as having been modified recently. A triggered update includes only routes that have the RRTF_CHANGED flag set.

Figure 1-46 shows an example image of **route6d**'s routing table for the network topology given in Figure 1-41 (page 50). It is assumed all routers exchange routes using RIPng; router A advertised the default route (`::/0`) with a metric of 1 at 15:32; router B advertised the network prefix of the lower-most link (`2001:db8:0:2000::/64`) with a metric of 1 two minutes later. Also assume the FreeBSD router, running **route6d**, is processing the RIPng response message from router B.

The first `riprt{}` entry is for the route being processed. The **route6d** daemon adds the metric of the receiving link to the advertised metric, and sets the `rip6_metric` member to the result value. Since this route is newly advertised, the RRTF_CHANGED flag is set in the `rrt_rflags` member, prompting a triggered update. The `rrt_t` member is set to the current time, 15:32.[4] It should also be noted that the gateway address (`rrt_gw`) embeds the link identifier (2) in the address. This is necessary because this address is passed to the kernel via the routing socket, which requires the embedded form as explained in Section 1.8.1.

The second entry is for the default route advertised by router A. The same description for the first entry naturally applies to this entry, but the `rrt_rflags` member is cleared because this route entry has already been installed and advertised as an update.

The last entry is the interface direct route for the local link prefix of `2001:db8:0:1000::/64`. The **route6d** daemon makes this entry on startup time by examining each local address and its prefix (this procedure is not described in this book). The `rrt_gw` member is set to the local address for the daemon's convenience. The metric of this route is set to 1 by default, which is used as the metric of the route in RIPng response messages sent from this router. An interface direct route is considered a static route, so the `rrt_t` member is set to 0.

1.11.3   Structures for Local Interfaces

The **route6d** daemon builds a list of local network interfaces at startup time and uses the parameters of each interface in the RIPng protocol operations. The `ifc{}` structure, as defined in Listing 1-14, describes the per interface data structure maintained in **route6d** for this purpose.

---

4. This value is actually an integer, but it is represented in the more intuitive form for readability.

FIGURE 1-46

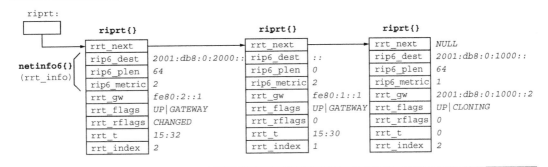

*A routing table snapshot of **route6d** for the topology shown in Figure 1-41. The RTF_ and RRTF_ prefixes
for the values of the* rrt_flags *and* rrt_rflags *members are omitted for brevity.*

Listing 1-14
—————————————————————————————————— route6d.c

```
111     struct  ifc {                          /* Configuration of an interface */
112             char    *ifc_name;             /* if name */
113             struct  ifc *ifc_next;
114             int     ifc_index;             /* if index */
115             int     ifc_mtu;               /* if mtu */
116             int     ifc_metric;            /* if metric */
117             u_int   ifc_flags;             /* flags */
118             short   ifc_cflags;            /* IFC_XXX */
119             struct  in6_addr ifc_mylladdr; /* my link-local address */
120             struct  sockaddr_in6 ifc_ripsin; /* rip multicast address */
121             struct  iff *ifc_filter;       /* filter structure */
122             struct  ifac *ifc_addr;        /* list of AF_INET6 addresses */
123             int     ifc_joined;            /* joined to ff02::9 */
124     };
```
—————————————————————————————————— route6d.c

The ifc_name member contains the name of the interface, e.g., fxp0. ifc_index contains
the interface index that was assigned by the kernel at the time when it was installed into the
system. ifc_mtu contains the link MTU value, for example, 1500 is the typical value for Ethernet
interfaces.

The ifc_next member points to the next ifc{} entry of the interface list. The head entry
is pointed to by a global variable named ifc.

The ifc_metric member contains the additional cost of accessing the network; in the
route6d implementation, the metric for a route is calculated as the sum of the hop count and
the value of ifc_metric.

The ifc_flags member contains the interface flags, such as IFF_UP, indicating the interface is operational. IFF_MULTICAST indicates the interface is capable of receiving and transmitting multicast packets. On the other hand, ifc_cflags defines implementation-specific
attributes of this interface. The only flag defined for ifc_cflags is IFC_CHANGED, which is
used to indicate that a route associated with the interface (e.g., a direct route corresponding to
a local address) has been modified recently and a RIPng update may need to be sent.

The ifc_mylladdr member stores a link-local address of the interface. This is used to
detect the case where an incoming RIPng message is sent from this local router. ifc_ripsin
is a template socket address structure of the all-rip-routers multicast group address (ff02::9)

and is used to send a RIPng response message to this group. Since this address has a link-local scope and different interfaces usually belong to different links, this structure is maintained per interface basis. The link index is set in this structure on initialization (see Listing 1-26, page 79).

The `ifc_filter` member contains a list of filters that are configured for this interface. Section 1.11.4 explains the `iff{}` structure in more detail. `ifc_addr` contains a list of IPv6 addresses configured on this interface. `ifc_joined` is a flag variable. When set, it indicates **route6d** has joined the all-rip-routers multicast group on the given interface.

The `ifac{}` structure constructs the address list linked in the `ifc{}` structure. The definition of this structure is shown in Listing 1-15.

Listing 1-15

```
                                                          route6d.c
126     struct  ifac {                      /* Adddress associated to an interface */
127             struct  ifc *ifa_conf;      /* back pointer */
128             struct  ifac *ifa_next;
129             struct  in6_addr ifa_addr;     /* address */
130             struct  in6_addr ifa_raddr;    /* remote address, valid in p2p */
131             int     ifa_plen;           /* prefix length */
132     };
                                                          route6d.c
```

Each `ifac{}` structure holds one interface address. `ifa_conf` is a back pointer to `ifc{}` to which it belongs. `ifa_next` points to the next interface address. `ifa_addr` contains the actual interface address. `ifa_raddr` contains the address of the remote node if the interface referenced by `ifa_conf` is a point-to-point interface. `ifa_plen` has the prefix length for `ifa_addr`.

Figure 1-47 depicts the relationship among these data structures for the FreeBSD router shown in Figure 1-41 (page 50). It is assumed in this figure that both the ne0 and ne1 interfaces have a link-local address `fe80::2`. This configuration is valid because these interfaces belong to different links.

It should also be noted that the interface list contains an `ifc{}` structure for a loopback interface lo0. This interface is not used for normal RIPng protocol operation, so most of the structure members are omitted in the figure. But it may be used as the imaginary outgoing interface for route aggregation (which is not described in this chapter), and must be configured in this list.

1.11.4   route6d Route Filter Entry

The `iff{}` structure, shown in Listing 1-16, describes a route filter configured for a given interface.

Listing 1-16

```
                                                          route6d.c
134     struct  iff {
135             int     iff_type;
136             struct  in6_addr iff_addr;
137             int     iff_plen;
138             struct  iff *iff_next;
139     };
                                                          route6d.c
```

The `iff_type` member specifies the type of filter, which is described by a single ASCII character corresponding to a command line option shown in Table 1-8 (page 66); the supported

FIGURE 1-47

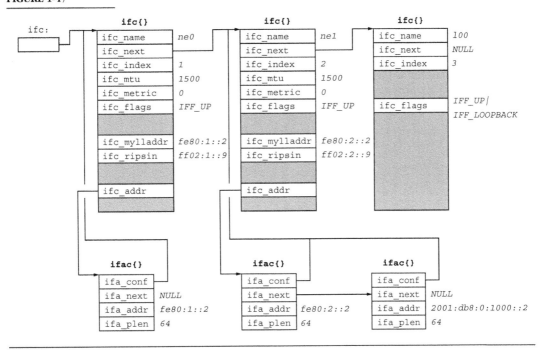

Interface and address list structures for the router shown in Figure 1-41. Some flags of the
`ifc_flags` *member are omitted for brevity.*

TABLE 1-9

iff_type	**route6d** *option*	*Description*
A	−A	Route aggregation filter
L	−L	Inbound route filter
O	−O	Outbound route filter

Route filter types supported in ***route6d***.

filter types are summarized in Table 1-9. The `iff_addr` and `iff_plen` members define the
IPv6 prefix to which this filter entry applies. `iff_next` points to the next filter.

For example, consider in Figure 1-41 (page 50) that the administrator wants to apply the
following route filtering policies:

- Only the default route is accepted on interface ne0.

- Only routes that belong to prefix `2001:db8::/48` are advertised on interface ne0.

Then the **route6d** daemon would be invoked as follows:

```
# route6d -L::/0,ne0 -O2001:db8::/48,ne0
```

Figure 1-48 shows the internal data structures for this configuration.

1.11.5 Subroutines and Global Variables

The **route6d** implementation relies on various utility functions and global variables, and some of them are frequently referred to in the code narrations in the next couple of sections. This subsection provides a short summary of these for convenience. Table 1-10 summarizes subroutines commonly used in the implementation; Table 1-11 summarizes some major global variables; Table 1-12 provides the description of supporting macro functions.

FIGURE 1-48

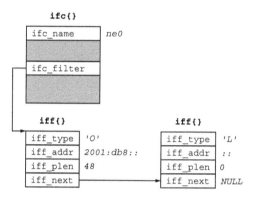

Data structures specifying route filtering entries.

TABLE 1-10

Function name	Function prototype and description
addroute()	int addroute(struct riprt *rrt, const struct in6_addr *gw, struct ifc *ifcp); Installs a **route6d**'s route entry pointed to by rrt into the kernel via a routing socket. gw actually points to rrt->gw but is passed as a separate constant parameter so that it not modified in this function. ifcp is only used for logging. Returns 0 on success; otherwise returns −1.
delroute()	int delroute(struct netinfo6 *np, struct in6_addr *gw); Deletes a route for the prefix identified by np from the kernel via a routing socket command. gw is also passed to the kernel as a hint, but it does not have any effect because the BSD kernel does not use this information to delete a route. Returns 0 on success; otherwise returns −1.
applyplen()	void applyplen(struct in6_addr *ia, int plen); Zero-clears the rightmost 128−plen bits of the given IPv6 address ia. For example, if ia is 2001:db8:1:2::abcd and plen is 64, ia is modified to 2001:db8:1:2:: in this function.

TABLE 1-10 (*Continued*)

Function name	Function prototype and description
iff_find()	`struct iff *iff_find(struct ifc *ifcp, int type);` Searches the filter list of `ifcp` (see Listing 1-14) for an entry that matches `type`. Returns a pointer to the matched entry if one is found, otherwise NULL.

rtsearch()	`struct riprt *rtsearch(struct netinfo6 *np,`
	`                      struct riprt **prev);`
	
	Searches the **route6d** routing table for an entry that has the same prefix as that specified in `np`. Returns a pointer to the entry on success; returns NULL on failure. `prev` is not used in the code covered in this book.

fatal()	`void fatal(const char *fmt, ...);` Called when a nonrecoverable error occurs. Makes a final log message based on the function arguments and exits.

*Commonly used subroutines for **route6d**.*

TABLE 1-11

Name	Type	Description
ripsock	int	The file descriptor for the socket sending and receiving RIPng messages. The socket is not bound to any address and listens on UDP port 521.
ripbuf	struct rip6 *	A global buffer with the constant size of RIP6_MAXMTU (1500) bytes, which is allocated in the initialization phase of **route6d**. This variable is represented as a pointer of the rip6{} structure and is commonly used to hold outgoing RIPng messages by various routines of **route6d**.

*Major **route6d** global variables referred to in this chapter.*

1.12   Interface Configuration

On startup, the **route6d** daemon collects information about each interface on the local node, including the link-level multicasting capability, IPv6 addresses configured on the interface, and the link MTU. The address information is also used to obtain the subnet prefix for the link to which the interface is attached, which will subsequently be advertised in RIPng

TABLE 1-12

Macro name and argument	Description
`IN6_LINKLOCAL_IFINDEX(a)`	Extracts the link index assuming it is embedded in address a (a pointer to `in6_addr{}`) in the form described in Section 1.8.1 and returns it as an integer.
`SET_IN6_LINKLOCAL_IFINDEX(a, id)`	Embeds an integer link ID `id` into address a (a pointer to `in6_addr{}`).
`RIPSIZE(n)`	Returns the number of bytes needed to construct a RIPng message containing n RTEs. This can be computed using a transformation of Equation (1.1) (page 14).

*Commonly used macro definitions for **route6d**.*

response messages. The collected information is maintained in such data structures as shown in Figure 1-47 (page 71).

This initialization process is performed by the `ifconfig()` function described in Section 1.12.1. The `ifconfig()` function then calls a dedicated subroutine named `ifconfig1()`, which handles an IPv6 address configured on the interface. The `ifconfig()` function is also called when a new address is configured or an existing address is deleted while the **route6d** daemon is running. But for simplicity this section focuses on the initialization procedure.

1.12.1 `ifconfig()` Function

Function `ifconfig()` is called at the **route6d** daemon startup phase to install usable interfaces into the daemon's internal table. The all-rip-routers multicast group membership is established over each usable interface.

Listing 1-17

————————————————————————————————————— route6d.c

```
1423    void
1424    ifconfig()
1425    {
1426            struct ifaddrs *ifap, *ifa;
1427            struct ifc *ifcp;
1428            struct ipv6_mreq mreq;
1429            int s;
1430
1431            if ((s = socket(AF_INET6, SOCK_DGRAM, 0)) < 0) {
1432                    fatal("socket");
1433                    /*NOTREACHED*/
1434            }
1435
1436            if (getifaddrs(&ifap) != 0) {
1437                    fatal("getifaddrs");
1438                    /*NOTREACHED*/
1439            }
```

————————————————————————————————————— route6d.c

1431–1434 A socket is created here and is passed to function `ifconfig1()` for interfacing with the kernel.

1436–1439 Function `getifaddrs()` is called to retrieve the list of available system interface addresses. The retrieved list is stored in `ifap`. Since the memory is dynamically allocated inside `getifaddrs()`, a subsequent call to `freeifaddrs()` at the end of this function is necessary to free that memory (see Listing 1-21).

Listing 1-18

── route6d.c

```
1441            for (ifa = ifap; ifa; ifa = ifa->ifa_next) {
1442                    if (ifa->ifa_addr->sa_family != AF_INET6)
1443                            continue;
1444                    ifcp = ifc_find(ifa->ifa_name);
1445                    /* we are interested in multicast-capable interfaces */
1446                    if ((ifa->ifa_flags & IFF_MULTICAST) == 0)
1447                            continue;
```

── route6d.c

1441–1447 Each interface address in the list is examined to determine whether an IPv6 address is configured on the interface, and whether the interface is multicast capable. The interface is bypassed if any of the aforementioned conditions is not satisfied.

    Function `ifc_find()` is called to search through the internal interface table of the **route6d** daemon to determine if the interface in question has already been installed previously. Note that the call to function `ifc_find()` may be relocated to after the check for interface multicast capability for efficiency reasons.

Listing 1-19

── route6d.c

```
1448                if (!ifcp) {
1449                        /* new interface */
1450                        if ((ifcp = MALLOC(struct ifc)) == NULL) {
1451                                fatal("malloc: struct ifc");
1452                                /*NOTREACHED*/
1453                        }
1454                        memset(ifcp, 0, sizeof(*ifcp));
1455                        ifcp->ifc_index = -1;
1456                        ifcp->ifc_next = ifc;
1457                        ifc = ifcp;
1458                        nifc++;
1459                        ifcp->ifc_name = allocopy(ifa->ifa_name);
1460                        ifcp->ifc_addr = 0;
1461                        ifcp->ifc_filter = 0;
1462                        ifcp->ifc_flags = ifa->ifa_flags;
1463                        trace(1, "newif %s <%s>\n", ifcp->ifc_name,
1464                                ifflags(ifcp->ifc_flags));
1465                        if (!strcmp(ifcp->ifc_name, LOOPBACK_IF))
1466                                loopifcp = ifcp;
```

── route6d.c

1448–1458 If the interface corresponding to this address has not been installed in the interface table maintained by the **route6d** daemon, a new `ifc{}` structure is created and is initialized here. The interface index `ifc_index` is set to −1 and it will be initialized in function ifconfig1() (Section 1.12.2). The new interface is then added into the interface list. The global counter `nifc` is incremented to account for the additional entry.

1459–1462 The `ifc_name` and the `ifc_flags` members are initialized with the values retrieved through `getifaddrs()`. The `allocopy()` function (not described in this book) copies the given interface name to `ifc_name` after allocating necessary memory.

1465–1466 The pointer reference `loopifcp` is initialized here if the given interface is a loopback interface. The loopback interface is used to install a special route into the kernel routing table for the purpose of route aggregation (details of aggregation is outside the scope of this book).

Listing 1-20
```
                                                               route6d.c
1467                     } else {
1468                             /* update flag, this may be up again */
1469                             if (ifcp->ifc_flags != ifa->ifa_flags) {
1470                                     trace(1, "%s: <%s> -> ", ifcp->ifc_name,
1471                                             ifflags(ifcp->ifc_flags));
1472                                     trace(1, "<%s>\n", ifflags(ifa->ifa_flags));
1473                                     ifcp->ifc_cflags |= IFC_CHANGED;
1474                             }
1475                             ifcp->ifc_flags = ifa->ifa_flags;
1476                     }
                                                               route6d.c
```

1467–1476 If the interface is found in the list, the interface flags are updated because the state of the interface may have changed since it was installed, in which case the change flag `IFC_CHANGED` is set. Typically a change in the interface state will trigger an unsolicited RIPng message to be sent.

Listing 1-21
```
                                                               route6d.c
1477                     ifconfig1(ifa->ifa_name, ifa->ifa_addr, ifcp, s);
1478                     if ((ifcp->ifc_flags & (IFF_LOOPBACK | IFF_UP)) == IFF_UP
1479                         && 0 < ifcp->ifc_index && !ifcp->ifc_joined) {
1480                             mreq.ipv6mr_multiaddr = ifcp->ifc_ripsin.sin6_addr;
1481                             mreq.ipv6mr_interface = ifcp->ifc_index;
1482                             if (setsockopt(ripsock, IPPROTO_IPV6, IPV6_JOIN_GROUP,
1483                                 &mreq, sizeof(mreq)) < 0) {
1484                                     fatal("IPV6_JOIN_GROUP");
1485                                     /*NOTREACHED*/
1486                             }
1487                             trace(1, "join %s %s\n", ifcp->ifc_name, RIP6_DEST);
1488                             ifcp->ifc_joined++;
1489                     }
1490             }
1491             close(s);
1492             freeifaddrs(ifap);
1493     }
                                                               route6d.c
```

1477 The function `ifconfig1()` is called to store the address `ifa` into `ifcp`, which is an instance of the `ifc{}` structure. It also completes the initialization of `ifcp` when it is newly created in this function.

1478–1489 If the interface is operational and the **route6d** daemon has not joined the all-rip-
routers multicast group on that interface, then function setsockopt() is called to join
the multicast group over the interface given in ifc_index. The ifc_joined variable
is set to indicate that the group membership has been established.

1491–1492 The temporary socket is closed here. The memory returned from the call to
getifaddrs() is freed here as well.

1.12.2 `ifconfig1()` Function

The function ifconfig1() is called by ifconfig() to install an IPv6 address configured on
the given interface. It also completes the initialization of a newly allocated interface structure.

Listing 1-22
route6d.c
```
1495    void
1496    ifconfig1(name, sa, ifcp, s)
1497            const char *name;
1498            const struct sockaddr *sa;
1499            struct  ifc *ifcp;
1500            int     s;
1501    {
1502            struct  in6_ifreq ifr;
1503            const struct sockaddr_in6 *sin6;
1504            struct  ifac *ifa;
1505            int     plen;
1506            char    buf[BUFSIZ];
```
route6d.c

1495–1500 On input, name points to the name of the interface; sa points to the interface
address; ifcp points to the interface; s is the socket that was created in the function
ifconfig() and is used for retrieving additional information about the given interface
from the kernel.

Listing 1-23
route6d.c
```
1508            sin6 = (const struct sockaddr_in6 *)sa;
1509            if (IN6_IS_ADDR_SITELOCAL(&sin6->sin6_addr) && !lflag)
1510                    return;
1511            ifr.ifr_addr = *sin6;
1512            strncpy(ifr.ifr_name, name, sizeof(ifr.ifr_name));
1513            if (ioctl(s, SIOCGIFNETMASK_IN6, (char *)&ifr) < 0) {
1514                    fatal("ioctl: SIOCGIFNETMASK_IN6");
1515                    /*NOTREACHED*/
1516            }
1517            plen = sin6mask2len(&ifr.ifr_addr);
1518            if ((ifa = ifa_match(ifcp, &sin6->sin6_addr, plen)) != NULL) {
1519                    /* same interface found */
1520                    /* need check if something changed */
1521                    /* XXX not yet implemented */
1522                    return;
1523            }
```
route6d.c

1508–1510 The lflag variable controls whether to exchange site-local prefixes, which is set
to non-zero if and only if the −l command line option is specified (see the note about the
−L option associated with Table 1-8 on page 66).

If this option is disabled and the given address has a site-local scope, the `ifconfig1()`
function returns immediately. Note `ifc_index` still has the value −L for the given interface structure.

1511–1517 The `ioctl()` call is issued here to retrieve the network mask associated with
the given address, and then `sin6mask2len()` converts the mask to the prefix length
by counting the leftmost consecutive bits on. The prefix length is saved in `plen` for a
subsequent call to `ifa_match()`.

1518–1523 The `ifa_match()` function (not described in this book) matches the given
address and the prefix length against all of the addresses that have been assigned to
the interface. The function returns here if a match is found.

Listing 1-24
── route6d.c
```
1524                /*
1525                 * New address is found
1526                 */
1527                if ((ifa = MALLOC(struct ifac)) == NULL) {
1528                        fatal("malloc: struct ifac");
1529                        /*NOTREACHED*/
1530                }
1531                memset(ifa, 0, sizeof(*ifa));
1532                ifa->ifa_conf = ifcp;
1533                ifa->ifa_next = ifcp->ifc_addr;
1534                ifcp->ifc_addr = ifa;
1535                ifa->ifa_addr = sin6->sin6_addr;
1536                ifa->ifa_plen = plen;
```
── route6d.c

1527–1536 A new interface address structure `ifac{}` is allocated and initialized here. The
new structure is linked into the address list. The new address is stored in the `ifa_addr`
field.

Listing 1-25
── route6d.c
```
1537                if (ifcp->ifc_flags & IFF_POINTOPOINT) {
1538                        ifr.ifr_addr = *sin6;
1539                        if (ioctl(s, SIOCGIFDSTADDR_IN6, (char *)&ifr) < 0) {
1540                                fatal("ioctl: SIOCGIFDSTADDR_IN6");
1541                                /*NOTREACHED*/
1542                        }
1543                        ifa->ifa_raddr = ifr.ifr_dstaddr.sin6_addr;
1544                        inet_ntop(AF_INET6, (void *)&ifa->ifa_raddr, buf, sizeof(buf));
1545                        trace(1, "found address %s/%d -- %s\n",
1546                                inet6_n2p(&ifa->ifa_addr), ifa->ifa_plen, buf);
1547                } else {
1548                        trace(1, "found address %s/%d\n",
1549                                inet6_n2p(&ifa->ifa_addr), ifa->ifa_plen);
1550                }
```
── route6d.c

1537–1547 For a point-to-point interface, the remote address is retrieved by issuing the
`SIOCGIFDSTADDR_IN6` command to the `ioctl()` function. The remote address of the
point-to-point link is stored in the `ifa_raddr` field.

Listing 1-26

```
1551                 if (ifcp->ifc_index < 0 && IN6_IS_ADDR_LINKLOCAL(&ifa->ifa_addr)) {
1552                         ifcp->ifc_mylladdr = ifa->ifa_addr;
1553                         ifcp->ifc_index = IN6_LINKLOCAL_IFINDEX(ifa->ifa_addr);
1554                         memcpy(&ifcp->ifc_ripsin, &ripsin, ripsin.ss_len);
1555                         SET_IN6_LINKLOCAL_IFINDEX(ifcp->ifc_ripsin.sin6_addr,
1556                                 ifcp->ifc_index);
1557                         setindex2ifc(ifcp->ifc_index, ifcp);
1558                         ifcp->ifc_mtu = getifmtu(ifcp->ifc_index);
1559                         if (ifcp->ifc_mtu > RIP6_MAXMTU)
1560                                 ifcp->ifc_mtu = RIP6_MAXMTU;
1561                         if (ioctl(s, SIOCGIFMETRIC, (char *)&ifr) < 0) {
1562                                 fatal("ioctl: SIOCGIFMETRIC");
1563                                 /*NOTREACHED*/
1564                         }
1565                         ifcp->ifc_metric = ifr.ifr_metric;
1566                         trace(1, "\tindex: %d, mtu: %d, metric: %d\n",
1567                                 ifcp->ifc_index, ifcp->ifc_mtu, ifcp->ifc_metric);
1568                 } else
1569                         ifcp->ifc_cflags |= IFC_CHANGED;
1570         }
```

1551–1552 An interface must have a link-local address assigned to it in order for it to be usable by the **route6d** daemon because all of the unsolicited RIPng response packets must be sent using a link-local address. Even though multiple link-local addresses may be configured on an interface, only one is necessary for **route6d**'s operation and it is stored in `ifc_mylladdr`.

> In fact, perhaps unintentionally, `ifc_mylladdr` is not used to send messages.

1553 The interface index is retrieved from the link-local address, which is stored in the third and fourth bytes of the `in6_addr{}` structure.

> This is a bad practice. First, a link index is not always equal to an interface index in terms of the IPv6 scoped address architecture [RFC4007]. Second, even if these are equal, an application should not use the KAME-specific embedded index in link-local addresses as noted in Section 1.8.1 wherever possible. In this case, the actual index can be taken from the interface information with the return value of `getifaddrs()` (see Listing 1-17), which should be used instead.

1554 The global variable `ripsin` is a placeholder structure that is initialized to store the all-rip-routers multicast address at startup time. The contents of the variable are copied into the `ifc_ripsin` member of the `ifc{}` structure being currently configured.

1555–1556 These lines embed the interface index into the IPv6 address field of `ifc_ripsin`, which is not only a bad practice (see note above) but also meaningless. The address stored in the `ifc_ripsin` member is only used for the `sendmsg()` system call and for the `IPV6_JOIN_GROUP` socket option, which are APIs for a "normal application" and do not require the embedded form (recall Figure 1-43, page 54); for `sendmsg()`, `sin6_scope_id` should simply work. For the `IPV6_JOIN_GROUP` option, the interface index stored in `ifcp` can be passed in the socket option argument without embedding the index into the address.

1557 Function `setindex2ifc()` (not described in this book) configures a separate array called `index2ifc` so that the array entry of this interface index points to the newly created `ifc{}` structure. This array is used so that the appropriate `ifc{}` structure can be efficiently identified by the index.

Figure 1-49 illustrates the relationship between the list of `ifc{}` structures shown in Figure 1-47 (page 71) and the `index2ifc` array. A global variable `nindex2ifc` stores the number of array entries. If a given interface index is invalid, the corresponding `index2ifc` array entry points to NULL. Note that `index2ifc[0]` always points to NULL because interface indices begin with 1.

1558–1560 The local function `getifmtu()` is called to retrieve the MTU of the link to which the interface is attached via a system call (not described in this book). The link MTU is stored in `ifc_mtu`. The `RIP6_MAXMTU` (1500) is an artificial limit, which is introduced by the **route6d** implementation and is not part of the specification.

1561–1565 The `SIOCGIFMETRIC` command is issued through `ioctl()` to retrieve the additional network costs for external routes. Note that the `ioctl()` call is actually not necessary because the routing metric information has already been retrieved in the call to `getifmtu()`. `ifc_metric` is discussed in more detail in Listing 1-41 (Section 1.13.2).

1569 If the code reaches here, that is because this function is processing a new interface address. The `IFC_CHANGED` flag is set to indicate the change condition and possibly trigger a RIPng response packet to be sent soon.

FIGURE 1-49

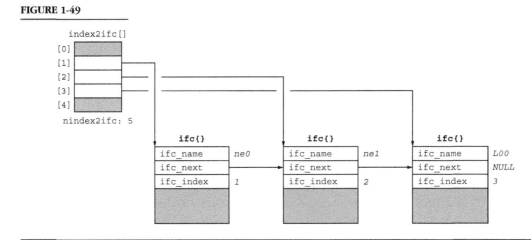

Relationship between `ifc{}` *list and* `index2ifc` *array.*

1.13 RIPng Protocol Operation

This section provides detailed descriptions of RIPng protocol processing of the **route6d** implementation. Figure 1-50 shows function call graphs involved in the processing. After initialization, **route6d** first sends out a RIPng request message on every available interface to ask neighbor routers for their routing table contents. This is done by the sendrequest() function. The **route6d** daemon then waits for incoming RIPng messages in an infinite loop. The riprecv() function is called on the receipt of a message and processes the messages depending on the command, that is, request or response.

A request message is handled in riprequest(). If the request asks for the whole routing table, riprequest() calls the ripsend() function with the RRTF_SENDANYWAY flag to indicate the response should be sent to any interface; normally **routed** does not send a response to a loopback interface not to confuse itself. On the other hand, if the request asks for the route for specific destinations, riprequest() generates the corresponding response by itself and passes it to the sendpacket() function to transmit the final packet to the network.

A response message is mainly handled in the riprecv() function. It updates the routing table based on the contents of the response message, and calls ripsend() with the RRTF_CHANGED flag if a triggered update is necessary.

A separate function named ripalarm() is called from the infinite loop about every 30 seconds to send response message for regular updates.

FIGURE 1-50

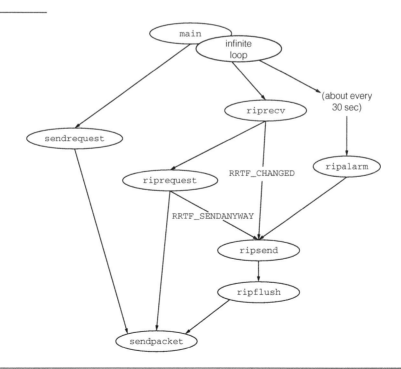

Functions that perform RIPng protocol operation.

The ripsend() function handles various cases of generating a response message. It examines the routing table entries and builds the appropriate response message considering configured route filtering and applying the split horizon algorithm. The ripflush() function is a simple subroutine of ripsend(), which just passes a single response message to the sendpacket() function.

The sendpacket() function sets up an ancillary data object for the given response message that specifies the outgoing interface and sends out the message to the network via the RIPng (AF_INET6 UDP) socket.

The following subsections explain the details of the functions shown in Figure 1-50 except main(), ripflush() and sendpacket(), which are pretty trivial and not actually relevant to the RIPng protocol operation.

1.13.1 sendrequest() Function

The sendrequest() function, shown in Listing 1-27, is called to send out a RIPng request message asking for the whole routing table of the receiver over a given interface.

Listing 1-27
route6d.c

```
1359   /*
1360    * Send all routes request packet to the specified interface.
1361    */
1362   void
1363   sendrequest(ifcp)
1364         struct ifc *ifcp;
1365   {
1366         struct netinfo6 *np;
1367         int error;
1368
1369         if (ifcp->ifc_flags & IFF_LOOPBACK)
1370                 return;
1371         ripbuf->rip6_cmd = RIP6_REQUEST;
1372         np = ripbuf->rip6_nets;
1373         memset(np, 0, sizeof(struct netinfo6));
1374         np->rip6_metric = HOPCNT_INFINITY6;
1375         tracet(1, "Send rtdump Request to %s (%s)\n",
1376                 ifcp->ifc_name, inet6_n2p(&ifcp->ifc_ripsin.sin6_addr));
1377         error = sendpacket(&ifcp->ifc_ripsin, RIPSIZE(1));
1378         if (error == EAFNOSUPPORT) {
1379                 /* Protocol not supported */
1380                 tracet(1, "Could not send rtdump Request to %s (%s): "
1381                         "set IFF_UP to 0\n",
1382                         ifcp->ifc_name, inet6_n2p(&ifcp->ifc_ripsin.sin6_addr));
1383                 ifcp->ifc_flags &= ~IFF_UP;      /* As if down for AF_INET6 */
1384         }
1385         ripbuf->rip6_cmd = RIP6_RESPONSE;
1386   }
```
route6d.c

1369–1370 Since the request is expected to be sent to other neighbor routers, it is suppressed on a loopback interface.

1371–1374 A request message asking for a full table dump (the destination prefix is ::/0 and an infinite metric) is built in the global buffer ripbuf. The other fields of the message were set in the initialization phase of **route6d** (not described in this book).

1377–1384 The `sendpacket()` function is called to send the response packet to the all-rip-routers multicast address (`ff02::9`) from the interface identified by `ifcp`. If sending the packet fails with an error of `EAFNOSUPPORT`, it means that interface does not allow IPv6 communication (some interfaces only allow IPv4 communication). The **route6d** daemon detects the failure at an early stage and disables the interface for the RIPng operation.

1385 The **route6d** daemon never sends a request message after this initial set of requests. The command field of the global buffer is thus reset to `RIP6_RESPONSE`.

In fact, this function is called in a loop examining all interfaces, and rewriting the command field should be deferred after the loop.

1.13.2 `riprecv()` Function

The `riprecv()` function is called to process received RIPng packets. The kernel routing table may be modified as a result of the RIPng response packet processing. `riprecv()` may call function `ripsend()` to send triggered updates if necessary.

Receive Packet

Listing 1-28

```
                                                              route6d.c
1079    void
1080    riprecv()
1081    {
1082            struct  ifc *ifcp, *ic;
1083            struct  sockaddr_in6 fsock;
1084            struct  in6_addr nh;    /* next hop */
1085            struct  rip6 *rp;
1086            struct  netinfo6 *np, *nq;
1087            struct  riprt *rrt;
1088            int     len, nn, need_trigger, idx;
1089            char    buf[4 * RIP6_MAXMTU];
1090            time_t  t;
1091            struct msghdr m;
1092            struct cmsghdr *cm;
1093            struct iovec iov[2];
1094            u_char cmsgbuf[256];
1095            struct in6_pktinfo *pi;
1096            struct iff *iffp;
1097            struct in6_addr ia;
1098            int ok;
1099            time_t t_half_lifetime;
1100
1101            need_trigger = 0;
                                                              route6d.c
```

1079–1101 The local variable `need_trigger` serves as an indicator of whether to generate a triggered update. When response packet processing completes, if `need_trigger` is set to 1 then a triggered update will be sent, provided that delay requirement is satisfied.

Listing 1-29

── route6d.c

```
1103              m.msg_name = (caddr_t)&fsock;
1104              m.msg_namelen = sizeof(fsock);
1105              iov[0].iov_base = (caddr_t)buf;
1106              iov[0].iov_len = sizeof(buf);
1107              m.msg_iov = iov;
1108              m.msg_iovlen = 1;
1109              cm = (struct cmsghdr *)cmsgbuf;
1110              m.msg_control = (caddr_t)cm;
1111              m.msg_controllen = sizeof(cmsgbuf);
1112              if ((len = recvmsg(ripsock, &m, 0)) < 0) {
1113                      fatal("recvmsg");
1114                      /*NOTREACHED*/
1115              }
1116              idx = 0;
1117              for (cm = (struct cmsghdr *)CMSG_FIRSTHDR(&m);
1118                   cm;
1119                   cm = (struct cmsghdr *)CMSG_NXTHDR(&m, cm)) {
1120                      if (cm->cmsg_level == IPPROTO_IPV6 &&
1121                          cm->cmsg_type == IPV6_PKTINFO) {
1122                              pi = (struct in6_pktinfo *)(CMSG_DATA(cm));
1123                              idx = pi->ipi6_ifindex;
1124                              break;
1125                      }
1126              }
```

── route6d.c

1103–1115 The `recvmsg()` system call requires the caller to supply a `msghdr{}` structure that describes storage for receiving both data and control information. The function `recvmsg()` is called once the `msghdr{}` is built. On return from the `recvmsg()` call, `fsock` will contain the source address of the packet, which is the address of the originator of the RIPng packet. `len` holds the number of bytes read from the socket.

1117–1126 The **route6d** daemon is interested in receiving the packet information that includes the packet destination address and the interface on which the packet arrived. `idx` will store the interface index if the `IPV6_PKTINFO` ancillary data object is present. See Chapter 7 of *IPv6 Core Protocols Implementation* for more details about this object.

Listing 1-30

── route6d.c

```
1127              if (idx && IN6_IS_ADDR_LINKLOCAL(&fsock.sin6_addr))
1128                      SET_IN6_LINKLOCAL_IFINDEX(fsock.sin6_addr, idx);
```

── route6d.c

1127–1128 If the receiving interface index is known, and the request packet came from a link-local address, then the interface index is embedded into the address. This is necessary because this address can be passed to the kernel as the gateway address of a route entry and the kernel expects the embedded form (see Section 1.8.1), although this *necessary evil* should be deferred until it is really necessary, that is, until installing a route with this address into the kernel.

Listing 1-31

── route6d.c

```
1130              nh = fsock.sin6_addr;
1131              nn = (len - sizeof(struct rip6) + sizeof(struct netinfo6)) /
1132                      sizeof(struct netinfo6);
1133              rp = (struct rip6 *)buf;
1134              np = rp->rip6_nets;
```

── route6d.c

1130–1134 nh holds the next hop address, which is the source address of the received packet. The number of RTEs that are present in the message is calculated according to the formula given in Equation 1.1 (page 14). rp points to the beginning of the RIPng packet header. np points to the beginning of the RTE list.

Figure 1-51 shows how these variables are set for a RIPng response message containing a route entry for prefix 2001:db8:1111::/48 with the metric of 3.

Handle Request

Listing 1-32

— route6d.c

```
1136            if (rp->rip6_vers !=  RIP6_VERSION) {
1137                    trace(1, "Incorrect RIP version %d\n", rp->rip6_vers);
1138                    return;
1139            }
1140            if (rp->rip6_cmd == RIP6_REQUEST) {
1141                    if (idx && idx < nindex2ifc) {
1142                            ifcp = index2ifc[idx];
1143                            riprequest(ifcp, np, nn, &fsock);
1144                    } else {
1145                            riprequest(NULL, np, nn, &fsock);
1146                    }
1147                    return;
1148            }
```

— route6d.c

1136–1139 Currently the only defined version is RIPng version 1 as explained in Section 1.4.1. riprecv() returns here if version validation fails.

1140–1148 This if block processes an incoming RIPng request message. The index of the arrival interface is usually provided in the interface table of the **route6d** daemon, but there are some exceptional cases: the kernel may fail to allocate the ancillary data object, in which case the message is received by the daemon without an interface index, although the daemon should then discard the message rather than try to deal with the missing

FIGURE 1-51

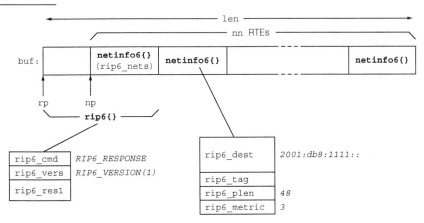

Relationship between a RIPng response message and **route6d** *implementation parameters.*

information; or, the packet may be received on an interface on which no IPv6 address is configured, although this is a very unlikely scenario. In either case, `riprequest()` is called to generate and transmit a RIPng response.

Response Validation

The rest of this function processes a RIPng response message.

Listing 1-33

── route6d.c
```
1150                    if (!IN6_IS_ADDR_LINKLOCAL(&fsock.sin6_addr)) {
1151                            trace(1, "Packets from non-ll addr: %s\n",
1152                               inet6_n2p(&fsock.sin6_addr));
1153                            return;          /* Ignore packets from non-link-local addr */
1154                    }
```
── route6d.c

1150–1154 If the source address of a response message is not a link-local address, it was likely to be sent in response to a RIPng request generated from an off-link router. The main purpose of such a request is that a management station conducts routing analysis within the autonomous system. Since the current **route6d** implementation does not send RIPng requests to off-link nodes, and the RIPng specification requires on-link routers to send both regular and triggered updates using a link-local address as the source address, the current **route6d** implementation ignores response packets that have non–link-local source addresses.

> [RFC2080] also specifies that a valid response must be sent from the RIPng port (521) and that the hop limit of a regular or triggered update must be 255, but this implementation does not check these conditions, which is a bug.

Listing 1-34

── route6d.c
```
1155            idx = IN6_LINKLOCAL_IFINDEX(fsock.sin6_addr);
1156            ifcp = (idx < nindex2ifc) ? index2ifc[idx] : NULL;
1157            if (!ifcp) {
1158                    trace(1, "Packets to unknown interface index %d\n", idx);
1159                    return;          /* Ignore it */
1160            }
1161            if (IN6_ARE_ADDR_EQUAL(&ifcp->ifc_mylladdr, &fsock.sin6_addr))
1162                    return;          /* The packet is from me; ignore */
1163            if (rp->rip6_cmd != RIP6_RESPONSE) {
1164                    trace(1, "Invalid command %d\n", rp->rip6_cmd);
1165                    return;
1166            }
```
── route6d.c

1155 This line assumes that the index of the receiving interface was embedded in Listing 1-30 and retrieves it from the address. This code is actually pointless; if the index was given in ancillary data, it should simply be used here; otherwise, since the kernel does not embed the index (recall Figure 1-43, page 54), the retrieved value will not be a valid index.

1156–1166 As long as the valid index is available, it should match an `ifc{}` structure in the interface table. Otherwise the packet is ignored.

1161–1162 Depending on configuration, though less likely, outgoing multicast packets may be looped back. The packet is ignored if it was sent by the local router.

1163–1165 RIPng version 1 defines only the request and response commands. Any other command is invalid and causes the packet to be ignored (note that the request case was covered in Listing 1-32).

Listing 1-35

route6d.c
```
1168            /* -N: no use */
1169            if (iff_find(ifcp, 'N') != NULL)
1170                    return;
```
route6d.c

1169–1170 The -N option may be specified when invoking the **route6d** daemon. The arguments to the -N option is a list of interfaces, which specifies those interfaces that should be excluded from RIPng operation. Function `iff_find()` searches **route6d**'s interface table to determine if the given interface belongs to the exclusion list. Any RIPng packet received over these excluded interfaces is ignored.

The -N option allows a router running **route6d** to choose on which of the attached networks RIPng will be run.

Listing 1-36

route6d.c
```
1172            tracet(1, "Recv(%s): from %s.%d info(%d)\n",
1173                    ifcp->ifc_name, inet6_n2p(&nh), ntohs(fsock.sin6_port), nn);
1174
1175            t = time(NULL);
1176            t_half_lifetime = t - (RIP_LIFETIME/2);
```
route6d.c

1175–1176 The current time is stored in the variable t, which will be used to either set the time in a new route or update an existing entry. t_half_lifetime is used for deciding if a newly discovered equal cost route should replace an existing one. This heuristic is discussed in the description of Listing 1-45 (pages 93–94).

Process RTE: Reject Invalid Routes

Listing 1-37

route6d.c
```
1177            for (; nn; nn--, np++) {
1178                    if (np->rip6_metric == NEXTHOP_METRIC) {
1179                            /* modify neighbor address */
1180                            if (IN6_IS_ADDR_LINKLOCAL(&np->rip6_dest)) {
1181                                    nh = np->rip6_dest;
1182                                    SET_IN6_LINKLOCAL_IFINDEX(nh, idx);
1183                                    trace(1, "\tNexthop: %s\n", inet6_n2p(&nh));
1184                            } else if (IN6_IS_ADDR_UNSPECIFIED(&np->rip6_dest)) {
1185                                    nh = fsock.sin6_addr;
```

```
1186                                    trace(1, "\tNexthop: %s\n", inet6_n2p(&nh));
1187                            } else {
1188                                    nh = fsock.sin6_addr;
1189                                    trace(1, "\tInvalid Nexthop: %s\n",
1190                                            inet6_n2p(&np->rip6_dest));
1191                            }
1192                            continue;
1193                    }
```
_____ route6d.c

1177 Each of the RTEs in the response is examined. An RTE carries the next hop address if
the RTE has a metric value of 0xff. In this case, the next hop address must be a link-local
address as required by the specification (see Section 1.4.1). If the next hop address is
unspecified, or if the next hop is a non link-local address, then the source of the response
packet should be taken as the next hop. In any case, the next hop address is saved in
variable nh. Processing continues on to the next RTE.

Listing 1-38
_____ route6d.c
```
1194                    if (IN6_IS_ADDR_MULTICAST(&np->rip6_dest)) {
1195                            trace(1, "\tMulticast netinfo6: %s/%d [%d]\n",
1196                                    inet6_n2p(&np->rip6_dest),
1197                                    np->rip6_plen, np->rip6_metric);
1198                            continue;
1199                    }
1200                    if (IN6_IS_ADDR_LOOPBACK(&np->rip6_dest)) {
1201                            trace(1, "\tLoopback netinfo6: %s/%d [%d]\n",
1202                                    inet6_n2p(&np->rip6_dest),
1203                                    np->rip6_plen, np->rip6_metric);
1204                            continue;
1205                    }
1206                    if (IN6_IS_ADDR_LINKLOCAL(&np->rip6_dest)) {
1207                            trace(1, "\tLink Local netinfo6: %s/%d [%d]\n",
1208                                    inet6_n2p(&np->rip6_dest),
1209                                    np->rip6_plen, np->rip6_metric);
1210                            continue;
1211                    }
1212                    /* may need to pass sitelocal prefix in some case, however*/
1213                    if (IN6_IS_ADDR_SITELOCAL(&np->rip6_dest) && !lflag) {
1214                            trace(1, "\tSite Local netinfo6: %s/%d [%d]\n",
1215                                    inet6_n2p(&np->rip6_dest),
1216                                    np->rip6_plen, np->rip6_metric);
1217                            continue;
1218                    }
```
_____ route6d.c

1194–1211 The IPv6 prefix field in the RTE is being validated. The following three types of
prefix are invalid. The RTE is ignored if the address part of the prefix is of these types.

- Multicast address
- Loopback address
- Link-local address

Technically, simply checking the address part is not enough because a short prefix
length may effectively change the type of the address. For example, if rip6_dest is
::1 and rip6_plen is 0, it actually means ::/0 (the default route). A default route
would usually be considered a valid route, but this implementation could reject it.

1213 By default the `lflag` is not set and **route6d** does not exchange site-local routes with other routers. See the description about Listing 1-23 (page 77) for more details on the `lflag`.

Listing 1-39

```
                                                                  route6d.c
1219                         trace(2, "\tnetinfo6: %s/%d [%d]",
1220                                 inet6_n2p(&np->rip6_dest),
1221                                 np->rip6_plen, np->rip6_metric);
1222                         if (np->rip6_tag)
1223                                 trace(2, "  tag=0x%04x", ntohs(np->rip6_tag) & 0xffff);
1224                         if (dflag >= 2) {
1225                                 ia = np->rip6_dest;
1226                                 applyplen(&ia, np->rip6_plen);
1227                                 if (!IN6_ARE_ADDR_EQUAL(&ia, &np->rip6_dest))
1228                                         trace(2, " [junk outside prefix]");
1229                         }
                                                                  route6d.c
```

1222 The route tag stored in `rip6_tag` is kept intact; it must be preserved by the receiving router and it is redistributed with the route. The route tag must have consistent semantics among all of the routers that run RIPng in the autonomous system. As explained in Section 1.4.1, the receiving router must preserve the tag and redistribute it unmodified.

Process RTE: Apply Inbound Filter

Listing 1-40

```
                                                                  route6d.c
1231                /*
1232                 * -L: listen only if the prefix matches the configuration
1233                 */
1234                ok = 1;          /* if there's no L filter, it is ok */
1235                for (iffp = ifcp->ifc_filter; iffp; iffp = iffp->iff_next) {
1236                        if (iffp->iff_type != 'L')
1237                                continue;
1238                        ok = 0;
1239                        if (np->rip6_plen < iffp->iff_plen)
1240                                continue;
1241                        /* special rule: ::/0 means default, not "in /0" */
1242                        if (iffp->iff_plen == 0 && np->rip6_plen > 0)
1243                                continue;
1244                        ia = np->rip6_dest;
1245                        applyplen(&ia, iffp->iff_plen);
1246                        if (IN6_ARE_ADDR_EQUAL(&ia, &iffp->iff_addr)) {
1247                                ok = 1;
1248                                break;
1249                        }
1250                }
1251                if (!ok) {
1252                        trace(2, "  (filtered)\n");
1253                        continue;
1254                }
                                                                  route6d.c
```

The `-L` option may be specified when invoking the **route6d** daemon (see Table 1-8 on page 66).

The `-L` option can be specified multiple times to configure multiple filter entries. When filter entries are specified, only those prefixes that are covered by any of the filter entries will be accepted.

1235–1237 Each configured filter is examined to find the -L option.

1238–1240 If the prefix length of the advertised route is smaller than the prefix length of filter, the advertised prefix cannot match the filter prefix and is ignored.

1242–1243 The ::/0 prefix is a special prefix filter when it is given as an argument to the -L option. This prefix is the default route, which does not mean accepting all prefixes. The default route condition is checked here. The advertised prefix is filtered if the default route is expected but the advertised route is not.

1244–1249 Now the advertised prefix length is equal to or longer than the length of the filter prefix. The advertised prefix is accepted if it is covered by the filter prefix. This condition is confirmed by calling applyplen() to mask the advertised prefix so that the trailing bit will be zero-cleared and then comparing the whole 128 bits of the two prefixes by the IN6_ARE_ADDR_EQUAL() macro.

1251–1254 The ok variable indicates whether the advertised prefix can be ignored; if so, the function returns without further processing.

Process RTE: Update Routing Table

Listing 1-41

——route6d.c
```
1256                    trace(2, "\n");
1257                    np->rip6_metric++;
1258                    np->rip6_metric += ifcp->ifc_metric;
1259                    if (np->rip6_metric > HOPCNT_INFINITY6)
1260                        np->rip6_metric = HOPCNT_INFINITY6;
```
——route6d.c

1257–1258 The RIPng specification discusses the metric as being either a simple hop count or a value that is set by an administrator. In the FreeBSD operating system, the ifc_metric value is defined as the additional cost of the network that may be set by the administrator using the **ifconfig** command. In other words, the metric is incremented by at least one hop and then the additional cost of ifc_metric is added. By default the value of ifc_metric is 0. For example, issuing the ifconfig command gives the following:

```
fxp0: flags=8843<UP,BROADCAST,RUNNING,SIMPLEX,MULTICAST> mtu 1500
        inet6 fe80::213:20ff:fea9:6e71%fxp0 prefixlen 64 scopeid 0x2
        inet 192.0.2.1 netmask 0xffffff00 broadcast 192.0.2.255
        ether 00:13:20:a9:6e:71
        media: Ethernet autoselect (100baseTX)
        status: active
```

After issuing the command

```
ifconfig. fxp0 metric 2
```

the output shows

```
fxp0: flags=8843<UP,BROADCAST,RUNNING,SIMPLEX,MULTICAST> metric 2 mtu 1500
        inet6 fe80::213:20ff:fea9:6e71%fxp0 prefixlen 64 scopeid 0x2
        inet 192.0.2.1 netmask 0xffffff00 broadcast 192.0.2.255
        ether 00:13:20:a9:6e:71
        media: Ethernet autoselect (100baseTX)
        status: active
```

The metric value is shown in the first line of the output.

1259–1260 The metric `rip6_metric` is set to 16 (`HOPCNT_INFINITY6`) if its value becomes larger than 16, effectively invalidating the advertised prefix.

Listing 1-42

route6d.c

```
1262                  applyplen(&np->rip6_dest, np->rip6_plen);
1263                  if ((rrt = rtsearch(np, NULL)) != NULL) {
```

route6d.c

1262–1263 The destination prefix is extracted according to the advertised prefix length. The local function `rtsearch()` is called to search **route6d**'s routing table for the given prefix. If found, information in the routing entry is updated.

Figure 1-52 depicts how an advertised route is processed when it is already in **route6d**'s routing table. Each number in the figure represents one decision path. In the code description to follow, we will use the term *decision path* and a set of numbers enclosed in parentheses to refer to the decision path implemented by a code segment. For example, a decision path (1, 2) indicates that the code segment implements decision paths 1 and 2 shown in the figure.

Listing 1-43

route6d.c

```
1264          if (rrt->rrt_t == 0)
1265                  continue;        /* Intf route has priority */
1266          nq = &rrt->rrt_info;
1267          if (nq->rip6_metric > np->rip6_metric) {
1268                  if (rrt->rrt_index == ifcp->ifc_index &&
1269                      IN6_ARE_ADDR_EQUAL(&nh, &rrt->rrt_gw)) {
1270                          /* Small metric from the same
   gateway */
1271                          nq->rip6_metric = np->rip6_metric;
1272                  } else {
1273                          /* Better route found */
1274                          rrt->rrt_index = ifcp->ifc_index;
1275                          /* Update routing table */
1276                          delroute(nq, &rrt->rrt_gw);
1277                          rrt->rrt_gw = nh;
1278                          *nq = *np;
1279                          addroute(rrt, &nh, ifcp);
1280                  }
1281                  rrt->rrt_rflags |= RRTF_CHANGED;
1282                  rrt->rrt_t = t;
1283                  need_trigger = 1;
```

route6d.c

— Line 1270 is broken here for layout reasons. However, it is a single line of code.

1264–1265 The advertised route is bypassed if the same route is already present as a static route in the local **route6d**'s routing table (recall `rrt_t` is set to 0 for static routes as explained for Listing 1-12). This property implies that the statically configured route overwrites any dynamically advertised route, which serves as a way to implement route policy.

1266 Variable `nq` points to the route in **route6d**'s routing table, which will be referred to as the *stored route* in the following discussion.

FIGURE 1-52

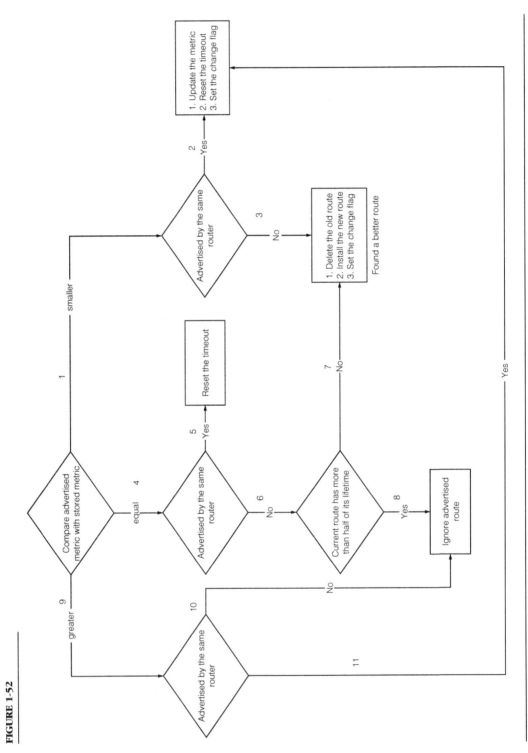

Processing advertised route.

1267–1280 If the advertised route has a smaller metric value, then

- the metric of the stored route is updated if the advertised route and the stored route came from the same router. This segment of code implements the decision paths (1, 2).
- the advertised route is a better route if the route was advertised by a different router. In this case, both the next hop address and the arrival interface is updated. Other advertised value is updated in the stored route at line 1279. Since the previously stored route had a different next hop, the local function delroute() is called to remove the previous route from the kernel routing table. Then the local function addroute() is called to add the same route but with the new next hop into the kernel routing table. This segment of code implements the decision paths (1, 3).

1281–1282 In either case the RRTF_CHANGED flag is marked in rrt_rtflags to reflect that the stored route has been updated. need_trigger is set so that a triggered update may be generated once the input processing is done. The stored route is also given a new lifetime.

Listing 1-44
————————————————————————— route6d.c

```
1284                } else if (nq->rip6_metric < np->rip6_metric &&
1285                        rrt->rrt_index == ifcp->ifc_index &&
1286                        IN6_ARE_ADDR_EQUAL(&nh, &rrt->rrt_gw)) {
1287                    /* Got worse route from same gw */
1288                    nq->rip6_metric = np->rip6_metric;
1289                    rrt->rrt_t = t;
1290                    rrt->rrt_rflags |= RRTF_CHANGED;
1291                    need_trigger = 1;
```
————————————————————————— route6d.c

1284–1291 If an advertised route has a larger metric value than that of the stored route, then

- the metric of the stored route is updated if the advertised route and the stored route came from the same router. The route lifetime is reset and the change flag is set. This segment of code implements the decision paths (9, 11).
- advertised route is simply ignored because the stored route is a better route. This segment of code implements the decision paths (9, 10).

Listing 1-45
————————————————————————— route6d.c

```
1292                } else if (nq->rip6_metric == np->rip6_metric &&
1293                        np->rip6_metric < HOPCNT_INFINITY6) {
1294                    if (rrt->rrt_index == ifcp->ifc_index &&
1295                        IN6_ARE_ADDR_EQUAL(&nh, &rrt->rrt_gw)) {
1296                        /* same metric, same route from
same gw */
1297                        rrt->rrt_t = t;
1298                    } else if (rrt->rrt_t < t_half_lifetime) {
1299                        /* Better route found */
1300                        rrt->rrt_index = ifcp->ifc_index;
1301                        /* Update routing table */
1302                        delroute(nq, &rrt->rrt_gw);
1303                        rrt->rrt_gw = nh;
1304                        *nq = *np;
```

```
1305                                     addroute(rrt, &nh, ifcp);
1306                                     rrt->rrt_rflags |= RRTF_CHANGED;
1307                                     rrt->rrt_t = t;
1308                             }
1309                     }
1310                     /*
1311                      * if nq->rip6_metric == HOPCNT_INFINITY6 then
1312                      * do not update age value.  Do nothing.
1313                      */
```
————————————————————————————————————— route6d.c

— Line 1296 is broken here for layout reasons. However, it is a single line of code.

1292–1309 The advertised route has the same metric as that of the stored route and the route
is a reachable route. The stored route is simply given a new lifetime and no other changes
are made. This segment of code implements the decision paths (4, 5). If a different router
advertised the route and the stored route has less than half of its lifetime left, then the stored
route is updated similarly to what was done in lines 1273–1279 as given in the description
for the code block of lines 1267–1280 (Listing 1-43). This segment of code implements the
decision paths (4, 6, 7). Switching to a new route when the stored route is at least halfway
to its expiration is a useful heuristic to avoid sticking to a dead route while suppressing
excessive route flapping and frequent triggered updates. This is a recommended heuristic
to RIPng implementations by [RFC2080].

Listing 1-46

————————————————————————————————————— route6d.c
```
1314                     } else if (np->rip6_metric < HOPCNT_INFINITY6) {
1315                             /* Got a new valid route */
1316                             if ((rrt = MALLOC(struct riprt)) == NULL) {
1317                                     fatal("malloc: struct riprt");
1318                                     /*NOTREACHED*/
1319                             }
1320                             memset(rrt, 0, sizeof(*rrt));
1321                             nq = &rrt->rrt_info;
1322
1323                             rrt->rrt_same = NULL;
1324                             rrt->rrt_index = ifcp->ifc_index;
1325                             rrt->rrt_flags = RTF_UP|RTF_GATEWAY;
1326                             rrt->rrt_gw = nh;
1327                             *nq = *np;
1328                             applyplen(&nq->rip6_dest, nq->rip6_plen);
1329                             if (nq->rip6_plen == sizeof(struct in6_addr) * 8)
1330                                     rrt->rrt_flags |= RTF_HOST;
1331
1332                             /* Put the route to the list */
1333                             rrt->rrt_next = riprt;
1334                             riprt = rrt;
1335                             /* Update routing table */
1336                             addroute(rrt, &nh, ifcp);
1337                             rrt->rrt_rflags |= RRTF_CHANGED;
1338                             need_trigger = 1;
1339                             rrt->rrt_t = t;
1340                     }
1341             }
```
————————————————————————————————————— route6d.c

1314–1320 This `else` block corresponds to the big `if` block starting in Listing 1-42, indicating
that the advertised route is not in **route6d**'s routing table. A route entry `riprt{}` is thus
allocated to store this new route.

1321–1330 `rrt_same` is currently not used by the implementation. `rrt_index` is initialized
to the index of the receiving interface. `rrt_gw` is initialized with the next hop address

that was saved in nh. The RTF_UP and the RTF_GATEWAY flags are saved in rrt_flags only for installing the route into the kernel routing table. Content of the RTE is copied into new route entry. Function applyplen() is called to extract the prefix according to the prefix length and save the extracted value into rip6_dest. The advertised route is a host route if the prefix length is 128, in which case the RTF_HOST flag is set in rrt_flags appropriately.

1333–1336 The new route entry is inserted into **route6d**'s routing table. Then addroute() is called to install this route into the kernel's routing table.

1337–1339 The RRTF_CHANGED flag is set to reflect the fact that the route entry is newly updated. need_trigger is set to 1 because a triggered update needs to be sent on all attached interfaces. The expiration time is then set for the new route entry.

Initiate Triggered Update

Listing 1-47

```
                                                              route6d.c
1342            /* XXX need to care the interval between triggered updates */
1343            if (need_trigger) {
1344                    if (nextalarm > time(NULL) + RIP_TRIG_INT6_MAX) {
1345                            for (ic = ifc; ic; ic = ic->ifc_next) {
1346                                    if (ifcp->ifc_index == ic->ifc_index)
1347                                            continue;
1348                                    if (ic->ifc_flags & IFF_UP)
1349                                            ripsend(ic, &ic->ifc_ripsin,
1350                                                    RRTF_CHANGED);
1351                            }
1352                    }
1353                    /* Reset the flag */
1354                    for (rrt = riprt; rrt; rrt = rrt->rrt_next)
1355                            rrt->rrt_rflags &= ~RRTF_CHANGED;
1356            }
1357    }
                                                              route6d.c
```

1343–1344 A triggered update will be sent immediately if the next regular update is beyond a delay of 5 (RIP_TRIG_INT6_MAX) seconds. The global nextalarm variable records the time when the next regular update will be sent.

> This code does not really conform to the protocol specification. [RFC2080] requires that an initial triggered update be delayed for a random interval between 1 and 5 seconds, and that subsequent updates also be delayed until this interval elapses. The idea is to accumulate as many triggered updates as possible before sending a response message containing all the updates in order to reduce overhead and maximize bandwidth utilization. This implementation does not impose the random delay.

1345–1352 Function ripsend() is called to send the update packet on all of the running interfaces except the one on which the response arrived. A running interface has the IFF_UP flag. Since the RRTF_CHANGED flag is given as an argument, ripsend() will send only those routes that carry this change flag, in other words, it will send a triggered update.

1354–1355 The RRTF_CHANGE flag is cleared for all of the recently updated routes once
ripsend() returns.

1.13.3 riprequest() Function

Function riprequest() is called to generate a response message for a given request.

Listing 1-48

```
                                                                         route6d.c
1391    void
1392    riprequest(ifcp, np, nn, sin6)
1393            struct ifc *ifcp;
1394            struct netinfo6 *np;
1395            int nn;
1396            struct sockaddr_in6 *sin6;
1397    {
1398            int i;
1399            struct riprt *rrt;
1400
1401            if (!(nn == 1 && IN6_IS_ADDR_UNSPECIFIED(&np->rip6_dest) &&
1402                np->rip6_plen == 0 && np->rip6_metric == HOPCNT_INFINITY6)) {
1403                    /* Specific response, don't split-horizon */
1404                    trace(1, "\tRIP Request\n");
1405                    for (i = 0; i < nn; i++, np++) {
1406                            rrt = rtsearch(np, NULL);
1407                            if (rrt)
1408                                    np->rip6_metric = rrt->rrt_info.rip6_metric;
1409                            else
1410                                    np->rip6_metric = HOPCNT_INFINITY6;
1411                    }
1412                    (void)sendpacket(sin6, RIPSIZE(nn));
1413                    return;
1414            }
1415            /* Whole routing table dump */
1416            trace(1, "\tRIP Request -- whole routing table\n");
1417            ripsend(ifcp, sin6, RRTF_SENDANYWAY);
1418    }
                                                                         route6d.c
```

1392–1396 On input ifcp points to the receiving interface. np points to the first RTE in the
received message. nn holds the number of RTEs that are present in the request message.
sin6 points to the destination to where the response message is to be sent.

1401–1414 The requester is asking for the entire routing table if there is exactly one RTE, the
destination prefix is ::/0, and the metric is infinity. The if statement on lines 1401 and
1402 tests to see if the conditions of sending the entire routing table are met. If not, then
each of the RTEs in the request message is processed one by one. Function rtsearch()
is called to look up the destination prefix in the local routing table by exact matching(*).
If an entry is found then the metric value of that entry is stored in the RTE. Otherwise, the
metric is set to infinity (16) to indicate the route is missing in the router's routing table.

> (*): It is not clear from the specification [RFC2080] whether this should be an exact
> match or a longest prefix match.

Function sendpacket() is called to transmit the response packet once all of the RTEs
have been processed.

1417 Function ripsend() is called to send the entire routing table.

1.13.4 `ripsend()` Function

Function `ripsend()` is called to generate and transmit a RIPng response packet. A RIPng response packet is generated for one of the following reasons:

- A router sends its entire routing table every 30 seconds (with some random offset).

- A router sends a response packet due to triggered updates.

- A router sends the entire routing table due to an explicit request.

Function `riprequest()` handles the case where **route6d** daemon sends a response packet in reply to an explicit query of specific IPv6 destination prefixes (see Section 1.13.3).

Listing 1-49

```
                                                              route6d.c
786     /*
787      * Generate RIP6_RESPONSE packets and send them.
788      */
789     void
790     ripsend(ifcp, sin6, flag)
791             struct  ifc *ifcp;
792             struct  sockaddr_in6 *sin6;
793             int flag;
794     {
795             struct  riprt *rrt;
796             struct  in6_addr *nh;   /* next hop */
797             int     maxrte;
                                                              route6d.c
```

789–793 On input, `ifcp` points to the interface associated with a directly attached network on which the response would be sent. `sin6` points to the destination address of the response packet. `flag` contains the output filter flags.

Listing 1-50

```
                                                              route6d.c
799             if (qflag)
800                     return;
                                                              route6d.c
```

799–800 The local node is in the quiet mode, which only listens to RIPng advertisements if the `qflag` is set to 1. In this case, `ripsend()` returns here without taking further action.

Listing 1-51

```
                                                              route6d.c
802             if (ifcp == NULL) {
803                     /*
804                      * Request from non-link local address is not
805                      * a regular route6d update.
806                      */
807                     maxrte = (IFMINMTU - sizeof(struct ip6_hdr) -
808                                 sizeof(struct udphdr) -
809                                 sizeof(struct rip6) + sizeof(struct netinfo6)) /
810                                 sizeof(struct netinfo6);
811                     nrt = 0; np = ripbuf->rip6_nets; nh = NULL;
812                     for (rrt = riprt; rrt; rrt = rrt->rrt_next) {
813                             if (rrt->rrt_rflags & RRTF_NOADVERTISE)
814                                     continue;
815                             /* Put the route to the buffer */
816                             *np = rrt->rrt_info;
```

```
817                           np++; nrt++;
818                           if (nrt == maxrte) {
819                                   ripflush(NULL, sin6);
820                                   nh = NULL;
821                           }
822                   }
823                   if (nrt)          /* Send last packet */
824                           ripflush(NULL, sin6);
825                   return;
826           }
```
                                                                        _____route6d.c

802–826 The `ifcp` pointer may be NULL if the kernel was not able to allocate an ancillary
data object to return the received packet information back to the caller of `recvmsg()`
(see Listing 1-32, page 85).

The code comment sounds as if the packet comes from an off-link node in this case,
but this is not always correct; `ifcp` can be NULL for an on-link request, too. Even if
the packet is sent from an off-link node, the protocol specification does not require such
requests to be processed differently, so the code in the rest of this block does not conform
to the specification. In particular, skipping the split horizon algorithm and configured
route filters for an on-link request will cause an undesirable routing effect and should be
considered a bug. This block of code should therefore be removed and the caller should
make sure that a valid `ifp` pointer is provided. Further discussion on the rest of the block is
omitted.

Listing 1-52
                                                                        _____route6d.c

```
828           if ((flag & RRTF_SENDANYWAY) == 0 &&
829               (qflag || (ifcp->ifc_flags & IFF_LOOPBACK)))
830                   return;
```
                                                                        _____route6d.c

828–830 The response packet is not sent on the loopback interface unless the
`RRTF_SENDANYWAY` flag is set by the caller.[5] This flag is set when **route6d** is sending a response message to a request (see Listing 1-48), in which case another process in
the local node, such as a monitoring process, may have sent the request and it must be
responded to.

Listing 1-53
                                                                        _____route6d.c

```
832           /* -N: no use */
833           if (iff_find(ifcp, 'N') != NULL)
834                   return;
```
                                                                        _____route6d.c

832–834 As discussed in Listing 1-35 (page 87), the -N option prevents **route6d** from advertising RIPng routes on specific interfaces. The `ripsend()` function returns here if
`iff_find()` indicates that the given interface `ifcp` is in the exclusion list.

---

5. The check on `qflag` is redundant because it is already performed on line 799 of Listing 1-50.

Listing 1-54

```
                                                           route6d.c
836              /* -T: generate default route only */
837              if (iff_find(ifcp, 'T') != NULL) {
838                      struct netinfo6 rrt_info;
839                      memset(&rrt_info, 0, sizeof(struct netinfo6));
840                      rrt_info.rip6_dest = in6addr_any;
841                      rrt_info.rip6_plen = 0;
842                      rrt_info.rip6_metric = 1;
843                      rrt_info.rip6_metric += ifcp->ifc_metric;
844                      rrt_info.rip6_tag = htons(routetag & 0xffff);
845                      np = ripbuf->rip6_nets;
846                      *np = rrt_info;
847                      nrt = 1;
848                      ripflush(ifcp, sin6);
849                      return;
850              }
                                                           route6d.c
```

837–850 The `-T` option instructs **route6d** to generate only a default route on a given interface. If function `iff_find()` determines the `-T` option applies to the given interface represented by `ifcp`, then a default route is built and is sent by `ripflush()`.

The global variable `routetag` is initialized by the `-t` option, which specifies a route tag to be assigned to all routes that are originated by the local **route6d** daemon.

Again, the route metric is the sum of the hop count and the `ifc_metric` value. The hop count is set to 1.

Listing 1-55

```
                                                           route6d.c
852              maxrte = (ifcp->ifc_mtu - sizeof(struct ip6_hdr) -
853                      sizeof(struct udphdr) -
854                      sizeof(struct rip6) + sizeof(struct netinfo6)) /
855                      sizeof(struct netinfo6);
                                                           route6d.c
```

852–855 `maxrte` is calculated according to the formula given by Equation 1.1 (page 14). The link MTU is retrieved from the output interface.

> Computing `maxrte` based on the link MTU may not be reasonable when this response message is sent as a result of a request message (i.e., not a regular or triggered update), because in this case the packet may be sent off-link and there may be an intermediate link with a smaller MTU. It should be safer to use the IPv6 minimum link MTU (1280 bytes) for off-link destinations.

Listing 1-56

```
                                                           route6d.c
857              nrt = 0; np = ripbuf->rip6_nets; nh = NULL;
858              for (rrt = riprt; rrt; rrt = rrt->rrt_next) {
859                      if (rrt->rrt_rflags & RRTF_NOADVERTISE)
860                              continue;
                                                           route6d.c
```

857 Variables `nrt` and `np` are globally accessible in `route6d.c` and are shared with other routines; `nrt` is the number of RTEs contained in the response message, and `np` points to the `netinfo6{}` structure that is currently built in the message buffer. Both variables will be updated as the message construction proceeds. A global buffer `ripbuf` (see Table 1-11, page 73) is used as a work space to construct the response message. When non-NULL, `nh` points to an `in6_addr{}` structure of the next hop address of particular route destinations.

858 Each entry in the routing table (`rrt`) is now examined in the `for` loop; some are used to add an RTE in the response message, and others are filtered based on the filtering configuration or the property of the route. Figure 1-53 shows the relationship between the routing table and the actual response message with the initial setting of related parameters.

859–860 Any route that is explicitly marked with the `RRTF_NOADVERTISE` flag will not be advertised and is bypassed here.

Listing 1-57
—— route6d.c
```
862                    /* Need to check filter here */
863                    if (out_filter(rrt, ifcp) == 0)
864                            continue;
```
—— route6d.c

863–864 The function `out_filter()` (not described in this book) is called to determine if an additional filter on the output interface applies to the route. A return value of 0 indicates `out_filter()` has filtered the route, so the route is bypassed.

Listing 1-58
—— route6d.c
```
866                    /* Check split horizon and other conditions */
867                    if (tobeadv(rrt, ifcp) == 0)
868                            continue;
```
—— route6d.c

FIGURE 1-53
—————————————

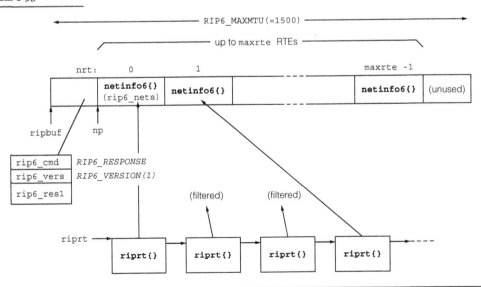

Constructing RIPng response message.

867–868 The `tobeadv()` function (not described in this book) examines the given route and determines if the route should be filtered by the split horizon algorithm, or if the route should be filtered because it is a manually installed route with the *reject* or *blackhole* flag. In these cases `tobeadv()` returns 0, and this route entry is ignored.

Listing 1-59
_____ route6d.c
```
870                         /* Only considers the routes with flag if specified */
871                         if ((flag & RRTF_CHANGED) &&
872                             (rrt->rrt_rflags & RRTF_CHANGED) == 0)
873                                 continue;
```
_____ route6d.c

871–873 If `ripsend()` is currently called to send triggered updates, which is indicated by the RRTF_CHANGED flag (see Listing 1-47), then only those routes that have been modified recently will be included in this response, while all other routes are bypassed.

Listing 1-60
_____ route6d.c
```
875                         /* Check nexthop */
876                         if (rrt->rrt_index == ifcp->ifc_index &&
877                             !IN6_IS_ADDR_UNSPECIFIED(&rrt->rrt_gw) &&
878                             (rrt->rrt_rflags & RRTF_NH_NOT_LLADDR) == 0) {
879                                 if (nh == NULL || !IN6_ARE_ADDR_EQUAL(nh, &rrt->
   rrt_gw)) {
880                                         if (nrt == maxrte - 2)
881                                                 ripflush(ifcp, sin6);
882                                         np->rip6_dest = rrt->rrt_gw;
883                                         if (IN6_IS_ADDR_LINKLOCAL(&np->rip6_dest))
884                                                 SET_IN6_LINKLOCAL_IFINDEX(np->
   rip6_dest, 0);
885                                         np->rip6_plen = 0;
886                                         np->rip6_tag = 0;
887                                         np->rip6_metric = NEXTHOP_METRIC;
888                                         nh = &rrt->rrt_gw;
889                                         np++; nrt++;
890                                 }
```
_____ route6d.c
− *Lines 879 and 884 are broken here for layout reasons. However, these are a single line of code.*

876–878 This block of the code checks to see if the next hop address should be explicitly specified as a separate RTE and includes the RTE when necessary. The purpose of such explicit next hop information is to optimize a redundant forwarding path within a single link. Consider the network topology shown in Figure 1-54, where routers A and B exchange routes via RIPng while router C does not advertise any routes by itself. It is also assumed that router C is connected to a different network identified by the prefix `2001:db8:1::/48` and router A configures a static route to the network. Since router B does not know how to route packets to `2001:db8:1::/48`, router A must advertise this route. Router A could advertise the route just like other routes so that router B would forward subsequent packets to router A, but router A can tell B the better path by the use of next hop RTE with a link-local address of C in the shared link.

Usually the `tobeadv()` function filters a route entry if its outgoing interface is equal to the interface to which the RIPng response is going to be sent; so if the `if` condition on

FIGURE 1-54

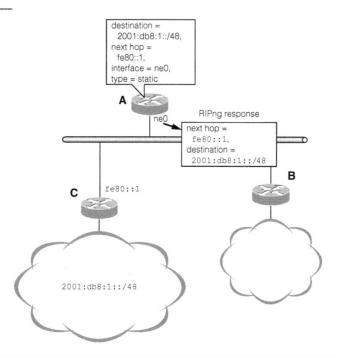

Forwarding path optimization by the use of next hop specification in RIPng response.

line 876 is met, it is likely to be a statically configured route which should be advertised with an explicit next hop. [RFC2080] requires the next hop address to be a link-local address, which is checked in the subsequent conditions of the `if` statement.

There are two other, probably unintended cases where these conditions hold when the `tobeadv()` function skips filtering by the split horizon algorithm. One case is that the route was learned from another router on the link via RIPng. The other case is that the route is a direct route to the interface associated with an address configured on the interface.

But supporting these cases does not really make sense. The first case is to disable split horizon, but in that case the route should simply be readvertised as a route from this router, rather than specifying the next hop. In the second case, `rrt_gw` is not a link-local address (recall the example shown in Figure 1-46, page 69), and will be treated as the unspecified address by the receiver; it does not make sense because the purpose of the explicit next hop is to optimize the forwarding path for the destination.

This block of code should be revised so that only the intended cases will be covered.

879 Variable `nh` remembers the current next hop. If it is currently not specified or a different next hop is specified, a new next hop RTE must be included.

880–881 A buffer space for at least two RTEs must be available, one for setting the next hop, the other for at least one route entry to which the next hop applies. The `ripflush()` function is called to transmit the accumulated routes if the space is insufficient. Note that `ripflush()` will reset `np` and `nrt`.

882–890 The RTE is filled with the next hop information as shown in Figure 1-12 (page 13).

Listing 1-61

——— route6d.c

```
891                     } else if (nh && (rrt->rrt_index != ifcp->ifc_index ||
892                                !IN6_ARE_ADDR_EQUAL(nh, &rrt->rrt_gw) ||
893                                rrt->rrt_rflags & RRTF_NH_NOT_LLADDR)) {
894                             /* Reset nexthop */
895                             if (nrt == maxrte - 2)
896                                     ripflush(ifcp, sin6);
897                             memset(np, 0, sizeof(struct netinfo6));
898                             np->rip6_metric = NEXTHOP_METRIC;
899                             nh = NULL;
900                             np++; nrt++;
901                     }
```

——— route6d.c

891–900 The `else` case holds if the route goes to a different link or the route is configured with a non link-local gateway address, which is probably statically configured. If, in addition, an explicit next hop is specified, it is reset here to the unspecified address, meaning this local router. It will allow the receiving routers to use the link-local address of the local router as the next hop for the advertised routes.

> The latter part of the `else if` condition should always hold and is redundant; it should suffice to check `nh`. This check may have intended to allow the local router to specify itself for a route entry with a non link-local address, but this code does not fully implement the possible intent because this block is effective only when a next hop was previously specified.

Listing 1-62

——— route6d.c

```
903                             /* Put the route to the buffer */
904                             *np = rrt->rrt_info;
905                             np++; nrt++;
906                             if (nrt == maxrte) {
907                                     ripflush(ifcp, sin6);
908                                     nh = NULL;
909                             }
910                     }
911             if (nrt)            /* Send last packet */
912                     ripflush(ifcp, sin6);
913     }
```

——— route6d.c

904–909 The route is copied into the output buffer and if the number of accumulated routes has reached the maximum, `ripflush()` is called to transmit the RIPng response message.

911–912 The remaining portion of the output buffer, if any, is sent out by `ripflush()`.

1.13.5 `ripalarm()` Function

The `ripalarm()` function is invoked about every 30 seconds (with some random offsets) to transmit the entire routing table. The route lifetime (RIP_LIFETIME, 180 seconds) and holddown time (RIP_HOLDDOWN, 30 seconds) are updated in this function, which makes sense because these are multiples of this call interval.

Listing 1-63

```
                                                               route6d.c
563    void
564    ripalarm()
565    {
566            struct  ifc *ifcp;
567            struct  riprt *rrt, *rrt_prev, *rrt_next;
568            time_t  t_lifetime, t_holddown;
569
570            /* age the RIP routes */
571            rrt_prev = 0;
572            t_lifetime = time(NULL) - RIP_LIFETIME;
573            t_holddown = t_lifetime - RIP_HOLDDOWN;
574            for (rrt = riprt; rrt; rrt = rrt_next) {
575                    rrt_next = rrt->rrt_next;
576
577                    if (rrt->rrt_t == 0) {
578                            rrt_prev = rrt;
579                            continue;
580                    }
581                    if (rrt->rrt_t < t_holddown) {
582                            if (rrt_prev) {
583                                    rrt_prev->rrt_next = rrt->rrt_next;
584                            } else {
585                                    riprt = rrt->rrt_next;
586                            }
587                            delroute(&rrt->rrt_info, &rrt->rrt_gw);
588                            free(rrt);
589                            continue;
590                    }
591                    if (rrt->rrt_t < t_lifetime)
592                            rrt->rrt_info.rip6_metric = HOPCNT_INFINITY6;
593                    rrt_prev = rrt;
594            }
595            /* Supply updates */
596            for (ifcp = ifc; ifcp; ifcp = ifcp->ifc_next) {
597                    if (ifcp->ifc_index > 0 && (ifcp->ifc_flags & IFF_UP))
598                            ripsend(ifcp, &ifcp->ifc_ripsin, 0);
599            }
600            alarm(ripinterval(SUPPLY_INTERVAL6));
601    }
                                                               route6d.c
```

572–573 Since `rrt_t` is not updated after its initialization, `t_lifetime` and `t_holddown` calculate the lifetime and holddown times in the reverse to determine expiration.

574–575 Every entry in the **route6d** routing table is examined to see if one of the two timers has expired.

577–579 A route entry that has `rrt_t` being 0 indicates a static route entry. Static route entries do not expire and are bypassed in this function.

581–590 If the holddown timer has expired for a route entry, function `delroute()` is called to delete this route entry from the kernel routing table. The memory associated with the deleted route entry is freed. If `rrt_prev` is NULL, then the first entry in the routing table is being deleted, so `riprt` is also updated.

591–592 If the route entry has expired, its metric is set to infinity (metric of 16) indicating the destination is no longer reachable.

596–599 A RIPng response message is generated for each directly connected network. The function `ripsend()` is called to send the RIPng response message on each active interface. Since the message is a regular update, the response message is sent to the all-rip-routers multicast address.

600 The interval timer is re-armed here. The `ripinterval()` function provides the timer interval based on the requirement of [RFC2080] to avoid synchronized updates among multiple routers. Specifically, it returns the standard interval (`SUPPLY_INTERVAL6`, which is 30) ±*randomtime* where *randomtime* is between 0 and 15. It also sets the global variable `nextalarm` to the next expiration time of the timer (see Listing 1-47 on page 95).

1.14 Routing Operation Using route6d

This section discusses the IPv6 routing operation using **route6d**. In a FreeBSD/KAME box, the **route6d** daemon can be started from the `rc` script executed at boot time, thereby enabling the routing and forwarding functions of the box whenever the box restarts. The configuration parameters of the program and other related information such as address information could be specified from the terminal application directly, but it is more usual to define these configuration parameters in the `/etc/rc.conf` file and use the `rc` script to start the daemon.

The detailed usage of the **route6d** program is not discussed in this book. Table 1-8 (page 66) provided some command line options of **route6d**. For further details, the manual page of **route6d** should be consulted using the UNIX **man** command. The manual page is installed as `/usr/local/v6/man/man8/route6d.8.gz`.

As discussed in Section 1.4, the RIPng protocol is not designed to operate for a large and complex IPv6 network. This section discusses RIPng operation for the following simple network configurations.

1 A leaf network

2 A simple loop network

3 A hierarchical network

1.14.1 A Leaf Network

The simplest case of operating **route6d** is the case where there is only one local subnet. Figure 1-55 shows the network configuration used in this subsection.

The network prefix of the leaf network is `2001:db8:0:1000::/64`. There is one router which connects the network and the upstream network. In this case, all routing information will come from the upstream router. The **route6d** program on the boundary router needs to advertise the routing information of the leaf network so that packets sent to this leaf network will be forwarded properly. In this configuration, the routing information for `2001:db8:0:1000::/64` needs to be advertised from the router.

FIGURE 1-55

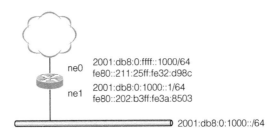

neo   2001:db8:0:ffff::1000/64
       fe80::211:25ff:fe32:d98c

ne1   2001:db8:0:1000::1/64
       fe80::202:b3ff:fe3a:8503

2001:db8:0:1000::/64

A leaf network.

When operating a router, all address configurations on the interfaces of the router must be done manually. In this case, we will assign 2001:db8:0:1000::1 on the ne1 interface and 2001:db8:0:ffff::1000 on the ne0 interface of the router.

The following command sequence will complete all of the configuration for this case.

```
# ifconfig ne1 2001:db8:0:1000::1/64
# ifconfig ne1 2001:db8:0:1000::/64 anycast
# ifconfig ne0 2001:db8:0:ffff::1000/64
# ifconfig ne0 2001:db8:0:ffff::/64 anycast
# route6d
```

The **ifconfig** command assigns an interface address and at the same time the network direct route is added statically in the routing table maintained in the kernel. In the above case, 2001:db8:0:1000::/64 and 2001:db8:0:ffff::/64 are added after assigning addresses. The two anycast addresses mean the subnet-router anycast address for the subnet prefix, which all IPv6 routers must configure (see Chapter 2 of *IPv6 Core Protocols Implementation*). The address consists of the network prefix and an all-zero interface identifier.

Listing 1-64 shows the routing table after the address assignment. Note that some lines are intentionally omitted from the output described in the listing because these are unnecessary in the following discussion.

Listing 1-64

── Direct route information

```
% netstat -rn -f inet6
Routing tables

Internet6:
Destination                      Gateway               Flags      Netif Expire
2001:db8:0:1000::                00:02:b3:3a:85:03     UHL        lo0 =>
2001:db8:0:1000::/64             link#1                UC         ne1 =>
2001:db8:0:1000::1               00:02:b3:3a:85:03     UHL        lo0
2001:db8:0:ffff::                00:11:25:32:d9:8c     UHL        lo0 =>
2001:db8:0:ffff::/64             link#2                UC         ne0 =>
2001:db8:0:ffff::1000            00:11:25:32:d9:8c     UHL        lo0
fe80::%ne1/64                    link#1                UC         ne1
fe80::202:b3ff:fe3a:8503%ne1     00:02:b3:3a:85:03     UHL        lo0
fe80::%ne0/64                    link#1                UC         ne0
fe80::211:25ff:fe32:d98c%ne0     00:11:25:32:d9:8c     UHL        lo0
...
```

── Direct route information

There are two network routes in the routing table. One is 2001:db8:0:1000::/64 via ne1 and the other is 2001:db8:0:ffff::/64 via ne0, which are both installed during address configuration processes. At this time, the router can only reach those two networks since it does not have any route information to other networks.

On invocation, **route6d** starts receiving routing information from other RIPng programs connected through its network interfaces. Also, it starts sending routing information it has in its routing table. Listing 1-65 shows the routing table after the **route6d** program started.

Listing 1-65

─── Routing table after routing information exchange

```
% netstat -rn -f inet6
Routing tables

Internet6:
Destination                         Gateway                           Flags    Netif Expire
default                             fe80::202:b3ff:fe3a:87d9%ne0      UGc      ne0
2001:db8:0:1000::                   00:02:b3:3a:85:03                 UHL      lo0  =>
2001:db8:0:1000::/64                link#1                            UC       ne1  =>
2001:db8:0:1000::1                  00:02:b3:3a:85:03                 UHL      lo0
2001:db8:0:2000::/64                fe80::202:b3ff:fe3a:87d9%ne0      UGc      ne0
2001:db8:0:3000::/64                fe80::202:b3ff:fe3a:87d9%ne0      UGc      ne0
2001:db8:0:ffff::                   00:11:25:32:d9:8c                 UHL      lo0  =>
2001:db8:0:ffff::/64                link#2                            UC       ne0  =>
2001:db8:0:ffff::1000               00:11:25:32:d9:8c                 UHL      lo0
fe80::%ne1/64                       link#1                            UC       ne1
fe80::202:b3ff:fe3a:8503%ne1        00:02:b3:3a:85:03                 UHL      lo0
fe80::%ne0/64                       link#2                            UC       ne0
fe80::211:25ff:fe32:d98c%ne0        00:11:25:32:d9:8c                 UHL      lo0
...
```

─── Routing table after routing information exchange

We see three new routing entries in the example. The first one is a routing entry for the default route. All packets received on this router will be forwarded to `fe80::202:b3ff:fe3a:87d9%ne0` if there is no more specific routing information against the destination address of the packets. `fe80::202:b3ff:fe3a:87d9%ne0` is given via RIPng response messages, which is usually the source address of the message but can also be specified as an explicit next hop address. The other two are the routing information for the `2001:db8:0:2000::/64` and `2001:db8:0:3000::/64` subnets. Note that such specific routing information may not appear when route aggregation takes place. In this case, these two specific routes can be aggregated to the default route. Whether the routing information is aggregated or not depends on the configuration of upstream routers.

All of the above configurations can also be done by setting up the `/etc/rc.conf` file. Once the configuration is confirmed to be correct, `rc.conf` should be prepared so that the same configuration will be done whenever the router reboots. Listing 1-66 shows a sample `rc.conf` file for this configuration.

Listing 1-66

─── `rc.conf` file for the leaf network case

```
ipv6_enable="YES"
ipv6_gateway_enable="YES"
ipv6_router_enable="YES"
ipv6_ifconfig_ne0="2001:db8:0:ffff::1000/64"
ipv6_ifconfig_ne0_alias0="2001:db8:0:ffff::/64 anycast"
ipv6_ifconfig_ne1="2001:db8:0:1000::1/64"
ipv6_ifconfig_ne1_alias0="2001:db8:0:1000::/64 anycast"
rtadvd_enable="YES"
rtadvd_interface="ne1"
```

─── `rc.conf` file for the leaf network case

The `ipv6_gateway_enable` variable enables the IPv6 forwarding function. A node never forwards packets unless the variable is set to YES. The `ipv6_router_enable` variable enables a routing daemon program. The default routing daemon program is **route6d**. The following `ifconfig_*` variables set interface addresses as described in the example above. The last two `rtadvd_*` variables are not discussed in this section, but they are usually required for router configurations. A router starts sending Router Advertisement messages when the `rtadvd_enable` variable is set to YES. The message is used by IPv6 hosts to autoconfigure their IPv6 addresses and to install a default router. The `rtadvd_interface` variable specifies the network interfaces to which the messages are sent. This example configuration just specifies ne1 since it is the only interface to the leaf network where Router Advertisements are necessary.

1.14.2   A Simple Loop Network

The **route6d** daemon can handle several networks which make a loop topology. As have already been discussed, however, RIPng is not designed to support a very complex network. Such a loop network should therefore be as simple as possible. Figure 1-56 is a sample loop network discussed in this section.

There are two networks in the sample network, one is `2001:db8:0:1000::/64` and the other is `2001:db8:0:1001::/64`. The two routers B and C construct a network loop. The loop network is connected to the outside network via router A.

In this case, there are two routes from router B to reach the outside network. One route is router A via the ne0 interface and the other is router C via the ne1 interface. Similarly, router C has two routes. If router B chooses to send all packets which are destined to the outside network to router C and router C chooses router B to send packets for outside networks, packets can

FIGURE 1-56

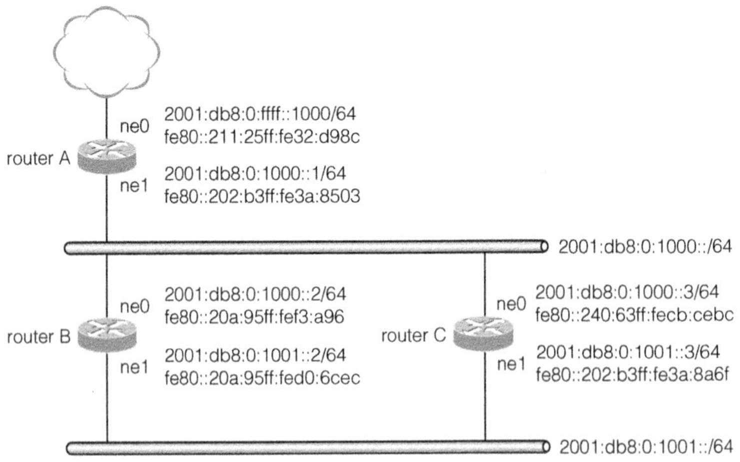

A simple loop network.

never reach their destination. RIPng handles such a case and installs proper route information based on the route information received from neighbor routers.

In this particular case, routers B and C will have the following route information.

```
router B:
  2001:db8:0:1000::/64 -> ne0
  2001:db8:0:1001::/64 -> ne1
  default -> router A via ne0

router C:
  2001:db8:0:1000::/64 -> ne0
  2001:db8:0:1001::/64 -> ne1
  default -> router A via ne0          .
```

In the above expression, -> denotes that the packets covered by the prefix information on the left-hand side are sent or forwarded to the network interface or the node written on the right-hand side.

The startup configuration in the /etc/rc.conf file for this network is shown in Listing 1-67.

Listing 1-67

—————————————————————————————— rc.conf files for a loop network

```
router A:
ipv6_enable="YES"
ipv6_gateway_enable="YES"
ipv6_router_enable="YES"
ipv6_ifconfig_ne0="2001:db8:0:ffff::1000/64"
ipv6_ifconfig_ne0_alias0="2001:db8:0:ffff::/64 anycast"
ipv6_ifconfig_ne1="2001:db8:0:1000::1/64"
ipv6_ifconfig_ne1_alias0="2001:db8:0:1000::/64 anycast"
rtadvd_enable="YES"
rtadvd_interface="ne1"

router B:
ipv6_enable="YES"
ipv6_gateway_enable="YES"
ipv6_router_enable="YES"
ipv6_ifconfig_ne0="2001:db8:0:1000::2/64"
ipv6_ifconfig_ne0_alias0="2001:db8:0:1000::/64 anycast"
ipv6_ifconfig_ne1="2001:db8:0:1001::2/64"
ipv6_ifconfig_ne1_alias0="2001:db8:0:1001::/64 anycast"
rtadvd_enable="YES"
rtadvd_interface="ne0 ne1"

router C:
ipv6_enable="YES"
ipv6_gateway_enable="YES"
ipv6_router_enable="YES"
ipv6_ifconfig_ne0="2001:db8:0:1000::3/64"
ipv6_ifconfig_ne0_alias0="2001:db8:0:1000::/64 anycast"
ipv6_ifconfig_ne1="2001:db8:0:1001::3/64"
ipv6_ifconfig_ne1_alias0="2001:db8:0:1001::/64 anycast"
rtadvd_enable="YES"
rtadvd_interface="ne0 ne1"
```

—————————————————————————————— rc.conf files for a loop network

Once the routing information becomes stable, each router will have the routing table shown in Listing 1-68.

Listing 1-68

_____ Routing table after exchanging routing information

```
router A% netstat -rn -f inet6
Routing tables

Internet6:
Destination                          Gateway                             Flags    Netif Expire
default                              fe80::202:b3ff:fe3a:87d9%ne0        UGc      ne0
2001:db8:0:1000::                    00:02:b3:3a:85:03                   UHL      lo0 =>
2001:db8:0:1000::/64                 link#1                              UC       ne1 =>
2001:db8:0:1000::1                   00:02:b3:3a:85:03                   UHL      lo0
2001:db8:0:1001::/64                 fe80::20a:95ff:fef3:a96%ne1         UGc      ne1
2001:db8:0:ffff::                    00:11:25:32:d9:8c                   UHL      lo0 =>
2001:db8:0:ffff::/64                 link#2                              UC       ne0 =>
2001:db8:0:ffff::1000                00:11:25:32:d9:8c                   UHL      lo0
fe80::%ne1/64                        link#1                              UC       ne1
fe80::202:b3ff:fe3a:8503%ne1         00:02:b3:3a:85:03                   UHL      lo0
fe80::%ne0/64                        link#2                              UC       ne0
fe80::211:25ff:fe32:d98c%ne0         00:11:25:32:d9:8c                   UHL      lo0
...


router B% netstat -rn -f inet6
Routing tables

Internet6:
Destination                          Gateway                             Flags    Netif Expire
default                              fe80::202:b3ff:fe3a:8503%ne0        UGc      ne0
2001:db8:0:1000::                    00:0a:95:f3:0a:96                   UHL      lo0 =>
2001:db8:0:1000::/64                 link#1                              UC       ne0 =>
2001:db8:0:1000::2                   00:0a:95:f3:0a:96                   UHL      lo0
2001:db8:0:1001::                    00:0a:95:d0:6c:ec                   UHL      lo0 =>
2001:db8:0:1001::/64                 link#2                              UC       ne1 =>
2001:db8:0:1001::2                   00:0a:95:d0:6c:ec                   UHL      lo0
fe80::%ne1/64                        link#1                              UC       ne1
fe80::20a:95ff:fed0:6cec%ne1         00:0a:95:d0:6c:ec                   UHL      lo0
fe80::%ne0/64                        link#2                              UC       ne0
fe80::20a:95ff:fef3:a96%ne0          00:0a:95:f3:0a:96                   UHL      lo0
...


router C% netstat -rn -f inet6
Routing tables

Internet6:
Destination                          Gateway                             Flags    Netif Expire
default                              fe80::202:b3ff:fe3a:8503%ne0        UGc      ne0
2001:db8:0:1000::                    00:40:63:cb:ce:bc                   UHL      lo0 =>
2001:db8:0:1000::/64                 link#1                              UC       ne0 =>
2001:db8:0:1000::3                   00:40:63:cb:ce:bc                   UHL      lo0
2001:db8:0:1001::                    00:02:b3:3a:8a:6f                   UHL      lo0 =>
2001:db8:0:1001::/64                 link#2                              UC       ne1 =>
2001:db8:0:1001::3                   00:02:b3:3a:8a:6f                   UHL      lo0
fe80::%ne1/64                        link#1                              UC       ne1
fe80::202:b3ff:fe3a:8a6f%ne1         00:02:b3:3a:8a:6f                   UHL      lo0
fe80::%ne0/64                        link#2                              UC       ne0
fe80::240:63ff:fecb:cebc%ne0         00:40:63:cb:ce:bc                   UHL      lo0
...
```

_____ Routing table after exchanging routing information

Router A forwards all packets whose destination address is neither
2001:db8:0:1000::/64 nor 2001:db8:0:1001::/64 to the ne0 interface as a default
route. Packets sent to 2001:db8:0:1000::/64 or 2001:db8:0:1001::/64 can be forwarded to either router B or router C. In this case, router B is chosen.

Each of routers B and C has two direct route entries. These routers are connected to
2001:db8:0:1000::/64 and 2001:db8:0:1001::/64 directly and have routes to them

via the ne0 and ne1 interfaces, respectively. The route to other networks is set to router A whose address is `fe80::202:b3ff:fe3a:8503` through the ne0 interface as a default route.

1.14.3   A Hierarchical Network

When many subnetworks need to exchange route information, the entire network must be carefully designed. Basically, each entry of routing information is generated per one subnetwork; 100 routing entries will be generated for 100 networks by default. When considering routing information exchange, however, it is better if the number of routing entries can be reduced for efficiency. A routing entry can be aggregated when routing prefixes from downstream networks can be included in one larger routing prefix. For example, prefixes `2001:db8:0:1::/64` to `2001:db8:0:ff::/64` can be aggregated to `2001:db8:0::/56`. Note, however, that the less specific routing entry, e.g., `2001:db8:0:1::/64` in this case, must not be used in other networks.

Figure 1-57 shows a sample hierarchical network where route aggregation is effective. The topology has 6 leaf networks. The three subnet prefixes on the left-hand side are `2001:db8:0:1::/64, 2001:db8:0:2::/64` and `2001:db8:0:3::/64`, which are reached via routers D, E and F, respectively. The three subnet prefixes on the right-hand side are `2001:db8:0:101::/64, 2001:db8:0:102::/64` and `2001:db8:0:103::/64` that can be reached via routers G, H and I, respectively. The first three networks are connected to router B and the latter three are connected to router C. Routers B and C are connected to router A.

In this case, there will be 6 routing entries without route aggregation, but the first three routes can actually be aggregated to `2001:db8:0::/56` and the latter three can be aggregated to `2001:db8:0:100::/56` (unless the other addresses covered in the aggregated prefix are used

FIGURE 1-57

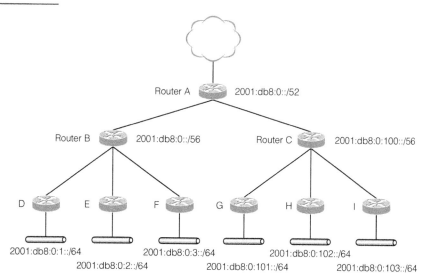

A hierarchical network.

elsewhere). These two aggregated routes are also aggregated to `2001:db8:0::/52` at router
A (likewise). As a result, the 6 routing entries can be aggregated to only 1 entry. Yet another
network can be added without increasing the number of route entries using this hierarchical
network. For example, adding a subnet with prefix `2001:db8:0:4::/64` under router B does
not increase the number of advertised route entries from router B since the new route information
is aggregated by the router. There can be at most 256 subnetworks under routers B and C without
any additional route information advertised from router B or C to the upstream router. Similarly, a
new second-level router can be added under router A without causing additional route information
advertised from this router. It suffices to introduce a new router which advertises, for example,
`2001:db8:200::/56` under router A, since router A aggregates all route information covered
by `2001:db8:0::/52`.

The `-A` command line option of **route6d** is used to aggregate route entries. In the example
shown in Figure 1-57, router B should invoke **route6d** as follows.

```
# route6d -A2001:db8:0::/56,ne0
```

The interface name after the aggregated prefix specifies the interface to which the aggregated routing information is advertised. Similarly, routers A and C need to specify
`2001:db8:0::/52` and `2001:db8:0:100::/56` for the `-A` option, respectively.

Listing 1-69 shows the corresponding startup configuration for router B.

Listing 1-69

_____ `rc.conf` files for a hierarchical network

```
ipv6_enable="YES"
ipv6_gateway_enable="YES"
ipv6_router_enable="YES"
ipv6_router_flags="-A2001:db8:0::/56,ne0"
```
_____ `rc.conf` files for a hierarchical network

In this example, router B does not have a global IPv6 address on the upstream interface.
Since interior routing protocols can generally run using link-local addresses only, a global prefix
does not have to be assigned to networks that do not contain IPv6 hosts.

IPv6 Multicasting

2.1   Introduction

IP multicasting is one of the key technologies for the next generation of the Internet. In fact, IPv6 basic features such as the Neighbor Discovery protocol actively and effectively use multicasting as shown in Chapter 5 of *IPv6 Core Protocols Implementation*, "Neighbor Discovery and Stateless Address Autoconfiguration." Meantime, increasing network bandwidth makes applications such as video streaming more realistic, which then makes IP multicasting more important.

Although the basic notion of multicasting is common to both IPv4 and IPv6, IPv6 multicasting brings several new characteristics based on operational experiences gained from the IPv4 counterpart. For example, IPv6 explicitly limits the scope of a multicast address by using a fixed address field (see Chapter 2 of the *Core Protocols* book, "IPv6 Addressing Architecture"), whereas in IPv4 the scope was specified by means of TTL (Time To Live) of a multicast packet.

> The notion of explicit multicast scoping (called *administratively scoped multicast*) was introduced in IPv4 multicasting subsequently. The IPv6 multicast scope can be regarded as a built-in extension of administrative scoping.

In addition, the wider address space of IPv6 eases multicast group management. As shown in Chapter 2 of the *Core Protocols* book, the IPv6 multicast address format allows users to allocate and manage a wide range of groups by themselves without fear of collisions. All of these points indicate multicasting is and will be more effective in IPv6.

This chapter discusses details about IPv6 multicasting, especially on multicast routing mechanisms. We first explain the basic technical background of IP multicasting, focusing on protocols

FIGURE 2-1

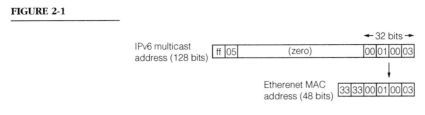

IPv6 to Ethernet multicast address mapping.

specific to IPv6. It includes both the host-to-router protocol and multicast routing protocols. We then describe the KAME kernel code that implements these standard protocols. Finally, we show some examples of IPv6 multicast operation using application programs provided in the KAME implementation.

2.2   IPv6 Multicast Address to Layer-2 Multicast Address Mapping

IPv6 takes a similar approach on mapping an IPv4 multicast address to a Layer-2 multicast address. The exact mapping algorithm depends on the media type. In the case of Ethernet, the method of mapping an IPv6 multicast address to an Ethernet multicast address is to prepend the value of 0x3333 to the last four bytes of the IPv6 multicast address to form a 48-bit Ethernet multicast address. For example, the multicast address for DHCPv6 servers assigned by the IANA, ff05::1:3, is mapped into Ethernet MAC address 33-33-00-00-01-03 as shown in Figure 2-1.

2.3   Multicast Listener Discovery Protocol

The *Multicast Listener Discovery* (MLD) protocol is the multicast group management protocol for IPv6 and is used to exchange group information between multicast hosts and routers. The MLD protocol was designed based on IGMP, the Internet Group Management Protocol for IPv4, and the protocol specification is the same in many points. Unlike IGMP, however, MLD is defined as part of ICMPv6, while IGMP is defined as a separate transport layer protocol.

MLD messages are generally sent with an IPv6 link-local source IP address. The hop limit is always 1, preventing the forwarding of MLD messages by a router. A Router Alert Hop-by-Hop option (see Chapter 3 of *IPv6 Core Protocols Implementation*, "Internet Protocol version 6") accompanies each MLD message: the reason behind it will be explained in Section 2.3.2.

Currently, two versions of MLD are defined: version 1 of MLD (MLDv1) [RFC2710] is based on version 2 of IGMP (IGMPv2), and version 2 of MLD (MLDv2) [RFC3810] is based on version 3 of IGMP (IGMPv3).

Similar to IGMPv2, MLDv1 consists of three types of messages: *Multicast Listener Query, Multicast Listener Report,* and *Multicast Listener Done.* These message types correspond to the IGMPv2 Membership Query, Membership Report, and Leave Group message types, respectively.

This book mainly focuses on MLDv1, although Section 2.4.5 will provide some more background of MLDv2. In the rest of this chapter, the term "MLD" generally means MLDv1 for brevity unless explicitly noted otherwise, even when the corresponding discussion applies to MLDv2 as well. In some cases, it is necessary to distinguish the different versions of MLD, and they are explictly referred to as MLDv1 or MLDv2.

2.3.1 MLD Protocol Message Format

MLD protocol messages have the ICMPv6 message format shown in Figure 2-2. The format is common to all MLD (v1 and v2) message types.

The length of any MLDv1 message must not be larger than 24 bytes. The sender must not transmit any MLDv1 message larger than 24 bytes; the receiver ignores any bytes passing this limit. This behavior of the receiver ensures upper-compatibility with future extensions of the protocol. In fact, MLDv2 uses larger packets with minimum compatibility with MLDv1.

MLD messages are identified by the ICMPv6 Type field as given in Table 2-1.

The Multicast Listener Query message can be classified into two query types: the *general Query* for a router to learn multicast addresses that have active listeners, and the (multicast-address) *specific Query* for membership in a particular multicast address on a given link.

The *Code* field has the value of 0. The *Checksum* field contains the ICMPv6 checksum value. The *Reserved* field must be set to 0 by the sender and is ignored by receivers.

The *Maximum Response Delay* field is given in units of milliseconds. This field specifies the maximum time a host can delay before sending a report back to the querying router. This field is meaningful only to Query messages, and it is set to 0 by the sender and is ignored by the receivers in the other types of MLD messages. The Maximum Response Delay controls the time between the time the last member of a multicast group stops listening and routers reflect that information in multicast routing. The Maximum Response Delay also controls the burstiness of the MLD traffic on the link.

FIGURE 2-2

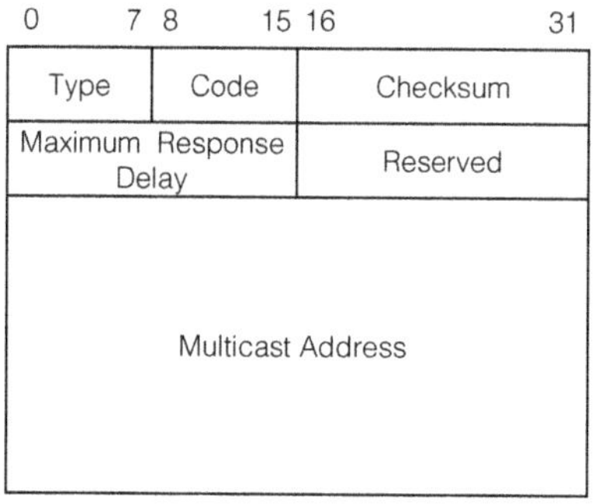

MLD message format.

TABLE 2-1

ICMPv6 message type	*MLD message type*
130	Multicast Listener Query
131	Multicast Listener Report
132	Multicast Listener Done

The *Multicast Address* field is set to 0 (the IPv6 unspecified address) in a general Query message, or a specific multicast address in an address specific Query message. In a Report message, the Multicast Address field contains the multicast address on which the sender is listening. In a Done message, the Multicast Address field contains the multicast address from which the sender is departing.

2.3.2   Router Alert Option

A node sends the Multicast Listener Report and Done messages to the multicast groups of which the node is already a member. The Router Alert option prompts a receiving router to examine the MLD messages even if these messages may be of no interest to the router at the IP layer, since it may be of interest to upper layer protocols or applications within the router. The sender ensures by including the Router Alert option in a Hop-by-Hop Options header with each MLD message that the MLD message processing is carried out by the receiving router.

The IPv6 Router Alert option, as defined in [RFC2711], reserves the value of 0 to specify an MLD packet (see also Chapter 3 of *IPv6 Core Protocols Implementation*).

2.3.3   Source Address Selection

The requirement that the source address of the MLD messages must be an IPv6 link-local address may be problematic during the boot-up time of the transmitting node.

A node configures a link-local address on an interface and begins the Duplicate Address Detection (DAD; see Chapter 5 of the *Core Protocols* book) procedure on the address right after the node enables that interface for IPv6 communication. This link-local address is called *tentative* while DAD is in progress. The operation of the DAD algorithm relies on the node joining the solicited-node multicast group of the tentative address, resulting in the transmission of a Multicast Listener Report message for that group. Unfortunately, the transmitting interface does not yet have a valid (i.e., nontentative) link-local address, in which case the Report message could not be sent.

A problem arises when an MLD-snooping switching device connects the nodes on the link. Such a switching device snoops for multicast packets on the link, but since no Report message was ever transmitted, the switching device blocks the Neighbor Solicitation and Neighbor Advertisement messages that otherwise would have allowed the configuring node to detect the duplicate address condition if and when it occurred on the link.

[RFC3590] loosens the source address requirement to prevent the above scenario. Nodes are allowed to send both the Report and Done messages with the unspecified address as the source address when no valid link-local address is available on the sending interface.

2.3.4   Destination Address Selection

Table 2-2 summarizes the MLD message types and the associated packet destination addresses.

2.3.5   MLD Querier

Hosts report multicast group memberships to routers by responding to both general and specific Query messages. The identity of the router that sent the Query messages is not important to the hosts; what is important to the hosts is to receive the Query messages. As such, just

TABLE 2-2

MLD message type	Packet destination address
General Query message	`ff02::1` (link-local All-Nodes multicast address)
Multicast-Address-Specific Query	Same as the address specified by Multicast Address field
Report message	Same as the address specified by Multicast Address field
Done message	`ff02::2` (link-local All-Routers multicast address)

TABLE 2-3

Variable	Default value
Robustness variable	2
Query Interval	125 s
Query Response Interval	10000 (10 s)
Multicast Listener Interval	(Robustness-var * Query Interval) + Query Response Interval
Other Querier Present Interval	(Robustness-var * Query Interval) + (0.5 * Query Response Interval)
Startup Query Interval	0.25 * Query Interval
Startup Query Count	Robustness variable
Last Listener Query Interval	1000 (1 s)
Last Listener Query Count	Robustness variable
Unsolicited Report Interval	10 s

a single router per link generating the Query messages suffices. This router is called the *(MLD) Querier*. A Querier generates periodic general Query messages on the link to solicit and learn the multicast addresses that have memberships.

A router can assume the role of either a Querier or a non-Querier. Each router on startup assumes the Querier role but participates in a Querier election process. The process converges to elect the router having the smallest IPv6 address. For brevity, we assume a router is the Querier in the succeeding MLD discussions.

2.3.6 Operational Variables

Table 2-3 lists configurable variables that affect the MLD operation.

The *Robustness variable* should be set with a value that reflects the expected packet loss characteristics of the link. This variable must not be 0 and should not be 1.

The *Query Interval* is the inter packet gap between consecutive general Query messages sent by the Querier.

The *Query Response Interval* is the value inserted into the Maximum Delay Response field of the MLD message. The smaller the value is the faster the hosts will send the reports, possibly resulting in a burst of MLD packets.

The *Multicast Listener Interval* specifies the amount of time that must elapse before a router decides that there are no more listeners in a particular group.

The *Other Querier Present Interval* specifies the amount of time that a router must wait before determining whether it should be the Querier.

The *Startup Query Interval* is the inter packet gap between consecutive general Query messages sent by a router that assumes the Querier role on startup.

The *Startup Query Count* specifies the number of queries separated by the Startup Query Interval, which may be transmitted by a router assuming the Querier role on startup.

The *Last Listener Query Interval* is the value inserted into the Maximum Response Delay field of multicast address specific Query messages sent in response to Done messages. The interval value also specifies the inter packet gap for the specific Query messages.

The *Last Listener Query Count* is the number of specific Query messages sent by a router before it assumes there are no more listeners in the multicast group queried.

The *Unsolicited Report Interval* specifies the inter packet gap between consecutive initial Report messages sent by a node expressing its interest in a multicast group.

2.3.7 MLD Join Process

An IPv6 host joins a multicast group by sending a Multicast Listener Report message destined to the multicast address of interest. A multicast router is configured to accept all multicast packets from the link. The router recognizes the MLD packets through the Hop-by-Hop Router Alert option and passes these MLD messages to the upper layer. The multicast routing process within the router accepts and starts forwarding these multicast packets to the reported group according to the routing protocol it deploys.

A host that is a member of a group also receives Report messages sent to the group by other hosts joining the group. The receiving host then remembers that there is another host joining the group. The existence of the other group members affects the leave process described in Section 2.3.8.

Figure 2-3 gives an example of the join process. In this example, host H2 has already joined the multicast group ff05::1:3. Host H1 is starting up and joins the same group by sending out the Report message indicating its interest in the ff05::1:3 group. Both the router and H2 receive the Report message, and H2 remembers there is another group member.

FIGURE 2-3

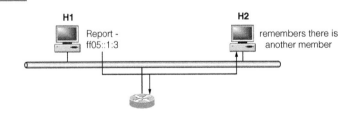

Joining a group.

2.3.8 MLD Leave Process

When a host is going to leave a multicast group and is the last node that sent a Multicast Listener Report message for the group (this can be detected by whether or not the host has heard a Report from another node for the group), it notifies the router of the departure by sending a Multicast Listener Done message to the All-Routers multicast group address (`ff02::2`).

Assume in the previous example that H1 did not receive any Report message from other nodes. Then H1 is the last member that sent a Report for `ff05::1:3`. Since H2 is aware of the presence of another listener (H1) being a member in that group, it will not generate a Done message if it leaves the group first. On the other hand, if H1 leaves the group before H2, it will notify the router with a Done message sent to the All-Routers multicast address (`ff02::2`).

The router responds to the Done message from H1 with a multicast-address specific Query. H2 responds to the Query with a Report message, indicating there is still a listener present. The router thus continues the multicast packet forwarding for this group. Figure 2-4 illustrates this scenario.

The router responds to the Done message by sending out Last Listener Query Count number of multicast-address specific Query messages, each separated by the Last Listener Query Interval seconds. If the departing node is the last member of the group, the router will not receive any Report. The router will cease forwarding multicast packets for the group once the transmissions complete without receiving any Report message. Continuing with the previous example, this progression takes place when H2 leaves the group as depicted in Figure 2-5.

FIGURE 2-4

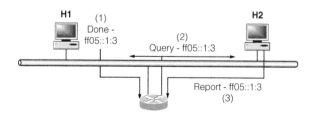

Leaving a group.

FIGURE 2-5

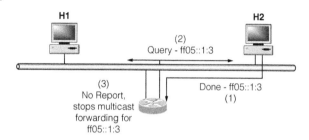

Last node leaving a group.

2.4 Multicast Routing Fundamentals

Routing and forwarding in multicast are quite different from unicast. First, since there are typically multiple recipients of a single original packet, the packet's delivery path has many branches, making the entire path a distribution tree. Secondly, unlike unicast routing, the source address information has an important role in forwarding multicast packets. Additionally, behavior of receiving nodes directly affects routing information via the host-to-router protocol such as MLD.

This section provides a brief overview of the general background of multicast routing, and gives an introduction to Protocol Independent Multicast (PIM), today's most popular multicast routing protocol. While most of the discussions are not specific to IPv6, these will help understand later sections of this chapter, especially for those who are not familiar with this field.

2.4.1 Reverse Path Forwarding

The *Reverse Path Forwarding* (RPF) algorithm is a fundamental notion of multicast routing. It verifies whether a multicast packet is received on the interface to which the router would forward a unicast packet to the source of the multicast packet. The RPF algorithm prevents forwarding loops by checking the source of the multicast packet and the incoming interface (IIF), permitting a router to accept a multicast packet only if the packet comes from the appropriate interface. The router then forwards this multicast packet onto some or all of the other interfaces. Multicast routing protocol and local multicast group membership determine the list of outgoing interfaces onto which the router fans out the multicast packet.

Figure 2-6 illustrates the basic concept of RPF. In Figure 2-6(a), a multicast packet of source S and group G (denoted as <S, G>) arrives on the correct IIF, and the router forwards the packet to the other interfaces assuming these interfaces are part of the correct outgoing interface list for group G. In Figure 2-6(b), a multicast packet arrives on the wrong IIF so the router discards the packet due to RPF failure.

FIGURE 2-6

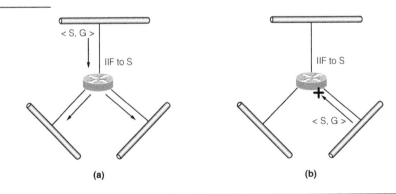

(a)   (b)

Basic concept of Reverse Path Forwarding.

Note that group G does not have any effect on performing the RPF check. It is only meaningful when the forwarding router determines the outgoing interfaces.

2.4.2 Multicast Routing Models

There are several models to realize multicast routing. This book will concentrate on two major models, which the target implementation of this book supports: the *flood and prune* model and the *explicit-join* model. Multicast routing protocols based on these models are often called a *dense* mode protocol and a *sparse* mode protocol, respectively.

The following description is not specific to IPv6 multicast routing, but we assume the MLD protocol as the group membership protocol to be specific.

Flood and Prune Model

In the flood and prune model, multicast routers first "flood" multicast packets in the entire network. That is, the routers forward multicast packets to all interfaces except the incoming one based on RPF.

When the packet is delivered to a router that attaches to a leaf network, the router makes a decision based on whether any receivers have informed the router of their existence via the MLD protocol.

If no receivers exist, the "prune" procedure starts. The router at the leaf network sends a *prune* message (the details may differ among protocols) to the upstream router based on RPF. If a router receives a prune message and no other routers or hosts request the multicast reception, it stops forwarding multicast packets for the group to the arrival interface of the prune message. Additionally, when the router stops forwarding for all possible outgoing interfaces, it then sends the prune message to its upstream router.

By repeating the procedure, the packet distribution converges to the ideal form: packets are delivered to all receivers, and to the receivers only. The resulting forwarding paths form a distribution tree for the pair of source and group addresses.

Figure 2-7 illustrates the flooding process. The arrows represent the flooding paths. There are four hosts in this routing domain: a multicast source S and three receivers, H1 to H3.

Initially, multicast packets from host S are flooded throughout the entire domain including network N2 even though there are no membership nodes on N2.

Then the prune stage starts as shown in Figure 2-8. During the pruning stage, router R3 sends a prune message upstream because R3 has no downstream routers and there are no group members on N2. Since R3 is the only downstream router of R2, R2 also sends a prune message upstream. R1 will stop forwarding the multicast packets to R2 once it receives the prune message from R2. R1 will not propagate a prune message upstream because R1 has one other downstream router, R4, with active group memberships.

The shaded region of the network in Figure 2-8 will be excluded from the multicast forwarding tree once the pruning process completes.

Explicit-Join Model

Flood and prune is a simple mechanism, and works nicely in some environments. In particular, it is advantageous that no special configuration is needed other than enabling the corresponding multicast routing protocol. But it also has disadvantages. First, flood and prune is not suitable for larger scale networks due to its flooding. Secondly, with this model a certain number of

FIGURE 2-7

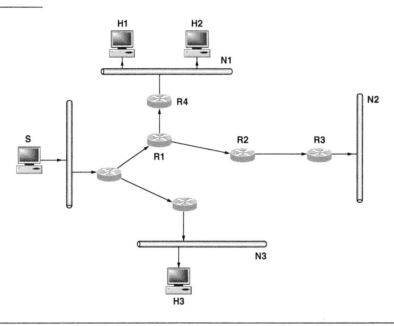

Dense mode operation—flooding.

FIGURE 2-8

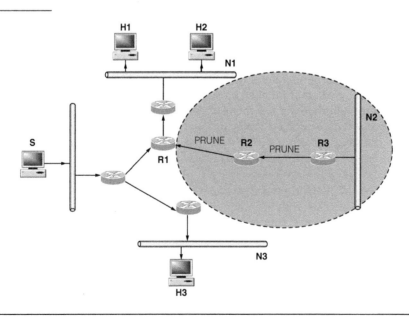

Dense mode operation—pruning.

packets must be sent on every single link (except the ones excluded by RPF). Depending on the volume of the packets and the link bandwidth, even the short period of unnecessary packets may be undesirable.

The explicit-join model explores a totally different way to solve these problems. In this model, when a router receives a Multicast Listener Report from a leaf network, it sends a *join* message (the details of which depend on the multicast routing protocol) for the group address toward the root node of multicast delivery tree, based on RPF. The root node can be an originating node of packets for the multicast address or a special router, often called a *core*, located between the originating node and the leaf nodes. For simplicity, the case with a core is mainly explained here, but the essential point is generally the same. Each router on the way to the core forwards the join message to the core, remembering the interest about the group downstream. When the join message arrives at the core, a packet distribution path for the specified multicast group is established.

Figure 2-9 shows the process of establishing a distribution path in the explicit-join model. In this example, two hosts, H1 and H2, are joining a multicast group. When the adjacent routers to H1 and H2, R4 and R5, receive Report messages from these hosts, the routers send join messages toward the core router.

Note that it is not trivial how these routers know the direction to the core router. This is one difficult issue of the explicit-join model with a core router, which will be revisited at the end of this section.

Continuing with the example, assume host S begins multicast packet transmissions to the group (Figure 2-10). The first hop multicast router (R1) will forward these packets to the core router. The core is a special router, so each routing protocol provides a way to determine its address. How the packets are forwarded from the first-hop router to the core also depends on the routing protocol. Once the core receives the packet, it can simply distribute the packet along

FIGURE 2-9

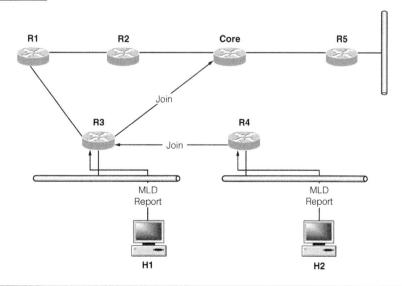

Establishing a distribution path in the explicit-join model.

with the path already established (if any). In fact, in Figure 2-10 the core does not forward the packets toward router R5 since no receiver exists in the leaf network attached to R5. This way the packets are only sent on the links where the packets are necessary, and the problems in the flood and prune model are solved or at least mitigated.

Note that the packet distribution path through the core from host S to host H2 or H3 is not the optimal path, which is the path via the link connecting R1 and R3. One of the problems associated with the explicit-join model using a core router is that the core may not be on every optimal path between the source and other group members.

In addition, the dependence on a core router may be problematic in that the core router can be a single point of failure. While particular routing protocols may offer remedies such as [PIMSM-BSR], [RFC3446] and [RFC4610], these proposals have their own issues, such as con-vergence delay or higher router load. Further details of these issues and solutions are beyond the scope of this book; for simplicity a single core will generally be assumed in the following discussion.

Another difficult issue in the explicit-join model is how each router knows the address of the core router. The examples shown in Figures 2-9 and 2-10 implicitly assumed each router somehow knew the address, but routing protocols using the explicit-join model actually need to provide methods for this purpose: the address information can be manually configured into each participating router, may be available through a dynamic discovery process [PIMSM-BSR], or can even be embedded in the corresponding multicast address [RFC3446]. Further discussion on core discovery is beyond the scope of this book. In the rest of this chapter, the address of a core router is generally assumed to be given in *some way*.

FIGURE 2-10

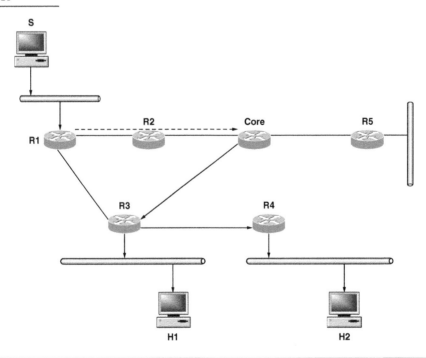

Packet distribution along with the distribution path in the explicit-join model.

2.4.3 Protocol Independent Multicast

Protocol Independent Multicast, PIM, is a major multicast routing protocol for IPv4, and is the only protocol for IPv6 available in the real world. PIM basically requires that all routers in a routing domain support the protocol, and, unlike DVMRP (Distance Vector Multicast Routing Protocol [RFC1075]), PIM does not require tunneling for bypassing routers that do not support the protocol.

PIM version 2, the current version of PIM, supports multiple network protocols: the packet format and the specification support both IPv4 and IPv6 (and even other or future network protocols).

PIM is called "Protocol Independent" because it is independent from protocols to perform RPF for multicast forwarding and for PIM message exchanges. Within PIM, only multicast group information is exchanged among routers. Typically, routing information given by the unicast routing protocol used in the multicast routing domain is simply used to perform RPF.

Figure 2-11 shows how an IPv6 multicast group address is encoded in PIM messages.

Address Family specifies the PIM address family of the Multicast Address field of this encoded address. A value of 2 is assigned to IPv6 by IANA.

Encoding Type specifies the type of encoding used within the specified address family. The value of 0 is reserved and represents the native encoding used by the address family.

B called the *Bidirectional PIM* bit. The definition and usage of this bit is beyond the scope of this book.

Reserved must be set to zero by the sender and ignored by the receiver.

Z called the *Admin Scope Zone* bit. The definition and usage of this bit is beyond the scope of this book.

Mask length 8-bits in length, and specifies the number of contiguous bits starting from the left-most bit position. When applied to the Group Multicast Address, it gives the corresponding range of multicast groups.

Group Multicast Address holds the multicast group address. This field is 16 bytes in size when carrying an IPv6 multicast address.

There are two types of PIM protocol: the *PIM Sparse Mode* (PIM-SM) protocol [RFC4601], and the *PIM Dense Mode* (PIM-DM) protocol [RFC3973]. The following description

FIGURE 2-11

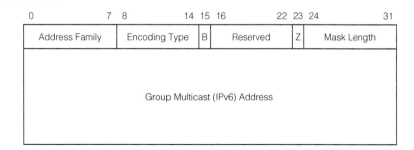

PIM encoding of IPv6 multicast address.

provides some key concepts of each PIM protocol, which are essential to understanding the relevant code description in the later sections of this chapter. The complexity of the protocols, however, warrants a separate book (such as [Wil00]) to discuss the protocols in full detail.

PIM Dense Mode

PIM-DM operates on the flood and prune model. Initially, multicast packets are flooded throughout the entire PIM routing domain with the PIM-DM protocol. Unnecessary delivery paths to leaf networks that are without any group memberships are then pruned from the forwarding tree using the PIM Join/Prune messages. This process has been illustrated in Figures 2-7 and 2-8 in Section 2.4.2.

One important difference of PIM from DVMRP is the need for the *assert* mechanism. Since PIM does not care about network topology, a multicast packet can be duplicated in a single link in the flooding stage. This is detected by PIM routers because the packet arrives on an outgoing interface, and then each router sends a *PIM Assert* message on the receiving interface. Each router receives Assert messages from other routers, and one of the routers is elected as the "winner" by comparing the preference or metric associated with the unicast routing protocol toward the source or comparing source IP addresses as a tie-breaker (the details of the election process is beyond the scope of this book and is omitted). Once the winner is determined, only the winner router will forward packets for the source and group pair on to the link. The other router sends *Join/Prune* messages upward to prune the unnecessary path if necessary.

Figure 2-12 illustrates a situation when the PIM assert mechanism is necessary to eliminate packet duplication. In this figure, routers R1 and R2 both receive a multicast packet from source S. Both R1 and R2 forward the packet downstream to host H, resulting in two copies

FIGURE 2-12

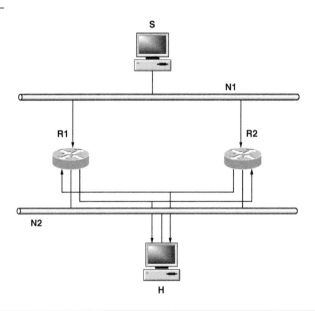

Multicast packet duplication detected.

FIGURE 2-13

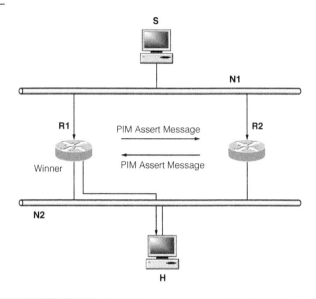

PIM assert procedure.

of the packet appearing on network N2. Both routers detect this packet duplication condition from the multicast packet that arrives on the outgoing interface that was used for transmission of the same packet previously. The two routers then enter the election process by sending out PIM Assert messages as shown in Figure 2-13.

In this example, the PIM assert procedure elects router R1 as the winner. From then on, R1 has the responsibility of forwarding packets from S to the multicast group on N2.

PIM Sparse Mode

PIM-SM operates on the explicit-join model. In PIM-SM, a core router is called a *Rendezvous Point* (RP). When a router recognizes a host joining a multicast group, it sends a PIM Join/Prune message containing the multicast group address toward the RP for the group address. The Join/Prune message is forwarded to the RP based on the RPF with regard to the RP's address, making or updating status for the group in each router.

This process will establish a packet distribution tree (called the *shared tree*) for the group from the RP to leaf networks. It is called "shared" because the same tree is used for all sources to the group.

When a multicast source sends a multicast packet to a particular group, the first hop router encapsulates the packets inside a *PIM Register* message, and forwards the Register message to the RP through unicast routing. The RP then decapsulates the original multicast packet and distributes it along the shared tree.

Figure 2-14 shows the packet format of a PIM Register message.

Version contains the PIM version number 2.

FIGURE 2-14

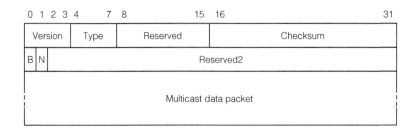

PIM Register message format.

Type specifies the type of PIM message. For the PIM Register message, the Type field has the value of 1.

Reserved and Reserved2 must be set to zero by the sender and ignored by the receiver.

Checksum the standard IP checksum covering the entire PIM message except the Multicast Data Packet section of the Register message. The checksum calculation is different depending on whether the PIM message is carried over IPv4 or IPv6. Details of the IPv6 case will be described in Section 2.4.4.

B called the *Border* bit. The definition and usage of this bit are beyond the scope of this book.

N called the *Null-Register* bit. A Register message with this bit on is called a Null-Register message. Unlike normal Register messages, a Null-Register message is exchanged just for a keep alive purpose between the first hop router and the RP, and does not encapsulate a multicast packet.

Multicast data packet holds the original multicast packet sent by the source.

Figure 2-15 illustrates an example of the multicast packet distribution based on the PIM-SM protocol.

In this example, when multicast source S sends out a multicast packet to a particular group, the first hop router R1 encapsulates the packet into a PIM Register message and forwards it to the RP as a unicast packet. The RP decapsulates the Register message and forwards the original multicast packet along the shared tree to the host members residing on the leaf networks.

2.4.4   IPv6 Specific Issues about PIM

Whereas the PIM base protocol is designed to be agnostic about IP versions, there were several issues specific to IPv6 found through implementation and operational experiences. Those issues were then addressed in later versions of the protocol specification. The following summarizes such issues.

Upstream Determination

PIM "neighbors," that is, PIM routers that share a single link, identify each other by periodically exchanging *PIM Hello* messages. The source address of the Hello message is used as the identifier of the sender. In the case of IPv6, this address is always a link-local unicast address because

FIGURE 2-15

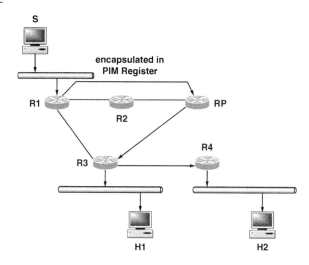

PIM-SM packet distribution scheme.

FIGURE 2-16

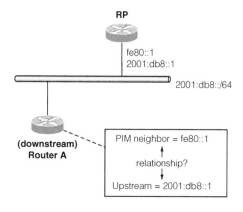

PIM upstream determination with multiple addresses.

the protocol specification requires that most PIM messages including Hello have a link-local source address.

A PIM router also identifies the neighbor's address that is the upstream router in RPF using the unicast routing protocol. Those two addresses are usually the same for the same neighbor. Even though IPv6 allows a node's interface to have multiple addresses, all IPv6 interior routing protocols use link-local addresses for exchanging routes (see, for example, Section 1.4.2), and an interface typically has only one link-local address.

Unfortunately, however, this is not always the case. Figure 2-16 shows one common exceptional case. In this example, the RP's address shares a subnet prefix (`2001:db8::/64`) with downstream routers.

Assume the RP's link-local address in this link is `fe80::1`, and a downstream router A tries to send a PIM Join/Prune message toward the RP. The RPF upstream is the RP itself in this case, and the upstream address is an RP's global address, `2001:db8::1`. For sending a PIM Join/Prune message, router A needs to include the link-local address for the upstream router in the message. However, the downstream router cannot know it is `fe80::1`, because there is no explicit information that combines the link-local and global addresses.

To address this problem, the IETF decided to introduce an additional option to the PIM Hello message, called the *(Interface) Address List* option. This option simply lists additional addresses other than the link-local address that the router sending the Hello message assigns to the outgoing interface. In the above example, this option would contain `2001:db8::1`. Since the source address of the Hello message is the link-local address (`fe80::1`), router A can now identify the link-local address of the upstream router, i.e., the RP.

This issue was found in early experiments with KAME's IPv6 multicast routing operation, and the Interface Address List option was first introduced as an experimental option specific to KAME's implementation. It has then been incorporated into the protocol specification, and an official option number (24) is now assigned.

> The PIM implementation described in this book uses the old, experimental option type. Later versions of the implementation supports the official type number as well.

Checksum Calculation

Each PIM message has a common header part, which contains a checksum field. In a former version of the protocol specification, the checksum was calculated through the message data only, that is, without a pseudo-IP header. This is reasonable for IPv4, because IPv4 has an IP layer checksum. Even though the IPv4 header of a PIM message is corrupted, the corruption is detected in the IP layer checksum validation of the receiving node and the message is discarded.

In contrast, IPv6 does not have an IP layer checksum as explained in Chapter 3 of *IPv6 Core Protocols Implementation*: Since PIM depends on some fields of the IP header of a PIM message, corruption of such fields might have a serious effect on protocol execution of PIM. For example, if the source address field of a Hello message is corrupted, the receiving node will register an invalid PIM neighbor.

Therefore, recent versions of the specification state that the PIM checksum for IPv6 uses a pseudo-IPv6 header like the checksum for other transport layer protocols over IPv6 (see Chapter 6 of the *Core Protocols* book, "Transport Layer Implications"). This issue was first identified through KAME's implementation experience of PIM for IPv6 and was addressed in the implementation. The change has then been incorporated into the standard specification.

2.4.5 IPv6 Multicast Future—MLDv2 and SSM

A challenging task in widely deploying PIM-SM is the issue of how to distribute the RP address throughout the PIM routing domain reliably and in time. Manual configuration at each router has the obvious scalability problem.

The IETF has defined a standard RP address distribution mechanism [PIMSM-BSR], but the method is based on flooding and still has limitation in scalability. Another standard that is specific to IPv6 [RFC3956] eliminates the scalability issue with the general distribution mechanism by embedding the address of the RP into the corresponding IPv6 multicast address. But it causes another limitation in that the RP address must be in a specific form to be embedded in the multicast address.

Meanwhile, applications such as Internet TV and Internet Radio based on IP multicasting have the characteristic of having a single packet source. In such cases, if a single distribution tree can be established from the source to the leaf nodes, an RP is not necessary in the first place.

Revised multicast specifications can provide such a possibility. For example, MLDv2, a revised version of MLD, allows a host to specify both the source for a particular multicast group as well as the group itself. Source Specific Multicast (SSM) [RFC4607] is a new notion in multicast routing that allows routers to establish a distribution tree from a single source only. PIM-SM can be easily adapted to SSM; for example, when a router receives a multicast group join request with a source address via MLDv2, the router can simply send the PIM Join/Prune message toward the source directly, instead of toward the RP.

The coverage of these new specifications are beyond the scope of this book; readers are encouraged to investigate these standards on their own merits.

2.5 Code Introduction

The KAME implementation of IPv6 multicasting supports both the host and the router aspects of the protocols. Figure 2-17 provides an overview of the architecture of the KAME multicast implementation.

The host aspect of the MLD protocol is implemented in the kernel. User applications access the host services related to IPv6 multicasting through the Basic Socket API as defined in

FIGURE 2-17

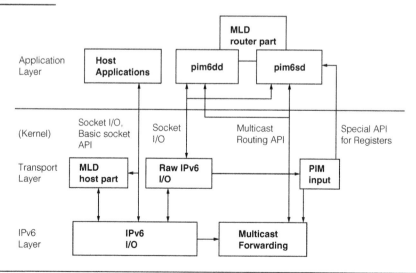

KAME multicast implementation architecture.

[RFC3493]. Multicast packet forwarding, which is an essential function of a multicast router, is also implemented in the kernel. The router aspect of MLD is part of the PIM-DM and PIM-SM routing daemons, **pim6dd** and **pim6sd**, respectively.

The **pim6sd** daemon was developed based on **pimd**, a reference implementation of the IPv4 PIM-SM daemon developed by the University of Southern California (USC). This USC implementation of PIM-SM included a special API to process PIM Register messages. The KAME's implementation in this part was also derived from USC's implementation. The **pim6sd** daemon was first ported from **pimd** by a separate individual developer, Mickael Hoerdt, who contributed the implementation to the KAME project. The KAME project then maintained **pim6sd** with bug fixes and function enhancements. In August 2005, the development effort was transfered to the mcast-tools project of SourceForge,[1] and has continued in mcast-tools since then.

In the following sections, we will describe in detail the kernel side of the KAME implementation on MLD, multicast forwarding, and some parts of the PIM protocol processing. We will refer to the files listed in Table 2-4 throughout the discussion.

TABLE 2-4

File name	Description
`netinet/icmp6.h`	Definitions of the MLD header and protocol constants
`netinet6/in6_var.h`	MLD listener structure
`netinet6/mld6.c`	MLD protocol processing functions
`netinet6/pim6.h`	PIM header definition
`netinet6/pim6_var.h`	Additional structure definitions and `sysctl` objects
`netinet6/ip6_mroute.h`	Internal data structure definitions for IPv6 multicasting routing
`netinet6/ip6_mrouter.c`	IPv6 multicast routing functions

Files discussed in this chapter. All files are located under `${KAME}/kame/sys/`.

TABLE 2-5

`icmp6_ifstat{}` *member*	*SNMP variable*	*Description*
`ifs6_in_mldquery`	`ipv6IfIcmpInGroupMembQueries`	# of input MLD queries
`ifs6_in_mldreport`	`ipv6IfIcmpInGroupMembResponses`	# of input Report messages
`ifs6_in_mlddone`	`ipv6IfIcmpInGroupMembReductions`	# of input Done messages
`ifs6_out_mldquery`	`ipv6IfIcmpOutGroupMembQueries`	# of output Query messages
`ifs6_out_mldreport`	`ipv6IfIcmpOutGroupMembResponses`	# of output Report messages
`ifs6_out_mlddone`	`ipv6IfIcmpOutGroupMembReductions`	# of output Done messages

ICMPv6 statistics related to MLD.

---

1. http://sourceforge.net/projects/mcast-tools/

Statistics

ICMPv6 MIB [RFC2466] contains statistics variables for incoming and outgoing MLD messages as shown in Table 2-5. `ifs6_in_xxx` variables are actually incremented in the `icmp6_input()` function, and do not appear in this chapter.

These variables can be seen by the `netstat -p icmp6 -s` command with the `-I` command line option specifying the interface. The following is an example output for interface named `fxp0`:

```
% netstat -p icmp6 -s -I fxp0
icmp6 on fxp0:
  ...
        25857 input MLD querys
        0 input MLD reports
        0 input MLD dones
  ...
        0 output MLD querys
        51655 output MLD reports
        0 output MLD dones
```

[RFC3019] defines MIB variables specific to the MLD protocol, but this implementation currently does not support any of the MIB variables.

2.6   MLD Implementation

Figure 2-18 depicts relationships among various MLD functions. These functions generally work on `in6_multi{}` structures, each of which maintains kernel internal parameters of a multicast group address that the node joins.

There are three major paths in MLD protocol processing. One is handling inbound MLD messages by the `mld6_input()` function. The second path is to join or leave a multicast group as a result of a socket option (Chapter 7 of *IPv6 Core Protocols Implementation*, "Socket API Extensions") or as a side effect of configuring a unicast address (Chapter 2 of the *Core Protocols* book). These operations are performed by the `mld6_start_listening()` and `mld6_stop_listening()` functions, respectively. The last one is timer processing for the `in6_multi{}` structures. A common single timer is used for all the structures, whose expiration handler is the `mld6_fasttimeo()` function. It is a fast timeout hander and is called every 200ms.

2.6.1   Types and Structures

Table 2-6 shows standard macro names for MLD message types defined in [RFC3542](*).

TABLE 2-6

Name	Type	Description
MLD_LISTENER_QUERY	130	Multicast Listener Query
MLD_LISTENER_REPORT	131	Multicast Listener Report
MLD_LISTENER_DONE	132	Multicast Listener Done

MLD type values.

FIGURE 2-18

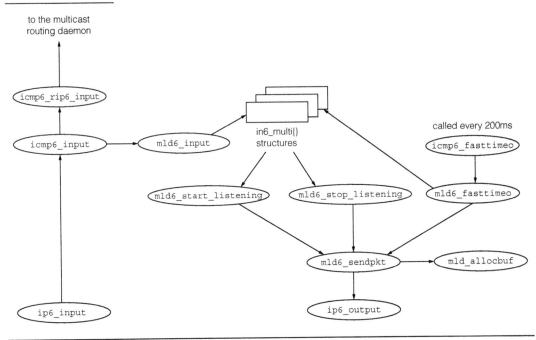

Relationship between MLD functions.

(*) [RFC3542] defines `MLD_LISTENER_REDUCTION` for Type 132, but it does not match the actual message type name as explained in Chapter 7 of the *Core Protocols* book. The KAME kernel implementation uses the nonstandard, but more intuitive macro name.

[RFC3542] also defines a template structure of MLD messages, the `mld_hdr{}` structure as shown in Listing 2-1. This is a straightforward implementation of the header format defined in Figure 2-2, but it begins with an instance of the `icmp6_hdr{}` structure, since MLD messages are defined as ICMPv6 messages. Shortcut macros are defined to get access to MLD-specific message fields.

Listing 2-1
—— icmp6.h

```
225    struct mld_hdr {
226           struct icmp6_hdr          mld_icmp6_hdr;
227           struct in6_addr           mld_addr; /* multicast address */
228    } __attribute__((__packed__));
....
241    /* shortcut macro definitions */
242    #define mld_type mld_icmp6_hdr.icmp6_type
243    #define mld_code mld_icmp6_hdr.icmp6_code
244    #define mld_cksum    mld_icmp6_hdr.icmp6_cksum
245    #define mld_maxdelay mld_icmp6_hdr.icmp6_data16[0]
246    #define mld_reserved mld_icmp6_hdr.icmp6_data16[1]
```
—— icmp6.h

FIGURE 2-19

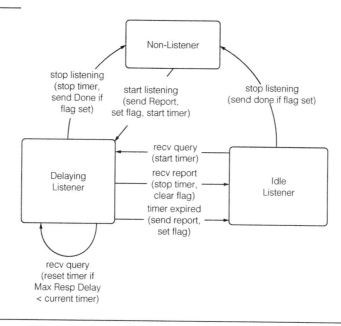

MLD listener state transition diagram.

MLD Listener State Transition

[RFC2710] defines three states for a "listener" (host) of a particular multicast group address with the MLD protocol operations: *Non-Listener*, *Delaying Listener*, and *Idle Listener*. A listener also has a flag indicating whether it is the member who sent the last Report message for the group on the link, and a timer delaying a Report message for the group.

Figure 2-19 is a state transition diagram between these states. Each arrow indicates the state transition associated with a label representing the event that causes the transition and the actions that take place for the transition. For example, the arrow from the Non-Listener state to the Delaying Listener state means when a listener starts listening to a multicast group, it sends a Report message, sets the flag, and starts the timer.

For brevity, we do not provide a comprehensive description of the states and the transition events, but these should be pretty trivial. The precise definitions can be found in [RFC2710].

In the KAME implementation, the information of a listener is represented in the `in6_multi{}` structure (Listing 2-2). The two structure members are relevant here: `in6m_state` and `in6m_timer` (see Chapter 2 of *IPv6 Core Protocols Implementation* for the other structure members). `in6m_state` can be either `MLD_OTHERLISTENER` or `MLD_IREPORTEDLAST`, which means a different listener or this listener sent the latest Report, respectively. `in6m_timer` is a counter of listener's timer with the granularity of 200ms(*). If the value of this member is 0, it means the timer is disabled.

Listing 2-2

```
                                                             in6_var.h
560    struct  in6_multi {
561            LIST_ENTRY(in6_multi) in6m_entry; /* list glue */
562            struct   sockaddr_in6 in6m_sa;   /* IP6 multicast address */
```

```
563        struct   ifnet *in6m_ifp;         /* back pointer to ifnet */
567        struct   ifmultiaddr *in6m_ifma; /* back pointer to ifmultiaddr */
569        u_int    in6m_refcount;          /* # membership claims by sockets */
570        u_int    in6m_state;             /* state of the membership */
571        u_int    in6m_timer;             /* MLD6 listener report timer */
572        struct   router6_info *in6m_rti; /* router info */
573        struct   in6_multi_source *in6m_source;  /* filtered source list */
574   };
```
                                                                    ————in6_var.h

(*) The timer granularity is coarse compared to the protocol specification, which suggests using the system's highest clock granularity. However, this implementation uses the coarse timer because when this code was first written the target version of BSD did not support fine-grained and scalable kernel timers; the "fast timeout" timers called every 200ms were the only reasonable choice when there might be a large number of timers. Later versions of the MLD implementation use more fine-grained timers for each entry.

In this implementation, the Non-Listener state is represented as the nonexistence of the `in6_multi{}` structure. Otherwise, if the timer is running, i.e., `in6m_timer` has a non-zero value, the listener is in the Delaying state; otherwise, it is in the Idle state.

2.6.2 `mld6_init()` Function

The `mld6_init()` function is called from the `icmp6_init()` function via the protocol initialization switch table stored in the `inet6sw` array. The `mld6_init()` function initializes many common variables used by other MLD routines.

Listing 2-3
                                                                    ————mld6.c
```
255   void
256   mld6_init()
257   {
258          static u_int8_t hbh_buf[8];
259          struct ip6_hbh *hbh = (struct ip6_hbh *)hbh_buf;
260          u_int16_t rtalert_code = htons((u_int16_t)IP6OPT_RTALERT_MLD);
261
262          static struct sockaddr_in6 all_nodes_linklocal0;
263          static struct sockaddr_in6 all_routers_linklocal0;
267
268          mld_group_timers_are_running = 0;
269          mld_interface_timers_are_running = 0;
270          mld_state_change_timers_are_running = 0;
271
272          /* ip6h_nxt will be fill in later */
273          hbh->ip6h_len = 0;         /* (8 >> 3) - 1 */
274
275          /* XXX: grotty hard coding... */
276          hbh_buf[2] = IP6OPT_PADN;        /* 2 byte padding */
277          hbh_buf[3] = 0;
278          hbh_buf[4] = IP6OPT_RTALERT;
279          hbh_buf[5] = IP6OPT_RTALERT_LEN - 2;
280          bcopy((caddr_t)&rtalert_code, &hbh_buf[6], sizeof(u_int16_t));
```

```
281
282            all_nodes_linklocal0.sin6_family = AF_INET6;
283            all_nodes_linklocal0.sin6_len = sizeof(struct sockaddr_in6);
284            all_nodes_linklocal0.sin6_addr = in6addr_linklocal_allnodes;
285
286            all_nodes_linklocal = &all_nodes_linklocal0;
287
288            all_routers_linklocal0.sin6_family = AF_INET6;
289            all_routers_linklocal0.sin6_len = sizeof(struct sockaddr_in6);
290            all_routers_linklocal0.sin6_addr = in6addr_linklocal_allrouters;
291
292            all_routers_linklocal = &all_routers_linklocal0;
293
302            init_ip6pktopts(&ip6_opts);
303            ip6_opts.ip6po_hbh = hbh;
```

(MLDv2 specific code: omitted)

```
306     }
```
——mld6.c

262–263 These variables are templates of commonly used link-local addresses (see lines 282–292 below).

268–270 Some timer-related variables are initialized. The last two variables are used for MLDv2.

272–280 MLD packets must have a Hop-by-Hop Options header containing a Router Alert option. Variable hbh is initialized as the common template of this extension header. A 2-byte padding before the actual option is necessary in meeting the alignment requirement of the Router Alert option (see Chapter 3 of *IPv6 Core Protocols Implementation*). The first 2 bytes of the option specify the option type and its length, followed by the option value specifying MLD Router Alert in the network byte order.

282–292 The link-local address structure templates are filled in and are pointed by file scope pointer variables `all_nodes_linklocal` and `all_routers_linklocal` for later use (see Section 2.6.3 for example usage).

302–303 `ip6_opts` is a file scope variable for storing the Hop-by-Hop Options header initialized above, and will be attached to MLD packets to be sent. The function `init_ip6pktopts()` initializes the structure and sets the corresponding member to point to `hbh`.

2.6.3 Joining a Group: `mld6_start_listening()` Function

The `mld6_start_listening()` function is called when the local node joins a multicast group specified by function parameter `in6m`. This function performs the state transition from Non-Listener to Delaying Listener in Figure 2-19.

Listing 2-4
——mld6.c
```
352    void
358    mld6_start_listening(in6m)
359            struct in6_multi *in6m;
361    {
```

```
367          struct sockaddr_in6 all_sa;
371          int s = splnet();
373
374          /*
375           * This function must not be called before mld6_init().
376           * We've once experienced the violation of the order, so we put an
377           * explicit assertion here.
378           */
379          if (all_nodes_linklocal == NULL)
380                  panic("mld6_start_listening: called too early");
381
382          /*
383           * RFC2710 page XX:
384           * The node never sends a Report or Done for the link-scope all-nodes
385           * address.
386           * MLD messages are never sent for multicast addresses whose scope is 0
387           * (reserved) or 1 (node-local).
388           */
389          all_sa = *all_nodes_linklocal;
390          if (in6_addr2zoneid(in6m->in6m_ifp, &all_sa.sin6_addr,
391              &all_sa.sin6_scope_id) ||
392              in6_embedscope(&all_sa.sin6_addr, &all_sa)) {
393                  /* XXX: this should not happen! */
394                  in6m->in6m_timer = 0;
395                  in6m->in6m_state = MLD_OTHERLISTENER;
396          }
397          if (SA6_ARE_ADDR_EQUAL(&in6m->in6m_sa, &all_sa) ||
398              IPV6_ADDR_MC_SCOPE(&in6m->in6m_sa.sin6_addr) <
399              IPV6_ADDR_SCOPE_LINKLOCAL) {
404                  in6m->in6m_timer = 0;
405                  in6m->in6m_state = MLD_OTHERLISTENER;
406          } else {
422                      mld6_sendpkt(in6m, MLD_LISTENER_REPORT, NULL);
423                      in6m->in6m_timer =
424                          MLD_RANDOM_DELAY
    (MLD_UNSOLICITED_REPORT_INTERVAL *
425                                      PR_FASTHZ);
426                      in6m->in6m_state = MLD_IREPORTEDLAST;
427                      mld_group_timers_are_running = 1;
429          }
430          splx(s);
431  }
```
── mld6.c

— Line 424 is broken here for layout reasons. However, it is a single line of code.

367–371 Network level interrupts must be disabled by splnet() because the mld6_start_listening() function is usually invoked by a user process, and the function modifies in6m, which can also be referred to in the input path.

375–380 The entire code in this file assumes mld6_init() must be called first, where all_nodes_linklocal is initialized. An unexpected state may cause a severe bad effect if this is not the case. Calling panic here would prevent the situation.

389–396 A local variable all_sa is initialized so that it specifies the All-Nodes link-local multicast address with the proper scope zone ID set for the joining interface. Note that link-local addresses are generally ambiguous within a node and must always be associated with its zone ID for proper operation. The KAME kernel ensures this by maintaining an IPv6 address in the form of the sockaddr_in6{} structure with the appropriate zone ID via the initialization by the in6_addr2zoneid() and in6_embedscope() functions. It should be noted that the sockaddr_in6{} structure may have different contents depending on the interface even if its address part is a constant. This is the reason a local variable must be used here rather than a constant structure. The initialization should always succeed as long as the given interface is valid, but if it happens to fail, the `in6m` entry transits to the Idle state.

See Chapter 2 of *IPv6 Core Protocols Implementation* for more details about this conversion.

397–406 [RFC2710] states that an MLD message must not be sent for the link-scope All-Nodes multicast address or for multicast addresses that have either 0 (reserved) or 1 (interface-local) scope. In either case, the `in6m` entry transits to the Idle state.

422 The `in6m` entry is passed to the `mld6_sendpkt()` function (Section 2.6.7) where a Report message is sent on the corresponding interface.

423–427 [RFC2710] requires the initial Report message to be repeated with a random delay up to `MLD_UNSOLICITED_REPORT_INTERVAL` (10) seconds. The random delay is calculated as follows: `PR_FASTHZ` is 5, which corresponds to the system's "fast timeouts" called every 200ms. The `MLD_RANDOM_DELAY` macro returns a random integer value between 1 and 50 (inclusive), and the `in6m_timer` member is set to this value. The `mld6_fasttimeo()` function will decrement this value by 1 every time it is called. When `in6m_timer` is decremented to 0, the timer expires. Since this node has just sent a Report message, the state of this entry is reset to `MLD_IREPORTEDLAST`. Finally, the global variable `mld_group_timers_are_running` is set to 1 to indicate the system needs to maintain MLD timers.

2.6.4 Leaving a Group: `mld6_stop_listening()` Function

The `mld6_stop_listening()` function is called when a node leaves a multicast group and performs the state transition to Non-Listener in Figure 2-19. It sends a Multicast Listener Done message if it sent the latest Report message for the group.

Listing 2-5

```
                                                                  ─mld6.c
433     void
434     mld6_stop_listening(in6m)
435             struct in6_multi *in6m;
436     {
437             struct sockaddr_in6 all_sa, allrouter_sa;
438
439             all_sa = *all_nodes_linklocal;
440             if (in6_addr2zoneid(in6m->in6m_ifp, &all_sa.sin6_addr,
441                 &all_sa.sin6_scope_id) ||
442                 in6_embedscope(&all_sa.sin6_addr, &all_sa)) {
443                     /* XXX: this should not happen! */
444                     return;
445             }
446             /* XXX: necessary when mrouting */
447             allrouter_sa = *all_routers_linklocal;
448             if (in6_addr2zoneid(in6m->in6m_ifp, &allrouter_sa.sin6_addr,
449                 &allrouter_sa.sin6_scope_id)) {
450                     /* XXX impossible */
451                     return;
452             }
453             if (in6_embedscope(&allrouter_sa.sin6_addr, &allrouter_sa)) {
454                     /* XXX impossible */
455                     return;
456             }
457
```

```
458            if (in6m->in6m_state == MLD_IREPORTEDLAST &&
459                !SA6_ARE_ADDR_EQUAL(&in6m->in6m_sa, &all_sa) &&
460                IPV6_ADDR_MC_SCOPE(&in6m->in6m_sa.sin6_addr) >
461                IPV6_ADDR_SCOPE_INTFACELOCAL) {
462                    mld6_sendpkt(in6m, MLD_LISTENER_DONE, &allrouter_sa);
463            }
464    }
```
_____mld6.c

439–452 all_sa is set to the All-Nodes link-local address. Similarly, allrouter_sa is set
to the All-Routers link-local address. Function in6_embedscope() embeds the corresponding link zone ID into the 128-bit IPv6 address, which is the general form of scoped
addresses in the KAME IPv6 stack (see Chapter 2 of *IPv6 Core Protocols Implementation*).

458–463 If the node is responsible for sending a Multicast Listener Done message, indicated by
its status, the multicast address is not the All-Nodes link-local address, and the multicast
scope is larger than the interface-local scope, then mld6_sendpkt() is called to send
an actual MLD message. The destination is the All-Routers multicast address.

2.6.5   Input Processing: mld6_input() Function

The mld6_input() function is called by the icmp6_input() function (Chapter 4 of the
Core Protocols book). It processes incoming MLD messages and maintains the corresponding
listener state accordingly.

Packet Validation

Listing 2-6
_____mld6.c

```
466    void
467    mld6_input(m, off)
468            struct mbuf *m;
469            int off;
470    {
471            struct ip6_hdr *ip6 = mtod(m, struct ip6_hdr *);
472            struct mld_hdr *mldh;
473            struct ifnet *ifp = m->m_pkthdr.rcvif;
474            struct in6_multi *in6m = NULL;
475            struct sockaddr_in6 all_sa, mc_sa;
477            struct ifmultiaddr *ifma;
481            int timer = 0;                    /* timer value in the MLD query header */

490            IP6_EXTHDR_CHECK(m, off, sizeof(*mldh),);
491            mldh = (struct mld_hdr *)(mtod(m, caddr_t) + off);

503            /* source address validation */
504            ip6 = mtod(m, struct ip6_hdr *); /* in case mpullup */
505            if (!(IN6_IS_ADDR_LINKLOCAL(&ip6->ip6_src) ||
506                IN6_IS_ADDR_UNSPECIFIED(&ip6->ip6_src))) {
507    #if 0                                    /* do not log in an input path */
508                    log(LOG_INFO,
509                        "mld6_input: src %s is not link-local (grp=%s)\n",
510                        ip6_sprintf(&ip6->ip6_src),
511                        ip6_sprintf(&mldh->mld_addr));
512    #endif
513                    /*
514                     * spec (RFC2710) does not explicitly
515                     * specify to discard the packet from a non link-local
516                     * source address. But we believe it's expected to do so.
517                     */
```

```
518                         m_freem(m);
519                         return;
520                 }
521
522                 /* convert the multicast address into a full sockaddr form */
523                 bzero(&mc_sa, sizeof(mc_sa));
524                 mc_sa.sin6_family = AF_INET6;
525                 mc_sa.sin6_len = sizeof(mc_sa);
526                 mc_sa.sin6_addr = mldh->mld_addr;
527                 if (in6_addr2zoneid(ifp, &mc_sa.sin6_addr, &mc_sa.sin6_scope_id) ||
528                     in6_embedscope(&mc_sa.sin6_addr, &mc_sa)) {
529                         /* XXX: this should not happen! */
530                         m_freem(m);
531                         return;
532                 }
```
                                                                              ————mld6.c

490–491 The IP6_EXTHDR_CHECK() macro ensures that the first mbuf (m) contains the
packet portion from the IPv6 header to the end of the MLD header for later operations
(see Chapter 1 of *IPv6 Core Protocols Implementation* for the relevant discussion).

503–520 The source address of an MLD message must be a link-local address or the unspecified
address, according to [RFC3590] (see Section 2.3.3). The code drops the packet if the
source address is neither of them. Although it may look like the correct implementation
of [RFC3590], it does not actually conform to the specification: the RFC clarifies that the
special case of the unspecified source address is for MLD snooping switches and specifies
that hosts and routers simply discard such MLD messages. That is, the implementation
should drop the message with the unspecified source address. This inconsistency was
fixed in later versions of KAME snapshots.

In addition, the kernel logging about an unexpected source address is explicitly
disabled because a flood of such unexpected messages may consume an unacceptable
portion of system log files.

522–532 mc_sa is a sockaddr_in6{} structure initialized with the 128-bit multicast address
retrieved from the MLD message. The appropriate multicast scope zone ID is determined
from the receiving interface and is embedded into the address as the general form in the
kernel.

Process Query

Listing 2-7
                                                                              ————mld6.c
```
545             /*
546              * In the MLD specification, there are 3 states and a flag.
547              *
548              * In Non-Listener state, we simply don't have a membership record.
549              * In Delaying Listener state, our timer is running (in6m->in6m_timer)
550              * In Idle Listener state, our timer is not running (in6m->in6m_timer==0)
551              *
552              * The flag is in6m->in6m_state, it is set to MLD_OTHERLISTENER if
553              * we have heard a report from another member, or MLD_IREPORTEDLAST
554              * if we sent the last report.
555              */
556             switch (mldh->mld_type) {
557             case MLD_LISTENER_QUERY:
558                     if (ifp->if_flags & IFF_LOOPBACK)
559                             break;
```

```
560
561                     if (!IN6_IS_ADDR_UNSPECIFIED(&mldh->mld_addr) &&
562                          !IN6_IS_ADDR_MULTICAST(&mldh->mld_addr))
563                          break;           /* print error or log stat? */
564
565                     all_sa = *all_nodes_linklocal;
566                     if (in6_addr2zoneid(ifp, &all_sa.sin6_addr,
567                          &all_sa.sin6_scope_id) ||
568                          in6_embedscope(&all_sa.sin6_addr, &all_sa)) {
569                          /* XXX: this should not happen! */
570                          break;
571                     }
```
                                                                                        _____mld6.c

558–559 The message was sent by the local node and is looped back if the receiving interface
is a loopback interface. The message is discarded in this case.

561–564 The message is discarded if neither the unspecified address nor a multicast address
is specified.

565 all_sa is set to the All-Nodes link-local address for later use.

Listing 2-8
                                                                                        _____mld6.c
```
604                 /*
605                  * - Start the timers in all of our membership records
606                  *   that the query applies to for the interface on
607                  *   which the query arrived excl. those that belong
608                  *   to the "all-nodes" group (ff02::1).
609                  * - Restart any timer that is already running but has
610                  *   A value longer than the requested timeout.
611                  * - Use the value specified in the query message as
612                  *   the maximum timeout.
613                  */
614
615                 /*
616                  * XXX: System timer resolution is too low to handle Max
617                  * Response Delay, so set 1 to the internal timer even if
618                  * the calculated value equals to zero when Max Response
619                  * Delay is positive.
620                  */
621                 timer = ntohs(mldh->mld_maxdelay) * PR_FASTHZ / MLD_TIMER_SCALE;
622                 if (timer == 0 && mldh->mld_maxdelay)
623                          timer = 1;
624
625
629                 for (ifma = LIST_FIRST(&ifp->if_multiaddrs);
630                          ifma;
631                          ifma = LIST_NEXT(ifma, ifma_link))
640                 {
642                          if (ifma->ifma_addr->sa_family != AF_INET6)
643                               continue;
644                          in6m = (struct in6_multi *)ifma->ifma_protospec;
646
647                          if (SA6_ARE_ADDR_EQUAL(&in6m->in6m_sa, &all_sa) ||
648                               IPV6_ADDR_MC_SCOPE(&in6m->in6m_sa.sin6_addr) <
649                               IPV6_ADDR_SCOPE_LINKLOCAL)
650                               continue;
651
652                          if (!IN6_IS_ADDR_UNSPECIFIED(&mldh->mld_addr) &&
653                               !IN6_ARE_ADDR_EQUAL(&mldh->mld_addr,
654                                                   &in6m->in6m_sa.sin6_addr))
655                               continue;
656
```

```
657                              if (timer == 0) {
661                                      /* send a report immediately */
662                                      mld6_sendpkt(in6m, MLD_LISTENER_REPORT, NULL);
663                                      in6m->in6m_timer = 0; /* reset timer */
664                                      in6m->in6m_state = MLD_IREPORTEDLAST;
665                              } else if (in6m->in6m_timer == 0 || /*idle state*/
666                                      in6m->in6m_timer > timer) {
670                                      in6m->in6m_timer = MLD_RANDOM_DELAY(timer);
671                                      mld_group_timers_are_running = 1;
672                              }
673                      }
689                      break;
```
_____ mld6.c

621–623 The timer interval is calculated based on the received value specified by the Maximum Response Delay field. It is converted to the timer count for the granularity of 200ms, and is set in the variable timer. If the advertised delay is positive but less than 200, timer is set to 0, effectively disabling the timer. In such a case, the variable is adjusted to 1 to activate the timer.

629–650 Each IPv6 multicast group address that the node has joined on the receiving interface is examined. The All-Nodes link-local multicast group and group addresses whose scope is smaller than link-local are ignored.

652–655 A query of the unspecified address as the multicast group is a general Query (Section 2.3.1) that matches all group addresses. Otherwise, only the matching multicast group is considered.

657–672 A Multicast Listener Report is sent immediately if the query has a 0 Maximum Response Delay. The timer is reset and the flag is set to MLD_IREPORTEDLAST. Otherwise, if the multicast entry is in the Idle state or a shorter timer value is specified, the timer is restarted. It corresponds to the state transition from Idle to Delaying Listener or the loop within the Delaying Listener state in Figure 2-19. A random factor is added to the timer value to avoid Report message flooding. The global variable mld_group_timers_are_running indicates there are active timers and the MLD timer function needs to service these timers.

Process MLD Report

Listing 2-9
_____ mld6.c

```
737             case MLD_LISTENER_REPORT:
738                     /*
739                      * For fast leave to work, we have to know that we are the
740                      * last person to send a report for this group.  Reports
741                      * can potentially get looped back if we are a multicast
742                      * router, so discard reports sourced by me.
743                      * Note that it is impossible to check IFF_LOOPBACK flag of
744                      * ifp for this purpose, since ip6_mloopback pass the physical
745                      * interface to looutput.
746                      */
747                     if (m->m_flags & M_LOOP) /* XXX: grotty flag, but efficient */
748                             break;
749
750                     if (!IN6_IS_ADDR_MULTICAST(&mldh->mld_addr))
751                             break;
752
753                     /*
754                      * If we belong to the group being reported, stop
```

```
755                            * our timer for that group.
756                            */
757                           IN6_LOOKUP_MULTI(&mc_sa, ifp, in6m);
758                           if (in6m) {
759                                   in6m->in6m_timer = 0; /* transit to idle state */
760                                   in6m->in6m_state = MLD_OTHERLISTENER; /* clear flag */
761                           }
762                           break;
763                   default:
764       #if 0
765                           /*
766                            * this case should be impossible because of filtering in
767                            * icmp6_input().  But we explicitly disabled this part
768                            * just in case.
769                            */
770                           log(LOG_ERR, "mld6_input: illegal type(%d)", mldh->mld_type);
771       #endif
772                           break;
773                   }
774
775           m_freem(m);
776       }
```
                                                                                            ———mld6.c

737–748 If a Report message from a different node is received, the receiving node is not
responsible for sending Done messages any more. This case is easy for a host, since it does
not loop its own Report messages back to itself (see Listing 2-13 following), which means
a received Report always comes from a different node. However, a multicast router needs
to loop transmitting Report messages to itself so that the multicast routing daemon can
notice the local listener, which may confuse the processing. The M_LOOP flag is examined
in order to avoid this scenario. As commented, checking the IFF_LOOPBACK flag on the
receiving interface does not work, since the packet is looped back via ip6_mloopback()
and the receiving interface is set to the physical outgoing interface, which may not have
the IFF_LOOPBACK flag.

   If the packet is detected as being looped back, it is silently discarded.

750–752 The Multicast Address field of a Report message must carry a multicast address.
Otherwise, the packet is invalid and is simply discarded.

757–762 The IN6_LOOKUP_MULTI() macro checks if the local node has joined the reported
multicast group. If so, the state for this group is moved to Idle by clearing the entry
timer. In addition, now that this node is not the listener who sent the latest Report, the
in6m_state member is changed to MLD_OTHERLISTENER.

763–773 The mld6_input() function is only called by function icmp6_input() when
the MLD message type is either Multicast Listener Query or Report. As such, the default
switch case should not happen.

775 There is no need to keep the packet because the packet is copied in function
icmp6_input() to be sent to applications when necessary and can be freed here.

2.6.6 mld6_fasttimeo() Function

The mld6_fasttimeo() function is responsible for processing MLD timers. Unfortunately,
this function is unnecessarily complicated by the support for MLDv2. We will only discuss code
related to MLDv1 in this section.

Listing 2-10

```
778    void
779    mld6_fasttimeo()
780    {
781            struct in6_multi *in6m;
782            struct in6_multistep step;
783            struct ifnet *ifp = NULL;
793            int s;
794
795            /*
796             * Quick check to see if any work needs to be done, in order
797             * to minimize the overhead of fasttimo processing.
798             */
799            if (!mld_group_timers_are_running && !mld_interface_timers_are_running
800                && !mld_state_change_timers_are_running)
801                    return;
802
806            s = splnet();
808
```

(MLDv2 specific code: omitted)

```
837            mld_group_timers_are_running = 0;
843            IN6_FIRST_MULTI(step, in6m);
844            if (in6m == NULL) {
845                    splx(s);
846                    return;
847            }
848            ifp = in6m->in6m_ifp;
849            while (in6m != NULL) {
850                    if (in6m->in6m_timer == 0)
851                            goto next_in6m; /* do nothing */
852
853                    --in6m->in6m_timer;
854                    if (in6m->in6m_timer > 0) {
855                            mld_group_timers_are_running = 1;
856                            goto bypass_state_transition;
857                    }
```

(MLDv2 specific code: omitted)

```
864                            mld6_sendpkt(in6m, MLD_LISTENER_REPORT, NULL);
865                            in6m->in6m_state = MLD_IREPORTEDLAST;
```

(MLDv2 specific code: omitted)

```
884
885            bypass_state_transition:
933            next_in6m:
934                    IN6_NEXT_MULTI(step, in6m);
935            }
936
944            splx(s);
945    }
```

799–801 The timer processing completes if the local node is not responsible for reporting any multicast groups the node is joining. Only the `mld_group_timers_are_running` variable is relevant to MLDv1.

806 Network level interrupts must be disabled by `splnet()` because the same list can be referred to in the packet input path.

837–935 The code is unnecessarily complicated due to the support for MLDv2, which is omitted
in the discussion. The original logic is straightforward: every multicast group entry that
enables the timer is examined; the entry timer counter decrements by 1, and, if the timer
expires and the local node is responsible for sending the Report, `mld6_sendpkt()` is
called to send the message. Since this node has just sent a Report message, `in6m_state`
is changed to `MLD_IREPORTEDLAST`. If an entry that has a positive timer value remains
in the list, `mld6_timers_are_running` is set to 1, indicating timer processing needs
to be continued.

2.6.7 `mld6_sendpkt()` Function

The `mld6_sendpkt()` function is responsible for performing the actual transmission of MLD
messages.

Listing 2-11
                                                                                                           ————mld6.c
```
974     static void
975     mld6_sendpkt(in6m, type, dst)
976             struct in6_multi *in6m;
977             int type;
978             const struct sockaddr_in6 *dst;
979     {
980             struct mbuf *mh;
981             struct mld_hdr *mldh;
982             struct ip6_hdr *ip6 = NULL;
983             struct ip6_moptions im6o;
984             struct ifnet *ifp = in6m->in6m_ifp;
985             struct in6_ifaddr *ia = NULL;
986             struct sockaddr_in6 src_sa, dst_sa;
987
996             /*
997              * At first, find a link local address on the outgoing interface
998              * to use as the source address of the MLD packet.
999              * We do not reject tentative addresses for MLD report to deal with
1000             * the case where we first join a link-local address.
1001             */
1002            if ((ia = in6ifa_ifpforlinklocal(ifp, ignflags)) == NULL)
1003                    return;
1004            if ((ia->ia6_flags & IN6_IFF_TENTATIVE))
1005                    ia = NULL;
```
                                                                                                           ————mld6.c

Source Address Selection

996–1005 [RFC3590] specifies that an MLD message must use a link-local address as the
source address if the node has a valid link-local address on the outgoing interface
(Section 2.3.3). Function `in6ifa_ifpforlinklocal()` is called to see this condition. The output process fails if there is no valid link-local address found; note that
`in6ifa_ipfforlinklocal()` may return a tentative address (i.e., an address being
checked about uniqueness by Duplicate Address Detection; see Chapter 5 of *IPv6 Core
Protocols Implementation*), which must be regarded as not available in this context. The
unspecified address will be used as the source address in this case.

Listing 2-12

——mld6.c
```
1007            /* Allocate two mbufs to store IPv6 header and MLD header */
1008            mldh = mld_allocbuf(&mh, MLD_MINLEN, in6m, type);
1009            if (mldh == NULL)
1010                    return;
1011
1012            /* fill src/dst here */
1013            ip6 = mtod(mh, struct ip6_hdr *);
1014            ip6->ip6_src = ia ? ia->ia_addr.sin6_addr : in6addr_any;
1015            ip6->ip6_dst = dst ? dst->sin6_addr : in6m->in6m_sa.sin6_addr;
1016
1017            /* set packet addresses in a full sockaddr_in6 form */
1018            bzero(&src_sa, sizeof(src_sa));
1019            bzero(&dst_sa, sizeof(dst_sa));
1020            src_sa.sin6_family = dst_sa.sin6_family = AF_INET6;
1021            src_sa.sin6_len = dst_sa.sin6_len = sizeof(struct sockaddr_in6);
1022            src_sa.sin6_addr = ip6->ip6_src;
1023            dst_sa.sin6_addr = ip6->ip6_dst;
1024            /*
1025             * in6_addr2zoneid() and ip6_setpktaddrs() are called at actual
1026             * advertisement time
1027             */
1028            if (in6_addr2zoneid(ifp, &src_sa.sin6_addr, &src_sa.sin6_scope_id) ||
1029                in6_addr2zoneid(ifp, &dst_sa.sin6_addr, &dst_sa.sin6_scope_id)) {
1030                    /* XXX: impossible */
1031                    m_free(mh);
1032                    return;
1033            }
1034            if (!ip6_setpktaddrs(mh, &src_sa, &dst_sa)) {
1035                    m_free(mh);
1036                    return;
1037            }
```
——mld6.c

Allocate Mbuf

1007–1010 The function `mld_allocbuf()` creates a chain of two mbufs: one contains the IPv6 header, and the other contains the MLD header. The reason for creating two mbufs is because a Hop-by-Hop Options header will be inserted later in `ip6_output()`, where using the chain of mbufs is more convenient as explained in Chapter 3 of the *Core Protocols* book. When `mld_allocbuf()` succeeds, variable `mh` points to the head of the chain, and `mldh` points to the MLD header in the second mbuf.

Set Addresses

1012–1015 A valid nontentative link-local address is chosen for the source address if available; otherwise, the unspecified address is used instead. The destination address is set to the address given by the caller if available; otherwise, the destination address is set to the multicast address for which the MLD message is sent. The former case applies to the Multicast Listener Done messages, which are sent to the All-Routers link-local multicast address regardless of the group address given.

1017–1037 Variables `src_sa` and `dst_sa` are `sockaddr_in6{}` structures that are set to the source and destination addresses of the packet respectively, with each address containing the appropriate scope zone index. The zone indices are determined from the scope of the addresses and the outgoing interface. The function `in6_addr2zoneid()` embeds the zone index into the addresses. The function `ip6_setpktaddrs()` attaches the `sockaddr_in6{}` structures to the mbuf.

Listing 2-13

mld6.c

```
1039            mldh->mld_addr = in6m->in6m_sa.sin6_addr;
1040            in6_clearscope(&mldh->mld_addr); /* XXX */
1041
1042            mldh->mld_cksum = in6_cksum(mh, IPPROTO_ICMPV6, sizeof(struct ip6_hdr),
1043                                  MLD_MINLEN);
1044
1045            /* construct multicast option */
1046            bzero(&im6o, sizeof(im6o));
1047            im6o.im6o_multicast_ifp = ifp;
1048            im6o.im6o_multicast_hlim = 1;
1049
1050            /*
1051             * Request loopback of the report if we are acting as a multicast
1052             * router, so that the process-level routing daemon can hear it.
1053             */
1054            im6o.im6o_multicast_loop = (ip6_mrouter != NULL);
```

mld6.c

Complete the Packet

1039–1043 The Multicast Address field of the MLD message is filled in with the address of the given multicast group as the function parameter in6m. Since a scope zone index may be embedded in the address, that space in the address must be zero-cleared before the packet is sent on the wire. Finally, in6_cksum() calculates the checksum over the complete MLD header and stores the checksum value into the checksum field.

Construct Multicast Options

1045–1054 Several packet transmission options are set in im6o, an instance of the ip6_moptions{} structure. The im6o_multicast_ifp field contains the outgoing interface, and the im6o_multicast_hlim field contains the packet hop limit, which is 1 as specified in [RFC2710]. im6o_multicast_loop controls the packet loopback behavior. Typically, an MLD message is not looped back to the transmitting node. But if the transmitting node is acting as a multicast router, the message must be looped back to the local node so that the multicast routing daemon can notice the local listener.

Listing 2-14

mld6.c

```
1056            /* increment output statictics */
1057            icmp6stat.icp6s_outhist[type]++;
1058            icmp6_ifstat_inc(ifp, ifs6_out_msg);
1059            switch (type) {
1060            case MLD_LISTENER_QUERY:
1061                    icmp6_ifstat_inc(ifp, ifs6_out_mldquery);
1062                    break;
1063            case MLD_LISTENER_REPORT:
1064                    icmp6_ifstat_inc(ifp, ifs6_out_mldreport);
1065                    break;
1066            case MLD_LISTENER_DONE:
1067                    icmp6_ifstat_inc(ifp, ifs6_out_mlddone);
1068                    break;
1069            }
1070
1071            ip6_output(mh, &ip6_opts, NULL, ia ? 0 : IPV6_UNSPECSRC, &im6o, NULL
1073                        ,NULL
1075                        );
1076    }
```

mld6.c

Statistics Update

1057–1069 ICMPv6 and MLD MIB variables are updated. It should be noted that most of them are interface-specific and need the outgoing interface.

Send Packet

1071–1076 The mbuf containing the message is passed to function `ip6_output()` for transmission. A special flag `IPV6_UNSPESRC` is set as a function argument if the source address is the unspecified address. This flag prevents `ip6_output()` from misinterpreting the packet as being invalid (see Chapter 3 of *IPv6 Core Protocols Implementation*).

2.6.8 `mld_allocbuf()` Function

The `mld_allocbuf()` function is a subroutine of the `mld6_sendpkt()` function. It allocates memory for the outgoing MLD message and partially initializes the header.

> You may notice that the function naming is inconsistent: only this function has the prefix `mld_` while the other MLD-related functions begin with `mld6_`. This is due to a historical reason: the other functions were first implemented when no standard API was defined. Then the advanced API specification [RFC3542] introduced the convention of the prefix `mld_` for MLD-related definitions. The function `mld_allocbuf()` was implemented after that, following the standard convention. Later versions of KAME snapshot has resolved this inconsistency by changing the prefix to `mld_` for all the other functions.

Listing 2-15

———mld6.c

```
1078    static struct mld_hdr *
1079    mld_allocbuf(mh, len, in6m, type)
1080            struct mbuf **mh;
1081            int len;
1082            struct in6_multi *in6m;
1083            int type;
1084    {
1085            struct mbuf *md;
1086            struct mld_hdr *mldh;
1087            struct ip6_hdr *ip6;
1088
1089            /*
1090             * Allocate mbufs to store ip6 header and MLD header.
1091             * We allocate 2 mbufs and make chain in advance because
1092             * it is more convenient when inserting the hop-by-hop option later.
1093             */
1094            MGETHDR(*mh, M_DONTWAIT, MT_HEADER);
1095            if (*mh == NULL)
1096                    return NULL;
1097            MGET(md, M_DONTWAIT, MT_DATA);
```

(MLDv2 specific code: omitted)

```
1108            if (md == NULL) {
1109                    m_free(*mh);
1110                    *mh = NULL;
```

```
1111                     return NULL;
1112             }
1113             (*mh)->m_next = md;
1114             md->m_next = NULL;
1115
1116             (*mh)->m_pkthdr.rcvif = NULL;
1117             (*mh)->m_pkthdr.len = sizeof(struct ip6_hdr) + len;
1118             (*mh)->m_len = sizeof(struct ip6_hdr);
1119             MH_ALIGN(*mh, sizeof(struct ip6_hdr));
1120
1121             /* fill in the ip6 header */
1122             ip6 = mtod(*mh, struct ip6_hdr *);
1123             bzero(ip6, sizeof(*ip6));
1124             ip6->ip6_flow = 0;
1125             ip6->ip6_vfc &= ~IPV6_VERSION_MASK;
1126             ip6->ip6_vfc |= IPV6_VERSION;
1127             /* ip6_plen will be set later */
1128             ip6->ip6_nxt = IPPROTO_ICMPV6;
1129             /* ip6_hlim will be set by im6o.im6o_multicast_hlim */
1130             /* ip6_src/dst will be set by mld_sendpkt() or mld_sendbuf() */
1131
1132             /* fill in the MLD header as much as possible */
1133             md->m_len = len;
1134             mldh = mtod(md, struct mld_hdr *);
1135             bzero(mldh, len);
1136             mldh->mld_type = type;
1137             return mldh;
1138     }
```
                                                                                ―mld6.c

1094–1097 As explained in `mld6_sendpkt()`, two separate mbufs are allocated for constructing an outgoing MLD message. The `M_DONTWAIT` flag is set for memory allocation because this routine can be called within an interrupt context.

1108–1114 The two mbufs are linked together if the allocation was successful.

1116–1130 The first mbuf contains the IPv6 header. Only the version field and the next header field in the IPv6 header are initialized here because other fields will be set either in function `mld6_sendpkt()` or in function `ip6_output()`.

1132–1137 The second mbuf contains the MLD header. Only the MLD message type field is set here.

2.7   IPv6 Multicast Interface: `mif6{}` Structure

The KAME kernel maintains a separate data structure for interfaces that are used in multicast forwarding. These interfaces are called *multicast interfaces*. The corresponding notion in the IPv4 multicast routing implementation is called *virtual interfaces*, since the implementation was originally developed for DVMRP, which used tunneling to bypass routers that do not support the protocol. Since DVMRP is not defined for IPv6 multicast routing, there is no need for the built-in notion of virtual interfaces in the IPv6 implementation, and the interfaces are simply called multicast interfaces.

Yet a special interface, called the *Register interface*, is reserved for the PIM Register message processing. The Register interface is implemented as an `ifnet{}` structure just like any other network interface. The Register interface, however, is only available in the IPv6 multicast forwarding code, i.e., `ip6_mroute.c`, and is not linked in the global `ifnet{}` chain(*).

(*) Recent versions of FreeBSD link the Register structure into the global chain as a side effect of calling common initialization functions for ifnet{} structures.

An IPv6 multicast interface corresponds to one network interface in the kernel, and stores information specific to multicast forwarding. The set of multicast interfaces is a subset of the entire network interfaces installed in the kernel with one exception, the Register interface.

Each multicast interface is described by an instance of the mif6{} structure. The structure definition is given in Listing 2-16.

Listing 2-16
_____ip6_mroute.h
```
205   /*
206    * The kernel's multicast-interface structure.
207    */
208   struct mif6 {
209           u_char          m6_flags;       /* MIFF_ flags defined above       */
210           u_int           m6_rate_limit;  /* max rate                        */
211   #ifdef notyet
212           struct tbf      *m6_tbf;         /* token bucket structure at intf. */
213   #endif
214           struct in6_addr m6_lcl_addr;    /* local interface address         */
215           struct ifnet    *m6_ifp;        /* pointer to interface            */
216           u_quad_t m6_pkt_in;     /* # pkts in on interface         */
217           u_quad_t m6_pkt_out;    /* # pkts out on interface        */
218           u_quad_t m6_bytes_in;   /* # bytes in on interface        */
219           u_quad_t m6_bytes_out;  /* # bytes out on interface       */
221           struct route m6_route;/* cached route if this is a tunnel */
225   #ifdef notyet
226           u_int           m6_rsvp_on;     /* RSVP listening on this vif */
227           struct socket   *m6_rsvpd;      /* RSVP daemon socket */
228   #endif
229   };
```
_____ip6_mroute.h

The only currently defined flag for the m6_flags member is the MIFF_REGISTER flag, which marks the multicast interface as being the Register interface. The m6_ifp member points to the corresponding network interface or the Register interface. The m6_pkt_in, m6_pkt_out, m6_bytes_in and m6_bytes_out members are per-interface statistics variables used by the routing daemon. The other members of the structure are not in use by the KAME IPv6 implementation at the time of this writing.

Figure 2-20 shows the relationship between data structures and global variables related to multicast interfaces. All mif6{} structures are stored in a global array named mif6table. This array currently has a fixed size of 64. The number of configured mif6{} structures is stored in a file-scope global variable nummifs. When the Register interface is configured, the corresponding array index in mif6table is stored in a file-scope global variable reg_mif_num. The ifnet{} structure for the Register interface is statically allocated via a global variable of multicast_register_if. Note that the if_index member of the Register interface is set to the array index in mif6table, which is irrelevant to the normal ifnet{} structure that has the same index.

FIGURE 2-20

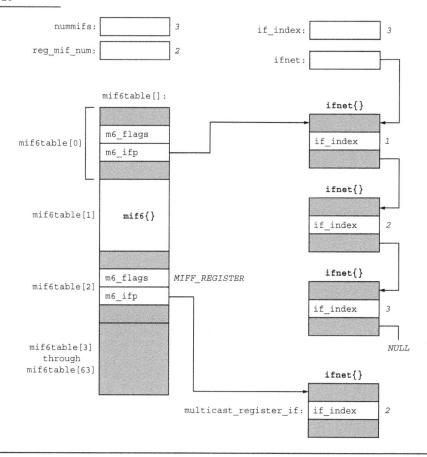

IPv6 multicast interface structures and related global variables.

2.8   IPv6 Multicast Routing API

The IPv6 multicast routing daemons manipulate the forwarding information maintained in the kernel via socket options and through `ioctl` commands. Figure 2-21 shows call graphs of the related functions.

Table 2-7 summarizes socket options used by the multicast routing daemon. These are effectively only available on an ICMPv6 socket as we will see in Section 2.8.2.

Table 2-8 summarizes `ioctl` commands used by the multicast routing daemon.

2.8.1   `ip6_mrouter_set()` Function

The `ip6_mrouter_set()` function handles the set operation of socket options related to multicast routing sent from the routing daemon.

FIGURE 2-21

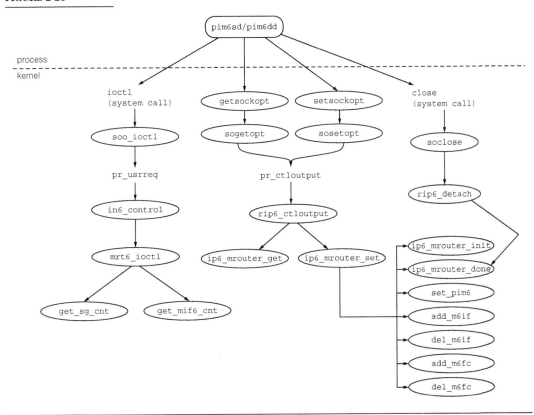

Multicast routing API call graph.

TABLE 2-7

optname	*optval type*	*Function*	*Description*
MRT6_INIT		ip6_mrouter_init	Start multicast routing
MRT6_DONE		ip6_mrouter_done	Shut down multicast routing
MRT6_ADD_MIF	struct mif6ctl	add_m6if	Add multicast interface
MRT6_DEL_MIF	mifi_t	del_m6if	Delete multicast interface
MRT6_ADD_MFC	struct mf6cctl	add_m6fc	Add forwarding cache entry
MRT6_DEL_MFC	struct mf6cctl	del_m6fc	Delete forwarding cache entry
MRT6_PIM	int	set_pim6	Toggle PIM routing

Multicast routing socket options.

TABLE 2-8

Command	Argument type	Function	Description
SIOCGETSGCNT_IN6	struct sioc_sg_req6	get_sg_cnt	Get multicast forwarding statistics
SIOCGETMIFCNT_IN6	struct sioc_mif_req6	get_mif6_cnt	Get statistics for a multicast interface

Multicast routing ioctl *commands.*

Listing 2-17

ip6_mroute.c
```
313    int
314    ip6_mrouter_set(so, sopt)
315            struct socket *so;
316            struct sockopt *sopt;
317    {
318            int        error = 0;
319            struct mbuf *m;
320
321            if (so != ip6_mrouter && sopt->sopt_name != MRT6_INIT)
322                    return (EACCES);
323
324            if ((error = soopt_getm(sopt, &m)) != 0) /* XXX */
325                    return (error);
326            if ((error = soopt_mcopyin(sopt, m)) != 0) /* XXX */
327                    return (error);
328
329            switch (sopt->sopt_name) {
330            case MRT6_INIT:
331    #ifdef MRT6_OINIT
332            case MRT6_OINIT:
333    #endif
334                    error = ip6_mrouter_init(so, m, sopt->sopt_name);
335                    break;
336            case MRT6_DONE:
337                    error = ip6_mrouter_done();
338                    break;
339            case MRT6_ADD_MIF:
340                    error = add_m6if(mtod(m, struct mif6ctl *));
341                    break;
342            case MRT6_DEL_MIF:
343                    error = del_m6if(mtod(m, mifi_t *));
344                    break;
345            case MRT6_ADD_MFC:
346                    error = add_m6fc(mtod(m, struct mf6cctl *));
347                    break;
348            case MRT6_DEL_MFC:
349                    error = del_m6fc(mtod(m, struct mf6cctl *));
350                    break;
351            case MRT6_PIM:
352                    error = set_pim6(mtod(m, int *));
353                    break;
354            default:
355                    error = EOPNOTSUPP;
356                    break;
357            }
358
359            (void)m_freem(m);
360            return (error);
361    }
```
ip6_mroute.c

321–322 The first command issued by the routing daemon must be MRT6_INIT. As will be
seen shortly, the socket pointer on which this option is set is stored in ip6_mrouter.
Any other socket options must be specified on this socket.

324–327 Function soopt_getm() allocates an mbuf for the socket command and command
options. Function soopt_mcopyin() transfers the command and its options to the newly
created mbuf. These utility functions are used here to provide better portability to other
BSD variants than FreeBSD.

329–361 An appropriate function is called for each specific option. These functions are
described in the succeeding subsections. The temporary mbuf is freed and the error code
is returned to the caller.

Note: This code has a bug. It can pass the mbuf to the subroutine function even if the data is
too short for the specific option; the length must be checked beforehand. This bug is fixed
in a later version of the KAME kernel.

2.8.2 ip6_mrouter_init() Function

The ip6_mrouter_init() function enables multicast routing in the kernel.

Listing 2-18

                                                                                        ip6_mroute.c
```
530     /*
531      * Enable multicast routing
532      */
533     static int
534     ip6_mrouter_init(so, m, cmd)
535             struct socket *so;
536             struct mbuf *m;
537             int cmd;
538     {
539             int *v;
540
548             if (so->so_type != SOCK_RAW ||
549                 so->so_proto->pr_protocol != IPPROTO_ICMPV6)
550                     return EOPNOTSUPP;
551
552             if (!m || (m->m_len != sizeof(int *)))
553                     return ENOPROTOOPT;
554
555             v = mtod(m, int *);
556             if (*v != 1)
557                     return ENOPROTOOPT;
```
                                                                                        ip6_mroute.c

548–553 The multicast routing socket options must be issued on an ICMPv6 socket. The socket
option must be present and the option value must be an integer. An appropriate error is
returned if one of the conditions is not met.

The ENOPROTOOPT code is not an appropriate error for an invalid argument. EINVAL would
have been a better choice.

555–557 The integer value specifies the kernel version supporting IPv6 multicast routing. The only currently available kernel version is 1. Any other version number is an error and the `ENOPROTOOPT` error code is returned.

Listing 2-19

```
                                                                          ip6_mroute.c
559            if (ip6_mrouter != NULL) return EADDRINUSE;
560
561            ip6_mrouter = so;
562            ip6_mrouter_ver = cmd;
563
564            bzero((caddr_t)mf6ctable, sizeof(mf6ctable));
565            bzero((caddr_t)n6expire, sizeof(n6expire));
566
567            pim6 = 0;/* used for stubbing out/in pim stuff */
568
570            callout_reset(&expire_upcalls_ch, EXPIRE_TIMEOUT,
571                expire_upcalls, NULL);
583
584            return 0;
585    }
                                                                          ip6_mroute.c
```

559 The check on `ip6_mrouter` variable is for avoiding repeated initialization.

561–567 The global variable `ip6_mrouter` points to the socket corresponding to the routing daemon that is performing the kernel multicast routing initialization. `ip6_mrouter_ver` remembers the socket option command to provide backward compatibility (see Listing 2-54). Variable `pim6` is reset to 0 to disable multicast packet forwarding until the routing daemon explicitly starts PIM routing.

570–571 Function `callout_reset()` starts a new timer identified by a file-scope global variable `expire_upcalls_ch`. The timer expires every 250 ms and invokes function `expire_upcalls()` (Section 2.9.3) to process stale events.

2.8.3 `ip6_mrouter_get()` Function

The `ip6_mrouter_get()` function is called from `rip6_ctloutput()` to perform the get operation of multicast routing socket options.

Listing 2-20

```
                                                                          ip6_mroute.c
392    int
393    ip6_mrouter_get(so, sopt)
394            struct socket *so;
395            struct sockopt *sopt;
396    {
397            int error = 0;
398
399            if (so != ip6_mrouter) return EACCES;
400
401            switch (sopt->sopt_name) {
402                    case MRT6_PIM:
403                            error = sooptcopyout(sopt, &pim6, sizeof(pim6));
404                            break;
405            }
406            return (error);
407    }
                                                                          ip6_mroute.c
```

399 Only the active routing daemon is allowed to issue the get operation; otherwise, an error of EACCES is returned.

401–405 The only available option for the get operation is MRT6_PIM that corresponds to the pim6 variable. This variable has a binary value indicating whether PIM routing is enabled. Function sooptcopyout() copies the value of pim6 into the socket option structure to be returned to the application.

> This function should actually return an error code for get options other than MRT6_PIM. Later versions of the kernel return an error of EOPNOTSUPP in such cases.

2.8.4 set_pim6() Function

The set_pim6() function, shown in Listing 2-21, is called by function ip6_mrouter_set() when the routing daemon starts or stops PIM routing. pim6 is set to the given binary value, which can only be either 0 or 1.

Listing 2-21

ip6_mroute.c

```
518    static int
519    set_pim6(i)
520          int *i;
521    {
522          if ((*i != 1) && (*i != 0))
523                return EINVAL;
524
525          pim6 = *i;
526
527          return 0;
528    }
```

ip6_mroute.c

2.8.5 add_m6if() Function

The add_m6if() function adds a multicast interface into the kernel via the MRT6_ADD_MIF socket option. The option argument is a pointer to the mif6ctl{} structure, which is defined in Listing 2-22.

Listing 2-22

ip6_mroute.h

```
101    struct mif6ctl {
102          mifi_t      mif6c_mifi;       /* the index of the mif to be added   */
103          u_char      mif6c_flags;      /* MIFF_ flags defined below          */
104          u_short     mif6c_pifi;       /* the index of the physical IF */
105    #ifdef notyet
106          u_int       mif6c_rate_limit; /* max rate                           */
107    #endif
108    };
```

ip6_mroute.h

mif6c_mifi specifies the index of the multicast interface to be created. The mif6c_flags member specifies attributes of the interface. The only available flag in this implementation

is MIFF_REGISTER, which means the specified interface should be the Register interface.
mif6c_pifi specifies the interface index of the corresponding physical interface.

Through the following listings, we will see the details of the add_m6if() function.

Listing 2-23

```
_____ ip6_mroute.c
700     /*
701      * Add a mif to the mif table
702      */
703     static int
704     add_m6if(mifcp)
705            struct mif6ctl *mifcp;
706     {
707            struct mif6 *mifp;
708            struct ifnet *ifp;
712            int error, s;
713     #ifdef notyet
714            struct tbf *m_tbf = tbftable + mifcp->mif6c_mifi;
715     #endif
716
717            if (mifcp->mif6c_mifi >= MAXMIFS)
718                    return EINVAL;
719            mifp = mif6table + mifcp->mif6c_mifi;
720            if (mifp->m6_ifp)
721                    return EADDRINUSE; /* XXX: is it appropriate? */
722            if (mifcp->mif6c_pifi == 0 || mifcp->mif6c_pifi > if_index)
723                    return ENXIO;
724            /*
725             * XXX: some OSes can remove ifp and clear ifindex2ifnet[id]
726             * even for id between 0 and if_index.
727             */
729            ifp = ifnet_byindex(mifcp->mif6c_pifi);
733            if (ifp == NULL)
734                    return ENXIO;
_____ ip6_mroute.c
```

717–718 If the given interface index is out of range, an error of EINVAL will be returned.

719–721 If the interface corresponding to the given index is in use in the interface table,
mif6table, an error of EADDRINUSE will be returned. The error code was derived
from the IPv4 multicast routing implementation, but may not be appropriate for IPv6 as
indicated by the comment at line 721. The error code was reasonable for IPv4 multicast
routing, since the interface was specified by an address. In this code for IPv6, however,
the interface is specified by an integer index, for which the error may not really make
sense.

719–734 If the index of the physical interface specified by mif6c_pifi is out of range, an
error of ENXIO will be returned. Even if the index is in the valid range, the corresponding
interface may not exist when the system allows dynamic addition or deletion of interfaces.
An error of ENXIO will be returned in such cases.

Listing 2-24

```
_____ ip6_mroute.c
736            if (mifcp->mif6c_flags & MIFF_REGISTER) {
737                    ifp = &multicast_register_if;
738
739                    if (reg_mif_num == (mifi_t)-1) {
```

```
743                              ifp->if_name = "register_mif";
745                              ifp->if_flags |= IFF_LOOPBACK;
746                              ifp->if_index = mifcp->mif6c_mifi;
747                              reg_mif_num = mifcp->mif6c_mifi;
748                              if (inet6domain.dom_ifattach) {
749                                      ifp->if_afdata[AF_INET6]
750                                          = inet6domain.dom_ifattach(ifp);
751                              }
752                      }
753
754              } /* if REGISTER */
```
_____ ip6_mroute.c

736–754 The `ifnet{}` data structure represented by `multicast_register_if` is
initialized if the new multicast interface is designated as the Register interface. Some of the
structure members are initialized here if the Register interface is seen for the first time. The
`if_index` member is set to the multicast interface index, although this may not be really
appropriate because this index value may conflict with that of a "real" interface. The interface attachment function for the `AF_INET6` domain, `in6_domifattach()`, performs
IPv6 specific initialization for this new interface. The global variable `reg_mif_num` is set
for tracking the Register interface.

Listing 2-25
_____ ip6_mroute.c

```
755              else {
756                      /* Make sure the interface supports multicast */
757                      if ((ifp->if_flags & IFF_MULTICAST) == 0)
758                              return EOPNOTSUPP;
759
763                      s = splnet();
766                      error = if_allmulti(ifp, 1);
776                      splx(s);
777                      if (error)
778                              return error;
779              }
```
_____ ip6_mroute.c

755–758 The physical interface must have link-level multicast capability in order for a multicast
interface to operate over it. Otherwise, an error of `EOPNOTSUPP` is returned.

763–778 Function `if_allmulti()` puts the interface into the multicast promiscuous mode
so that the router can receive and forward multicast packets not directly destined for it.

Listing 2-26
_____ ip6_mroute.c

```
784              s = splnet();
786              mifp->m6_flags      = mifcp->mif6c_flags;
787              mifp->m6_ifp        = ifp;
788      #ifdef notyet
789              /* scaling up here allows division by 1024 in critical code */
790              mifp->m6_rate_limit = mifcp->mif6c_rate_limit * 1024 / 1000;
791      #endif
792              /* initialize per mif pkt counters */
793              mifp->m6_pkt_in    = 0;
794              mifp->m6_pkt_out   = 0;
795              mifp->m6_bytes_in  = 0;
796              mifp->m6_bytes_out = 0;
```

```
797             splx(s);
798
799             /* Adjust nummifs up if the mifi is higher than nummifs */
800             if (nummifs <= mifcp->mif6c_mifi)
801                     nummifs = mifcp->mif6c_mifi + 1;
802
811             return 0;
812     }
```
——— ip6_mroute.c

784–812 The multicast interface flags, the pointer to the physical interface, and the packet
counters are initialized. The global variable `nummifs` is adjusted if necessary to contain
the highest index value among the existing multicast interfaces.

2.8.6 `del_m6if()` Function

The `del_m6if()` function deletes a multicast interface from the kernel via the `MRT6_DEL_MIF`
socket option. It takes the multicast interface index as the key for the entry to be deleted.

Listing 2-27

——— ip6_mroute.c
```
814     /*
815      * Delete a mif from the mif table
816      */
817     static int
818     del_m6if(mifip)
819             mifi_t *mifip;
820     {
821             struct mif6 *mifp = mif6table + *mifip;
822             mifi_t mifi;
823             struct ifnet *ifp;
827             int s;
828
829             if (*mifip >= nummifs)
830                     return EINVAL;
831             if (mifp->m6_ifp == NULL)
832                     return EINVAL;
833
837             s = splnet();
839
840             if (mifp->m6_flags & MIFF_REGISTER && reg_mif_num != (mifi_t) -1) {
841                     reg_mif_num = -1;
842                     if (inet6domain.dom_ifdetach) {
843                             ifp = &multicast_register_if;
844                             inet6domain.dom_ifdetach(ifp, ifp->if_afdata[AF_INET6]);
845                             ifp->if_afdata[AF_INET6] = NULL;
846                     }
847             }
```
——— ip6_mroute.c

817–832 An error of `EINVAL` is returned if either the given multicast interface index is out of
the range or the multicast interface has not been initialized.

837–847 If the Register interface is being deleted, global variable `reg_mif_num` is reset
to indicate the system does not have the Register interface installed. In addition, the
`inet6domain.dom_ifdetach` function is called to clean up the IPv6 specific
parameters stored in the `ifnet{}` structure associated with the interface.

Listing 2-28

ip6_mroute.c

```
848            if (!(mifp->m6_flags & MIFF_REGISTER)) {
849                    /*
850                     * XXX: what if there is yet IPv4 multicast daemon
851                     *       using the interface?
852                     */
853                    ifp = mifp->m6_ifp;
854
856                    if_allmulti(ifp, 0);
862            }
863
864    #ifdef notyet
865            bzero((caddr_t)qtable[*mifip], sizeof(qtable[*mifip]));
866            bzero((caddr_t)mifp->m6_tbf, sizeof(*(mifp->m6_tbf)));
867    #endif
868            bzero((caddr_t)mifp, sizeof (*mifp));
869
870            /* Adjust nummifs down */
871            for (mifi = nummifs; mifi > 0; mifi--)
872                    if (mif6table[mifi - 1].m6_ifp)
873                            break;
874            nummifs = mifi;
875
876            splx(s);
882
883            return 0;
884    }
```

ip6_mroute.c

848–862 For a physical interface, the function `if_allmulti()` is called with the second argument being 0 to disable the multicast promiscuous mode on the interface. This operation is erroneous in a dual stack environment where IPv4 multicast routing is running in parallel with IPv6 multicast routing: the disabling operation takes place regardless of whether there is another application that requires the promiscuous mode (the IPv4 multicast routing daemon in this case), thereby interfering with the other application.

864–884 The memory occupied by the deleted multicast interface is zero-cleared. The global variable `nummifs` is adjusted to the next highest index value found in the multicast interface table.

2.8.7 `ip6_mrouter_done()` Function

The multicast routing daemon calls `ip6_mrouter_done()` to disable kernel multicast routing and perform necessary cleanups. This function is also called when the corresponding socket is closed, either explicitly or implicitly as a result of process termination, so that the things will be cleaned up even if the multicast routing daemon terminates without performing the cleanup procedure.

Listing 2-29

ip6_mroute.c

```
587    /*
588     * Disable multicast routing
589     */
590    int
591    ip6_mrouter_done()
```

```
592    {
593            mifi_t mifi;
594            int i;
595            struct ifnet *ifp;
596            struct in6_ifreq ifr;
597            struct mf6c *rt;
598            struct rtdetq *rte;
599            int s;
600
604            s = splnet();
606
607            /*
608             * For each phyint in use, disable promiscuous reception of all IPv6
609             * multicasts.
610             */
611    #ifdef INET
612    #ifdef MROUTING
613            /*
614             * If there is still IPv4 multicast routing daemon,
615             * we remain interfaces to receive all muliticasted packets.
616             * XXX: there may be an interface in which the IPv4 multicast
617             * daemon is not interested...
618             */
619            if (!ip_mrouter)
620    #endif
621    #endif
622            {
623                    for (mifi = 0; mifi < nummifs; mifi++) {
624                            if (mif6table[mifi].m6_ifp &&
625                                !(mif6table[mifi].m6_flags & MIFF_REGISTER)) {
626                                    ifr.ifr_addr.sin6_family = AF_INET6;
627                                    ifr.ifr_addr.sin6_addr = in6addr_any;
628                                    ifp = mif6table[mifi].m6_ifp;
629                                    (*ifp->if_ioctl)(ifp, SIOCDELMULTI,
630                                                (caddr_t)&ifr);
631                            }
632                    }
633            }
```
——ip6_mroute.c

604 Network level interrupts must be disabled by `splnet()` to prevent multicast forwarding during the cleanup procedure.

607–633 This part of the code tries to disable the multicast promiscuous mode for each physical interface used for IPv6 multicast routing. It does not actually work as intended, however, since on FreeBSD it is not possible to disable the promiscuous mode by directly issuing the `SIOCDELMULTI` command. The `if_allmulti()` function must be used as we saw in Listing 2-28.

It also tries to address the issue for a dual-stack multicast router described in Listing 2-28 by issuing the `ioctl` command only when it is not acting as an IPv4 multicast router. As commented, however, this should actually be done in a more fine-grained manner. Ideally, the code should check to see whether each particular interface is used in IPv4 multicast routing so that the promiscuous mode is disabled only if it is not.

Listing 2-30
——ip6_mroute.c
```
634    #ifdef notyet
635            bzero((caddr_t)qtable, sizeof(qtable));
636            bzero((caddr_t)tbftable, sizeof(tbftable));
637    #endif
```

```
638              bzero((caddr_t)mif6table, sizeof(mif6table));
639              nummifs = 0;
640
641              pim6 = 0; /* used to stub out/in pim specific code */
642
644              callout_stop(&expire_upcalls_ch);
650
651              /*
652               * Free all multicast forwarding cache entries.
653               */
654              for (i = 0; i < MF6CTBLSIZ; i++) {
655                      rt = mf6ctable[i];
656                      while (rt) {
657                              struct mf6c *frt;
658
659                              for (rte = rt->mf6c_stall; rte != NULL; ) {
660                                      struct rtdetq *n = rte->next;
661
662                                      m_free(rte->m);
663                                      free(rte, M_MRTABLE);
664                                      rte = n;
665                              }
666                              frt = rt;
667                              rt = rt->mf6c_next;
668                              free(frt, M_MRTABLE);
669                      }
670              }
671
672              bzero((caddr_t)mf6ctable, sizeof(mf6ctable));
```
── *ip6_mroute.c*

634–641 The multicast routing interface table is cleared and the PIM routing is disabled.

644 The function `callout_stop()` cancels the timer identified by variable `expire_upcalls_ch`.

654–672 The `for` loop goes through the entire hash buckets of the multicast forwarding cache entries (see Section 2.9). The inner `while` loop examines each hash entry in a single bucket, discards all pending packets at the entry and releases the entry itself. Finally, the forwarding cache table is zero-cleared.

Listing 2-31
── *ip6_mroute.c*
```
674              /*
675               * Reset register interface
676               */
677              if (inet6domain.dom_ifdetach) {
678                      ifp = &multicast_register_if;
679                      if (ifp->if_afdata[AF_INET6])
680                              inet6domain.dom_ifdetach(ifp, ifp->if_afdata[AF_INET6]);
681                      ifp->if_afdata[AF_INET6] = NULL;
682              }
683              reg_mif_num = -1;
684
685              ip6_mrouter = NULL;
686              ip6_mrouter_ver = 0;
687
688              splx(s);
694
695              return 0;
696      }
```
── *ip6_mroute.c*

674–683 The `dom_ifdetach` member of the `inet6domain{}` structure points to the `in6_domifdetach()` function, which handles IPv6 specific interface cleanups. Then the global variable `reg_mif_num` is reset to indicate there is no virtual Register interface in the system.

685 `ip6_mrouter` is reset to NULL to indicate there is no active IPv6 multicast routing daemon attached in the system that performs multicast routing functions.

2.8.8 `mrt6_ioctl()` Function

The `mrt6_ioctl()` function, shown below, is called from `in6_control()` to provide IPv6 multicast routing-related statistics to interested applications. The `get_mif6_cnt()` function will be described in the next subsection, while the description of `get_sg_cnt()` will be deferred until Section 2.9.4.

Listing 2-32

———————————————————————————————— ip6_mroute.c
```
434    int
435    mrt6_ioctl(cmd, data)
436           int cmd;
437           caddr_t data;
438    {
439
440           switch (cmd) {
441           case SIOCGETSGCNT_IN6:
442                  return (get_sg_cnt((struct sioc_sg_req6 *)data));
443           case SIOCGETMIFCNT_IN6:
444                  return (get_mif6_cnt((struct sioc_mif_req6 *)data));
445           default:
446                  return (EINVAL);
447           }
448    }
```
———————————————————————————————— ip6_mroute.c

2.8.9 `get_mif6_cnt()` Function

The `get_mif6_cnt()` function returns statistics for the given multicast interface.

Listing 2-33

———————————————————————————————— ip6_mroute.c
```
483    static int
484    get_mif6_cnt(req)
485           struct sioc_mif_req6 *req;
486    {
487           mifi_t mifi = req->mifi;
488
489           if (mifi >= nummifs)
490                  return EINVAL;
491
492           req->icount = mif6table[mifi].m6_pkt_in;
493           req->ocount = mif6table[mifi].m6_pkt_out;
494           req->ibytes = mif6table[mifi].m6_bytes_in;
495           req->obytes = mif6table[mifi].m6_bytes_out;
496
497           return 0;
498    }
```
———————————————————————————————— ip6_mroute.c

487–497 The multicast interface index specified by the application is validated. An error of `EINVAL` is returned if the index is out of range. The index refers to an entry in the multicast interface table, and the statistics from this entry are copied into the storage provided by the application.

2.9   IPv6 Multicast Forwarding Cache

Since the routing mechanism for multicast is different from that for unicast in that it is based on both the source address (for RPF) and the destination group address, a separate data structure is used to store IPv6 multicast forwarding information, called the *multicast forwarding cache*. Each cache entry contains a source and destination (group) address pair for a specific multicast flow, the incoming interface, and a set of outgoing interfaces for the destination multicast group. Each cache entry facilitates the necessary information for running the RPF algorithm.

Listing 2-34 gives the precise definition of the `mf6c{}` structure, the forwarding cache entry.

Listing 2-34

―――ip6_mroute.h
```
234    struct mf6c {
235            struct sockaddr_in6  mf6c_origin;     /* IPv6 origin of mcasts    */
236            struct sockaddr_in6  mf6c_mcastgrp;   /* multicast group associated*/
237            mifi_t               mf6c_parent;     /* incoming IF              */
238            struct if_set        mf6c_ifset;      /* set of outgoing IFs */
239
240            u_quad_t             mf6c_pkt_cnt;    /* pkt count for src-grp    */
241            u_quad_t             mf6c_byte_cnt;   /* byte count for src-grp   */
242            u_quad_t             mf6c_wrong_if;   /* wrong if for src-grp     */
243            int                  mf6c_expire;     /* time to clean entry up   */
244            struct timeval       mf6c_last_assert;/* last time I sent an assert*/
245            struct rtdetq        *mf6c_stall;     /* pkts waiting for route */
246            struct mf6c          *mf6c_next;      /* hash table linkage */
247    };
```
―――ip6_mroute.h

The `mf6c_origin` and `mf6c_mcastgrp` members specify the source and the group addresses of this entry. The `mf6c_parent` member holds the index of the incoming interface and `mf6c_ifset` holds the index set of outgoing interfaces for the destination multicast group.

The `mf6c_pkt_cnt`, `mf6c_byte_cnt`, and `mf6c_wrong_if` members are statistics variables.

The `mf6c_expire` member specifies the lifetime for this entry. When the entry is created, `mf6c_expire` is set to UPCALL_EXPIRE (6), which means 1.5 seconds. It decrements by one each time the timer function `expire_upcalls()` is called. The cache entry is deleted when `mf6c_expire` reaches 0.

The `mf6c_last_assert` member is not used for now.

`mf6c_stall` is the packet queue accumulating the outgoing packets while waiting for the cache entry to be completed with full routing information. The packet queue consists of a list of the `rtdetq{}` structure, which is shown in Listing 2-35. This structure contains the mbuf of the waiting packet and a pointer to the incoming interface of the packet.

Listing 2-35

ip6_mroute.h
```
255    struct rtdetq {              /* XXX: rtdetq is also defined in ip_mroute.h */
256        struct mbuf          *m;              /* A copy of the packet        */
257        struct ifnet         *ifp;            /* Interface pkt came in on    */
258    #ifdef UPCALL_TIMING
259        struct timeval       t;               /* Timestamp */
260    #endif /* UPCALL_TIMING */
261        struct rtdetq        *next;
262    };
```
ip6_mroute.h

Multicast forwarding cache entries are stored in a hash table whose key is the pair of the source (mfc6_origin) and the group (mf6c_mcastgrp) addresses. The hash table is an array of pointers to the mf6c{} structure containing 256 array entries.

The hash value is calculated by the MF6CHASH() macro, which is defined in Listing 2-36.

Listing 2-36

ip6_mroute.c
```
204    #define MF6CHASH(a, g) MF6CHASHMOD((a).s6_addr32[0] ^ (a).s6_addr32[1] ^ \
205                                       (a).s6_addr32[2] ^ (a).s6_addr32[3] ^ \
206                                       (g).s6_addr32[0] ^ (g).s6_addr32[1] ^ \
207                                       (g).s6_addr32[2] ^ (g).s6_addr32[3])
208
```
ip6_mroute.c

The MF6CHASHMOD() macro simply provides the reminder by dividing the hash value by 256, the table size.

Figure 2-22 shows the relationship between various data structures regarding forwarding cache entries.

The routing daemon shares a common control structure with the kernel to add or delete a cache entry. The control structure, mf6cctl{}, contains the basic routing information of a forwarding cache entry described by an mf6c{} structure. Listing 2-37 shows the exact definition of the mf6cctl{} structure.

Listing 2-37

ip6_mroute.h
```
115    struct mf6cctl {
116        struct sockaddr_in6 mf6cc_origin;         /* IPv6 origin of mcasts */
117        struct sockaddr_in6 mf6cc_mcastgrp; /* multicast group associated */
118        mifi_t          mf6cc_parent;   /* incoming ifindex */
119        struct if_set   mf6cc_ifset;    /* set of forwarding ifs */
120    };
```
ip6_mroute.h

2.9.1 add_m6fc() Function

The add_m6fc() function allows the caller to add a forwarding cache entry into the kernel via the MRT6_ADD_MFC socket option.

FIGURE 2-22

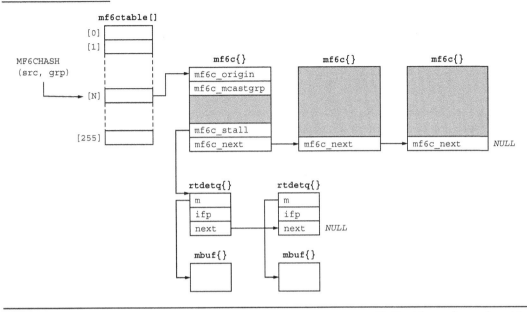

Multicast forwarding cache entries.

Find and Update Entry

Listing 2-38

————————————————————————————————————— ip6_mroute.c

```
886    /*
887     * Add an mfc entry
888     */
889    static int
890    add_m6fc(mfccp)
891           struct mf6cctl *mfccp;
892    {
893           struct mf6c *rt;
894           u_long hash;
895           struct rtdetq *rte;
896           u_short nstl;
897           int s;
898
899           MF6CFIND(mfccp->mf6cc_origin.sin6_addr,
900                    mfccp->mf6cc_mcastgrp.sin6_addr, rt);
901
902           /* If an entry already exists, just update the fields */
903           if (rt) {
911
915                   s = splnet();
917                   rt->mf6c_parent = mfccp->mf6cc_parent;
918                   rt->mf6c_ifset = mfccp->mf6cc_ifset;
919                   splx(s);
920                   return 0;
921           }
```

————————————————————————————————————— ip6_mroute.c

889–921 The `MF6CFIND()` macro searches the hash table for an active forwarding cache entry that matches the given source and destination address pair. If a cache entry is found, the source interface and the set of outgoing interfaces are retrieved from the control structure to update the cache entry. This function terminates here in this case.

> The code contains a bug. The `MF6CFIND()` macro must be guarded by `splnet()`.

The definition of the `MF6CFIND()` macro is given in Listing 2-39. This is a straight-forward implementation of a hash search, but it should be noted that an entry that has a stalled packet is bypassed. This means `MF6CFIND()` returns a complete cache entry only.

Listing 2-39
── ip6_mroute.c
```
214   #define MF6CFIND(o, g, rt) do { \
215           struct mf6c *_rt = mf6ctable[MF6CHASH(o,g)]; \
216           rt = NULL; \
217           mrt6stat.mrt6s_mfc_lookups++; \
218           while (_rt) { \
219                   if (IN6_ARE_ADDR_EQUAL(&_rt->mf6c_origin.sin6_addr, &(o)) && \
220                       IN6_ARE_ADDR_EQUAL(&_rt->mf6c_mcastgrp.sin6_addr, &(g)) && \
221                       (_rt->mf6c_stall == NULL)) { \
222                           rt = _rt; \
223                           break; \
224                   } \
225                   _rt = _rt->mf6c_next; \
226           } \
227           if (rt == NULL) { \
228                   mrt6stat.mrt6s_mfc_misses++; \
229           } \
230   } while (/*CONSTCOND*/ 0)
```
── ip6_mroute.c

Update Stalled Entry

Listing 2-40
── ip6_mroute.c
```
923           /*
924            * Find the entry for which the upcall was made and update
925            */
929           s = splnet();
931           hash = MF6CHASH(mfccp->mf6cc_origin.sin6_addr,
932                           mfccp->mf6cc_mcastgrp.sin6_addr);
933           for (rt = mf6ctable[hash], nstl = 0; rt; rt = rt->mf6c_next) {
934                   if (IN6_ARE_ADDR_EQUAL(&rt->mf6c_origin.sin6_addr,
935                                           &mfccp->mf6cc_origin.sin6_addr) &&
936                       IN6_ARE_ADDR_EQUAL(&rt->mf6c_mcastgrp.sin6_addr,
937                                           &mfccp->mf6cc_mcastgrp.sin6_addr) &&
938                       (rt->mf6c_stall != NULL)) {
939
940                           if (nstl++)
941                                   log(LOG_ERR,
942                                   "add_m6fc: %s o %s g %s p %x dbx %p\n",
943                                   "multiple kernel entries",
944                                   ip6_sprintf(&mfccp->mf6cc_origin.sin6_addr),
945                                   ip6_sprintf(&mfccp->
   mf6cc_mcastgrp.sin6_addr),
```

```
946                                     mfccp->mf6cc_parent, rt->mf6c_stall);

957                       rt->mf6c_origin     = mfccp->mf6cc_origin;
958                       rt->mf6c_mcastgrp   = mfccp->mf6cc_mcastgrp;
959                       rt->mf6c_parent     = mfccp->mf6cc_parent;
960                       rt->mf6c_ifset      = mfccp->mf6cc_ifset;
961                       /* initialize pkt counters per src-grp */
962                       rt->mf6c_pkt_cnt    = 0;
963                       rt->mf6c_byte_cnt   = 0;
964                       rt->mf6c_wrong_if   = 0;
965
966                       rt->mf6c_expire = 0;          /* Don't clean this guy up */
967                       n6expire[hash]--;
```
── ip6_mroute.c
— *Line 945 is broken here for layout reasons. However, it is a single line of code.*

929–946 Now the search is performed for an incomplete cache entry, which has stalled packets
queued at the `mf6c_stall` structure member. The `MF6CHASH()` macro calculates the
hash value for a given address pair. Variable `nstl` tracks the number of cache entries
having the same source and group address pair. There should be no more than one entry
in the hash bucket for the same address pair; if this condition is not met, it should indicate
a kernel bug, and an error message is logged.

957–967 The cache entry is updated with the information provided by the control structure.
The statistics counters are cleared. The cache entry is now considered complete. Setting
`mf6c_expire` to 0 marks the cache entry as a permanent entry that will never time out;
this entry will only be deleted by the multicast routing daemon. The corresponding entry
in the `n6expire` table is decremented to indicate that the number of entries needed to be
checked by the timer function, `expire_upcalls()`, decreases by one. The `n6expire`
table serves as an optimization for the timer function to show which hash table entries do
not require expiration checks (see Section 2.9.3).

Listing 2-41
── ip6_mroute.c
```
969                       /* free packets Qed at the end of this entry */
970                       for (rte = rt->mf6c_stall; rte != NULL; ) {
971                               struct rtdetq *n = rte->next;
972                               ip6_mdq(rte->m, rte->ifp, rt);
973                               m_freem(rte->m);
974   #ifdef UPCALL_TIMING
975                               collate(&(rte->t));
976   #endif /* UPCALL_TIMING */
977                               free(rte, M_MRTABLE);
978                               rte = n;
979                       }
980                       rt->mf6c_stall = NULL;
981               }
982       }
```
── ip6_mroute.c

969–981 Function `ip6_mdq()` is called to perform delayed forwarding for the stalled packets.
Unlike the case in `ip6_mforward()` (see Listing 2-50), the packet does not have to
be kept, and the remaining mbuf must be freed here. The `mf6c_stall` field is reset to
empty.

Insert New Entry

Listing 2-42

———ip6_mroute.c

```
984           /*
985            * It is possible that an entry is being inserted without an upcall
986            */
987           if (nstl == 0) {
997
998                   for (rt = mf6ctable[hash]; rt; rt = rt->mf6c_next) {
999
1000                          if (IN6_ARE_ADDR_EQUAL(&rt->mf6c_origin.sin6_addr,
1001                                          &mfccp->mf6cc_origin.sin6_addr)&&
1002                                  IN6_ARE_ADDR_EQUAL(&rt->mf6c_mcastgrp.sin6_addr,
1003                                          &mfccp->mf6cc_mcastgrp.sin6_addr)) {
1004
1005                                  rt->mf6c_origin      = mfccp->mf6cc_origin;
1006                                  rt->mf6c_mcastgrp    = mfccp->mf6cc_mcastgrp;
1007                                  rt->mf6c_parent      = mfccp->mf6cc_parent;
1008                                  rt->mf6c_ifset            = mfccp->mf6cc_ifset;
1009                                  /* initialize pkt counters per src-grp */
1010                                  rt->mf6c_pkt_cnt     = 0;
1011                                  rt->mf6c_byte_cnt    = 0;
1012                                  rt->mf6c_wrong_if    = 0;
1013
1014                                  if (rt->mf6c_expire)
1015                                          n6expire[hash]--;
1016                                  rt->mf6c_expire      = 0;
1017                          }
1018                  }
```

———ip6_mroute.c

987–1018 The value of `nstl` is zero if no entry in the multicast forwarding cache matches
the address pair. This also means the `for` loop is meaningless; all the cases where such
an entry exists were covered in the former part of this function. This code was probably
introduced directly from the IPv4 multicast routing implementation. At that time there was
a notion of the origin (source) mask, which complicated the match algorithm and caused
some minor exceptions.

Listing 2-43

———ip6_mroute.c

```
1019                  if (rt == NULL) {
1020                          /* no upcall, so make a new entry */
1021                          rt = (struct mf6c *)malloc(sizeof(*rt), M_MRTABLE,
1022                                          M_NOWAIT);
1023                          if (rt == NULL) {
1024                                  splx(s);
1025                                  return ENOBUFS;
1026                          }
1027
1028                          /* insert new entry at head of hash chain */
1029                          rt->mf6c_origin      = mfccp->mf6cc_origin;
1030                          rt->mf6c_mcastgrp    = mfccp->mf6cc_mcastgrp;
1031                          rt->mf6c_parent      = mfccp->mf6cc_parent;
1032                          rt->mf6c_ifset            = mfccp->mf6cc_ifset;
1033                          /* initialize pkt counters per src-grp */
1034                          rt->mf6c_pkt_cnt     = 0;
1035                          rt->mf6c_byte_cnt    = 0;
1036                          rt->mf6c_wrong_if    = 0;
1037                          rt->mf6c_expire      = 0;
1038                          rt->mf6c_stall = NULL;
```

```
1039
1040                                  /* link into table */
1041                                  rt->mf6c_next  = mf6ctable[hash];
1042                                  mf6ctable[hash] = rt;
1043                          }
1044              }
1045              splx(s);
1046              return 0;
1047      }
```
——— ip6_mroute.c

1019–1047 At this point, `rt` must be NULL (again, the `if` condition is redundant). A new cache entry is created and initialized with the values provided in the control structure. Then the new entry created area inserted into the corresponding hash table.

2.9.2 `del_m6fc()` Function

The `del_m6fc()` function allows the caller to remove a multicast forwarding cache entry from the kernel via the `MRT6_DEL_MFC` socket option.

Listing 2-44

——— ip6_mroute.c
```
1076      /*
1077       * Delete an mfc entry
1078       */
1079      static int
1080      del_m6fc(mfccp)
1081              struct mf6cctl *mfccp;
1082      {
1083              struct sockaddr_in6         origin;
1084              struct sockaddr_in6         mcastgrp;
1085              struct mf6c                 *rt;
1086              struct mf6c                 **nptr;
1087              u_long                 hash;
1088              int s;
1089
1090              origin = mfccp->mf6cc_origin;
1091              mcastgrp = mfccp->mf6cc_mcastgrp;
1092              hash = MF6CHASH(origin.sin6_addr, mcastgrp.sin6_addr);
1093
1104              s = splnet();
1106
1107              nptr = &mf6ctable[hash];
1108              while ((rt = *nptr) != NULL) {
1109                      if (IN6_ARE_ADDR_EQUAL(&origin.sin6_addr,
1110                                              &rt->mf6c_origin.sin6_addr) &&
1111                          IN6_ARE_ADDR_EQUAL(&mcastgrp.sin6_addr,
1112                                              &rt->mf6c_mcastgrp.sin6_addr) &&
1113                          rt->mf6c_stall == NULL)
1114                              break;
1115
1116                      nptr = &rt->mf6c_next;
1117              }
1118              if (rt == NULL) {
1119                      splx(s);
1120                      return EADDRNOTAVAIL;
1121              }
1122
1123              *nptr = rt->mf6c_next;
1124              free(rt, M_MRTABLE);
1125
1126              splx(s);
```

```
1127
1128            return 0;
1129      }
```

1076–1092 The macro MF6CHASH() searches the multicast forwarding cache for the given
source and destination address pair.

1104–1129 The chain in the hash table bucket is traversed and searched for a matching entry.
Incomplete cache entries, i.e., cache entries with packets queued waiting for forwarding,
are ignored because these entries will eventually expire and will be removed by the timer
function. Variable nptr holds the address of the mf6c_next field of the previous entry
in the list until a match is found, which simplifies the list update procedure. The error
EADDRNOTAVAIL is returned for a failed search. Otherwise, the cache entry is removed
from the hash table and its associated memory is freed.

2.9.3 expire_upcalls() Function

The expire_upcalls() function is responsible for removing expired cache entries from the
kernel multicast forwarding table. The entire cache table is examined for expired entries.

Listing 2-45

```
1434    static void
1435    expire_upcalls(unused)
1436           void *unused;
1437    {
1438           struct rtdetq *rte;
1439           struct mf6c *mfc, **nptr;
1440           int i;
1441           int s;
1442
1446           s = splnet();
1448           for (i = 0; i < MF6CTBLSIZ; i++) {
1449                   if (n6expire[i] == 0)
1450                           continue;
1451                   nptr = &mf6ctable[i];
1452                   while ((mfc = *nptr) != NULL) {
1453                           rte = mfc->mf6c_stall;
1454                           /*
1455                            * Skip real cache entries
1456                            * Make sure it wasn't marked to not expire
        (shouldn't happen)
1457                            * If it expires now
1458                            */
1459                           if (rte != NULL &&
1460                               mfc->mf6c_expire != 0 &&
1461                               --mfc->mf6c_expire == 0) {
1468                                   /*
1469                                    * drop all the packets
1470                                    * free the mbuf with the pkt, if, timing info
1471                                    */
1472                                   do {
1473                                           struct rtdetq *n = rte->next;
1474                                           m_freem(rte->m);
1475                                           free(rte, M_MRTABLE);
1476                                           rte = n;
1477                                   } while (rte != NULL);
1478                                   mrt6stat.mrt6s_cache_cleanups++;
1479                                   n6expire[i]--;
```

```
1480
1481                                        *nptr = mfc->mf6c_next;
1482                                        free(mfc, M_MRTABLE);
1483                            } else {
1484                                        nptr = &mfc->mf6c_next;
1485                            }
1486                    }
1487            }
1488            splx(s);
1490            callout_reset(&expire_upcalls_ch, EXPIRE_TIMEOUT,
1491                    expire_upcalls, NULL);
1498    }
```
                                                                        ————ip6_mroute.c

— *Line 1456 is broken here for layout reasons. However, it is a single line of code.*

1446 Network level interrupts must be disabled by splnet() during access to the hash table because the table can be accessed in the packet input processing code for multicast forwarding.

1448–1452 The for loop goes through all the hash buckets of mf6ctable, and the inner while loop examines every forwarding cache entry linked in the given bucket. Before entering the while loop, the number of cache entries needed to be checked are tested. If no entry needs the check, the entire check for the buckets can be skipped.

1453–1461 If the cache entry has a stalled packet, a timer is running for the entry, and the timer counter just decrements to 0, then the entry must be removed.

1472-1482 All stalled packets stored in the cache entry are freed. The number of entries to be checked decrements by 1, since this entry is now going to be removed.

1490–1491 callout_reset() resets the timer so that this function will be called again in 250 ms.

2.9.4   get_sg_cnt() Function

The get_sg_cnt() function returns multicast forwarding-related statistics for a given pair of the source and group addresses.

Listing 2-46
                                                                        ————ip6_mroute.c

```
453     static int
454     get_sg_cnt(req)
455             struct sioc_sg_req6 *req;
456     {
457             struct mf6c *rt;
458             int s;
459
463             s = splnet();
465             MF6CFIND(req->src.sin6_addr, req->grp.sin6_addr, rt);
466             splx(s);
467             if (rt != NULL) {
468                     req->pktcnt = rt->mf6c_pkt_cnt;
469                     req->bytecnt = rt->mf6c_byte_cnt;
470                     req->wrong_if = rt->mf6c_wrong_if;
471             } else
472                     return (ESRCH);
476
477             return 0;
478     }
```
                                                                        ————ip6_mroute.c

463–472 The `MF6CFIND()` macro looks for a forwarding cache entry for a pair of source and group addresses provided by the application. When an entry is found, the values of the statistics parameters are copied into the storage space given by the application. An error of `ESRCH` is returned if an entry is not found in the cache.

2.10 IPv6 Multicast Forwarding

As mentioned in Section 2.9, multicast packet forwarding is different from the mechanism deployed in unicast packet forwarding. One apparent difference in the implementation is that an arriving multicast packet is not discarded even if there is no matching multicast forwarding cache entry for this packet. Instead, the function `ip6_mforward()` creates a cache entry and queues the packet in it. `ip6_mforward()` then notifies the multicast routing daemon and queries the daemon to complete the cache entry; this procedure is called *upcall* in the BSD kernel implementation.

The routing daemon transfers the requested information into the kernel via the `MRT6_ADD_MFC` socket option. Additional multicast packets of the same source and destination group may be queued while waiting for the daemon to finish the task. All queued packets are dequeued and forwarded toward the leaf networks once the necessary information is set in the cache by the routing daemon.

If the routing daemon fails to update the cache information within a reasonable amount of time (e.g., due to a lost message), the `expire_upcalls()` function purges the stale entries.

Figure 2-23 summarizes the whole procedure performed in the KAME kernel, assuming the routing daemon is the **pim6sd** daemon.

FIGURE 2-23

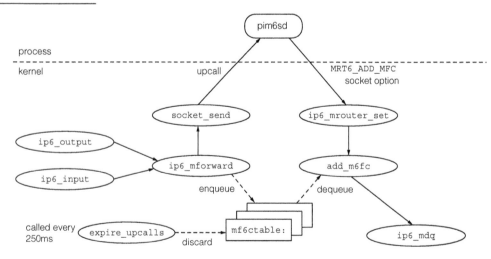

IPv6 multicast forwarding upcall.

Information communicated from the kernel code to the routing daemon in an upcall is carried inside the `mrt6msg{}` data structure. Listing 2-47 shows the exact definition of this structure.

Listing 2-47

```
──────────────────────────────────────────────────────────────── ip6_mroute.h
struct mrt6msg {
#define MRT6MSG_NOCACHE          1
#define MRT6MSG_WRONGMIF         2
#define MRT6MSG_WHOLEPKT         3        /* used for user level encap*/
        u_char      im6_mbz;             /* must be zero            */
        u_char      im6_msgtype;         /* what type of message    */
        u_int16_t   im6_mif;             /* mif rec'd on            */
        u_int32_t   im6_pad;             /* padding for 64bit arch  */
        struct in6_addr  im6_src, im6_dst;
};
──────────────────────────────────────────────────────────────── ip6_mroute.h
```

The value of the `im6_msgtype` member can be one of `MRT6MSG_NOCACHE`, `MRT6MSG_WRONGMIF`, or `MRT6MSG_WHOLEPKT`. `MRT6MSG_NOCACHE` indicates to the routing daemon that the kernel does not have a cache entry for the source and group address pair; `MRT6MSG_WRONGMIF` indicates the message arrived on the wrong interface according to the RPF algorithm; `MRT6MSG_WHOLEPKT` indicates the message is a complete packet including the IPv6 header which is used for sending a PIM Register message.

Structure member `im6_src` contains the packet source address and `im6_dst` contains the address of the destination group. Member `im6_mif` contains the multicast interface index on which the multicast packet arrived.

As will be seen in the code described in Section 2.10.1, this structure is generally overlaid onto the IPv6 header of the forwarded packet. The structure definition ensures that the source and destination (group) address fields of the packet can be transparently used in the `im6_src` and `im6_dst` members of this structure.

On the other hand, the **pim6dd** and **pim6sd** daemons receive this message on an ICMPv6 socket for the MLD operations, which means the message is represented as an ICMPv6 message for these daemons. These daemon implementations employ a risky way of demultiplexing the upcall messages and the MLD messages; they prevent the ICMPv6 socket from receiving a normal ICMPv6 packet with the type being 0 by setting a reception filter using the `ICMP6_FILTER` socket option, and regard received "ICMPv6" messages with type 0 as upcall messages. This works because the ICMPv6 filter does not affect the delivery path of upcall messages. Figure 2-24 illustrates the relationship between these structures.

2.10.1   `ip6_mforward()` **Function**

The `ip6_mforward()` function is the main routine for forwarding IPv6 multicast packets. Figure 2-25 provides an overview of the function call graphs for the forwarding process.

As shown in the figure, there are two possible paths to `ip6_mforward()`: from `ip6_input()` and from `ip6_output()`. The path from `ip6_input()` is the usual forwarding case. The `ip6_mforward()` searches the forwarding cache table and forwards the packet to the specified set of outgoing interfaces according to the matching cache entry. Note that this case includes forwarding an encapsulated packet in a PIM Register message, which

FIGURE 2-24

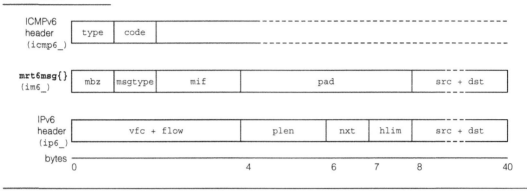

Overlaying for the `mrt6msg{}` *structure.*

FIGURE 2-25

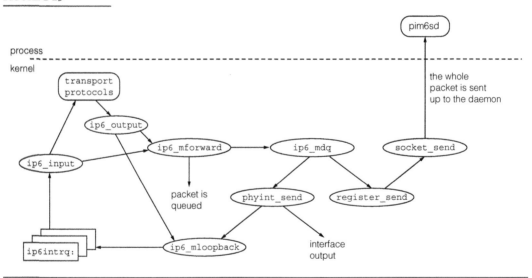

`ip6_mforward()` *procedure.*

will be detailed in Section 2.10.6. On the other hand, the `ip6_output()` function calls `ip6_mforward()` when a local application on a multicast router originates a multicast packet.

In either case, if local listeners exist on different interfaces from the incoming (in the case of `ip6_input()`) or originating (in the case of `ip6_output()`) interface, the `ip6_mloopback()` function will be called and the packet is looped back to the local listener application(s).

We now see the details of the ip6_mforward() function through the following listings.

Validation

Listing 2-48

```
1149    /*
1150     * IPv6 multicast forwarding function. This function assumes that the packet
1151     * pointed to by "ip6" has arrived on (or is about to be sent to) the interface
1152     * pointed to by "ifp", and the packet is to be relayed to other networks
1153     * that have members of the packet's destination IPv6 multicast group.
1154     *
1155     * The packet is returned unscathed to the caller, unless it is
1156     * erroneous, in which case a non-zero return value tells the caller to
1157     * discard it.
1158     */
1159
1160    int
1161    ip6_mforward(ip6, ifp, m)
1162            struct ip6_hdr *ip6;
1163            struct ifnet *ifp;
1164            struct mbuf *m;
1165    {
1166            struct mf6c *rt;
1167            struct mif6 *mifp;
1168            struct mbuf *mm;
1169            int s;
1170            mifi_t mifi;
```

1160–1164 Function parameter ip6 points to the received IPv6 header, ifp is the receiving interface, and m is the mbuf containing the multicast packet.

Listing 2-49

```
1182            /*
1183             * Don't forward a packet with Hop limit of zero or one,
1184             * or a packet destined to a local-only group.
1185             */
1186            if (ip6->ip6_hlim <= 1 || IN6_IS_ADDR_MC_INTFACELOCAL(&ip6->ip6_dst) ||
1187                IN6_IS_ADDR_MC_LINKLOCAL(&ip6->ip6_dst))
1188                    return 0;
1189            ip6->ip6_hlim--;
1190
1191            /*
1192             * Source address check: do not forward packets with unspecified
1193             * source. It was discussed in July 2000, on ipngwg mailing list.
1194             * This is rather more serious than unicast cases, because some
1195             * MLD packets can be sent with the unspecified source address
1196             * (although such packets must normally set 1 to the hop limit field).
1197             */
1198            if (IN6_IS_ADDR_UNSPECIFIED(&ip6->ip6_src)) {
1199                    ip6stat.ip6s_cantforward++;
1200                    if (ip6_log_time + ip6_log_interval < time_second) {
1201                            ip6_log_time = time_second;
1202                            log(LOG_DEBUG,
1203                                "cannot forward "
1204                                "from %s to %s nxt %d received on %s\n",
1205                                ip6_sprintf(&ip6->ip6_src),
1206                                ip6_sprintf(&ip6->ip6_dst),
```

```
1207                              ip6->ip6_nxt,
1208                              m->m_pkthdr.rcvif ?
1209                              if_name(m->m_pkthdr.rcvif) : "?");
1210                      }
1211              return 0;
1212          }
```
_____ ip6_mroute.c

1186–1189 A packet with the hop limit of 1 or less is invalid and is discarded according to [RFC2460]. If the destination address is an interface-local or link-local multicast address, the packet must not be forwarded to interfaces other than the incoming one, and is discarded here.

> The case of link-local scope is not as trivial as it might look. As explained in Chapter 2 of *IPv6 Core Protocols Implementation*, a router should not discard a *unicast* packet to be forwarded simply because the destination address has the link-local scope; rather, it must forward the packet toward the appropriate next hop as long as the packet stays in the same link. In case of *multicast*, however, the packets should be directly delivered to the local receivers, and the router should not forward the packet back to the incoming link due to the RPF check. The code behavior is thus justified.

1191–1212 [RFC3513] as well as its successor, [RFC4291], state that a packet with the unspecified source address must not be forwarded by a router; such packets are discarded here. The code comment is based on a previous specification, [RFC2373], where it was not clear for a router how to handle such packets.

Lookup Forwarding Cache

Listing 2-50
_____ ip6_mroute.c

```
1214          /*
1215           * Determine forwarding mifs from the forwarding cache table
1216           */
1220          s = splnet();
1222          MF6CFIND(ip6->ip6_src, ip6->ip6_dst, rt);

1223
1224          /* Entry exists, so forward if necessary */
1225          if (rt) {
1226                  splx(s);
1227                  return (ip6_mdq(m, ifp, rt));
```
_____ ip6_mroute.c

1220 Network level interrupts must be disabled by `splnet()` during any access to the forwarding cache table. In fact, this is one common case where the cache entry is called at the network interrupt level, but the protection by `splnet()` is still necessary since this function can also be called in an output path.

1222 The `MF6CFIND()` macro (Listing 2-39) searches for the matching cache entry in the table for the source and group address pair. The search result is stored in `rt`.

1224–1227 If a cache entry is found, it is passed to `ip6_mdq()`, where the packet will be copied and forwarded to the outgoing interfaces. `m` must not be freed here, since the caller may use it for local delivery (in `ip6_input()`) or the transmission on the originating interface (in `ip6_output()`).

The remaining code of the `ip6_mforward()` function is executed when a multicast forwarding cache entry is not found for the given source and group address pair.

Copy Packet

Listing 2-51
―― ip6_mroute.c

```
1228                } else {
1229                        /*
1230                         * If we don't have a route for packet's origin,
1231                         * Make a copy of the packet &
1232                         * send message to routing daemon
1233                         */
1234
1235                        struct mbuf *mb0;
1236                        struct rtdetq *rte;
1237                        u_long hash;
1244
1245                        mrt6stat.mrt6s_no_route++;
1252
1253                        /*
1254                         * Allocate mbufs early so that we don't do extra work if we
1255                         * are just going to fail anyway.
1256                         */
1257                        rte = (struct rtdetq *)malloc(sizeof(*rte), M_MRTABLE,
1258                                                        M_NOWAIT);
1259                        if (rte == NULL) {
1260                                splx(s);
1261                                return ENOBUFS;
1262                        }
1263                        mb0 = m_copy(m, 0, M_COPYALL);
1264                        /*
1265                         * Pullup packet header if needed before storing it,
1266                         * as other references may modify it in the meantime.
1267                         */
1268                        if (mb0 &&
1269                            (M_READONLY(mb0) || mb0->m_len < sizeof(struct ip6_hdr)))
1270                                mb0 = m_pullup(mb0, sizeof(struct ip6_hdr));
1271                        if (mb0 == NULL) {
1272                                free(rte, M_MRTABLE);
1273                                splx(s);
1274                                return ENOBUFS;
1275                        }
```
―― ip6_mroute.c

1257–1263 The `rtdetq{}` structure is allocated to queue the packet while the upcall is being made. A local copy of the incoming packet is made, which will be held in a new cache entry. The original packet stored in `m` will possibly be used by the caller.

1265–1275 Function `m_pullup()` is called to preprocess the packet such that the IPv6 header is in contiguous memory space and is writable. `m_pullup()` may require an additional mbuf, and the packet is discarded if the allocation fails.

Send Callup

Listing 2-52

————————————————————————————————————ip6_mroute.c
```
1277                          /* is there an upcall waiting for this packet? */
1278                          hash = MF6CHASH(ip6->ip6_src, ip6->ip6_dst);
1279                          for (rt = mf6ctable[hash]; rt; rt = rt->mf6c_next) {
1280                              if (IN6_ARE_ADDR_EQUAL(&ip6->ip6_src,
1281                                                     &rt->mf6c_origin.sin6_addr) &&
1282                                  IN6_ARE_ADDR_EQUAL(&ip6->ip6_dst,
1283                                                     &rt->mf6c_mcastgrp.sin6_addr) &&
1284                                  (rt->mf6c_stall != NULL))
1285                                  break;
1286                          }
```
————————————————————————————————————ip6_mroute.c

1277–1286 A search is performed in the multicast forwarding cache to determine if there is an outstanding upcall made previously for the same source and group address pair. No further processing is necessary if such an entry exists. This situation occurs when multiple packets of the same multicast stream arrive before the forwarding cache entry becomes complete.

Listing 2-53

————————————————————————————————————ip6_mroute.c
```
1288                          if (rt == NULL) {
1289                              struct mrt6msg *im;
1290      #ifdef MRT6_OINIT
1291                              struct omrt6msg *oim;
1292      #endif
1293
1294                              /* no upcall, so make a new entry */
1295                              rt = (struct mf6c *)malloc(sizeof(*rt), M_MRTABLE,
1296                                                        M_NOWAIT);
1297                              if (rt == NULL) {
1298                                  free(rte, M_MRTABLE);
1299                                  m_freem(mb0);
1300                                  splx(s);
1301                                  return ENOBUFS;
1302                              }
```
————————————————————————————————————ip6_mroute.c

1288–1302 If the pair is not found in the table, a new cache entry is allocated.

Listing 2-54

————————————————————————————————————ip6_mroute.c
```
1303                          /*
1304                           * Make a copy of the header to send to the user
1305                           * level process
1306                           */
1307                          mm = m_copy(mb0, 0, sizeof(struct ip6_hdr));
1308
1309                          if (mm == NULL) {
1310                              free(rte, M_MRTABLE);
1311                              m_freem(mb0);
1312                              free(rt, M_MRTABLE);
1313                              splx(s);
1314                              return ENOBUFS;
1315                          }
```

```
1316
1317                               /*
1318                                * Send message to routing daemon
1319                                */
1320                               sin6.sin6_addr = ip6->ip6_src;
1321
1322                               im = NULL;
1323   #ifdef MRT6_OINIT
1324                               oim = NULL;
1325   #endif
1326                               switch (ip6_mrouter_ver) {
1327   #ifdef MRT6_OINIT
1328                               case MRT6_OINIT:
1329                                       oim = mtod(mm, struct omrt6msg *);
1330                                       oim->im6_msgtype = MRT6MSG_NOCACHE;
1331                                       oim->im6_mbz = 0;
1332                                       break;
1333   #endif
1334                               case MRT6_INIT:
1335                                       im = mtod(mm, struct mrt6msg *);
1336                                       im->im6_msgtype = MRT6MSG_NOCACHE;
1337                                       im->im6_mbz = 0;
1338                                       break;
1339                               default:
1340                                       free(rte, M_MRTABLE);
1341                                       m_freem(mb0);
1342                                       free(rt, M_MRTABLE);
1343                                       splx(s);
1344                                       return EINVAL;
1345                               }
```
—— ip6_mroute.c

1307–1315 Function m_copy() copies the IPv6 header of the original packet into a new mbuf,
which will be sent to the routing daemon shortly.

1318–1345 A file-scope global variable sin6 is an AF_INET6 socket address structure.
It is set to the source address of the multicast packet, and passed to the routing
daemon as the source address of the upcall. But the KAME implementation of the routing daemons, namely **pim6sd** and **pim6dd**, currently do not use this value. Variable
im is an mrt6msg{} structure (Listing 2-47) carrying information needed by the routing
daemon for completing the forwarding cache entry. The im6_msgtype member is set
to MRT6MSG_NOCACHE, indicating the kernel does not find a multicast forwarding cache
entry for the pair of the source and group addresses.

The different cases for ip6_mrouter_ver are considered to provide backward
compatibility to old applications. This book only considers the MRT6_INIT case, which
corresponds to the latest applications.

Listing 2-55
—— ip6_mroute.c

```
1353                               for (mifp = mif6table, mifi = 0;
1354                                    mifi < nummifs && mifp->m6_ifp != ifp;
1355                                    mifp++, mifi++)
1356                                       ;
1357
1358                               switch (ip6_mrouter_ver) {
```

```
1359    #ifdef MRT6_OINIT
1360                            case MRT6_OINIT:
1361                                    oim->im6_mif = mifi;
1362                                    break;
1363    #endif
1364                            case MRT6_INIT:
1365                                    im->im6_mif = mifi;
1366                                    break;
1367                            }
1368
1369                            if (socket_send(ip6_mrouter, mm, &sin6) < 0) {
1370                                    log(LOG_WARNING, "ip6_mforward: ip6_mrouter "
1371                                        "socket queue full\n");
1372                                    mrt6stat.mrt6s_upq_sockfull++;
1373                                    free(rte, M_MRTABLE);
1374                                    m_freem(mb0);
1375                                    free(rt, M_MRTABLE);
1376                                    splx(s);
1377                                    return ENOBUFS;
1378                            }
1379
1380                            mrt6stat.mrt6s_upcalls++;
```
——— ip6_mroute.c

1353–1367 The index value of the incoming interface in mif6table is retrieved, and the im6_mif member is set to that index value.

1369–1380 Function socket_send() (Section 2.10.5) passes the upcall message to the routing daemon, and updates the corresponding statistics variable.

Initialize Cache Entry

Listing 2-56
——— ip6_mroute.c

```
1382                            /* insert new entry at head of hash chain */
1383                            bzero(rt, sizeof(*rt));
1384                            rt->mf6c_origin.sin6_family = AF_INET6;
1385                            rt->mf6c_origin.sin6_len = sizeof(struct sockaddr_in6);
1386                            rt->mf6c_origin.sin6_addr = ip6->ip6_src;
1387                            rt->mf6c_mcastgrp.sin6_family = AF_INET6;
1388                            rt->mf6c_mcastgrp.sin6_len = sizeof(struct sockaddr_in6);
1389                            rt->mf6c_mcastgrp.sin6_addr = ip6->ip6_dst;
1390                            rt->mf6c_expire = UPCALL_EXPIRE;
1391                            n6expire[hash]++;
1392                            rt->mf6c_parent = MF6C_INCOMPLETE_PARENT;
1393
1394                            /* link into table */
1395                            rt->mf6c_next  = mf6ctable[hash];
1396                            mf6ctable[hash] = rt;
1397                            /* Add this entry to the end of the queue */
1398                            rt->mf6c_stall = rte;
```
——— ip6_mroute.c

1382–1398 The new cache entry is initialized with the packet source and destination group address. The mf6c_parent member is set to MF6C_INCOMPLETE_PARENT, essentially preventing the cache entry from being used in making forwarding decisions(*). The mf6c_expire field is set to the default allowable value for the completion of the upcall before deleting the incomplete cache entry. The newly initialized entry is inserted

into the forwarding hash table. The received packet is queued in the `mf6c_stall`
member.

(*) This trick is probably unnecessary, since the stalled packet should take the same role.

Enqueue the Packet

Listing 2-57

```
                                                                        ip6_mroute.c
1399                    } else {
1400                            /* determine if q has overflowed */
1401                            struct rtdetq **p;
1402                            int npkts = 0;
1403
1404                            for (p = &rt->mf6c_stall; *p != NULL; p = &(*p)->next)
1405                                    if (++npkts > MAX_UPQ6) {
1406                                            mrt6stat.mrt6s_upq_ovflw++;
1407                                            free(rte, M_MRTABLE);
1408                                            m_freem(mb0);
1409                                            splx(s);
1410                                            return 0;
1411                                    }
1412
1413                            /* Add this entry to the end of the queue */
1414                            *p = rte;
1415                    }
1416
1417                    rte->next = NULL;
1418                    rte->m = mb0;
1419                    rte->ifp = ifp;
1420  #ifdef UPCALL_TIMING
1421                    rte->t = tp;
1422  #endif /* UPCALL_TIMING */
1423
1424                    splx(s);
1425
1426                    return 0;
1427            }
1428    }
                                                                        ip6_mroute.c
```

1399–1415 If a multicast forwarding cache entry exists but does not have complete information
to forward the packet, the packet being forwarded is inserted at the end of the stall queue
of the entry. If the queue is full, i.e., there are MAX_UPQ6 (4) packets in the queue, the
newly created queue entry and the associated packet are discarded.

1417–1427 The rest of the `rtdetq{}` structure members are initialized, and this function
successfully returns.

2.10.2   `ip6_mdq()` Function

The `ip6_mdq()` function forwards a given multicast packet to each of the outgoing interfaces
given in the multicast forwarding cache entry. This function also performs the RPF check.

Perform RPF

Listing 2-58

———ip6_mroute.c

```
1500    /*
1501     * Packet forwarding routine once entry in the cache is made
1502     */
1503    static int
1504    ip6_mdq(m, ifp, rt)
1505            struct mbuf *m;
1506            struct ifnet *ifp;
1507            struct mf6c *rt;
1508    {
1509            struct ip6_hdr *ip6 = mtod(m, struct ip6_hdr *);
1510            mifi_t mifi, iif;
1511            struct mif6 *mifp;
1512            int plen = m->m_pkthdr.len;
1513            struct sockaddr_in6 src_sa, dst_sa, s0, d0;
1514
1515    /*
1516     * Macro to send packet on mif.  Since RSVP packets don't get counted on
1517     * input, they shouldn't get counted on output, so statistics keeping is
1518     * separate.
1519     */
1520
1521    #define MC6_SEND(ip6, mifp, m, s, d) do {                          \
1522                    if ((mifp)->m6_flags & MIFF_REGISTER)             \
1523                            register_send((ip6), (mifp), (m), (s), (d));\
1524                    else                                             \
1525                            phyint_send((ip6), (mifp), (m), (s), (d)); \
1526    } while (/*CONSTCOND*/ 0)
```

———ip6_mroute.c

1521–1526 The MC6_SEND() macro determines the correct output function to forward a multi-cast packet. The output function is either register_send() or phyint_send(). If the packet is forwarded to a PIM RP encapsulated in a Register message, register_send() directs the complete packet to the routing daemon for encapsulation. The encapsulated packet is sent as a unicast packet by the routing daemon. The phyint_send() output function transmits the packet directly to the network.

Listing 2-59

———ip6_mroute.c

```
1528            /*
1529             * Don't forward if it didn't arrive from the parent mif
1530             * for its origin.
1531             */
1532            mifi = rt->mf6c_parent;
1533            if ((mifi >= nummifs) || (mif6table[mifi].m6_ifp != ifp)) {
1534                    /* came in the wrong interface */
1542                    mrt6stat.mrt6s_wrong_if++;
1543                    rt->mf6c_wrong_if++;
```

———ip6_mroute.c

1528–1543 Variable mifi is the multicast interface identifier of the "parent" interface of this forwarding cache entry, that is, the correct incoming interface according to RPF. Variable ifp points to the incoming interface of the packet. According to the principle of RPF, these two interfaces must be the same. Otherwise, the succeeding code performs error handling with incrementing counters.

Listing 2-60

_____ ip6_mroute.c
```
1544                       /*
1545                        * If we are doing PIM processing, and we are forwarding
1546                        * packets on this interface, send a message to the
1547                        * routing daemon.
1548                        */
1549                       /* have to make sure this is a valid mif */
1550                       if (mifi < nummifs && mif6table[mifi].m6_ifp)
1551                               if (pim6 && (m->m_flags & M_LOOP) == 0) {
1552                                       /*
1553                                        * Check the M_LOOP flag to avoid an
1554                                        * unnecessary PIM assert.
1555                                        * XXX: M_LOOP is an ad-hoc hack...
1556                                        */
1557                                       static struct sockaddr_in6 sin6 =
1558                                       { sizeof(sin6), AF_INET6 };
1559
1560                                       struct mbuf *mm;
1561                                       struct mrt6msg *im;
1562     #ifdef MRT6_OINIT
1563                                       struct omrt6msg *oim;
1564     #endif
1565
1566                                       mm = m_copy(m, 0, sizeof(struct ip6_hdr));
1567                                       if (mm &&
1568                                           (M_READONLY(mm) ||
1569                                           mm->m_len < sizeof(struct ip6_hdr)))
1570                                               mm = m_pullup(mm,sizeof
     (struct ip6_hdr));
1571                                       if (mm == NULL)
1572                                               return ENOBUFS;
1573
1574     #ifdef MRT6_OINIT
1575                                       oim = NULL;
1576     #endif
1577                                       im = NULL;
1578                                       switch (ip6_mrouter_ver) {
1579     #ifdef MRT6_OINIT
1580                                       case MRT6_OINIT:
1581                                               oim = mtod(mm, struct omrt6msg *);
1582                                               oim->im6_msgtype = MRT6MSG_WRONGMIF;
1583                                               oim->im6_mbz = 0;
1584                                               break;
1585     #endif
1586                                       case MRT6_INIT:
1587                                               im = mtod(mm, struct mrt6msg *);
1588                                               im->im6_msgtype = MRT6MSG_WRONGMIF;
1589                                               im->im6_mbz = 0;
1590                                               break;
1591                                       default:
1592                                               m_freem(mm);
1593                                               return EINVAL;
1594                                       }
```
_____ ip6_mroute.c
_ Line 1570 is broken here for layout reasons. However, it is a single line of code.

1544–1551 If this router uses PIM as the multicast routing protocol, the fact that the packet on
the wrong interface should be reported to the routing daemon to initiate the PIM assert
mechanism (see Figures 2-12 and 2-13). This should only be done if the mbuf for the
packet does not have the M_LOOP flag, that is, if the packet is not looped back.

To understand why this check is necessary, consider the following scenario: a local
listener for a multicast group on the multicast router joins the group on a multicast interface
whose index is 1. A packet to the group address arrives on multicast interface 2, which

FIGURE 2-26

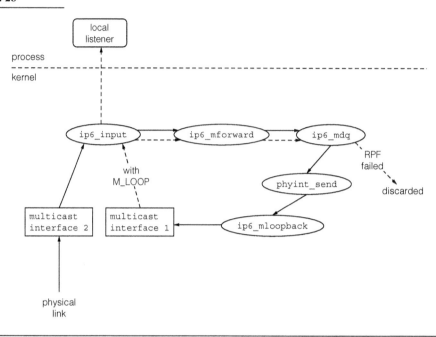

Preventing unnecessary PIM assert in loopback delivery.

we assume is the correct incoming interface for the packet's source address. As shown in Figure 2-25, the packet is looped back via the `ip6_mloopback()` function, and is passed to `ip6_mdq()` again, but with the `M_LOOP` flag being set. Since the "incoming interface" (index 1) is different from the correct one (index 2), the PIM assert mechanism would be triggered without the check at line 1551. Figure 2-26 illustrates this scenario based on the correct code.

1557–1572 `m_copy()` makes a copy of the IPv6 header of the received packet. Function `m_pullup()` ensures that the entire IPv6 header is in contiguous writable memory.

1574–1594 Pointer `im` treats the memory location of the IPv6 header as if it were the `mrt6msg{}` structure. The message type is set to `MRT6MSG_WRONGMIF`, indicating that the cause of the upcall notification is due to receiving a packet on the incorrect interface according to the RPF algorithm.

Listing 2-61

```
                                                                    ip6_mroute.c
1596                          for (mifp = mif6table, iif = 0;
1597                               iif < nummifs && mifp &&
1598                                       mifp->m6_ifp != ifp;
1599                               mifp++, iif++)
1600                                  ;
1601
1602                          switch (ip6_mrouter_ver) {
1603    #ifdef MRT6_OINIT
```

```
1604                                     case MRT6_OINIT:
1605                                             oim->im6_mif = iif;
1606                                             sin6.sin6_addr = oim->im6_src;
1607                                             break;
1608    #endif
1609                                     case MRT6_INIT:
1610                                             im->im6_mif = iif;
1611                                             sin6.sin6_addr = im->im6_src;
1612                                             break;
1613                                     }
1614
1615                                     mrt6stat.mrt6s_upcalls++;
1616
1617                                     if (socket_send(ip6_mrouter, mm, &sin6) < 0) {
1622                                             ++mrt6stat.mrt6s_upq_sockfull;
1623                                             return ENOBUFS;
1624                                     }       /* if socket Q full */
1625                             }               /* if PIM */
1626                     return 0;
1627             }                       /* if wrong iif */
```
———————————————————————————————— ip6_mroute.c

1596–1613 The multicast interface index of the incoming interface is identified and stored in the control structure.

1615–1627 The `socket_send()` function passes the control information to the routing daemon. The multicast packet is not forwarded regardless of whether the router is running the PIM protocol or not. Note that this function returns 0 in this case. This is necessary so that the ultimate caller of this function such as `ip6_input()` can proceed for local delivery in the scenario shown in Figure 2-26.

Transmit Packet

Listing 2-62
———————————————————————————————— ip6_mroute.c
```
1629            /* If I sourced this packet, it counts as output, else it was input. */
1630            if (m->m_pkthdr.rcvif == NULL) {
1631                    /* XXX: is rcvif really NULL when output?? */
1632                    mif6table[mifi].m6_pkt_out++;
1633                    mif6table[mifi].m6_bytes_out += plen;
1634            } else {
1635                    mif6table[mifi].m6_pkt_in++;
1636                    mif6table[mifi].m6_bytes_in += plen;
1637            }
1638            rt->mf6c_pkt_cnt++;
1639            rt->mf6c_byte_cnt += plen;
```
———————————————————————————————— ip6_mroute.c

1629–1639 Per packet statistics counters are incremented, based on whether the packet is originated (in case `rcvif` is NULL) or is being forwarded.

Technically, it is not guaranteed that `rcvif` is NULL in the output path, depending on how to make the mbuf that stores the outgoing packet. In this particular version of the implementation, however, this assumption holds, since `ip6_output()`, the only caller in the output path, resets `rcvif` to NULL before calling `ip6_mforward()` (see Chapter 3 of *IPv6 Core Protocols Implementation*).

Listing 2-63

── ip6_mroute.c

```
1641          /*
1642           * For each mif, forward a copy of the packet if there are group
1643           * members downstream on the interface.
1644           */
1645          if (ip6_getpktaddrs(m, &s0, &d0))
1646                  return (-1);        /* XXX: impossible */
1647          /* make a local copies to reuse */
1648          src_sa = s0;
1649          dst_sa = d0;
1650          for (mifp = mif6table, mifi = 0; mifi < nummifs; mifp++, mifi++) {
1651                  if (IF_ISSET(mifi, &rt->mf6c_ifset)) {
1652                          u_int32_t dscopeout, sscopeout;
1653
1654                          /*
1655                           * check if the outgoing packet is going to break
1656                           * a scope boundary.
1657                           * XXX For packets through PIM register tunnel
1658                           * interface, we believe a routing daemon.
1659                           */
1660                          if (!(mif6table[rt->mf6c_parent].m6_flags &
1661                              MIFF_REGISTER) &&
1662                              !(mif6table[mifi].m6_flags & MIFF_REGISTER)) {
1663                                  if (in6_addr2zoneid(mif6table[mifi].m6_ifp,
1664                                                      &ip6->ip6_dst,
1665                                                      &dscopeout) ||
1666                                      in6_addr2zoneid(mif6table[mifi].m6_ifp,
1667                                                      &ip6->ip6_src,
1668                                                      &sscopeout) ||
1669                                      dst_sa.sin6_scope_id != dscopeout ||
1670                                      src_sa.sin6_scope_id != sscopeout) {
1671                                          ip6stat.ip6s_badscope++;
1672                                          continue;
1673                                  }
1674                          }
1675
1676                          mifp->m6_pkt_out++;
1677                          mifp->m6_bytes_out += plen;
1678                          MC6_SEND(ip6, mifp, m, &src_sa, &dst_sa);
1679                  }
1680          }
1681          /* recover the packet addresses */
1682          if (!ip6_setpktaddrs(m, &src_sa, &dst_sa))
1683                  return (-1);
1684          return 0;
1685  }
```

── ip6_mroute.c

1644–1649 Function `ip6_getpktaddrs()` copies the source and destination group
addresses of the packet in the form of the socket address structure into `s0` and `d0`,
respectively, for later use.

1650–1651 The entire multicast interfaces are traversed. The `IF_ISSET()` macro checks to
see if a multicast interface belongs to the list of outgoing interfaces for this pair of source
and group addresses specified by the cache entry.

1660–1673 The forwarded packet must not break the scope zone with regard to the source
or destination address. This code block performs the boundary check if neither the
incoming nor the outgoing interface is the Register interface. `dscopeout` is the scope
zone index with regard to the outgoing interface and the scope types of the destination address. If this is not equal to the original zone index of the destination address,
the packet is going to break the zone boundary of the destination address and must be

FIGURE 2-27

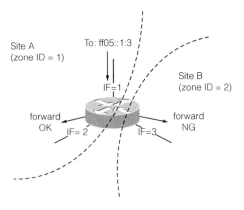

Scope zone check in multicast forwarding.

discarded. A similar check must be made for the source address. As commented, this check must also be performed for an encapsulated packet in a PIM Register message. But the current implementation simply trusts that the routing daemon handles this case appropriately.

Figure 2-27 shows an example of the scope zone check for the destination address. The forwarding router connects to two sites, A and B, whose site zone indices in the router are 1 and 2, respectively. When the router tries to forward a packet to a site-local multicast address ff05::1:3 received on interface 1, which belongs to site A, the router can forward it to interface 2, but not to interface 3. In the latter case, since dscopeout is 2 and the sin6_scope_id member of dst_sa is 1, the check at line 1669 rejects this forwarding.

1676–1679 The MC6_SEND() macro transmits the packet using the appropriate function as described in Listing 2-58.

1681–1683 The original packet may be used for local delivery, in which case the source and destination addresses should be stored in the form of the socket address structure in the mbuf. Function ip6_setpktaddrs() restores the original source and destination addresses back into the packet, just in case these are lost in MC6_SEND().

2.10.3 phyint_send() Function

The phyint_send() function makes a copy of the original packet, and sends the copy out to the given multicast interface.

Listing 2-64

—— ip6_mroute.c

```
1687    static void
1688    phyint_send(ip6, mifp, m, src, dst)
1689        struct ip6_hdr *ip6;
1690        struct mif6 *mifp;
```

```
1691        struct mbuf *m;
1692        struct sockaddr_in6 *src, *dst;
1693    {
1694            struct mbuf *mb_copy;
1695            struct ifnet *ifp = mifp->m6_ifp;
1696            int error = 0;
1700            int s = splnet();          /* needs to protect static "ro" below. */
1702    #ifdef NEW_STRUCT_ROUTE
1703            static struct route ro;
1704    #else
1705            static struct route_in6 ro;
1706    #endif
1707            struct          in6_multi *in6m;
1708            u_long linkmtu;
1709
1710            /*
1711             * Make a new reference to the packet; make sure that
1712             * the IPv6 header is actually copied, not just referenced,
1713             * so that ip6_output() only scribbles on the copy.
1714             */
1715            mb_copy = m_copy(m, 0, M_COPYALL);
1716            if (mb_copy &&
1717                (M_READONLY(mb_copy) || mb_copy->m_len < sizeof(struct ip6_hdr)))
1718                    mb_copy = m_pullup(mb_copy, sizeof(struct ip6_hdr));
1719            if (mb_copy == NULL) {
1720                    splx(s);
1721                    return;
1722            }
1723            /* set MCAST flag to the outgoing packet */
1724            mb_copy->m_flags |= M_MCAST;
```
── ip6_mroute.c

1710–1724 m_copy() makes a full copy of the original packet. The copy is necessary because the packet may be sent through the ip6_output() function, where some header fields will be modified; thus, the packet cannot be shared among the various processing functions.

Listing 2-65

── ip6_mroute.c
```
1726            /*
1727             * If we sourced the packet, call ip6_output since we may divide
1728             * the packet into fragments when the packet is too big for the
1729             * outgoing interface.
1730             * Otherwise, we can simply send the packet to the interface
1731             * sending queue.
1732             */
1733            if (m->m_pkthdr.rcvif == NULL) {
1734                    struct ip6_moptions im6o;
1735
1736                    im6o.im6o_multicast_ifp = ifp;
1737                    /* XXX: ip6_output will override ip6->ip6_hlim */
1738                    im6o.im6o_multicast_hlim = ip6->ip6_hlim;
1739                    im6o.im6o_multicast_loop = 1;
1740                    error = ip6_output(mb_copy, NULL, &ro,
1741                                       IPV6_FORWARDING, &im6o, NULL
1743                                       , NULL
1745                                       );
1746
1752                    splx(s);
1753                    return;
1754            }
```
── ip6_mroute.c

1726–1754 If this node, which is acting as a multicast router, is originating the multicast packet, the packet is sent to `ip6_output()`, because the packet may need to be fragmented if it is too large for the outgoing link. Note that the logic is different from IPv4 here; since IPv6 routers do not fragment forwarded packets, `ip6_output()` does not have to be called for the forwarding case. In other words, this is an exceptional case for IPv6 multicast forwarding. The `IPV6_FORWARDING` flag is specified as an argument to `ip6_output()` so that it will not call `ip6_mforward()` again. See Chapter 3 of *IPv6 Core Protocols Implementation* about how this flag works in `ip6_output()`.

Listing 2-66

—————————————————————————————— ip6_mroute.c

```
1756            /*
1757             * If we belong to the destination multicast group
1758             * on the outgoing interface, loop back a copy.
1759             */
1760            /*
1761             * Does not have to check source info, as it's alreay covered by
1762             * ip6_input
1763             */
1764            IN6_LOOKUP_MULTI(dst, ifp, in6m);
1765            if (in6m != NULL) {
1766                    if (ip6_setpktaddrs(m, src, dst))
1767                            ip6_mloopback(ifp, m, dst);
1768            }
```

—————————————————————————————— ip6_mroute.c

1756–1768 If the local node is a member of the destination multicast group on the outgoing interface, function `ip6_mloopback()` inserts a copy of the forwarded packet in the input queue of the outgoing interface. Note that since the outgoing interface is never equal to the original incoming interface, the packet is not going to be duplicated. The function `ip6_setpktaddrs()` attaches the socket address form of the source and destination addresses to the packet, since the addresses in the IPv6 header may not contain enough information to disambiguate address scope zones. `ip6_mloopback()` will make its own copy for the local delivery, and m is still valid after this process.

Listing 2-67

—————————————————————————————— ip6_mroute.c

```
1769            /*
1770             * Put the packet into the sending queue of the outgoing interface
1771             * if it would fit in the MTU of the interface.
1772             */
1773            linkmtu = IN6_LINKMTU(ifp);
1774            if (mb_copy->m_pkthdr.len <= linkmtu || linkmtu < IPV6_MMTU) {
1775                    /*
1776                     * We just call if_output instead of nd6_output here, since
1777                     * we need no ND for a multicast forwarded packet...right?
1778                     */
1779                    error = (*ifp->if_output)(ifp, mb_copy,
1780                        (struct sockaddr *)dst, NULL);
```

—————————————————————————————— ip6_mroute.c

1769–1780 The packet is passed to the interface output function if the packet fits in the link
MTU of the outgoing interface. The link-layer driver is responsible for link-level packet
fragmentation and reassembly if the MTU is smaller than the minimum value defined in
[RFC2460] (1280 bytes). In reality, however, no FreeBSD drivers support this functionality,
and the packet will most likely be dropped in this case.

   As noted above, the forwarded packet does not have to be passed to `ip6_output()`,
unlike IPv4 multicast forwarding. The code could call the `nd6_output()` function as in
`ip6_forward()` (see Chapter 3 of *IPv6 Core Protocols Implementation*). As commented,
however, the call to `nd6_output()` causes effectively the same result as the direct call to
the interface output function, since a multicast packet does not require link-layer address
resolution, which is the main purpose of `nd6_output()`.

Listing 2-68
```
                                                                    ip6_mroute.c
1786            } else {
1787    #ifdef MULTICAST_PMTUD
1788                    icmp6_error(mb_copy, ICMP6_PACKET_TOO_BIG, 0, linkmtu);
1789    #else
1800                    m_freem(mb_copy); /* simply discard the packet */
1801    #endif
1802            }
1803
1804            splx(s);
1805    }
                                                                    ip6_mroute.c
```

1786–1805 The specification [RFC4443] requires that an ICMPv6 Packet Too Big error
message be returned when the packet is too large for the outgoing link, regardless of whether the packet is unicasted or multicasted. But experiences gained from
deploying the IPv4 multicast network have indicated that sending the error message
can be harmful: it was found that careless multicast applications sent large packets,
causing implosion of the ICMP error messages. The situation was sometimes even
worse when the error messages were filtered, in which case the application simply
kept sending large packets and the ICMP implosion did not stop while the application was running. The KAME implementation thus follows the specification only
when the `MULTICAST_PMTUD` compilation option is enabled, which is disabled by
default. Otherwise, the packet is simply discarded without generating an ICMPv6 error
message.

2.10.4 `register_send()` Function

The `register_send()` function is a PIM-specific routine. It is called from `ip6_mdq()`
via the `MC6_SEND()` macro when the outgoing interface is the PIM Register interface. The
function `socket_send()` transfers this packet to the routing daemon, where the packet will
be encapsulated in a PIM Register message and sent to the RP as a unicast packet. Figure 2-28
shows a typical processing flow of forwarding a packet encapsulated in a Register message to
the RP.

Listing 2-69

```
                                                              ip6_mroute.c
1807   static int
1808   register_send(ip6, mif, m, src, dst)
1809          struct ip6_hdr *ip6;
1810          struct mif6 *mif;
1811          struct mbuf *m;
1812          struct sockaddr_in6 *src;
1813          struct sockaddr_in6 *dst; /* XXX currently unused */
1814   {
1815          struct mbuf *mm;
1816          int i, len = m->m_pkthdr.len;
1817          struct mrt6msg *im6;
1818
1824          ++pim6stat.pim6s_snd_registers;
1825
1826          /* Make a copy of the packet to send to the user level process */
1827          MGETHDR(mm, M_DONTWAIT, MT_HEADER);
1828          if (mm == NULL)
1829                  return ENOBUFS;
1830          mm->m_pkthdr.rcvif = NULL;
1831          mm->m_data += max_linkhdr;
1832          mm->m_len = sizeof(struct ip6_hdr);
                                                              ip6_mroute.c
```

1826–1832 A new packet header is created for the routing daemon with a reserved space for
the link-layer header. The reserved space is actually meaningless, though. Since the packet
will be sent to the routing daemon, the reserved space will not be used. Also, it is not
really safe to set the size of the packet header to the size of the `ip6_hdr{}` structure;
the correct value is the size of the `mrt6msg{}` structure. Although the sizes of the two
structures are the same by design as shown in Figure 2-24, relying on such an implicit
assumption is not good practice.

FIGURE 2-28

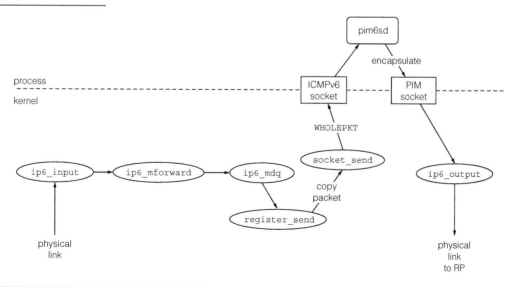

Processing flow of forwarding a packet with Register encapsulation.

Listing 2-70

```
1834              if ((mm->m_next = m_copy(m, 0, M_COPYALL)) == NULL) {
1835                      m_freem(mm);
1836                      return ENOBUFS;
1837              }
1838              i = MHLEN - M_LEADINGSPACE(mm);
1839              if (i > len)
1840                      i = len;
1841              mm = m_pullup(mm, i);
1842              if (mm == NULL)
1843                      return ENOBUFS;
1844      /* TODO: check it! */
1845              mm->m_pkthdr.len = len + sizeof(struct ip6_hdr);
```

1834–1845 m_copy() makes a complete copy of the original multicast packet. Unlike the other upcall cases, a full copy is necessary because the packet will then be encapsulated and forwarded by the routing daemon.

Listing 2-71

```
1847              /*
1848               * Send message to routing daemon
1849               */
1850              im6 = mtod(mm, struct mrt6msg *);
1851              im6->im6_msgtype       = MRT6MSG_WHOLEPKT;
1852              im6->im6_mbz           = 0;
1853
1854              im6->im6_mif = mif - mif6table;
1855
1856              /* iif info is not given for reg. encap.n */
1857              mrt6stat.mrt6s_upcalls++;
1858
1859              if (socket_send(ip6_mrouter, mm, src) < 0) {
1865                      ++mrt6stat.mrt6s_upq_sockfull;
1866                      return ENOBUFS;
1867              }
1868              return 0;
1869      }
```

1810–1832 The control message to the routing daemon has a message type of MRT6MSG_WHOLEPKT, indicating to the routing daemon to forward this multicast packet in a PIM Register message. The multicast interface index is actually unused by the routing daemon. socket_send() passes the message to the routing daemon like any other notification messages.

2.10.5 socket_send() Function

The socket_send() function, shown in Listing 2-72, can be called from ip6_mforward(), ip6_mdq() and register_send() to pass notification messages regarding multicast routing to the routing daemon. In the register_send() case, the information carried by the notification message contains an entire multicast packet so that the routing daemon can encapsulate the packet into a PIM Register message and send it to the RP.

The socket_send() function simply appends the mbuf that contains the information to the special socket allocated by the routing daemon, and then wakes up the daemon. Note that the inbound processing at the ICMPv6 layer is bypassed even though the "packet" is appended to an ICMPv6 socket.

Listing 2-72

———————————————————————————————————— ip6_mroute.c
```
1131    static int
1132    socket_send(s, mm, src)
1133            struct socket *s;
1134            struct mbuf *mm;
1135            struct sockaddr_in6 *src;
1136    {
1137            if (s) {
1138                    if (sbappendaddr(&s->so_rcv,
1139                                    (struct sockaddr *)src,
1140                                    mm, (struct mbuf *)0) != 0) {
1141                            sorwakeup(s);
1142                            return 0;
1143                    }
1144            }
1145            m_freem(mm);
1146            return -1;
1147    }
```
———————————————————————————————————— ip6_mroute.c

2.10.6 `pim6_input()` Function

The `pim6_input()` function is called as the upper layer input routine from `ip6_input()` for the next header value of 103 (`IPPROTO_PIM`). Even though this function partly deals with the PIM protocol, it is defined in `ip6_mroute.c`, since some other parts of the input processing code relate to multicast forwarding.

Figure 2-29 shows call graphs for incoming PIM message processing, focusing on the `pim6_input()` function.

The minimum header part of PIM messages is defined as the `pim{}` structure as shown in Listing 2-73. This is a straightforward implementation of the first four bytes of Figure 2-14.

Listing 2-73

———————————————————————————————————— pim6.h
```
43    struct pim {
52            u_char  pim_ver:4,       /* PIM version */
53                    pim_type:4;      /* PIM type    */
55            u_char  pim_rsv;         /* Reserved */
56            u_short pim_cksum;       /* IP style check sum */
57    };
```
———————————————————————————————————— pim6.h

Length Validation

Listing 2-74

———————————————————————————————————— ip6_mroute.c
```
1871    /*
1872     * PIM sparse mode hook
1873     * Receives the pim control messages, and passes them up to the listening
1874     * socket, using rip6_input.
1875     * The only message processed is the REGISTER pim message; the pim header
1876     * is stripped off, and the inner packet is passed to register_mforward.
1877     */
```

```
1878    int
1879    pim6_input(mp, offp, proto)
1880            struct mbuf **mp;
1881            int *offp, proto;
1882    {
1883            struct pim *pim; /* pointer to a pim struct */
1884            struct ip6_hdr *ip6;
1885            int pimlen;
1886            struct mbuf *m = *mp;
1887            int minlen;
1888            int off = *offp;
1889
1890            ++pim6stat.pim6s_rcv_total;
1891
1892            ip6 = mtod(m, struct ip6_hdr *);
1893            pimlen = m->m_pkthdr.len - *offp;
1894
1895            /*
1896             * Validate lengths
1897             */
1898            if (pimlen < PIM_MINLEN) {
1899                    ++pim6stat.pim6s_rcv_tooshort;
1904                    m_freem(m);
1905                    return (IPPROTO_DONE);
1906            }
```
                                                                ip6_mroute.c

FIGURE 2-29

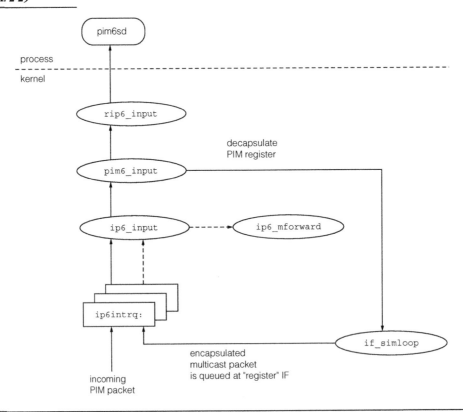

Incoming PIM message processing.

1878–1906 The function parameter offp contains the offset value from the beginning of the
IPv6 header to the beginning of the PIM header. Any PIM message must have at least
PIM_MINLEN (8) bytes; otherwise, the message is discarded.

Technically, the check here is too restrictive according to the latest protocol specification
[RFC4601] because a PIM Hello message can be just 4 bytes long. This check made sense for
a former version of the specification [RFC2362], where a Hello message always included at
least one option and the check condition held.

Listing 2-75

ip6_mroute.c

```
1908             /*
1909              * if the packet is at least as big as a REGISTER, go ahead
1910              * and grab the PIM REGISTER header size, to avoid another
1911              * possible m_pullup() later.
1912              *
1913              * PIM_MINLEN         == pimhdr + u_int32 == 8
1914              * PIM6_REG_MINLEN    == pimhdr + reghdr + eip6hdr == 4 + 4 + 40
1915              */
1916             minlen = (pimlen >= PIM6_REG_MINLEN) ? PIM6_REG_MINLEN : PIM_MINLEN;

1917
1918             /*
1919              * Make sure that the IP6 and PIM headers in contiguous memory, and
1920              * possibly the PIM REGISTER header
1921              */
1923             IP6_EXTHDR_CHECK(m, off, minlen, IPPROTO_DONE);
1924             /* adjust pointer */
1925             ip6 = mtod(m, struct ip6_hdr *);
1926
1927             /* adjust mbuf to point to the PIM header */
1928             pim = (struct pim *)((caddr_t)ip6 + off);
```

ip6_mroute.c

1916 The minimum packet length depending on the PIM message type is calculated and stored
in minlen. For a Register message, the minimum length is the sum of the size of the
common part of the message (see Figure 2-14) and the size of the inner IPv6 header. For
the other types of messages, the minimum length is PIM_MINLEN (except in the rare case
noted above).

1923–1928 The IP6_EXTHDR_CHECK() macro ensures that the first mbuf contains the whole
data from the IPv6 header to the minimum length of the PIM message. Pointers ip6 and
pim are then set to point to the IPv6 and PIM headers, respectively.

Checksum Calculation

Listing 2-76

ip6_mroute.c

```
1937     #define PIM6_CHECKSUM
1938     #ifdef PIM6_CHECKSUM
1939             {
1940                     int cksumlen;
1941
```

```
1942                        /*
1943                         * Validate checksum.
1944                         * If PIM REGISTER, exclude the data packet
1945                         */
1946                        if (pim->pim_type == PIM_REGISTER)
1947                                cksumlen = PIM_MINLEN;
1948                        else
1949                                cksumlen = pimlen;
1950
1951                        if (in6_cksum(m, IPPROTO_PIM, off, cksumlen)) {
1952                                ++pim6stat.pim6s_rcv_badsum;
1958                                m_freem(m);
1959                                return (IPPROTO_DONE);
1960                        }
1961                }
1962    #endif /* PIM_CHECKSUM */
```
——— ip6_mroute.c

1937–1962 Whereas the upper layer checksum should usually cover the entire message, the checksum for a Register message is only calculated for the PIM header to reduce the encapsulation overhead, as required by the specification. The specification also requires that the implementation accept the checksum covered by the entire message for a Register message for interoperability reasons, but the current implementation does not conform to the requirement. This simplification should do no harm in practice, though, because the interoperability concern is to provide backward compatibility to some old PIM implementations that compute the checksum for the entire Register message; IPv6 implementations are sufficiently new, and there is no known implementation that has the compatibility issue.

It is worth noting that the checksum computation is performed by the in6_cksum() function, which uses the pseudo header used by other transport layer protocols for computing the checksum. This is different from the case for IPv4 PIM, as explained in Section 2.4.4.

Version Number Validation

Listing 2-77
——— ip6_mroute.c

```
1964                /* PIM version check */
1965                if (pim->pim_ver != PIM_VERSION) {
1966                        ++pim6stat.pim6s_rcv_badversion;
1972                        m_freem(m);
1973                        return (IPPROTO_DONE);
1974                }
```
——— ip6_mroute.c

1964–1974 The current version of PIM is version 2 (PIM_VERSION). A packet is discarded if the version field of the PIM header does not match the current version number. Backward compatibility regarding the version is not an issue here, because the previous version does not support multiple address families, i.e., IPv6 is not supported by PIMv1.

PIM Register Message Processing

A PIM Register message needs special consideration: it can be regarded as a PIM protocol message and also as a multicast packet to be forwarded. A copy of the packet will be passed

to the application, which is usually the PIM routing daemon. The original packet is sent back
to the multicast forwarding code as if it came from the "imaginary" Register interface.

Figure 2-30 summarizes various message headers and parameters involved in the procedure
described below.

Listing 2-78

```
                                                                              ip6_mroute.c
1976            if (pim->pim_type == PIM_REGISTER) {
1977                    /*
1978                     * since this is a REGISTER, we'll make a copy of the register
1979                     * headers ip6+pim+u_int32_t+encap_ip6, to be passed up to the
1980                     * routing daemon.
1981                     */
1982                    static struct sockaddr_in6 dst = { sizeof(dst), AF_INET6 };
1983
1984                    struct mbuf *mcp;
1985                    struct ip6_hdr *eip6;
1986                    u_int32_t *reghdr;
1987                    int rc;
1988
1989                    ++pim6stat.pim6s_rcv_registers;
1990
1991                    if ((reg_mif_num >= nummifs) || (reg_mif_num == (mifi_t) -1)) {
1998                            m_freem(m);
1999                            return (IPPROTO_DONE);
2000                    }
                                                                              ip6_mroute.c
```

1991–2000 The packet is discarded if the Register interface is not configured. This can happen,
for example, if multicast routing has not been enabled. While the Register interface index
should be in the correct range as long as it has a non-negative value, the code checks the
upper boundary as well for safety.

FIGURE 2-30

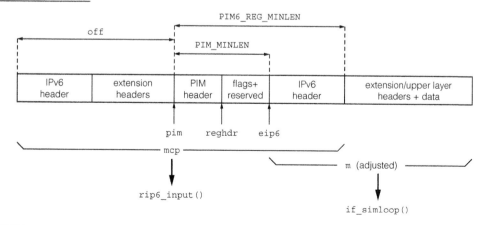

Handling a PIM Register message.

Listing 2-79

```
2002                    reghdr = (u_int32_t *)(pim + 1);
2003
2004                    if ((ntohl(*reghdr) & PIM_NULL_REGISTER))
2005                            goto pim6_input_to_daemon;
```

2002–2005 The `PIM_NULL_REGISTER` constant is a flag bit for testing the Null-Register bit of the Register message (see Figure 2-14). If this bit is on, meaning this is a Null-Register message, it does not involve forwarding, and the rest of the processing can be skipped.

Listing 2-80

```
2007                    /*
2008                     * Validate length
2009                     */
2010                    if (pimlen < PIM6_REG_MINLEN) {
2011                            ++pim6stat.pim6s_rcv_tooshort;
2012                            ++pim6stat.pim6s_rcv_badregisters;
2019                            m_freem(m);
2020                            return (IPPROTO_DONE);
2021                    }
2022
2023                    eip6 = (struct ip6_hdr *) (reghdr + 1);
```

2007–2021 The packet is silently discarded if the PIM message has less than the minimum required length for a Register message. The minimum Register message length (`PIM6_REG_MINLEN`) is 48 bytes, which contains the common part of a Register message and the IPv6 header of the inner multicast packet. `eip6` safely points to the top of the inner IPv6 header after the minimum length validation.

Listing 2-81

```
2034                    /* verify the version number of the inner packet */
2035                    if ((eip6->ip6_vfc & IPV6_VERSION_MASK) != IPV6_VERSION) {
2036                            ++pim6stat.pim6s_rcv_badregisters;
2042                            m_freem(m);
2043                            return (IPPROTO_NONE);
2044                    }
2045
2046                    /* verify the inner packet is destined to a mcast group */
2047                    if (!IN6_IS_ADDR_MULTICAST(&eip6->ip6_dst)) {
2048                            ++pim6stat.pim6s_rcv_badregisters;
2056                            m_freem(m);
2057                            return (IPPROTO_DONE);
2058                    }
```

Inner Header Validation

2034–2044 The inner packet must at least have the right IPv6 version number.

The check is actually unnecessary because `ip6_input()` will also perform the same validation.

2047–2058 A PIM Register message, except a Null-Register, must contain a valid IPv6 multicast packet. The packet is discarded if the destination address is not an IPv6 multicast address.

Listing 2-82

```
                                                             ip6_mroute.c
2060                     /*
2061                      * make a copy of the whole header to pass to the daemon later.
2062                      */
2063                     mcp = m_copy(m, 0, off + PIM6_REG_MINLEN);
2064                     if (mcp == NULL) {
2070                             m_freem(m);
2071                             return (IPPROTO_DONE);
2072                     }
                                                             ip6_mroute.c
```

2060–2072 `mcp` is a copy of the packet to be sent to the routing daemon. Since the routing daemon needs only the necessary routing information, only the minimum length of the Register message needs to be copied.

Listing 2-83

```
                                                             ip6_mroute.c
2074                     /*
2075                      * forward the inner ip6 packet; point m_data at the inner ip6.
2076                      */
2077                     m_adj(m, off + PIM_MINLEN);
2088
2091                     rc = if_simloop(mif6table[reg_mif_num].m6_ifp, m,
2092                                     dst.sin6_family, NULL);
2103
2104                     /* prepare the register head to send to the mrouting daemon */
2105                     m = mcp;
2106             }
2107
2108     /*
2109      * Pass the PIM message up to the daemon; if it is a register message
2110      * pass the 'head' only up to the daemon. This includes the
2111      * encapsulator ip6 header, pim header, register header and the
2112      * encapsulated ip6 header.
2113      */
2114  pim6_input_to_daemon:
2115     rip6_input(&m, offp, proto);
2116     return (IPPROTO_DONE);
2117  }
                                                             ip6_mroute.c
```

2077–2105 The Register message is stripped off to obtain the inner packet, which is the original multicast packet to be forwarded by the receiving router. `PIM_MINLEN` is 8 bytes, containing the common part of a Register message. The original multicast packet is passed to `if_simploop()`, which will transfer the packet back to the IPv6 input queue. The incoming interface will be set as if the packet came from the virtual Register interface.

2108–2116 The original PIM message (the adjusted part of the packet in the case of Register) is passed to the routing daemon via `rip6_input()`. The upper layer checksum will not be calculated in `rip6_input()` unless the routing daemon explicitly requires the kernel to calculate the checksum via a socket option as we saw in Chapter 6 of *IPv6 Core Protocols Implementation*, but it is safe since it was done in this function.

2.11   IPv6 Multicast Operation

We conclude this chapter with some concrete examples of IPv6 multicast operation and descriptions of several utility programs related to multicasting and multicast routing. The description of each utility is not comprehensive and we encourage the reader to read the manual pages for further details.

2.11.1   ifmcstat Command

The **ifmcstat** command allows a system administrator to check whether a node is listening to a particular multicast group. The **ifmcstat** command needs access to the kernel memory and requires the super user privilege to run the command.

The following is a sample output from this command executed on an IPv6 router that also serves as a DHCPv6 server. The `-f inet6` option instructs the **ifmcstat** utility to print IPv6-related information only; without this option, **ifmcstat** would output both IPv4 and IPv6 group addresses.

```
# ifmcstat -f inet6

fxp0:
        inet6 fe80::2e0:18ff:fe98:f19d%fxp0
        inet6 2001:db8:0:4819:2e0:18ff:fe98:f19d
        inet6 2001:db8:0:4819::
        inet6 2001:db8:0:8002:2e0:18ff:fe98:f19d
        inet6 2001:db8:0:8002::
                group ff05::1:3 refcnt 1
                    mcast-macaddr 33:33:00:01:00:03 multicnt 1
                group ff02::1:2%fxp0 refcnt 1
                    mcast-macaddr 33:33:00:01:00:02 multicnt 1
                group ff02::9%fxp0 refcnt 1
                    mcast-macaddr 33:33:00:00:00:09 multicnt 1
                group ff02::2%fxp0 refcnt 1
                    mcast-macaddr 33:33:00:00:00:02 multicnt 1
```

ifmcstat displays the group membership information on a per interface basis beginning with the interface name. The command first lists the unicast and anycast addresses assigned to the interface. You may notice that there are two subnet-router anycast addresses: `2001:db8:0:4819::` and `2001:db8:0:8002::`.

Multicast group address information follows the list of unicast addresses. Each line beginning with the keyword `group` shows an IPv6 multicast group address to which the node is listening on the interface, and corresponds to an `in6_multi{}` data structure. Since the sample router is a DHCPv6 server, it joins the All_DHCP_Servers address, `ff05::1:3`, and the All_DHCP_Relay_Agents_and_Servers address, `ff02::1:2` (Section 4.2.3). Similarly, since the node is a router, it joins the All-Routers address `ff02::2`, and joins the all-rip-routers address `ff02::9` for running the RIPng routing protocol (Section 1.4.2).

`refcnt` shows the value of the `in6m_refcount` member of the corresponding `in6_multi{}` structure, which is meaningless for FreeBSD. FreeBSD manages multicast groups through an address family independent structure, `ifmultiaddr{}`, which has its own reference counter and is shown as `multicnt` in the preceding output.

Lines beginning with the keyword `mcast-macaddr` show the corresponding Layer-2 multicast address for a Layer-3 group address. The interface used in this example is an Ethernet interface, and it can be easily checked that the corresponding Layer-2 addresses conform to the mapping described in Section 2.2.

2.11.2   Enable IPv6 Multicast Routing

No special kernel configuration is necessary to enable IPv6 multicast routing, while the kernel should be rebuilt with the `MROUTING` option to enable IPv4 multicast routing in the traditional BSD kernel. The difference comes from the view that multicasting is not special anymore.

An IPv6 multicast router should also function as a unicast router (recall that a multicast router must join the All-Routers multicast address and process the Router Alert Hop-by-Hop option). Enabling unicast routing can be done either by rebuilding the kernel with the `GATEWAY6` option, or by executing the following **sysctl** command:

```
# sysctl -w net.inet6.ip6.forwarding=1
```

2.11.3   pim6dd and pim6sd Routing Daemons

The **pim6dd** and **pim6sd** routing daemons are almost configuration free. These daemons can be started by simply invoking the command. For example,

```
# /usr/local/v6/sbin/pim6dd
```

The **pim6sd** daemon requires that a configuration file exist in the system due to an implementation constraint, which is `/etc/pim6sd.conf` by default.[2] An empty configuration file is accepted. A major exception is a PIM-SM RP because a PIM router needs to be configured explicitly to function as an RP. The following line should be added to the configuration file to enable a PIM-SM router as an RP.

```
cand_rp;
```

Additionally, there should normally be one special router called the *bootstrap router* in order to distribute the RP address (the mechanism is beyond the scope of this book and is not explained in this chapter). The easiest way is to let the RP act as the bootstrap router as well, which should be done by adding the following line to the configuration file:

```
cand_bootstrap_router;
```

In the rest of this chapter, we will concentrate on the **pim6sd** operation, although most of the information can easily apply to **pim6dd**. Our discussion will focus on the network topology given in Figure 2-31. Routers A and C are FreeBSD-based PCs that run **pim6sd**, which are the main concern in the following discussion. In Figure 2-31, ne0, ne1, etc., refer to interface names in a router.

2.11.4   pim6stat Output

The **pim6stat** command displays the internal status of a running **pim6sd** process. **pim6stat** requires the super user privilege to execute the command. Assuming there are two hosts

---

2. In mcast-tools (see Section 2.5), the default path name of the configuration file is
`/usr/local/etc/pim6sd.conf`.

FIGURE 2-31

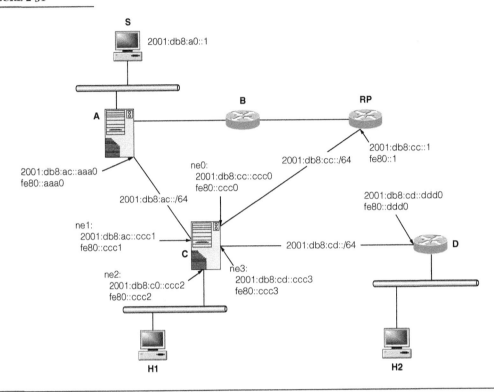

Sample network topology of PIM operations.

(i.e., H1 and H2 in Figure 2-31) joining a multicast group `ff05::1:3` but there is no multicast traffic yet, the output from **pim6stat** at Router C would be like this:

```
Multicast Interface Table
  Mif   PhyIF  Local-Address/Prefixlen                          Scope Flags
  0      ne0  2001:db8:cc::ccc0/64                               0     DR PIM
              fe80::ccc0/64                                      1
              Timers: PIM hello = 0:05, MLD query = 0:50
              possible MLD version = 1
  1      ne1  2001:db8:ac::ccc1/64                               0     DR PIM
              fe80::ccc1/64                                      2
              Timers: PIM hello = 0:05, MLD query = 0:50
              possible MLD version = 1
  2      ne2  2001:db8:c0::ccc2/64                               0     DR PIM QRY NO-NBR
              fe80::ccc2/64                                      3
              Timers: PIM hello = 0:20, MLD query = 1:05
              possible MLD version = 1
  3      ne3  2001:db8:cd::ccc3/64                               0     PIM QRY
              fe80::ccc3/64                                      4
              Timers: PIM hello = 0:05, MLD query = 0:50
              possible MLD version = 1
  4    regist fe80::cccc/64                                      1     REGISTER
              Timers: PIM hello = 0:00, MLD query = 0:00
              possible MLD version = 1

PIM Neighbor List
```

```
     Mif  PhyIF Address                           Timer
     0      ne0 fe80::1                            85
                2001:db8:cc::1
     1      ne1 fe80::aaa1                         40
                2001:db8:ac::aaa1
     3      ne3 fe80::ddd0                         55
                2001:db8:cd::ddd0

  MLD Querier List
     Mif  PhyIF Address                     Timer           Last
     0      ne0 fe80::1                     145             41m27s
     1      ne1 fe80::aaa1                  85              40m49s
     2      ne2 fe80::ccc2                  255             43m14s
     3      ne3 fe80::ddd0                  160             42m35s

  Reported MLD Group
     Mif  PhyIF Group/Source
     0      ne2 ff05::1:3
                (any source)

  Multicast Routing Table
  ------------------------------(*,G)----------------------------
  IN6ADDR_ANY     ff05::1:3      2001:db8:cc::1 WC RP
  Joined    oifs: ...j.
  Pruned    oifs: .....
  Leaves    oifs: ..l..
  Asserted oifs: .....
  Outgoing oifs: ..oo.
  Incoming     : I....
  Upstream nbr: fe80::1

  TIMERS: Entry=0 JP=45 RS=0 Assert=0
     MIF   0   1   2   3   4   5   6   7   8   9
       0   0   0   0   0   0   0   0   0   0   0
       1   0   0   0   0   0   0   0   0   0   0
       2   0   0   0

  ------------------------(*,*,RP)--------------------------
  Number of Groups: 3
  Number of Cache MIRRORs: 0

  --------------------------RP-Set----------------------------
  Current BSR address: 2001:db8:cc::1 Prio: 10 Timeout: 120
  RP-address(Upstream)/Group prefix         Prio Hold Age
  2001:db8:cc::1(fe80::1%ne0)
       ff00::/8                               0    150  130
```

The first section of the **pim6stat** output lists the multicast interfaces with the local address assigned on each interface. The `Flags` field gives additional information on each interface: `QRY` means the router is acting as an MLD querier on the corresponding link. `NO-NBR` means there are no other PIM routers on the link. It is common to have both the `NO-NBR` flag and the `QRY` flag set at the same time. `DR` means the router is the PIM *designated router* on the link (the concept of designated router is not discussed in this book).

The second section of the output shows a list of PIM neighbor routers on each multicast interface attached to the router. Each PIM neighbor router is recognized by a link-local address, but each router also notifies each other of global addresses (if any) on the corresponding interface in order to improve the robustness of RPF (see Section 2.4.4). The list of global addresses is shown, following the link-local addresses.

The third section of the output is a list of the current MLD queriers.

The fourth section of the output is a list of recognized multicast groups that have listeners reported via MLD.

Then the internal routing table (cache) of **pim6sd** follows. In this example, there is only one entry for the group `ff05::1:3`. In this entry, the first line beginning with `IN6ADDR_ANY` means this entry is for a shared tree for the group `ff05::1:3` with `2001:db:cc::1` as the RP address. The next section of the entry shows per interface information. Each line describes the status of each interface in terms of a particular PIM event, such as a joining or pruning event. In this example, the first line means this router (C) receives a join message on interface 3 (from router D). The third line means there is a listener (H1) for the group on the link attached to interface 2. The fifth line means incoming packets should be sent on interfaces 3 and 4. And finally, the sixth line means packets for this group should come from interface 0 (toward the RP), which should be determined by the RPF algorithm.

The last section of the output provides information on the RP and the bootstrap router. In this example, the address of RP is `2001:db8:cc::1`, and the upstream router's link-local address toward the RP is `fe80::1` on the link attached to ne0. The multicast prefix `ff00::/8` means this RP is responsible for all valid multicast addresses.

The **pim6stat** command also works for **pim6dd** by specifying the `-d` command line option.

2.11.5   netstat Command

Now assume sender S starts sending multicast packets to group `ff05::1:3`. Each PIM router creates an appropriate multicast forwarding cache (or an equivalent state depending on the implementation) and forwards the packets. Executing the **netstat** command with the `-g` option allows a user to view the multicast forwarding cache.

```
# netstat -g
```

For example, an output of **netstat -g** at router A would be as follows:

```
IPv6 Multicast Forwarding Cache
  Origin              Group          Packets Waits In-Mif  Out-Mifs
  2001:db8:a0::1      ff05::1:3      10      0     0       3
```

This means one forwarding cache entry exists for the source address `2001:db8:a0::1` and the group address `ff05::1:3` pair. Router A has forwarded 10 packets for this multicast flow, and there are no packets waiting for a cache entry to be established. The incoming multicast interface is interface ne0. The only outgoing interface is the Register interface, which is identified by the multicast interface index of 3.

Similarly, **netstat -g** would contain the following part at router C:

```
IPv6 Multicast Forwarding Cache
  Origin              Group          Packets Waits In-Mif Out-Mifs
  2001:db8:a0::1      ff05::1:3      5       0     0      2  3
```

Since router C has two outgoing interfaces, ne2 and ne3, the list of the outgoing interfaces is shown as "2 3".

3

DNS for IPv6

3.1   Introduction

The Domain Name System (DNS) is one of the most fundamental components of today's Internet. In fact, most Internet applications, including e-mail and WWW, depend on the DNS in some way. This is also the case for applications that support IPv6 and for new IPv6 specific applications.

DNS is flexible enough to support IPv6 with straightforward extensions. Still, there are some nontrivial issues regarding IPv6. This is partly because the DNS itself is an Internet application, and the use of the DNS over IPv6 introduces a new level of complexities which are not seen with only IPv4. Also, there are known misbehaviors in some existing DNS implementations that handle IPv6 extensions to the DNS in an inappropriate way, causing trouble not only for IPv6 users but also for those who do not use IPv6. It is therefore important for all kinds of Internet users and developers to understand how the DNS operates with IPv6.

This chapter describes the DNS protocol specification and implementation, focusing on IPv6-specific topics. It begins with a general description of the DNS protocol, followed by an explanation of extensions for IPv6 along with discussions on IPv6-specific issues. Next, it describes KAME's DNS resolver (client) implementation, highlighting its support for IPv6. This part concludes the implementation description of the getaddrinfo() library function as a continuation of Chapter 7 of *IPv6 Core Protocols Implementation*. Together, these two chapters will provide a comprehensive view of the complicated library. The latter half of this chapter talks about BIND, the most widely deployed DNS server implementation. It describes how to operate DNS with IPv6 using the latest version of BIND, BIND9, as well as explains common pitfalls and issues that come from implementation characteristics of BIND9.

3.2   Basics of DNS Definitions and Protocols

This section provides some basic background to help understand the later discussion in this chapter. It explains fundamental concepts of the DNS, which are not specific to IPv6, so that those who are not familiar with the DNS can better understand the rest of this chapter. To understand the DNS in more detail, other materials cited in the text are recommended. Beginners may also want to consult general guides about the DNS such as [Liu06].

3.2.1   DNS, Domains, and Zones

DNS is a global database system which provides a mapping from a host name[1] (such as `www.kame.example`) to an IP address (such as `192.0.2.1` or `2001:db8::1`), or vice versa. It is a distributed and hierarchical system, ensuring coherency as well as avoiding a single point of failure. The results of database lookups are often cached, reducing network traffic and server load, and increasing lookup efficiency.

From the data structure point of view, the database system of the DNS is represented as a labeled tree called the *domain name space*. Figure 3-1 shows a part of the tree structure. The strings associated with tree nodes are called DNS *labels*, which consist of alphabets, numeric numbers, and the dash character (-). A *domain* is a sub-tree whose root is an arbitrary node in the entire tree. The *domain name* of a domain is a string concatenating all labels from the domain's root to the root of the entire name space, separated with periods.

In Figure 3-1, example, wide, ftp, and www are labels. Strings `ftp.kame.net.`, `wide.example.`, and `jp.` are domain names. Technically, the terminating period is a part of a domain name, but it is often omitted when the context makes it clear. For example, people often say the `example` domain, instead of the `example.` domain, as does this chapter.

As will soon be seen, domains starting at a top level (i.e., near the root) are particularly important for DNS operation. These domains are generally called *Top Level Domains* (TLDs), and TLDs are often referred to by specific names. The entire name space is called the *root domain*, and some common first-level domains are called *generic top level domains* or gTLDs. Examples of gTLDs are the `com`, `net`, and `org` domains. At the first level, there are also per-country domain names, which are called *country code top level domains* (or ccTLDs). There is no technical difference between gTLDs and ccTLDs in terms of the DNS protocol; the difference is in who manages the corresponding name space.

An arbitrary connected subset of the name space can be a notion called a *zone*. Every node in the name space belongs to one and only one of the zones, which allows a zone to define an administration boundary of a particular part of the name space. Note that a zone is not necessarily a sub-tree, and does not necessarily equal the domain of the same name. In fact, the corresponding zones for most top-level domains are not equal to the domains; in particular, the root zone effectively consists of the root node only.

Each zone is served by one or more *nameservers*. A nameserver of a zone maintains domain names within the zone, and responds to database queries for the names. Nameservers are often called *authoritative (DNS) servers*. Nameservers of the root zone and gTLD zones are called the *root servers* and the *gTLD servers*, respectively. One single nameserver can serve

---

1. In the DNS, a *host* commonly means any Internet node including a router. This chapter follows that convention.

FIGURE 3-1

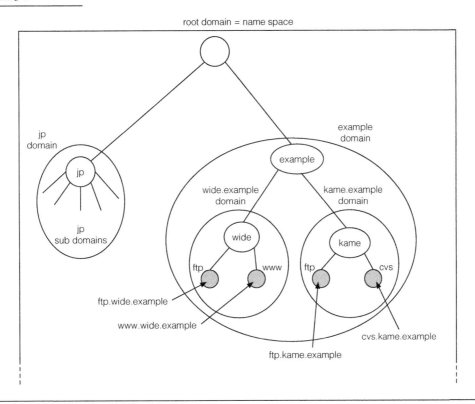

root domain = name space

jp
domain

example
domain

jp

example

jp
sub domains

wide.example
domain

kame.example
domain

wide

kame

ftp

www

ftp

cvs

ftp.wide.example

www.wide.example

cvs.kame.example

ftp.kame.example

Structure of the domain name space.

for multiple different zones. For example, `com` and `net` zones are served by the same set of nameservers.

Many zones have more than one authoritative server, particularly in the case of top-level zones, to provide redundancy and improve stability. Usually only one of them maintains the *master* database, which is called the *primary* (or master) server of the zone. Other nameservers, called *secondary* (or slave) servers, periodically synchronize with the primary server to provide coherent behavior. This process is called a *zone transfer*.

There are several techniques to make the zone transfer mechanism more timely and efficient, but the details of those techniques are beyond the scope of this book.

In general, an upper level (called *parent*) zone *delegates* the administration authority for some lower-level domains to lower level (called *child*) zones. Figure 3-2 shows an example of the delegation relationship. In this example, the authority for the `example` domain is delegated to a separate zone from the root zone. The `example` domain contains several subdomains, each of which forms a separate zone. That is, the `example` zone is not equal to the `example` domain. This also applies to the `com` zone and domain. On the other hand, the `kame.example` and

FIGURE 3-2

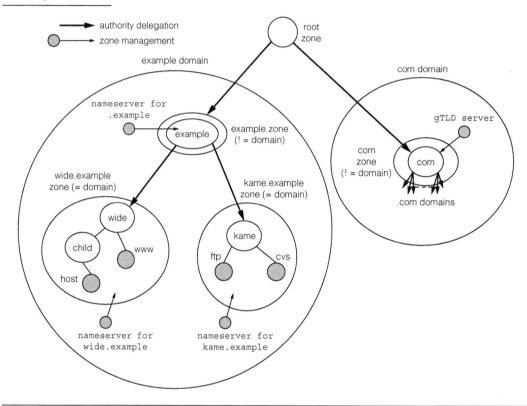

Example of zone delegation.

wide.example domains are each managed with the same single authority, even though the wide.example domain contains a subdomain, child.wide.example. In these cases, the zone equals the domain.

3.2.2 Resource Records and Zone Files

Resource records (often abbreviated as *RRs*) are database entries in the DNS. When it is obvious from the context, a resource record will be referred to as just a *record* in the rest of this chapter. A resource record consists of the following six fields:

NAME A domain name, which is a lookup key for this resource record. This field is also referred to as *owner name.*

TYPE The type of the resource record (2 bytes). For example, a type A record means a mapping from a domain name to an IPv4 address.

CLASS The identifier of a protocol family or instance of a protocol (2 bytes). For normal DNS operation, only the *IN* (Internet) class is used.

TTL The *time to live* of this resource record represented in seconds (4 bytes). This determines how long a resource record is allowed to exist in a cache.

RDLENGTH The length of RDATA represented in bytes (2 bytes).

RDATA Type dependent data. For a type A resource record, RDATA is an IPv4 address (and RDLENGTH is 4).

Some of the fields have a fixed length, which is specified in the above description. These fields appear in this order in DNS messages.

Table 3-1 shows a list of some major resource records. A set of the resource records constructs a zone. In a valid zone, there must be exactly one SOA resource record and one or more NS records that represent the authoritative servers of the zone. The NAME field of these records must be the zone's name, which corresponds to the topmost node in the zone.

A *zone file* (or a master file) is a textual representation of a zone as a set of resource records. In a zone file, each record of the zone is represented in the following format:

```
NAME   [<TTL>] [<CLASS>] <TYPE> <RDATA>
```

or

```
NAME   [<CLASS>] [<TTL>] <TYPE> <RDATA>
```

For example, an A record specifying a mapping from www.kame.example to 192.0.2.1 with the TTL of 3600 seconds can be represented as follows:

```
www.kame.example. 3600 IN A 192.0.2.1
```

TTL and CLASS can be omitted. In particular, the CLASS field will often be omitted in the examples in the rest of this chapter, since they are all of the IN class.

TABLE 3-1

Type	RDLENGTH	RDATA	Description
A	4	An IPv4 address	Provides a mapping from a host name (the owner name) to an IPv4 address.
NS	variable	A domain name	Provides a host (nameserver) name of a zone's authoritative server.
CNAME	variable	A domain name	Defines an alias of the owner name, that is, the RDATA of a CNAME RR is another name of the owner name.
SOA	variable	Seven-tuple values	Defines zone's property.
PTR	variable	A domain name	Points to some location in the name space. The RDATA of a PTR RR has no official semantics in the DNS protocol definition, but it commonly provides a mapping from an IP address to a host name.
MX	variable	A set of a 16-bit integer and a domain name	Provides a host name of a mail server for a domain specified by the owner name. The integer defines the preference among multiple servers.
AAAA	16	An IPv6 address	Provides a mapping from a host name (the owner name) to an IPv6 address. More details of the AAAA RR will be discussed in Section 3.3.1.

Major resource records.

FIGURE 3-3

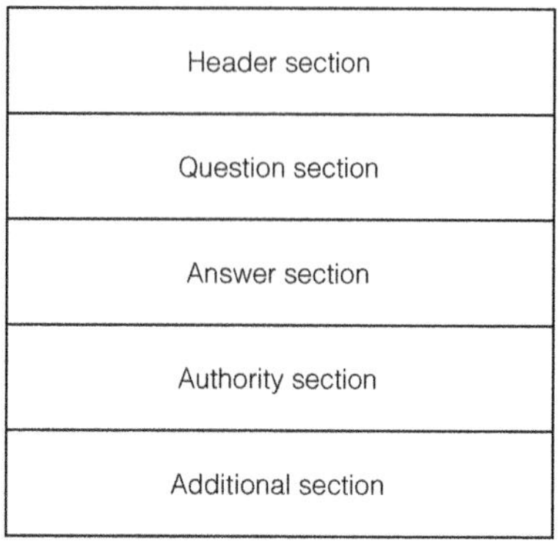

Header section
Question section
Answer section
Authority section
Additional section

DNS packet format.

Multiple resource records for the same owner name, class, and type can usually coexist in a single zone with some exceptions such as SOA and CNAME records. The entire set of resource records that share the same owner name, class, and type is called a *resource record set*, which is often abbreviated to *RRset*.`

3.2.3   DNS Transaction and Packet Format

From the database transaction point of view, DNS is a network protocol based on the server-client model, in which servers are nameservers, and clients are called *resolvers*. A server waits for queries on the well-known UDP and TCP ports of 53. A resolver first sends a query over UDP, rather than TCP, to the well-known port of an appropriate server as required in [RFC1123], and the server sends a response to the client over UDP. TCP is used for some special cases such as zone transfer or when the message is too large to carry over UDP (see Section 3.3.4).

Regardless of whether it is carried over UDP or TCP, a DNS query or response begins with a common Header section.[2] Other sections follow as shown in Figure 3-3, some of which may be empty.

Each section that follows the Header section carries the following information per [RFC1034]:

Question Carries the query name

Answer Carries the answer resource records to the query name

Authority Carries resource records which describe authoritative servers. The nameserver information that has the authority of the response is provided in this section.

Additional Carries resource records which may be helpful in using the records in the other sections.

Figure 3-4 details the format of the Header section.

---

2. More precisely, a DNS message carried by TCP has a prefix with a two-byte length field before the Header section.

FIGURE 3-4

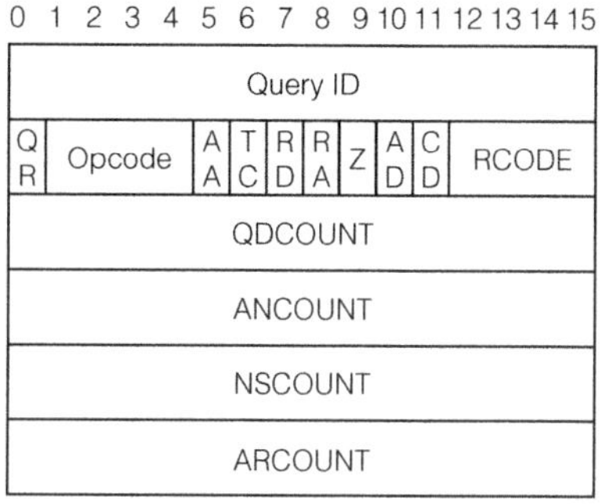

```
 0  1  2  3  4  5  6  7  8  9 10 11 12 13 14 15
┌───────────────────────────────────────────┐
│                  Query ID                   │
├──┬────────┬──┬──┬──┬─┬──┬──┬───────────────┤
│Q │ Opcode │A │T │R │Z│R │A │C│    RCODE     │
│R │        │A │C │D │ │A │D │D│              │
├──┴────────┴──┴──┴──┴─┴──┴──┴───────────────┤
│                  QDCOUNT                     │
├─────────────────────────────────────────────┤
│                  ANCOUNT                     │
├─────────────────────────────────────────────┤
│                  NSCOUNT                     │
├─────────────────────────────────────────────┤
│                  ARCOUNT                     │
└─────────────────────────────────────────────┘
```

DNS Header section format.

[RFC1035] defines some fields of the Header section as follows:

Query ID A 16-bit identifier assigned by the program that generates a query. This identifier is copied to the corresponding reply and can be used by the requester to match up replies to outstanding queries.

QR A 1-bit field that specifies whether this message is a query (0), or a response (1).

OPCODE A 4-bit field that specifies the type of query in this message. This value is usually zero, which means a standard query.

AA *Authoritative Answer* bit. This bit is only valid in responses, and specifies that the responding nameserver have an authority for the domain name in the Question section.

TC *TrunCation* bit. This specifies that this message was truncated due to a length greater than that permitted on the transmission channel (see Section 3.3.4).

RD *Recursion Desired* bit. This bit may be set in a query and is copied into the response. When set, it directs the responding server to pursue the query recursively (see Section 3.2.4 for recursive query).

RA *Recursion Available* bit. This bit is set or cleared in a response and denotes whether recursive query support is available in the responding server.

Z Reserved for future use. This field must be zero in all queries and responses.

RCODE A 4-bit *Response Code*. This field is set as part of responses. The available RCODE values are listed in Table 3-2.

QDCOUNT An unsigned 16-bit integer specifying the number of entries in the Question section.

ANCOUNT An unsigned 16-bit integer specifying the number of resource records in the Answer section.

NSCOUNT An unsigned 16-bit integer specifying the number of (nameserver) resource records in the Authority section.

ARCOUNT An unsigned 16-bit integer specifying the number of resource records in the Additional section.

TABLE 3-2

Value	Description
0	No error condition.
1	*Format Error*—The server was unable to interpret the query.
2	*Server Failure*—The server was unable to process this query due to a problem with the name-server.
3	*Name Error*—Meaningful only for responses from an authoritative nameserver, this code signifies that the domain name of any resource record type referenced in the query does not exist. This code is also known as *NXDOMAIN*, the term derived from widely deployed implementations.
4	*Not Implemented*—The server does not support the requested kind of query.
5	*Refused*—The server refuses to perform the specified operation for policy reasons.
6–15	Reserved for future use.

DNS response codes.

FIGURE 3-5

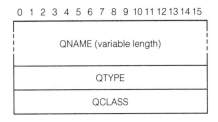

DNS Question section format.

In addition, [RFC2535] defines the **AD** and **CD** bits for the security extensions to the DNS (DNSSEC). DNSSEC is beyond the scope of this book; therefore, these bits are not referred to in the following discussion.

The format of the Question section is shown in Figure 3-5. This section is simple and intuitive: *QNAME* is a domain name of the query or response, and *QTYPE* and *QCLASS* specify the type and class of the queried resource records, respectively.

Each of the remaining sections consists of a sequence of 0 or 1 or more resource records as indicated in the corresponding COUNT field of the header.

3.2.4   Name Resolution and Caching

Name resolution (or simply resolution) is the lookup process in the DNS. Resolution of an IP address from a host name is called *forward resolution* or *forward lookup*; resolution of a host name from an IP address is called a *reverse resolution* or *reverse lookup*. Likewise, a subset of the domain name space that is used for forward resolution is often called the *forward tree*, and a subset for reverse resolution is sometimes called the *reverse tree*; the mapping provided by the DNS for forward and reverse resolution is called *forward mapping* and *reverse mapping*, respectively.

How does a resolver perform the resolution process? Before answering the question, the notion of caching should be introduced. A resolver implemented in a host operating system, often called a *stub resolver*, usually does not send a query directly to authoritative DNS servers. Instead, it uses a more powerful resolver, called *recursive (or iterative) resolver* or *caching server*, which performs the essential part of name resolution. It thus makes more sense to describe the resolution process with a caching server.

Figure 3-6 shows examples of the name resolution process with stub resolvers and a caching server. The stub resolvers only interact with the caching server, and the caching server communicates with authoritative servers. Queries from a stub resolver to the caching server set the RD bit of the Header section, asking the caching server to perform the full resolution process, and are called *recursive queries*. Also, the procedure that the caching server performs is sometimes called *recursive resolution*.

The following describes a common resolution process, as shown in Figure 3-6.

1. Stub resolver A sends a recursive query for name `www.kame.example` to the caching server.

2. The caching server begins the recursive resolution process with a root server by sending a nonrecursive query for `www.kame.example` to the root server.

> *Note*: To resolve the bootstrap problem, the addresses of the root servers are usually provided as a *hint* zone file or hardcoded in the caching server implementation. The example shown in Figure 3-6 assumes the hint is provided as a file named `root.cache`.

3. In general, when an authoritative server receives a query for a domain name, it searches for the zone that best matches the queried name, and, if found, responds with the corresponding

FIGURE 3-6

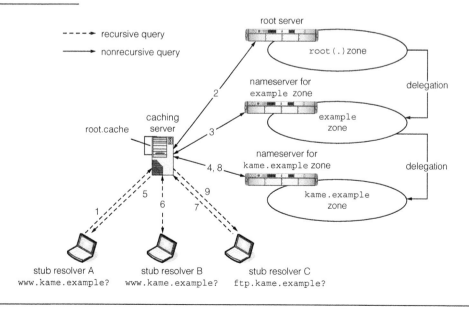

Recursive name resolution process.

resource records stored in the zone. The response may be a determinate one stored in the zone or, in case the queried name belongs to a zone for which the server does not have authority, a referral to the another zone.

In this example, since the root zone delegates the authority for the `example` domain to the `example` zone, the root server returns a referral, in the form of an NS RRset in the Authority section, to the caching server. The NS RRset would be described as follows:

```
example. 3600 NS ns1.example.
example. 3600 NS ns2.example.
```

This means the nameservers that maintain the delegated zone are identified by the name of `ns1.example` and `ns2.example`. As shown in the next steps, the caching server will then need to send queries to these servers, so it will need to know the IP (v4 or v6) addresses of these names. Although the addresses would be given via A and AAAA resource records of these names, the records belong to the `example` domain that the caching server is now going to explore.

To resolve the chicken and egg problem, the nameserver at the parent zone (the root server in this case) maintains a copy of such A and AAAA RRsets[3] associated with each NS record for delegation from the parent zone, and includes these A or AAAA RRsets in the Additional section. For example, the Additional section of the referral answer would be something like this:

```
ns1.example. 3600 A 192.0.2.1
ns2.example. 3600 A 192.0.2.2
```

This way the caching server can send further queries to the nameservers of the delegated zone. These A or AAAA resource records are called *glue (resource) records*.

4. The caching server caches the result, and sends the same query to one of the specified authoritative servers. Again, since the `example` zone delegates the authority of the `kame.example` domain to the `kame.example` zone, it in turn returns a referral (NS RRset) with glue records for the child zone.

5. The caching server caches the result, and sends the same query to a specified authoritative server of the `kame.example` zone. This time, the authoritative server has a record for the query name in its zone file, and sends the result to the caching server.

6. The caching server caches the result, and forwards it to stub resolver A.

7. Next, assume that a different stub resolver (B) asks the caching server for the same name `www.kame.example`. Since the caching server has already cached the result, it simply returns the cached response without asking the authoritative servers.

8. Finally, another stub resolver (C) asks a slightly different name `ftp.kame.example`.

9. The caching server does not have a cache for this name, but knows where to ask for names under the `kame.example` domain (as a result of step 4). It can directly query

---

3. Technically, this does not necessarily have to be an exact copy; it can be a subset of the RRsets stored in the child zone.

an authoritative server of the `kame.example` zone, and the authoritative server returns a response from its zone file.

10. The caching server caches the result, and forwards it to stub resolver C.

3.3 IPv6-Related Topics about DNS

This section gives IPv6-related definitions, protocol, and issues regarding DNS. It also clarifies which version of the protocol specification should be used in the actual operation today; some of the proposed standards have been obsoleted, and the standardization process has caused confusion among operators. The clarification will provide a clear guideline on the possibly confusing point.

3.3.1 AAAA Resource Record

In order to convert a host name to IPv6 addresses, a separate resource record AAAA (pronounced as *quad-A*) is defined. The format and use of the AAAA resource record are very similar to those of the traditional A record, and are easy to understand.

Listing 3-1 shows an example of A and AAAA resource records for the same single host name `www.kame.example`. That is, to represent a mapping from a host name to an IPv6 address, we can simply use the AAAA record instead of the A record and specify the IPv6 address as RDATA.

Listing 3-1

```
www.kame.example.    3600 A       192.0.2.1
www.kame.example.    3600 AAAA    2001:db8::1
```

Notice that in the above resource records the IN class is assumed and omitted as noted in Section 3.2.2. Even though AAAA records provide forward mappings of a different version of Internet protocol (i.e., IPv6), they are used in conjunction with the same class as A records. It also applies to reverse mappings described in Section 3.3.2.

3.3.2 DNS Reverse Tree for IPv6

For those who are familiar with IPv4 DNS operation, it is easy to understand the basic mechanism to construct a reverse DNS tree for IPv6 addresses because it is essentially the same as that used for IPv4 addresses. A single resource record provides a mapping from an IPv6 address to a host name. The owner name of the record is derived from the address and a well-known name space, `ip6.arpa`. To construct the rest of the owner name, the IPv6 address is first divided into a series of 4-bit pieces, from the least significant 4 bits to the most significant 4 bits, separated by periods. This is called the *nibble* format.

For example, the owner name of the IPv6 address shown in Listing 3-1 for the reverse mapping should be described as follows:

```
1.0.0.0.0.0.0.0.0.0.0.0.0.0.0.0.0.0.0.0.0.0.0.0.8.b.d.0.1.0.0.2.ip6.arpa.
```

The type of the resource record commonly used for the reverse mapping is PTR, just as for the IPv4 (in-addr.arpa) case.

As a result, a complete format of the resource record for the reverse mapping of this address is as follows:

```
1.0.0.0.0.0.0.0.0.0.0.0.0.0.0.0.0.0.0.0.0.0.0.0.0.8.b.d.0.1.0.0.2.ip6.arpa.
3600 PTR www.kame.example.*
```

FIGURE 3-7

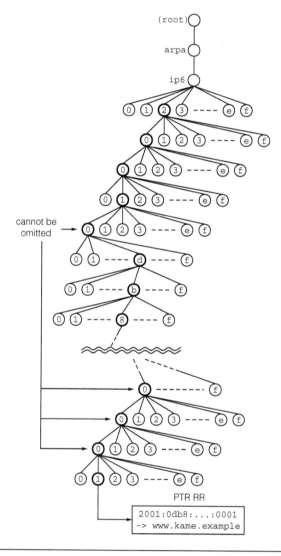

DNS reverse tree for IPv6 reverse mapping.

---

* Line is broken here for layout reasons. However, it is a single line of resource record.

Figure 3-7 illustrates how the owner name of this PTR record is represented in the DNS name space. As shown in the figure, each level under the `ip6.arpa` domain contains sixteen single-character labels, 0, 1, ..., and `f`. The labels in thicker circles correspond to the owner name, `1.0.0...0.1.0.0.2.ip6.arpa`.

It should also be noted that the labels corresponding to leading zeros in each 16-bit chunk of the IPv6 address cannot be omitted in the DNS representation. This also applies to intermediate consecutive zeros that can be compressed into `::` in the textual representation. For example, the IPv6 address used in this example is normally represented as `2001:db8::1`, where the leading zero of `0db8` in the second 16-bit chunk is omitted. But it must appear in the DNS representation as noted in Figure 3-7; otherwise, it would share the domain name with different addresses such as `2001:db80:...`. It does not make sense since these two addresses are most likely allocated to different organizations, and these organizations would like to manage the corresponding DNS reverse tree separately.

3.3.3 IPv6 Transport for DNS

The transport carrying DNS data is, by design, independent of its content. That is, a DNS query or response that contains IPv4-related data such as an A resource record or a PTR record under the `in-addr.arpa` domain can be carried over either IPv4 or IPv6. Similarly, a DNS query or response containing IPv6-related data can be carried over either IPv6 or IPv4.

In practice, however, it may sometimes be desirable to have the same network protocol for both the DNS transport and the content. For example, if an application wants to resolve a AAAA resource record for a host name, it is likely that the application wants to use IPv6 to communicate with the host and that IPv6 connectivity is provided for that purpose. Since IPv4 connectivity may or may not be provided, it may make much more sense to try IPv6 transport for the DNS transaction.

Unfortunately, there are still DNS servers that are not reachable over IPv6. In particular, none of the root servers is *practically* IPv6 reachable; some of the servers have actual IPv6 connectivity, but these addresses are not visible in the public name space as of October 2006. More specifically, none of the root server names have a AAAA resource record, partly due to the packet size issue which will be explained in Section 3.3.4. Still, the situation is improving; a number of gTLD and ccTLD servers have been supporting IPv6 and are actually reachable over IPv6. The IPv6 addresses of these servers have been published as glue resource records in the root zone since July 2004. There is even an ongoing effort to publish the capability of IPv6 transport at the root servers.

3.3.4 Packet Size Issue and EDNS0

In the old days of IPv4, a constant of 512 bytes had been widely used as the default buffer size of applications. Apparently from the convention, [RFC791] defines 576 bytes as the minimum size of datagram which any host is required to be able to handle, with consideration for room for the IPv4 header, IPv4 options (if any), and the transport layer header. The DNS specification [RFC1035] also limits the size of a DNS message carried by UDP to 512 bytes, excluding the IPv4 and UDP headers so that any DNS message can be safely accepted at the receiver with the conventional receiving buffer size.

An obvious consequence of this upper limit is that a UDP DNS packet cannot contain a large number of resource records. This subsequently imposes an operational limitation in terms of the number of nameservers of each zone; since the corresponding A or AAAA RRsets must be included in the Additional section as glue records when delegation occurs from the parent zone, this limitation indicates that the number of IP (v4 or v6) addresses of the nameservers is limited. Even though the querier could then switch to TCP, it is much more expensive and should be avoided as much as possible.

Meanwhile, it is generally beneficial to have more nameservers serve a zone for stability as long as these servers are adequately managed and working. This is the case particularly for top-level domain servers, since the availability of these servers is crucial for the name resolution procedure as indicated in Figure 3-6 (page 215).

The number of IP addresses of top-level domain servers is therefore chosen carefully so that responses sent by these servers will fit in the limited size of UDP DNS packets as well as ensuring maximum availability of these servers. For example, the number of root DNS servers is currently 13, as is the number of some gTLD servers, each of which can have only one single IPv4 address. This means it is hard to add IPv6 addresses to such top-level domain servers without reducing the number of servers.

Notes:

(1) There are other techniques to provide both higher availability and relatively smaller responses [Abl03, Abl04]. In general, these techniques share a single IP address with multiple physical server equipments, thereby reducing the number of necessary addresses. Many root servers actually use this technique today.

(2) Technically, the limitation of the number of (addresses of) root servers does not stem from the delegation issue because there is no delegation to the root zone. But the general rationale applies to the root servers as well.

To see an example of this, assume that we had sent a DNS query for an A resource record of a host name `www.kame.net` to a root server in June 2004, when no gTLD servers had a AAAA record. The **dig** utility (see Section 3.5.7 for the usage of **dig**) that performed this query would have then produced the following response:

```
;; QUESTION SECTION:
;www.kame.net. IN  A

;; AUTHORITY SECTION:
net.              172800   IN   NS   A.GTLD-SERVERS.net.
net.              172800   IN   NS   G.GTLD-SERVERS.net.
net.              172800   IN   NS   H.GTLD-SERVERS.net.
net.              172800   IN   NS   C.GTLD-SERVERS.net.
net.              172800   IN   NS   I.GTLD-SERVERS.net.
net.              172800   IN   NS   B.GTLD-SERVERS.net.
net.              172800   IN   NS   D.GTLD-SERVERS.net.
net.              172800   IN   NS   L.GTLD-SERVERS.net.
net.              172800   IN   NS   F.GTLD-SERVERS.net.
net.              172800   IN   NS   J.GTLD-SERVERS.net.
net.              172800   IN   NS   K.GTLD-SERVERS.net.
net.              172800   IN   NS   E.GTLD-SERVERS.net.
net.              172800   IN   NS   M.GTLD-SERVERS.net.

;; ADDITIONAL SECTION:
A.GTLD-SERVERS.net. 172800   IN   A    192.5.6.30
G.GTLD-SERVERS.net. 172800   IN   A    192.42.93.30
H.GTLD-SERVERS.net. 172800   IN   A    192.54.112.30
C.GTLD-SERVERS.net. 172800   IN   A    192.26.92.30
```

```
I.GTLD-SERVERS.net. 172800   IN   A   192.43.172.30
B.GTLD-SERVERS.net. 172800   IN   A   192.33.14.30
D.GTLD-SERVERS.net. 172800   IN   A   192.31.80.30
L.GTLD-SERVERS.net. 172800   IN   A   192.41.162.30
F.GTLD-SERVERS.net. 172800   IN   A   192.35.51.30
J.GTLD-SERVERS.net. 172800   IN   A   192.48.79.30
K.GTLD-SERVERS.net. 172800   IN   A   192.52.178.30
E.GTLD-SERVERS.net. 172800   IN   A   192.12.94.30
M.GTLD-SERVERS.net. 172800   IN   A   192.55.83.30

;; Query time: 122 msec
;; SERVER: 202.12.27.33#53(m.root-servers.net)
;; WHEN: Thu Jun 10 22:56:41 2004
;; MSG SIZE  rcvd: 459
```

Look at the last line. It indicates the response size is 459 bytes.[4]

In October 2004, a couple of AAAA resource records for the net (and com) servers were registered in the root zone. Since then, the response could be as follows:

```
;; QUESTION SECTION:
;www.kame.net. IN  A

;; AUTHORITY SECTION:
net.            172800   IN   NS   A.GTLD-SERVERS.net.
net.            172800   IN   NS   G.GTLD-SERVERS.net.
net.            172800   IN   NS   H.GTLD-SERVERS.net.
net.            172800   IN   NS   C.GTLD-SERVERS.net.
net.            172800   IN   NS   I.GTLD-SERVERS.net.
net.            172800   IN   NS   B.GTLD-SERVERS.net.
net.            172800   IN   NS   D.GTLD-SERVERS.net.
net.            172800   IN   NS   L.GTLD-SERVERS.net.
net.            172800   IN   NS   F.GTLD-SERVERS.net.
net.            172800   IN   NS   J.GTLD-SERVERS.net.
net.            172800   IN   NS   K.GTLD-SERVERS.net.
net.            172800   IN   NS   E.GTLD-SERVERS.net.
net.            172800   IN   NS   M.GTLD-SERVERS.net.

;; ADDITIONAL SECTION:
A.GTLD-SERVERS.net. 172800   IN   AAAA2001:503:a83e::2:30
A.GTLD-SERVERS.net. 172800   IN   A   192.5.6.30
G.GTLD-SERVERS.net. 172800   IN   A   192.42.93.30
H.GTLD-SERVERS.net. 172800   IN   A   192.54.112.30
C.GTLD-SERVERS.net. 172800   IN   A   192.26.92.30
I.GTLD-SERVERS.net. 172800   IN   A   192.43.172.30
B.GTLD-SERVERS.net. 172800   IN   AAAA2001:503:231d::2:30
B.GTLD-SERVERS.net. 172800   IN   A   192.33.14.30
D.GTLD-SERVERS.net. 172800   IN   A   192.31.80.30
L.GTLD-SERVERS.net. 172800   IN   A   192.41.162.30
F.GTLD-SERVERS.net. 172800   IN   A   192.35.51.30
J.GTLD-SERVERS.net. 172800   IN   A   192.48.79.30
K.GTLD-SERVERS.net. 172800   IN   A   192.52.178.30
E.GTLD-SERVERS.net. 172800   IN   A   192.12.94.30
M.GTLD-SERVERS.net. 172800   IN   A   192.55.83.30

;; Query time: 12 msec
;; SERVER: 202.12.27.33#53(202.12.27.33)
;; WHEN: Sat May 14 23:24:18 2005
;; MSG SIZE  rcvd: 515
```

However, this actually should not happen (unless TCP is used for the DNS transport) because the response size (515 bytes) would exceed the maximum value of 512 bytes.

---

4. The message size is the length of the response in its wire-format, which is different from the number of characters contained in the textual output of **dig**.

TABLE 3-3

Field name	Description
NAME	Empty (the root domain)
TYPE	41 (OPT)
CLASS	Sender's UDP payload size
TTL	Extended RCODE and flags
RDLEN	The length of RDATA
RDATA	A pair of attribute and value

The OPT resource record for EDNS0.

The difference of the size is 56 bytes. It means each AAAA record needs an additional 28 bytes, which consist of 2 bytes of domain name (compressed),[5] 2 bytes of record type (AAAA), 2 bytes of record class (IN), 4 bytes of TTL, 2 bytes of data length (16), and 16 bytes of the data (the IPv6 address).

If we could agree on reducing the number of top level-domain servers, we would be able to add IPv6 addresses to those servers. But this is not always a feasible option due to the need for ensuring high availability of these servers.

The IETF developed a way to resolve the issue through a protocol extension called *EDNS0*, *Extension Mechanisms for DNS (version 0)* [RFC2671]. EDNS0 defines a new resource record, the OPT record. This is a pseudo-record in that it does not appear in the DNS database. The format of the OPT record is shown in Table 3-3.

The semantics of the class field is redefined, and represents the receiving buffer size of the sender. If the client has a buffer larger than 512 bytes and supports EDNS0, the client will include the OPT resource record in a query with its buffer size; if the server also supports EDNS0, it will fill in the response up to the specified buffer size of the client.

Most DNS servers that do not support EDNS0 simply return a response with an error code if it receives a query containing an OPT record. The client will then fall back to the traditional query without EDNS0. Thanks to this fallback mechanism, caching server operators usually do not have to care about the existence of the OPT record or interoperability issues regarding EDNS0.

3.3.5   Misbehaving DNS Servers against AAAA

The AAAA resource record has been in the standard specification for quite a long period, and most DNS server implementations correctly handle it. Yet there are known authoritative DNS implementations that do not treat the AAAA record in the expected way and do harm in actual operation. [RFC4074] details such misbehavior.

---

5. The notion of name compression is beyond the scope of this book. In this context, it is enough to understand that the DNS standard defines a name compression scheme that can reduce the size of a DNS packet.

FIGURE 3-8

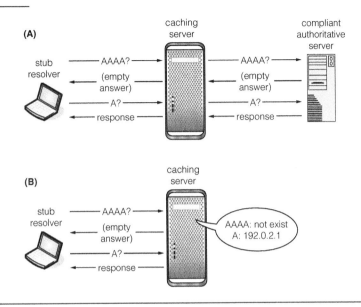

Compliant behavior when AAAA RR does not exist.

Most dual stack network applications try to resolve both IPv4 and IPv6 addresses for the host name of a given communication peer, and send DNS queries for both A and AAAA records. As described in Figure 3-6 (page 215), queries are sent to the corresponding authoritative DNS servers, usually via a caching DNS server.

The problem with misbehaving authoritative servers occurs when the query name has an A record but does not have a AAAA record. The expected scenario with a compliant authoritative server is shown in part (A) of Figure 3-8; it returns a successful response with an empty Answer section, indicating the query name does not have a AAAA record, but *may* have other types of resource records of the same name. Compliant behavior optimizes succeeding transactions; since the caching server remembers the result per resource record type, it can return an empty answer for succeeding queries for the AAAA record while returning the correct response for the A record without asking the authoritative server again (part (B) of Figure 3-8).

On the other hand, misbehaving authoritative servers cause various types of problems as summarized below.

Ignore AAAA Queries

Some authoritative servers respond to queries for an A record correctly, but ignore queries for a AAAA record. Naive implementations of the stub resolver, including the one implemented in BSD's resolver library, send queries for A and AAAA records sequentially, each with a certain amount of waiting time. Such resolver implementations thus need to endure unnecessary timeouts (Figure 3-9).

Return Name Error

Other misbehaving authoritative servers respond to any query for a AAAA record with a Response Code of Name Error (also known as NXDOMAIN), which indicates that no resource

FIGURE 3-9

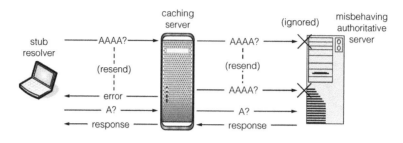

Misbehaving DNS server that ignores AAAA queries.

FIGURE 3-10

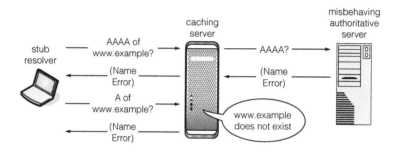

Misbehaving DNS server that returns a response with Name Error.

record of *any type* exists for the queried name. Once the caching server receives and caches this response, it will return the negative response regardless of the resource record type without asking the authoritative server. As a result, the application calling the stub resolver cannot make any communication even if the queried name has an A record and IPv4 connectivity is provided (Figure 3-10). If the stub resolver in Figure 3-10 sent the query for an A record first, it would get a valid positive response; however, the succeeding query for a AAAA record would create the negative cache in the caching server, and subsequent queries for the same name will still fail. So simply changing the query order is not a complete solution to this problem.

Return Other Erroneous Codes

Some other authoritative DNS servers return a response with a Response Code of Not Implemented, Server Failure, or Format Error to a AAAA query. This behavior is not valid, but most stub resolvers that send AAAA queries first fall back to A queries of the same name in this case. Thus, this behavior is relatively harmless. As major caching servers such as BIND-based servers do not cache the fact that the queried host name has no AAAA record, it results in increasing the load on the authoritative server and wasting network bandwidth; these caching servers send AAAA queries to the authoritative server whenever they receive a AAAA query for the name from the stub resolver.

FIGURE 3-11

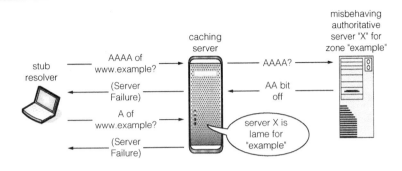

Misbehaving DNS server that makes a lame delegation.

Make *Lame* Delegation

This type of authoritative server returns an authoritative response to A queries, but returns an *inauthoritative* response to AAAA queries (i.e., the AA bit is not set in the response), causing a situation called a *lame delegation*. Some older versions of BIND8 (BIND version 8) caching servers can suffer from this behavior, since it will stop using a remote DNS server for some period once it detects that the server is lame. These BIND8 caching servers simply return a response with the Response Code of Server Failure for queries in the zone which is managed by the *lame* authoritative server throughout the period. In this case, the stub resolver will never be able to get the correct response even if it falls back from AAAA query to A query after receiving the error. Figure 3-11 depicts this situation.

Whereas some of the issues can be mitigated at the resolver or the caching server side (see, for example, Section 3.5.5), this is primarily a problem of authoritative servers, which are what should really be fixed. Efforts are being made to improve the situation [Suz06], but it is generally difficult to get access to the operators of a misbehaving server and have them fix it due to various reasons, including confidentiality concerns. Wider collaboration among users, implementors, and operators is therefore necessary.

3.3.6 Obsolete Standards

The IETF once defined a *successor* of the DNS standards for IPv6 described in Sections 3.3.1 and 3.3.2 [RFC2672, RFC2673, RFC2874].[6] In the set of the new proposals, a new resource record, A6, was defined for forward mapping. For reverse mapping, a new type of DNS labels called *bit-string labels* (or often called *bit labels*) were introduced. Another new resource record, DNAME, was used in conjunction with bit-string labels to implement the counterpart of A6 for reverse mapping.

Roughly speaking, the goal of these new definitions was to divide an IPv6 address into several chunks corresponding to the hierarchical address architecture and to represent each chunk as a single A6 record. It was originally expected that these would make IPv6 renumbering easier in terms of the DNS.

---

6. More precisely, they were *proposed standards*, which are at the first stage of the IETF standardization hierarchy.

It then turned out, however, that the expected benefit did not outweigh the complexity of the process to deal with the new definitions. In particular, the resolution procedure with these definitions would require radical changes in the stub resolver, and it was not trivial to deploy the changes in existing stub resolver implementations.

After a long and heated discussion, the IETF finally decided to cancel the migration to these new definitions [RFC3363]. Even though the IETF officially said the new definitions became *experimental*, it was actually a wording compromise, and these definitions were essentially *deprecated*. In fact, BIND 9.3 has removed most parts of the support for A6 and bit-string labels that were available in previous versions.

Thus, the details of A6 record and bit-string labels are no longer of interest, and this book will concentrate on the old and future definitions described in the earlier sections. The authors do not necessarily discourage curious readers from *experiencing* A6 or bit-string labels as long as they understand it is effectively deprecated rather than just categorized as experimental. However, it would generally be more advisable to concentrate on other issues regarding the technology deployed (or expected to be deployed) in the real world.

It should be noted that not all the contents that defined the deprecated standards are obsolete. First, `ip6.arpa`, the common name space for IPv6 reverse mapping defined as a replacement of an old well-known name `ip6.int`, is still and will be used for this purpose [RFC3152], even though it was first introduced with the now-deprecated standard [RFC2874]. In fact, Regional Internet Registries (RIRs) that had maintained the `ip6.int` zones stopped the service in June 2006, and IANA also removed the delegation for the `ip6.int` domain from the `int` zone almost at the same time. The `ip6.arpa` domain thus has become the only effective well-known domain suffix for IPv6 reverse mapping.

second, [RFC3363] does not necessarily deprecate the general use of DNAME. It only deprecates the counterpart of A6 for IPv6 reverse mapping in conjunction with bit-string labels. Other future standards, which may or may not be directly related to IPv6, can use DNAME for other purposes. Although [RFC4294] states that IPv6 nodes that need to resolve names are *NOT RECOMMENDED* to support the DNAME record, it should be interpreted as applicable to the limited usage.

3.4   Implementation of IPv6 DNS Resolver

This section describes KAME's stub resolver implementation,[7] concentrating on its IPv6-related part. Files listed in Table 3.4 are covered in this section.

This section describes the resolver implementation along with the usage of the `getaddrinfo()` and `getnameinfo()` library functions, the most commonly used API for name resolution in IPv6 applications. Figure 3-12 shows the relationship between resolver library routines used by `getaddrinfo()` and `getnameinfo()`. Shaded functions are described in this series of books: the `getaddrinfo()` and `getnameinfo()` functions were discussed in Chapter 7 of *IPv6 Core Protocols Implementation*, "Socket API Extensions"; the rest of the functions are described in this section. This section thus concludes the entire story of these library functions that began in the *Core Protocols* book, and provides complete understanding of the complex implementation.

---

7. In fact, the base resolver implementation was derived from a BIND library, which is not a product of KAME.

TABLE 3-4

File	Description
arpa/nameser_compat.h	DNS Header section structure
arpa/netdb.h	Internal state structure of the resolver library for getaddrinfo()
resolv.h	Public state structure of the resolver library
getaddrinfo.c	DNS resolver routines used by getaddrinfo()
name6.c	A DNS resolver routine used by getnameinfo()
resolv/res_init.c	Generic initialization routine of the resolver library
resolv/res_send.c	General library routines for DNS transactions

Files in this section. Header files (.h) are located under ${KAME}/freebsd4/include/ and program files (.c) are under ${KAME}/kame/kame/libinet6/.

FIGURE 3-12

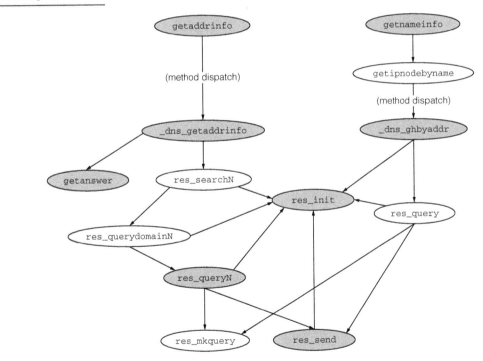

Relationship between resolver library routines.

Revisiting getaddrinfo() and getnameinfo() Functions

Before detailing the resolver library routines, it would be helpful to review the getaddrinfo() and getnameinfo() functions briefly, because these are the top-level API functions about which most application developers are concerned. The getaddrinfo() function is a name to address conversion function; it takes a host name such as `www.kame.net` (as well as other input arguments) and returns one or more IP (v4 or v6) addresses, such as `203.178.141.194` or `2001:200:0:8002:203:47ff:fea5:3085`, depending on the arguments.

One major characteristic of `getaddrinfo()` is that its interface is independent of particular network protocols, namely IPv4 or IPv6, and even other or future protocols. The `getaddrinfo()` function returns a chain of the `addrinfo{}` structure (Listing 3-2), and the chain can contain addresses of different network protocols if the calling application indicates `getaddrinfo()` that it accepts addresses of any protocol.

Listing 3-2

```
struct addrinfo {
        int     ai_flags;       /* AI_PASSIVE, AI_CANONNAME, AI_NUMERICHOST */
        int     ai_family;      /* PF_xxx */
        int     ai_socktype;    /* SOCK_xxx */
        int     ai_protocol;    /* 0 or IPPROTO_xxx for IPv4 and IPv6 */
        size_t  ai_addrlen;     /* length of ai_addr */
        char    *ai_canonname;  /* canonical name for hostname */
        struct  sockaddr *ai_addr;      /* binary address */
        struct  addrinfo *ai_next;      /* next structure in linked list */
};
```

The `ai_addr` member points to a memory space that stores a network address in the form of general socket address structure; the application can transparently use the result by passing it to other protocol-independent system calls such as `sendto()`. If the application needs to behave differently depending on the protocol, it can refer to the `ai_family` member of the structure. In the previous example of `www.kame.net`, most `getaddrinfo()` implementations will return the chain shown in Figure 3-13 by default.

FIGURE 3-13

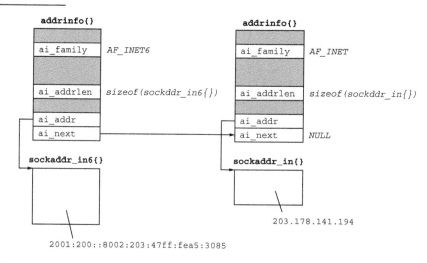

Example of `addrinfo{}` *chain returned by* `getaddrinfo()`*.*

The `getnameinfo()` function provides the reverse mapping service; it converts a binary form of an IPv4 or IPv6 address to a textual host name. This function also has a protocol-independent interface: it takes a generic `sockaddr{}` structure as an input argument and performs the conversion on it. The application does not even have to be aware of which protocol of address is stored in the structure.

3.4.1 `_dns_getaddrinfo()` Function

As seen in Chapter 7 of *IPv6 Core Protocols Implementation*, when the `getaddrinfo()` implementation tries to map a host name to addresses, it uses multiple services that provide the mapping, including the DNS, local `/etc/hosts` file, and at times NIS (Network Information Service). This implementation first consults the `/etc/host.conf` file to determine the preference between the services, and calls method functions associated with the services in the preferred order. The `_dns_getaddrinfo()` function is the method function for the DNS, which is described in this subsection.

The `res_target{}` Structure

The `getaddrinfo()` function often tries to resolve several types of DNS resource records for a single call, usually A for IPv4 and AAAA for IPv6, and combines the entire results to return to the caller. The `_dns_getaddrinfo()` function and its subroutines maintain a separate structure, `res_target{}`, to hold the resolution context for each resource record until the whole process is completed. While the structure is publicly defined in `/usr/include/netdb.h`, it is not normally expected to be referred to from applications.

The definition of the `res_target{}` structure is shown in Listing 3-3.

Listing 3-3
                                                                    ____netdb.h

```
struct res_target {
        struct res_target *next;
        const char *name;         /* domain name */
        int qclass, qtype;        /* class and type of query */
        u_char *answer;           /* buffer to put answer */
        int anslen;               /* size of answer buffer */
        int n;                    /* result length */
};
```
                                                                    ____netdb.h

While multiple resource records are being resolved, the corresponding `res_target{}` structures are concatenated as a chain. The `next` member of the structure is a pointer to the next entry of the chain.

The `name` member takes no significant role in this implementation.

The `qclass` and `qtype` members are the DNS class and type for corresponding queries, respectively.

The `answer` member points to a buffer space to store DNS responses, and `anslen` specifies the total size of the buffer. The length of the actual response packet will be stored in the last member of the `res_target{}` structure, `n`.

The `_dns_getaddrinfo()` function also uses a supplemental structure called `querybuf{}`. This is essentially a buffer to store a DNS response, but is defined as a union so that it can also be used as the header of a DNS packet.

Listing 3-4

```
                                                              ──getaddrinfo.c
247     #define MAXPACKET           (64*1024)
248
249     typedef union {
250             HEADER hdr;
251             u_char buf[MAXPACKET];
252     } querybuf;
                                                              ──getaddrinfo.c
```

The `hdr` member of the union will be used when the resolver library parses the DNS packet header part. This does not necessarily have to be part of a union, though. Simply casting to the `HEADER` type from the opaque buffer would also work. The use of the union is probably a matter of taste.

The `HEADER` type is shown in Listing 3-5.[8] It is a straightforward representation of the Header section format shown in Figure 3-4 (page 213).

Listing 3-5

```
                                                              ──nameser_compat.h
64      typedef struct {
65              unsigned        id :16;          /* query identification number */

67                              /* fields in third byte */
68              unsigned        qr: 1;           /* response flag */
69              unsigned        opcode: 4;       /* purpose of message */
70              unsigned        aa: 1;           /* authoritive answer */
71              unsigned        tc: 1;           /* truncated message */
72              unsigned        rd: 1;           /* recursion desired */
73                              /* fields in fourth byte */
74              unsigned        ra: 1;           /* recursion available */
75              unsigned        unused :1;       /* unused bits (MBZ as of 4.9.3a3) */
76              unsigned        ad: 1;           /* authentic data from named */
77              unsigned        cd: 1;           /* checking disabled by resolver */
78              unsigned        rcode :4;        /* response code */

....(little endian case: omitted)

94                              /* remaining bytes */
95              unsigned        qdcount :16;     /* number of question entries */
96              unsigned        ancount :16;     /* number of answer entries */
97              unsigned        nscount :16;     /* number of authority entries */
98              unsigned        arcount :16;     /* number of resource entries */
99      } HEADER;
                                                              ──nameser_compat.h
```

In Listing 3-4, the size of the buffer is 64K bytes, which is the maximum size of DNS packets that this resolver implementation may receive. This size is sufficiently large because the possible maximum size is represented in the CLASS field of the EDNS0 OPT record for UDP or the length field of the prefix for TCP (see footnote 2 on page 212), which are both a two-byte field specifying the size in bytes.

Figure 3-14 clarifies the relationship between the `res_target{}` structure and the `querybuf{}` union. The shaded portion of the `querybuf{}` union is a DNS response packet. The `HFIXEDSZ` constant is defined in `nameser_compat.h` as the fixed size of the Header section (12 bytes), which will often be referred to in the code narrations below.

The details of the `_dns_getaddrinfo()` function will be seen through the following listings.

---

8. This listing only shows the big endian case since it should be more intuitive.

FIGURE 3-14

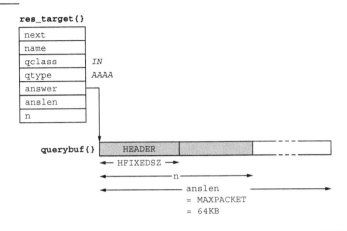

Relationship between the res_target{} *structure and the* querybuf{} *union.*

Initialization

Listing 3-6

getaddrinfo.c

```
4455    static int
4456    _dns_getaddrinfo(pai, hostname, res)
4457            const struct addrinfo *pai;
4458            const char *hostname;
4459            struct addrinfo **res;
4460    {
4461            struct addrinfo *ai;
4462            querybuf *buf, *buf2;
4463            const char *name;
4464            struct addrinfo sentinel, *cur;
4465            struct res_target q, q2;
4466
4467            memset(&q, 0, sizeof(q2));
4468            memset(&q2, 0, sizeof(q2));
4469            memset(&sentinel, 0, sizeof(sentinel));
4470            cur = &sentinel;
4471
4472            buf = malloc(sizeof(*buf));
4473            if (!buf) {
4474                    h_errno = NETDB_INTERNAL;
4475                    return NULL;
4476            }
4477            buf2 = malloc(sizeof(*buf2));
4478            if (!buf2) {
4479                    free(buf);
4480                    h_errno = NETDB_INTERNAL;
4481                    return NULL;
4482            }
```

getaddrinfo.c

4469–4482 Variable sentinel will store the result when name resolution succeeds. Two separate buffers of the type querybuf are allocated for queries of both A and AAAA resource records.

Set Up the Context

Listing 3-7

                                                                    ————getaddrinfo.c
```
4484            switch (pai->ai_family) {
4485            case AF_UNSPEC:
4486                    /* prefer IPv6 */
4487                    q.name = name;
4488                    q.qclass = C_IN;
4489                    q.qtype = T_AAAA;
4490                    q.answer = buf->buf;
4491                    q.anslen = sizeof(buf->buf);
4492                    q.next = &q2;
4493                    q2.name = name;
4494                    q2.qclass = C_IN;
4495                    q2.qtype = T_A;
4496                    q2.answer = buf2->buf;
4497                    q2.anslen = sizeof(buf2->buf);
4498                    break;
4499            case AF_INET:
4500                    q.name = name;
4501                    q.qclass = C_IN;
4502                    q.qtype = T_A;
4503                    q.answer = buf->buf;
4504                    q.anslen = sizeof(buf->buf);
4505                    break;
4506            case AF_INET6:
4507                    q.name = name;
4508                    q.qclass = C_IN;
4509                    q.qtype = T_AAAA;
4510                    q.answer = buf->buf;
4511                    q.anslen = sizeof(buf->buf);
4512                    break;
4513            default:
4514                    free(buf);
4515                    free(buf2);
4516                    return EAI_FAIL;
4517            }
```
                                                                    ————getaddrinfo.c

4484–4517 The `ai_family` member of `pai` is copied from the same member of the `hints` (i.e., the third) argument of `getaddrinfo()`. This resolver implementation supports the following three families:

AF_UNSPEC In this case, the caller of `getaddrinfo()` indicates it will accept addresses of any protocol, whether they are IPv4 or IPv6 addresses. The `_dns_getaddrinfo()` function then tries to provide the possible maximum set of addresses, that is, all available IPv4 and IPv6 addresses, and a chain of the `res_target{}` structures is needed to send queries for both A and AAAA resource records (Figure 3-15). The backend resolver routine will send out DNS queries, following this chain (Listing 3-21, page 244), so queries for AAAA resource records will be sent first, followed by queries for A records.

The `C_xxx` and `T_xxx` constants are commonly used in the resolver implementation. The former specifies the class of a resource record, and only `C_IN`, specifying the IN class, appears in the discussion of this chapter. The latter specifies the type of the record: `T_A` and `T_AAAA` specify the A and AAAA types, respectively. These constants are defined in `nameser_compat.h`.

FIGURE 3-15

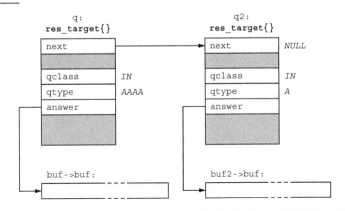

A chain of res_target{} *for the* AF_UNSPEC *case.*

The resolver library provided in FreeBSD 5.4 and later has changed the order of the res_target{} chain so that queries for A record will be sent out first. According to the release note, it intends to avoid the trouble caused by misbehaving authoritative servers that respond to AAAA queries with a response with the Name Error Response Code (Section 3.3.5). Unfortunately, this is only a partial solution to this problem as explained in that section.

AF_INET In this case, only IPv4 addresses are requested. A single entry of res_target{} is set up with the qtype member specifying the A resource record type.

AF_INET6 In this case, only IPv6 addresses are requested. A single entry of res_target{} is set up with the qtype member specifying the AAAA resource record type.

If an unsupported address family is specified, an error of EAI_FAIL is returned. (This case is actually caught earlier, though. See the description for the getaddrinfo() function in Chapter 7 of *IPv6 Core Protocols Implementation.*)

This code has a bug: the name member of q and q2 is set to point to variable name, but it is not initialized as can be seen in Listing 3-6, and will be passed to other functions in Listing 3-8 (via variable q) and Listing 3-9. Even though this bug actually does no harm since the called routines do not refer to the uninitialized value, it should be fixed. This is in fact corrected in recent versions of FreeBSD's resolver library.

Sending DNS Queries

Listing 3-8

getaddrinfo.c

```
4518             if (res_searchN(hostname, &q) < 0) {
4519                     free(buf);
4520                     free(buf2);
```

```
4521                         return EAI_NONAME;
4522                 }
```
_____ getaddrinfo.c

4518–4522 The `res_searchN()` function sends DNS queries as specified in the `res_target{}` chain starting at q, collecting answers in the buffer of each chain element. If this returns a fatal error, the processing is terminated and an error of `EAI_NONAME` is returned, which can happen when, for example, all queries are timed out.

Parse the Responses

Listing 3-9
_____ getaddrinfo.c

```
4523            ai = getanswer(buf, q.n, q.name, q.qtype, pai);
4524            if (ai) {
4525                    cur->ai_next = ai;
4526                    while (cur && cur->ai_next)
4527                            cur = cur->ai_next;
4528            }
4529            if (q.next) {
4530                    ai = getanswer(buf2, q2.n, q2.name, q2.qtype, pai);
4531                    if (ai)
4532                            cur->ai_next = ai;
4533            }
```
_____ getaddrinfo.c

4523–4533 The `getanswer()` function parses the DNS responses stored in the `res_target{}` elements, and constructs a chain of `addrinfo{}` structures from the responses. If both of the `res_target{}` elements were used and have responses, the two `addrinfo{}` chains are concatenated.

Post Process

Listing 3-10
_____ getaddrinfo.c

```
4534            free(buf);
4535            free(buf2);
4536            if (sentinel.ai_next == NULL)
4537                    switch (h_errno) {
4538                    case HOST_NOT_FOUND:
4539                            return EAI_NONAME;
4540                    case TRY_AGAIN:
4541                            return EAI_AGAIN;
4542                    default:
4543                            return EAI_FAIL;
4544                    }
4545            *res = sentinel.ai_next;
4546            return 0;
4547    }
```
_____ getaddrinfo.c

4534–4546 Temporary buffers are released. If the resulting `addrinfo{}` chain is empty, an error code for `getaddrinfo()` is returned. The code value is determined according to the value of h_errno, or `EAI_FAIL` when h_errno is unset. If resolution succeeded, the constructed `addrinfo{}` chain is set in the res variable, and 0 is returned indicating success.

3.4.2 `getanswer()` Function

The `getanswer()` function is called from the `_dns_getaddrinfo()` function to parse a DNS response, extracts the required RDATA, and constructs a chain of `addrinfo{}` structures corresponding to the response. It is one of the final steps of the entire implementation of the `getaddrinfo()` function. Following is a detailed description of the `getanswer()` function along with a concrete example of DNS response to a query for a AAAA resource record of the name `www.kame.example`. It is assumed in this case that the response packet contains one CNAME record and two AAAA records as follows:

```
www.kame.example. CNAME turtle.kame.example.
turtle.kame.example. AAAA 2001:db8::1
turtle.kame.example. AAAA 2001:db8::2
```

(The class and TTL fields are omitted for brevity.)

Another assumption in this example is that the caller of `getaddrinfo()` specifies the `AI_CANONNAME` flag in the hints structure. Since the response contains a CNAME record, the first entry of the resulting `addrinfo{}` chain should point to the string `turtle.kame.example` from its `ai_canonname` member.

Listing 3-11

getaddrinfo.c

```
4257    static struct addrinfo *
4258    getanswer(answer, anslen, qname, qtype, pai)
4259            const querybuf *answer;
4260            int anslen;
4261            const char *qname;
4262            int qtype;
4263            const struct addrinfo *pai;
```

getaddrinfo.c

4257–4263 The `answer` argument points to a buffer that stores the DNS response; `anslen` is the length of the response (recall Figure 3-14, page 231). The `qname` variable is effectively unused (see Listing 3-14); `qtype` is either `T_A` or `T_AAAA`, depending on whether this is a response to a query for an A or a AAAA resource record. The `pai` argument points to the `addrinfo{}` structure that is a template for the expected result.

Listing 3-12

getaddrinfo.c

```
4264    {
4265            struct addrinfo sentinel, *cur;
4266            struct addrinfo ai;
4267            const struct afd *afd;
4268            char *canonname;
4269            const HEADER *hp;
4270            const u_char *cp;
4271            int n;
4272            const u_char *eom;
4273            char *bp, *ep;
4274            int type, class, ancount, qdcount;
4275            int haveanswer, had_error;
4276            char tbuf[MAXDNAME];
4277            int (*name_ok) __P((const char *));
4278            char hostbuf[8*1024];
4279
4280            memset(&sentinel, 0, sizeof(sentinel));
4281            cur = &sentinel;
```

```
4282
4283            canonname = NULL;
4284            eom = answer->buf + anslen;
4285            switch (qtype) {
4286            case T_A:
4287            case T_AAAA:
4288            case T_ANY:        /*use T_ANY only for T_A/T_AAAA lookup*/
4289                    name_ok = res_hnok;
4290                    break;
4291            default:
4292                    return (NULL);   /* XXX should be abort(); */
4293            }
```
_____getaddrinfo.c

4280–4291 The variable sentinel is a dummy structure for constructing the returned chain
of addrinfo{} structures; canonname will usually point to a query name, but when
the response contains a CNAME record it will point to a domain name string corresponding to the RDATA of the CNAME. If multiple CNAME records are used to make
a chain, the terminating RDATA will be used. The res_hnok function pointer, pointed to
by name_ok, will be used to verify whether domain names contained in the response
are syntactically valid (the details of the syntax check is out of scope of this book).
The default case should never happen since qtype must be either T_A or T_AAAA;
the same note will apply to other portions of this function described below and will not be
repeated.

Listing 3-13
_____getaddrinfo.c

```
4294            /*
4295             * find first satisfactory answer
4296             */
4297            hp = &answer->hdr;
4298            ancount = ntohs(hp->ancount);
4299            qdcount = ntohs(hp->qdcount);
4300            bp = hostbuf;
4301            ep = hostbuf + sizeof hostbuf;
4302            cp = answer->buf + HFIXEDSZ;
4303            if (qdcount != 1) {
4304                    h_errno = NO_RECOVERY;
4305                    return (NULL);
4306            }
```
_____getaddrinfo.c

4297–4302 First, the QDCOUNT and ANCOUNT fields of the Header section are extracted
from the response and set in local variables. Variable cp points to the end of the Header
section, that is, the start of the query name in the Question section. The hostbuf buffer
is a temporary work space that stores domain names found in the response. Pointer bp is
initialized to point to the head of the buffer and will be adjusted as the response processing
proceeds; ep is set to point to the end of the buffer to avoid an overrun.

4303–4306 Within the currently standardized specifications, there should be exactly one query
name in a normal response (see the discussion in [EDNS1]). Otherwise, the response is
bogus and is discarded here.

Listing 3-14
_____getaddrinfo.c

```
4307            n = dn_expand(answer->buf, eom, cp, bp, ep - bp);
4308            if ((n < 0) || !(*name_ok)(bp)) {
```

```
4309                     h_errno = NO_RECOVERY;
4310                     return (NULL);
4311             }
4312             cp += n + QFIXEDSZ;
4313             if (qtype == T_A || qtype == T_AAAA || qtype == T_ANY) {
4314                     /* res_send() has already verified that the query name is the
4315                      * same as the one we sent; this just gets the expanded name
4316                      * (i.e., with the succeeding search-domain tacked on).
4317                      */
4318                     n = strlen(bp) + 1;                 /* for the \0 */
4319                     if (n >= MAXHOSTNAMELEN) {
4320                             h_errno = NO_RECOVERY;
4321                             return (NULL);
4322                     }
4323                     canonname = bp;
4324                     bp += n;
4325                     /* The qname can be abbreviated, but h_name is now absolute. */
4326                     qname = canonname;
4327             }
```
——getaddrinfo.c

4307–4311 The dn_expand() function expands the wire-format domain name pointed to
by cp and appends the name to the hostbuf buffer (pointed to by bp) as a string.
If the expansion function found an error, as indicated by a negative return value, or the
resulting string is not a valid name, then parsing the response fails and this function returns
NULL.

4312–4327 The rest of the Question section is of no interest and can be skipped; referring
to Figure 3-5 (page 214), the size of the Question section is the sum of the length of
the query name (n) and the fixed size of the type and class fields (4 bytes, the value of
the QFIXEDSZ constant). The query name is used to initialize canonname. The variable
qname is in fact initialized here because it has not been used so far and the if condition at
line 4313 always holds. Also, the code comment on line 4325 was derived from old resolver
code that based this implementation, where h_name appeared, and does not make sense
here.

Figure 3-16 depicts the processing of this code listing for the concrete example.

FIGURE 3-16

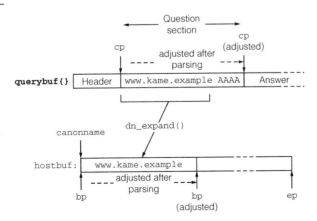

Question section processing of getanswer().

Next, get answer() examines each resource record in the Answer section. This part is a big loop and is hard to understand due to its size and unnecessary case analysis. Listing 3-15 shows a simplified outline of the loop to help understand the subsequent detailed discussion. Each resource record is processed at each iteration of the `while` loop. After examining the owner name by the `dn_expand()` function, the resource record type is checked to see if this is an alias (CNAME) or the expected record type (A or AAAA). If this record is an alias, `dn_expand()` extracts its RDATA (a domain name) and saves it in `canonname` for later use. Otherwise, a corresponding `addrinfo{}` structure is created and filled in using the RDATA of the A or AAAA record. This procedure is repeated unless a fatal error happens, in which case `had_error` is set to non-0.

Listing 3-15

```
                                                                        getaddrinfo.c
4330            while (acount-- > 0 && cp < eom && !had_error) {
4331                    n = dn_expand(answer->buf, eom, cp, bp, ep - bp);
                        (examine the owner name)
4348                    if (...
4349                        type == T_CNAME) {
4350                            n = dn_expand(answer->buf, eom, cp, tbuf, sizeof tbuf);
                                (save RDATA of CNAME in canonname)
4365                            continue;
4366                        }

                        (handle A or AAAA RR,
                         construct addrinfo entry for the RR)

4438                    if (!had_error)
4439                            haveanswer++;
4440            }
                                                                        getaddrinfo.c
```

Now the following listings contain more details of this processing.

Listing 3-16

```
                                                                        getaddrinfo.c
4328            haveanswer = 0;
4329            had_error = 0;
4330            while (acount-- > 0 && cp < eom && !had_error) {
4331                    n = dn_expand(answer->buf, eom, cp, bp, ep - bp);
4332                    if ((n < 0) || !(*name_ok)(bp)) {
4333                            had_error++;
4334                            continue;
4335                    }
4336                    cp += n;                        /* name */
4337                    type = _getshort(cp);
4338                    cp += INT16SZ;                  /* type */
4339                    class = _getshort(cp);
4340                    cp += INT16SZ + INT32SZ;        /* class, TTL */
4341                    n = _getshort(cp);
4342                    cp += INT16SZ;                  /* len */
4343                    if (class != C_IN) {
4344                            /* XXX - debug? syslog? */
4345                            cp += n;
4346                            continue;               /* XXX - had_error++ ? */
4347                    }
                                                                        getaddrinfo.c
```

4328–4329 Two local variables `haveanswer` and `had_error` remember the intermediate status of parsing. The former increments each time a requested resource record is found while the latter increments when an error occurs.

4330–4347 The `while` loop goes through the entire Answer section, examining the resource records contained in the section one by one. The `dn_expand()` function extracts the owner name of the record being parsed. The type and class values are copied in `type` and `class`, respectively, in host byte order. The class must be IN; otherwise the response is bogus because this should be a response to a query in the IN class, but the processing continues in case the remaining records are a requested answer. The TTL is not used in this function and is simply skipped.

The `INT16SZ` and `INT32SZ` constants have the obvious value—2 and 4.

Listing 3-17

getaddrinfo.c

```
4348                    if ((qtype == T_A || qtype == T_AAAA || qtype == T_ANY) &&
4349                        type == T_CNAME) {
4350                            n = dn_expand(answer->buf, eom, cp, tbuf, sizeof tbuf);
4351                            if ((n < 0) || !(*name_ok)(tbuf)) {
4352                                    had_error++;
4353                                    continue;
4354                            }
4355                            cp += n;
4356                            /* Get canonical name. */
4357                            n = strlen(tbuf) + 1;   /* for the \0 */
4358                            if (n > ep - bp || n >= MAXHOSTNAMELEN) {
4359                                    had_error++;
4360                                    continue;
4361                            }
4362                            strlcpy(bp, tbuf, ep - bp);
4363                            canonname = bp;
4364                            bp += n;
4365                            continue;
4366                    }
4367                    if (qtype == T_ANY) {
4368                            if (!(type == T_A || type == T_AAAA)) {
4369                                    cp += n;
4370                                    continue;
4371                            }
4372                    } else if (type != qtype) {
....
4380                            cp += n;
4381                            continue;                   /* XXX - had_error++ ? */
4382                    }
```

getaddrinfo.c

4348–4366 If the type of this record is CNAME, RDATA is a domain name (see Table 3-1, page 211), which is converted to a string by `dn_expand()`. On success of conversion, it is saved in the `hostbuf` buffer starting at `bp`, and `canonname` is adjusted to point to this name. This processing indicates `canonname` will point to RDATA of CNAMEs when multiple CNAMEs make a chain of aliases in the response.

Figure 3-17 shows related data structures at this point of code for the concrete example. Note that `canonname` is now adjusted to point to `turtle.kame.net`, which corresponds to RDATA of the CNAME record.

4367–4381 Any other record types except the queried type are of no interest, and the record is ignored.

FIGURE 3-17

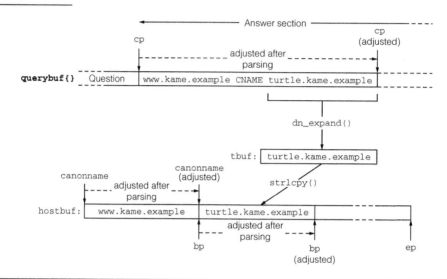

CNAME record processing.

Listing 3-18

getaddrinfo.c

```
4383                    switch (type) {
4384                    case T_A:
4385                    case T_AAAA:
4386                            if (strcasecmp(canonname, bp) != 0) {
....
4391                                    cp += n;
4392                                    continue;        /* XXX - had_error++ ? */
4393                            }
4394                            if (type == T_A && n != INADDRSZ) {
4395                                    cp += n;
4396                                    continue;
4397                            }
4398                            if (type == T_AAAA && n != IN6ADDRSZ) {
4399                                    cp += n;
4400                                    continue;
4401                            }
....
4412                            if (!haveanswer) {
4413                                    int nn;
4414
4415                                    canonname = bp;
4416                                    nn = strlen(bp) + 1;    /* for the \0 */
4417                                    bp += nn;
4418                            }
4419
4420                            /* don't overwrite pai */
4421                            ai = *pai;
4422                            ai.ai_family = (type == T_A) ? AF_INET : AF_INET6;
4423                            afd = find_afd(ai.ai_family);
4424                            if (afd == NULL) {
4425                                    cp += n;
4426                                    continue;
4427                            }
4428                            cur->ai_next = get_ai(&ai, afd, (const char *)cp);
4429                            if (cur->ai_next == NULL)
4430                                    had_error++;
```

```
4431                        while (cur && cur->ai_next)
4432                                cur = cur->ai_next;
4433                        cp += n;
4434                        break;
4435                default:
4436                        abort();
4437                }
4438                if (!had_error)
4439                        haveanswer++;
4440        }
```
getaddrinfo.c

4383–4401 The owner name of an A or a AAAA record should be identical (modulo letter case) to the query name or to the last RDATA of CNAME chain if a CNAME is contained. Otherwise, this record is not what the querier wants to get and is ignored. As commented, this may be better regarded as an error.

4394–4400 Both A and AAAA records have fixed RDATA lengths. If the length is not correct, the record is ignored. This should probably be treated as a fatal error, though, because the packet is clearly broken in this case.

4412–4418 If this is the first record of requested type, canonname is adjusted to point to the owner name string for this record. Pointer bp is moved to the end of the name so that the space pointed to by canonname can be used later (note that the buffer space starting at the address pointed to by bp can be overridden by dn_expand()).

4420–4436 The find_afd() and get_ai() functions allocate a new addrinfo{} structure with the address corresponding to this record, which is pointed to by cp. These functions were described in Chapter 7 of *IPv6 Core Protocols Implementation*. On success, the new addrinfo{} structure is appended to the list starting at sentinel (see Listing 3-12).

In the while statement at line 4431, the check for variable cur is redundant because it cannot be NULL in this code.

Figure 3-18 shows the result of this processing for the first AAAA record of the example response. The ai_canonname member of the addrinfo{} structure is still NULL at this point.

4438–4439 Finally, state variable haveanswer increments if no error has happened.

Listing 3-19

getaddrinfo.c
```
4441        if (haveanswer) {
4442                if (!canonname)
4443                        (void)get_canonname(pai, sentinel.ai_next, qname);
4444                else
4445                        (void)get_canonname(pai, sentinel.ai_next, canonname);
4446                h_errno = NETDB_SUCCESS;
4447                return sentinel.ai_next;
4448        }
4449
4450        h_errno = NO_RECOVERY;
4451        return NULL;
4452 }
```
getaddrinfo.c

FIGURE 3-18

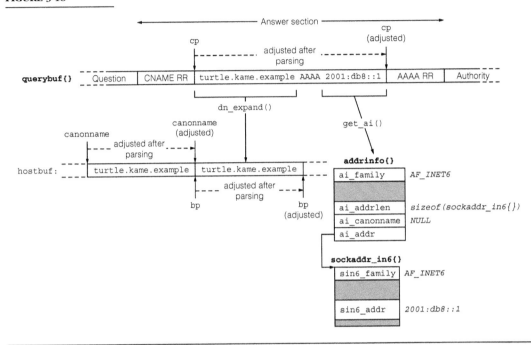

Constructing an addrinfo{} *structure from AAAA RR.*

4441–4445 If any requested answer is found, whether or not error happened, the
get_canonname() function copies the string pointed to by canonname into the first
entry of the addrinfo{} chain when AI_CANONNAME is specified as a hint. Note that
in this implementation canonname is always set to a non-NULL pointer, so the condition
of the if statement on line 4442 is always false.

The complete addrinfo{} chain to be returned to the caller for the example is
shown in Figure 3-19.

> The get_canonname() function copies the name only to the given addrinfo{}
> structure specified as the second argument, rather than to the entire chain. This is
> correct at this point per [RFC3493], since the specification does not require copying
> the canonical name to the addrinfo{} structures in the chain other than the first
> one, but this is actually not enough. Since the getaddrinfo() implementation may
> reorder the addrinfo{} chain as explained in Chapter 7 of the *Core Protocols* book,
> it must ensure that the first structure of the resulting chain stores the canonical name.
> The current implementation does not ensure this condition, which is a bug.

4446–4447 Finally, the global h_errno variable[9] is set to indicate a success, and the
addrinfo{} chain constructed in this function is returned.

---

9. This *variable* is thread-specific data, rather than a global variable, in recent versions of FreeBSD.

FIGURE 3-19

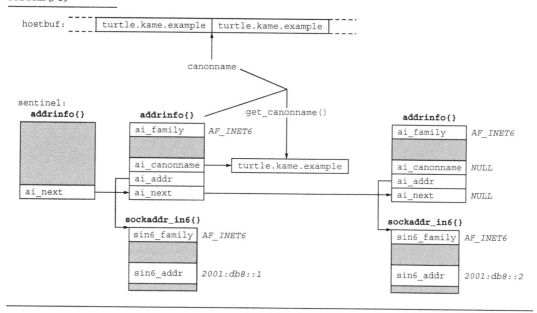

Completing the addrinfo{} *chain by filling in* ai_canonname.

4450–4451 If no requested record is found, h_errno is set to an error code and NULL is returned to the caller.

3.4.3 res_queryN() Function

The res_queryN() function sends DNS queries based on the res_target{} chain built in the _dns_getaddrinfo() function.

Initialization

Listing 3-20

```
                                                                  getaddrinfo.c
4741    static int
4742    res_queryN(name, target)
4743            const char *name;          /* domain name */
4744            struct res_target *target;
4745    {
4746            u_char buf[MAXPACKET];
4747            HEADER *hp;
4748            int n;
4749            struct res_target *t;
4750            int rcode;
4751            int ancount;
4752
4753            rcode = NOERROR;
4754            ancount = 0;
4755
4756            if ((_res.options & RES_INIT) == 0 && res_init() == -1) {
4757                    h_errno = NETDB_INTERNAL;
4758                    return (-1);
4759            }
                                                                  getaddrinfo.c
```

4756–4759 If the resolver routine is not yet initialized, `res_init()` is called to perform the initialization. Global variable `_res` contains resolver configuration parameters and the state of an outstanding query. This structure will be described in Section 3.4.4.

Send Queries

Listing 3-21
getaddrinfo.c

```
4761             for (t = target; t; t = t->next) {
4762                     int class, type;
4763                     u_char *answer;
4764                     int anslen;
4765
4766                     hp = (HEADER *)(void *)t->answer;
4767                     hp->rcode = NOERROR;          /* default */
4768
4769                     /* make it easier... */
4770                     class = t->qclass;
4771                     type = t->qtype;
4772                     answer = t->answer;
4773                     anslen = t->anslen;
4778
4779                     n = res_mkquery(QUERY, name, class, type, NULL, 0, NULL,
4780                         buf, sizeof(buf));
4781                     if (n <= 0) {
4786                             h_errno = NO_RECOVERY;
4787                             return (n);
4788                     }
4789                     n = res_send(buf, n, answer, anslen);
     ....
4800
4801                     if (n < 0 || hp->rcode != NOERROR || ntohs(hp->ancount) == 0) {
4802                             rcode = hp->rcode;       /* record most recent error */
4808                             continue;
4809                     }
4810
4811                     ancount += ntohs(hp->ancount);
4812
4813                     t->n = n;
4814             }
```
getaddrinfo.c

4761–4789 The `for` loop goes through the entire `res_target{}` chain, each of which corresponds to a particular type of DNS query. The `res_mkquery()` function builds a query message based on the class, type and host name, and stores the message in `buf`. The `res_send()` function then sends the query to the configured servers, waits for responses, and stores the result, if any, in `answer`.

> Recall the construction of the `res_target{}` chain in `_dns_getaddrinfo()` when `AF_UNSPEC` is specified for `getaddrinfo()`: the first element is for type AAAA and the second one is for type A. This ordering of the chain and the `for` loop in this function explain the ordering of DNS queries sent from the resolver library.

4801–4810 If `res_send()` fails, the Response Code indicates an erroneous result, or the Answer section is empty, then the possible error code is temporarily stored in `rcode`. The processing continues to the next `res_target{}` entry, if any.

It is particularly important to continue to the next entry rather than terminate the whole resolution when the response comes from a misbehaving authoritative server described in Section 3.3.5. For example, even if the Response Code indicates Server Failure for a AAAA query, it may be specific to that type of query, in which case a query for an A record may succeed and should be tried.

4811–4813 If `res_send()` succeeds, the counter `account` is increased by the number of resource records stored in the Answer section (`hp->account`). This value will be used in Listing 3-22 to determine whether any answer is returned throughout the resolution process.

Check Result

Listing 3-22

getaddrinfo.c

```
4816            if (account == 0) {
4817                    switch (rcode) {
4818                    case NXDOMAIN:
4819                            h_errno = HOST_NOT_FOUND;
4820                            break;
4821                    case SERVFAIL:
4822                            h_errno = TRY_AGAIN;
4823                            break;
4824                    case NOERROR:
4825                            h_errno = NO_DATA;
4826                            break;
4827                    case FORMERR:
4828                    case NOTIMP:
4829                    case REFUSED:
4830                    default:
4831                            h_errno = NO_RECOVERY;
4832                            break;
4833                    }
4834                    return (-1);
4835            }
4836            return (account);
4837    }
```

getaddrinfo.c

4816–4835 If no answer has been received (i.e., `account` is 0), the error code of the DNS is converted to a resolver error code, which is stored in `h_errno`, and −1 is returned to the caller as an indication of an erroneous result.

4836 On success this function returns the value of `account`, which is larger than 0.

3.4.4   Resolver State Structure

The resolver library maintains a common structure, `__res_state{}`, to keep the context of name resolution, including the addresses of caching servers and query timeout parameters.

Listing 3-23

resolv.h

```
 98    struct __res_state {
 99            int     retrans;        /* retransmition time interval */
100            int     retry;          /* number of times to retransmit */
101            u_long  options;        /* option flags - see below. */
102            int     nscount;        /* number of name servers */
103            struct sockaddr_in
```

```
104                nsaddr_list[MAXNS];          /* address of name server */
105     #define nsaddr  nsaddr_list[0]          /* for backward compatibility */
106                u_short  id;                 /* current message id */
107                char     *dnsrch[MAXDNSRCH+1]; /* components of domain to search */
108                char     defdname[256];      /* default domain (deprecated) */
109                u_long   pfcode;             /* RES_PRF_ flags - see below. */
110                unsigned ndots:4;            /* threshold for initial abs. query */
111                unsigned nsort:4;            /* number of elements in sort_list[] */
112                char     unused[3];
113                struct {
114                        struct in_addr   addr;
115                        u_int32_t        mask;
116                } sort_list[MAXRESOLVSORT];
117                char     pad[72];            /* on an i386 this means 512b total */
118     };
```
                                                                ———— resolv.h

The members of the structure that are referred to in the succeeding discussion are as follows: the `retrans` member is the initial timeout value of queries, and `retry` is the number of query retransmissions per each caching server when the resolver gets no responses. The `nsaddr_list` member is an array of `sockaddr_in{}` structures containing the IPv4 addresses of caching servers. The `sort_list` member stores IPv4 network prefixes or masks to sort the result of name resolution.

FreeBSD's resolver library described in this chapter uses a global instance of this structure, `_res`, to manage the resolver state. This variable is defined in the `res_init.c` file as shown in Listing 3-24.

Listing 3-24
                                                                ———— res_init.c

```
129     struct _res_state _res
        ....
133                 ;
```
                                                                ———— res_init.c

Since the size of `sockaddr_in{}` is smaller than that of `sockaddr_in6{}`, the `nsaddr_list` array cannot hold IPv6 addresses. A separate extended state structure to support IPv6, `_res_state_ext{}`, is defined for this purpose, as described in Listing 3-25. Likewise, the `sort_list` member is also extended in `_res_state_ext{}` to support IPv6 prefixes, but this book does not talk about the extension for `sort_list` because `getaddrinfo()`, which is of primary interest as a higher layer name resolution function, does not use the list.

Listing 3-25
                                                                ———— resolv.h

```
121     /*
122      * replacement of _res_state, separated to keep binary compatibility.
123      */
124     struct _res_state_ext {
125             struct sockaddr_storage nsaddr_list[MAXNS];
126             struct {
127                     int     af;                 /* address family for addr, mask */
128                     union {
129                             struct   in_addr ina;
130                             struct   in6_addr in6a;
131                     } addr, mask;
132             } sort_list[MAXRESOLVSORT];
133     };
```
                                                                ———— resolv.h

In the new structure, the `nsaddr_list` member is an array of the `sockaddr_storage{}` structures so that the list can support any types of addresses that the implementation supports, including IPv6 addresses.

The reason for using a separate structure is to provide backward *binary* compatibility as indicated in the code comment. If the `_res_state{}` structure was extended to contain IPv6 addresses, it would increase the size of the structure. Then application binary code that refers to the old definition of `_res_state{}` would not work as intended when dynamically linked with the new resolver library, because the application allocates a space for the structure in its data section and the new library could possibly override an invalid area in that section (Figure 3-20). Providing a separate structure while keeping the size of the original avoids this scenario. Although this is generally trouble with exported symbols and a dynamically linked library, rather than an IPv6-specific issue, this type of trouble is a common pitfall in porting existing code to support IPv6 due to the difference of address size. It should thus be worth noting here.

Like `_res_state{}`, the resolver library provides global instances of the `_res_state_ext{}`, `_res_ext`, which is also defined in `res_init.c`:

Listing 3-26

—— res_init.c
```
135     struct _res_state_ext _res_ext;
```
—— res_init.c

The `_res` and `_res_ext` variables are visible to applications by including `resolv.h`, although applications rarely touch these variables by themselves.

In this implementation, these global variables are shared by multiple threads without protection by a lock, and thus this library is not thread-safe. As noted in Chapter 7 of *IPv6 Core Protocols Implementation*, the KAME implementation of `getaddrinfo()` is not thread-safe partly because the underlying resolver library is not thread-safe, and the use of the global variables is the main reason for this.

FIGURE 3-20

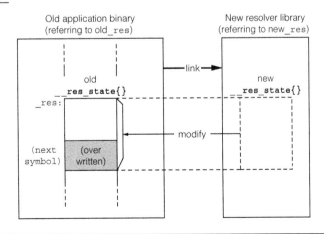

Binary backward compatibility issue about the size of `_res`.

Recent versions of FreeBSD solved this problem by ensuring that the instances referred to by _res and _res_ext are thread-specific.

3.4.5 `res_init()` Function

The res_init() function sets up a resolver library context mainly from the /etc/resolv.conf file. It is quite a large function, most of which is not directly related to IPv6. The following listings show the portions of this function that are of interest for IPv6-related discussions.

Set Up the Default Server

Listing 3-27
```
                                                                    res_init.c
159    int
160    res_init()
161    {
162            register FILE *fp;
163            register char *cp, **pp;
164            register int n;
165            char buf[MAXDNAME];
166            int nserv = 0;    /* number of nameserver records read from file */
 ....
196            if (!_res.retrans)
197                    _res.retrans = RES_TIMEOUT;
198            if (!_res.retry)
199                    _res.retry = 4;
 ....
222            _res.nscount = 1;
 ....
213            _res.nsaddr.sin_addr.s_addr = INADDR_ANY;
215            _res.nsaddr.sin_family = AF_INET;
216            _res.nsaddr.sin_port = htons(NAMESERVER_PORT);
217            _res.nsaddr.sin_len = sizeof(struct sockaddr_in);
219            if (sizeof(_res_ext.nsaddr) >= _res.nsaddr.sin_len)
220                    memcpy(&_res_ext.nsaddr, &_res.nsaddr, _res.nsaddr.sin_len);
 ....
                                                                    res_init.c
```

213–220 The nsaddr member, which is actually the first member of the nsaddr_list array (see Listing 3-24), is set to the all-zero IPv4 address by default. This means that the *localhost* will be used as the caching server when no servers are specified in the configuration file.

Read the Configuration File

Listing 3-28
```
                                                                    res_init.c
272            if ((fp = fopen(_PATH_RESCONF, "r")) != NULL) {
278                    /* read the config file */
279                    while (fgets(buf, sizeof(buf), fp) != NULL) {
280                            /* skip comments */
281                            if (*buf == ';' || *buf == '#')
282                                    continue;
 ....
                                                                    res_init.c
```

272–282 `_PATH_RESCONF` is a predefined constant specifying the `/etc/resolv.conf` file. Each line of this file specifies a particular parameter of the resolver library. Lines beginning with a semicolon or a pound-character are comments and are ignored.

Configure a Caching Server Address

Listing 3-29

_____*res_init.c*

```
334                        /* read nameservers to query */
335                        if (MATCH(buf, "nameserver") && nserv < MAXNS) {
337                            char *q;
338                            struct addrinfo hints, *res;
339                            char pbuf[NI_MAXSERV];
343
344                            cp = buf + sizeof("nameserver") - 1;
345                            while (*cp == ' ' || *cp == '\t')
346                                cp++;
348                            if ((*cp == '\0') || (*cp == '\n'))
349                                continue;
350                            for (q = cp; *q; q++) {
351                                if (isspace(*q)) {
352                                    *q = '\0';
353                                    break;
354                                }
355                            }
356                            memset(&hints, 0, sizeof(hints));
357                            hints.ai_flags = AI_NUMERICHOST;
358                            hints.ai_socktype = SOCK_DGRAM;
359                            snprintf(pbuf, sizeof(pbuf), "%d", NAMESERVER_PORT);
360                            if (getaddrinfo(cp, pbuf, &hints, &res) == 0 &&
361                                    res->ai_next == NULL) {
362                                if (res->ai_addrlen <=
sizeof(_res_ext.nsaddr_list[nserv])) {
363                                    memcpy(&_res_ext.nsaddr_list[nserv], res->ai_addr,
364                                        res->ai_addrlen);
365                                } else {
366                                    memset(&_res_ext.nsaddr_list[nserv], 0,
367                                        sizeof(_res_ext.nsaddr_list[nserv]));
368                                }
369                                if (res->ai_addrlen <=
sizeof(_res.nsaddr_list[nserv])) {
370                                    memcpy(&_res.nsaddr_list[nserv], res->ai_addr,
371                                        res->ai_addrlen);
372                                } else {
373                                    memset(&_res.nsaddr_list[nserv], 0,
374                                        sizeof(_res.nsaddr_list[nserv]));
375                                }
376                                nserv++;
377                            }
378                            if (res)
379                                freeaddrinfo(res);
391                            continue;
392                        }
....
522                    }
523                    if (nserv > 1)
524                        _res.nscount = nserv;
....
```

_____*res_init.c*

— *Lines 362 and 369 are broken here for layout reasons. However, they are a single line of code.*

335–355 If the line begins with `nameserver`, it specifies the address of a DNS caching server. The address should be a numeric IPv4 or IPv6 address.

356–361 The getaddrinfo() function tries to convert the specified string to a socket address structure with the well-known port number for DNS, 53. Note that the AI_NUMERICHOST flag is specified in the hints structure. Without this flag, this call to getaddrinfo() might cause another call to this function recursively, resulting in an indefinite iteration of calls and a stack overflow.

362–392 If the next nsaddr_list entry of _res_ext{} has enough space to store the conversion result, the socket address structure is copied into the entry; otherwise that entry is zero-cleared. The next nsaddr_list entry of _res is filled in a similar fashion. Since the result must be either an IPv4 or IPv6 address, the entry in _res_ext{} should actually have enough space; the else case at line 365 is explicitly considered just for safety. On the other hand, the entry in _res does not have enough space to contain a sockaddr_in6{} structure, and it will be cleared in this case.

523–524 The nscount member of _res is set to the total number of configured caching server addresses.

Exiting

Listing 3-30

```
─────────────────────────────────────────────────────res_init.c
528            (void) fclose(fp);
529        }

 ....

568            _res.options |= RES_INIT;
569            return (0);
570    }
─────────────────────────────────────────────────────res_init.c
```

568–569 The RES_INIT flag is set in the options member to indicate that initialization has been completed.

Example of Server Configuration

Suppose that there are two caching server addresses, one for IPv4 and the other for IPv6. Then the configuration in the /etc/resolv.conf file would be as follows:

```
nameserver 192.0.2.1
nameserver 2001:db8::1234
```

Figure 3-21 depicts the contents of the _res{} and _res_ext{} structures after the initialization in the res_init() function. Since _res{} cannot store IPv6 addresses as caching servers, the second element of the nsaddr_list array is zero-cleared. On the other hand, _res_ext{} can have any type of addresses, and the second element of the nsaddr_list array is the socket address structure for the IPv6 address 2001:db8::1234. The list elements are actually sockaddr_storage{} structures, and usually have a trailing free area.

As will be shown in Section 3.4.6, the zero-cleared second element of nsaddr_list in _res{} indicates that the corresponding element in _res_ext{} should be used.

3.4.6 res_send() Function

The res_send() function is a primitive of the resolver libraries, in that it sends a DNS query for a particular type and waits for a response. This function is big, and a full line-by-line description

FIGURE 3-21

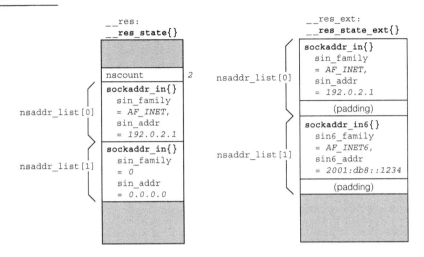

Global state structures when both IPv4 and IPv6 addresses are specified in the /etc/resolv.conf *file.*

would be lengthy. Since most of the function is a common general process of the DNS and is not directly related to IPv6, this section will describe selected portions of this function, concentrating on the main topic of this chapter. Specifically, the discussion will focus on a common simple scenario where one or more UDP queries are sent to one or more caching servers and no special resolver options are specified; TCP queries will not be considered.

Overview

Listing 3-31 is an overview of the entire structure of the res_send() function focusing on network operations (line indentation is modified for readability). This function essentially consists of two big nested for loops. In the inner loop (lines 391 through 941), res_send() iterates through all configured caching servers. A UDP socket is created for UDP transaction, which is then connected to the selected server address so that the socket can receive ICMP errors. Next, res_send() sends the query message given by the caller over the socket, and waits for a response in the select() system call. If a response is returned, it is stored in the buffer pointed to by ans and is parsed. This function returns with the length of the response message once it gets a valid response. If res_send() cannot get a valid response from any of the configured servers, the above procedure is repeated with the configured retry times at most in the outer for loop or until the total timeout period has passed (not shown in this overview code). On failure, this function returns −1 to indicate the error.

Listing 3-31

————————————————————————————————————res_send.c

```
356    int
357    res_send(buf, buflen, ans, anssiz)
358          const u_char *buf;
359          int buflen;
360          u_char *ans;
361          int anssiz;
362    {
```
(local variables, initialization)

```
387                /*
388                 * Send request, RETRY times, or until successful
389                 */
390                for (try = 0; try < _res.retry; try++) {
391                    for (ns = 0; ns < _res.nscount; ns++) {
```

(server selection)

```
453                    if (v_circuit) {
```

(TCP transaction: omitted)

```
605                    } else {
606                        /*
607                         * Use datagrams.
608                         */
    ....
618                        s = socket(af, SOCK_DGRAM, 0);
    ....
672                        if (connect(s, nsap, salen) < 0) {
```

(error handling)

```
678                            goto next_ns;
679                        }
    ....
682                        if (send(s, (char*)buf, buflen, 0) != buflen) {
```

(error handling)

```
686                            goto next_ns;
687                        }
    ....
756                        n = select(s+1, &dsmask, (fd_set *)NULL,
757                                (fd_set *)NULL, &timeout);
    ....
783                        if (n == 0) {
```

(Timeout handling)

```
791                            goto next_ns;
792                        }
    ....
795                        resplen = recvfrom(s, (char*)ans, anssiz, 0,
796                                    (struct sockaddr *)&from, &fromlen);
```

(Validate and parse response)

```
937
938                    }
939                return (resplen);
940    next_ns: ;
941            } /*foreach ns*/
942        } /*foreach retry*/
```

(Cleanup for error cases)

```
951        return (-1);
952    }
```
——— res_send.c

Below are more detailed descriptions of the res_send() implementation.

Initialization

Listing 3-32

——— res_send.c
```
356    int
357    res_send(buf, buflen, ans, anssiz)
```

```
358              const u_char *buf;
359              int buflen;
360              u_char *ans;
361              int anssiz;
362      {
363              HEADER *hp = (HEADER *) buf;
364              HEADER *anhp = (HEADER *) ans;
365              int gotsomewhere, connreset, terrno, try, v_circuit, resplen, ns;
366              register int n;
367              u_int badns;          /* XXX NSMAX can't exceed #/bits in this var */
368              int changeserver = 0;
369              struct sockaddr_storage newnsap;
370
371              if ((_res.options & RES_INIT) == 0 && res_init() == -1) {
372                      /* errno should have been set by res_init() in this case. */
373                      return (-1);
374              }
375              if (anssiz < HFIXEDSZ) {
376                      errno = EINVAL;
377                      return (-1);
378              }
379              DprintQ((_res.options & RES_DEBUG) || (_res.pfcode & RES_PRF_QUERY),
380                      (stdout, ";; res_send()\n"), buf, buflen);
381              v_circuit = (_res.options & RES_USEVC) || buflen > PACKETSZ;
382              gotsomewhere = 0;
383              connreset = 0;
384              terrno = ETIMEDOUT;
385              badns = 0;
```
                                                                                _____res_send.c

371–385 If the resolver state, _res, has not been initialized, res_init() will be called to do the initial setup. In the intended call path described here, however, this does not happen because res_queryN() should have done this (recall Listing 3-20, page 243). If v_circuit is set to non-zero, it means TCP should be used as the DNS packet transport, but that is not considered in this book.

Server Address Setup

Listing 3-33
                                                                                _____res_send.c
```
387              /*
388               * Send request, RETRY times, or until successful
389               */
390              for (try = 0; try < _res.retry; try++) {
391                  for (ns = 0; ns < _res.nscount; ns++) {
392                          struct sockaddr *nsap = get_nsaddr(ns);
394                          socklen_t salen;
398
399                          if (nsap->sa_len)
400                                  salen = nsap->sa_len;
402                          else if (nsap->sa_family == AF_INET6)
403                                  salen = sizeof(struct sockaddr_in6);
405                          else if (nsap->sa_family == AF_INET)
406                                  salen = sizeof(struct sockaddr_in);
407                          else
408                                  salen = 0;          /*unknown, die on connect*/
```
                                                                                _____res_send.c

390–391 The number of query retransmissions is determined by two parameters: the number of server addresses and the number of retries per server. The nscount member of _res{} specifies the former, and the retry member specifies the latter.

392–408 The get_nsaddr() function (Listing 3-42, page 259) returns the address of the caching server that is indexed by the function argument (ns in this case). In this implementation, there are actually two possible address families: `AF_INET6` for IPv6 and `AF_INET` for IPv4. The variable `salen` is set to the length of the corresponding socket address structure.

Check Bad Server

Listing 3-34

```
                                                                _____ res_send.c
410        same_ns:
411                    if (badns & (1 << ns)) {
412                            res_close();
413                            goto next_ns;
414                    }
                                                                _____ res_send.c
```

411–414 The variable `badns` is a bit mask that records *bad* caching servers. A server is recorded as *bad* when a socket operation has failed, the server has returned a bogus response, or the server has returned a fatal error. These cases will be shown later in this function. If the current server is known to be bad, `res_close()` releases any temporary resources for the communication with the server, including an open socket, and exits from the inner loop.

Setup Socket

Listing 3-35

```
                                                                _____ res_send.c
    . . . .
453                    if (v_circuit) {

    . . . .

605                    } else {
606                            /*
607                             * Use datagrams.
608                             */
609                            struct timeval timeout, finish, now;
610                            fd_set dsmask;
611                            struct sockaddr_storage from;
612                            int fromlen;
613
614                            if ((s < 0) || vc || (af != nsap->sa_family)) {
615                                    if (vc)
616                                            res_close();
617                                    af = nsap->sa_family;
618                                    s = socket(af, SOCK_DGRAM, 0);
619                                    if (s < 0) {
```
(error handling (omitted))
```
632                                    }
633    #ifdef IPV6_USE_MIN_MTU
634                                    if (af == AF_INET6) {
635                                            const int yes = 1;
636                                            (void)setsockopt(s, IPPROTO_IPV6,
637                                                IPV6_USE_MIN_MTU, &yes,
638                                                sizeof(yes));
639                                    }
640    #endif
641                                    connected = 0;
642                            }
                                                                _____ res_send.c
```

453–632 As noted in listing 3-35, we only consider the case where `v_circuit` is 0 and thus UDP transport is used. If no open socket exists, TCP has been used as the transport (in which case `vc` is set to 1), or different address family was previously used, then a new socket is created. Additionally, if TCP was previously used, the socket is closed beforehand.

> It may look safer in the different address family case to try to close the old socket as well as in switching from TCP, but this code is actually workable since in this case the previous socket has already been closed in error handling.

634–642 If this is an `AF_INET6` socket, the `IPV6_USE_MIN_MTU` option is enabled so that large queries are always fragmented at the IPv6 minimum MTU, which is 1280 bytes including the IPv6 and UDP header (see Chapter 7 of *IPv6 Core Protocols Implementation*). This option is set because performing path MTU discovery does not really make sense for a normal DNS transaction where only a few UDP packets are involved.

> In practice, this does not matter for two reasons. First, the length of DNS data packets over UDP is limited to 512 bytes unless EDNS0 is used (Section 3.3.4), and thus it is very unlikely for UDP query packets to exceed the minimum MTU. Second, even if EDNS0 is used, a DNS query sent from a stub resolver to a caching server is usually small enough to fit in the minimum MTU size.

Connect Socket and Send Query

Listing 3-36

```
                                                              res_send.c
643                     /*
644                      * On a 4.3BSD+ machine (client and server,
645                      * actually), sending to a nameserver datagram
646                      * port with no nameserver will cause an
647                      * ICMP port unreachable message to be returned.
648                      * If our datagram socket is "connected" to the
649                      * server, we get an ECONNREFUSED error on the next
650                      * socket operation, and select returns if the
651                      * error message is received.  We can thus detect
652                      * the absence of a nameserver without timing out.
653                      * If we have sent queries to at least two servers,
654                      * however, we don't want to remain connected,
655                      * as we wish to receive answers from the first
656                      * server to respond.
657                      *
658                      * When the option "insecure1" is specified, we'd
659                      * rather expect to see responses from an "unknown"
660                      * address.  In order to let the kernel accept such
661                      * responses, do not connect the socket here.
662                      * XXX: or do we need an explicit option to disable
663                      * connecting?
664                      */
665                     if (!(_res.options & RES_INSECURE1) &&
666                         (_res.nscount == 1 || (try == 0 && ns == 0))) {
667                             /*
668                              * Connect only if we are sure we won't
669                              * receive a response from another server.
670                              */
671                             if (!connected) {
672                                     if (connect(s, nsap, salen) < 0) {
```

```
673                                              Aerror(stderr,
674                                                      "connect(dg)",
675                                                      errno, nsap);
676                                              badns |= (1 << ns);
677                                              res_close();
678                                              goto next_ns;
679                                      }
680                                      connected = 1;
681                              }
682                      if (send(s, (char*)buf, buflen, 0) != buflen) {
683                              Perror(stderr, "send", errno);
684                              badns |= (1 << ns);
685                              res_close();
686                              goto next_ns;
687                      }
```
——————————————————————————————————————— res_send.c

665–681 If there is only one possible caching server to try or this is the first try of the first caching server (note that we assume no resolver option is specified in `_res.options` in this discussion), which is assumed in this simplified scenario, then the UDP socket is connected to the caching server's address. As commented in lines 643 to 664, connecting the socket will help receive ICMP errors when the destination is unreachable for some reason and help detect the erroneous case quickly.

682–687 The query packet is then sent to the server. If any of these socket operations fails, this server is marked as *bad*, and the next possible server will be tried immediately.

Wait for Response

Listing 3-37
——————————————————————————————————————— res_send.c

```
688                      } else {
```

(atypical case (omitted))

```
734                      }
735
736                      /*
737                       * Wait for reply
738                       */
739                      timeout.tv_sec = (_res.retrans << try);
740                      if (try > 0)
741                              timeout.tv_sec /= _res.nscount;
742                      if ((long) timeout.tv_sec <= 0)
743                              timeout.tv_sec = 1;
744                      timeout.tv_usec = 0;
```

(setting for error handling (omitted))

```
748      wait:
749                      if (s < 0 || s >= FD_SETSIZE) {
750                              Perror(stderr, "s out-of-bounds", EMFILE);
751                              res_close();
752                              goto next_ns;
753                      }
754                      FD_ZERO(&dsmask);
755                      FD_SET(s, &dsmask);
756                      n = select(s+1, &dsmask, (fd_set *)NULL,
757                              (fd_set *)NULL, &timeout);
```
——————————————————————————————————————— res_send.c

739–757 The resolver waits for a response from the server using the `select()` system call. It only watches the socket it opened (variable `s`), and waits for a period determined by the retries and the number of servers.

By default, the `retrans` parameter, which is the base timeout, is set to 5 (sec), and the `retry` parameter, the upper limit of retries for each caching server, is set to 4.

Handle Timeout

Listing 3-38

```
                                                                ____res_send.c
758                             if (n < 0) {

(error handling (omitted))

782                             }
783                             if (n == 0) {
784                                     /*
785                                      * timeout
786                                      */
787                                     Dprint(_res.options & RES_DEBUG,
788                                            (stdout, ";; timeout\n"));
789                                     gotsomewhere = 1;
790                                     res_close();
791                                     goto next_ns;
792                             }
                                                                ____res_send.c
```

783–792 If the `select()` call indicates a timeout, the current socket is closed and the next caching server will be tried. Note that the server is not regarded as *bad* in this case, and thus can be tried again later.

Receive and Validate Response

Listing 3-39

```
                                                                ____res_send.c
793                             errno = 0;
794                             fromlen = sizeof(from);
795                             resplen = recvfrom(s, (char*)ans, anssiz, 0,
796                                                (struct sockaddr *)&from, &fromlen);
797                             if (resplen <= 0) {
798                                     Perror(stderr, "recvfrom", errno);
799                                     res_close();
800                                     goto next_ns;
801                             }
802                             gotsomewhere = 1;
803                             if (resplen < HFIXEDSZ) {
804                                     /*
805                                      * Undersized message.
806                                      */
807                                     Dprint(_res.options & RES_DEBUG,
808                                            (stdout, ";; undersized: %d\n",
809                                             resplen));
810                                     terrno = EMSGSIZE;
811                                     badns |= (1 << ns);
812                                     res_close();
813                                     goto next_ns;
814                             }
                                                                ____res_send.c
```

793–814 At this point, some data from the receiving socket is available. If the `recvfrom()`
call fails or the received data is not large enough to contain a DNS response, the socket
is closed and the next caching server will be tried. In the latter case, the original server is
marked as *bad*.

Handle Exceptions

Listing 3-40

```
                                                                    res_send.c
```

(response validation (omitted))

```
861                     if (anhp->rcode == SERVFAIL ||
862                         anhp->rcode == NOTIMP ||
863                         anhp->rcode == REFUSED) {
864                             DprintQ(_res.options & RES_DEBUG,
865                                     (stdout, "server rejected query:\n"),
866                                     ans, (resplen>anssiz)?anssiz:resplen);
867                             badns |= (1 << ns);
868                             res_close();
869                             /* don't retry if called from dig */
870                             if (!_res.pfcode)
871                                     goto next_ns;
872                     }
873                     if (!(_res.options & RES_IGNTC) && anhp->tc) {
```

(truncation, and fall back to TCP (omitted))

```
887                     }
888             } /*if vc/dg*/
    ....
```

```
                                                                    res_send.c
```

861–872 If the response provides a Response Code of Server Failure (`SERVFAIL`), Not Implemented (`NOTIMP`), or Refused (`REFUSED`), each indicates some error, the current caching
server is marked as *bad*, and the next server will be tried.

873–887 If the TC (TrunCation) bit is on in the response, it means the response was too large
to fit in a UDP packet. In this case, the resolver will fall back to TCP transport. Since it
rarely happens in a usual environment, and the callback mechanism complicates the code,
it is omitted in this description.

Exiting

Listing 3-41

```
                                                                    res_send.c
```

```
939                     return (resplen);
940         next_ns: ;
941             } /*foreach ns*/
942         } /*foreach retry*/
943         res_close();
944         if (!v_circuit)
945                 if (!gotsomewhere)
946                         errno = ECONNREFUSED;       /* no nameservers found */
947                 else
948                         errno = ETIMEDOUT;          /* no answer obtained */
949         else
950                 errno = terrno;
951         return (-1);
952     }
```

```
                                                                    res_send.c
```

939–942 If the response looks valid so far, the transaction succeeds in the level of `res_send()`.
The length of the response is returned to the caller. The response packet is stored in the
buffer pointed to by `ans`, which was provided by the caller.

943–952 If all retries for all caching servers have failed and the socket is still open, the socket
is closed, and −1 is returned to indicate the failure.

Functions `get_nsaddr()` and `res_close()` are shown below, which are subroutines
called from the `res_send()` function.

Listing 3-42
─── res_send.c

```
194    static struct sockaddr *
195    get_nsaddr(n)
196         size_t n;
197    {
198
199         if (!_res.nsaddr_list[n].sin_family) {
200                /*
201                 * - _res_ext.nsaddr_list[n] holds an address that is larger
202                 *   than struct sockaddr, and
203                 * - user code did not update _res.nsaddr_list[n].
204                 */
205                return (struct sockaddr *)&_res_ext.nsaddr_list[n];
206         } else {
207                /*
208                 * - user code updated _res.nsaddr_list[n], or
209                 * - _res.nsaddr_list[n] has the same content as
210                 *   _res_ext.nsaddr_list[n].
211                 */
212                return (struct sockaddr *)&_res.nsaddr_list[n];
213         }
214    }
```
─── res_send.c

199–213 If the nth address is an IPv4 address, it is stored in the `nsaddr_list` of the base
`_res{}` structure; otherwise, it is stored in the external `_res_ext{}` structure. Function
`get_nsaddr()` returns an appropriate pointer to the socket address structure according
to the value of the `sin_family` member in the `_res{}` structure.

Listing 3-43
─── res_send.c

```
961    void
962    res_close()
963    {
964         if (s >= 0) {
965                (void) close(s);
966                s = -1;
967                connected = 0;
968                vc = 0;
969                af = 0;
970         }
971    }
```
─── res_send.c

964–970 The global socket variable `s` is closed if it is still open, and is reset to −1. Other global
parameters are also reinitialized.

3.4.7   IPv6 Reverse Lookup: `_dns_ghbyaddr()` Function

The `_dns_ghbyaddr()` function is called from `getipnodebyaddr()` as a backend of
`getnameinfo()`. It constructs DNS query names for reverse mapping of a given IPv4 or
IPv6 address, sends queries, and waits for a response through the `res_query()`
function.

Ignore Link-Local Addresses

Listing 3-44

————————————————————————————————————name6.c

```
1443    static struct hostent *
1444    _dns_ghbyaddr(const void *addr, int addrlen, int af, int *errp)
1445    {
1446            int n;
1447            struct hostent *hp;
1448            u_char c, *cp;
1449            char *bp;
1450            struct hostent hbuf;
1451            int na;
1453            static const char hex[] = "0123456789abcdef";
1455            querybuf *buf;
1456            char qbuf[MAXDNAME+1];
1457            char *hlist[2];
1458            char *tld6[] = { "ip6.arpa", "ip6.int", NULL };
1459            char *tld4[] = { "in-addr.arpa", NULL };
1460            char **tld;
1461
1463            /* XXX */
1464            if (af == AF_INET6 && IN6_IS_ADDR_LINKLOCAL((struct in6_addr *)addr))
1465                    return NULL;
```

————————————————————————————————————name6.c

1464–1465 If the given address is an IPv6 link-local address, a negative response is returned
without sending DNS queries. This check is actually meaningless, because all callers of
the function do the same check in this implementation.

Set Up the TLD

Listing 3-45

————————————————————————————————————name6.c

```
1468            switch (af) {
1470            case AF_INET6:
1471                    tld = tld6;
1472                    break;
1474            case AF_INET:
1475                    tld = tld4;
1476                    break;
1477            default:
1478                    return NULL;
1479            }
```

————————————————————————————————————name6.c

1468–1479 The variable `tld` is an array of strings, whose elements specify the common domain
name suffix(es) for reverse lookups. For IPv6, `ip6.arpa` is first used, and then `ip6.int`
will be tried. For IPv4, `in-addr.arpa` is used.

It does not make sense to try ip6.int anymore because the use of this domain has been deprecated as explained in Section 3.3.6. Any query about the name under this domain simply results in a negative response. The resolver library provided in recent versions of BSD variants, including FreeBSD, now only tries the ip6.arpa domain.

Set Up the Resolver Context

Listing 3-46

```
                                                                    ____name6.c
1481             if ((_res.options & RES_INIT) == 0) {
1482                     if (res_init() < 0) {
1483                             *errp = h_errno;
1484                             return NULL;
1485                     }
1486             }
                                                                    ____name6.c
```

1481–1486 If this is the first time the resolver library is used, res_init() is called to initialize the resolver context, _res{} and _res_ext{}.

Initialize Other Variables

Listing 3-47

```
                                                                    ____name6.c
1487             memset(&hbuf, 0, sizeof(hbuf));
1488             hbuf.h_name = NULL;
1489             hbuf.h_addrtype = af;
1490             hbuf.h_length = addrlen;
1491             na = 0;
1492
1493             buf = malloc(sizeof(*buf));
1494             if (buf == NULL) {
1495                     *errp = NETDB_INTERNAL;
1496                     return NULL;
1497             }
                                                                    ____name6.c
```

1487–1491 The variable hbuf is an instance of the standard hostent{} structure to store a temporary result within this function. The variable na is actually unused and can be ignored.

1493–1497 The variable buf points to a querybuf{} union, which is the same as the one used for the _dns_getaddrinfo() function (see Listing 3-4, page 230).

Build and Send Queries

Listing 3-48

```
                                                                    ____name6.c
1498             for (/* nothing */; *tld; tld++) {
1499                     /*
1500                      * XXX assumes that MAXDNAME is big enough - error checks
1501                      * has been made by callers
1502                      */
1503                     n = 0;
1504                     bp = qbuf;
```

```
1505                    cp = (u_char *)addr+addrlen-1;
1506                    switch (af) {
1508                    case AF_INET6:
1509                            for (; n < addrlen; n++, cp--) {
1510                                    c = *cp;
1511                                    *bp++ = hex[c & 0xf];
1512                                    *bp++ = '.';
1513                                    *bp++ = hex[c >> 4];
1514                                    *bp++ = '.';
1515                            }
1516                            strcpy(bp, *tld);
1517                            break;
1519                    case AF_INET:
1520                            for (; n < addrlen; n++, cp--) {
1521                                    c = *cp;
1522                                    if (c >= 100)
1523                                            *bp++ = '0' + c / 100;
1524                                    if (c >= 10)
1525                                            *bp++ = '0' + (c % 100) / 10;
1526                                    *bp++ = '0' + c % 10;
1527                                    *bp++ = '.';
1528                            }
1529                            strcpy(bp, *tld);
1530                            break;
1531                    }
1532
1533                    n = res_query(qbuf, C_IN, T_PTR, buf->buf, sizeof buf->buf);
```
                                                                                     ————name6.c

1498–1505 The `for` loop goes through all possible domain suffixes for reverse lookups; `bp` points to the head of the buffer containing the query name; `cp` is set to point to the end of the address.

1506–1517 If an IPv6 address is given, it is converted into the nibble format explained in Section 3.3.2 as follows: each single byte of the address is divided into the uppermost 4 bits and the lowermost 4 bits. Then each 4-bit chunk (i.e., a nibble) is converted into the corresponding ASCII hexadecimal character. Finally, the two characters are concatenated with periods as delimiters, where the lower part of the character leads. For example, one byte of 0x8a is converted to the string `"a.8."` in the inner `for` loop. The `for` loop repeats this process for the entire address, concatenating the latest string to the previous result. Then the well-known domain string is appended at the end of the name.

Note that the inner `for` loop starts at the end of the IPv6 address and the pointer `cp` moves backward as the loop continues. Figures 3-22 and 3-23 illustrate an example of this process for the IPv6 address `2001:db8:...:abcd`. Figure 3-22 shows the intermediate state when the last 2 bytes of the address are parsed, which corresponds to the first 2 cycles of the loop. Figure 3-23 depicts the final query name at the completion of the process with the domain suffix of `ip6.arpa`.

> It is redundant to repeat the process of the inner `for` loop in every iteration of the outer `for` loop because `af` and `addr` are invariant throughout the outer loop. This should be done as common initialization before entering the outer `for` loop.

1519–1531 A similar process is taken for an IPv4 address except that each byte is converted into a decimal number. For example, it converts an IPv4 address `203.178.141.194` into the domain name `194.141.178.203.in-addr.arpa`.

FIGURE 3-22

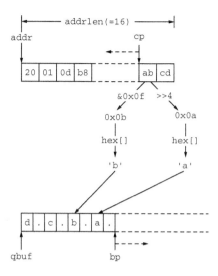

Building query name for an IPv6 reverse lookup.

FIGURE 3-23

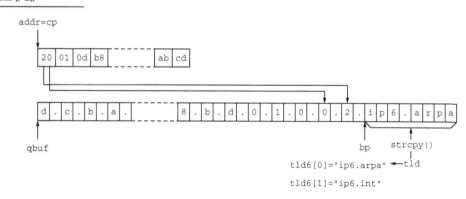

Complete query name for an IPv6 reverse lookup.

1533 `res_query()` constructs a DNS query message, sends it to caching servers, and waits for a response. The actual process is done in the backend functions, `res_mkquery()` and `res_send()` (see Figure 3-12, page 227). As shown in the arguments, the class of the query is IN and the type is PTR.

Collect Answer

Listing 3-49

name6.c

```
1534            if (n < 0) {
1535                    *errp = h_errno;
1536                    continue;
```

```
1537                       }
1538                       hp = getanswer(buf, n, qbuf, T_PTR, &hbuf, errp);
1539                       if (!hp)
1540                               continue;
1541                       hbuf.h_addrtype = af;
1542                       hbuf.h_length = addrlen;
1543                       hbuf.h_addr_list = hlist;
1544                       hlist[0] = (char *)addr;
1545                       hlist[1] = NULL;
1546                       return _hpcopy(&hbuf, errp);
1547            }
```
———————————————————————————————— name6.c

1534–1536 If `res_query()` fails for some reason, it should return a negative value and `h_errno` should have an error code. The error code is temporarily stored in `*errp`, and the next top-level domain will be tried, if any.

One common error here is "host not found," which corresponds to the Name Error code of the DNS. In this case, `h_errno` should have been set to `HOST_NOT_FOUND`. The details of the `res_query()` function are omitted here, but the logic is almost the same as that of `res_queryN()` (Section 3.4.3).

1538–1546 The `getanswer()` function analyzes the response and constructs the result in a `hostent{}` structure passed from `_dns_ghbyaddr()` as the fifth argument (a pointer to `hbuf`). It returns a non-NULL pointer (which should actually be the pointer to `hbuf`) on success, in which case the `hostent{}` structure is filled with other parameters. Finally, `_hpcopy()` will allocate memory for a new `hostent{}` structure, copy the result stored in `hbuf` to the new structure, and return the pointer to the new one. The resulting pointer is then the return value of `_dns_ghbyaddr()` itself.

> Here is a serious bug. The temporary buffer pointed to by `buf` must be released before exiting. A memory leak occurs every time this function is called. In particular, every call to `getnameinfo()` that involves DNS reverse lookups can cause a memory leak. This has been fixed in later versions of the library code.

Error Handling

Listing 3-50
———————————————————————————————— name6.c
```
1548           free(buf);
1549           return NULL;
1550     }
```
———————————————————————————————— name6.c

1548–1549 If queries failed for all possible domain suffixes, the temporary buffer to store DNS responses is released and a NULL pointer is returned to indicate the failure.

3.5   IPv6 DNS Operation with BIND

BIND (Berkeley Internet Name Domain) is the most widely used implementation of DNS. It is developed by Internet Systems Consortium, Inc. (ISC), and is available as free software at ISC's Web site, http://www.isc.org/bind/. BIND is also available at ISC's FTP site, ftp://ftp.isc.org/isc/.

Right now, two major versions of BIND are mainly used: versions 8 and 9 (called BIND8 and BIND9, respectively).

All versions of BIND9 provide IPv6 transport support, as do 8.4 and later versions of BIND8. The implementation status of IPv6 content is a bit complicated. As seen in Section 3.3.6, some new standards of DNS contents for IPv6 were introduced and then deprecated. Some versions of BIND support the deprecated standard, and some others do not, as per the recent change in standardization. In any case, however, it is generally advisable to use the latest versions. The standardization status is now mature, and the latest implementations have already caught up to the latest standards.

Recall that three types of elements are commonly used in DNS operation: authoritative servers, caching servers, and stub resolvers. Any BIND package contains all three elements. A single network daemon called **named** provides the server function. The **named** daemon can act as an authoritative only server, a caching only server, and a server supporting both the roles simultaneously. On the other hand, a separate portable resolver library, often called *libbind*, provides the stub resolver function. The libbind library is actually adopted in many operating systems including BSD variants, and, in fact, the library routines seen in Section 3.4 were derived from libbind. Conversely, some IPv6 extensions to the original libbind developed by the KAME project were merged back into recent libbind implementations.

The rest of this chapter will concentrate on the server side of BIND, primarily BIND9. It is the recommended version by ISC, particularly for advanced features such as IPv6 support. The support for IPv6 in BIND8 was provided for users who cannot upgrade to BIND9 for some reason, and is more limited than the IPv6 support in BIND9.[10]

The latest release version of BIND9, as of this writing, is 9.3, and is the main focus of this chapter. The IPv6 support has been massively improved since 9.2, especially about the transport support. For example, BIND9 servers could not listen on a selected subset of IPv6 addresses for queries until 9.3. Also, BIND 9.2 was already in maintenance mode when the IETF obsoleted some IPv6 related protocol standards (Section 3.3.6), and still contains the deprecated protocol features.

3.5.1 Overview of BIND9

As already explained, BIND9 is the latest major release of BIND. While the configuration syntax is mostly compatible to BIND8, the implementation is totally different. In fact, BIND9 was designed and implemented from scratch. No code fragment in prior versions was used in the BIND9 implementation; the only exception is the stub resolver implementation, which is a copy of the corresponding part of BIND8. The stub resolver routines based on the BIND8 code is provided with the BIND9 package for the convenience of system developers who want to use the BIND9 program in their system while incorporating the resolver library to the same system.

In terms of technical features, BIND9 has the following characteristics:

- Full compliance to the latest DNS protocol standards
- IPv6 support, both for transport and contents

---

10. However, most basic configurations for BIND9 are compatible with those for BIND8 in terms of the IPv6 support. Many examples described in this book would also work for BIND8.

- Support for the DNS security extension (DNSSEC)
- Views, which can virtually provide multiple servers based on some properties of queries (e.g., source and/or destination address)
- Thread-based software architecture for better support for multiprocessor machines

3.5.2 Getting BIND9

BIND9 is, just like prior versions of BIND, open source software and is provided at ISC's Web and FTP site free of charge. It is distributed under a BSD-style license, so users can freely modify the source code.

BIND9 is available at the following URL via FTP: ftp://ftp.isc.org/isc/bind9/*VERSION*/ bind-*VERSION*.tar.gz *VERSION* is 9.x.y where x and y are the major and minor versions within BIND9. For example, the source code of version 9.3.3 is available at ftp://ftp.isc.org/isc/bind9/ 9.3.3/bind-9.3.3.tar.gz

In the following discussion, if the BIND9 implementation is referred to as 9.x, the description applies to all 9.x.y versions. Minor versions are specified only when that particular version has some special behavior.

3.5.3 Building and Installing BIND9

BIND9 is highly portable, and it is usually easy to build and install. For many major operating systems, the installation procedure simply consists of the following steps:

```
#unpack the package
  % gzcat bind-9.3.3.tar.gz | tar xf -
#build programs
  % cd bind-9.3.3
  % ./configure
  % make
#install programs as a super user
  % su
  # make install
```

The `configure` script should normally work fine without any command line options unless the user wants to specify nondefault install paths. In particular, IPv6 transport support is enabled by default; if there is any reason for disabling IPv6 transport, the `--disable-ipv6` option should be specified for `configure`. The `configure` script also supports the `--with-kame` option. It was introduced when BSD did not officially support IPv6 so that BIND9 could be built on a KAME-patched BSD system for IPv6 transport, but this option is now meaningless. It should also be noted that the `--disable-ipv6` option only affects the transport protocol for DNS transactions, and is irrelevant to the contents exchanged in the transactions. For example, even if the `--disable-ipv6` option is specified, **named** will return AAAA resource records if it has the records of the query name.

On FreeBSD, which is the base operating system used in this book, the BIND9 programs will be installed under `/usr/local/bin` and `/usr/local/sbin` by the above procedure. In particular, the **named** daemon should be available as `/usr/local/sbin/named`.

BIND9 has been incorporated in FreeBSD as a base component since 5.3-RELEASE. This can be confirmed by invoking `/usr/sbin/named` with the `-v` command line option.

3.5.4   Configuring BIND9 for IPv6 Operation

This section provides a brief overview of configuring a BIND9 server to support IPv6. Although Section 3.5.6 also provides a complete configuration that can be used in actual operation, neither section intends to provide a comprehensive description of BIND configuration; they concentrate on describing the IPv6-related parts. A general description of BIND configuration is beyond the scope of this book. Those who need such information should consult other references such as [Liu06] and [Liu02].

The `named.conf` Configuration File

The BIND9 **named** daemon usually requires a configuration file. If BIND9 is built as a separate package as previously shown, the default path to the file is `/usr/local/etc/named.conf`. For those operating systems that incorporate BIND9 in their base systems, the default path depends on the system. On FreeBSD, it is `/etc/namedb/named.conf`.

The configuration file can specify a number of run-time parameters for **named** to operate and define zones for which the server has the authority. It consists of one or more *statements*, each of which often contains multiple substatements. Table 3-5 shows a summary of major statements used in the configuration file. These statements will appear in the succeeding examples.

Address Match Lists

To control DNS transport, an *address match list* is often required. In particular, an address match list is used to specify local IPv4 or IPv6 addresses to accept DNS queries. In general, an address match list can contain IPv4 addresses, IPv4 prefixes, IPv6 addresses, or IPv6 prefixes.

When a link-local IPv6 address or prefix is specified in an address match list, its link identifier must be given as well with the "%" notation. See Chapter 2 of *IPv6 Core Protocols Implementation*, "IPv6 Addressing Architecture," for more details on this notation. In this case, the BIND9 implementation assumes a one-to-one mapping between links and interfaces like the KAME implementation, and interface names can be used as a link identifier. For example, a link-local address `fe80::1` on the link attached to interface fxp0 is represented as `fe80::1%fxp0`. Similarly, the prefix that contains all link-local addresses on this link is represented as `fe80::%fxp0/10`.

Some predefined keywords can also be used as an address match list element. Keyword `any` matches any possible address in the context, and `none` does not match any address. Keyword

TABLE 3-5

Statement	Description
options	Specifies run-time operational parameters, including local IP addresses for incoming queries.
controls	Specifies control channel interfaces.
zone	Defines zones for which the server has the authority.
view	Defines a view (see Section 3.5.1).
server	Specifies nondefault parameters for a particular remote server.

Major statements for the `named.conf` *file.*

`localhost` matches all (IPv4 and IPv6) addresses configured on the system, and `localnets` matches all (IPv4 and IPv6) addresses covered by prefixes of local subnets.

Some systems do not provide a way to determine local IPv6 subnet prefixes, and on them `localnets` has the same effect as `localhost` in terms of IPv6. Fortunately, FreeBSD provides this information and `localnets` works for IPv6 as expected.

Most of the above description is a new feature of BIND 9.3. Before 9.3, you could specify only `any` or `none` as local addresses to accept queries (see later). Also, `localhost` and `localnets` worked only for IPv4 addresses.

Enable Accepting IPv6 Queries

By default, **named** does not accept DNS queries over IPv6. The `listen-on-v6` option is used to allow such queries. It should be specified in the `options` statement and/or in `view` statements.

The `listen-on-v6` option takes an address match list containing IPv6 addresses or prefixes. The easiest way to accept queries over IPv6 is to add the following line in an appropriate place:

```
listen-on-v6 { any; };
```

More specific configurations are also available. For example, to limit the local address that accepts queries to the loopback address only, the following configuration should be used instead:

```
listen-on-v6 { ::1; };
```

Access Control

BIND9 **named** supports several options for access control purposes. These options generally take an address match list as an argument. Since an address match list equally accepts IPv4 and IPv6 addresses or prefixes, access control based on IPv6 addresses can be done just as access control based on IPv4 addresses.

For example, the following configuration limits the source address of a DNS query to the addresses that match `192.0.2.0/24` or `2001:db8:1::/64`:

```
allow-query { 192.0.2.0/24; 2001:db8:1::/64; };
```

A common access control policy for a caching server is to limit the source of the query to its local subnets. It can be done with the following configuration:

```
allow-query { localnets; };
```

Recall that `localnets` matches both IPv4 and IPv6 addresses of local subnets.

The same configuration notation applies to the following options: `allow-notify`, `allow-transfer`, `allow-recursion`, and `allow-update-forwarding`.

Source Address Specification

BIND9 allows the user to specify a particular source address for some DNS transport operations. The configuration options for this purpose are separated for IPv4 and IPv6. In general, options for IPv6 transport have the naming convention `xxx-source-v6` where `xxx` identifies a particular operation. The usage is the same as that of the corresponding options for IPv4.

For example, in order to specify `2001:db8::1` as the source address of DNS queries sent from the system, the following should be added:

```
query-source-v6 address 2001:db8::1;
```

Similarly, the following option specifies the IPv6 address `2001:db8::2` as the source address for zone transfers:

```
transfer-source-v6 2001:db8::2;
```

The same notation also applies to the options `notify-source-v6` and `alt-transfer-source-v6`.

Server Address Specifications

In some cases, the IP address(es) of a remote DNS server must be specified in the configuration file. For example, to perform zone transfer, the IP address(es) of the master (primary) server must be specified in a zone-specific configuration. Both IPv4 and IPv6 addresses can be specified for these cases.

The following is an example of the zone transfer case. It specifies an IPv4 address `192.0.2.1` and an IPv6 address `2001:db8::1` as master (primary) servers of a zone for which this system is acting as a slave (secondary):

```
masters { 192.0.2.1; 2001:db8::1; };
```

In a `masters` statement an arbitrary number of IPv4 or IPv6 addresses can be specified. Of course, it can consist of addresses of a single address family, either IPv4 or IPv6.

This notation works for `also-notify`, `forwarders`, and `dual-stack-servers`.

Similarly, either an IPv4 or an IPv6 address can be specified for a `server` statement, which defines characteristics of a particular remote server. For example, the following specifies not to use EDNS0 with the server that has an IPv6 address `2001:db8::1`:

```
server 2001:db8::1 {
       edns no;
};
```

Other IPv6-Related Options

The following are other options that are related to the IPv6 operation.

`preferred-glue` This option specifies the preference of glue resource records when not all of them can be stored in a single UDP response due to the size limitation (see Section 3.3.4). For example, consider a zone `kame.example` that contains the following delegation:

```
child.kame.example.       NS     ns001.child.kame.example.
                                 ns002.child.kame.example.
...
                                 ns009.child.kame.example.
ns001.child.kame.example. A      192.0.2.1
                          AAAA 2001:db8::1
...
ns009.child.kame.example. A      192.0.2.9
                          AAAA 2001:db8::9
```

That is, there are nine nameservers for a delegated zone `child.kame.example`, each of which has one A and one AAAA glue resource records.

The default limitation of UDP responses is usually too small to store all the glue resource records. By default, a BIND9 server returns some A records and some AAAA records when it returns a delegation to the `child.kame.example` zone. But if the following line is specified in the `options` statement:

```
preferred-glue A;
```

then the response would contain all the A resource records and (possibly) some AAAA resource records.

Similarly, if the following line is specified:

```
preferred-glue AAAA;
```

then the response would probably contain as many AAAA records as possible and no A records.

> This is a new feature in BIND 9.3. BIND 9.2 does not support this option.

Today it is generally advisable to specify the A record for `preferred-glue`. In fact, since most of the DNS (caching) server implementations that support IPv6 transport also support EDNS0 and responses to such servers will always contain a full set of glue records, this preference effectively does not have any negative impact on the caching servers; the cost at the authoritative server to handle the preference should be negligible. On the other hand, preferring A records will help older implementations that do not support IPv6 transport or EDNS0 when a response is large and some glue records must be omitted. In this case glue records of type A are clearly much more useful than AAAA glue records for these caching servers.

dual-stack-servers This option specifies the *last resort* forwarder for a single stack (i.e., either only IPv4 or only IPv6) caching server. Unlike the `forwarders` option, the caching server system normally tries to resolve names by itself in a recursive manner. However, if the system detects that a remote server cannot be reached due to address family mismatch (e.g., when the local system only has IPv4 connectivity but the remote server only has AAAA glue records), a forwarder specified in `dual-stack-servers` that has the missing connectivity will be used. This option does not have any effect on a dual stack node.

> Note that in this context *dual stack* means the system can open both AF_INET and AF_INET6 sockets. This is always the case for the generic FreeBSD kernel even if the node does not have an IP address for the corresponding address family. Therefore, **named** must either be built with `--disable-ipv6` or be invoked with the `-4` option (see below for this option) in order to act as an *IPv4-only* node; similarly, **named** must be invoked with the `-6` option in order to act as an *IPv6-only* node. Otherwise, it will be treated as a dual stack node and `dual-stack-servers` will not work as expected.

FIGURE 3-24

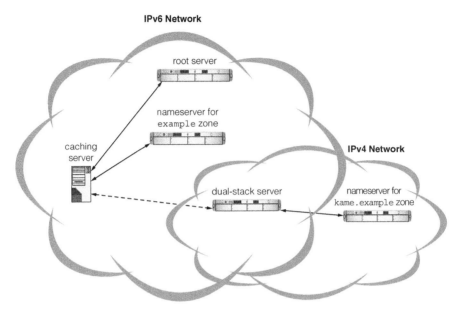

- - - - → recursive query
——————→ nonrecursive query

IPv6 Network

root server

nameserver for
example zone

caching
server

IPv4 Network

dual-stack server

nameserver for
kame.example zone

Name resolution with a dual-stack forwarding server.

Figure 3-24 shows an example usage of a dual-stack forwarder. Recall the resolution procedure given in Figure 3-6 (page 215), and assume the caching server is located in an IPv6-only network. In Figure 3-24 it is also assumed that the root server and the authoritative server of the example zone is reachable via IPv6, but the authoritative server of the kame.example zone is in an IPv4-only network.

In this case, the caching server can follow the delegation by directly sending (nonrecursive) queries to the root and the example zone servers. But since it cannot reach the kame.example zone server due to the IP version mismatch, the caching server contacts the kame.example zone server via the dual-stack forwarder with a recursive query.

This is a new feature in BIND 9.3. BIND 9.2 does not support this option.

Obsolete Options

The following options were used to work around some IPv6 related issues, but the use of these options on BIND 9.3 is now generally discouraged.

match-mapped-addresses This option specifies that when **named** matches an IPv4 address with address match list entries, it must automatically generate the IPv4-mapped IPv6 address corresponding to the IPv4 address and match the IPv6 address as well as the original IPv4 address. This option was introduced to work around the security issue described in Chapter 7 of *IPv6 Core Protocols Implementation*. Later versions of BIND9 **named** disable IPv4 communication over an `AF_INET6` socket by specifying the `IPV6_V6ONLY` socket option (see also the *Core Protocols* book), which effectively makes this option obsolete. Issues about this option will be discussed in more detail in Section 3.5.5.

allow-v6-synthesis This option was introduced to provide a migration method to forward lookups using the A6 resource record and reverse lookups using bit labels and the DNAME resource record. However, the migration was canceled by the standardization procedure as explained in Section 3.3.6, and this option has no use accordingly.

Command Line Options to Specify Transport

A couple of command line options are available to limit the network protocol for DNS transport:

- `-4` specifies that only IPv4 should be used
- `-6` specifies that only IPv6 should be used

For example, if **named** is invoked as follows:

```
/usr/local/sbin/named -4;
```

then IPv6 will never be used as the DNS transport even if **named** is built with IPv6 support and the system has IPv6 connectivity. In addition, **named** will not listen on IPv6 addresses for incoming queries regardless of how the `listen-on-v6` option is specified.

This option is useful when the network connectivity of a particular protocol, especially IPv6, is known to be poor but **named** cannot be rebuilt with the `--disable-ipv6` option (see Section 3.5.3) for some reason. Note that there are no other run-time options or configuration statements to disable the use of IPv4 or IPv6 for queries sent from the system; `listen-on` or `listen-on-v6` only restricts incoming queries.

The same note for the `--disable-ipv6` build option applies to the `-4` and `-6` run-time options; they only affect the transport protocol for DNS transactions, and are irrelevant to the contents exchanged in the transactions.

> The `--disable-ipv6` build option and the `-6` command line option cannot coexist for an obvious reason. If **named** is built with `--disable-ipv6` and is invoked with the `-6` option, it will immediately quit with an error message. On the other hand, IPv6-specific configuration statements and options such as `listen-on-v6` are simply ignored on a **named** process built with `--disable-ipv6`.

Control Channel

The **named** daemon can be controlled via a control channel with the administrative command, **rndc**. The **named** and **rndc** processes communicate with each other over a TCP connection. Either IPv4 or IPv6 can be used for this purpose.

In BIND 9.2, there was a well-known pitfall on the control channel that made **named** refuse a connection from **rndc**. This could happen with the following configuration for **named** in `named.conf` to set up the channel:

```
controls {
        inet 127.0.0.1 port 953
        allow { 127.0.0.1; } keys { "rndc-key"; };
};
```

This means **named** will listen on a TCP socket bound to IPv4 address `127.0.0.1` and port 953, and accept control commands from `127.0.0.1` with a secret key named `rndc-key`.

With this configuration, if the following is specified in `rndc.conf`, which is the default configuration file name for the **rndc** command:

```
options {
        default-key "rndc-key";
        default-server localhost;
        default-port 953;
};
```

then the **rndc** command will try to resolve the name `localhost` to an IP (v4 or v6) address. In many operating systems, the result is a list of addresses, whose first element is the loopback IPv6 address, `::1`. The **rndc** command of BIND 9.2 tries only the first element of the list, and the connection setup attempt will fail with a "Connection refused" error because the server is configured to accept IPv4 connections only.

To avoid this type of mismatch, it is recommended to specify the IP address in `rndc.conf`:

```
default-server 127.0.0.1;
```

BIND 9.3 does not have this problem, since the **rndc** command now tries all possible addresses when a host name is specified as the server.

Of course, an IPv6 address can also be specified in the `controls` statement. The following is a common configuration of control channels on a dual-stack server node:

```
controls {
        inet 127.0.0.1 port 953
        allow { 127.0.0.1; } keys { "rndc-key"; };
        inet ::1 port 953
        allow { ::1; } keys { "rndc-key"; };
};
```

Zone Files

There is nothing special to configuring DNS zone files containing IPv6 related resource records. In particular, to store an IPv6 address for a host name in an existing zone, it is enough just to add the corresponding AAAA resource record in the zone file. For example, assuming that we have authority for the zone `kame.example`, the following line should be added to the zone file to store an IPv6 address `2001:db8:1234:abcd::1` for a host name `www.kame.example`:

```
www.kame.example. AAAA 2001:db8:1234:abcd::1
```

To set up a reverse mapping for an IPv6 prefix, a separate zone under the `ip6.arpa` domain corresponding to the prefix must be created. For example, if a site

manages a prefix `2001:db8:1234:abcd::/64`, the corresponding `ip6.arpa` zone is
`d.c.b.a.4.3.2.1.8.b.d.0.1.0.0.2.ip6.arpa`.

Just like a zone for IPv4 reverse mapping, this `ip6.arpa` zone will usually only contain SOA,
NS, and PTR resource records. For example, the reverse mapping for `www.kame.example` in
the preceding example is represented in this zone as follows:

```
1.0.0.0.0.0.0.0.0.0.0.0.0.0.0.0 PTR www.kame.example.
```

> Previously, the obsolete well-known domain suffix for IPv6 reverse mapping, `ip6.int`,
> coexisted with `ip6.arpa`, and resolver implementations varied: some only used `ip6.int`,
> and others only tried `ip6.arpa`. Zone administrators therefore needed to provide con-
> sistent contents for both the domains. Fortunately, today's administrators can forget
> `ip6.int` because this domain has been removed from the `int` zone as explained in
> Section 3.3.6.

3.5.5 Implementation-Specific Notes

This section discusses various issues that stem from implementation characteristics of BIND9
and may confuse a system administrator. Most of them are related to IPv6 transport for DNS
transactions, rather than DNS contents for IPv6 such as AAAA resource records. Some issues are
even irrelevant to the DNS protocol per se, but they are common pitfalls in the actual operation
that have confused administrators and should be worth discussing here.

AF_INET6 Sockets for DNS Transactions

Figure 3-25 shows a simplified image of the BIND9 **named** daemon process, focusing on
sockets used for DNS transactions along with major modules and internal databases. It is
assumed that this server has two IPv4 addresses, `127.0.0.1` and `192.0.2.1`, and several
IPv6 addresses. The sockets shown in the figure are created as a result of including the
following in the `options` statement in the configuration file:

```
listen-on { any; };
listen-on-v6 { any; };
```

although the first line is assumed by default and can be omitted.

On startup the BIND9 **named** daemon loads authoritative zone files and maintains the
contents as in-memory *zone databases*. It also creates a *cache database* in memory to store the
results of the name resolution initiated by this process. The daemon accepts incoming queries
sent to its UDP or TCP sockets bound to port 53, finds an appropriate answer from its zone
or cache database, and returns the response from the socket that received the query. If the
answer to a query is not cached in the cache database and requires recursive name resolution,
the internal resolver module performs DNS transactions with external authoritative servers. The
sockets used for recursive resolution are bound to ephemeral ports by default; in Figure 3-25
ports 3001 and 3002 are assumed to be chosen.

FIGURE 3-25

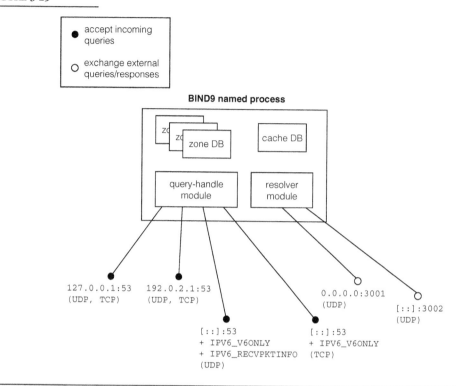

BIND9 process image with AF_INET and AF_INET6 sockets.

It should be noted that the AF_INET6 UDP socket, used to accept incoming queries, is a wildcard socket regarding the address; that is, it is not bound to any specific address.[11] On the other hand, each AF_INET socket has to be bound to a specific address configured on this host to ensure that the source address of the response packet to a query equals the destination address of the corresponding query packet, which is assumed by the client. On the AF_INET6 UDP socket, this can be ensured with a single wildcard socket, thanks to the IPV6_RECVPKTINFO socket option. The receiving process can get the destination address of the query in an IPV6_PKTINFO ancillary data item associated with the received data and can specify that address to be the source address of the response packet by including an IPV6_PKTINFO item with that address.

It is beneficial to use a wildcard socket with the IPV6_RECVPKTINFO socket option because a node can often have more IPv6 addresses than IPv4 addresses; it at least has the loop-back address, ::1, and a link-local address on each interface. Handling all of these addresses on a single socket will contribute to reducing system resources and may also help improve performance, particularly when the node has many IPv6 addresses.

---

11. This is the case only when any is specified for listen-on-v6. If a specific listening IPv6 address is specified, an AF_INET6 socket bound to that specific address is created.

It is also helpful to handle all queries on a single wildcard socket when the node renumbers its addresses. The explicitly bound `AF_INET` sockets cannot receive queries to a newly configured address, so the BIND9 **named** daemon periodically checks the node's addresses to update the sockets appropriately. This means there may be a time-lag between the time a new address is configured and the time the daemon can listen on that address for accepting queries. This time-lag does not exist for IPv6 addresses because the `AF_INET6` socket is not bound to a specific address.

One subtle issue regarding this approach is that the wildcard socket may be overridden by the other `AF_INET6` socket used by the resolver module. For example, assume the node shown in Figure 3-25 has a global IPv6 address `2001:db8::1` and the system administrator specifies that address with a UDP port of 53 as the source address and port of external queries as follows:

```
query-source-v6 address 2001:db8::1 port 53;
```

Then incoming queries will be delivered to the more specific socket and dropped in the resolver module, which is only interested in response messages (Figure 3-26(A)).

BIND 9.3 and later avoid this problem by sharing the socket for external queries with the query-handle module when that socket can conflict with the listening socket as shown in Figure 3-26(B). When the socket is shared, response messages to the address-port pair are delivered to the query-handle module, and then forwarded to the resolver module. This setting is automatically done in the implementation, and the administrator does not have to add any specific configuration options to deal with such cases.

FIGURE 3-26

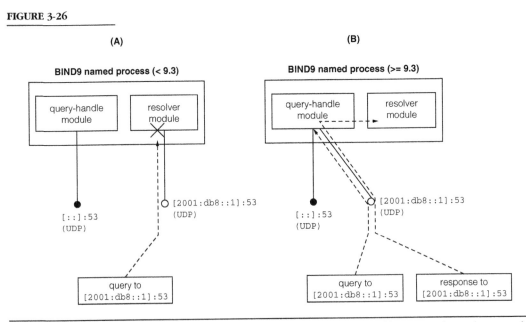

Conflict between wildcard listening socket and query socket.

One last issue is results from IPv6 socket API using IPv4-mapped IPv6 addresses. Since BIND9 uses wildcard listening sockets for incoming queries over IPv6, it may accept queries carried over IPv4 on those sockets as represented in the form of IPv4-mapped IPv6 addresses, unless the `IPV6_V6ONLY` socket option with a non-zero option value is specified on the sockets. BIND9 prior to version 9.3 does not set this socket option and causes various confusing difficulties.

First, Linux does not allow an `AF_INET6` wildcard socket and an `AF_INET` socket bound to a specific IPv4 address to coexist for the same TCP port.[12] This means the scenario shown at the beginning of this section (Figure 3-25) will fail for Linux running BIND9 **named** prior to 9.3 with the following warning messages:

```
Oct 05 20:39:24.728 listening on IPv6 interfaces, port 53
Oct 05 20:39:24.729 listening on IPv4 interface lo, 127.0.0.1#53
Oct 05 20:39:24.729 binding TCP socket: address in use
Oct 05 20:39:24.729 listening on IPv4 interface eth0, 192.0.2.1#53
Oct 05 20:39:24.729 binding TCP socket: address in use
```

But these errors are not regarded as fatal, and the process starts working. This situation is shown in Figure 3-27(A).

Assume further that this server acts as a primary authoritative server of a zone and the source of zone transfers is limited to `192.0.2.2`. This is done by including the following line to the corresponding `zone` statement of the configuration file:

```
allow-transfer { 192.0.2.2; };
```

The legitimate secondary server will eventually need to transfer zone contents and make a TCP connection from `192.0.2.2` to `192.0.2.1`. But since the corresponding `AF_INET` TCP socket failed to be opened and Linux accepts IPv4 packets on a wildcard `AF_INET6` socket by default, this connection is made via the `AF_INET6` socket. The remote address of the connection for the accepting server is represented as the IPv4-mapped IPv6 address `::ffff:192.0.2.2` in this case, which does not *literally* match the specified address (`192.0.2.2`) that is allowed to make the transfer, so the server rejects this attempt with the following log message:

```
Oct 05 20:51:31.838 client ::ffff:192.0.2.2#60618: zone transfer 'kame.example/IN' denied
```

Figure 3-27(B) depicts this situation.

This can be avoided by setting the `match-mapped-addresses` option to `yes` in the configuration file (Figure 3-27(C)). With this option enabled, **named** internally converts the IPv4-mapped IPv6 address into the corresponding IPv4 address represented as a 32-bit integer, and then compares it with the address specified in the `allow-transfer` statement. Since these two addresses *semantically* match, the transfer request is accepted.

But the kludge with the `match-mapped-addresses` option does not really solve the fundamental problem that the expected TCP sockets could not be opened at startup time and

---

12. More precisely, Linux prevents the attempt of binding the `AF_INET` socket when the `AF_INET6` socket is in the listening state. A Linux expert told the authors that a possible rationale of this restriction is to avoid a tricky inconsistency in identifying the accepting socket when the `AF_INET6` socket is accepting a connection that would also match the `AF_INET` socket while the `AF_INET` socket is being bound (the details are not actually related to IPv6 and are out of the scope of this book). Whatever the reason, this implementation-specific restriction not only breaks the protocol but is also inconvenient because it is common for server applications to bind a socket and listen on it as a single set of operations.

FIGURE 3-27

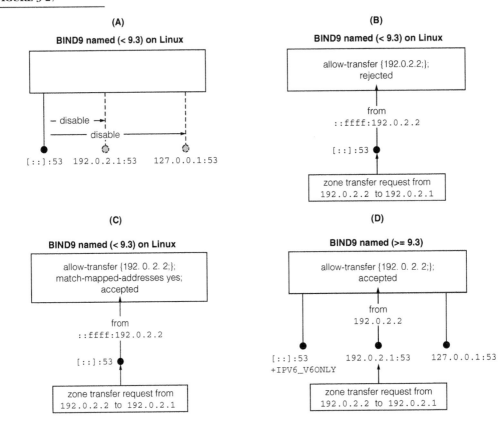

Problem in zone transfer on a Linux BIND9 server.

an IPv4 connection is made on an `AF_INET6` socket; it can be the source of other problems due to the use of IPv4-mapped IPv6 addresses.

There is in fact another problematic case that `match-mapped-addresses` cannot remedy. Suppose that the administrator wants to disallow accepting DNS queries over IPv4 while accepting queries over IPv6 to any local IPv6 addresses. The following configuration may look correct for this purpose:

```
listen-on { none; };
listen-on-v6 { any; };
```

This seemingly reasonable configuration actually has a hole if the **named** version is prior to 9.3 and the operating system allows IPv4 communication via an `AF_INET6` socket using IPv4-mapped IPv6 addresses, however the `match-mapped-addresses` option is specified. In this case, the server will at least accept any DNS queries carried over TCP/IPv4. Whether queries over UDP/IPv4 are accepted depends on the OS implementation of the `IPV6_RECVPKTINFO` socket option. If this option works for IPv4 packets, in which case the corresponding ancillary data item contains the local IPv4 address in the form of IPv4-mapped IPv6 addresses, the UDP query will be accepted and the reply packet will be returned to the sender (which is the case for Solaris). On BSD variants and Linux, `IPV6_RECVPKTINFO` is not effective for IPv4 packets received on the `AF_INET6` socket and the query is dropped at an early stage of the query examination procedure of **named**.

The authors emphasized the risk of relying on IPv4-mapped IPv6 addresses in applications in Chapter 7 of *IPv6 Core Protocols Implementation*. All the above issues should prove that the concerns are real. Fortunately, the `IPV6_V6ONLY` socket option provides a perfect solution to these problems. The recommended solution for DNS operators who want to use IPv6 is thus to use a newer version of BIND9—9.3 or later. As explained above, newer versions of **named** enable this socket option for `AF_INET6` sockets. In addition, the Linux kernel allows the `AF_INET` TCP socket with specific IPv4 addresses to be configured as a positive side effect of this option. Consequently, the problem of zone transfer disappears as shown in Figure 3-27(D).

Handling Misbehaving *Lame* Servers

Section 3.3.5 pointed out that old versions of the BIND8 caching server cause problems with misbehaving authoritative servers that behave as a *lame* server for AAAA queries even if the zone is properly configured (in this case, the authoritative server correctly responds to A queries with the AA bit on).

The caching server implementation contained in BIND9 and newer versions of BIND8 do not have this problem. BIND9 prior to 9.4 (9.4 is a release candidate as of this writing) tries to send queries to a lame server if there is no other choice; the caching server implementation in BIND 8.3.5 and later behave in the same manner.

Figure 3-28 describes how this countermeasure works for the same situation shown in Figure 3-11 (page 225). Even though the information that server X is lame is cached in step (1) of the figure, the caching server tries the server as the last resort option. This helps resolve querying for an A record under the problematic domain (step (2)), but is still suboptimal in that it makes the cached information effectively useless (step (3)). The caching server still tries to avoid the *lame* server if there are other compliant servers for the zone, but zone administrators using such a misbehaving server tend to use the same implementation for all nameservers of their zone, resulting in the situation where all servers are *lame*.

BIND 9.4 further optimizes the solution. It caches the lame server information per the combination of query name, type and class, and suppresses queries to known lame servers for each combination. This can provide the expected result for existing resource records while reducing unnecessary traffic due to the last resort queries to the misbehaving servers.

Figure 3-29 highlights the difference between the two types of work around. A query for an A resource record is not susceptible to the misbehaving server because the query type does not match the one in the cached information as shown in step (2) of the figure. In addition, the caching server can safely suppress external queries for the AAAA record that are very likely to fail, thanks to the per-type cache (step (3)).

It should still be emphasized that what must be fixed is the misbehaving authoritative server; authoritative server implementors should not rely on the optional workaround at the caching server side.

Remote Server Selection and Send Error Handling

The BIND9 caching server implementation maintains a *smoothed round trip time* (SRTT) for each remote authoritative server address to determine in which order the caching server should

FIGURE 3-28

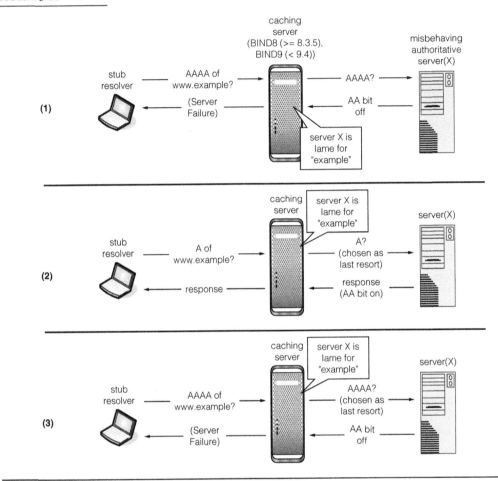

Work around misbehaving lame server by last resort queries.

try the authoritative servers of a given zone [Som03].[13] The selection algorithm prefers remote servers with smaller SRTT values since they should be more responsive than others. In particular, it ensures that a server that is likely to be down or unreachable will not be tried first for some period, thereby making the entire resolution process faster.

Here is an example of server address selection. Assume a caching server tries to resolve a name under the `example` domain and gets the following response from the root server:

```
example.   NS ns1.example.
example.   NS ns2.example.

ns1.example.   A    192.0.2.1
ns1.example.   AAAA 2001:db8::1
ns2.example.   A    192.0.2.2
ns2.example.   AAAA 2001:db8::2
```

13. As noted in [Som03], older versions of BIND9 did not use an SRTT.

FIGURE 3-29

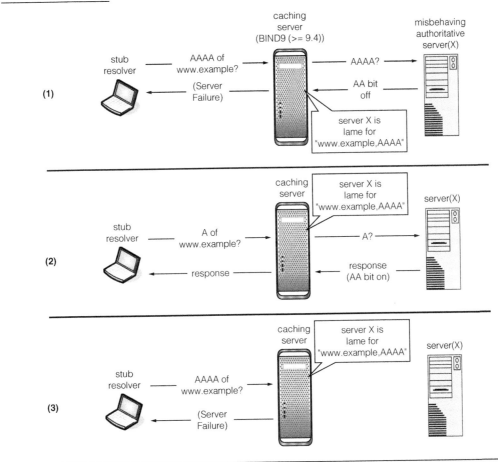

Work around misbehaving lame server with per-type lame information.

Also suppose the current SRTT values of each address are the ones shown with the glue records, which are 15ms, 10ms, 20ms, and 30ms (from top to bottom).

Then the address selection routine in the BIND9 implementation constructs a temporary data structure corresponding to these addresses with their known SRTT values as follows: the names of the nameservers (i.e., the RDATA of the NS records) compose a list, and each entry of the list is also a list of IPv4 and IPv6 addresses (i.e., the RDATA of the glue A and AAAA records). Each entry of the address list also stores the known SRTT value of the address.

Next the address selection routine sorts the addresses as follows:

- It first sorts the list of addresses for each nameserver in ascending order regarding SRTT. That is, the *nearest* address will be placed at the head of the list.

- Then the routine sorts the list of the nameservers based on the SRTT of the head entry of their address lists.

This processing results in the ordering shown in Figure 3-30.

The next step is to choose an address in this list for an outgoing query. It begins with the head entry of the address list in the head entry of the nameserver list. The chosen address entry is marked, and is used as the destination address of the query. The entry of the nameserver list that contains the chosen address is remembered for possible retries of the same query. In the second try, due to some failure in the first attempt, the search moves to the entry next to the recorded entry of the nameserver list and chooses the first unmarked address entry within its internal address list. Again, the chosen address entry is marked, and this address is used as the source address. When the search reaches the end of the nameserver list, it moves back to the head entry of the list and finds the first unmarked entry within its internal address list.

As a result, the first query will be sent to 2001:db8::1. If it fails due to an erroneous response or timeout, 192.0.2.2, 192.0.2.1, and 2001:db8::2 will be tried in this order. It should be noted that the second query will be sent to 192.0.2.2, while its SRTT is larger than that of 192.0.2.1. This probably comes from the observation that the same server name (such as ns1.example) is likely to specify the same server, and that if one of the addresses does not work others will likely not either.

Sending a query to the selected address may fail for various reasons. One common reason is that the querying server runs a dual-stack kernel supporting both IPv4 and IPv6 but does not have IPv6 connectivity. Usually the server implementation will notice the failure from the result of the sending system call (which is sendmsg() in the case of BIND9) and can move to a different address quickly. In addition, the SRTT of the address for which sendmsg() fails is penalized so that the preference level of this address for succeeding queries will be lowered.

The BIND9 implementation initializes the SRTT of each server address with a random value. Considering that some top-level authoritative servers have IPv6 addresses (i.e., AAAA glue records), as was seen in Section 3.3.4, it means that an IPv6 address can be the first

FIGURE 3-30

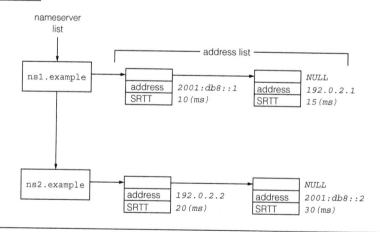

Sort result of remote nameservers.

candidate even on a caching server without IPv6 connectivity. The immediate fall-back described above is thus crucial for smooth operation. In fact, until versions 9.2.5 and 9.3.1, BIND9 did not handle erroneous results of `sendmsg()`, occasionally causing a few seconds of delay in name resolution under the `com` domain. This was a well-known problem for some time.

Note: There are still subtle points here. First, if the IPv6 stack supports the *on-link assumption*, which assumes all IPv6 destinations are on-link when no router is present (see Chapter 5 of *IPv6 Core Protocols Implementation*, "Neighbor Discovery and Stateless Address Autoconfiguration"), the send operation will not get an immediate error; it will only fail after a timeout during Neighbor Discovery. The fall back mechanism would then not work as expected. Fortunately, this assumption is disabled by default in BSD-variant systems including FreeBSD, and has been completely removed from more recent versions.

Second, even if all of the above are fixed, BIND9 cannot get an error of the `sendmsg()` call as an immediate result on some systems such as Solaris. In such systems an error occurring at the network layer can only be delivered in an asynchronous fashion, and only to a connected socket. Since BIND9 uses a nonconnected socket for outgoing queries so that it can efficiently support multiple destinations on a single socket, the erroneous result is effectively discarded. Unfortunately, the only effective workaround for such systems, except for getting IPv6 connectivity, is to disable the support for IPv6 transport by the `-4` command line option (for 9.3 or later) or by rebuilding the package with `--disable-ipv6`.

3.5.6 Complete Configuration Example

This section provides a small but complete set of DNS configurations with BIND9 for a site providing some IPv6 network services so that it can be used as a template in real world operation. Assume IPv6 networks shown in Figure 3-31. The left-hand side of the figure is a middle-scale IPv6 site (e.g., a corporate network). It has an IPv6 prefix `2001:db8:1234::/48`, and its own domain name `kame.example`. Within this domain there is a subdomain named `child.kame.example`. This site has at least two IPv6 subnets, `2001:db8:1234:abcd::/64` and `2001:db8:1234:5678::/64`. The site provides a mail (SMTP) server and a WWW server in the former subnet.

The right-hand side of the figure is another IPv6 network with a single subnet of `2001:db8:ffff::/64`. It also has a domain name `turtle.example`.

Several DNS zones are defined for this topology that are interrelated as summarized in Figure 3-32.

The top level of the `kame.net` domain constructs a single separate DNS zone of the same name, whose authoritative nameserver is `ns.kame.example`. The subdomain `child.kame.example` is represented as a separate zone delegated from the `kame.example` zone. Its authoritative nameserver is `ns.child.kame.example`.

The other domain, `turtle.example`, consists of a single DNS zone of the same name, whose authoritative nameserver is `ns.turtle.example`. The nameserver `ns.kame.example` serves as a secondary nameserver for this zone.

FIGURE 3-31

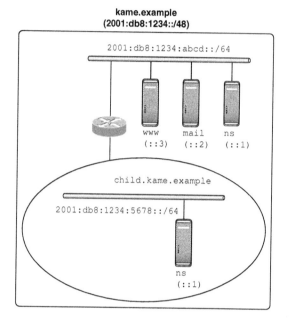
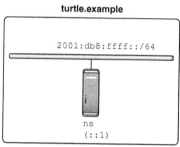

Network topology for the DNS configuration sample.

Listing 3-51 is the BIND9 configuration file of the top level network. In order to accept IPv6 queries, the `listen-on-v6` option is explicitly specified in the `options` statement.

Listing 3-51

```
options {
        listen-on-v6 { any; };
};

key "rndc-key" {
        algorithm hmac-md5;
        secret "/fODhw+VkG66TaSRHIeEMA==";
};

controls {
        inet 127.0.0.1 port 953
        allow { 127.0.0.1; } keys { "rndc-key"; };
        inet ::1 port 953
        allow { ::1; } keys { "rndc-key"; };
};

zone "kame.example" {
        type master;
        file "kame-example.zone";
};

zone "turtle.example" {
        type slave;
        masters { 2001:db8:ffff::1; };
```

```
        file "turtle.zone.bak";
};

zone "4.3.2.1.8.b.d.0.1.0.0.2.ip6.arpa" {
        type master;
        file "2001:db8:1234::.zone";
};

zone "localhost" {
        type master;
        file "localhost.zone";
};

zone "1.0.0.0.0.0.0.0.0.0.0.0.0.0.0.0.0.0.0.0.0.0.0.0.0.0.0.0.0.0.0.0.ip6.arpa" {
        type master;
        file "loopback-v6.zone";
};
```

The `key` and `controls` statements are for the control channel, and are not part of DNS protocol operation. One important note is that the secret value is provided only for reference and should not be copied to actual configuration files. In the real operation, the administrator should use a separate configuration utility named **rndc-confgen**, which automatically generates a secret key that is highly likely to be unique.

The rest of the file is zone configurations for which this nameserver has authority. Most of them are configurations as a primary (master) server. The only exception is for the `turtle.example` zone, in which the primary (master) server's IPv6 address, `2001:db8:ffff::1`, is specified in the masters list.

FIGURE 3-32

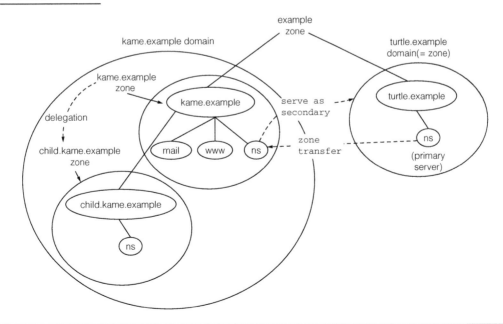

DNS zones for the sample network.

The `kame-example.zone` file (Listing 3-52) is the zone file of the forward tree for the zone `kame.example`. According to the network configuration, it has one MX resource record whose RDATA is `mail.kame.example`. The host name of the mail server has A and AAAA resource records, corresponding to the IPv4 and IPv6 addresses. Similarly, the WWW server has one IPv4 address and one IPv6 address, which correspond to the A and AAAA resource records. The second NS resource record specifies the authority delegation for the subdomain `child.kame.example` whose authoritative nameserver is named `ns.child.kame.example`. The nameserver also has IPv4 and IPv6 addresses, so both the A and AAAA glue records are provided.

Listing 3-52

```
                                                                      kame-example.zone
$TTL 86400          ; 1 day

@                   IN SOA  root.kame.example. ns.kame.example. (
                                  2005081601 ; serial
                                  7200       ; refresh (2 hours)
                                  3600       ; retry (1 hour)
                                  2592000    ; expire (4 weeks 2 days)
                                  1200       ; minimum (20 minutes)
                                  )
                    NS      ns
                    MX      10 mail

ns                  A       192.0.2.1
                    AAAA    2001:db8:1234:abcd::1
mail                A       192.0.2.2
                    AAAA    2001:db8:1234:abcd::2
www                 A       192.0.2.3
                    AAAA    2001:db8:1234:abcd::3

child               NS      ns.child
ns.child            A       192.0.2.4
                    AAAA    2001:db8:1234:5678::1
                                                                      kame-example.zone
```

The reverse mapping zone is also defined for the prefix `2001:db8:1234::/48` (Listing 3-53). This zone file contains three PTR records that correspond to the servers used in the forward mapping example.

Listing 3-53

```
                                                                      2001:db8:1234::.zone
$TTL 86400          ; 1 day

@                   SOA     root.kame.example. ns.kame.example. (
                                  2005101100 ; serial
                                  7200       ; refresh (2 hours)
                                  3600       ; retry (1 hour)
                                  2592000    ; expire (4 weeks 2 days)
                                  1200       ; minimum (20 minutes)
                                  )
                    NS      ns.kame.example.

1.0.0.0.0.0.0.0.0.0.0.0.0.0.0.0.d.c.b.a PTR      ns.kame.example.
2.0.0.0.0.0.0.0.0.0.0.0.0.0.0.0.d.c.b.a PTR      mail.kame.example.
3.0.0.0.0.0.0.0.0.0.0.0.0.0.0.0.d.c.b.a PTR      www.kame.example.

8.7.6.5             NS      ns.child.kame.example.
                                                                      2001:db8:1234::.zone
```

Like the forward zone, the authority is delegated to a separate server `ns.child.kame.example` for the subdomain corresponding to the IPv6 prefix `2001:db8:1234:5678::/64`.

In this example of the `named.conf` file, the forward and reverse zones for the `localhost` variants are also provided, which is a widely deployed practice. These define *isolated* zones that map the host name `localhost` to `127.0.0.1` and `::1`, and vice versa. There is basically nothing special in these configurations except that they are not officially delegated in the global DNS name space. However, it should be noted that the zone name for the reverse mapping of `::1` corresponds to the entire address; a common misconfiguration has been deployed where the zone is `0.0.0.0.0.0.0.0.0.0.0.0.0.0.0.0.0.0.0.0.0.0.0.0.0.0.0.0.0.0.0.0.ip6.arpa` (containing 31 zeros), which corresponds to `::/124`, and the zone file has a single resource record:

```
1       PTR     localhost.
```

Technically, this is wrong because this zone also contains the names that correspond to `::2`, `::3`, etc., which do not have any special semantics in the IPv6 address architecture [RFC4291]. If these addresses are assigned to someone or for some special purposes in the future, an application will try to resolve the host name for these addresses and will be confused with the result of `localhost`. Even though such an assignment will be less likely to happen, it should be better to configure things proactively to avoid possible confusion.

3.5.7   `dig` and `host` Utilities

BIND packages contain useful management tools for DNS operation. The most powerful tool is **dig**, which can generate various types of queries, send them to an arbitrary server, and dump the response.

The **dig** command provided in BIND9 fully supports IPv6 transport and content. For example, with the following command line arguments, **dig** will send a query for an A resource record of `www.kame.example` to `2001:db8::1`:

```
% dig @2001:db8::1 www.kame.example
```

Type A is the default resource record to be queried and can be omitted.

The **dig** command even accepts a link-local IPv6 address with its link zone specified as the nameserver address. The following example will send the same query to `fe80::1` on the link attached to the interface fxp0:

```
% dig @fe80::1%fxp0 www.kame.example
```

To ask for a AAAA resource record, the record type must be specified somewhere in the command line:

```
% dig @2001:db8::1 AAAA www.kame.example
```

The resource record type is case insensitive, and `aaaa` should also work.

A query for the reverse map can also be generated with a proper set of arguments. The following example could send a reverse map query for the IPv6 address `2001:db8::1234` using the well-known domain suffix `ip6.arpa`:

```
% dig @2001:db8::1 PTR
4.3.2.1.0.0.0.0.0.0.0.0.0.0.0.0.0.0.0.0.0.0.0.0.0.0.8.b.d.0.1.0.0.2.ip6.arpa*
```

The problem of this notation is that it is too long and difficult to type. The **dig** command thus provides a shortcut with the -x option to generate a query for reverse mapping. With this option, the previous example will be as follows:

```
% dig @2001:db8::1 -x 2001:dn8::1234
```

Note that even the resource record type (PTR) can be omitted.

In some cases, we may have to send queries with the obsolete well-known domain, `ip6.int`, for debugging purposes for example. The -i option in conjunction with the -x option can make this possible with the shortcut:

```
% dig @2001:db8::1 -i -x 2001:db8::1234
```

This is equivalent to:

```
% dig @2001:db8::1 PTR
4.3.2.1.0.0.0.0.0.0.0.0.0.0.0.0.0.0.0.0.0.0.0.0.0.0.8.b.d.0.1.0.0.2.ip6.int*
```

It should be noted that the -x option is context sensitive. In these examples, the address `2001:db8::1234` is the argument of the -x option and must be placed just after the option. Additionally, when the -i option is used, it must appear before the -x option.

The **dig** command is a very powerful tool that can provide various types of information, but a simpler result is often all that is needed. The **host** command can be used for that purpose. It uses the same backend routines as **dig**, but only shows a simple form of the Answer section of the result.

For example, the following command execution shows IPv4 and IPv6 addresses of the domain name `www.kame.example` and (possibly) the name of MX (if it exists) of that domain name.

```
% host www.kame.example
```

Reverse lookup can also be done just by specifying the IPv6 address:

```
% host 2001:db8::1
```

By default, the **host** command uses the `ip6.arpa` domain for IPv6 reverse lookup. The -i option can be used to specify the `ip6.int` domain like **dig**, but this option is probably less useful; a lookup attempt under `ip6.int` is now almost meaningless except for debugging in some limited cases, where the operator would prefer the detailed output from **dig**.

---

* Lines are broken here for layout reasons. However, they are a single line of command input.

DHCPv6

4.1 Introduction

Autoconfiguration is an important feature of IPv6 as already emphasized in other chapters of this series of books. The Neighbor Discover protocol (Chapter 5 of *IPv6 Core Protocols Implementation*) has a significant role in this area, through the stateless address autoconfiguration mechanism and by providing the addresses of the default routers.

However, autoconfiguration is not only a matter of configuring addresses and default routers, but also of getting any other higher level information. One common and important example is the address of a recursive (caching) DNS server. The Neighbor Discovery protocol is intended to provide information specific to the network (and in some cases lower) layer, and cannot provide this type of higher level information.[1]

Meanwhile, the large address space that IPv6 can provide each end user creates a new challenge for *site-level autoconfiguration*. When home network users connect the local networks to their Internet Service Providers (ISPs) and are allocated blocks of IPv6 addresses, how can these home users configure the entire local networks? In particular, the elimination of NAT as a result of introducing IPv6 means that the gateway to the ISP must act as a router. In the context of autoconfiguration, this also means we need automatic router configuration.

Dynamic Host Configuration Protocol for IPv6 (DHCPv6), with its simple but powerful mechanism, fills in all the missing pieces, and, in some areas, is the only standardized solution.

---

1. In fact, there is a proposal to provide recursive DNS server addresses via Neighbor Discovery [RA-DNSDISC], but it has not been standardized as an RFC at the time of this writing.

This chapter discusses all the details of DHCPv6. It is organized as follows: Section 4.2 provides the technical background for DHCPv6, including the protocol specification and common usage models. The succeeding sections describe KAME's implementation of DHCPv6 along with detailed examples of how the protocol works. These sections also discuss other details of the protocol specification which Section 4.2 does not cover. Section 4.8 concludes this chapter by showing operation examples of the KAME implementation for some common scenarios.

Since the DHCPv6 protocol is very similar to its IPv4 counterpart, the traditional DHCP, this chapter will often mention the IPv4 version of DHCP as well. In order to avoid confusion, the term *DHCPv4* will be used to refer to the IPv4 version of the protocol. In some cases, *DHCP* will still be used, but it will always refer to DHCPv6.

4.2   Overview of the DHCPv6 Protocol

The DHCPv6 protocol is essentially identical to DHCPv4 in the following ways:

- Both protocols are based on the client-server model.

- The objective of the protocols is to provide network configuration information from a server to a client. In particular, the primary goal is to allocate one or more IP addresses to the client during its initialization procedure.

- If the client and the server are located in different networks and cannot communicate with each other directly due to the lack of an initial address at the client, relaying nodes, called *relay agents*, forward packets between the client and the server.

- Both protocols use UDP as the data transport.

Those who are familiar with DHCPv4 should thus be able to understand the DHCPv6 protocol quite easily. At the same time, however, the DHCPv6 protocol introduced many improvements over DHCPv4, based on implementation and operational experiences gained from DHCPv4. Also, the difference in the background technology between IPv4 and IPv6 has introduced new applications of this protocol.

The following subsections provide a simplified but comprehensive description of the DHCPv6 protocol, commenting on the major differences from DHCPv4,[2] beginning with common use cases of DHCPv6, then describing detailed protocol specification. The last subsection concludes with a summary of the differences between DHCPv4 and DHCPv6.

4.2.1   Cases for DHCPv6

This subsection describes three common use cases of DHCPv6: address allocation, prefix delegation, and stateless services.

Address Allocation

The primary usage of DHCPv6 is to allocate IPv6 addresses to a client. This is conceptually the same as the main role of DHCPv4; a server is configured with a block of IPv6 addresses to lease, and clients ask the server for some of those addresses to configure their network interfaces.

---

2.   These comments are for those who are familiar with the DHCPv4 protocol and can be safely ignored by others.

Although this is the original goal of the DHCPv6 protocol, it is somewhat less important than the same provision of DHCPv4; in IPv6, there is another mechanism for a host to configure its IPv6 addresses automatically: stateless address autoconfiguration. In fact, the node requirement document for IPv6 [RFC4294] categorizes address allocation by DHCPv6 as an optional feature while the support for stateless autoconfiguration is mandatory.

Still, there is a demand for address allocation by DHCPv6. For example, in an enterprise network, the network administrator may not want to allow arbitrary hosts to have access to the network autonomously and may want to enforce DHCPv6 for controlling accessibility or for accounting purposes.

Another important difference between DHCPv4 and DHCPv6 is that DHCPv6 does not provide information about the address of a default router or the prefix length of an allocated address. In DHCPv4, these are provided through the *router option* and the *subnet mask option*. DHCPv6 could also provide these types of configuration information using separate options; there is no protocol requirement that precludes the introduction of such options. In IPv6, however, such information does not have to be provided via DHCPv6, because Router Advertisement provides the same information without requiring a server or additional message exchanges.

One may still have a reason for providing those types of information through DHCPv6. For instance, a network administrator might want to provide different hosts with different router addresses for load-balancing or access control purposes. In fact, similar discussions have occurred several times in the IETF. However, none of these discussions have ever convinced the community about the need for these options. Thus, the lack of such options should be considered to be a deliberate choice in the design of DHCPv6, not an open issue that needs further debate.

A common scenario for a host configuring itself using DHCPv6 is as follows: first, it creates an IPv6 link-local address using the stateless address autoconfiguration mechanism (see Chapter 5 of *IPv6 Core Protocols Implementation*). Then it starts a DHCPv6 exchange to configure a global IPv6 address on its interface. In parallel with that, the host also uses the Neighbor Discovery protocol to configure default routes and on-link prefixes which define the subnet addresses. A concrete example of this operation is provided in Section 4.8.8.

The DHCPv6 address allocation procedure is described in the base protocol specification [RFC3315].

Prefix Delegation

Another important application of DHCPv6 is the prefix delegation function from an upstream ISP to a customer site.

Figure 4-1 shows the entire system architecture of a typical example using this feature. A customer site—for example a home or small-office network—is connected to an ISP over a digital subscriber line (DSL). A small router at the customer site, often called a *Customer Premises Equipment* (CPE), is the gateway to the ISP. The CPE is connected to a *Provider Edge* (PE) device over a point-to-point link on the DSL. It has another network interface to the internal link of the customer network (in this example, it is assumed that the customer has only one internal link directly attached to the CPE). The PE terminates a very large number of access lines to customers and acts as a gateway to the ISP's backbone network and then to the Internet.

Prefix delegation in this system works as follows: when the CPE and PE establish the point-to-point link, the PE identifies the owner of the line (e.g., by matching the PPP user name against

FIGURE 4-1

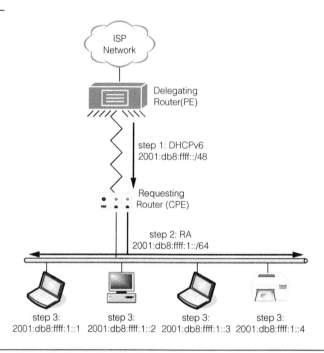

A common scenario of automatic site configuration using DHCPv6 prefix delegation.

its customer database), and chooses an IPv6 prefix for the customer network. The length of the prefix often used is 48 bits. This means that the customer site can have up to 65,535 subnets with today's standard subnet prefix length, 64 bits. In this example, the prefix is assumed to be `2001:db8:ffff::/48`. The CPE and PE then perform the prefix delegation procedure over DHCPv6 as defined in [RFC3633], and the 48-bit prefix is delegated to the customer site (Figure 4-1, step 1).

The CPE produces a longer prefix out of the delegated prefix to use as the subnet prefix of its internal network. In this simple network topology, the CPE can do that autonomously: for example, it can simply choose an arbitrary 16-bit integer (e.g., "1") and generate a 64-bit subnet prefix, `2001:db8:ffff:1::/64`, without risk of address collision.

Once the subnet prefix is determined, the CPE starts sending Router Advertisements (RA) that contain a Prefix Information option for that prefix (Figure 4-1, step 2). End hosts connecting to the link can then configure themselves with IPv6 addresses using the standard stateless address autoconfiguration mechanism (Figure 4-1, step 3).

Note that there is no need for manual configuration at the customer side except in the initial contract procedure with the ISP; the CPE and end hosts configure themselves completely in an autonomous fashion. Users do not need any knowledge about IPv6 or DHCPv6. All they need to do is to physically connect the CPE and the end hosts appropriately. This can therefore be considered *plug-and-play* at the site level.

In prefix delegation, the CPE acts as a DHCPv6 client, and the PE is the DHCPv6 server. However, since both the PE and CPE are usually routers, [RFC3633] defines more precise terms to use when describing these components. The CPE is referred to as a *requesting router*, and the PE is referred to as the *delegating router*.

This special terminology may naturally lead to the question of why a *host configuration* protocol is used to configure *routers*. There was actually a discussion about this point in the IETF, but the consensus was to ignore the superficial oddity. In essence, DHCP is a client-server protocol which provides some configuration information. It makes sense in IPv6, which allows end users to have many addresses, to use the protocol on a wider scale; the application of the protocol to routers is a natural consequence of that expansion. Besides, this type of overloading has already been pretty common in DHCPv4: a NAT router is not a *host* either, but it is frequently configured with a public IPv4 address via DHCPv4.

Stateless Services

Address allocation and prefix delegation are both *stateful* in that the server maintains the allocated addresses or delegated prefixes per client, processes renewal requests, expires outdated information, and so on. In addition to the stateful mode, DHCPv6 supports *stateless* service, with which the client can get configuration information other than its IP address in a lighter weight method.

For example, IPv6 addresses of recursive DNS servers (also known as *DNS caching servers* as often used in Chapter 3, or simply *DNS servers* from the end user's point of view) are as important for an end host as its IP addresses. Since DNS server addresses are usually common to all hosts, a mechanism providing this information does not have to be stateful.

[RFC3736] specifies a subset of the full DHCPv6 specification for the stateless services, and gives guidance for an implementation that supports only stateless service. This way, an implementor can consider providing a compliant implementation that only supports the lightweight subset of services.

The stateless subset can provide various types of other configuration information including recursive DNS server addresses. In fact, this (as well as the full set of DHCPv6) is the only standardized mechanism to provide this information to IPv6 hosts.[3]

DHCPv4 provides a similar service using the DHCPINFORM message, but it is less useful than the stateless service of DHCPv6. Since there is no general and automatic mechanism to allocate an IPv4 address other than DHCPv4 and since IP addresses are crucial configuration information for most hosts requiring autoconfiguration, it makes more sense to provide the other information as well as IPv4 addresses via stateful, namely normal, DHCPv4 operation.

4.2.2 Definitions about DHCPv6

Several key definitions of DHCPv6 terms which are commonly used throughout this chapter are listed here.

DHCP Unique Identifier

A *DHCP Unique Identifier* (DUID) is variable length data which uniquely identifies each individual DHCPv6 client or server. This is similar to the client or server identifier in DHCPv4, but is designed to ensure better uniqueness of the identifier among all clients and servers.

---

3. A *proposal* using RA exists as noted in Section 4.1.

A DUID is an opaque, variable length piece of data in terms of DHCPv6 message handling. That is, the only comparison that a DHCP client or a server can do between two DUIDs is to test to see if they are equal. However, [RFC3315] defines a standard format of DUIDs in order to help ensure that DUIDs are unique.

A DUID begins with a 2-byte *type* field, followed by type-specific variable length data. [RFC3315] defines the following three types:

1. DUID-LLT: Link-layer address plus time

2. DUID-EN: Vendor-assigned unique ID based on Enterprise Number

3. DUID-LL: Link-layer address

Figure 4-2 shows the format of a DUID-LLT.

hardware type A 16-bit hardware type reserved by the IANA. For example, type 1 means an Ethernet device.

time A 32-bit unsigned integer. This is the timestamp in seconds of the point when this DUID was generated since midnight (UTC), January 1, 2000, modulo 2^{32}.

link-layer address The link-layer address of a network device on the node generating this DUID. The type of the device is specified in the hardware type field.

Because the generation time is included in the identifier, a DUID-LLT is very likely to be unique. [RFC3315] recommends that all general purpose devices—such as personal computers—which have nonvolatile storage use this type of DUID. The hardware for the generation of the DUID can be independent of the DHCPv6 operation on the node. For example, a DHCPv6 message can be sent on a different interface than the interface on whose link-layer address the DUID is based.

Figure 4-3 shows the format of a DUID-EN.

enterprise-number A 32-bit integer maintained by the IANA which uniquely identifies a particular vendor.

identifier Variable length data specific to each vendor.

A DUID-EN is supposed to be used by a manufacturer of network devices and should identify one particular device provided by that manufacturer. Like a DUID-LLT, a DUID-EN

FIGURE 4-2

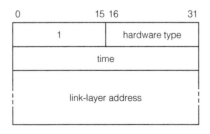

Format of DUID-LLT.

FIGURE 4-3

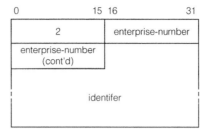

Format of DUID-EN.

FIGURE 4-4

```
0               15 16              31
 ┌────────────────┬────────────────┐
 │       3        │  hardware type │
 ├────────────────┴────────────────┤
 │                                 │
 │        link-layer address       │
 │                                 │
 └─────────────────────────────────┘
```

Format of DUID-LL.

is also expected to be highly unique, because the IANA controls the uniqueness of the enterprise-number, and the enterprise can control the uniqueness of the identifier.

Figure 4-4 shows the format of a DUID-LL.

hardware type A 16-bit hardware type reserved by the IANA. For example, type 1 means an Ethernet device.

link-layer address The link-layer address of a network device on the node generating this DUID. The type of the device is specified in the hardware type field.

A DUID-LL is similar to DUID-LLT but does not contain the time field. This is for a device which has a permanently connected network interface with a link-layer address and does not have nonvolatile storage for storing the generation time. A network interface embedded in a device chip is a common example of such interfaces. [RFC3315] prohibits the use of a DUID-LL if it is not clear whether the network interface is permanently connected to the device and the device does not have volatile storage; in this case, a DUID-LLT should be used even if the generation time cannot be reused.

Throughout this chapter, a DUID will be represented as a colon-separated hexadecimal sequence where each separated part is composed of two hexadecimal values. For example, a DUID-EN 0x0200090CC084D303000912 is represented as 02:00:09:0C:C0:84:D3:03:00:09:12. This notation is also used in implementation description and configuration examples later in this chapter.

Identity Association

An *Identity Association* (IA) is a conceptual structure that identifies a set of DHCPv6 configuration information. Each IA is identified by a 32-bit identifier (*Identity Association Identifier*, IAID). An IAID must uniquely identify one particular IA within each client.

The notion of an IA was introduced in DHCPv6 because of the property of IPv6 that an interface can have multiple IP addresses. The primary goal of IAs is to define multiple *identities* within a single client, each of which is associated with a different IPv6 address. For example, consider a client acting as "virtual hosts" which provide multiple services with different IPv6 addresses. If the client wants to configure itself with these addresses using DHCPv6, it would associate each address with a separate IA.

Multiple IPv6 addresses can also be associated with a single IA. For instance, a host in a multihomed site that provides a single service may have a single IA containing multiple addresses.

The *lease* duration is managed per IA, not per address. That is, DHCPv6 exchanges for renewal of allocated configuration information are performed per IA. While each address also has the notion of lifetimes, which have the same semantics as those defined in the context of stateless address autoconfiguration [RFC2462], these lifetimes do not affect DHCPv6 exchanges.

For controlling the renewal timing, each IA has two parameters, *T1* and *T2*. Section 4.2.3 will describe how these parameters work with regard to the renewal operation.

Whereas [RFC3315] defines an IA as a collection of *addresses* assigned to a client, the notion can be naturally extended to other types of configuration information with lease duration. In fact, [RFC3633] extends the notion to a set of prefixes delegated to a requesting router. This term will be used in the general sense throughout this chapter.

[RFC3315] and [RFC3633] define the following three types of IA:

Identity association for non-temporary addresses (IA_NA) An IA_NA defines a set of normal, that is, not temporary, IPv6 addresses to be allocated for a client's interface. Addresses in an IA_NA are expected to be for a client's interface. Addresses in an IA_NA are expected to be used as long as the client wants to renew these addresses as necessary.

Identity association for temporary addresses (IA_TA) An IA_TA defines a set of temporary IPv6 addresses to be allocated for a client's interface, where *temporary* refers to the privacy extension as defined in [RFC3041] (see also Chapter 5 of *IPv6 Core Protocols Implementation*). Due to the nature of temporary addresses, an IA_TA does not have the T1 and T2 parameters and is not expected to be renewed.

Identity association for prefix delegation (IA_PD) An IA_PD defines a set of IPv6 prefixes to be allocated from a delegating router to a requesting router for prefix delegation. Like IA_NA, an IA_PD is expected to be renewed using the T1 and T2 parameters.

Binding

A *binding* is a conceptual structure maintained by a server, which represents particular configuration information currently assigned to a client.

For configuration information associated with an IA, the binding is identified by the tuple of <client's DUID, IA-type, IAID>, where *IA-type* is one of IA_NA, IA_TA, and IA_PD. This chapter discusses only bindings associated with IAs.

For configuration information independent of an IA, the binding is identified by the client's DUID.

4.2.3 DHCPv6 Message Exchanges

This subsection describes the main part of the DHCPv6 protocol, concentrating on message exchanges.

DHCPv6 Messages

Figure 4-5 shows the common part of DHCPv6 messages exchanged between a client and a server. Unlike DHCPv4, most information, even that related to allocated addresses, is provided as an option, and therefore the common part is very simple.

msg-type An 8-bit integer identifying the DHCP message type. Unlike DHCPv4, where message types are also specified in a DHCP option, the type of a DHCPv6 message is identified by the separate field.

transaction-id The transaction ID for this message exchange. A transaction ID is a 24-bit integer. The transaction ID is chosen by the initiator of an exchange (which is usually a client). The responder (which is usually a server) copies the ID to the response. When the initiator receives the response, it matches the ID in order to identify the corresponding exchange.

options Options carried in this message. Some available options are described in Section 4.2.4.

Unlike DHCPv4, separate DHCPv6 message types are defined for communication between relay agents and servers. Figure 4-6 shows the format of these messages.

msg-type Either 12 (Relay-forward) or 13 (Relay-reply) (see ahead).

hop-count This field is only meaningful in a Relay-forward message, and indicates the number of relay agents that have relayed this message. This prevents the message from being forwarded in an infinite loop.

link-address A global address that will be used by the server to identify the link on which the client is located.

peer-address The address of the client or relay agent from which the message that is to be relayed was received. This is set in a Relay-forward message, and is used in a Relay-reply message to forward the message back toward the client.

FIGURE 4-5

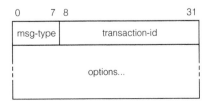

Format of DHCPv6 messages between a client and a server.

FIGURE 4-6

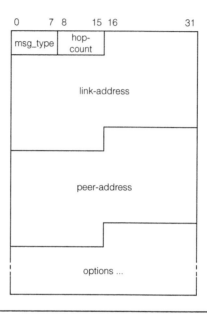

Format of DHCPv6 messages between relay agents and servers.

options This field contains DHCPv6 options specific to relay agent operation. A Relay Message option must always be included.

Section 4.3 (Figures 4-31 and 4-37) will show how these fields are used with concrete examples.

All values in any DHCPv6 message field or in any DHCPv6 option field (which can be interpreted by nodes with different native word ordering) are in network byte order. It is also noteworthy that DHCPv6 options and fields are aligned on byte boundaries. This means, for example, that an implementation processing a received DHCPv6 message cannot assume that a multibyte option is aligned at its natural boundary.

Table 4-1 summarizes the DHCPv6 messages that are defined in [RFC3315].

Message Transport

All DHCPv6 messages are carried in IPv6 UDP packets. The following well-known IPv6 addresses and UDP ports are used in DHCPv6 exchanges:

- All_DHCP_Relay_Agents_and_Servers (ff02::1:2): The well-known link-scope multicast address for relay agents and servers. All relay agents and servers must join this group on the interface accepting incoming messages.

- All_DHCP_Servers (ff05::1:3): The well-known site-scope multicast address for servers. All servers must join this group on the interface accepting incoming messages.

- UDP port 546: The well-known UDP port that clients listen on.

- UDP port 547: The well-known UDP port that servers and relay agents listen on.

TABLE 4-1

Type	Name	Description
1	Solicit	Sent by a client to find available DHCPv6 servers. This is similar to the DHCPv4 DHCPDISCOVER message.
2	Advertise	Sent by a server in response to a Solicit message with configuration information. This is similar to the DHCPv4 DHCPOFFER message.
3	Request	Sent by a client to a particular server to perform resource (e.g., address) allocation. This is similar to the DHCPv4 DHCPREQUEST message.
4	Confirm	Sent by a client when it may have moved to a different link in order to check whether the prefix of allocated addresses (if any) is still valid. There is no corresponding DHCPv4 message; DHCPv4 clients use the DHCPREQUEST message for this purpose.
5	Renew	Sent by a client to the server that has allocated a configuration resource to renew the use of that resource. There is no corresponding DHCPv4 message; DHCPv4 clients use the DHCPREQUEST message for this purpose.
6	Rebind	Sent by a client to servers to renew an allocated information resource when the attempt using Renew messages fails. There is no corresponding DHCPv4 message; DHCPv4 clients use the DHCPREQUEST message for this purpose.
7	Reply	Sent by a server in response to various messages from a client, mainly for confirming or rejecting the request that the client made. This is similar to the DHCPv4 DHCPACK message.
8	Release	Sent by a client to the server that allocated a configuration resource in order to inform the server that the resource can be released. This is similar to the DHCPv4 DHCPRELEASE message.
9	Decline	Sent by a client when it detects that an allocated address is already in use. It informs the server that the address cannot be used. This is similar to the DHCPv4 DHCPDECLINE message.
10	Reconfigure	Sent by a server to initiate exchanges starting with a Renew or Information-request message. It forces the client to refresh the information allocated to it. This is similar to the DHCPv4 DHCPFORCERENEW message.
11	Information-request	Sent by a client for the stateless service. This is similar to the DHCPv4 DHCPINFORM message.
12	Relay-forward	Sent by a relay agent, encapsulating a message from a client to the server. There is no corresponding DHCPv4 message; DHCPv4 relay agents just modify a field of the original message and forward the message without any encapsulation.
13	Relay-reply	Sent by a server, encapsulating a message returned to a client through relay agents. There is no corresponding DHCPv4 message.

DHCPv6 messages.

A DHCPv6 client sends any DHCPv6 messages to the All_DHCP_Relay_Agents_and_Servers multicast address unless the client and a server have agreed to use unicast exchanges through the Server Unicast option(*). If the client and servers reside on the same link, the servers directly receive the message and, if necessary, respond to it. Otherwise, a relay agent accepts the message, encapsulates it in a Relay-forward message, and forwards it toward the servers. In this case, the relay agent may send the message to the All_DHCP_Servers, or to the unicast address of a particular server if it is configured with the address.

(*) This is one major difference from DHCPv4. For example, a DHCPREQUEST message of DHCPv4 is often sent to the server's unicast address. The reason for the difference probably comes from the difference between broadcasting and multicasting. In DHCPv4, a client must either broadcast or unicast a message on the link, and broadcasting is generally expensive. In the design of DHCPv6, a dedicated multicast address is assigned for this service, and the effect can be localized. Multicasting a Renew message by default is also advantageous if it is forwarded by a relay agent and the server takes some special action depending on the contents of the Relay-forward message, e.g., the link-address field for processing a Renew message.

When sending to the All_DHCP_Relay_Agents_and_Servers multicast address, a client must use a link-local address as the source address of the packet, regardless of whether it has a global address. Remember, a link-local address is always configured autonomously through the stateless autoconfiguration mechanism and can be considered very stable. Therefore, the use of a link-local address for the packet's source is generally a good idea in an operation dealing with address allocation, in which the address in question can be unstable or even invalid during the operation.

Message Retransmission

Since DHCPv6 messages are carried over UDP, which is not a reliable transport, messages can be lost. Also, in some cases, the intended recipient of a message may be down and cannot receive the message. The initiator of a DHCPv6 exchange, usually a client, may need to resend the same message in these cases.

The timing of resending messages is controlled by the following parameters:

IRT Initial retransmission time

MRC Maximum retransmission count

MRT Maximum retransmission time

MRD Maximum retransmission duration

IRT is the initial timeout period during which the message sender waits for a response. If IRT seconds elapse, the sender retransmits the same message (with the same transaction ID) and waits for a response for a new period. The new period is 2 times the previous one, as long as it does not exceed MRT, in which case MRT is used for the retransmission period. If MRC is not zero, the sender attempts the transmission MRC times at most (including the first transmission); if MRD is not zero, the sender attempts retransmission until MRD seconds have elapsed since the first transmission; if both MRC and MRD are zero, the sender keeps retransmitting the message until it receives an expected response.

The actual retransmission period includes a random factor for avoiding collision with other synchronized senders. For simplicity, however, this random factor is often not taken into account in the following discussion. Table 4-2 summarizes these parameters for different DHCPv6 messages.

Figure 4-7 shows an example of retransmission with these parameters for the Request message. The client first waits for 1 second (IRT). If it does not receive a Reply within this period, it resends the message and waits for 2 seconds (IRT * 2). Eventually, the retransmission period will reach MRT (30 seconds), and, if the client still cannot get a Reply, it gives up retransmission after the tenth (MRC) transmission.

Message Exchanges

The DHCPv6 protocol consists of various types of message exchanges. The exchanges for some common scenarios will be described next. The description below refers to some specific DHCPv6 options before showing the definition in Section 4.2.4. Although the meaning of these options should be obvious from the context, it may be necessary for the reader to refer to the definitions in some cases.

TABLE 4-2

Message Type	*IRT(sec)*	*MRC(times)*	*MRT(sec)*	*MRD(sec)*
Solicit	1	0	120	0
Request	1	10	30	0
Confirm	1	0	4	10
Renew	10	0	600	(*1)
Rebind	10	0	600	(*2)
Release	1	5	0	0
Decline	1	5	0	0
Reconfigure	2	0	8	0
Information-request	1	0	120	0

Message retransmission parameters.

*1 Remaining time until T2.

*2 Remaining time until valid lifetimes of all addresses or prefixes have expired.

FIGURE 4-7

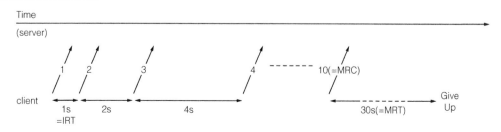

Retransmission of the Request message.

Exchanges for Address Allocation

A client starts DHCPv6 exchanges for address allocation with a Solicit message specifying an IA_TA or IA_NA for which the client wants to configure addresses. Servers receiving the Solicit message consult their local configurations, determine whether they can allocate addresses for the IA, and return Advertise messages containing their offers. When a server prepares the Advertise message, it attempts to send the same options that it will send to the client in its Reply message if the client chooses this server. This allows the client to compare the options and addresses advertised by different DHCP servers and choose the set of options and addresses that fit its particular needs.

In practice, the contents of the Advertise message may not matter much; the client may simply choose the server that sends the first Advertise message as long as the server has the same preference (see the description of the Preference option in Section 4.2.4). The KAME's client implementation behaves this way, as will be described in Section 4.4.3.

After sending the Solicit message, the client collects Advertise messages for about 1 second (with a random factor for avoiding synchronization with other clients). Then the client selects the most preferred server based on the contents of the Advertise messages and sends a Request message to the selected server, including the server's DUID and the offered IA.

The Request message is usually sent to the All_DHCP_Relay_Agents_and_Servers multicast address, and multiple servers can receive the request message. However, only the selected server continues the processing of the message—the others discard it because the DUID does not match.

The selected server makes a local binding for the tuple of <client's DUID, IA-type, IAID>, and returns a Reply message to the client. The Reply message includes the IA and associated addresses with lifetimes.

When the client receives the Reply message, it configures itself with the IA (and the associated addresses) in the Reply message. The uniqueness of the addresses on the client's link is confirmed by the Duplicate Address Detection procedure (see Chapter 5 of *IPv6 Core Protocols Implementation*). After the confirmation, the client can start using the addresses for further communication.

Figure 4-8 depicts the above procedure. In this figure, two servers, server1 and server2, respond to the Solicit message, and the client selects server1.

This initial procedure is not a time-consuming process in the usual sense. In some special cases, however, it may be desirable and possible to minimize the configuration delay. For example, a nomadic device which frequently moves from one link to another (e.g., a cellular phone) may even want to avoid the delay for collecting Advertisement messages from multiple servers.

This can be done using the Rapid Commit option. If the client includes this option in the Solicit message, and the responding server is configured to accept it, the server immediately makes a binding and responds with a Reply message (Figure 4-9).

The use of the Rapid Commit option primarily assumes an environment where at most one server is available for the client (e.g., where the client is directly connected to a server over a point-to-point link). Although the protocol does not necessarily prohibit the use of this option with multiple servers, it would cause problems as discussed in [RFC3315] and is thus inadvisable.

FIGURE 4-8

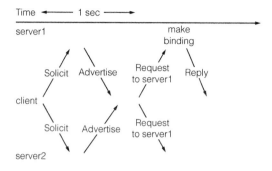

Initial message exchanges for address allocation.

FIGURE 4-9

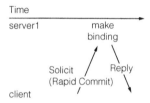

Initial exchanges with the Rapid Commit option.

Renewal of Addresses

Each IA_NA contained in the Request message includes parameters T1 and T2, which control per-IA timing of the renewal procedure.

When T1 seconds have passed since the client received the Request message, the client sends a Renew message to the server, including the IA and the server's DUID. If the server's policy allows the renewal request (which should be the usual case), the server updates its internal binding and responds with a Reply message containing the IA with (possibly) new T1 and T2 parameters, and associated addresses with (possibly) new lifetimes. The client receives the Reply message, and updates the lifetimes of the addresses of the IA.

As in the case of the Request and Reply exchanges, the Renew message may be received by other servers, but it is discarded because the DUID does not match. Figure 4-10 shows the above exchanges.

If the client does not receive a Reply message in response to a Renew message within a certain period, it resends the message until it gets a Reply, increasing the resend period. However, if T2 seconds have passed since the Reply message to the Request arrived, and the client has not received a Reply to its Renew messages, then the client gives up resending the Renew message and starts sending a Rebind message.

The content of the Rebind message is almost the same as that of the Renew message but does not contain the server's DUID, and can be processed by any server. In fact, the silence of

FIGURE 4-10

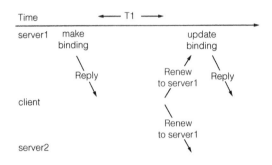

Address renewal using a Renew message.

FIGURE 4-11

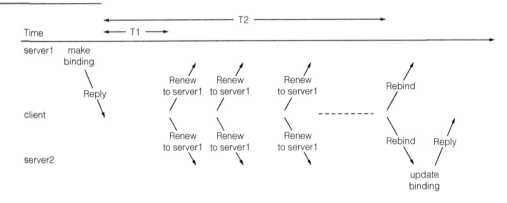

Address renewal using a Rebind message.

the server likely means it is down due to some reason and cannot be fixed in a short time, so it does not make sense to stick to that particular server.

If one of the (other) servers has enough information to renew the binding, it will respond to the Rebind message with a Reply message containing the IA and the associated addresses, and its DUID.

The client receives the Reply message, and updates the address as it did with the Reply to the Renew message. This procedure is shown in Figure 4-11. In this case, server1 has not been responding to Renew messages, so the client switches to a Rebind message. An alternate server, server2, responds to the Rebind message.

Note that the alternate server can respond to the Rebind message only when it has information about the binding established by another server (server1 in this example). This means the bindings on the two servers must be synchronized by some out-of-band mechanism. [RFC3315] does not specify such a mechanism, and it is currently implementation dependent.

It should also be noted that there is no strong requirement on the relationship between the address lifetimes and T1 or T2 of the corresponding IA. For example, if T1 for an IA is 1 day, but the preferred lifetime of an address associated with the IA is 12 hours, the address will be *deprecated* (in terms of [RFC2462]; see also Chapter 5 of *IPv6 Core Protocols Implementation*) in 12 hours because no renewal procedure takes place before the preferred lifetime expires. [RFC3315] recommends T1 of an IA be smaller than the shortest preferred lifetime of addresses associated with the IA, but this is not a mandatory requirement.

Other Exchanges for Address Allocation

A client can spontaneously release some or all of the allocated addresses in an IA by sending a Release message to the server. The server, upon receipt of the Release message, removes the addresses specified in the message from the corresponding binding, and returns a Reply message to the client. The server can then allocate the released addresses to other clients.

Recall that the client performs Duplicate Address Detection (DAD) for the allocated addresses upon receipt of a Reply message to Request. If this procedure detects that a different node on the link is already using any of the addresses, the client cannot use those duplicate addresses. In addition, the client informs the server of the duplication by sending a Decline message including the IA and the duplicate addresses. Upon receipt of the Decline message, the server marks the addresses *duplicated* and will not use those for further allocation. The server then returns a Reply message to the client. Figure 4-12 shows this procedure.

[RFC3315] does not specify what the client should do after the exchange of Decline and Reply messages. Perhaps it will need to restart the procedure from a Solicit message or another Request message to the same or other server.

When a client detects that it may have moved to a new link (e.g., when it detects a change of wireless access points), the client sends a Confirm message containing the IA for the interface which may now connect to a new link, along with all the addresses in the IA. Since the client may now be in a different network, the Confirm message must not contain the DUID of the server that allocated the IA.

When a server in the possibly new link receives the Confirm message, it examines the addresses in the message, and detects whether those are valid for the client's current link. If they are still valid, the server returns a Reply message containing a Status Code option with the code of Success (see Table 4-3 on page 315). Otherwise, it returns a Reply message containing a Status Code option with the code of NotOnLink.

FIGURE 4-12

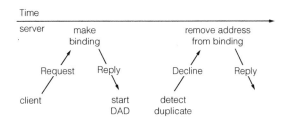

Decline and Reply exchanges for duplicate addresses.

FIGURE 4-13

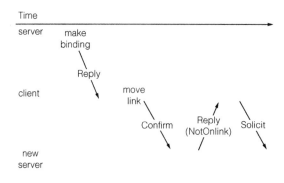

Confirming addresses in a new link.

In the latter case, the client must stop using the addresses which are now invalid, and must restart the address allocation procedure from a Solicit message in the new network. Figure 4-13 shows the procedure in the case where the client actually moves to a new link.

Exchanges for Prefix Delegation

DHCPv6 message exchanges for prefix delegation are mostly the same as those for address allocation described before with the following minor exceptions:

- The Confirm and Decline messages are not used for prefix delegation.

- When the requesting router (i.e., the DHCPv6 client) detects that it may have attached to a new uplink, it uses Rebind and Reply exchanges to confirm the previous binding, instead of using the Confirm message.

Server-initiated Exchanges

DHCPv6 exchanges are normally initiated by a client as shown in the previous descriptions. In some cases, however, a server may want to indicate the need for new exchanges to the client. For example, when a site is going to renumber its network, allocated addresses may become invalid before the scheduled renewal time and the server may want to force the client to renumber through DHCPv6.

The server can initiate new exchanges by sending a Reconfigure message. It includes a Reconfigure Message option, which specifies whether the client should respond to the message with a Renew message or an Information-request message (normally the Renew message is specified, as will soon be explained below). In case of the renumbering of allocated addresses or prefixes, the Reconfigure message also includes the corresponding IA.

Due to the intrusive nature of the Reconfigure message, [RFC3315] mandates the use of the DHCPv6 authentication mechanism for ensuring the validity of the message, thereby avoiding denial of service or other security attacks. A client must discard any Reconfigure message which does not include an Authentication option or does not pass authentication verification. The DHCPv6 authentication mechanism will be described later in this section.

FIGURE 4-14

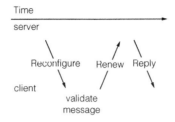

Server-initiated exchanges with a Reconfigure message.

Upon receipt of a valid Reconfigure message, the client starts new message exchanges based on the content of the Reconfigure message. If the Reconfigure Message option specifies the Renew message and an IA is contained in the message, the client starts Renew-Reply exchanges for the IA as if time T1 has passed for that IA. The server responds to the Renew message with a Reply message, which likely contains some new configuration information. Figure 4-14 shows the exchanges starting from a Reconfigure message.

Exchanges for the Stateless Services

For the stateless DHCPv6 service—that is, getting configuration information that does not need per-client binding—Information-request and Reply exchanges are used.

These exchanges are simple: the client sends an Information-request message, usually without including the DUID of any particular server. Servers receive the message, and respond with a Reply message containing any stateless configuration information.

Unfortunately, this simple mechanism has turned out to be insufficient in practice, due to the lack of *renewal* operation. Even though such stateless configuration information normally does not require renewal, updates on the information may still happen. For example, if a site has been renumbered with its IPv6 addresses, the recursive DNS server addresses will have to be changed accordingly. However, [RFC3315] does not include an automatic way that allows the client to update the stale information.

In theory, the server could initiate exchanges for updating previous information by sending a Reconfigure message. In practice, however, this is not really feasible, since in order to send a Reconfigure message the server must retain information about each individual client and cannot be stateless any more.

In order to fill in the requirement gap, the IETF has standardized a new DHCPv6 option, called the Information Refresh Time (IRT) option, for the Information-request and Reply exchanges [RFC4242]. This option specifies the interval with which the client needs to perform another exchange of Information-request and Reply messages so that the client can update the information with no more delay than the refresh interval.

An implementation that supports this option also has the notion of a default refresh time. Even if the Reply message to Information-request does not include an Information Refresh Time option, the client will perform another exchange about every 24 hours.

FIGURE 4-15

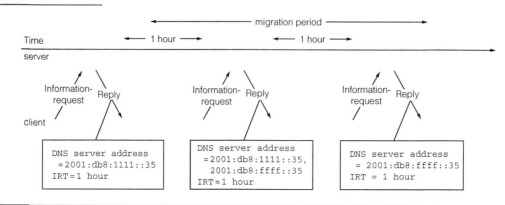

Renumbering procedure for stateless exchanges.

Figure 4-15 shows an example of exchanges with the Information Refresh Time option. In the first exchange, the Reply to the Information-request message contains a recursive DNS server address, 2001:db8:1111::35, and an Information Refresh Time option with the interval of 1 hour. Then the site starts renumbering, and the DNS server will have a new address, 2001:db8:ffff::35. During the migration period, both the old and new addresses are valid. In about 1 hour, the client starts the second exchange. This time, the two addresses of the recursive DNS server are provided. Eventually, the Reply message will contain the new address only, and then the site can stop using the old address(es).

The Information Refresh Time option works well for this type of *planned renumbering*. Yet this is not sufficient; there is no way to update the information due to *unplanned renumbering* such as changing a server and its address due to unexpected failure. How to deal with such unplanned renumbering is a subject of future study.

Exchanges with Authentication

DHCPv6 has a built-in security mechanism between a client and a server(*) in its base protocol specification. This security mechanism primarily aims to ensure integrity of DHCPv6 messages (particularly ones from a server to a client). It does not provide any confidentiality for message contents.

(*) [RFC3315] does not define a dedicated mechanism for authenticating communication between a relay agent and a server or between relay agents. It suggests the use of IP security (IPsec, see Chapter 6) for this purpose.

Overall, the integrity in the DHCPv6 security mechanism is ensured based on the HMAC (Keyed Hashing for Message Authentication Code) protocol [RFC2104]: the client and the server share some secret value as a *key*, compute the digest of each DHCPv6 message with the key and a cryptographically strong hash algorithm, and attach it to the message as the digital signature of the message. The receiver of the message validates its content by computing the digest using the same key and the hash algorithm, and by comparing the computed value and the value stored in the message.

[RFC3315] defines two variations of the mechanism: (1) the *delayed authentication protocol* and (2) the *reconfigure key protocol*. Both protocols use a special-purpose DHCPv6 option—the Authentication option—as a common framework.

In the delayed authentication protocol, it is assumed that the client and the server(s) share the key beforehand by some out-of-band method. The client includes an Authentication option in the Solicit message without including any authentication information. This indicates its desire to use the delayed authentication protocol for further exchanges. The server(s) identifies an appropriate key from its local configuration, and responds with an Advertise (or Reply with a Rapid Commit option) message containing an Authentication option with the HMAC digest. The client verifies the validity of the Advertise message using its preconfigured key, and accepts the message if it is properly verified. All further messages between the client and the server must be authenticated this way. Figure 4-16 shows message exchanges using the delayed authentication protocol.

On the other hand, the reconfigure key protocol is used specifically to secure a Reconfigure message. In this protocol, the client and the server do not have to share a key beforehand. When the server sends the first Reply message (likely to a Request message) to the client, the server chooses a key for the client, and includes the key in the Reply message. If the server then wants to send a Reconfigure message to the client and it cannot use any other authentication mechanism, it computes the HMAC digest of the key for the reconfigure key protocol and includes it in the Reconfigure message as a part of an Authentication option. The client verifies the Reconfigure message using the key that was included in the Reply message. Figure 4-17 shows message exchanges including a Reconfigure message with the reconfigure key protocol.

Note that the key is sent to the client in the first Reply message without being encrypted. Thus, if an attacker can snoop between the server and the client, it can steal the key and mount an attack using a Reconfigure message with the *valid* HMAC digest. The reconfigure key protocol is thus not entirely secure, and that is why [RFC3315] states that this protocol be used only when there is not another mechanism available.

Nevertheless, the reconfigure key protocol has its own value. The most important advantage is that the server and the client do not have to share the key beforehand. Key distribution

FIGURE 4-16

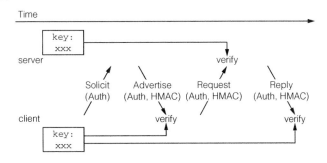

DHCPv6 message exchanges using the delayed authentication protocol.

FIGURE 4-17

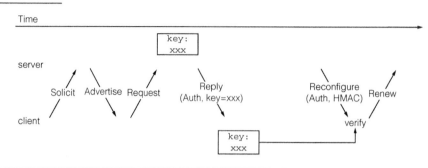

DHCPv6 message exchanges using the reconfigure key protocol.

is a difficult challenge in any security mechanisms, not just for DHCPv6, and a fully secure mechanism often is not feasible because of this issue. The compromise in the reconfigure key protocol is thus considered as a tradeoff between feasibility and the level of security.

Exchanges with Relay Agents

If there is no server on a link to which a client is attached, the client needs to contact servers via a DHCPv6 relay agent. The basic notion of relay agents is the same as that of relay agents in DHCPv4, but unlike DHCPv4, separate types of messages are used for communication between servers and relay agents.

When a relay agent receives a message from a client, it creates a Relay-forward message containing a Relay Message option which encapsulates the original message from the client. The relay agent then sends the Relay-forward message toward the available server(s), either to the All_DHCP_Servers multicast address or to a preconfigured unicast address.

The server receives the Relay-forward message, extracts the encapsulated original message in the Relay Message option, and processes the original message. The server then makes a response to the original message, encapsulates it in a Relay-reply message using the Relay Message option, and sends the Relay-reply message to the relay agent.

Finally, the relay agent extracts the response encapsulated in the Relay Message option, and forwards it to the client. It should be noted that a relay agent does not have to maintain any state for a message exchange between a client and a server. The Relay-reply message contains information about how to forward the response toward the client. Thus, a relay agent implementation can be very lightweight, as will be seen in Section 4.6. Figure 4-18 shows this procedure for a Solicit-Advertise exchange.

Multiple relay agents can be used between the client and the server, in which case Relay-forward or Relay-reply messages are nested accordingly. Unlike DHCPv4, the server does not have to return the response directly to the relay agent that is closest to the client, thanks to the separate Relay-reply message.

4.2.4 Summary of DHCPv6 Options

As shown in Section 4.2.3, most protocol operations of DHCPv6 are realized through its options. This subsection summarizes some of the DHCPv6 options that are currently officially defined.

FIGURE 4-18

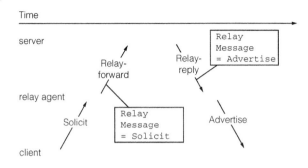

Solicit-Advertise exchange via a relay agent.

FIGURE 4-19

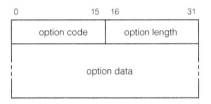

Common format of DHCPv6 options.

There have been other proposals for new DHCPv6 options, and some of them are currently under discussion in the IETF. Rather than adding those new options here, this section concentrates on those that are specified in [RFC3315], i.e., the base DHCPv6 specification, and some others that are of particular interest in this chapter. Most of the new options not described here just carry some new configuration information (e.g., NTP server addresses), which are quite straightforward and understandable.

All DHCPv6 options begin with commonly formatted fields, as shown in Figure 4-19.

option code A 16-bit unsigned integer identifying a particular option.

option length A 16-bit unsigned integer. This is the length of the option data field in bytes.

option data The data for the option. The format of this field depends on each option.

Below are detailed descriptions of each option along with their common fields.

Client Identifier

Option Code: 1

Length: n

Data: client DUID (n bytes)

The Client Identifier option contains variable-length opaque data which should uniquely identify a particular client.

Server Identifier

Option Code: 2

Length: n

Data: server DUID (n bytes)

The Server Identifier option contains variable-length opaque data which should uniquely identify a particular server. Unlike the same option of DHCPv4 (whose data is an IPv4 address), this option takes variable length data.

Identity Association for Non-temporary Addresses (IA_NA)

Option Code: 3

Length: n

Data: IAID (4 bytes)

                T1 (4 bytes)

                T2 (4 bytes)

                IA_NA options (n − 12 bytes)

The IA_NA option specifies an IA for a set of nontemporary (i.e., normal) IPv6 addresses. IAID is the identifier of the IA. T1 and T2 are time parameters represented in seconds, specifying the renewal timing of this IA (see Section 4.2.3). A value 0xffffffff has a special meaning of infinity; if T1 is set to this value, the correspondent timeout never happens. IA_NA options contain suboptions specific to this IA. IA Address options (described later) are often included in the options field.

Identity Association for Temporary Addresses (IA_TA)

Option Code: 4

Length: n

Data: IAID (4 bytes)

                IA_TA options (n − 4 bytes)

The IA_TA option specifies an IA for a set of temporary IPv6 addresses. IAID is the identifier of the IA. IA_TA options contain suboptions specific to this IA. IA Address options are often included in the options field. Note that neither the T1 nor T2 field is contained in this option. Since temporary addresses are used for privacy and are frequently changed in a short period, they are not expected to be renewed.

IA Address

Option Code: 5

Length: n

Data: IPv6 address (16 bytes)

                preferred-lifetime (4 bytes)

                valid-lifetime (4 bytes)

                IAaddr-options (n − 24 bytes)

The IA Address option carries parameters of an IPv6 address allocated to a client. This option can only appear as a suboption of an IA_NA or IA_TA option. The preferred and valid lifetimes have the same semantics as defined in [RFC2462] (see also Chapter 5 of *IPv6 Core Protocols Implementation*).

Option Request

Option Code:	6
Length:	2 * number of codes
Data:	list of option codes (2 bytes each)

The Option Request option lists options that a client wants to get from a server. Each 2-byte field contains the option code of a particular DHCPv6 option.

Preference

Option Code:	7
Length:	1
Data:	8-bit integer

The Preference option represents the server preference for the client to use to select a server. Higher values have higher preference. Value 255 has the special meaning that the client must immediately select the server which has this value.

Elapsed Time

Option Code:	8
Length:	2
Data:	16-bit integer

The Elapsed Time option is included in messages from the client and represents the elapsed time since the first message of one set of exchanges (e.g., Request and Reply) in hundredths of a second (2 bytes). This is a hint for servers other than the one the client is sending messages to, so that they can determine when the server currently responsible for the client is down and another server needs to take over the session (if possible).

Relay Message

Option Code:	9
Length:	n
Data:	relay message (n bytes)

The Relay Message option is used in a Relay-forward or Relay-reply message to encapsulate another DHCPv6 message. The option data is a complete DHCPv6 message starting with the common header.

Option Code 10

This was previously reserved for an option called Server Message option, which was deprecated during standardization.

Authentication

Option Code: 11

Length: n

Data: protocol (1 byte)

algorithm (1 byte)

replay detection method (RDM) (1 byte)

replay detection information (8 bytes)

authentication information (n − 11 bytes)

The Authentication option carries parameters for the DHCPv6 authentication mechanism.

The protocol field specifies the authentication protocol. Currently the following protocols are available:

2 delayed authentication protocol

3 reconfigure key protocol

The algorithm field specifies the algorithm used for message authentication. Currently, the only defined value is 1, which specifies HMAC-MD5.

The RDM field specifies the method for preventing replay attacks. Currently, the only defined value is 0, which means using a monotonically increasing counter.

The replay detection information stores data depending on the replay detection method. If the RDM field is 0, this field is simply regarded as a monotonically increasing 64-bit unsigned integer (modulo 2^{64}).

The authentication information field is protocol dependent, and can be empty depending on the protocol and the state of authentication.

For the delayed authentication protocol, the authentication information field, if not empty, is as follows:

DHCP realm A variable length opaque value which identifies the key.

key ID A 32-bit integer which identifies a particular key with the DHCP realm.

HMAC-MD5 The message authentication code for the entire DHCPv6 message.

In the delayed authentication protocol, servers and clients identify a particular key using the tuple of <DHCP realm, client DUID, key ID>.

For the reconfigure key protocol, the authentication information field is always provided as follows:

Type A 1-byte integer specifying the semantics of the Value field:

1 Reconfigure Key value (used in Reply message).

2 HMAC-MD5 digest of the message (used in Reconfigure message).

Value 128-bit data as specified by the type field.

Server Unicast

Option Code: 12

Length: 16

Data: a unicast IPv6 address of the server

The Server Unicast option indicates that the client can send messages directly to the server's unicast address. The data is a server's unicast address to which the client should send messages.

Status Code

Option Code:	13
Length:	n
Data:	status-code (2 byte)
	status-message (n − 2 bytes)

The Status Code option indicates the result of a DHCPv6 exchange. A Status Code option can appear in the top level option field of a DHCPv6 message or in the option field of another option. In the former case, it indicates the result of the entire exchange. In the latter case, it indicates the result about that particular option, e.g., one specific IA. Status-message is an optional data field, which is a UTF-8 encoded string as readable information of that code.

Table 4-3 summarizes the status codes currently defined in [RFC3315] and [RFC3633].

Rapid Commit

Option Code:	14
Length:	0
Data:	none

The Rapid Commit option indicates a shortcut exchange between the client and server. If this option is included in a Solicit message and the server is configured to accept it, the server will respond directly to the message with a Reply message, not Advertise, and make a corresponding binding.

TABLE 4-3

Name	Code	Description
Success	0	Success.
UnspecFail	1	Failure for an unspecified reason. This status code can be sent by either a client or a server.
NoAddrsAvail	2	An error indicating the server has no addresses available to allocate to the IA(s).
NoBinding	3	An error indicating the binding specified by the client is not available at the server side.
NotOnLink	4	An error indicating the prefix for the address is not appropriate for the link to which the client is attached.
UseMulticast	5	An error indicating the client has sent a message to a unicast address without permission, forcing the client to send further messages to the server using a multicast address.
NoPrefixAvail	6	An error indicating the delegating router has no prefixes available to allocate to the IAPD(s).

DHCPv6 status codes.

User Class

Option Code: 15

Length: n

Data: user-class-data (n bytes)

The User Class option identifies a *class* or a set of classes of the client. One example of classes would be different divisions in a corporate network: each division could be a class. This option is used by the server to provide different configuration information on a per-class basis. The data field of the User Class option consists of one or more instances of *user class data*, each of which starts with a 2-byte length field followed by an opaque data field.

Vendor Class

Option Code: 16

Length: n

Data: enterprise-number (4 bytes)

              vendor-class-data (n − 4 bytes)

The Vendor Class option identifies the vendor of the device on which the client DHCPv6 process is running. The enterprise-number field is a 32-bit integer maintained by the IANA which uniquely identifies a particular vendor. The vendor-class-data field consists of one or more instances of *vendor class data*, each of which starts with a 2-byte length field followed by an opaque data field.

Vendor-specific Information

Option Code: 17

Length: n

Data: enterprise-number (4 bytes)

              option-data (n − 4 bytes)

The Vendor-specific Information option carries optional data specific to a particular vendor, and can be used for vendor-specific purposes by clients manufactured by that vendor (or those that want to support these particular options). Such a client typically includes an Option Request option containing an option code specifying this option and a Vendor Class option identifying the vendor. If the server supports options for the specific vendor, it will return requested information.

The vendor is uniquely identified by the enterprise-number field, which is a 32-bit integer maintained by the IANA. The option-data field consists of a sequence of code, length, and data fields. Each sequence is represented as follows:

code A 2-byte integer which identifies one vendor-specific option.

length A 2-byte integer which specifies the length of the data field in bytes.

data The code-specific data.

Code values in the option-data field are vendor specific; the IANA does not maintain these values.

Interface-Id

Option Code: 18

Length: n

Data: interface-id (n bytes)

The Interface-Id option is set by a relay agent in order to identify the receiving interface of a message from a client (or other relay agent closer to a client). This is an opaque value which can only be meaningful to that relay agent. The server simply copies this option when it constructs the corresponding Relay-reply message, and this option is eventually used by the relay agent to identify the outgoing interface on which a decapsulated message is sent.

Reconfigure Message

Option Code: 19

Length: 1

Data: 5: Renew message

                11: Information-request message

The Reconfigure Message option can only appear in a Reconfigure message, and it indicates with which type of message the receiving client should respond to the Reconfigure message. If the option value is 5, the client should respond with a Renew message; if it is 11, the client should respond with an Information-request message.

Reconfigure Accept

Option Code: 20

Length: 0

Data: none

The Reconfigure Accept option can be sent by either a client or a server. When sent by a client, this option means the client is willing to accept a Reconfigure message. When sent by a server, it means the server wants the receiving client to accept a Reconfigure message (in the future). However, [RFC3315] does not specify the relationship between the existence or nonexistence of this option and the behavior for the Reconfigure message. For example, it is not clear whether a client can or should accept a Reconfigure message if it has not included this option in previous messages.

DNS Recursive Name Server

Option Code: 23

Length: 16 * number of addresses

Data: list of IPv6 addresses

The DNS Recursive Name Server option lists IPv6 addresses of DNS recursive servers. This option is defined in [RFC3646].

Domain Search List

> Option Code: 24
>
> Length: n
>
> Data: n characters (list of domain names)

The Domain Search List option lists domain names which can be used by the client host to resolve DNS names. This option is defined in [RFC3646].

Identity Association for Prefix Delegation (IA_PD)

> Option Code: 25
>
> Length: n
>
> Data: IAID (4 bytes)
>
>   T1 (4 bytes)
>
>   T2 (4 bytes)
>
>   IA_PD options (n − 12 bytes)

The IA_PD option specifies an IA for a set of IPv6 prefixes. IAID is the identifier of the IA. T1 and T2 are time parameters represented in seconds, specifying the renewal timing of this IA. IA_PD Prefix options are often included in the options field.

IA_PD Prefix

> Option Code: 26
>
> Length: n
>
> Data: preferred-lifetime (4 bytes)
>
>   valid-lifetime (4 bytes)
>
>   prefix-length (1 byte)
>
>   IPv6-prefix (16 bytes)
>
>   IA-prefix options (n − 25 bytes)

The IA_PD Prefix option carries parameters of an IPv6 prefix allocated to a client. This option can only appear as a suboption of an IA_PD option. The IPv6-prefix and prefix-length fields define the IPv6 prefix: the former is the address portion and the latter is the prefix length in bits. The values of the preferred and valid lifetime fields are expected to be included in Router Advertisements sent by the requesting router.

Information Refresh Time

> Option Code: 32
>
> Length: 4
>
> Data: 32-bit integer

The Information Refresh Time option specifies the interval in seconds after which the client needs to perform another exchange of Information-request and Reply messages.

4.2.5   Interaction with Neighbor Discovery

Although [RFC2461] and [RFC2462] indicate interaction between the Neighbor Discovery protocol and DHCPv6 through the M and O flags of the Router Advertisement message, the specification is too vague to implement. In fact, it is not even clear whether the protocol corresponding to these flags is DHCPv6, some other mechanisms, or both.

This is partly because when Neighbor Discovery was standardized, the DHCPv6 specification was still in flux, and the documents that were finished first could not be specific about DHCPv6. The IETF then started clarification work on the interaction during a revision process of the Neighbor Discovery specifications, but failed to make clear consensus due to much controversy. Therefore, this book discusses DHCPv6 as being independent of its interaction with Neighbor Discovery.

4.2.6   Comparison to DHCPv4

Following is a summary of the major differences between DHCPv4 and DHCPv6, most of which were mentioned in the preceding subsections.

- DHCPv6 is designed with the ability to allocate multiple addresses on a single interface of a client. The notion of Identity Association was introduced for this purpose. On the other hand, DHCPv4 can only allocate one address in a single DHCPv4 session.

- As a UDP service, DHCPv4 is part of the bootstrap protocol (BOOTP). DHCPv6 is a separate UDP service.

- DHCPv6 introduces separate message types (e.g., Renew or Rebind) depending on the role of exchanges.

- DHCPv6 introduces separate message types for the communication between relay agents and servers. This allows response messages from a server to be relayed by multiple agents. In DHCPv4, the server must send the response directly to the relay agent closest to the client, even if the corresponding message from the client was relayed by multiple agents.

- In DHCPv6, there is no need for the use of the unspecified address (::) as the source address of DHCPv6 messages because of the use of link-local addresses. A DHCPv4 client needs to use 0.0.0.0 as the source address for initial communication with a server.

- DHCPv6 uses separate multicast addresses for sending messages to servers or relay agents, thereby avoiding expensive broadcasting. DHCPv4 requires the use of link-level broadcasting.

- DHCPv6 explicitly introduces likely unique identifiers for clients and servers (DUIDs). In DHCPv4, a server is identified as an IPv4 address, which at times might not necessarily be globally unique.

- DHCPv6 adopts 16-bit integers for the option code and length fields which allow for a larger number or larger size of options. In DHCPv4, these fields are 8-bit integers.

- By design, there is no router option in DHCPv6 (see the description about address allocation in Section 4.2.1). Similarly, there is no subnet mask (or prefix length) option in DHCPv6.

4.3 Code Introduction

This section and the following three sections describe KAME's DHCPv6 implementation, providing a solid understanding of how the protocol works. Unlike the implementation description in many other chapters of this series of books, the target code is the 20050509 version of the KAME snapshots. The newer version is used because the standardization of the DHCPv6 protocol was not completed when the code base was chosen for the other chapters, and the implementation at that time was immature. In addition, the newer version supports IPv6 address allocation, the primary goal of the DHCPv6 protocol, making it more suitable as a reference.

Still, the implementation is incomplete in some areas. Specifically, it does not support the following DHCPv6 messages: Confirm, Decline, and Reconfigure. It also does not implement the Reconfigure Key authentication protocol, nor does it implement some of the standard DHCPv6 options.

This implementation includes the three major components of the protocol: a client, a server, and a relay agent. The client and the relay agent implementations can be used in a practical environment, but the server implementation for stateful resource allocation (i.e., address allocation and prefix delegation) should be treated as just a reference. In particular, it does not support the notion of address or prefix pools, and the allocated resources must be explicitly preconfigured with the clients' identifiers. This is not a reasonable requirement in the actual operation. Providing stateless configuration information using Information-request and Reply exchanges does work well with the current server implementation, however.

Although this section provides a fairly comprehensive description of the entire implementation in terms of the DHCPv6 protocol operation, there are still many undocumented parts. In fact, the whole implementation includes many other miscellaneous features, such as configuration parsers, run-time operation via control channels, hash calculation routines for authentication, logging, and so on. For clarity, when the meaning is obvious from the context, the definitions for some data structures referenced in the text are omitted. All of the definitions are available in the full source code.

Files listed in Table 4-4 are covered in this chapter. All files are located under the `dhcp6` directory that can be found by unpacking the `kame-dhcp6-20050509.tgz` archive file contained on the companion web site (see the Preface).

4.3.1 Common Data Structures and Routines

Here is a brief review of the various data structures commonly used by the client, server, and relay agent implementations, and related routines regarding the structures.

Variable Length Buffers

Listing 4-1 contains the `duid{}` and `dhcp6_vbuf{}` structures. They are both data types that implement variable-length data.

TABLE 4-4

File	Description
auth.h	Internal structure for DHCPv6 authentication keys
config.h	Structures containing configuration information
dhcp6.h	Structures for DHCPv6 protocol operation
dhcp6c_ia.h	IA definition for the client
addrconf.c	IPv6 address configuration by DHCPv6
dhcp6c.c	Main routines of the client
dhcp6c_ia.c	IA operations for the client
dhcp6relay.c	Relay agent routines
dhcp6s.c	Server routines

Files discussed in this chapter.

Listing 4-1

—— dhcp6.h

```
90    struct duid {
91            size_t duid_len;         /* length */
92            char *duid_id;           /* variable length ID value (must be opaque) */
93    };

95    struct dhcp6_vbuf {              /* generic variable length buffer */
96            int dv_len;
97            caddr_t dv_buf;
98    };
```

—— dhcp6.h

The following functions are common routines for manipulating these structures:

```
int duidcpy(struct duid *dst, struct duid *src);
```

Description: Copy DUID `src` to `dst`. Necessary memory is allocated in this function.

```
int duidcmp(struct duid *d1, struct duid *d2);
```

Description: Compare two DUID structures, d1 and d2. It returns 0 if those two are identical, and non-zero if not.

```
void duidfree(struct duid *duid);
```

Description: Free the memory that was allocated for `duid`.

```
int dhcp6_vbuf_copy(struct dhcp6_vbuf *dst, struct dhcp6_vbuf *src);
```

Description: Copy the source buffer `src` to `dst`. Necessary memory is allocated in this function.

```
void dhcp6_vbuf_free(struct dhcp6_vbuf *vbuf);
```

Description: Free the memory that was allocated for `vbuf`.

List Structure

The DHCPv6 protocol specification uses complex data structures. Many of them contain variable-length data, and in some cases implementations need to deal with nested structures. This implementation introduces a dedicated data structure, `dhcp6_list{}`, to manipulate this complex data.

The `dhcp6_list{}` structure itself is a standard BSD tail-queue structure. List elements are the `dhcp6_listval{}` structure shown in Listing 4-2.

Listing 4-2
dhcp6.h

```
128     struct dhcp6_listval {
129             TAILQ_ENTRY(dhcp6_listval) link;
130
131             dhcp6_listval_type_t type;
132
133             union {
134                     int uv_num;
135                     u_int16_t uv_num16;
136                     struct in6_addr uv_addr6;
137                     struct dhcp6_prefix uv_prefix6;
138                     struct dhcp6_statefuladdr uv_statefuladdr6;
139                     struct dhcp6_ia uv_ia;
140                     struct dhcp6_vbuf uv_vbuf;
141             } uv;
142
143             struct dhcp6_list sublist;
144     };
145     #define val_num uv.uv_num
146     #define val_num16 uv.uv_num16
147     #define val_addr6 uv.uv_addr6
148     #define val_ia uv.uv_ia
149     #define val_prefix6 uv.uv_prefix6
150     #define val_statefuladdr6 uv.uv_statefuladdr6
151     #define val_vbuf uv.uv_vbuf
```
dhcp6.h

131 A `dhcp6_listval{}` structure can contain various types of DHCPv6-related data. The type of data is specified by its `type` member.

133–141 This union is the main value of the element. Some of the union members are allowed only for particular types. For example, the `uv_ia` member is effective only for the `DHCP6_LISTVAL_IAPD` and `DHCP6_LISTVAL_IANA` types (see Table 4-5).

143 When needed, the `sublist` member is an associated list for this list element. This member is used to construct a nested data structure.

145–151 `val_xxx` macros are shortcuts to get access to the union members.

Table 4-5 summarizes possible element types.

The following functions are common routines for manipulating the list framework:

```
int dhcp6_copy_list(struct dhcp6_list *dst, struct dhcp6_list *src);
```

Description: Copy the entire list from `src` to `dst`. Necessary memory is allocated in this function.

```
void dhcp6_clear_list(struct dhcp6_list *head);
```

Description: Free the entire list, including sublists (if any).

TABLE 4-5

Type value	Union member (val_)	Description
DHCP6_LISTVAL_NUM	num	Normal integers
DHCP6_LISTVAL_STCODE	num16	DHCPv6 Status Code
DHCP6_LISTVAL_ADDR6	addr6	Generic IPv6 address
DHCP6_LISTVAL_IAPD	ia	IA_PD
DHCP6_LISTVAL_PREFIX6	prefix6	IPv6 prefix
DHCP6_LISTVAL_IANA	ia	IA_NA
DHCP6_LISTVAL_STATEFULADDR6	statefuladdr6	IPv6 address with lifetimes
DHCP6_LISTVAL_VBUF	vbuf	Variable length data in general

Elements of dhcp6_listval{}.

```
struct dhcp6_listval *dhcp6_find_listval(struct dhcp6_list *head,
                                         dhcp6_listval_type_t type,
                                         void *val,
                                         int option);\vspace*{0.6pt}
```

Description: Search list head for value val with type type. option is a flag for customizing the search operation. If the MATCHLIST_PREFIXLEN flag is set, the address part of prefixes are ignored.

```
struct dhcp6_listval *dhcp6_add_listval(struct dhcp6_list *head,
                                        dhcp6_listval_type_t type,
                                        void *val,
                                        struct dhcp6_list *sublist);
```

Description: Add a list element val with type type to the end of list head. If sublist is non-NULL, a copy of it is created and stored in the sublist member of the new element. When necessary, memory for the new element is allocated in this function.

```
void dhcp6_clear_listval(struct dhcp6_listval *lv);
```

Description: Free the list element lv, including the sublist (if it exists).

DHCPv6 Options

The dhcp6_optinfo{} structure (Listing 4-3) represents a set of DHCPv6 options in a single DHCPv6 message. Due to the complexity of the wire format of the options, it does not make sense to deal with the raw data in the protocol implementation. This structure is therefore used as an easily accessible internal representation of the wire format data.

For the most part, the meaning of the members should be obvious from their names and in-line comments, although a couple of notes might make things clearer:

- The authflags and the following members are related to the Authentication option. The authflags member specifies how this option should be handled. Currently the only supported value is DHCP6OPT_AUTHFLAG_NOINFO, meaning that no Authentication information is included.

- The aiu_reconfig member of the authinfo{} union is intended for the reconfigure key protocol, but it is not currently implemented.

Listing 4-3

_____dhcp6.h

```
153    struct dhcp6_optinfo {
154            struct duid clientID;           /* DUID */
155            struct duid serverID;           /* DUID */
156
157            int rapidcommit;        /* bool */
158            int pref;                       /* server preference */
159            int32_t elapsed_time;           /* elapsed time (from client to
    server only) */
160            int64_t refreshtime;            /* info refresh time for stateless
    options */
161
162            struct dhcp6_list iapd_list; /* list of IA_PD */
163            struct dhcp6_list iana_list; /* list of IA_NA */
164            struct dhcp6_list reqopt_list; /* options in option request */
165            struct dhcp6_list stcode_list; /* status code */
166            struct dhcp6_list sip_list; /* SIP server list */
167            struct dhcp6_list sipname_list; /* SIP server domain list */
168            struct dhcp6_list dns_list; /* DNS server list */
169            struct dhcp6_list dnsname_list; /* Domain Search list */
170            struct dhcp6_list ntp_list; /* NTP server list */
171            struct dhcp6_list prefix_list; /* prefix list */
172
173            struct dhcp6_vbuf relay_msg; /* relay message */
174    #define relaymsg_len relay_msg.dv_len
175    #define relaymsg_msg relay_msg.dv_buf
176
177            struct dhcp6_vbuf ifidopt; /* Interface-id */
178    #define ifidopt_len ifidopt.dv_len
179    #define ifidopt_id ifidopt.dv_buf
180
181            u_int authflags;
182    #define DHCP6OPT_AUTHFLAG_NOINFO        0x1
183            int authproto;
184            int authalgorithm;
185            int authrdm;
186            /* the followings are effective only when NOINFO is unset */
187            u_int64_t authrd;
188            union {
189                    struct {
190                            u_int32_t keyid;
191                            struct dhcp6_vbuf realm;
192                            int offset; /* offset to the HMAC field */
193                    } aiu_delayed;
194                    struct {
195                            int type;
196                            int offset; /* offset to the HMAC field */
197                            char val[16]; /* key value */
198                    } aiu_reconfig;
199            } authinfo;
200    #define delayedauth_keyid authinfo.aiu_delayed.keyid
201    #define delayedauth_realmlen authinfo.aiu_delayed.realm.dv_len
202    #define delayedauth_realmval authinfo.aiu_delayed.realm.dv_buf
203    #define delayedauth_offset authinfo.aiu_delayed.offset
204    #define reconfigauth_type authinfo.aiu_reconfig.type
205    #define reconfigauth_offset authinfo.aiu_reconfig.offset
206    #define reconfigauth_val authinfo.aiu_reconfig.val
207    };
```

_____dhcp6.h

— *Lines 159 and 160 are broken here for layout reasons. However, they are a single line of code.*

Two major routines are often used for the `dhcp6_option{}` structure:

```
int dhcp6_get_options(struct dhcp6opt *p,
                      struct dhcp6opt *ep,
                      struct dhcp6_optinfo *optinfo);
```

Description: Parse wire-format DHCPv6 options and construct the corresponding `dhcp6_optinfo{}` structure. Arguments `p` and `ep` specify the head and end of the options, and argument `optinfo` is the target structure.

```
int dhcp6_set_options(int type,
                      struct dhcp6opt *optbp,
                      struct dhcp6opt *optep,
                      struct dhcp6_optinfo *optinfo);
```

Description: Make wire-format DHCPv6 options from a given `optinfo{}` structure. The argument `type` specifies the type of the DHCPv6 message which contains the options. This is necessary since the type may restrict the use of some options. The argument `optinfo` is the source structure.

Figure 4-20 illustrates the relationship between DHCPv6 options in wire format and the corresponding `dhcp6_optinfo{}` structure, and how the two subroutines work with these data structures. In this example, there are two IA_PD options, one for IAID 100 and the other for IAID 200. The former contains two prefixes, while the latter has no prefix and includes a Status Code option indicating an error condition. The corresponding data structures are represented as a linked list on the `iapd_list` member of the `dhcp6_optinfo{}` structure. The two IA_PD options are represented as a list of `dhcp6_listval{}` structures, both of which contain sublists for prefixes or the Status Code option.

FIGURE 4-20

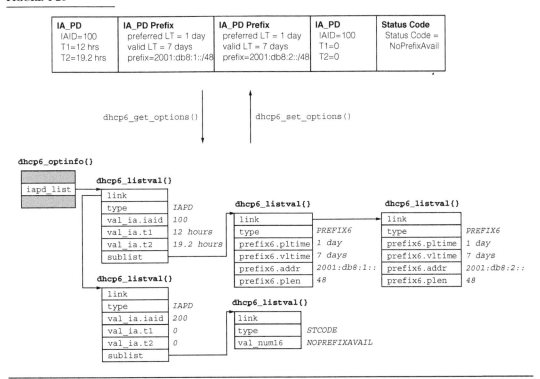

Relationship between wire-format DHCPv6 options and the `dhcp6_optinfo{}` *structure.*

Timers

The DHCPv6 protocol often requires the use of timeouts. The `dhcp6_timer{}` structure, shown in Listing 4-4, is used as a general timer entry to implement timeouts.

Listing 4-4

```
                                                                                dhcp6.h
43    struct dhcp6_timer {
44            LIST_ENTRY(dhcp6_timer) link;
45
46            struct timeval tm;
47
48            struct dhcp6_timer *(*expire) __P((void *));
49            void *expire_data;
50    };
                                                                                dhcp6.h
```

44–49 The `tm` member is the time when this timer entry expires. The `expire` and `expire_data` members define the timer handler for this entry; when this timer expires, the function pointed to by `expire` is called with an argument of `expire_data`.

The following are the most commonly-used timer routines:

```
struct dhcp6_timer *dhcp6_add_timer(
    struct dhcp6_timer *(*timeout) __P((void *));
    void *timeodata);
```

Description: Create a new timer with the timer handler function `timeout` and its argument `timeodata`.

```
void dhcp6_remove_timer(struct dhcp6_timer **timer);
```

Description: Remove the timer pointed to by *`timer`.

```
void dhcp6_set_timer(struct timeval *tm,
                     struct dhcp6_timer *timer);
```

Description: Start or restart the timer with an interval of `tm`.

```
struct timeval *dhcp6_check_timer();
```

Description: Check the expiration for each timer in the process. If any timer has expired, this function calls the expire function.

4.4   Client Implementation

Figure 4-21 shows an overview of the functioning of the client implementation. After initialization, the process goes into an infinite loop in the `client6_mainloop()` function, waiting for a socket or timer event.

Many client actions start as a result of timer expiration, due to an initial random delay or the expiration of a retransmission timer. The `dhcp6_check_timer()` function checks the client's timers, and calls the timer handler function when a timer expires. The `client6_timo()` function is a general timer for the client; it initiates the transmission of the first message after a random delay of Solicit or Information-request. All packets being resent after a timeout are also sent via this function. On the other hand, the `ia_timo()` function handles the state transition of an IA, and sends a Renew or Rebind message to update the configuration information.

The `client6_recv()` function receives responses from the server, and calls the `client6_recvadvert()` or `client6_recvreply()` function, depending on the message

FIGURE 4-21

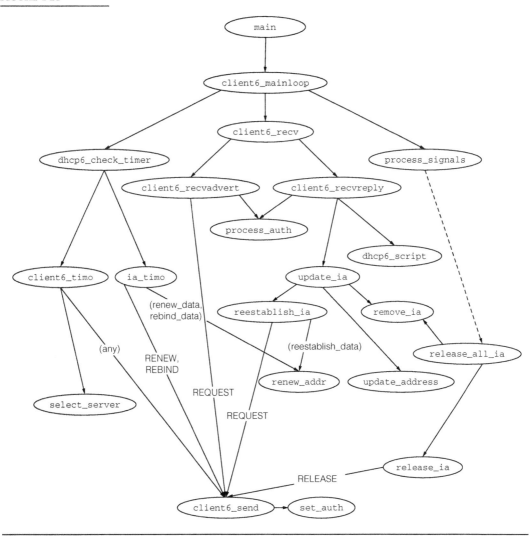

An overview of the client processes.

type. If the received message contains a DHCPv6 Authentication option, the `process_auth()` function is called to authenticate the message.

The `client6_recvreply()` function handles an incoming Reply message. It calls the `dhcp6_script()` function for further processing of stateless configuration information such as DNS recursive server addresses. For stateful information, the `update_ia()` function processes the Reply message, and creates or updates the IA contained in the Reply. For address allocation, the `update_address()` function, called from `update_ia()`, creates or updates the addresses allocated by the server.

Upon receiving a SIGTERM signal, the client releases all internal resources allocated by the server, including addresses or prefixes, and sends a Release message for each released IA. The `process_signals()` function starts this process.

All messages from the client are generated and sent from the `client6_send()` function (each arrow to this function is labeled with the message names which the corresponding call can make). If the client uses DHCPv6 authentication, the `set_auth()` function prepares the necessary parameters for the Authentication option.

4.4.1   Client-Specific Data Structures

First, here is a brief review of client-specific data structures.

The `dhcp6_if{}` structure, shown below, contains per-interface configuration parameters used by the client and the server, but it is described in this section since most of its members are only used by the client.

Listing 4-5

―――config.h
```
36    /* per-interface information */
37    struct dhcp6_if {
38            struct dhcp6_if *next;
39
40            /* timer for the interface */
41            struct dhcp6_timer *timer;
42
43            /* event queue */
44            TAILQ_HEAD(, dhcp6_event) event_list;
45
46            /* static parameters of the interface */
47            char *ifname;
48            unsigned int ifid;
49            u_int32_t linkid;        /* to send link-local packets */
50
51            /* configuration parameters */
52            u_long send_flags;
53            u_long allow_flags;
54    #define DHCIFF_INFO_ONLY 0x1
55    #define DHCIFF_RAPID_COMMIT 0x2
56
57            int server_pref;        /* server preference (server only) */
58
59            char *scriptpath;       /* path to config script (client only) */
60
61            struct dhcp6_list reqopt_list;
62            struct ia_conflist iaconf_list;
63
64            /* authentication information */
65            int authproto;                  /* protocol */
66            /* the followings are valid only if authproto is not UNDEF */
67            int authalgorithm;      /* algorithm */
68            int authrdm;                    /* replay attack detection method */
69    };
```
―――config.h

36–69 The `timer` member points to a per-interface timer, which is used to implement the Information Refresh timer for stateless configuration information. The `event_list` member is a list of `dhcp6_event{}` structures (described later). Each structure corresponds to an ongoing message exchange between the client and the server on the interface. The `send_flags` member is only for the client. It specifies some special behavior when sending packets. Currently, only two flags are available:

DHCIFF_INFO_ONLY Send Information-request messages only
DHCIFF_RAPID_COMMIT Include the Rapid Commit option in Solicit messages

The `allow_flags` member is only for the server. It specifies the server's policy for some types of messages. Currently, the only available flag is DHCIFF_RAPID_COMMIT, which means the server will honor the Rapid Commit option in a Solicit message; if this flag is not set, the server responds as if no Rapid Commit option had been included in the Solicit message.

The `server_pref` member is specific to the server. It specifies the server's preference value when explicitly configured.

The `scriptpath` member is specific to the client and specifies the path to a script file, which is invoked with stateless information (such as recursive DNS server addresses). The `reqopt_list` and `iaconf_list` members are specific to the client. The former is a list of options which will be included in outgoing messages as Option Request options. The latter corresponds to the client's local configuration of requested IAs. This is a list of `ia_conf{}` structures, which will be described later.

The rest of this structure specifies authentication parameters configured for the client.

The `dhcp6_event{}` structure is shown in Listing 4-6. As explained previously, this structure represents a single exchange between the client and the server.

Listing 4-6

_____config.h
```
 83   struct dhcp6_event {
 84           TAILQ_ENTRY(dhcp6_event) link;
 85
 86           struct dhcp6_if *ifp;
 87           struct dhcp6_timer *timer;
 88
 89           struct duid serverid;
 90
 91           struct timeval tv_start; /* timestamp when the 1st msg is sent */
 92
 93           /* internal timer parameters */
 94           long retrans;
 95           long init_retrans;
 96           long max_retrans_cnt;
 97           long max_retrans_time;
 98           long max_retrans_dur;
 99           int timeouts;              /* number of timeouts */
100
101           u_int32_t xid;             /* current transaction ID */
102           int state;
103
104           /* list of known servers */
105           struct dhcp6_serverinfo *current_server;
106           struct dhcp6_serverinfo *servers;
107
108           /* authentication parameters */
109           struct authparam *authparam;
110
111           TAILQ_HEAD(, dhcp6_eventdata) data_list;
112   };
```
_____config.h

83–91 The `ifp` member specifies the corresponding `dhcp6_if{}` structure. The `timer` member is a timer associated with this event, which usually specifies a timeout for receiving a response from the server. If the event is associated with a particular server (e.g., when it is used for a Request message to one particular server), the `serverid` member specifies the server's DUID. The `tv_start` member keeps the time when the first message for this event was sent (see Section 4.4.4).

93–99 The members from `retrans` to `timeouts` are timeout parameters for this event (see Table 4-2, page 301). The first member (`retrans`) is the retransmission period including a random delay. The succeeding four members correspond to IRT (Initial retransmission time), MRC (Maximum retransmission count), MRT (Maximum retransmission time), and MRD (Maximum retransmission duration). The `timeout` member is the number of timeouts that have expired for this event, which is also the number of retransmissions.

101–102 The `xid` member is the transaction ID of the message associated with this event and which is expected in the response. The `state` member basically identifies which type of messages are sent with this event. Possible states are DHCP6S_INIT, DHCP6S_SOLICIT, DHCP6S_INFOREQ, DHCP6S_REQUEST, DHCP6S_RENEW, DHCP6S_REBIND, and DHCP6S_RELEASE.

DHCP6S_INIT is a special state. It means that the initial message is pending for a random period. The rest of the members correspond to one particular DHCPv6 message type, which should be obvious from the state name.

104–111 The `current_server` and `servers` members are used to maintain multiple servers when the client is accepting DHCPv6 Advertise messages from multiple servers while trying to select the best server. When DHCPv6 authentication is used, the `authparam` member contains various authentication parameters, such as the authentication protocol or the latest replay detection counter. Finally, the `data_list` member stores a list of configuration information to be requested to the server, such as IA parameters of addresses or prefixes.

The `ia_conf{}` structure, defined in Listing 4-7, represents the client's local configuration for a particular IA. An `ia_conf{}` structure is also used to maintain run-time information about the IA allocated by the server.

Listing 4-7
_____config.h
```
159    struct ia_conf {
160            TAILQ_ENTRY(ia_conf) link;
161            /*struct ia_conf *next;*/
162            iatype_t type;
163            u_int32_t iaid;
164
165            TAILQ_HEAD(, ia) iadata; /* struct ia is an opaque type */
166
167            /* type dependent values follow */
168    };
```
_____config.h

161–163 The `type` and `iaid` parameters are common to any type of IA. The IA types supported by the current implementation are IATYPE_NA and IATYPE_PD, meaning IA_NA and IA_PD, respectively.

165 The `iadata` member is an opaque variable, which is used as run-time data.

As commented in the definition of the `ia_conf{}` structure, each particular type of IA has its specific configuration structure, `iapd_conf{}` and `iana_conf{}` shown in Listing 4-8. These structures share the same "header," which is an `ia_conf{}` structure. The `iapd_conf{}` structure contains a list of prefixes (`iapd_prefix_list`) for which the client wants delegations. It also includes the local configuration parameters for the local network (`iapd_pif_list`). This will be clarified in the description about the `prefix-interface` statement for the example of prefix delegation configuration shown in Section 4.8.4.

On the other hand, the `iana_conf{}` structure contains a list of addresses which the client wants to be allocated.

Listing 4-8

```
                                                                              config.h
170    struct iapd_conf {
171            struct ia_conf iapd_ia;
172
173            /* type dependent values follow */
174            struct dhcp6_list iapd_prefix_list;
175            struct pifc_list iapd_pif_list;
176    };
....
181    struct iana_conf {
182            struct ia_conf iana_ia;
183
184            /* type dependent values follow */
185            struct dhcp6_list iana_address_list;
186    };
                                                                              config.h
```

Global Variables

Table 4-6 summarizes major global variables specific to the client implementation.

Example

Here is an example of a client configuration. Assume there is a DHCPv6 client that wants to get the following configuration parameters:

- IPv6 addresses. This client would like to have these addresses allocated: `2001:db8:1234::1` and `2001:db8:abcd::a`. For these addresses, the client uses two IAs whose IAIDs are 100 and 200.

TABLE 4-6

Name	Type	Description
`client_duid`	`struct duid`	Client's DUID.
`insock`	`int`	The file descriptor for the socket receiving inbound packets. The socket listens on UDP port 546.
`outsock`	`int`	The file descriptor for the socket sending outbound packets. This socket is also bound to port 546, since there is a server implementation that rejects packets from a client with a different port.
`sa6_allagent`	`struct sockaddr_in6 *`	A socket address structure initialized with (UDP) port 547 of the All_DHCP_Relay_Agents_and_Servers multicast group (`ff02::1:2`). This is used as a template of the destination address for sending a DHCPv6 message.

Global variables of the client implementation.

- Recursive DNS server addresses
- DNS domain search list

Figure 4-22 shows the related data structures when this client is going to send a Solicit message with the above preferences. The data pointed to by the `iaconf_list` and `reqopt_list` members of the `dhcp6_if{}` structure represents the client's local configuration. In order to send a Solicit message, a `dhcp6_event{}` structure is associated with the `dhcp6_if{}` structure, which contains the IA-related parameters derived from the client's configuration stored in the `iana_conf{}` structures.

Note that the client specifies two separate IAs for the two desired addresses. The client could also specify the addresses in a single IA, but then the client may get only one address, because the addresses specified in a Solicit message can be used by the server just as a hint; the server may not even respect the number of addresses specified. By specifying multiple IAs, the client explicitly requests multiple addresses (even though the actual addresses allocated may be different from the desired ones).

4.4.2 `client6_mainloop()` Function

Once the DHCPv6 client finishes configuring itself, it enters the `client6_mainloop()` function, which loops indefinitely, handling all the DHCPv6 protocol events.

Listing 4-9 shows this function. It is not complicated: it first checks asynchronous events, for example, signals and timers, and then waits for socket events using the `select()` system call. If a DHCPv6 packet arrives, the function is resumed from the `select()` call, and calls the `client6_recv()` function. The `w` variable contains the time until the next timer expires, so if no packets arrive before that time, `select()` returns anyway. The `client6_mainloop()` function repeats indefinitely.

Listing 4-9

dhcp6c.c

```
560    static void
561    client6_mainloop()
562    {
563            struct timeval *w;
564            int ret, maxsock;
565            fd_set r;
566
567            while(1) {
568                    if (sig_flags)
569                            process_signals();
570
571                    w = dhcp6_check_timer();
572
573                    FD_ZERO(&r);
574                    FD_SET(insock, &r);
575                    maxsock = insock;
576                    if (ctlsock >= 0) {
577                            FD_SET(ctlsock, &r);
578                            maxsock = (insock > ctlsock) ? insock : ctlsock;
579                            (void)dhcp6_ctl_setreadfds(&r, &maxsock);
580                    }
581
582                    ret = select(maxsock + 1, &r, NULL, NULL, w);
583
584                    switch (ret) {
585                    case -1:
```

```
586                             if (errno != EINTR) {
587                                     dprintf(LOG_ERR, FNAME, "select: %s",
588                                             strerror(errno));
589                                     exit(1);
590                             }
591                             continue;
592                     case 0:         /* timeout */
593                             break;          /* dhcp6_check_timer() will treat
    the case */
594                     default:
595                             break;
596                     }
597                     if (FD_ISSET(insock, &r))
598                             client6_recv();
599                     if (ctlsock >= 0) {
600                             if (FD_ISSET(ctlsock, &r)) {
601                                     (void)dhcp6_ctl_acceptcommand(ctlsock,
602                                             client6_do_ctlcommand);
603                             }
604                             (void)dhcp6_ctl_readcommand(&r);
605                     }
606             }
607     }
```
_____dhcp6c.c

— *Lines 593 are broken here for layout reasons. However, they are a single line of code.*

4.4.3 `client6_timo()` Function

The `client6_timo()` function, following, is the timer handler routine for a single client event, which usually corresponds to one set of message exchanges between the client and the server(s), e.g., exchanges of the Request and Reply messages, and implements necessary random delay for the first message or resending timeout messages.

Check Retransmission Limit

Listing 4-10
_____dhcp6c.c

```
851     struct dhcp6_timer *
852     client6_timo(arg)
853             void *arg;
854     {
855             struct dhcp6_event *ev = (struct dhcp6_event *)arg;
856             struct dhcp6_if *ifp;
857             int state = ev->state;
858
859             ifp = ev->ifp;
860             ev->timeouts++;
861
862             /*
863              * Unless MRC is zero, the message exchange fails once the client has
864              * transmitted the message MRC times.
865              * [RFC3315 14.]
866              */
867             if (ev->max_retrans_cnt && ev->timeouts >= ev->max_retrans_cnt) {
868                     dprintf(LOG_INFO, FNAME, "no responses were received");
869                     dhcp6_remove_event(ev);
870
871                     if (state == DHCP6S_RELEASE)
872                             check_exit();
873
874                     return (NULL);
875             }
```
_____dhcp6c.c

FIGURE 4-22

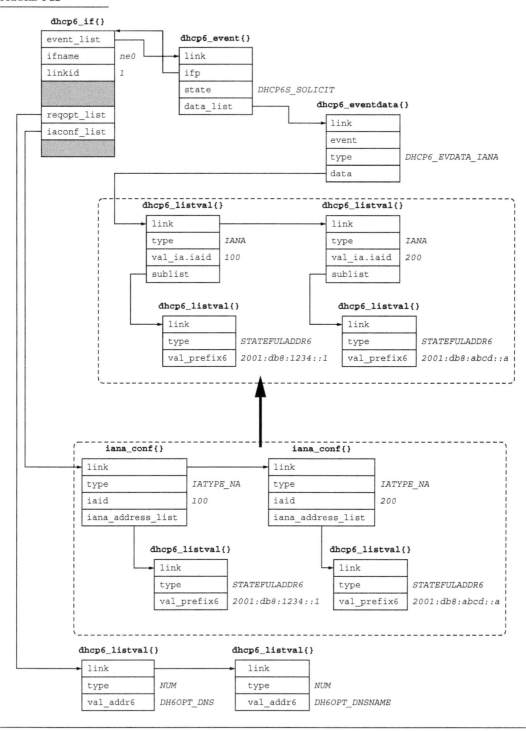

Client configuration structures when sending Solicit.

859–875 If the maximum number of retransmissions is specified for this event, as is the case
for the Request, Release, and Decline messages (although the last one is not supported in
this implementation), it is compared against the number of retransmissions made so far.
If it reaches the limit, the event processing is terminated unsuccessfully. In particular, if
the associated event is Release-Reply exchanges, the `check_exit()` function is called
to see whether the whole process can be stopped.

Change Event State and Send Message

Listing 4-11

```
                                                                              dhcp6c.c
877          switch(ev->state) {
878          case DHCP6S_INIT:
879                  ev->timeouts = 0; /* indicate to generate a new XID. */
880                  if ((ifp->send_flags & DHCIFF_INFO_ONLY) || infreq_mode)
881                          ev->state = DHCP6S_INFOREQ;
882                  else {
883                          ev->state = DHCP6S_SOLICIT;
884                          if (construct_confdata(ifp, ev)) {
885                                  dprintf(LOG_ERR, FNAME, "can't send solicit");
886                                  exit(1); /* XXX */
887                          }
888                  }
889                  dhcp6_set_timeoparam(ev); /* XXX */
890                  /* fall through */
891          case DHCP6S_REQUEST:
892          case DHCP6S_RELEASE:
893          case DHCP6S_INFOREQ:
894                  client6_send(ev);
895                  break;
896          case DHCP6S_RENEW:
897          case DHCP6S_REBIND:
898                  if (!TAILQ_EMPTY(&ev->data_list))
899                          client6_send(ev);
900                  else {
901                          dprintf(LOG_INFO, FNAME,
902                              "all information to be updated was canceled");
903                          dhcp6_remove_event(ev);
904                          return (NULL);
905                  }
906                  break;
                                                                              dhcp6c.c
```

877–889 If this routine is called during the `DHCP6S_INIT` state, it means the random delay
for the initial transmission is over. The message to be sent depends on the local configuration: if the client is running in the Information-request only mode, an Information-
request message is sent; otherwise a Solicit message is sent. In the latter case the
`construct_confdata()` function builds IAs to be included in the Solicit message from
the client's configuration (see Figure 4-22, page 334). The `dhcp6_set_timeoparam()`
function resets new parameters for the new message (initial and maximum timeouts).

891–895 For sending a Solicit, Request, Release, or Information-request message, the
`client6_send()` function is simply called with the associated event structure.

896–906 For a Renew or Rebind message, if the event has data to be updated (e.g., an
address to be renewed), the `client6_send()` function sends the corresponding message. Otherwise, the event is simply canceled without sending any message. The latter
case can happen, for example, when time T2 for an IA has passed while the client is

sending Renew messages, and it now needs to send a Rebind message. In this case, the
ia_timo() function (Section 4.4.12) cancels the old event while keeping the associated
timer.

Resend Solicit or Send New Request

Listing 4-12

```
                                                                              dhcp6c.c
907            case DHCP6S_SOLICIT:
908                    if (ev->servers) {
909                            /*
910                             * Send a Request to the best server.
911                             * Note that when we set Rapid-commit in Solicit,
912                             * but a direct Reply has been delayed (very much),
913                             * the transition to DHCP6S_REQUEST (and the change of
914                             * transaction ID) will invalidate the reply even if it
915                             * ever arrives.
916                             */
917                            ev->current_server = select_server(ev);
918                            if (ev->current_server == NULL) {
919                                    /* this should not happen! */
920                                    dprintf(LOG_NOTICE, FNAME,
921                                        "can't find a server");
922                                    exit(1); /* XXX */
923                            }
924                            if (duidcpy(&ev->serverid,
925                                &ev->current_server->optinfo.serverID)) {
926                                    dprintf(LOG_NOTICE, FNAME,
927                                        "can't copy server ID");
928                                    return (NULL); /* XXX: better recovery? */
929                            }
930                            ev->timeouts = 0;
931                            ev->state = DHCP6S_REQUEST;
932                            dhcp6_set_timeoparam(ev);
933
934                            if (ev->authparam != NULL)
935                                    free(ev->authparam);
936                            ev->authparam = ev->current_server->authparam;
937                            ev->current_server->authparam = NULL;
938
939                            if (construct_reqdata(ifp,
940                                &ev->current_server->optinfo, ev)) {
941                                    dprintf(LOG_NOTICE, FNAME,
942                                        "failed to construct request data");
943                                    break;
944                            }
945                    }
946                    client6_send(ev);
947                    break;
948            }
                                                                              dhcp6c.c
```

907–929 If this routine is called under the DHCP6S_SOLICIT state and the client has already
received any Advertise messages during this state, the select_server() function is
called to choose the best server for the client. The current logic of the server selection
is very simple: it picks up a server that has the highest priority, without considering the
information that the server is offering. Then the server's identifier is copied to the event
structure.

930–937 The client now sends a Request message to the selected server. The event state and
timeout parameters are updated accordingly. From now on, authentication parameters (if
provided) given by the server will be used.

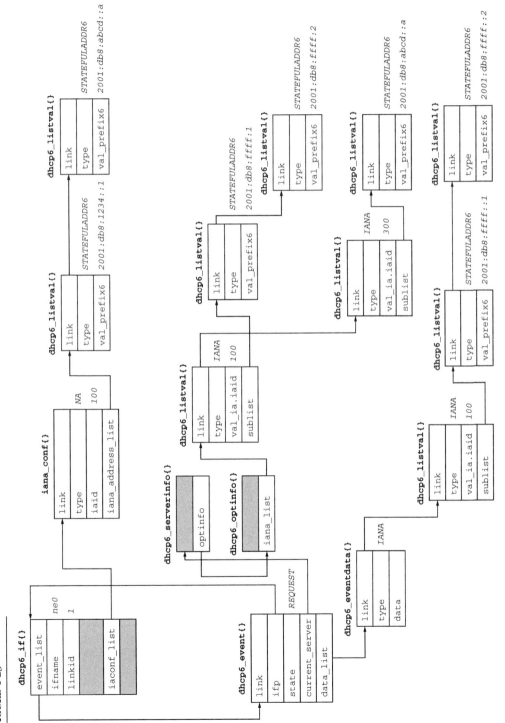

FIGURE 4-23

Construct request data.

939–945 The `construct_reqdata()` function copies each IA returned by the server into the event data list whose IAID matches one of the IAIDs in the client's local configuration.

Figure 4-23 depicts an example of this procedure. The client configuration is the same as that in Figure 4-22. The Advertise message from the selected server contains two IAs, one with the IAID of 100 and the other with the IAID of 300. Since the client did not include an IA with the ID of 300 in the Solicit message, it only copies the IAs whose ID is 100(*). Note also that the addresses in the Request message (`2001:db8:ffff::1` and `2001:db8:ffff::2`) are not included in the client's configuration list or in the Solicit message. The client should still accept the offer, since the addresses in the Solicit message are just hints for the server, and it is legitimate for the server to allocate different addresses.

(*) This is an artificial example. A compliant server would not include such an IA in the Advertise message that was not included in the corresponding Solicit message.

946 The `client6_send()` function resends a Solicit message (if this is just a timeout of the previous Solicit message) or sends a Request message.

Reset Timer

Listing 4-13

_____ dhcp6c.c
```
950            dhcp6_reset_timer(ev);
951
952            return (ev->timer);
953    }
```
_____ dhcp6c.c

950–952 The `dhcp6_reset_timer()` function updates the timeout value for the event based on the new timeout parameters (which may have been changed due to a state transition), as specified in Section 14 of [RFC3315]. The `dhcp6_reset_timer()` function then resets the internal timer based on the new timeout. Returning a non-NULL timer pointer tells the caller that the timer is still valid.

4.4.4 `client6_send()` Function

The `client6_send()` function follows. It sends a DHCPv6 message to a server or servers. The message type depends on its argument, `ev`.

Set Message Type

Listing 4-14

_____ dhcp6c.c
```
1195    void
1196    client6_send(ev)
1197            struct dhcp6_event *ev;
1198    {
1199            struct dhcp6_if *ifp;
1200            char buf[BUFSIZ];
1201            struct sockaddr_in6 dst;
1202            struct dhcp6 *dh6;
1203            struct dhcp6_optinfo optinfo;
```

```
1204            ssize_t optlen, len;
1205            struct dhcp6_eventdata *evd;
1206
1207            ifp = ev->ifp;
1208
1209            dh6 = (struct dhcp6 *)buf;
1210            memset(dh6, 0, sizeof(*dh6));
1211
1212            switch(ev->state) {
1213            case DHCP6S_SOLICIT:
1214                    dh6->dh6_msgtype = DH6_SOLICIT;
1215                    break;
1216            case DHCP6S_REQUEST:
1217                    dh6->dh6_msgtype = DH6_REQUEST;
1218                    break;
1219            case DHCP6S_RENEW:
1220                    dh6->dh6_msgtype = DH6_RENEW;
1221                    break;
1222            case DHCP6S_REBIND:
1223                    dh6->dh6_msgtype = DH6_REBIND;
1224                    break;
1225            case DHCP6S_RELEASE:
1226                    dh6->dh6_msgtype = DH6_RELEASE;
1227                    break;
1228            case DHCP6S_INFOREQ:
1229                    dh6->dh6_msgtype = DH6_INFORM_REQ;
1230                    break;
1231            default:
1232                    dprintf(LOG_ERR, FNAME, "unexpected state");
1233                    exit(1);         /* XXX */
1234            }
```
─── dhcp6c.c

1212–1234 The type of message is determined by the event state, which is mapped in a straight-forward manner.

Select Transaction ID

Listing 4-15
─── dhcp6c.c

```
1236            if (ev->timeouts == 0) {
1237                    /*
1238                     * A client SHOULD generate a random number that cannot easily
1239                     * be guessed or predicted to use as the transaction ID for
1240                     * each new message it sends.
1241                     *
1242                     * A client MUST leave the transaction-ID unchanged in
1243                     * retransmissions of a message. [RFC3315 15.1]
1244                     */
1245    #ifdef HAVE_ARC4RANDOM
1246                    ev->xid = arc4random() & DH6_XIDMASK;
1247    #else
1248                    ev->xid = random() & DH6_XIDMASK;
1249    #endif
1250                    dprintf(LOG_DEBUG, FNAME, "a new XID (%x) is generated",
1251                        ev->xid);
1252            }
1253            dh6->dh6_xid &= ~ntohl(DH6_XIDMASK);
1254            dh6->dh6_xid |= htonl(ev->xid);
1255            len = sizeof(*dh6);
```
─── dhcp6c.c

1236–1255 If this is the first message of the exchange, a new transaction ID, a 24-bit integer, is randomly generated. The generated value is stored in the message's transaction-id field

in network byte order. The message length is initialized to the length of the fixed part of
DHCPv6 messages.

Set Options

Listing 4-16

_____dhcp6c.c

```
1257          /*
1258           * construct options
1259           */
1260          dhcp6_init_options(&optinfo);
1261
1262          /* server ID */
1263          switch (ev->state) {
1264          case DHCP6S_REQUEST:
1265          case DHCP6S_RENEW:
1266          case DHCP6S_RELEASE:
1267                  if (duidcpy(&optinfo.serverID, &ev->serverid)) {
1268                          dprintf(LOG_ERR, FNAME, "failed to copy server ID");
1269                          goto end;
1270                  }
1271                  break;
1272          }
1273
1274          /* client ID */
1275          if (duidcpy(&optinfo.clientID, &client_duid)) {
1276                  dprintf(LOG_ERR, FNAME, "failed to copy client ID");
1277                  goto end;
1278          }
1279
1280          /* rapid commit (in Solicit only) */
1281          if (ev->state == DHCP6S_SOLICIT &&
1282              (ifp->send_flags & DHCIFF_RAPID_COMMIT)) {
1283                  optinfo.rapidcommit = 1;
1284          }
1285
1286          /* elapsed time */
1287          if (ev->timeouts == 0) {
1288                  gettimeofday(&ev->tv_start, NULL);
1289                  optinfo.elapsed_time = 0;
1290          } else {
1291                  struct timeval now, tv_diff;
1292                  long et;
1293
1294                  gettimeofday(&now, NULL);
1295                  tv_sub(&now, &ev->tv_start, &tv_diff);
1296
1297                  /*
1298                   * The client uses the value 0xffff to represent any elapsed
1299                   * time values greater than the largest time value that can be
1300                   * represented in the Elapsed Time option.
1301                   * [RFC3315 22.9.]
1302                   */
1303                  if (tv_diff.tv_sec >= (MAX_ELAPSED_TIME / 100) + 1) {
1304                          /*
1305                           * Perhaps we are nervous too much, but without this
1306                           * additional check, we would see an overflow in 248
1307                           * days (of no responses).
1308                           */
1309                          et = MAX_ELAPSED_TIME;
1310                  } else {
1311                          et = tv_diff.tv_sec * 100 + tv_diff.tv_usec / 10000;
1312                          if (et >= MAX_ELAPSED_TIME)
1313                                  et = MAX_ELAPSED_TIME;
1314                  }
```

```
1315                          optinfo.elapsed_time = (int32_t)et;
1316              }
1317
1318              /* option request options */
1319              if (ev->state != DHCP6S_RELEASE &&
1320                  dhcp6_copy_list(&optinfo.reqopt_list, &ifp->reqopt_list)) {
1321                      dprintf(LOG_ERR, FNAME, "failed to copy requested options");
1322                      goto end;
1323              }
1324
1325              /* configuration information specified as event data */
1326              for (evd = TAILQ_FIRST(&ev->data_list); evd;
1327                   evd = TAILQ_NEXT(evd, link)) {
1328                      switch(evd->type) {
1329                      case DHCP6_EVDATA_IAPD:
1330                              if (dhcp6_copy_list(&optinfo.iapd_list,
1331                                  (struct dhcp6_list *)evd->data)) {
1332                                      dprintf(LOG_NOTICE, FNAME,
1333                                          "failed to add an IAPD");
1334                                      goto end;
1335                              }
1336                              break;
1337                      case DHCP6_EVDATA_IANA:
1338                              if (dhcp6_copy_list(&optinfo.iana_list,
1339                                  (struct dhcp6_list *)evd->data)) {
1340                                      dprintf(LOG_NOTICE, FNAME,
1341                                          "failed to add an IAPD");
1342                                      goto end;
1343                              }
1344                              break;
1345                      default:
1346                              dprintf(LOG_ERR, FNAME, "unexpected event data (%d)",
1347                                  evd->type);
1348                              exit(1);
1349                      }
1350              }
```
_____ dhcp6c.c

1260 The optinfo variable is the structure which contains option information for the message. The dhcp6_init_options() function initializes the structure.

1263–1272 For those messages that require a Server Identifier option, the event structure should contain the identifier, and it is copied to the option structure.

1274–1278 The client's identifier is copied to the option structure, which will be used as the Client Identifier option. Although the specification does not require an Information-request message to have that option, this implementation simply includes the option for all messages.

1280–1284 If the client is configured to use the Rapid Commit option and this is a Solicit message, the use of the option is specified in the option structure.

1286–1289 If this is the first message of the exchange, the current time is recorded in the tv_start member of the event structure, which will be the base of the Elapsed Time option value when the same message needs to be resent. The initial value of the Elapsed Time option is set to 0.

1290–1316 When the same message is resent after a timeout, the Elapsed Time option value is set to the time since the first message was sent in hundredths of a second (10^{-2} seconds). Since the elapsed time is a 16-bit unsigned integer, the maximum possible value is 65,535, which is approximately 11 minutes. This is not large enough to ensure that the elapsed value does not exceed the maximum. Thus, if the real elapsed time is larger than the maximum value, the elapsed time field is set to the maximum value.

1318–1323 The list of requested options configured in the client is copied to the option structure as an Option Request option.

1325–1350 If the event structure contains a nonempty data list, the list elements are copied to the option structure as corresponding DHCPv6 options. Possible options in this implementation are the IA_PD option for prefix delegation and the IA_NA option for address allocation.

Authenticate Message

Listing 4-17

dhcp6c.c

```
1352            /* authentication information */
1353            if (set_auth(ev, &optinfo)) {
1354                    dprintf(LOG_INFO, FNAME,
1355                        "failed to set authentication option");
1356                    goto end;
1357            }
```

dhcp6c.c

1352–1357 The `set_auth()` function sets parameters for DHCPv6 authentication if the client is configured to use this feature, and for some message types, if the client and server have negotiated a session key. The `set_auth()` function will be described in Section 4.7.2.

Encode Options

Listing 4-18

dhcp6c.c

```
1359            /* set options in the message */
1360            if ((optlen = dhcp6_set_options(dh6->dh6_msgtype,
1361                (struct dhcp6opt *)(dh6 + 1),
1362                (struct dhcp6opt *)(buf + sizeof(buf)), &optinfo)) < 0) {
1363                    dprintf(LOG_INFO, FNAME, "failed to construct options");
1364                    goto end;
1365            }
1366            len += optlen;
```

dhcp6c.c

1359–1366 The `dhcp6_set_options()` function converts the option structure to wire format in the output buffer, and returns the length of the options as stored in the output buffer. If authentication parameters are set in the option structure, it calculates the offset from the head of the options to the HMAC-MD5 field of the corresponding Authentication option and stores the offset back in the option structure. For the delayed authentication protocol, the offset will be set in the `delayedauth_offset` macro member of the `dhcp6_optinfo{}` structure (Listing 4-3, page 324). The HMAC-MD5 field is set to zero at this point. Figure 4-24 shows this procedure.

FIGURE 4-24

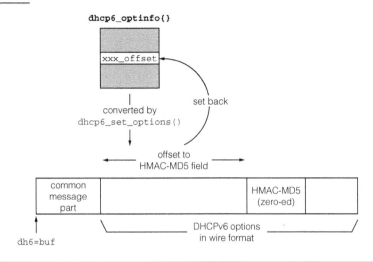

Setting DHCPv6 options with authentication information.

Calculate HMAC

Listing 4-19

—— dhcp6c.c
```
1368              /* calculate MAC if necessary, and put it to the message */
1369              if (ev->authparam != NULL) {
1370                      switch (ev->authparam->authproto) {
1371                      case DHCP6_AUTHPROTO_DELAYED:
1372                              if (ev->authparam->key == NULL)
1373                                      break;
1374
1375                              if (dhcp6_calc_mac((char *)dh6, len,
1376                                  optinfo.authproto, optinfo.authalgorithm,
1377                                  optinfo.delayedauth_offset + sizeof(*dh6),
1378                                  ev->authparam->key)) {
1379                                      dprintf(LOG_WARNING, FNAME,
1380                                          "failed to calculate MAC");
1381                                      goto end;
1382                              }
1383                              break;
1384                      default:
1385                              break;          /* do nothing */
1386                      }
1387              }
```
—— dhcp6c.c

1368–1387 If the message is to be authenticated using the delayed authentication protocol, the
dhcp6_set_options() function should have set the delayedauth_offset member
of the option structure to the offset of the HMAC-MD5 field. The dhcp6_calc_mac()
function calculates the HMAC digest for the entire DHCPv6 message using the key parameters in the event structure and stores the value in the appropriate place in the message
identified by the offset (i.e., in the HMAC-MD5 field of the Authentication option).

Send Packet

Listing 4-20
_____dhcp6c.c

```
1389              /*
1390               * Unless otherwise specified in this document or in a document that
1391               * describes how IPv6 is carried over a specific type of link (for link
1392               * types that do not support multicast), a client sends DHCP messages
1393               * to the All_DHCP_Relay_Agents_and_Servers.
1394               * [RFC3315 Section 13.]
1395               */
1396              dst = *sa6_allagent;
1397              dst.sin6_scope_id = ifp->linkid;
1398
1399              if (sendto(outsock, buf, len, 0, (struct sockaddr *)&dst,
1400                  ((struct sockaddr *)&dst)->sa_len) == -1) {
1401                      dprintf(LOG_ERR, FNAME,
1402                          "transmit failed: %s", strerror(errno));
1403                      goto end;
1404              }
1405
1406              dprintf(LOG_DEBUG, FNAME, "send %s to %s",
1407                  dhcp6msgstr(dh6->dh6_msgtype), addr2str((struct sockaddr *)&dst));
1408
1409      end:
1410              dhcp6_clear_options(&optinfo);
1411              return;
1412      }
```
_____dhcp6c.c

1389–1404 This implementation does not support unicast transport of DHCPv6 messages, and all messages from the client are sent to the All_DHCP_Relay_Agents_and_Servers multicast address (ff02::1:2). To disambiguate the link of the link-local multicast address, the sin6_scope_id member is set to the link ID, which is identified at initialization and is set in the interface structure.

4.4.5 client6_recv() **Function**

The client6_recv() function processes received DHCPv6 messages, and dispatches message-specific routines.

Receive Packet

Listing 4-21
_____dhcp6c.c

```
1437    static void
1438    client6_recv()
1439    {
1440            char rbuf[BUFSIZ], cmsgbuf[BUFSIZ];
1441            struct msghdr mhdr;
1442            struct iovec iov;
1443            struct sockaddr_storage from;
1444            struct dhcp6_if *ifp;
1445            struct dhcp6opt *p, *ep;
1446            struct dhcp6_optinfo optinfo;
1447            ssize_t len;
1448            struct dhcp6 *dh6;
1449            struct cmsghdr *cm;
1450            struct in6_pktinfo *pi = NULL;
1451
1452            memset(&iov, 0, sizeof(iov));
```

```
1453                memset(&mhdr, 0, sizeof(mhdr));
1454
1455                iov.iov_base = (caddr_t)rbuf;
1456                iov.iov_len = sizeof(rbuf);
1457                mhdr.msg_name = (caddr_t)&from;
1458                mhdr.msg_namelen = sizeof(from);
1459                mhdr.msg_iov = &iov;
1460                mhdr.msg_iovlen = 1;
1461                mhdr.msg_control = (caddr_t)cmsgbuf;
1462                mhdr.msg_controllen = sizeof(cmsgbuf);
1463                if ((len = recvmsg(insock, &mhdr, 0)) < 0) {
1464                        dprintf(LOG_ERR, FNAME, "recvmsg: %s", strerror(errno));
1465                        return;
1466                }
1467
1468                /* detect receiving interface */
1469                for (cm = (struct cmsghdr *)CMSG_FIRSTHDR(&mhdr); cm;
1470                        cm = (struct cmsghdr *)CMSG_NXTHDR(&mhdr, cm)) {
1471                        if (cm->cmsg_level == IPPROTO_IPV6 &&
1472                            cm->cmsg_type == IPV6_PKTINFO &&
1473                            cm->cmsg_len == CMSG_LEN(sizeof(struct in6_pktinfo))) {
1474                                pi = (struct in6_pktinfo *)(CMSG_DATA(cm));
1475                        }
1476                }
1477                if (pi == NULL) {
1478                        dprintf(LOG_NOTICE, FNAME, "failed to get packet info");
1479                        return;
1480                }
```
── dhcp6c.c

1452–1480 The `msghdr{}` structure, `mhdr`, is initialized, and then the `recvmsg()` system call receives the packet with it. The `IPV6_RECVPKTINFO` socket option (see Chapter 7 of *IPv6 Core Protocols Implementation*, "Socket API Extensions") was specified at initialization for this socket, so the `msghdr{}` should contain an ancillary data item of the `IPV6_PKTINFO` type. The ancillary data information is crucial because the DHCPv6 protocol is oriented heavily around the network interface.

Identify the Local Configuration

Listing 4-22

── dhcp6c.c

```
1482                if ((ifp = find_ifconfbyid((unsigned int)pi->ipi6_ifindex)) == NULL) {
1483                        dprintf(LOG_INFO, FNAME, "unexpected interface (%d)",
1484                            (unsigned int)pi->ipi6_ifindex);
1485                        return;
1486                }
```
── dhcp6c.c

1482–1486 The `find_ifconfbyid()` function returns the local interface configuration structure, `ifp`, based on the identifier of the incoming interface.

Initial Process

Listing 4-23

── dhcp6c.c

```
1487
1488                if (len < sizeof(*dh6)) {
1489                        dprintf(LOG_INFO, FNAME, "short packet (%d bytes)", len);
1490                        return;
1491                }
1492
```

```
1493            dh6 = (struct dhcp6 *)rbuf;
1494
1495            dprintf(LOG_DEBUG, FNAME, "receive %s from %s on %s",
1496                dhcp6msgstr(dh6->dh6_msgtype),
1497                addr2str((struct sockaddr *)&from), ifp->ifname);
1498
1499            /* get options */
1500            dhcp6_init_options(&optinfo);
1501            p = (struct dhcp6opt *)(dh6 + 1);
1502            ep = (struct dhcp6opt *)((char *)dh6 + len);
1503            if (dhcp6_get_options(p, ep, &optinfo) < 0) {
1504                    dprintf(LOG_INFO, FNAME, "failed to parse options");
1505                    return;
1506            }
```
── dhcp6c.c

1488–1506 After the minimum length validation, the `dhcp6_get_options()` function parses
the DHCPv6 options from the message and converts them into local data structures.

Dispatch Subroutine

Listing 4-24
── dhcp6c.c

```
1508            switch(dh6->dh6_msgtype) {
1509            case DH6_ADVERTISE:
1510                    (void)client6_recvadvert(ifp, dh6, len, &optinfo);
1511                    break;
1512            case DH6_REPLY:
1513                    (void)client6_recvreply(ifp, dh6, len, &optinfo);
1514                    break;
1515            default:
1516                    dprintf(LOG_INFO, FNAME, "received an unexpected message (%s) "
1517                        "from %s", dhcp6msgstr(dh6->dh6_msgtype),
1518                        addr2str((struct sockaddr *)&from));
1519                    break;
1520            }
1521
1522            dhcp6_clear_options(&optinfo);
1523            return;
1524    }
```
── dhcp6c.c

1508–1520 In the current implementation, the supported message types by the client are Advertise and Reply (i.e., Reconfigure is not implemented). The corresponding subroutines are
called for further processing.

4.4.6 `client6_recvadvert()` Function

The `client6_recvadvert()` function handles incoming Advertise messages.

Find the Event

Listing 4-25
── dhcp6c.c

```
1526    static int
1527    client6_recvadvert(ifp, dh6, len, optinfo)
1528            struct dhcp6_if *ifp;
```

```
1529                struct dhcp6 *dh6;
1530                ssize_t len;
1531                struct dhcp6_optinfo *optinfo;
1532        {
1533                struct dhcp6_serverinfo *newserver, **sp;
1534                struct dhcp6_event *ev;
1535                struct dhcp6_eventdata *evd;
1536                struct authparam *authparam = NULL, authparam0;
1537
1538                /* find the corresponding event based on the received xid */
1539                ev = find_event_withid(ifp, ntohl(dh6->dh6_xid) & DH6_XIDMASK);
1540                if (ev == NULL) {
1541                        dprintf(LOG_INFO, FNAME, "XID mismatch");
1542                        return (-1);
1543                }
```
_____ dhcp6c.c

1538–1543 An Advertise message must be sent from a DHCPv6 server in response to a Solicit message from the client. The corresponding Solicit message is identified by the transaction ID. The find_event_withid() function searches the list of events on the receiving interface for one that matches the ID in the received Advertise message. If no event is found, the received message is discarded.

Packet Validation

Listing 4-26
_____ dhcp6c.c

```
1545                /* packet validation based on Section 15.3 of RFC3315. */
1546                if (optinfo->serverID.duid_len == 0) {
1547                        dprintf(LOG_INFO, FNAME, "no server ID option");
1548                        return (-1);
1549                } else {
1550                        dprintf(LOG_DEBUG, FNAME, "server ID: %s, pref=%d",
1551                            duidstr(&optinfo->serverID),
1552                            optinfo->pref);
1553                }
1554                if (optinfo->clientID.duid_len == 0) {
1555                        dprintf(LOG_INFO, FNAME, "no client ID option");
1556                        return (-1);
1557                }
1558                if (duidcmp(&optinfo->clientID, &client_duid)) {
1559                        dprintf(LOG_INFO, FNAME, "client DUID mismatch");
1560                        return (-1);
1561                }
```
_____ dhcp6c.c

1545–1561 The next part of this function performs packet validation checks based on the protocol specification:

- An Advertise message must contain a Server Identifier option
- An Advertise message must contain a Client Identifier option, and it must match the client's DUID.

If any of the checks fail, the packet is discarded.

Process Authentication

Listing 4-27

```
1563              /* validate authentication */
1564              authparam0 = *ev->authparam;
1565              if (process_auth(&authparam0, dh6, len, optinfo)) {
1566                      dprintf(LOG_INFO, FNAME, "failed to process authentication");
1567                      return (-1);
1568              }
```

1564–1568 The `process_auth()` function handles an Authentication option in the Advertise message if it was included, and authenticates the message according to the authentication algorithm being used.

Check the Case of No Prefix or Address

Listing 4-28

```
1570          /*
1571           * The requesting router MUST ignore any Advertise message that
1572           * includes a Status Code option containing the value NoPrefixAvail
1573           * [RFC3633 Section 11.1].
1574           * Likewise, the client MUST ignore any Advertise message that includes
1575           * a Status Code option containing the value NoAddrsAvail.
1576           * [RFC3315 Section 17.1.3].
1577           * We only apply this when we are going to request an address or
1578           * a prefix.
1579           */
1580          for (evd = TAILQ_FIRST(&ev->data_list); evd;
1581              evd = TAILQ_NEXT(evd, link)) {
1582              u_int16_t stcode;
1583              char *stcodestr;
1584
1585              switch (evd->type) {
1586              case DHCP6_EVDATA_IAPD:
1587                      stcode = DH6OPT_STCODE_NOPREFIXAVAIL;
1588                      stcodestr = "NoPrefixAvail";
1589                      break;
1590              case DHCP6_EVDATA_IANA:
1591                      stcode = DH6OPT_STCODE_NOADDRSAVAIL;
1592                      stcodestr = "NoAddrsAvail";
1593                      break;
1594              default:
1595                      continue;
1596              }
1597              if (dhcp6_find_listval(&optinfo->stcode_list,
1598                  DHCP6_LISTVAL_STCODE, &stcode, 0)) {
1599                      dprintf(LOG_INFO, FNAME,
1600                          "advertise contains %s status", stcodestr);
1601                      return (-1);
1602              }
1603          }
```

1580–1603 For prefix delegation or address allocation, when a server cannot provide the requested configuration it will return a Status Code option with the code value of No-PrefixAvail or NoAddrsAvail in an Advertise message respectively. In this case, that Advertise message is ignored.

Unexpected Advertise

Listing 4-29
_____dhcp6c.c
```
1605            if (ev->state != DHCP6S_SOLICIT ||
1606                (ifp->send_flags & DHCIFF_RAPID_COMMIT) || infreq_mode) {
1607                    /*
1608                     * We expected a reply message, but do actually receive an
1609                     * Advertise message.  The server should be configured not to
1610                     * allow the Rapid Commit option.
1611                     * We process the message as if we expected the Advertise.
1612                     * [RFC3315 Section 17.1.4]
1613                     */
1614                    dprintf(LOG_INFO, FNAME, "unexpected advertise");
1615                    /* proceed anyway */
1616            }
```
_____dhcp6c.c

1605–1616 If the client has sent a Solicit message with a Rapid Commit option, it expects an immediate Reply, omitting Advertise and Request exchanges. The client may still receive an Advertise message when the server does not accept rapid commit. In this case, that Advertise message will be accepted.

Remember the Server

Listing 4-30
_____dhcp6c.c
```
1618            /* ignore the server if it is known */
1619            if (find_server(ev, &optinfo->serverID)) {
1620                    dprintf(LOG_INFO, FNAME, "duplicated server (ID: %s)",
1621                        duidstr(&optinfo->serverID));
1622                    return (-1);
1623            }
1624
1625            /* keep the server */
1626            if ((newserver = malloc(sizeof(*newserver))) == NULL) {
1627                    dprintf(LOG_WARNING, FNAME,
1628                        "memory allocation failed for server");
1629                    return (-1);
1630            }
1631            memset(newserver, 0, sizeof(*newserver));
1632
1633            /* remember authentication parameters */
1634            newserver->authparam = ev->authparam;
1635            newserver->authparam->flags = authparam0.flags;
1636            newserver->authparam->prevrd = authparam0.prevrd;
1637            newserver->authparam->key = authparam0.key;
1638
1639            /* allocate new authentication parameter for the soliciting event */
1640            if ((authparam = new_authparam(ev->authparam->authproto,
1641                ev->authparam->authalgorithm, ev->authparam->authrdm)) == NULL) {
1642                    dprintf(LOG_WARNING, FNAME, "memory allocation failed "
1643                        "for authentication parameters");
1644                    free(newserver);
1645                    return (-1);
1646            }
1647            ev->authparam = authparam;
1648
1649            /* copy options */
1650            dhcp6_init_options(&newserver->optinfo);
1651            if (dhcp6_copy_options(&newserver->optinfo, optinfo)) {
1652                    dprintf(LOG_ERR, FNAME, "failed to copy options");
1653                    if (newserver->authparam != NULL)
```

```
1654                          free(newserver->authparam);
1655                  free(newserver);
1656                  return (-1);
1657          }
1658          if (optinfo->pref != DH6OPT_PREF_UNDEF)
1659                  newserver->pref = optinfo->pref;
1660          newserver->active = 1;
1661          for (sp = &ev->servers; *sp; sp = &(*sp)->next) {
1662                  if ((*sp)->pref != DH6OPT_PREF_MAX &&
1663                      (*sp)->pref < newserver->pref) {
1664                          break;
1665                  }
1666          }
1667          newserver->next = *sp;
1668          *sp = newserver;
```
_____ dhcp6c.c

1618–1623 Responding servers are recorded in the event structure. If the sending server is already stored, this Advertise message is simply ignored.

1625–1660 Otherwise, a new dhcp6_serverinfo{} structure is allocated, and the information that was sent by the server, including advertised options and authentication information, are copied to that structure.

> In this implementation, active does not mean anything; it is always nonzero.

1661–1668 The new server information is inserted in the list of servers that have responded to the initial Solicit message. This list is sorted by the server preference. Figure 4-25 shows related data structures at this point. As was seen in Listing 4-12 (page 336), the client6_timo() function will eventually pick up the first entry of the server list to send a Request message as it has the highest priority.

FIGURE 4-25

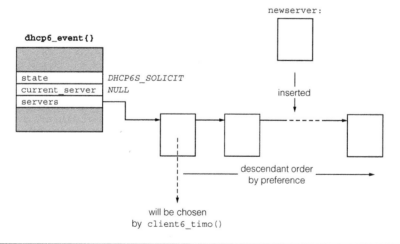

Adding a server on receipt of DHCPv6 Advertise.

Immediate Request

Listing 4-31
———dhcp6c.c
```
1670             if (newserver->pref == DH6OPT_PREF_MAX) {
1671                     /*
1672                      * If the client receives an Advertise message that includes a
1673                      * Preference option with a preference value of 255, the client
1674                      * immediately begins a client-initiated message exchange.
1675                      * [RFC3315 Section 17.1.2]
1676                      */
1677                     ev->current_server = newserver;
1678                     if (duidcpy(&ev->serverid,
1679                         &ev->current_server->optinfo.serverID)) {
1680                             dprintf(LOG_NOTICE, FNAME, "can't copy server ID");
1681                             return (-1); /* XXX: better recovery? */
1682                     }
1683                     if (construct_reqdata(ifp, &ev->current_server->optinfo, ev)) {
1684                             dprintf(LOG_NOTICE, FNAME,
1685                                 "failed to construct request data");
1686                             return (-1); /* XXX */
1687                     }
1688
1689                     ev->timeouts = 0;
1690                     ev->state = DHCP6S_REQUEST;
1691
1692                     free(ev->authparam);
1693                     ev->authparam = newserver->authparam;
1694                     newserver->authparam = NULL;
1695
1696                     client6_send(ev);
1697
1698                     dhcp6_set_timeoparam(ev);
1699                     dhcp6_reset_timer(ev);
```
———dhcp6c.c

1670–1699 If the server specifies the maximum preference for itself in the Advertise message, the server selection procedure is completed immediately, and this server is chosen. Some information on this server is copied to the event structure for later use. The `construct_reqdata()` function sets up DHCPv6 options for a Request message, and the message is sent by the `client_send()` function. Finally, the timer corresponding to this event is reset for Request-Reply exchanges.

Reset Timer

Listing 4-32
———dhcp6c.c
```
1700             } else if (ev->servers->next == NULL) {
1701                     struct timeval *rest, elapsed, tv_rt, tv_irt, timo;
1702
1703                     /*
1704                      * If this is the first advertise, adjust the timer so that
1705                      * the client can collect other servers until IRT elapses.
1706                      * XXX: we did not want to do such "low level" timer
1707                      *      calculation here.
1708                      */
1709                     rest = dhcp6_timer_rest(ev->timer);
1710                     tv_rt.tv_sec = (ev->retrans * 1000) / 1000000;
1711                     tv_rt.tv_usec = (ev->retrans * 1000) % 1000000;
1712                     tv_irt.tv_sec = (ev->init_retrans * 1000) / 1000000;
1713                     tv_irt.tv_usec = (ev->init_retrans * 1000) % 1000000;
1714                     timeval_sub(&tv_rt, rest, &elapsed);
1715                     if (TIMEVAL_LEQ(elapsed, tv_irt))
```

```
1716                        timeval_sub(&tv_irt, &elapsed, &timo);
1717            else
1718                        timo.tv_sec = timo.tv_usec = 0;
1719
1720            dprintf(LOG_DEBUG, FNAME, "reset timer for %s to %d.%06d",
1721                ifp->ifname, (int)timo.tv_sec, (int)timo.tv_usec);
1722
1723            dhcp6_set_timer(&timo, ev->timer);
1724        }
1725
1726        return (0);
1727    }
```
—— dhcp6c.c

1700–1724 If the server's preference is unspecified or is not the maximum, the client will still need to wait for Advertise messages from other servers. The event timer is reset accordingly.

4.4.7 `client6_recvreply()` Function

The `client6_recvreply()` function processes DHCPv6 Reply messages in response to various messages that the client sent.

Initialization and Validation

Listing 4-33

—— dhcp6c.c
```
1744    static int
1745    client6_recvreply(ifp, dh6, len, optinfo)
1746        struct dhcp6_if *ifp;
1747        struct dhcp6 *dh6;
1748        ssize_t len;
1749        struct dhcp6_optinfo *optinfo;
1750    {
1751        struct dhcp6_listval *lv;
1752        struct dhcp6_event *ev;
1753        int state;
1754
1755        /* find the corresponding event based on the received xid */
1756        ev = find_event_withid(ifp, ntohl(dh6->dh6_xid) & DH6_XIDMASK);
1757        if (ev == NULL) {
1758            dprintf(LOG_INFO, FNAME, "XID mismatch");
1759            return (-1);
1760        }
1761
1762        state = ev->state;
1763        if (state != DHCP6S_INFOREQ &&
1764            state != DHCP6S_REQUEST &&
1765            state != DHCP6S_RENEW &&
1766            state != DHCP6S_REBIND &&
1767            state != DHCP6S_RELEASE &&
1768            (state != DHCP6S_SOLICIT ||
1769             !(ifp->send_flags & DHCIFF_RAPID_COMMIT))) {
1770            dprintf(LOG_INFO, FNAME, "unexpected reply");
1771            return (-1);
1772        }
1773
1774        /* A Reply message must contain a Server ID option */
1775        if (optinfo->serverID.duid_len == 0) {
1776            dprintf(LOG_INFO, FNAME, "no server ID option");
1777            return (-1);
1778        }
```

```
1779
1780            /*
1781             * DUID in the Client ID option (which must be contained for our
1782             * client implementation) must match ours.
1783             */
1784            if (optinfo->clientID.duid_len == 0) {
1785                    dprintf(LOG_INFO, FNAME, "no client ID option");
1786                    return (-1);
1787            }
1788            if (duidcmp(&optinfo->clientID, &client_duid)) {
1789                    dprintf(LOG_INFO, FNAME, "client DUID mismatch");
1790                    return (-1);
1791            }
1792
1793            /* validate authentication */
1794            if (process_auth(ev->authparam, dh6, len, optinfo)) {
1795                    dprintf(LOG_INFO, FNAME, "failed to process authentication");
1796                    return (-1);
1797            }
```
——dhcp6c.c

1751–1797 The first part of this function is almost the same as that of the
client6_recvadvert() function: it checks the validity of the incoming message
based on the protocol specification. As noted in the comment, since this implementation always includes a Client Identifier option in messages from the client, the Reply
message must contain a copy of this option as per Section 15.10 of [RFC3315].

Process Rapid Commit Case

Listing 4-34
——dhcp6c.c

```
1799            /*
1800             * If the client included a Rapid Commit option in the Solicit message,
1801             * the client discards any Reply messages it receives that do not
1802             * include a Rapid Commit option.
1803             * (should we keep the server otherwise?)
1804             * [RFC3315 Section 17.1.4]
1805             */
1806            if (state == DHCP6S_SOLICIT &&
1807                (ifp->send_flags & DHCIFF_RAPID_COMMIT) &&
1808                !optinfo->rapidcommit) {
1809                    dprintf(LOG_INFO, FNAME, "no rapid commit");
1810                    return (-1);
1811            }
```
——dhcp6c.c

1799–1811 If the client's state is DHCP6S_SOLICIT, and the client is configured to include a
Rapid Commit option in Solicit messages, the Reply message must be a response to the
"rapid-commit" version of Solicit, which must include a Rapid Commit option. Otherwise,
the packet is discarded.

Process Status Codes

Listing 4-35
——dhcp6c.c

```
1813            /*
1814             * The client MAY choose to report any status code or message from the
1815             * status code option in the Reply message.
```

```
1816              * [RFC3315 Section 18.1.8]
1817              */
1818             for (lv = TAILQ_FIRST(&optinfo->stcode_list); lv;
1819                  lv = TAILQ_NEXT(lv, link)) {
1820                 dprintf(LOG_INFO, FNAME, "status code: %s",
1821                     dhcp6_stcodestr(lv->val_num16));
1822             }
```
——— dhcp6c.c

1813–1822 The protocol specification does not require a particular action for a Status Code
option included in a Reply message, except for printing informational messages. This
implementation simply logs the status codes.

Process Stateless Options

Listing 4-36
——— dhcp6c.c
```
1824             if (!TAILQ_EMPTY(&optinfo->dns_list)) {
1825                 struct dhcp6_listval *d;
1826                 int i = 0;
1827
1828                 for (d = TAILQ_FIRST(&optinfo->dns_list); d;
1829                      d = TAILQ_NEXT(d, link), i++) {
1830                     info_printf("nameserver[%d] %s",
1831                         i, in6addr2str(&d->val_addr6, 0));
1832                 }
1833             }
1834
1835             if (!TAILQ_EMPTY(&optinfo->dnsname_list)) {
1836                 struct dhcp6_listval *d;
1837                 int i = 0;
1838
1839                 for (d = TAILQ_FIRST(&optinfo->dnsname_list); d;
1840                      d = TAILQ_NEXT(d, link), i++) {
1841                     info_printf("Domain search list[%d] %s",
1842                         i, d->val_vbuf.dv_buf);
1843                 }
1844             }
1845
1846             if (!TAILQ_EMPTY(&optinfo->ntp_list)) {
1847                 struct dhcp6_listval *d;
1848                 int i = 0;
1849
1850                 for (d = TAILQ_FIRST(&optinfo->ntp_list); d;
1851                      d = TAILQ_NEXT(d, link), i++) {
1852                     info_printf("NTP server[%d] %s",
1853                         i, in6addr2str(&d->val_addr6, 0));
1854                 }
1855             }
1856
1857             if (!TAILQ_EMPTY(&optinfo->sip_list)) {
1858                 struct dhcp6_listval *d;
1859                 int i = 0;
1860
1861                 for (d = TAILQ_FIRST(&optinfo->sip_list); d;
1862                      d = TAILQ_NEXT(d, link), i++) {
1863                     info_printf("SIP server address[%d] %s",
1864                         i, in6addr2str(&d->val_addr6, 0));
1865                 }
1866             }
1867
1868             if (!TAILQ_EMPTY(&optinfo->sipname_list)) {
1869                 struct dhcp6_listval *d;
1870                 int i = 0;
1871
```

```
1872                        for (d = TAILQ_FIRST(&optinfo->sipname_list); d;
1873                            d = TAILQ_NEXT(d, link), i++) {
1874                                info_printf("SIP server domain name[%d] %s",
1875                                    i, d->val_vbuf.dv_buf);
1876                        }
1877                }
1878
1879                /*
1880                 * Call the configuration script, if specified, to handle various
1881                 * configuration parameters.
1882                 */
1883                if (ifp->scriptpath != NULL && strlen(ifp->scriptpath) != 0) {
1884                        dprintf(LOG_DEBUG, FNAME, "executes %s", ifp->scriptpath);
1885                        client6_script(ifp->scriptpath, state, optinfo);
1886                }
```
—— dhcp6c.c

1824–1886 If the reply message contains stateless options, which are basically just advertised by the server and any state of which are not maintained at the server side, and the client is configured with a script file for the options, the `client6_script()` function is called to execute the script. There is nothing special in this function: it simply sets some environment variables corresponding to the stateless options, and executes the specified program (script) as a child process. A concrete example of how this can be used will be seen in Sections 4.8.4 and 4.8.8.

Setup Refresh Timer

Listing 4-37
—— dhcp6c.c
```
1888    #ifdef USE_DH6OPT_REFRESHTIME
1889            /*
1890             * Set refresh timer for configuration information specified in
1891             * information-request.  If the timer value is specified by the server
1892             * in an information refresh time option, use it; use the protocol
1893             * default otherwise.
1894             */
1895            if (state == DHCP6S_INFOREQ) {
1896                    int64_t refreshtime = DHCP6_IRT_DEFAULT;
1897
1898                    if (optinfo->refreshtime != DH6OPT_REFRESHTIME_UNDEF)
1899                            refreshtime = optinfo->refreshtime;
1900
1901                    ifp->timer = dhcp6_add_timer(client6_expire_refreshtime, ifp);
1902                    if (ifp->timer == NULL) {
1903                            dprintf(LOG_WARNING, FNAME,
1904                                "failed to add timer for refresh time");
1905                    } else {
1906                            struct timeval tv;
1907
1908                            tv.tv_sec = (long)refreshtime;
1909                            tv.tv_usec = 0;
1910
1911                            if (tv.tv_sec < 0) {
1912                                    /*
1913                                     * XXX: tv_sec can overflow for an
1914                                     * unsigned 32bit value.
1915                                     */
1916                                    dprintf(LOG_WARNING, FNAME,
1917                                        "refresh time is too large: %lu",
1918                                        (u_int32_t)refreshtime);
1919                                    tv.tv_sec = 0x7fffffff;        /* XXX */
1920                            }
1921
```

```
1922                               dhcp6_set_timer(&tv, ifp->timer);
1923                       }
1924               } else if (optinfo->refreshtime != DH6OPT_REFRESHTIME_UNDEF) {
1925                       /*
1926                        * draft-ietf-dhc-lifetime-02 clarifies that refresh time
1927                        * is only used for information-request and reply exchanges.
1928                        */
1929                       dprintf(LOG_INFO, FNAME,
1930                           "unexpected information refresh time option (ignored)");
1931               }
1932   #endif /* USE_DH6OPT_REFRESHTIME */
```
                                                                              ————————dhcp6c.c

1895–1923 If this Reply message is a response to an Information-Request message and it contains the Information Refresh Time option, a separate timer with the specified timeout value is set up so that the client can resend the Information-Request message for updating the stateless information. Note that the timer is set up even if the Information Refresh Time option is not contained, in which case the timeout value is set to the protocol default (DHCP6_IRT_DEFAULT, which is 1 day).

1924–1931 [RFC4242] specifies that this option is only used for a Reply to Information-Request. An Information Refresh Time option included in any other message is ignored.

Process *Stateful* Information

Listing 4-38
                                                                              ————————dhcp6c.c
```
1934               /* update stateful configuration information */
1935               if (state != DHCP6S_RELEASE) {
1936                       update_ia(IATYPE_PD, &optinfo->iapd_list, ifp,
1937                           &optinfo->serverID, ev->authparam);
1938                       update_ia(IATYPE_NA, &optinfo->iana_list, ifp,
1939                           &optinfo->serverID, ev->authparam);
1940               }
```
                                                                              ————————dhcp6c.c

1934–1940 If this Reply message is a response to any DHCPv6 message other than a Release message, it typically contains some information on *stateful* configuration parameters, that is, IPv6 addresses or prefixes allocated by the server. The update_ia() function updates the state of the IA for the information corresponding to the Reply message.

Release Completion

Listing 4-39
                                                                              ————————dhcp6c.c
```
1942           dhcp6_remove_event(ev);
1943
1944           if (state == DHCP6S_RELEASE) {
1945                   /*
1946                    * When the client receives a valid Reply message in response
1947                    * to a Release message, the client considers the Release event
1948                    * completed, regardless of the Status Code option(s) returned
1949                    * by the server.
1950                    * [RFC3315 Section 18.1.8]
1951                    */
1952                   check_exit();
1953           }
1954
1955           dprintf(LOG_DEBUG, FNAME, "got an expected reply, sleeping.");
```

```
1956
1957            if (infreq_mode) {
1958                    exit_ok = 1;
1959                    free_resources(NULL);
1960                    unlink(pid_file);
1961                    check_exit();
1962            }
1963            return (0);
1964    }
```
_____ dhcp6c.c

1944–1953 If this Reply message is a response to a Release message, the client can simply stop processing, regardless of the actual result of this exchange that may be indicated in a Status Code option. The `check_exit()` function determines whether there are outstanding tasks on this client, perhaps for a different interface or another IA, and terminates the process if not.

1957–1963 If this client is running in the "Information-request only" mode (specified by the `-1` command line option), it simply exits after the initial exchange of Information-request and Reply messages. Otherwise, the processing continues for next events.

4.4.8 Processing Identity Association

One major job of a DHCPv6 client is to manage configuration resources allocated by the server, which are associated with Identity Associations (IAs). We are going to see the implementation of this part, beginning with some data structures specific to IA processing.

The `ia{}` structure is shown in Listing 4-40. It manages the state of allocated resources of a particular IA. It corresponds to one particular `ia_conf{}` structure, which represents the client's configuration of this IA, via its `iadata` member (see Listing 4-7, page 330).

Listing 4-40
_____ dhcp6c_ia.c

```
54   struct ia {
55           TAILQ_ENTRY(ia) link;
56
57           /* back pointer to configuration */
58           struct ia_conf *conf;
59
60           /* common parameters of IA */
61           u_int32_t t1;                   /* duration for renewal */
62           u_int32_t t2;                   /* duration for rebind  */
63
64           /* internal parameters for renewal/rebinding */
65           iastate_t state;
66           struct dhcp6_timer *timer;
67           struct dhcp6_eventdata *evdata;
68
69           /* DHCP related parameters */
70           struct dhcp6_if *ifp;           /* DHCP interface */
71           struct duid serverid;           /* the server ID that provided this IA */
72
73           /* control information shared with each particular config routine */
74           struct iactl *ctl;
75
76           /* authentication parameters for transaction with servers on this IA */
77           struct authparam *authparam;
78   };
```
_____ dhcp6c_ia.c

55–77 The `link` member is effectively unused because there can actually be only one `ia{}` structure for an IA. The `conf` member points to the corresponding `ia_conf{}` structure. The `t1` and `t2` members are the T1 and T2 time parameters for this IA, specified by the server or calculated internally when unspecified. The following three members control timers for sending Renew or Rebind messages for this IA. There are three states: *ACTIVE* (`IAS_ACTIVE`), *RENEW* (`IAS_RENEW`), and *REBIND* (`IAS_REBIND`). When an IA is newly created, its state is set to ACTIVE, and a new timer is set with the duration of T1 seconds. When the timer expires, the state is changed to RENEW, and a Renew-Reply exchange starts. If the exchange does not succeed for T2 – T1 seconds, the state is then changed to REBIND, and a Rebind-Reply exchange takes place. The `evdata` member stores temporary data for the Renew or Rebind messages. This process will be described in Section 4.4.12. The `ctl` member is a set of parameters depending on the IA type (addresses or prefixes), which is described in Listing 4-41. If the DHCPv6 session between the client and the server is authenticated using the Authentication option, the `authparam` member keeps authentication-related parameters.

Figure 4-26 summarizes state transitions of an IA. Each arrow indicates a state transition associated with a label representing the event that causes the transition and the actions that take place for the transition. For example, the arrow from ACTIVE to RENEW means that when

FIGURE 4-26

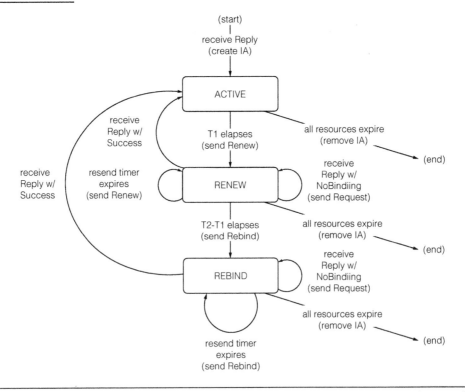

State transition diagram of an IA.

T1 time of the IA has passed since the IA entered in the ACTIVE state, the client will send a Renew message and the state of the IA will change to RENEW.

Some of the transition paths were explained previously. In addition, if a Renew or Rebind message is responded to with a successful Reply message, the IA is reestablished and its state becomes ACTIVE again. On the other hand, if the IA in the Reply message contains a NoBinding status code, the client will send a Request message to ask the server to reestablish the binding. This will be described in Listing 4-46 (pages 361–362). The Renew or Rebind message will be resent until the client receives a corresponding Reply message, whether successful or not.

It should be noted that an IA itself does not have an expiration timer. An IA is regarded as expired when all associated resources such as IPv6 addresses expire. Until then, the client will keep resending Renew or Rebind messages.

Many procedures having to do with an IA are independent of the type of IA, e.g., whether it is for addresses or for prefixes. This implementation thus uses a common structure, the `iactl{}` structure shown in Listing 4-41, as type-independent interfaces to type specific operations. This structure is essentially a set of method functions, corresponding to the IA-related operations. The usage of these methods will be described in the succeeding subsections (4.4.9 through 4.4.13).

Listing 4-41

—— dhcp6c_ia.h

```
34   struct iactl {
35          struct ia *iactl_ia;          /* back pointer to IA */
36
37          /* callback function called when something may happen on the IA */
38          void (*callback) __P((struct ia *));
39
40          /* common methods: */
41          int (*isvalid) __P((struct iactl *));
42          u_int32_t (*duration) __P((struct iactl *));
43          int (*renew_data) __P((struct iactl *, struct dhcp6_ia *,
44              struct dhcp6_eventdata **, struct dhcp6_eventdata *));
45          int (*rebind_data) __P((struct iactl *, struct dhcp6_ia *,
46              struct dhcp6_eventdata **, struct dhcp6_eventdata *));
47          int (*release_data) __P((struct iactl *, struct dhcp6_ia *,
48              struct dhcp6_eventdata **, struct dhcp6_eventdata *));
49          int (*reestablish_data) __P((struct iactl *, struct dhcp6_ia *,
50              struct dhcp6_eventdata **, struct dhcp6_eventdata *));
51          void (*cleanup) __P((struct iactl *));
52   };
```

—— dhcp6c_ia.h

4.4.9 `update_ia()` Function

The `update_ia()` function, called from `client6_recvreply()`, processes IAs in a DHCPv6 reply message.

Identify Local Configuration

Listing 4-42

—— dhcp6c_ia.c

```
93   void
94   update_ia(iatype, ialist, ifp, serverid, authparam)
95          iatype_t iatype;
96          struct dhcp6_list *ialist;
97          struct dhcp6_if *ifp;
98          struct duid *serverid;
99          struct authparam *authparam;
```

```
100   {
101           struct ia *ia;
102           struct ia_conf *iac;
103           struct iapd_conf *iapdc;
104           struct iana_conf *ianac;
105           struct dhcp6_listval *iav, *siav;
106           struct timeval timo;
107
108           for (iav = TAILQ_FIRST(ialist); iav; iav = TAILQ_NEXT(iav, link)) {
109                   /* if we're not interested in this IA, ignore it. */
110                   if ((iac = find_iaconf(&ifp->iaconf_list, iatype,
111                       iav->val_ia.iaid)) == NULL) {
112                           continue;
113                   }
```
_____ dhcp6c_ia.c

109–113 An IA is chosen and sent to the server by the client, and the server uses it to make
a new binding. This means that a received IA must always match one in the client's local
configurations. The find_iaconf() function identifies the local configuration based on
the received IA. If no configuration is found, the IA is ignored.

Parameter Validation

Listing 4-43
_____ dhcp6c_ia.c

```
115                   /* validate parameters */
116                   /*
117                    * If a client receives an IA_NA with T1 greater than T2, and
118                    * both T1 and T2 are greater than 0, the client discards the
119                    * IA_NA option and processes the remainder of the message as
120                    * though the server had not included the invalid IA_NA option.
121                    * [RFC331522.4]
122                    * We apply the same rule to IA_PD as well.
123                    */
124                   if (iav->val_ia.t2 != 0 && iav->val_ia.t1 > iav->val_ia.t2) {
125                           dprintf(LOG_INFO, FNAME,
126                               "invalid IA: T1(%lu) > T2(%lu)",
127                               iav->val_ia.t1, iav->val_ia.t2);
128                           continue;
129                   }
```
_____ dhcp6c_ia.c

124–129 The TI and T2 parameters control the timing of renewing allocated information.
[RFC3315] requires that T1 not be greater than T2 or T2 be zero, as also described in
the code comment. If these are not met, this IA is ignored.

Find or Make a Local IA

Listing 4-44
_____ dhcp6c_ia.c

```
131                   /* locate the local IA or make a new one */
132                   ia = get_ia(iatype, ifp, iac, iav, serverid);
133                   if (ia == NULL) {
134                           dprintf(LOG_WARNING, FNAME, "failed to get an IA "
135                               "type: %s, ID: %u", iastr(iac->type), iac->iaid);
136                           continue;
137                   }
```
_____ dhcp6c_ia.c

131–137 The `get_ia()` function searches the local list of IAs for a local `ia{}` structure corresponding to the received IA. If no local IA exists (which is the case when the client first receives a DHCPv6 Reply to a DHCPv6 Request), it creates a new one.

Record Authentication

Listing 4-45

```
─────────────────────────────────────────────────────dhcp6c_ia.c
139                     /* update authentication parameters */
140                     if (update_authparam(ia, authparam)) {
141                             dprintf(LOG_WARNING, FNAME, "failed to update "
142                                 "authentication param for IA "
143                                 "type: %s, ID: %u", iastr(iac->type), iac->iaid);
144                             remove_ia(ia);
145                             continue;
146                     }
─────────────────────────────────────────────────────dhcp6c_ia.c
```

140–146 If authentication parameters are provided in an Authentication option, the `update_authparam()` function records the latest replay detection information in the local IA.

> It is probably not a good idea to maintain the replay detection information per IA, since multiple sets of exchanges with the same server for different IAs may take place, and the per-IA replay information may cause confusion in validating received messages, or can even make a replay attack possible. This information should be maintained per server.

Update Configuration Information

Listing 4-46

```
─────────────────────────────────────────────────────dhcp6c_ia.c
148                     /* update IA configuration information */
149                     for (siav = TAILQ_FIRST(&iav->sublist); siav;
150                         siav = TAILQ_NEXT(siav, link)) {
151                         switch (siav->type) {
152                         case DHCP6_LISTVAL_PREFIX6:
153                             /* add or update the prefix */
154                             iapdc = (struct iapd_conf *)iac;
155                             if (update_prefix(ia, &siav->val_prefix6,
156                                 &iapdc->iapd_pif_list, ifp, &ia->ctl,
157                                 callback)) {
158                                     dprintf(LOG_NOTICE, FNAME,
159                                         "failed to update a prefix %s/%d",
160                                         in6addr2str(&siav->
val_prefix6.addr, 0),
161                                             siav->val_prefix6.plen);
162                             }
163                             break;
164                         case DHCP6_LISTVAL_STATEFULADDR6:
165                             ianac = (struct iana_conf *)iac;
166                             if (update_address(ia, &siav->val_statefuladdr6,
167                                 ifp, &ia->ctl, callback)) {
168                                     dprintf(LOG_NOTICE, FNAME,
169                                         "failed to update an address %s",
170                                         in6addr2str(&siav->
val_statefuladdr6.addr, 0));
```

```
171                                        }
172                                        break;
173                          case DHCP6_LISTVAL_STCODE:
174                                  dprintf(LOG_INFO, FNAME,
175                                      "status code for %s-%lu: %s",
176                                      iastr(iatype), iav->val_ia.iaid,
177                                      dhcp6_stcodestr(siav->val_num16));
178                                  if ((ia->state == IAS_RENEW ||
179                                      ia->state == IAS_REBIND) &&
180                                      siav->val_num16 ==
      DH6OPT_STCODE_NOBINDING) {
181                                          /*
182                                           * For each IA in the original Renew or
183                                           * Rebind message, the client
184                                           * sends a Request message if the IA
185                                           * contained a Status Code option
186                                           * with the NoBinding status.
187                                           * [RFC3315 18.1.8]
188                                           * XXX: what about the PD case?
189                                           */
190                                          dprintf(LOG_INFO, FNAME,
191                                              "receive NoBinding against "
192                                              "renew/rebind for %s-%lu",
193                                              iastr(ia->conf->type),
194                                              ia->conf->iaid);
195                                          reestablish_ia(ia);
196                                          goto nextia;
197                                  }
198                                  break;
199                          default:
200                                  dprintf(LOG_ERR, FNAME, "impossible case");
201                                  goto nextia;
202                          }
203                  }
```
——dhcp6c_ia.c

— Lines 160, 170, and 180 are broken here for layout reasons. However, they are a single line of code.

148–172 All configuration information contained in the received IA is examined. For prefix delegation (when an IA_PD Prefix option is included), the update_prefix() function processes or updates the corresponding local prefix. Similarly, for address allocation (when an IA Address option is included), the update_address() function processes or updates the corresponding local address.

The callback() function, which is not described in this book, will be called when some of the allocated resources associated with the IA are removed. This function will then check that the IA still has a valid resource, and if not, it removes the IA. This processing corresponds to the state transition to "end" in Figure 4-26 (on page 358).

173–198 If the IA option received in response to a Renew or Rebind message contains a NoBinding status code, it means the server has lost the binding for some reason (perhaps due to a crash and a reboot, etc.). In this case, the client falls back to sending a Request message to the server in order to establish a new binding.

Adjust Timeout Parameters

Listing 4-47
——dhcp6c_ia.c

```
205                  /* see if this IA is still valid.  if not, remove it. */
206                  if (ia->ctl == NULL || !(*ia->ctl->isvalid)(ia->ctl)) {
207                          dprintf(LOG_DEBUG, FNAME, "IA %s-%lu is invalidated",
```

```
208                              iastr(ia->conf->type), ia->conf->iaid);
209                      remove_ia(ia);
210                      continue;
211              }
212
213              /* if T1 or T2 is 0, determine appropriate values locally. */
214              if (ia->t1 == 0 || ia->t2 == 0) {
215                      u_int32_t duration;
216
217                      if (ia->ctl && ia->ctl->duration)
218                              duration = (*ia->ctl->duration)(ia->ctl);
219                      else
220                              duration = 1800; /* 30min. XXX: no rationale */
221
222                      if (ia->t1 == 0) {
223                              if (duration == DHCP6_DURATITION_INFINITE)
224                                      ia->t1 = DHCP6_DURATITION_INFINITE;
225                              else
226                                      ia->t1 = duration / 2;
227                      }
228                      if (ia->t2 == 0) {
229                              if (duration == DHCP6_DURATITION_INFINITE)
230                                      ia->t2 = DHCP6_DURATITION_INFINITE;
231                              else
232                                      ia->t2 = duration * 4 / 5;
233                      }
234
235                      /* make sure T1 <= T2 */
236                      if (ia->t1 > ia->t2)
237                              ia->t1 = ia->t2 * 5 / 8;
238
239                      dprintf(LOG_INFO, FNAME, "T1(%lu) and/or T2(%lu) "
240                          "is locally determined", ia->t1, ia->t2);
241              }
242
243              /*
244               * Be proactive for too-small timeout values.  Note that
245               * the adjusted values may make some information expire
246               * without renewal.
247               */
248              if (ia->t2 < DHCP6_DURATITION_MIN) {
249                      dprintf(LOG_INFO, FNAME, "T1 (%lu) or T2 (%lu) "
250                          "is too small", ia->t1, ia->t2);
251                      ia->t2 = DHCP6_DURATITION_MIN;
252                      ia->t1 = ia->t2 * 5 / 8;
253                      dprintf(LOG_INFO, "", "  adjusted to %lu and %lu",
254                          ia->t1, ia->t2);
255              }
```
                                                                    ___dhcp6c_ia.c

205–211 The received IA option may invalidate the local IA. For example, if the valid lifetime of a delegated prefix or an allocated address is 0 in the IA option, the prefix or address is removed. If the IA contains no address or prefix as a result of this operation, the `isvalid` method of this IA indicates the IA is now invalid (this can happen if the lifetimes for the addresses or prefixes are all 0). In this case the client removes the IA from the interface, and starts a new DHCPv6 session; this happens in the `remove_ia()` function.

213–233 If either timeout parameter T1 or T2 is 0, the client is expected to choose an appropriate value for that parameter by itself. The specification does not provide any guidance on how to choose the parameters in this case; this implementation reuses the specification recommendations [RFC3315] for the server that T1 and T2 be basically 0.5 and 0.8 times the shortest preferred lifetime of the addresses belonging to this IA, respectively. If the

shortest preferred lifetime is 0xffffffff, meaning infinity, the corresponding timeout values
are also set to infinity.

235–241 If only one of T1 and T2 is 0, T1 might become larger than T2 as a result of the
adjustment. In this case, T1 is readjusted in order to make sure that it is less than T2. The
ratio derived from the recommended relationship described above (5:8) applies. Note that
this is not stipulated in the specification but is an implementation-specific behavior.

248–255 In order to avoid a storm of Renew-Reply exchanges, this implementation introduces an implementation-specific minimum value (30 seconds) of T2. If the advertised
or adjusted value is smaller than the minimum, T2 is reset to the minimum value, and
T1 is also adjusted accordingly. In this case, T1, the timeout period for the next Renew
message to be sent, is reset to about 18 seconds.

Reset Timer

Listing 4-48
dhcp6c_ia.c

```
257                     /* set up a timer for this IA. */
258                     if (ia->t1 == DHCP6_DURATITION_INFINITE) {
259                             if (ia->timer)
260                                     dhcp6_remove_timer(&ia->timer);
261                     } else {
262                             if (ia->timer == NULL)
263                                     ia->timer = dhcp6_add_timer(ia_timo, ia);
264                             if (ia->timer == NULL) {
265                                     dprintf(LOG_ERR, FNAME,
266                                         "failed to add IA timer");
267                                     remove_ia(ia); /* XXX */
268                                     continue;
269                             }
270                             timo.tv_sec = ia->t1;
271                             timo.tv_usec = 0;
272                             dhcp6_set_timer(&timo, ia->timer);
273                     }
```
dhcp6c_ia.c

257–273 If T1 is infinite, the timer for this IA is canceled. Otherwise, a new timer is set to the
value of T1 for sending the next Renew message.

Become Active

Listing 4-49
dhcp6c_ia.c

```
274
275                             ia->state = IAS_ACTIVE;
276
277             nextia:
278                     ;
279             }
280     }
```
dhcp6c_ia.c

275 The state of this IA is set to ACTIVE, indicating renewal has succeeded (either by a Renew-
Reply or Rebind-Reply exchange).

4.4.10 `update_address()` **Function**

The `update_address()` function is called from `update_ia()` to actually configure or
update the corresponding addresses in an IA_NA. As was seen in Section 4.4.9, a similar function, `update_prefix()`, is used for the counterpart of prefix delegation. Since the essential
behavior in terms of the DHCPv6 protocol is almost the same, this book just concentrates on
the address allocation case.

This routine maintains a per-IA(NA) structure, `iactl_na{}`, and associated structures,
`statefuladdr{}`, corresponding to the addresses in the IA_NA. These structures follow.

Listing 4-50

———addrconf.c
```
61    TAILQ_HEAD(statefuladdr_list, statefuladdr);
62    struct iactl_na {
63            struct iactl common;
64            struct statefuladdr_list statefuladdr_head;
65    };

76    struct statefuladdr {
77            TAILQ_ENTRY (statefuladdr) link;
78
79            struct dhcp6_statefuladdr addr;
80            time_t updatetime;
81            struct dhcp6_timer *timer;
82            struct iactl_na *ctl;
83            struct dhcp6_if *dhcpif;
84    };
```
———addrconf.c

61–84 The `iactl_na{}` structure consists of the common control structure and a list of
`statefuladdr{}` structures. The `statefuladdr{}` structure contains address parameters including the valid and preferred lifetimes and an associated timer.

Next are the details of the `update_address()` function.

Lifetime Validation

Listing 4-51

———addrconf.c
```
102   int
103   update_address(ia, addr, dhcpifp, ctlp, callback)
104           struct ia *ia;
105           struct dhcp6_statefuladdr *addr;
106           struct dhcp6_if *dhcpifp;
107           struct iactl **ctlp;
108           void (*callback)__P((struct ia *));
109   {
110           struct iactl_na *iac_na = (struct iactl_na *)*ctlp;
111           struct statefuladdr *sa;
112           int sacreate = 0;
113           struct timeval timo;
114
115           /*
116            * A client discards any addresses for which the preferred
117            * lifetime is greater than the valid lifetime.
118            * [RFC3315 22.6]
119            */
120           if (addr->vltime != DHCP6_DURATITION_INFINITE &&
121               (addr->pltime == DHCP6_DURATITION_INFINITE ||
```

```
122                    addr->pltime > addr->vltime)) {
123                        dprintf(LOG_INFO, FNAME, "invalid address %s: "
124                            "pltime (%lu) is larger than vltime (%lu)",
125                            in6addr2str(&addr->addr, 0),
126                            addr->pltime, addr->vltime);
127                        return (-1);
128                }
```
—— addrconf.c

120–128 If the preferred lifetime of the address is greater than the valid lifetime, this address is ignored.

Create Control Structure

Listing 4-52
—— addrconf.c
```
130            if (iac_na == NULL) {
131                if ((iac_na = malloc(sizeof(*iac_na))) == NULL) {
132                        dprintf(LOG_NOTICE, FNAME, "memory allocation failed");
133                        return (-1);
134                }
135                memset(iac_na, 0, sizeof(*iac_na));
136                iac_na->iacna_ia = ia;
137                iac_na->iacna_callback = callback;
138                iac_na->iacna_isvalid = isvalid_addr;
139                iac_na->iacna_duration = duration_addr;
140                iac_na->iacna_cleanup = cleanup_addr;
141                iac_na->iacna_renew_data =
142                    iac_na->iacna_rebind_data =
143                    iac_na->iacna_release_data =
144                    iac_na->iacna_reestablish_data = renew_addr;
145
146                TAILQ_INIT(&iac_na->statefuladdr_head);
147                *ctlp = (struct iactl *)iac_na;
148            }
```
—— addrconf.c

130–148 When this function is first called for the IA_NA, the associated control structure, `iac_na`, is NULL. A new one is allocated and the pointers to the method functions are set.

Create Address Structure

Listing 4-53
—— addrconf.c
```
150            /* search for the given address, and make a new one if it fails */
151            if ((sa = find_addr(&iac_na->statefuladdr_head, addr)) == NULL) {
152                if ((sa = malloc(sizeof(*sa))) == NULL) {
153                        dprintf(LOG_NOTICE, FNAME, "memory allocation failed");
154                        return (-1);
155                }
156                memset(sa, 0, sizeof(*sa));
157                sa->addr.addr = addr->addr;
158                sa->ctl = iac_na;
159                TAILQ_INSERT_TAIL(&iac_na->statefuladdr_head, sa, link);
160                sacreate = 1;
161            }
```
—— addrconf.c

150–161 The `find_addr()` subroutine searches for a `statefuladdr{}` structure corresponding to the address being processed in the IA_NA. If this fails, it indicates that this is a new address, and a new structure is allocated.

Set or Update Address Parameters

Listing 4-54

———addrconf.c
```
163             /* update the timestamp of update */
164             sa->updatetime = time(NULL);
165
166             /* update the prefix according to addr */
167             sa->addr.pltime = addr->pltime;
168             sa->addr.vltime = addr->vltime;
169             sa->dhcpif = dhcpifp;
170             dprintf(LOG_DEBUG, FNAME, "%s an address %s pltime=%lu, vltime=%lu",
171                 sacreate ? "create" : "update",
172                 in6addr2str(&addr->addr, 0), addr->pltime, addr->vltime);
```
———addrconf.c

163–172 The valid and preferred lifetimes are copied to the local structure, along with a pointer to the interface on which the address is configured.

Configure Address

Listing 4-55

———addrconf.c
```
174             if (sa->addr.vltime != 0)
175                     na_ifaddrconf(IFADDRCONF_ADD, sa);
```
———addrconf.c

174–175 If the valid lifetime is not zero, the `na_ifaddrconf()` function installs the address into the kernel or updates the lifetimes of the address. The `na_ifaddrconf()` function, through its subroutine, issues the `SIOCAIFADDR_IN6` command of the `ioctl()` system call with the given address and lifetimes.

Unfortunately, this does not work as intended when updating an existing address; the kernel implementation described in this book does not update the lifetimes of an existing address. See the `in6_update_ifa()` function described in Chapter 2 of *IPv6 Core Protocols Implementation*, "IPv6 Addressing Architecture." The kernel implementation should be fixed for DHCPv6 to work correctly.

Invalidate Expired Address

Listing 4-56

———addrconf.c
```
177             /*
178              * If the new vltime is 0, this address immediately expires.
179              * Otherwise, set up or update the associated timer.
180              */
```

```
181              switch (sa->addr.vltime) {
182              case 0:
183                      remove_addr(sa);
184                      break;
```
_____addrconf.c

181–184 If the new valid lifetime is zero, the `remove_addr()` function removes this address
from the list in the `iactl_na{}` structure and from the kernel, and stops the timer (if
running) for the address. Note that this procedure is also done when the address is first
created.

Create or Update Timer

Listing 4-57
_____addrconf.c

```
185              case DHCP6_DURATITION_INFINITE:
186                      if (sa->timer)
187                              dhcp6_remove_timer(&sa->timer);
188                      break;
189              default:
190                      if (sa->timer == NULL) {
191                              sa->timer = dhcp6_add_timer(addr_timo, sa);
192                              if (sa->timer == NULL) {
193                                      dprintf(LOG_NOTICE, FNAME,
194                                          "failed to add stateful addr timer");
195                                      remove_addr(sa); /* XXX */
196                                      return (-1);
197                              }
198                      }
199                      /* update the timer */
200                      timo.tv_sec = sa->addr.vltime;
201                      timo.tv_usec = 0;
202
203                      dhcp6_set_timer(&timo, sa->timer);
204                      break;
205              }
206
207              return (0);
208      }
```
_____addrconf.c

185–188 If the new valid lifetime is infinite, this address never expires. The associated timer,
if running, is no longer necessary and is stopped. Note that this timer is specific to
this particular address. A separate timer is running for the IA containing this address
as long as the IA has a finite T1 value, and renewing the IA on the timer expiration may reduce the address lifetime. In that case the address timer will be enabled
again.

189–204 Otherwise, if a timer for the address is not running, it is restarted with the timeout
value of the new valid lifetime. When the timer expires the `addr_timo()` function,
which is not described in this book, will be called as the timer handler and remove the
address from the kernel and from the client process. The `addr_timo()` will also call the
`callback` function passed to this function (see Listing 4-51 on pages 365–366), which
will subsequently remove the IA if all addresses associated with the IA have expired, as
was explained in Listing 4-46 (pages 361–362).

> The kernel would also automatically remove the address from the system on the expiration of the valid lifetime as shown in Chapter 5 of *IPv6 Core Protocols Implementation*, but the DHCPv6 client implementation does not assume the specific kernel behavior and explicitly removes it.

Example

Here is a concrete example. Recall the request from the client shown in Figure 4-23 (page 337) with the assumption that the server responded with the following configuration information at September 1, 0:00:

IA-type: IANA

IAID: 100

T1: 12 hours

T2: 19.2 hours

Address 1: `2001:db8:ffff::1`, preferred lifetime = 7 days, valid lifetime = 30 days

Address 2: `2001:db8:ffff::2`, preferred lifetime = 1 day, valid lifetime = 7 days

(The T1 and T2 times are derived from the specification recommendation that T1 be .5 times the shortest preferred lifetime (1 day) and T2 be .8 times the shortest preferred lifetime).

Then the data structures shown in Figure 4-27 will be constructed by the client.

According to the timer settings, the `ia_timo()` function will be called in 12 hours, and a Renew-Reply exchange will start at that point. If the exchange does not go well, the timer for Address 2 will eventually expire (in one week) and the `addr_timo()` function (not described in this book) will be called to remove this address.

4.4.11 `reestablish_ia()` Function

The `reestablish_ia()` function is called from the `update_ia()` function when the server includes a Status Code option with the code of NoBinding for a particular IA.

State Check

Listing 4-58

——dhcp6c_ia.c
```
306     static void
307     reestablish_ia(ia)
308             struct ia *ia;
309     {
310             struct dhcp6_ia iaparam;
311             struct dhcp6_event *ev;
312             struct dhcp6_eventdata *evd;
313
314             dprintf(LOG_DEBUG, FNAME, "re-establishing IA: %s-%lu",
315                 iastr(ia->conf->type), ia->conf->iaid);
316
317             if (ia->state != IAS_RENEW && ia->state != IAS_REBIND) {
318                     dprintf(LOG_ERR, FNAME, "internal error (invalid IA status)");
319                     exit(1);        /* XXX */
320             }
```
——dhcp6c_ia.c

FIGURE 4-27

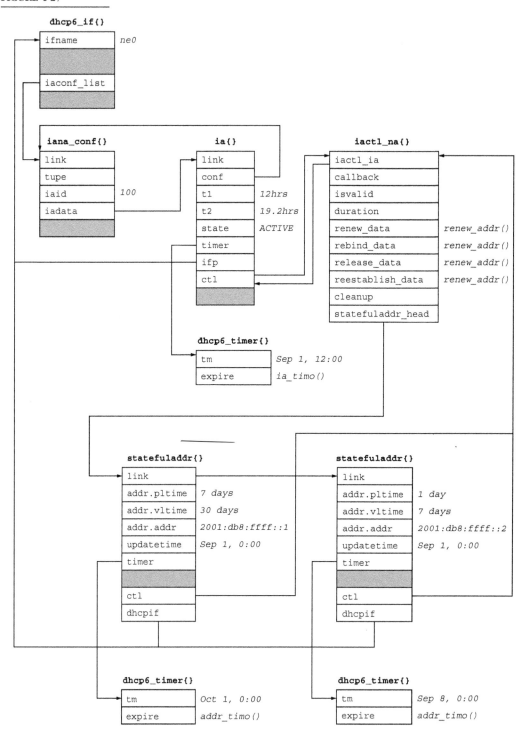

Data structures related to address allocation.

317–320 This should only happen in response to a Renew or Rebind message, and should be ignored in any other cases.

> *Note*: This check is almost redundant, since it is explicitly ensured by the caller.

Discard Old Event Data

Listing 4-59

———————————————————————————————————————dhcp6c_ia.c
```
322             /* cancel the current event for the prefix. */
323             if (ia->evdata) {
324                     TAILQ_REMOVE(&ia->evdata->event->data_list, ia->evdata, link);
325                     if (ia->evdata->destructor)
326                             ia->evdata->destructor(ia->evdata);
327                     else
328                             free(ia->evdata);
329                     ia->evdata = NULL;
330             }
331
332             /* we don't need a timer for the IA (see comments in ia_timo()) */
333             if (ia->timer)
334                     dhcp6_remove_timer(&ia->timer);
```
———————————————————————————————————————dhcp6c_ia.c

322–330 If the IA happens to have associated event data, it is released.

> This probably does not happen in this scenario. The code seems to be just copied from the `ia_timo()` function (described in Listing 4-65 on page 374).

333–334 Sending Renew or Rebind messages for this IA is now meaningless (since the server says that it has lost the binding), and the associated timer, if running, is removed.

Create Event

Listing 4-60

———————————————————————————————————————dhcp6c_ia.c
```
336             if ((ev = dhcp6_create_event(ia->ifp, DHCP6S_REQUEST)) == NULL) {
337                     dprintf(LOG_NOTICE, FNAME, "failed to create a new event");
338                     goto fail;
339             }
340             TAILQ_INSERT_TAIL(&ia->ifp->event_list, ev, link);
341
342             if ((ev->timer = dhcp6_add_timer(client6_timo, ev)) == NULL) {
343                     dprintf(LOG_NOTICE, FNAME,
344                         "failed to create a new event timer");
345                     goto fail;
346             }
347
348             if ((evd = malloc(sizeof(*evd))) == NULL) {
349                     dprintf(LOG_NOTICE, FNAME,
350                         "failed to create a new event data");
351                     goto fail;
352             }
353             memset(evd, 0, sizeof(*evd));
354             evd->event = ev;
```

```
355            TAILQ_INSERT_TAIL(&ev->data_list, evd, link);
356
357            if (duidcpy(&ev->serverid, &ia->serverid)) {
358                    dprintf(LOG_NOTICE, FNAME, "failed to copy server ID");
359                    goto fail;
360            }
361
362            iaparam.iaid = ia->conf->iaid;
363            iaparam.t1 = ia->t1;
364            iaparam.t2 = ia->t2;
365
366            if (ia->ctl && ia->ctl->reestablish_data) {
367                    if ((*ia->ctl->reestablish_data)(ia->ctl, &iaparam,
368                        &ia->evdata, evd)) {
369                            dprintf(LOG_NOTICE, FNAME,
370                                "failed to make reestablish data");
371                            goto fail;
372                    }
373            }
```
—— dhcp6c_ia.c

336–355 A new event for resending Request messages is created and inserted in the client's event list. An associated timer for the event and a separate event data structure are also allocated. The latter is then linked to the data list of the event structure.

357–360 The server's identifier is copied to the event structure, which is used in the Server Identifier option in the Request message.

366–373 If the IA has the corresponding `reestablish_data` method, it is called and sets parameters specific to this IA in the event data. This is always the case in this implementation. In the case of address allocation, the method function is the `renew_addr()` function, which will be described in Listing 4-64. The method function builds a list of prefixes or addresses corresponding to the IA to be included in the Request message.

Set Authentication Parameters

Listing 4-61
—— dhcp6c_ia.c
```
375            if (ia->authparam != NULL) {
376                    if ((ev->authparam = copy_authparam(ia->authparam)) == NULL) {
377                            dprintf(LOG_WARNING, FNAME,
378                                "failed to copy authparam");
379                            goto fail;
380                    }
381            }
```
—— dhcp6c_ia.c

375–381 If authentication parameters are recorded in the IA, they are copied to the event structure and will be used in an Authentication option in the Request message.

Reset Timer

Listing 4-62
—— dhcp6c_ia.c
```
383            ev->timeouts = 0;
384            dhcp6_set_timeoparam(ev);
385            dhcp6_reset_timer(ev);
```
—— dhcp6c_ia.c

383–385 The `dhcp6_set_timeoparam()` function sets appropriate timeout parameters specific to the Request message as specified in [RFC3315]. Specifically, IRT is set to 10 seconds, MRT to 30 seconds, and MRC to 10 times. Then the `dhcp6_reset_timer()` function starts the timer for the event.

Send Packet

Listing 4-63

_____dhcp6c_ia.c

```
387             ia->evdata = evd;
388
389             client6_send(ev);
390
391             return;
392
393     fail:
394             if (ev)
395                     dhcp6_remove_event(ev);
396
397             return;
398     }
```
_____dhcp6c_ia.c

389 The `client6_send()` function sends the Request message to the server.

The `renew_addr()` function, shown in Listing 4-64, is called from several routines related to IA_NA operation, including `reestablish_ia()`, as the corresponding method in order to construct the data structure for a Request, Renew, Rebind, or Release message. There is also a similar function for the prefix delegation case, but this section concentrates on address allocation as noted in the `update_address()` function.

The behavior of this function is actually simple. It makes a copy of the addresses for the given IA_NA, and sets it as the event data structure.

Listing 4-64

_____addrconf.c

```
291     static int
292     renew_addr(iac, iaparam, evdp, evd)
293             struct iactl *iac;
294             struct dhcp6_ia *iaparam;
295             struct dhcp6_eventdata **evdp, *evd;
296     {
297             struct iactl_na *iac_na = (struct iactl_na *)iac;
298             struct statefuladdr *sa;
299             struct dhcp6_list *ial = NULL, pl;
300
301             TAILQ_INIT(&pl);
302             for (sa = TAILQ_FIRST(&iac_na->statefuladdr_head); sa;
303                 sa = TAILQ_NEXT(sa, link)) {
304                     if (dhcp6_add_listval(&pl, DHCP6_LISTVAL_STATEFULADDR6,
305                         &sa->addr, NULL) == NULL)
306                             goto fail;
307             }
308
309             if ((ial = malloc(sizeof(*ial))) == NULL)
310                     goto fail;
311             TAILQ_INIT(ial);
312             if (dhcp6_add_listval(ial, DHCP6_LISTVAL_IANA, iaparam, &pl) == NULL)
313                     goto fail;
314             dhcp6_clear_list(&pl);
```

```
315
316             evd->type = DHCP6_EVDATA_IANA;
317             evd->data = (void *)ial;
318             evd->privdata = (void *)evdp;
319             evd->destructor = na_renew_data_free;
320
321             return (0);
322
323     fail:
324             dhcp6_clear_list(&pl);
325             if (ial)
326                     free(ial);
327             return (-1);
328     }
```
_____addrconf.c

4.4.12 `ia_timo()` Function

The `ia_timo()` function is the timer handler function for an IA maintained in the client, and is
called via the `dhcp6_check_timer()` function when the IA needs to be updated by a Renew
or Rebind message. This function also changes the internal state of the IA.

Discard Old Event Data

Listing 4-65
_____dhcp6c_ia.c
```
547     static struct dhcp6_timer *
548     ia_timo(arg)
549             void *arg;
550     {
551             struct ia *ia = (struct ia *)arg;
552             struct dhcp6_ia iaparam;
553             struct dhcp6_event *ev;
554             struct dhcp6_eventdata *evd;
555             struct timeval timo;
556             int dhcpstate;
557
558             dprintf(LOG_DEBUG, FNAME, "IA timeout for %s-%lu, state=%s",
559                 iastr(ia->conf->type), ia->conf->iaid, statestr(ia->state));
560
561             /* cancel the current event for the prefix. */
562             if (ia->evdata) {
563                     TAILQ_REMOVE(&ia->evdata->event->data_list, ia->evdata, link);
564                     if (ia->evdata->destructor)
565                             ia->evdata->destructor(ia->evdata);
566                     else
567                             free(ia->evdata);
568                     ia->evdata = NULL;
569             }
```
_____dhcp6c_ia.c

561–569 If the IA has associated event data (which is the case when this function is called for
   a Rebind message), it is released.

State Transition

Listing 4-66
_____dhcp6c_ia.c
```
571             switch (ia->state) {
572             case IAS_ACTIVE:
573                     ia->state = IAS_RENEW;
```

```
574                       dhcpstate = DHCP6S_RENEW;
575                       timo.tv_sec = ia->t1 < ia->t2 ? ia->t2 - ia->t1 : 0;
576                       timo.tv_usec = 0;
577                       dhcp6_set_timer(&timo, ia->timer);
578                       break;
579               case IAS_RENEW:
580                       ia->state = IAS_REBIND;
581                       dhcpstate = DHCP6S_REBIND;
582
583                       /*
584                        * We need keep DUID for sending Release in this state.
585                        * But we don't need a timer for the IA.  We'll just wait for a
586                        * reply for the REBIND until all associated configuration
587                        * parameters for this IA expire.
588                        */
589                       dhcp6_remove_timer(&ia->timer);
590                       break;
591               default:
592                       dprintf(LOG_ERR, FNAME, "invalid IA state (%d)",
593                           (int)ia->state);
594                       return (NULL);          /* XXX */
595               }
```
——— dhcp6c_ia.c

571–578 If the current state of the IA is ACTIVE, it is changed to RENEW, indicating that a Renew-Reply exchange is being performed between the client and the server. The associated timer is reset to T2 − T1, so that the next transition to REBIND will take place in T2 seconds after the time when the IA was established.

> The update_ia() function ensures T2 >= T1, and the check at line 575 is actually redundant.

579–590 If the current state is RENEW, the new state is set to REBIND, indicating that Rebind-Reply exchanges are being performed between the client and servers. In this state, the original server information is meaningless for sending a Rebind message, but it is still kept in the structure in case it is necessary to send a Release message while the IA is in this state. As mentioned in the comments, the per-IA timer is no longer necessary and is removed.

Create Event

Listing 4-67
——— dhcp6c_ia.c

```
597               if ((ev = dhcp6_create_event(ia->ifp, dhcpstate)) == NULL) {
598                       dprintf(LOG_NOTICE, FNAME, "failed to create a new event");
599                       goto fail;
600               }
601               TAILQ_INSERT_TAIL(&ia->ifp->event_list, ev, link);
602
603               if ((ev->timer = dhcp6_add_timer(client6_timo, ev)) == NULL) {
604                       dprintf(LOG_NOTICE, FNAME,
605                           "failed to create a new event timer");
606                       goto fail;
607               }
608
609               if ((evd = malloc(sizeof(*evd))) == NULL) {
610                       dprintf(LOG_NOTICE, FNAME,
611                           "failed to create a new event data");
612                       goto fail;
```

```
613              }
614              memset(evd, 0, sizeof(*evd));
615              evd->event = ev;
616              TAILQ_INSERT_TAIL(&ev->data_list, evd, link);
617
618              if (ia->state == IAS_RENEW) {
619                      if (duidcpy(&ev->serverid, &ia->serverid)) {
620                              dprintf(LOG_NOTICE, FNAME, "failed to copy server ID");
621                              goto fail;
622                      }
623              }
624
625              iaparam.iaid = ia->conf->iaid;
626              iaparam.t1 = ia->t1;
627              iaparam.t2 = ia->t2;
628              switch(ia->state) {
629              case IAS_RENEW:
630                      if (ia->ctl && ia->ctl->renew_data) {
631                              if ((*ia->ctl->renew_data)(ia->ctl, &iaparam,
632                                  &ia->evdata, evd)) {
633                                      dprintf(LOG_NOTICE, FNAME,
634                                          "failed to make renew data");
635                                      goto fail;
636                              }
637                      }
638                      break;
639              case IAS_REBIND:
640                      if (ia->ctl && ia->ctl->rebind_data) {
641                              if ((*ia->ctl->rebind_data)(ia->ctl, &iaparam,
642                                  &ia->evdata, evd)) {
643                                      dprintf(LOG_NOTICE, FNAME,
644                                          "failed to make rebind data");
645                                      goto fail;
646                              }
647                      }
648                      break;
649              default:
650                      break;
651              }
```
─── *dhcp6c_ia.c*

597–616 A new event for (re)sending Renew or Rebind messages is created and inserted in the client's event list. An associated timer for the event and a separate event data structure are also allocated. The event data structure is then linked to the data list of the event structure.

618–623 If the new state is RENEW, the server's identifier is copied to the event structure. This is used in the Server Identifier option in the Renew message.

625–651 If the IA has the corresponding `renew` or `rebind` method (this is always the case in this implementation, as already mentioned), it is called and sets parameters specific to this IA in the event data.

Reset Timer

Listing 4-68
─── *dhcp6c_ia.c*

```
653              ev->timeouts = 0;
654              dhcp6_set_timeoparam(ev);
655              dhcp6_reset_timer(ev);
```
─── *dhcp6c_ia.c*

653–655 The `dhcp6_set_timeoparam()` function sets appropriate timeout parameters specific to the event state. Specifically, IRT is set to 10 seconds, and MRT to 600 seconds for either Renew or Rebind. Then the `dhcp6_reset_timer()` function starts the timer for the event.

Set Authentication Parameters

Listing 4-69

_____dhcp6c_ia.c

```
657                 if (ia->authparam != NULL) {
658                         if ((ev->authparam = copy_authparam(ia->authparam)) == NULL) {
659                                 dprintf(LOG_WARNING, FNAME,
660                                     "failed to copy authparam");
661                                 goto fail;
662                         }
663                 }
```

_____dhcp6c_ia.c

657–663 If authentication parameters are recorded in the IA, they are copied to the event structure and will be used in an Authenticate option in the Renew or Rebind message.

Send Packet

Listing 4-70

_____dhcp6c_ia.c

```
665             ia->evdata = evd;
666
667             switch(ia->state) {
668             case IAS_RENEW:
669             case IAS_REBIND:
670                     client6_send(ev);
671                     break;
672             case IAS_ACTIVE:
673                     /* what to do? */
674                     break;
675             }
676
677             return (ia->timer);
678
679     fail:
680             if (ev)
681                     dhcp6_remove_event(ev);
682
683             return (NULL);
684     }
```

_____dhcp6c_ia.c

665–675 The `client6_send()` function sends a Renew or Rebind message for the IA, depending on its state.

Example

Figure 4-28 shows an example of data structures constructed in the timeout routine. This example is based on the scenario described in Figure 4-27 on page 370. When the timer for the IA expires at 12:00, the `ia_timo()` function is called. It constructs the event structures, copying the IAID from the `iana_conf{}` structure, and constructing the list of addresses to be renewed in the event data derived from the list in the `iactl_na{}` structure via the `renew_addr()` method function. Then the state of the `ia{}` structure is changed to RENEW, and the associated timer is reset so that it will expire at 19:12 (which corresponds to the T2 time of the IA).

FIGURE 4-28

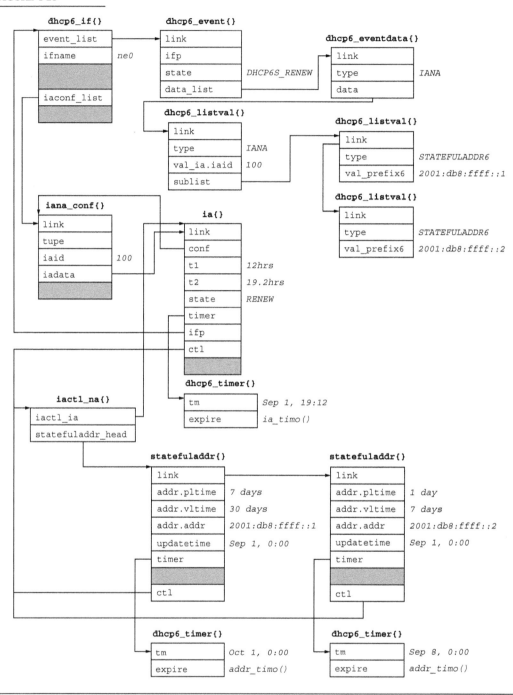

Data structures for a Renew message.

4.4.13   Release Resources

Upon receipt of the SIGTERM signal or of the *stop* command from a control channel, the client releases all configuration information and, if appropriate, sends corresponding Release messages.

This process starts with the `release_all_ia()` function, which is called from the main loop via the `process_signals()` function when a signal is received.

Listing 4-71

```
                                                                    dhcp6c_ia.c
412   void
413   release_all_ia(ifp)
414           struct dhcp6_if *ifp;
415   {
416           struct ia_conf *iac;
417           struct ia *ia, *ia_next;
418
419           for (iac = TAILQ_FIRST(&ifp->iaconf_list); iac;
420                iac = TAILQ_NEXT(iac, link)) {
421                   for (ia = TAILQ_FIRST(&iac->iadata); ia; ia = ia_next) {
422                           ia_next = TAILQ_NEXT(ia, link);
423
424                           (void)release_ia(ia);
425
426                           /*
427                            * The client MUST stop using all of the addresses
428                            * being released as soon as the client begins the
429                            * Release message exchange process.
430                            * [RFC3315 Section 18.1.6]
431                            */
432                           remove_ia(ia);
433                   }
434           }
435   }
                                                                    dhcp6c_ia.c
```

419–434 For each IA configured on the given interface, the `release_ia()` function (described in Listing 4-72) sends a Release message to the server. As commented, the configuration resources for the IA must be removed from the system once the Release message is sent; otherwise, the server might reallocate the resource to a different client, resulting in duplicate allocation. The `remove_ia()` function handles this action.

> The inner `for` loop is actually redundant because there must be at most one IA for a given `ia_conf{}` structure as noted in Listing 4-40 (page 357).

Listing 4-72 shows the `release_ia()` function.

Listing 4-72

```
                                                                    dhcp6c_ia.c
437   static int
438   release_ia(ia)
439           struct ia *ia;
440   {
441           struct dhcp6_ia iaparam;
```

```
442              struct dhcp6_event *ev;
443              struct dhcp6_eventdata *evd;
444
445              dprintf(LOG_DEBUG, FNAME, "release an IA: %s-%lu",
446                  iastr(ia->conf->type), ia->conf->iaid);
447
448              if ((ev = dhcp6_create_event(ia->ifp, DHCP6S_RELEASE))
449                  == NULL) {
450                      dprintf(LOG_NOTICE, FNAME, "failed to create a new event");
451                      goto fail;
452              }
453              TAILQ_INSERT_TAIL(&ia->ifp->event_list, ev, link);
454
455
456              if ((ev->timer = dhcp6_add_timer(client6_timo, ev)) == NULL) {
457                      dprintf(LOG_NOTICE, FNAME,
458                          "failed to create a new event timer");
459                      goto fail;
460              }
461
462              if (duidcpy(&ev->serverid, &ia->serverid)) {
463                      dprintf(LOG_NOTICE, FNAME, "failed to copy server ID");
464                      goto fail;
465              }
466
467              if ((evd = malloc(sizeof(*evd))) == NULL) {
468                      dprintf(LOG_NOTICE, FNAME,
469                          "failed to create a new event data");
470                      goto fail;
471              }
472              memset(evd, 0, sizeof(*evd));
473              iaparam.iaid = ia->conf->iaid;
474              /* XXX: should we set T1/T2 to 0?  spec is silent on this. */
475              iaparam.t1 = ia->t1;
476              iaparam.t2 = ia->t2;
477
478              if (ia->ctl && ia->ctl->release_data) {
479                      if ((*ia->ctl->release_data)(ia->ctl, &iaparam, NULL, evd)) {
480                              dprintf(LOG_NOTICE, FNAME,
481                                  "failed to make release data");
482                              goto fail;
483                      }
484              }
485              TAILQ_INSERT_TAIL(&ev->data_list, evd, link);
486
487              ev->timeouts = 0;
488              dhcp6_set_timeoparam(ev);
489              dhcp6_reset_timer(ev);
490
491              if (ia->authparam != NULL) {
492                      if ((ev->authparam = copy_authparam(ia->authparam)) == NULL) {
493                              dprintf(LOG_WARNING, FNAME,
494                                  "failed to copy authparam");
495                              goto fail;
496                      }
497              }
498
499              client6_send(ev);
500
501              return (0);
502
503     fail:
504              if (ev)
505                      dhcp6_remove_event(ev);
506
507              return (-1);
508     }
```

Create event

448–460 A new event for resending Release messages is created and inserted in the client's event list. An associated timer for the event is also allocated.

462–465 The server identifier is copied from the IA to the event.

467–485 A separate event data structure is also allocated, and the `release_data` method for the IA constructs IA-dependent data for the Release message. In the case of address allocation, the method function is `renew_addr()` (Listing 4-64, pages 373–374), just as for Renew or Rebind. The event data structure is linked to the data list of the event structure.

Reset timer

487–489 The `dhcp6_set_timeoparam()` function sets appropriate timeout parameters specific to the Release message. Specifically, IRT is set to 1 second and MRC to 5 times. Then the `dhcp6_reset_timer()` function starts the timer for the event.

Set authentication parameters

491–497 If authentication parameters are recorded in the IA, they are copied to the event structure and will be used in an Authentication option in the Release message.

Send packet

499 The `client6_send()` function sends the Release message to the server.

The `remove_ia()` function is shown in Listing 4-73. It simply frees all data structures for the given IA. During the procedure, this function calls the `cleanup` method specific to the IA type. In the case of address allocation, the method function frees all address structures, calling the `remove_addr()` function to delete the address from the kernel.

Listing 4-73

dhcp6c_ia.c

```
510    static void
511    remove_ia(ia)
512            struct ia *ia;
513    {
514            struct ia_conf *iac = ia->conf;
515            struct dhcp6_if *ifp = ia->ifp;
516
517            dprintf(LOG_DEBUG, FNAME, "remove an IA: %s-%lu",
518                iastr(ia->conf->type), ia->conf->iaid);
519
520            TAILQ_REMOVE(&iac->iadata, ia, link);
521
522            duidfree(&ia->serverid);
523
524            if (ia->timer)
525                    dhcp6_remove_timer(&ia->timer);
526
527            if (ia->evdata) {
528                    TAILQ_REMOVE(&ia->evdata->event->data_list, ia->evdata, link);
529                    if (ia->evdata->destructor)
530                            ia->evdata->destructor(ia->evdata);
531                    else
532                            free(ia->evdata);
533                    ia->evdata = NULL;
534            }
```

```
535
536            if (ia->ctl && ia->ctl->cleanup)
537                    (*ia->ctl->cleanup)(ia->ctl);
538
539            if (ia->authparam != NULL)
540                    free(ia->authparam);
541
542            free(ia);
543
544            (void)client6_start(ifp);
545    }
```
                                                                    dhcp6c_ia.c

4.5 Server Implementation

Figure 4-29 shows an overview of the entire process of the server implementation. After initialization, the process goes into an infinite loop in the server6_mainloop() function, waiting for a message from a client.

FIGURE 4-29

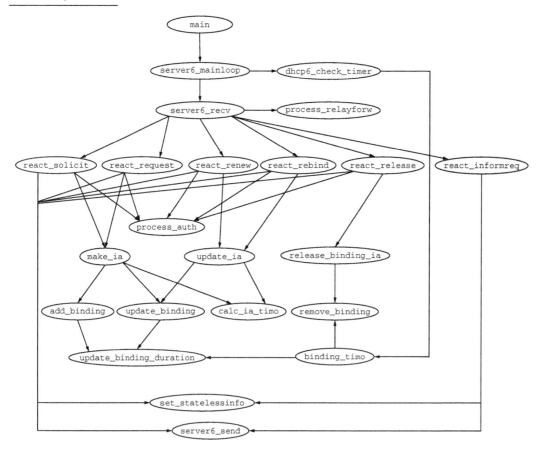

An overview of the server processes.

The common task for the server is to receive a message from a client, process it, and respond with a Reply message. This task starts from the `server6_recv()` function, which calls one of the `react_xxx()` functions corresponding to the message type. If the message is sent via a relay agent, the `process_relayforw()` function is first called and decapsulates the message into the original one sent from the client.

All `react_xxx()` functions except `react_informreq()`, which handles Information-request messages, call the `process_auth()` function to process DHCPv6 authentication. The Information-request message can also contain an Authentication option, but since the specification on this usage is not very clear yet (see [DHCP6AUTH]), this implementation does not support that option for Information-request messages.

The `react_solicit()` and `react_request()` functions process Solicit and Request messages, respectively. These call the `make_ia()` function to see if the server can allocate the requested resource for the received IA and to create bindings for the resources when possible.

The `react_renew()` and `react_rebind()` functions process Renew and Rebind messages, respectively. These messages are usually sent to update an existing binding for the specified IAs, and the `update_ia()` function performs this task.

The `react_release()` function handles Release messages. It calls the `release_binding_ia()` function, which then calls the `remove_binding()` function, in order to remove the corresponding bindings for the IAs in the Release message.

Bindings are also removed as a result of timer expiration, when, for example, the client does not try to renew the resource for a long period. The `binding_timo()` function, the timer handler for each binding, is called in this case, and this function in turn calls the `remove_binding()` function.

On success, the `react_xxx()` functions usually call the `server6_send()` function in order to respond to the received message with a Reply message. Before then, these functions also call the `set_statelessinfo()` function, which includes stateless configuration information that the server can provide in the Reply message. The `react_informreq()` function, which handles Information-request messages, essentially calls only these two functions.

Server Specific Data Structures

As previously explained, the `dhcp6_if{}` structure (Listing 4-5, page 328) is used by both the client and the server.

The `host_conf{}` structure, shown in Listing 4-74, represents per-host (client) configuration parameters. Most of its members are set at initialization from the server's configuration file.

Listing 4-74

config.h

```
189    /* per-host configuration */
190    struct host_conf {
191            struct host_conf *next;
192
193            char *name;                  /* host name to identify the host */
194            struct duid duid;        /* DUID for the host */
195
196            /* prefixes to be delegated to the host */
197            struct dhcp6_list prefix_list;
198            /* address to be assigned for the host */
```

```
199             struct dhcp6_list addr_list;
200
201             /* secret key shared with the client for delayed authentication */
202             struct keyinfo *delayedkey;
203             /* previous replay detection value from the client */
204             int saw_previous_rd;        /* if we remember the previous value */
205             u_int64_t previous_rd;
206     };
```
config.h

193–194 The name and duid members identify the corresponding client. In fact, name is just an arbitrary string and is only meaningful in log messages. The duid member is the DUID of the client.

196–199 The prefix_list and addr_list are preconfigured lists of prefixes and addresses to be allocated to the client.

201–205 The delayedkey member specifies the secret key shared with the client for DHCPv6 authentication, if configured. The saw_previous_rd and previous_rd members are run-time variables for replay protection in DHCPv6 authentication.

The dhcp6_binding{} structure, shown in Listing 4-75, represents a single DHCPv6 binding.

Listing 4-75

dhcp6s.c

```
 85     struct dhcp6_binding {
 86             TAILQ_ENTRY(dhcp6_binding) link;
 87
 88             dhcp6_bindingtype_t type;
 89
 90             /* identifier of the binding */
 91             struct duid clientid;
 92             /* additional identifiers for IA-based bindings */
 93             int iatype;
 94             u_int32_t iaid;
 95
 96             /*
 97              * configuration information of this binding,
 98              * which is type-dependent.
 99              */
100             union {
101                     struct dhcp6_list uv_list;
102             } val;
103     #define val_list val.uv_list
104
105             u_int32_t duration;
106             time_t updatetime;
107             struct dhcp6_timer *timer;
108     };
```
dhcp6s.c

86–107 Bindings are managed in a single list. A dhcp6_binding{} structure is a single entry of the list linked with its link member. The current implementation only supports bindings for IAs, and the type member is always DHCP6_BINDING_IA. The clientid, iatype, and iaid members represent the index of this binding: <DUID, IA-type, IAID>. In the current implementation, iatype must be either DHCP6_LISTVAL_IAPD (for IA_PD) or DHCP6_LISTVAL_IANA (for IA_NA). The val_list *member* (the union is actually redundant) is a list of binding data records, that is, a list of addresses or prefixes.

The rest of the members control the timer for this binding: `duration` specifies the timer interval, `updatetime` is the timestamp at which this binding is renewed by the client, and `timer` points to the actual timer object.

Global Variables

Table 4-7 summarizes major global variables specific to the server implementation.

Example

Figure 4-30 shows an example of server configurations.

This server is configured so that it will serve at least two clients: **kame** and **usagi**(*), whose DUIDs are XX:XX: ... and YY:YY: ..., respectively. For client **kame**, this server will allocate IPv6 addresses `2001:db8:ffff::1` (with the preferred and valid lifetimes being 7 days and 30 days) and `2001:db8:ffff::2` (with the preferred and valid lifetimes being 1 day and 7 days). For client **usagi**, the server will delegate an IPv6 prefix `2001:db8:1234::/48` (with the preferred valid lifetimes being 30 days and 90 days).

> (*) Client name **kame** is derived from the KAME project, of course. Similarly, **usagi** is derived from the *USAGI project*, which is also a subgroup of the WIDE project, working on IPv6 implementation for Linux. KAME and USAGI mean turtles and rabbits, respectively. The project name *USAGI* was also inspired by a famous fable by Aesop.

In addition to the per-client configurations, the server is also configured with stateless (i.e., client-independent) configuration information: two recursive DNS server addresses and a DNS domain search list.

TABLE 4-7

Name	Type	Description
insock	int	The file descriptor for the socket receiving inbound packets. The socket listens on UDP port 547. The server listens to the All_DHCP_Relay_Agents_and_Servers and All_DHCP_Servers multicast groups (`ff02::1:2` and `ff05::1:3`) through this socket.
outsock	int	The file descriptor for the socket sending outbound packets. This socket is initially not bound to any port or address.
server_duid	struct duid	Server's DUID.
dnslist	struct dhcp6_list	List of recursive DNS server addresses.
dnsnamelist	struct dhcp6_list	DNS search list.
siplist	struct dhcp6_list	List of SIP server addresses.
sipnamelist	struct dhcp6_list	List of SIP server domain names.
ntplist	struct dhcp6_list	List of NTP server addresses.

Global variables of the server implementation.

FIGURE 4-30

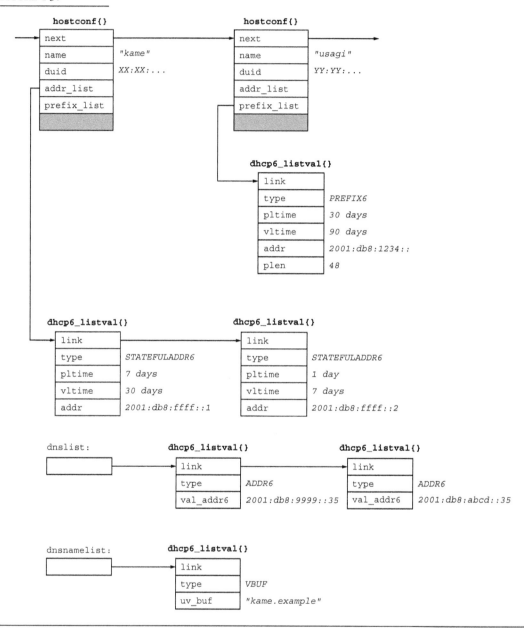

Server configuration example.

4.5.1 `server6_mainloop()` Function

The `server6_mainloop()` function, shown in Listing 4-76, is the main loop of the server. This function is pretty simple. In each iteration of the infinite loop, the `dhcp6_check_timer()` function is first called to examine expired timers, for each of which the associated callback function is called. Then the server watches the receiving socket (insock) until a message arrives or a new timer expires. When a new DHCPv6 message arrives, the server6_recv() function is called to process the message.

The discussions below ignore the operation on the control socket (ctlsock), since it is not directly relevant to protocol operation.

Listing 4-76
_____dhcp6s.c

```
538    static void
539    server6_mainloop()
540    {
541            struct timeval *w;
542            int ret;
543            fd_set r;
544            int maxsock;
545
546
547            while (1) {
548                    w = dhcp6_check_timer();
549
550                    FD_ZERO(&r);
551                    FD_SET(insock, &r);
552                    maxsock = insock;
553                    if (ctlsock >= 0) {
554                            FD_SET(ctlsock, &r);
555                            maxsock = (insock > ctlsock) ? insock : ctlsock;
556                            (void)dhcp6_ctl_setreadfds(&r, &maxsock);
557                    }
558
559                    ret = select(maxsock + 1, &r, NULL, NULL, w);
560                    switch (ret) {
561                    case -1:
562                            dprintf(LOG_ERR, FNAME, "select: %s",
563                                strerror(errno));
564                            exit(1);
565                            /* NOTREACHED */
566                    case 0:                        /* timeout */
567                            break;
568                    default:
569                            break;
570                    }
571
572                    if (FD_ISSET(insock, &r))
573                            server6_recv(insock);
574                    if (ctlsock >= 0) {
575                            if (FD_ISSET(ctlsock, &r)) {
576                                    (void)dhcp6_ctl_acceptcommand(ctlsock,
577                                        server6_do_ctlcommand);
578                            }
579                            (void)dhcp6_ctl_readcommand(&r);
580                    }
581            }
582    }
```
_____dhcp6s.c

4.5.2 server6_recv() Function

The server6_recv() function, shown on page 388, is the entry point of processing DHCPv6 messages in the server implementation.

Receive Message

Listing 4-77

_____dhcp6s.c

```
785    static void
786    server6_recv(s)
787          int s;
788    {
789          ssize_t len;
790          struct sockaddr_storage from;
791          int fromlen;
792          struct msghdr mhdr;
793          struct iovec iov;
794          char cmsgbuf[BUFSIZ];
795          struct cmsghdr *cm;
796          struct in6_pktinfo *pi = NULL;
797          struct dhcp6_if *ifp;
798          struct dhcp6 *dh6;
799          struct dhcp6_optinfo optinfo;
800          struct dhcp6opt *optend;
801          struct relayinfolist relayinfohead;
802          struct relayinfo *relayinfo;
803
804          TAILQ_INIT(&relayinfohead);
805
806          memset(&iov, 0, sizeof(iov));
807          memset(&mhdr, 0, sizeof(mhdr));
808
809          iov.iov_base = rdatabuf;
810          iov.iov_len = sizeof(rdatabuf);
811          mhdr.msg_name = &from;
812          mhdr.msg_namelen = sizeof(from);
813          mhdr.msg_iov = &iov;
814          mhdr.msg_iovlen = 1;
815          mhdr.msg_control = (caddr_t)cmsgbuf;
816          mhdr.msg_controllen = sizeof(cmsgbuf);
817
818          if ((len = recvmsg(insock, &mhdr, 0)) < 0) {
819                  dprintf(LOG_ERR, FNAME, "recvmsg: %s", strerror(errno));
820                  return;
821          }
822          fromlen = mhdr.msg_namelen;
```

_____dhcp6s.c

804–822 The arriving message is read by the `recvmsg()` system call. The message is stored in `rdatabuf`, and ancillary data is stored in `cmsgbuf`.

Identify the Interface

Listing 4-78

_____dhcp6s.c

```
824          for (cm = (struct cmsghdr *)CMSG_FIRSTHDR(&mhdr); cm;
825              cm = (struct cmsghdr *)CMSG_NXTHDR(&mhdr, cm)) {
826                  if (cm->cmsg_level == IPPROTO_IPV6 &&
827                      cm->cmsg_type == IPV6_PKTINFO &&
828                      cm->cmsg_len == CMSG_LEN(sizeof(struct in6_pktinfo))) {
829                          pi = (struct in6_pktinfo *)(CMSG_DATA(cm));
830                  }
831          }
832          if (pi == NULL) {
833                  dprintf(LOG_NOTICE, FNAME, "failed to get packet info");
834                  return;
835          }
```

```
836                 if ((ifp = find_ifconfbyid((unsigned int)pi->ipi6_ifindex)) == NULL) {
837                         dprintf(LOG_INFO, FNAME, "unexpected interface (%d)",
838                             (unsigned int)pi->ipi6_ifindex);
839                         return;
840                 }
```
_____dhcp6s.c

824–840 The ancillary data should contain an item of `IPV6_PKTINFO`, specifying the arrival interface and the destination address. The `find_ifconfbyid()` function compares the arrival interface to the interface configured for the server (given as a command line argument). If the message is received on an unexpected interface, it is discarded.

> Discarding messages on an unexpected interface is not a protocol requirement, but an implementation-dependent limitation.

Initial Validation

Listing 4-79
_____dhcp6s.c

```
842             dh6 = (struct dhcp6 *)rdatabuf;
843
844             if (len < sizeof(*dh6)) {
845                     dprintf(LOG_INFO, FNAME, "short packet (%d bytes)", len);
846                     return;
847             }
848
849             dprintf(LOG_DEBUG, FNAME, "received %s from %s",
850                 dhcp6msgstr(dh6->dh6_msgtype),
851                 addr2str((struct sockaddr *)&from));
852
853             /*
854              * A server MUST discard any Solicit, Confirm, Rebind or
855              * Information-request messages it receives with a unicast
856              * destination address.
857              * [RFC3315 Section 15.]
858              */
859             if (!IN6_IS_ADDR_MULTICAST(&pi->ipi6_addr) &&
860                 (dh6->dh6_msgtype == DH6_SOLICIT ||
861                 dh6->dh6_msgtype == DH6_CONFIRM ||
862                 dh6->dh6_msgtype == DH6_REBIND ||
863                 dh6->dh6_msgtype == DH6_INFORM_REQ)) {
864                     dprintf(LOG_INFO, FNAME, "invalid unicast message");
865                     return;
866             }
867
868             /*
869              * A server never receives a relay reply message.  Since relay
870              * replay messages will annoy option parser below, we explicitly
871              * reject them here.
872              */
873             if (dh6->dh6_msgtype == DH6_RELAY_REPLY) {
874                     dprintf(LOG_INFO, FNAME, "relay reply message from %s",
875                         addr2str((struct sockaddr *)&from));
876                     return;
877
878             }
```
_____dhcp6s.c

842–847 The message should contain the common part of DHCPv6 messages.

853–866 If the message's destination is an IPv6 unicast address and the message must not be unicasted, the packet is discarded.

868–878 A Relay-reply message can only be received by a relay agent (relaying a message from a server to a client). If a Relay-reply message is somehow received by a client or server, it must be ignored.

> A Relay-reply message would eventually be discarded in Listing 4-82 even without this check. But this implementation explicitly rejects this message in order for the dhcp6_get_options() function called in Listing 4-81 to not be bothered with the Relay Message option included in the Relay-reply message.

Process Relay-forward Message

Listing 4-80

```
                                                                      dhcp6s.c
880              optend = (struct dhcp6opt *)(rdatabuf + len);
881              if (dh6->dh6_msgtype == DH6_RELAY_FORW) {
882                      if (process_relayforw(&dh6, &optend, &relayinfohead,
883                          (struct sockaddr *)&from)) {
884                              goto end;
885                      }
886                      /* dh6 and optend should have been updated. */
887              }
                                                                      dhcp6s.c
```

880–887 If the message type is Relay-forward, it encapsulates (perhaps recursively) the original message from the client, which must be decapsulated before further processing. The process_relayforw() function does this job. On success, variable dh6 will point to the head of the original message, and optend will point to the tail of its options field. Variable relayinfohead will keep the (possibly) nested structure of Relay-forward messages, which will be used to construct a Reply message later (see Section 4.5.12).

Parse Options

Listing 4-81

```
                                                                      dhcp6s.c
889              /*
890               * parse and validate options in the message
891               */
892              dhcp6_init_options(&optinfo);
893              if (dhcp6_get_options((struct dhcp6opt *)(dh6 + 1),
894                  optend, &optinfo) < 0) {
895                      dprintf(LOG_INFO, FNAME, "failed to parse options");
896                      goto end;
897              }
                                                                      dhcp6s.c
```

889–897 The dhcp6_get_options() function parses options in the message, building internal data structures corresponding to the options in variable optinfo.

Process Message

Listing 4-82

─── dhcp6s.c

```
899         switch (dh6->dh6_msgtype) {
900         case DH6_SOLICIT:
901              (void)react_solicit(ifp, dh6, len, &optinfo,
902                  (struct sockaddr *)&from, fromlen, &relayinfohead);
903              break;
904         case DH6_REQUEST:
905              (void)react_request(ifp, pi, dh6, len, &optinfo,
906                  (struct sockaddr *)&from, fromlen, &relayinfohead);
907              break;
908         case DH6_RENEW:
909              (void)react_renew(ifp, pi, dh6, len, &optinfo,
910                  (struct sockaddr *)&from, fromlen, &relayinfohead);
911              break;
912         case DH6_REBIND:
913              (void)react_rebind(ifp, dh6, len, &optinfo,
914                  (struct sockaddr *)&from, fromlen, &relayinfohead);
915              break;
916         case DH6_RELEASE:
917              (void)react_release(ifp, pi, dh6, len, &optinfo,
918                  (struct sockaddr *)&from, fromlen, &relayinfohead);
919              break;
920         case DH6_INFORM_REQ:
921              (void)react_informreq(ifp, dh6, len, &optinfo,
922                  (struct sockaddr *)&from, fromlen, &relayinfohead);
923              break;
924         default:
925              dprintf(LOG_INFO, FNAME, "unknown or unsupported msgtype (%s)",
926                  dhcp6msgstr(dh6->dh6_msgtype));
927              break;
928         }
```

─── dhcp6s.c

899–928 An appropriate subroutine is called based on the message type, in which per-message processing takes place.

Cleanup

Listing 4-83

─── dhcp6s.c

```
930         dhcp6_clear_options(&optinfo);
931
932     end:
933         while ((relayinfo = TAILQ_FIRST(&relayinfohead)) != NULL) {
934              TAILQ_REMOVE(&relayinfohead, relayinfo, link);
935              free_relayinfo(relayinfo);
936         }
937
938         return;
939     }
```

─── dhcp6s.c

930–936 Temporary data structures for DHCPv6 options and the information of Relay-forward messages (if any) are released.

4.5.3 `process_relayforw()` Function

The `process_relayforw()` function decapsulates a Relay-forward message (or a chain of Relay-forward messages) until the original message from the client is found.

Validation

Listing 4-84

——dhcp6s.c

```
954     static int
955     process_relayforw(dh6p, optendp, relayinfohead, from)
956             struct dhcp6 **dh6p;
957             struct dhcp6opt **optendp;
958             struct relayinfolist *relayinfohead;
959             struct sockaddr *from;
960     {
961             struct dhcp6_relay *dh6relay = (struct dhcp6_relay *)*dh6p;
962             struct dhcp6opt *optend = *optendp;
963             struct relayinfo *relayinfo;
964             struct dhcp6_optinfo optinfo;
965             int len;
966
967         again:
968             len = (void *)optend - (void *)dh6relay;
969             if (len < sizeof (*dh6relay)) {
970                     dprintf(LOG_INFO, FNAME, "short relay message from %s",
971                         addr2str(from));
972                     return (-1);
973             }
974             dprintf(LOG_DEBUG, FNAME,
975                 "dhcp6 relay: hop=%d, linkaddr=%s, peeraddr=%s",
976                 dh6relay->dh6relay_hcnt,
977                 in6addr2str(&dh6relay->dh6relay_linkaddr, 0),
978                 in6addr2str(&dh6relay->dh6relay_peeraddr, 0));
```

——dhcp6s.c

968–978 The part of the message considered must be large enough to store the common part of a Relay-forward message. Otherwise, the packet is discarded.

Parse and Validate Options

Listing 4-85

——dhcp6s.c

```
980             /*
981              * parse and validate options in the relay forward message.
982              */
983             dhcp6_init_options(&optinfo);
984             if (dhcp6_get_options((struct dhcp6opt *)(dh6relay + 1),
985                 optend, &optinfo) < 0) {
986                     dprintf(LOG_INFO, FNAME, "failed to parse options");
987                     return (-1);
988             }
989
990             /* A relay forward message must include a relay message option */
991             if (optinfo.relaymsg_msg == NULL) {
992                     dprintf(LOG_INFO, FNAME, "relay forward from %s "
993                         "without a relay message", addr2str(from));
994                     return (-1);
995             }
996
997             /* relay message must contain a DHCPv6 message. */
998             len = optinfo.relaymsg_len;
999             if (len < sizeof (struct dhcp6)) {
1000                    dprintf(LOG_INFO, FNAME,
1001                        "short packet (%d bytes) in relay message", len);
1002                    return (-1);
1003            }
```

——dhcp6s.c

980–988 The dhcp6_get_options() function parses options in this particular Relay-forward message.

990–995 If a Relay Message option is not included for this Relay-forward message, the packet is discarded.

997–1003 The option data of the Relay Message option must be a valid DHCPv6 message. If it is too short for a DHCPv6 message, the packet is discarded.

Remember the Relay Information

Listing 4-86

```
                                                                    dhcp6s.c
1005            if ((relayinfo = malloc(sizeof (*relayinfo))) == NULL) {
1006                    dprintf(LOG_ERR, FNAME, "failed to allocate relay info");
1007                    return (-1);
1008            }
1009            memset(relayinfo, 0, sizeof (*relayinfo));
1010
1011            relayinfo->hcnt = dh6relay->dh6relay_hcnt;
1012            memcpy(&relayinfo->linkaddr, &dh6relay->dh6relay_linkaddr,
1013                sizeof (relayinfo->linkaddr));
1014            memcpy(&relayinfo->peeraddr, &dh6relay->dh6relay_peeraddr,
1015                sizeof (relayinfo->peeraddr));
1016
1017            if (dhcp6_vbuf_copy(&relayinfo->relay_msg, &optinfo.relay_msg))
1018                    goto fail;
1019            if (optinfo.ifidopt_id &&
1020                dhcp6_vbuf_copy(&relayinfo->relay_ifid, &optinfo.ifidopt)) {
1021                    goto fail;
1022            }
1023
1024            TAILQ_INSERT_HEAD(relayinfohead, relayinfo, link);
                                                                    dhcp6s.c
```

1005–1022 A new relayinfo{} structure is allocated, and some parameters of this Relay-forward message are stored in it. Listing 4-87 gives the definition of the relayinfo{} structure.

  If the Relay-forward message contains an Interface-Id option, it is also stored in relayinfo{}. This will be used later for constructing a chain of Relay-reply messages when the server builds a Reply message. Note that the option data of the Relay message option must also be copied, even though it is not necessary when responding, since the data space will soon be released (at line 1026 in Listing 4-88).

> At the time of this writing, Interface-Id is the only option that is to be copied into the corresponding Relay-reply message according to the specification, but future specifications may require a new relay-agent specific option that must be copied to the Relay-reply message.

1024 The new relayinfo{} structure is then added to the list started at relayinfohead.

Listing 4-87

_____dhcp6s.c
```
111    struct relayinfo {
112            TAILQ_ENTRY(relayinfo) link;
113
114            u_int hcnt;                    /* hop count */
115            struct in6_addr linkaddr; /* link address */
116            struct in6_addr peeraddr; /* peer address */
117            struct dhcp6_vbuf relay_ifid; /* Interface ID (if provided) */
118            struct dhcp6_vbuf relay_msg; /* relay message */
119    };
120    TAILQ_HEAD(relayinfolist, relayinfo);
```
_____dhcp6s.c

Move to the Inner Message

Listing 4-88

_____dhcp6s.c
```
1026            dhcp6_clear_options(&optinfo);
1027
1028            optend = (struct dhcp6opt *)(relayinfo->relay_msg.dv_buf + len);
1029            dh6relay = (struct dhcp6_relay *)relayinfo->relay_msg.dv_buf;
1030
1031            if (dh6relay->dh6relay_msgtype != DH6_RELAY_FORW) {
1032                    *dh6p = (struct dhcp6 *)dh6relay;
1033                    *optendp = optend;
1034                    return (0);
1035            }
1036
1037            goto again;
1038
1039    fail:
1040            free_relayinfo(relayinfo);
1041            dhcp6_clear_options(&optinfo);
1042
1043            return (-1);
1044    }
```
_____dhcp6s.c

1026–1029 The options for the Relay-forward message are not used any more and released.
Variables dh6relay and optend are adjusted so that the former points to the head of
the encapsulated message and the latter points to its end.

1031–1037 If the encapsulated message is not another Relay-forward, the process has successfully completed. Variables dh6p and optendp are updated for the caller. Otherwise, the
same process is repeated for the next Relay-forward message.

Example

To understand this procedure, consider a concrete example (see Figure 4-31). Suppose that the
server receives a Solicit message via two relay agents (the *Original message* at the left side of
the figure).

The process_relayforw() function first parses the outermost Relay-forward message.
It allocates a relayinfo{} structure and sets its members according to the Relay-forward
message. The inner Relay-forward message is copied and set in the relay_msg member of the
relay_info{} structure.

FIGURE 4-31

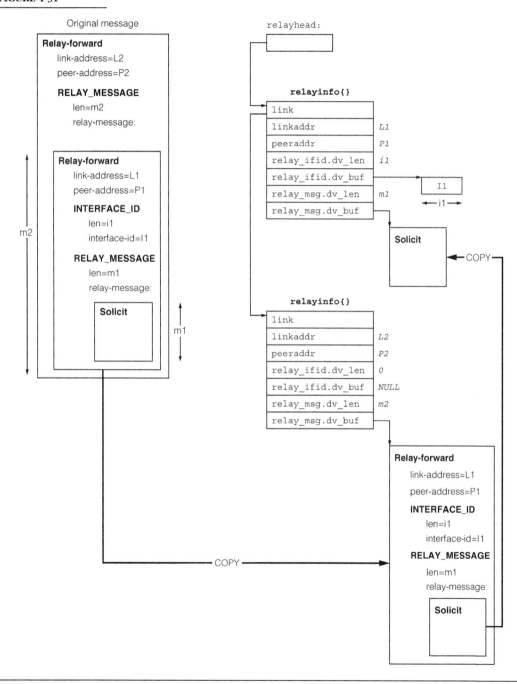

Decapsulation of a Relay-forward message.

The process_relayforw() function repeats the procedure for the copied message. It creates another relayinfo{} structure, sets its members according to the copied (inner) Relay-forward message. This Relay-forward message contains an Interface-Id option, which is converted into a vbuf type and set in the relay_ifid member of relayinfo{}. The Solicit message encapsulated in the inner Relay-forward message is then copied and set in the relay_msg member of relayinfo{}. Finally, the second relayinfo{} structure is linked at the head of the list from relayhead. Note that the relayinfo{} structure corresponding to the inner message is placed before the structure for the outermost message. This ordering is important when this list is used to build a Reply message (see Section 4.5.12).

4.5.4 react_solicit() Function

The react_solicit() function processes a DHCPv6 Solicit message from a client.

Identify the Client

Listing 4-89

dhcp6s.c

```
1098    static int
1099    react_solicit(ifp, dh6, len, optinfo, from, fromlen, relayinfohead)
1100            struct dhcp6_if *ifp;
1101            struct dhcp6 *dh6;
1102            ssize_t len;
1103            struct dhcp6_optinfo *optinfo;
1104            struct sockaddr *from;
1105            int fromlen;
1106            struct relayinfolist *relayinfohead;
1107    {
1108            struct dhcp6_optinfo roptinfo;
1109            struct host_conf *client_conf;
1110            int resptype, do_binding = 0, error;
1111
1112            /*
1113             * Servers MUST discard any Solicit messages that do not include a
1114             * Client Identifier option.
1115             * [RFC3315 Section 15.2]
1116             */
1117            if (optinfo->clientID.duid_len == 0) {
1118                    dprintf(LOG_INFO, FNAME, "no client ID option");
1119                    return (-1);
1120            } else {
1121                    dprintf(LOG_DEBUG, FNAME, "client ID %s",
1122                        duidstr(&optinfo->clientID));
1123            }
1124
1125            /* get per-host configuration for the client, if any. */
1126            if ((client_conf = find_hostconf(&optinfo->clientID))) {
1127                    dprintf(LOG_DEBUG, FNAME, "found a host configuration for %s",
1128                        client_conf->name);
1129            }
```

dhcp6s.c

1112–1123 If the Solicit message does not contain a Client Identifier option, the message is discarded.

1125–1129 The find_hostconf() function looks for the configuration information for the client by the client identifier. It is possible that no information is found, particularly when the server provides stateless DHCPv6 services only.

Build Options for Response

Listing 4-90

_____ dhcp6s.c

```
1131            /*
1132             * configure necessary options based on the options in solicit.
1133             */
1134            dhcp6_init_options(&roptinfo);
1135
1136            /* process authentication */
1137            if (process_auth(dh6, len, client_conf, optinfo, &roptinfo)) {
1138                    dprintf(LOG_INFO, FNAME, "failed to process authentication "
1139                        "information for %s",
1140                        clientstr(client_conf, &optinfo->clientID));
1141                    goto fail;
1142            }
1143
1144            /* server identifier option */
1145            if (duidcpy(&roptinfo.serverID, &server_duid)) {
1146                    dprintf(LOG_ERR, FNAME, "failed to copy server ID");
1147                    goto fail;
1148            }
1149
1150            /* copy client information back */
1151            if (duidcpy(&roptinfo.clientID, &optinfo->clientID)) {
1152                    dprintf(LOG_ERR, FNAME, "failed to copy client ID");
1153                    goto fail;
1154            }
1155
1156            /* preference (if configured) */
1157            if (ifp->server_pref != DH6OPT_PREF_UNDEF)
1158                    roptinfo.pref = ifp->server_pref;
1159
1160            /* add other configuration information */
1161            if (set_statelessinfo(DH6_SOLICIT, &roptinfo)) {
1162                    dprintf(LOG_ERR, FNAME,
1163                        "failed to set other stateless information");
1164                    goto fail;
1165            }
```

_____ dhcp6s.c

1134 Options in the response message (Advertise or Reply) will be built in the `roptinfo{}` structure. The following lines are just a straightforward implementation of the DHCPv6 specification.

1136–1142 If necessary and possible, the `process_auth()` function examines the authentication information provided by the client, and sets relevant options in `roptinfo`. The details of authentication processing will be seen in Section 4.7.4.

1144–1148 The server's DUID is copied to `roptinfo` from the server's local configuration.

1150–1154 The client's DUID, which was specified in the Solicit message, is copied back to `roptinfo`.

1156–1158 If the server is configured with a particular preference, it is specified in `roptinfo` as the value for the Preference option.

1160–1165 The `set_statelessinfo()` function sets configuration information in `roptinfo` for stateless information, i.e., information that does not have the notion of lease or binding. One common example of such information is a list of DNS recursive server addresses.

The implementation of set_statelessinfo() is pretty trivial, so a line-by-line description of this function is not provided here. As of this writing, the following information can be set in this function:

- SIP server addresses
- SIP server domain names
- DNS recursive server addresses
- DNS search list
- NTP server addresses (the support for this information was experimental when this code was written due to immature status of standardization. Today [RFC4075] defines a DHCPv6 option to provide SNTP server addresses).
- (in a Reply to Information-request) Information refresh time

While the included information could be adjusted according to the Option Request option in the Solicit message (if included), this implementation simply sets all possible information.

Prepare *Stateful* Information

Listing 4-91

——dhcp6s.c
```
1167          /*
1168           * see if we have information for requested options, and if so,
1169           * configure corresponding options.
1170           */
1171          if (optinfo->rapidcommit && (ifp->allow_flags & DHCIFF_RAPID_COMMIT))
1172                  do_binding = 1;
1173
1174          /*
1175           * The delegating router MUST include an IA_PD option, identifying any
1176           * prefix(es) that the delegating router will delegate to the
1177           * requesting router.  [RFC3633 Section 11.2]
1178           */
1179          if (!TAILQ_EMPTY(&optinfo->iapd_list)) {
1180                  int found = 0;
1181                  struct dhcp6_list conflist;
1182                  struct dhcp6_listval *iapd;
1183
1184                  TAILQ_INIT(&conflist);
1185
1186                  /* make a local copy of the configured prefixes */
1187                  if (client_conf &&
1188                      dhcp6_copy_list(&conflist, &client_conf->prefix_list)) {
1189                          dprintf(LOG_NOTICE, FNAME,
1190                              "failed to make local data");
1191                          goto fail;
1192                  }
1193
1194                  for (iapd = TAILQ_FIRST(&optinfo->iapd_list); iapd;
1195                      iapd = TAILQ_NEXT(iapd, link)) {
1196                          /*
1197                           * find an appropriate prefix for each IA_PD,
1198                           * removing the adopted prefixes from the list.
1199                           * (dhcp6s cannot create IAs without client config)
1200                           */
1201                          if (client_conf &&
1202                              make_ia(iapd, &conflist, &roptinfo.iapd_list,
1203                              client_conf, do_binding) > 0)
1204                                  found = 1;
1205                  }
1206
```

```
1207                         dhcp6_clear_list(&conflist);
1208
1209                     if (!found) {
1210                             /*
1211                              * If the delegating router will not assign any
1212                              * prefixes to any IA_PDs in a subsequent Request from
1213                              * the requesting router, the delegating router MUST
1214                              * send an Advertise message to the requesting router
1215                              * that includes a Status Code option with code
1216                              * NoPrefixAvail.
1217                              * [dhcpv6-opt-prefix-delegation-01 Section 10.2]
1218                              */
1219                             u_int16_t stcode = DH6OPT_STCODE_NOPREFIXAVAIL;
1220
1221                             if (dhcp6_add_listval(&roptinfo.stcode_list,
1222                                 DHCP6_LISTVAL_STCODE, &stcode, NULL) == NULL)
1223                                     goto fail;
1224                     }
1225             }
1226
1227         if (!TAILQ_EMPTY(&optinfo->iana_list)) {
1228                 int found = 0;
1229                 struct dhcp6_list conflist;
1230                 struct dhcp6_listval *iana;
1231
1232                 TAILQ_INIT(&conflist);
1233
1234                 /* make a local copy of the configured addresses */
1235                 if (client_conf &&
1236                     dhcp6_copy_list(&conflist, &client_conf->addr_list)) {
1237                         dprintf(LOG_NOTICE, FNAME,
1238                             "failed to make local data");
1239                         goto fail;
1240                 }
1241
1242                 for (iana = TAILQ_FIRST(&optinfo->iana_list); iana;
1243                     iana = TAILQ_NEXT(iana, link)) {
1244                         /*
1245                          * find an appropriate address for each IA_NA,
1246                          * removing the adopted addresses from the list.
1247                          * (dhcp6s cannot create IAs without client config)
1248                          */
1249                         if (client_conf &&
1250                             make_ia(iana, &conflist, &roptinfo.iana_list,
1251                             client_conf, do_binding) > 0)
1252                                 found = 1;
1253                 }
1254
1255                 dhcp6_clear_list(&conflist);
1256
1257                 if (!found) {
1258                         u_int16_t stcode = DH6OPT_STCODE_NOADDRSAVAIL;
1259
1260                         if (dhcp6_add_listval(&roptinfo.stcode_list,
1261                             DHCP6_LISTVAL_STCODE, &stcode, NULL) == NULL)
1262                                 goto fail;
1263                 }
1264         }
```

——— dhcp6s.c

1167–1172 If the received Solicit message includes a Rapid Commit option and the server is configured to accept it, do_binding is set to 1 so that new bindings for requested information (addresses or prefixes) will be established later in this function.

1174–1192 If the Solicit message includes IA_PD options, soliciting a server which can delegate IPv6 prefixes, and the configuration information for the client was found (see Listing 4-89), the server makes a local copy of the specified IA_PD options. Since the current server implementation cannot delegate prefixes from a pool, the configuration information for the client is crucial for further processing.

1194–1207 For each IA_PD option, the make_ia() function tries to find a prefix in the client's configuration which can be delegated to the client and match the requested prefix (if particular prefixes are specified in IA_PD). Normally, make_ia() just searches for a prefix and does not create any state at this moment. If do_binding is non-zero (i.e., the Solicit message includes a Rapid Commit option), however, it will immediately make a binding between the found prefix and the client. Function make_ia() returns the number of found prefixes. If it is greater than 0, it means at least one prefix is found.

1209–1225 If no prefix is found, a Status Code option with a code of NoPrefixAvail is set in roptinfo.

> This part follows a draft version of the specification, which is slightly different from [RFC3633]. [RFC3633] requires that in this case the server (delegating router) include the IA_PD option with no prefixes and with a Status Code option of NoPrefixAvail inside the IA_PD option. But the RFC's behavior is not very consistent with the corresponding specification for the client (requesting router). Section 11.1 of [RFC3633] reads:
>
> > The requesting router MUST ignore any Advertise message that includes a Status Code option containing the value NoPrefixAvail, with the exception that the requesting router MAY display the associated status message to the user.
>
> It only mentions a Status Code option and does not mention IA_PD option(s). If the server fully conforms to the RFC's behavior, it can confuse the client, especially when the Solicit message (and Advertise in response to it) includes multiple IA_PD options. Therefore, this implementation purposely leaves this behavior as it was according to an old version of the specification. Although this is only an issue in a relatively minor erroneous case, it should be clarified in the standardization community.

1227–1264 The similar procedure is taken for IA_NA options, which solicit a server that can assign (nontemporary) IPv6 addresses. However, there is no consistency issue when no address is found to be assigned: The server can simply include a Status Code option with a code of NoAddrsAvail (this is another reason that the behavior described in [RFC3633] seems odd).

Send Response

Listing 4-92

```
                                                                                    dhcp6s.c
1266            if (optinfo->rapidcommit && (ifp->allow_flags & DHCIFF_RAPID_COMMIT)) {
1267                    /*
1268                     * If the client has included a Rapid Commit option and the
1269                     * server has been configured to respond with committed address
1270                     * assignments and other resources, responds to the Solicit
1271                     * with a Reply message.
1272                     * [RFC3315 Section 17.2.1]
1273                     */
1274                    roptinfo.rapidcommit = 1;
1275                    resptype = DH6_REPLY;
1276            } else
1277                    resptype = DH6_ADVERTISE;
```

```
1278
1279                error = server6_send(resptype, ifp, dh6, optinfo, from, fromlen,
1280                               &roptinfo, relayinfohead, client_conf);
1281        dhcp6_clear_options(&roptinfo);
1282        return (error);
1283
1284    fail:
1285        dhcp6_clear_options(&roptinfo);
1286        return (-1);
1287    }
```
_____ dhcp6s.c

1266–1275 If the received Solicit message includes a Rapid Commit option and the server is configured to accept it, the server sends a Reply message with a Rapid Commit option in response to the Solicit message.

1276–1277 Otherwise, the server returns an Advertise message to the client.

1279–1280 The server6_send() function builds the actual response packet and sends it to the wire.

4.5.5 react_request() Function

This subsection, the react_request() function, processes a Request message from a client. Many parts of the processing are similar to the react_solicit() function, in which case it will be referred to rather than repeating the points.

Validation

Listing 4-93
_____ dhcp6s.c
```
1289    static int
1290    react_request(ifp, pi, dh6, len, optinfo, from, fromlen, relayinfohead)
1291        struct dhcp6_if *ifp;
1292        struct in6_pktinfo *pi;
1293        struct dhcp6 *dh6;
1294        ssize_t len;
1295        struct dhcp6_optinfo *optinfo;
1296        struct sockaddr *from;
1297        int fromlen;
1298        struct relayinfolist *relayinfohead;
1299    {
1300        struct dhcp6_optinfo roptinfo;
1301        struct host_conf *client_conf;
1302
1303        /* message validation according to Section 15.4 of RFC3315 */
1304
1305        /* the message must include a Server Identifier option */
1306        if (optinfo->serverID.duid_len == 0) {
1307            dprintf(LOG_INFO, FNAME, "no server ID option");
1308            return (-1);
1309        }
1310        /* the contents of the Server Identifier option must match ours */
1311        if (duidcmp(&optinfo->serverID, &server_duid)) {
1312            dprintf(LOG_INFO, FNAME, "server ID mismatch");
1313            return (-1);
1314        }
1315        /* the message must include a Client Identifier option */
1316        if (optinfo->clientID.duid_len == 0) {
1317            dprintf(LOG_INFO, FNAME, "no server ID option");
1318            return (-1);
1319        }
```
_____ dhcp6s.c

1305–1319 A Request message must contain a Server Identifier option and it must match the identifier of the receiving server. A Request message must also contain a Client Identifier option. If any of the requirements are not met, the message is discarded.

Build Options for Reply and Identify Client

Listing 4-94

——dhcp6s.c

```
1321            /*
1322             * configure necessary options based on the options in request.
1323             */
1324            dhcp6_init_options(&roptinfo);
1325
1326            /* server identifier option */
1327            if (duidcpy(&roptinfo.serverID, &server_duid)) {
1328                    dprintf(LOG_ERR, FNAME, "failed to copy server ID");
1329                    goto fail;
1330            }
1331            /* copy client information back */
1332            if (duidcpy(&roptinfo.clientID, &optinfo->clientID)) {
1333                    dprintf(LOG_ERR, FNAME, "failed to copy client ID");
1334                    goto fail;
1335            }
1336
1337            /* get per-host configuration for the client, if any. */
1338            if ((client_conf = find_hostconf(&optinfo->clientID))) {
1339                    dprintf(LOG_DEBUG, FNAME,
1340                        "found a host configuration named %s", client_conf->name);
1341            }
1342
1343            /* process authentication */
1344            if (process_auth(dh6, len, client_conf, optinfo, &roptinfo)) {
1345                    dprintf(LOG_INFO, FNAME, "failed to process authentication "
1346                        "information for %s",
1347                        clientstr(client_conf, &optinfo->clientID));
1348                    goto fail;
1349            }
```

——dhcp6s.c

1324–1349 This part is the same as in the `react_solicit()` function.

Handle Unexpected Unicast Request

Listing 4-95

——dhcp6s.c

```
1351            /*
1352             * When the server receives a Request message via unicast from a
1353             * client to which the server has not sent a unicast option, the server
1354             * discards the Request message and responds with a Reply message
1355             * containing a Status Code option with value UseMulticast, a Server
1356             * Identifier option containing the server's DUID, the Client
1357             * Identifier option from the client message and no other options.
1358             * [RFC3315 18.2.1]
1359             * (Our current implementation never sends a unicast option.)
1360             * Note: a request message encapsulated in a relay server option can be
1361             * unicasted.
1362             */
1363            if (!IN6_IS_ADDR_MULTICAST(&pi->ipi6_addr) &&
1364                TAILQ_EMPTY(relayinfohead)) {
1365                    u_int16_t stcode = DH6OPT_STCODE_USEMULTICAST;
1366
1367                    dprintf(LOG_INFO, FNAME, "unexpected unicast message from %s",
1368                        addr2str(from));
```

```
1369                         if (dhcp6_add_listval(&roptinfo.stcode_list,
1370                             DHCP6_LISTVAL_STCODE, &stcode, NULL) == NULL) {
1371                                 dprintf(LOG_ERR, FNAME, "failed to add a status code");
1372                                 goto fail;
1373                         }
1374                         server6_send(DH6_REPLY, ifp, dh6, optinfo, from,
1375                             fromlen, &roptinfo, relayinfohead, client_conf);
1376                         goto end;
1377                 }
```
_____dhcp6s.c

1351–1377 If the message is sent via unicast directly from the client (i.e., not relayed via a
relay agent), the procedure is terminated. The server responds with a Reply message
which only contains a Status Code option with a code of UseMulticast. Note that a unicast
Request message is not necessarily invalid protocol-wise; the client can use unicast if the
server and the client have negotiated about the unicast capability by the Server Unicast
option. However, this implementation does not support this option (yet), and this cannot
happen.

Delegate Prefix

Listing 4-96
_____dhcp6s.c
```
1379           /*
1380            * See if we have to make a binding of some configuration information
1381            * for the client.
1382            */
1383
1384           /*
1385            * When a delegating router receives a Request message from a
1386            * requesting router that contains an IA_PD option, and the delegating
1387            * router is authorized to delegate prefix(es) to the requesting
1388            * router, the delegating router selects the prefix(es) to be delegated
1389            * to the requesting router.
1390            * [RFC3633 Section 12.2]
1391            */
1392           if (!TAILQ_EMPTY(&optinfo->iapd_list)) {
1393                   struct dhcp6_list conflist;
1394                   struct dhcp6_listval *iapd;
1395
1396                   TAILQ_INIT(&conflist);
1397
1398                   /* make a local copy of the configured prefixes */
1399                   if (client_conf &&
1400                       dhcp6_copy_list(&conflist, &client_conf->prefix_list)) {
1401                           dprintf(LOG_NOTICE, FNAME,
1402                               "failed to make local data");
1403                           goto fail;
1404                   }
1405
1406                   for (iapd = TAILQ_FIRST(&optinfo->iapd_list); iapd;
1407                       iapd = TAILQ_NEXT(iapd, link)) {
1408                           /*
1409                            * Find an appropriate prefix for each IA_PD,
1410                            * removing the adopted prefixes from the list.
1411                            * The prefixes will be bound to the client.
1412                            */
1413                           if (make_ia(iapd, &conflist, &roptinfo.iapd_list,
1414                               client_conf, 1) == 0) {
1415                                   /*
1416                                    * We could not find any prefixes for the IA.
1417                                    * RFC3315 specifies to include NoAddrsAvail
1418                                    * for the IA in the address configuration
1419                                    * case (Section 18.2.1).  We follow the same
```

```
1420                          * logic for prefix delegation as well.
1421                          */
1422                         if (make_ia_stcode(DHCP6_LISTVAL_IAPD,
1423                             iapd->val_ia.iaid,
1424                             DH6OPT_STCODE_NOPREFIXAVAIL,
1425                             &roptinfo.iapd_list)) {
1426                                 dprintf(LOG_NOTICE, FNAME,
1427                                     "failed to make an option list");
1428                                 dhcp6_clear_list(&conflist);
1429                                 goto fail;
1430                         }
1431                 }
1432         }
1433
1434         dhcp6_clear_list(&conflist);
1435 }
```
_____dhcp6s.c

1379–1435 If the Request message contains IA_PD options, the server (delegating router) tries
to find an appropriate prefix for each IA_PD and makes a new binding for the client
(requesting router). The process is almost the same as that of react_solicit(), but this
time the fifth argument of make_ia() function is always 1, indicating that a new binding
must be established. Another difference is that when make_ia() fails for a particular
IA_PD the server calls the make_ia_stcode() function in order to create an IA_PD
option containing a Status Code option with a code of NoPrefixAvail. [RFC3633] does not
specify the server behavior in this case, but this implementation uses the same logic as is
used for address allocation, as described in [RFC3315] (see below).

Allocate Address

Listing 4-97
_____dhcp6s.c

```
1437         if (!TAILQ_EMPTY(&optinfo->iana_list)) {
1438                 struct dhcp6_list conflist;
1439                 struct dhcp6_listval *iana;
1440
1441                 TAILQ_INIT(&conflist);
1442
1443                 /* make a local copy of the configured prefixes */
1444                 if (client_conf &&
1445                     dhcp6_copy_list(&conflist, &client_conf->addr_list)) {
1446                         dprintf(LOG_NOTICE, FNAME,
1447                             "failed to make local data");
1448                         goto fail;
1449                 }
1450
1451                 for (iana = TAILQ_FIRST(&optinfo->iana_list); iana;
1452                     iana = TAILQ_NEXT(iana, link)) {
1453                         /*
1454                          * Find an appropriate address for each IA_NA,
1455                          * removing the adopted addresses from the list.
1456                          * The addresses will be bound to the client.
1457                          */
1458                         if (make_ia(iana, &conflist, &roptinfo.iana_list,
1459                             client_conf, 1) == 0) {
1460                                 if (make_ia_stcode(DHCP6_LISTVAL_IANA,
1461                                     iana->val_ia.iaid,
1462                                     DH6OPT_STCODE_NOADDRSAVAIL,
1463                                     &roptinfo.iana_list)) {
1464                                         dprintf(LOG_NOTICE, FNAME,
1465                                             "failed to make an option list");
1466                                         dhcp6_clear_list(&conflist);
1467                                         goto fail;
```

```
1468                                        }
1469                                    }
1470                                }
1471
1472                        dhcp6_clear_list(&conflist);
1473                    }
```
——dhcp6s.c

1437–1473 Likewise, if the Request message contains IA_NA options, the server tries to find an appropriate address for each IA_NA to be allocated to the client and makes a new binding. If the make_ia() function fails for a particular IA_NA, the server calls the make_ia_stcode() function in order to create an IA_NA option containing a Status Code option with a code of NoAddrsAvail.

Add Stateless Options

Listing 4-98
——dhcp6s.c

```
1475                /*
1476                 * If the Request message contained an Option Request option, the
1477                 * server MUST include options in the Reply message for any options in
1478                 * the Option Request option the server is configured to return to the
1479                 * client.
1480                 * [RFC3315 18.2.1]
1481                 * Note: our current implementation always includes all information
1482                 * that we can provide.  So we do not have to check the option request
1483                 * options.
1484                 */
1485    #if 0
1486            for (opt = TAILQ_FIRST(&optinfo->reqopt_list); opt;
1487                 opt = TAILQ_NEXT(opt, link)) {
1488                    ;
1489            }
1490    #endif
1491
1492                /*
1493                 * Add options to the Reply message for any other configuration
1494                 * information to be assigned to the client.
1495                 */
1496            if (set_statelessinfo(DH6_REQUEST, &roptinfo)) {
1497                    dprintf(LOG_ERR, FNAME,
1498                        "failed to set other stateless information");
1499                    goto fail;
1500            }
```
——dhcp6s.c

1475–1500 All possible stateless configuration information is set in roptinfo. This part is the same as react_solicit().

Send Reply

Listing 4-99
——dhcp6s.c

```
1501
1502            /* send a reply message. */
1503            (void)server6_send(DH6_REPLY, ifp, dh6, optinfo, from, fromlen,
1504                &roptinfo, relayinfohead, client_conf);
1505
1506    end:
1507            dhcp6_clear_options(&roptinfo);
1508            return (0);
1509
```

```
1510    fail:
1511            dhcp6_clear_options(&roptinfo);
1512            return (-1);
1513    }
```
_____dhcp6s.c

1502–1504 The `server6_send()` function makes a Reply message containing the options
built so far, and sends it back to the client.

4.5.6 `make_ia()` Function

The `make_ia()` function is called from the `react_solicit()` and `react_request()`
functions. It tries to find an IA for a particular client, considering the server's configuration and
the client's request. If the fifth argument, `do_binding`, is not 0, this function will also make a
binding between the client and the IA that was found.

Update Existing Binding

Listing 4-100
_____dhcp6s.c

```
2334    static int
2335    make_ia(spec, conflist, retlist, client_conf, do_binding)
2336            struct dhcp6_listval *spec;
2337            struct dhcp6_list *conflist, *retlist;
2338            struct host_conf *client_conf;
2339            int do_binding;
2340    {
2341            struct dhcp6_binding *binding;
2342            struct dhcp6_list ialist;
2343            struct dhcp6_listval *specia;
2344            struct dhcp6_ia ia;
2345            int found = 0;
2346
2347            /*
2348             * If we happen to have a binding already, update the binding and
2349             * return it.  Perhaps the request is being retransmitted.
2350             */
2351            if ((binding = find_binding(&client_conf->duid, DHCP6_BINDING_IA,
2352                spec->type, spec->val_ia.iaid)) != NULL) {
2353                    struct dhcp6_list *blist = &binding->val_list;
2354                    struct dhcp6_listval *bia, *v;
2355
2356                    dprintf(LOG_DEBUG, FNAME, "we have a binding already: %s",
2357                        bindingstr(binding));
2358
2359                    update_binding(binding);
2360
2361                    memset(&ia, 0, sizeof(ia));
2362                    ia.iaid = spec->val_ia.iaid;
2363                    /* determine appropriate T1 and T2 */
2364                    calc_ia_timo(&ia, blist, client_conf);
2365                    if (dhcp6_add_listval(retlist, spec->type, &ia, blist)
2366                        == NULL) {
2367                            dprintf(LOG_NOTICE, FNAME,
2368                                "failed to copy binding info");
2369                            return (0);
2370                    }
2371
2372                    /* remove bound values from the configuration */
2373                    for (bia = TAILQ_FIRST(blist); bia;
2374                        bia = TAILQ_NEXT(bia, link)) {
2375                            if ((v = dhcp6_find_listval(conflist,
2376                                bia->type, &bia->uv, 0)) != NULL) {
```

```
2377                                    found++;
2378                                    TAILQ_REMOVE(conflist, v, link);
2379                                    dhcp6_clear_listval(v);
2380                            }
2381                    }
2382
2383                    return (found);
2384            }
```
_____dhcp6s.c

2347–2359 If there is already a binding between the requested IA and the client, the
`update_binding()` function is called to update the IA (resetting the timer for the IA),
as if it is just being established. While this is not a normal scenario, it can still occur, e.g.,
if the server has already received and processed the same Request message but the Reply
message was lost, making the client resend the message.

> Updating the IA unconditionally is probably not a good idea. This should be limited
> to when `do_binding` is non-zero.

2361–2370 A new local template, `ia`, is initialized, and passed to the `calc_ia_timo()`
function, which sets appropriate T1 and T2 values for the IA based on the binding just
found. A new list value for the IA is then inserted to the return list (`retlist`).

2372–2381 For each bound parameter (i.e., an address or a prefix), if the server's configuration
for the client contains the parameter, it is removed from the configuration, so that it will
not be reused. In this loop, the number of matched parameters is counted and stored in
the variable `found`.

2383 The process is completed. The number of matched parameters is returned.

> Simply returning the number of parameters is probably not a good idea if it is zero. In
> this case, the server should probably go to the following steps.

Find Appropriate Configuration

Listing 4-101

_____dhcp6s.c
```
2386            /*
2387             * trivial case:
2388             * if the configuration is empty, we cannot make any IA.
2389             */
2390            if (TAILQ_EMPTY(conflist))
2391                    return (0);
2392
2393            TAILQ_INIT(&ialist);
2394
2395            /* First, check if we can meet the client's requirement */
2396            for (specia = TAILQ_FIRST(&spec->sublist); specia;
2397                specia = TAILQ_NEXT(specia, link)) {
2398                    /* try to find an IA that matches the spec best. */
2399                    if (make_match_ia(specia, conflist, &ialist))
2400                            found++;
2401            }
2402            if (found == 0) {
2403                    struct dhcp6_listval *v;
2404
```

```
2405                        /* use the first IA in the configuration list */
2406                        v = TAILQ_FIRST(conflist);
2407                        if (dhcp6_add_listval(&ialist, v->type, &v->uv, NULL)) {
2408                                found = 1;
2409                                TAILQ_REMOVE(conflist, v, link);
2410                                dhcp6_clear_listval(v);
2411                        }
2412                }
2413        if (found) {
2414                memset(&ia, 0, sizeof(ia));
2415                ia.iaid = spec->val_ia.iaid;
2416                /* determine appropriate T1 and T2 */
2417                calc_ia_timo(&ia, &ialist, client_conf);
2418
2419                /* make a binding for the set if necessary */
2420                if (do_binding) {
2421                        if (add_binding(&client_conf->duid, DHCP6_BINDING_IA,
2422                                spec->type, spec->val_ia.iaid, &ialist) == NULL) {
2423                                dprintf(LOG_NOTICE, FNAME,
2424                                        "failed to make a binding");
2425                                found = 0;
2426                        }
2427                }
2428                if (found) {
2429                        /* make an IA for the set */
2430                        if (dhcp6_add_listval(retlist, spec->type,
2431                                &ia, &ialist) == NULL)
2432                                found = 0;
2433                }
2434                dhcp6_clear_list(&ialist);
2435        }
2436
2437        return (found);
2438 }
```
_____ dhcp6s.c

2390–2391 If the server's configuration for the client is empty, the server obviously cannot find an IA for the client.

2395–2401 If the client specifies particular parameters (addresses or prefixes) for the IA, the make_match_ia() function tries to find an appropriate match in the server's configuration for each of the specified parameters. For an address, make_match_ia() performs exact matching; for a prefix, it first tries to find an exact match (i.e., the address part of the prefixes is identical and one prefix length equals the other), and then tries to find a configuration parameter that only matches the prefix length. If a parameter is found, the matched parameter is removed from the server's configuration, and the parameter values are copied in a new local list, ialist.

2402–2412 If no parameter is found in the server's configuration or the client does not specify any particular parameters, the head entry of the configuration list is picked up, and its value is copied to ialist.

2413–2417 If something was found in the previous procedure, the calc_ia_timo() function sets T1 and T2 for the IA.

2419–2427 If making a new binding is required at this point, the add_binding() function is called to make it.

2428–2434 If everything is okay, the chosen IA, which contains the actual parameters, is copied to the return list.

2437 The number of parameters is returned; if it is zero, it means a failure.

The `calc_ia_timo()` function, shown in Listing 4-102, is called from various routines including the `make_ia()` function.

Listing 4-102

———dhcp6s.c

```
2483    static void
2484    calc_ia_timo(ia, ialist, client_conf)
2485            struct dhcp6_ia *ia;
2486            struct dhcp6_list *ialist; /* this should not be empty */
2487            struct host_conf *client_conf; /* unused yet */
2488    {
2489            struct dhcp6_listval *iav;
2490            u_int32_t base = DHCP6_DURATITION_INFINITE;
2491            int iatype;
2492
2493            iatype = TAILQ_FIRST(ialist)->type;
2494            for (iav = TAILQ_FIRST(ialist); iav; iav = TAILQ_NEXT(iav, link)) {
2495                    if (iav->type != iatype) {
2496                            dprintf(LOG_ERR, FNAME,
2497                                "assumption failure: IA list is not consistent");
2498                            exit (1); /* XXX */
2499                    }
2500                    switch (iatype) {
2501                    case DHCP6_LISTVAL_PREFIX6:
2502                    case DHCP6_LISTVAL_STATEFULADDR6:
2503                            if (base == DHCP6_DURATITION_INFINITE ||
2504                                iav->val_prefix6.pltime < base)
2505                                    base = iav->val_prefix6.pltime;
2506                            break;
2507                    }
2508            }
2509
2510            switch (iatype) {
2511            case DHCP6_LISTVAL_PREFIX6:
2512            case DHCP6_LISTVAL_STATEFULADDR6:
2513                    /*
2514                     * Configure the timeout parameters as recommended in
2515                     * Section 22.4 of RFC3315 and Section 9 of RFC3633.
2516                     * We could also set the parameters to 0 if we let the client
2517                     * decide the renew timing (not implemented yet).
2518                     */
2519                    if (base == DHCP6_DURATITION_INFINITE) {
2520                            ia->t1 = DHCP6_DURATITION_INFINITE;
2521                            ia->t2 = DHCP6_DURATITION_INFINITE;
2522                    } else {
2523                            ia->t1 = base / 2;
2524                            ia->t2 = (base * 4) / 5;
2525                    }
2526                    break;
2527            }
2528    }
```
———dhcp6s.c

2493–2508 The `for` loop goes through the list of prefixes or addresses of the IA given to this function and identifies the one that has the smallest preferred lifetime.

2510–2527 If all the prefixes or addresses have an infinite preferred lifetime, both T1 and T2 are set to infinity. Otherwise, T1 is set to 0.5 times the shortest preferred hboxlifetime, and T2 is set to 0.8 times the shortest preferred lifetime, as recommended in [RFC3315].

Example

Figures 4-32 through 4-35 depict the steps of making an IA to be returned to the client in response to a Solicit or Request message. This example assumes the server configuration shown in Figure 4-30 (page 386) and that the client sends a Request message as shown in Figure 4-27 (page 370).

Step 1 (Figure 4-32): In the `react_request()` function, the list of addresses for the client, stored in the `client_conf{}` structure, is copied to `conflist`. Variable `spec` points

FIGURE 4-32

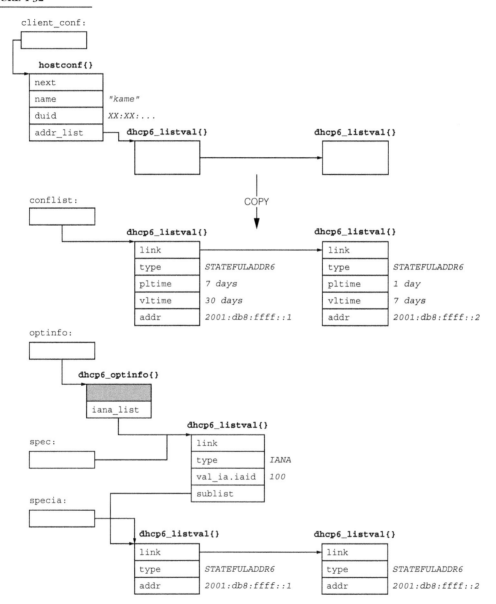

to the IA requested by the client in the Request message. In the `make_ia()` function, the variable `specia` goes through the sublist of the IA. The first entry of the list matches the first entry of `conflist` (`2001:db8:ffff::1`).

Step 2 (Figure 4-33): A new list entry for the matched address is created and inserted in variable `ialist` in the `make_match_ia()` function. The matched entry in `conflist` is

FIGURE 4-33

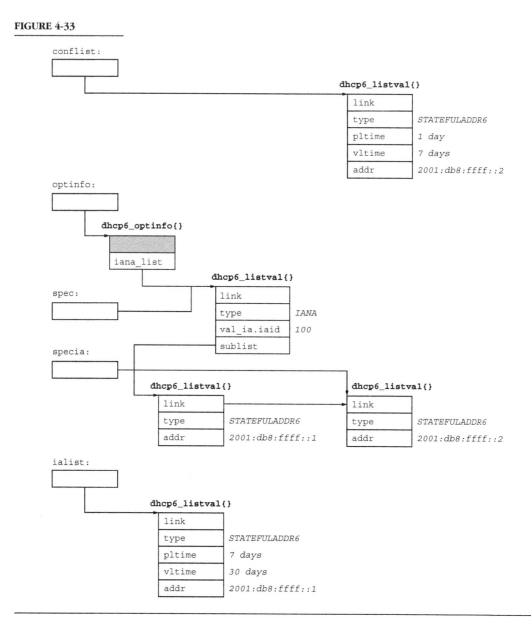

Creation of returned IA, step 2.

removed (in order to avoid a duplicate match later). The variable `specia` then proceeds to the second entry of the configured address list, which matches the remaining entry in `conflist` (`2001:db8:ffff::2`).

Step 3 (Figure 4-34): The same procedure is done for the second address, and `conflist` becomes empty.

Step 4 (Figure 4-35): A separate structure for the IA that the server has allocated to the client is created based on the IA parameters stored in the variable `spec` and the list of addresses starting from `ialist`. It is appended to the tail of the variable `retlist`, which will be included in the Reply message.

The `add_binding()` function, a subroutine of `make_ia()`, is shown in Listing 4-103.

FIGURE 4-34

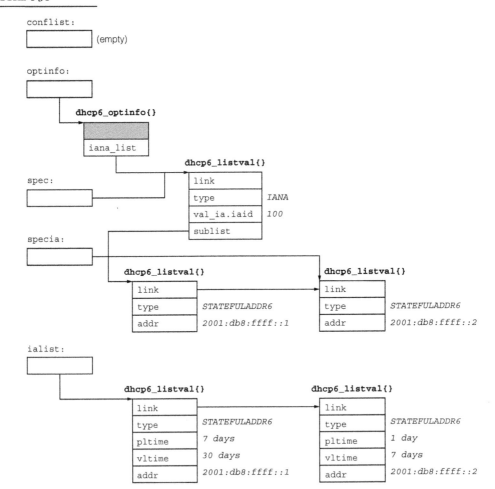

Creation of returned IA, step 3.

FIGURE 4-35

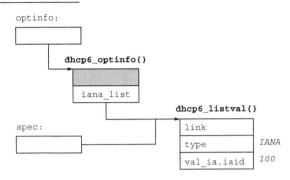

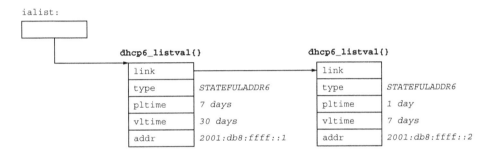

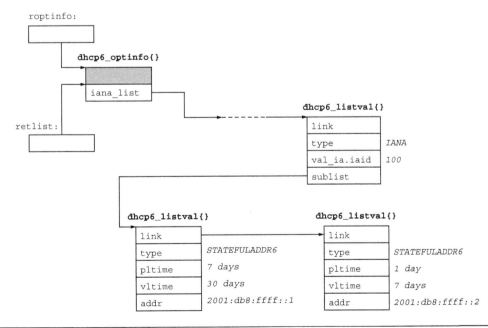

Creation of returned IA, step 4.

Listing 4-103

```
                                                                        dhcp6s.c
2588    static struct dhcp6_binding *
2589    add_binding(clientid, btype, iatype, iaid, val0)
2590            struct duid *clientid;
2591            dhcp6_bindingtype_t btype;
2592            int iatype;
2593            u_int32_t iaid;
2594            void *val0;
2595    {
2596            struct dhcp6_binding *binding = NULL;
2597            u_int32_t duration = DHCP6_DURATITION_INFINITE;
2598
2599            if ((binding = malloc(sizeof(*binding))) == NULL) {
2600                    dprintf(LOG_NOTICE, FNAME, "failed to allocate memory");
2601                    return (NULL);
2602            }
2603            memset(binding, 0, sizeof(*binding));
2604            binding->type = btype;
2605            if (duidcpy(&binding->clientid, clientid)) {
2606                    dprintf(LOG_NOTICE, FNAME, "failed to copy DUID");
2607                    goto fail;
2608            }
2609            binding->iatype = iatype;
2610            binding->iaid = iaid;
2611
2612            /* construct configuration information for this binding */
2613            switch (btype) {
2614            case DHCP6_BINDING_IA:
2615                    TAILQ_INIT(&binding->val_list);
2616                    if (dhcp6_copy_list(&binding->val_list,
2617                        (struct dhcp6_list *)val0)) {
2618                            dprintf(LOG_NOTICE, FNAME,
2619                                "failed to copy binding data");
2620                            goto fail;
2621                    }
2622                    break;
2623            default:
2624                    dprintf(LOG_ERR, FNAME, "unexpected binding type(%d)", btype);
2625                    goto fail;
2626            }
2627
2628            /* calculate duration and start timer accordingly */
2629            binding->updatetime = time(NULL);
2630            update_binding_duration(binding);
2631            if (binding->duration != DHCP6_DURATITION_INFINITE) {
2632                    struct timeval timo;
2633
2634                    binding->timer = dhcp6_add_timer(binding_timo, binding);
2635                    if (binding->timer == NULL) {
2636                            dprintf(LOG_NOTICE, FNAME, "failed to add timer");
2637                            goto fail;
2638                    }
2639                    timo.tv_sec = (long)duration;
2640                    timo.tv_usec = 0;
2641                    dhcp6_set_timer(&timo, binding->timer);
2642            }
2643
2644            TAILQ_INSERT_TAIL(&dhcp6_binding_head, binding, link);
2645
2646            dprintf(LOG_DEBUG, FNAME, "add a new binding %s", bindingstr(binding));
2647
2648            return (binding);
2649
2650      fail:
2651            if (binding)
2652                    free_binding(binding);
2653            return (NULL);
2654    }
                                                                        dhcp6s.c
```

2599–2610 A new binding structure is allocated, the binding type (which must be DHCP6_BINDING_IA) is initialized, and the IA type (IA_NA or IA_PD) and IAID are set in the structure. The client identifier of this binding is also copied.

2612–2626 The variable val0 should contain the list of addresses or prefixes for the binding, depending on the IA type. The entire list is copied to the binding structure.

2629–2642 The updatetime member of the structure is initialized with the creation time. The update_binding_duration() function calculates the nearest time for this IA at which some action needs to be taken. For both addresses and prefixes, update_binding_duration() returns the remaining time until the shortest valid lifetime of the addresses or prefixes expires. If the client does not succeed in the renewal of the binding by then, that address or prefix will be removed from the binding. Finally, the corresponding timer for this binding is started.

Figure 4-36 shows an example of the procedure for the add_binding() function, assuming the same situation as in the previous examples. It is assumed in this example that this happens on September 1, at 0:00, just as in the example shown in Figure 4-27 (page 370).

First, a new dhcp6_binding{} structure is created. The client's DUID is copied from the server's configuration structure, client_conf, and the type of IA and IAID are copied from the client's request message (the variable spec in the make_ia() function). The variable val0 (which is referred to as ialist in the make_ia() function) specifies the list of addresses to be allocated to the client. The entire list is copied and set in the val_list member of the dhcp6_binding{} structure. The update_binding_duration() identifies the shortest valid lifetime of the addresses (7 days), and sets the duration member to this value. A timer for this binding is also created with the duration, which will expire on September 8, 0:00 with the timer handler function of binding_timo().

When everything is set up, the new dhcp6_binding{} structure is added to the tail of the binding list, dhcp6_binding_head.

Listing 4-104 shows the update_binding() function. This function is simple: It just resets updatetime to the current time, and resets the timer for the binding with the duration calculated by the update_binding_duration() function.

Listing 4-104

```
2680    static void
2681    update_binding(binding)
2682            struct dhcp6_binding *binding;
2683    {
2684            struct timeval timo;
2685
2686            dprintf(LOG_DEBUG, FNAME, "update binding %s for %s",
2687                bindingstr(binding), duidstr(&binding->clientid));
2688
2689            /* update timestamp and calculate new duration */
2690            binding->updatetime = time(NULL);
2691            update_binding_duration(binding);
2692
2693            /* if the lease duration is infinite, there's nothing to do. */
2694            if (binding->duration == DHCP6_DURATITION_INFINITE)
2695                    return;
2696
2697            /* reset the timer with the duration */
```

```
2698            timo.tv_sec = (long)binding->duration;
2699            timo.tv_usec = 0;
2700            dhcp6_set_timer(&timo, binding->timer);
2701    }
```
                                                                            ———————dhcp6s.c

FIGURE 4-36

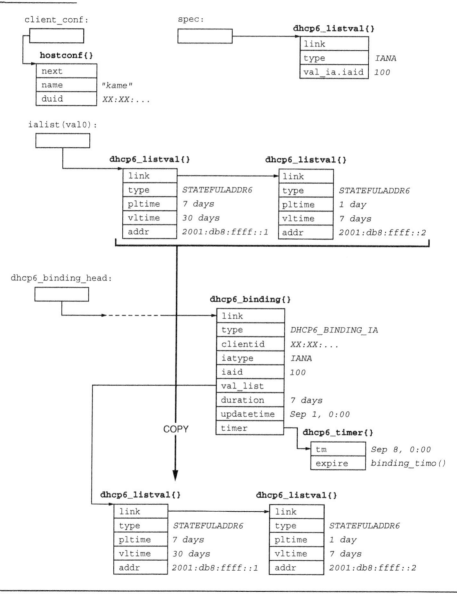

Adding a new binding.

4.5.7 `react_renew()` Function

The `react_renew()` function processes a Renew message from a client and updates bindings corresponding to the Renew message.

Validation

Listing 4-105

```
1515    static int
1516    react_renew(ifp, pi, dh6, len, optinfo, from, fromlen, relayinfohead)
1517            struct dhcp6_if *ifp;
1518            struct in6_pktinfo *pi;
1519            struct dhcp6 *dh6;
1520            ssize_t len;
1521            struct dhcp6_optinfo *optinfo;
1522            struct sockaddr *from;
1523            int fromlen;
1524            struct relayinfolist *relayinfohead;
1525    {
1526            struct dhcp6_optinfo roptinfo;
1527            struct dhcp6_listval *ia;
1528            struct host_conf *client_conf;
1529
1530            /* message validation according to Section 15.6 of RFC3315 */
1531
1532            /* the message must include a Server Identifier option */
1533            if (optinfo->serverID.duid_len == 0) {
1534                    dprintf(LOG_INFO, FNAME, "no server ID option");
1535                    return (-1);
1536            }
1537            /* the contents of the Server Identifier option must match ours */
1538            if (duidcmp(&optinfo->serverID, &server_duid)) {
1539                    dprintf(LOG_INFO, FNAME, "server ID mismatch");
1540                    return (-1);
1541            }
1542            /* the message must include a Client Identifier option */
1543            if (optinfo->clientID.duid_len == 0) {
1544                    dprintf(LOG_INFO, FNAME, "no server ID option");
1545                    return (-1);
1546            }
```

1530–1546 A valid Renew message must contain a Server Identifier option and it must match the identifier of the receiving server. A Renew message must also contain a Client Identifier option. If any of these requirements are not met, the message is discarded.

Build Options for Reply, Identify Client, Handle Unexpected Unicast Message

Listing 4-106

```
1548            /*
1549             * configure necessary options based on the options in request.
1550             */
1551            dhcp6_init_options(&roptinfo);
1552
1553            /* server identifier option */
1554            if (duidcpy(&roptinfo.serverID, &server_duid)) {
1555                    dprintf(LOG_ERR, FNAME, "failed to copy server ID");
1556                    goto fail;
1557            }
1558            /* copy client information back */
```

```
1559            if (duidcpy(&roptinfo.clientID, &optinfo->clientID)) {
1560                    dprintf(LOG_ERR, FNAME, "failed to copy client ID");
1561                    goto fail;
1562            }
1563
1564            /* get per-host configuration for the client, if any. */
1565            if ((client_conf = find_hostconf(&optinfo->clientID))) {
1566                    dprintf(LOG_DEBUG, FNAME,
1567                        "found a host configuration named %s", client_conf->name);
1568            }
1569
1570            /* process authentication */
1571            if (process_auth(dh6, len, client_conf, optinfo, &roptinfo)) {
1572                    dprintf(LOG_INFO, FNAME, "failed to process authentication "
1573                        "information for %s",
1574                        clientstr(client_conf, &optinfo->clientID));
1575                    goto fail;
1576            }
1577
1578            /*
1579             * When the server receives a Renew message via unicast from a
1580             * client to which the server has not sent a unicast option, the server
1581             * discards the Request message and responds with a Reply message
1582             * containing a status code option with value UseMulticast, a Server
1583             * Identifier option containing the server's DUID, the Client
1584             * Identifier option from the client message and no other options.
1585             * [RFC3315 18.2.3]
1586             * (Our current implementation never sends a unicast option.)
1587             */
1588            if (!IN6_IS_ADDR_MULTICAST(&pi->ipi6_addr) &&
1589                TAILQ_EMPTY(relayinfohead)) {
1590                    u_int16_t stcode = DH6OPT_STCODE_USEMULTICAST;
1591
1592                    dprintf(LOG_INFO, FNAME, "unexpected unicast message from %s",
1593                        addr2str(from));
1594                    if (dhcp6_add_listval(&roptinfo.stcode_list,
1595                        DHCP6_LISTVAL_STCODE, &stcode, NULL) == NULL) {
1596                            dprintf(LOG_ERR, FNAME, "failed to add a status code");
1597                            goto fail;
1598                    }
1599                    server6_send(DH6_REPLY, ifp, dh6, optinfo, from,
1600                        fromlen, &roptinfo, relayinfohead, client_conf);
1601                    goto end;
1602            }
```
                                                                                    _____dhcp6s.c

1548–1602 This part is the same as the `react_request()` function (see Section 4.5.5).

Update Bindings

Listing 4-107
                                                                                    _____dhcp6s.c

```
1604            /*
1605             * Locates the client's binding and verifies that the information
1606             * from the client matches the information stored for that client.
1607             */
1608            for (ia = TAILQ_FIRST(&optinfo->iapd_list); ia;
1609                ia = TAILQ_NEXT(ia, link)) {
1610                    if (update_ia(DH6_RENEW, ia, &roptinfo.iapd_list, optinfo))
1611                            goto fail;
1612            }
1613            for (ia = TAILQ_FIRST(&optinfo->iana_list); ia;
1614                ia = TAILQ_NEXT(ia, link)) {
1615                    if (update_ia(DH6_RENEW, ia, &roptinfo.iana_list, optinfo))
1616                            goto fail;
1617            }
```
                                                                                    _____dhcp6s.c

1604–1612 For each IA_PD in the Renew message (if any), the `update_ia()` function locates the corresponding binding, updates it, and puts the updated IA_PD on the return list.

1613–1617 Likewise, the binding for each IA_NA is updated, and the updated information is put on the return list.

Set Stateless Options

Listing 4-108

———dhcp6s.c
```
1619                /* add other configuration information */
1620                if (set_statelessinfo(DH6_RENEW, &roptinfo)) {
1621                        dprintf(LOG_ERR, FNAME,
1622                           "failed to set other stateless information");
1623                        goto fail;
1624                }
```
———dhcp6s.c

1619–1624 The `set_statelessinfo()` function sets configuration information in `roptinfo` for stateless information. See Listing 4-90 (page 397).

Send Reply

Listing 4-109

———dhcp6s.c
```
1626                (void)server6_send(DH6_REPLY, ifp, dh6, optinfo, from, fromlen,
1627                    &roptinfo, relayinfohead, client_conf);
1628
1629      end:
1630            dhcp6_clear_options(&roptinfo);
1631            return (0);
1632
1633      fail:
1634            dhcp6_clear_options(&roptinfo);
1635            return (-1);
1636    }
```
———dhcp6s.c

1626–1627 The `server6_send()` function builds a Reply message in response to the Renew message just processed, and sends it to the client.

4.5.8 `react_rebind()` Function

The `react_rebind()` function processes a Rebind message from a client and updates the bindings that correspond to the Rebind message.

Validation

Listing 4-110

———dhcp6s.c
```
1638    static int
1639    react_rebind(ifp, dh6, len, optinfo, from, fromlen, relayinfohead)
1640            struct dhcp6_if *ifp;
1641            struct dhcp6 *dh6;
1642            ssize_t len;
1643            struct dhcp6_optinfo *optinfo;
1644            struct sockaddr *from;
1645            int fromlen;
```

```
1646            struct relayinfolist *relayinfohead;
1647      {
1648            struct dhcp6_optinfo roptinfo;
1649            struct dhcp6_listval *ia;
1650            struct host_conf *client_conf;
1651
1652            /* message validation according to Section 15.7 of RFC3315 */
1653
1654            /* the message must include a Client Identifier option */
1655            if (optinfo->clientID.duid_len == 0) {
1656                    dprintf(LOG_INFO, FNAME, "no server ID option");
1657                    return (-1);
1658            }
1659
1660            /* the message must not include a server Identifier option */
1661            if (optinfo->serverID.duid_len) {
1662                    dprintf(LOG_INFO, FNAME, "server ID option is included in "
1663                        "a rebind message");
1664                    return (-1);
1665            }
```
                                                                    ————dhcp6s.c

1652–1665 A valid Rebind message must contain a Client Identifier option. Unlike a Renew message, a Rebind message must *not* contain a Server Identifier option, since it is sent to a multicast address when the server that previously sent Reply messages is down for a long period. If any of the requirements are not met, the Rebind message is discarded.

Build Options for Reply, Identify Client, Handle Unexpected Unicast Message

Listing 4-111
                                                                    ————dhcp6s.c

```
1667            /*
1668             * configure necessary options based on the options in request.
1669             */
1670            dhcp6_init_options(&roptinfo);
1671
1672            /* server identifier option */
1673            if (duidcpy(&roptinfo.serverID, &server_duid)) {
1674                    dprintf(LOG_ERR, FNAME, "failed to copy server ID");
1675                    goto fail;
1676            }
1677            /* copy client information back */
1678            if (duidcpy(&roptinfo.clientID, &optinfo->clientID)) {
1679                    dprintf(LOG_ERR, FNAME, "failed to copy client ID");
1680                    goto fail;
1681            }
1682
1683            /* get per-host configuration for the client, if any. */
1684            if ((client_conf = find_hostconf(&optinfo->clientID))) {
1685                    dprintf(LOG_DEBUG, FNAME,
1686                        "found a host configuration named %s", client_conf->name);
1687            }
1688
1689            /* process authentication */
1690            if (process_auth(dh6, len, client_conf, optinfo, &roptinfo)) {
1691                    dprintf(LOG_INFO, FNAME, "failed to process authentication "
1692                        "information for %s",
1693                        clientstr(client_conf, &optinfo->clientID));
1694                    goto fail;
1695            }
```
                                                                    ————dhcp6s.c

1667–1695 This part is the same as the react_request() function (see Section 4.5.5).

Update Bindings

Listing 4-112

―――dhcp6s.c
```
1697            /*
1698             * Locates the client's binding and verifies that the information
1699             * from the client matches the information stored for that client.
1700             */
1701            for (ia = TAILQ_FIRST(&optinfo->iapd_list); ia;
1702                 ia = TAILQ_NEXT(ia, link)) {
1703                    if (update_ia(DH6_REBIND, ia, &roptinfo.iapd_list, optinfo))
1704                            goto fail;
1705            }
1706            for (ia = TAILQ_FIRST(&optinfo->iana_list); ia;
1707                 ia = TAILQ_NEXT(ia, link)) {
1708                    if (update_ia(DH6_REBIND, ia, &roptinfo.iana_list, optinfo))
1709                            goto fail;
1710            }
1711
1712            /*
1713             * If the returned iapd_list is empty, we do not have an explicit
1714             * knowledge about validity nor invalidity for any IA_PD information
1715             * in the Rebind message.  In this case, we should rather ignore the
1716             * message than to send a Reply with empty information back to the
1717             * client, which may annoy the recipient.  However, if we have at least
1718             * one useful information, either positive or negative, based on some
1719             * explicit knowledge, we should reply with the responsible part.
1720             */
1721            if (TAILQ_EMPTY(&roptinfo.iapd_list)) {
1722                    dprintf(LOG_INFO, FNAME, "no useful information for a rebind");
1723                    goto fail;           /* discard the rebind */
1724            }
```
―――dhcp6s.c

1697–1710 This part is mostly the same as the react_renew() function (see Section 4.5.7). For a Rebind message, however, if the update_ia() function cannot find a binding for an IA, it simply ignores the IA.

1712–1724 If, as a result of the update procedure, the list of IA_PD options becomes empty, which means the update_ia() function could not find a binding for any IA_PD, then the Rebind message is discarded. This behavior is not explicitly described in the protocol specification, but if this server sent a Reply with an empty IA_PD list, the client would resend a Rebind message as described in the specification. This scenario is undesirable when another server which has valid bindings is responding more slowly than this server; the client would continue resending Rebind messages, and the IA_PD would eventually expire. This implementation-specific behavior avoids this scenario.

> The same action should actually be taken for IA_NA options, but this is not implemented. One subtle and difficult issue here is that the Rebind message contains both IA_PD and IA_NA options, and the server has bindings for only one of them. Some protocol-wise clarification will be necessary. In practice, however, this does not matter much, since prefix delegation and address allocation are mostly orthogonal services and do not usually happen concurrently between the same client and server.

Set Stateless Options and Send Reply

Listing 4-113

── dhcp6s.c

```
1726            /* add other configuration information */
1727            if (set_statelessinfo(DH6_REBIND, &roptinfo)) {
1728                    dprintf(LOG_ERR, FNAME,
1729                        "failed to set other stateless information");
1730                    goto fail;
1731            }
1732
1733            (void)server6_send(DH6_REPLY, ifp, dh6, optinfo, from, fromlen,
1734                &roptinfo, relayinfohead, client_conf);
1735
1736            dhcp6_clear_options(&roptinfo);
1737            return (0);
1738
1739    fail:
1740            dhcp6_clear_options(&roptinfo);
1741            return (-1);
1742    }
```

── dhcp6s.c

1726–1737 The rest of this function is the same as `react_renew()`.

Next, the `update_ia()` function is shown, which is called from `react_renew()` and `react_rebind()` and updates the binding corresponding to the specified IA.

Get Host Configuration

Listing 4-114

── dhcp6s.c

```
1945    static int
1946    update_ia(msgtype, iap, retlist, optinfo)
1947            int msgtype;
1948            struct dhcp6_listval *iap;
1949            struct dhcp6_list *retlist;
1950            struct dhcp6_optinfo *optinfo;
1951    {
1952            struct dhcp6_binding *binding;
1953            struct host_conf *client_conf;
1954
1955            /* get per-host configuration for the client, if any. */
1956            if ((client_conf = find_hostconf(&optinfo->clientID))) {
1957                    dprintf(LOG_DEBUG, FNAME,
1958                        "found a host configuration named %s", client_conf->name);
1959            }
```

── dhcp6s.c

1955–1959 The `find_hostconf()` function searches the server's local configuration for information about the client, which, if found, will be used as an argument to the `calc_ia_timo()` function at the end of this function (Listing 4-118, page 426).

> This part is actually redundant, since the caller of this function should already have the information and could pass it to this function.

Erroneous Case: No Binding

Listing 4-115

――dhcp6s.c
```
1961              if ((binding = find_binding(&optinfo->clientID, DHCP6_BINDING_IA,
1962                  iap->type, iap->val_ia.iaid)) == NULL) {
1963                      /*
1964                       * Behavior in the case where the delegating router cannot
1965                       * find a binding for the requesting router's IA_PD as
1966                       * described in RFC3633 Section 12.2.  It is derived from
1967                       * Sections 18.2.3 and 18.2.4 of RFC3315, and the two sets
1968                       * of behavior are identical.
1969                       */
1970                      dprintf(LOG_INFO, FNAME, "no binding found for %s",
1971                          duidstr(&optinfo->clientID));
1972
1973                      switch (msgtype) {
1974                      case DH6_RENEW:
1975                              /*
1976                               * If the delegating router cannot find a binding for
1977                               * the requesting router's IA_PD the delegating router
1978                               * returns the IA_PD containing no prefixes with a
1979                               * Status Code option set to NoBinding in the Reply
1980                               * message.
1981                               */
1982                              if (make_ia_stcode(iap->type, iap->val_ia.iaid,
1983                                  DH6OPT_STCODE_NOBINDING, retlist)) {
1984                                      dprintf(LOG_NOTICE, FNAME,
1985                                          "failed to make an option list");
1986                                      return (-1);
1987                              }
1988                              break;
1989                      case DH6_REBIND:
1990                              /*
1991                               * If it can be determined the prefixes are not
1992                               * appropriate from the delegating router's explicit
1993                               * configuration, it MAY send a Reply message to
1994                               * the requesting router containing the IA_PD with the
1995                               * lifetimes of the prefixes in the IA_PD set to zero.
1996                               *
1997                               * If unable to determine, the Rebind message is
1998                               * discarded.
1999                               *
2000                               * XXX: it is not very clear what the explicit
2001                               * configuration means.  Thus, we always discard the
2002                               * message.
2003                               */
2004                              return (-1);
2005                      default:        /* XXX: should be a bug */
2006                              dprintf(LOG_ERR, FNAME, "impossible message type %s",
2007                                  dhcp6msgstr(msgtype));
2008                              return (-1);
2009              }
```
――dhcp6s.c

1961–1971 The `find_binding()` function identifies the local binding for the specified IA. This should usually succeed, but can fail, e.g., if the server has lost the binding due to rebooting or an unexpected timeout. The behavior in this case is only defined in [RFC3315], but it should also apply to the prefix delegation usage. This code does not differentiate these two cases.

1973–1988 If the IA is specified in a Renew message, it means this server has allocated the IA for the client but has lost the binding. In this case, an IA option (IA_NA or IA_PD) for the specified IA is built in the return list which contains a Status Code option with the code of NoBinding. Then the client will send a Request message for the IA to reestablish it (see Section 4.4.11).

1989–2004 On the other hand, if the IA is specified in a Rebind message, the things are more complicated. The server cannot verify that it has allocated the IA to the client (note that a Rebind message does not contain a Server Identifier option), and it cannot determine that the address or the prefix is not appropriate for the client simply because it does not have a corresponding binding. Thus, this implementation simply discards the Rebind message without returning any Reply message.

> In general, a server cannot respond to a Rebind message for sure unless it has allocated the IA or the binding information is shared with the allocating server by some out-of-band mechanism (see Section 4.2.3). If the server that has allocated the IA does not work for a long period and the other servers do not share the binding information, there is nothing for the client to do other than let the IA expire.

Update Binding

Listing 4-116
── dhcp6s.c

```
2010            } else {         /* we found a binding */
2011                    struct dhcp6_list ialist;
2012                    struct dhcp6_listval *lv;
2013                    struct dhcp6_prefix prefix;
2014                    struct dhcp6_statefuladdr saddr;
2015                    struct dhcp6_ia ia;
2016
2017                    TAILQ_INIT(&ialist);
2018                    update_binding(binding);
```
── dhcp6s.c

2010–2018 If the binding is found, its timeout parameter is updated by the `update_binding()` function (Listing 4-104, pages 415–416).

> This code updates the binding regardless of the content of the received IA. The specification requires that the client include all addresses assigned to the IA in a Renew or Rebind message, but it does not clearly specify how the server should react if some of the addresses in the server's binding are not included in the IA.

Update the IA for the Client

Listing 4-117
── dhcp6s.c

```
2020                    /* see if each information to be renewed is still valid. */
2021                    for (lv = TAILQ_FIRST(&iap->sublist); lv;
2022                         lv = TAILQ_NEXT(lv, link)) {
2023                            struct dhcp6_listval *blv;
2024
2025                            switch (iap->type) {
2026                            case DHCP6_LISTVAL_IAPD:
2027                                    if (lv->type != DHCP6_LISTVAL_PREFIX6)
```

```
2028                                            continue;
2029
2030                            prefix = lv->val_prefix6;
2031                            blv = dhcp6_find_listval(&binding->val_list,
2032                                DHCP6_LISTVAL_PREFIX6, &prefix, 0);
2033                            if (blv == NULL) {
2034                                    dprintf(LOG_DEBUG, FNAME,
2035                                        "%s/%d is not found in %s",
2036                                        in6addr2str(&prefix.addr, 0),
2037                                        prefix.plen, bindingstr(binding));
2038                                    prefix.pltime = 0;
2039                                    prefix.vltime = 0;
2040                            } else {
2041                                    prefix.pltime =
2042                                        blv->val_prefix6.pltime;
2043                                    prefix.vltime =
2044                                        blv->val_prefix6.vltime;
2045                            }
2046
2047                            if (dhcp6_add_listval(&ialist,
2048                                DHCP6_LISTVAL_PREFIX6, &prefix, NULL)
2049                                == NULL) {
2050                                    dprintf(LOG_NOTICE, FNAME,
2051                                        "failed  to copy binding info");
2052                                    dhcp6_clear_list(&ialist);
2053                                    return (-1);
2054                            }
2055                            break;
2056                    case DHCP6_LISTVAL_IANA:
2057                            if (lv->type != DHCP6_LISTVAL_STATEFULADDR6)
2058                                    continue;
2059
2060                            saddr = lv->val_statefuladdr6;
2061                            blv = dhcp6_find_listval(&binding->val_list,
2062                                DHCP6_LISTVAL_STATEFULADDR6, &saddr, 0);
2063                            if (blv == NULL) {
2064                                    dprintf(LOG_DEBUG, FNAME,
2065                                        "%s is not found in %s",
2066                                        in6addr2str(&saddr.addr, 0),
2067                                        bindingstr(binding));
2068                                    saddr.pltime = 0;
2069                                    saddr.vltime = 0;
2070                            } else {
2071                                    saddr.pltime =
2072                                        blv->val_statefuladdr6.pltime;
2073                                    saddr.vltime =
2074                                        blv->val_statefuladdr6.pltime;
2075                            }
2076
2077                            if (dhcp6_add_listval(&ialist,
2078                                DHCP6_LISTVAL_STATEFULADDR6, &saddr, NULL)
2079                                == NULL) {
2080                                    dprintf(LOG_NOTICE, FNAME,
2081                                        "failed  to copy binding info");
2082                                    dhcp6_clear_list(&ialist);
2083                                    return (-1);
2084                            }
2085                            break;
2086                    default:
2087                            dprintf(LOG_ERR, FNAME, "unsupported IA type");
2088                            return (-1); /* XXX */
2089                    }
2090            }
```
——dhcp6s.c

2021–2085 Each prefix or address in the IA is examined, one by one. If it is still valid in the
binding, the valid and preferred lifetimes (which are common for prefixes and addresses)

are updated with the configured parameters in the binding. Otherwise, these lifetimes are set to 0, telling the client that it is no longer valid.

Create a Response IA

Listing 4-118

dhcp6s.c

```
2092                        memset(&ia, 0, sizeof(ia));
2093                        ia.iaid = binding->iaid;
2094                        /* determine appropriate T1 and T2 */
2095                        calc_ia_timo(&ia, &ialist, client_conf);
2096
2097                        if (dhcp6_add_listval(retlist, iap->type,
2098                            &ia, &ialist) == NULL) {
2099                                dhcp6_clear_list(&ialist);
2100                                return (-1);
2101                        }
2102                        dhcp6_clear_list(&ialist);
2103                }
2104
2105        return (0);
2106    }
```

dhcp6s.c

2092–2102 A new IA for the specified binding is created with the updated list of prefixes or addresses from the previous procedure. The T1 and T2 times are recalculated with the latest prefixes or addresses by the `calc_ia_timo()` function. The new IA is then linked in the return list.

4.5.9 `binding_timo()` Function

The `binding_timo()` function is the timeout handler for bindings, which will be called from the `server6_mainloop()` function via the `dhcp6_check_timer()` function. Typically, at least one address or prefix of the binding expires and is removed from the binding when this function is called.

Listing 4-119

dhcp6s.c

```
2738    static struct dhcp6_timer *
2739    binding_timo(arg)
2740            void *arg;
2741    {
2742            struct dhcp6_binding *binding = (struct dhcp6_binding *)arg;
2743            struct dhcp6_list *ia_list = &binding->val_list;
2744            struct dhcp6_listval *iav, *iav_next;
2745            time_t now = time(NULL);
2746            u_int32_t past, lifetime;
2747            struct timeval timo;
2748
2749            past = (u_int32_t)(now >= binding->updatetime ?
2750                now - binding->updatetime : 0);
2751
2752            switch (binding->type) {
2753            case DHCP6_BINDING_IA:
2754                    for (iav = TAILQ_FIRST(ia_list); iav; iav = iav_next) {
2755                            iav_next = TAILQ_NEXT(iav, link);
2756
2757                            switch (binding->iatype) {
2758                            case DHCP6_LISTVAL_IAPD:
2759                            case DHCP6_LISTVAL_IANA:
```

```
2760                                    lifetime = iav->val_prefix6.vltime;
2761                                    break;
2762                            default:
2763                                    dprintf(LOG_ERR, FNAME, "internal error: "
2764                                        "unknown binding type (%d)",
2765                                        binding->iatype);
2766                                    return (NULL); /* XXX */
2767                            }
2768
2769                            if (lifetime != DHCP6_DURATITION_INFINITE &&
2770                                lifetime <= past) {
2771                                    dprintf(LOG_DEBUG, FNAME, "bound prefix %s/%d"
2772                                        " in %s has expired",
2773                                        in6addr2str(&iav->val_prefix6.addr, 0),
2774                                        iav->val_prefix6.plen,
2775                                        bindingstr(binding));
2776                                    TAILQ_REMOVE(ia_list, iav, link);
2777                                    dhcp6_clear_listval(iav);
2778                            }
2779                    }
2780
2781                    /* If all IA parameters have expired, remove the binding. */
2782                    if (TAILQ_EMPTY(ia_list)) {
2783                            remove_binding(binding);
2784                            return (NULL);
2785                    }
2786
2787                    break;
2788            default:
2789                    dprintf(LOG_ERR, FNAME, "unknown binding type %d",
2790                        binding->type);
2791                    return (NULL);          /* XXX */
2792            }
2793
2794            update_binding_duration(binding);
2795
2796            /* if the lease duration is infinite, there's nothing to do. */
2797            if (binding->duration == DHCP6_DURATITION_INFINITE)
2798                    return (NULL);
2799
2800            /* reset the timer with the duration */
2801            timo.tv_sec = (long)binding->duration;
2802            timo.tv_usec = 0;
2803            dhcp6_set_timer(&timo, binding->timer);
2804
2805            return (binding->timer);
2806    }
```

─── dhcp6s.c

Calculate the time passed

2749–2750 The variable `past` is set to the amount of time which has passed since the previous update of this binding.

Remove expired entry

2752–2779 For each element of the binding list (an address or a prefix), if its valid lifetime is not infinite and is shorter than or equal to the variable `past`, that element has expired and is removed from the list.

2781–2785 If the binding list becomes empty, the binding itself is considered as having expired. The `remove_binding()` function performs any necessary cleanups.

Restart timer

2794–2805 Since some of the addresses or prefixes are removed from the binding, the duration to the next timeout may also change. The `update_binding_duration()` function recalculates the duration using the remaining addresses or prefixes, and the timer is restarted with the new period.

The `remove_binding()` function, shown in Listing 4-120, is very simple. It just stops the timer if it is running, and frees any allocated memory resources for the binding.

Listing 4-120

```
─────────────────────────────────────────────────────────────── dhcp6s.c
2703    static void
2704    remove_binding(binding)
2705            struct dhcp6_binding *binding;
2706    {
2707            dprintf(LOG_DEBUG, FNAME, "remove a binding %s",
2708                bindingstr(binding));
2709
2710            if (binding->timer)
2711                    dhcp6_remove_timer(&binding->timer);
2712
2713            TAILQ_REMOVE(&dhcp6_binding_head, binding, link);
2714
2715            free_binding(binding);
2716    }
─────────────────────────────────────────────────────────────── dhcp6s.c
```

4.5.10 `react_release()` Function

The `react_release()` function processes a Release message from a client and removes any bindings corresponding to the message.

Validation

Listing 4-121

```
─────────────────────────────────────────────────────────────── dhcp6s.c
1744    static int
1745    react_release(ifp, pi, dh6, len, optinfo, from, fromlen, relayinfohead)
1746            struct dhcp6_if *ifp;
1747            struct in6_pktinfo *pi;
1748            struct dhcp6 *dh6;
1749            ssize_t len;
1750            struct dhcp6_optinfo *optinfo;
1751            struct sockaddr *from;
1752            int fromlen;
1753            struct relayinfolist *relayinfohead;
1754    {
1755            struct dhcp6_optinfo roptinfo;
1756            struct dhcp6_listval *ia;
1757            struct host_conf *client_conf;
1758            u_int16_t stcode;
1759
1760            /* message validation according to Section 15.9 of RFC3315 */
1761
1762            /* the message must include a Server Identifier option */
1763            if (optinfo->serverID.duid_len == 0) {
1764                    dprintf(LOG_INFO, FNAME, "no server ID option");
1765                    return (-1);
1766            }
1767            /* the contents of the Server Identifier option must match ours */
```

```
1768            if (duidcmp(&optinfo->serverID, &server_duid)) {
1769                    dprintf(LOG_INFO, FNAME, "server ID mismatch");
1770                    return (-1);
1771            }
1772            /* the message must include a Client Identifier option */
1773            if (optinfo->clientID.duid_len == 0) {
1774                    dprintf(LOG_INFO, FNAME, "no server ID option");
1775                    return (-1);
1776            }
```
_____dhcp6s.c

1760–1776 A valid Release message must contain a Server Identifier option and it must match the identifier of the receiving server. A Release message must also contain a Client Identifier option. If any of these requirements are not met, the message is discarded.

Build Options for Reply, Identify Client, Handle Unexpected Unicast Message

Listing 4-122
_____dhcp6s.c

```
1778            /*
1779             * configure necessary options based on the options in request.
1780             */
1781            dhcp6_init_options(&roptinfo);
1782
1783            /* server identifier option */
1784            if (duidcpy(&roptinfo.serverID, &server_duid)) {
1785                    dprintf(LOG_ERR, FNAME, "failed to copy server ID");
1786                    goto fail;
1787            }
1788            /* copy client information back */
1789            if (duidcpy(&roptinfo.clientID, &optinfo->clientID)) {
1790                    dprintf(LOG_ERR, FNAME, "failed to copy client ID");
1791                    goto fail;
1792            }
1793
1794            /* get per-host configuration for the client, if any. */
1795            if ((client_conf = find_hostconf(&optinfo->clientID))) {
1796                    dprintf(LOG_DEBUG, FNAME,
1797                        "found a host configuration named %s", client_conf->name);
1798            }
1799
1800            /* process authentication */
1801            if (process_auth(dh6, len, client_conf, optinfo, &roptinfo)) {
1802                    dprintf(LOG_INFO, FNAME, "failed to process authentication "
1803                        "information for %s",
1804                        clientstr(client_conf, &optinfo->clientID));
1805                    goto fail;
1806            }
1807
1808            /*
1809             * When the server receives a Release message via unicast from a
1810             * client to which the server has not sent a unicast option, the server
1811             * discards the Release message and responds with a Reply message
1812             * containing a Status Code option with value UseMulticast, a Server
1813             * Identifier option containing the server's DUID, the Client
1814             * Identifier option from the client message and no other options.
1815             * [RFC3315 18.2.6]
1816             * (Our current implementation never sends a unicast option.)
1817             */
1818            if (!IN6_IS_ADDR_MULTICAST(&pi->ipi6_addr) &&
1819                TAILQ_EMPTY(relayinfohead)) {
1820                    u_int16_t stcode = DH6OPT_STCODE_USEMULTICAST;
1821
1822                    dprintf(LOG_INFO, FNAME, "unexpected unicast message from %s",
1823                        addr2str(from));
```

```
1824                        if (dhcp6_add_listval(&roptinfo.stcode_list,
1825                            DHCP6_LISTVAL_STCODE, &stcode, NULL) == NULL) {
1826                                dprintf(LOG_ERR, FNAME, "failed to add a status code");
1827                                goto fail;
1828                        }
1829                        server6_send(DH6_REPLY, ifp, dh6, optinfo, from,
1830                            fromlen, &roptinfo, relayinfohead, client_conf);
1831                        goto end;
1832                }
```
——dhcp6s.c

1778–1832 This part is the same as the `react_request()` function (see Section 4.5.5).

Remove Bindings

Listing 4-123

——dhcp6s.c
```
1834            /*
1835             * Locates the client's binding and verifies that the information
1836             * from the client matches the information stored for that client.
1837             */
1838            for (ia = TAILQ_FIRST(&optinfo->iapd_list); ia;
1839                ia = TAILQ_NEXT(ia, link)) {
1840                    if (release_binding_ia(ia, &roptinfo.iapd_list, optinfo))
1841                            goto fail;
1842            }
1843            for (ia = TAILQ_FIRST(&optinfo->iana_list); ia;
1844                ia = TAILQ_NEXT(ia, link)) {
1845                    if (release_binding_ia(ia, &roptinfo.iana_list, optinfo))
1846                            goto fail;
1847            }
```
——dhcp6s.c

1834–1842 For each IA_PD in the Release message, if any, the `release_binding_ia()` function locates the corresponding binding and removes it. If no binding is found for the IA, `release_binding_ia()` builds an IA (IA_PD) option for the IA containing a Status Code option with the code of NoBinding and adds it to the return list.

1843–1847 Likewise, the binding for each IA_NA is removed.

Set Status Code

Listing 4-124

——dhcp6s.c
```
1849            /*
1850             * After all the addresses have been processed, the server generates a
1851             * Reply message and includes a Status Code option with value Success.
1852             * [RFC3315 Section 18.2.6]
1853             */
1854            stcode = DH6OPT_STCODE_SUCCESS;
1855            if (dhcp6_add_listval(&roptinfo.stcode_list,
1856                DHCP6_LISTVAL_STCODE, &stcode, NULL) == NULL) {
1857                    dprintf(LOG_NOTICE, FNAME, "failed to add a status code");
1858                    goto fail;
1859            }
```
——dhcp6s.c

1849–1859 As the comment indicates, a separate Status Code option with the code of Success is added to the Reply message.

Send Reply

Listing 4-125

———————————————————————————————————dhcp6s.c

```
1860
1861              (void)server6_send(DH6_REPLY, ifp, dh6, optinfo, from, fromlen,
1862                  &roptinfo, relayinfohead, client_conf);
1863
1864     end:
1865              dhcp6_clear_options(&roptinfo);
1866              return (0);
1867
1868     fail:
1869              dhcp6_clear_options(&roptinfo);
1870              return (-1);
1871     }
```

———————————————————————————————————dhcp6s.c

1861–1862 The `server6_send()` function constructs a Reply message and sends it to the client. Note that a Reply message sent in response to Release does not contain any additional configuration information, such as stateless options.

The `release_binding_ia()` function, shown below, is called from the `react_release()` function.

Listing 4-126

———————————————————————————————————dhcp6s.c

```
2108    static int
2109    release_binding_ia(iap, retlist, optinfo)
2110            struct dhcp6_listval *iap;
2111            struct dhcp6_list *retlist;
2112            struct dhcp6_optinfo *optinfo;
2113    {
2114            struct dhcp6_binding *binding;
2115
2116            if ((binding = find_binding(&optinfo->clientID, DHCP6_BINDING_IA,
2117                iap->type, iap->val_ia.iaid)) == NULL) {
2118                    /*
2119                     * For each IA in the Release message for which the server has
2120                     * no binding information, the server adds an IA option using
2121                     * the IAID from the Release message and includes a Status Code
2122                     * option with the value NoBinding in the IA option.
2123                     */
2124                    if (make_ia_stcode(iap->type, iap->val_ia.iaid,
2125                        DH6OPT_STCODE_NOBINDING, retlist)) {
2126                            dprintf(LOG_NOTICE, FNAME,
2127                                "failed to make an option list");
2128                            return (-1);
2129                    }
2130            } else {
2131                    struct dhcp6_listval *lv, *lvia;
2132
2133                    /*
2134                     * If the IAs in the message are in a binding for the client
2135                     * and the addresses in the IAs have been assigned by the
2136                     * server to those IAs, the server deletes the addresses from
2137                     * the IAs and makes the addresses available for assignment to
2138                     * other clients.
2139                     * [RFC3315 Section 18.2.6]
2140                     * RFC3633 is not very clear about the similar case for IA_PD,
2141                     * but we apply the same logic.
2142                     */
2143                    for (lv = TAILQ_FIRST(&iap->sublist); lv;
```

```
2144                              lv = TAILQ_NEXT(lv, link)) {
2145                                  if ((lvia = find_binding_ia(lv, binding)) != NULL) {
2146                                      switch (binding->iatype) {
2147                                      case DHCP6_LISTVAL_IAPD:
2148                                          dprintf(LOG_DEBUG, FNAME,
2149                                              "bound prefix %s/%d "
2150                                              "has been released",
2151                                              in6addr2str(&lvia->
     val_prefix6.addr,
2152                                              0),
2153                                              lvia->val_prefix6.plen);
2154                                          break;
2155                                      case DHCP6_LISTVAL_IANA:
2156                                          dprintf(LOG_DEBUG, FNAME,
2157                                              "bound address %s "
2158                                              "has been released",
2159                                              in6addr2str(&lvia->
     val_prefix6.addr,
2160                                              0));
2161                                          break;
2162                                      }

2164                                      TAILQ_REMOVE(&binding->val_list, lvia, link);
2165                                      dhcp6_clear_listval(lvia);
2166                                      if (TAILQ_EMPTY(&binding->val_list)) {
2167                                          /*
2168                                           * if the binding has become empty,
2169                                           * stop procedure.
2170                                           */
2171                                          remove_binding(binding);
2172                                          return (0);
2173                                      }
2174                                  }
2175                              }
2176                          }

2178                  return (0);
2179      }
```
_____ dhcp6s.c

— Lines 2151 and 2159 are broken here for layout reasons. However, they are a single line of code.

Erroneous case: no binding

2116–2129 If the server does not find a binding that matches the parameters specified in the Release message, it builds in the return list a corresponding IA option (IA_NA or IA_PD) including a Status Code option with the code of NoBinding.

Release resources

2130–2165 For each address or prefix of the IA in the Release message, it is removed and released from the server's binding, if it is contained in the binding list.

2166–2173 If the binding list becomes empty, the binding itself is also released by the `remove_binding()` function (see Listing 4-120, page 428).

4.5.11 `react_informreq()` Function

The `react_informreq()` function processes an Information-request message from a client.

Validation

Listing 4-127

---
dhcp6s.c

```
1873    static int
1874    react_informreq(ifp, dh6, len, optinfo, from, fromlen, relayinfohead)
1875            struct dhcp6_if *ifp;
1876            struct dhcp6 *dh6;
1877            ssize_t len;
1878            struct dhcp6_optinfo *optinfo;
1879            struct sockaddr *from;
1880            int fromlen;
1881            struct relayinfolist *relayinfohead;
1882    {
1883            struct dhcp6_optinfo roptinfo;
1884            int error;
1885
1886            /*
1887             * An IA option is not allowed to appear in an Information-request
1888             * message.  Such a message SHOULD be discarded.
1889             * [RFC3315 Section 15]
1890             */
1891            if (!TAILQ_EMPTY(&optinfo->iapd_list)) {
1892                    dprintf(LOG_INFO, FNAME,
1893                        "information request contains an IA_PD option");
1894                    return (-1);
1895            }
1896            if (!TAILQ_EMPTY(&optinfo->iana_list)) {
1897                    dprintf(LOG_INFO, FNAME,
1898                        "information request contains an IA_NA option");
1899                    return (-1);
1900            }
1901
1902            /* if a server identifier is included, it must match ours. */
1903            if (optinfo->serverID.duid_len &&
1904                duidcmp(&optinfo->serverID, &server_duid)) {
1905                    dprintf(LOG_INFO, FNAME, "server DUID mismatch");
1906                    return (-1);
1907            }
```

---
dhcp6s.c

1886–1900 If an IA option (IA_PD or IA_NA in this implementation) is contained in the Information-request message, the message is discarded.

1902–1907 An Information-request message may contain a Server Identifier option. If it does, the identifier must match that of the receiving server; otherwise the message is discarded.

Build Options for Reply

Listing 4-128

---
dhcp6s.c

```
1909            /*
1910             * configure necessary options based on the options in request.
1911             */
1912            dhcp6_init_options(&roptinfo);
1913
1914            /* server identifier option */
1915            if (duidcpy(&roptinfo.serverID, &server_duid)) {
1916                    dprintf(LOG_ERR, FNAME, "failed to copy server ID");
1917                    goto fail;
```

```
1918                    }
1919
1920                    /* copy client information back (if provided) */
1921                    if (optinfo->clientID.duid_id &&
1922                        duidcpy(&roptinfo.clientID, &optinfo->clientID)) {
1923                            dprintf(LOG_ERR, FNAME, "failed to copy client ID");
1924                            goto fail;
1925                    }
1926
1927                    /* set stateless information */
1928                    if (set_statelessinfo(DH6_INFORM_REQ, &roptinfo)) {
1929                            dprintf(LOG_ERR, FNAME,
1930                                "failed to set other stateless information");
1931                            goto fail;
1932                    }
```
                                                                                          _____ dhcp6s.c

1914–1925 The server identifier will be included in a Server Identifier option of the Reply
message. If the Information-request message contains a Client Identifier option, it will be
copied back to the Reply message.

1927–1932 The `set_statelessinfo()` function sets stateless configuration information in
the option structure for the Reply message. If the information refresh time is configured
in the server, it will be included in the Information Refresh Time option.

Send Packet

Listing 4-129
                                                                                          _____ dhcp6s.c

```
1934                error = server6_send(DH6_REPLY, ifp, dh6, optinfo, from, fromlen,
1935                    &roptinfo, relayinfohead, NULL);
1936
1937                dhcp6_clear_options(&roptinfo);
1938                return (error);
1939
1940        fail:
1941                dhcp6_clear_options(&roptinfo);
1942                return (-1);
1943        }
```
                                                                                          _____ dhcp6s.c

1934–1935 The `server6_send()` function builds a Reply message and sends it back to the
client.

4.5.12 `server6_send()` Function

The `server6_send()` function is shown below. This is the final stage of the server's message
processing.

Construct the Response Header

Listing 4-130
                                                                                          _____ dhcp6s.c

```
2181    static int
2182    server6_send(type, ifp, origmsg, optinfo, from, fromlen,
2183        roptinfo, relayinfohead, client_conf)
2184            int type;
2185            struct dhcp6_if *ifp;
```

```
2186              struct dhcp6 *origmsg;
2187              struct dhcp6_optinfo *optinfo, *roptinfo;
2188              struct sockaddr *from;
2189              int fromlen;
2190              struct relayinfolist *relayinfohead;
2191              struct host_conf *client_conf;
2192       {
2193              char replybuf[BUFSIZ];
2194              struct sockaddr_in6 dst;
2195              int len, optlen;
2196              int relayed = 0;
2197              struct dhcp6 *dh6;
2198              struct relayinfo *relayinfo;
2199
2200              if (sizeof(struct dhcp6) > sizeof(replybuf)) {
2201                      dprintf(LOG_ERR, FNAME, "buffer size assumption failed");
2202                      return (-1);
2203              }
2204
2205              dh6 = (struct dhcp6 *)replybuf;
2206              len = sizeof(*dh6);
2207              memset(dh6, 0, sizeof(*dh6));
2208              dh6->dh6_msgtypexid = origmsg->dh6_msgtypexid;
2209              dh6->dh6_msgtype = (u_int8_t)type;
```
——— dhcp6s.c

2205–2209 The type of response packet is either an Advertise (in response to a Solicit without a Rapid Commit option) or a Reply message. The transaction ID is copied from the corresponding message from the client.

Set Options

Listing 4-131

——— dhcp6s.c
```
2211              /* set options in the reply message */
2212              if ((optlen = dhcp6_set_options(type, (struct dhcp6opt *)(dh6 + 1),
2213                  (struct dhcp6opt *)(replybuf + sizeof(replybuf)), roptinfo)) < 0) {
2214                      dprintf(LOG_INFO, FNAME, "failed to construct reply options");
2215                      return (-1);
2216              }
2217              len += optlen;
```
——— dhcp6s.c

2211–2217 The dhcp6_set_options() function sets the prepared options in the response packet.

Added Authentication Information

Listing 4-132

——— dhcp6s.c
```
2219              /* calculate MAC if necessary, and put it to the message */
2220              switch (roptinfo->authproto) {
2221              case DHCP6_AUTHPROTO_DELAYED:
2222                      if (client_conf == NULL || client_conf->delayedkey == NULL) {
2223                              /* This case should have been caught earlier */
2224                              dprintf(LOG_ERR, FNAME, "authentication required "
2225                                  "but not key provided");
2226                              break;
2227                      }
2228                      if (dhcp6_calc_mac((char *)dh6, len, roptinfo->authproto,
2229                          roptinfo->authalgorithm,
2230                          roptinfo->delayedauth_offset + sizeof(*dh6),
```

```
2231                        client_conf->delayedkey)) {
2232                            dprintf(LOG_WARNING, FNAME, "failed to calculate MAC");
2233                            return (-1);
2234                        }
2235                    break;
2236            default:
2237                    break;                        /* do nothing */
2238                }
```
_____dhcp6s.c

2219–2238 If the Reply message needs to be authenticated by the delayed authentication
protocol and a key is configured for the client, the dhcp6_calc_mac() function computes the HMAC of the message using the key. The procedure is the same as in the client;
see Section 4.4.4 for more details.

Construct Relay-reply Chain

Listing 4-133
_____dhcp6s.c

```
2240                /* construct a relay chain, if necessary */
2241                for (relayinfo = TAILQ_FIRST(relayinfohead); relayinfo;
2242                    relayinfo = TAILQ_NEXT(relayinfo, link)) {
2243                    struct dhcp6_optinfo relayopt;
2244                    struct dhcp6_vbuf relaymsgbuf;
2245                    struct dhcp6_relay *dh6relay;
2246
2247                    relayed = 1;
2248                    dhcp6_init_options(&relayopt);
2249
2250                    relaymsgbuf.dv_len = len;
2251                    relaymsgbuf.dv_buf = replybuf;
2252                    if (dhcp6_vbuf_copy(&relayopt.relay_msg, &relaymsgbuf))
2253                        return (-1);
2254                    if (relayinfo->relay_ifid.dv_buf &&
2255                        dhcp6_vbuf_copy(&relayopt.ifidopt,
2256                        &relayinfo->relay_ifid)) {
2257                            dhcp6_vbuf_free(&relayopt.relay_msg);
2258                            return (-1);
2259                    }
2260
2261                    /* we can safely reuse replybuf here */
2262                    dh6relay = (struct dhcp6_relay *)replybuf;
2263                    memset(dh6relay, 0, sizeof (*dh6relay));
2264                    dh6relay->dh6relay_msgtype = DH6_RELAY_REPLY;
2265                    dh6relay->dh6relay_hcnt = relayinfo->hcnt;
2266                    memcpy(&dh6relay->dh6relay_linkaddr, &relayinfo->linkaddr,
2267                        sizeof (dh6relay->dh6relay_linkaddr));
2268                    memcpy(&dh6relay->dh6relay_peeraddr, &relayinfo->peeraddr,
2269                        sizeof (dh6relay->dh6relay_peeraddr));
2270
2271                    len = sizeof(*dh6relay);
2272                    if ((optlen = dhcp6_set_options(DH6_RELAY_REPLY,
2273                        (struct dhcp6opt *)(dh6relay + 1),
2274                        (struct dhcp6opt *)(replybuf + sizeof(replybuf)),
2275                        &relayopt)) < 0) {
2276                            dprintf(LOG_INFO, FNAME,
2277                                "failed to construct relay message");
2278                            dhcp6_clear_options(&relayopt);
2279                            return (-1);
2280                    }
2281                    len += optlen;
2282
2283                    dhcp6_clear_options(&relayopt);
2284                }
```
_____dhcp6s.c

2240–2259 If the list starting from `relayinfohead` is not empty, it means the original message was relayed via an intermediate relay agent. A new option context is initialized in the variable `relayopt`, and the message is encapsulated in a Relay Message option. If the corresponding Relay-forward message contained an Interface-Id option, it is copied into the variable `relayopt`.

2261–2269 Most of the Relay-reply message header is copied from the corresponding Relay-forward message stored in the `relayinfo{}` structure. The hop count does not have any meaning in a Relay-reply message, but it is also copied from the Reply-forward message, as described in [RFC3315]. The contents of `replybuf` were already copied into the Relay Message option, and the buffer can be reused for the Relay-reply message.

2271–2284 The `dhcp6_set_options()` encodes the options in the buffer, then the option information can be released.

Figures 4-37 and 4-38 show an example of this procedure for a response to the message shown in Figure 4-31 (page 395). In the first iteration of the `for` loop, the first (inner) Relay-reply message is created using the original Reply message and the information stored in the head member of the `relayinfo` list (Figure 4-37).

FIGURE 4-37

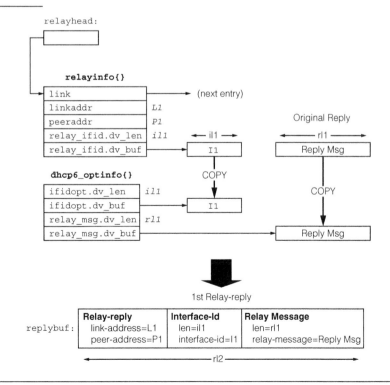

Construction of a Relay-reply chain: first step.

The second iteration of the `for` loop repeats the same procedure for the first Relay-reply message just created and the second entry of the `relayinfo` list, resulting in the actual outgoing message, which is the second (outermost) Relay-reply message (Figure 4-38).

Figure 4-39 depicts the resulting Relay-reply message that is to be sent out by the server.

FIGURE 4-38

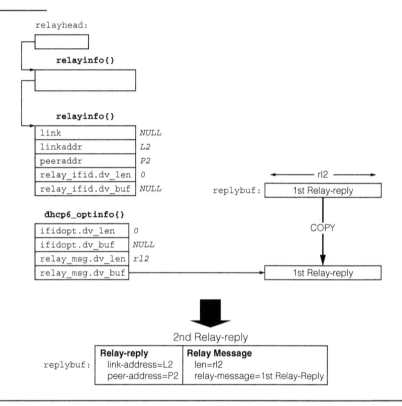

Construction of a Relay-reply chain: second step.

FIGURE 4-39

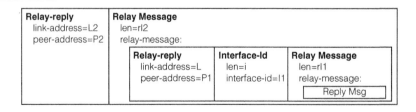

Complete outgoing packet containing a Relay-reply chain.

Send Packet

Listing 4-134

```
                                                                            dhcp6s.c
2286            /* specify the destination and send the reply */
2287            dst = relayed ? *sa6_any_relay : *sa6_any_downstream;
2288            dst.sin6_addr = ((struct sockaddr_in6 *)from)->sin6_addr;
2289            dst.sin6_scope_id = ((struct sockaddr_in6 *)from)->sin6_scope_id;
2290            if (transmit_sa(outsock, (struct sockaddr *)&dst,
2291                replybuf, len) != 0) {
2292                    dprintf(LOG_ERR, FNAME, "transmit %s to %s failed",
2293                        dhcp6msgstr(type), addr2str((struct sockaddr *)&dst));
2294                    return (-1);
2295            }
2296
2297            dprintf(LOG_DEBUG, FNAME, "transmit %s to %s",
2298                dhcp6msgstr(type), addr2str((struct sockaddr *)&dst));
2299
2300            return (0);
2301    }
                                                                            dhcp6s.c
```

2287–2300 If the original message was relayed from a relay agent, the response packet is sent to the relay agent's well-known port (UDP port 547); otherwise, it is sent to the client's well-known port (UDP port 546). The destination address of the packet is the client's address or the address of the relay agent that sent a Relay-forward message to the server.

The packet is then sent out on the outbound socket.

4.6 Relay Agent Implementation

The relay agent implementation is straightforward as shown in its function call graph (Figure 4-40). After initialization, it waits for messages in an infinite loop in the `relay6_loop()` function. When a message arrives, the `relay6_recv()` function is called from the loop, which has two subroutines. The `relay_to_server()` function handles messages from a client or another relay agent located at the *downstream* side, encapsulates the message into a Relay-forward message, and forwards it to a server or another relay agent located at the *upstream* side. The `relay_to_client()` function performs the opposite process: It receives messages from a server or another relay agent located at the upstream side, decapsulates the message, and forwards the inner message to a client or another relay agent located at the downstream side.

Global Variables

Table 4-8 summarizes the major global variables specific to the relay agent implementation.

4.6.1 `relay6_loop()` Function

The `relay6_loop()` function is the main loop of the relay agent implementation.

FIGURE 4-40

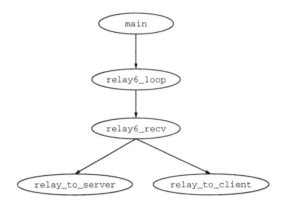

An overview of the relay agent implementation.

TABLE 4-8

Name	Type	Description
ssock	int	The file descriptor of the socket for communicating with servers or other relay agents located closer to the servers. The socket listens on UDP port 546. It is not bound to any address by default, but the relay agent can be configured with a particular address for binding the socket.
csock	int	The file descriptor of the socket for communicating with clients or other relay agents located closer to the clients. The socket listens on UDP port 547. The relay agent listens to the All_DHCP_Relay_Agents_and_Servers multicast group (ff02::1:2) through this socket.
sa6_server	struct sockaddr_in6	A socket address structure bound to UDP port 547. By default, it is also set to the All_DHCP_Servers multicast address (ff05::1:3), but it can be configured with a global unicast address of a server or another relay agent. This structure is used as a template for the destination address when sending a DHCPv6 message upstream toward a server.
sa6_client	struct sockaddr_in6	A socket address structure bound to UDP port 546. This structure is used as a template for the destination address when sending a DHCPv6 message downstream toward a client.

Global variables of the relay agent implementation.

Listing 4-135

```
458   static void
459   relay6_loop()
460   {
461           fd_set readfds;
462           int e;
463
464           while(1) {
465                   /* we'd rather use FD_COPY here, but it's not POSIX friendly */
466                   FD_ZERO(&readfds);
467                   FD_SET(csock, &readfds);
468                   FD_SET(ssock, &readfds);
469
470                   e = select(maxfd + 1, &readfds, NULL, NULL, NULL);
471                   switch(e) {
472                   case 0:                    /* impossible in our situation */
473                           errx(1, "select returned 0");
474                                   /* NOTREACHED */
475                   case -1:
476                           err(1, "select");
477                                   /* NOTREACHED */
478                   default:
479                           break;
480                   }
481
482                   if (FD_ISSET(csock, &readfds))
483                           relay6_recv(csock, 1);
484
485                   if (FD_ISSET(ssock, &readfds))
486                           relay6_recv(ssock, 0);
487           }
488   }
```

464–487 In an infinite loop, the relay agent watches the client side socket (csock) and the server side socket (ssock) using the select() system call. If a packet arrives on one of the sockets, the relay6_recv() function is called to process the packet.

4.6.2 relay6_recv() Function

The relay6_recv() function is shown below. It receives a DHCPv6 packet from a socket and calls the appropriate subroutine depending on the message type.

Receive Packet

Listing 4-136

```
490   static void
491   relay6_recv(s, fromclient)
492           int s, fromclient;
493   {
494           ssize_t len;
495           struct sockaddr_storage from;
496           struct in6_pktinfo *pi = NULL;
497           struct cmsghdr *cm;
498           struct dhcp6 *dh6;
499           char ifname[IF_NAMESIZE];
500
501           rmh.msg_control = (caddr_t)rmsgctlbuf;
```

```
502              rmh.msg_controllen = rmsgctllen;
503
504              rmh.msg_name = &from;
505              rmh.msg_namelen = sizeof (from);
506
507              if ((len = recvmsg(s, &rmh, 0)) < 0) {
508                      dprintf(LOG_WARNING, FNAME, "recvmsg: %s", strerror(errno));
509                      return;
510              }
511
512              dprintf(LOG_DEBUG, FNAME, "from %s, size %d",
513                  addr2str((struct sockaddr *)&from), len);
514
515              if (((struct sockaddr *)&from)->sa_family != AF_INET6) {
516                      dprintf(LOG_WARNING, FNAME,
517                          "non-IPv6 packet is received (AF %d) ",
518                          ((struct sockaddr *)&from)->sa_family);
519                      return;
520              }
```
——dhcp6relay.c

501–520 The `recvmsg()` system call receives packets with ancillary data. On success, the source of the packet must be an IPv6 address, so the address family check should be redundant.

Retrieve Ancillary Data

Listing 4-137
——dhcp6relay.c
```
522              /* get optional information as ancillary data (if available) */
523              for (cm = (struct cmsghdr *)CMSG_FIRSTHDR(&rmh); cm;
524                   cm = (struct cmsghdr *)CMSG_NXTHDR(&rmh, cm)) {
525                      if (cm->cmsg_level != IPPROTO_IPV6)
526                              continue;
527
528                      switch(cm->cmsg_type) {
529                      case IPV6_PKTINFO:
530                              pi = (struct in6_pktinfo *)CMSG_DATA(cm);
531                              break;
532                      }
533              }
534              if (pi == NULL) {
535                      dprintf(LOG_WARNING, FNAME,
536                          "failed to get the arrival interface");
537                      return;
538              }
539              if (if_indextoname(pi->ipi6_ifindex, ifname) == NULL) {
540                      dprintf(LOG_WARNING, FNAME,
541                          "if_indextoname(id = %d): %s",
542                          pi->ipi6_ifindex, strerror(errno));
543                      return;
544              }
```
——dhcp6relay.c

522–544 Unless an unexpected error (e.g., memory shortage) happens in the kernel, the ancillary data should contain the `IPV6_PKTINFO` item, which specifies the destination address of the packet and the packet's incoming interface. If this item is not contained in the ancillary data, the relay agent cannot perform any further processing and the packet is discarded.

Length Validation

Listing 4-138

```
                                                              ——————dhcp6relay.c
546        /* packet validation */
547        if (len < sizeof (*dh6)) {
548                dprintf(LOG_INFO, FNAME, "short packet (%d bytes)", len);
549                return;
550        }
                                                              ——————dhcp6relay.c
```

547–550 If the received packet is not large enough to contain the minimal DHCPv6 packet (i.e., the type and transaction ID), the packet is discarded.

Process Packets

Listing 4-139

```
                                                              ——————dhcp6relay.c
552        dh6 = (struct dhcp6 *)rdatabuf;
553        dprintf(LOG_DEBUG, FNAME, "received %s from %s",
554            dhcp6msgstr(dh6->dh6_msgtype), addr2str((struct sockaddr *)&from));
555
556        /*
557         * Relay the packet according to the type.  A client message or
558         * a relay forward message is forwarded to servers (or other relays),
559         * and a relay reply message is forwarded to the intended client.
560         */
561        if (fromclient) {
562                switch (dh6->dh6_msgtype) {
563                case DH6_SOLICIT:
564                case DH6_REQUEST:
565                case DH6_CONFIRM:
566                case DH6_RENEW:
567                case DH6_REBIND:
568                case DH6_RELEASE:
569                case DH6_DECLINE:
570                case DH6_INFORM_REQ:
571                case DH6_RELAY_FORW:
572                        relay_to_server(dh6, len, (struct sockaddr_in6 *)&from,
573                            ifname, htonl(pi->ipi6_ifindex));
574                        break;
575                case DH6_RELAY_REPLY:
576                        /*
577                         * The server may send a relay reply to the client
578                         * port.
579                         * XXX: need to clarify the port issue
580                         */
581                        relay_to_client((struct dhcp6_relay *)dh6, len,
582                            (struct sockaddr *)&from);
583                        break;
584                default:
585                        dprintf(LOG_INFO, FNAME,
586                            "unexpected message (%s) on the client side "
587                            "from %s", dhcp6msgstr(dh6->dh6_msgtype),
588                            addr2str((struct sockaddr *)&from));
589                        break;
590                }
591        } else {
592                if (dh6->dh6_msgtype != DH6_RELAY_REPLY) {
593                        dprintf(LOG_INFO, FNAME,
594                            "unexpected message (%s) on the server side"
595                            "from %s", dhcp6msgstr(dh6->dh6_msgtype),
596                            addr2str((struct sockaddr *)&from));
```

```
597                              return;
598                      }
599                      relay_to_client((struct dhcp6_relay *)dh6, len,
600                          (struct sockaddr *)&from);
601              }
602      }
```

561–574 If the DHCPv6 packet arrives at the client side port and is one of Solicit, Request, Confirm, Renew, Rebind, Release, Decline, or Information-request, it came from a client, and must be forwarded to servers or another relay agent toward the servers. Although this implementation set of DHCPv6 does not support some of the message types, that does not matter for a relay agent because it does not have to interpret the message content.

575–583 The DHCPv6 specification does not specify to which port the server or an upstream relay agent should send a Relay-reply message. But at least for a Reconfigure message, which is sent spontaneously by the server, and a Relay-reply message relayed from another relay agent, the message is likely to be sent to the relay agent's well-known port, because in these cases the sender does not have any other information on the port(*). On the other hand, when the server sends a Relay-reply message in response to a Relay-forward message sent from this agent, the server may send it back to the source port of the Relay-forward message. The relay agent should be prepared for either case.

(*) In this sense, the comment in the code is not really appropriate.

584–590 Otherwise, the packet is discarded.

591–601 If the packet arrives at the server side socket, it must be a Relay-reply message; otherwise, the packet is discarded. If it is a Relay-reply message, it is relayed to a client or another relay agent toward the client.

4.6.3 `relay_to_server()` Function

The `relay_to_server()` function, which forwards a message from a client to servers or another intermediate relay agent toward the servers, is shown below.

Construct Options

Listing 4-140

```
650      static void
651      relay_to_server(dh6, len, from, ifname, ifid)
652              struct dhcp6 *dh6;
653              ssize_t len;
654              struct sockaddr_in6 *from;
655              char *ifname;
656              unsigned int ifid;
657      {
658              struct dhcp6_optinfo optinfo;
659              struct dhcp6_relay *dh6relay;
660              struct in6_addr linkaddr;
661              struct prefix_list *p;
662              int optlen, relaylen;
```

```
663              int cc;
664              struct msghdr mh;
665              static struct iovec iov[2];
666              u_char relaybuf[sizeof (*dh6relay) + BUFSIZ];
667              struct in6_pktinfo pktinfo;
668              char ctlbuf[CMSG_SPACE(sizeof (struct in6_pktinfo))
669                  + CMSG_SPACE(sizeof (int))];
670
671              /*
672               * Prepare a relay forward option.
673               */
674              dhcp6_init_options(&optinfo);
675
676              /* Relay message */
677              if ((optinfo.relaymsg_msg = malloc(len)) == NULL) {
678                      dprintf(LOG_WARNING, FNAME,
679                          "failed to allocate memory to copy the original packet: "
680                          "%s", strerror(errno));
681                      goto out;
682              }
683              optinfo.relaymsg_len = len;
684              memcpy(optinfo.relaymsg_msg, dh6, len);
685
686              /* Interface-id.  We always use this option. */
687              if ((optinfo.ifidopt_id = malloc(sizeof (ifid))) == NULL) {
688                      dprintf(LOG_WARNING, FNAME,
689                          "failed to allocate memory for IFID: %s", strerror(errno));
690                      goto out;
691              }
692              optinfo.ifidopt_len = sizeof (ifid);
693              memcpy(optinfo.ifidopt_id, &ifid, sizeof (ifid));
```
_____dhcp6relay.c

671–674 The relay agent is now going to encapsulate the original DHCPv6 message in a Relay-forward message. A new option context, initialized by the `dhcp6_init_options()` function, is necessary for this process.

676–684 The main part of the Relay-forward message is the Relay Message option that contains the entire original message. A separate buffer is allocated into which the original message is copied, and is set in the option data field of the Relay Message option.

686–693 The DHCPv6 specification does not require a relay agent to include an Interface-Id option in a Relay-forward message. However, this implementation always includes this option, since it will help when processing the Relay-reply message later (see Section 4.6.4). The content of the Interface-Id option is opaque data whose semantics are only meaningful for the generating relay agent. This implementation simply uses the numeric interface identifier as the value of Interface-Id.

Construct Relay-forward Message

Listing 4-141
_____dhcp6relay.c
```
695              /*
696               * Construct a relay forward message.
697               */
698              memset(relaybuf, 0, sizeof (relaybuf));
699
700              dh6relay = (struct dhcp6_relay *)relaybuf;
701              memset(dh6relay, 0, sizeof (*dh6relay));
702              dh6relay->dh6relay_msgtype = DH6_RELAY_FORW;
703              memcpy(&dh6relay->dh6relay_peeraddr, &from->sin6_addr,
704                  sizeof (dh6relay->dh6relay_peeraddr));
```

```
705
706              /* find a global address to fill in the link address field */
707              memset(&linkaddr, 0, sizeof (linkaddr));
708              for (p = TAILQ_FIRST(&global_prefixes); p; p = TAILQ_NEXT(p, plink)) {
709                      if (getifaddr(&linkaddr, ifname, &p->paddr.sin6_addr,
710                                  p->plen, 1, IN6_IFF_INVALID) == 0) /* found */
711                              break;
712              }
713              if (p == NULL) {
714                      dprintf(LOG_NOTICE, FNAME,
715                          "failed to find a global address on %s", ifname);
716
717                      /*
718                       * When relaying a message from a client, we need a global
719                       * link address.
720                       * XXX: this may be too strong for the stateless case, but
721                       * the DHCPv6 specification seems to require the behavior.
722                       */
723                      if (dh6->dh6_msgtype != DH6_RELAY_FORW)
724                              goto out;
725              }
```
———dhcp6relay.c

695–704 The source address of the original message is copied to the peer address field of the Relay-forward message.

706–725 The DHCPv6 specification requires that a relay agent, when relaying a message from a client (not from another relay agent), specify in the link-address field a global or (now deprecated) site-local address which identifies the incoming link of the original message. The global variable `global_prefixes`, which is initialized at invocation, is a list of the global prefixes in use by the relay agent. This version of the implementation has actually only one prefix in this list: `2000::/3`.

The `for` loop goes through the prefix list, trying to find an address that matches any of the prefixes and is configured on the local interface attached to the link. If no such address is found and the relay agent is relaying a message from a client, the relay agent gives up relaying the packet.

This behavior may look reasonable, and it should in fact work well in most cases. Yet it is possible that the relay agent does not have a global or site-local address on the interface to the link where the client resides: In theory, the relay agent can assign a non-link-local address only on a different interface to communicate with servers and configure only a link-local address on the interface toward the client. Consider the network topology shown in Figure 4-41. A router acting as a DHCPv6 relay agent connects a PPP link where a DHCPv6 client resides to an Ethernet link where a DHCPv6 server resides. The relay agent configures its PPP interface only with a link-local address, but it can still have global connectivity with the global address assigned on the Ethernet interface. With this configuration, when the relay agent receives a DHCPv6 message from the client, this implementation will drop it since the search for a global address on the receiving (PPP) interface fails.

This is obviously undesirable, and the behavior is in fact too restrictive because the specification does not require this address to be derived from the addresses configured on the relay agent. However, the local addresses are the only available information for this implementation that can be used as the link-address, and there is nothing else for it to do in this case.

FIGURE 4-41

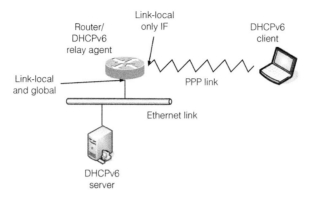

Relay agent configuration causing failure in link-address detection.

As commented in the code, since the link-address information will often be useless for stateless configuration information, it might be better to behave differently based on the DHCPv6 message type. The implementation could also have a configuration option so that the administrator can manually specify the appropriate link-address which is independent from the relay agent's local addresses. In any case, the restriction in the current implementation suggests an implicit operational requirement for a relay agent that a non-link-local address be configured on each interface that may receive a message from a client.

Listing 4-142

```
                                                                    dhpc6relay.c
727          if (dh6->dh6_msgtype == DH6_RELAY_FORW) {
728                  struct dhcp6_relay *dh6relay0 = (struct dhcp6_relay *)dh6;
729
730                  /* Relaying a Message from a Relay Agent */
731
732                  /*
733                   * If the hop-count in the message is greater than or equal to
734                   * HOP_COUNT_LIMIT, the relay agent discards the received
735                   * message.
736                   * [RFC3315 Section 20.1.2]
737                   */
738                  if (dh6relay0->dh6relay_hcnt >= DHCP6_RELAY_HOP_COUNT_LIMIT) {
739                          dprintf(LOG_INFO, FNAME, "too many relay forwardings");
740                          goto out;
741                  }
742
743                  dh6relay->dh6relay_hcnt = dh6relay0->dh6relay_hcnt + 1;
744
745                  /*
746                   * We can keep the link-address field 0, regardless of the
747                   * scope of the source address, since we always include
748                   * interface-ID option.
749                   */
750          } else {
751                  /* Relaying a Message from a Client */
752                  memcpy(&dh6relay->dh6relay_linkaddr, &linkaddr,
753                      sizeof (dh6relay->dh6relay_linkaddr));
```

```
754                            dh6relay->dh6relay_hcnt = 0;
755                    }
756
757            relaylen = sizeof (*dh6relay);
758            if ((optlen = dhcp6_set_options(DH6_RELAY_FORW,
759                (struct dhcp6opt *)(dh6relay + 1),
760                (struct dhcp6opt *)(relaybuf + sizeof (relaybuf)),
761                &optinfo)) < 0) {
762                    dprintf(LOG_INFO, FNAME,
763                        "failed to construct relay options");
764                    goto out;
765            }
766            relaylen += optlen;
```
── dhpc6relay.c

727–749 If the message being relayed is a Relay-forward message, which indicates it was sent from another relay agent, the hop-count field of the message must be examined. If it reaches the specification limit (32), the packet cannot be relayed further and is discarded. Otherwise, the hop-count field is incremented.

As commented, the link-address field is left zero; the Interface-Id option, which is always included in this implementation, should have enough information for identifying the appropriate link.

750–755 If the message was sent from a client, the global address found above is assigned to the link-address field. The hop-count field is initialized to zero.

> [RFC3315] mentions the case where the link-address field is set to a non-zero address, depending on the source address of the received Relay-forward message packet. This implementation does not adopt it without breaking the specification by always including the Interface-Id option.

757–766 The dhcp6_set_options() function sets the prepared option in the new Relay-forward message.

Figure 4-42 summarizes the construction process of the Relay-forward message based on the original message via the relay agent's internal data structure.

Send Packet

Listing 4-143

── dhcp6relay.c
```
768            /*
769             * Forward the message.
770             */
771            memset(&mh, 0, sizeof (mh));
772            iov[0].iov_base = relaybuf;
773            iov[0].iov_len = relaylen;
774            mh.msg_iov = iov;
775            mh.msg_iovlen = 1;
776            mh.msg_name = &sa6_server;
777            mh.msg_namelen = sizeof (sa6_server);
778            if (IN6_IS_ADDR_MULTICAST(&sa6_server.sin6_addr)) {
779                    memset(&pktinfo, 0, sizeof (pktinfo));
780                    pktinfo.ipi6_ifindex = relayifid;
781                    if (make_msgcontrol(&mh, ctlbuf, sizeof (ctlbuf),
782                        &pktinfo, mhops)) {
783                            dprintf(LOG_WARNING, FNAME,
```

```
784                              "failed to make message control data");
785                         goto out;
786                    }
787            }
788
789         if ((cc = sendmsg(ssock, &mh, 0)) < 0) {
790                 dprintf(LOG_WARNING, FNAME,
791                     "sendmsg %s failed: %s",
792                     addr2str((struct sockaddr *)&sa6_server), strerror(errno));
793         } else if (cc != relaylen) {
794                 dprintf(LOG_WARNING, FNAME,
795                     "failed to send a complete packet to %s",
796                     addr2str((struct sockaddr *)&sa6_server));
797         } else {
798                 dprintf(LOG_DEBUG, FNAME,
799                     "relay a message to a server %s",
800                     addr2str((struct sockaddr *)&sa6_server));
801         }
802
803     out:
804         dhcp6_clear_options(&optinfo);
805     }
```
——— dhcp6relay.c

768–787 The global variable `sa6_server` stores the address which was initialized in the `relay6_init()` function, specifying the destination address of all Relay-forward packets. It is typically the All_DHCP_Servers multicast address (`ff05::1:3`), but can also be a

FIGURE 4-42

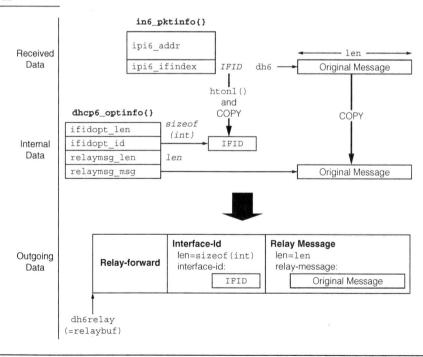

Construction of Relay-forward message.

unicast address when explicitly specified by the -s option on the command line (see also
the relay agent operation example in Section 4.8.8).

When sa6_server specifies a multicast address, the outgoing interface is also
specified as an IPV6_PKTINFO ancillary data item. This interface is given as a command line argument, whose interface is stored in the global relayifid variable. The
make_msgcontrol() function sets the ancillary data item in the message header, mh.

789–801 The message is then sent on the server side socket.

4.6.4 relay_to_client() Function

The relay_to_client() function is shown below, which implements the opposite side of
processing done by the relay_to_server() function described in the previous section.

Parse Options

Listing 4-144

```
                                                                    dhcp6relay.c
807     static void
808     relay_to_client(dh6relay, len, from)
809             struct dhcp6_relay *dh6relay;
810             ssize_t len;
811             struct sockaddr *from;
812     {
813             struct dhcp6_optinfo optinfo;
814             struct sockaddr_in6 peer;
815             unsigned int ifid;
816             char ifnamebuf[IFNAMSIZ];
817             int cc;
818             struct msghdr mh;
819             struct in6_pktinfo pktinfo;
820             static struct iovec iov[2];
821             char ctlbuf[CMSG_SPACE(sizeof (struct in6_pktinfo))];
822
823             dprintf(LOG_DEBUG, FNAME,
824                 "dhcp6 relay reply: hop=%d, linkaddr=%s, peeraddr=%s",
825                 dh6relay->dh6relay_hcnt,
826                 in6addr2str(&dh6relay->dh6relay_linkaddr, 0),
827                 in6addr2str(&dh6relay->dh6relay_peeraddr, 0));
828
829             /*
830              * parse and validate options in the relay reply message.
831              */
832             dhcp6_init_options(&optinfo);
833             if (dhcp6_get_options((struct dhcp6opt *)(dh6relay + 1),
834                 (struct dhcp6opt *)((char *)dh6relay + len), &optinfo) < 0) {
835                     dprintf(LOG_INFO, FNAME, "failed to parse options");
836                     return;
837             }
838
839             /* A relay reply message must include a relay message option */
840             if (optinfo.relaymsg_msg == NULL) {
841                     dprintf(LOG_INFO, FNAME, "relay reply message from %s "
842                         "without a relay message", addr2str(from));
843                     goto out;
844             }
845
846             /* minimum validation for the inner message */
847             if (optinfo.relaymsg_len < sizeof (struct dhcp6)) {
848                     dprintf(LOG_INFO, FNAME, "short relay message from %s",
849                         addr2str(from));
```

```
850                    goto out;
851            }
```
──dhcp6relay.c

829–851 The dhcp6_init_options() function examines the DHCPv6 options contained
in the received Relay-reply message. A valid Relay-reply message must contain a Relay
Message option, and the packet is discarded if it is not present. Additionally, the Relay
Message option must contain a complete DHCPv6 message. If the option data is too short
to contain a common DHCPv6 header, the packet is discarded.

Determine and Set the Client-Side Interface

Listing 4-145
──dhcp6relay.c

```
853            /*
854             * Extract interface ID which should be included in relay reply
855             * messages to us.
856             */
857            ifid = 0;
858            if (optinfo.ifidopt_id) {
859                    if (optinfo.ifidopt_len != sizeof (ifid)) {
860                            dprintf(LOG_INFO, FNAME,
861                                "unexpected length (%d) for Interface ID from %s",
862                                optinfo.ifidopt_len, addr2str(from));
863                            goto out;
864                    } else {
865                            memcpy(&ifid, optinfo.ifidopt_id, sizeof (ifid));
866                            ifid = ntohl(ifid);
867
868                            /* validation for ID */
869                            if ((if_indextoname(ifid, ifnamebuf)) == NULL) {
870                                    dprintf(LOG_INFO, FNAME,
871                                        "invalid interface ID: %x", ifid);
872                                    goto out;
873                            }
874                    }
875            } else {
876                    dprintf(LOG_INFO, FNAME,
877                        "Interface ID is not included from %s", addr2str(from));
878                    /*
879                     * the responding server should be buggy, but we deal with it.
880                     */
881            }
882
883            /*
884             * If we fail, try to get the interface from the link address.
885             */
886            if (ifid == 0 &&
887                !IN6_IS_ADDR_UNSPECIFIED(&dh6relay->dh6relay_linkaddr) &&
888                !IN6_IS_ADDR_LINKLOCAL(&dh6relay->dh6relay_linkaddr)) {
889                    if (getifidfromaddr(&dh6relay->dh6relay_linkaddr, &ifid))
890                            ifid = 0;
891            }
892
893            if (ifid == 0) {
894                    dprintf(LOG_INFO, FNAME, "failed to determine relay link");
895                    goto out;
896            }
```
──dhcp6relay.c

853–856 The next step of the processing is to determine the client side interface to which the
message encapsulated in the Relay Message option should be forwarded. Typically, the
destination address of the relayed message is the client's link-local address, and the relay

agent cannot determine the appropriate interface just from this address itself due to the ambiguity of link-local addresses.

857–874 The Relay-reply message should normally contain an Interface-Id option, since this relay agent implementation always includes this option (see the previous section) and the DHCPv6 specification requires the server to copy this option in the corresponding Relay-reply message. The value of this option is opaque, and it is just the interface identifier in this implementation. The `if_indextoname()` function checks whether the value specifies a valid interface. If it is invalid, the packet is discarded.

875–891 If the responding server is not fully compliant with the specification, the expected Interface-Id option might not be included. Also, even a compliant server can spontaneously send a Relay-reply message without an Interface-Id option when it encapsulates a Reconfigure message. In this case, this implementation tries to identify the appropriate interface from the link-address field of the Relay-reply message. If the address is not the unspecified address, and the `getifidfromaddr()` function (not described in this book) successfully finds the interface on which the given address is configured, that interface will be used.

893–896 If all the attempts fail, the relay agent gives up forwarding the message.

Make and Send Relay Packet

Listing 4-146

————————————————————————————————————dhcp6relay.c

```
897
898                peer = sa6_client;
899                memcpy(&peer.sin6_addr, &dh6relay->dh6relay_peeraddr,
900                    sizeof (peer.sin6_addr));
901                if (IN6_IS_ADDR_LINKLOCAL(&peer.sin6_addr))
902                    peer.sin6_scope_id = ifid; /* XXX: we assume a 1to1 map */
903
904                /* construct a message structure specifying the outgoing interface */
905                memset(&mh, 0, sizeof (mh));
906                iov[0].iov_base = optinfo.relaymsg_msg;
907                iov[0].iov_len = optinfo.relaymsg_len;
908                mh.msg_iov = iov;
909                mh.msg_iovlen = 1;
910                mh.msg_name = &peer;
911                mh.msg_namelen = sizeof (peer);
912                memset(&pktinfo, 0, sizeof (pktinfo));
913                pktinfo.ipi6_ifindex = ifid;
914                if (make_msgcontrol(&mh, ctlbuf, sizeof (ctlbuf), &pktinfo, 0)) {
915                    dprintf(LOG_WARNING, FNAME,
916                        "failed to make message control data");
917                    goto out;
918                }
919
920                /* send packet */
921                if ((cc = sendmsg(csock, &mh, 0)) < 0) {
922                    dprintf(LOG_WARNING, FNAME,
923                        "sendmsg to %s failed: %s",
924                        addr2str((struct sockaddr *)&peer), strerror(errno));
925                } else if (cc != optinfo.relaymsg_len) {
926                    dprintf(LOG_WARNING, FNAME,
927                        "failed to send a complete packet to %s",
928                        addr2str((struct sockaddr *)&peer));
```

```
929              } else {
930                  dprintf(LOG_DEBUG, FNAME,
931                      "relay a message to a client %s",
932                      addr2str((struct sockaddr *)&peer));
933              }
934
935      out:
936          dhcp6_clear_options(&optinfo);
937          return;
938      }
```
——dhcp6relay.c

904–933 If everything is processed correctly, the relay agent forwards the option data
(`optinfo.relaymsg_msg`) of the Relay Message option to the client-side link as a
separate DHCPv6 message. The destination of the relayed packet is copied from the peer
address field of the received Relay-reply message. The identified link (which also specifies
the interface) is specified as the outgoing interface in the `ipi6_ifindex` member of the
`in6_pktinfo{}` structure.

Figure 4-43 summarizes the processing of a Relay-reply message described so far, assuming
it contains a valid Interface-Id option. The resulting data structure is used as argument to the
`sendmsg()` system call.

FIGURE 4-43

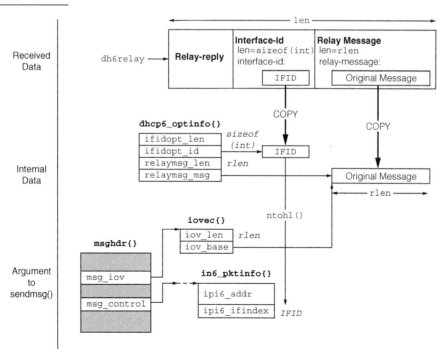

Processing of a Relay-reply message to forward an encapsulated message toward the client.

4.7   Implementation of DHCPv6 Authentication

This section provides a review of the implementation of DHCPv6 authentication more closely. As was seen in Figure 4-21 (page 327) and Figure 4-29 (page 382), the client and the server call their own `process_auth()` function to process an Authentication option in the incoming message, if it is present. In addition, the client implementation calls the `set_auth()` function to prepare an Authentication option for outgoing messages.

4.7.1   Data Structures Related to DHCPv6 Authentication

First, this subsection introduces some data structures specific to DHCPv6 authentication. The next listing shows the parameters of a key shared between a server and a client, which is a straightforward implementation of the protocol specification.

Listing 4-147

auth.h

```
34    /* secret key information for delayed authentication */
35    struct keyinfo {
36          struct keyinfo *next;
37
38          char *name;             /* key name */
39
40          char *realm;            /* DHCP realm */
41          size_t realmlen;        /* length of realm */
42          u_int32_t keyid;        /* key ID */
43          char *secret;           /* binary key */
44          size_t secretlen;       /* length of the key */
45          time_t expire;          /* expiration time (0 means forever) */
46    };
```

auth.h

36–45 The `name` member is readable identifier of the key, which is only used for logging purposes. The `realm` and `realmlen` members define a variable length data string for the DHCP realm of this key. The `keyid` member is the 32-bit key identifier. The `secret` and `secretlen` members define a variable length data string for the actual key value. The `expire` member is the time when this key expires, which is represented as the number of seconds since the Epoch (00:00:00 UTC, January 1, 1970). As noted in the comment, a special value of 0 means that this key never expires.

The `authparam{}` structure, shown in Listing 4-148, is a client-specific data structure to maintain run-time parameters for a DHCPv6 authentication session.

Listing 4-148

config.h

```
71    /* run-time authentication parameters */
72    struct authparam {
73          int authproto;
74          int authalgorithm;
75          int authrdm;
76          struct keyinfo *key;
77          int flags;
78    #define AUTHPARAM_FLAGS_NOPREVRD        0x1
79
80          u_int64_t prevrd;        /* previous RD value provided by the peer */
81    };
```

config.h

73–80 The first three members specify the protocol, algorithm, and replay detection method used in this session. The `key` member identifies the secret key shared with the server. The `flags` member records non-default information regarding the authentication session. The only flag currently defined is `AUTHPARAM_FLAGS_NOPREVRD`, which means the client does not have any information about the replay detection context of the server. In this implementation, this is always the case for the first message (which is usually the first Advertise message sent in response to a Solicit message) from the server in a DHCPv6 session. Finally, the `prevrd` member records the previous replay detection value sent by the server. If the `AUTHPARAM_FLAGS_NOPREVRD` is set, this member is meaningless.

Figure 4-44 depicts how these structures are used in a common client processing. When the client starts a DHCPv6 session with authentication, it first creates an `authparam{}` structure based on its local configuration information, and sets some minimal authentication parameters in a Solicit message. The client then receives an Advertise message, which is supposed to contain authentication information specified by the server. The client identifies the `keyinfo{}` structure in its local configuration that matches the authentication information contained in the Advertise message, and attaches it in the `authparam{}` structure.

From now on, the complete `authparam{}` structure with a valid `keyinfo{}` will be used to verify incoming messages and to authenticate outgoing messages. For incoming messages, replay detection (RD) value is recorded in the `authparam{}` structure and updated as message exchanges proceed for replay protection. This implementation initially does not have any knowledge about the RD value, so the value of the first incoming message (Advertise in this example) is unconditionally recorded in the `authparam{}` structure.

4.7.2 `set_auth()` Function

The `set_auth()` function is called from the `client6_send()` function in order to set up an Authentication option based on the client's configuration and authentication state.

FIGURE 4-44

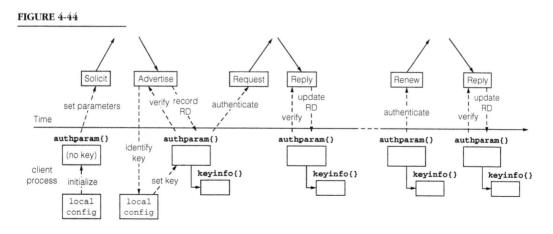

DHCPv6 authentication processing in the client implementation.

Copy Base Parameters

Listing 4-149

———dhcp6c.c

```
2108    static int
2109    set_auth(ev, optinfo)
2110            struct dhcp6_event *ev;
2111            struct dhcp6_optinfo *optinfo;
2112    {
2113            struct authparam *authparam = ev->authparam;
2114
2115            if (authparam == NULL)
2116                    return (0);
2117
2118            optinfo->authproto = authparam->authproto;
2119            optinfo->authalgorithm = authparam->authalgorithm;
2120            optinfo->authrdm = authparam->authrdm;
```

———dhcp6c.c

2115–2120 The `authparam` variable should always be non-NULL, but is explicitly checked for safety. The common parameters of protocol, algorithm, and replay detection method (`rdm`) are copied from `authparam` into the option information.

Case without Authentication

Listing 4-150

———dhcp6c.c

```
2122            switch (authparam->authproto) {
2123            case DHCP6_AUTHPROTO_UNDEF: /* we simply do not need authentication */
2124                    return (0);
```

———dhcp6c.c

2122–2124 If the client is not configured to use authentication, processing is completed.

Authentication for Information-request

Listing 4-151

———dhcp6c.c

```
2125            case DHCP6_AUTHPROTO_DELAYED:
2126                    if (ev->state == DHCP6S_INFOREQ) {
2127                            /*
2128                             * In the current implementation, delayed
2129                             * authentication for Information-request and Reply
2130                             * exchanges doesn't work.  Specification is also
2131                             * unclear on this usage.
2132                             */
2133                            dprintf(LOG_WARNING, FNAME, "delayed authentication "
2134                                "cannot be used for Information-request yet");
2135                            return (-1);
2136                    }
```

———dhcp6c.c

2126–2136 Currently, this implementation does not support DHCPv6 authentication for Information-request messages, since the protocol specification is not very clear about its usage as pointed out in [DHCP6AUTH].

Authentication for Solicit

Listing 4-152

_____dhcp6c.c

```
2138                    if (ev->state == DHCP6S_SOLICIT) {
2139                            optinfo->authflags |= DHCP6OPT_AUTHFLAG_NOINFO;
2140                            return (0); /* no auth information is needed */
2141                    }
```

_____dhcp6c.c

2138–2141 The only authentication protocol available in this implementation is the delayed
authentication protocol. For Solicit messages, the client only needs to indicate its intent to
use the protocol, and does not include authentication information in the Authentication
option.

Set Authentication Parameters

Listing 4-153

_____dhcp6c.c

```
2143                    if (authparam->key == NULL) {
2144                            dprintf(LOG_INFO, FNAME,
2145                                "no authentication key for %s",
2146                                dhcp6_event_statestr(ev));
2147                            return (-1);
2148                    }
2149
2150                    if (dhcp6_validate_key(authparam->key)) {
2151                            dprintf(LOG_INFO, FNAME, "key %s is invalid",
2152                                authparam->key->name);
2153                            return (-1);
2154                    }
2155
2156                    if (get_rdvalue(optinfo->authrdm, &optinfo->authrd,
2157                        sizeof(optinfo->authrd))) {
2158                            dprintf(LOG_ERR, FNAME, "failed to get a replay "
2159                                "detection value");
2160                            return (-1);
2161                    }
2162
2163                    optinfo->delayedauth_keyid = authparam->key->keyid;
2164                    optinfo->delayedauth_realmlen = authparam->key->realmlen;
2165                    optinfo->delayedauth_realmval =
2166                        malloc(optinfo->delayedauth_realmlen);
2167                    if (optinfo->delayedauth_realmval == NULL) {
2168                            dprintf(LOG_ERR, FNAME, "failed to allocate memory "
2169                                "for authentication realm");
2170                            return (-1);
2171                    }
2172                    memcpy(optinfo->delayedauth_realmval, authparam->key->realm,
2173                        optinfo->delayedauth_realmlen);
2174
2175                    break;
2176            default:
2177                    dprintf(LOG_ERR, FNAME, "unsupported authentication protocol "
2178                        "%d", authparam->authproto);
2179                    return (-1);
2180            }
2181
2182            return (0);
2183    }
```

_____dhcp6c.c

2143–2148 If a secret key is not available for this message, it should mean the client has decided not to use authentication after having received an Advertise message even though it requested authentication in the Solicit message. As will be seen in the process_auth() function following, this implementation does not support this operation. Thus, the key member is usually non-NULL.

2150–2154 If the key has expired, authentication fails.

2156–2161 The get_rdvalue() function provides a replay detection counter, depending on the method (authrdm) and the counter size. In this implementation, the only supported method is a 64-bit monotonically increasing counter. The get_rdvalue() function actually returns the current time in an NTP-format timestamp, as suggested in [RFC3315]. (Technically, the new counter should be determined by taking into account the previous value, so that the new one is indeed "greater" than the previous one.)

2163–2175 The key ID and the DHCP realm are copied to the option information.

4.7.3   process_auth() Function (Client Side)

The client's process_auth() function processes the Authentication option, if it is included in the message from a server, and authenticates the message.

The Case without Authentication

Listing 4-154

```
                                                                    dhcp6c.c
1982    static int
1983    process_auth(authparam, dh6, len, optinfo)
1984            struct authparam *authparam;
1985            struct dhcp6 *dh6;
1986            ssize_t len;
1987            struct dhcp6_optinfo *optinfo;
1988    {
1989            struct keyinfo *key = NULL;
1990            int authenticated = 0;
1991
1992            switch (optinfo->authproto) {
1993            case DHCP6_AUTHPROTO_UNDEF:
1994                    /* server did not provide authentication option */
1995                    break;
                                                                    dhcp6c.c
```

1992–1995 If the protocol is *Undefined* (DHCP6_AUTHPROTO_UNDEF), it means the received message does not contain an Authentication option. Whether or not this is acceptable for the client will be checked in Listing 4-160.

Process Unexpected Cases

Listing 4-155

```
                                                                    dhcp6c.c
1996            case DHCP6_AUTHPROTO_DELAYED:
1997                    if ((optinfo->authflags & DHCP6OPT_AUTHFLAG_NOINFO)) {
1998                            dprintf(LOG_INFO, FNAME, "server did not include "
1999                                "authentication information");
2000                            break;
2001                    }
```

```
2002
2003                        if (optinfo->authalgorithm != DHCP6_AUTHALG_HMACMD5) {
2004                                dprintf(LOG_INFO, FNAME, "unknown authentication "
2005                                    "algorithm (%d)", optinfo->authalgorithm);
2006                                break;
2007                        }
2008
2009                        if (optinfo->authrdm != DHCP6_AUTHRDM_MONOCOUNTER) {
2010                                dprintf(LOG_INFO, FNAME,"unknown RDM (%d)",
2011                                    optinfo->authrdm);
2012                                break;
2013                        }
```
——dhcp6c.c

1997–2013 This `case` block handles the delayed authentication protocol. If the Authentication option does not contain authentication information, or the algorithm or the replay detection method is unknown, then the message is regarded as unauthenticated.

Replay Detection

Listing 4-156
——dhcp6c.c
```
2015                        /*
2016                         * Replay protection.  If we do not know the previous RD value,
2017                         * we accept the message anyway (XXX).
2018                         */
2019                        if ((authparam->flags & AUTHPARAM_FLAGS_NOPREVRD)) {
2020                                dprintf(LOG_WARNING, FNAME, "previous RD value is "
2021                                    "unknown (accept it)");
2022                        } else {
2023                                if (dhcp6_auth_replaycheck(optinfo->authrdm,
2024                                    authparam->prevrd, optinfo->authrd)) {
2025                                        dprintf(LOG_INFO, FNAME,
2026                                            "possible replay attack detected");
2027                                        break;
2028                                }
2029                        }
```
——dhcp6c.c

2019–2021 If this is the first message using authentication in the DHCPv6 session, this implementation does not have any information about the last replay detection counter from the server (ideally, the client should record the latest counter in nonvolatile storage). Thus, the client accepts any counter at the risk of being susceptible to a replay attack.

2022–2029 The `dhcp6_auth_replaycheck()` function checks if the replay detection counter in the received message is newer than the previously received value stored in `authparam`. If not, the message is regarded as unauthenticated.

Key Identification

Listing 4-157
——dhcp6c.c
```
2030
2031                        /* identify the secret key */
2032                        if ((key = authparam->key) != NULL) {
2033                                /*
2034                                 * If we already know a key, its identification should
2035                                 * match that contained in the received option.
2036                                 * (from Section 21.4.5.1 of RFC3315)
2037                                 */
```

```
2038                         if (optinfo->delayedauth_keyid != key->keyid ||
2039                             optinfo->delayedauth_realmlen != key->realmlen ||
2040                             memcmp(optinfo->delayedauth_realmval, key->realm,
2041                             key->realmlen) != 0) {
2042                                 dprintf(LOG_INFO, FNAME,
2043                                     "authentication key mismatch");
2044                                 break;
2045                         }
2046                     } else {
2047                         key = find_key(optinfo->delayedauth_realmval,
2048                             optinfo->delayedauth_realmlen,
2049                             optinfo->delayedauth_keyid);
2050                         if (key == NULL) {
2051                             dprintf(LOG_INFO, FNAME, "failed to find key "
2052                                 "provided by the server (ID: %x)",
2053                                 optinfo->delayedauth_keyid);
2054                             break;
2055                         } else {
2056                             dprintf(LOG_DEBUG, FNAME, "found key for "
2057                                 "authentication: %s", key->name);
2058                         }
2059                         authparam->key = key;
2060                     }
2061
2062                     /* check for the key lifetime */
2063                     if (dhcp6_validate_key(key)) {
2064                         dprintf(LOG_INFO, FNAME, "key %s has expired",
2065                             key->name);
2066                         break;
2067                     }
```
                                                                    ———————— dhcp6c.c

2031–2045 If a key (shared secret) is already set for the session, it must match the key specified in the message; the key ID and the DHCP realm must be identical. If the two keys do not match, the message is regarded as unauthenticated.

2046–2060 The `find_key()` function searches for a key in the client's local configuration that matches the key parameters in the received message. If no local key is found, the message is regarded as unauthenticated. Otherwise, it is stored in the `authparam{}` structure.

2062–2067 If the key has already expired, the message is regarded as unauthenticated.

Authenticate Message

Listing 4-158

                                                                    ———————— dhcp6c.c
```
2069                     /* validate MAC */
2070                     if (dhcp6_verify_mac((char *)dh6, len, optinfo->authproto,
2071                         optinfo->authalgorithm,
2072                         optinfo->delayedauth_offset + sizeof(*dh6), key) == 0) {
2073                             dprintf(LOG_DEBUG, FNAME, "message authentication "
2074                                 "validated");
2075                             authenticated = 1;
2076                     } else {
2077                             dprintf(LOG_INFO, FNAME, "invalid message "
2078                                 "authentication");
2079                     }
2080
2081                     break;
```
                                                                    ———————— dhcp6c.c

2070–2079 If the key is still valid, the `dhcp6_verify_mac()` function computes the HMAC digest of the message using the key, and verifies whether it matches the digest stored in the message. The variable `authenticated` is set to 1 only when the verification succeeds.

Unsupported Protocol

Listing 4-159

_____ dhcp6c.c

```
2082            default:
2083                    dprintf(LOG_INFO, FNAME, "server sent unsupported "
2084                        "authentication protocol (%d)", optinfo->authproto);
2085                    break;
2086            }
```

_____ dhcp6c.c

2082–2085 If the authentication protocol specified by the server is not supported by the client, the message is regarded as unauthenticated.

Post Authentication Process

Listing 4-160

_____ dhcp6c.c

```
2088            if (authenticated == 0) {
2089                    if (authparam->authproto != DHCP6_AUTHPROTO_UNDEF) {
2090                            dprintf(LOG_INFO, FNAME, "message not authenticated "
2091                                "while authentication required");
2092
2093                            /*
2094                             * Right now, we simply discard unauthenticated
2095                             * messages.
2096                             */
2097                            return (-1);
2098                    }
2099            } else {
2100                    /* if authenticated, update the "previous" RD value */
2101                    authparam->prevrd = optinfo->authrd;
2102                    authparam->flags &= ~AUTHPARAM_FLAGS_NOPREVRD;
2103            }
2104
2105            return (0);
2106    }
```

_____ dhcp6c.c

2088–2098 If the message was regarded as unauthenticated due to one of the above reasons and the client wanted to use DHCPv6 authentication, the message is discarded. Note that this implementation does not differentiate between the case where the message HMAC verification fails and the other failure cases (e.g., where the message does not contain an Authentication option). While the protocol specification differentiates between them and allows the client to accept the latter in some cases, this implementation just refuses all such cases.

2099–2103 If the message was successfully authenticated, the latest replay detection counter is recorded and the `NOPREVRD` flag is cleared, indicating the client now has the latest counter.

4.7.4 `process_auth()` Function (Server Side)

The server's `process_auth()` function processes the Authentication option, if it is included in the message from the client, and authenticates the message. This function is almost the same as the client's version, but still includes some server-specific behaviors.

Figure 4-45 shows a common processing scenario of DHCPv6 authentication with the server implementation. The server initializes the `host_conf{}` structure (Listing 4-74, pages 383–384) for every client with the key information (if specified) `keyinfo{}` at startup time.

When the server receives a Solicit message from a clint, it identifies the corresponding `host_conf{}` structure for the client. If the Solicit message indicates the client wants to use DHCPv6 authentication and a valid `keyinfo{}` structure is associated with `host_conf{}`, the server authenticates the returned Advertise message using the key information.

Succeeding exchanges will be authenticated using these structures. The server keeps track of the received replay detection (RD) value in the `host_conf{}` structure for replay protection. Like the client case, this server implementation does not have any knowledge about the initial RD value, so the RD value that the server sees first time is recorded unconditionally.

Message without Authentication

Listing 4-161

_____dhcp6s.c

```
2857    static int
2858    process_auth(dh6, len, client_conf, optinfo, roptinfo)
2859            struct dhcp6 *dh6;
2860            ssize_t len;
2861            struct host_conf *client_conf;
2862            struct dhcp6_optinfo *optinfo, *roptinfo;
2863    {
2864            u_int8_t msgtype = dh6->dh6_msgtype;
2865            int authenticated = 0;
2866            struct keyinfo *key;
2867
2868            /*
2869             * if the client wanted DHCPv6 authentication, check if a secret
2870             * key is available for the client.
2871             */
2872            switch (optinfo->authproto) {
2873            case DHCP6_AUTHPROTO_UNDEF:
2874                    /*
2875                     * The client did not include authentication option.  What if
2876                     * we had sent authentication information?  The specification
2877                     * is not clear, but we should probably accept it, since the
2878                     * client MAY ignore the information in advertise messages.
2879                     */
2880                    return (0);
```

_____dhcp6s.c

2872–2880 If the received message does not contain an Authentication option, the server simply accepts the result and continues processing. As commented, this applies to the case where the client previously included an Authentication option and the server has responded to the message with an authenticated message.

FIGURE 4-45

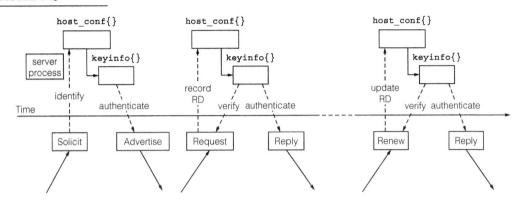

DHCPv6 authentication processing in the server implementation.

Unexpected Cases

Listing 4-162

```
                                                                    dhcp6s.c
2881              case DHCP6_AUTHPROTO_DELAYED:
2882                  if (optinfo->authalgorithm != DHCP6_AUTHALG_HMACMD5) {
2883                      dprintf(LOG_INFO, FNAME, "unknown authentication "
2884                          "algorithm (%d) required by %s",
2885                          optinfo->authalgorithm,
2886                          clientstr(client_conf, &optinfo->clientID));
2887                      break;          /* give up with this authentication */
2888                  }
2889
2890                  if (optinfo->authrdm != DHCP6_AUTHRDM_MONOCOUNTER) {
2891                      dprintf(LOG_INFO, FNAME,
2892                          "unknown RDM (%d) required by %s",
2893                          optinfo->authrdm,
2894                          clientstr(client_conf, &optinfo->clientID));
2895                      break;          /* give up with this authentication */
2896                  }
                                                                    dhcp6s.c
```

2882–2896 For the delayed authentication protocol, which is the only protocol supported in this implementation, the supported authentication algorithm is HMAC-MD5 and the replay detection method is the use of a monotonically increasing counter. If anything else is specified, the message is regarded as unauthenticated.

Find a Key

Listing 4-163

```
                                                                    dhcp6s.c
2898                  /* see if we have a key for the client */
2899                  if (client_conf == NULL || client_conf->delayedkey == NULL) {
2900                      dprintf(LOG_INFO, FNAME, "client %s wanted "
2901                          "authentication, but no key found",
2902                          clientstr(client_conf, &optinfo->clientID));
2903                      break;
```

```
2904                    }
2905                    key = client_conf->delayedkey;
2906                    dprintf(LOG_DEBUG, FNAME, "found key %s for client %s",
2907                        key->name, clientstr(client_conf, &optinfo->clientID));
```
── dhcp6s.c

2898–2907 If the server is configured with a shared secret for the client, that key is used to
authenticate the message. Otherwise, the message is regarded as unauthenticated.

The Solicit Case
Listing 4-164
── dhcp6s.c
```
2909              if (msgtype == DH6_SOLICIT) {
2910                      if (!(optinfo->authflags & DHCP6OPT_AUTHFLAG_NOINFO)) {
2911                              /*
2912                               * A solicit message should not contain
2913                               * authentication information.
2914                               */
2915                              dprintf(LOG_INFO, FNAME,
2916                                  "authentication information "
2917                                  "provided in solicit from %s",
2918                                  clientstr(client_conf,
2919                                  &optinfo->clientID));
2920                              /* accept it anyway. (or discard?) */
2921                      }
```
── dhcp6s.c

2909–2921 A Solicit message is not expected to contain authentication information. However,
the specification is not clear about what to do if it is included, and so this implementation
just logs the fact and proceeds.

Replay Protection
Listing 4-165
── dhcp6s.c
```
2922              } else {
2923                      /* replay protection */
2924                      if (!client_conf->saw_previous_rd) {
2925                              dprintf(LOG_WARNING, FNAME,
2926                                  "previous RD value for %s is unknown "
2927                                  "(accept it)", clientstr(client_conf,
2928                                  &optinfo->clientID));
2929                      } else {
2930                              if (dhcp6_auth_replaycheck(optinfo->authrdm,
2931                                  client_conf->previous_rd,
2932                                  optinfo->authrd)) {
2933                                      dprintf(LOG_INFO, FNAME,
2934                                          "possible replay attack detected "
2935                                          "for client %s",
2936                                          clientstr(client_conf,
2937                                          &optinfo->clientID));
2938                                      break;
2939                              }
2940                      }
```
── dhcp6s.c

2922–2940 For messages other than Solicit, the replay protection method is performed. If
the server does not have any information about the last replay detection counter from

the client, it accepts any counter (similar to the case for the client implementation in
Listing 4-156, page 459). Otherwise, the dhcp6_auth_replaycheck() function does
the replay protection check, and if it fails the message is regarded as unauthenticated.

Authentication without Information

Listing 4-166

```
                                                                              dhcp6s.c
2942                    if ((optinfo->authflags & DHCP6OPT_AUTHFLAG_NOINFO)) {
2943                            dprintf(LOG_INFO, FNAME,
2944                                "client %s did not provide authentication "
2945                                "information in %s",
2946                                clientstr(client_conf, &optinfo->clientID),
2947                                dhcp6msgstr(msgtype));
2948                            break;
2949                    }
                                                                              dhcp6s.c
```

2942–2949 When an Authentication option is included in messages other than Solicit, it must
contain authentication information. If not, the message is regarded as unauthenticated.

Key Identification and Validation

Listing 4-167

```
                                                                              dhcp6s.c
2951                    /*
2952                     * The client MUST use the same key used by the server
2953                     * to generate the authentication information.
2954                     * [RFC3315 Section 21.4.4.3]
2955                     * The RFC does not say what the server should do if
2956                     * the client breaks this rule, but it should be
2957                     * natural to interpret this as authentication failure.
2958                     */
2959                    if (optinfo->delayedauth_keyid != key->keyid ||
2960                        optinfo->delayedauth_realmlen != key->realmlen ||
2961                        memcmp(optinfo->delayedauth_realmval, key->realm,
2962                        key->realmlen) != 0) {
2963                            dprintf(LOG_INFO, FNAME, "authentication key "
2964                                "mismatch with client %s",
2965                                clientstr(client_conf,
2966                                &optinfo->clientID));
2967                            break;
2968                    }
2969
2970                    /* check for the key lifetime */
2971                    if (dhcp6_validate_key(key)) {
2972                            dprintf(LOG_INFO, FNAME, "key %s has expired",
2973                                key->name);
2974                            break;
2975                    }
                                                                              dhcp6s.c
```

2951–2968 If a key (shared secret) is configured for the client, it must match the key specified
in the message. Otherwise, the message is regarded as unauthenticated.

2970–2975 If the key for the client has already expired, the message is regarded as
unauthenticated.

Authenticate Message

Listing 4-168

```
                                                                            dhcp6s.c
2977                        /* validate MAC */
2978                        if (dhcp6_verify_mac((char *)dh6, len,
2979                            optinfo->authproto, optinfo->authalgorithm,
2980                            optinfo->delayedauth_offset + sizeof(*dh6), key)
2981                            == 0) {
2982                                dprintf(LOG_DEBUG, FNAME,
2983                                    "message authentication validated for "
2984                                    "client %s", clientstr(client_conf,
2985                                    &optinfo->clientID));
2986                        } else {
2987                                dprintf(LOG_INFO, FNAME, "invalid message "
2988                                    "authentication");
2989                                break;
2990                        }
2991                }
                                                                            dhcp6s.c
```

2977–2990 The `dhcp6_verify_mac()` function computes the HMAC of the message using the key, and verifies whether it matches the HMAC value stored in the message. If it does not match, the message is regarded as unauthenticated.

Prepare Authentication Reply

Listing 4-169

```
                                                                            dhcp6s.c
2993                roptinfo->authproto = optinfo->authproto;
2994                roptinfo->authalgorithm = optinfo->authalgorithm;
2995                roptinfo->authrdm = optinfo->authrdm;
2996
2997                if (get_rdvalue(roptinfo->authrdm, &roptinfo->authrd,
2998                    sizeof(roptinfo->authrd))) {
2999                        dprintf(LOG_ERR, FNAME, "failed to get a replay "
3000                            "detection value for %s",
3001                            clientstr(client_conf, &optinfo->clientID));
3002                        break;          /* XXX: try to recover? */
3003                }
3004
3005                roptinfo->delayedauth_keyid = key->keyid;
3006                roptinfo->delayedauth_realmlen = key->realmlen;
3007                roptinfo->delayedauth_realmval =
3008                    malloc(roptinfo->delayedauth_realmlen);
3009                if (roptinfo->delayedauth_realmval == NULL) {
3010                        dprintf(LOG_ERR, FNAME, "failed to allocate memory "
3011                            "for authentication realm for %s",
3012                            clientstr(client_conf, &optinfo->clientID));
3013                        break;
3014                }
3015                memcpy(roptinfo->delayedauth_realmval, key->realm,
3016                    roptinfo->delayedauth_realmlen);
3017
3018                authenticated = 1;
3019
3020                break;
                                                                            dhcp6s.c
```

2993–2995 The protocol, algorithm, and replay detection method are copied from the received message to the option information for the response (Advertise or Reply) message.

2997–3003 The `get_rdvalue()` function provides a replay detection counter for the Reply message.

3005–3016 The key ID and DHCP realm are copied from the server's configuration to the option information.

Unsupported Protocol

Listing 4-170

```
                                                                    dhcp6s.c
3021            default:
3022                    dprintf(LOG_INFO, FNAME, "client %s wanted authentication "
3023                        "with unsupported protocol (%d)",
3024                        clientstr(client_conf, &optinfo->clientID),
3025                        optinfo->authproto);
3026                    return (-1);          /* or simply ignore it? */
3027            }
                                                                    dhcp6s.c
```

3021–3027 If the authentication protocol specified by the client is not supported, the message is simply discarded. Recall, for example, that the `react_solicit()` function discards the packet if `process_auth()` returns −1 (Listing 4-90, page 397).

Post Authentication Process

Listing 4-171

```
                                                                    dhcp6s.c
3029            if (authenticated == 0) {
3030                    if (msgtype != DH6_SOLICIT) {
3031                            /*
3032                             * If the message fails to pass the validation test,
3033                             * the server MUST discard the message.
3034                             * [RFC3315 Section 21.4.5.2]
3035                             */
3036                            return (-1);
3037                    }
3038            } else {
3039                    /* Message authenticated.  Update RD counter. */
3040                    if (msgtype != DH6_SOLICIT && client_conf != NULL) {
3041                            client_conf->previous_rd = optinfo->authrd;
3042                            client_conf->saw_previous_rd = 1;
3043                    }
3044            }
3045
3046            return (0);
3047    }
                                                                    dhcp6s.c
```

3029–3037 If a message other than Solicit was regarded as unauthenticated due to one of the above reasons, it must be discarded.

3038–3044 If the message is not Solicit and was successfully authenticated, the latest replay detection counter is recorded. The `saw_previous_rd` member is set in the client configuration, indicating that the server now has the latest.

4.8   DHCPv6 Operation

This section shows examples of DHCPv6 operation on some common usages with KAME's implementation.

The implementation consists of the following programs:

- **dhcp6c**, the DHCPv6 client daemon
- **dhcp6s**, the DHCPv6 server daemon
- **dhcp6relay**, the DHCPv6 relay agent daemon
- **dhcp6ctl**, a supplemental tool for run-time control of **dhcp6c** and **dhcp6s**

Each program has several command line options. In addition, **dhcp6c** and **dhcp6s** require configuration files that specify lots of parameters. Instead of providing a complete reference to the options or configuration file notation, this section concentrates on concrete examples of major operational cases. For a comprehensive reference, the manual pages contained in the implementation archive (see Section 4.8.1) should be consulted.

4.8.1   Building the DHCPv6 Implementation

KAME's DHCPv6 implementation is included in its weekly snapshot kits, which are built through the build and installation procedure of the entire kit. However, the code in this chapter is based on a separate snapshot version than the version used in other chapters. Thus, a description of how to build and install the programs as a separate package is given here.

1. Unpack the archive contained on the companion web site (see the Preface) and go to the program directory:

   ```
   % gzcat kame-dhcp6-20050509.tgz | tar xf -
   % cd dhcp6
   ```

2. Configure the package:

   ```
   % ./configure --with-opt-refreshtime=32
   ```

   As can be seen, this step requires a configuration option. When the implementation described in this chapter was written, the Information Refresh Time option was not standardized and did not get an official type number (32). It must therefore be specified explicitly via the configuration option.

3. Build the package:

   ```
   % make
   ```

   There should be no problems with this step.

4. Install the package as a super user:

   ```
   % su
   Password: (type in the root password)
   # make install
   ```

   This will install all the programs under `/usr/local/sbin/`.

In the rest of this chapter, it is assumed that the programs were installed using these steps.

In December 2005, the development effort was transferred to the WIDE-DHCPv6 project of SourceForge (http://sourceforge.net/projects/wide-dhcpv6/). The DHCPv6 implementation in the KAME snapshot was then removed in March 2006, but the development has continued in the SourceForge project.

4.8.2 Configuring a DUID

A DHCPv6 client or server needs its DUID for the protocol operation. The user does not have to configure the ID by hand: **dhcp6c** and **dhcp6s** automatically generate their type 1 DUIDs (DUID-LLT, Section 4.2.2) on their first invocation, and store them in volatile files, /var/db/dhcp6c_duid and /var/db/dhcp6s_duid.

One possible problem regarding DUIDs is that the server may need to be configured with the client's DUIDs (see Section 4.8.3). The only effective way to know the DUID of a particular client at the server is to run the program in full debugging mode (with the -D option) and look at the logs when the server receives a DHCPv6 message from the client.

For example, a server which receives a request message from a client would produce the following log:

```
Apr/05/2005 23:16:07: server6_recv: received solicit from fe80::203:47ff:fea5:3085%fxp0
Apr/05/2005 23:16:07: dhcp6_get_options: get DHCP option client ID, len 14
Apr/05/2005 23:16:07:   DUID: 00:01:00:01:09:5f:93:76:00:03:47:a5:30:85
```

This means the client's DUID is represented as 00:01:00:01:09:5f:93:76:00:03:47:a5:30:85. If the server is to be configured to allocate any stateful resources for this client, it should contain the following line in the corresponding host statement (see Section 4.8.3 for more details):

```
duid 00:01:00:01:09:5f:93:76:00:03:47:a5:30:85;
```

4.8.3 Configuring the DHCPv6 Server

Recall the example shown in Figure 4-30 (page 386). This subsection provides configuration examples of **dhcp6s** using that example.

The **dhcp6s** daemon requires a configuration file, /usr/local/etc/dhcp6s.conf, which contains the server's configuration information. The configuration file consists of a sequence of statements, each terminated by a semi-colon (;). Statements are composed of tokens separated by white space; white space can be any combination of blanks, tabs and new lines. In some cases a set of statements is combined with a pair of brackets, and is regarded as a single token. Lines beginning with "#" are comments.

Per-host Stateful Configuration

Regarding the configuration for host **kame** in Figure 4-30, the dhcp6s.conf file should contain the following lines:

```
host kame {
        duid 00:01:00:01:09:5f:93:76:00:03:47:a5:30:85;
        address 2001:db8:ffff::1 86400 604800;
        address 2001:db8:ffff::2 604800 2592000;
};
```

where the DUID of this client is assumed to be 00:01:....:30:85. The above configuration means the server can assign two IPv6 addresses to the client named **kame**, 2001:db8:ffff::1 and 2001:db8:ffff::2. The preferred and valid lifetimes of the first address are 1 day and 7 days, and the lifetimes of the second address are 7 days and 30 days; the lifetimes are represented in seconds in the configuration file.

Similarly, the following lines mean the server will delegate a prefix 2001:db8:1234::/48 to the client named **usagi** (assuming its DUID is 00:01:....:f1:9d), with the preferred and valid lifetimes being 30 days and 90 days (represented in seconds).

```
host usagi {
        duid 00:01:00:01:09:3c:91:d9:00:e0:18:98:f1:9d;
        prefix 2001:db8:1234::/48 2592000 7776000;
};
```

Finally, the following lines in the `dhcp6s.conf` file configures stateless configuration information which is to be provided to any clients:

```
option domain-name-servers 2001:db8:9999::35 2001:db8:abcd::35;
option domain-name "kame.example";
```

Again, this corresponds to the example shown in Figure 4-30, that is, two recursive DNS server addresses and a DNS search list.

4.8.4   Configuring the DHCPv6 Client

Like **dhcp6s**, the **dhcp6c** daemon requires a configuration file, `/usr/local/etc/dhcp6c.conf`. The basic syntactic notation is the same as that for **dhcp6s**.

Configuration for Address Allocation

The following is a common configuration example for a client which is going to be allocated IPv6 addresses on the interface "ne0".

```
interface ne0 {
        send ia-na 100;
};
id-assoc na 100 { };
```

This configuration defines an IA_NA with the IAID of 100 and specifies to include this IA_NA in Solicit messages. That particular value of IAID does not have any meaning; it can be an arbitrary number as long as it is unique within the client. The IA_NA definition contains an empty parameter, since a DHCPv6 client normally does not care about the address(es) actually allocated.

If the client wants to get more than one address, it needs to specify multiple IAs. Here is a sample configuration for a client that wants to get at least two addresses:

```
interface ne0 {
        send ia-na 100;
        send ia-na 200;
};
id-assoc na 100 { };
id-assoc na 200 { };
```

Though less common, if the client wants to tell its preference about the assigned address(es) to the server, it can include particular addresses in the Solicit message by specifying those in the corresponding `id-assoc` statement. The following is a configuration example for the client's preference shown in Figure 4-22 (page 334).

```
interface ne0 {
        send ia-na 100;
        send ia-na 200;
};
id-assoc na 100 {
        address 2001:db8:1234::1 0;
};
id-assoc na 200 {
        address 2001:db8:abcd::a 0;
};
```

The decimal number at the end of each address indicates the client's preference on the preferred lifetime of the address (represented in seconds). In this example, zero is specified, which means the client does not have any preference.

As explained in Figure 4-27 (page 370), it is important to specify multiple IAs in the last two examples. On the other hand, the following configuration example is almost meaningless although it is still valid.

```
interface ne0 {
        send ia-na 100;
};
id-assoc na 100 {
        address 2001:db8:1234::1 0;
        address 2001:db8:abcd::a 0;
};
```

Configuration for Prefix Delegation

The basic concept of configuring prefix delegation is the same as that of address allocation: defining an IA_PD with some parameters and specifying the IA_PD in the `interface` statement.

This is a typical example of a client's configuration for prefix delegation:

```
interface tun0 {
        send ia-pd 200;
};
id-assoc pd 200 {
        prefix-interface ne0 {
                sla-id 1;
        };
};
```

In the `id-assoc` statement, `pd` specifies this is an IA_PD, and 200 is its IAID. The main difference from the previous examples is that the `id-assoc` statement contains a `prefix-interface` statement. This is necessary because, in prefix delegation, the requesting router (DHCPv6 client) usually subnets a delegated prefix for its local links.

Figure 4-46 shows the network topology for a requesting router which would have this configuration. The requesting router has (at least) two interfaces: a PPP interface (`tun0`), which is connected to the uplink to the delegating router (upstream provider), and an Ethernet interface, `ne0` (the *prefix-interface*), which is connected to the local network.

The requesting router is usually delegated a block of prefixes which can be subnetted. The delegated prefix is conventionally 48 bits in length, and the requesting router subnets the large

FIGURE 4-46

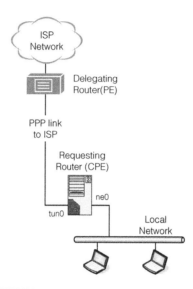

Network topology for a requesting router.

prefix into one or more subnet prefixes whose length is 64. The `sla-id` statement defines each subnet prefix by filling in the remaining 16 bits. For example, if the delegated prefix is `2001:db8:1234::/48`, the 64-bit prefix `2001:db8:1234:1::/64` will be assigned on the link attached to interface `ne0`.

A more complicated configuration can be specified with this notation. For instance, for a requesting router which has two local interfaces, `ne0` and `ne1` (Figure 4-47), a configuration which allows the requesting router to subnet the delegated prefix to those local links is as follows:

```
id-assoc pd 200 {
        prefix-interface ne0 {
                sla-id 1;
        };
        prefix-interface ne1 {
                sla-id 2;
        };
};
```

With this configuration and the example prefix shown above, the other link which attaches to `ne1` will have a different 64-bit prefix, `2001:db8:1234:2::/64`.

The requesting router can have an even more complicated topology which consists of multiple local links connected via other internal routers (Figure 4-48). In such a topology, the requesting router needs to tell the other router(s) how to assign the subnet prefix from the delegated prefix. Unfortunately, this is not a trivial task, and the current implementation does not yet support this level of complexity.

Finally, a requesting router can indicate its preference about the delegated prefix(es) by specifying particular prefix(es) in the `id-assoc` statement. The following configuration

FIGURE 4-47

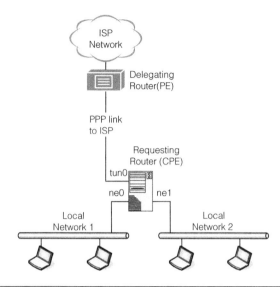

Requesting router with two local interfaces.

FIGURE 4-48

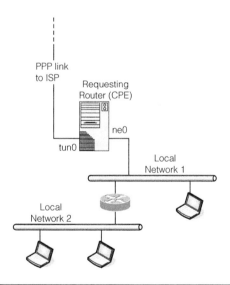

Network topology of multiple local networks connected by a separate router.

example means the requesting router wants to be delegated a particular prefix, `2001:db8:1234::/48`, without any preference about its preferred lifetime.

```
id-assoc pd 200 {
        prefix 2001:db8:1234::/48 0;
        ...;
};
```

Configuration for Stateless Services

If the client does not have to be assigned an IPv6 address or prefix but wants to get other configuration information such as recursive DNS server addresses, it can use Information-request and Reply exchanges, which are more lightweight.

The following configuration specifies that these exchanges should be performed on interface ne0. No Solicit messages will be sent in this case.

```
interface ne0 {
        information-only;
};
```

Configuring the Script File

The **dhcp6c** daemon handles address- or prefix-related configuration information within its process. For example, it installs an allocated IPv6 address in the kernel by itself.

For other configuration information, the daemon does nothing except execute an external script, since how the information should be processed may vary among users. Regarding recursive DNS server addresses, one may want to override the `/etc/resolv.conf` file with the address provided by the DHCPv6 server, or just pass it to a separate process (e.g., a local DNS caching/forwarding server).

The script file is specified by the `script` statement. Here is an example showing the usage of this statement:

```
interface ne0 {
        ....
        script "/usr/local/sbin/dhcp6c-script";
};
```

For security reasons, several restrictions are imposed on the script path. First, it must be an absolute path from the root directory (i.e., it must begin with "/"). Second, the path name must be a regular file; in particular, it cannot be a symbolic link. And finally, the owner of the script must be the same user who runs the **dhcp6c** daemon—usually a super user.

The `script` statement can be used with address allocation, prefix delegation, or stateless services.

Following is an example of a shell script that will reflect configuration information for recursive DNS server addresses and DNS search list provided via DHCPv6 in the host's `/etc/resolv.conf` file.

```
#!/bin/sh

rm /etc/resolv.conf
if [ ! -z $new_domain_name ]; then
        echo search $new_domain_name >> /etc/resolv.conf
fi
for nameserver in $new_domain_name_servers; do
        echo nameserver $nameserver >>/etc/resolv.conf
done
```

4.8.5   Configuring the DHCPv6 Relay Agent

There is no need to configure **dhcp6relay** with a configuration file. Its minor configuration parameters can be specified as command line options.

4.8.6 Configuring DHCPv6 Authentication

In order to enable DHCPv6 authentication, the client and the server must be configured with the same secret key. The key is specified in each configuration file by the `keyinfo` statement as follows:

```
keyinfo kamekey {
        realm "kame.example";
        keyid 1;
        secret "yHShgx8gdo20EIgxi6oO1w==";
};
```

The key name (`kamekey`), the string(*) following the keyword `keyinfo`, is an arbitrary string identifying that particular key. It does not affect the client behavior, but is used by the client to associate with the relevant client information (see below). The key name can be different in the server and the client.

(*) the configuration parser in the current implementation does not accept the dash (−) character as a part of a string.

The server and client must share all the other parameters of the `keyinfo` statement. The value of the `secret` statement is the shared secret in the form of the BASE-64 encoding. If the operating system has the openssl package (this is the case for FreeBSD), one convenient way to produce a key file is to use the output of the following command:

```
% openssl rand -base64 16
```

It should be obvious, but when a configuration file contains a `keyinfo` statement, the file must not be readable to anyone except those involved with the DHCPv6 operation. Also, the exact value of secret shown in the above example must not be used in actual operation.

In addition to the key information, the server and client must also be configured with information on how to use the authentication protocol.

The following is a configuration example for a client which enables DHCPv6 authentication. It is a modification to the configuration for address allocation shown at the beginning of Section 4.8.4.

```
interface ne0 {
        send ia-na 100;
        send authentication kameauth;
};
authentication kameauth {
        protocol delayed;
};
```

In the `interface` statement, the second `send` statement specifies that the client wants to use DHCPv6 authentication for exchanges on this interface. The name `kameauth` is used for the details of authentication, and is defined by the `authentication` statement with the same name. It simply specifies the use of the delayed authentication protocol.

The client does not have to associate the key information with any other local configuration. It will be matched automatically when the client receives messages from a server containing an Authentication option.

On the other hand, the server needs to associate the key information to a particular client. The following example is an extension to the one shown in Section 4.8.3, and means that if the client includes an Authentication option for the delayed authentication protocol in a Solicit message, **dhcp6s** will perform the authentication protocol for succeeding message exchanges using the key named kamekey.

```
host kame {
        duid 00:01:00:01:09:5f:93:76:00:03:47:a5:30:85;
        address 2001:db8:ffff::1/128 86400 604800;
        address 2001:db8:ffff::2/128 604800 2592000;
        delayedkey kamekey;
};
```

4.8.7   Configuring Control Command Keys

In order to control the behavior of a running server or client via a control channel, the running process and the control command (**dhcp6ctl**) must share a secret key.

The key file must consist of a single line, in which the secret value is written in the form of the BASE-64 encoding. As shown in Section 4.8.6, one convenient way to produce a key file is as follows:

```
# openssl rand -base64 16 > /usr/local/etc/dhcp6sctlkey
(for the server key file)

# openssl rand -base64 16 > /usr/local/etc/dhcp6cctlkey
(for the client key file)
```

Note that these files must not be readable to anyone except DHCPv6 administrators, so that an unauthorized user cannot control the running process.

In a common (and recommended) case where the control command is run on the same node which runs the running process, the same key file can be shared by the process and the control command, since the default file path is the same.

Control key files are not mandatory for invoking a client or a server. If you do not need to control the process run-time, you can omit this configuration procedure. In fact, the current implementation does not support very many operations—it provides the framework for future extensions. Thus, examples using the **dhcp6ctl** command will not be shown in this book.

4.8.8   Operation of DHCPv6 Services

This section describes operational examples of three major DHCPv6 services: address allocation, prefix delegation, and the stateless service providing DNS-related information. They will also provide concrete examples of how to use the DHCPv6 relay agent in some common scenarios.

Operation of Address Allocation

Assume a simple network topology for an example of address allocation (Figure 4-49). That is, there is a single link where a server and a client reside. The server also acts as the default router to external networks.

The server configuration file, dhcp6s.conf, should be as follows, and is a summary of Section 4.8.3.

FIGURE 4-49

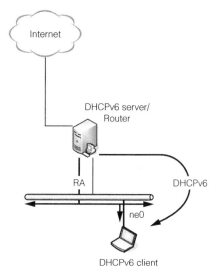

Network topology for address allocation.

```
host kame {
      duid 00:01:00:01:09:5f:93:76:00:03:47:a5:30:85;
      address 2001:db8:ffff::1/128 86400 604800;
      address 2001:db8:ffff::2/128 604800 2592000;
};

option domain-name-servers 2001:db8:9999::35 2001:db8:abcd::35;
option domain-name "kame.example";
```

In addition, the server node, while acting as a router, needs to be configured to send Router Advertisements. Assuming that the natural 64-bit prefix length of the configured addresses is the on-link prefix, the following is the configuration file for KAME's Router Advertisement daemon, **rtadvd**:

```
ne0:\
      :addr="2001:db8:ffff::":prefixlen#64:pinfoflags="l":
```

The **rtadvd** daemon will advertise prefix 2001:db8:ffff::/64 with the L-bit on and the A-bit off. When the A-bit is set to off, it indicates this prefix is *not* to be used for stateless address autoconfiguration. It is also noteworthy that the M flag is not set in Router Advertisement messages when performing address allocation using DHCPv6. As mentioned in Section 4.2.5, the relationship between the M or O flag and DHCPv6 services is still not clear, and thus the operation is described independently from these flags.

On the other hand, the client configuration file, dhcp6c.conf, should be as follows:

```
interface ne0 {
      send ia-na 100;
      script "/usr/local/sbin/dhcp6c-script";
};
id-assoc na 100 { };
```

where the dhcp6c-script script is assumed to be the one shown in Section 4.8.4.

The first step of the operation is to start the DHCPv6 server and the **rtadvd** daemon with an argument of the listening interface:

```
server# dhcp6s ne0
server# rtadvd ne0
```

Now the client is ready to start:

```
client# ifconfig ne0 up
client# dhcp6c ne0
```

In this example, the interface is explicitly enabled beforehand, since the **dhcp6c** daemon does not do this automatically.

Unless something is misconfigured, the client host will soon get all its necessary configuration information. First, it will have a global IPv6 address allocated via DHCPv6:

```
client% ifconfig -L ne0 inet6 ne0:
flags=8843<UP,BROADCAST,RUNNING,SIMPLEX,MULTICAST> mtu 1500 inet6
fe80::202:b3ff:fe64:8e0e%ne0 prefixlen 64 scopeid 0x1 inet6
2001:db8:ffff::1 prefixlen 128 pltime 86398 vltime 604798
```

The preferred and valid lifetimes of the global address are almost the same as those received via DHCPv6. The small difference comes from the time lag between address allocation and the invocation of the `ifconfig` command.

> The client will eventually try to renew the address by Renew and Reply exchanges. As explained in Section 4.4.10, however, the lifetimes of the address in the kernel will not be updated even if the exchanges succeed. Therefore, the address will be deprecated in about 86,400 seconds, and will expire in about 604,800 seconds, regardless of the DHCPv6 operation.

The client host will also have the default route and the direct route for the on-link prefix:

```
client% netstat -rn -f inet6
[...]
default                          fe80::1%ne0 UGc ne0
[...]
2001:db8:ffff::/64               link#1    UC  ne0
```

These are provided via Router Advertisements.

Finally, the client will have recursive DNS server addresses and a DNS search list in its `/etc/resolv.conf` file:

```
client% cat /etc/resolv.conf
search kame.example.
nameserver 2001:db8:9999::35
nameserver 2001:db8:abcd::35
```

These are received via DHCPv6, and the `resolv.conf` file is modified by the `dhcp6c-script` script.

Operation of Prefix Delegation

The network topology shown in Figure 4-46 (page 472) is a common example for prefix delegation. A user network is connected to an ISP via a CPE. CPE and PE are directly connected over a PPPoE (PPP over Ethernet) link. CPE is also attached to an Ethernet link, which is the user's local network.

A sample configuration of the server (PE as the delegating router) derived from Section 4.8.3 is as follows:

```
host usagi {
        duid 00:01:00:01:09:3c:91:d9:00:e0:18:98:f1:9d;
        prefix 2001:db8:1234::/48 2592000 7776000;
};
option domain-name-servers 2001:db8:9999::35 2001:db8:abcd::35;
```

The `domain-name-servers` option is specified assuming the ISP provides recursive DNS services to its customers.

This is an example configuration of the client (CPE as the requesting router):

```
interface tun0 {
        send ia-pd 200;
};
id-assoc pd 200 {
        prefix-interface ne0 {
                sla-id 1;
        };
};
```

This is the same configuration that was shown in Section 4.8.4.

In addition to the DHCPv6 configuration, the requesting router also needs to send Router Advertisements on to the local Ethernet link. With the combination of KAME's DHCPv6 and Router Advertisement implementations, there is no need for explicit configuration for the **rtadvd** daemon.

Before doing prefix delegation, a PPPoE link needs to be established between the requesting router and the delegating router. For simplicity, however, the configuration details of PPPoE are not described here, and an already established link is assumed.

To start the delegating router, the **dhcp6s** daemon can be simply invoked with the PPPoE interface as its command-line argument:

```
dlgtrtr# dhcp6s tun0
```

At the requesting router, the **rtadvd** daemon should be invoked first, followed by the DHCPv6 client:

```
reqrtr# rtadvd ne0
reqrtr# dhcp6c tun0
```

If everything was set up correctly, the prefix `2001:db8:1234::/48` will be delegated to the requesting router, which will then make a longer prefix based on the delegated one, `2001:db8:1234:1::/64`, and assign an IPv6 address using the longer prefix on the interface to the local network.

The **rtadvd** daemon will learn the prefix through a routing socket, and automatically start advertising the prefix via Router Advertisement messages.

Figure 4-50 depicts this procedure. The **dhcp6c** daemon receives a DHCPv6 Reply message on interface `tun0` containing the IPv6 prefix `2001:db8:1234::/48` delegated to the requesting router. It opens a separate UDP/IPv6 socket and calls the `ioctl()` system call for assigning a derived address `2001:db8:1234::1/64` to its local interface, `ne0`. The new address and the prefix are automatically reported to the routing socket that the **rtadvd** daemon watches.

FIGURE 4-50

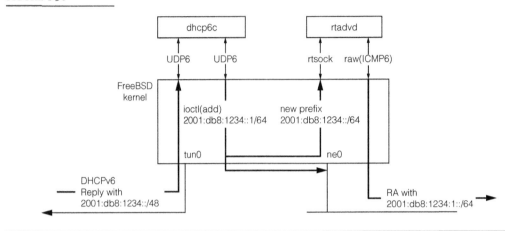

*Inter-process relationship between **dhcp6c** and **rtadvd**.*

Then the daemon makes a new Router Advertisement message, including the new prefix, and sends it to an IPv6 raw (ICMPv6) socket.

User hosts attached to the link will then perform stateless address auto-configuration for configuring global IPv6 addresses. The hosts will also get the default router address from the Router Advertisements.

DNS related and other configuration information can be provided for the hosts via the stateless subset of DHCPv6 (Information-request and Reply exchanges). In this case, the requesting router would also act as a stateless DHCPv6 server, responding to Information-request messages.

Unlike the example of address allocation described above, the lifetimes of the address are set to infinity, regardless of the valid and preferred lifetimes of the corresponding delegated prefix. This is an intentional implementation-specific behavior. In fact, [RFC3633] does not specify the relationship between the address lifetimes of the requesting router and the lifetimes of the delegated prefix. This implementation prefers a tighter control about the stability of the address, depending on further DHCPv6 exchanges for prefix delegation, rather than leaving the management of the lifetime to the kernel.

Yet the implementation does not fully conform to [RFC3633]. The specification requires that the requesting router copy the lifetimes of the delegated prefix to those of prefixes advertised via Router Advertisements. However, the **rtadvd** daemon actually sets the lifetimes to the default values defined by the specification (7 days for the preferred lifetime and 30 days for the valid lifetime).

Although this does not cause a problem during normal operation, it can be troubling when the delegated site renumbers. The lifetimes of the old (expiring) prefix should be decreasing to zero during the renumbering procedure, but there is no automatic way to change the advertised prefix lifetimes from the **rtadvd** daemon.

Operation of Stateless Services

Operation of the stateless subset of DHCPv6 via Information-request and Reply exchanges is simple.

The client should have the following in its `dhcp6c.conf` file:

```
interface ne0 {
        information-only;
        script "/usr/local/sbin/dhcp6c-script";
};
```

and the `dhcp6c-script` file shown in Section 4.8.4 should be placed in the `/usr/local/sbin/` directory.

As seen in the previous cases, the client can be invoked with an interface name, e.g.,

```
client# dhcp6c ne0
```

Information-request messages will then be sent on interface ne0. If the server is properly configured with some recursive DNS server addresses and a DNS search list, a Reply message containing those addresses and the search list will be returned, and the client's `/etc/resolv.conf` file will be adjusted as described in the address allocation example.

Operation of Relay Agent

One simple but useful case of a DHCPv6 relay agent is to connect two links by a relay agent (which also acts as a router). Figure 4-51 shows this type of network topology.

In this case, the **dhcp6relay** daemon should be invoked as follows:

```
relay# dhcp6relay -r ne1 ne0
```

FIGURE 4-51

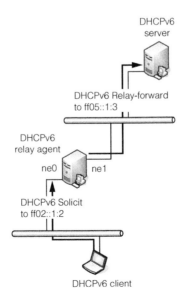

Network topology where a relay agent and a server share a link.

FIGURE 4-52

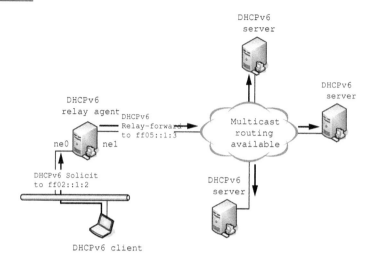

Network topology with a relay agent using multicast routing to reach servers.

FIGURE 4-53

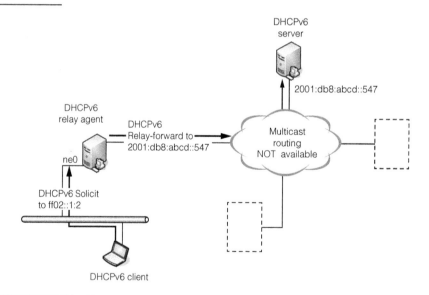

Network topology with a relay agent using unicast messages to reach a server.

The -r option specifies the interface to which Relay-forward messages are to be sent. The mandatory command-line argument, ne0, specifies the listening interface attached to the link where clients reside (multiple listening interfaces can be specified if necessary).

When a client sends a DHCPv6 message (e.g., Solicit) to ff02::1:2, the relay agent receives the packet on interface ne0, encapsulates it in a Relay-forward message, and sends it to `ff05::1:3` on interface `ne1`. Since the relay agent and the server reside on the same link, the server can receive the Relay-forward message directly, and responds to the original message from the client via the relay agent.

When the server and the relay agent do not share a link, a more complicated configuration is necessary. If IPv6 multicast routing is available on the network containing the server and the relay agent, the **dhcp6relay** daemon can be invoked exactly as shown above. The Relay-forward message from the relay agent will be delivered to the server using the multicast routing infrastructure. If more than one server exists in the multicast routing domain, each server will receive a copy of the Relay-forward message as shown in Figure 4-52.

On the other hand, if the server and the relay agent do not share a link and IPv6 multicast routing is not available, the relay agent must be configured with a global unicast address of the server using the `-s` option:

```
relay# dhcp6relay -s 2001:db8:abcd::547 ne0
```

(where the server is assumed to have a unicast address of `2001:db8:abcd::547`).

In this case, the Relay-forward message will be sent directly to the server via its unicast address, and the server will respond to the client's message through the relay agent (Figure 4-53).

In general, it is desirable to use the well-known multicast address for redundancy and for robustness against server renumbering. Unfortunately, multicast routing may not always be available; the explicit manual configuration of a unicast address is a common workaround in such a case.

5 Mobile IPv6

5.1 Introduction

Mobile IPv6 is a mobility support protocol for IPv6 at the network layer. The specification was standardized at the IETF in June 2004. The standardization process was quite slow compared to the basic IPv6 specification. The initial working group draft of Mobile IPv6 was submitted in 1996, which compares favorably with the first IPv6 draft specification which was proposed to the IPng working group in 1995. The reason for the delay in the standardization of Mobile IPv6 was the need to solve security issues associated with the protocol. Mobile IPv6 enables IPv6 nodes to send or receive packets whose source address does not match the network prefix to which they are currently attached. That is, nodes have to use a type of source spoofing technique. In the early version of the specification, the protocol required the use of IPsec to ensure the source address was valid. However, when we consider the real situation—a mobile node may communicate with many other nodes for which it does not have any identification information—using IPsec is almost impossible.

The IESG rejected the proposal from the Mobile IPv6 working group to standardize the protocol specification at that time, and insisted the working group propose a procedure to securely validate the source address of a mobile node. The Mobile IPv6 working group started a discussion to solve the problem in 2000 and finally developed a loose address ownership mechanism called the return routability procedure (discussed in Section 5.5.1) in 2002. The specification was accepted by the IESG and published as [RFC3775] in 2004.

The KAME project originally used the Mobile IPv6 stack that was contributed by Ericsson. The project started to implement its own Mobile IPv6 stack in 2001, during the middle of the second term of the KAME activity. KAME implemented several versions of Mobile IPv6 to follow and validate the latest specification. The code discussed in this chapter is based on the KAME snapshot released in July 2004. At that time, the specification had already been accepted as an RFC and the code was mature.

After KAME completed the first version of their Mobile IPv6 code, they started to redesign the architecture of the mobility stack. In the new architecture most of the signal processing tasks are moved to user space, compared to the first version of Mobile IPv6 where the code was implemented in the kernel. The design is similar to the BSD Routing Socket mechanism, which separates the routing information exchange and forwarding mechanisms, with exchanging routing information in the user space and forwarding in the kernel space. There are many benefits to this design. It makes it easier to develop complicated signal processing code since developers can utilize many advanced debugging programs and techniques, while the packet processing performance is not reduced, since it is done in the kernel. Extending or replacing some of the signal processing mechanisms is also easier, which makes it possible to add support for new mobility protocols or to adapt some part of the functions to user needs. Reducing the amount of kernel modification is important when we consider merging the developed code into the original BSDs. Unfortunately, we do not discuss the new stack in this book, since the code had not reached the quality level required for a reference implementation at the time this book was written. The code is still under development.

In this chapter, we first introduce the basic procedures of Mobile IPv6. Next, we discuss how the KAME Mobile IPv6 stack implements the specification in detail and briefly explain the usage of the stack.

5.2 Mobile IPv6 Overview

Mobile IPv6 adds the mobility function to IPv6. Mobile IPv6 is specified in [RFC3775] and [RFC3776]. An IPv6 host which supports the Mobile IPv6 function can move around the IPv6 Internet(*). The host which supports Mobile IPv6 can change its point of attachment to the IPv6 Internet whenever it wants. If a host does not support Mobile IPv6, all the existing connections on the host are terminated when it changes its point of attachment. A connection between two nodes is maintained by the pairing of the source address and the destination address. Since the IPv6 address of an IPv6 node is assigned based on the prefix of the network, the assigned address on a given network becomes invalid when the host leaves that network and attaches itself to another network. The reason for this problem came from the nature of IP addresses. An IP address has two meanings, one is the identifier of the node, and the other is the location information of the node. It would not be a big problem as long as IP nodes do not move around the Internet frequently, because, in that case, the location information would not change frequently and we could use location information as the identifier of a node. However, recent progress of communication technologies and small computers made it possible for IP nodes to move around. It is getting harder and harder to treat location information as an identifier, because the location information frequently changes.

(*) There is ongoing work to extend the Mobile IPv6 specification to support the IPv4 Internet [MIP6-NEMO-V4TRAVERSAL]. With this extension, a Mobile IPv6 mobile node can attach to the IPv4 Internet keeping the existing connections with its IPv6 peer nodes. In addition, the mobile node can use a fixed IPv4 address to communicate with other IPv4 nodes regardless of the IP version of the network to which the node is attached.

As such the basic idea of Mobile IPv6 is to provide a second IPv6 address to an IPv6 host as an identifier in addition to the address that is usually assigned to the node from the attached network as a locator. The second address is fixed to the home position of the host and never changes even if the host moves. The fixed address is called a "home address." As long as the host uses its home address as its connection information, the connection between the host and other nodes will not be terminated when the mobile host moves.

The concept of a home address provides another useful feature to a host that supports Mobile IPv6. Any IPv6 nodes on the Internet can access a host which supports Mobile IPv6 by specifying its home address, regardless of the location of the host. Such a feature will make it possible to create a roaming server. Since the home address of the roaming server never changes, we can constantly reach the server at the home address. For example, anyone could run a web server application on a notebook computer which supports Mobile IPv6 and everyone could access it without any knowledge of where the computer is located.

5.2.1 Types of Nodes

The Mobile IPv6 specification defines three types of nodes. The first type is the *mobile node*, which has the capability of moving around IPv6 networks without breaking existing connections while moving. A mobile node is assigned a permanent IPv6 address called a *home address*. A home address is an address assigned to the mobile node when it is attached to the *home network* and through which the mobile node is always reachable, regardless of its location on an IPv6 network. Because the mobile node is always assigned the home address, it is always logically connected to the home link. When a mobile node leaves its home network and attaches to another network, the node will get another address called a *care-of address*, which is assigned from the newly attached network. This network, which is not a home network, is called a *foreign network* or a *visited network*. A mobile node does not use a care-of address as an endpoint address when communicating with other nodes, since the address may change when the mobile node changes its point of attachment.

A second Mobile IPv6 node type is the *home agent*, which acts as a support node on the home network for Mobile IPv6 mobile nodes. A home agent is a router which has a proxy function for mobile nodes while they are away from home. The destination address of packets sent to mobile nodes are set to the home addresses of the mobile nodes. A home agent intercepts all packets which are addressed to the mobile node's home address, and thus delivered to the home network, on behalf of the mobile nodes.

This forwarding mechanism is the core feature provided by the Mobile IPv6 protocol. All IPv6 nodes which want to communicate with a mobile node can use the home address of the mobile node as a destination address, regardless of the current location of the mobile node. Those packets sent from an IPv6 node to the home address of a mobile node are delivered to the home network by the Internet routing mechanism where the home agent of the mobile node receives the packets and forwards the packets appropriately. For the reverse direction, a mobile node uses its home address as a source address when sending packets. However, a mobile cannot directly send packet nodes whose source address is a home address from its current location if it is away from home, since source addresses are not topologically correct. Sending a packet whose source address is out of the range of the network address of the sender node is a common technique when an attacker tries to hide its location when he is attacking a specific node. Such a packet may be considered as an attack. Because of this reason, the first hop router may drop such topologically incorrect packets to avoid the risk of the source spoofing attack. To solve this problem, a mobile node uses the IPv6 in IPv6 encapsulation technology. All packets sent from a mobile node while away from home are sent to its home agent using the encapsulation mechanism. The home agent decapsulates the packets and forwards them as if the packets were sent from the home network.

A third type of Mobile IPv6 node is called the *correspondent node*. A correspondent node is an IPv6 node that communicates with a mobile node. A correspondent node does not have to be Mobile IPv6-capable, other than supporting the IPv6 protocol; any IPv6 node can be a correspondent node. Since the Mobile IPv6 specification provides a backward compatibility to all IPv6 nodes which do not support Mobile IPv6, all IPv6 nodes can communicate with mobile nodes without any modification. However, as we have described in the previous paragraph, all packets between a mobile node and a correspondent node must be forwarded basically by the home agent of the mobile node. This process is sometimes redundant, especially when a correspondent node and a mobile node are located on topologically near networks. To solve this redundancy, Mobile IPv6 provides an optimization mechanism called the *route optimization* mechanism which a correspondent node may support. A mobile node can send packets directly to a correspondent node using the care-of address of the mobile node as a source address. The information of the home address of a mobile node is carried by the newly defined option for the Destination Options Header. Also, a correspondent node can send packets directly to the care-of address of a mobile node. In this case, the information of the home address is carried by the Routing Header. For a general discussion about IPv6 Extension Headers, refer to Chapter 3 of *IPv6 Core Protocol Implementation*, "Internet Protocol version 6."

A correspondent node may itself be a mobile node. In this case, two moving nodes can communicate with each other without terminating their sessions regardless of their points of attachment to the Internet.

5.2.2   Basic Operation of Mobile IPv6

A mobile node uses a home address when communicating with other nodes. When a mobile node moves from one network to another network, the node sends a message called a *Binding Update* to its home agent. The message includes the care-of address and the home address of the mobile node. Such information is called *binding information*, since it binds a care-of address to the home address of a mobile node.

When a home agent receives the message and accepts the contents of the message, the home agent replies with a *Binding Acknowledgment* message to indicate that the Binding Update message is accepted. The home agent creates a bi-directional tunnel connection from its address to the care-of address of the mobile node. A mobile node also creates a bi-directional tunnel connection from its care-of address to the home agent when it receives the acknowledgment message. After the successful tunnel creation, all packets sent to the home address of the mobile node are intercepted by the home agent at the home network and tunneled to the mobile node. Also, all packets originated at the mobile node are tunneled to its home agent and forwarded from its home network to destination nodes. Figure 5-1 shows the concept.

The communication path between a mobile node and a peer node described in Figure 5-1 sometimes may not be optimal. Figure 5-2 shows the worst case: A mobile node and a correspondent node are on the same network. The packets exchanged between them are always sent to the home network of the mobile nodes, even if they are directly accessible to each other

FIGURE 5-1

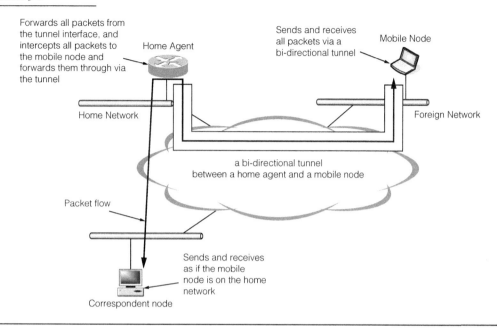

Forwards all packets from the tunnel interface, and intercepts all packets to the mobile node and forwards them through via the tunnel

Home Agent

Sends and receives all packets via a bi-directional tunnel

Mobile Node

Home Network

Foreign Network

a bi-directional tunnel between a home agent and a mobile node

Packet flow

Sends and receives as if the mobile node is on the home network

Correspondent node

Bi-directional tunneling.

FIGURE 5-2

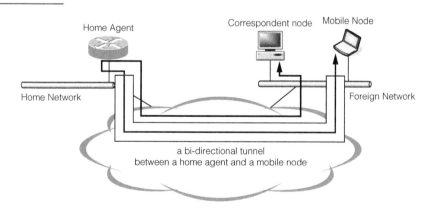

Home Agent

Correspondent node

Mobile Node

Home Network

Foreign Network

a bi-directional tunnel between a home agent and a mobile node

The worst case of bi-directional tunneling.

using the local network. For example, when two people whose mobile nodes are originally located in Japan visit the United States, their traffic always traverses the Pacific Ocean.

If a peer node supports the route optimization mechanism defined in the Mobile IPv6 specification, the mobile node and the peer node can communicate directly without detouring through the home agent. To optimize the route, the mobile node sends a Binding Update message to the peer node. After it receives the message, the peer node sends packets directly to the care-of address of the mobile node. The packets also contain a Routing Header which specifies their final destination which is set to the home address of the mobile node. The packets are routed directly to the care-of address of the mobile node. The mobile node receives the packets and finds the packets have a Routing Header and performs Routing Header processing, which involves swapping the destination address in the packets' IPv6 header and the home address carried in the Routing Header. The mobile node forwards the packets to the final destination which is the home address at this point, and the packets are delivered to the mobile node itself. When the mobile node sends packets to the peer node, the mobile node sets its care-of address as a source address of the packets and inserts its home address into a Destination Options Header. The peer node swaps the care-of address and the home address when it receives those packets, and processes the packets as if they were sent from the home address. Figure 5-3 shows the procedure.

As you may notice, a Binding Update message is quite a dangerous message. If a node accepts the message without any verification, an attacker can easily redirect packets sent to the mobile node to the attacker. To prevent this attack, the message is protected in the following two ways:

1. A Binding Update message to a home agent is protected by the IPsec mechanism.

2. A Binding Update message to a correspondent node is protected by the return routability procedure described in Section 5.5.1.

FIGURE 5-3
_____

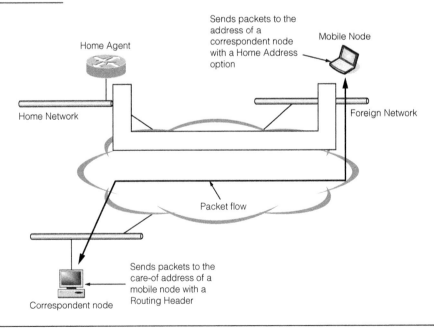

Optimized communication between a mobile node and a correspondent node.

The IPsec mechanism is strong enough to prevent this type of attack and we can use the technology between a mobile node and a home agent. However, it is difficult to use the IPsec mechanism between a mobile node and a correspondent node, since the IPsec mechanism requires both nodes to be in the same administrative domain. We can assume that a home agent and a mobile node can share such a secret since they are managed by the same administrative domain in most cases. However, there is usually no such relationship between a mobile node and a correspondent node.

> There is an ongoing action to use the IPsec mechanism between a mobile node and a correspondent node [MIP6-CN-IPSEC].

The Mobile IPv6 specification defines a new method of creating a shared secret between a mobile node and a correspondent node. The procedure is called the *return routability* procedure. When a mobile node sends a Binding Update message, the most important thing is to provide a way to prove to the correspondent node that the care-of address and home address are owned by the same mobile node. The return routability procedure provides such an address ownership proof mechanism.

A mobile node sends two messages: One message is sent from its home address and the other message is sent from its care-of address. Respectively, the messages are called a *Home Test Init* message and a *Care-of Test Init* message. A correspondent node replies to both messages with a *Home Test* message to the first and a *Care-of Test* message to the second. These reply messages include values for tokens which are computed from addresses of the mobile node and secret information which is only kept in the correspondent node. A mobile node generates a shared secret from the token values and puts a signature in a Binding Update message using the shared secret. This mechanism ensures that the home address and the care-of address are assigned to the same mobile node. Figure 5-4 shows the procedure. Section 5.4 contains a detailed discussion of Mobile IPv6 operation.

5.3 Header Extension

[RFC3775] defines new extension headers and several new types and options for existing headers for Mobile IPv6. The specification also defines some header formats of Neighbor Discovery [RFC2461] which are modified for Mobile IPv6. The following is a list of new or modified headers and options. The detailed description of each header and option will be discussed in Sections 5.3.2 to 5.3.7.

Home Address option The Home Address option is a newly defined destination option which carries the home address of a mobile node when packets are sent from a mobile node.

Type 2 Routing Header The Type 2 Routing Header is a newly defined routing header type which carries a home address of a mobile node when packets are sent from a home agent or a correspondent node to a mobile node.

Mobility Header The Mobility Header is a newly defined Extension Header which carries the signaling information of the Mobile IPv6 protocol.

FIGURE 5-4

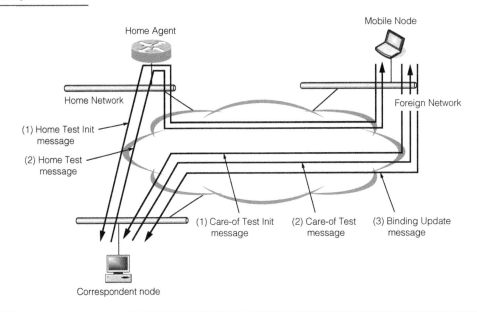

The return routability procedure.

Router Advertisement message The Router Advertisement message is modified to include a flag which indicates whether a router has the home agent function or not.

Prefix Information option The Prefix Information option is one of the Neighbor Discovery options used to distribute prefix information of a network from a router to other nodes connected to the network. In Mobile IPv6, a home agent includes its address in this option as a part of the prefix information. All home agents on the same home network can know all addresses of home agents of the network by listening to this option.

Home Agent Information option The Home Agent Information option is a newly defined Neighbor Discovery option which carries the lifetime and preference information of a home agent.

Advertisement Interval option The Advertisement Interval option is a newly defined Neighbor Discovery option which carries the interval value between unsolicited Router Solicitation messages sent from a router.

Dynamic Home Agent Address Discovery Request/Reply messages The Dynamic Home Agent Address Discovery Request and Reply messages are newly defined ICMPv6 message types which provide the mechanism to discover the addresses of home agents for a mobile node when the mobile node is away from home.

Mobile Prefix Solicitation/Advertisement messages The Mobile Prefix Solicitation and Advertisement messages are newly defined ICMPv6 message types used to solicit/deliver the prefix information of a home network to a mobile node while the mobile node is away from home.

5.3.1 Alignment Requirements

Some Extension Headers and Options have alignment requirements when placing these headers in a packet. Basically, the header or option fields are placed at a natural boundary, that is, fields of n bytes in length are placed at multiples of n bytes from the start of the packet. The reason for such a restriction is for performance; accessing the natural boundary is usually faster. For example, the Home Address Option (Figure 5-5) has $8n + 6$ alignment requirements, that puts the home address field on an 8-byte boundary.

5.3.2 Home Address Option

The *Home Address* option is a newly defined Destination option. The alignment requirement of the Home Address option is $8n + 6$. The format of the Home Address option is shown in Figure 5-5. This option is used to specify the home address of a mobile node when the mobile node sends packets while it is away from home. It is used in the following three cases.

1. When a mobile node sends a Binding Update message
2. When a mobile node communicates with peers with route optimization
3. When a mobile node sends a Mobile Prefix Solicitation message

A mobile node never sends packets with its source address set to its home address directly while it is away from home, since such a source address is topologically incorrect and may be dropped by an intermediate router because of the Ingress Filtering posed on that router. When sending a packet, a mobile node needs to perform one of following procedures.

- Send a packet using a bi-directional tunnel created between a mobile node and its home agent.

- Use the Home Address option which includes the home address of the mobile node with the source address of the packet set to the care-of address of the mobile node.

The *Type* field is 0xC9. The first 2 bits of an option type number determine the action taken on the receiving node when the option is not supported, as discussed in Chapter 3 of *IPv6 Core*

FIGURE 5-5

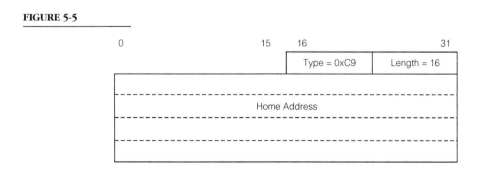

Home Address option.

Protocols Implementation. In this case, the first 2 bits are both set. This means that if a node does not recognize the option, the following actions must be taken:

- The packet which includes the option must be dropped.
- An ICMPv6 Parameter Problem message must be sent if the destination address of the incoming packet is not a multicast address.

This provides a mechanism to detect whether a peer supports the Home Address option. If the peer does not support the option, the mobile node cannot use the route optimization mechanism.

The *Length* field is set to 16. The *Home Address* field contains a home address of a mobile node.

5.3.3 Type 2 Routing Header

The *Type 2 Routing Header* is a newly defined routing header type for Mobile IPv6. This Routing Header is used by a home agent or a correspondent node to carry a home address of a mobile node when packets are sent to the mobile node. The format of the Type 2 Routing Header is shown in Figure 5-6.

The Type 2 Routing Header is used in the following three cases:

1. When a node sends a Binding Acknowledgment message
2. When a home agent or a correspondent is performing route optimization
3. When a home agent sends a Mobile Prefix Advertisement message

A packet whose destination address is a home address of a mobile node is never delivered to the mobile node directly when the mobile node is away from home. Such a packet is delivered to the home network of the mobile node.

A node needs to use a Type 2 Routing Header if it wants to send packets directly to a mobile node which is away from home. In this case, the destination address of the packet is set to the care-of address of the mobile node. The home address is carried in the Type 2 Routing Header. A packet is delivered directly to the care-of address of the mobile node, and the mobile

FIGURE 5-6

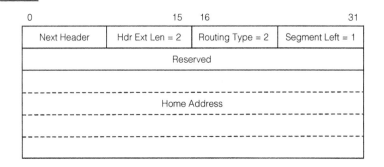

Type 2 Routing Header.

node processes the Type 2 Routing Header and delivers the packet to the home address, which is the mobile node itself.

The *Next Header* field is set to the protocol number of the following header. The *Hdr Ext Len* field is fixed at 2, since the length of the Type 2 Routing Header is fixed. The *Routing Type* field is set to 2. The *Segments Left* field is initialized to 1. The *Home Address* field contains one IPv6 address which is the home address of the mobile node. The usage of this header is very restrictive. We can only specify one intermediate node as a home address. A mobile node which receives this header drops the packet if there is more than one intermediate node specified. Also, the address in the Type 2 Routing Header and the destination address of the IPv6 packet must belong to the same mobile node. That is, the packet can only be forwarded to the mobile node itself.

A new type number is required for Mobile IPv6 in order to make it easy to support Mobile IPv6 on firewall software. In the early stages of the Mobile IPv6 standardization, a Type 0 Routing Header was used instead of a Type 2 Routing Header. However, many people thought that it would be difficult to distinguish between using a Type 0 Routing Header for carrying a Mobile IPv6 home address or carrying a Routing Header that is being used as a method to perform source routing. We need to pay attention to the usage of source routing, since such forwarding is sometimes used as a method for attacking other nodes. Firewall vendors may drop all packets with a Type 0 Routing Header to decrease the risk of such attacks. It is much easier for those vendors to pass only Mobile IPv6 data if we have a new routing header type number for the exclusive use of Mobile IPv6.

5.3.4 Mobility Header

The *Mobility Header* is a newly introduced extension header to carry Mobile IPv6 signaling messages. The format of the Mobility Header is shown in Figure 5-7. The format of the header is based on the usual extension header format.

The *Payload Proto* field indicates the following header. The field is equivalent to the Next Header field of other extension headers; however, the current specification does not allow the Mobility Header to be followed by other extension headers or by transport headers. That is, the Mobility Header must always be the last header in the header chain of an IPv6 packet. The reason for this restriction is to simplify the interaction between the IPsec mechanism and Mobile IPv6. Some signaling messages used by the Mobile IPv6 protocol must be protected by

FIGURE 5-7

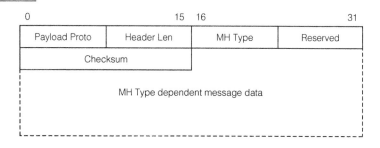

Mobility Header.

the IPsec mechanism. It is impossible to protect the Mobility Header if other headers follow it, because with the current IPsec specification we cannot apply IPsec policies to the intermediate extension headers. Currently, the *Payload Proto* field is always set to 58 (IPV6-NONXT) which indicates there is no next header. The *Header Len* field indicates the length of a Mobility Header in units of 8 bytes excluding the first 8 bytes. The *MH Type* field indicates the message type of the Mobility Header. Currently, 8 kinds of Mobility Header types are defined. Table 5-1 shows all Mobility Header types. The *Reserved* field is reserved for future use. The *Checksum* field stores the checksum value of a Mobility Header message. The algorithm used to compute the checksum value is the same as is used for ICMPv6. The rest of the header is defined depending on the Mobility Header type value. Also, the Mobility Header may have some options called *mobility options*.

Binding Refresh Request Message

The *Binding Refresh Request (BRR)* message is used when a correspondent needs to extend the lifetime of binding information for a mobile node. A mobile node that has received a Binding Refresh Request message should send a Binding Update message to the correspondent node to update the binding information held in the correspondent node. The format of the Binding Refresh Request message is shown in Figure 5-8.

TABLE 5-1

Type	Description
0	Binding Refresh Request: requests a mobile node to resend a Binding Update message to update binding information.
1	Home Test Init: starts the return routability procedure for a home address of a mobile node.
2	Care-of Test Init: starts the return routability procedure for a care-of address of a mobile node.
3	Home Test: a response message to the Home Test Init message.
4	Care-of Test: a response message to the Care-of Test Init message.
5	Binding Update: sends a request to create binding information between a home address and a care-of address of a mobile node.
6	Binding Acknowledgment: a response message to the Binding Update message.
7	Binding Error: notifies an error related to the signal processing of the Mobile IPv6 protocol.

Mobility Header types.

FIGURE 5-8

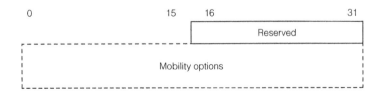

Binding Refresh Request message.

The Binding Refresh Request message is sent from a correspondent node to a mobile node. The source address of the IPv6 packet is the address of the correspondent node which is sending the Binding Refresh Request message. The destination address of the IPv6 packet is the home address of a mobile node, which is requested to resend a Binding Update message. The Binding Refresh Request message must have neither a Type 2 Routing Header nor a Home Address option. That is, the message is tunneled by the home agent to the destination mobile node, if the destination mobile node is away from home. Currently, no mobility options are defined for the Binding Refresh Request message.

Home Test Init Message

The *Home Test Init (HoTI)* message is used to initiate the return routability procedure. The format of the Home Test Init message is shown in Figure 5-9.

The Home Test Init message is sent from a mobile node to a correspondent node when the mobile node wants to optimize the path between itself and the correspondent node. The source address of the IPv6 packet is the home address of the mobile node and the destination address of the IPv6 packet is the address of the correspondent node.

The *Home Init Cookie* field is filled with a random value generated in the mobile node. The cookie is used to match a Home Test Init message and a Home Test message, which is sent from a correspondent node in response to the Home Test Init message. The Home Test Init message must have neither a Type 2 Routing Header nor a Home Address option. The Home Test Init message is always tunneled from a mobile node to its home agent and forwarded to a correspondent node. Currently, no mobility options are defined for the HoTI message.

Care-of Test Init Message

The *Care-of Test Init (CoTI)* message is used to initiate the return routability procedure. The format of the Care-of Test Init message is shown in Figure 5-10.

The Care-of Test Init message is sent from a mobile node to a correspondent node when a mobile node wants to optimize the path between itself and the correspondent node. The source address of the IPv6 packet is the care-of address of the mobile node and the destination address of the IPv6 packet is the address of the correspondent node.

The *Care-of Init Cookie* is filled with a random value generated in the mobile node. The cookie is used to match a Care-of Test Init message and a Care-of Test message,

FIGURE 5-9

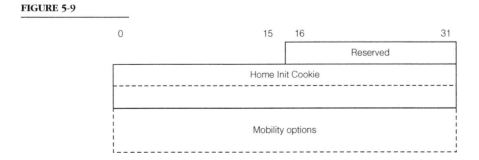

Home Test Init message.

FIGURE 5-10

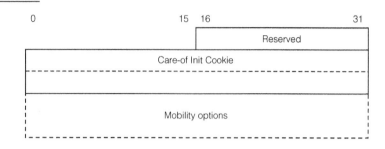

Care-of Test Init message.

FIGURE 5-11

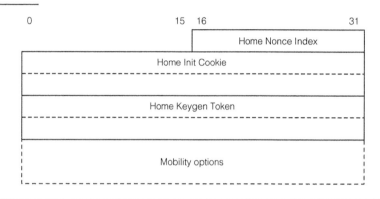

Home Test message.

which is sent from the correspondent node in response to the Care-of Test Init message. A Care-of Test Init message must have neither a Type 2 Routing Header nor a Home Address option. A Care-of Test Init message is always directly sent from a mobile node to a correspondent node. Currently, no mobility options are defined for the Care-of Test Init message.

Home Test Message

The *Home Test (HoT)* message is used as a reply to a Home Test Init message sent from a mobile node to a correspondent node. This message includes a token which is used to compute a shared secret to protect the Binding Update message. The format of the Home Test message is shown in Figure 5-11.

The Home Test message is sent from a correspondent node to a mobile node as a response to a Home Test Init message which was previously sent from the mobile node. The source address of the IPv6 packet is the address of the correspondent node and the destination address is the home address of the mobile node.

The *Home Nonce Index* indicates an index value of the nonce value in the home nonce array which is maintained in the correspondent node. The *Home Init Cookie* is a copy of the value of the *Home Init Cookie* field of the corresponding Home Test Init message. A mobile node can match a previously sent Home Test Init message and the received Home Test message by comparing the cookie values. If there is no corresponding Home Test Init message, the received Home Test message is dropped. The *Home Keygen Token* is a token value which is used to compute a shared secret to secure the Binding Update message. The algorithm used is described in Section 5.5.1. Currently, no mobility options are defined for the Home Test message.

Care-of Test Message

The *Care-of Test (CoT)* message is used as a reply to a Care-of Test Init message sent from a mobile node to a correspondent node. This message includes a token value which is used to compute a shared secret to protect the Binding Update message. The format of the Care-of Test message is shown in Figure 5-12.

   The Care-of Test message is sent from a correspondent node to a mobile node as a response to the Care-of Test Init message which was previously sent from the mobile node. The source address of the IPv6 packet is the address of the correspondent node and the destination address is the care-of address of the mobile node.

   The *Care-of Nonce Index* indicates the index value of the nonce value in the care-of nonce array which is maintained in the correspondent node. The *Care-of Init Cookie* is a copy of the value of the *Care-of Init Cookie* field of the corresponding Care-of Test Init message. A mobile node can match a previously sent Care-of Test Init message and the received Care-of Test message by comparing the cookie values. The *Care-of Keygen Token* is a token value which is used to compute a shared secret to secure the Binding Update message later. The algorithm used is described in Section 5.5.1. Currently, no mobility options are defined for the Care-of Test message.

Binding Update Message

The *Binding Update (BU)* message is used by a mobile node to notify a correspondent node or a home agent of the binding information of a care-of address and a home address of the mobile node. A mobile node sends the Binding Update message with its care-of address and its home address whenever it changes its point of attachment to the Internet and changes its

FIGURE 5-12

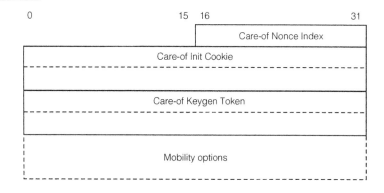

Care-of Test message.

care-of address. The node which receives the message will create an entry to keep the binding information. Figure 5-13 shows the Binding Update message.

The Binding Update message is sent from a mobile node to a home agent or a correspondent node. The source address of the IPv6 packet is the care-of address of the mobile node and the destination address is the address of the home agent or the correspondent node. To include the information of the home address of the mobile node, the Binding Update message contains a Destination Options Header which has a Home Address option as described in Section 5.3.2.

The *Sequence Number* field contains a sequence number for a Binding Update message to avoid a replay attack. The *flag* fields of the Binding Update message may contain the flags described in Table 5-2.

The *Lifetime* field specifies the proposed lifetime of the binding information. When a Binding Update message is used for home registration, the value must not be greater than the remaining lifetime of either the home address or the care-of address of the mobile node which is sending the Binding Update message. The value is in units of 4 seconds.

The Binding Update message may have the following mobility options.

- The Binding Authorization Data option

- The Nonce Indices option

- The Alternate Care-of Address option

Each option is described in Section 5.3.5.

FIGURE 5-13

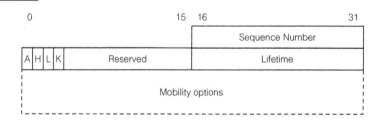

Binding Update message.

TABLE 5-2

Flag	Description
A	*Acknowledge*: requires a Binding Acknowledgment message as a response to a Binding Update message. When the H flag is set, the A flag must be set. Note that a Binding Acknowledgment message may be sent to indicate an error even if the A flag is not set.
H	*Home Registration*: means that this Binding Update message is a message for home registration.
L	*Link-local Address Compatibility*: means that the link-local address of a mobile node has the same interface ID with its home address.
K	*Key Management Mobility Capability*: means the IKE SA information survives on movements.

The flags of the Binding Update message.

Binding Acknowledgment Message

The *Binding Acknowledgment (BA)* message is sent as a response to a Binding Update message sent from a mobile node. The format of the Binding Acknowledgment message is shown in Figure 5-14.

A Binding Acknowledgment message is sent from a home agent or a correspondent node to a mobile node. The source address of the Binding Acknowledgment message is the address of the home agent or the correspondent node and the destination address is the care-of address of the mobile node. To deliver a Binding Acknowledgment message to the home address of a mobile node which is away from home, a Type 2 Routing Header, which contains the home address of the mobile node, is necessary.

The *Status* field specifies the result of the processing of the received Binding Update message. Table 5-3 is a list of currently specified status codes. The field immediately after the

FIGURE 5-14

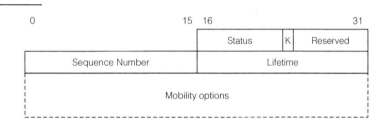

Binding Acknowledgment message.

TABLE 5-3

Code	Description
0	Binding Update accepted
1	Accepted but prefix discovery necessary
128	Reason unspecified
129	Administratively prohibited
130	Insufficient resources
131	Home registration not supported
132	Not home subnet
133	Not home agent for this mobile node
134	Duplicate Address Detection failed
135	Sequence number out of window
136	Expired home nonce index
137	Expired care-of nonce index
138	Expired nonces
139	Registration type change disallowed

The status codes of the Binding Acknowledgment message.

Status field is the flag field. Currently only the K flag is defined. Table 5-4 describes the K flag. The *Sequence Number* field indicates the copy of the last valid sequence number which was contained in the last Binding Update message. The field is also used as an indicator of the latest sequence number when a mobile node sends a Binding Update message with a smaller sequence number value. This situation may occur when a mobile node reboots and loses the sequence number information of recent binding information. The *Lifetime* field indicates the approved lifetime for the binding information. Even if a mobile node requests a large lifetime value in the *Lifetime* field in the Binding Update message, the requested lifetime is not always approved by the receiving node. The actual lifetime can be determined by the node which receives the Binding Update message.

The Binding Acknowledgment message may have the following mobility options.

• The Binding Authorization Data option

• The Binding Refresh Advice option

Each option is described in Section 5.3.5.

Binding Error Message

The *Binding Error (BE)* message is used to indicate an error which occurs during the mobility signaling processing. The format of a Binding Error message is shown in Figure 5-15.

TABLE 5-4

Flag	Description
K	Key Management Mobility Capability means the IKE SA information cannot survive on movements.

The flag of the Binding Acknowledgment message.

FIGURE 5-15

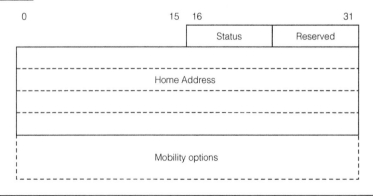

Binding Error Message.

The Binding Error message is sent from a node which supports Mobile IPv6. The source address of the IPv6 packet is the address of the node which sends the Binding Error message. The Binding Error message must have neither a Type 2 Routing Header nor a Home Address option.

The *Status* field indicates the kind of error as described in Table 5-5. The *Home Address* field contains the home address of a mobile node if the packet which causes the error is sent from a mobile node. Otherwise, the field contains an unspecified address. Currently, no mobility options are defined for the Binding Error message.

5.3.5 Mobility Options

The Mobility Options are the options used with the Mobility Header to provide supplemental information. Figure 5-16 shows the format of the Mobility Option.

The Mobility Option format is the same format used by the Hop-by-Hop options and Destination options. The first byte indicates the type of the option. The second byte indicates the length of the following data. Currently 6 options are defined as described in Table 5-6.

TABLE 5-5

Status	Description
1	A Home Address option is received without existing binding information
2	Unrecognized Mobility Header type value is received

The status value of a Binding Error message.

FIGURE 5-16

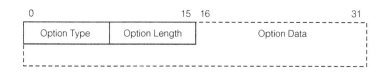

Mobility Option.

TABLE 5-6

Type	Description
0	Pad1
1	PadN
2	Binding Refresh Advice
3	Alternate Care-of address
4	Nonce indices
5	Binding Authorization data

Mobility Options.

Pad1 Option

The *Pad1* option is used when one byte of padding is needed to meet the alignment requirements of other Mobility Options. This option does not have any effect and must be ignored on
the receiver side. The format of the Pad1 option is a special format which does not meet the
standard format described in Figure 5-16. Figure 5-17 shows the format of the Pad1 option.

PadN Option

The *PadN* option is used when two or more bytes of padding are needed to meet the alignment
requirements of other Mobility Options. This option does not have any effect and must be
ignored on the receiver side. The format of the PadN option is described in Figure 5-18.

The *Option Length* field is set to the size of the required padding length minus 2. The
Option Data field consists of a zero cleared byte stream whose length is the required padding
size minus 2. A receiver must ignore the contents of the *Option Data* field when processing this
option.

Binding Refresh Advice Option

The *Binding Refresh Advice* option is used to specify the recommended interval between Binding Update messages for updating the binding information. The option is used with the Binding
Acknowledgment message which is sent from a home agent to a mobile node which the home
agent serves. The format of the Binding Refresh Advice option is shown in Figure 5-19. The
alignment requirement of the Binding Refresh Advice option is $2n$.

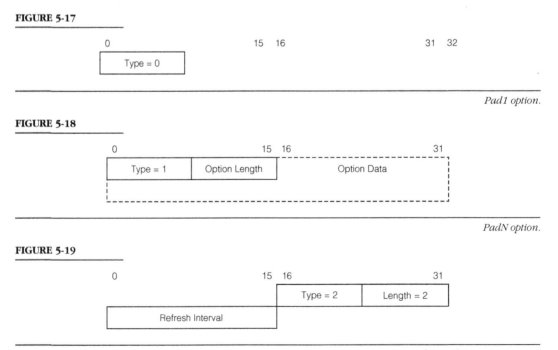

FIGURE 5-17

Pad1 option.

FIGURE 5-18

PadN option.

FIGURE 5-19

Binding Refresh Advice option.

The *Length* field is set to 2. The *Refresh Interval* field indicates the interval value. The value is specified in units of 4 seconds.

Alternate Care-of Address Option

The *Alternate Care-of Address* option is used in two cases with the Binding Update message. The first case is when a mobile node wants to bind its home address to an address other than the source address of the Binding Update message. Usually, the source address of the IPv6 packet is used as a care-of address, if the Alternate Care-of Address option does not exist. The second case is to protect the care-of address information from on-path attackers. The Binding Update message for home registration must be protected by an IPsec ESP or AH. However, the ESP does not protect the IPv6 header itself. That is, the source address, which is used as a care-of address, is not protected by the ESP. Adding this option to a Binding Update message will protect the care-of address information, since this option is included in a Mobility Header and the Mobility Header is covered by the ESP. If we use the AH, the option can be omitted. The format of the Alternate Care-of Address option is shown in Figure 5-20. The alignment requirement of the Alternate Care-of Address option is $8n + 6$.

The *Length* field is set to 16 which is the length of an IPv6 address. The *Alternate Care-of Address* field contains the address which should be used as a care-of address instead of the source address of the Binding Update message.

Nonce Indices Option

The *Nonce Indices* option is used to specify nonce values which are used to compute the Authenticator value specified by the Binding Authorization Data option. This option is used with the Binding Authorization Data option. The alignment requirement of the Nonce Indices option is $2n$. The format of the Nonce Indices option is shown in Figure 5-21.

FIGURE 5-20

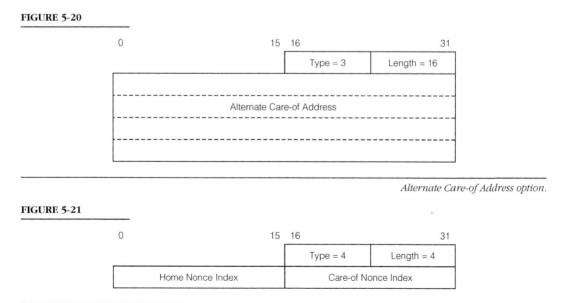

Alternate Care-of Address option.

FIGURE 5-21

Nonce Indices option.

FIGURE 5-22

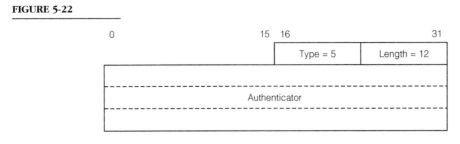

The *Length* field is set to 4. The value of the *Home Nonce Index* and *Care-of Nonce Index* fields are copied from the *Home Nonce Index* field of the Home Test message and *Care-of Nonce Index* field of the Care-of Test message which a mobile node has previously received.

Binding Authorization Data Option

The *Binding Authorization Data* option stores a hash value computed over the Binding Update or the Binding Acknowledgment message. The option does not have any alignment requirement, however, because it has to be placed at the end of the message, it eventually has an $8n + 2$ requirement. The format of the Binding Authorization Data option is shown in Figure 5-22.

The *Length* field depends on the length of the *Authenticator* field. At this moment, the length is 12 because the procedure to compute the authenticator produces a 96-bit authenticator value. The algorithm used for this computation is discussed in Section 5.5.1.

5.3.6 Neighbor Discovery Messages

The Mobile IPv6 specification modifies the Router Advertisement message and the Prefix Information option so that we can distribute information about a home agent. Two new Neighbor Discovery options are introduced.

Router Advertisement Message

The *Router Advertisement* message is modified to include the newly defined Home Agent flag. Figure 5-23 shows the modified Router Advertisement message.

The H flag in the flags field is added. A router which is acting as a Mobile IPv6 home agent must specify the H flag so that other home agents can detect there is another home agent on the same network. This information is used on each home agent when creating a list of home agent addresses. The mechanism is described in Section 5.7. A-mobile node may use this option to create the list of home agents when it is at home.

Prefix Information Option

The *Prefix Information* option is an option defined in [RFC2461]. The option is used with the Router Advertisement message to distribute the prefix information to the nodes on the attached network. Figure 5-24 shows the format of this option.

In [RFC2461], this option only carries the information of the prefix part. In the Mobile IPv6 specification, the option is modified to include the address of the home agent including the

FIGURE 5-23

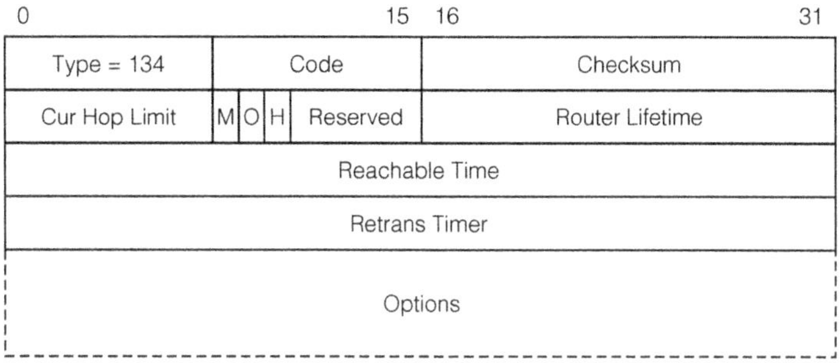

Modified Router Advertisement message.

FIGURE 5-24

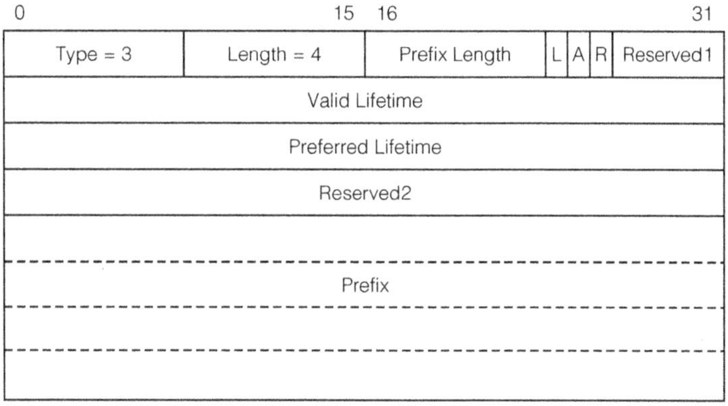

Prefix Information option.

interface identifier part. The R flag is added in the flags field for that purpose. If the R flag is set, the Prefix field includes a full IPv6 address of the home agent, not only the prefix part. A node which receives this option with the R flag can discover the address of a home agent on the network. This information is used when each home agent creates a list of home agent addresses. The mechanism is described in Section 5.7.

Advertisement Interval Option

The *Advertisement Interval* option is used to supply the interval at which Router Advertisement messages are sent from a home agent. The Router Advertisement message is used as a hint of the reachability of the router. A mobile node assumes it has not moved to other networks as long as the same router is reachable on the attached network. A mobile node can detect the unreachability of a router by listening for the Router Advertisement message, since a router periodically sends these messages. However, such detection is usually difficult since the interval between Router Advertisement messages varies on each network. This option explicitly supplies the interval between Router Advertisement messages. The interval is set to a lower value than the usual IPv6 Router Advertisement messages. A mobile node can determine a router is unreachable if the router does not send a Router Advertisement message for the period specified in this option. The format of the Advertisement Interval option is shown in Figure 5-25.

The *Type* field is set to 7. The *Length* field is fixed at 1. The *Reserved* field must be cleared by the sender and must be ignored by the receiver. The *Advertisement Interval* field is a 32-bit unsigned integer which specifies the interval value between Router Advertisement messages in units of 1 second.

Home Agent Information Option

The *Home Agent Information* option is a newly defined Neighbor Discovery option to distribute the information of a home agent. This option is used with the Router Advertisement message sent from a home agent. The format of the Home Agent Information option is shown in Figure 5-26.

The *Type* field is set to 8. The *Length* field is fixed at 1. The *Reserved* field must be cleared by the sender, and must be ignored by the receiver. The *Home Agent Preference* field specifies the preference value of a home agent which sends this option. The value is a 16-bit unsigned integer. Higher values mean the home agent is more preferable. This value is used to order the addresses of the home agent list which is maintained on each home agent on the home network. The home agent list is sent to a mobile node when the mobile node requests the latest list of home agents. The *Home Agent Lifetime* field contains the lifetime of the home agent. The value is a 16-bit unsigned integer and stored in units of 1 second. This value specifies how long the router can provide the home agent service. If there is no Home Agent Information option sent by a home agent, the preference value is considered 0 and the lifetime is considered the same value as the router lifetime.

FIGURE 5-25

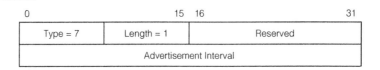

Advertisement Interval option.

FIGURE 5-26

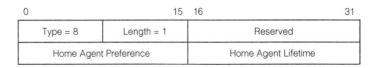

Home Agent Information option.

5.3.7 ICMPv6 Messages

The Mobile IPv6 specification defines 4 new types of the ICMPv6 message.

Dynamic Home Agent Address Discovery Request

A mobile node sometimes requests the latest list of home agents on its home network. When requesting the list, a mobile node sends the *Dynamic Home Agent Address Discovery Request* message, which is a newly defined ICMPv6 message. The format of the Dynamic Home Agent Address Discovery Request message is shown in Figure 5-27.

The source address of the IPv6 packet is the care-of address of a mobile node. The destination address is the *home agent anycast address*. The algorithm to construct the home agent anycast address is shown in Figure 5-28. There are two patterns to compute the anycast address; One is for the prefix whose prefix length is 64 and the other is for the prefix whose prefix length is not 64. The home agent anycast address is a combination of a prefix and the anycast identifier `ffff:ffff:ffff:ffff:ffff:ffff:ffff:fffe`, which is reserved for the home agent anycast address. The important point when generating the anycast address is if the prefix length is 64, the interface identifier part of the generated anycast address must satisfy the EUI-64 requirements. That is, the universal/local bit must be cleared since the anycast address may be assigned to multiple home agents. In this case we must use `fdff:ffff:ffff:fffe` as an anycast identifier. The interface identifier of the home agent anycast address is defined in [RFC2526].

The *Type* field is set to 144. The *Code* field is set to 0. No other code value is defined. The *Checksum* field is a checksum value computed as specified in the ICMPv6 specification [RFC2463]. The *Identifier* field contains an identifier to match the request message and the reply message. The *Reserved* field must be cleared by the sender and must be ignored by the receiver. The procedure of Dynamic Home Agent Address Discovery is discussed in Section 5.7.

Dynamic Home Agent Address Discovery Reply

The *Dynamic Home Agent Address Discovery Reply* message is used as a response message to the Dynamic Home Agent Address Discovery Request message. Each home agent maintains the list of home agents on its home network by listening to Router Advertisement messages sent by other home agents and updating the list as necessary. When a home agent receives a Dynamic Home Agent Address Discovery Request message, the node will reply to the mobile node that has sent the request message with a Dynamic Home Agent Address Discovery Reply message including the latest list of home agents. The format of the Dynamic Home Agent Address Discovery Reply message is shown in Figure 5-29.

FIGURE 5-27

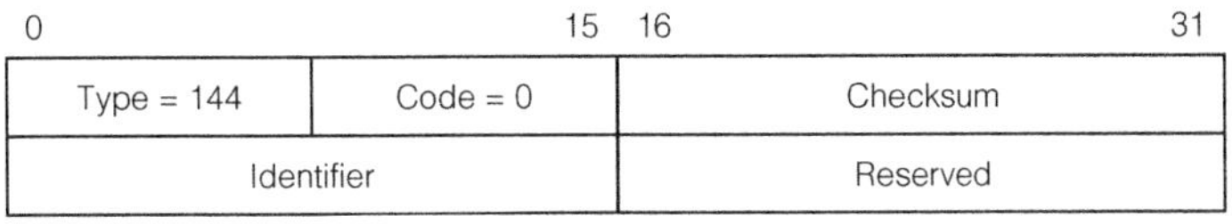

0	15	16	31
Type = 144	Code = 0	Checksum	
Identifier		Reserved	

Dynamic Home Agent Address Discovery Request message.

FIGURE 5-28

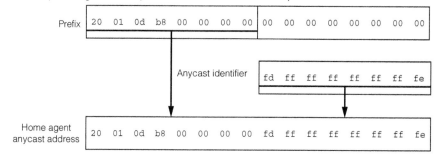

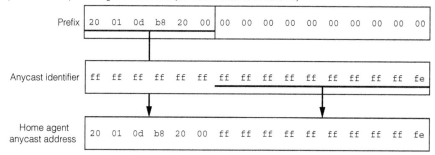

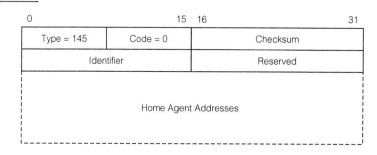

Computation of the home agent anycast address.

FIGURE 5-29

<table>
<tr><td colspan="2">0</td><td>15</td><td>16</td><td>31</td></tr>
</table>

Type = 145	Code = 0	Checksum
Identifier		Reserved
Home Agent Addresses		

Dynamic Home Agent Address Discovery Reply message.

The source address of the IPv6 packet is set to one of the addresses of the home agent which replies to this message. The source address must be an address recognized as the home agent's address because a mobile node may use the source address as the home agent's address in the following Mobile IPv6 signaling process. The destination address is copied from the source address field of a Dynamic Home Agent Address Discovery Request message.

The *Type* field is set to 145. The *Code* field is set to 0. No other code values are defined. The *Checksum* field is a checksum value computed as specified in the ICMPv6 specification [RFC2463]. The value of the *Identifier* field is copied from the *Identifier* field of the corresponding Dynamic Home Agent Address Discovery Request message. The *Reserved* field must be cleared by the sender and must be ignored by the receiver. The *Home Agent Addresses* field contains the list of addresses of home agents on the home network. The order of the list is decided based on the preference value of each home agent. To avoid fragmentation of the message, the maximum number of addresses in the list is restricted to not exceed the path MTU value from a home agent to a mobile node. The procedure of Dynamic Home Agent Address Discovery is discussed in Section 5.7.

Mobile Prefix Solicitation

The *Mobile Prefix Solicitation* message is a newly defined ICMPv6 message which is sent when a mobile node wants to know the latest prefix information on its home network. This message is typically sent to extend the lifetime of the home address before it expires. The format of the Mobile Prefix Solicitation message is shown in Figure 5-30.

The source address of the IPv6 packet is set to the current care-of address of the mobile node. The destination address is set to the address of the home agent with which the mobile node is currently registered. This message must contain the Home Address option to carry the home address of the mobile node. This message should be protected by the IPsec ESP header to prevent the information from being modified by attackers.

The *Type* field is set to 146. The *Code* field is set to 0. No other code values are defined. The *Checksum* field is a checksum value computed as specified in the ICMPv6 specification [RFC2463]. The *Identifier* field contains a random value which is used to match the solicitation message and the advertisement message. The *Reserved* field is cleared by the sender and must be ignored by the receiver.

Mobile Prefix Advertisement

The *Mobile Prefix Advertisement* message is a newly defined ICMPv6 message which is used to supply the prefix information of a home network to mobile nodes. This message is used as a response message to a Mobile Prefix Solicitation message sent from a mobile node. Also, this message may be sent from a home agent to each mobile node which has registered with the home agent to notify the mobile node of updates to the prefix information of the home network, even if the mobile nodes do not request the information explicitly. The format of the Mobile Prefix Advertisement message is shown in Figure 5-31.

FIGURE 5-30

0		15 16	31
Type = 146	Code = 0	Checksum	
Identifier		Reserved	

Mobile Prefix Solicitation message.

FIGURE 5-31

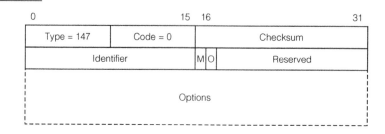

Mobile Prefix Advertisement message.

The source address of the IPv6 packet is one of the addresses of the home agent. The destination address is copied from the source address field of the Mobile Prefix Solicitation message if the message is in response to a solicitation message. Otherwise, the destination address is the registered care-of address of a mobile node. A Type 2 Routing Header must be included in this message to contain the home address of a mobile node. This message should be protected by the IPsec ESP header to prevent being modified by attackers.

The *Type* field is set to 147. The *Code* field is set to 0. No other code values are defined. The *Checksum* field is a checksum value computed as specified in the ICMPv6 specification [RFC2463]. If this message is in response to a solicitation message, the value of the *Identifier* field is copied from the *Identifier* field of the Mobile Solicitation message. If the message is not a response message, this field can be set to any value. A mobile node which receives a Mobile Prefix Advertisement which has an unmatched identifier should send the Mobile Prefix Solicitation message to confirm the prefix information. The M and O flags are copied from the configuration of a home network. That is, if the home network is being operated with a managed address configuration mechanism (e.g., DHCPv6), the M flag is set. Also if the home network provides stateful configuration parameters (e.g., DNS server addresses via DHCPv6), the O flag is set. Currently, the exact processing procedure of these flags is not defined in the Mobile IPv6 specification. A future document will define the exact processing mechanism. The *Reserved* field must be cleared by the sender and must be ignored by the receiver. This message will have the modified Prefix Information option described in Section 5.3.6.

5.4 Procedure of Mobile IPv6

In this section, we discuss the detailed procedure of the Mobile IPv6 protocol operation.

5.4.1 Protocol Constants and Variables

Table 5-7 shows a list of the variables used in the Mobile IPv6 protocol. Some of these variables are constant while others may have their values modified.

5.4.2 Home Registration

When a mobile node is at home, the node acts as a fixed IPv6 node. Figure 5-32 shows the situation.

TABLE 5-7

Name	*Description*
INITIAL_DHAAD_TIMEOUT	The initial timeout value when retransmitting a Dynamic Home Agent Address Discovery Request message. (Constant: 3 seconds)
DHAAD_RETRIES	The maximum number of retries for a Dynamic Home Agent Address Discovery Request message (Constant: 4 times)
InitialBindackTimeoutFirstReg	The initial timeout value when retransmitting a Binding Update message when a mobile node moves from a home network to a foreign network for the first time. (Configurable: default to 1.5 seconds)
INITIAL_BINDACK_TIMEOUT	The initial timeout value when retransmitting a Binding Update message when updating the existing binding information of a peer node. (Constant: 1 second)
MAX_BINDACK_TIMEOUT	The maximum timeout value for retransmitting a Binding Update message. (Constant: 32 seconds)
MAX_UPDATE_RATE	The maximum number of Binding Update messages which a mobile node can send in 1 second. (Constant: 3 times)
MAX_NONCE_LIFETIME	The maximum lifetime of nonce values. (Constant: 240 seconds)
MAX_TOKEN_LIFETIME	The maximum lifetime of Keygen Token values. (Constant: 210 seconds)
MAX_RR_BINDING_LIFETIME	The maximum lifetime for binding information created by the Return Routability procedure. (Constant: 420 seconds)
MaxMobPfxAdvInterval	The maximum interval value between Mobile Prefix Advertisement messages. (Modifiable: default to 86,400 seconds)
MinMobPfxAdvInterval	The minimum interval value between Mobile Prefix Advertisement messages. (Modifiable: default to 600 seconds)
PREFIX_ADV_TIMEOUT	The timeout value when retransmitting a Mobile Prefix Advertisement message. (Constant: 3 seconds)
PREFIX_ADV_RETRIES	The maximum number of retransmissions of Mobile Prefix Advertisement messages. (Constant: 3 times)
MinDelayBetweenRAs	The minimum interval value between Router Advertisement messages. (Modifiable: default to 3 seconds, minimum 0.03 seconds)

Protocol constants and variables.

A mobile node gets its IPv6 addresses from its home network. The addresses assigned on the home network are called home addresses. When a mobile node sends a packet, the source address of the packet is set to one of the home addresses of the mobile node. The destination address of the packet is the address of the peer node. When the peer node sends a packet to

FIGURE 5-32

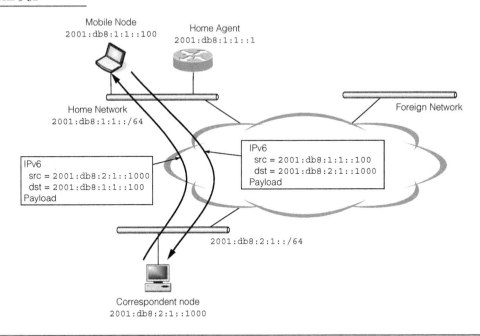

Packet exchange while a mobile node is home.

the mobile node, the source and the destination address are set to the peer address and the home address respectively.

When a mobile node moves to a foreign network, the mobile node will get address(es) from the foreign network. These addresses are called care-of addresses. If the mobile node detects that it is on a foreign network, the node creates an entry that keeps the state of the mobile node and maintains it. The entry is called a *binding update list* entry. It contains the information of the home address and one of the care-of addresses of the node, the lifetime of the entry, and so on. The detailed contents of this entry is discussed in Section 5.11.29.

The mobile node sends a Binding Update message to its home agent to notify the home agent of its current location. The source address of the message is set to the care-of address picked from the list of available care-of addresses. The destination address is the address of the home agent. The message also includes a Home Address option which contains the home address of the mobile node. This message must be protected by the IPsec ESP mechanism.

When a home agent receives a Binding Update message, it adds the information to its internal database. The information kept in a home agent is called a *binding cache* (the detailed structure of this information is discussed in Section 5.11.28). The home agent replies with a Binding Acknowledgment message in response to the Binding Update message. If the mobile node does not receive the acknowledgment message, it re-sends a Binding Update message until it gets an acknowledgment message. This procedure is called *Home registration*. Figure 5-33 shows the procedure.

A Binding Update message includes a sequence number. If a home agent already has a corresponding binding cache entry and the sequence number of the received Binding Update

FIGURE 5-33

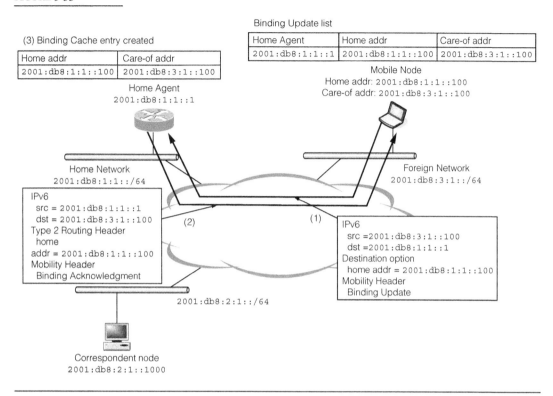

Binding Update list

Home Agent	Home addr	Care-of addr
2001:db8:1:1::1	2001:db8:1:1::100	2001:db8:3:1::100

(3) Binding Cache entry created

Home addr	Care-of addr
2001:db8:1:1::100	2001:db8:3:1::100

Home Agent
2001:db8:1:1::1

Mobile Node
Home addr: 2001:db8:1:1::100
Care-of addr: 2001:db8:3:1::100

Home Network
2001:db8:1:1::/64

Foreign Network
2001:db8:3:1::/64

IPv6
  src = 2001:db8:1:1::1
  dst = 2001:db8:3:1::100
Type 2 Routing Header
  home
addr = 2001:db8:1:1::100
Mobility Header
  Binding Acknowledgment

(2)

(1)

IPv6
  src = 2001:db8:3:1::100
  dst = 2001:db8:1:1::1
Destination option
  home addr = 2001:db8:1:1::100
Mobility Header
  Binding Update

2001:db8:2:1::/64

Correspondent node
2001:db8:2:1::1000

Sending binding messages.

message is smaller than the sequence number kept in the cache entry, the home agent returns a Binding Acknowledgment message with an error status of 135 and the latest sequence number. The mobile node re-sends a Binding Update message with a correct sequence number to complete home registration. The comparison of sequence numbers is based on modulo 2^{16}, since the sequence number is represented as a 16-bit variable. For example, if the current sequence number is 10015, then the numbers 0 though 10014 and 42783 through 65535 are considered less than 10015 (Figure 5-34).

A mobile node must set the H and A flags to indicate that it is requesting home registration when it registers its current location with its home agent. In addition to the flags, a mobile node must set the L flag if the home address of the mobile node has the same interface identifier as is used in its link-local address. Setting the L flag will create a binding cache entry for the link-local address of the mobile node and protect that address from being used by other nodes on its home network.

When a mobile node sets the A flag, the node re-sends a Binding Update message until it receives a Binding Acknowledgment message. The initial retransmission timeout value is determined based on whether this registration is the first home registration or if it is updating the home registration entry. If the message is for the first home registration, the initial retransmission timeout is set to `InitialBindackTimeoutFirstReg` seconds. Otherwise, the initial retransmission timeout is `INITIAL_BINDACK_TIMEOUT` seconds. The difference is due to running

FIGURE 5-34

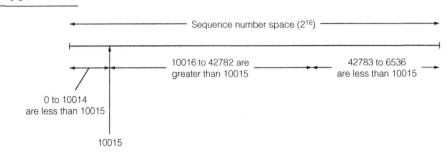

Sequence number comparison.

the DAD procedure at the home agent. The first time a mobile node registers its location, the home agent must make sure that the home address (and the link-local address, if the L flag is set) is not used on the home network by some other node by performing the DAD procedure. Usually the DAD procedure takes 1 second. This is why the initial timeout must be greater than 1 second. The timeout value is increased exponentially on every retransmission with the maximum retransmission timeout being `MAX_BINDACK_TIMEOUT` seconds. If a mobile node does not receive a Binding Acknowledgment after the last retransmission, the mobile node may perform a Dynamic Home Agent Address Discovery to find another home agent on the home network.

A Binding Update message includes an Alternate Care-of Address option to protect the care-of address information. The Binding Update message is protected by an ESP IPsec header, but the ESP header does not cover the source address field of an IPv6 header which contains the care-of address of a mobile node. A mobile node needs to put its care-of address in the Alternate Care-of Address option as a part of the Binding Update message in order for it to be covered by the ESP header.

The lifetime field of a Binding Update message is set to the smaller lifetime of either the care-of address or the home address of a mobile node. If a home agent accepts the requested lifetime, the acknowledgment message includes the same value. A home agent can reduce the lifetime based on the local policy of the home agent. A Binding Acknowledgment message may include a Binding Refresh Advice option.

A mobile node maintains its binding update list entry for home registration by sending a Binding Update message periodically.

5.4.3 Bi-directional Tunneling

When a mobile node and a home agent complete the exchange of the binding information, these nodes create a tunnel connection between them. The endpoint addresses of the tunnel connection are the address of the home agent and the care-of address of the mobile node. This tunnel connection is used to hide the location of the mobile node from correspondent nodes. The peer node does not notice whether the mobile node is at home or in any foreign networks. Note that the packets sent to the link-local address of the mobile node are not forwarded to the

FIGURE 5-35

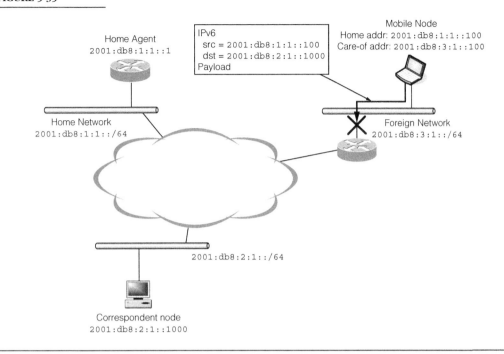

Topologically incorrect packets may be dropped.

mobile node even if the L flag is set in the Binding Update message from the mobile node. The flag is used to protect the link-local address to be used with other nodes on the home link but not to be used to forward the link-local packets to other links.

A mobile node usually uses its home address as a logical endpoint address when sending packets. This ensures that the communication between a mobile node and other nodes survives when the mobile node moves from one network to another network, since a home address never changes. However, a mobile node cannot simply send a packet with its source address set to the home address of the node. Such a packet is topologically incorrect and the router which serves the foreign network may discard the packet based on its local security policy. Figure 5-35 shows the procedure.

To avoid this problem, a mobile node sends packets whose source address is the home address of the node by using the tunnel connection created between the mobile node and its home agent. Figure 5-36 shows the procedure.

A packet is encapsulated within another IPv6 header whose source and destination addresses are the care-of address of the mobile node and the address of mobile node's home agent respectively. The packet is de-capsulated at the home agent, and the home agent forwards the packet to the final destination. The packet looks as if it is being sent from a node which is attached to the home network.

When a correspondent node sends packets to the mobile node, the tunnel connection is also used in reverse direction. All packets whose destination address is the home address of

FIGURE 5-36

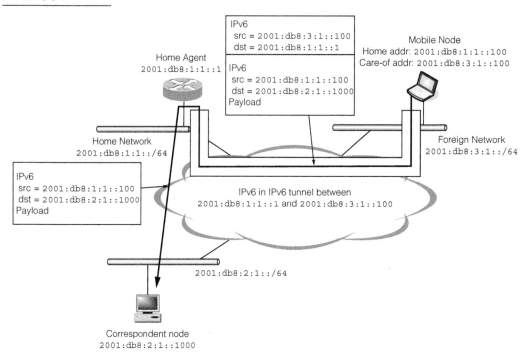

Sending packets by a tunnel connection from a mobile node to a home agent.

the mobile node are delivered to the home network of the mobile node. These packets are intercepted by the home agent of the mobile node, if the home agent has a valid binding cache entry for the mobile node, and sent to the mobile node using IPv6 in IPv6 tunneling. The source and destination addresses of the outer IPv6 header are the address of the home agent and the care-of address of the mobile node respectively. Figure 5-37 shows the flow.

5.4.4 Intercepting Packets for a Mobile Node

A home agent needs to intercept packets sent to a mobile node which the home agent is serving, and then needs to forward these packets using a tunnel connection between the home agent and the mobile node.

To receive packets which are sent to a mobile node, a home agent utilizes the proxy Neighbor Discovery mechanism. When a home agent creates a binding cache entry after receiving a Binding Update message from a mobile node, the home agent starts responding to Neighbor Solicitation messages sent to the home address or the solicited node multicast address of the home address. The home agent replies with a Neighbor Advertisement message in response to these solicitation messages. In the advertisement message, the home agent includes its own link-layer address as a target link-layer address. As a result, all packets sent to the home address of the mobile node are sent to the link-layer address of the home agent. The home agent forwards the received packets to the tunnel connection constructed between the home agent and

FIGURE 5-37

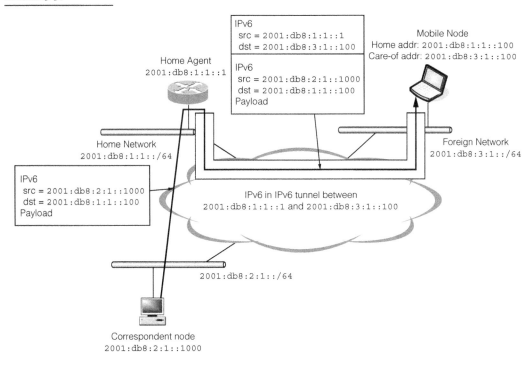

Sending packets by a tunnel connection from a home agent to a mobile node.

the mobile node as described in the previous section. Figure 5-38 shows the behavior of the proxy Neighbor Discovery mechanism.

5.4.5   Returning Home

When a mobile node returns home, it must clear any of its binding information registered on a home agent and correspondent nodes. The procedure to de-register binding information is almost the same as that of registering the information. The message used to de-register the binding is a Binding Update message.

First of all, a mobile node must send a Binding Update message to its home agent. The source address of the message must be a care-of address of a mobile node; however, in this case, the source address is set to the home address of a mobile node, since the care-of address and the home address are the same when a mobile node is home. The message also contains a Home Address option which contains the home address. The lifetime field is set to 0 to indicate de-registration. Also, the message contains an Alternate Care-of Address option to hold a care-of address (which is a home address in this case). The message must be protected by the IPsec ESP mechanism.

In some situations, a mobile node may not know the link-layer address of its home agent, which is necessary when sending a packet to the home agent. In this case, a mobile node must perform the Neighbor Discovery procedure, but we need to take care of one thing. If a home agent has a valid binding cache entry for the mobile node's link-local address, the mobile

FIGURE 5-38

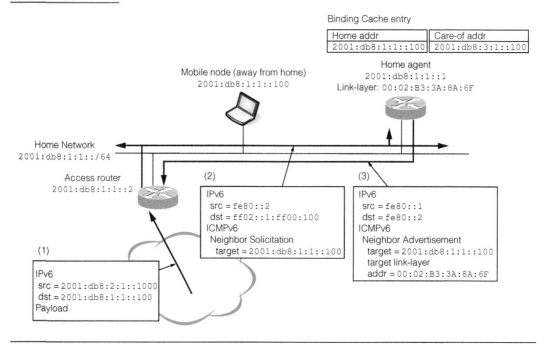

Intercepting packets.

node cannot use its link-local address during the Neighbor Discovery procedure because the home agent is acting as a proxy server of the address. Such usage may be considered address duplication. When a mobile node needs to resolve the link-layer address of its home agent when returning home, it sends a Neighbor Solicitation message from an unspecified address. When the home agent receives such a solicitation message, it replies with a Neighbor Advertisement message to an all-node multicast address as described in the Neighbor Discovery specification [RFC2461]. A mobile node can learn the link-layer address of the home agent by listening to the advertisement message.

If a home agent accepts the Binding Update message, it replies with a Binding Acknowledgment message. A home agent also stops its proxy function for the mobile node and shuts down the tunnel connection between the home agent and the mobile node. Finally it removes the binding cache entry for the mobile node.

A mobile node also shuts down the tunnel connection between itself and its home agent after receiving a Binding Acknowledgment message from its home agent. This procedure is called *home de-registration*.

There is a possibility that the signaling messages may be dropped because of communication errors. If a Binding Update message sent from a mobile node for de-registration is lost, the mobile node will re-send another Binding Update message until it receives a Binding Acknowledgment message. If a Binding Acknowledgment message is lost, the situation is slightly complicated, because the binding cache entry for the mobile node which sent a de-registration message has already been removed from the home agent when the Binding Acknowledgment message was sent. The mobile node will re-send a Binding Update message because it has not received a corresponding Binding Acknowledgment message. When a home agent receives a

Binding Update message for de-registration from a mobile node but it does not have a corresponding binding cache entry, it will reply to the mobile node with a Binding Acknowledgment message with status code 133. When a mobile node which has returned home receives a Binding Acknowledgment message with status code 133, the mobile node should consider that the acknowledgment message has been lost and complete the de-registration procedure.

A mobile node may de-register its address from its home agent even when it does not return to home (for example, when the mobile node stops its mobility function on a foreign network). In this case, a similar procedure is used to de-register the address. The Binding Update message sent from the mobile node will have a different home address and care-of address but the lifetime field will be set to 0. The home agent will remove its binding cache entry and stop intercepting packets for the mobile node.

5.5   Route Optimization

When a mobile node communicates with other nodes, all packets are forwarded by a home agent if the mobile node is away from home. This causes a communication delay, especially if the mobile node and its peer node are located on networks that are topologically close and the home agent is far away. The worst case is when both nodes are on the same network.

The Mobile IPv6 specification provides a solution for this problem. If the peer node supports the Mobile IPv6 correspondent node function, the path between a mobile node and the peer node can be optimized. To optimize the path, a mobile node sends a Binding Update message to the correspondent node. The message must not have the H and L flags set because the message is not requesting home registration. The A flag may be set; however, it is not mandatory. If the A flag is set, a correspondent node replies with a Binding Acknowledgment message in response to the Binding Update message. Note that even if the A flag is not set, a correspondent node must reply to the mobile node with a Binding Acknowledgment message when an error occurs during the message processing except in the authentication error case.

A Binding Update message must be protected by the return routability procedure, discussed in the next section. The message must contain a Binding Authorization Data option. The option contains a hash value of the Binding Update message, which is computed with the shared secret generated as a result of the return routability procedure. If the hash value is incorrect, the message is dropped. Similarly, a Binding Acknowledgment message sent from a correspondent node must include a Binding Authorization Data option to protect the contents.

Once the exchange of a Binding Update message (and a Binding Acknowledgment message, if the A flag is set) has completed, a mobile node starts exchanging route optimized packets with a correspondent node. The source address field of the packets is set to the care-of address of the mobile node. The mobile node cannot set the source address to its home address directly, since intermediate routers may drop a packet whose source address is not topologically correct to prevent source spoofing attacks. The home address information is kept in a Home Address option of a Destination Options header of the packet.

When a correspondent node receives a packet which has a Home Address option, it checks to see if it has a binding cache entry related to the home address. If there is no such entry, the correspondent node responds with a Binding Error message with status code 0. A mobile node needs to re-send a Binding Update message to create a binding cache entry in the correspondent node if it receives a Binding Error message. This validation procedure prevents any malicious nodes from using forged care-of addresses on behalf of the legitimate mobile node.

If the Home Address option is valid, the correspondent node accepts the incoming packet and swaps the home address in the option and the source address of the packet. As a result, the packets passed to the upper layer protocols have the home address as the source address. The upper layer protocols and applications need not care about any address changes for the mobile node since this address swap is done in the IPv6 layer.

When a correspondent node sends a packet to a mobile node, it uses the Type 2 Routing Header. A home address of a mobile node is put in the Routing Header and the destination address of the IPv6 packet is set to the care-of address of the mobile node. The packet does not go to the home network. Instead, the packet is routed to the foreign network where the mobile node is currently attached, since the destination address is set to the care-of address. The processing of a Type 2 Routing Header is similar to the processing of a Type 0 Routing Header except for some validation checks. A mobile node checks that the Routing Header contains only one address in the intermediate nodes field and ensures that the address is assigned to the mobile node itself. If the address specified in the Routing Header is not an address of the mobile node, the mobile node discards the packet, as the packet may be an attempt to force the mobile node to forward the packet. A mobile node drops any packets which contain an invalid Type 2 Routing Header.

5.5.1   Return Routability

A mobile node and a correspondent node need to share secret information before exchanging binding information. When a mobile node sends a Binding Update message, it computes a hash value of the message, using the shared information, and puts the value in the message. A correspondent node verifies the hash value by recomputing it, and drops the packet if the value computed on the correspondent node and the value specified in the message are different. In the same manner, a Binding Acknowledgment message sent from a correspondent node to a mobile node is protected by the hash mechanism. The shared information is created by the return routability procedure. In this section, we discuss the detailed procedure of the return routability mechanism.

5.5.2   Sending Initial Messages

Only a mobile node can initiate the return routability procedure. When a mobile node wants to start route optimized communication, it sends two initial messages. One is a Home Test Init message and the other is a Care-of Test Init message. There is no strict specification as to when a mobile node should send these messages. A mobile node can initiate the procedure whenever it needs to optimize the route. In the KAME implementation, for example, a mobile node sends these messages when the mobile node receives a packet from a correspondent node via a bi-directional tunnel between the mobile node and its home agent.

A Home Test Init message is sent from the home address of a mobile node. As we discussed already, such a packet whose source address is a home address cannot be sent directly from a foreign network. A Home Test Init message is sent through a tunnel connection between a mobile node and its home agent. A correspondent node will receive the message as if it were sent from the home network of the mobile node.

A Care-of Test Init message is sent from the care-of address of a mobile node. This message can be sent directly from a foreign network.

Both messages contain a random value called a cookie. The cookie in a Home Test Init message is called the Home Init Cookie and the cookie in a Care-of Test Init message is called the Care-of Test Init Cookie. These cookie values are used to match messages which a mobile node receives in response to the Home Test Init/Care-of Test Init messages from the correspondent node.

Figure 5-39 shows the packet flow of the Home Test Init and Care-of Test Init message.

5.5.3 Responding to Initial Messages

When a correspondent node which supports the return routability procedure receives a Home Test Init or a Care-of Test Init message from a mobile node, the correspondent node replies to the mobile node with a Home Test message and a Care-of Test message.

A Home Test message is sent to the home address of a mobile node. The message is delivered to the home network of the mobile node and intercepted by the home agent of the mobile node. The mobile node receives the message from a tunnel connection between the node and its home agent.

A Care-of Test message is sent to the care-of address of a mobile node directly.

FIGURE 5-39

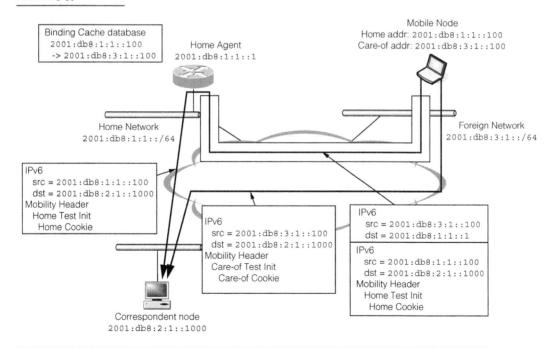

The Home Test Init and the Care-of Test Init message flow.

Both messages contain a copy of the cookie value which is contained in the Home Test Init/Care-of Test Init message, so that a mobile node can check to see if the received messages are sent in response to the initial messages.

A Home Test and a Care-of Test message have two other pieces of information: the nonce index and the Keygen Token. A correspondent node keeps an array of nonce values and node keys. The nonce index values specify the nonce values in the array. The nonce values and the node key values are never exposed outside of a correspondent node. This information must be kept in the correspondent node. The Keygen Token is computed from a nonce value and a node key using the following algorithms.

$$\text{Home Keygen Token} = First(64, HMAC\_SHA1(K_{cn},$$
$$(\textit{the home address of a mobile node}$$
$$|\textit{the nonce specified by the home nonce index}$$
$$|0)))$$
$$\text{Care-of Keygen Token} = First(64, HMAC\_SHA1(K_{cn},$$
$$(\textit{the care-of address of a mobile node}$$
$$|\textit{the nonce specified by the care-of nonce index}$$
$$|1)))$$

where,

'|' denotes concatenation,

First (x, y) function returns the first x bits from y,

HMAC_SHA1 (*key, data*) function returns

a HMAC SHA-1 hash value against '*data*' using '*key*' as a key,

K_{cn} is a node key of a correspondent node.

These tokens are used to generate a shared secret which is used to compute the hash values of a Binding Update message on a mobile node and a Binding Acknowledgment message on a correspondent node. To prevent a replay attack, a correspondent node must generate a new nonce value and node key and revoke the old nonce value and node key periodically. The maximum lifetime of all nonce values is restricted to MAX_NONCE_LIFETIME seconds. The lifetime of generated tokens is also restricted to MAX_TOKEN_LIFETIME seconds.

The array that keeps the nonce values and node keys are shared between mobile nodes with which the correspondent node is communicating. In theory, it is possible to use different values per mobile node, however it introduces a vulnerability in management of the values. That is, a malicious node can easily consume the memory of the correspondent node sending bogus Home Test Init or Care-of Test Init messages with a lot of fake mobile node's addresses.

When a mobile node sends a Binding Update message, it includes nonce index values. A correspondent node must keep the history of these values and must be able to regenerate Keygen Tokens from the index values.

Figure 5-40 shows the packet flow of the Home Test and the Care-of Test messages.

FIGURE 5-40

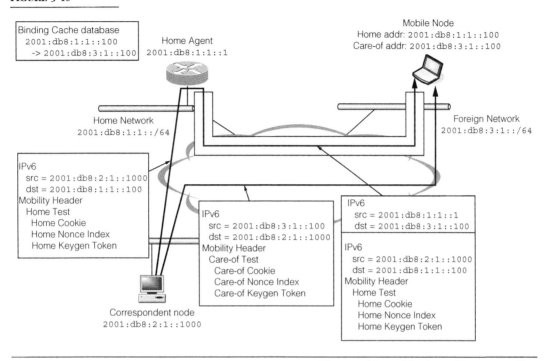

The Home Test and the Care-of Test message flow.

5.5.4 Computing a Shared Secret

A shared secret is computed as follows:

$$K_{bm} = SHA1(home\ keygen\ token\ |\ care\text{-}of\ keygen\ token)$$
$$\dots (\text{if a mobile node is at a foreign network})$$

    or

$$K_{bm} = SHA1(home\ keygen\ token)$$
$$\dots (\text{if a mobile node is at home})$$

where,

    '|' denotes concatenation of data,

    K_{bm} is a shared secret computed from token values,

    $SHA1(data)$ computes a SHA-1 hash value against '*data*',

Depending on the location of a mobile node, the shared secret is computed differently. If a mobile node is in a foreign network, the secret is computed from both a Home Keygen Token and a Care-of Keygen Token. If a mobile node is at home, only a Home Keygen Token is used, because the home address and the care-of address of the mobile node are the same. In this case, we need to check only one of them. The procedure when returning to home is discussed in Section 5.5.7.

A mobile node computes a hash value using the secret information computed above. The algorithm is as follows:

$$\begin{aligned}
\textit{Mobility Data} &= \textit{the care-of address of a mobile node} \\
&\quad | \textit{the address of a correspondent node} \\
&\quad | \textit{the Mobility Header message} \\
\textit{Authenticator} &= \textit{First}(96, \textit{HMAC\_SHA1}(K_{bm}, \textit{Mobility Data}))
\end{aligned}$$

where,

'|' denotes concatenation of data,

'*the Mobility Header message*' is either a Binding Update

or a Binding Acknowledgment message,

First(*x, y*) function returns the first x bits from y,

HMAC_SHA1(*key, data*) computes a HMAC SHA-1 hash value

against '*data*' using '*key*' as a key.

The hash value is called an Authenticator. The original data of the hash value consists of a care-of address, a home address, and a Mobility Header message. When sending a Binding Update message, the Mobility Header message is the contents of the Binding Update message. When computing the hash value, all mobility options are included as a part of the Mobility Header, except the Authenticator field of the Binding Authorization Data option. The checksum field of a Mobility Header message is considered zero and it must be cleared before computing the hash value.

5.5.5 Verifying Message

A mobile node sends a Binding Update message with a Binding Authorization Data option which includes the Authenticator value computed by the procedure described in the previous paragraph and a Nonce Index option which contains the home nonce index and the care-of nonce index which have been used when generating a shared secret to compute the Authenticator. When creating a Binding Update message as a result of the return routability procedure, the lifetime of the binding information is limited to `MAX_RR_BINDING_LIFETIME` seconds.

When a correspondent node receives a Binding Update message, it first checks the existence of a Binding Authorization Data option and a Nonce Index option. If these options do not exist, the message is dropped.

The correspondent node generates a Home Keygen Token and a Care-of Keygen Token from the nonce index values included in the Nonce Index option of the incoming Binding Update message. From the tokens, the correspondent node can generate the shared secret which was used by the mobile node when it created the Binding Update message. A correspondent node verifies the message by computing a hash value of the message using the same algorithm described previously. If the result is different from the Authenticator value of the Binding Authorization Data option which was computed in the mobile node, the incoming message is dropped.

In some cases, a mobile node may use older nonce index values which a correspondent node has not kept any more. In this case, the correspondent node replies with a Binding Acknowledgment message with a status code 136 to 138 (see Table 5-3) which indicates the specified nonce index is not valid. The mobile node which receives such an error status performs the return routability procedure to get the latest nonce values.

If the incoming Binding Update message is valid, the correspondent node creates a binding cache entry for the mobile node and, if the A flag is set in the Binding Update message, replies with a Binding Acknowledgment message. The Binding Acknowledgment message also includes a Binding Authorization Data option and a Nonce Index option to protect the message. Figure 5-41 describes the packet flow of the Binding Update and the Binding Acknowledgment messages between a mobile node and a correspondent node.

5.5.6 Security Considerations

The return routability procedure provides an authorization mechanism for mobile nodes to inject binding cache entries to correspondent nodes. A correspondent node can ensure that the home address and the care-of address provided by a Binding Update message are bound to a single mobile node. But it cannot determine who the mobile node is.

For the purpose of route optimization, the provided feature is sufficient. The problem when creating a binding cache entry is that if an attacker can create a binding cache entry with the home address of a victim mobile node and the care-of address of the attacker, all traffic to the

FIGURE 5-41

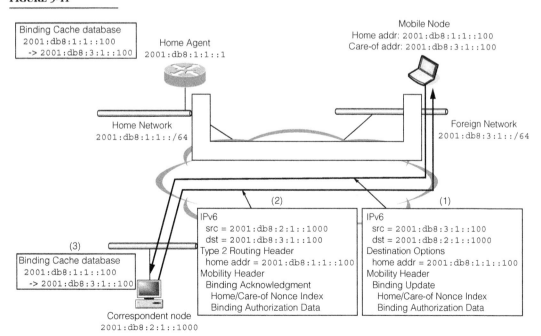

Exchanging binding information between a mobile node and a correspondent node.

victim node is routed to the attacker. The return routability procedure at least prevents this problem.

The messages exchanged between a mobile node and a correspondent node are protected by a hash function. The tokens used to generate a shared secret are exchanged by the Home Test and Care-of Test messages. That means anyone can generate the shared secret once he acquires these tokens. The Mobile IPv6 specification stipulates that the tunnel connection between a mobile node and a home agent used to send or receive the Home Test Init and the Home Test messages must be protected by the IPsec ESP mechanism. This is done by using the IPsec tunnel mode communication between them. As a result, an attacker cannot eavesdrop on the contents of the Home Test message that includes a Home Keygen Token value; however, the path between the home network of the mobile node and the correspondent node is not protected. If the attacker is on this path, the Home Keygen Token value can be examined.

To generate a shared secret, an attacker must get both a Home Keygen Token and a Care-of Keygen Token. One possible way to get both the tokens is to attach to the network between the home agent and the correspondent node of the victim mobile node. In this case, the attacker can eavesdrop on the Home Keygen token sent to the victim and can request a Care-of Keygen token by sending a faked Care-of Test Init message from the attacker's address. However, even if the attacker can get access to such a network, the situation is no worse than the normal IPv6 (not Mobile IPv6) communication. If the attacker can get access between two nodes, it can do more than just examine traffic, as with a Man-in-the-middle attack.

5.5.7 De-Register Binding for Correspondent Nodes

After successful home de-registration as discussed in Section 5.4.5, a mobile node may perform the return routability procedure for all correspondent nodes for which it has binding update list entries. The return routability procedure from a home network is slightly different from the procedure done in a foreign network since the care-of address and the home address of a mobile node are the same. In this case, a mobile node and correspondent nodes only exchange a Home Test Init and a Home Test message and a shared secret is generated only from a Home Keygen Token as described in Section 5.5.1. These messages are not tunneled to the home agent because the tunnel link has already been destroyed by the home de-registration procedure performed before this return routability procedure.

5.5.8 Backward Compatibility

When we consider deploying a new technology, we need to take care of the backward compatibility with legacy nodes. Mobile IPv6 will not be deployed if it cannot communicate with many old IPv6 nodes that do not understand it.

To ensure backward compatibility, the Mobile IPv6 specification defines a tunnel mechanism. A mobile node can send and receive packets using a tunnel between a mobile node and its home agent, as if the mobile node were at home. As long as a mobile node uses the tunnel, no backward compatibility issues occur.

However, as we have already discussed, a mobile node may initiate the return routability procedure to optimize the route between itself and a correspondent node. A mobile node cannot know beforehand if the peer node, with which the mobile node is currently communicating, supports Mobile IPv6. So, a mobile node may send a Home Test Init or a Care-of Test Init message, even if the peer node does not support Mobile IPv6. These messages use the Mobility Header, which is a new extension header introduced by the Mobile IPv6 specification. The old

FIGURE 5-42

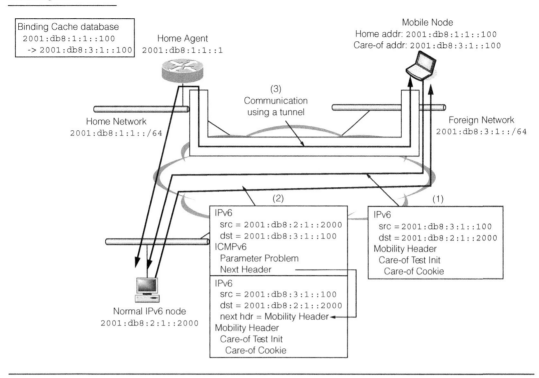

An ICMPv6 message generation from a non-Mobile IPv6 node.

IPv6 nodes do not know of the extension header and cannot recognize the protocol number (in this case, 135). When a node receives an unrecognized protocol number, the node will generate an ICMPv6 Parameter Problem message with code 2 indicating that the incoming packet has an unrecognized next header value. The ICMPv6 message also indicates the position where an error occurred. In this case, the error messages point to the next header field of the header located before the Mobility Header. The generation of an ICMPv6 message for an unrecognized header is defined in the IPv6 base specification. We can assume all IPv6 nodes have this functionality.

If a mobile receives an ICMPv6 Parameter Problem message with code 2, and the error position indicates the protocol number of a Mobility Header, the mobile node stops performing the return routability procedure and uses only tunnel communication. Figure 5-42 shows the packet exchange.

5.6   Movement Detection

When a mobile node attaches to a network, it must detect whether or not it has moved. There are several pieces of information which can be used to detect the movement of a node. The Mobile IPv6 specification talks about a basic movement detection method which uses Neighbor Unreachability Detection of a default router of a mobile node. As described in the Neighbor Discovery specification, an IPv6 node keeps a list of default routers on the attached network. If the routers become unreachable, it can be assumed that the node is attached to a different network.

When performing Neighbor Unreachability Detection for default routers, we need to take care of one thing. The Neighbor Unreachability Detection is done by sending a Neighbor Solicitation message to the target router. Usually, the address of the target router is a link-local address, since a normal Router Advertisement does not contain the global address of the router. A node usually does not know the global address of routers. However, a link-local address is unique only on a single link. This means that even if a mobile node moves from one network to another network, the mobile node may not be able to detect the unreachability of the default router if routers on the different links use the same link-local address. A mobile node needs to utilize other information as much as possible.

One of the other pieces of information which can be used for the unreachability detection is a global address from a Prefix Information option which is extended by the Mobile IPv6 specification. If a Router Advertisement message contains the extension, a mobile node should perform Neighbor Unreachability Detection against the global address. Of course, this can be used only with routers that support Mobile IPv6 extension.

Another method is collecting all prefix information on a network. The prefix value is unique to each network. In this method, a mobile node keeps collecting prefix information. If prefix information which was advertised before can no longer be seen, the node may have moved to another network. The important thing is that the mobile node must not decide its movement by receiving only one advertisement message because there may be several routers which advertise different prefix information on the network. In that case, a single router advertisement does not show the entire network information.

There is no standard way of detecting movement of a mobile node. It is highly implementation dependent.

The IETF DNA working group is trying to enhance the detection mechanism so that mobile nodes can detect their location or movement faster and more precisely.

5.7　Dynamic Home Agent Address Discovery

A mobile node may not know the address of its home agent when it wants to send a Binding Update message for home registration. For example, if a mobile node reboots on a foreign network, there is no information about the home agent unless such information is pre-configured.

The Dynamic Home Agent Address Discovery mechanism is used to get the address information of home agents when a mobile node is in a foreign network. A mobile node sends a Dynamic Home Agent Address Discovery request message when it needs to know the address of its home agent. The source address of the message is a care-of address of a mobile node and the destination address of the message is a home agent anycast address which can be computed from the home prefix. This message does not contain a Home Address option, since this message may be sent before the first home registration is completed. A mobile node cannot use its home address before home registration is completed.

On the home network, home agents maintain the list of global addresses of all home agents on the home network by listening to each other's Router Advertisement messages. As described in Section 5.3.6, a home agent advertises its global address with a modified Prefix Information option. Figure 5-45 shows the concept.

FIGURE 5-43

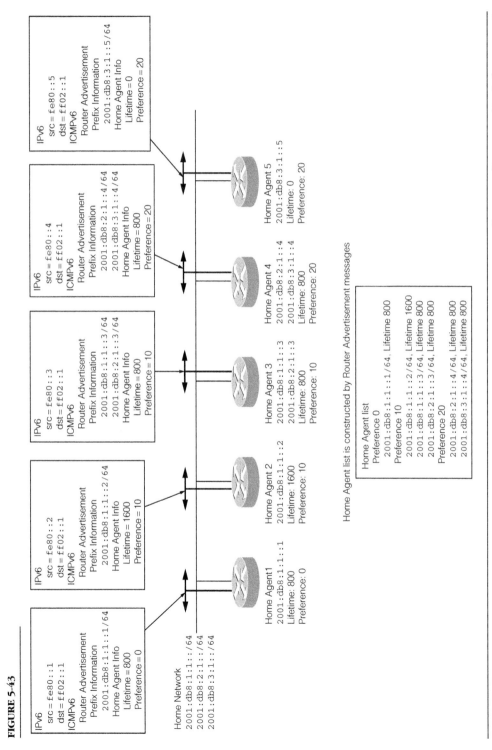

Home agent list generated in the home network.

Every home agent has a special anycast address called a home agent anycast address which is computed as described previously in Figure 5-28. A Dynamic Home Agent Address Discovery request message is delivered to one of the home agents in a home network thanks to the anycast address mechanism. The home agent which receives the message will reply to the mobile node with a Dynamic Home Agent Address Discovery reply message containing all of the home agent addresses which the home agent currently knows. The address list is ordered by the preference value of each home agent. If there are multiple home agents with the same preference value, the addresses should be ordered randomly every time for load balancing. To avoid packet fragmentation, the total length of the message must be smaller than the path MTU to the mobile node. If the list is too long to include in one packet, the home agents which have low preference values are excluded from the reply message. Figure 5-44 shows the procedure.

If a mobile node does not receive a reply message, the node will resend a request message. The initial timeout value for the retransmission is INITIAL_DHAAD_TIMEOUT seconds. The timeout value is increased exponentially at every retransmission. The maximum number of retransmissions is restricted to DHAAD_RETRIES times.

FIGURE 5-44

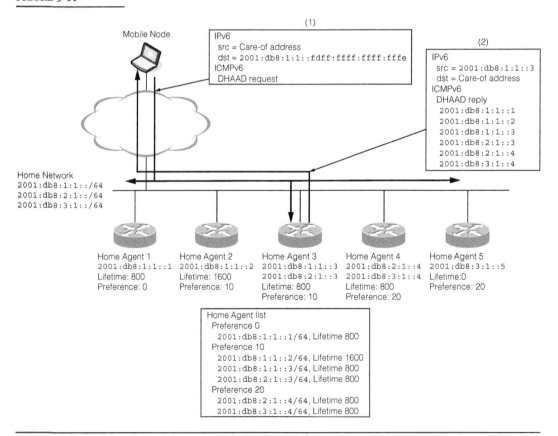

Replying to a Dynamic Home Agent Address Discovery Reply message.

In theory, the Home Agent Address Discovery mechanism can be used as a mechanism to notify mobile nodes of available home agents on its home network. However, as we discuss in Section 5.9, adding/removing the home agent causes IPsec configuration problems. In the recent discussion at the IETF, the dynamic home agent assignment and security setup are considered as part of other infrastructure-based mechanisms [RFC4640].

5.8 Mobile Prefix Solicitation/Advertisement

An IPv6 address has a lifetime value. The lifetime is derived from the lifetime of the prefix. If the home address of a mobile node is going to expire, the mobile node sends a Mobile Prefix Solicitation message to get the latest information about home prefixes. The source address of the message is set to the care-of address of the mobile node. The destination of the message is the address of the home agent with which the mobile node is currently registered. The message must include a Home Address option which contains the home address of the mobile node (i.e., a Mobile Prefix Solicitation message can be sent only after successful home registration). Since the home registration procedure requires the information of a home network, this prefix discovery mechanism cannot be used to find the home prefixes when a mobile node is booting up on a foreign network, but can only be used to know new home prefixes or deprecated home prefixes.

When a home agent receives a Mobile Prefix Solicitation message from a mobile node, the node must reply to the mobile node with a Mobile Prefix Advertisement message. The source address of the message must be the destination address of the corresponding solicitation message. The destination address of the message must be the source address of the corresponding solicitation message, that is, the care-of address of a mobile node. A Type 2 Routing Header that contains the home address of a mobile node must exist. The list of modified Prefix Information options follows the advertisement message header.

Unlike the Router Advertisement messages, the list of Prefix Information options sent from the home agents on the same home network must be consistent. To make sure of the consistency, every home agent must be configured to have the same prefix information of its home network, or must listen to Router Advertisement messages from other home agents and construct a merged list of prefix information. A mobile node sends a solicitation message to the home agent with which the mobile node is currently registered. If the prefix information returned in response to the solicitation message differs for each home agent, the mobile node may incorrectly consider that some prefix information has disappeared.

A home agent may send a Mobile Prefix Advertisement message even if a mobile node does not request the prefix information in the following cases:

- The state of the flags of the home prefix which a mobile node is using changes.
- The valid or preferred lifetime of a home prefix is reconfigured.
- A new home prefix is added.
- The state of the flags or lifetime values of a home prefix which is not used by any mobile node changes.

When either of the first two conditions occur, a home agent must send an unsolicited Mobile Prefix Advertisement. When the third condition occurs, a home agent should send an unsolicited Mobile Prefix Advertisement message. When the last condition occurs, a home agent may send the message. A mobile node updates its prefix information and home addresses derived from updated prefixes when it receives this unsolicited Mobile Prefix Advertisement.

When sending an advertisement message, a home agent must follow the following scheduling algorithm to avoid network congestion:

- If a mobile node sends a solicitation message, a home agent sends an advertisement message immediately.

- Otherwise, a home agent schedules the next transmission time as follows:

$$MaxScheduleDelay = MIN(MaxMobPfxAdvInterval, preferred\ lifetime)$$
$$RandomDelay = MinMobPfxAdvInterval$$
$$+ (RANDOM()\ \%$$
$$ABS(MaxScheduleDelay - MinMobPfxAdvInterval))$$

where,

$MIN(a, b)$ returns the smaller of a or b,

$RANDOM()$ generates a random value from 0 to the maximum possible integer value,

$ABS(a)$ returns an absolute value of a.

The next advertisement will be sent after *RandomDelay* seconds.

When a mobile node receives an unsolicited Mobile Prefix Advertisement message, it must send a Mobile Prefix Solicitation message as an acknowledgment of that message. Otherwise, a home agent will resend the unsolicited advertisement message every PREFIX_ADV_TIMEOUT seconds. The maximum number of retransmissions is restricted to PREFIX_ADV_RETIRES times. The Mobile Prefix Solicitation and Advertisement message should be protected by the IPsec mechanism.

In theory, the Mobile Prefix Solicitation/Advertisement mechanism can be used as a mechanism to renumber the home network of mobile nodes, however, as discussed in Section 5.9, renumbering the home addresses has IPsec configuration problems. A mobile node and its home agent must negotiate which home address should be used and the IPsec policy database on both nodes need to be updated because the database has home address information. The Mobile IPv6 specification does not specify any address transition procedure in its base specification.

5.9   Relationship with IPsec

Mobile IPv6 uses the IPsec mechanism to protect the Mobile IPv6 signaling messages. The specifications on how to protect messages are defined in [RFC3776].

The messages directly exchanged between a mobile node and a home agent are protected by the IPsec transport mode mechanism. The Binding Update and Binding Acknowledgment messages must be protected by the IPsec ESP or AH header. The Mobile Prefix Solicitation and Advertisement messages should be protected by the IPsec mechanism.

The messages exchanged between a mobile node and a correspondent node, and relayed by the home agent, are protected by the IPsec tunnel mode mechanism. The Home Test Init and Home Test messages must be protected by the IPsec ESP header with the IPsec tunnel mode. As we will show in this section, the tunnel mode policy entries must be able to support the Mobility Header type specific policy rule. More precisely, it must be able to send and receive the Home Test Init and Home Test messages only via the IPsec tunnel. This is necessary when two mobile nodes communicate with route optimization. If a mobile node cannot specify the Home Test Init/Home Test messages as policy specification, a Binding Update message to the other mobile node (this node is actually treated as a correspondent node) is incorrectly tunneled to the home agent of the mobile node that is sending the Binding Update message.

Note that the Dynamic Home Agent Address Discovery Request and Reply messages cannot be protected because the mobile node does not know the home agent address before exchanging these messages. The address information is required to set up the IPsec security policy database to protect messages.

Tables 5-8 and 5-9 summarize the policy entries required for a mobile node and a home agent.

The Security Associations for each policy can be configured by a manual operation. The IKE mechanism can be used to create these Security Associations dynamically, however, it requires a modification to the IKE program. Usually, the addresses of a Security Association IKE configures are derived from the addresses which are used to perform the IKE negotiation. In the Mobile IPv6 case, when a mobile node moves from its home network to a foreign network, the home address cannot be used until the home registration procedure has been completed. But we need a Security Association between the home address and the home agent address to complete the home registration procedure. The IKE program must use a care-of address for IKE negotiation and create a Security Association for addresses which are not used in the IKE negotiation. Currently, few IKE implementations support this function.

There are other problems which are caused by the design of the IPsec policy configuration mechanism. The IPsec policy configuration is usually static, however in the Mobile IPv6 operation we need to change policies in the following situations:

- When a new home agent is installed.
  — A mobile node needs to install new transport and tunnel mode policy entries for the new home agent.

- When a renumbering occurs.
  — A mobile node and a home agent need to update their home prefix information in the policy database.

The use of IPsec with Mobile IPv6 has many unresolved issues. More research is required to achieve flexible operation of the combination of these technologies.

TABLE 5-8

Mode	IPsec protocol	Target source	Target destination	Target protocol	Tunnel source	Tunnel destination
Transport	ESP (or AH)	Home address	Home agent	MH (Binding Update)	–	–
Transport	ESP (or AH)	Home agent	Home address	MH (Binding Acknowledgment)	–	–
Transport	ESP (or AH)	Home address	Home agent	ICMPv6 (Mobile Prefix Solicitation)	–	–
Transport	ESP (or AH)	Home agent	Home address	ICMPv6 (Mobile Prefix Advertisement)	–	–
Tunnel	ESP	Home address	Any	MH (Home Test Init)	Care-of address	Home agent
Tunnel	ESP	Any	Home address	MH (Home Test)	Home agent	Care-of address

Security policy entries required for a mobile node.

TABLE 5-9

Mode	IPsec protocol	Target source	Target destination	Target protocol	Tunnel source	Tunnel destination
Transport	ESP (or AH)	Home agent	Home address	MH (Binding Update)	–	–
Transport	ESP (or AH)	Home address	Home agent	MH (Binding Acknowledgment)	–	–
Transport	ESP (or AH)	Home agent	Home address	ICMPv6 (Mobile Prefix Solicitation)	–	–
Transport	ESP (or AH)	Home address	Home agent	ICMPv6 (Mobile Prefix Advertisement)	–	–
Tunnel	ESP	Any	Home address	MH (Home Test Init)	Home agent	Care-of address
Tunnel	ESP	Home address	Any	MH (Home Test)	Care-of address	Home agent

Security policy entries required for a home agent.

5.10 Code Introduction

In this section, we describe the detailed Mobile IPv6 code implemented as a part of the KAME distribution. Note that the code we quote in this chapter is newer than the other code quoted in other chapters. In this book, most of the code fragments other than those in this chapter are copied from the snapshot code generated on April 21, 2003; however, the code used in this chapter is based on the snapshot code generated on July 12, 2004. We decided to use the latest Mobile IPv6 code as much as possible, since the Mobile IPv6 code was incomplete when we started writing this book. There are some inconsistent parts between this chapter and other chapters. One big difference is the way to keep address information of IPv6 packets in the kernel. The code discussed in this chapter refers to the IPv6 source and destination address fields to access address information, while the information is stored in the `ip6_aux{}` structure separately in older codes discussed in other chapters. We believe such inconsistency will not confuse readers in understanding the implementation of Mobile IPv6, since the framework of the KAME code itself has not been modified drastically.

5.10.1 Statistics

Statistics are stored in the `mip6stat{}` structure. Table 5-10 describes the statistics variables.

TABLE 5-10

mip6sta{}member	*Description*
`mip6s_mobility`	# of Mobility Header packets received.
`mip6s_omobility`	# of Mobility Header packets sent.
`mip6s_hoti`	# of Home Test Init packets received.
`mip6s_ohoti`	# of Home Test Init packets sent.
`mip6s_coti`	# of Care-of Test Init packets received.
`mip6s_ocoti`	# of Care-of Test Init packets sent.
`mip6s_hot`	# of Home Test packets received.
`mip6s_ohot`	# of Home Test packets sent.
`mip6s_cot`	# of Care-of Test packets received.
`mip6s_ocot`	# of Care-of Test packets sent.
`mip6s_bu`	# of Binding Update received.
`mip6s_obu`	# of Binding Update sent.
`mip6s_ba`	# of Binding Acknowledgment received.
`mip6s_ba_hist[0...255]`	Histogram based on the status code of Binding Acknowledgment received.
`mip6s_oba`	# of Binding Acknowledgment sent.
`mip6s_oba_hist[0...255]`	Histogram based on the status code of Binding Acknowledgment sent.

Continued

TABLE 5-10 (*Continued*)

mip6sta{ }member	*Description*
`mip6s_br`	# of Binding Refresh Request received.
`mip6s_obr`	# of Binding Refresh Request sent.
`mip6s_be`	# of Binding Error received.
`mip6s_be_hist [0...255]`	Histogram based on the status code of Binding Error received.
`mip6s_obe`	# of Binding Error sent.
`mip6s_obe_hist[0...255]`	Histogram based on the status code of Binding Error sent.
`mip6s_hao`	# of Home Address option received.
`mip6s_unverifiedhao`	# of received Home Address options which do not have corresponding binding cache information.
`mip6s_ohao`	# of Home Address option sent.
`mip6s_rthdr2`	# of Type 2 Routing Header received.
`mip6s_orthdr2`	# of Type 2 Routing Header sent.
`mip6s_revtunnel`	# of packets which came from bi-directional tunnel.
`mip6s_orevtunnel`	# of packets which are sent to bi-directional tunnel.
`mip6s_checksum`	# of Mobility Header packets in which checksum value was incorrect.
`mip6s_payloadproto`	# of Mobility Header packets in which payload protocol number is other than `IPV6-NONXT`.
`mip6s_unknowntype`	# of Mobility Header packets in which type value is unknown.
`mip6s_nohif`	# of packets in which destination address is not my home address.
`mip6s_nobue`	# of packets which have no corresponding binding update information.
`mip6s_hinitcookie`	# of Home Test packets in which cookie does not match the stored cookie.
`mip6s_cinitcookie`	# of Care-of Test packets in which cookie does not match the stored cookie.
`mip6s_unprotected`	# of Binding Update/Binding Acknowledgment packets which are not protected by IPsec.
`mip6s_haopolicy`	# of Binding Update/Binding Acknowledgment packets in which HAO is not protected by IPsec or Authentication Data suboption.
`mip6s_rrauthfail`	# of failure of the Return Routability procedure.
`mip6s_seqno`	# of failure of sequence number mismatch.
`mip6s_paramprobhao`	# of ICMPv6 Parameter Problem packets against HAO option.
`mip6s_paramprobmh`	# of ICMPv6 Parameter Problem packets against Mobility Header packets.
`mip6s_invalidcoa`	# of packets which care-of address was not acceptable.
`mip6s_invalidopt`	# of packets which contained invalid mobility options.
`mip6s_circularrefered`	# of Binding Update packets which requests binding a care-of address of one node with a home address of another node.

Mobile IPv6 statistics.

5.11 Mobile IPv6 Related Structures

In this section we introduce all structures used by the Mobile IPv6 stack.

As discussed in Section 5.3.4, a new extension header, Mobility Header, is introduced in [RFC3775]. Mobility Header has a type field to specify different message types based on each message's function. In [RFC3775] 8 type values are defined. Each message format is described in Sections 5.11.2 to 5.11.10. Mobility Header may have option data as discussed in Section 5.3.5. The related structures are described in Sections 5.11.11 to 5.11.16.

The message format of the Home Address option and the Type 2 Routing Header (Sections 5.3.2 and 5.3.3), which are used for route optimized communication, are described in Sections 5.11.18 and 5.11.19.

[RFC3775] extends some Neighbor Discovery messages as discussed in Section 5.3.6. The extended Neighbor Discovery structures are described in Sections 5.11.20 to 5.11.23.

The Dynamic Home Agent Address Discovery messages discussed in Section 5.3.7 are used to discover the addresses of a mobile node's home agent. The message formats are described in Sections 5.11.24 and 5.11.25.

Finally, the Mobile Prefix Solicitation/Advertisement message formats used to distribute home prefix information from a home agent to a mobile node are described in Sections 5.11.26 and 5.11.27.

Section 5.11 also describes some internal structures that are not related to any messages defined in [RFC3775]. These structures are used for the kernel internal use.

5.11.1 Files

Table 5-11 shows the files that define Mobile IPv6 related structures.

5.11.2 Mobility Header Message—`ip6_mh{}` Structure

The `ip6_mh{}` structure defined in `ip6mh.h` represents the Mobility Header (Section 5.3.4) described in Listing 5-1. The structure definitions of protocol headers and options are documented in [RFC4584].

TABLE 5-11

File	Description
`${KAME}/kame/sys/net/if_hif.h`	Home virtual interface structures
`${KAME}/kame/sys/netinet/icmp6.h`	Dynamic Home Agent Address Discovery and Mobile Prefix Solicitation/Advertisement structures
`${KAME}/kame/sys/netinet/ip6.h`	Home Address option structure
`${KAME}/kame/sys/netinet/ip6mh.h`	Mobility Header structures
`${KAME}/kame/sys/netinet6/mip6_var.h`	All structures which are used in the Mobile IPv6 stack
`${KAME}/kame/kame/had/halist.h`	Home agent information structure used by the home agent side

Files that define Mobile IPv6 related structures.

Listing 5-1

—— ip6mh.h
```
36        struct ip6_mh {
37                u_int8_t  ip6mh_proto;      /* following payload protocol (for PG) */
38                u_int8_t  ip6mh_len;        /* length in units of 8 octets */
39                u_int8_t  ip6mh_type;       /* message type */
40                u_int8_t  ip6mh_reserved;
41                u_int16_t ip6mh_cksum;      /* sum of IPv6 pseudo-header and MH */
42                /* followed by type specific data */
43        } __attribute__((__packed__));
```
—— ip6mh.h

36–43 The `ip6_mh{}` structure is the base structure for all the Mobility Headers. `ip6mh_proto` is a protocol number of an upper layer protocol which follows the Mobility Header. At this moment, the RFC specifies that there should not be any upper layer protocol headers after Mobility Headers. This field should be always set to `IPV6-NONXT` (decimal 58), which means there are no following headers. This field can be considered a reserved field for future use in piggy-backing the mobility signals on upper layer packets. `ip6mh_len` is the length of a Mobility Header in units of 8 bytes, not including the first 8 bytes. `ip6mh_type` indicates the message type. Currently, 8 message types are defined. Table 5-12 shows the

TABLE 5-12

Name	Value	Description
IP6_MH_TYPE_BRR	0	Binding Refresh Request message: sent from a correspondent node to a mobile node when it wants to extend its binding lifetime.
IP6_MH_TYPE_HOTI	1	Home Test Init message: sent from a mobile node to a correspondent node when it initiates the return routability procedure to confirm the home address ownership and reachability.
IP6_MH_TYPE_COTI	2	Care-of Test Init message: sent from a mobile node to a correspondent node when it initiates the return routability procedure to confirm the care-of address ownership and reachability.
IP6_MH_TYPE_HOT	3	Home Test message: sent from a correspondent node to a mobile node in response to a Home Test Init message.
IP6_MH_TYPE_COT	4	Care-of Test message: sent from a correspondent node to a mobile node in response to a Care-of Test Init message.
IP6_MH_TYPE_BU	5	Binding Update message: sent from a mobile node to a home agent or a correspondent node to inform binding information between the home and care-of address of the mobile node.
IP6_MH_TYPE_BACK	6	Binding Acknowledgment message: sent from a home agent or a correspondent node in response to a Binding Update message. Note that the KAME Mobile IPv6 correspondent node does not send this message except in error cases.
IP6_MH_TYPE_BERROR	7	Binding Error message: sent when an error occurs while a node is processing Mobile IPv6 messages.
IP6_MH_TYPE_MAX	7	(maximum type value)

MH type numbers.

current message types. `ip6mh_reserved` is a reserved field for future use. This field should be zero cleared when sending, and must be ignored when receiving. `ip6mh_cksum` keeps the checksum value of an MH message. The computation procedure is the same as the one for the ICMPv6 message.

5.11.3 Binding Refresh Request Message—`ip6_mh_binding_request{}` Structure

The `ip6_mh_binding_request{}` structure represents the Binding Refresh Request message described in Figure 5-8 of Section 5.3.4. Listing 5-2 shows the definition of the `ip6_mh_binding_request{}` structure.

Listing 5-2

—————————————————————————————————— ip6mh.h

```
61      struct ip6_mh_binding_request {
62              struct ip6_mh ip6mhbr_hdr;
63              u_int16_t      ip6mhbr_reserved;
64              /* followed by mobility options */
65      } __attribute__((__packed__));
66      #ifdef _KERNEL
67      #define ip6mhbr_proto ip6mhbr_hdr.ip6mh_proto
68      #define ip6mhbr_len ip6mhbr_hdr.ip6mh_len
69      #define ip6mhbr_type ip6mhbr_hdr.ip6mh_type
70      #define ip6mhbr_reserved0 ip6mhbr_hdr.ip6mh_reserved
71      #define ip6mhbr_cksum ip6mhbr_hdr.ip6mh_cksum
72      #endif /* _KERNEL */
```

—————————————————————————————————— ip6mh.h

61–72 The `ip6mhbr_hdr` field is common for all Mobility Header messages. To make it easy to access the member fields in `ip6mhbr_hdr`, some macros are defined in lines 67–71. Note that these shortcuts, bracketed by the `_KERNEL` macro, can be used only from the inside kernel. Any application program which uses the header fields must use the `ip6mhbr_hdr` member field for compatibility. In the Binding Refresh Request message, the type number, `ip6mhbr_type`, is set to `IP6_MH_TYPE_BRR`. The `ip6mhbr_reserved` field is reserved for future use. A sender must clear this field when sending a message, and a receiver must ignore this field.

5.11.4 Home Test Init Message—`ip6_mh_home_test_init{}` Structure

The `ip6_mh_home_test_init{}` structure represents the Home Test Init message described in Figure 5-9 of Section 5.3.4. Listing 5-3 shows the definition of the `ip6_mh_home_test_init{}` structure.

Listing 5-3

—————————————————————————————————— ip6mh.h

```
75      struct ip6_mh_home_test_init {
76              struct ip6_mh ip6mhhti_hdr;
77              u_int16_t      ip6mhhti_reserved;
78              union {
79                      u_int8_t  __cookie8[8];
80                      u_int32_t __cookie32[2];
81              } __ip6mhhti_cookie;
82              /* followed by mobility options */
83      } __attribute__((__packed__));
```

```
84      #ifdef _KERNEL
85      #define ip6mhhti_proto ip6mhhti_hdr.ip6mh_proto
86      #define ip6mhhti_len ip6mhhti_hdr.ip6mh_len
87      #define ip6mhhti_type ip6mhhti_hdr.ip6mh_type
88      #define ip6mhhti_reserved0 ip6mhhti_hdr.ip6mh_reserved
89      #define ip6mhhti_cksum ip6mhhti_hdr.ip6mh_cksum
90      #define ip6mhhti_cookie8 __ip6mhhti_cookie.__cookie8
91      #endif /* _KERNEL */
92      #define ip6mhhti_cookie __ip6mhhti_cookie.__cookie32
```
─── ip6mh.h

75–92 The `ip6mhhti_hdr` field is common to all Mobility Header messages. There are 5 macro definitions for shortcut access to the common header part in lines 85–89. Also, there are two other macros to access the cookie value. The API specification only defines `ip6mhhti_cookie`, which is used to access the values in a unit of 32 bits. There are some cases where it is more convenient if we can access the value in an 8-bit unit. The `ip6mhhti_cookie8` macro is provided for this purpose. `ip6mhhti_type` is set to `IP6_MH_TYPE_HOTI`. `ip6mhhti_cookie` is an 8-byte cookie value which is generated in a mobile node to bind a Home Test Init message and a Home Test message. Two reserved fields (`ip6mhhti_reserved0` and `ip6mhti_reserved`) must be cleared by the sender and must be ignored by the receiver.

5.11.5   Care-of Test Init Message—`ip6_mh_careof_test_init{}` Structure

The `ip6_mh_careof_test_init{}` structure represents the Care-of Test Init message described in Figure 5-10 of Section 5.3.4. Listing 5-4 shows the definition of the `ip6_mh_careof_test_init{}` structure.

Listing 5-4
─── ip6mh.h

```
95      struct ip6_mh_careof_test_init {
96              struct ip6_mh ip6mhcti_hdr;
97              u_int16_t       ip6mhcti_reserved;
98              union {
99                      u_int8_t   __cookie8[8];
100                     u_int32_t  __cookie32[2];
101             } __ip6mhcti_cookie;
102             /* followed by mobility options */
103     } __attribute__((__packed__));
104     #ifdef _KERNEL
105     #define ip6mhcti_proto ip6mhcti_hdr.ip6mh_proto
106     #define ip6mhcti_len ip6mhcti_hdr.ip6mh_len
107     #define ip6mhcti_type ip6mhcti_hdr.ip6mh_type
108     #define ip6mhcti_reserved0 ip6mhcti_hdr.ip6mh_reserved
109     #define ip6mhcti_cksum ip6mhcti_hdr.ip6mh_cksum
110     #define ip6mhcti_cookie8 __ip6mhcti_cookie.__cookie8
111     #endif /* _KERNEL */
112     #define ip6mhcti_cookie __ip6mhcti_cookie.__cookie32
```
─── ip6mh.h

95–112 The `ip6mhcti_hdr` field is common to all Mobility Header messages. The structure is almost the same as the `ip6_mh_home_test_init{}` structure. The only difference is the name of its member fields. In the Home Test Init message, `ip6mhhti_` is used as a prefix for each member field, while `ip6mhcti_` is used in the Care-of Test Init message.

5.11.6 Home Test Message—`ip6_mh_home_test{}` Structure

The `ip6_mh_home_test{}` structure represents the Home Test message described in Figure 5-11 of Section 5.3.4. Listing 5-5 shows the definition of the `ip6_mh_home_test{}` structure.

Listing 5-5

```
──────────────────────────────────────────────────────────────────ip6mh.h
115    struct ip6_mh_home_test {
116            struct ip6_mh ip6mhht_hdr;
117            u_int16_t     ip6mhht_nonce_index; /* idx of the CN nonce list array */
118            union {
119                    u_int8_t  __cookie8[8];
120                    u_int32_t __cookie32[2];
121            } __ip6mhht_cookie;
122            union {
123                    u_int8_t  __keygen8[8];
124                    u_int32_t __keygen32[2];
125            } __ip6mhht_keygen;
126            /* followed by mobility options */
127    } __attribute__((__packed__));
128    #ifdef _KERNEL
129    #define ip6mhht_proto ip6mhht_hdr.ip6mh_proto
130    #define ip6mhht_len ip6mhht_hdr.ip6mh_len
131    #define ip6mhht_type ip6mhht_hdr.ip6mh_type
132    #define ip6mhht_reserved0 ip6mhht_hdr.ip6mh_reserved
133    #define ip6mhht_cksum ip6mhht_hdr.ip6mh_cksum
134    #define ip6mhht_cookie8 __ip6mhht_cookie.__cookie8
135    #define ip6mhht_keygen8 __ip6mhht_keygen.__keygen8
136    #endif /* _KERNEL */
137    #define ip6mhht_cookie __ip6mhht_cookie.__cookie32
138    #define ip6mhht_keygen __ip6mhht_keygen.__keygen32
──────────────────────────────────────────────────────────────────ip6mh.h
```

115–138 The `ip6mhht_hdr` field is common for all Mobility Header messages. The `ip6_mh_home_test{}` structure also has several shortcuts, which can be used only in the kernel, to access the member fields in the common part of the MH message. In the Home Test message, the type number (`ip6mhht_type`) is set to `IP6_MH_TYPE_HOT`, the `ip6mhht_cookie` field is used to store the cookie value which is sent from a mobile node in the Home Test Init message. The cookie value is copied from the Home Test Init message to the Home Test message. A mobile node uses the cookie value to determine if the received Home Test message was sent in response to a Home Test Init message which the mobile node sent previously. The `ip6mhht_keygen` field contains the keygen token value which is computed inside a correspondent node using secret information from the correspondent node. The `ip6mhht_cookie8` and `ip6mhht_keygen8` fields are provided as methods to access the cookie and token values as byte arrays.

5.11.7 Care-of Test Message—`ip6_mh_careof_test{}` Structure

The `ip6_mh_careof_test{}` structure represents the Care-of Test message described in Figure 5-12 of Section 5.3.4. Listing 5-6 shows the definition of the `ip6_careof_test{}` structure.

Listing 5-6

```
──────────────────────────────────────────────────────────────────ip6mh.h
141    struct ip6_mh_careof_test {
142            struct ip6_mh ip6mhct_hdr;
```

```
143              u_int16_t     ip6mhct_nonce_index; /* idx of the CN nonce list array */
144              union {
145                      u_int8_t  __cookie8[8];
146                      u_int32_t __cookie32[2];
147              } __ip6mhct_cookie;
148              union {
149                      u_int8_t  __keygen8[8];
150                      u_int32_t __keygen32[2];
151              } __ip6mhct_keygen;
152              /* followed by mobility options */
153      } __attribute__((__packed__));
154      #ifdef _KERNEL
155      #define ip6mhct_proto ip6mhct_hdr.ip6mh_proto
156      #define ip6mhct_len ip6mhct_hdr.ip6mh_len
157      #define ip6mhct_type ip6mhct_hdr.ip6mh_type
158      #define ip6mhct_reserved0 ip6mhct_hdr.ip6mh_reserved
159      #define ip6mhct_cksum ip6mhct_hdr.ip6mh_cksum
160      #define ip6mhct_cookie8 __ip6mhct_cookie.__cookie8
161      #define ip6mhct_keygen8 __ip6mhct_keygen.__keygen8
162      #endif /* _KERNEL */
163      #define ip6mhct_cookie __ip6mhct_cookie.__cookie32
164      #define ip6mhct_keygen __ip6mhct_keygen.__keygen32
```
                                                                              ip6mh.h

141–164 The `ip6mhct_hdr` field is common for all Mobility Header messages. This structure is almost identical to the `ip6_mh_home_test{}` structure. The difference is the name of each member field. In the `ip6_mh_careof_test{}` structure, each member field has `ip6mhct_` as a prefix, while the `ip6_mh_home_test{}` structure uses `ip6mhht_`. The `ip6mhct_cookie` and `ip6mhct_keygen` fields are equivalent to the `ip6mhht_cookie` and `ip6mht_keygen` fields. The `ip6mhct_cookie` field stores the cookie value sent from a mobile node in the Care-of Test Init message. The `ip6mhct_keygen` field stores the token value which is used to compute the shared secret between the correspondent node and the mobile node. The `ip6mhct_cookie8` and `ip6mhct_keygen8` fields point to the same contents as do the `ip6mhct_cookie` and `ip6mhct_keygen` fields, but they allow access to the fields as byte streams.

5.11.8 Binding Update Message—`ip6_mh_binding_update{}` Structure

The `ip6_mh_binding_update{}` structure represents the Binding Update message described in Figure 5-13 of Section 5.3.4. Listing 5-7 shows the definition of the `ip6_mh_binding_update{}` structure.

Listing 5-7
                                                                              ip6mh.h

```
167      struct ip6_mh_binding_update {
168              struct ip6_mh ip6mhbu_hdr;
169              u_int16_t     ip6mhbu_seqno;    /* sequence number */
170              u_int16_t     ip6mhbu_flags;    /* IP6MU_* flags */
171              u_int16_t     ip6mhbu_lifetime; /* in units of 4 seconds */
172              /* followed by mobility options */
173      } __attribute__((__packed__));
174      #ifdef _KERNEL
175      #define ip6mhbu_proto ip6mhbu_hdr.ip6mh_proto
176      #define ip6mhbu_len ip6mhbu_hdr.ip6mh_len
177      #define ip6mhbu_type ip6mhbu_hdr.ip6mh_type
178      #define ip6mhbu_reserved0 ip6mhbu_hdr.ip6mh_reserved
179      #define ip6mhbu_cksum ip6mhbu_hdr.ip6mh_cksum
180      #endif /* _KERNEL */
```
                                                                              ip6mh.h

167–180 The `ip6mhbu_hdr` field is common for all Mobility Header messages. As with the other messages, there are macro definitions to access inside members of the `ip6mhbu_hdr` field. The `ip6mhbu_type` field is set to `IP6_MH_TYPE_BU`. The `ip6mhbu_seqno` field keeps a sequence number of the binding information, which is used to prevent a replay attack from malicious nodes. A mobile node must increase the sequence number when sending a Binding Update message. The home agent of the mobile node will discard any messages that have an old sequence number. (See Section 5.4.2 for the procedure and Listing 5-59 for its implementation.)

The `ip6mhbu_flags` field keeps the flag values of the message. Currently, there are 4 flags in the specification. Table 5-2 (page 500) describes the flags and their meanings. Table 5-13 shows the list of macros for the flags. `IP6MU_CLONED` macro is a special macro which is used to represent the internal state of binding information. `IP6MU_CLONED` flag is set when a home agent receives a BU message with the L flag set. The home agent will create two binding entries when it accepts the message. One is to bind the home address and the care-of address of the mobile node. The other is to bind the link-local address (which is generated automatically using the interface identifier part of the home address) and the care-of address of the mobile node to protect the link-local address of the mobile node. The latter binding cache entry will have `IP6MU_CLONED` flag set to mark that the entry is created as a side effect of the L flag. This flag is an implementation-dependent flag and should never be sent to the wire with any Mobility messages.

The `ip6mhbu_lifetime` field indicates the proposed lifetime of the binding information. The value is units of 4 seconds to allow for a mobile node to specify a longer time with smaller data. A mobile node sets the value based on the remaining lifetimes of its home and care-of addresses. Note that the value is just a proposal from the mobile node to the node receiving the Binding Update message. The actual approved lifetime may be reduced from the proposed lifetime based on the local policy of the recipient node.

5.11.9 Binding Acknowledgment Message—`ip6_mh_binding_ack{}` Structure

The `ip6_mh_binding_ack{}` structure represents the Binding Acknowledgment message described in Figure 5-14 of Section 5.3.4. Listing 5-8 shows the definition of the `ip6_mh_binding_ack{}` structure.

TABLE 5-13

Name	Description
IP6MU_ACK	Acknowledgment (The A flag)
IP6MU_HOME	Home Registration (The H flag)
IP6MU_LINK	Link-Local Address Compatibility (The L flag)
IP6MU_KEY	Key Management Mobility Capability (The K flag)
IP6MU_CLONED	(internal use only) means the binding information is generated by the L flag processing.

Macro definitions for flags of Binding Update message.

TABLE 5-14

Name	Description
IP6_MH_BA_KEYM	Key Management Mobility Capability (the K flag)

Macro definitions for the Binding Acknowledgment flag field.

Listing 5-8

```
199     struct ip6_mh_binding_ack {
200             struct ip6_mh ip6mhba_hdr;
201             u_int8_t      ip6mhba_status;    /* status code */
202             u_int8_t      ip6mhba_flags;
203             u_int16_t     ip6mhba_seqno;     /* sequence number */
204             u_int16_t     ip6mhba_lifetime; /* in units of 4 seconds */
205             /* followed by mobility options */
206     } __attribute__((__packed__));
207     #ifdef _KERNEL
208     #define ip6mhba_proto ip6mhba_hdr.ip6mh_proto
209     #define ip6mhba_len ip6mhba_hdr.ip6mh_len
210     #define ip6mhba_type ip6mhba_hdr.ip6mh_type
211     #define ip6mhba_reserved0 ip6mhba_hdr.ip6mh_reserved
212     #define ip6mhba_cksum ip6mhba_hdr.ip6mh_cksum
213     #endif /* _KERNEL */
```

199–213 The `ip6mhba_hdr` is common for all Mobility Header messages. Similar to other messages, some macros are defined to make it easy to access the members of the `ip6mhba_hdr` field. The `ip6mhba_type` field is set to `IP6_MH_TYPE_BACK`, the `ip6mhba_status` field indicates the result of processing a Binding Update message. Table 5-15 shows all the status codes defined in [RFC3775] which can be contained in the `ip6mhba_status` field. The `ip6mhba_flags` field is the flags. Currently, only the `IP6_MH_BA_KEYM` flag is defined as described in Table 5-14. `ip6mhba_seqno` is the latest sequence number for binding information stored in a correspondent node or a home agent. `ip6mhba_lifetime` indicates the approved lifetime for the binding information. A mobile node requests the lifetime of binding information by specifying field `ip6mhbu_lifetime` in a Binding Update message; however, the requested value is not always appropriate. A node which receives a Binding Update decides the proper lifetime and sets the value in the `ip6mhba_lifetime` field. The value is units of 4 seconds (that is, the value 100 means 400 seconds).

5.11.10 Binding Error Message—`ip6_mh_binding_error{}` Structure

The `ip6_mh_binding_error{}` structure represents a Binding Error message described in Figure 5-15 of Section 5.3.4. Listing 5-9 shows the definition of the `ip6_mh_binding_error{}` structure.

Listing 5-9

```
236     struct ip6_mh_binding_error {
237             struct ip6_mh   ip6mhbe_hdr;
238             u_int8_t        ip6mhbe_status;          /* status code */
```

```
239                 u_int8_t           ip6mhbe_reserved;
240                 struct in6_addr ip6mhbe_homeaddr;
241                 /* followed by mobility options */
242         } __attribute__((__packed__));
243         #ifdef _KERNEL
244         #define ip6mhbe_proto ip6mhbe_hdr.ip6mh_proto
245         #define ip6mhbe_len ip6mhbe_hdr.ip6mh_len
246         #define ip6mhbe_type ip6mhbe_hdr.ip6mh_type
247         #define ip6mhbe_reserved0 ip6mhbe_hdr.ip6mh_reserved
248         #define ip6mhbe_cksum ip6mhbe_hdr.ip6mh_cksum
249         #endif /* _KERNEL */
```
—— ip6mh.h

236–249 The `ip6mhbe_hdr` field is common for all MH messages. As with the other messages, some macros are defined to make it easy to access the members of field `ip6mhbe_hdr`. The `ip6mhbe_type` field is set to `IP6_MH_TYPE_BERROR`, the `ip6mhbe_status` field indicates the reason for the error. Table 5-16 shows the list of macro names for the status codes currently defined. The `ip6mhbe_homeaddr` field contains the home address of the mobile node which caused this error, if the home address is known, otherwise this field is set to the unspecified address.

TABLE 5-15

Name	Description
IP6_MH_BAS_ACCEPTED	Binding Update is accepted.
IP6_MH_BAS_PRFX_DISCOV	Binding Update is accepted, but need to perform the prefix discovery procedure.
IP6_MH_BAS_ERRORBASE	(internal use) The base value which indicated error status.
IP6_MH_BAS_UNSPECIFIED	Binding Update is rejected.
IP6_MH_BAS_PROHIBIT	Administratively prohibited.
IP6_MH_BAS_INSUFFICIENT	Insufficient resources.
IP6_MH_BAS_HA_NOT_SUPPORTED	Home registration function is not provided.
IP6_MH_BAS_NOT_HOME_SUBNET	Binding Update is received on another network interface which is not a home subnet.
IP6_MH_BAS_NOT_HA	Binding Update was sent to a wrong home agent.
IP6_MH_BAS_DAD_FAILED	Duplicate Address Detection for home address of a mobile node failed.
IP6_MH_BAS_SEQNO_BAD	The sequence number specified in a Binding Update message is smaller than the number stored in the binding information on a correspondent node or a home agent.
IP6_MH_BAS_HOME_NI_EXPIRED	Home Nonce Index is already expired.
IP6_MH_BAS_COA_NI_EXPIRED	Care-of Nonce Index is already expired.
IP6_MH_BAS_NI_EXPIRED	Both Home/Care-of Nonce Index are expired.
IP6_MH_BAS_REG_NOT_ALLOWED	A mobile node tried to change its registration type (home registration/not home registration).

Macro definitions for the Binding Acknowledgment status field.

TABLE 5-16

Name	Description
IP6_MH_BES_UNKNOWN_HAO	The home address which was included in the received packet was not valid.
IP6_MH_BES_UNKNOWN_MH	The type number of the received MH message was unknown.

Macro definitions for the Binding Error status field.

TABLE 5-17

Name	Description
IP6_MHOPT_PAD1	Pad1. The padding option to fill one byte space.
IP6_MHOPT_PADN	PadN. The padding option to fill from 2 bytes to 253 bytes space.
IP6_MHOPT_BREFRESH	Binding Refresh Advice. The option contains the suggested interval to resend a Binding Update message to update the binding.
IP6_MHOPT_ALTCOA	Alternate Care-of Address. The option contains the care-of address which should be used as the care-of address instead of the address specified in the source address field of the Binding Update message.
IP6_MHOPT_NONCEID	Nonce Indices. The option contains indices of Home Nonce and Care-of Nonce to specify nonce values which are used to authenticate Binding Update and Binding Acknowledgment messages.
IP6_MHOPT_BAUTH	Binding Authorization Data. The option contains the computed hash value of Binding Update and Binding Acknowledgment message.

Mobility options.

5.11.11 Mobility Option Message Structures

Mobility Options carry additional information in addition to the base Mobility Header messages. Currently, 6 options are defined. Table 5-17 shows the macro names for these option types. Each option has already been explained in Section 5.3.5.

5.11.12 Mobility Option Message—`ip6_mh_opt{}` Structure

The `ip6_mh_opt{}` structure is a generic structure for all mobility options.

Listing 5-10

—— ip6mh.h

```
256     struct ip6_mh_opt {
257             u_int8_t ip6mhopt_type;
258             u_int8_t ip6mhopt_len;
259             /* followed by option data */
260     } __attribute__((__packed__));
```

—— ip6mh.h

256–260 The `ip6mhopt_type` field specifies the type number of the option. The `ip6mhopt_len` field indicates the length of the option excluding the first two bytes (ip6mhopt_type and ip6mhopt_len). This structure is also used for the PadN mobility option. When used as a PadN option, the ip6mhopt_type field is set to IP6_MHOPT_PADN and the ip6mhopt_len field is set to the length of the required padding minus 2 bytes.

5.11.13 Binding Refresh Advice Option—ip6_mh_opt_refresh_advice{} Structure

The ip6_mh_opt_refresh_advice{} structure represents the Binding Refresh Advice option.

Listing 5-11

```
                                                                          ip6mh.h
271     struct ip6_mh_opt_refresh_advice {
272             u_int8_t ip6mora_type;
273             u_int8_t ip6mora_len;
274             u_int8_t ip6mora_interval[2];    /* Refresh Interval (units of 4 sec)
275     } __attribute__((__packed__));
                                                                          ip6mh.h
```

271–275 The ip6mora_type field is set to IP6_MHOPT_BREFRESH. The ip6mora_len field is set to 2. The ip6mora_interval field indicates the suggested interval value to use when resending a Binding Update message to update the binding information. The interval value is specified in units of 4 seconds.

In the recent specification, the ip6mora_interval field is defined as u_int16_t.

5.11.14 Alternate Care-of Address Option—ip6_mh_opt_altcoa{} Structure

The ip6_mh_opt_altcoa{} structure represents the Alternate Care-of Address option.

Listing 5-12

```
                                                                          ip6mh.h
278     struct ip6_mh_opt_altcoa {
279             u_int8_t ip6moa_type;
280             u_int8_t ip6moa_len;
281             u_int8_t ip6moa_addr[16];         /* Alternate Care-of Address */
282     } __attribute__((__packed__));
                                                                          ip6mh.h
```

278–282 The ip6moa_type field is set to IP6_MHOPT_ALTCOA. The ip6moa_len field is set to 16. The ip6moa_addr field contains an IPv6 address which should be used as a care-of address. Usually, the address specified in the IPv6 source address field of a Binding Update message is used as a care-of address in the mobility processing. This option specifies an alternate care-of address to be used as a care-of address. For example, when a mobile node has two network interfaces, interface A and B, and the node needs to register the address of interface B as a care-of address, using interface A to send a Binding Update message, the mobile node sets interface A's address to the IPv6 source address field and specifies interface B's address as an Alternate Care-of Address option.

5.11.15   Nonce Index Option—`ip6_mh_opt_nonce_index{}` Structure

The `ip6_mh_opt_nonce_index{}` structure represents the Nonce Indices option.

Listing 5-13

```
                                                                      ip6mh.h
285    struct ip6_mh_opt_nonce_index {
286            u_int8_t ip6moni_type;
287            u_int8_t ip6moni_len;
288            union {
289                    u_int8_t __nonce8[2];
290                    u_int16_t __nonce16;
291            } __ip6moni_home_nonce;
292            union {
293                    u_int8_t __nonce8[2];
294                    u_int16_t __nonce16;
295            } __ip6moni_coa_nonce;
296    } __attribute__((__packed__));
297    #ifdef _KERNEL
298    #define ip6moni_home_nonce8 __ip6moni_home_nonce.__nonce8
299    #define ip6moni_coa_nonce8 __ip6moni_coa_nonce.__nonce8
300    #endif /* _KERNEL */
301    #define ip6moni_home_nonce __ip6moni_home_nonce.__nonce16
302    #define ip6moni_coa_nonce __ip6moni_coa_nonce.__nonce16
                                                                      ip6mh.h
```

285–302 This option is used with the Binding Authorization Data option. The `ip6moni_type` field is set to `IP6_MH_OPT_NONCE_ID`, and the `ip6moni_len` field is set to 4. The `ip6moni_home_nonce` field contains the index of the home nonce value of the nonce array maintained by the correspondent node to which a mobile node is sending this option. `ip6moni_coa_nonce` contains the index to the care-of nonce value of the nonce array which is kept on a correspondent node. The index values for each nonce value have been passed to a mobile node by the Home Test and Care-of Test messages. The nonce values are random numbers periodically generated on a correspondent node to associate the Home Test/Care-of Test messages and the Binding Update message generated based on those messages. The `ip6moni_home_nonce8` and `ip6moni_coa_nonce8` fields provide a way to access those values as a byte array. These shortcuts can be used only inside the kernel.

5.11.16   Authentication Data Option—`ip6_mh_opt_auth_data{}` Structure

The `ip6_mh_opt_auth_data{}` structure represents a Binding Authorization Data option which is used with the Nonce Indices option.

Listing 5-14

```
                                                                      ip6mh.h
304    /* Binding Authorization Data */
305    struct ip6_mh_opt_auth_data {
306            u_int8_t ip6moad_type;
307            u_int8_t ip6moad_len;
308            /* followed by authenticator data */
309    } __attribute__((__packed__));
                                                                      ip6mh.h
```

304–309 The `ip6moad_type` field is set to `IP6_MHOPT_BAUTH`, and the `ip6moad_len` field is set to 12 because the size of authenticator data computed by the return routability procedure (Section 5.16.6) is 12 bytes.

5.11.17   The Internal Mobility Option—`mip6_mobility_options{}` Structure

As described in Section 5.3.5, 4 mobility options, except padding options, are defined in the Mobile IPv6 specification. The `mip6_mobility_options{}` structure is an internal structure which is used when parsing the mobility options included in a Mobility Header message and can be seen in Listing 5-15.

Listing 5-15

```
                                                                 mip6_var.h
310     struct mip6_mobility_options {
311             u_int16_t valid_options;          /* shows valid options in this
    structure */
312             struct in6_addr mopt_altcoa;          /* Alternate CoA */
313             u_int16_t       mopt_ho_nonce_idx;    /* Home Nonce Index */
314             u_int16_t       mopt_co_nonce_idx;    /* Care-of Nonce Index */
315             caddr_t mopt_auth;                    /* Authenticator */
316             u_int16_t       mopt_refresh;         /*  Refresh Interval */
317     };
318
319     #define MOPT_ALTCOA     0x0001
320     #define MOPT_NONCE_IDX  0x0002
321     #define MOPT_AUTHDATA   0x0004
322     #define MOPT_REFRESH    0x0008
                                                                 mip6_var.h
```
— Line 311 is broken here for layout reasons. However, it is a single line of code.

311–316 The `valid_options` field is a bit field which indicates what kind of options are contained in the structure. The macros defined in lines 319–322 are used to specify which option value is included. If multiple options exist in one Mobility Header, the logical *OR* of each value is stored in the `valid_options` field. The `mopt_altcoa` field contains the address value from the Alternate Care-of Address option. The `mopt_ho_nonce_idx` and `mopt_co_nonce_idx` fields store the home and care-of nonce index which are contained in the Nonce Index option. The `mopt_auth` field points to the address of the Binding Authorization Data option if the option exists. The `mopt_refresh` field contains the value specified in the Binding Refresh Advice option.

5.11.18   Home Address Option—`ip6_opt_home_address{}` Structure

The `ip6_opt_home_address{}` structure represents the Home Address option described in Section 5.3.2 and is shown in Listing 5-16.

Listing 5-16

```
                                                                 ip6.h
232     struct ip6_opt_home_address {
233             u_int8_t ip6oh_type;
234             u_int8_t ip6oh_len;
235             u_int8_t ip6oh_addr[16];/* Home Address */
236             /* followed by sub-options */
237     } __attribute__((__packed__));
                                                                 ip6.h
```

232–237 The `ip6oh_type` field is an option type, in which 0xC9 is used to indicate the Home Address option. The `ip6oh_len` field is the length of the value of this option, and its value is set to 16. The `ip6oh_addr` field contains the home address of a mobile node. At this moment the Home Address option does not have any options.

5.11.19 Type 2 Routing Header—`ip6_rthdr2{}` Structure

The `ip6_rthdr2{}` structure represents the Type 2 Routing Header described in Section 5.3.3. Listing 5-17 shows the definition of the `ip6_rthdr2{}` structure.

Listing 5-17

```
                                                                  ip6.h
259    struct ip6_rthdr2 {
260           u_int8_t  ip6r2_nxt;            /* next header */
261           u_int8_t  ip6r2_len;            /* always 2 */
262           u_int8_t  ip6r2_type;           /* always 2 */
263           u_int8_t  ip6r2_segleft;        /* 0 or 1 */
264           u_int32_t  ip6r2_reserved;      /* reserved field */
265           /* followed by one struct in6_addr */
266    } __attribute__((__packed__));
                                                                  ip6.h
```

259–266 The `ip6_rthdr2{}` structure is similar to the `ip6_rthdr0{}` structure which represents a Type 0 Routing Header. The `ip6r2_nxt` field contains the protocol number which follows immediately after this header. The `ip6r2_len` contains the length of this header excluding the first 8 bytes. The value is specified in units of 8 bytes. Since the Type 2 Routing Header contains only one address field of an intermediate node, the `ip6r2_len` field is always set to 2. The `ip6r2_type` field contains the type of this routing header and is set to 2. The `ip6r2_segleft` field is the number of unprocessed intermediate nodes. The value is always initialized to 1. The `ip6r2_reserved` field is cleared by the sender and must be ignored by the receiver. An IPv6 address, which is the home address of a mobile node, follows this structure immediately.

5.11.20 The Modified Router Advertisement Message—`nd_router_advert{}` Structure

As described in Section 5.3.6, a new flag for the Router Advertisement message is defined to advertise that the router is a home agent. Listing 5-18 shows the definition of the `nd_router_advert{}` structure.

Listing 5-18

```
                                                                  icmp6.h
326    struct nd_router_advert {       /* router advertisement */
327           struct icmp6_hdr      nd_ra_hdr;
328           u_int32_t             nd_ra_reachable;    /* reachable time */
329           u_int32_t             nd_ra_retransmit;   /* retransmit timer */
330           /* could be followed by options */
331    } __attribute__((__packed__));
332
333    #define nd_ra_type             nd_ra_hdr.icmp6_type
334    #define nd_ra_code             nd_ra_hdr.icmp6_code
335    #define nd_ra_cksum            nd_ra_hdr.icmp6_cksum
336    #define nd_ra_curhoplimit      nd_ra_hdr.icmp6_data8[0]
337    #define nd_ra_flags_reserved   nd_ra_hdr.icmp6_data8[1]
                                                                  icmp6.h
```

326–337 The definition of the `nd_router_advert{}` structure is described in Section 5.6.2 of *IPv6 Core Protocols Implementation*. Mobile IPv6 extends the flag values used by the `nd_ra_flags_reserved` field by defining one new flag.

TABLE 5-18

Name	Description
ND_RA_FLAG_MANAGED	The link provides a managed address configuration mechanism.
ND_RA_FLAG_OTHER	The link provides other stateful configuration mechanisms.
ND_RA_FLAG_HOME_AGENT	The router is a home agent.

Router Advertisement flags.

TABLE 5-19

Name	Description
ND_OPT_PI_FLAG_ONLINK	The prefix can be considered as an onlink prefix.
ND_OPT_PI_FLAG_AUTO	The prefix information can be used for the stateless address autoconfiguration.
ND_OPT_PI_FLAG_ROUTER	The nd_opt_pi_prefix field specifies the address of a home agent.

Prefix Information flags.

Table 5-18 shows the flags used in nd_router_advert structure. The ND_RA_FLAG_HOME_AGENT is the newly defined flag which indicates that the router is a home agent. By examining this flag, a receiver of a Router Advertisement message can know if the sender of the message node is a home agent or not.

5.11.21 The Modified Prefix Information Option—nd_opt_prefix_info{} Structure

As described in Section 5.3.6, Mobile IPv6 modifies the nd_opt_prefix_info{} structure to carry the address of a home agent in a Router Advertisement message. Listing 5-19 shows the definition of the nd_opt_prefix_info{} structure.

Listing 5-19

—— icmp6.h

```
488     struct nd_opt_prefix_info {      /* prefix information */
489            u_int8_t           nd_opt_pi_type;
490            u_int8_t           nd_opt_pi_len;
491            u_int8_t           nd_opt_pi_prefix_len;
492            u_int8_t           nd_opt_pi_flags_reserved;
493            u_int32_t          nd_opt_pi_valid_time;
494            u_int32_t          nd_opt_pi_preferred_time;
495            u_int32_t          nd_opt_pi_reserved2;
496            struct in6_addr nd_opt_pi_prefix;
497     } __attribute__((__packed__));
```

—— icmp6.h

488–497 The definition of the nd_opt_prefix_info{} structure is described in Section 5.7.2 of *IPv6 Core Protocols Implementation*. Mobile IPv6 extends the flag values used by nd_opt_pi_flags_reserved by defining one new flag.

Table 5-19 shows the available flags for the nd_opt_prefix_info{} structure. The ND_OPT_PI_FLAG_ROUTER flag is the newly defined flag to specify the address of a home agent. A receiver node of a Router Advertisement message can obtain the address of a home agent from the Prefix Information Option that has this flag.

5.11.22   Advertisement Interval Option—`nd_opt_adv_interval{}` Structure

The `nd_opt_adv_interval{}` structure represents the Advertisement Interval option described in Section 5.3.6. Listing 5-20 shows the definition of the Advertisement Interval option.

Listing 5-20

── icmp6.h

```
518     struct nd_opt_adv_interval {    /* Advertisement interval option */
519             u_int8_t           nd_opt_ai_type;
520             u_int8_t           nd_opt_ai_len;
521             u_int16_t          nd_opt_ai_reserved;
522             u_int32_t          nd_opt_ai_interval;
523     } __attribute__((__packed__));
```

── icmp6.h

518–523 The `nd_opt_ai_type` field is set to 7 which indicates the option type for the Advertisement Interval. The `nd_opt_ai_len` field is set to 1. The `nd_opt_ai_reserved` field is cleared by the sender and must be ignored by the receiver. The `nd_opt_ai_interval` field specifies the interval between the Router Advertisement message in units of a second.

5.11.23   Home Agent Information Option—`nd_opt_homeagent_info{}` Structure

The `nd_opt_homeagent_info{}` structure represents the Home Agent Information option described in Section 5.3.6. Listing 5-21 shows the definition of the `nd_opt_homeagent_info{}` structure.

Listing 5-21

── icmp6.h

```
525     struct nd_opt_homeagent_info {  /* Home Agent info */
526             u_int8_t           nd_opt_hai_type;
527             u_int8_t           nd_opt_hai_len;
528             u_int16_t          nd_opt_hai_reserved;
529             u_int16_t          nd_opt_hai_preference;
530             u_int16_t          nd_opt_hai_lifetime;
531     } __attribute__((__packed__));
```

── icmp6.h

525–531 `nd_opt_hai_type` is set to 8, which indicates the Home Agent Information option. `nd_opt_hai_len` is fixed to 1. `nd_opt_hai_reserved` is cleared by the sender and must be ignored by the receiver. `nd_opt_hai_preference` indicates the preference value of the home agent which is sending this option. `nd_opt_hai_lifetime` indicates the time that this home agent can provide the home agent functions in units of 1 second.

5.11.24 Dynamic Home Agent Address Discovery Request Message—`mip6_dhaad_req{}` Structure

The `mip6_dhaad_req{}` structure represents the Dynamic Home Agent Address Discovery Request message described in Section 5.3.7. Listing 5-22 shows the definition of the `mip6_dhaad_req{}` structure.

Listing 5-22

```
                                                             ──icmp6.h
420      struct mip6_dhaad_req {       /* HA Address Discovery Request */
421              struct icmp6_hdr      mip6_dhreq_hdr;
422      } __attribute__((__packed__));

424      #define mip6_dhreq_type       mip6_dhreq_hdr.icmp6_type
425      #define mip6_dhreq_code       mip6_dhreq_hdr.icmp6_code
426      #define mip6_dhreq_cksum      mip6_dhreq_hdr.icmp6_cksum
427      #define mip6_dhreq_id         mip6_dhreq_hdr.icmp6_data16[0]
428      #define mip6_dhreq_reserved   mip6_dhreq_hdr.icmp6_data16[1]
                                                             ──icmp6.h
```

420–428 The `mip6_dhaad_req{}` structure uses the standard ICMPv6 header `icmp6_hdr{}`. The `mip6_dhreq_type` field is set to 144, which indicates a Dynamic Home Agent Address Discovery Request. The `mip6_dhreq_code` field is set to 0. The `mip6_dhreq_cksum` field contains the checksum value computed in the same way as the ICMPv6 checksum. The `mip6_dhreq_id` field is a random identifier set by the sender to match request messages with reply messages. The `mip6_dhreq_reserved` field must be cleared by the sender and must be ignored by the receiver.

5.11.25 Dynamic Home Agent Address Discovery Reply Message—`mip6_dhaad_rep{}` Structure

The `mip6_dhaad_rep{}` structure represents the Dynamic Home Agent Address Discovery Reply message described in Section 5.3.7. Listing 5-23 shows the definition of the `mip6_dhaad_rep{}` structure.

Listing 5-23

```
                                                             ──icmp6.h
430      struct mip6_dhaad_rep {       /* HA Address Discovery Reply */
431              struct icmp6_hdr      mip6_dhrep_hdr;
432              /* could be followed by home agent addresses */
433      } __attribute__((__packed__));

435      #define mip6_dhrep_type       mip6_dhrep_hdr.icmp6_type
436      #define mip6_dhrep_code       mip6_dhrep_hdr.icmp6_code
437      #define mip6_dhrep_cksum      mip6_dhrep_hdr.icmp6_cksum
438      #define mip6_dhrep_id         mip6_dhrep_hdr.icmp6_data16[0]
439      #define mip6_dhrep_reserved   mip6_dhrep_hdr.icmp6_data16[1]
                                                             ──icmp6.h
```

430–439 The `mip6_dhaad_rep{}` structure uses the standard ICMPv6 header `icmp6_hdr{}`. The `mip6_dhrep_type` is set to 145 to indicate the message is a Dynamic Home Agent Address Discovery Reply message. The `mip6_dhrep_code` field is set to 0. The `mip6_dhrep_cksum` is the checksum value computed in the same way as the ICMPv6 checksum. The `mip6_dhrep_id` field is the identifier copied from the `mip6_dhreq_id` field in the `mip6_dhaad_req{}` structure to match this reply message with the request message. The `mip6_dhrep_reserved` field must be cleared by the sender and must be ignored by the receiver. The address(es) of the home agent(s) of the home network follows just after this structure.

5.11.26 Mobile Prefix Solicitation Message—`mip6_prefix_solicit{}` Structure

The `mip6_prefix_solicit{}` structure represents the Mobile Prefix Solicitation message described in Section 5.3.7. Listing 5-24 shows the definition of the `mip6_prefix_solicit{}` structure.

Listing 5-24

icmp6.h

```
441     struct mip6_prefix_solicit {     /* Mobile Prefix Solicitation */
442             struct icmp6_hdr         mip6_ps_hdr;
443     } __attribute__((__packed__));

445     #define mip6_ps_type             mip6_ps_hdr.icmp6_type
446     #define mip6_ps_code             mip6_ps_hdr.icmp6_code
447     #define mip6_ps_cksum            mip6_ps_hdr.icmp6_cksum
448     #define mip6_ps_id               mip6_ps_hdr.icmp6_data16[0]
449     #define mip6_ps_reserved         mip6_ps_hdr.icmp6_data16[1]
```

icmp6.h

441–449 The `mip6_prefix_solicit{}` structure uses the standard ICMPv6 header `icmp6_hdr{}`. The `mip6_ps_type` is set to 146, which indicates the Mobile Prefix Solicitation. The `mip6_ps_code` field is set to 0. The `mip6_ps_cksum` field is the checksum value computed in the same manner as the ICMPv6 checksum. The `mip6_ps_id` field is a random value set by the sender to match request messages and reply messages. The `mip6_ps_reserved` field must be cleared by the sender and must be ignored by the receiver.

5.11.27 Mobile Prefix Advertisement Message—`mip6_prefix_advert{}` Structure

The `mip6_prefix_advert{}` structure represents the Mobile Prefix Advertisement message described in Section 5.3.7. Listing 5-25 shows the definition of the `mip6_prefix_advert{}` structure.

Listing 5-25

icmp6.h

```
451     struct mip6_prefix_advert {      /* Mobile Prefix Advertisement */
452             struct icmp6_hdr         mip6_pa_hdr;
453             /* followed by options */
454     } __attribute__((__packed__));

456     #define mip6_pa_type             mip6_pa_hdr.icmp6_type
457     #define mip6_pa_code             mip6_pa_hdr.icmp6_code
458     #define mip6_pa_cksum            mip6_pa_hdr.icmp6_cksum
459     #define mip6_pa_id               mip6_pa_hdr.icmp6_data16[0]
460     #define mip6_pa_flags_reserved   mip6_pa_hdr.icmp6_data16[1]
```

icmp6.h

451–460 The `mip6_prefix_advert{}` structure uses the standard ICMPv6 header structure defined as `icmp6_hdr{}`. The `mip6_pa_type` field is set to 147, which indicates the Mobile Prefix Advertisement. The `mip6_pa_code` field is set to 0. The `mip6_pa_cksum` field is the checksum value computed in the same manner as the ICMPv6 checksum. The `mip6_pa_id` is the identifier copied from the `mip6_ps_id` field of the `mip6_prefix_solicit{}` structure to match the reply message with the request message. The `mip6_pa_flags_reserved` field may contain flags as defined in Table 5-20.

5.11.28 Binding Cache Entry—`mip6_bc{}` Structure

The `mip6_bc{}` structure represents the binding information, called *binding cache*, which is stored on a correspondent node or a home agent. Listing 5-26 shows the definition of the `mip6_bc{}` structure.

Listing 5-26

```
                                                                        mip6_var.h
91      struct mip6_bc {
92              LIST_ENTRY(mip6_bc)     mbc_entry;
93              struct in6_addr         mbc_phaddr;     /* peer home address */
94              struct in6_addr         mbc_pcoa;       /* peer coa */
95              struct in6_addr         mbc_addr;       /* my addr (needed?) */
96              u_int8_t                mbc_status;     /* BA statue */
97              u_int8_t                mbc_send_ba;    /* nonzero means BA should be
   sent */
98              u_int32_t               mbc_refresh;    /* Using for sending BA */
99              u_int16_t               mbc_flags;      /* recved BU flags */
100             u_int16_t               mbc_seqno;      /* recved BU seqno */
101             u_int32_t               mbc_lifetime;   /* recved BU lifetime */
102             time_t                  mbc_expire;     /* expiration time of this BC. */
103             u_int8_t                mbc_state;      /* BC state */
104             struct ifnet            *mbc_ifp;       /* ifp that the BC belongs to. */
105                                                     /* valid only when BUF_HOME. */
106             const struct encaptab   *mbc_encap;     /* encapsulation from MN */
107             void                    *mbc_dad;       /* dad handler */
108             time_t                  mbc_mpa_exp;    /* expiration time for sending
   MPA */
109                                                     /* valid only when BUF_HOME. */
110             struct mip6_bc          *mbc_llmbc;
111             u_int32_t               mbc_refcnt;
112             u_int                   mbc_brr_sent;

114             struct callout          mbc_timer_ch;

118     };
                                                                        mip6_var.h
```

— *Lines 97 and 108 are broken here for layout reasons. However, they are a single line of code.*

TABLE 5-20

Name	Description
`MIP6_PA_FLAG_MANAGED`	Set if the home network provides the managed address configuration.
`MIP6_PA_FLAG_OTHER`	Set if the home network provides the other stateful autoconfiguration parameters.

Flags used in Mobile Prefix Advertisement.

91–118 The `mip6_bc{}` structure is defined as a list element. The `mbc_entry` field links the list of binding cache entries that is managed as a hash table. The implementation is discussed in Section 5.16.3.

The `mbc_phaddr` field is a home address of a mobile node and the `mbc_pcoa` field is a care-of address of the same mobile node. The `mbc_addr` field is the address which received the Binding Update message from the mobile node.

The `mbc_status` field keeps the status code of the Binding Acknowledgment message sent to the mobile node in response to the Binding Update message from the mobile node. The `mbc_send_ba` field is an internal flag that indicates whether the Binding Acknowledgment message should be sent after the processing of the Binding Update message has finished. The `mbc_refresh` field is used to store the refresh advice value, which is used by the Binding Refresh Advice option. The `mbc_flags` field contains a copy of flags which is set in the Binding Update message. Table 5-13 (page 545) shows the list of flags. The `IP6MU_CLONED` flag is used only in the `mip6_bc{}` structure. The `mbc_seqno` field is a copy of the valid sequence number which was most recently received. The `mbc_lifetime` field is an approved lifetime for this binding cache entry. `mbc_expire` indicates the absolute time that this binding cache expires.

The `mbc_state` field indicates the internal state of this cache. Table 5-21 shows the list of state values. The `mbc_ifp` field points to the network interface to which this cache belongs. The interface must be the same interface to as the `mbc_addr` is assigned. The `mbc_encap` field is a pointer to the `encaptab{}` structure which represents the bi-directional tunneling between a home agent and a mobile node. The `mbc_dad` field is used when a home agent is performing the DAD process for the home address of a mobile node. The `mbc_mpa_exp` field is intended to be used for unsolicited Mobile Prefix Advertisements, but the member is not currently used. The `mbc_llmbc` field is a pointer to another `mip6_bc{}` structure which keeps the binding information for the link-local address of the mobile node whose care-of address is the same as the address of this binding cache. The `mbc_refcnt` field is a reference counter for this cache. The value is set to 1 when no other entry refers to this entry. The value increases when other binding cache entries point to this entry using the `mbc_llmbc` field. The `mbc_brr_sent` field stores the number of BRR messages sent to the mobile node to update the cache information. Once the cache is updated, the field is cleared. The `mbc_timer_ch` field is the handler of the timer entry for this cache.

TABLE 5-21

Name	*Description*
`MIP6_BC_FSM_STATE_BOUND`	Binding is valid.
`MIP6_BC_FSM_STATE_WAITB`	Binding is valid, but the node should send BRR messages.
`MIP6_BC_FSM_STATE_WAITB2`	Binding is valid, but this entry will be removed at the next timer call.

List of state of a binding cache.

5.11.29 Binding Update List Entry—`mip6_bu{}` Structure

The `mip6_bu{}` structure represents the binding information kept on a mobile node. Such information is called a *binding update list entry*. Listing 5-27 shows the definition of the `mip6_bu{}` structure.

Listing 5-27

```
                                                                        mip6_var.h
150     struct mip6_bu {
151            LIST_ENTRY(mip6_bu) mbu_entry;
152            struct in6_addr     mbu_paddr;       /* peer addr of this BU */
153            struct in6_addr     mbu_haddr;       /* HoA */
154            struct in6_addr     mbu_coa;         /* CoA */
155            u_int16_t           mbu_lifetime;    /* BU lifetime */
156            u_int16_t           mbu_refresh;     /* refresh frequency */
157            u_int16_t           mbu_seqno;       /* sequence number */
158            u_int16_t           mbu_flags;       /* BU flags */
159            mip6_cookie_t       mbu_mobile_cookie;
160            u_int16_t           mbu_home_nonce_index;
161            mip6_home_token_t   mbu_home_token; /* home keygen token */
162            u_int16_t           mbu_careof_nonce_index;
163            mip6_careof_token_t mbu_careof_token; /* careof keygen token */
164            u_int8_t            mbu_pri_fsm_state; /* primary fsm state */
165            u_int8_t            mbu_sec_fsm_state; /* secondary fsm state */
166            time_t              mbu_expire;      /* expiration time of this BU */
167            time_t              mbu_retrans;     /* retrans/refresh timo value */
168            u_int8_t            mbu_retrans_count;
169            time_t              mbu_failure;     /* failure timo value */
170            u_int8_t            mbu_state;       /* local status */
171            struct hif_softc    *mbu_hif;        /* back pointer to hif */
172            const struct encaptab *mbu_encap;
173     };
                                                                        mip6_var.h
```

150–173 The `mip6_bu{}` structure is defined as a list element. The `mbu_entry` field links the list of binding update entries. A mobile node may have more than one binding update list. Each binding update list is kept in an hif virtual interface structure, which is described in Section 5.11.32. The `mbu_paddr` field is an address of a correspondent node or a home agent, for which this binding update list entry is created. The `mbu_haddr` and `mbu_coa` fields are a home address and a care-of address of this mobile node.

The `mbu_lifetime` field is the lifetime and indicates the time for which this binding information is valid. The `mbu_refresh` field is the time at which the mobile node should update its binding information by sending a Binding Update message. These fields are represented in units of 1 second. The `mbu_seqno` field is a sequence number for this binding information and is incremented when a mobile node sends a Binding Update message to the correspondent node or the home agent specified by the address `mbu_paddr`. The `mbu_flags` field keeps the flags for this binding information. Table 5-13 (page 545) shows the list of flag values. The `mbu_mobile_cookie` field is a cookie value which is used in the Home Test Init and the Care-of Test Init messages. The `mbu_home_nonce_index` and `mbu_home_token` fields contain the home nonce index and the home keygen token sent with a Home Test message from a correspondent node. The `mbu_careof_nonce_index` and `mbu_careof_token` fields contain the value of the care-of nonce index and the care-of keygen token sent with a Care-of Test message.

The `mbu_pri_fsm_state` and `mbu_sec_fsm_state` fields indicate the current state of this binding update list entry. The former stores the state of registration of the binding information, the latter stores the state of the return routability procedure for the binding information. The list of states is described in Tables 5-22 and 5-23.

The `mbu_expire` field is the time at which this binding update list entry expires. The `mbu_retrans` field is the time at which the retransmission timer of the binding update list entry expires. The `mbu_retrans_count` is the number of retransmissions used to compute the exponential backoff for retransmissions. The `mbu_failure` field is the time when the binding update list entry is disabled to prevent infinite retries in the case of disaster; however, this timeout mechanism is not utilized currently.

The `mbu_state` field is the internal state of this binding update list entry. Table 5-24 shows the list of states. The `mbu_hif` field is a pointer to the hif virtual interface to which this binding update list entry belongs. The `mbu_encap` field is a pointer to the `encaptab{}` structure which represents the bi-directional tunnel between a mobile node and its home agent.

TABLE 5-22

Name	Description
MIP6_BU_PRI_FSM_STATE_IDLE	Initial state.
MIP6_BU_PRI_FSM_STATE_RRINIT	Performing the RR procedure. No registration exists.
MIP6_BU_PRI_FSM_STATE_RRREDO	Performing the RR procedure for re-registration. A valid registration exists.
MIP6_BU_PRI_FSM_STATE_RRDEL	Performing the RR procedure for de-registration.
MIP6_BU_PRI_FSM_STATE_WAITA	Waiting a Binding Acknowledgment message. No registration exists.
MIP6_BU_PRI_FSM_STATE_WAITAR	Waiting a Binding Acknowledgment message for re-registration. A valid registration exists.
MIP6_BU_PRI_FSM_STATE_WAITD	Waiting a Binding Acknowledgment message for de-registration.
MIP6_BU_PRI_FSM_STATE_BOUND	Registration completed.

List of states for registration.

TABLE 5-23

Name	Description
MIP6_BU_SEC_FSM_STATE_START	Initial state.
MIP6_BU_SEC_FSM_STATE_WAITHC	Waiting Home Test and Care-of Test messages.
MIP6_BU_SEC_FSM_STATE_WAITH	Waiting Home Test message.
MIP6_BU_SEC_FSM_STATE_WAITC	Waiting Care-of Test message.

List of states for the Return Routability procedure.

TABLE 5-24

Name	Description
MIP6_BU_STATE_DISABLE	The peer node does not support Mobile IPv6.
MIP6_BU_STATE_FIREWALLED	The peer address is behind a firewall. Not discussed in this book.
MIP6_BU_STATE_NEEDTUNNEL	(MIP6_BU_STATE_DISABLE|MIP6_BU_STATE_FIREWALLED)

Internal states of a binding update list entry.

5.11.30 Home Agent Entry—`mip6_ha{}` structure

The `mip6_ha{}` structure represents the information a mobile node knows about home agents. In the KAME implementation, the list of home agents is created either by receiving Dynamic Home Agent Address Discovery reply messages or by listening to Router Advertisement messages. Listing 5-28 shows the `mip6_ha{}` structure.

Listing 5-28

———mip6_var.h

```
256     struct mip6_ha {
257             TAILQ_ENTRY(mip6_ha) mha_entry;
258             struct in6_addr     mha_addr ;     /* lladdr or global addr */
259             u_int8_t            mha_flags;     /* RA flags */
260             u_int16_t           mha_pref;      /* home agent preference */
261             u_int16_t           mha_lifetime;  /* router lifetime */
262             time_t              mha_expire;
263
264             time_t              mha_timeout;   /* next timeout time. */
265             long                mha_ntick;
....
267             struct callout      mha_timer_ch;
....
271     };
272     TAILQ_HEAD(mip6_ha_list, mip6_ha);
```

———mip6_var.h

256–271 The `mip6_ha{}` structure is defined as a list. The list structure is defined as the `mip6_ha_list{}` structure on line 272. The `mha_entry` field links the `mip6_ha{}` structures. The `mha_addr` field is the IPv6 address of a home agent. The `mha_flags` field is a copy of the flag which is advertised in Router Advertisement messages sent by this home agent. The `mha_pref` field is the value of the home agent preference advertised in the Home Agent Information option. If Router Advertisement messages from this home agent do not contain the Home Agent Information option, the default value 0 is used. The `mha_lifetime` field is the lifetime of this home agent advertised by the Home Agent Information option. If Router Advertisement messages from this home agent do not contain the Home Agent Information option, the value of the router lifetime specified in a Router Advertisement message is used. The `mha_expire` field indicates the time at which the lifetime of this home agent expires. The `mha_timeout` and `mha_ntick` fields indicate the time left to the next timeout. The `mha_timer_ch` field is a handle for the kernel timer mechanism.

5.11.31   Prefix Entry—`mip6_prefix{}` Structure

A mobile node receives prefix information via two methods: one by receiving Router Advertisement messages which contain Prefix Information options, and the other by receiving Mobile Prefix Advertisement messages which contain prefixes for the home network. The prefix information is stored as the `mip6_prefix{}` structure. Listing 5-29 shows the `mip6_prefix{}` structure.

Listing 5-29

_____mip6_var.h

```
279     struct mip6_prefix {
280             LIST_ENTRY(mip6_prefix) mpfx_entry;
281             struct in6_addr         mpfx_prefix;
282             u_int8_t                mpfx_prefixlen;
283             u_int32_t               mpfx_vltime;
284             time_t                  mpfx_vlexpire;
285             u_int32_t               mpfx_pltime;
286             time_t                  mpfx_plexpire;
287             struct in6_addr         mpfx_haddr;
288             LIST_HEAD(mip6_prefix_ha_list, mip6_prefix_ha) mpfx_ha_list;
289             int                     mpfx_refcnt;
290
291             int                     mpfx_state;
292             time_t                  mpfx_timeout;
293             long                    mpfx_ntick;
....
295             struct callout          mpfx_timer_ch;
....
299     };
300     LIST_HEAD(mip6_prefix_list, mip6_prefix);
```

_____mip6_var.h

279–299 The `mip6_prefix{}` structure is defined as a list on line 300. The `mpfx_entry` field makes a list of the `mip6_prefix{}` instances. The `mpfx_prefix` and `mpfx_prefixlen` fields indicate the values of IPv6 prefix and prefix length respectively. The `mpfx_vltime` and `mpfx_vlexpire` fields indicate the valid lifetime of the prefix and the time when the valid lifetime expires. The `mpfx_pltime` and `mpfx_plexpire` fields indicate the preferred lifetime of the prefix and the time when the preferred lifetime expires. The `mpfx_ha_list` field is a list of `mip6_prefix_ha{}` instances. The `mip6_prefix_ha` field indicates the home agent that advertises this prefix information. The structure is described later. The `mpfx_refcnt` field is a reference count for this instance. The `mip6_prefix` instance is pointed to by the `mip6_prefix_ha{}` structure. The instance is used to manage the lifetime of this instance. The instance will be removed when the reference count becomes zero. The `mpfx_state` field indicates the current state of this prefix information. Table 5-25 shows the possible states. This state is used to decide when a mobile node should send a Mobile Prefix Solicitation to update the information of this prefix. The `mpfx_timeout` and `mpfx_ntick` fields indicate the time left to the next timeout. The `mpfx_timer_ch` field is a handle for the kernel timer mechanism.

TABLE 5-25

Name	Description
MIP6_PREFIX_STATE_PREFERRED	The lifetime left of this prefix is longer than the preferred lifetime.
MIP6_PREFIX_STATE_EXPIRING	The lifetime left of this prefix is longer than the valid lifetime.

The list of state of `mip6_prefix{}` *structure.*

The `mip6_prefix_ha{}` structure is a supplement structure to bind prefix information to the home agent which advertises the prefix. Listing 5-30 shows the definition.

Listing 5-30

————————————————————————————————————mip6_var.h
```
274     struct mip6_prefix_ha {
275             LIST_ENTRY(mip6_prefix_ha) mpfxha_entry;
276             struct mip6_ha              *mpfxha_mha;
277     };
```
————————————————————————————————————mip6_var.h

275–277 The `mpfxha_entry` field links the list of `mip6_prefix_ha{}` instances, which are used in the `mip6_prefix{}` structure. The `mpfxha_mha` field points to an instance of a home agent.

Figure 5-45 describes the relationship between the prefix information structures and home agent information structures. In the figure, there are 3 prefixes (Prefix 2001:db8:100::/64, 2001:db8:101::/64 and 2001:db8:200::/64) and 3 home agents (2001:db8:100::1, 2001:db8:101::1 and 2001:db8:200::1). Prefix 2001:db8:100::/64 is advertised by Home Agents 2001:db8:100::1 and 2001:db8:101::1. To point to these two home agents from the prefix instance, it has two instances of the `mip6_prefix_ha{}` structure in the `mpfx_ha_list`. Prefix 2001:db8:200::/64 is advertised by Home Agent 2001:db8:200::1, and its `mpfx_ha_list` has one instance of the `mip6_prefix_ha{}` structure to point to the home agent. Prefix 2001:db8:101::/64 is almost the same as Prefix 2001:db8:100::/64. All instances of the `mip6_prefix{}` structure are linked together. The head structure of the prefix list is the `mip6_prefix_list{}` structure defined on line 300 in Listing 5-29. Similarly, all instances of the `mip6_ha{}` structure are linked together. The head structure of the home agent list is the `mip6_ha_list{}` structure from line 272 in Listing 5-28.

5.11.32 Home Virtual Interface—`hif_softc{}` Structure

In the KAME Mobile IPv6 implementation, the home address of a mobile node is assigned to the hif virtual interface while the mobile node is away from home. The hif interface represents the home network of a mobile node and keeps related information, such as home prefixes. Listing 5-31 shows the definition of the `hif_softc{}` structure.

564

FIGURE 5-45

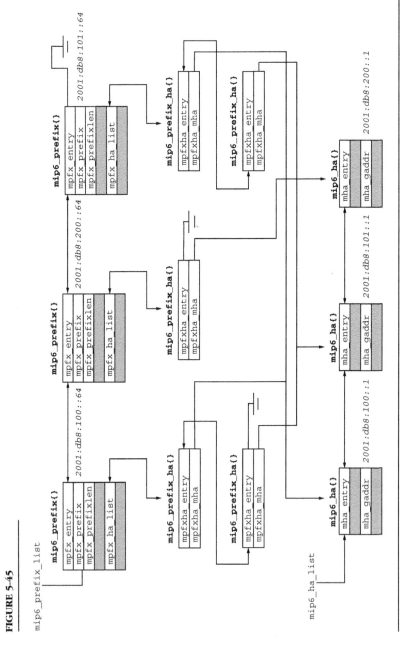

Home agent list generated in the home network.

Listing 5-31

_____if_hif.h
```
100     struct hif_softc {
101             struct ifnet hif_if;
102             LIST_ENTRY(hif_softc)  hif_entry;
103             int                    hif_location;           /* cur location */
104             int                    hif_location_prev;      /* XXX */
105             struct in6_ifaddr      *hif_coa_ifa;
106             struct hif_site_prefix_list hif_sp_list;
107             struct mip6_bu_list    hif_bu_list;            /* list of BUs */
108             struct hif_prefix_list hif_prefix_list_home;
109             struct hif_prefix_list hif_prefix_list_foreign;
110             u_int16_t              hif_dhaad_id;
111             long                   hif_dhaad_lastsent;
112             u_int8_t               hif_dhaad_count;
113             u_int16_t              hif_mps_id;
114             long                   hif_mps_lastsent;
115             struct in6_addr        hif_ifid;
116     };
```
_____if_hif.h

100–116 The `hif_if` field is an instance of the `ifnet{}` structure to provide basic ifnet features. The `hif_location` and `hif_location_prev` fields store the current and previous positions of a mobile node. The fields take one of the values described in Table 5-26. The `hif_coa_ifa` field points to the instance of the `in6_ifaddr{}` structure which contains the current care-of address. The `hif_sp_list` field is a list of the `hif_site_prefix{}` instances which contains the prefixes which are considered intranet prefixes to provide hints for initiation of the return routability procedure. We do not discuss the `hif_sp_list` field and its related functions in this book, since they are KAME-specific experimental codes and are beyond the specification. The `hif_bu_list` field is a list of instances of the `mip6_bu{}` structure which belong to this interface. The `hif_prefix_list_home` and `hif_prefix_list_foreign` fields are the list of prefixes of a home network and foreign networks respectively. A mobile node can detect that it is home or foreign by comparing its current care-of address and these prefixes. The `hif_dhaad_id` field stores the last used identifier of the Dynamic Home Agent Address Discovery Request message. The `hif_dhaad_lastsent` field is the time when the last Dynamic Home Agent Address Discovery Request message has been sent. The `hif_dhaad_count` field contains the number of Dynamic Home Agent Address Discovery Request messages. The value is used to perform the exponential backoff calculation done when retransmitting the message. The `hif_mps_id` and `hif_mps_lastsent` fields have the same meaning as the `hif_dhaad_id` and `hif_dhaad_lastsent` fields for the Mobile Prefix Solicitation message. The `hif_ifid` field stores the interface

TABLE 5-26

Name	Description
HIF_LOCATION_UNKNOWN	Location is unknown.
HIF_LOCATION_HOME	The node is at home network.
HIF_LOCATION_FOREIGN	The node is at foreign network.

Location.

FIGURE 5-46

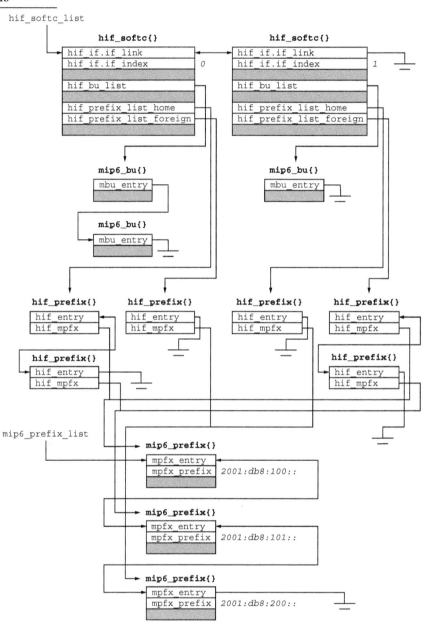

Relationship between `hif_softc{}` *and other structures.*

identifier of this virtual interface. In the KAME implementation, the home address of a mobile node is generated in the similar manner to that of the stateless address autoconfiguration mechanism. In this mechanism, the mobile node needs to generate a unique identifier value that is used for its lower 64-bit part of the address. The `hif_ifid` field keeps the unique identifier generated from the MAC address of the network interface of the node, and it is used as a part of the home address when the node assigns the home address to this virtual interface the first time.

The `hif_prefix{}` structure is used in the `hif_softc{}` structure.

Listing 5-32
```
                                                                    if_hif.h
87      struct hif_prefix {
88              LIST_ENTRY(hif_prefix) hpfx_entry;
89              struct mip6_prefix     *hpfx_mpfx;
90      };
91      LIST_HEAD(hif_prefix_list, hif_prefix);
                                                                    if_hif.h
```

87–90 The `hpfx_entry` field makes a list of `hif_prefix{}` structures, represented as the `hif_prefix_list` structure defined on line 91. The `hpfx_mpfx` field is a pointer to the `mip6_prefix{}` structure, which contains the prefix information kept in a mobile node. The `mip6_prefix{}` structure is discussed in Section 5.11.31.

Figure 5-46 describes the relationship between the `hif_softc{}` structure and other related structures. In this figure, there are two hif virtual interfaces. The mobile node keeps information about 3 prefix entries as a list of `mip6_prefix_list`. Two of those prefixes are home prefixes of the first hif interface. These two prefixes are considered foreign prefixes for the second interface. Another prefix is a foreign prefix for the first interface, and a home prefix for the second interface.

5.12 Macro and Type Definitions

The KAME Mobile IPv6 stack defines several types to increase the readability of the source code. Table 5-27 shows the type definitions for the Mobile IPv6 stack. Table 5-28 shows some constant definitions used by the Mobile IPv6 stack. Table 5-29 shows some utility macros used in the Mobile IPv6 stack.

TABLE 5-27

Type name	Description
mip6_nonce_t	8-byte unsigned integer array which represents a nonce value.
mip6_nodekey_t	20-byte unsigned integer array which represents a nodekey value.
mip6_cookie_t	8-byte unsigned integer array which represents a cookie value.
mip6_home_token_t	8-byte unsigned integer array which represents a home keygen token value.
mip6_careof_token_t	8-byte unsigned integer array which represents a care-of keygen token value.

New types introduced in Mobile IPv6.

TABLE 5-28

Name	Value	Description
`MIP6_REFRESH_MINLIFETIME`	2	Minimum allowed refresh interval.
`MIP6_REFRESH_LIFETIME_RATE`	50	The percentage used when a mobile node calculates refresh interval time from the life-time of a binding ack, when a home agent does not specify refresh interval.
`MIP6_MAX_NONCE_LIFE`	240	The lifetime of nonces generated by a correspondent node.
`MIP6_COOKIE_SIZE`	8	The size of a cookie value in bytes.
`MIP6_HOME_TOKEN_SIZE`	8	The size of a home keygen token value in bytes.
`MIP6_CAREOF_TOKEN_SIZE`	8	The size of a care-of keygen token value in bytes.
`MIP6_NONCE_SIZE`	8	The size of a nonce value in bytes.
`MIP6_NODEKEY_SIZE`	20	The size of a nodekey in bytes.
`MIP6_NONCE_HISTORY`	10	The number of old nonces kept in a correspondent node. Older nonces are removed from a correspondent node and considered as invalid.
`MIP6_KBM_LEN`	20	The size of a key length shared by a mobile node and a correspondent node.
`MIP6_AUTHENTICATOR_LEN`	12	The size of authentication data in Binding Update/Acknowledgment messages.
`MIP6_MAX_RR_BINDING_LIFE`	420	The maximum lifetime of binding information created by the return routability procedure.
`MIP6_NODETYPE_CORRESPONDENT_NODE`	0	Indicates the node is a correspondent node. Used by the `mip6ctl_nodetype` global variable.
`MIP6_NODETYPE_MOBILE_NODE`	1	Indicates the node is a mobile node. Used by the `mip6ctl_nodetype` global variable.
`MIP6_NODETYPE_HOME_AGENT`	2	Indicates the node is a home agent. Used by the `mip6ctl_nodetype` global variable.
`MIP6_BU_TIMEOUT_INTERVAL`	1	The interval between calls to the timer function for binding update list entries.

Constants.

TABLE 5-29

Name	Description
`GET_NETVAL_S`(*addr*, *value*)	Copies 2 bytes of data from the memory space specified by *addr* to *value*. `GET_NETVAL_*` macros are intended to provide an easy way to write multiple bytes on processor architecture which have alignment restrictions.
`GET_NETVAL_L`(*addr*, *value*)	Same as `GET_NETVAL_S`(), but the length of data is 4 bytes.
`SET_NETVAL_S`(*addr*, *value*)	Writes 2 bytes of data to the memory specified by *addr* from *value*.
`SET_NETVAL_L`(*addr*, *value*)	Same as `SET_NETVAL_S`(), but the length of data is 4 bytes.
`MIP6_LEQ`(*a*, *b*)	Compares *a* and *b* using modulo 2^{16}.
`MIP6_PADLEN`(*off*, *x*, *y*)	Computes the length of padding required for Destination/Mobility options. *off* is the offset from the head of the Destination Options header or Mobility header. *x* and *y* represent the alignment requirement (e.g., if the requirement is $8n + 6$, *x* is 8 and *y* is 6).
`MIP6_IS_BC_DAD_WAIT`(*bc*)	Returns true, if the specified binding cache entry is waiting for DAD completion, otherwise, it returns false.
`MIP6_IS_BU_BOUND_STATE`(*bu*)	Returns true, if the specified binding update list entry is registered successfully, otherwise, it returns false.
`MIP6_IS_BU_WAITA_STATE`(*bu*)	Returns true, if the specified binding update list entry is waiting for a Binding Acknowledgment message, otherwise, it returns false.
`MIP6_IS_BU_RR_STATE`(*bu*)	Returns true, if the specified binding update list entry is performing the return routability procedure.
`MIP6_BU_DEFAULT_REFRESH_INTERVAL`(*lifetime*)	Computes refresh interval time from the specified lifetime.
`MIP6_IS_MN`	Returns true, if a node is a mobile node.
`MIP6_IS_HA`	Returns true, if a node is a home agent.
`MIP6_DEBUG`((*msg*))	Prints a debug message based on when global variable `mip6ctl_debug` is set to true (see Table 5-30). The `mip6ctl_debug` variable is a configurable variable through the **sysctl** program.

Utility macros.

5.13   Global Variables

In the Mobile IPv6 code, the global variables listed in Table 5-30 are used.

5.14   Utility Functions

There are 2 utility functions which are used from various locations in the Mobile IPv6 code. In this section, we discuss these utility functions. Table 5-31 contains the list of functions.

5.14.1   Files

Table 5-32 shows the files that implement utility functions.

5.14.2   Creation of IPv6 Header

In the Mobile IPv6 code, we need to create IPv6 headers frequently. The `mip6_create_ip6hdr()` function provides a handy way to create an IPv6 header.

Listing 5-33

_____mip6_cncore.c
```
471     struct mbuf *
472     mip6_create_ip6hdr(src, dst, nxt, plen)
473             struct in6_addr *src;
474             struct in6_addr *dst;
475             u_int8_t nxt;
476             u_int32_t plen;
477     {
478             struct ip6_hdr *ip6; /* ipv6 header. */
479             struct mbuf *m; /* a pointer to the mbuf containing ipv6 header. */
480             u_int32_t maxlen;
481
482             maxlen = sizeof(*ip6) + plen;
483             MGETHDR(m, M_DONTWAIT, MT_HEADER);
484             if (m && (max_linkhdr + maxlen >= MHLEN)) {
485                     MCLGET(m, M_DONTWAIT);
486                     if ((m->m_flags & M_EXT) == 0) {
487                             m_free(m);
488                             return (NULL);
489                     }
490             }
491             if (m == NULL)
492                     return (NULL);
493             m->m_pkthdr.rcvif = NULL;
494             m->m_data += max_linkhdr;
495
496             /* set mbuf length. */
497             m->m_pkthdr.len = m->m_len = maxlen;
```
_____mip6_cncore.c

471–476 The `mip6_create_ip6hdr()` function has four parameters. The `src` and `dst` parameters are used as source and destination addresses for the generated IPv6 header. The `nxt` and `plen` parameters are the next header value and payload length of the generated IPv6 header respectively.

480–497 An mbuf is allocated by calling the `MGETHDR()` macro. If the allocated mbuf does not have enough length for the requested payload value, then the mbuf is reallocated by requesting a new mbuf as a cluster mbuf via a call to the `MCLGET()` macro. If allocation of

TABLE 5-30

Name	Description (related node types)
struct hif_softc_list hif_softc_list	The list of home virtual network entries (MN)
struct mip6_bc_list mip6_bc_list	The list of binding cache entries (CN, HA)
struct mip6_prefix_list mip6_prefix_list	The list of prefix entries (MN)
struct mip6_ha_list mip6_ha_list	The list of home agent entries (MN)
u_int16_t nonce_index	The current nonce index (CN)
mip6_nonce_t mip6_nonce[]	The array which keeps the list of nonce (CN)
mip6_nonce_t *nonce_head	A pointer to the current nonce value which is kept in the mip6_nonce[] array (CN)
mip6_nodekey_t mip6_nodekey[]	The array which keeps the list of nodekeys (CN)
u_int16_t mip6_dhaad_id	The identifier which was used when a Dynamic Home Agent Address Discovery request message was recently sent (MN)
u_int16_t mip6_mps_id	The identifier which was used when a Mobile Prefix Solicitation message was recently sent (MN)
struct mip6_unuse_hoa_list mip6_unuse_hoa	The list of addresses or port numbers for which we should use a care-of address when we send packets to the destination (MN)
int mip6ctl_nodetype	The type of the node (CN, HA, MN)
int mip6ctl_use_ipsec	A switch to enable/disable IPsec signal protection (HA, MN)
int mip6ctl_debug	A switch to enable/disable printing debug messages (CN, HA, MN)
u_int32_t mip6ctl_bc_maxlifetime	The maximum lifetime of binding cache entries for correspondent nodes (CN)
u_int32_t mip6ctl_hrbc_maxlifetime	The maximum lifetime of binding cache entries for home registration information (HA)
u_int32_t mip6ctl_bu_maxlifetime	The maximum lifetime of binding update entries for correspondent nodes (MN)
u_int32_t mip6ctl_hrbu_maxlifetime	The maximum lifetime of binding update entries for home registration information (MN)
struct mip6_preferred_ifnames mip6_preferred_ifnames	The list of interface names used when choosing a care-of address. They are ordered by preference (MN)
struct mip6stat mip6stat	Mobile IPv6 related statistics (CN, HA, MN)

Global variables.

571

TABLE 5-31

Name	Description
`mip6_create_ip6hdr()`	Create an IPv6 header as a mbuf.
`mip6_cksum()`	Compute a checksum value for MH messages.

Utility functions.

TABLE 5-32

File	Description
`${KAME}/kame/sys/netinet/ip6.h`	IPv6 header structure
`${KAME}/kame/sys/netinet/ip6mh.h`	Mobility Header structures
`${KAME}/kame/sys/netinet6/mip6_var.h`	All structures which are used in the Mobile IPv6 stack
`${KAME}/kame/sys/netinet6/mip6_cncore.c`	Implementation of utility functions

Files that implement utility functions.

a cluster mbuf also fails, a NULL pointer is returned. On line 494 (in listing 5-33), unused space whose length is `max_linkhdr` is created. This trick will avoid the overhead of another memory allocation when we prepend a link-layer protocol header later. The `max_linkhdr` variable is set to 16 by default. The size of the mbuf (`m_len`) and the header length information, `m_pkthdr.len`, are initialized to the sum of the IPv6 header and payload length.

Listing 5-34

———`mip6_cncore.c`

```
499              /* fill an ipv6 header. */
500              ip6 = mtod(m, struct ip6_hdr *);
501              ip6->ip6_flow = 0;
502              ip6->ip6_vfc &= ~IPV6_VERSION_MASK;
503              ip6->ip6_vfc |= IPV6_VERSION;
504              ip6->ip6_plen = htons((u_int16_t)plen);
505              ip6->ip6_nxt = nxt;
506              ip6->ip6_hlim = ip6_defhlim;
507              ip6->ip6_src = *src;
508              ip6->ip6_dst = *dst;
509
510              return (m);
511      }
```

———`mip6_cncore.c`

500–510 After the successful allocation of an mbuf, the IPv6 header information is filled. The payload length, `ip6_plen`, is set to `plen` as specified in the parameter list; however, this value will be updated during the output processing of the packet.

5.14.3 Checksum Computation

The Mobility Header has a checksum field to detect corruption of signaling data. The algorithm to compute the checksum is same as the one used for TCP, UDP and ICMPv6 checksum computation.

In TCP, UDP and ICMPv6, the `in6_cksum()` function provides the computation method. However, the same function cannot be used here to compute the MH checksum, since the `in6_cksum()` function assumes that the packet is passed as an mbuf structure. In the Mobile IPv6 code, a normal memory block is used to prepare MH messages instead of the mbuf structure as in other extension headers. The KAME code processes extension headers with normal memory blocks, not with mbufs, in its output processing. See Chapter 3 of *IPv6 Core Protocols Implementation*, "Internet Protocol version 6." The MH processing code also utilizes normal memory blocks in its output processing since it is treated as one of the extension headers. The `mip6_cksum()` function provides a function to compute the checksum value for MH messages. Most of the `mip6_cksum()` function is copied from the `in6_cksum()` function.

Listing 5-35

———mip6_cncore.c

```
2677    #define ADDCARRY(x)   (x > 65535 ? x -= 65535 : x)
2678    #define REDUCE do {l_util.l = sum; sum = l_util.s[0] + l_util.s[1];
    ADDCARRY(sum);} while(0);
2679    int
2680    mip6_cksum(src, dst, plen, nh, mobility)
2681            struct in6_addr *src;
2682            struct in6_addr *dst;
2683            u_int32_t plen;
2684            u_int8_t nh;
2685            char *mobility;
2686    {
```

———mip6_cncore.c

— Line 2678 is broken here for layout reasons. However, it is a single line of code.

2679–2685 The `mip6_cksum()` function has five parameters. The `src` and `dst` parameters are the source and destination addresses of the MH message. The `plen` and nh parameters are the payload length and the next header value of the MH message. In the MH case, the `nxt` parameter is always set to IPPROTO_MH. The `mobility` parameter is a pointer to the memory that contains the MH message.

Listing 5-36

———mip6_cncore.c

```
2687            int sum, i;
2688            u_int16_t *payload;
2689            union {
2690                    u_int16_t uphs[20];
2691                    struct {
2692                            struct in6_addr uph_src;
2693                            struct in6_addr uph_dst;
2694                            u_int32_t uph_plen;
2695                            u_int8_t uph_zero[3];
2696                            u_int8_t uph_nh;
2697                    } uph_un __attribute__((__packed__));
2698            } uph;
2699            union {
2700                    u_int16_t s[2];
2701                    u_int32_t l;
2702            } l_util;
```

———mip6_cncore.c

FIGURE 5-47

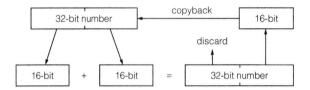

The REDUCE macro.

2687–2702 Two structured variables are declared in the declaration section. One is uph which indicates the pseudo header used for checksum computation, the other is l_util which represents 4 bytes of data as an array of two 16-bit or one 32-bit variable. The l_util variable is used by the REDUCE macro. The REDUCE macro extracts two 16-bit numbers from one 32-bit number and adds those two 16-bit numbers. The result is copied back to the original 32-bit variable again. Figure 5-47 shows the algorithm in the REDUCE macro.

Listing 5-37

_____mip6_cncore.c

```
2704            bzero(&uph, sizeof(uph));
2705            uph.uph_un.uph_src = *src;
2706            in6_clearscope(&uph.uph_un.uph_src);
2707            uph.uph_un.uph_dst = *dst;
2708            in6_clearscope(&uph.uph_un.uph_dst);
2709            uph.uph_un.uph_plen = htonl(plen);
2710            uph.uph_un.uph_nh = nh;
2711
2712            sum = 0;
2713            for (i = 0; i < 20; i++) {
2714                    REDUCE;
2715                    sum += uph.uphs[i];
2716            }
2717            payload = (u_int16_t *)mobility;
2718            for (i = 0; i < (plen / 2); i++) {
2719                    REDUCE;
2720                    sum += *payload++;
2721            }
```

_____mip6_cncore.c

2704–2712 The pseudo header information is filled with the parameters passed to function mip6_cksum() and the 1's complement sum is computed over the pseudo header and the MH message contents.

Listing 5-38

_____mip6_cncore.c

```
2722            if (plen % 2) {
2723                    union {
2724                            u_int16_t s;
2725                            u_int8_t c[2];
```

```
2726                    } last;
2727                    REDUCE;
2728                    last.c[0] = *(char *)payload;
2729                    last.c[1] = 0;
2730                    sum += last.s;
2731            }
2732
2733            REDUCE;
2734            return (~sum & 0xffff);
2735    }
2736    #undef ADDCARRY
2737    #undef REDUCE
```
——mip6_cncore.c

2722–2734 If the payload length of the MH message is odd, one byte is appended to the end
of the message. The last byte is treated as 0 in the checksum computation. Finally, the 1's
complement of the computed result is returned as the checksum value.

5.15   Common Mobility Header Processing

Because the function of a mobile node and a home agent/correspondent node significantly
differs, only a little part of the code that is related to Mobility Header input and error generation
processing is shared. In this section, we discuss these functions.

5.15.1   Files

Table 5-33 shows the related files.

5.15.2   Mobility Header Input

The signaling information used by Mobile IPv6 is carried by the Mobility Header which is a
newly introduced extension header. The Mobility Header was initially designed to be followed
by upper layer protocols, like TCP or UDP; however, the final specification defines it as a final
header with no following headers as explained in Section 5.3.4.

  To accept this new extension header, the protocol switch array for IPv6, inet6sw[], is
extended as shown in Listing 5-39.

TABLE 5-33

File	Description
${KAME}/kame/sys/netinet/ip6.h	IPv6 header structure
${KAME}/kame/sys/netinet6/in6_proto.c	Mobility Header protocol switch structure
${KAME}/kame/sys/netinet/ip6mh.h	Mobility Header structures
${KAME}/kame/sys/netinet6/mobility6.c	Entry point of Mobility Header input processing
${KAME}/kame/sys/netinet6/mip6_var.h	All structures which are used in the Mobile IPv6 stack

Files related to Mobility Header input processing.

Listing 5-39
_____in6_proto.c

```
409     #ifdef MIP6
410     { SOCK_RAW,        &inet6domain,      IPPROTO_MH,PR_ATOMIC|PR_ADDR,
411       mobility6_input,        0,                 0,                  0,
412       0,
413       0,              0,                 0,                 0,
....
417       &nousrreqs,
....
419     },
420     #endif /* MIP6 */
```
_____in6_proto.c

410–419 The Mobility Header is defined as a raw socket protocol in the inet6 domain. The protocol number is IPPROTO_MH, decimal 135. All received Mobility Header packets are processed via the mobility6_input() function.

The Mobility Header should be accessible from user space programs via a raw socket to allow application level header management. The KAME Mobile IPv6 code does not provide that function with this version. It can receive but cannot send messages through the raw socket. The latest KAME Mobile IPv6 code, which has been totally rewritten, processes all Mobility Header messages in user space programs using a raw socket.

Listing 5-40
_____mobility6.c

```
108     int
109     mobility6_input(mp, offp, proto)
110             struct mbuf **mp;
111             int *offp, proto;
112     {
113             struct mbuf *m = *mp;
114             struct m_tag *n; /* for ip6aux */
115             struct ip6_hdr *ip6;
116             struct ip6_mh *mh;
117             int off = *offp, mhlen;
118             int sum;
....
122             ip6 = mtod(m, struct ip6_hdr *);
123
124             /* validation of the length of the header */
....
126             IP6_EXTHDR_CHECK(m, off, sizeof(*mh), IPPROTO_DONE);
127             mh = (struct ip6_mh *)(mtod(m, caddr_t) + off);
```
_____mobility6.c

108–127 The mobility6_input() function has three parameters.

- The mp parameter is a double pointer to an mbuf structure which contains the input packet.
- The offp parameter is the offset from the head of the IPv6 packet to the head of Mobility Header.
- The proto parameter is the protocol number to be processed. (In this case, the number is 135, IPPROTO_MH.)

The IP6_EXTHDR_CHECK() macro makes sure that the content of the Mobility Header is located in contiguous memory. If the IP6_EXTHDR_CHECK() macro fails, IPPROTO_DONE is returned to terminate the input processing. The mh variable, which is a pointer to an ip6_mh{} structure, is initialized to the address offset by off bytes. We can access the internal data of the input Mobility Header using the mh variable.

Listing 5-41

_____mobility6.c

```
133                mhlen = (mh->ip6mh_len + 1) << 3;
134                if (mhlen < IP6M_MINLEN) {
135                        /* too small */
136                        ip6stat.ip6s_toosmall++;
137                        /* 9.2 discard and SHOULD send ICMP Parameter Problem */
138                        icmp6_error(m, ICMP6_PARAM_PROB,
139                                    ICMP6_PARAMPROB_HEADER,
140                                    (caddr_t)&mh->ip6mh_len - (caddr_t)ip6);
141                        return (IPPROTO_DONE);
142                }
143
144                if (mh->ip6mh_proto != IPPROTO_NONE) {
....
147                        /* 9.2 discard and SHOULD send ICMP Parameter Problem */
148                        mip6stat.mip6s_payloadproto++;
149                        icmp6_error(m, ICMP6_PARAM_PROB,
150                                    ICMP6_PARAMPROB_HEADER,
151                                    (caddr_t)&mh->ip6mh_proto - (caddr_t)ip6);
152                        return (IPPROTO_DONE);
153                }
```

_____mobility6.c

133–152 This part performs some validation of the input packet. If the length of the Mobility Header is smaller than the minimal value (IP6M_MINLEN = 8), an ICMPv6 Parameter Problem error is sent and the packet is discarded. The problem pointer of the error packet is set to the length field, ip6mh_len. If the payload protocol number is not IPPROTO_NONE, no next header value, an ICMPv6 Parameter Problem error is sent and the packet is discarded. Currently, the Mobile IPv6 specification does not allow piggybacking any kind of upper layer headers after a Mobility Header. The problem pointer of the ICMPv6 error packet is set to the payload protocol field, ip6mh_proto in the ip6_mh{} structure.

Listing 5-42

_____mobility6.c

```
155                /*
156                 * calculate the checksum
157                 */
....
159                IP6_EXTHDR_CHECK(m, off, mhlen, IPPROTO_DONE);
160                mh = (struct ip6_mh *)(mtod(m, caddr_t) + off);
   ....
166                if ((sum = in6_cksum(m, IPPROTO_MH, off, mhlen)) != 0) {
   ....
171                        m_freem(m);
   ....
p173:                      return (IPPROTO_DONE);
174                }
```

_____mobility6.c

155–174 After header validation is finished, the checksum value is checked. At this point, memory contiguity is assured only for the ip6_mh{} structure. To compute the checksum value, we need to make sure the entire Mobility Header message is placed in contiguous memory. Before performing checksum validation, the IP6_EXTHDR_CHECK() macro is called to make sure that the input message is located in contiguous memory. The in6_cksum() function computes the checksum value. If the checksum field, ip6mh_cksum, contains the correct value, the returned value of in6_cksum() will be 0. If the checksum verification fails, the packet is discarded.

Listing 5-43

_____mobility6.c
```
176              off += mhlen;
177
178              /* XXX sanity check. */
179
180              switch (mh->ip6mh_type) {
181              case IP6_MH_TYPE_HOTI:
182                      if (mip6_ip6mhi_input(m, (struct ip6_mh_home_test_init *)mh,
183                          mhlen) != 0)
184                              return (IPPROTO_DONE);
185                      break;
186
187              case IP6_MH_TYPE_COTI:
188                      if (mip6_ip6mci_input(m, (struct ip6_mh_careof_test_init *)mh,
189                          mhlen) != 0)
190                              return (IPPROTO_DONE);
191                      break;
192
193      #if defined(MIP6) && defined(MIP6_MOBILE_NODE)
194              case IP6_MH_TYPE_HOT:
195                      if (!MIP6_IS_MN)
196                              break;
197                      if (mip6_ip6mh_input(m, (struct ip6_mh_home_test *)mh,
198                          mhlen) != 0)
199                              return (IPPROTO_DONE);
200                      break;
201
202              case IP6_MH_TYPE_COT:
203                      if (!MIP6_IS_MN)
204                              break;
205                      if (mip6_ip6mc_input(m, (struct ip6_mh_careof_test *)mh,
206                          mhlen) != 0)
207                              return (IPPROTO_DONE);
208                      break;
209
210              case IP6_MH_TYPE_BRR:
211                      if (!MIP6_IS_MN)
212                              break;
213                      if (mip6_ip6mr_input(m, (struct ip6_mh_binding_request *)mh,
214                          mhlen) != 0)
215                              return (IPPROTO_DONE);
216                      break;
217
218              case IP6_MH_TYPE_BACK:
219                      if (!MIP6_IS_MN)
220                              break;
221                      if (mip6_ip6ma_input(m, (struct ip6_mh_binding_ack *)mh,
222                          mhlen) != 0)
223                              return (IPPROTO_DONE);
224                      break;
225
226              case IP6_MH_TYPE_BERROR:
227                      if (mip6_ip6me_input(m, (struct ip6_mh_binding_error *)mh,
228                          mhlen) != 0)
```

```
229                              return (IPPROTO_DONE);
230                      break;
231      #endif /* MIP6 && MIP6_MOBILE_NODE */
232
233          case IP6_MH_TYPE_BU:
234                  if (mip6_ip6mu_input(m, (struct ip6_mh_binding_update *)mh,
235                      mhlen) != 0)
236                          return (IPPROTO_DONE);
237                  break;
```
——mobility6.c

180–237 Each Mobility Header type has its own processing function. In this `switch` clause, the corresponding functions are called based on the message type value. All processing functions have three parameters: The first is a double pointer to the mbuf which contains the input packet: the second is a pointer to the head of the Mobility Header message; and the third is the length of the message. Table 5-34 shows the functions for each Mobility Header type.

Listing 5-44

——mobility6.c
```
239          default:
240                  /*
241                   * if we receive a MH packet which type is unknown,
242                   * send a binding error message.
243                   */
244                  n = ip6_findaux(m);
245                  if (n) {
246                          struct ip6aux *ip6a;
247                          struct in6_addr src, home;
248
249                          ip6a = (struct ip6aux *) (n + 1);
250                          src = ip6->ip6_src;
251                          if ((ip6a->ip6a_flags & IP6A_HASEEN) != 0) {
252                                  home = ip6->ip6_src;
253                                  if ((ip6a->ip6a_flags & IP6A_SWAP) != 0) {
254                                          /*
255                                           * HAO exists and swapped
256                                           * already at this point.
257                                           * send a binding error to CoA
258                                           * of the sending node.
259                                           */
260                                          src = ip6a->ip6a_coa;
261                                  } else {
262                                          /*
263                                           * HAO exists but not swapped
264                                           * yet.
265                                           */
266                                          home = ip6a->ip6a_coa;
267                                  }
268                          } else {
269                                  /*
270                                   * if no HAO exists, the home address
271                                   * field of the binding error message
272                                   * must be an unspecified address.
273                                   */
274                                  home = in6addr_any;
275                          }
276                          (void)mobility6_send_be(&ip6->ip6_dst, &src,
277                              IP6_MH_BES_UNKNOWN_MH, &home);
278                  }
279                  mip6stat.mip6s_unknowntype++;
280                  break;
281          }
```
——mobility6.c

TABLE 5-34

Type	Function name
IP6_MH_TYPE_HOTI	mip6_ip6mhi_input()
IP6_MH_TYPE_COTI	mip6_ip6mci_input()
IP6_MH_TYPE_HOT	mip6_ip6mh_input()
IP6_MH_TYPE_COT	mip6_ip6mc_input()
IP6_MH_TYPE_BRR	mip6_ip6mr_input()
IP6_MH_TYPE_BACK	mip6_ip6ma_input()
IP6_MH_TYPE_BERROR	mip6_ip6me_input()
IP6_MH_TYPE_BU	mip6_ip6mu_input()

Input processing functions for Mobility Header messages.

TABLE 5-35

Name	Description
IP6A_HASEEN	The packet contains a Home Address option.
IP6A_SWAP	The source and home addresses specified in a Home Address option have been swapped.

Flags of ip6aux{} structure used for Mobile IPv6.

239–281 If a node receives a Mobility Header message which has a type value other than those listed in Table 5-34, the node sends a Binding Error message.

The destination address of a Binding Error message must be set to the IPv6 source address (which was seen on the wire) of the incoming packet. That is, if the packet contains a Home Address option, and the home and source addresses have been swapped at this point, the addresses have to be recovered before the swapping. The IP6A_HASEEN flag, which is in the ip6aux{} structure, indicates that the packet has a Home Address option and was processed before. Table 5-35 shows the flags extended for Mobile IPv6. The IP6A_SWAP flag is set when a Home Address option is processed and the source and home addresses have been swapped. The IP6A_SWAP flag is valid only if the IP6A_HASEEN flag is set. If the IP6A_SWAP flag is set, we need to use the address stored in the ip6aux{} structure, which was the source address while the packet was on the wire; otherwise, we can use the address stored in the source address field of the incoming IPv6 header. A Binding Error message also contains the home address of the incoming packet if the packet has a Home Address option. The home address field of a Binding Error message, ip6mhbe_homeaddr, is set to an unspecified address if the incoming packet does not have a Home Address option.

The mobility6_send_be() function generates a Binding Error message. This function is described in Section 5.15.3.

Listing 5-45

```
282
283                    /* deliver the packet to appropriate sockets */
284                    if (mobility6_rip6_input(&m, *offp) == IPPROTO_DONE) {
285                            /* in error case, IPPROTO_DONE is returned. */
286                            return (IPPROTO_DONE);
287                    }
288
289                    *offp = off;
290
291                    return (mh->ip6mh_proto);
292            }
```

283–292 All Mobility Header messages are delivered into user space through a raw
socket. The `mobility6_rip6_input()` function sends the messages to every
opened raw socket which is waiting for Mobility Header messages. Note that the
comment on line 285 is wrong. Since we do not have any upper layer protocol headers after the Mobility Header, `mobility6_rip6_input()` always returns
`IPPROTO_DONE`. We can finish packet processing after we have finished the Mobility
Header processing.

5.15.3 Generating Binding Error Messages

When there is any error condition while processing Mobile IPv6 signaling messages,
a Binding Error message is sent to the sender of the packet which caused the error.
The `mobility6_send_be()` function generates a Binding Error packet and sends the packet
to the source of the error.

Listing 5-46

```
297     int
298     mobility6_send_be(src, dst, status, home)
299             struct in6_addr *src;
300             struct in6_addr *dst;
301             u_int8_t status;
302             struct in6_addr *home;
303     {
304             struct mbuf *m;
305             struct ip6_pktopts opt;
306             int error = 0;
307
308             /* a binding message must be rate limited. */
309             if (mobility6_be_ratelimit(dst, home, status))
310                     return (0); /* rate limited. */
```

297–302 The `mobility6_send_be()` function has four parameters: The `src` and `dst`
parameters are the source and destination addresses of the Binding Error message to be
generated, the `status` parameter is a status code of the Binding Error message, and the
`home` parameter is the home address that is set to the home address field of the Binding
Error message. Table 5-16 (page 548) shows the available codes.

309–310 Sending   Binding   Error   messages   must   be   rate   limited.   The
`mobility6_be_ratelimit()` function returns whether we can send a Binding
Error message or not, based on the rate limitation algorithm we use. Function
`mobility6_be_ratelimit()` is discussed in Section 5.15.4.

Listing 5-47
                                                                                    _____mobility6.c

```
312                 ip6_initpktopts(&opt);
313
314                 m = mip6_create_ip6hdr(src, dst, IPPROTO_NONE, 0);
315                 if (m == NULL)
316                         return (ENOMEM);
317
318                 error = mip6_ip6me_create(&opt.ip6po_mh, src, dst, status, home);
319                 if (error) {
320                         m_freem(m);
321                         goto free_ip6pktopts;
322                 }
323
324                 /* output a binding missing message. */
....
326                 error = ip6_output(m, &opt, NULL, 0, NULL, NULL
....
328                                         , NULL
....
330                                         );
331                 if (error)
332                         goto free_ip6pktopts;
333
334         free_ip6pktopts:
335                 if (opt.ip6po_mh)
336                         FREE(opt.ip6po_mh, M_IP6OPT);
337
338                 return (error);
339         }
```
                                                                                    _____mobility6.c

314–322 The `mip6_create_ip6hdr()` function creates an IPv6 header based on the specified parameters. The `mip6_ip6me_create()` function creates a Binding Error message with the specified parameters and stores the message in the instance of the
`ip6_pktopts{}` structure given as the first parameter, `opt.ip6po_mh` in this case.
Function `mip6_ip6me_create()` is discussed in Section 5.15.5.

324–338 Since Mobility Header packets do not have any upper layer headers, we can simply
call the `ip6_output()` function with a Mobility Header only as a packet option to
send the packet. The Mobility Header message must be freed by the caller, since the
`ip6_output()` function does not free packet option information.

5.15.4   Rate Limitation of Binding Error Messages

To avoid flooding the network with error messages, the sending rate of Binding Error messages
is limited.

Listing 5-48

```
                                                          mobility6.c
341     static int
342     mobility6_be_ratelimit(dst, hoa, status)
343         const struct in6_addr *dst;     /* not used at this moment */
344         const struct in6_addr *hoa;     /* not used at this moment */
345         const int status;               /* not used at this moment */
346     {
347         int ret;
348
349         ret = 0;        /* okay to send */
350
351         /* PPS limit */
352         if (!ppsratecheck(&ip6me_ppslim_last, &ip6me_pps_count,
353             ip6me_ppslim)) {
354             /* The packet is subject to rate limit */
355             ret++;
356         }
357
358         return ret;
359     }
                                                          mobility6.c
```

341–359 The `mobility6_be_ratelimit()` function decides whether we can send a Binding Error message, based on the system rate limit parameter. Currently the rate limitation code does not take into account any information about the source or destination address of the Binding Error message to be sent. In the current algorithm, Binding Error messages are limited to the number specified by the `ip6me_ppslim` global variable per second. The `ppsratecheck()` function returns true if the number of packets has not reached the limit, otherwise it returns false. The `ip6me_ppslim_last` global variable keeps the start time of the one limitation unit time to count the number of error messages sent in 1 second. The `ip6me_pps_count` variable keeps the number of messages we sent after `ip6me_ppslim_last`. If `ip6me_pps_count` exceeds the `ip6me_ppslim` variable, we must not send the packet. The `ip6me_ppslim_last` and `ip6me_pps_count` variables are updated in the `ppsratecheck()` function. Figure 5-48 shows the mechanism.

5.15.5 Creation of Binding Error Message

A Binding Error message is created by calling the `mip6_ip6me_create()` function.

FIGURE 5-48

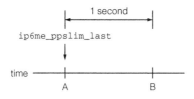

ip6me_pps_count = the number of packets sent between A and B

ppsratecheck() mechanism.

Listing 5-49

————————————————————————————mip6_cncore.c

```
2574    int
2575    mip6_ip6me_create(pktopt_mobility, src, dst, status, addr)
2576            struct ip6_mh **pktopt_mobility;
2577            struct in6_addr *src;
2578            struct in6_addr *dst;
2579            u_int8_t status;
2580            struct in6_addr *addr;
2581    {
2582            struct ip6_mh_binding_error *ip6me;
2583            int ip6me_size;
2584
2585            *pktopt_mobility = NULL;
2586
2587            ip6me_size = sizeof(struct ip6_mh_binding_error);
2588
2589            MALLOC(ip6me, struct ip6_mh_binding_error *,
2590                    ip6me_size, M_IP6OPT, M_NOWAIT);
2591            if (ip6me == NULL)
2592                    return (ENOMEM);
2593
2594            bzero(ip6me, ip6me_size);
2595            ip6me->ip6mhbe_proto = IPPROTO_NONE;
2596            ip6me->ip6mhbe_len = (ip6me_size >> 3) - 1;
2597            ip6me->ip6mhbe_type = IP6_MH_TYPE_BERROR;
2598            ip6me->ip6mhbe_status = status;
2599            ip6me->ip6mhbe_homeaddr = *addr;
2600            in6_clearscope(&ip6me->ip6mhbe_homeaddr);
2601
2602            /* calculate checksum. */
2603            ip6me->ip6mhbe_cksum = mip6_cksum(src, dst, ip6me_size, IPPROTO_MH,
2604                (char *)ip6me);
2605
2606            *pktopt_mobility = (struct ip6_mh *)ip6me;
2607
2608            return (0);
2609    }
```

————————————————————————————mip6_cncore.c

2574–2580 The mip6_ip6me_create() function has five parameters. The pktopt_mobility is a pointer to the ip6po_mh field of the ip6_pktopts{} structure, the src and dst parameters are the IPv6 addresses which are used as source and destination addresses of a Binding Error message and the status and addr parameters are the status code and the home address included in the Binding Error message.

2587–2592 A Binding Error message is passed to the ip6_output() function as a packet option. Memory is allocated based on the packet format of a Binding Error message. If memory allocation fails, an error is returned.

2594–2608 The contents of a Binding Error message are filled. Care has to be taken when setting the length of the message since the length of an extension header is specified in units of 8 bytes. If the home address information passed by the caller has an embedded scope identifier, it must be cleared by calling the in6_clearscope() function. The checksum computation is done by the mip6_cksum() function, which serves the same function as the in6_cksum() function. The difference is that in6_cksum() takes the mbuf as a parameter, while mip6_cksum() takes address information as an in6_addr{} structure. The created Binding Error message is set to the ip6po_mh field.

5.15.6   Mobility Header Message Delivery to Raw Sockets

All Mobility Header messages are delivered to raw sockets. A user space program can receive
Mobility Header messages by opening a raw socket specifying `IPPROTO_MH` as a protocol. The
delivery to raw sockets is implemented in the `mobility6_rip6_input()` function.

Listing 5-50

——mobility6.c
```
361     static int
362     mobility6_rip6_input(mp, off)
363             struct mbuf **mp;
364             int off;
365     {
366             struct mbuf *m = *mp;
367             struct ip6_hdr *ip6;
368             struct ip6_mh *mh;
369             struct sockaddr_in6 fromsa;
370             struct in6pcb *in6p;
371             struct in6pcb *last = NULL;
372             struct mbuf *opts = NULL;
373
374             ip6 = mtod(m, struct ip6_hdr *);
....
377             mh = (struct ip6_mh *)((caddr_t)ip6 + off);
....
386             /*
387              * XXX: the address may have embedded scope zone ID, which should be
388              * hidden from applications.
389              */
390             bzero(&fromsa, sizeof(fromsa));
391             fromsa.sin6_family = AF_INET6;
392             fromsa.sin6_len = sizeof(struct sockaddr_in6);
393             if (in6_recoverscope(&fromsa, &ip6->ip6_src, m->m_pkthdr.rcvif) != 0) {
394                     m_freem(m);
395                     return (IPPROTO_DONE);
396             }
```
——mobility6.c

361–364 The `mobility6_rip6_input()` function has two parameters. The `mp` parameter
is a pointer to the packet which contains the Mobility Header message to be delivered
and the `off` parameter is the offset from the head of the IPv6 header to the head of the
Mobility Header.

377 Since the contiguous memory check has already been done in the initial part of the input
processing, the pointer to the Mobility Header can be set to the `mh` variable without any
validation.

386–396 The source address of the Mobility Header message is set to the variable `fromsa`. In
the KAME implementation, the address used in the kernel may have an embedded scope
identifier. The `fromsa` variable is used to communicate the source address to user space
programs. This code makes sure that the scope identifier is cleared, since we must not
pass addresses which have embedded scope identifiers to user space programs.

Listing 5-51

——mobility6.c
```
399             LIST_FOREACH(in6p, &ripcb, inp_list)
    ....
```

```
408                    {
....
410                              if ((in6p->inp_vflag & INP_IPV6) == 0)
411                                      continue;
....
414                              if (in6p->inp_ip_p != IPPROTO_MH)
....
418                                      continue;
419                              if (!IN6_IS_ADDR_UNSPECIFIED(&in6p->in6p_laddr) &&
420                                  !IN6_ARE_ADDR_EQUAL(&in6p->in6p_laddr, &ip6->ip6_dst))
421                                      continue;
422                              if (!IN6_IS_ADDR_UNSPECIFIED(&in6p->in6p_faddr) &&
423                                  !IN6_ARE_ADDR_EQUAL(&in6p->in6p_faddr, &ip6->ip6_src))
424                                      continue;
425                              if (last) {
426                                      struct  mbuf *n = NULL;
427
428                                      /*
429                                       * Recent network drivers tend to allocate a single
430                                       * mbuf cluster, rather than to make a couple of
431                                       * mbufs without clusters.  Also, since the IPv6 code
432                                       * path tries to avoid m_pullup(), it is highly
433                                       * probable that we still have an mbuf cluster here
434                                       * even though the necessary length can be stored in an
435                                       * mbuf's internal buffer.
436                                       * Meanwhile, the default size of the receive socket
437                                       * buffer for raw sockets is not so large.  This means
438                                       * the possibility of packet loss is relatively higher
439                                       * than before.  To avoid this scenario, we copy the
440                                       * received data to a separate mbuf that does not use
441                                       * a cluster, if possible.
442                                       * XXX: it is better to copy the data after stripping
443                                       * intermediate headers.
444                                       */
445                                      if ((m->m_flags & M_EXT) && m->m_next == NULL &&
446                                          m->m_len <= MHLEN) {
447                                              MGET(n, M_DONTWAIT, m->m_type);
448                                              if (n != NULL) {
....
453                                                      m_dup_pkthdr(n, m);
....
457                                                      bcopy(m->m_data, n->m_data, m->m_len);
458                                                      n->m_len = m->m_len;
459                                              }
460                                      }
461                                      if (n != NULL ||
462                                          (n = m_copy(m, 0, (int)M_COPYALL)) != NULL) {
463                                              if (last->in6p_flags & IN6P_CONTROLOPTS)
464                                                      ip6_savecontrol(last, n, &opts);
465                                              /* strip intermediate headers */
466                                              m_adj(n, off);
467                                              if (sbappendaddr(&last->in6p_socket->so_rcv,
468                                                  (struct sockaddr *)&fromsa, n, opts)
469                                                  == 0) {
470                                                      /* should notify about lost packet */
471                                                      m_freem(n);
472                                                      if (opts) {
473                                                              m_freem(opts);
474                                                      }
475                                              } else
476                                                      sorwakeup(last->in6p_socket);
477                                              opts = NULL;
478                                      }
479                              }
480                              last = in6p;
```

```
481                     }
482                     if (last) {
483                             if (last->in6p_flags & IN6P_CONTROLOPTS)
484                                     ip6_savecontrol(last, m, &opts);
485                             /* strip intermediate headers */
486                             m_adj(m, off);
487
488                             /* avoid using mbuf clusters if possible (see above) */
489                             if ((m->m_flags & M_EXT) && m->m_next == NULL &&
490                                 m->m_len <= MHLEN) {
491                                     struct mbuf *n;
492
493                                     MGET(n, M_DONTWAIT, m->m_type);
494                                     if (n != NULL) {
....
499                                             m_dup_pkthdr(n, m);
....
503                                             bcopy(m->m_data, n->m_data, m->m_len);
504                                             n->m_len = m->m_len;
505
506                                             m_freem(m);
507                                             m = n;
508                                     }
509                             }
510                             if (sbappendaddr(&last->in6p_socket->so_rcv,
511                                 (struct sockaddr *)&fromsa, m, opts) == 0) {
512                                     m_freem(m);
513                                     if (opts)
514                                             m_freem(opts);
515                             } else
516                                     sorwakeup(last->in6p_socket);
517                     } else {
518                             m_freem(m);
519                             ip6stat.ip6s_delivered--;
520                     }
521                     return IPPROTO_DONE;
522             }
```
                                                                            ———— mobility6.c

399–424 The Protocol Control Block (PCB) entries for raw sockets are kept in the ripcb
variable as a list of PCB entries. Each PCB entry is checked to determine if the Mobility
Header message should be delivered to the PCB entry. The following PCB entries are
skipped because they have nothing to do with this processing.

- The version is not IPv6.
- The protocol is not Mobility Header (IPPROTO_MH).
- The local address of the PCB entry does not match the destination address of the
  incoming Mobility Header packet.
- The foreign address of the PCB entry does not match the source address of the incoming
  Mobility Header packet.

445–460 If the incoming packet is stored in a cluster mbuf, but the size is smaller than the
mbuf size of a non-cluster mbuf, a new non-cluster mbuf is created and the contents are
copied to the non-cluster mbuf to avoid exhaustion of cluster mbufs.

461–477 If the above code fails and a copy of the incoming packet has not been created, the
m_copy() function is called to copy the mbuf which keeps the incoming packet. If the
copy is created, it is delivered to the raw socket of the current PCB entry that is being processed. The ip6_savecontrol() function extracts packet information and stores it in

the `opts` variable. A user needs to specify required information using the socket API if the user wants to use packet information in the program. The `ip6_savecontrol()` function is discussed in Chapter 7 of *IPv6 Core Protocols Implementation*, "Socket API Extensions." Before putting the Mobility Header message in the socket with the `sbappendaddr()` function, the IPv6 header and other extension headers have to be removed by the `m_adj()` function if it exists. The `sbappendaddr()` function appends the Mobility Header message to the tail of the socket buffer which is bound to this PCB entry. To give a user program the source address of a packet, the value of the `fromsa` variable is passed. In addition, the saved packet information, `opt`, is passed to function `sbappendaddr()`. If the call to function `sbappendaddr()` succeeds, the `sorwakeup()` function is called to notify the socket that there is unreceived data in the socket buffer. If the call fails, the copied Mobility Header message and packet information are freed.

482–517 This code is almost the same as the code written on lines 461–477, but handles the last PCB entry in the raw PCB entry list. The difference from the previous code is that we need not copy the incoming packet since we do not have any other PCB entry to be processed. We can directly modify the original packet to deliver the data.

518–521 If there are no raw PCB entries in the kernel, the incoming mbuf is simply freed. After all the PCB entries have been processed, `IPPROTO_DONE` is returned to indicate the delivery has finished. There is no need to return a value other than `IPPROTO_DONE`, since the Mobility Header does not have any upper layer protocols. Incoming packet processing can be finished after Mobility Header processing is finished.

5.16 Home Agent and Correspondent Node

A home agent is a special router located on a home network to support mobile nodes. A home agent has the following capabilities.

- Maintaining binding information for home registration.

- Intercepting and forwarding packets sent to the home addresses of mobile nodes using the IPv6 in IPv6 encapsulating mechanism.

- Forwarding packets sent from mobile nodes using the IPv6 in IPv6 encapsulating mechanism to the final destination of those packets.

A correspondent node may have the capability to perform the route optimization procedure described in Section 5.5. Such a node has the following capabilities.

- Receiving binding information for route optimized communication.

- Performing direct communication with mobile nodes using the Home Address Option and the Type 2 Routing Header.

A home agent also has the capabilities to perform route optimization. The above functions are implemented as the binding cache mechanism that keeps information about mobile nodes. We describe the mechanism in this section for both a home agent and a correspondent node that supports route optimization at the same time, since those two types of nodes share pieces of code.

TABLE 5-36

File	Description
${KAME}/kame/sys/netinet/icmp6.h	Dynamic Home Agent Address Discovery and Mobile Prefix Solicitation/Advertisement structures
${KAME}/kame/sys/netinet/ip6.h	Home Address option structure
${KAME}/kame/sys/netinet/ip6mh.h	Mobility Header structures
${KAME}/kame/sys/netinet6/dest6.c	Processing code of the Home Address option
${KAME}/kame/sys/netinet6/mip6_var.h	All structures which are used in the Mobile IPv6 stack
${KAME}/kame/sys/netinet6/mip6_cncore.c	Implementation of correspondent node functions
${KAME}/kame/sys/netinet6/mip6_hacore.c	Implementation of home agent functions
${KAME}/kame/sys/netinet6/mip6_icmp6.c	Implementation of ICMPv6 message related processing
${KAME}/kame/sys/netinet6/ip6_forward.c	Sending packets to the bi-directional tunnel on a home agent side
${KAME}/kame/sys/netinet6/ip6_output.c	Insertion of extension headers for Mobile IPv6 signaling
${KAME}/kame/kame/had/halist.h	Home agent information structure used by the home agent side
${KAME}/kame/kame/had/halist.c	Home Agent information management
${KAME}/kame/kame/had/haadisc.c	Implementation of the Dynamic Home Agent Address Discovery mechanism of the home agent side
${KAME}/kame/kame/had/mpa.c	Implementation of the Mobile Prefix Solicitation and Advertisement mechanism of the home agent side

Files for home agent and route optimization functions.

5.16.1 Files

Table 5-36 shows the files used by a home agent and route optimization functions.

5.16.2 Binding Update Message Input

A mobile node sends its binding information via the Binding Update message, which is a Mobility Header message. A Binding Update message is dispatched to the `mip6_ip6mu_input()` function from the `mobility6_input()` function.

Listing 5-52

```
                                                                mip6_cncore.c
2002    #define IS_REQUEST_TO_CACHE(lifetime, hoa, coa)  \
2003         (((lifetime) != 0) &&                       \
2004          (!IN6_ARE_ADDR_EQUAL((hoa), (coa))))
```

```
2005      int
2006      mip6_ip6mu_input(m, ip6mu, ip6mulen)
2007              struct mbuf *m;
2008              struct ip6_mh_binding_update *ip6mu;
2009              int ip6mulen;
2010      {
2011              struct ip6_hdr *ip6;
2012              struct m_tag *mtag;
2013              struct ip6aux *ip6a = NULL;
2014              u_int8_t isprotected = 0;
2015              struct mip6_bc *mbc;
2016
2017              int error = 0;
2018              u_int8_t bu_safe = 0;    /* To accept bu always without authentication,
          this value is set to non-zero */
2019              struct mip6_mobility_options mopt;
2020              struct mip6_bc bi;
2021
2022              mip6stat.mip6s_bu++;
2023              bzero(&bi, sizeof(bi));
2024              bi.mbc_status = IP6_MH_BAS_ACCEPTED;
2025              /*
2026               * we send a binding ack immediately when this binding update
2027               * is not a request for home registration and has an ACK bit
2028               * on.
2029               */
2030              bi.mbc_send_ba = ((ip6mu->ip6mhbu_flags & IP6MU_ACK)
2031                  && !(ip6mu->ip6mhbu_flags & IP6MU_HOME));
```
──*mip6_cncore.c*

— Line 2018 is broken here for layout reasons. However, it is a single line of code.

2006–2031 The `mip6_ip6mu_input()` function has three parameters. The `m` parameter is a
pointer to the mbuf which contains a Binding Update message, the `ip6mu` and `ip6mulen`
parameters are pointers to the head of the Binding Update message and the length of the
message respectively.

The variable `bi`, which is an instance of the `mip6_bc{}` structure, is used as a
temporary buffer for the binding information which will be stored in the node. The
`mbc_send_ba` variable is a flag which indicates whether the node needs to reply to the
mobile node that has sent this Binding Update message with a Binding Acknowledgment
message in this function. A Binding Update message for home registration must have the
A (Acknowledge) flag set. If the input message has the H (Home registration) flag set but
does not have the A flag set, the `mbc_send_ba` variable is set to true to send a Binding
Acknowledgment message to the sender to indicate an error.

Listing 5-53
──*mip6_cncore.c*

```
2045              ip6 = mtod(m, struct ip6_hdr *);
2046              bi.mbc_addr = ip6->ip6_dst;
2047
2048              /* packet length check. */
2049              if (ip6mulen < sizeof(struct ip6_mh_binding_update)) {
  ....
2054                      ip6stat.ip6s_toosmall++;
2055                      /* send ICMP parameter problem. */
2056                      icmp6_error(m, ICMP6_PARAM_PROB, ICMP6_PARAMPROB_HEADER,
2057                          (caddr_t)&ip6mu->ip6mhbu_len - (caddr_t)ip6);
2058                      return (EINVAL);
2059              }
2060
2061              bi.mbc_flags = ip6mu->ip6mhbu_flags;
```

```
2062
2063     #ifdef M_DECRYPTED        /* not openbsd */
2064             if (((m->m_flags & M_DECRYPTED) != 0)
2065                 || ((m->m_flags & M_AUTHIPHDR) != 0)) {
2066                     isprotected = 1;
2067             }
2068     #endif
```
_____ mip6_cncore.c

2045–2059 The length of the incoming packet must be greater than the size of an
`ip6_mh_binding_update{}` structure, otherwise an ICMPv6 Parameter Problem message will be sent. The code value is set to `ICMP6_PARAMPROB_HEADER` to indicate that
the header is invalid and the problem pointer points to the length field of the Binding
Update message.

2064–2067 The KAME IPsec stack adds the `M_DECRYPTED` mbuf flag if the packet was
encrypted by the ESP mechanism. The stack also adds the `M_AUTHIPHDR` mbuf flag
if the packet was protected by an AH. The Mobile IPv6 specification requires that
Binding Update messages for home registration must be protected by ESP or AH. The
`isprotected` variable is used later when we perform the home registration procedure.

Listing 5-54
_____ mip6_cncore.c

```
2075             bi.mbc_pcoa = ip6->ip6_src;
2076             mtag = ip6_findaux(m);
2077             if (mtag == NULL) {
2078                     m_freem(m);
2079                     return (EINVAL);
2080             }
2081             ip6a = (struct ip6aux *) (mtag + 1);
2082             if (((ip6a->ip6a_flags & IP6A_HASEEN) != 0) &&
2083                 ((ip6a->ip6a_flags & IP6A_SWAP) != 0)) {
2084                     bi.mbc_pcoa = ip6a->ip6a_coa;
2085             }
```
_____ mip6_cncore.c

2075–2085 The care-of address of the mobile node is extracted from the incoming Binding
Update packet and is stored in the Home Address Option at this point. We can copy
the address from the auxiliary mbuf, since the address has already been copied to the
auxiliary mbuf during the Destination Option processing discussed in Section 5.16.15. The
exception is a Binding Update message for home de-registration. In the de-registration
case, the Home Address option may not exist, in which case the source address of the
IPv6 header is considered a care-of address.

Listing 5-55
_____ mip6_cncore.c

```
2087             if (!mip6ctl_use_ipsec && (bi.mbc_flags & IP6MU_HOME)) {
2088                     bu_safe = 1;
2089                     goto accept_binding_update;
2090             }
2091
2092             if (isprotected) {
2093                     bu_safe = 1;
2094                     goto accept_binding_update;
2095             }
2096             if ((bi.mbc_flags & IP6MU_HOME) == 0)
```

```
2097                    goto accept_binding_update;    /* Must be checked its safety
2098                                                     * with RR later */
2099
2100              /* otherwise, discard this packet. */
2101              m_freem(m);
2102              mip6stat.mip6s_haopolicy++;
2103              return (EINVAL);
```
_____mip6_cncore.c

2087–2090 The `mip6ctl_use_ipsec` variable is a configurable variable which can be set using the **sysctl** program. A Binding Update message is accepted even if it is not protected by IPsec when the `mip6ctl_use_ipsec` variable is set to false.

2092–2097 If the Binding Update message is protected by the IPsec mechanism, the message is accepted, otherwise, the validity is checked later by return routability information if the message is for route optimization and is not for home registration.

2100–2103 Any other Binding Update messages are silently discarded.

Listing 5-56
_____mip6_cncore.c

```
2105      accept_binding_update:
2106
2107              /* get home address. */
2108              bi.mbc_phaddr = ip6->ip6_src;
2109
2110              if ((error = mip6_get_mobility_options((struct ip6_mh *)ip6mu,
2111                      sizeof(*ip6mu), ip6mulen, &mopt))) {
2112                  /* discard. */
2113                  m_freem(m);
2114                  mip6stat.mip6s_invalidopt++;
2115                  return (EINVAL);
2116              }
2117
2118              if (mopt.valid_options & MOPT_ALTCOA)
2119                  bi.mbc_pcoa = mopt.mopt_altcoa;
2120
2121              if (IN6_IS_ADDR_MULTICAST(&bi.mbc_pcoa) ||
2122                  IN6_IS_ADDR_UNSPECIFIED(&bi.mbc_pcoa) ||
2123                  IN6_IS_ADDR_V4MAPPED(&bi.mbc_pcoa) ||
2124                  IN6_IS_ADDR_V4COMPAT(&bi.mbc_pcoa) ||
2125                  IN6_IS_ADDR_LOOPBACK(&bi.mbc_pcoa)) {
2126                  /* discard. */
2127                  m_freem(m);
2128                  mip6stat.mip6s_invalidcoa++;
2129                  return (EINVAL);
2130              }
```
_____mip6_cncore.c

2108 The home address of a mobile node is stored in the source address field of the IPv6 header. As already described, the address may be the same as the care-of address when the Binding Update message is for home de-registration.

2110–2130 A mobile node may specify an alternate care-of address when it wants to use an address other than the address specified in the source address field of a Binding Update message. The source address is taken as a care-of address unless the mobile node explicitly specifies it is not. The alternate address is carried in the option field of the Binding Update message. The `mip6_get_mobility_options()` function extracts all options contained in a Mobility message. The function is discussed in Section 5.16.4. If the message has an Alternate Care-of Address mobility option, the specified address in the option is

set as a care-of address. The care-of address must be a global unicast address. We discard
the packet if the care-of address is not a global unicast address.

Listing 5-57

```
                                                                    mip6_cncore.c
2132              if ((mopt.valid_options & MOPT_AUTHDATA) &&
2133                  ((mopt.mopt_auth + IP6MOPT_AUTHDATA_SIZE) -
(caddr_t)ip6mu < ip6mulen)) {
2134                      /* Auth. data options is not the last option */
2135                      /* discard. */
2136                      m_freem(m);
2137                      /* XXX Statistics */
2138                      return (EINVAL);
2139              }
2140
2141
2142              if ((mopt.valid_options & (MOPT_AUTHDATA | MOPT_NONCE_IDX)) &&
2143                  (ip6mu->ip6mhbu_flags & IP6MU_HOME)) {
2144                      /* discard. */
2145                      m_freem(m);
....
2147                      return (EINVAL);
2148              }
                                                                    mip6_cncore.c
```

— *Line 2133 is broken here for layout reasons. However, it is a single line of code.*

2132–2148 When a mobile node tries to optimize the path to a correspondent node, the node
needs to send a Binding Update message with an Authentication Data mobility option.
[RFC3775] says that the option must be the last option in the message. If the option is not
located at the end of options, the packet is discarded.

   The packet is discarded if a mobile node uses an Authentication Data mobility option
in a home registration request.

Listing 5-58

```
                                                                    mip6_cncore.c
2150              bi.mbc_seqno = ntohs(ip6mu->ip6mhbu_seqno);
2151              bi.mbc_lifetime = ntohs(ip6mu->ip6mhbu_lifetime) << 2;
    /* units of 4 secs */
2152              /* XXX Should this check be done only when this bu is confirmed
    with RR ? */
2153              if (bi.mbc_lifetime > MIP6_MAX_RR_BINDING_LIFE)
2154                      bi.mbc_lifetime = MIP6_MAX_RR_BINDING_LIFE;
2155
2156              if (IS_REQUEST_TO_CACHE(bi.mbc_lifetime, &bi.mbc_phaddr, &bi.mbc_pcoa)
2157                  && mip6_bc_list_find_withphaddr(&mip6_bc_list, &bi.mbc_pcoa)) {
2158                      /* discard */
2159                      m_freem(m);
2160                      mip6stat.mip6s_circularrefered++;        /* XXX */
2161                      return (EINVAL);
2162              }
2163              if (!bu_safe &&
2164                  mip6_is_valid_bu(ip6, ip6mu, ip6mulen, &mopt, &bi.mbc_phaddr,
2165                      &bi.mbc_pcoa, IS_REQUEST_TO_CACHE(bi.mbc_lifetime,
2166                          &bi.mbc_phaddr, &bi.mbc_pcoa), &bi.mbc_status)) {
....
2170                      /* discard. */
2171                      m_freem(m);
2172                      mip6stat.mip6s_rrauthfail++;
```

```
2173                    if (bi.mbc_status >= IP6_MH_BAS_HOME_NI_EXPIRED &&
2174                        bi.mbc_status <= IP6_MH_BAS_NI_EXPIRED) {
2175                            bi.mbc_send_ba = 1;
2176                            error = EINVAL;
2177                            goto send_ba;
2178                    }
2179                    return (EINVAL);
2180            }
```
——mip6_cncore.c

— *Lines 2151 and 2152 are broken here for layout reasons. However, they are a single line of code.*

2150–2151 A sequence number and lifetime are extracted from the incoming Binding Update message. Both values are stored in network byte order. We need to shift the lifetime value by 2 bits, since the value is specified in units of 4 seconds.

2153–2162 The KAME implementation restricts the lifetime of all binding cache information to `MIP6_MAX_RR_BINDING_LIFE` seconds. As the macro name says, the lifetime limitation should be applied to the binding cache entries created by the return routability procedure. In the home registration case, the lifetime of a binding cache can be larger than `MIP6_MAX_RR_BINDING_LIFE`; however, the current implementation does not consider this case and limits the lifetime of all entries to `MIP6_MAX_RR_BINDING_LIFE`.

2156–2162 A care-of address cannot also be a home address of other binding information. Such a binding may cause unwanted loop conditions.

2163–2180 The `mip6_is_valid_bu()` function checks if the Binding Update message is protected by the return routability procedure discussed in Section 5.17.23. If the message is not protected by the IPsec mechanism or the `use_ipsec` sysctl switch is turned off (`bu_safe` is false), we call `mip6_is_valid_bu()`. The function returns a non-zero value if the message is not acceptable. In this case, the node returns a Binding Acknowledgment message with an error status. The error status is decided by the `mip6_is_valid_bu()` function.

Listing 5-59
——mip6_cncore.c

```
2182            /* ip6_src and HAO has been already swapped at this point. */
2183            mbc = mip6_bc_list_find_withphaddr(&mip6_bc_list, &bi.mbc_phaddr);
2184            if (mbc != NULL) {
2185                    /* check a sequence number. */
2186                    if (MIP6_LEQ(bi.mbc_seqno, mbc->mbc_seqno)) {
....
2192                            /*
2193                             * the seqno of this binding update is smaller than the
2194                             * corresponding binding cache.  we send TOO_SMALL
2195                             * binding ack as an error.  in this case, we use the
2196                             * coa of the incoming packet instead of the coa
2197                             * stored in the binding cache as a destination
2198                             * addrress.  because the sending mobile node's coa
2199                             * might have changed after it had registered before.
2200                             */
2201                            bi.mbc_status = IP6_MH_BAS_SEQNO_BAD;
2202                            bi.mbc_seqno = mbc->mbc_seqno;
2203                            bi.mbc_send_ba = 1;
2204                            error = EINVAL;
2205
2206                            /* discard. */
2207                            m_freem(m);
```

```
2208                         mip6stat.mip6s_seqno++;
2209                         goto send_ba;
2210                 }
```
————————————————————————————————————— mip6_cncore.c

2182–2210 A Binding Update message has a sequence number field to detect an out-of-sequence packet. We need to check to see if the sequence number of the incoming Binding Update message is greater than the sequence number of the existing binding cache entry. To compare the sequence numbers, the MIP6_LEQ() macro is used. The comparison algorithm is described in Figure 5-34 of Section 5.4.2. If the sequence number of the incoming message is equal to or smaller than the existing one, the incoming Binding Update message is discarded. The node needs to reply to the message sender with a Binding Acknowledgment message with error code IP6_MH_BAS_SEQNO_BAD, so that the message sender can catch up to the latest sequence number and resend a Binding Update message with a valid sequence number.

Listing 5-60

————————————————————————————————————— mip6_cncore.c
```
2211                 if ((bi.mbc_flags & IP6MU_HOME) ^ (mbc->mbc_flags &
        IP6MU_HOME)) {
2212                         /* 9.5.1 */
2213                         bi.mbc_status = IP6_MH_BAS_REG_NOT_ALLOWED;
2214                         bi.mbc_send_ba = 1;
2215                         error = EINVAL;
2216
2217                         /* discard. */
2218                         m_freem(m);
2219                         goto send_ba;
2220                 }
2221         }
```
————————————————————————————————————— mip6_cncore.c

— Line 2211 is broken here for layout reasons. However, it is a single line of code.

2211–2221 A mobile node cannot change the home registration flag (the H flag) of the existing binding cache entry. If there is a binding cache entry which corresponds to the incoming Binding Update message, and the H flag of the message differs from the H flag of the binding cache entry, the message is discarded. In this case the node replies a Binding Acknowledgment message with the error code IP6_MH_BAS_REG_NOT_ALLOWED.

Listing 5-61

————————————————————————————————————— mip6_cncore.c
```
2223             if (ip6mu->ip6mhbu_flags & IP6MU_HOME) {
2224                     /* request for the home (un)registration. */
2225                     if (!MIP6_IS_HA) {
2226                             /* this is not a homeagent. */
2227                             /* XXX */
2228                             bi.mbc_status = IP6_MH_BAS_HA_NOT_SUPPORTED;
2229                             bi.mbc_send_ba = 1;
2230                             goto send_ba;
2231                     }
2232
2233     #ifdef MIP6_HOME_AGENT
2234                     /* limit the max duration of bindings. */
2235                     if (mip6ctl_hrbc_maxlifetime > 0 &&
2236                         bi.mbc_lifetime > mip6ctl_hrbc_maxlifetime)
2237                             bi.mbc_lifetime = mip6ctl_hrbc_maxlifetime;
2238
```

```
2239                      if (IS_REQUEST_TO_CACHE(bi.mbc_lifetime, &bi.mbc_phaddr, &
     bi.mbc_pcoa)) {
2240                              if (mbc != NULL && (mbc->mbc_flags & IP6MU_CLONED)) {
....
2244                                      /* XXX */
2245                              }
2246                              if (mip6_process_hrbu(&bi)) {
....
2250                                      /* continue. */
2251                              }
2252                      } else {
2253                              if (mbc == NULL || (mbc->mbc_flags & IP6MU_CLONED)) {
2254                                      bi.mbc_status = IP6_MH_BAS_NOT_HA;
2255                                      bi.mbc_send_ba = 1;
2256                                      goto send_ba;
2257                              }
....
2265                              if (mip6_process_hurbu(&bi)) {
....
2269                                      /* continue. */
2270                              }
2271                      }
2272      #endif /* MIP6_HOME_AGENT */
```
——mip6_cncore.c
— *Line 2239 is broken here for layout reasons. However, it is a single line of code.*

2223–2231 If the incoming Binding Update message has the H flag on, the message is
for home registration or home de-registration. A node must return an error with
IP6_MH_BAS_HA_NOT_SUPPORTED status, if the node is not acting as a home agent.

2235–2272 The lifetime of a binding cache entry for home registration cannot be longer
than the value stored in the mip6ctl_hrbc_maxlifetime variable. The
mip6ctl_hrbc_maxlifetime variable is tunable; a user can change the value with
the **sysctl** command. A mobile node uses a Binding Update message for both home registration and de-registration. We can check to see if the message is for registration or
de-registration with the following two conditions.

- If the lifetime requested is 0, the message is for de-registration.
- If the home address and the care-of address which are included in the message are the
  same, the message is for de-registration.

If the message is for home registration, the mip6_process_hrbu() function is called,
which performs the home registration procedure. The code fragment from 2240 to 2245 is
intended for error handling when there is a binding cache entry for the same mobile node
and the entry has the CLONED flag set. There is no error processing code right now. If the
message is for home de-registration, the mip6_process_hurbu() function is called,
which performs the home de-registration procedure. If there is a binding cache entry for
the mobile node which sent the incoming Binding Update message and the cache entry has
the CLONED flag set, a Binding Acknowledgment message with IP6_MH_BAS_NOT_HA
status is sent.

Listing 5-62
——mip6_cncore.c
```
2273              } else {
2274                      /* request to cache/remove a binding for CN. */
```

```
2275                        if (IS_REQUEST_TO_CACHE(bi.mbc_lifetime, &bi.mbc_phaddr, &
    bi.mbc_pcoa)) {
2276                                int bc_error;
2277
2278                                if (mbc == NULL)
2279                                        bc_error = mip6_bc_register(&bi.mbc_phaddr,
2280                                                        &bi.mbc_pcoa,
2281                                                        &bi.mbc_addr,
2282                                                        ip6mu->ip6mhbu_flags,
2283                                                        bi.mbc_seqno,
2284                                                        bi.mbc_lifetime);
2285                                else
2286                                  /* Update a cache entry */
2287                                        bc_error = mip6_bc_update(mbc, &bi.mbc_pcoa,
2288                                                        &bi.mbc_addr,
2289                                                        ip6mu->ip6mhbu_flags,
2290                                                        bi.mbc_seqno,
2291                                                        bi.mbc_lifetime);
2292                        } else {
2293                                mip6_bc_delete(mbc);
2294                        }
2295                }
```
──mip6_cncore.c

— Line 2275 is broken here for layout reasons. However, it is a single line of code.

2274–2291 If the H flag is not set in the incoming Binding Update message, the request is
sent to a correspondent node. If the message is a request to register the binding information, then the `mip6_bc_register()` or `mip6_bc_update()` function is called. The
`mip6_bc_register()` function creates a new binding cache entry and is called when
there is no binding cache entry corresponding to the incoming Binding Update message.
The `mip6_bc_update()` function is used to update the existing binding cache entry.

2293 If the incoming message is a request to remove the existing binding cache information,
the `mip6_bc_delete()` function is called to remove the corresponding binding cache
entry.

Listing 5-63

──mip6_cncore.c
```
2297    send_ba:
2298            if (bi.mbc_send_ba) {
2299                    int ba_error;
2300
2301                    ba_error = mip6_bc_send_ba(&bi.mbc_addr, &bi.mbc_phaddr,
2302                                    &bi.mbc_pcoa, bi.mbc_status, bi.mbc_seqno,
2303                                    bi.mbc_lifetime, bi.mbc_refresh, &mopt);
2304                    if (ba_error) {
.... (log the error)
2308                    }
2309            }
2310
2311            return (error);
2312    }
```
──mip6_cncore.c

2297–2311 We need to send back a Binding Acknowledgment message in certain cases:

- There is an error in processing a Binding Update message.
- The Binding Update message is for home registration/de-registration.

If one of the conditions listed above matches, the `mbc_send_ba` variable is set to 1. The
`mip6_bc_send_ba()` function creates a Binding Acknowledgment message and sends
it to the appropriate destination. If the sending process fails, an error is logged and packet
processing is continued.

TABLE 5-37

Name	Description
mip6_bc_create()	Create an mip6_bc structure
mip6_bc_delete()	Delete an mip6_bc structure
mip6_bc_list_insert()	Insert an mip6_bc structure to the list
mip6_bc_list_remove()	Remove an mip6_bc structure from the list
mip6_bc_list_find_withphaddr()	Search an mip6_bc structure from the list which has the specified home address
mip6_bc_settimer()	Set a timer to call the timeout function
mip6_bc_timer()	The function called when a timer expires

Binding cache entry management functions.

5.16.3 Binding Cache Entry Management

A binding cache entry is represented by the mip6_bc{} structure. In an IPv6 node, binding cache entries are managed as a list of mip6_bc{} entries. The Mobile IPv6 stack provides several access methods for the structure and list. Table 5-37 shows the list of access functions.

Creating a mip6_bc{} Structure

A mip6_bc{} structure is created by the mip6_bc_create() function.

Listing 5-64

```
                                                          mip6_cncore.c
750     struct mip6_bc *
751     mip6_bc_create(phaddr, pcoa, addr, flags, seqno, lifetime, ifp)
752             struct in6_addr *phaddr;
753             struct in6_addr *pcoa;
754             struct in6_addr *addr;
755             u_int8_t flags;
756             u_int16_t seqno;
757             u_int32_t lifetime;
758             struct ifnet *ifp;
759     {
760             struct mip6_bc *mbc;
....
765             MALLOC(mbc, struct mip6_bc *, sizeof(struct mip6_bc),
766                     M_TEMP, M_NOWAIT);
767             if (mbc == NULL) {
....
771                     return (NULL);
772             }
773             bzero(mbc, sizeof(*mbc));
774
775             mbc->mbc_phaddr = *phaddr;
776             mbc->mbc_pcoa = *pcoa;
777             mbc->mbc_addr = *addr;
778             mbc->mbc_flags = flags;
779             mbc->mbc_seqno = seqno;
780             mbc->mbc_lifetime = lifetime;
781             mbc->mbc_state = MIP6_BC_FSM_STATE_BOUND;
```

```
782              mbc->mbc_mpa_exp = time_second; /* set to current time to send mpa as
    soon as created it */
783              mbc->mbc_ifp = ifp;
784              mbc->mbc_llmbc = NULL;
785              mbc->mbc_refcnt = 0;
....
789              callout_init(&mbc->mbc_timer_ch);
....
793              mbc->mbc_expire = time_second + lifetime;
794              /* sanity check for overflow */
795              if (mbc->mbc_expire < time_second)
796                      mbc->mbc_expire = 0x7fffffff;
797              mip6_bc_settimer(mbc, mip6_brr_time(mbc));
798
799              if (mip6_bc_list_insert(&mip6_bc_list, mbc)) {
800                      FREE(mbc, M_TEMP);
801                      return (NULL);
802              }
803
804              return (mbc);
805      }
```
_____ mip6_cncore.c

— Line 782 is broken here for layout reasons. However, it is a single line of code.

750–759 The mip6_bc_create() function has seven parameters. The phaddr and pcoa parameters are respectively the home address and the care-of address of the communication peer, the addr parameter is the IPv6 address of this node, the flags, seqno and lifetime parameters are information which is included in the incoming Binding Update message. The ifp parameter is the network interface of this node on which the Binding Update message has been received.

765–796 Memory is allocated for the mip6_bc{} structure and each member variable is filled with parameters specified in the parameter list of the function. The mbc_state variable is initialized with MIP6_BC_FSM_STATE_BOUND which means the lifetime left is long enough. The mbc_mpa_exp variable is not currently used. The callout_init() function initializes the timer routine related to the timer handler mbc_timer_ch. Each entry has its own timer handler to manage its timeouts. The mbc_expire variable is set to the time when the lifetime of this entry expires. The variable is set to 0x7fffffff if the value overflows the limitation of the time_t type.

797 The mip6_bc_settimer() function schedules the next timeout for the entry. The mip6_brr_time() function returns the time when the node should send a Binding Refresh Request message to the mobile node of this entry so that the entry does not expire. The timer function for a binding cache entry is called when the time specified to send a Binding Refresh Request message has passed.

799–804 The mip6_bc_list_insert() function inserts the mip6_bc{} instance in the list specified by the first parameter of the mip6_bc_list_insert() function. NULL will be returned if the insertion fails, otherwise, the pointer to the new instance of mip6_bc{} structure is returned.

Deleting the mip6_bc{} Structure

The mip6_bc_delete() function removes an instance of the mip6_bc{} structure from mip6_bc_list.

Listing 5-65

```
                                                              mip6_cncore.c
854    static int
855    mip6_bc_delete(mbc)
856            struct mip6_bc *mbc;
857    {
858            int error;
859
860            /* a request to delete a binding. */
861            if (mbc) {
862                    error = mip6_bc_list_remove(&mip6_bc_list, mbc);
863                    if (error) {
....
867                            return (error);
868                    }
869            } else {
870                    /* There was no Binding Cache entry */
871                    /* Is there someting to do ? */
872            }
873
874            return (0);
875    }
                                                              mip6_cncore.c
```

854–857 The mip6_bc_delete() function takes a pointer of the mip6_bc{} instance as
the parameter mbc.

861–874 The mip6_bc_list_remove() function is called to remove the entry if mbc is not a
NULL pointer, otherwise nothing happens. The mip6_bc_delete() function returns to 0
when the removal succeeded, or returns an error code of the mip6_bc_list_remove()
function if any error occurs when removing the entry.

Inserting the mip6_bc{} Structure to List

The mip6_bc_list_insert() function inserts a newly created instance of the mip6_bc{}
structure to the mip6_bc_list.

Listing 5-66

```
                                                              mip6_cncore.c
877    static int
878    mip6_bc_list_insert(mbc_list, mbc)
879            struct mip6_bc_list *mbc_list;
880            struct mip6_bc *mbc;
881    {
882            int id = MIP6_BC_HASH_ID(&mbc->mbc_phaddr);
883
884            if (mip6_bc_hash[id] != NULL) {
885                    LIST_INSERT_BEFORE(mip6_bc_hash[id], mbc, mbc_entry);
886            } else {
887                    LIST_INSERT_HEAD(mbc_list, mbc, mbc_entry);
888            }
889            mip6_bc_hash[id] = mbc;
890
891            mbc->mbc_refcnt++;
892
893            return (0);
894    }
                                                              mip6_cncore.c
```

877–894 The mip6_bc_list_insert() function has 2 parameters. The mbc_list
parameter is a pointer to the list of mip6_bc{} structures and usually points to the

FIGURE 5-49

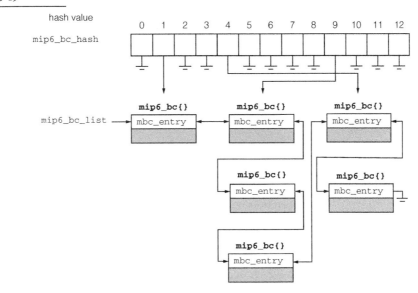

The Hashed list structure of the `mip6_bc{}` *structure.*

`mip6_bc_list` global variable. The `mbc` parameter is a pointer to the newly created instance of the `mip6_bc` structure. The list of `mip6_bc{}` structures is maintained as a hashed list. The `MIP6_BC_HASH_ID()` macro computes the hash ID of the `mip6_bc{}` instance based on the peer home address, `mbc_phaddr`. If there is an `mip6_bc{}` instance which has the same hash ID in the `mip6_bc_list` already, the new instance is inserted before the existing instance, otherwise, the new instance is inserted at the head of the `mip6_bc_list`. Figure 5-49 shows the structure of the hashed list. In the figure, three different hash IDs (1, 4, 9) are active. The Hash Index 1 points to the first `mip6_bc{}` instance in the `mip6_bc_list`. The Hash Index 9 points to the second `mip6_bc{}` instance. The third and fourth instances have the same hash value with the second instance. The Hash Index 4 points to the fifth instance and the last instance also has the same hash value.

Removing the `mip6_bc{}` Structure from List

The `mip6_bc_list_remove()` function removes the specified `mip6_bc{}` instance from the `mip6_bc_list`.

Listing 5-67

```
                                                              mip6_cncore.c
896     int
897     mip6_bc_list_remove(mbc_list, mbc)
898             struct mip6_bc_list *mbc_list;
899             struct mip6_bc *mbc;
900     {
901             int error = 0;
902             int id;
903
```

```
904               if ((mbc_list == NULL) || (mbc == NULL)) {
905                       return (EINVAL);
906               }
907
908               id = MIP6_BC_HASH_ID(&mbc->mbc_phaddr);
909               if (mip6_bc_hash[id] == mbc) {
910                       struct mip6_bc *next = LIST_NEXT(mbc, mbc_entry);
911                       if (next != NULL &&
912                           id == MIP6_BC_HASH_ID(&next->mbc_phaddr)) {
913                               mip6_bc_hash[id] = next;
914                       } else {
915                               mip6_bc_hash[id] = NULL;
916                       }
917               }
```
———mip6_cncore.c

896–899 The `mip6_bc_list_remove()` function has 2 parameters. The `mbc_list`
parameter is a pointer to the list of `mip6_bc{}` structures and usually points to the
`mip6_bc_list` global variable. The `mbc` parameter is a pointer to the instance of the
`mip6_bc{}` structure to be removed.

908–917 We need to rehash the hash table of the `mip6_bc{}` list, since removing an entry
may cause inconsistency in the hash table.

Listing 5-68
———mip6_cncore.c
```
919               mbc->mbc_refcnt--;
920               if (mbc->mbc_flags & IP6MU_CLONED) {
921                       if (mbc->mbc_refcnt > 1)
922                               return (0);
923               } else {
924                       if (mbc->mbc_refcnt > 0)
925                               return (0);
926               }
927               mip6_bc_settimer(mbc, -1);
928               LIST_REMOVE(mbc, mbc_entry);
```
———mip6_cncore.c

920–926 The `IP6MU_CLONED` flag is a special internal flag which indicates that the `mip6_bc{}`
instance is cloned as a result of a Binding Update message with the Link-local compatibility
bit (the L bit). Only home agents have such entries which have the L bit on.

Every `mip6_bc{}` instance has a reference count. The entry is released only when
there are no references from other instances. The exception is a cloned entry. A cloned
entry has 2 references initially. One is a reference as a list entry, the other is a reference from the original entry which clones the entry. An entry is released when the
reference counter goes to 1, if `IP6MU_CLONED` is set. Otherwise, it is released when
the reference count goes to 0.

927–928 The `mip6_bc_settimer()` function controls the timer for the entry. Specifying -1
stops the timer function. After stopping the timer, the entry is removed from the list. At
this point, the entry itself is not released.

Listing 5-69
———mip6_cncore.c
```
929       #ifdef MIP6_HOME_AGENT
930               if (mbc->mbc_flags & IP6MU_HOME) {
931                       if (MIP6_IS_BC_DAD_WAIT(mbc)) {
```

```
932                                  mip6_dad_stop(mbc);
933                          } else {
934                                  error = mip6_bc_proxy_control(&mbc->mbc_phaddr,
935                                      &mbc->mbc_addr, RTM_DELETE);
936                                  if (error) {
 ....
942                                  }
943                                  error = mip6_tunnel_control(MIP6_TUNNEL_DELETE,
944                                      mbc, mip6_bc_encapcheck, &mbc->mbc_encap);
945                                  if (error) {
 ....
951                                  }
952                          }
953                  }
954      #endif /* MIP6_HOME_AGENT */
955              FREE(mbc, M_TEMP);
956
957              return (error);
958      }
```

_mip6_cncore.c

929–954 If a node is acting as a home agent, then the proxy Neighbor Discovery and tunneling for the mobile node needs to be stopped. The `MIP6_IS_BC_DAD_WAIT()` macro checks to see if the entry has finished the DAD procedure. If the DAD procedure of the entry is incomplete, the entry can simply be released since the proxy/tunnel service has not started yet. If the DAD procedure has finished, the proxy service has to be stopped by calling the `mip6_bc_proxy_control()` function and the tunneling service has to be stopped by calling the `mip6_tunnel_control()` function.

955–957 If an error occurs, the memory used for the entry is released and the error code is returned.

Looking Up the `mip6_bc{}` Structure

The `mip6_bc_list_find_withphaddr()` function is used when we need to find a certain `mip6_bc{}` instance from the `mip6_bc_list` by its peer home address.

Listing 5-70

_mip6_cncore.c

```
960      struct mip6_bc *
961      mip6_bc_list_find_withphaddr(mbc_list, haddr)
962              struct mip6_bc_list *mbc_list;
963              struct in6_addr *haddr;
964      {
965              struct mip6_bc *mbc;
966              int id = MIP6_BC_HASH_ID(haddr);
967
968              for (mbc = mip6_bc_hash[id]; mbc;
969                  mbc = LIST_NEXT(mbc, mbc_entry)) {
970                      if (MIP6_BC_HASH_ID(&mbc->mbc_phaddr) != id)
971                              return NULL;
972                      if (IN6_ARE_ADDR_EQUAL(&mbc->mbc_phaddr, haddr))
973                              break;
974              }
975
976              return (mbc);
977      }
```

_mip6_cncore.c

960–963 The `mip6_bc_list_find_withphaddr()` function has 2 parameters. The `mbc_list` parameter is a pointer to the list of `mip6_bc{}` structures and usually points to the `mip6_bc_list` global variable. The `haddr` parameter is the home address of the `mip6_bc{}` entry we are looking for.

968–976 As described in Listing 5-66, the `mip6_bc_list` variable is maintained as a hashed list. The hash ID is computed from the home address specified as the second parameter, and the hash list of binding cache entries is checked to find the target entry by comparing `haddr` and `mbc_phaddr` variables.

Timer Processing of the `mip6_bc{}` Structure

The `mip6_bc_settimer()` sets the next timeout of an `mip6_bc{}` instance. The `mip6_bc_timer()` function will be called when the timer of the entry expires.

Listing 5-71

———mip6_cncore.c

```
815     void
816     mip6_bc_settimer(mbc, t)
817             struct mip6_bc *mbc;
818             int t;  /* unit: second */
819     {
820             long tick;
821             int s;
822
    ....
826             s = splnet();
    ....
828
829             if (t != 0) {
830                     tick = t * hz;
831                     if (t < 0) {
    ....
833                             callout_stop(&mbc->mbc_timer_ch);
    ....
839                     } else {
    ....
841                             callout_reset(&mbc->mbc_timer_ch, tick,
842                                 mip6_bc_timer, mbc);
    ....
848                     }
849             }
850
851             splx(s);
852     }
```

———mip6_cncore.c

815–818 The `mip6_bc_settimer()` has 2 parameters. The `mbc` parameter is a pointer to the `mip6_bc{}` instance whose timer is set, and the `t` parameter is the time until the next timeout event in seconds.

829–849 The `t` parameter can be a negative value, in which case, the timer configuration is cleared by calling the `callout_stop()` function. Otherwise, the next timeout event is set by calling the `callout_reset()` function.

Listing 5-72
_____mip6_cncore.c

```
1256     static void
1257     mip6_bc_timer(arg)
1258             void *arg;
1259     {
1260             int s;
1261             u_int brrtime;
1262             struct mip6_bc *mbc = arg;
  ....
1270             s = splnet();
  ....
1272
1273             switch (mbc->mbc_state) {
1274             case MIP6_BC_FSM_STATE_BOUND:
1275                     mbc->mbc_state = MIP6_BC_FSM_STATE_WAITB;
1276                     mbc->mbc_brr_sent = 0;
1277                     /* No break; */
1278             case MIP6_BC_FSM_STATE_WAITB:
1279                     if (mip6_bc_need_brr(mbc) &&
1280                         (mbc->mbc_brr_sent < mip6_brr_maxtries)) {
1281                             brrtime = mip6_brr_time(mbc);
1282                             if (brrtime == 0) {
1283                                     mbc->mbc_state = MIP6_BC_FSM_STATE_WAITB2;
1284                             } else {
1285                                     mip6_bc_send_brr(mbc);
1286                             }
1287                             mip6_bc_settimer(mbc, mip6_brr_time(mbc));
1288                             mbc->mbc_brr_sent++;
1289                     } else {
1290                             mbc->mbc_state = MIP6_BC_FSM_STATE_WAITB2;
1291                             mip6_bc_settimer(mbc, mbc->mbc_expire - time_second);
1292                     }
1293                     break;
1294             case MIP6_BC_FSM_STATE_WAITB2:
1295     #ifdef MIP6_HOME_AGENT
1296                     if (mbc->mbc_flags & IP6MU_CLONED) {
1297                             /*
1298                              * cloned entry is removed
1299                              * when the last referring mbc
1300                              * is removed.
1301                              */
1302                             break;
1303                     }
1304                     if (mbc->mbc_llmbc != NULL) {
1305                             /* remove a cloned entry. */
1306                             if (mip6_bc_list_remove(
1307                                 &mip6_bc_list, mbc->mbc_llmbc) != 0) {
  ....
1312                             }
1313                     }
1314     #endif /* MIP6_HOME_AGENT */
1315                     mip6_bc_list_remove(&mip6_bc_list, mbc);
1316                     break;
1317             }
1318
1319             splx(s);
1320     }
```

_____mip6_cncore.c

1256–1258 The mip6_bc_timer() function has one parameter which specifies a pointer to the mip6_bc{} instance whose timer expired.

1273–1277 An mip6_bc{} structure has three states as described in Table 5-21 (page 558). When the state is BOUND, it is changed to WAITB when the timer expires.

1278–1286 When the state is `WAITB`, a Binding Refresh Request message is sent. The `mip6_bc_need_brr()` function checks the current TCP connections to see if there is any TCP connection related to this `mip6_bc{}` entry. The `mip6_brr_maxtries` variable is an upper limit on the number of Binding Refresh Request messages to be sent; its default value is 2. If `mip6_bc_need_brr()` returns true and `mbc_brr_sent` is smaller than `mip6_brr_maxtries`, then a Binding Refresh Request message is sent: The `mip6_brr_time()` function returns the time when the next Binding Refresh Request message should be sent. If `mip6_brr_time()` returns 0, the state is changed to `WAITB2`; otherwise, a Binding Refresh Request message is sent by the `mip6_bc_send_brr()` function.

1287–1288 The next timeout event is scheduled by calling the `mip6_bc_settimer()` function and a counter which tracks the number of Binding Refresh Request messages sent is incremented.

1290–1291 If `mip6_bc_need_brr()` returns false, the state is changed to `WAITB2` and the next timeout is set to the time when the entry expires.

1294–1316 If the state is `WAITB2`, the entry is removed. When removing an entry, cloned entries must also be considered. These entries must be removed after all references from other `mip6_bc{}` instances are removed. A cloned entry is referenced to by the `mbc_llmbc` member variable of the `mip6_bc{}` structure. If the entry is not a cloned entry and the entry has a valid `mbc_llmbc` pointer, the cloned entry is removed or the reference counter of the cloned entry is decremented as discussed in Section 5.16.3. Figure 5-50 shows the state transition diagram of a binding cache entry.

5.16.4   Mobility Options Processing

Some mobility messages have optional parameters at the end of the message. These options are called mobility options. The options are encoded in the Type-Length-Value (TLV) format. The `mip6_get_mobility_options()` parses the options and sets the values of each option in the `mip6_mobility_options{}` structure.

Listing 5-73

```
                                                            ─────mip6_cncore.c
2611    int
2612    mip6_get_mobility_options(ip6mh, hlen, ip6mhlen, mopt)
2613            struct ip6_mh *ip6mh;
2614            int hlen, ip6mhlen;
2615            struct mip6_mobility_options *mopt;
2616    {
2617            u_int8_t *mh, *mhend;
2618            u_int16_t valid_option;
2619
2620            mh = (caddr_t)(ip6mh) + hlen;
2621            mhend = (caddr_t)(ip6mh) + ip6mhlen;
2622            mopt->valid_options = 0;
                                                            ─────mip6_cncore.c
```

2611–2616 The `mip6_get_mobility_options()` function has 4 parameters. The `ip6mh` parameter is a pointer to the head of the incoming Mobility Header message; the `hlen`

FIGURE 5-50

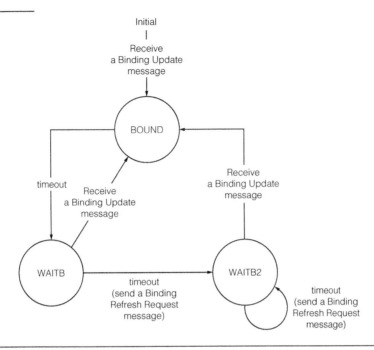

The state transition diagram of a binding cache entry.

parameter is the size of the message excluding the option area; the `ip6mhlen` parameter is the size of the message including the options area; and the `mopt` parameter is a pointer to the `mip6_mobility_options{}` structure which stores the result of this function.

2620–2622 The `mh` and `mhend` variables point to the head of the option area and the tail of the option area respectively. The `valid_options` variable is a bitfield which indicates what kind of options are stored in the `mip6_mobility_options{}` structure.

Listing 5-74

mip6_cncore.c

```
2624    #define check_mopt_len(mopt_len)            \
2625            if (*(mh + 1) != mopt_len) goto bad;
2626
2627            while (mh < mhend) {
2628                    valid_option = 0;
2629                    switch (*mh) {
2630                            case IP6_MHOPT_PAD1:
2631                                    mh++;
2632                                    continue;
2633                            case IP6_MHOPT_PADN:
2634                                    break;
2635                            case IP6_MHOPT_ALTCOA:
2636                                    check_mopt_len(16);
2637                                    valid_option = MOPT_ALTCOA;
2638                                    bcopy(mh + 2, &mopt->mopt_altcoa,
```

```
2639                                        sizeof(mopt->mopt_altcoa));
2640                                break;
2641                        case IP6_MHOPT_NONCEID:
2642                                check_mopt_len(4);
2643                                valid_option = MOPT_NONCE_IDX;
2644                                GET_NETVAL_S(mh + 2, mopt->mopt_ho_nonce_idx);
2645                                GET_NETVAL_S(mh + 4, mopt->mopt_co_nonce_idx);
2646                                break;
2647                        case IP6_MHOPT_BAUTH:
2648                                valid_option = MOPT_AUTHDATA;
2649                                mopt->mopt_auth = mh;
2650                                break;
2651                        case IP6_MHOPT_BREFRESH:
2652                                check_mopt_len(2);
2653                                valid_option = MOPT_REFRESH;
2654                                GET_NETVAL_S(mh + 2, mopt->mopt_refresh);
2655                                break;
2656                        default:
2657                                /*        '... MUST quietly ignore ... (6.2.1)'
....
2661                                 */
2662                                break;
2663                        }
2664
2665                mh += *(mh + 1) + 2;
2666                mopt->valid_options |= valid_option;
2667            }
2668
2669    #undef check_mopt_len
2670
2671            return (0);
2672
2673      bad:
2674            return (EINVAL);
2675    }
```

─── mip6_cncore.c

2624–2625 The `check_mopt_len()` macro validates the option length. This macro terminates the `mip6_get_mobility_options()` function if the received option length does not match the length as specified in [RFC3775].

2627–2663 Each option is parsed based on its option type number stored in the first byte of the option. If the option type is one of `IP6_MHOPT_ALTCOA`, `IP6_MHOPT_NONCEID` or `IP6_MHOPT_BREFRESH`, the option values are copied to the corresponding member fields of the `mip6_mobility_options{}` structure. The macro `GET_NETVAL_S()` provides a safe operation to copy 2 bytes of data even when the data is not aligned as the processor architecture permits. If the option type is `IP6_MHOPT_BAUTH`, the address of the option is stored in the `mopt_auth` member variable. Unknown options are ignored.

2665–2666 The pointer is incremented as specified in the option length field to proceed to the next mobility option, and the `valid_options` variable is updated to indicate the structure has a valid option value.

5.16.5 Validation of Binding Update Message for Correspondent Node

When a correspondent node receives a Binding Update message, the node needs to validate whether or not the message is acceptable. The validation is done by the `mip6_is_valid_bu()` function.

Listing 5-75

——————————————————————————————mip6_cncore.c
```
1527    int
1528    mip6_is_valid_bu(ip6, ip6mu, ip6mulen, mopt, hoa, coa, cache_req, status)
1529            struct ip6_hdr *ip6;
1530            struct ip6_mh_binding_update *ip6mu;
1531            int ip6mulen;
1532            struct mip6_mobility_options *mopt;
1533            struct in6_addr *hoa, *coa;
1534            int cache_req;  /* true if this request is cacheing */
1535            u_int8_t *status;
1536    {
```
——————————————————————————————mip6_cncore.c

1527–1535 The mip6_is_valid_bu() function has eight parameters. The ip6 and ip6mu parameters are pointers to the head of the incoming IPv6 packet and Binding Update message respectively; the ip6mulen parameter is the size of the Binding Update message; the mopt parameter is a pointer to the instance of the mip6_mobility_option{} structure which holds received options; the hoa and coa parameters indicate the home and care-of addresses of the mobile node which sent this Binding Update message; the cache_req parameter is a boolean value which indicates that this message is for registration or for de-registration; and the status parameter is space to store the status code which is used when sending a Binding Acknowledgment message.

Listing 5-76

——————————————————————————————mip6_cncore.c
```
1537            u_int8_t key_bm[MIP6_KBM_LEN]; /* Stated as 'Kbm' in the spec */
1538            u_int8_t authdata[SHA1_RESULTLEN];
1539            u_int16_t cksum_backup;
1540
1541            *status = IP6_MH_BAS_ACCEPTED;
1542            /* Nonce index & Auth. data mobility options are required */
1543            if ((mopt->valid_options & (MOPT_NONCE_IDX | MOPT_AUTHDATA))
1544                != (MOPT_NONCE_IDX | MOPT_AUTHDATA)) {
....
1549                    return (EINVAL);
1550            }
1551            if ((*status = mip6_calculate_kbm_from_index(hoa, coa,
1552                mopt->mopt_ho_nonce_idx, mopt->mopt_co_nonce_idx,
1553                !cache_req, key_bm))) {
1554                    return (EINVAL);
1555            }
1556
1557            cksum_backup = ip6mu->ip6mhbu_cksum;
1558            ip6mu->ip6mhbu_cksum = 0;
1559            /* Calculate authenticator */
1560            if (mip6_calculate_authenticator(key_bm, authdata, coa, &ip6->ip6_dst,
1561                (caddr_t)ip6mu, ip6mulen,
1562                (u_int8_t *)mopt->mopt_auth + sizeof(struct ip6_mh_opt_auth_data)
    - (u_int8_t *)ip6mu,
1563                MOPT_AUTH_LEN(mopt) + 2)) {
1564                    return (EINVAL);
1565            }
1566
1567            ip6mu->ip6mhbu_cksum = cksum_backup;
1568
1569            return (bcmp(mopt->mopt_auth + 2, authdata, MOPT_AUTH_LEN(mopt)));
1570    }
```
——————————————————————————————mip6_cncore.c

– Line 1562 is broken here for layout reasons. However, it is a single line of code.

1541–1555 A Binding Update message to a correspondent node must include the nonce index and authentication data mobility options. An error is returned if the incoming packet does not have these options. The `mip6_calculate_kbm_from_index()` function computes the K_{bm} value from home address, care-of address, home nonce and care-of nonce. The result is stored in the `key_mb` variable.

1557–1565 The   authentication   data   value   is   verified.   The `mip6_calculate_authenticator()` function computes the value of the authentication data field using the K_{bm} computed previously. The result will be stored in `authdata`, the second parameter of the function. Note that we need to clear the checksum field of a Mobility Header message before computing the authentication data value, since the sender of a Binding Update message clears the field when computing the authentication value.

1567–1569 After finishing the validation of authentication data, the function recovers the checksum field and returns the result of the comparison of the authentication data value sent as an option value (the `mopt_auth` member variable), and the verified value (the `authdata` variable).

5.16.6 K_{bm} and Authorization Data Computation

As described in Section 5.5, a Binding Update message and a Binding Acknowledgment message must have an authentication data mobility option to protect them. The content of the authentication data is a hash value based on HMAC-SHA1. The key of the hash function is computed by the `mip6_calculate_kbm_from_index()` function and the value is computed by the `mip6_calculate_authenticator()` function.

Listing 5-77

———mip6_cncore.c

```
1572    int
1573    mip6_calculate_kbm_from_index(hoa, coa, ho_nonce_idx, co_nonce_idx,
    ignore_co_nonce, key_bm)
1574            struct in6_addr *hoa;
1575            struct in6_addr *coa;
1576            u_int16_t ho_nonce_idx; /* Home Nonce Index */
1577            u_int16_t co_nonce_idx; /* Care-of Nonce Index */
1578            int ignore_co_nonce;
1579            u_int8_t *key_bm;       /* needs at least MIP6_KBM_LEN bytes */
1580    {
```

———mip6_cncore.c

– Line 1573 is broken here for layout reasons. However, it is a single line of code.

1572–1579 The `mip6_calculate_kbm_from_index()` function has 6 parameters. The `hoa` and `coa` parameters are the home and care-of addresses of a Binding Update message; the `ho_nonce_idx` and `co_nonce_idx` parameters are indices which indicate the home and care-of nonces which are used to compute the key (K_{bm}). The `ignore_co_nonce` parameter is a flag which is set when de-registering from home network. When a mobile node is home, the care-of nonce is ignored since the home and care-of addresses are the same address. The variable `key_bm` points to the address where the key value is stored.

Listing 5-78

```
                                                                   ___mip6_cncore.c
1581            int stat = IP6_MH_BAS_ACCEPTED;
1582            mip6_nonce_t home_nonce, careof_nonce;
1583            mip6_nodekey_t home_nodekey, coa_nodekey;
1584            mip6_home_token_t home_token;
1585            mip6_careof_token_t careof_token;
1586
1587            if (mip6_get_nonce(ho_nonce_idx, &home_nonce) != 0) {
....
1592                    stat =IP6_MH_BAS_HOME_NI_EXPIRED;
1593            }
1594            if (!ignore_co_nonce &&
1595                mip6_get_nonce(co_nonce_idx, &careof_nonce) != 0){
....
1600                    stat = (stat == IP6_MH_BAS_ACCEPTED) ?
1601                        IP6_MH_BAS_COA_NI_EXPIRED : IP6_MH_BAS_NI_EXPIRED;
1602            }
1603            if (stat != IP6_MH_BAS_ACCEPTED)
1604                    return (stat);
                                                                   ___mip6_cncore.c
```

1587–1604 The `mip6_get_nonce()` function finds a nonce value based on the index number provided as the first parameter. The function returns true when the index has already been expired and is invalid. `IP6_MH_BAS_HOME_NI_EXPIRED` is set as a status value if the home nonce index is invalid.

If the message is for de-registration, the `ignore_co_nonce` variable is set to true and the care-of nonce can be ignored. If the `ignore_co_nonce` variable is false, the `mip6_get_nonce()` function is called to check whether the care-of nonce index is valid. If both home and care-of nonce indices are invalid, `IP6_MH_BA_NI_EXPIRED` is set as a status value. If only the care-of nonce index is invalid, `IP6_MH_BA_COA_NI_EXPIRED` is set as a status value.

`IP6_MH_BAS_ACCEPTED` is set as a status value if both nonce indices are valid.

Listing 5-79

```
                                                                   ___mip6_cncore.c
1610            if ((mip6_get_nodekey(ho_nonce_idx, &home_nodekey) != 0) ||
1611                    (!ignore_co_nonce &&
1612                        (mip6_get_nodekey(co_nonce_idx, &coa_nodekey) != 0))) {
....
1617                    return (IP6_MH_BAS_NI_EXPIRED);
1618            }
....
1624            /* Calculate home keygen token */
1625            if (mip6_create_keygen_token(hoa, &home_nodekey, &home_nonce, 0,
1626                    &home_token)) {
....
1631                    return (IP6_MH_BAS_UNSPECIFIED);
1632            }
....
1637            if (!ignore_co_nonce) {
1638                    /* Calculate care-of keygen token */
1639                    if (mip6_create_keygen_token(coa, &coa_nodekey, &careof_nonce,
1640                        1, &careof_token)) {
....
```

```
1645                             return (IP6_MH_BAS_UNSPECIFIED);
1646                     }
....
1650             }
1651
1652             /* Calculate K_bm */
1653             mip6_calculate_kbm(&home_token, ignore_co_nonce ? NULL : &careof_token,
1654                 key_bm);
....
1658
1659             return (IP6_MH_BAS_ACCEPTED);
1660     }
```
                                                                    _____mip6_cncore.c

1610–1618 The `mip6_get_nodekey()` function finds a nodekey value based on the index value specified as the first parameter. Nonce and nodekey management is discussed in Section 5.16.14. Nodekeys for the home and care-of addresses are stored in the `home_nodekey` and the `coa_nodekey` variables. If any error occurs while getting nodekey values, `IP6_MH_BAS_NI_EXPIRED` is returned.

1625–1650 The `mip6_create_keygen_token()` function computes a keygen token based on home and care-of addresses, nodekey and nonce values. The function is described later in this section. If computing these tokens meets any error, then `IP6_MH_BAS_UNSPECIFIED` is returned.

1653–1659 K_{bm} value is computed from keygen tokens by calling the `mip6_calculate_kbm()` function. This function is described later in this section.

Listing 5-80
                                                                    _____mip6_cncore.c

```
1429    int
1430    mip6_create_keygen_token(addr, nodekey, nonce, hc, token)
1431            struct in6_addr *addr;
1432            mip6_nodekey_t *nodekey;
1433            mip6_nonce_t *nonce;
1434            u_int8_t hc;
1435            void *token;               /* 64 bit */
1436    {
1437            /* keygen token = HMAC_SHA1(Kcn, addr | nonce | hc) */
1438            HMAC_CTX hmac_ctx;
1439            u_int8_t result[HMACSIZE];
1440
1441            hmac_init(&hmac_ctx, (u_int8_t *)nodekey,
1442                    sizeof(mip6_nodekey_t), HMAC_SHA1);
1443            hmac_loop(&hmac_ctx, (u_int8_t *)addr, sizeof(struct in6_addr));
1444            hmac_loop(&hmac_ctx, (u_int8_t *)nonce, sizeof(mip6_nonce_t));
1445            hmac_loop(&hmac_ctx, (u_int8_t *)&hc, sizeof(hc));
1446            hmac_result(&hmac_ctx, result, sizeof(result));
1447            /* First64 */
1448            bcopy(result, token, 8);
1449
1450            return (0);
1451    }
```
                                                                    _____mip6_cncore.c

1430–1435 The `mip6_create_keygen_token()` function has five parameters. The `addr` parameter is an IPv6 address which is either the home or the care-of address of a Mobility

Header message, the `hc` parameter is a decimal value either 0 or 1. 0 is specified if `addr` is a home address and 1 is specified if `addr` is a care-of address. The parameter `token` points to the address in which the computed keygen token is stored.

1438–1450 Keygen token is a hash value computed over the concatenation of a nodekey, a home or care-of address, a nonce value and 0 or 1 based on the kind of address. The algorithm (HMAC-SHA1), used to compute the hash value, generates 128-bit data. Only the first 64 bits of data is used for a keygen token, since it needs only 64-bit data.

Listing 5-81

```
                                                                      mip6_cncore.c
1662    void
1663    mip6_calculate_kbm(home_token, careof_token, key_bm)
1664            mip6_home_token_t *home_token;
1665            mip6_careof_token_t *careof_token;      /* could be null */
1666            u_int8_t *key_bm;           /* needs at least MIP6_KBM_LEN bytes */
1667    {
1668            SHA1_CTX sha1_ctx;
1669            u_int8_t result[SHA1_RESULTLEN];
1670
1671            SHA1Init(&sha1_ctx);
1672            SHA1Update(&sha1_ctx, (caddr_t)home_token, sizeof(*home_token));
1673            if (careof_token)
1674                    SHA1Update(&sha1_ctx, (caddr_t)careof_token,
1675            SHA1Final(result, &sha1_ctx);
1676            /* First 128 bit */
1677            bcopy(result, key_bm, MIP6_KBM_LEN);
1678    }
                                                                      mip6_cncore.c
```
— Line 1674 is broken here for layout reasons. However, it is a single line of code.

1663–1666 The `mip6_calculate_kbm()` function has three parameters. The `home_token` and `careof_token` parameters are the keygen tokens for the home and the care-of addresses, and the `key_bm` parameter stores the computed K_{bm} value.

1668–1677 The K_{bm} value is computed using the SHA1 hash algorithm over the concatenated data of a home keygen token and a care-of keygen token. Note that a care-of keygen token may not be specified when performing de-registering from the home network. The first 128 bits of the computed data (which are 196 bits long) are copied as a K_{bm} value.

Listing 5-82

```
                                                                      mip6_cncore.c
1690    int
1691    mip6_calculate_authenticator(key_bm, result, addr1, addr2, data, datalen,
1692        exclude_offset, exclude_data_len)
1693            u_int8_t *key_bm;                   /* Kbm */
1694            u_int8_t *result;
1695            struct in6_addr *addr1, *addr2;
1696            caddr_t data;
1697            size_t datalen;
1698            int exclude_offset;
1699            size_t exclude_data_len;
1700    {
1701            HMAC_CTX hmac_ctx;
1702            int restlen;
1703            u_int8_t sha1_result[SHA1_RESULTLEN];
```

```
1704
1705                /* Calculate authenticator (5.5.6) */
1706                /* MAC_Kbm(addr1, | addr2 | (BU|BA) ) */
1707                hmac_init(&hmac_ctx, key_bm, MIP6_KBM_LEN, HMAC_SHA1);
1708                hmac_loop(&hmac_ctx, (u_int8_t *)addr1, sizeof(*addr1));
....
1712                hmac_loop(&hmac_ctx, (u_int8_t *)addr2, sizeof(*addr2));
....
1716                hmac_loop(&hmac_ctx, (u_int8_t *)data, exclude_offset);
....
1721                /* Exclude authdata field in the mobility option to calculate authdata
1722                   But it should be included padding area */
1723                restlen = datalen - (exclude_offset + exclude_data_len);
1724                if (restlen > 0) {
1725                        hmac_loop(&hmac_ctx,
1726                                data + exclude_offset + exclude_data_len,
1727                                restlen);
....
1732                }
1733                hmac_result(&hmac_ctx, sha1_result, sizeof(sha1_result));
1734                /* First(96, sha1_result) */
1735                bcopy(sha1_result, result, MIP6_AUTHENTICATOR_LEN);
....
1739
1740                return (0);
1741    }
```
_____mip6_cncore.c

1690–1699 The mip6_calculate_authenticator() function has eight parameters. The
key_bm parameter is the K_{bm} value computed by the mip6_calculate_kbm()
function; the result parameter points to the memory in which the computed authentication data is stored; the addr1 and addr2 parameters are the care-of and the
destination addresses of the Mobility Header message which will be protected; the data
and datalen parameters specify the address of the Mobility Header message and size
respectively; and the exclude_offset and exclude_data_len parameters specify
the region of the authentication data itself located in the Mobility Header message. The
region must not be included in computation. Figure 5-51 shows the meanings of each
parameter.

1707–1716 The computation algorithm we use is HMAC-SHA1. We first compute two addresses
specified as parameters and the Mobility Header message before the region which is
excluded.

FIGURE 5-51

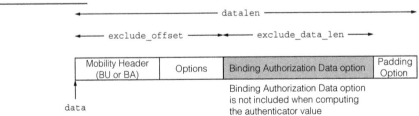

Calculation of the authenticator value.

1723–1740 The specification says that the authentication data should be placed as the last mobility option, however, there is a possibility that there is a padding option after the authentication data. The `restlen` variable indicates the length to the end of the Mobility Header message after the authentication data. The length of the authentication data is 96 bits, whereas the result of HMAC-SHA1 computation will be 128 bits. The first 96 bits are taken as the authentication data value.

5.16.7 Managing Binding Cache Entry as Correspondent Node

After receiving a valid Binding Update message from a mobile node, a correspondent node will create a binding cache entry to perform the route optimization. The procedure for registering the binding information is implemented in the `mip6_bc_register()` function, and the procedure for updating is implemented in the `mip6_bc_update()` function.

Adding Binding Cache Entry

The `mip6_bc_register()` function is used by a correspondent node to create a new binding cache entry.

Listing 5-83

```
                                                              mip6_cncore.c
979     static int
980     mip6_bc_register(hoa, coa, dst, flags, seqno, lifetime)
981             struct in6_addr *hoa;
982             struct in6_addr *coa;
983             struct in6_addr *dst;
984             u_int16_t flags;
985             u_int16_t seqno;
986             u_int32_t lifetime;
987     {
988             struct mip6_bc *mbc;
989
990             /* create a binding cache entry. */
991             mbc = mip6_bc_create(hoa, coa, dst, flags, seqno, lifetime,
992                 NULL);
993             if (mbc == NULL) {
....
998                     return (ENOMEM);
999             }
1000
1001            return (0);
1002    }
                                                              mip6_cncore.c
```

979–987 The `mip6_bc_register()` function has six parameters. The `hoa` and `coa` parameters are the home and care-of addresses of the mobile node which sent the Binding Update message; the `dst` parameter is the IPv6 address of the correspondent node; the `flags` and `seqno` parameters are copies of the flags and seqno fields of the incoming Binding Update message; and the `lifetime` parameter is the lifetime of the binding cache entry. As discussed in Section 5.11.8, a correspondent node may not always create a binding cache entry with the lifetime requested by the mobile node. The actual lifetime may be shortened by the correspondent node.

991–1001 The `mip6_bc_register()` function simply calls the `mip6_bc_create()` function to create a binding cache entry. It returns ENOMEM error when `mip6_bc_create()` cannot create a new binding cache entry; otherwise, it returns to 0.

Updating Binding Cache Entry

The `mip6_bc_update()` function is used by a correspondent node to update the information of an existing binding cache entry.

Listing 5-84

_____mip6_cncore.c

```
1004     static int
1005     mip6_bc_update(mbc, coa, dst, flags, seqno, lifetime)
1006             struct mip6_bc *mbc;
1007             struct in6_addr *coa;
1008             struct in6_addr *dst;
1009             u_int16_t flags;
1010             u_int16_t seqno;
1011             u_int32_t lifetime;
1012     {
....
1014             struct timeval mono_time;
....
1018             microtime(&mono_time);
....
1020             /* update a binding cache entry. */
1021             mbc->mbc_pcoa = *coa;
1022             mbc->mbc_flags = flags;
1023             mbc->mbc_seqno = seqno;
1024             mbc->mbc_lifetime = lifetime;
1025             mbc->mbc_expire = mono_time.tv_sec + mbc->mbc_lifetime;
1026             /* sanity check for overflow */
1027             if (mbc->mbc_expire < mono_time.tv_sec)
1028                     mbc->mbc_expire = 0x7fffffff;
1029             mbc->mbc_state = MIP6_BC_FSM_STATE_BOUND;
1030             mip6_bc_settimer(mbc, -1);
1031             mip6_bc_settimer(mbc, mip6_brr_time(mbc));
1032
1033             return (0);
1034     }
```

_____mip6_cncore.c

1004–1011 The `mip6_bc_update()` function has six parameters, most of which have the same meanings as the `mip6_bc_register()` function. The home address of a mobile node never changes when updating other information. The first parameter of the function is a pointer to the address of the related binding cache entry. The rest of parameters are the same as the `mip6_bc_register()` function.

1018 The `microtime()` function returns the current time in the first parameter. This value is used to compute the expiration time of the binding cache entry.

1021–1029 Based on the parameters of the `mip6_bc_update()` function, the information stored in the existing binding cache entry is updated. Note that we need to take care of the overflow of the `mbc_expire` field, since it is a 32-bit signed integer. The `mip6_bc_update()` function is called when a correspondent node receives a valid Binding Update message. The `mbc_state` field is set to MIP6_BC_FSM_STATE_BOUND which indicates that the entry is valid and usable.

1030–1031 When a node receives a Binding Update message, it needs to reset the pending timer event. The next timeout is set to the time when the node needs to send a Binding Refresh Request message.

Calculating Next Timeout of Binding Refresh Request Message

The `mip6_brr_time()` function returns the time at which a node needs to send a Binding Refresh Request message.

Listing 5-85

_____mip6_cncore.c

```
1228    u_int
1229    mip6_brr_time(mbc)
1230            struct mip6_bc *mbc;
1231    {
....
1236            switch (mbc->mbc_state) {
1237            case MIP6_BC_FSM_STATE_BOUND:
1238                    if (mip6_brr_mode == MIP6_BRR_SEND_EXPONENT)
1239                            return ((mbc->mbc_expire - mbc->mbc_lifetime / 2)
    - time_second);
1240                    else
1241                            return ((mbc->mbc_expire -
1242                                    mip6_brr_tryinterval * mip6_brr_maxtries)
    - time_second);
1243                    break;
1244            case MIP6_BC_FSM_STATE_WAITB:
1245                    if (mip6_brr_mode == MIP6_BRR_SEND_EXPONENT)
1246                            return (mbc->mbc_expire - time_second) / 2;
1247                    else
1248                            return (mip6_brr_tryinterval < mbc->mbc_expire
    - time_second
1249                                    ? mip6_brr_tryinterval : mbc->mbc_expire
    - time_second);
1250                    break;
1251            }
1252
1253            return (0); /* XXX; not reach */
1254    }
```

_____mip6_cncore.c

— *Lines 1239, 1242, 1248, and 1249 are broken here for layout reasons. However, they are a single line of code.*

1228–1230 The function has only one parameter `mbc`, which points to the address of the binding cache entry to be updated by the Binding Refresh Request message.

1236–1250 A binding cache entry has a state field which indicates the current state as described in Table 5-21 on page 558. The computation is slightly different depending on the state and the mode specified as the `mip6_brr_mode` variable. Table 5-38 shows the available values for the `mip6_brr_mode` global variable. The default value of the `mip6_brr_mode` variable is hard-coded to `MIP6_BRR_SEND_EXPONENT` and we need to modify `mip6_cncore.c` if we want to change the mode. When `mip6_brr_mode` is set to `MIP6_BRR_SEND_EXPONENT`, a correspondent node will try to send Binding Refresh Request messages repeatedly with an exponential timeout. When `mip6_brr_mode` is set to `MIP6_BRR_SEND_LINER`, the message will be sent at a constant interval. Figure 5-52 shows the calculation algorithm. The interval between each try when the mode is `MIP6_BRR_SEND_LINER` is specified as the

TABLE 5-38

Name	Description
MIP6_BRR_SEND_EXPONENT	Try to send a Binding Refresh Request message exponentially, e.g., when 1/2, 3/4, 7/8, … of lifetime is elapsed.
MIP6_BRR_SEND_LINER	Try to send a Binding Refresh Request message at a constant interval.

The mode of `mip6_brr_mode`.

FIGURE 5-52

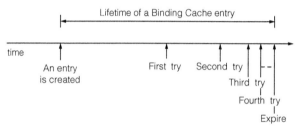

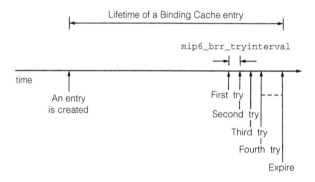

The calculation of time for when to send a Binding Refresh Request message.

`mip6_brr_tryinterval` variable which is 10 seconds by default. Note that Figure 5-52 describes four retries to make it easy to understand the difference between the `MIP6_BRR_SEND_EXPONENT` mode and the `MIP6_BRR_SEND_LINER` mode; however, the KAME implementation only tries twice since `mip6_brr_maxtries` is set to 2.

5.16.8 Sending Binding Refresh Request Message

A correspondent node can send a Binding Refresh Request message to extend the lifetime of current binding information between a mobile node and the correspondent node. In the KAME

Mobile IPv6, a correspondent node sends the message only when there is more than one TCP connection between those nodes. This means that the binding information between those nodes is kept as long as there is communication using TCP, otherwise the binding information will be removed when the lifetime of the binding information expires.

Listing 5-86

─── *mip6_cncore.c*

```
1187     static int
1188     mip6_bc_need_brr(mbc)
1189             struct mip6_bc *mbc;
1190     {
1191             int found;
1192             struct in6_addr *src, *dst;
....
1194             struct inpcb *inp;
....
1200             found = 0;
1201             src = &mbc->mbc_addr;
1202             dst = &mbc->mbc_phaddr;
1203
....
1205             for (inp = LIST_FIRST(&tcb); inp; inp = LIST_NEXT(inp, inp_list)) {
1206                     if ((inp->inp_vflag & INP_IPV6) == 0)
1207                             continue;
1208                     if (IN6_ARE_ADDR_EQUAL(src, &inp->in6p_laddr)
1209                         && IN6_ARE_ADDR_EQUAL(dst, &inp->in6p_faddr)) {
1210                             found++;
1211                             break;
1212                     }
1213             }
....
1224
1225             return (found);
1226     }
```

─── *mip6_cncore.c*

1187–1226 The `mip6_bc_need_brr()` function takes one parameter `mbc` which points to the binding cache entry to be checked to determine whether the lifetime of the entry has to be extended.

In the loop between lines 1205 and 1213, all TCP protocol control block (`tcb`) entries are checked to find a matching entry in which the local address and foreign address are the same as the local and peer addresses in the `mbc` entry. If there is at least one entry that matches the condition, the code tries to keep the binding information.

The current implementation does not take into account other upper layer connections. If there is no TCP connection between a mobile node and a correspondent node, the cache entry between them will be removed when the lifetime expires, even if they are exchanging other types of data (e.g., UDP datagrams). If the communication continues after expiration of the related binding cache, the mobile node will perform the return routability procedure again and a new cache entry will be created.

Creation and Sending of Binding Refresh Request Message

A correspondent node or a home agent may send a Binding Refresh Request message before a binding cache information expires. Sending a Binding Refresh Request message is implemented in the `mip6_bc_send_brr()` function.

Listing 5-87

_____mip6_cncore.c
```
1132    static int
1133    mip6_bc_send_brr(mbc)
1134            struct mip6_bc *mbc;
1135    {
1136            struct mbuf *m;
1137            struct ip6_pktopts opt;
1138            int error;
```
_____mip6_cncore.c

1133–1134 The mip6_bc_send_brr() function has a pointer to the instance of the mip6_bc{} structure in which information is going to expire soon.

Listing 5-88

_____mip6_cncore.c
```
1140            ip6_initpktopts(&opt);
1141
1142            m = mip6_create_ip6hdr(&mbc->mbc_addr, &mbc->mbc_phaddr, IPPROTO_NONE,
1143                0);
1144            if (m == NULL) {
....
1148                    return (ENOMEM);
1149            }
1150
1151            error = mip6_ip6mr_create(&opt.ip6po_mh, &mbc->mbc_addr,
1152                &mbc->mbc_phaddr);
1153            if (error) {
....
1158                    m_freem(m);
1159                    goto free_ip6pktopts;
1160            }
```
_____mip6_cncore.c

1140 A Binding Refresh Request message is passed to the ip6_output() function as a packet option. The in6_initpktopts() function initializes the ip6_pktopts{} structure.

1142–1160 An IPv6 header is created by the mip6_create_ip6hdr() function with a source address set to the correspondent or home agent and a destination address set to the address of a mobile node. The mip6_ip6mr_create() function will fill the contents of a Binding Refresh Request message.

Listing 5-89

_____mip6_cncore.c
```
1162            error = ip6_output(m, &opt, NULL, 0, NULL, NULL
....
1164                            , NULL
....
1166                            );
1167            if (error) {
....
1171                    goto free_ip6pktopts;
1172            }
1173
1174    free_ip6pktopts:
```

```
1175                if (opt.ip6po_mh)
1176                        FREE(opt.ip6po_mh, M_IP6OPT);
1177
1178                return (error);
1179        }
```
——mip6_cncore.c

1162–1176 The `ip6_output()` function is called to send the Binding Refresh Request message. The packet option created for the message must be released before completing the function.

Listing 5-90
——mip6_cncore.c
```
2542    static int
2543    mip6_ip6mr_create(pktopt_mobility, src, dst)
2544            struct ip6_mh **pktopt_mobility;
2545            struct in6_addr *src;
2546            struct in6_addr *dst;
2547    {
2548            struct ip6_mh_binding_request *ip6mr;
2549            int ip6mr_size;
```
——mip6_cncore.c

2542–2546 The `mip6_ip6mr_create()` function creates a Binding Refresh Request message. The function has three parameters: The `pktopt_mobility` parameter is a pointer to the address of the `pktopt_mobility{}` structure in which the created message is stored, the `src` parameter is the address of a correspondent node or a home agent, and the `dst` parameter is the home address of a mobile node.

Listing 5-91
——mip6_cncore.c
```
2551            *pktopt_mobility = NULL;
2552
2553            ip6mr_size = sizeof(struct ip6_mh_binding_request);
2554
2555            MALLOC(ip6mr, struct ip6_mh_binding_request *,
2556                    ip6mr_size, M_IP6OPT, M_NOWAIT);
2557            if (ip6mr == NULL)
2558                    return (ENOMEM);
2559
2560            bzero(ip6mr, ip6mr_size);
2561            ip6mr->ip6mhbr_proto = IPPROTO_NONE;
2562            ip6mr->ip6mhbr_len = (ip6mr_size >> 3) - 1;
2563            ip6mr->ip6mhbr_type = IP6_MH_TYPE_BRR;
2564
2565            /* calculate checksum. */
2566            ip6mr->ip6mhbr_cksum = mip6_cksum(src, dst, ip6mr_size, IPPROTO_MH,
2567                    (char *)ip6mr);
2568
2569            *pktopt_mobility = (struct ip6_mh *)ip6mr;
2570
2571            return (0);
2572    }
```
——mip6_cncore.c

2551–2558 Memory is allocated to store the message content.

2560–2569 A Binding Refresh Request message is built. The next header (`ip6mhbr_proto`) is
set to `IPPROTO_NONE`, which means there is no next header. The type (`ip6mhbr_type`)
is set to `IP6_MH_TYPE_BRR` which indicates a Binding Refresh Request message.
`ip6mhbr_cksum` is filled with the return value of the `mip6_cksum()` function which
computes the checksum value of a Mobility Header.

5.16.9   Home Registration Processing

When a node is acting as a home agent, it receives a Binding Update message for home registration from mobile nodes. The basic procedure for home registration is the same as the procedure
for the binding cache creation procedure which is done in a correspondent node. The main
difference is a home agent needs to perform the following two additional tasks:

- Set up proxy Neighbor Discovery for the mobile node

- Create an IPv6 in IPv6 tunnel to the mobile node

Home registration is implemented in the `mip6_process_hrbu()` function. The overview
of the home registration process is described in Section 5.4.2.

Listing 5-92

———*mip6_hacore.c*
```
87      int
88      mip6_process_hrbu(bi)
89              struct mip6_bc *bi;
90      {
91              struct sockaddr_in6 addr_sa;
92              struct ifaddr *destifa = NULL;
93              struct ifnet *destifp = NULL;
94              struct nd_prefix *pr, *llpr = NULL;
95              struct ifnet *hifp = NULL;
96              struct in6_addr lladdr;
97              struct mip6_bc *llmbc = NULL;
98              struct mip6_bc *mbc = NULL;
99              struct mip6_bc *prim_mbc = NULL;
100             u_int32_t prlifetime = 0;
101             int busy = 0;
....
106             bi->mbc_status = IP6_MH_BAS_ACCEPTED;
107
108             /* find the interface which the destination address belongs to. */
109             bzero(&addr_sa, sizeof(addr_sa));
110             addr_sa.sin6_len = sizeof(addr_sa);
111             addr_sa.sin6_family = AF_INET6;
112             addr_sa.sin6_addr = bi->mbc_addr;
113             /* XXX ? */
114             if (in6_recoverscope(&addr_sa, &addr_sa.sin6_addr, NULL))
115                     panic("mip6_process_hrbu: recovering scope");
116             if (in6_embedscope(&addr_sa.sin6_addr, &addr_sa))
117                     panic("mip6_process_hrbu: embedding scope");
118             destifa = ifa_ifwithaddr((struct sockaddr *)&addr_sa);
119             if (!destifa) {
120                     bi->mbc_status = IP6_MH_BAS_NOT_HOME_SUBNET;
121                     bi->mbc_send_ba = 1;
122                     return (0); /* XXX is 0 OK? */
123             }
124             destifp = destifa->ifa_ifp;
```
———*mip6_hacore.c*

87–89 The `mip6_process_hrbu()` function has one parameter `bi` which is a pointer to an instance of the `mip6_bc{}` structure. The `bi` parameter is a pointer to a template of a binding cache entry that will be activated as a result of this function.

106 A home agent must reply to the mobile node with a Binding Acknowledgment message when it receives a home registration request. The `mbc_status` variable is filled with an error status code if an error occurs. The default value is `IP6_MH_BAS_ACCEPTED` which means that the registration succeeded.

109–124 The `destifa` variable will point to the network interface on which the Binding Update message was received. The destination address of the message is kept in the `mbc_addr` member variable. The instance of the `in6_ifaddr{}` structure that is related to the address is searched by calling the `ifa_ifwithaddr()` function. An error reply will be sent to the mobile node with the `IP6_MH_BAS_NOT_HOME_SUBNET` status code if the home agent failed to find the address to which the received message was sent. The `in6_ifaddr{}` structure has a pointer to the network interface structure. The pointer to `destifp` is kept for later use.

Listing 5-93

mip6_hacore.c

```
126                 /* find the home ifp of this homeaddress. */
127                 for (pr = nd_prefix.lh_first; pr; pr = pr->ndpr_next) {
128                         if (pr->ndpr_ifp != destifp)
129                                 continue;
130                         if (in6_are_prefix_equal(&bi->mbc_phaddr,
131                                 &pr->ndpr_prefix.sin6_addr, pr->ndpr_plen)) {
132                                 hifp = pr->ndpr_ifp; /* home ifp. */
133                                 prlifetime = pr->ndpr_vltime;
134                         }
135                 }
136                 if (hifp == NULL) {
137                         /*
138                          * the haddr0 doesn't have an online prefix.  return a
139                          * binding ack with an error NOT_HOME_SUBNET.
140                          */
141                         bi->mbc_status = IP6_MH_BAS_NOT_HOME_SUBNET;
142                         bi->mbc_send_ba = 1;
143                         return (0); /* XXX is 0 OK? */
144                 }
```

mip6_hacore.c

127–144 When sending a Binding Acknowledgment message, a home agent needs to check the remaining lifetime of the home prefix which is assigned to the mobile node. If the remaining lifetime is too short, the home agent needs to notify the mobile node to update the prefix information. The `for` loop on line 127 searches the home prefix information of the network interface specified by the `destifp` variable and stores the valid lifetime in the `prlifetime` variable.

If no home related prefix information is found, an error message with the `IP6_MH_BAS_NOT_HOME_SUBNET` status code is sent.

Listing 5-94

mip6_hacore.c

```
146                 /* find the link-local prefix of the home ifp. */
147                 if ((bi->mbc_flags & IP6MU_LINK) != 0) {
```

```
148                     for (pr = nd_prefix.lh_first; pr; pr = pr->ndpr_next) {
149                         if (hifp != pr->ndpr_ifp) {
150                             /* this prefix is not a home prefix. */
151                             continue;
152                         }
153                         /* save link-local prefix. */
154                         if (IN6_IS_ADDR_LINKLOCAL(&pr->ndpr_prefix.sin6_addr)){
155                             llpr = pr;
156                             continue;
157                         }
158                     }
159                 }
```
_____ mip6_hacore.c

147–159 We also need to take care of the link-local prefix if the received Binding Update message has the L flag (IP6MU_LINK) set. In the loop defined on line 148, we determine whether there is link-local prefix information on the network interface on which the home prefix is assigned. If such a prefix is found, the pointer to the prefix is stored to the llpr variable for later use.

Listing 5-95
_____ mip6_hacore.c

```
161                 if (prlifetime < 4) {    /* lifetime in units of 4 sec */
....
166                     bi->mbc_status = IP6_MH_BAS_UNSPECIFIED;
167                     bi->mbc_send_ba = 1;
168                     bi->mbc_lifetime = 0;
169                     bi->mbc_refresh = 0;
170                     return (0); /* XXX is 0 OK? */
171                 }
172                 /* sanity check */
173                 if (bi->mbc_lifetime < 4) {
....
179                     return (0); /* XXX is 0 OK? */
180                 }
181
182                 /* adjust lifetime */
183                 if (bi->mbc_lifetime > prlifetime) {
184                     bi->mbc_lifetime = prlifetime;
185                     bi->mbc_status = IP6_MH_BAS_PRFX_DISCOV;
186                 }
```
_____ mip6_hacore.c

161–186 The lifetime field stored in the mip6_bc{} structure is represented in units of 4 seconds. If the remaining prefix lifetime is less than 4 seconds, the Binding Update message is rejected and an error message with the IP6_MH_BAS_UNSPECIFIED status code is returned.

The mbc_lifetime variable keeps the lifetime requested by the mobile node which sent the Binding Update message. A Binding Update message whose lifetime is less than 4 seconds is also rejected.

A home agent replies with a Binding Acknowledgment message with the IP6_MH_BAS_PRFX_DISCOV status code if the home prefix lifetime is shorter than the lifetime of the binding information. A mobile node will perform Mobile Prefix Solicitation when receiving the status code to get the latest prefix information.

Listing 5-96

_____mip6_hacore.c
```
188          /*
189           * - L=0: defend the given address.
190           * - L=1: defend both the given non link-local unicast (home)
191           *         address and the derived link-local.
192           */
193          /*
194           * at first, check an existing binding cache entry for the
195           * link-local.
196           */
197          if ((bi->mbc_flags & IP6MU_LINK) != 0 && llpr != NULL) {
198                  mip6_create_addr(&lladdr,
199                      (const struct in6_addr *)&bi->mbc_phaddr, llpr);
200                  llmbc = mip6_bc_list_find_withphaddr(&mip6_bc_list, &lladdr);
201                  if (llmbc == NULL) {
202                          /*
203                           * create a new binding cache entry for the
204                           * link-local.
205                           */
206                          llmbc = mip6_bc_create(&lladdr, &bi->mbc_pcoa,
207                              &bi->mbc_addr, bi->mbc_flags, bi->mbc_seqno,
208                              bi->mbc_lifetime, hifp);
209                          if (llmbc == NULL) {
210                                  /* XXX INSUFFICIENT RESOURCE error */
211                                  return (-1);
212                          }
213
214                          /* start DAD processing. */
215                          mip6_dad_start(llmbc);
216                  } else if (MIP6_IS_BC_DAD_WAIT(llmbc)) {
217                          llmbc->mbc_pcoa = bi->mbc_pcoa;
218                          llmbc->mbc_seqno = bi->mbc_seqno;
219                          busy++;
220                  } else {
221                          /*
222                           * update the existing binding cache entry for
223                           * the link-local.
224                           */
225                          llmbc->mbc_pcoa = bi->mbc_pcoa;
226                          llmbc->mbc_flags = bi->mbc_flags;
227                          llmbc->mbc_seqno = bi->mbc_seqno;
228                          llmbc->mbc_lifetime = bi->mbc_lifetime;
229                          llmbc->mbc_expire
230                                  = time_second + llmbc->mbc_lifetime;
231                          /* sanity check for overflow. */
232                          if (llmbc->mbc_expire < time_second)
233                                  llmbc->mbc_expire = 0x7fffffff;
234                          llmbc->mbc_state = MIP6_BC_FSM_STATE_BOUND;
235                          mip6_bc_settimer(llmbc, -1);
236                          mip6_bc_settimer(llmbc, mip6_brr_time(llmbc));
237                          /* modify encapsulation entry */
238                          /* XXX */
239                          if (mip6_tunnel_control(MIP6_TUNNEL_CHANGE, llmbc,
240                              mip6_bc_encapcheck, &llmbc->mbc_encap)) {
241                                  /* XXX error */
242                          }
243                  }
244                  llmbc->mbc_flags |= IP6MU_CLONED;
245          }
```
_____mip6_hacore.c

197–215 The existing binding cache entry of the link-local address of the mobile node is examined. If a mobile node specified the L flag, we look up the corresponding binding cache entry on line 220. The `mip6_create_addr()` function creates a link-local address

from the interface identifier part of the IPv6 address passed as a second parameter and
the prefix passed as the third parameter.

    If there is no existing cache entry for the link-local address, a binding cache entry is
created by calling the `mip6_bc_create()` function and the DAD procedure is initiated
to make sure that the link-local address is not duplicated.

216–219 If there is an existing entry, and the entry is in DAD wait status, only the care-of
address and sequence number of the existing entry information are updated. This code
applies when a home agent receives a Binding Update message to a certain address while
performing the DAD procedure on the address.

220–244 If there is an existing entry, all information in the binding cache entry is updated with
the received information. The updated information is the care-of address, flags, sequence
number, lifetime and registration status. Note that the overflow of expiration time of the
cache information must be checked because the expiration date is represented as a 32-bit
signed integer. The timer function also has to be scheduled to reflect the current lifetime.
This occurs on lines 235–236. Finally, the `mip6_tunnel_control()` function is called
to update the care-of address of the mobile node, which is the endpoint address of the
IPv6 in IPv6 tunnel between the home agent the mobile node.

Listing 5-97

——mip6_hacore.c

```
247                     /*
248                      * next, check an existing binding cache entry for the unicast
249                      * (home) address.
250                      */
251             mbc = mip6_bc_list_find_withphaddr(&mip6_bc_list, &bi->mbc_phaddr);
252             if (mbc == NULL) {
253                     /* create a binding cache entry for the home address. */
254                     mbc = mip6_bc_create(&bi->mbc_phaddr, &bi->mbc_pcoa,
255                         &bi->mbc_addr, bi->mbc_flags, bi->mbc_seqno,
256                         bi->mbc_lifetime, hifp);
257                     if (mbc == NULL) {
258                             /* XXX STATUS_RESOUCE */
259                             return (-1);
260                     }
261
262                     /* mark that we should do DAD later in this function. */
263                     prim_mbc = mbc;
264
265                     /*
266                      * if the request has IP6MU_LINK flag, refer the
267                      * link-local entry.
268                      */
269                     if (bi->mbc_flags & IP6MU_LINK) {
270                             mbc->mbc_llmbc = llmbc;
271                             llmbc->mbc_refcnt++;
272                     }
273             } else if (MIP6_IS_BC_DAD_WAIT(mbc)) {
274                     mbc->mbc_pcoa = bi->mbc_pcoa;
275                     mbc->mbc_seqno = bi->mbc_seqno;
276                     busy++;
277             } else {
278                     /*
279                      * update the existing binding cache entry for the
280                      * home address.
281                      */
282                     mbc->mbc_pcoa = bi->mbc_pcoa;
```

```
283                         mbc->mbc_flags = bi->mbc_flags;
284                         mbc->mbc_seqno = bi->mbc_seqno;
285                         mbc->mbc_lifetime = bi->mbc_lifetime;
286                         mbc->mbc_expire = time_second + mbc->mbc_lifetime;
287                         /* sanity check for overflow. */
288                         if (mbc->mbc_expire < time_second)
289                                 mbc->mbc_expire = 0x7fffffff;
290                         mbc->mbc_state = MIP6_BC_FSM_STATE_BOUND;
291                         mip6_bc_settimer(mbc, -1);
292                         mip6_bc_settimer(mbc, mip6_brr_time(mbc));
293
294                         /* modify the encapsulation entry. */
295                         if (mip6_tunnel_control(MIP6_TUNNEL_CHANGE, mbc,
296                                 mip6_bc_encapcheck, &mbc->mbc_encap)) {
297                                 /* XXX UNSPECIFIED */
298                                 return (-1);
299                         }
300                 }
```
—— mip6_hacore.c

251–272 After checking the link-local address, the home address (which is always a global
address) of the mobile node is processed. If there is no existing binding cache entry for
the home address, then a new binding cache entry is created. If the mobile node specified
the L flag in the Binding Update message, a pointer to the binding cache entry of the
link-local address is kept in the `llmbc` variable. The `llmbc` variable is set to the newly
created binding cache entry and its reference counter is incremented.

273–276 If the entry exists and is in DAD status, then the care-of address and the sequence
number are updated.

277–299 If the entry exists already, the cache information is updated in a fashion similar to
updating the information for the link-local cache entry.

Listing 5-98
—— mip6_hacore.c

```
302                 if (busy) {
....
305                         return(0);
306                 }
307
308                 if (prim_mbc) {
309                         /*
310                          * a new binding cache is created. start DAD
311                          * proccesing.
312                          */
313                         mip6_dad_start(prim_mbc);
314                         bi->mbc_send_ba = 0;
315                 } else {
316                         /*
317                          * a binding cache entry is updated.  return a binding
318                          * ack.
319                          */
320                         bi->mbc_refresh = bi->mbc_lifetime *
MIP6_REFRESH_LIFETIME_RATE / 100;
321                         if (bi->mbc_refresh < MIP6_REFRESH_MINLIFETIME)
322                                 bi->mbc_refresh = bi->mbc_lifetime <
MIP6_REFRESH_MINLIFETIME ?
323                                         bi->mbc_lifetime : MIP6_REFRESH_MINLIFETIME;
324                         bi->mbc_send_ba = 1;
325                 }
326
```

```
327          return (0);
328    }
```
_____mip6_hacore.c
— *Lines 320 and 322 are broken here for layout reasons. However, they are a single line of code.*

302–305 If the DAD procedure is incomplete, the `mip6_process_hrbu()` function is aborted. The remaining processing will be done after the current DAD operation has finished.

308–314 If a new home registration entry for the home address of the mobile node is created, the DAD procedure is initiated to make sure the address is not duplicated. The `mbc_send_ba` flag is set to 0 to suppress replying to a Binding Acknowledgment message, since it will be sent after the DAD procedure has completed.

316–324 If the existing binding cache information is being updated, a Binding Acknowledgment message can be sent immediately, since the DAD procedure should have finished when the first registration was performed.

A refresh interval is sent to the mobile node with the Binding Acknowledgment message. The refresh time is calculated based on the lifetime. The default value is half of the lifetime since `MIP6_REFRESH_LIFETIME_RATE` is defined as 50. The refresh time must be greater than the minimum value `MIP6_REFRESH_MINLIFETIME` (= 2).

5.16.10   The DAD Procedure

A home agent must ensure that the addresses that a mobile node requested to register are not duplicated on the home network before replying with a Binding Acknowledgment message. The Mobile IPv6 stack utilizes the core DAD functions implemented as a part of Neighbor Discovery (see Section 5.21 of *IPv6 Core Protocols Implementation*). The DAD functions for Mobile IPv6 are implemented in the following 6 functions:

- `mip6_dad_start()`
  Start a DAD procedure for a specified address.

- `mip6_dad_stop()`
  Cancel the running DAD procedure for a specified address.

- `mip6_dad_find()`
  Find a pointer to the running DAD procedure for a specified address.

- `mip6_dad_success()`
  A callback function which is called when the DAD procedure succeeds

- `mip6_dad_duplicated()`
  A wrapper function of `mip6_dad_error()`

- `mip6_dad_error()`
  A callback function which is called when DAD procedure fails

Starting the DAD Procedure

The `mip6_dad_start()` function is used by a home agent to initiate the DAD procedure for a given mobile node's address.

Listing 5-99

_____mip6_hacore.c

```
692    static int
693    mip6_dad_start(mbc)
694            struct  mip6_bc *mbc;
695    {
696            struct in6_ifaddr *ia;
697
698            if (mbc->mbc_dad != NULL)
699                    return (EEXIST);
700
701            MALLOC(ia, struct in6_ifaddr *, sizeof(*ia), M_IFADDR, M_NOWAIT);
702            if (ia == NULL)
703                    return (ENOBUFS);
704
705            bzero((caddr_t)ia, sizeof(*ia));
706            ia->ia_ifa.ifa_addr = (struct sockaddr *)&ia->ia_addr;
707            ia->ia_addr.sin6_family = AF_INET6;
708            ia->ia_addr.sin6_len = sizeof(ia->ia_addr);
709            ia->ia_ifp = mbc->mbc_ifp;
710            ia->ia6_flags |= IN6_IFF_TENTATIVE;
711            ia->ia_addr.sin6_addr = mbc->mbc_phaddr;
712            if (in6_addr2zoneid(ia->ia_ifp, &ia->ia_addr.sin6_addr,
713                            &ia->ia_addr.sin6_scope_id)) {
714                    FREE(ia, M_IFADDR);
715                    return (EINVAL);
716            }
717            in6_embedscope(&ia->ia_addr.sin6_addr, &ia->ia_addr);
718            IFAREF(&ia->ia_ifa);
719            mbc->mbc_dad = ia;
720            nd6_dad_start((struct ifaddr *)ia, 0);
721
722            return (0);
723    }
```

_____mip6_hacore.c

692–694 The `mip6_dad_start()` function has one parameter which specifies a binding cache entry and includes the address for the DAD procedure of the address.

698–699 The `mbc_dad` variable points to the `in6_ifaddr{}` instance which stores the address information that is being tested by the DAD procedure. No new DAD procedure is started if `mbc_dad` is set, since it means the DAD procedure for that address has already been launched.

701–719 Memory is allocated for an `in6_ifaddr{}` structure to store the address information. The flag variable, `ia6_flags`, of the instance needs to have the `IN6_IFF_TENTATIVE` flag set to indicate that the address is being tested by the DAD procedure.

720 The `nd6_dad_start()` function is called to start the DAD operation. The `mip6_dad_success()` or the `mip6_dad_error()` function will be called when the DAD operation is completed, depending on the result of the operation.

Stopping the DAD Procedure

The `mip6_dad_stop()` function stops the ongoing DAD procedure executed by the `mip6_dad_start()` function.

Listing 5-100

_____mip6_hacore.c

```
725    int
726    mip6_dad_stop(mbc)
```

```
727              struct  mip6_bc *mbc;
728      {
729              struct in6_ifaddr *ia = (struct in6_ifaddr *)mbc->mbc_dad;
730
731              if (ia == NULL)
732                      return (ENOENT);
733              nd6_dad_stop((struct ifaddr *)ia);
734              FREE(ia, M_IFADDR);
735              mbc->mbc_dad = NULL;
736              return (0);
737      }
```
_____ mip6_hacore.c

725–737 The `mip6_dad_stop()` function takes one parameter which points to a binding
cache entry. Nothing happens if the `mbc_dad` variable of the parameter is NULL, which
means no DAD procedure is running for this address, otherwise, the `nd6_dad_stop()`
function is called to stop the running DAD procedure. The `mbc_dad` variable is set to
NULL to indicate that no DAD procedure is being performed after stopping the DAD
procedure.

Listing 5-101
_____ mip6_hacore.c

```
739      struct ifaddr *
740      mip6_dad_find(taddr, ifp)
741              struct in6_addr *taddr;
742              struct ifnet *ifp;
743      {
744              struct mip6_bc *mbc;
745              struct in6_ifaddr *ia;
746
747              for (mbc = LIST_FIRST(&mip6_bc_list);
748                   mbc;
749                   mbc = LIST_NEXT(mbc, mbc_entry)) {
750                      if (!MIP6_IS_BC_DAD_WAIT(mbc))
751                              continue;
752                      if (mbc->mbc_ifp != ifp || mbc->mbc_dad == NULL)
753                              continue;
754                      ia = (struct in6_ifaddr *)mbc->mbc_dad;
755                      if (IN6_ARE_ADDR_EQUAL(&ia->ia_addr.sin6_addr, taddr))
756                              return ((struct ifaddr *)ia);
757              }
758
759              return (NULL);
760      }
```
_____ mip6_hacore.c

739–742 The `mip6_dad_find()` function has two parameters: The `taddr` parameter is the
address for which we are looking, and the `ifp` parameter is a pointer to the network
interface to which the address specified by the `taddr` variable belongs.

747–759 In the loop defined on line 747, all binding cache entries, which are performing DAD
and which belong to the same network interface as specified by `ifp`, are checked. If the
address stored in the `mbc_dad` variable and the `taddr` variable are the same address,
the address information is returned to the caller.

Finishing the DAD Procedure with Success

The `mip6_dad_success()` function is called when the DAD procedure succeeded and
performs remaining home registration procedures that must be done after the successful DAD
operation.

Listing 5-102

```
                                                                  mip6_hacore.c
762    int
763    mip6_dad_success(ifa)
764           struct ifaddr *ifa;
765    {
766           struct  mip6_bc *mbc = NULL;
767
768           for (mbc = LIST_FIRST(&mip6_bc_list);
769                mbc;
770                mbc = LIST_NEXT(mbc, mbc_entry)) {
771                   if (mbc->mbc_dad == ifa)
772                           break;
773           }
774           if (!mbc)
775                   return (ENOENT);
776
777           FREE(ifa, M_IFADDR);
778           mbc->mbc_dad = NULL;
779
780           /* create encapsulation entry */
781           mip6_tunnel_control(MIP6_TUNNEL_ADD, mbc, mip6_bc_encapcheck,
782               &mbc->mbc_encap);
783
784           /* add rtable for proxy ND */
785           mip6_bc_proxy_control(&mbc->mbc_phaddr, &mbc->mbc_addr, RTM_ADD);
786
787           /* if this entry has been cloned by L=1 flag, just return. */
788           if ((mbc->mbc_flags & IP6MU_CLONED) != 0)
789                   return (0);
790
791           /* return a binding ack. */
792           if (mip6_bc_send_ba(&mbc->mbc_addr, &mbc->mbc_phaddr, &mbc->mbc_pcoa,
793               mbc->mbc_status, mbc->mbc_seqno, mbc->mbc_lifetime,
794               mbc->mbc_lifetime / 2 /* XXX */, NULL)) {
....
800           }
801
802           return (0);
803    }
                                                                  mip6_hacore.c
```

762–764 The `mip6_dad_success()` function is called when the DAD procedure of the Neighbor Discovery mechanism has successfully completed. The parameter is a pointer to the `in6_ifaddr{}` structure which holds the address.

768–778 The code looks up the corresponding binding cache entry which has the address that has been successfully tested by the DAD procedure. Memory used to store the address information is released and the `mbc_dad` field is set to NULL to indicate that no DAD procedure is running for this cache entry.

781–785 After successful DAD, the home agent needs to set up a proxy Neighbor Discovery entry for the address of the mobile node and needs to create a tunnel to the mobile node. The `mip6_tunnel_control()` function (Section 5.17.25) and the `mip6_bc_proxy_control()` function (Section 5.16.11) implement these mechanisms.

788–802 A Binding Acknowledgment message is sent by calling the `mip6_bc_send_ba()` function, if the binding cache entry does not have the cloned (`IP6MU_CLONED`) flag. The cloned flag indicates that the entry has been created as a side effect of another binding cache creation. An acknowledgment message will be sent when the original cache entry is processed.

Error Handling of the DAD Procedure

The `mip6_dad_duplicated()` function is called when the node detects the duplicated address for the mobile node's address passed by the `mip6_dad_start()` function, and performs error processing.

Listing 5-103

_____mip6_hacore.c
```
805     int
806     mip6_dad_duplicated(ifa)
807             struct ifaddr *ifa;
808     {
809             return mip6_dad_error(ifa, IP6_MH_BAS_DAD_FAILED);
810     }
811
812     int
813     mip6_dad_error(ifa, err)
814             struct ifaddr *ifa;
815             int err;
816     {
817             struct mip6_bc *mbc = NULL, *llmbc = NULL;
818             struct mip6_bc *gmbc = NULL, *gmbc_next = NULL;
819             int error;
820
821             for (mbc = LIST_FIRST(&mip6_bc_list);
822                 mbc;
823                 mbc = LIST_NEXT(mbc, mbc_entry)) {
824                     if (mbc->mbc_dad == ifa)
825                             break;
826             }
827             if (!mbc)
828                     return (ENOENT);
829
830             FREE(ifa, M_IFADDR);
831             mbc->mbc_dad = NULL;
```
_____mip6_hacore.c

805–810 The `mip6_dad_duplicated()` simply calls the `mip6_dad_error()` function with the status code `IP6_MH_BAS_DAD_FAILED`. This function is called from the Neighbor Discovery mechanism when the DAD procedure detects address duplication.

812–815 The `mip6_dad_error()` function has two parameters: The `ifa` is a pointer to the address information on which the DAD procedure has detected an error while performing DAD, and the `err` parameter is a status code which is used when sending back a Binding Acknowledgment message to a mobile node.

821–828 The addresses on which a home agent is performing DAD operations are stored in the `mbc_dad` member variable of the `mip6_bc{}` structure. The `ENOENT` error is returned if there is no matching address in the binding cache list.

830–831 There is no need for the address information stored in `ifa` any longer. `mbc_dad` is set to NULL to indicate that the DAD procedure is not running anymore.

Listing 5-104

_____mip6_hacore.c
```
833             if ((mbc->mbc_flags & IP6MU_CLONED) != 0) {
834                     /*
835                      * DAD for a link-local address failed.  clear all
```

```
836                          * references from other binding caches.
837                          */
838                         llmbc = mbc;
839                         for (gmbc = LIST_FIRST(&mip6_bc_list);
840                              gmbc;
841                              gmbc = gmbc_next) {
842                                 gmbc_next = LIST_NEXT(gmbc, mbc_entry);
843                                 if (((gmbc->mbc_flags & IP6MU_LINK) != 0)
844                                     && ((gmbc->mbc_flags & IP6MU_CLONED) == 0)
845                                     && (gmbc->mbc_llmbc == llmbc)) {
846                                         gmbc_next = LIST_NEXT(gmbc, mbc_entry);
847                                         if (MIP6_IS_BC_DAD_WAIT(gmbc)) {
848                                                 mip6_dad_stop(gmbc);
849                                                 gmbc->mbc_llmbc = NULL;
850                                                 error = mip6_bc_list_remove(
851                                                     &mip6_bc_list, llmbc);
852                                                 if (error) {
....
856                                                         /* what should I do? */
857                                                 }
858
859                                                 /* return a binding ack. */
860                                                 mip6_bc_send_ba(&gmbc->mbc_addr,
861                                                     &gmbc->mbc_phaddr, &gmbc->mbc_pcoa,
862                                                     err, gmbc->mbc_seqno, 0, 0, NULL);
863
864                                                 /*
865                                                  * update gmbc_next, beacuse removing
866                                                  * llmbc may invalidate gmbc_next.
867                                                  */
868                                                 gmbc_next = LIST_NEXT(gmbc, mbc_entry);
869                                                 error = mip6_bc_list_remove(
870                                                     &mip6_bc_list, gmbc);
871                                                 if (error) {
....
875                                                         /* what should I do? */
876                                                 }
877                                         } else {
878                                                 /*
879                                                  * DAD for a lladdr failed, but
880                                                  * a related BC's DAD had been
881                                                  * succeeded.  does this happen?
882                                                  */
883                                         }
884                                 }
885                         }
886                         return (0);
```
──mip6_hacore.c

833 Lines 833–886 is the code for binding cache entries which are cloned by other binding cache entries.

839–862 The loop checks all binding cache entries which meet the following conditions:

- The entry has a cloned entry (IP6MU_LINK is set).
- The mbc_llmbc member variable is set to the entry which the DAD procedure failed.
- The entry is not a cloned entry (IP6MU_CLONED is not set).

In these cases, the original entry must be removed as well as the cloned entry, and a Binding Acknowledgment message is sent with an error status code. The Acknowledgment message is sent by the mip6_bc_send_ba() function.

868–876 A single cloned entry may be referred to by two or more binding cache entries. The loop continues to check other cache entries which should be removed. Note that

the gmbc_next variable must be updated before removing the entry from the binding
cache list, since removing a cloned entry (llmbc, in this case) may make the gmbc_next
pointer invalid.

Listing 5-105

```
                                                              mip6_hacore.c
887             } else {
888                     /*
889                      * if this binding cache has a related link-local
890                      * binding cache entry, decrement the refcnt of the
891                      * entry.
892                      */
893                     if (mbc->mbc_llmbc != NULL) {
894                             error = mip6_bc_list_remove(&mip6_bc_list,
895                                 mbc->mbc_llmbc);
896                             if (error) {
....
901                                     /* what should I do? */
902                             }
903                     }
904             }
                                                              mip6_hacore.c
```

893–904 The mip6_bc_list_remove() function is called to remove the cloned entry of
the entry that has a duplicated address. If the entry has a cloned entry, the mbc_llmbc
holds a pointer to the cloned entry. Calling mip6_bc_list_remove() will decrement
the reference count of the entry and will remove it if the reference count reaches 0.

Listing 5-106

```
                                                              mip6_hacore.c
906             /* return a binding ack. */
907             mip6_bc_send_ba(&mbc->mbc_addr, &mbc->mbc_phaddr, &mbc->mbc_pcoa, err,
908                 mbc->mbc_seqno, 0, 0, NULL);
909             error = mip6_bc_list_remove(&mip6_bc_list, mbc);
910             if (error) {
....
914                     /* what should I do? */
915             }
916
917             return (0);
918     }
                                                              mip6_hacore.c
```

907–917 After finishing the error processing of a DAD failure, a Binding Acknowledgment
message is sent to the mobile node to notify that its address is duplicated. The original
binding cache entry for the mobile node is removed here.

5.16.11   Proxy Neighbor Discovery Control

While a mobile node is away from home, the home agent of a mobile node receives all traffic
sent to the home address of the mobile node at the mobile node's home address and tunnels
the packets to its care-of address using an IPv6 in IPv6 tunnel. To receive packets whose
destination address is the home address of the mobile node, the home agent uses the proxy
Neighbor Discovery mechanism.

Listing 5-107

_____mip6_hacore.c

```
428     int
429     mip6_bc_proxy_control(target, local, cmd)
430             struct in6_addr *target;
431             struct in6_addr *local;
432             int cmd;
433     {
```

_____mip6_hacore.c

428–432 The `mip6_bc_proxy_control()` function has three parameters: The `target` parameter is a pointer to the address which will be proxied by a home agent, the `local` parameter is a pointer to the address of the home agent, and the `cmd` parameter specifies the operation. In this function, either `RTM_DELETE` to stop proxying or `RTM_ADD` to start proxying can be specified.

The information is stored in the routing subsystem as a routing entry. It is used by the home agent to reply to the nodes that query for the link-layer address of the mobile node by sending Neighbor Solicitation messages. The home agent replies with Neighbor Advertisement messages, adding its link-layer address as a destination link-layer address to receive all packets sent to the mobile node.

Listing 5-108

_____mip6_hacore.c

```
434             struct sockaddr_in6 target_sa, local_sa, mask_sa;
435             struct sockaddr_dl *sdl;
436             struct rtentry *rt, *nrt;
437             struct ifaddr *ifa;
438             struct ifnet *ifp;
439             int flags, error = 0;
440
441             /* create a sockaddr_in6 structure for my address. */
442             bzero(&local_sa, sizeof(local_sa));
443             local_sa.sin6_len = sizeof(local_sa);
444             local_sa.sin6_family = AF_INET6;
445             /* XXX */ in6_recoverscope(&local_sa, local, NULL);
446             /* XXX */ in6_embedscope(&local_sa.sin6_addr, &local_sa);
447
448             ifa = ifa_ifwithaddr((struct sockaddr *)&local_sa);
449             if (ifa == NULL)
450                     return (EINVAL);
451             ifp = ifa->ifa_ifp;
```

_____mip6_hacore.c

442–451 A `sockaddr_in6{}` instance, which stores the address of the home agent, is created. Lines 445–446 try to restore the scope identifier of the home address. It is impossible to decide the scope information of the address because the address information passed to this function does not have such information. If the home agent is operated with scoped addresses (such as the site-local addresses), the result will be unreliable. But this is not critical since the site-local addresses are deprecated and the home agent address which is used for proxying is usually a global address.

Listing 5-109

_____mip6_hacore.c

```
453             bzero(&target_sa, sizeof(target_sa));
454             target_sa.sin6_len = sizeof(target_sa);
```

```
455              target_sa.sin6_family = AF_INET6;
456              target_sa.sin6_addr = *target;
457              if (in6_addr2zoneid(ifp, &target_sa.sin6_addr,
458                      &target_sa.sin6_scope_id)) {
....
462                      return(EIO);
463              }
464              error = in6_embedscope(&target_sa.sin6_addr, &target_sa);
465              if (error != 0) {
466                      return(error);
467              }
```
                                                            _____mip6_hacore.c

453–467 A `sockaddr_in6{}` instance, which stores the address of a mobile node, is created.
The scope identifier should be the same as the address of the home agent which performs
proxying.

Listing 5-110
                                                            _____mip6_hacore.c

```
468              /* clear sin6_scope_id before looking up a routing table. */
469              target_sa.sin6_scope_id = 0;
470
471              switch (cmd) {
472              case RTM_DELETE:
....
474                      rt = rtalloc1((struct sockaddr *)&target_sa, 0, 0UL);
....
478                      if (rt)
479                              rt->rt_refcnt--;
480                      if (rt == NULL)
481                              return (0);
482                      if ((rt->rt_flags & RTF_HOST) == 0 ||
483                          (rt->rt_flags & RTF_ANNOUNCE) == 0) {
484                              /*
485                               * there is a rtentry, but is not a host nor
486                               * a proxy entry.
487                               */
488                              return (0);
489                      }
490                      error = rtrequest(RTM_DELETE, rt_key(rt), (struct sockaddr *)0,
491                          rt_mask(rt), 0, (struct rtentry **)0);
492                      if (error) {
....
497                      }
498                      rt = NULL;
499
500                      break;
```
                                                            _____mip6_hacore.c

469 The `sin6_scope_id` field of the `target_sa` is cleared before using it to look up a
routing entry. The `sin6_scope_id` field keeps scope information of the address and
the KAME code utilizes this field when it handles IPv6 addresses as `sockaddr_in6{}`
structures. The routing table is one of the exceptions that does not utilize the field because
of the design of the Radix tree implementation. The current Radix tree implementation of BSD operating systems only checks the address field when looking up a routing
entry. The scope information has to be embedded into the address field instead of the
`sin6_scope_id` field.

471–500 The RTM_DELETE command deletes the existing proxy Neighbor Discovery entry from the routing table. All proxy routing entries have the RTF_HOST and the RTF_ANNOUNCE flags set. If the entry found by rtalloc1() has these flags, the rtrequest() function is called with the RTM_DELETE command to remove the entry from the routing table.

Listing 5-111

──mip6_hacore.c

```
502                 case RTM_ADD:
....
504                         rt = rtalloc1((struct sockaddr *)&target_sa, 0, 0UL);
....
508                         if (rt)
509                                 rt->rt_refcnt--;
510                         if (rt) {
511                                 if (((rt->rt_flags & RTF_HOST) != 0) &&
512                                     ((rt->rt_flags & RTF_ANNOUNCE) != 0) &&
513                                     rt->rt_gateway->sa_family == AF_LINK) {
....
518                                         return (EEXIST);
519                                 }
520                                 if ((rt->rt_flags & RTF_LLINFO) != 0) {
521                                         /* nd cache exist */
522                                         rtrequest(RTM_DELETE, rt_key(rt),
523                                             (struct sockaddr *)0, rt_mask(rt), 0,
524                                             (struct rtentry **)0);
525                                         rt = NULL;
526                                 } else {
527                                         /* XXX Path MTU entry? */
....
533                                 }
534                         }
```

──mip6_hacore.c

502–525 If the command is RTM_ADD, the existing proxy Neighbor Discovery entry is removed first to avoid duplicated registration of a routing entry. A proxy entry has the RTF_LLINFO flag set indicating the entry has link-layer address information. Such an entry is removed before adding a new proxy entry for the same address.

527 Usually there is no routing entry for directly connected links other than link-layer address entries. If such entries exist, the code does nothing. In this case, the proxy Neighbor Discovery setup will fail. This special case is not supported.

Listing 5-112

──mip6_hacore.c

```
539                         /* sdl search */
540                 {
541                         struct ifaddr *ifa_dl;
542
543                         for (ifa_dl = ifp->if_addrlist.tqh_first; ifa_dl;
544                             ifa_dl = ifa_dl->ifa_list.tqe_next) {
545                                 if (ifa_dl->ifa_addr->sa_family == AF_LINK)
546                                         break;
547                         }
548
549                         if (!ifa_dl)
```

```
550                                        return (EINVAL);
551
552                        sdl = (struct sockaddr_dl *)ifa_dl->ifa_addr;
553                }
```
———————————————————————————————————————mip6_hacore.c

541–552 The `ifa_dl` variable is set to the link-layer address information of the home agent.
The link-layer address is kept as one of the interface addresses in the address list of the
`ifnet{}` structure. An error is returned if there is no address that can be used as a
destination link-layer address of the proxy entry.

Listing 5-113
———————————————————————————————————————mip6_hacore.c

```
556                        /* create a mask. */
557                        bzero(&mask_sa, sizeof(mask_sa));
558                        mask_sa.sin6_family = AF_INET6;
559                        mask_sa.sin6_len = sizeof(mask_sa);
560
561                        in6_prefixlen2mask(&mask_sa.sin6_addr, 128);
562                        flags = (RTF_STATIC | RTF_HOST | RTF_ANNOUNCE);
563
564                        error = rtrequest(RTM_ADD, (struct sockaddr *)&target_sa,
565                            (struct sockaddr *)sdl, (struct sockaddr *)&mask_sa, flags,
566                            &nrt);
567
568                        if (error == 0) {
569                                /* Avoid expiration */
570                                if (nrt) {
571                                        nrt->rt_rmx.rmx_expire = 0;
572                                        nrt->rt_refcnt--;
573                                } else
574                                        error = EINVAL;
575                        } else {
....
580                        }
```
———————————————————————————————————————mip6_hacore.c

556–580 A host mask (all bits set to 1) is created and the `rtrequest()` function with the
`RTM_ADD` command is called to insert the proxy Neighbor Discovery entry. The flags have
the `RTF_STATIC` flag set to indicate the entry is created statically, the `RTF_HOST` flag set
to indicate it is not a network route entry, and the `RTF_ANNOUNCE` flag set to indicate
this is a proxy entry. After the successful call to `rtrequest()`, the expiration time of the
entry is set to infinite, since the lifetime of this entry is managed by the Mobile IPv6 stack.

Listing 5-114
———————————————————————————————————————mip6_hacore.c

```
582                {
583                        /* very XXX */
584                        struct sockaddr_in6 daddr_sa;
585
586                        bzero(&daddr_sa, sizeof(daddr_sa));
587                        daddr_sa.sin6_family = AF_INET6;
588                        daddr_sa.sin6_len = sizeof(daddr_sa);
589                        daddr_sa.sin6_addr = in6addr_linklocal_allnodes;
590                        if (in6_addr2zoneid(ifp, &daddr_sa.sin6_addr,
591                            &daddr_sa.sin6_scope_id)) {
592                                /* XXX: should not happen */
```

```
        ....
597                                             error = EIO; /* XXX */
598                                 }
599                                 if (error == 0) {
600                                         error = in6_embedscope(&daddr_sa.sin6_addr,
601                                             &daddr_sa);
602                                 }
603                                 if (error == 0) {
604                                         nd6_na_output(ifp, &daddr_sa.sin6_addr,
605                                             &target_sa.sin6_addr, ND_NA_FLAG_OVERRIDE,
606                                             1, (struct sockaddr *)sdl);
607                                 }
608                         }
609
610                 break;
611
612         default:
        ....
617                 error = -1;
618                 break;
619         }
620
621         return (error);
622     }
```
                                                                     ————————————mip6_hacore.c

586–603 A Neighbor Advertisement message is sent to the all nodes link-local multicast address to inform all nodes that packets destined to the mobile node's home address should be sent to the link-layer address of the home agent. The message contains the mobile node's home address, the address of the home agent and the home agent's link-layer address. The flag of the message has the `ND_NA_FLAG_OVERRIDE` flag set which indicates that existing neighbor cache entries should be updated with the newly advertised information.

612–621 If the procedure succeeds, 0 is returned, otherwise an error code is returned.

5.16.12   Home De-Registration Procedure

When a home agent receives a message to de-register the home address of a mobile node, it removes the related binding cache entry from its binding cache list. In addition to this, a home agent needs to perform the following tasks:

- Stop proxying the home address of the mobile node.
- Destroy the IPv6 in IPv6 tunnel between the home agent and mobile node.

The overview of the de-registration processing is described in Section 5.4.5.

Listing 5-115
                                                                     ————————————mip6_hacore.c
```
330     int
331     mip6_process_hurbu(bi)
332             struct mip6_bc *bi;
333     {
```
                                                                     ————————————mip6_hacore.c

330–332 The de-registration process is implemented as the `mip6_process_hurbu()` function. The function has one parameter which points to a value containing binding information to be removed. The parameter is also used to store some information needed to send a Binding Acknowledgment message by the caller.

Listing 5-116

```
334            struct sockaddr_in6 addr_sa;
335            struct ifaddr *destifa = NULL;
336            struct ifnet *destifp = NULL;
337            struct mip6_bc *mbc;
338            struct nd_prefix *pr;
339            struct ifnet *hifp = NULL;
340            int error = 0;
341
342            /* find the interface which the destination address belongs to. */
343            bzero(&addr_sa, sizeof(addr_sa));
344            addr_sa.sin6_len = sizeof(addr_sa);
345            addr_sa.sin6_family = AF_INET6;
346            addr_sa.sin6_addr = bi->mbc_addr;
347            /* XXX ? */
348            if (in6_recoverscope(&addr_sa, &addr_sa.sin6_addr, NULL))
349                    panic("mip6_process_hrbu: recovering scope");
350            if (in6_embedscope(&addr_sa.sin6_addr, &addr_sa))
351                    panic("mip6_process_hrbu: embedding scope");
352            destifa = ifa_ifwithaddr((struct sockaddr *)&addr_sa);
353            if (!destifa) {
354                    bi->mbc_status = IP6_MH_BAS_NOT_HOME_SUBNET;
355                    bi->mbc_send_ba = 1;
356                    return (0); /* XXX is 0 OK? */
357            }
358            destifp = destifa->ifa_ifp;
```

343–358 The destifa variable is set to the network interface on which the Binding Update message arrived. Usually the mbuf contains a pointer to the interface on which the packet has arrived; however, in this case the information cannot be used because a different interface may receive the message when the home agent has multiple network interfaces. The stack needs to know which interface has the same address as the destination address of the Binding Update message. To get the interface on which the address is assigned, the ifa_ifwithaddr() function is used with the address of the home agent. A Binding Acknowledgment message with the status code IP6_MH_BAS_NOT_HOME_SUBNET is sent if there is no such interface.

Listing 5-117

```
360            /* find the home ifp of this homeaddress. */
361            for (pr = nd_prefix.lh_first; pr; pr = pr->ndpr_next) {
362                    if (pr->ndpr_ifp != destifp)
363                            continue;
364                    if (in6_are_prefix_equal(&bi->mbc_phaddr,
365                        &pr->ndpr_prefix.sin6_addr, pr->ndpr_plen)) {
366                            hifp = pr->ndpr_ifp; /* home ifp. */
367                    }
368            }
369            if (hifp == NULL) {
370                    /*
371                     * the haddr0 doesn't have an online prefix.  return a
372                     * binding ack with an error NOT_HOME_SUBNET.
```

```
373                             */
374                             bi->mbc_status = IP6_MH_BAS_NOT_HOME_SUBNET;
375                             bi->mbc_send_ba = 1;
376                             bi->mbc_lifetime = bi->mbc_refresh = 0;
377                             return (0); /* XXX is 0 OK? */
378                     }
```
———mip6_hacore.c

361–378 The home address must belong to the same network of the interface on which the destination address of the Binding Update message is assigned. In the `for` loop on line 361, all prefixes assigned to all interfaces are checked and the prefix which has the same prefix as the home address and which points to the same interface as `destifp` is picked. A Binding Acknowledgment message with `IP6_MH_BAS_NOT_HOME_SUBNET` is sent if there is no interface that has the same prefix as the home address of the mobile node.

Listing 5-118
———mip6_hacore.c
```
380                     /* remove a global unicast home binding cache entry. */
381                     mbc = mip6_bc_list_find_withphaddr(&mip6_bc_list, &bi->mbc_phaddr);
382                     if (mbc == NULL) {
383                             /* XXX panic */
384                             return (0);
385                     }
```
———mip6_hacore.c

381–385 The `mbc` variable is set to the binding cache entry for the home address of the mobile node which is specified as `bi->mbc_phaddr`.

Listing 5-119
———mip6_hacore.c
```
387                     /*
388                      * update the CoA of a mobile node.  this is needed to update
389                      * ipsec security policy databse addresses properly.
390                      */
391                     mbc->mbc_pcoa = bi->mbc_pcoa;
392
393                     /*
394                      * remove a binding cache entry and a link-local binding cache
395                      * entry, if any.
396                      */
397                     if ((bi->mbc_flags & IP6MU_LINK) &&  (mbc->mbc_llmbc != NULL)) {
398                             /* remove a link-local binding cache entry. */
399                             error = mip6_bc_list_remove(&mip6_bc_list, mbc->mbc_llmbc);
400                             if (error) {
....
404                                     bi->mbc_status = IP6_MH_BAS_UNSPECIFIED;
405                                     bi->mbc_send_ba = 1;
406                                     bi->mbc_lifetime = bi->mbc_refresh = 0;
407                                     return (error);
408                             }
409                     }
410                     error = mip6_bc_list_remove(&mip6_bc_list, mbc);
411                     if (error) {
....
415                             bi->mbc_status = IP6_MH_BAS_UNSPECIFIED;
416                             bi->mbc_send_ba = 1;
417                             bi->mbc_lifetime = bi->mbc_refresh = 0;
```

```
418                        return (error);
419             }
420
421             /* return BA */
422             bi->mbc_lifetime = 0;  /* ID-19 10.3.2. the lifetime MUST be 0. */
423             bi->mbc_send_ba = 1;     /* Need it ? */
424
425             return (0);
426     }
```
─── mip6_hacore.c

391 The current care-of address is updated with the address stored in the Binding Update message sent by the mobile node. In the de-registration case, the care-of address should be the home address.

397–409 A binding cache entry may have a cloned entry. Before releasing the cache entry, the cloned entry specified as mbc_llmbc has to be released by calling the mip6_bc_list_remove() function. If an error occurs during the release of the cloned entry, a Binding Acknowledgment message with a status code IP6_MH_BAS_UNSPECIFIED is sent.

410–425 The binding cache entry used for home registration is removed. The error status IP6_MH_BAS_UNSPECIFIED is returned when an error occurs. After the successful removal of the binding cache entry, the home agent will return a Binding Acknowledgment message with lifetime set to 0 to the mobile node which confirms de-registration.

5.16.13   Sending a Binding Acknowledgment Message

A home agent replies with a Binding Acknowledgment message in response to the Binding Update message for home registration of a mobile node. A correspondent node must reply with a Binding Acknowledgment message when a Binding Update message from a mobile node has the A (Acknowledgment) flag set or when it encounters any problem during the incoming Binding Update message processing.

The mip6_bc_send_ba() function creates a Binding Acknowledgment message and sends it.

Listing 5-120
─── mip6_cncore.c

```
1036    int
1037    mip6_bc_send_ba(src, dst, dstcoa, status, seqno, lifetime, refresh, mopt)
1038            struct in6_addr *src;
1039            struct in6_addr *dst;
1040            struct in6_addr *dstcoa;
1041            u_int8_t status;
1042            u_int16_t seqno;
1043            u_int32_t lifetime;
1044            u_int32_t refresh;
1045            struct mip6_mobility_options *mopt;
1046    {
```
─── mip6_cncore.c

1037–1045 Function mip6_bc_send_ba() has eight parameters. The src and dst parameters are the address of a sending node and the home address of a mobile node. These addresses are used as the source and destination addresses of the Binding Acknowledgment message which will be sent. The dstcoa parameter is the care-of address of the mobile node. The `status` parameter is a status code of the Acknowledgment message which must be one of the values described in Table 5-3 on page 501. The `seqno` parameter is a copy of the sequence number of the corresponding Binding Update message. The `lifetime` parameter is the lifetime of the binding cache information. The value will be greater than 0 when the incoming Binding Update message is for registration, and will be 0 when the message is for de-registration. The `refresh` parameter is the refresh interval value. The `mopt` parameter is a pointer to the `mip6_mobility_options{}` structure whose contents are extracted from the Binding Update message.

Listing 5-121

```
                                                                    _____mip6_cncore.c
1047            struct mbuf *m;
1048            struct ip6_pktopts opt;
1049            struct m_tag *mtag;
1050            struct ip6aux *ip6a;
1051            struct ip6_rthdr *pktopt_rthdr;
1052            int error = 0;
1053
1054            ip6_initpktopts(&opt);
1055
1056            m = mip6_create_ip6hdr(src, dst, IPPROTO_NONE, 0);
1057            if (m == NULL) {
....
1061                    return (ENOMEM);
1062            }
1063
1064            error =  mip6_ip6ma_create(&opt.ip6po_mh, src, dst, dstcoa,
1065                                status, seqno, lifetime, refresh, mopt);
1066            if (error) {
....
1070                    m_freem(m);
1071                    goto free_ip6pktopts;
1072            }
                                                                    _____mip6_cncore.c
```

1056–1072 An IPv6 packet for the Binding Acknowledgment message is prepared with the `mip6_create_ip6hdr()` function. The Binding Acknowledgment message is created as an instance of the `ip6_pktopt{}` structure by the `mip6_ip6ma_create()` function. If the creation of the headers fails, an error is returned.

Listing 5-122

```
                                                                    _____mip6_cncore.c
1074            /*
1075             * when sending a binding ack, we use rthdr2 except when
1076             * we are on the home link.
1077             */
1078            if (!IN6_ARE_ADDR_EQUAL(dst, dstcoa)) {
1079                    error = mip6_rthdr_create(&pktopt_rthdr, dstcoa, NULL);
1080                    if (error) {
....
1084                            m_freem(m);
1085                            goto free_ip6pktopts;
1086                    }
1087                    opt.ip6po_rthdr2 = pktopt_rthdr;
1088            }
```

```
1089
1090              mtag = ip6_findaux(m);
1091              if (mtag) {
1092                      ip6a = (struct ip6aux *)(mtag + 1);
1093                      ip6a->ip6a_flags |= IP6A_NOTUSEBC;
1094              }
```
——mip6_cncore.c

1078–1088 A Binding Acknowledgment message must contain a Type 2 Routing Header, except when the destination mobile node is attached to its home link. If dst (the home address of the mobile node) and dstcoa (the care-of address of the mobile node) are the same, the mobile node is at home. Otherwise, a Type 2 Routing Header is prepared with the mip6_rthdr_create() function.

1090–1094 When sending a Binding Acknowledgment message, binding cache entries are not used to insert a Type 2 Routing Header, since the header is already inserted above.

The IP6A_NOTUSEBC flag indicates that there is no need to look up binding cache information when sending the packet.

Listing 5-123
——mip6_cncore.c

```
1096      #ifdef MIP6_HOME_AGENT
1097              /* delete proxy nd entry temprolly */
1098              if ((status >= IP6_MH_BAS_ERRORBASE) &&
1099                  IN6_ARE_ADDR_EQUAL(dst, dstcoa)) {
1100                      struct mip6_bc *mbc;
1101
1102                      mbc = mip6_bc_list_find_withphaddr(&mip6_bc_list, dst);
1103                      if (mtag && mbc && mbc->mbc_flags & IP6MU_HOME &&
1104                          (mip6_bc_proxy_control(&mbc->mbc_phaddr, &mbc->mbc_addr,
         RTM_DELETE) == 0)) {
1105                              ip6a->ip6a_flags |= IP6A_TEMP_PROXYND_DEL;
1106                      }
1107              }
1108      #endif
```
——mip6_cncore.c

— Line 1104 is broken here for layout reasons. However, it is a single line of code.

1097–1107 The proxy Neighbor Discovery entry for the destination mobile node has to be disabled if the mobile node is at home and the status code is one of the error codes. If the entry is active, the Binding Acknowledgment message whose destination address is the address of the mobile node will be received by the sending node because of the proxy entry. Usually, the proxy Neighbor Discovery entry is removed before calling the mip6_bc_send_ba() function when no error occurs; however, when an error occurs, the entry still exists at this point. To avoid the loopback of the message, the entry has to be removed temporarily. The temporarily disabled entry will be restored after the message is sent (see Section 5.16.17).

Listing 5-124
——mip6_cncore.c

```
1112              error = ip6_output(m, &opt, NULL, 0, NULL, NULL
....
1114                              , NULL
```

```
      ....
1116                            );
1117           if (error) {
      ....
1121                   goto free_ip6pktopts;
1122           }
1123    free_ip6pktopts:
1124           if (opt.ip6po_rthdr2)
1125                   FREE(opt.ip6po_rthdr2, M_IP6OPT);
1126           if (opt.ip6po_mh)
1127                   FREE(opt.ip6po_mh, M_IP6OPT);
1128
1129           return (error);
1130    }
```
                                                            ————mip6_cncore.c

1112–1130 The Binding Acknowledgment message is sent via the `ip6_output()` function. The memory allocated for the Acknowledgment message and the Routing Header has to be released here since it is not released in `ip6_output()`.

Creation of a Binding Acknowledgment Message

The `mip6_ip6ma_create()` function will prepare a Binding Acknowledgment message.

Listing 5-125

                                                            ————mip6_cncore.c

```
2409    int
2410    mip6_ip6ma_create(pktopt_mobility, src, dst, dstcoa, status, seqno, lifetime,
2411       refresh, mopt)
2412           struct ip6_mh **pktopt_mobility;
2413           struct in6_addr *src;
2414           struct in6_addr *dst;
2415           struct in6_addr *dstcoa;
2416           u_int8_t status;
2417           u_int16_t seqno;
2418           u_int32_t lifetime;
2419           u_int32_t refresh;
2420           struct mip6_mobility_options *mopt;
2421    {
```
                                                            ————mip6_cncore.c

2409–2420 The `pktopt_mobility` parameter stores a pointer to the newly created message. Other parameters are the same as the paremeters of the `mip6_bc_send_ba()` function (see Listing 5-120).

Listing 5-126

                                                            ————mip6_cncore.c

```
2422           struct ip6_mh_binding_ack *ip6ma;
2423           struct ip6_mh_opt_refresh_advice *mopt_refresh = NULL;
2424           struct ip6_mh_opt_auth_data *mopt_auth = NULL;
2425           int need_refresh = 0;
2426           int need_auth = 0;
2427           int ip6ma_size, pad;
2428           int ba_size = 0, refresh_size = 0, auth_size = 0;
2429           u_int8_t key_bm[MIP6_KBM_LEN]; /* Stated as 'Kbm' in the spec */
2430           u_int8_t *p;
2431
2432           *pktopt_mobility = NULL;
```

```
2433
2434                ba_size = sizeof(struct ip6_mh_binding_ack);
2435                if (refresh > 3 && refresh < lifetime) {
2436                        need_refresh = 1;
2437                        ba_size += MIP6_PADLEN(ba_size, 2, 0);
2438                        refresh_size = sizeof(struct ip6_mh_opt_refresh_advice);
2439                } else {
2440                        refresh_size = 0;
2441                }
2442                if (mopt &&
2443                    ((mopt->valid_options & (MOPT_NONCE_IDX | MOPT_AUTHDATA)) ==
(MOPT_NONCE_IDX | MOPT_AUTHDATA)) &&
2444                    mip6_calculate_kbm_from_index(dst, dstcoa,
2445                        mopt->mopt_ho_nonce_idx, mopt->mopt_co_nonce_idx,
2446                        !IS_REQUEST_TO_CACHE(lifetime, dst, dstcoa), key_bm) == 0) {
2447                        need_auth = 1;
2448                        /* Since Binding Auth Option must be the last mobility option,
2449                            an implicit alignment requirement is 8n + 2.
2450                            (6.2.7) */
2451                        if (refresh_size)
2452                                refresh_size += MIP6_PADLEN(ba_size + refresh_size,
8, 2);
2453                        else
2454                                ba_size += MIP6_PADLEN(ba_size, 8, 2);
2455                        auth_size = IP6MOPT_AUTHDATA_SIZE;
2456                }
2457                ip6ma_size = ba_size + refresh_size + auth_size;
2458                ip6ma_size += MIP6_PADLEN(ip6ma_size, 8, 0);
```
———mip6_cncore.c

— Lines 2443 and 2452 are broken here for layout reasons. However, they are a single line of code.

2434–2458 The size of the Binding Acknowledgment message is calculated. Note that a Binding
Acknowledgment message may have options. In this case, the Binding Refresh Advice
option and the Binding Authorization Data option may exist. Each option has alignment
requirements. The Binding Refresh Advice option must meet the $2n$ requirement, and the
Binding Authorization Data option must meet the $8n + 2$ requirement.

When a correspondent sends a Binding Acknowledgment message, the message
must have a Binding Authorization Data option to protect the contents of the message.
The mechanism is the same as that for the creation of a Binding Authorization Data
option for a Binding Update message. On line 2444, the key data is computed by the
`mip6_calculate_kbm_from_index()` function.

Listing 5-127
———mip6_cncore.c
```
2460                MALLOC(ip6ma, struct ip6_mh_binding_ack *,
2461                        ip6ma_size, M_IP6OPT, M_NOWAIT);
2462                if (ip6ma == NULL)
2463                        return (ENOMEM);
2464                if (need_refresh) {
2465                        mopt_refresh = (struct ip6_mh_opt_refresh_advice *)
((u_int8_t *)ip6ma + ba_size);
2466                }
2467                if (need_auth)
2468                        mopt_auth = (struct ip6_mh_opt_auth_data *)
((u_int8_t *)ip6ma + ba_size + refresh_size);
2469
2470                bzero(ip6ma, ip6ma_size);
2471
2472                ip6ma->ip6mhba_proto = IPPROTO_NONE;
2473                ip6ma->ip6mhba_len = (ip6ma_size >> 3) - 1;
```

```
2474                ip6ma->ip6mhba_type = IP6_MH_TYPE_BACK;
2475                ip6ma->ip6mhba_status = status;
2476                ip6ma->ip6mhba_seqno = htons(seqno);
2477                ip6ma->ip6mhba_lifetime =
2478                        htons((u_int16_t)(lifetime >> 2));        /* units of 4 secs */
```
———mip6_cncore.c

— *Lines 2465 and 2468 are broken here for layout reasons. However, they are a single line of code.*

2460–2470 Memory is allocated and pointers to the mobility options are set.

2472–2478 Each field of the Binding Acknowledgment message is filled. The ip6mhba_proto
field must be IPPROTO_NONE since the message must be the last in the chain in the IPv6
packet. The length of the message is represented in units of 8 bytes and the lifetime in
units of 4 seconds.

Listing 5-128
———mip6_cncore.c
```
2480            /* padN */
2481            p = (u_int8_t *)ip6ma + sizeof(struct ip6_mh_binding_ack);
2482            if ((pad = ba_size - sizeof(struct ip6_mh_binding_ack)) >= 2) {
2483                    *p = IP6_MHOPT_PADN;
2484                    *(p + 1) = pad - 2;
2485            }
2486            if (refresh_size &&
2487                    ((p = (u_int8_t *)ip6ma + ba_size + sizeof(struct
    ip6_mh_opt_refresh_advice)),
2488                    (pad = refresh_size - sizeof(struct ip6_mh_opt_refresh_advice))
       >= 2)) {
2489                    *p = IP6_MHOPT_PADN;
2490                    *(p + 1) = pad - 2;
2491            }
2492            if (auth_size &&
2493                    ((p = (u_int8_t *)ip6ma + ba_size + refresh_size
    +IP6MOPT_AUTHDATA_SIZE),
2494                    (pad = auth_size - IP6MOPT_AUTHDATA_SIZE) >= 2)) {
2495                    *p = IP6_MHOPT_PADN;
2496                    *(p + 1) = pad - 2;
2497            }
2498            if (pad + (ip6ma_size - (ba_size + refresh_size + auth_size)) >= 2) {
2499                    *p = IP6_MHOPT_PADN;
2500                    *(p + 1) += ip6ma_size - (ba_size + refresh_size + auth_size)
                - 2;
2501            }
```
———mip6_cncore.c

— *Lines 2487, 2488, 2493, and 2500 are broken here for layout reasons. However, they are a single line of code.*

2481–2501 All the necessary padding data is added.

Listing 5-129
———mip6_cncore.c
```
2503            /* binding refresh advice option */
2504            if (need_refresh) {
2505                    mopt_refresh->ip6mora_type = IP6_MHOPT_BREFRESH;
2506                    mopt_refresh->ip6mora_len
2507                            = sizeof(struct ip6_mh_opt_refresh_advice) - 2;
2508                    SET_NETVAL_S(&mopt_refresh->ip6mora_interval, refresh >> 2);
2509            }
2510
2511            if (need_auth) {
2512                    /* authorization data processing. */
```

```
2513                       mopt_auth->ip6moad_type = IP6_MHOPT_BAUTH;
2514                       mopt_auth->ip6moad_len = IP6MOPT_AUTHDATA_SIZE - 2;
2515                       mip6_calculate_authenticator(key_bm, (caddr_t)(mopt_auth + 1),
2516                           dstcoa, src, (caddr_t)ip6ma, ip6ma_size,
2517                           ba_size + refresh_size + sizeof(struct
      ip6_mh_opt_auth_data),
2518                           IP6MOPT_AUTHDATA_SIZE - 2);
2519               }
```
_____mip6_cncore.c

— *Line 2517 is broken here for layout reasons. However, it is a single line of code.*

2504–2509 A Binding Refresh Advice option is created. The refresh interval is represented in units of 4 seconds.

2511–2519 A Binding Authorization Data option is created. The authentication data is computed by the `mip6_calculate_authenticator()` function with the key computed on line 2444.

Listing 5-130
_____mip6_cncore.c

```
2532
2533              /* calculate checksum. */
2534              ip6ma->ip6mhba_cksum = mip6_cksum(src, dst, ip6ma_size, IPPROTO_MH,
2535                  (char *)ip6ma);
2536
2537              *pktopt_mobility = (struct ip6_mh *)ip6ma;
2538
2539              return (0);
2540      }
```
_____mip6_cncore.c

2534–2539 Finally, the checksum value of the Binding Acknowledgment message is computed by the `mip6_cksum()` function. The created message is set to the `pktopt_mobility` parameter and returned to the caller.

Listing 5-131
_____mip6_cncore.c

```
645     int
646     mip6_rthdr_create(pktopt_rthdr, coa, opt)
647             struct ip6_rthdr **pktopt_rthdr;
648             struct in6_addr *coa;
649             struct ip6_pktopts *opt;
650     {
651             struct ip6_rthdr2 *rthdr2;
652             size_t len;
653
654             /*
655              * Mobile IPv6 uses type 2 routing header for route
656              * optimization. if the packet has a type 1 routing header
657              * already, we must add a type 2 routing header after the type
658              * 1 routing header.
659              */
660
661             len = sizeof(struct ip6_rthdr2) + sizeof(struct in6_addr);
662             MALLOC(rthdr2, struct ip6_rthdr2 *, len, M_IP6OPT, M_NOWAIT);
663             if (rthdr2 == NULL) {
664                     return (ENOMEM);
665             }
666             bzero(rthdr2, len);
```

```
667
668                /* rthdr2->ip6r2_nxt = will be filled later in ip6_output */
669                rthdr2->ip6r2_len = 2;
670                rthdr2->ip6r2_type = 2;
671                rthdr2->ip6r2_segleft = 1;
672                rthdr2->ip6r2_reserved = 0;
673                bcopy((caddr_t)coa, (caddr_t)(rthdr2 + 1), sizeof(struct in6_addr));
674                *pktopt_rthdr = (struct ip6_rthdr *)rthdr2;
....
678                return (0);
679        }
```
                                                                         ───mip6_cncore.c

645–649 The `mip6_rthdr_create()` function prepares a Type 2 Routing Header. The
`pktopt_rthdr` parameter stores the created Routing Header, while the `coa` parameter
is the care-of address of a mobile node which is set in the Routing Header. The `opt`
parameter is not used currently.

661–678 The length of the Type 2 Routing Header is fixed to 2. Memory to store the
`ip6_rthdr2{}` structure and the `in6_addr{}` structure is allocated. The type field,
`ip6r2_type`, is 2. The segment left field, `ip6r2_segleft`, is fixed to 1 since the header
only has one address. The care-of address is copied just after the header.

5.16.14   Nonce and Nodekey Management

A correspondent node must maintain the nonce and nodekey arrays to perform the return
routability procedure. Nonce and nodekey have associated lifetimes. The lifetime must be less
than 240 (`MIP6_MAX_NONCE_LIFE`) seconds as specified in [RFC3775]. The KAME implementation keeps the latest 10 nonces/nodekeys (`MIP6_NONCE_HISTORY`) as the `mip6_nonce`
and `mip6_nodekey` global variables. Figure 5-53 shows the structure of the nonce
array.

FIGURE 5-53

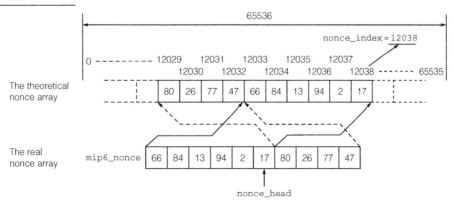

Nonce array management.

Listing 5-132

```
                                                            mip6_cncore.c
160    #define NONCE_UPDATE_PERIOD     (MIP6_MAX_NONCE_LIFE / MIP6_NONCE_HISTORY)
161    mip6_nonce_t mip6_nonce[MIP6_NONCE_HISTORY];
162    mip6_nodekey_t mip6_nodekey[MIP6_NONCE_HISTORY];        /* this is described
  as 'Kcn' in the spec */
163    u_int16_t nonce_index;              /* the idx value pointed by nonce_head */
164    mip6_nonce_t *nonce_head;           /* Current position of nonce on the array
  mip6_nonce */
                                                            mip6_cncore.c
```
— Lines 162 and 164 are broken here for layout reasons. However, they are a single line of code.

160–164 The `NONCE_UPDATE_PERIOD` macro represents the interval of nonce creation. The `mip6_nonce` and `mip6_nodekey` arrays hold this information. The `nonce_index` variable indicates the latest index of the nonce array. The `nonce_head` variable is a pointer to the latest nonce entry in the array.

The nonce management mechanism consists of the following functions.

- `mip6_update_nonce_nodekey()`
  A timer function to update the array.

- `mip6_create_nonce()`
  Generates a new nonce.

- `mip6_create_nodekey()`
  Generates a new nodekey.

- `mip6_get_nonce()`
  Retrieves a nonce from the array.

- `mip6_get_nodekey()`
  Retrieves a nodekey from the array.

Update Nonce and Nodekeys

The `mip6_update_nonce_nodekey()` function is called periodically to update the nonce and nodekey arrays.

Listing 5-133

```
                                                            mip6_cncore.c
1343    static void
1344    mip6_update_nonce_nodekey(ignored_arg)
1345            void    *ignored_arg;
1346    {
1347            int s;
1348
....
1352            s = splnet();
....
1355            callout_reset(&mip6_nonce_upd_ch, hz * NONCE_UPDATE_PERIOD,
1356                    mip6_update_nonce_nodekey, NULL);
....
1364            nonce_index++;
1365            if (++nonce_head >= mip6_nonce + MIP6_NONCE_HISTORY)
1366                    nonce_head = mip6_nonce;
1367
```

```
1368              mip6_create_nonce(nonce_head);
1369              mip6_create_nodekey(mip6_nodekey + (nonce_head - mip6_nonce));
1370
1371              splx(s);
1372       }
```
                                                                                      —————mip6_cncore.c

1343–1372 The interval is set to NONCE_UPDATE_PERIOD, which is 24 seconds in the KAME
implementation. The nonce_index variable is an unsigned 16-bit integer and is incremented by 1 every time a new nonce is generated. The nonce_head variable points to
the latest entry of the nonce array. The function calls the mip6_create_nonce() and
mip6_create_nodekey() functions before returning.

Generate Nonce and Nodekeys

The mip6_create_nonce() and mip6_create_nodekey() functions are called to
generate a new nonce and a nodekey.

Listing 5-134
                                                                                      —————mip6_cncore.c
```
1322    static void
1323    mip6_create_nonce(nonce)
1324            mip6_nonce_t *nonce;
1325    {
1326            int i;
1327
1328            for (i = 0; i < MIP6_NONCE_SIZE / sizeof(u_long); i++)
1329                    ((u_long *)nonce)[i] = random();
1330    }
1331
1332    static void
1333    mip6_create_nodekey(nodekey)
1334            mip6_nodekey_t *nodekey;
1335    {
1336            int i;
1337
1338            for (i = 0; i < MIP6_NODEKEY_SIZE / sizeof(u_long); i++)
1339                    ((u_long *)nodekey)[i] = random();
1340    }
```
                                                                                      —————mip6_cncore.c

1322–1330 The mip6_create_nonce() function takes one parameter to store the result.
In this function, the nonce is filled with a random value generated by the random()
function.

1332–1340 The mip6_create_nodekey() function is almost the same as the
mip6_create_nonce() function. It puts a random value into the pointer specified
in the parameter nodekey.

Retrieve Nonce and Nodekeys

The mip6_get_nonce() function returns the nonce value that is related to the specified index
value.

Listing 5-135
                                                                                      —————mip6_cncore.c
```
1374    int
1375    mip6_get_nonce(index, nonce)
```

```
1376              u_int16_t index;           /* nonce index */
1377              mip6_nonce_t *nonce;
1378     {
1379              int32_t offset;
1380
1381              offset = index - nonce_index;
1382              if (offset > 0) {
1383                      /* nonce_index was wrapped. */
1384                      offset = offset - 0xffff;
1385              }
1386
1387              if (offset <= -MIP6_NONCE_HISTORY) {
1388                      /* too old index. */
1389                      return (-1);
1390              }
1391
1392              if (nonce_head + offset < mip6_nonce)
1393                      offset = nonce_head - mip6_nonce - offset;
1394
1395              bcopy(nonce_head + offset, nonce, sizeof(mip6_nonce_t));
1396              return (0);
1397     }
```
                                                              ————————mip6_cncore.c

1374–1377 The `mip6_get_nonce()` function has two parameters: The `index` parameter is the index to the nonce being requested, and the `nonce` parameter is for the returned nonce value.

1381–1385 The KAME implementation keeps only 10 recent values. The offset from the head of the nonce array is calculated from the `index` parameter.

1387–1390 If the specified index is older than the last 10 nonce values, the nonce is invalid and not returned to the caller.

1392–1396 The nonce value specified by `index` is copied to the `nonce` variable.

Listing 5-136
                                                              ————————mip6_cncore.c

```
1399     int
1400     mip6_get_nodekey(index, nodekey)
1401              u_int16_t index;           /* nonce index */
1402              mip6_nodekey_t *nodekey;
1403     {
1404              int32_t offset;
1405              mip6_nodekey_t *nodekey_head;
1406
1407              offset = index - nonce_index;
1408              if (offset > 0) {
1409                      /* nonce_index was wrapped. */
1410                      offset = offset - 0xffff;
1411              }
1412
1413              if (offset <= -MIP6_NONCE_HISTORY) {
1414                      /* too old index. */
1415                      return (-1);
1416              }
1417
1418              if (nonce_head + offset < mip6_nonce)
1419                      offset = nonce_head - mip6_nonce - offset;
1420
1421              nodekey_head = mip6_nodekey + (nonce_head - mip6_nonce);
1422              bcopy(nodekey_head + offset, nodekey, sizeof(mip6_nodekey_t));
1423
```

```
1424              return (0);
1425      }
```
———————————————————————————————————————mip6_cncore.c

1399–1425 The code is almost the same as the `mip6_get_nonce()` function. The only difference is that the array referred to in this function is the nodekey array.

5.16.15   Receiving a Home Address Option

When a correspondent node communicates with a mobile node using route optimization, the correspondent node receives packets with a Home Address option. The option indicates the real source address of the mobile node; however, the correspondent node cannot believe it without verifying the validity of the address.

Destination Option Processing

The Home Address option is defined as a destination option. The option is processed in the `dest6_input()` function defined in `dest6.c` which is called as a part of extension header processing.

Listing 5-137
——dest6.c
```
127              /* search header for all options. */
128              for (optlen = 0; dstoptlen > 0; dstoptlen -= optlen, opt += optlen)
....
142      #ifdef MIP6
143              case IP6OPT_HOME_ADDRESS:
144                      /* HAO must appear only once */
145                      n = ip6_addaux(m);
146                      if (!n) {
147                              /* not enough core */
148                              goto bad;
149                      }
150                      ip6a = (struct ip6aux *) (n + 1);
151                      if ((ip6a->ip6a_flags & IP6A_HASEEN) != 0) {
152                              /* XXX icmp6 paramprob? */
153                              goto bad;
154                      }
```
——dest6.c

143–154 The loop defined on line 128 processes each destination option included in an incoming Destination Options header. The Home Address option can appear only once in an IPv6 packet. The `IP6A_HASEEN` flag is set in an auxiliary mbuf when the `dest6_input()` function processes a Home Address option. If the mbuf has the `IP6A_HASEEN` flag at this point, it means there is one more Home Address option in the packet.

Listing 5-138
——dest6.c
```
156                      haopt = (struct ip6_opt_home_address *)opt;
157                      optlen = haopt->ip6oh_len + 2;
158
159                      if (optlen != sizeof(*haopt)) {
....
```

```
161                         goto bad;
162                     }
163
164                     /* XXX check header ordering */
165
166                     bcopy(haopt->ip6oh_addr, &home,
167                         sizeof(struct in6_addr));
168
169                     bcopy(&home, &ip6a->ip6a_coa, sizeof(ip6a->ip6a_coa));
170                     ip6a->ip6a_flags |= IP6A_HASEEN;
```
                                                                        dest6.c

156–170 The length of the Home Address option must be the size of the
ip6_opt_home_address{} structure. If the length is correct, the address information
is copied to the home variable. The address is also copied to the auxiliary mbuf of the
input packet as the ip6a_coa variable. At this point, the source address of the IPv6
packet is the care-of address of a mobile node, and the address in the Home Address
option is the home address of the mobile node. These addresses will be swapped
when the validity of the addresses is verified.

Listing 5-139

                                                                        dest6.c
```
174                             /* check whether this HAO is 'verified'. */
175                             if ((mbc = mip6_bc_list_find_withphaddr(
176                                 &mip6_bc_list, &home)) != NULL) {
177                                 /*
178                                  * we have a corresponding binding
179                                  * cache entry for the home address
180                                  * includes in this HAO.
181                                  */
182                                 if (IN6_ARE_ADDR_EQUAL(&mbc->mbc_pcoa,
183                                     &ip6->ip6_src))
184                                         verified = 1;
185                             }
186                         /*
187                          * we have neither a corresponding binding
188                          * cache nor ESP header. we have no clue to
189                          * beleive this HAO is a correct one.
190                          */
191                         /*
192                          * Currently, no valid sub-options are
193                          * defined for use in a Home Address option.
194                          */
195
196                             break;
197     #endif /* MIP6 */
198                 default:                    /* unknown option */
....
204                             break;
205             }
206         }
```
                                                                        dest6.c

175–185 The pair of care-of and home addresses of the mobile node must be registered as a
binding cache entry. The existence of a cache for the same pair of addresses indicates that
the mobile node and the correspondent node have already performed the return routability
procedure, or the home registration procedure if the node is acting as a home agent of
the mobile node, and previously successfully exchanged a Binding Update message. In
this case, the home address stored in the Home Address option is valid.

187–190 Otherwise, the address has to be verified in other ways. If the packet is a Binding Update message for initial registration, there is no binding cache entry related to the home address. These packets are verified as follows:

- If the packet is for home registration, the packet must be secured by ESP. If the Home Address option contains an incorrect home address, the ESP processing will fail.

- If the packet is for registration to a correspondent node, the packet must contain a Binding Authorization Data option. In this case, the `mip6_ip6mu_input()` function will verify the validity of the option (see Section 5.16.5).

Listing 5-140

dest6.c

```
207
208     #ifdef MIP6
209             /* if haopt is non-NULL, we are sure we have seen fresh HA option */
210             if (verified)
211                     if (dest6_swap_hao(ip6, ip6a, haopt) < 0)
212                             goto bad;
213     #endif /* MIP6 */
214
215             *offp = off;
216             return (dstopts->ip6d_nxt);
217
218       bad:
219             m_freem(m);
220             return (IPPROTO_DONE);
221       }
```

dest6.c

210–212 The source address (which is the care-of address of the mobile node) and the address stored in the Home Address option (which is the home address of the mobile node) are swapped.

Note that if there is no existing binding cache entry for the incoming Binding Update message, the address swapping is done in the `ip6_input()` function (Listing 5-142). The detailed discussion will be done in Listings 5-143 to 5-147.

Swap Home Address and Source Address

The `dest6_swap_hao()` function swaps the source address of a received IPv6 header and the address stored in the Home Address option.

Listing 5-141

dest6.c

```
224     static int
225     dest6_swap_hao(ip6, ip6a, haopt)
226             struct ip6_hdr *ip6;
227             struct ip6aux *ip6a;
228             struct ip6_opt_home_address *haopt;
229     {
230
231             if ((ip6a->ip6a_flags & (IP6A_HASEEN | IP6A_SWAP)) != IP6A_HASEEN)
232                     return (EINVAL);
233
      ....
```

```
238                 bcopy(&ip6->ip6_src, &ip6a->ip6a_coa, sizeof(ip6a->ip6a_coa));
239                 bcopy(haopt->ip6oh_addr, &ip6->ip6_src, sizeof(ip6->ip6_src));
240                 bcopy(&ip6a->ip6a_coa, haopt->ip6oh_addr, sizeof(haopt->ip6oh_addr));
    ....
246                 ip6a->ip6a_flags |= IP6A_SWAP;
247
248                 return (0);
249         }
```
                                                                              ───dest6.c

224–228 The `dest6_swap_hao()` function has three parameters: The `ip6` parameter is a
pointer to the incoming IPv6 packet, the `ip6a` parameter is a pointer to the auxiliary
mbuf of the incoming packet, and the `haopt` parameter is a pointer to the Home Address
option.

231–232 If the addresses are already swapped, that is, the `IP6A_SWAP` flag is set, an error is
returned.

238–246 The care-of address and the home address are swapped. The `IP6A_SWAP` flag is set
to indicate that the addresses are swapped.

To handle the case that the Home Address option and the source address of the incoming
IPv6 header are not swapped in the destination option processing, the `ip6_input()` function
has to deal with swapping the addresses. The following code is quoted from `ip6_input()`.

Listing 5-142
                                                                          ───ip6_input.c

```
1092              while (nxt != IPPROTO_DONE) {
    ....
1136    #ifdef MIP6
1137                  if (dest6_mip6_hao(m, off, nxt) < 0)
1138                      goto bad;
    ....
1154    #endif /* MIP6 */
1155                  nxt = (*inet6sw[ip6_protox[nxt]].pr_input)(&m, &off, nxt);
1156              }
```
                                                                          ───ip6_input.c

1092–1156 The loop processes all extension headers inserted in an IPv6 packet. The
`dest6_mip6_hao()` function checks the next extension header to be processed, and
swaps the home and care-of addresses if the next header is an ESP, an AH, or a Binding
Update message. If the addresses are correct, the ESP or the AH processing succeeds,
otherwise, an error will occur while processing the ESP or AH. If the packet does not
have either ESP or AH but has a Binding Update message, the validation will be performed during the Binding Update message input processing (see Section 5.16.5). Any
bogus Binding Update messages in which addresses are forged can be safely dropped.

Swap Home Address and Source Address in Unverified Packet

The `dest6_mip6_hao()` function is called before processing every header chained in a
received IPv6 packet, and swaps the source address of the IPv6 packet and the address in
the Home Address option using the `dest6_swap_hao()` function when necessary.

Listing 5-143

_____dest6.c
```
282     int
283     dest6_mip6_hao(m, mhoff, nxt)
284             struct mbuf *m;
285             int mhoff, nxt;
286     {
287             struct ip6_hdr *ip6;
288             struct ip6aux *ip6a;
289             struct ip6_opt ip6o;
290             struct m_tag *n;
291             struct in6_addr home;
292             struct ip6_opt_home_address haopt;
293             struct ip6_mh mh;
294             int newoff, off, proto, swap;
295
296             /* XXX should care about destopt1 and destopt2.  in destopt2,
297                hao and src must be swapped. */
298             if ((nxt == IPPROTO_HOPOPTS) || (nxt == IPPROTO_DSTOPTS)) {
299                     return (0);
300             }
301             n = ip6_findaux(m);
302             if (!n)
303                     return (0);
304             ip6a = (struct ip6aux *) (n + 1);
305
306             if ((ip6a->ip6a_flags & (IP6A_HASEEN | IP6A_SWAP)) != IP6A_HASEEN)
307                     return (0);
```
_____dest6.c

282–285 The `dest6_mip6_hao()` function has three parameters: The `m` parameter is a pointer to the mbuf which contains the incoming packet, the `mhoff` parameter is the offset to the header to be processed, and the `nxt` parameter is the value of protocol number of the header to be processed.

298–306 There is no need to swap addresses before processing a Hop-by-Hop Options Header or a Destination Options Header, and there is nothing to do if the addresses have already been swapped.

Listing 5-144

_____dest6.c
```
309             ip6 = mtod(m, struct ip6_hdr *);
310             /* find home address */
311             off = 0;
312             proto = IPPROTO_IPV6;
313             while (1) {
314                     int nxt;
315                     newoff = ip6_nexthdr(m, off, proto, &nxt);
316                     if (newoff < 0 || newoff < off)
317                             return (0);      /* XXX */
318                     off = newoff;
319                     proto = nxt;
320                     if (proto == IPPROTO_DSTOPTS)
321                             break;
322             }
323             ip6o.ip6o_type = IP6OPT_PADN;
324             ip6o.ip6o_len = 0;
325             while (1) {
326                     newoff = dest6_nextopt(m, off, &ip6o);
327                     if (newoff < 0)
328                             return (0);      /* XXX */
329                     off = newoff;
```

```
330                         if (ip6o.ip6o_type == IP6OPT_HOME_ADDRESS)
331                             break;
332                     }
333                     m_copydata(m, off, sizeof(struct ip6_opt_home_address),
334                         (caddr_t)&haopt);
```
———dest6.c

312–333 A Home Address option is searched for in the incoming Destination Options header.
If there is a Home Address option, the contents are copied to the `haopt` variable.

Note that it is impossible to keep the pointer to the Home Address option in the
auxiliary area during the destination option processing at the `dest6_input()` function for later use, because such a pointer may become invalid when some part of the
packet is relocated by the `m_pullup()` function during processing other extension
headers.

Listing 5-145
———dest6.c

```
336                 swap = 0;
337                 if (nxt == IPPROTO_AH || nxt == IPPROTO_ESP)
338                     swap = 1;
339                 if (nxt == IPPROTO_MH) {
340                     m_copydata(m, mhoff, sizeof(mh), (caddr_t)&mh);
341                     if (mh.ip6mh_type == IP6_MH_TYPE_BU)
342                         swap = 1;
343                     else if (mh.ip6mh_type == IP6_MH_TYPE_HOTI ||
344                         mh.ip6mh_type == IP6_MH_TYPE_COTI)
345                         return (-1);
346                     else if (mh.ip6mh_type > IP6_MH_TYPE_MAX)
347                         swap = 1;          /* must be sent BE with
    UNRECOGNIZED_TYPE */
348                 }
```
———dest6.c

— Line 347 is broken here for layout reasons. However, it is a single line of code.

337–348 The addresses are swapped if the next header is either an ESP or an AH. The addresses
must also be swapped when the next header is an MH. There are three types of MH
messages which a correspondent node may receive: the Binding Update, Home Test Init
and Care-of Test Init messages. The addresses will not be swapped in the Home Test
Init and the Care-of Test Init cases and the code explicitly excludes these cases on lines
343–345. However, these conditions should not happen since these types of message must
not contain a Home Address option.

Listing 5-146
———dest6.c

```
350                 home = *(struct in6_addr *)haopt.ip6oh_addr;
351                 /*
352                  * reject invalid home-addresses
353                  */
354                 if (IN6_IS_ADDR_MULTICAST(&home) ||
355                     IN6_IS_ADDR_LINKLOCAL(&home) ||
356                     IN6_IS_ADDR_V4MAPPED(&home) ||
357                     IN6_IS_ADDR_UNSPECIFIED(&home) ||
358                     IN6_IS_ADDR_LOOPBACK(&home)) {
    ....
```

```
360                          if (!(nxt == IPPROTO_MH && mh.ip6mh_type == IP6_MH_TYPE_BU)) {
361                                  /* BE is sent only when the received packet is
362                                      not BU */
363                                  (void)mobility6_send_be(&ip6->ip6_dst, &ip6->ip6_src,
364                                      IP6_MH_BES_UNKNOWN_HAO, &home);
365                          }
366                          return (-1);
367                  }
```
———dest6.c

354–366 There are some kinds of addresses which cannot be used as a home address. These
prohibited addresses are explicitly excluded. A Binding Error message has to be sent when
an invalid type of home address is received, except in one case. An error message is not
sent if the incoming packet is a Binding Update message.[1]

Listing 5-147
———dest6.c

```
369                  if (swap) {
370                          int error;
371                          error = dest6_swap_hao(ip6, ip6a, &haopt);
372                          if (error)
373                                  return (error);
374                          m_copyback(m, off, sizeof(struct ip6_opt_home_address),
375                              (caddr_t)&haopt);                    /* XXX */
376                          return (0);
377                  }
378
379                  /* reject */
....
381                  mobility6_send_be(&ip6->ip6_dst, &ip6->ip6_src,
382                      IP6_MH_BES_UNKNOWN_HAO, &home);
383
384                  return (-1);
385          }
386      #endif /* MIP6 */
```
———dest6.c

369–384 The addresses are swapped. If the node receives a packet that has a Home Address
option while it does not have a binding cache entry related to the home address included
in the option, the code on lines 381–384 generates a Binding Error message to notify the
sender that the received packet has an unverified Home Address option.

Listing 5-148
———dest6.c

```
251      static int
252      dest6_nextopt(m, off, ip6o)
253              struct mbuf *m;
254              int off;
255              struct ip6_opt *ip6o;
256      {
257              u_int8_t type;
258
259              if (ip6o->ip6o_type != IP6OPT_PAD1)
260                      off += 2 + ip6o->ip6o_len;
261              else
```

---

1. The exception seems to have no meaning, perhaps due to misreading of the RFC.

```
262                        off += 1;
263              if (m->m_pkthdr.len < off + 1)
264                        return -1;
265              m_copydata(m, off, sizeof(type), (caddr_t)&type);
266
267              switch (type) {
268              case IP6OPT_PAD1:
269                        ip6o->ip6o_type = type;
270                        ip6o->ip6o_len = 0;
271                        return off;
272              default:
273                        if (m->m_pkthdr.len < off + 2)
274                                  return -1;
275                        m_copydata(m, off, sizeof(ip6o), (caddr_t)ip6o);
276                        if (m->m_pkthdr.len < off + 2 + ip6o->ip6o_len)
277                                  return -1;
278                        return off;
279              }
280     }
```
_____ dest6.c

251–280 The dest6_nextopt() function locates the next option stored in a Destination
Options Header beginning from the offset specified by the second parameter off, and
returns the offset of the next option. This function is used by the dest6_mip6_hao()
function to find a Home Address option.

5.16.16   Sending Packets to Mobile Nodes via Tunnel

When a node is acting as a home agent of a mobile node, it must intercept all packets sent
to the home address of the mobile node and tunnel them to the care-of address of the mobile
node using an IPv6 in IPv6 tunnel. The home agent will receive packets by using the proxy
Neighbor Discovery mechanism. Received packets are sent to the ip6_input() function, and
are passed to the ip6_forward() function since the destination address of these packets is
not the address of the home agent. In the ip6_forward() function, the packets are tunneled
to the mobile node based on the binding cache information.

Listing 5-149
_____ ip6_forward.c

```
137     void
138     ip6_forward(m, srcrt)
139              struct mbuf *m;
140              int srcrt;
141     {
....
403     #if defined(MIP6) && defined(MIP6_HOME_AGENT)
404              {
405                        /*
406                         * intercept and tunnel packets for home addresses
407                         * which we are acting as a home agent for.
408                         */
409                        struct mip6_bc *mbc;
410
411                        mbc = mip6_bc_list_find_withphaddr(&mip6_bc_list,
412                            &ip6->ip6_dst);
413                        if (mbc &&
414                            (mbc->mbc_flags & IP6MU_HOME) &&
415                            (mbc->mbc_encap != NULL)) {
```
_____ ip6_forward.c

411–415 When forwarding a packet, a home agent checks the binding cache entries to determine whether it has a matching cache entry for the forwarded packet. The following two conditions are checked before forwarding:

1. An entry exists and it is for home registration, that is, the `IP6MU_HOME` flag is set.

2. The IPv6 in IPv6 tunnel of the entry is active, that is, the `mbc_encap` variable is not NULL.

If the above two conditions are met, then the home agent tries to forward the packet to the mobile node associated with the binding cache entry using the tunnel.

Listing 5-150
```
                                                                    ip6_forward.c
416                     if (IN6_IS_ADDR_LINKLOCAL(&mbc->mbc_phaddr)
417                         || IN6_IS_ADDR_SITELOCAL(&mbc->mbc_phaddr)
418                         )
419                     {
420                             ip6stat.ip6s_cantforward++;
421                             if (mcopy) {
422                                     icmp6_error(mcopy, ICMP6_DST_UNREACH,
423                                         ICMP6_DST_UNREACH_ADDR, 0);
424                             }
425                             m_freem(m);
426                             return;
427                     }
428
429                     if (m->m_pkthdr.len > IPV6_MMTU) {
430                             u_long mtu = IPV6_MMTU;
....
432                             if (mcopy) {
433                                     icmp6_error(mcopy,
434                                         ICMP6_PACKET_TOO_BIG, 0, mtu);
435                             }
436                             m_freem(m);
437                             return;
438                     }
                                                                    ip6_forward.c
```

416–438 Some validation checks are done. If the home address of the mobile node is not in the proper scope, the home agent sends an ICMPv6 error message with a type of `ICMP6_DST_UNREACH`. This should not happen since the home agent checks the validity of the home address when accepting the home registration message for the home address.

The MTU size of the tunnel interface between a mobile node and a home agent is hard coded to the minimum MTU size. If the size of a forwarded packet exceeds the minimum MTU value, the home agent sends an ICMPv6 error with `ICMP6_PACKET_TOO_BIG` to perform the Path MTU Discovery procedure (see Section 4.3 of *IPv6 Core Protocols Implementation*).

Listing 5-151
```
                                                                    ip6_forward.c
440                     /*
441                      * if we have a binding cache entry for the
442                      * ip6_dst, we are acting as a home agent for
443                      * that node.  before sending a packet as a
```

```
444                            * tunneled packet, we must make sure that
445                            * encaptab is ready.  if dad is enabled and
446                            * not completed yet, encaptab will be NULL.
447                            */
448                           if (mip6_tunnel_output(&m, mbc) != 0) {
....
450                           }
451                           if (mcopy)
452                                   m_freem(mcopy);
453                           return;
454                   }
455               mbc = mip6_bc_list_find_withphaddr(&mip6_bc_list,
456                   &ip6->ip6_src);
457               if (mbc &&
458                   (mbc->mbc_flags & IP6MU_HOME) &&
459                   (mbc->mbc_encap != NULL)) {
460                       tunnel_out = 1;
461               }
462           }
463   #endif /* MIP6 && MIP6_HOME_AGENT */
```
── ip6_forward.c

448–453 The `mip6_tunnel_output()` function is called if the home address is valid.

455–461 When the home agent forwards a packet, the `tunnel_out` variable is set to true. This variable will be examined when sending an ICMPv6 redirect message later.

Listing 5-152
── ip6_forward.c
```
659               if (rt->rt_ifp == m->m_pkthdr.rcvif && !srcrt && ip6_sendredirects &&
660   #ifdef IPSEC
661               !ipsecrt &&
662   #endif
663   #ifdef MIP6
664               !tunnel_out &&
665   #endif
666               (rt->rt_flags & (RTF_DYNAMIC|RTF_MODIFIED)) == 0) {
```
(Redirect processing)
── ip6_forward.c

659–666 During forwarding, a packet may be re-sent to the same network interface. In this case, a router usually sends an ICMPv6 Redirect message to notify the sender that there is a better route. In the case of Mobile IPv6, this condition may happen even during normal operation. For example, a home agent will re-send a packet to the same interface if the home agent has only one network interface which is attached to the home network. Because of this, the home agent does not send a redirect message if `tunnel_out` is set to true.

Sending Packets in IPv6 in IPv6 Format

The `mip6_tunnel_output()` function encapsulates the packet addressed to a mobile node and passes it to the `ip6_output()` function.

Listing 5-153
── mip6_hacore.c
```
926   int
927   mip6_tunnel_output(mp, mbc)
928           struct mbuf **mp;    /* the original ipv6 packet */
```

```
929                 struct mip6_bc *mbc; /* the bc entry for the dst of the pkt */
930       {
931                 const struct encaptab *ep = mbc->mbc_encap;
932                 struct mbuf *m = *mp;
933                 struct in6_addr *encap_src = &mbc->mbc_addr;
934                 struct in6_addr *encap_dst = &mbc->mbc_pcoa;
935                 struct ip6_hdr *ip6;
936                 int len;
937
938                 if (ep->af != AF_INET6) {
....
942                         return (EFAULT);
943                 }
944
945                 /* Recursion problems? */
946
947                 if (IN6_IS_ADDR_UNSPECIFIED(encap_src)) {
....
951                         return (EFAULT);
952                 }
```
———mip6_hacore.c

926–929 The `mip6_tunnel_output()` function has two parameters: The `mp` parameter is a
double pointer to the mbuf in which the tunneled packet is stored, and the `mbc` parameter
is a pointer to the related binding cache entry.

938–952 The tunneling function only supports IPv6 in IPv6 tunnels. If the tunnel, represented
by the `encaptab{}` structure, does not support the IPv6 protocol family, forwarding
cannot be done. If the tunnel source address is not specified, the packet cannot be sent
through the tunnel.

Listing 5-154
———mip6_hacore.c
```
954               len = m->m_pkthdr.len; /* payload length */
955
956               if (m->m_len < sizeof(*ip6)) {
957                       m = m_pullup(m, sizeof(*ip6));
958                       if (!m) {
....
962                               return (ENOBUFS);
963                       }
964               }
965               ip6 = mtod(m, struct ip6_hdr *);
```
———mip6_hacore.c

956–965 Before accessing the internal member variables of the IPv6 header to be tunneled,
the contiguity of the header memory is verified. If the header is not contiguous, the
`m_pullup()` function is called to rearrange it. An error is returned if getting the header
into contiguous memory fails.

Listing 5-155
———mip6_hacore.c
```
967               /* prepend new, outer ipv6 header */
968               M_PREPEND(m, sizeof(struct ip6_hdr), M_DONTWAIT);
969               if (m && m->m_len < sizeof(struct ip6_hdr))
```

```
970                       m = m_pullup(m, sizeof(struct ip6_hdr));
971                   if (m == NULL) {
....
975                       return (ENOBUFS);
976                   }
```

967–976 The M_PREPEND() macro is called to prepare an extra IPv6 header for tunneling.

Listing 5-156

```
978                   /* fill the outer header */
979                   ip6 = mtod(m, struct ip6_hdr *);
980                   ip6->ip6_flow = 0;
981                   ip6->ip6_vfc &= ~IPV6_VERSION_MASK;
982                   ip6->ip6_vfc |= IPV6_VERSION;
....
986                   ip6->ip6_nxt = IPPROTO_IPV6;
987                   ip6->ip6_hlim = ip6_defhlim;
988                   ip6->ip6_src = *encap_src;
989
990                   /* bidirectional configured tunnel mode */
991                   if (!IN6_IS_ADDR_UNSPECIFIED(encap_dst))
992                       ip6->ip6_dst = *encap_dst;
993                   else {
....
997                       m_freem(m);
998                       return (ENETUNREACH);
999                   }
....
1004                  /*
1005                   * force fragmentation to minimum MTU, to avoid path MTU discovery.
1006                   * it is too painful to ask for resend of inner packet, to achieve
1007                   * path MTU discovery for encapsulated packets.
1008                   */
1009                  return (ip6_output(m, 0, 0, IPV6_MINMTU, 0, NULL
....
1011                                      , NULL
....
1013                                      ));
....
1021       }
```

978–1021 The fields of the outer IPv6 header are filled and the IPv6 in IPv6 packet is sent
via the ip6_output() function. The source and the destination addresses of the outer
header are taken from the tunnel information stored in the encaptab{} structure of the
binding cache entry.

5.16.17   Recovery of Temporarily Disabled Proxy Entry

When a home agent sends a Binding Acknowledgment message with an error status to a
mobile node which is attached to its home network, the home agent needs to disable the proxy
Neighbor Discovery entry for the mobile node temporarily; otherwise, the Binding Acknowledgment message sent to the mobile node will be caught by the home agent because of the proxy

Neighbor Discovery mechanism. The following two functions restore the proxy Neighbor Discovery entry of a particular binding cache entry which is temporarily disabled.

1. `mip6_restore_proxynd_entry()`
   Called from the `nd6_output()` function when the neighbor discovery entry for the home address of a mobile node is removed to restore the proxy entry.

2. `mip6_temp_deleted_proxy()`
   Finds a binding cache entry related to the IPv6 packet passed as its argument.

Listing 5-157

```
                                                           ─────mip6_hacore.c
624     struct mip6_bc *
625     mip6_restore_proxynd_entry(m)
626             struct mbuf *m;
627     {
628             struct mip6_bc *mbc;
629
630             mbc = mip6_temp_deleted_proxy(m);
631             if (mbc)
632                     mip6_bc_proxy_control(&mbc->mbc_phaddr, &mbc->mbc_addr,
   RTM_ADD);
633
634             return (mbc);
635     }
                                                           ─────mip6_hacore.c
```
— Line 632 is broken here for layout reasons. However, it is a single line of code.

624–635 The `mip6_restore_proxynd_entry()` function recovers the proxy Neighbor Discovery entry which is temporarily disabled in the `mip6_bc_send_ba()` function. The function takes one parameter which is a pointer to the mbuf which contains the IPv6 packet sent while proxy Neighbor Discovery is disabled. We use the `mip6_bc_proxy_control()` function to restore the proxy Neighbor Discovery entry. The binding cache entry which the `mip6_bc_proxy_control()` function requires can be obtained by calling the `mip6_temp_deleted_proxy()` function.

Listing 5-158

```
                                                           ─────mip6_hacore.c
637     struct mip6_bc *
638     mip6_temp_deleted_proxy(m)
639             struct mbuf *m;
640     {
641             struct ip6_hdr *ip6;
642             struct m_tag *mtag;
643             struct mip6_bc *mbc = NULL;
644             struct ip6aux *ip6a;
645
646             ip6 = mtod(m, struct ip6_hdr *);
647
648             mtag = ip6_findaux(m);
649             if (!mtag)
650                     return (NULL);
651             ip6a = (struct ip6aux *) (mtag + 1);
652
653             if (ip6a->ip6a_flags & IP6A_TEMP_PROXYND_DEL) {
654                     mbc = mip6_bc_list_find_withphaddr(&mip6_bc_list,
655                             &ip6->ip6_dst);
656                     ip6a->ip6a_flags &= ~IP6A_TEMP_PROXYND_DEL;
```

```
657                }
658
659                return (mbc);
660        }
```
_____mip6_hacore.c

637–660 The `mip6_temp_deleted_proxy()` function takes one parameter which is a
pointer to the IPv6 packet. This function checks the auxiliary mbuf specified as the parameter m and checks to see if the `IP6A_TEMP_PROXYND_DEL` flag is set. The flag indicates
that the proxy entry was temporarily disabled and needs to be restored. If the flag is set,
the `mip6_bc_list_find_withphaddr()` function is called to get the binding cache
entry related to the packet, and the binding cache entry is returned.

5.16.18   Receiving ICMPv6 Error Messages

A correspondent node may receive an ICMPv6 Destination Unreachable message when a mobile
node moves. Usually, a mobile node sends a Binding Update message when it moves; however,
the message may be lost and the correspondent node may not know the new care-of address of
the mobile node. In this case, the correspondent node sends packets to the old care-of address
of the mobile node and will receive an ICMPv6 error message. ICMPv6 messages are not reliable
and the node should not rely on them. As the binding information to the destination mobile
node has a lifetime even if the correspondent node does not receive either a Binding Update
message or an ICMPv6 error message, the information will be deleted shortly. ICMPv6 is used
as a supportive mechanism to reduce the detection time.

   ICMPv6 messages are processed in the `mip6_icmp6_input()` function, which is called
from the `icmp6_input()` function. (For more information on basic ICMPv6 message processing, see Chapter 4 of *IPv6 Core Protocols Implementation.*)

Listing 5-159
_____mip6_icmp6.c

```
129     int
130     mip6_icmp6_input(m, off, icmp6len)
131            struct mbuf *m;
132            int off;
133            int icmp6len;
134     {
135            struct ip6_hdr *ip6;
136            struct icmp6_hdr *icmp6;
137            struct mip6_bc *mbc;
138            struct in6_addr laddr, paddr;
```
_____mip6_icmp6.c

129–133 The `mip6_icmp6_input()` function has three parameters: The m parameter is a
pointer to the mbuf which contains the incoming ICMPv6 packet, the `off` parameter is an
offset from the head of the packet to the head of the ICMPv6 header, and the `icmp6len`
parameter is the length of the ICMPv6 message.

Listing 5-160
_____mip6_icmp6.c

```
147            /* header pullup/down is already done in icmp6_input(). */
148            ip6 = mtod(m, struct ip6_hdr *);
149            icmp6 = (struct icmp6_hdr *)((caddr_t)ip6 + off);
```

```
150
151                     switch (icmp6->icmp6_type) {
152                     case ICMP6_DST_UNREACH:
153                             /*
154                              * the contacting mobile node might move to somewhere.
155                              * in current code, we remove the corresponding
156                              * binding cache entry immediately.  should we be more
157                              * patient?
158                              */
159                             IP6_EXTHDR_CHECK(m, off, icmp6len, EINVAL);
160                             mip6_icmp6_find_addr(m, off, icmp6len, &laddr, &paddr);
161                             mbc = mip6_bc_list_find_withphaddr(&mip6_bc_list, &paddr);
162                             if (mbc && (mbc->mbc_flags & IP6MU_HOME) == 0) {
....
166                                     mip6_bc_list_remove(&mip6_bc_list, mbc);
167                             }
168                             break;
169
....    [code for a mobile node]
269                     }
270
271                     return (0);
272             }
```
                                                                    ————mip6_icmp6.c

152–168 If the type value is `ICMP6_DST_UNREACH`, the `mip6_icmp6_find_addr()` function is called to extract the source and destination addresses of the original packet which
caused the error. If a correspondent node has a binding cache entry for the address pair
extracted by function `mip6_icmp6_find_addr()`, the `mip6_bc_list_remove()` is
called to remove the entry since the entry is not valid anymore.

　　If the node is acting as a home agent, the node may have home registration entries.
Home registration entries are not removed even if ICMPv6 error messages are received.
A mobile node will continue to send a Binding Update message for its home registration
entry until the registration succeeds. The home agent has to keep the entry.

Find Source and Destination Addresses of the Original Packet

The `mip6_icmp6_find_addr()` function extracts the source and destination addresses of
the original packet stored in the ICMPv6 payload.

Listing 5-161
                                                                    ————mip6_icmp6.c

```
274     static void
275     mip6_icmp6_find_addr(m, icmp6off, icmp6len, local, peer)
276             struct mbuf *m;
277             int icmp6off;
278             int icmp6len; /* Total icmp6 payload length */
279             struct in6_addr *local; /* Local home address */
280             struct in6_addr *peer; /* Peer home address */
281     {
282             caddr_t icmp6;
283             struct ip6_opt_home_address *haddr_opt; /* Home Address option */
284             struct ip6_hdr *ip6;                    /* IPv6 header */
285             struct ip6_ext *ehdr;                   /* Extension header */
286             struct sockaddr_in6 local_sa, peer_sa;
287             struct ip6_rthdr2 *rh;                  /* Routing header */
288             u_int8_t *eopt, nxt, optlen;
```

```
289                    int off, elen, eoff;
290                    int rlen, addr_off;
```
———mip6_icmp6.c

274–280 The `mip6_icmp6_find_addr()` function has five parameters: The `m`, `icmp6off` and `icmp6len` parameters are the same as those of the `mip6_icmp6_input()` function. The `local` and `peer` parameters are the pointers to the memory which are used to store the source and destination addresses extracted from the ICMPv6 message.

Listing 5-162
———mip6_icmp6.c
```
292                    icmp6 = mtod(m, caddr_t) + icmp6off;
293                    off = sizeof(struct icmp6_hdr);
294                    ip6 = (struct ip6_hdr *)(icmp6 + off);
295                    nxt = ip6->ip6_nxt;
296                    off += sizeof(struct ip6_hdr);
297
298                    *local = ip6->ip6_src;
299                    *peer = ip6->ip6_dst;
```
———mip6_icmp6.c

292–296 An ICMPv6 message contains the original packet which caused the error immediately after the ICMPv6 header. The `ip6` variable points to the address of the original packet.

298–299 `local` and `peer` are initialized to the source and the destination addresses of the original IPv6 packet. These values may be updated later in this function if the original packet contains a Home Address option or a Routing Header.

Listing 5-163
———mip6_icmp6.c
```
301            /* Search original IPv6 header extensions for Routing Header type 0
302               and for home address option (if I'm a mobile node). */
303            while ((off + 2) < icmp6len) {
304                    if (nxt == IPPROTO_DSTOPTS) {
305                            ehdr = (struct ip6_ext *)(icmp6 + off);
306                            elen = (ehdr->ip6e_len + 1) << 3;
307                            eoff = 2;
308                            eopt = icmp6 + off + eoff;
309                            while ((eoff + 2) < elen) {
310                                    if (*eopt == IP6OPT_PAD1) {
311                                            eoff += 1;
312                                            eopt += 1;
313                                            continue;
314                                    }
315                                    if (*eopt == IP6OPT_HOME_ADDRESS) {
316                                            optlen = *(eopt + 1) + 2;
317                                            if ((off + eoff + optlen) > icmp6len)
318                                                    break;
319
320                                            haddr_opt = (struct
       ip6_opt_home_address *)eopt;
321                                            bcopy((caddr_t)haddr_opt->ip6oh_addr,
322                                                local, sizeof(struct in6_addr));
323                                            eoff += optlen;
324                                            eopt += optlen;
325                                            continue;
326                                    }
327                                    eoff += *(eopt + 1) + 2;
```

```
328                             eopt += *(eopt + 1) + 2;
329                         }
330                         nxt = ehdr->ip6e_nxt;
331                         off += (ehdr->ip6e_len + 1) << 3;
332                         continue;
333                     }
```
——mip6_icmp6.c

— Line 320 is broken here for layout reasons. However, it is a single line of code.

303 Extension headers of the original IPv6 packet which are contained in the incoming ICMPv6 message are examined.

304–328 If the original packet has a Destination Options Header, we need to check to see if there is a Home Address option. If a Home Address option exists, the home address is copied to the `local` variable as the source address of the original packet. All other options are skipped. The PAD1 option is skipped on lines 310–314, and other options are skipped on lines 327–328.

330–332 The `nxt` variable is set to the protocol number of the next extension header of the Destination Options Header, and the `off` variable is set to the offset of the next extension header.

Listing 5-164
——mip6_icmp6.c
```
334             if (nxt == IPPROTO_ROUTING) {
335                     rh = (struct ip6_rthdr2 *)(icmp6 + off);
336                     rlen = (rh->ip6r2_len + 1) << 3;
337                     if ((off + rlen) > icmp6len) break;
338                     if ((rh->ip6r2_type != 2) || (rh->ip6r2_len % 2)) {
339                             nxt = rh->ip6r2_nxt;
340                             off += (rh->ip6r2_len + 1) << 3;
341                             continue;
342                     }
343
344                     addr_off = 8 + (((rh->ip6r2_len / 2) - 1) << 3);
345                     bcopy((caddr_t)(icmp6 + off + addr_off), peer,
346                         sizeof(struct in6_addr));
347
348                     nxt = rh->ip6r2_nxt;
349                     off += (rh->ip6r2_len + 1) << 3;
350                     continue;
351             }
```
——mip6_icmp6.c

334–351 If the original packet has a Type 2 Routing Header, the address contained in the routing header is copied to the `peer` variable as the destination address of the original packet. Note that we do not deal with Type 0 Routing Headers, since the Type 0 Routing Header has nothing to do with Mobile IPv6.

The `nxt` and `off` variables are adjusted to the protocol value and the offset of the next extension header respectively.

Listing 5-165
——mip6_icmp6.c
```
352             if (nxt == IPPROTO_HOPOPTS) {
353                     ehdr = (struct ip6_ext *)(icmp6 + off);
354                     nxt = ehdr->ip6e_nxt;
```

```
355                         off += (ehdr->ip6e_len + 1) << 3;
356                         continue;
357                 }
358
359                 /* Only look at the unfragmentable part.  Other headers
360                    may be present but they are of no interest. */
361                 break;
362         }
```
                                                                    ——mip6_icmp6.c

352–357 Hop-by-Hop Options Headers are ignored since they contain no data related to
Mobile IPv6.

359–361 Only the Destination Options Header and (Type 2) Routing Header are checked. The
rest of the packet contains no data related to the source and destination addresses of the
original packet.

Listing 5-166
                                                                    ——mip6_icmp6.c
```
364                 local_sa.sin6_len = sizeof(local_sa);
365                 local_sa.sin6_family = AF_INET6;
366                 local_sa.sin6_addr = *local;
367                 /* XXX */
368                 in6_addr2zoneid(m->m_pkthdr.rcvif, &local_sa.sin6_addr,
369                     &local_sa.sin6_scope_id);
370                 in6_embedscope(local, &local_sa);
371
372                 peer_sa.sin6_len = sizeof(peer_sa);
373                 peer_sa.sin6_family = AF_INET6;
374                 peer_sa.sin6_addr = *peer;
375                 /* XXX */
376                 in6_addr2zoneid(m->m_pkthdr.rcvif, &peer_sa.sin6_addr,
377                     &peer_sa.sin6_scope_id);
378                 in6_embedscope(peer, &peer_sa);
379         }
```
                                                                    ——mip6_icmp6.c

364–378 The scope identifier of the address has to be recovered if the source or destination
address is a scoped address. The scope identifier is recovered from the information about
the interface on which the ICMPv6 packet arrived. Unfortunately, it is not always possible
to know the original scope identifier, since an error packet may come from a different
interface than the one on which the original packet arrived. The above mechanism is the
best effort to recover the information.

5.16.19   Home Agent List Management

The home agent list is managed by a user space daemon program called **had** on the home
agent side. The **had** program listens for Router Advertisement messages (Section 5.11.20) and
constructs the list of home agents on its home network. The program also responds to Dynamic
Home Agent Address Discovery request messages (Section 5.11.24) and Mobile Prefix Solicitation messages (Section 5.11.26) sent from a mobile node, and replies with Dynamic Home
Agent Address Discovery response messages (Section 5.11.25) and Mobile Prefix Advertisement
messages (Section 5.11.27) respectively.

In this section, we discuss the implementation of the **had** program briefly.

Home Agent Information Structures

The structures to keep home agent information are defined in `halist.h`.

Listing 5-167

halist.h

```
121     struct hagent_gaddr {
122             struct hagent_gaddr      *hagent_next_gaddr, *hagent_prev_gaddr;
123             struct hagent_gaddr      *hagent_next_expire, *hagent_prev_expire;
124             struct in6_addr          hagent_gaddr;
125             u_int8_t                 hagent_prefixlen;
126             struct hagent_flags {
127                     u_char           onlink : 1;
128                     u_char           autonomous : 1;
129                     u_char           router : 1;
130             } hagent_flags;
131             u_int32_t                hagent_vltime;
132             u_int32_t                hagent_pltime;
133             long                     hagent_expire;
134             long                     hagent_preferred;
135     };
```

halist.h

121–135 The `hagent_gaddr{}` structure represents the global address of a home agent. The `hagent_next_gaddr` and the `hagent_prev_gaddr` variables point to a list of `hagent_gaddr{}` structures in one `hagent_entry{}` structure described later. The `hagent_next_expire` and the `hagent_prev_expire` variables point to a list of `hagent_gaddr{}` structures ordered by lifetime. The list constructed by `hagent_next_expire` and `hagent_prev_expire` includes all `hagent_gaddr{}` instances kept in a node. The `hagent_gaddr` and the `hagent_prefixlen` variables are address and prefix length. The `hagent_flags` variable is a copy of the flags which are received in Router Advertisement messages. The `hagent_vltime` and `hagent_expire` variables are the valid lifetime and the time when the valid lifetime expires. The `hagent_pltime` and the `hagent_preferred` variables are the preferred lifetime and the time when the preferred lifetime expires respectively.

Listing 5-168

halist.h

```
138     struct hagent_entry {
139             struct hagent_entry      *hagent_next_expire, *hagent_prev_expire,
140                                      *hagent_next_pref, *hagent_prev_pref;
141             struct in6_addr          hagent_addr;
142             u_int16_t                hagent_pref;
143             u_int16_t                hagent_lifetime;
144             long                     hagent_expire;
145             struct hagent_gaddr      hagent_galist;
146     };
```

halist.h

138–146 The `hagent_entry{}` structure represents a home agent. The `hagent_next_expire` and the `hagent_prev_expire` variables construct a list of `hagent_entry{}` structures ordered by lifetime. The `hagent_next_pref` and `hagent_prev_pref` variables construct another list of `hagent_entry{}` structures ordered by the preference value. The `hagent_addr` variable is a link-local address of a home agent. The `hagent_pref` and the `hagent_lifetime` variables are the preference value and the lifetime respectively. The `hagent_expire` variable is the time when the lifetime expires. The `hagent_galist` variable is a pointer to the `hagent_gaddr{}` structure which contains a list of global addresses of this home agent.

Listing 5-169

halist.h

```
151     struct hagent_ifinfo {
152             struct hagent_entry        halist_pref;
153             int                        ifindex;
154             char                       ifname[IF_NAMESIZE];
155             struct ifaddrs             *linklocal;
156             struct hagent_ifa_pair     *haif_gavec;
157             int                        gavec_used;
158             int                        gavec_size;
159     };
160
161     #define GAVEC_INIT_SIZE            (16)
```

halist.h

151–159 The `hagent_ifinfo{}` structure represents a network interface on a home agent. The `halist_pref` variable is a pointer to the list of `hagent_entry{}` structures which contain home agent information on the interface. The `ifindex` and the `ifname` variables are the interface index and name, respectively. The `linklocal` variable is a pointer to the `ifaddrs{}` structure which contains a link-local address for the interface. The `haif_gavec` variable is a pointer to the array of `hagent_ifa_pair{}` structures which contains a pair of a global address and an anycast address of the interface. The `gavec_used` and the `gavec_size` variables are the number of entries used in the `haif_gavec{}` array and the number of allocated entries of the `haif_gavec{}` array.

Listing 5-170

halist.h

```
164     struct hagent_ifa_pair {
165             struct ifaddrs             *global;
166             struct ifaddrs             *anycast;
167     };
```

halist.h

164–167 The `hagent_ifa_pair{}` structure keeps a set of a global address and an anycast address.

Figures 5-54 and 5-55 show the relationship of the above structures.

Updating Home Agent Information

When a home agent receives a Router Advertisement message, the **had** program updates its internal information by extracting data related to the home agent management from the message.

FIGURE 5-54

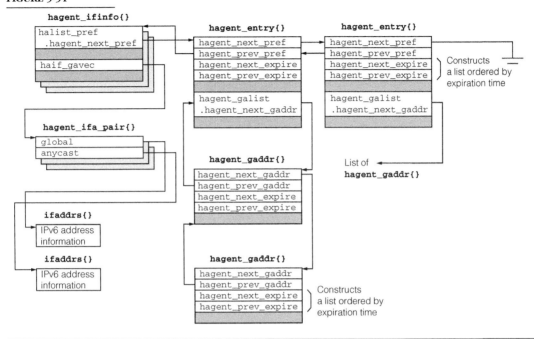

The relationship of the `hagent_ifinfo{}` and related structures.

FIGURE 5-55

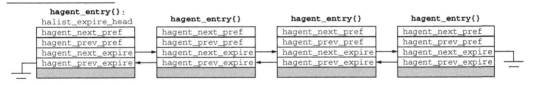

`hagent_next_pref` and `hagent_prev_pref` constructs a list of hagent_entry{} which is ordered by the preference value per hagent_ifinfo{}

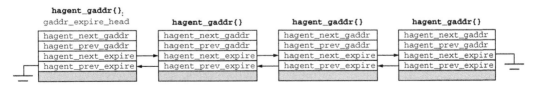

`hagent_next_gaddr` and `hagent_prev_gaddr` constructs a list of hagent_gaddr{} per hagent_entry{}

The global list of the `hagent_entry{}` and the `hagent_gaddr{}` structures.

Listing 5-171

```
                                                                  haadisc.c
607        static void
608        ra_input(len, ra, pinfo, from)
609            int len;
610            struct nd_router_advert *ra;
611            struct in6_pktinfo *pinfo;
612            struct sockaddr_in6 *from;
613        {
                                                                  haadisc.c
```

607–612 The `ra_input()` function is called when the **had** program receives a Router Advertisement message. The `len` parameter is the length of the message; the `ra` parameter is a pointer of the `nd_router_advert{}` structure which points to the head of the message; the `pinfo` parameter is a pointer to the `in6_pktinfo{}` structure which contains an interface index and hoplimit information; and the `from` parameter is the source address of the message.

Listing 5-172

```
                                                                  haadisc.c
623        haif = haif_find(pinfo->ipi6_ifindex);
624        if (haif == NULL) {
....
630            goto done;
631        }
                                                                  haadisc.c
```

623–631 The `haif_find()` function finds an instance of the `hagent_ifinfo{}` structure with the specified interface index value from the list of `hagent_ifinfo{}`. If there is no `hagent_ifinfo{}` structure which has the specified index value, the packet is dropped.

Listing 5-173

```
                                                                  haadisc.c
634        bzero(&ndopts, sizeof(union nd_opts));
635        nd6_option_init(ra + 1, len - sizeof(struct nd_router_advert), &ndopts);
636        if (nd6_options(&ndopts) < 0) {
....
638            goto done;
639        }
                                                                  haadisc.c
```

635–639 The `nd6_option_init()` and the `nd6_options()` functions do the same tasks as the functions which have the same names in the kernel. The contents of the options of the incoming Router Advertisement message are extracted into the `ndopts` variable.

Listing 5-174

```
                                                                  haadisc.c
641        /* Is this RA from some home agent or not? */
642        if (0 == (ra->nd_ra_flags_reserved & ND_RA_FLAG_HOME_AGENT)) {
```

```
643             /* IMPLID:MIP6HA#7 */
644             /*
645              * delete home agent list entry if it exists,
646              * because this router is not a home agent.
647              */
648             hal_delete(haif, &(from->sin6_addr));
649             goto done;
650         }
```
——haadisc.c

641–650 Every home agent must set the home agent flag, the ND_RA_FLAG_HOME_AGENT
flag, when sending a Router Advertisement message. If the received message does not
have the flag, and there is an entry for the router, the home agent removes the entry from
the list by calling the hal_delete() function since the node is not acting as a home
agent anymore. The hal_delete() function removes the hagent_entry{} instance
specified by its second parameter from the hagent_ifinfo{} structure specified by the
first parameter.

Listing 5-175

——haadisc.c
```
652             /* determine HA lifetime and preference */
653             /* IMPLID:MIP6HA#9 */
654             ha_lifetime = ntohs(ra->nd_ra_router_lifetime);
655             if (ndopts.nd_opts_hai) {
656                 ha_lifetime = ntohs(ndopts.nd_opts_hai->nd_opt_hai_lifetime);
657                 /* IMPLID:MIP6HA#10 */
658                 ha_pref = ntohs(ndopts.nd_opts_hai->nd_opt_hai_preference);
659             }
660
661             /* update and get home agent list entry */
662             halp = hal_update(pinfo->ipi6_ifindex, &from->sin6_addr, ha_lifetime,
    ha_pref);
663
664             if (!halp) {
665                 /*
666                  * no home agent list entry (deleted or cannot create)
667                  */
668                 goto done;
669             }
```
——haadisc.c
— *Line 662 is broken here for layout reasons. However, it is a single line of code.*

654–659 The lifetime of a home agent is considered the same as the lifetime of a router,
nd_ra_router_lifetime, unless the lifetime as a home agent is explicitly specified by the Home Agent Information option, nd_opt_hai_lifetime. The preference is set to 0 unless explicitly specified by the Home Agent Information option,
nd_opt_hai_preference.

662–669 The hal_update() function updates the home agent information of the specified
address as its second parameter.

Listing 5-176

——haadisc.c
```
671             /* proceee prefix information option in RA
672              * in order to accumlate home agent global address
673              * information in home agent list
674              */
675             if (ndopts.nd_opts_pi) {
676                 /*
```

```
677                    * parse prefix information option and
678                    * get global address(es) in it.
679                    */
680                   struct nd_opt_hdr *pt;
681                   struct nd_opt_prefix_info *pi;
682                   struct hagent_gaddr *lastp;
683                   /* tempolary global address list */
684                   struct hagent_gaddr newgaddrs;
```
.... (validation of prefix information option)
```
737                           if ((pi->nd_opt_pi_flags_reserved & ND_OPT_PI_FLAG_ROUTER) != 0) {
738                                   /* IMPLID:MIP6HA#14 */
739                                   lastp = hal_gaddr_add(halp, lastp, pi);
740                           }
741                   }
742                   /* replace home agent global address list to new one */
743                   if (newgaddrs.hagent_next_gaddr == NULL) goto done;
744                   hal_gaddr_last(halp, newgaddrs.hagent_next_gaddr);
     ....
750           }
751   done:
752   }
```
                                                                                    __haadisc.c

675–741 A Prefix Information option may include a global address for the home agent, in which case the option has the ND_OPT_PI_FLAG_ROUTER flag. The hal_gaddr_add() function collects the global addresses from the incoming Router Advertisement message and makes a list of addresses in the newgaddrs variable which is an instance of the hagent_gaddr{} structure. If the incoming message contains global addresses, the global address list of the home agent who sent the message is updated by the hal_gaddr_last() function.

Updating the hagent_entry{} Structure

The hagent_entry{} structure is updated when a home agent receives a Router Advertisement message. The update code is implemented as the hal_update() function.

Listing 5-177
                                                                                    __halist.c
```
131   struct hagent_entry *
132   hal_update(ifindex, ha_addr, ha_lifetime, ha_pref)
133       int ifindex;
134       struct in6_addr *ha_addr;
135       u_int16_t ha_lifetime;
136       u_int16_t ha_pref;
137   {
```
                                                                                    __halist.c

131–136 The hal_update() function updates the hagent_entry{} structure identified by the interface index specified by the first parameter and the address specified by the second parameter. The ha_lifetime and ha_pref parameters are the new values of the lifetime and preference of the home agent.

Listing 5-178
                                                                                    __halist.c
```
148       /* lookup home agent i/f info from ifindex */
149       haif = haif_find(ifindex);
150
151       if (!haif) {
```

```
      ....
153              goto err;
154         }
```
── halist.c

149–154 If a home agent does not have a `hagent_ifinfo{}` instance whose interface index is the same as the specified value as the `ifindex` parameter, it ignores the message.

Listing 5-179
── halist.c
```
156         /* lookup home agent entry from home agent list of specified i/f */
157         halp = hal_find(haif, ha_addr);
158
159         /* if HA entry exists, remove it from list first */
160         if (halp) {
      ....
164             /* remove from preference list */
165             if (halp->hagent_next_pref) {
166                 halp->hagent_next_pref->hagent_prev_pref
167                     = halp->hagent_prev_pref;
168             }
169             if (halp->hagent_prev_pref) {
170                 halp->hagent_prev_pref->hagent_next_pref
171                     = halp->hagent_next_pref;
172             }
173             halp->hagent_next_pref = halp->hagent_prev_pref = NULL;
174
175             /* remove from expire list */
176             if (halp->hagent_next_expire) {
177                 halp->hagent_next_expire->hagent_prev_expire
178                     = halp->hagent_prev_expire;
179             }
180             if (halp->hagent_prev_expire) {
181                 halp->hagent_prev_expire->hagent_next_expire
182                     = halp->hagent_next_expire;
183             }
184             halp->hagent_next_expire = halp->hagent_prev_expire = NULL;
185         }
```
── halist.c

157–185 If a home agent has a `hagent_entry{}` instance which matches the specified parameters, it first removes the entry from the list. The `hagent_entry{}` structure has two kinds of lists, one is a list ordered by the preference value, the other is ordered by lifetime. The entry is removed from both lists and the pointers which construct the lists are initialized with a NULL pointer.

Listing 5-180
── halist.c
```
187         if (ha_lifetime > 0) {
188             /* create list entry if not already exist */
189             if (! halp) {
190
191                 /* IMPLID:MIP6HA#13 */
192                 halp = malloc(sizeof (struct hagent_entry));
193                 if (halp) {
194                     bzero(halp, sizeof (struct hagent_entry));
195                     bcopy(ha_addr, &halp->hagent_addr, sizeof (struct in6_addr));
      ....
197                 }
198                 else {
```

```
        ....
200                              goto err;
201                    }
202              }
```

187–202 If `ha_lifetime` is a positive value and there is no existing `hagent_entry{}`
instance to update, the home agent creates a new `hagent_entry{}` instance.

Listing 5-181

```
204              /* IMPLID:MIP6HA#12 */
205              /* update parameters */
206              halp->hagent_pref = ha_pref;
207              halp->hagent_lifetime = ha_lifetime;
208              halp->hagent_expire = now + ha_lifetime;
```

206–208 Each element of the `hagent_entry{}` structure is updated with the specified
lifetime and preference values as parameters.

Listing 5-182

```
210              /* insert entry to preference list */
211              for (prevp = curp = haif->halist_pref.hagent_next_pref;
212                   curp; curp = curp->hagent_next_pref) {
213                  if (halp->hagent_pref > curp->hagent_pref) {
214                      halp->hagent_prev_pref = curp->hagent_prev_pref;
215                      halp->hagent_next_pref = curp;
216                      if (curp->hagent_prev_pref) {
217                          curp->hagent_prev_pref->hagent_next_pref = halp;
218                      }
219                      curp->hagent_prev_pref = halp;

221                      break;
222                  }
223                  prevp = curp;
224              }
225              if (! curp) {
226                  if (prevp) {
227                      /* append tail */
228                      prevp->hagent_next_pref = halp;
229                      halp->hagent_prev_pref = prevp;
230                  }
231                  else {
232                      /* insert head */
233                      haif->halist_pref.hagent_next_pref = halp;
234                      halp->hagent_prev_pref = &haif->halist_pref;
235                  }
236              }
```

211–223 The updated entry or the newly created entry is inserted into the list whose entries
are ordered by the preference value. Each pointer to the entry in the list is set to the `curp`
variable and compared to the updated/created entry, while `prevp` points to the previous
entry of the entry specified by the `curp`.

225–235 If `curp` is a NULL pointer and `prevp` has a valid pointer to the entry in the list, the updated/created entry will be inserted at the tail of the list. If `curp` and `prevp` are both NULL pointers, then it means the list is empty. The updated/new entry is inserted at the head of the list.

Listing 5-183

——*halist.c*

```
238                 /* insert entry to expire list */
239                 for (prevp = curp = halist_expire_head.hagent_next_expire;
240                     curp; curp = curp->hagent_next_expire) {
241                     if (curp->hagent_expire > halp->hagent_expire) {
242                         halp->hagent_prev_expire = curp->hagent_prev_expire;
243                         halp->hagent_next_expire = curp;
244                         if (curp->hagent_prev_expire) {
245                             curp->hagent_prev_expire->hagent_next_expire = halp;
246                         }
247                         curp->hagent_prev_expire = halp;
248
249                         break;
250                     }
251                     prevp = curp;
252                 }
253                 if (! curp) {
254                     if (prevp) {
255                         /* append tail */
256                         prevp->hagent_next_expire = halp;
257                         halp->hagent_prev_expire = prevp;
258                     }
259                     else {
260                         /* insert head */
261                         halist_expire_head.hagent_next_expire = halp;
262                         halp->hagent_prev_expire = &halist_expire_head;
263                     }
264                 }
265
266             }
```

——*halist.c*

238–266 The entry is also inserted into the other list ordered by the lifetime value.

Listing 5-184

——*halist.c*

```
267         else if (halp) { /* must be deleted */
268             /* IMPLID:MIP6HA#11 */
269             /* clear global address list */
270             hal_gaddr_clean(halp);
271             free(halp);
272             halp = NULL;
....
275         }
276
277     done:
....
284         return halp;
285     err:
....
288         halp = NULL;
289         goto done;
290     }
```

——*halist.c*

267–272 If the specified lifetime is 0, the entry will be removed. The `hal_gaddr_clean()` function removes all `hagent_gaddr{}` instances pointed to by the `hagent_galist` variable, which contains the list of global addresses of the home agent.

Sending a Dynamic Home Agent Address Discovery Reply Message

When the **had** program receives a Dynamic Home Agent Address Discovery request message from a mobile node, it replies with a Dynamic Home Agent Address Discovery reply message with home agent addresses of the home network of the mobile node as described in Section 5.7. Receiving and Replying to these messages is implemented in the `haad_request_input()` and the `haad_reply_output()` functions.

Listing 5-185

haadisc.c

```
900     static void
901     haad_request_input(len, haad_req, pi, src, type)
902         int len;
903         struct mip6_dhaad_req *haad_req;
904         struct in6_pktinfo *pi;
905         struct sockaddr_in6 *src;
906         int type;
907     {
908         u_int16_t msgid;
909         struct hagent_ifinfo *haif;
910         int ifga_index = -1;
```

haadisc.c

900–906 The `haad_request_input()` function is called when a mobile node receives a Dynamic Home Agent Address Discovery request message. The `len` parameter is the length of the message; the `haad_req` parameter is a pointer to the head of the incoming message; the `pi` parameter is a pointer to the `in6_pktinfo{}` structure which contains the destination address of the message; and the `type` parameter is the type number of the ICMPv6 message, which should be `MIP6_HA_DISCOVERY_REQUEST` in this case.

Listing 5-186

haadisc.c

```
912         msgid = haad_req->mip6_dhreq_id;
913
914         /* determine home link by global address */
915         haif = haif_findwithanycast(&pi->ipi6_addr, &ifga_index);
916
917         if (! haif) {
....
919             goto err;
920         }
921
922         /* send home agent address discovery response message */
923         haad_reply_output(msgid, src,
....
927                           &(pi->ipi6_addr),          /* anycast addr. */
....
929                           haif, type, ifga_index);
930     err:
931     }
```

haadisc.c

912 The identifier, `mip6_dhreq_id`, of the message which is included in the received Dynamic Home Agent Address Discovery request message must be copied to the reply message.

915–920 The destination address of the request message must be one of the addresses of the interface which is acting as the home network. If there is no `hagent_ifinfo{}` instance which has the address used as the destination address of the received Dynamic Home Agent Address Discovery request message, the home agent ignores the message. The `ifga_index` variable is passed to the `haif_findwithanycast()` function and updated in the function. The index will point to the entry in the `haif_gavec{}` array of `hagent_ifinfo{}` structures which has the address specified by the first parameter of the `haif_findwithanycast()` function.

923–929 The `haad_reply_output()` function sends a Dynamic Home Agent Address Discovery reply message.

Listing 5-187

```
                                                              haadisc.c
936     static void
937     haad_reply_output(msgid, coaddr, reqaddr, haif, type, ifga_index)
938         u_int16_t msgid;
939         struct sockaddr_in6 *coaddr;
940         struct in6_addr *reqaddr;
941         struct hagent_ifinfo *haif;
942         int type, ifga_index;
943     {
944         struct cmsghdr *cm;
945         struct in6_pktinfo *pi;
946         struct mip6_dhaad_rep *hap;
947         struct in6_addr *hagent_addr;
948         struct in6_addr src = in6addr_any;
949         int len, nhaa, count;
950         u_int8_t buf[IPV6_MMTU];
                                                              haadisc.c
```

936–942 The `haad_reply_output()` function has six parameters: The `msgid` parameter is an identifier which is included in the Dynamic Home Agent Address Discovery request message; the `coaddr` and `reqaddr` parameters are the care-of address of a mobile node and the destination address of the incoming request message, respectively; the `haif` parameter is a pointer to the `hagent_ifinfo{}` structure which indicates the incoming interface; the `type` parameter is the type number of the incoming ICMPv6 message, which is `MIP6_HA_DISCOVERY_REQUEST` in this case; and the `ifga_index` parameter is an index number to the `haif_gavec{}` array which contains the pair of global and anycast addresses of the home agent.

Listing 5-188

```
                                                              haadisc.c
959         if (haif->haif_gavec[ifga_index].global != NULL)
960             src = ((struct sockaddr_in6 *)(haif->
    haif_gavec[ifga_index].global->ifa_addr))->sin6_addr;
961
962         /* create ICMPv6 message */
963         hap = (struct mip6_dhaad_rep *)buf;
```

```
964         bzero(hap, sizeof (struct mip6_dhaad_rep));
965         hap->mip6_dhrep_type = MIP6_HA_DISCOVERY_REPLY;
966         hap->mip6_dhrep_code = 0;
967         hap->mip6_dhrep_cksum = 0;
968         hap->mip6_dhrep_id = msgid;
969         len = sizeof (struct mip6_dhaad_rep);
```
——haadisc.c

— *Line 960 is broken here for layout reasons. However, it is a single line of code.*

959–960 The global address that corresponds to the anycast address used as the destination
address of the incoming request message is used as a source address of the reply message.

963–969 All ICMPv6 message fields are filled. The identifier, `mip6_dhrep_id`, must be copied
from the identifier in the request message.

Listing 5-189
——haadisc.c
```
970         hagent_addr = (struct in6_addr *)(hap + 1);
971         count = (IPV6_MMTU - sizeof (struct ip6_hdr) -
972                 sizeof (struct mip6_dhaad_rep)) / sizeof (struct in6_addr);
973         /* pick home agent global addresses for this home address */
974          if ((nhaa = hal_pick(reqaddr, hagent_addr, &src, haif, count)) < 0) {
    ....
976            goto err;
977          }
978         if (IN6_IS_ADDR_UNSPECIFIED(&src))
979            goto err;
980         len += nhaa * sizeof (struct in6_addr);
```
——haadisc.c

970–977 The `hal_pick()` function constructs the payload part of a Dynamic Home Agent
Address Discovery reply message.

978–979 The `src` variable is set in the `hal_pick()` function to one of the global home agent
addresses which received the request message. If no source address is selected, the home
agent aborts replying to the message.

Listing 5-190
——haadisc.c
```
982         sndmhdr.msg_name = (caddr_t)coaddr;
983         sndmhdr.msg_namelen = coaddr->sin6_len;
984         sndmhdr.msg_iov[0].iov_base = (caddr_t)buf;
985         sndmhdr.msg_iov[0].iov_len = len;
986
987         cm = CMSG_FIRSTHDR(&sndmhdr);
988         /* specify source address */
989         cm->cmsg_level = IPPROTO_IPV6;
990         cm->cmsg_type = IPV6_PKTINFO;
991         cm->cmsg_len = CMSG_LEN(sizeof(struct in6_pktinfo));
992         pi = (struct in6_pktinfo *)CMSG_DATA(cm);
993         pi->ipi6_addr = src;
994         pi->ipi6_ifindex = 0; /* determined with routing table */
995
996         if ((len = sendmsg(sock, &sndmhdr, 0)) < 0) {
    ....
998            goto err;
999          }
```

```
1000    err:
1001    }
```
———haadisc.c

982–985 A destination address of the reply message must be the source address of the request
message. The `coaddr` variable is set as the destination address.

993–999 The created Dynamic Home Agent Address Discovery reply message is sent by the
`sendmsg()` system call from the source address selected by the `hal_pick()` function.

Constructing a Payload

The `hal_pick()` function constructs the payload of a Dynamic Home Agent Address Discovery
reply message.

Listing 5-191

———halist.c
```
803    int
804    hal_pick(req_addr, hagent_addrs, src_addr, haif, count)
805        struct in6_addr *req_addr;
806        struct in6_addr *hagent_addrs;
807        struct in6_addr *src_addr;
808        struct hagent_ifinfo *haif;
809        int count;
810    {
811        int naddr;
812        struct hagent_entry *hap, *selfhalp = NULL;
813        struct hagent_gaddr *ha_gaddr;
814        int found_src = 0;
```
———halist.c

803–809 The `hal_pick()` function has five parameters: The `req_addr` parameter is the
destination address of the request message; the `hagent_addrs` parameter is a pointer
to the memory space where the constructed payload is stored; the `src_addr` parameter
is the source address of the request message; the `haif` parameter is a pointer to the
`hagent_ifinfo{}` instance to which the request message is delivered; and the `count`
parameter is the maximum number of addresses to be listed in the payload.

Listing 5-192

———halist.c
```
816        /* shuffle home agent entries with same preference */
817        hal_shuffle(haif);
818
819        /* lookup self entry from home agent list */
820        if (haif->linklocal)
821            selfhalp = hal_find(haif, &((struct sockaddr_in6 *)(haif->linklocal->
   ifa_addr))->sin6_addr);
822
823        /* list all home agents in the home agent list of this interface */
824        for (naddr = 0, hap = haif->halist_pref.hagent_next_pref;
825            hap && naddr < count; hap = hap->hagent_next_pref) {
826            for (ha_gaddr = hap->hagent_galist.hagent_next_gaddr;
827                (ha_gaddr != NULL) && (naddr < count);
828                ha_gaddr = ha_gaddr->hagent_next_gaddr) {
829                *hagent_addrs = ha_gaddr->hagent_gaddr;
830                if (hap == selfhalp && found_src == 0) {
831                    *src_addr = *hagent_addrs;
```

```
832                      found_src++;
833                  }
834              hagent_addrs ++;
835              naddr ++;
836          }
837      }
838
839      return naddr;
840  }
```
———halist.c

— Line 821 is broken here for layout reasons. However, it is a single line of code.

817 The `hal_shuffle()` function randomly reorders the `hagent_entries` instances which have the same preference value. A mobile node will use the first address in the home agent address list. If there are multiple home agents in the home network, shuffling the addresses randomly will balance the load between home agents when there are many mobile nodes in the home network.

820–837 The global addresses of home agents, listed in the `halist_pref` variable of the `hagent_ifinfo{}` structure, are listed in the order of preference value. During the process, the `src_addr` variable is set to the global address of the home agent which received the request message.

5.16.20   Prefix List Management

When a home agent receives a Mobile Prefix Solicitation message, the node needs to reply with a Mobile Prefix Advertisement message as described in Section 5.8. The prefix information of a home network can be taken from the home agent list information which is maintained as a part of Dynamic Home Agent Address Discovery mechanism.

The current implementation only supports solicited request messages. The **had** program does not send an unsolicited Mobile Prefix Advertisement message.

5.16.21   Sending a Mobile Prefix Advertisement Message

The `mpi_solicit_input()` function is called when the **had** program receives a Mobile Prefix Solicitation message.

Listing 5-193
———mpa.c
```
122      void
123      mpi_solicit_input(pi, sin6_hoa, mps)
124          struct in6_pktinfo *pi;
125          struct sockaddr_in6 *sin6_hoa;
126          struct mip6_prefix_solicit *mps;
127      {
128          int ifga_index = -1;
129          struct in6_addr ha_addr;
130          struct hagent_ifinfo *haif;
131          struct in6_addr src;
132          int error;
```
———mpa.c

122–126 The `mpi_solicit_input()` function has three parameters: The `pi` parameter is a pointer to the `in6_pktinfo{}` instance which contains the destination address of the request message; the `sin6_hoa` parameter is the home address of the mobile node which sent the request message; and the `mps` parameter is a pointer to the head of the message.

Listing 5-194

_____mpa.c
```
137          ha_addr = pi->ipi6_addr;
138          /* determine a home link by the global address */
139          haif = haif_findwithunicast(&pi->ipi6_addr, &ifga_index);
140
141          if (!haif) {
....
143              goto err;
144          }
....
151          src = ha_addr;
152          mpi_advert_output(sin6_hoa, &src, haif, mps->mip6_ps_id);
153      err:
154      }
```
_____mpa.c

137–144 A Mobile Prefix Solicitation message is sent to the global unicast address of the home agent of a mobile node. The `haif_findwithunicast()` function finds the `hagent_ininfo{}` instance which has the specified unicast global address.

152 The `mpi_advert_output()` function sends a Mobile Prefix Advertisement message.

Listing 5-195

_____mpa.c
```
159      void
160      mpi_advert_output(dst_sa, src, haif, id)
161          struct sockaddr_in6 *dst_sa;          /* home addr of destination MN */
162          struct in6_addr *src;
163          struct hagent_ifinfo *haif;
164          u_int16_t id;
165      {
166          struct cmsghdr *cm;
167          struct nd_opt_prefix_info *prefix_info;
168          u_int8_t buf[IPV6_MMTU];
169          struct mip6_prefix_advert *map;
170          int len;
171          int count;
172          int npi;
173          struct in6_pktinfo *pi;
```
_____mpa.c

159–164 The `mpi_advert_output()` function has four parameters. The `dst_sa` parameter is the home address of the mobile node which sent the request message. The `src` parameter is the global unicast address of the home agent. The `haif` parameter is a pointer to the `hagent_ifinfo{}` instance. This parameter represents the network interface on which the request message arrived. The `id` parameter is the identifier which is contained in the request message.

Listing 5-196

_____mpa.c
```
175          /* create ICMPv6 message */
176          map = (struct mip6_prefix_advert *)buf;
177          bzero(map, sizeof (struct mip6_prefix_advert));
```

```
178              map->mip6_pa_type = MIP6_PREFIX_ADVERT;
179              map->mip6_pa_code = 0;
180
181              len = sizeof(struct mip6_prefix_advert);
182              prefix_info = (struct nd_opt_prefix_info *)&map[1];
183              /* count number of prefix informations --
   to make assurance (not in spec.) */
184              count = (IPV6_MMTU - sizeof (struct ip6_hdr) - /* XXX: should include the
   size of routing header*/
185                                    sizeof (struct mip6_prefix_advert)) / sizeof
   (struct nd_opt_prefix_info);
186
187              /* Pick home agent prefixes */
188              /* -- search by dest. address instead of Home Address */
189              if ((npi = pi_pick(src, prefix_info, haif, count)) < 0) {
....
191                  goto err;
192              }
```
―――*mpa.c*

― Lines 183, 184 and 185 are broken here for layout reasons. However, they are a single line of code.

176–179 Memory for the reply message is allocated and ICMPv6 header fields are filled in.

182–192 The `pi_pick()` function constructs the payload of the reply message and returns the number of prefix information entries which have been put into the payload. On lines 184–185, the maximum number of prefix information entries to be included is calculated. As the comment says, the stack should take into account the size of the Type 2 Routing Header, since a Mobile Prefix Advertisement message always has a Type 2 Routing header; however, the current code does not count the size at this moment. This is may be a bug in the code.

Listing 5-197
―――*mpa.c*
```
194              if(!npi)
195                  return;
196
197              len += npi * sizeof (struct nd_opt_prefix_info);
198
199              map->mip6_pa_cksum = 0;
200              map->mip6_pa_id = id;
201              sndmhdr.msg_name = (caddr_t)dst_sa;
202              sndmhdr.msg_namelen = dst_sa->sin6_len;
203              sndmhdr.msg_iov[0].iov_base = (caddr_t)buf;
204              sndmhdr.msg_iov[0].iov_len = len;
```
―――*mpa.c*

200–201 The identifier field, `mip6_pa_id`, must be copied from the identifier field of the corresponding solicitation message. The destination address of the advertisement message must be the home address of the mobile node, `dst_sa`, which sent the solicitation message.

Listing 5-198
―――*mpa.c*
```
206              cm = CMSG_FIRSTHDR(&sndmhdr);
207              /* specify source address */
208              cm->cmsg_level = IPPROTO_IPV6;
```

```
209            cm->cmsg_type = IPV6_PKTINFO;
210            cm->cmsg_len = CMSG_LEN(sizeof(struct in6_pktinfo));
211            pi = (struct in6_pktinfo *)CMSG_DATA(cm);
212            pi->ipi6_addr = *src;
213            pi->ipi6_ifindex = 0; /* determined with a routing table */
214
215            if ((len = sendmsg(sock, &sndmhdr, 0)) < 0) {
....
217                goto err;
218            }
219     err:
220        }
```
——————————————————————————————————————— mpa.c

212–215 The source address must be the destination address of the incoming solicitation message. The created advertisement message is sent by the `sendmsg()` system call.

5.16.22   Constructing the Payload

The `pi_pick()` function constructs the payload of a Mobile Prefix Advertisement message.

Listing 5-199

——————————————————————————————————————— mpa.c
```
225     int
226     pi_pick(home_addr, prefix_info, haif, count)
227         struct in6_addr *home_addr;
228         struct nd_opt_prefix_info *prefix_info;
229         struct hagent_ifinfo *haif;
230         int count;
231     {
232         int naddr;
233         struct hagent_entry *hap;
234         struct hagent_gaddr *ha_gaddr;
235         struct nd_opt_prefix_info *h_prefix_info;
236         struct timeval now;
237         u_int32_t vltime, pltime;
```
——————————————————————————————————————— mpa.c

225–230 The `pi_pick()` function has four parameters: The `home_addr` parameter is the home address of a mobile node; the `prefix_info` parameter is a pointer to the memory space where the payload is stored; the `haif` parameter is a pointer to the `hagent_ifinfo{}` instance which received the solicitation message; and the `count` parameter is the maximum amount of prefix information to be contained.

Listing 5-200

——————————————————————————————————————— mpa.c
```
239         h_prefix_info = prefix_info;
240         /* search home agent list and pick all prefixes */
241         for (naddr = 0, hap = haif->halist_pref.hagent_next_pref;
242             hap && naddr < count; hap = hap->hagent_next_pref) {
243             for (ha_gaddr = hap->hagent_galist.hagent_next_gaddr;
244                 (ha_gaddr != NULL) && (naddr < count);
245                 ha_gaddr = ha_gaddr->hagent_next_gaddr) {
246                 /* duplication check whether MPA includes duplicated prefixes */
247                 if (prefix_dup_check(h_prefix_info, ha_gaddr, naddr))
248                     /* duplicated prefix is included */
249                     continue;
```
——————————————————————————————————————— mpa.c

241–245 The prefix information is created from the global addresses of the home agent of the home network. The outer `for` loop checks all `hagent_entry{}` instances related to the home network and the inner `for` loop checks all global addresses of each `hagent_entry{}` instance.

247–249 The `prefix_dup_check()` function checks whether the global address specified by the `ha_gaddr` variable has already been included in the payload which is under construction. If the payload has the global address already, a duplicate prefix information entry is not included.

Listing 5-201

```
                                                                  mpa.c
251                 /* make prefix information */
252                 prefix_info->nd_opt_pi_type = ND_OPT_PREFIX_INFORMATION;
253                 prefix_info->nd_opt_pi_len = 4;
254                 prefix_info->nd_opt_pi_prefix_len = ha_gaddr->hagent_prefixlen;
255                 prefix_info->nd_opt_pi_flags_reserved = 0;
256
257                 if (ha_gaddr->hagent_flags.onlink)
258                     prefix_info->nd_opt_pi_flags_reserved |= ND_OPT_PI_FLAG_ONLINK;
259                 if (ha_gaddr->hagent_flags.autonomous)
260                     prefix_info->nd_opt_pi_flags_reserved |= ND_OPT_PI_FLAG_AUTO;
261                 if (ha_gaddr->hagent_flags.router)
262                     prefix_info->nd_opt_pi_flags_reserved |= ND_OPT_PI_FLAG_ROUTER;
                                                                  mpa.c
```

252–262 A prefix information entry is constructed as a form of the modified prefix information structure described in Section 5.3.6.

Listing 5-202

```
                                                                  mpa.c
264                 if (ha_gaddr->hagent_vltime || ha_gaddr->hagent_pltime)
265                     gettimeofday(&now, NULL);
266                 if (ha_gaddr->hagent_vltime == 0)
267                     vltime = ha_gaddr->hagent_expire;
268                 else
269                     vltime = (ha_gaddr->hagent_expire > now.tv_sec) ?
270                         ha_gaddr->hagent_expire - now.tv_sec : 0;
271                 if (ha_gaddr->hagent_pltime == 0)
272                     pltime = ha_gaddr->hagent_preferred;
273                 else
274                     pltime = (ha_gaddr->hagent_preferred > now.tv_sec) ?
275                         ha_gaddr->hagent_preferred - now.tv_sec : 0;
276                 if (vltime < pltime) {
277                     /*
278                      * this can happen if vltime is decrement but pltime
279                      * is not.
280                      */
281                     pltime = vltime;
282                 }
283                 prefix_info->nd_opt_pi_valid_time = htonl(vltime);
284                 prefix_info->nd_opt_pi_preferred_time = htonl(pltime);
285                 prefix_info->nd_opt_pi_reserved2 = 0;
286                 prefix_info->nd_opt_pi_prefix = ha_gaddr->hagent_gaddr;
287
288                 prefix_info ++;
289                 naddr ++;
290             }
```

```
291          }
292          return naddr;
293     }
```

264–282 The valid lifetime and the preferred lifetime are calculated based on the lifetime values of the global address from which the prefix information is derived. The lifetime values which are included in the prefix information will be the actual lifetimes. In other words, if the advertised lifetime was 1000 seconds, but the last Router Advertisement was 400 seconds ago, the lifetime of the Mobile Prefix Advertisement will be 600 seconds.

Note that the code when the lifetime values are 0 (that means infinite lifetime in the **had** program) is wrong. Lines 267 and 272 should be:

```
267                      vltime = ND6_INFINITE_LIFETIME;

272                      pltime = ND6_INFINITE_LIFETIME;
```

5.17   Mobile Node

A mobile node is an IPv6 node that can change its point of attachment to the Internet without disconnecting existing connections with other nodes. A mobile node has the following capabilities.

- Maintaining binding information to inform its home agent of its current location.

- Receiving and sending all the packets using the tunnel connection established between it and its home agent to hide its current location and provide transparent access to its communicating peer nodes.

- Performing the return routability procedure to communicate with nodes that support the route optimizaion function to avoid inefficient tunnel communication.

5.17.1   Files

Table 5-39 shows the files used by a mobile node.

5.17.2   Binding Update List Entry Management

A mobile node keeps a small amount of information called binding update list entry, which contains a mobile node's address, communicating node's address and other information representing the communication status between the two nodes. The information is used to keep the status of home registration or the status of route optimization between a mobile and a correspondent node.

There are six functions to manage binding update list entries.

- `mip6_bu_create()`
  Creates a binding update list entry.

- `mip6_bu_list_insert()`
  Inserts a binding update list entry into a binding update list.

TABLE 5-39

File	Description
`${KAME}/kame/sys/net/if_hif.h`	Home virtual interface structures
`${KAME}/kame/sys/net/if_hif.c`	Implementation of the home virtual interface
`${KAME}/kame/sys/netinet/icmp6.h;`	Dynamic Home Agent Address Discovery and Mobile Prefix Solicitation/Advertisement structures
`${KAME}/kame/sys/netinet/ip6.h`	Home Address option structure
`${KAME}/kame/sys/netinet/ip6mh.h`	Mobility Header structures
`${KAME}/kame/sys/netinet6/mip6_var.h`	All structures which are used in the Mobile IPv6 stack
`${KAME}/kame/sys/netinet6/mip6_mncore.c`	Implementation of mobile node functions
`${KAME}/kame/sys/netinet6/mip6_fsm.c`	The finite state machine of a binding update list entry
`${KAME}/kame/sys/netinet6/mip6_halist.c`	Home agent list management for a mobile node
`${KAME}/kame/sys/netinet6/mip6_prefix.c`	Prefix information management for a mobile node
`${KAME}/kame/sys/netinet6/mip6_icmp6.c`	Implementation of ICMPv6 message related processing
`${KAME}/kame/sys/netinet6/in6_src.c`	Implementation of the default address selection mechanism
`${KAME}/kame/sys/netinet6/ip6_output.c`	Insertion of extension headers for Mobile IPv6 signaling
`${KAME}/kame/sys/netinet6/nd6_rtr.c`	Gathering router information and prefix information
`${KAME}/kame/sys/netinet6/route6.c`	Implementation of the Type 2 Routing Header

Files used by a mobile node.

- `mip6_bu_list_remove()`
  Removes the specified entry from the list.

- `mip6_bu_list_remove_all()`
  Removes all binding update list entries from the list.

- `mip6_bu_list_find_home_registration()`
  Returns a pointer to the binding update list entry for home registration.

- `mip6_bu_list_find_withpaddr()`
  Returns a pointer to the binding update list entry which has the specified correspondent address.

Creating a Binding Update List Entry

A binding update list entry is created by the `mip6_bu_create()` function.

Listing 5-203

```
1482    static struct mip6_bu *
1483    mip6_bu_create(paddr, mpfx, coa, flags, sc)
1484            const struct in6_addr *paddr;
1485            struct mip6_prefix *mpfx;
1486            struct in6_addr *coa;
1487            u_int16_t flags;
1488            struct hif_softc *sc;
1489    {
1490            struct mip6_bu *mbu;
1491            u_int32_t coa_lifetime, cookie;
....
1496            MALLOC(mbu, struct mip6_bu *, sizeof(struct mip6_bu),
1497                    M_TEMP, M_NOWAIT);
1498            if (mbu == NULL) {
....
1502                    return (NULL);
1503            }
```

1482–1488 The `mip6_bu_create()` function has five parameters: The `paddr` parameter is a pointer to the address of a communicating node; the `mpfx` parameter is a pointer to the prefix information of the home address of a mobile node; the `coa` parameter is a pointer to the care-of address of the mobile node; the `flags` parameter is a combination of flags defined in Table 5-13 (on page 545); and the `sc` parameter is a pointer to the `hif_softc{}` instance which indicates the home network of the mobile node.

1496–1503 Memory is allocated for the binding update list entry.

Listing 5-204

```
1505            coa_lifetime = mip6_coa_get_lifetime(coa);
1506
1507            bzero(mbu, sizeof(*mbu));
1508            mbu->mbu_flags = flags;
1509            mbu->mbu_paddr = *paddr;
1510            mbu->mbu_haddr = mpfx->mpfx_haddr;
1511            if (sc->hif_location == HIF_LOCATION_HOME) {
1512                    /* un-registration. */
1513                    mbu->mbu_coa = mpfx->mpfx_haddr;
1514                    mbu->mbu_pri_fsm_state =
1515                            (mbu->mbu_flags & IP6MU_HOME)
1516                            ? MIP6_BU_PRI_FSM_STATE_WAITD
1517                            : MIP6_BU_PRI_FSM_STATE_IDLE;
1518            } else {
1519                    /* registration. */
1520                    mbu->mbu_coa = *coa;
1521                    mbu->mbu_pri_fsm_state =
1522                            (mbu->mbu_flags & IP6MU_HOME)
1523                            ? MIP6_BU_PRI_FSM_STATE_WAITA
1524                            : MIP6_BU_PRI_FSM_STATE_IDLE;
1525            }
1526            if (coa_lifetime < mpfx->mpfx_vltime) {
1527                    mbu->mbu_lifetime = coa_lifetime;
1528            } else {
1529                    mbu->mbu_lifetime = mpfx->mpfx_vltime;
1530            }
1531            if (mip6ctl_bu_maxlifetime > 0 &&
1532                mbu->mbu_lifetime > mip6ctl_bu_maxlifetime)
1533                    mbu->mbu_lifetime = mip6ctl_bu_maxlifetime;
```

1505 The lifetime of a binding update list entry is determined from the lifetime of a care-of and a home address. The `mip6_coa_get_lifetime()` function returns the lifetime of the specified address.

1507–1525 The member variables of the `mip6_bu{}` structure are set. The home address is copied from the prefix information provided by the `mpfx` parameter. The care-of address and registration status are set based on the current location of the mobile node. If the mobile node is at home (`sc->hif_location` is `HIF_LOCATION_HOME`), the care-of address is set to the home address of the mobile node. The registration status is set to the `WAITD` state if the binding update list entry is for home registration (that is, the `IP6MU_HOME` flag is set). This is when the mobile node returns home without a corresponding home registration entry. If the entry is not for home registration, the state is set to `IDLE`. If the mobile node is in a foreign network, the care-of address is set to the address specified as the `coa` parameter. The state is set to the `WAITA` status if the entry is for home registration; otherwise, it is set to `IDLE`.

1526–1533 The lifetime is set to the lifetime of the care-of address if the lifetime of the care-of address is greater than the lifetime of the home address (more precisely, the lifetime of the home prefix); otherwise, it is set to the lifetime of the home address.

1531–1533 `mip6ctl_bu_maxlifetime` is a global variable which is used to limit the lifetime of binding update list entries.

Listing 5-205

_____mip6_mncore.c
```
1534            mbu->mbu_expire = time_second + mbu->mbu_lifetime;
1535            /* sanity check for overflow */
1536            if (mbu->mbu_expire < time_second)
1537                    mbu->mbu_expire = 0x7fffffff;
1538            mbu->mbu_refresh = mbu->mbu_lifetime;
1539            /* Sequence Number SHOULD start at a random value */
1540            mbu->mbu_seqno = (u_int16_t)arc4random();
1541            cookie = arc4random();
1542            bcopy(&cookie, &mbu->mbu_mobile_cookie[0], 4);
1543            cookie = arc4random();
1544            bcopy(&cookie, &mbu->mbu_mobile_cookie[4], 4);
1545            mbu->mbu_hif = sc;
1546            /* *mbu->mbu_encap = NULL; */
1547            mip6_bu_update_firewallstate(mbu);
1548
1549            return (mbu);
1550    }
```
_____mip6_mncore.c

1534–1549 The expiration time of the binding update list entry is set. The code checks the overflow of the expiration time, since the time is represented as a 32-bit signed integer. The refresh time is set to the same value as the expiration time. The value may be overwritten by a Binding Acknowledgment message which will arrive later. The sequence number is initialized to a random number and the mobile cookie used for the return routability procedure is initialized to random numbers.

The `mip6_bu_update_firewallstate()` function is not discussed in this book, since the function is used for the KAME-specific experimental code for the firewall traversal mechanism.

Inserting a Binding Update List Entry to List

Binding update list entries are maintained as a list. Each `hif_softc{}` structure, which represents a home network, has a list constructed of binding update list entries which belong to the home network. Figure 5-46 (on page 566) shows the relationship between the `hif_softc{}` and `mip6_bu{}` structures.

Listing 5-206

```
                                                                  ──mip6_mncore.c
1552    static int
1553    mip6_bu_list_insert(bu_list, mbu)
1554            struct mip6_bu_list *bu_list;
1555            struct mip6_bu *mbu;
1556    {
1557            LIST_INSERT_HEAD(bu_list, mbu, mbu_entry);
1558
1559            if (mip6_bu_count == 0) {
....
1562                    mip6_bu_starttimer();
1563            }
1564            mip6_bu_count++;
1565
1566            return (0);
1567    }
                                                                  ──mip6_mncore.c
```

1552–1555 The `mip6_bu_list_insert()` function has two parameters: The `bu_list` parameter is a pointer to the list of binding update list entries kept in a `hif_softc{}` instance and the `mbu` parameter is a pointer to the binding update list entry to insert.

1557–1566 The `mip6_bu_starttimer()` function starts the timer function for binding update list entries when the first binding update list entry is inserted by the `LIST_INSERT_HEAD()` macro. The `mip6_bu_count` variable is the total number of binding update entries currently held by the mobile node. The variable is used to determine when to start and stop the timer function.

Removing a Binding Update List Entry from List

A binding update list entry is removed when its lifetime is expired. The `mip6_bu_list_remove()` function removes a binding update list entry from a list.

Listing 5-207

```
                                                                  ──mip6_mncore.c
1569    int
1570    mip6_bu_list_remove(mbu_list, mbu)
1571            struct mip6_bu_list *mbu_list;
1572            struct mip6_bu *mbu;
1573    {
1574            if ((mbu_list == NULL) || (mbu == NULL)) {
1575                    return (EINVAL);
1576            }
1577
1578            LIST_REMOVE(mbu, mbu_entry);
1579            FREE(mbu, M_TEMP);
1580
```

```
1581                    mip6_bu_count--;
1582                    if (mip6_bu_count == 0) {
1583                            mip6_bu_stoptimer();
    ....
1587                    }
1588
1589                    return (0);
1590    }
```
——mip6_mncore.c

1569–1572 The mip6_bu_list_remove() has two parameters: The mbu_list parameter is a pointer to the list which includes the entry to remove and the mbu parameter is a pointer to the binding update list entry.

1578–1589 The specified entry is removed by the LIST_REMOVE() macro and the memory used by the entry is released. The mip6_bu_count variable is decremented by 1 and the mip6_bu_stop_timer() function is called if the variable reaches 0, which means there is no binding update list entry.

Listing 5-208
——mip6_mncore.c

```
1592    int
1593    mip6_bu_list_remove_all(mbu_list, all)
1594            struct mip6_bu_list *mbu_list;
1595            int all;
1596    {
1597            struct mip6_bu *mbu, *mbu_next;
1598            int error = 0;
1599
1600            if (mbu_list == NULL) {
1601                    return (EINVAL);
1602            }
1603
1604            for (mbu = LIST_FIRST(mbu_list);
1605                 mbu;
1606                 mbu = mbu_next) {
1607                    mbu_next = LIST_NEXT(mbu, mbu_entry);
1608
1609                    if (!all &&
1610                        (mbu->mbu_flags & IP6MU_HOME) == 0 &&
1611                        (mbu->mbu_state & MIP6_BU_STATE_DISABLE) == 0)
1612                            continue;
1613
1614                    error = mip6_bu_list_remove(mbu_list, mbu);
1615                    if (error) {
    ....
1619                            continue;
1620                    }
1621            }
1622
1623            return (0);
1624    }
```
——mip6_mncore.c

1592–1595 The mip6_bu_list_remove_all() function is used to remove all the binding update list entries. The mbu_list parameter is a pointer to the list which contains the binding update list entries to remove. All the binding update list entries are removed if the all parameter is set to true; otherwise, all entries except for correspondent nodes which do not support the Mobile IPv6 function are removed.

1604–1623 All binding update list entries held in the `mbu_list` are released by the function `mip6_bu_list_remove()`. If the `all` variable is set to false, binding update list entries for correspondent nodes which have the `MIP6_BU_STATE_DISABLE` flag set (the flag means the node does not support Mobile IPv6) are not removed. Keeping the entries of non-Mobile IPv6 aware nodes will avoid unnecessary signaling to those nodes in later communications.

Looking Up a Binding Update List Entry

To retrieve a binding update list entry, the KAME Mobile IPv6 code provides two functions: The `mip6_bu_list_find_home_registration()` function will find the home registration entry and the `mip6_bu_list_find_withpaddr()` function will find the entry which matches the specified destination address.

Listing 5-209

——*mip6_mncore.c*

```
1626    struct mip6_bu *
1627    mip6_bu_list_find_home_registration(bu_list, haddr)
1628        struct mip6_bu_list *bu_list;
1629        struct in6_addr *haddr;
1630    {
1631        struct mip6_bu *mbu;
1632
1633        for (mbu = LIST_FIRST(bu_list); mbu;
1634            mbu = LIST_NEXT(mbu, mbu_entry)) {
1635            if (IN6_ARE_ADDR_EQUAL(&mbu->mbu_haddr, haddr) &&
1636                (mbu->mbu_flags & IP6MU_HOME) != 0)
1637                break;
1638        }
1639        return (mbu);
1640    }
```

——*mip6_mncore.c*

1626–1629 The `mip6_bu_list_find_home_registration()` function has two parameters: The `bu_list` parameter is a pointer to the list of binding update list entries and the `haddr` parameter is the home address of the target mobile node.

1633–1639 All binding update list entries contained in the `bu_list` are checked and the entry whose home address is the same as the `haddr` parameter and has the `IP6MU_HOME` flag set is returned.

Listing 5-210

——*mip6_mncore.c*

```
1648    struct mip6_bu *
1649    mip6_bu_list_find_withpaddr(bu_list, paddr, haddr)
1650        struct mip6_bu_list *bu_list;
1651        struct in6_addr *paddr;
1652        struct in6_addr *haddr;
1653    {
1654        struct mip6_bu *mbu;
1655
1656        /* sanity check. */
1657        if (paddr == NULL)
1658            return (NULL);
1659
1660        for (mbu = LIST_FIRST(bu_list); mbu;
1661            mbu = LIST_NEXT(mbu, mbu_entry)) {
```

```
1662                        if (IN6_ARE_ADDR_EQUAL(&mbu->mbu_paddr, paddr)
1663                            && ((haddr != NULL)
1664                                ? IN6_ARE_ADDR_EQUAL(&mbu->mbu_haddr, haddr)
1665                                : 1))
1666                                break;
1667                    }
1668            return (mbu);
1669    }
```
—— mip6_mncore.c

1648–1652 The mip6_bu_list_find_withpaddr() function has three parameters: The bu_list parameter is a pointer to the list of binding update list entries and the paddr and haddr parameters are the addresses of the correspondent node and the home address of the mobile node being searched. If the mobile node has multiple home addresses, there may be multiple entries for the same node that have different home addresses. To verify that there is at least one entry of the specified peer node, the haddr parameter can be a NULL pointer. In that case, the function returns the first entry whose peer address is the same as the paddr parameter.

1660–1668 All binding update list entries included in the bu_list are checked. If the haddr parameter is NULL, the first entry whose peer address, mbu_peer, is the same as the paddr parameter is returned. If the haddr parameter is not NULL, the entry whose peer, address, mbu_peer, is the same as paddr and whose home address, mbu_haddr, is the same as the haddr parameter is returned.

Timer Processing of the mip6_bu{} Structure

Similar to the mip6_bc{} structure, the mip6_bu{} structure has its timer function. The difference between the timer functions of the mip6_bc{} and mip6_bu{} structures is that the mip6_bc{} structure has a timer entry in each instance, while the mip6_bu{} structure shares one timer function among all the binding update list entries. This implementation design is due to historical reasons.

There are three functions related to the timer processing of the mip6_bu{} structure.

1. mip6_bu_starttimer()
   Start the timer function.

2. mip6_bu_stoptimer()
   Stop the timer function.

3. mip6_bu_timeout()
   Process periodical jobs needed to manage binding update list entries.

Listing 5-211
—— mip6_mncore.c
```
2294    static void
2295    mip6_bu_starttimer()
2296    {
    ....
2298            callout_reset(&mip6_bu_ch,
2299                    MIP6_BU_TIMEOUT_INTERVAL * hz,
2300                    mip6_bu_timeout, NULL);
    ....
2309    }
```
—— mip6_mncore.c

2294–2309 The `mip6_bu_starttimer()` function is called when the first binding update list entry is created on a mobile node. The function is also called from the `mip6_bu_timeout()` function to reset the timer. The interval to call the timer function is set to 1 second.

Listing 5-212

```
2311    static void
2312    mip6_bu_stoptimer()
2313    {
....
2315            callout_stop(&mip6_bu_ch);
....
2321    }
```

2311–2321 The `mip6_bu_stoptimer()` function stops the timer function. This function is called when all the binding update list entries have been removed.

Listing 5-213

```
2324    mip6_bu_timeout(arg)
2325            void *arg;
2326    {
2327            int s;
2328            struct hif_softc *sc;
2329            int error = 0;
....
2331            struct timeval mono_time;
....
2335            mono_time.tv_sec = time_second;
....
2341            s = splnet();
....
2343            mip6_bu_starttimer();
```

2323–2325 The `mip6_bu_timeout()` function is called periodically to process each binding update list entry kept by a mobile node.

2343 The `mip6_bu_starttimer()` function is called to schedule the next timeout.

Listing 5-214

```
2345            for (sc = LIST_FIRST(&hif_softc_list); sc;
2346                 sc = LIST_NEXT(sc, hif_entry)) {
2347                struct mip6_bu *mbu, *mbu_entry;
2348
2349                for (mbu = LIST_FIRST(&sc->hif_bu_list);
2350                     mbu != NULL;
2351                     mbu = mbu_entry) {
2352                        mbu_entry = LIST_NEXT(mbu, mbu_entry);
```

```
2353
2354                          /* check expiration. */
2355                          if (mbu->mbu_expire < mono_time.tv_sec) {
2356                                  if ((mbu->mbu_flags & IP6MU_HOME) != 0) {
2357                                          /*
2358                                           * the binding update entry for
2359                                           * the home registration
2360                                           * should not be removed.
2361                                           */
2362                                          mip6_bu_fsm(mbu,
2363                                                  MIP6_BU_PRI_FSM_EVENT_RETRANS_TIMER,
2364                                                  NULL);
2365                                  } else {
2366                                          error = mip6_bu_list_remove(
2367                                                  &sc->hif_bu_list, mbu);
2368                                          if (error) {
....
2373                                                  /* continue anyway... */
2374                                          }
2375                                          continue;
2376                                  }
2377                          }
2378
2379                          /* check if we need retransmit something. */
2380                          if ((mbu->mbu_state & MIP6_BU_STATE_NEEDTUNNEL) != 0)
2381                                  continue;
2382
2383                          /* check timeout. */
2384                          if ((mbu->mbu_retrans != 0)
2385                              && (mbu->mbu_retrans < mono_time.tv_sec)) {
2386                                  /* order is important. */
2387                                  if(MIP6_IS_BU_RR_STATE(mbu)) {
2388                                          /* retransmit RR signals. */
2389                                          error = mip6_bu_fsm(mbu,
2390                                                  MIP6_BU_SEC_FSM_EVENT_RETRANS_TIMER,
2391                                                  NULL);
2392                                  } else if (((mbu->mbu_flags & IP6MU_ACK) != 0)
2393                                      && MIP6_IS_BU_WAITA_STATE(mbu)) {
2394                                          /* retransmit a binding update
2395                                           * to register. */
2396                                          error = mip6_bu_fsm(mbu,
2397                                                  MIP6_BU_PRI_FSM_EVENT_RETRANS_TIMER,
2398                                                  NULL);
2399                                  } else if (MIP6_IS_BU_BOUND_STATE(mbu)) {
2400                                          /* retransmit a binding update
2401                                           * for to refresh binding. */
2402                                          error = mip6_bu_fsm(mbu,
2403                                                  MIP6_BU_PRI_FSM_EVENT_REFRESH_TIMER,
2404                                                  NULL);
2405                                  }
2406                                  if (error) {
....
2411                                          /* continue, anyway... */
2412                                  }
2413                          }
2414                  }
2415          }
2416
2417          splx(s);
2418  }
```

                                                            ————mip6_mncore.c

2345–2352 Each home network information entry (the instance of the `hif_softc{}` structure) has a list of binding update list entries. All of the `hif_softc{}` instances are visited
to process all binding update list entries included in each `hif_softc{}` instance.

2355–2377 The expiration time of the binding update list entry is checked. The timer function will remove the expired entry by calling the `mip6_bu_list_remove()` function if the entry is not for home registration. In the KAME implementation, home registration entries never expire. A mobile node will try to re-register its information to the home agent forever.

2380–2381 The retransmission procedure is skipped if the entry has been marked with the `MIP6_BU_STATE_NEEDTUNNEL` flag, that means the destination node does not support Mobile IPv6 and requires tunnel communication.

2384–2413 The retransmission timeout of each binding update list entry is checked. Based on the current state of the binding update list entry, a proper event is sent to the state machine operated in each binding update list entry. If the state is `MIP6_IS_BU_RR_STATE`, which means the entry is performing the return routability procedure, the `MIP6_BU_SEC_FSM_EVENT_RETRANS_TIMER` event is sent to retransmit required messages for the return routability procedure. If the state is `MIP6_IS_WAITA_STATE`, which means the entry is waiting for a Binding Acknowledgment message, and the entry has the `IP6MU_ACK` flag set, the `MIP6_BU_PRI_FSM_EVENT_RETRANS_TIMER` event is sent to retransmit a Binding Update message. If the state is `MIP6_IS_BU_BOUND_STATE`, which means the mobile node has successfully registered with the node being described, the `MIP6_BU_PRI_FSM_EVENT_REFRESH_TIMER` event is triggered to send a Binding Update message to extend the lifetime of the registered entry. The state machine will be discussed in Section 5.17.19.

5.17.3   Movement Detection

The most interesting part of a mobile node is the mechanism to detect its movement. The movement detection mechanism implemented by the KAME Mobile IPv6 is based on NUD (Neighbor Unreachability Detection) and the status change of care-of addresses. The basic idea is as follows:

1. Receive a Router Advertisement message.

2. Configure IPv6 addresses based on the received Router Advertisement.

3. Probe all routers by sending Neighbor Solicitation messages.

4. Wait for any status change of assigned IPv6 addresses.

5. Check the available care-of addresses.

6. Recognize movement if the old care-of address is not usable any more.

The overview is shown in Figure 5-56. In the KAME IPv6 implementation, the prefix and router information have a close relationship. When a router becomes unreachable, the related prefix is also marked as unusable. The care-of address constructed from the invalid prefix can no longer be used for communication anymore. When a mobile node detects that the current care-of address has become unusable, the node thinks it has moved to another network.

Probing Routers

Router Advertisement messages are processed by the `nd6_ra_input()` function.

FIGURE 5-56

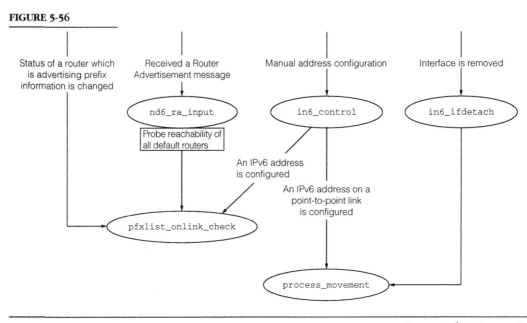

Movement detection overview.

Listing 5-215

_____ nd6_rtr.c

```
229     void
230     nd6_ra_input(m, off, icmp6len)
231             struct  mbuf *m;
232             int off, icmp6len;
233     {
  ....
436     #if defined(MIP6) && defined(MIP6_MOBILE_NODE)
437             if (MIP6_IS_MN) {
438                     /* check reachability of all routers. */
439                     mip6_probe_routers();
440             }
  ....
```
_____ nd6_rtr.c

437–440 If a node is acting as a mobile node and receives a Router Advertisement message,
the `mip6_probe_routers()` function is called to initiate NUD for all default routers
currently kept in the default router list of the mobile node.

Listing 5-216

_____ mip6_mncore.c

```
617     void
618     mip6_probe_routers(void)
619     {
620             struct llinfo_nd6 *ln;
621
622             ln = llinfo_nd6.ln_next;
623             while (ln && ln != &llinfo_nd6) {
```

```
624                     if ((ln->ln_router) &&
625                         ((ln->ln_state == ND6_LLINFO_REACHABLE) ||
626                          (ln->ln_state == ND6_LLINFO_STALE))) {
627                             ln->ln_asked = 0;
628                             ln->ln_state = ND6_LLINFO_DELAY;
629                             nd6_llinfo_settimer(ln, 0);
630                     }
631                     ln = ln->ln_next;
632             }
633     }
```
——mip6_mncore.c

617–633 The mip6_probe_routers() function changes the neighbor discovery state of
routers. The ln_router field of the llinfo_nd6{} structure indicates whether the entry
is for a router. If the entry is for a router and the state is either ND6_LLINFO_REACHABLE or
ND6_LLINFO_STALE, the state is changed to ND6_LLINFO_DELAY and the timer function
for the entry is called by setting the time to the next timeout to 0 second. The timer function
will be called soon and a Neighbor Solicitation message will be sent from the timer function because the state is ND6_LLINFO_DELAY. After the Neighbor Solicitation message
is sent, the state is changed to ND6_LLINFO_PROBE in the timer function. The detailed
state transition of a neighbor cache entry is discussed in Chapter 5 of *IPv6 Core Protocols
Implementation*.

   If routers are still reachable, the mobile node will receive Neighbor Advertisement messages from the routers. The state of each entry is updated to ND6_LLINFO_REACHABLE
when the mobile node receives the messages; otherwise, the entry is removed.

   This mechanism works only when the routers of the network to which the mobile
node attaches use the Router Advertisement message. If the care-of address of the mobile
node is assigned in other ways, such as a PPP link on a point-to-point network, address
availability is checked by the in6_control() function described in Listing 5-218.

Updating the Status of Addresses

The status of IPv6 addresses are changed in the following situations:

- A new prefix is advertised and a new address is configured.

- The lifetime of an address is expired.

- An address is removed manually.

- Routers become unreachable and addresses which are generated from the prefixes sent
  from the routers become detached.

When one of these events occurs, the KAME implementation checks the availability of
care-of addresses and re-registers a new care-of address if necessary.

Listing 5-217

——nd6_rtr.c
```
1654    void
1655    pfxlist_onlink_check()
1656    {
....
1827    #if defined(MIP6) && defined(MIP6_MOBILE_NODE)
1828            if (MIP6_IS_MN)
```

```
1829                    mip6_process_movement();
1830     #endif /* MIP6 && MIP6_MOBILE_NODE */
1831     }
```
── nd6_rtr.c

1654–1831 The `pfxlist_onlink_check()` function is called whenever a node needs to
check the latest status of the prefix information stored in the node. Based on the status of
each prefix, the statuses of addresses assigned to the node are also updated. At the end
of this function, the `mip6_process_movement()` function is called to verify whether
movement has occurred.

Listing 5-218
── in6.c

```
464      int
....
473      in6_control(so, cmd, data, ifp, p)
474              struct  socket *so;
475              u_long cmd;
476              caddr_t data;
477              struct ifnet *ifp;
478              struct proc *p;
....
480      {
....
823              case SIOCAIFADDR_IN6:
824              {
....
870                      if (pr0.ndpr_plen == 128) {
871      #if defined(MIP6) && defined(MIP6_MOBILE_NODE)
872                              if (MIP6_IS_MN)
873                                      mip6_process_movement();
874      #endif /* MIP6 && MIP6_MOBILE_NODE */
875                              break;  /* we don't need to install a host route. */
876                      }
....
```
── in6.c

823–876 When an address is manually configured, the `in6_control()` function is called as a
part of the address assignment procedure. In that case, the `SIOCAIFADDR_IN6` command
and required address information are passed to the function. In the corresponding code,
the `mip6_process_movement()` function is called only when the prefix length of the
assigned address is 128. Typically, this condition occurs when assigning an IPv6 address
on a Point-to-Point interface, such as a gif interface. Addresses which have a prefix length
less than 128 are handled by the `pfxlist_onlink_ckech()` function.

Listing 5-219
── in6_ifattach.c

```
957      void
958      in6_ifdetach(ifp)
959              struct ifnet *ifp;
960      {
....
1095     #if defined(MIP6) && defined(MIP6_MOBILE_NODE)
```

```
1096              if (MIP6_IS_MN)
1097                  mip6_process_movement();
1098     #endif /* MIP6 && MIP6_MOBILE_NODE */
1099     }
```
_____in6_ifattach.c

957–1099 The `in6_ifdetach()` function is called when a network interface is deleted, for
example, when removing a PCMCIA network card. In this case, all the addresses assigned
to the network interface are removed and the mobile node needs to check the latest status
of available care-of addresses.

Listing 5-220
_____mip6_mncore.c
```
641      void
642      mip6_process_movement(void)
643      {
644              struct hif_softc *sc;
645              int coa_changed = 0;
```
_____mip6_mncore.c

641–645 The `mip6_process_movement()` is called whenever a mobile node needs to
check the current location. A Binding Update message will be sent if the node detects
movement, otherwise, the function has no effect.

Listing 5-221
_____mip6_mncore.c
```
647              for (sc = LIST_FIRST(&hif_softc_list); sc;
648                  sc = LIST_NEXT(sc, hif_entry)) {
649                  hif_save_location(sc);
650                  coa_changed = mip6_select_coa(sc);
651                  if (coa_changed == 1) {
652                      if (mip6_process_pfxlist_status_change(sc)) {
653                          hif_restore_location(sc);
654                          continue;
655                      }
656                      if (mip6_register_current_location(sc)) {
657                          hif_restore_location(sc);
658                          continue;
659                      }
660                      mip6_bu_list_update_firewallstate(sc);
661                  } else
662                      hif_restore_location(sc);
663              }
664      }
```
_____mip6_mncore.c

647–663 The KAME implementation assigns one care-of address to each `hif_softc{}` instance
(meaning the home network). The loop defined on line 647 checks all the `hif_softc{}`
instances in a mobile node and calls the `mip6_select_coa()` function to choose the best
care-of address. The `mip6_select_coa()` function returns to 1 if a new care-of address is
chosen. In this case, the `mip6_process_pfxlist_status_change()` function is called
to determine the current location and the `mip6_register_current_location()`
function is called subsequently to register the current location by sending a Binding
Update message.

Listing 5-222

_____mip6_mncore.c

```
767     int
768     mip6_select_coa(sc)
769             struct hif_softc *sc;
770     {
771             int hoa_scope, ia_best_scope, ia_scope;
772             int ia_best_matchlen, ia_matchlen;
773             struct in6_ifaddr *ia, *ia_best;
774             struct in6_addr *hoa;
775             struct mip6_prefix *mpfx;
776             int i;
777
778             hoa = NULL;
779             hoa_scope = ia_best_scope = -1;
780             ia_best_matchlen = -1;
```
_____mip6_mncore.c

767–769 The `mip6_select_coa()` function has one parameter. The `sc` parameter is a
pointer to the `hif_softc{}` instance that indicates one of the home networks of a
mobile node.

Listing 5-223

_____mip6_mncore.c

```
782             /* get the first HoA registered to a certain home network. */
783             for (mpfx = LIST_FIRST(&mip6_prefix_list); mpfx;
784                 mpfx = LIST_NEXT(mpfx, mpfx_entry)) {
785                     if (hif_prefix_list_find_withmpfx(&sc->hif_prefix_list_home,
786                         mpfx) == NULL)
787                             continue;
788                     if (IN6_IS_ADDR_UNSPECIFIED(&mpfx->mpfx_haddr))
789                             continue;
790                     hoa = &mpfx->mpfx_haddr;
791                     hoa_scope = in6_addrscope(hoa);
792             }
```
_____mip6_mncore.c

782–784 One of the home addresses assigned to the home network, specified by the parameter
of the `mip6_select_coa()` function, is located. The `mip6_prefix_list` variable is
a list that keeps all prefix information which the mobile node currently has. Each prefix
information entry has an IPv6 address generated from the prefix. If the prefix is a home
prefix, then the address kept in the information is a home address.

785–791 If the prefix information currently being checked is not one of the home prefixes
of the `hif_softc{}` instance specified by the parameter, the prefix information is
ignored. The `hif_prefix_list_find_withmpfx()` function searches for a specified prefix information entry in the prefix list which is kept in the `hif_softc{}`
instance. The `hif_prefix_list_home` member variable holds all home prefixes of
a particular `hif_softc{}` instance. If a home prefix is found, the home address of
the prefix and its scope identifier are set based on the information stored in the prefix
information.

Listing 5-224

_____mip6_mncore.c

```
794             ia_best = NULL;
795             for (ia = in6_ifaddr; ia; ia = ia->ia_next) {
```

```
796                          ia_scope = -1;
797                          ia_matchlen = -1;
```
                                                                    _____mip6_mncore.c

794–797 The following code selects a new care-of address for a particular home network.
The algorithm is similar to the default source address selection algorithm implemented
as the `in6_selectsrc()` function discussed in Section 3.13.1 of *IPv6 Core Protocols
Implementation*. In the loop defined on line 795, all IPv6 addresses assigned to the mobile
node are checked to determine if there is a more appropriate address for use as a care-of
address than the current candidate.

Listing 5-225
                                                                    _____mip6_mncore.c
```
799                      /* IFT_HIF has only home addresses. */
800                      if (ia->ia_ifp->if_type == IFT_HIF)
801                          goto next;
802
803                      if (ia->ia6_flags &
804                          (IN6_IFF_ANYCAST
....
808                          /* | IN6_IFF_TENTATIVE */
809                          | IN6_IFF_DETACHED
810                          | IN6_IFF_DUPLICATED))
811                          goto next;
812
813                      /* loopback address cannot be used as a CoA. */
814                      if (IN6_IS_ADDR_LOOPBACK(&ia->ia_addr.sin6_addr))
815                          goto next;
816
817                      /* link-local addr as a CoA is impossible? */
818                      if (IN6_IS_ADDR_LINKLOCAL(&ia->ia_addr.sin6_addr))
819                          goto next;
820
821                      /* tempaddr as a CoA is not supported. */
822                      if (ia->ia6_flags & IN6_IFF_TEMPORARY)
823                          goto next;
```
                                                                    _____mip6_mncore.c

800–801 Addresses which cannot be used as a care-of address are excluded. The interface
type `IFT_HIF` means a virtual interface that represents a home network. The addresses
assigned to the virtual interface are home addresses and are never used as care-of
addresses.

803–811 An anycast address, detached address or duplicated address cannot be used as a
care-of address.

814–815 A loopback address cannot be used as a care-of address.

818–819 Using a link-local address as a care-of address is possible in theory; however, it is
almost meaningless since a packet whose source address is a link-local address cannot be
forwarded by routers.

821–823 An address which is generated based on the privacy extension specification [RFC3041]
can be used as a care-of address; however, the KAME implementation does not use such
addresses so that we can reduce the frequency of movement. The privacy extension

mechanism invalidates the autoconfigured address in a short time and generates a new autoconfigured address to make it difficult to bind the address and its user. If it is used as a care-of address, the stack has to send a new Binding Update message when a new privacy enhanced address is generated.

Listing 5-226

_____mip6_mncore.c

```
825                     /* prefer a home address. */
826                     for (mpfx = LIST_FIRST(&mip6_prefix_list); mpfx;
827                         mpfx = LIST_NEXT(mpfx, mpfx_entry)) {
828                             if (hif_prefix_list_find_withmpfx(
829                                 &sc->hif_prefix_list_home, mpfx) == NULL)
830                                     continue;
831                             if (IN6_ARE_ADDR_EQUAL(&mpfx->mpfx_haddr,
832                                 &ia->ia_addr.sin6_addr)) {
833                                     ia_best = ia;
834                                     goto out;
835                             }
836                     }
```
_____mip6_mncore.c

826–836 If an IPv6 address, which is the same as one of the home addresses, is assigned to a mobile node, the address is chosen as a care-of address. This means the mobile node has returned home.

Listing 5-227

_____mip6_mncore.c

```
838                     if (ia_best == NULL)
839                             goto replace;
840
841                     /* prefer appropriate scope. */
842                     ia_scope = in6_addrscope(&ia->ia_addr.sin6_addr);
843                     if (IN6_ARE_SCOPE_CMP(ia_best_scope, ia_scope) < 0) {
844                             if (IN6_ARE_SCOPE_CMP(ia_best_scope, hoa_scope) < 0)
845                                     goto replace;
846                             goto next;
847                     } else if (IN6_ARE_SCOPE_CMP(ia_scope, ia_best_scope) < 0) {
848                             if (IN6_ARE_SCOPE_CMP(ia_scope, hoa_scope) < 0)
849                                     goto next;
850                             goto replace;
851                     }
```
_____mip6_mncore.c

842–851 An address which has the same scope identifier as the home address is preferred. If the address being checked has the same scope identifier as the home address, the address is chosen as a new candidate care-of address. If the current candidate has the same scope identifier, the current candidate is kept. If both addresses have (or do not have) the same scope identifier, then other conditions are considered.

Listing 5-228

_____mip6_mncore.c

```
853                     /* avoid a deprecated address. */
854                     if (!IFA6_IS_DEPRECATED(ia_best) && IFA6_IS_DEPRECATED(ia))
855                             goto next;
```

```
856                          if (IFA6_IS_DEPRECATED(ia_best) && !IFA6_IS_DEPRECATED(ia))
857                                  goto replace;
```
—————————————————————————————————mip6_mncore.c

853–857 A deprecated address is not used as a care-of address. If the current candidate is deprecated, then the address currently being examined is chosen as a new candidate. If the address currently being examined is deprecated, then the current candidate is kept. If both address are (or are not) deprecated, then other conditions are checked.

Listing 5-229

—————————————————————————————————mip6_mncore.c
```
859                          /* prefer an address on an alive interface. */
860                          if ((ia_best->ia_ifp->if_flags & IFF_UP) &&
861                              !(ia->ia_ifp->if_flags & IFF_UP))
862                                  goto next;
863                          if (!(ia_best->ia_ifp->if_flags & IFF_UP) &&
864                              (ia->ia_ifp->if_flags & IFF_UP))
865                                  goto replace;
```
—————————————————————————————————mip6_mncore.c

860–865 An address which is assigned to the active interface is preferred.

Listing 5-230

—————————————————————————————————mip6_mncore.c
```
867                          /* prefer an address on a preferred interface. */
868                          for (i = 0; i < sizeof(mip6_preferred_ifnames.mip6pi_ifname);
869                              i++) {
870                                  if ((strncmp(if_name(ia_best->ia_ifp),
871                                      mip6_preferred_ifnames.mip6pi_ifname[i],
872                                      IFNAMSIZ) == 0)
873                                      && (strncmp(if_name(ia->ia_ifp),
874                                      mip6_preferred_ifnames.mip6pi_ifname[i],
875                                      IFNAMSIZ) != 0))
876                                          goto next;
877                                  if ((strncmp(if_name(ia_best->ia_ifp),
878                                      mip6_preferred_ifnames.mip6pi_ifname[i],
879                                      IFNAMSIZ) != 0)
880                                      && (strncmp(if_name(ia->ia_ifp),
881                                      mip6_preferred_ifnames.mip6pi_ifname[i],
882                                      IFNAMSIZ) == 0))
883                                          goto replace;
884                          }
```
—————————————————————————————————mip6_mncore.c

868–884 The KAME implementation provides a feature to set priorities among interfaces when selecting a care-of address. For example, a user can specify that the ne0 Ethernet interface is more preferable than the wi0 wireless network interface. The mip6_preferred_ifnames variable is a configurable variable for specifying the preference. The value can be set by using the I/O control mechanism (I/O control is discussed in Section 5.17.27). The variable keeps the interface names ordered by preference.

Listing 5-231

—————————————————————————————————mip6_mncore.c
```
886                          /* prefer a longest match address. */
887                          if (hoa != NULL) {
```

```
888                               ia_matchlen = in6_matchlen(&ia->ia_addr.sin6_addr,
889                                   hoa);
890                               if (ia_best_matchlen < ia_matchlen)
891                                       goto replace;
892                               if (ia_matchlen < ia_best_matchlen)
893                                       goto next;
894                       }
```
———mip6_mncore.c

887–894 An address which is similar to the home address is preferred. The `in6_matchlen()` function returns the number of bits which are the same from the MSB side between two addresses. The address which has a longer matching part is selected as a new candidate care-of address.

Listing 5-232
———mip6_mncore.c
```
896                       /* prefer same CoA. */
897                       if ((ia_best == sc->hif_coa_ifa)
898                           && (ia != sc->hif_coa_ifa))
899                               goto next;
900                       if ((ia_best != sc->hif_coa_ifa)
901                           && (ia == sc->hif_coa_ifa))
902                               goto replace;
```
———mip6_mncore.c

897–902 If the care-of address is changed, then the mobile node needs to re-register its care-of address to its home agent. Since a care-of address indicates the current topological location of the mobile node, frequent changes of care-of addresses may cause frequent path changes of traffic flow from the mobile node, which sometimes causes bad performance. To avoid the situation as much as possible, the KAME implementation tries to keep the current care-of address as long as the care-of address is available.

Listing 5-233
———mip6_mncore.c
```
904               replace:
905                       ia_best = ia;
906                       ia_best_scope = (ia_scope >= 0 ? ia_scope :
907                           in6_addrscope(&ia_best->ia_addr.sin6_addr));
908                       if (hoa != NULL)
909                               ia_best_matchlen = (ia_matchlen >= 0 ? ia_matchlen :
910                                   in6_matchlen(&ia_best->ia_addr.sin6_addr, hoa));
911               next:
912                       continue;
913               out:
914                       break;
915               }
916
917               if (ia_best == NULL) {
....
921                       return (0);
922               }
```
———mip6_mncore.c

904–910 The candidate care-of address is replaced with the address currently being examined.

917–922 If there is no proper care-of address, then the current status is kept until a usable care-of address becomes available.

Listing 5-234

```
924                 /* check if the CoA has been changed. */
925                 if (sc->hif_coa_ifa == ia_best) {
926                         /* CoA has not been changed. */
927                         return (0);
928                 }
929
930                 if (sc->hif_coa_ifa != NULL)
931                         IFAFREE(&sc->hif_coa_ifa->ia_ifa);
932                 sc->hif_coa_ifa = ia_best;
933                 IFAREF(&sc->hif_coa_ifa->ia_ifa);
....
938                 return (1);
939         }
```

925–928 If the care-of address has not been changed, the current status is kept.

930–938 If the care-of address has been changed, the pointer to the care-of address stored in the `hif_softc{}` instance is updated to the new care-of address. The function returns to 1 to notify the caller that the care-of address has been changed.

Listing 5-235

```
666     int
667     mip6_process_pfxlist_status_change(sc)
668             struct hif_softc *sc;
669     {
670             struct hif_prefix *hpfx;
671             struct sockaddr_in6 hif_coa;
672             int error = 0;
673
674             if (sc->hif_coa_ifa == NULL) {
....
678                     sc->hif_location = HIF_LOCATION_UNKNOWN;
679                     return (0);
680             }
681             hif_coa = sc->hif_coa_ifa->ia_addr;
682             if (in6_addr2zoneid(sc->hif_coa_ifa->ia_ifp,
683                     &hif_coa.sin6_addr, &hif_coa.sin6_scope_id)) {
684                     /* must not happen. */
685             }
686             if (in6_embedscope(&hif_coa.sin6_addr, &hif_coa)) {
687                     /* must not happen. */
688             }
```

666–669 The `mip6_process_pfxlist_status_change()` function has one parameter. The `sc` parameter is a pointer to the `hif_softc{}` instance which indicates the home network of a mobile node.

674–679 If the care-of address, `hif_coa_ifa`, is unknown, or has not been set yet, the location is considered as unknown (`HIF_LOCATION_UNKNOWN`).

682–688 The `hif_coa` variable, which is an instance of the `sockaddr_in6{}` structure, is created from the `hif_coa_ifa` variable, which is an instance of the `in6_ifaddr{}` structure.

Listing 5-236

_____mip6_mncore.c

```
690              sc->hif_location = HIF_LOCATION_UNKNOWN;
691              for (hpfx = LIST_FIRST(&sc->hif_prefix_list_home); hpfx;
692                  hpfx = LIST_NEXT(hpfx, hpfx_entry)) {
693                      if (in6_are_prefix_equal(&hif_coa.sin6_addr,
694                          &hpfx->hpfx_mpfx->mpfx_prefix,
695                          hpfx->hpfx_mpfx->mpfx_prefixlen)) {
696                              sc->hif_location = HIF_LOCATION_HOME;
697                              goto i_know_where_i_am;
698                      }
699              }
700              sc->hif_location = HIF_LOCATION_FOREIGN;
```

_____mip6_mncore.c

690–700 The code verifies whether the prefix of the current care-of address is the same as one of the home prefixes of the home network. If the prefix is one of the home prefixes, the mobile node is at home (`HIF_LOCATION_HOME`), otherwise, the mobile node is in a foreign network (`HIF_LOCATION_FOREIGN`).

Listing 5-237

_____mip6_mncore.c

```
701      i_know_where_i_am:
....
706              /*
707               * configure home addresses according to the home
708               * prefixes and the current location determined above.
709               */
710              error = mip6_haddr_config(sc);
711              if (error) {
....
715                      return (error);
716              }
717
718              return (0);
719      }
```

_____mip6_mncore.c

710–716 The `mip6_haddr_config()` function is called to configure home addresses based on the current location information stored in the `hif_softc{}` instance.

Listing 5-238

_____mip6_mncore.c

```
726      static int
727      mip6_register_current_location(sc)
728              struct hif_softc *sc;
729      {
730              int error = 0;
731
732              switch (sc->hif_location) {
733              case HIF_LOCATION_HOME:
```

```
734                        /*
735                         * we moved to home.  unregister our home address.
736                         */
737                        error = mip6_home_registration(sc);
738                        break;
739
740                case HIF_LOCATION_FOREIGN:
741                        /*
742                         * we moved to foreign.  register the current CoA to
743                         * our home agent.
744                         */
745                        /* XXX: TODO register to the old subnet's AR. */
746                        error = mip6_home_registration(sc);
747                        break;
748
749                case HIF_LOCATION_UNKNOWN:
750                        break;
751                }
752
753                return (error);
754        }
```
――― mip6_mncore.c

726–753 The `mip6_register_current_location()` function has one parameter. The `sc` parameter is a pointer to the `hif_softc{}` instance which represents the home network of a mobile node. The `mip6_register_current_location()` function performs any necessary tasks to register the current care-of address based on the current location stored in the `sc` parameter. At this moment, the function calls the `mip6_home_registration()` function when the location is either `HIF_LOCATION_HOME` or `HIF_LOCATION_FOREIGN`. The `mip6_home_registration()` function can handle both registration and de-registration requests. If the location is unknown, the function does nothing.

5.17.4 Configuring Home Addresses

When a mobile node detects movement, it configures home addresses based on the current location. The address configuration is implemented in the `mip6_haddr_config()` function and subsequent functions listed here.

- `mip6_haddr_config()`
  Manages all home address configuration.

- `mip6_attach_haddrs()`
  Removes all home addresses assigned to physical interfaces and configures all home addresses on the specified home virtual interface.

- `mip6_detach_haddrs()`
  Removes all home addresses assigned to the specified virtual interface.

- `mip6_add_haddrs()`
  Does the actual job of assigning home addresses.

- `mip6_remove_haddrs()`
  Does the actual job of removing home addresses.

- `mip6_remove_addr()`
  This generic function removes an IPv6 address from the specified network interface.

FIGURE 5-57

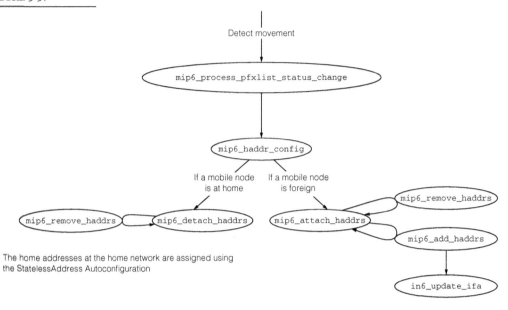

Call flow of home address configuration.

The call flow of these functions is illustrated in Figure 5-57.

Listing 5-239

_____mip6_mncore.c

```
941     static int
942     mip6_haddr_config(sc)
943             struct hif_softc *sc;
944     {
945             int error = 0;
946
947             switch (sc->hif_location) {
948             case HIF_LOCATION_HOME:
949                     /*
950                      * remove all home addresses attached to hif.
951                      * all physical addresses are assigned in a
952                      * address autoconfiguration manner.
953                      */
954                     error = mip6_detach_haddrs(sc);
955
956                     break;
957
958             case HIF_LOCATION_FOREIGN:
959                     /*
960                      * attach all home addresses to the hif interface.
961                      * before attach home addresses, remove home addresses
962                      * from physical i/f to avoid the duplication of
963                      * address.
964                      */
965                     error = mip6_attach_haddrs(sc);
966                     break;
967
968             case HIF_LOCATION_UNKNOWN:
969                     break;
```

```
970                 }
971
972                 return (error);
973         }
```

941–943 The `mip6_haddr_config()` function has one parameter, `sc`, which indicates the home network related to the home address to be configured. Based on the current location, the `mip6_attach_haddrs()` or the `mip6_detach_haddrs()` function is called. The former function removes all home addresses assigned to the corresponding virtual interface and configures them on the physical interface attached to the foreign network of the mobile node. The latter function does the opposite.

Listing 5-240

```
979       static int
980       mip6_attach_haddrs(sc)
981               struct hif_softc *sc;
982       {
983               struct ifnet *ifp;
984               int error = 0;
985
986               /* remove all home addresses for sc from phisical I/F. */
987               for (ifp = ifnet.tqh_first; ifp; ifp = ifp->if_list.tqe_next) {
988                       if (ifp->if_type == IFT_HIF)
989                               continue;
990
991                       error = mip6_remove_haddrs(sc, ifp);
992                       if (error) {
....
997                               return (error);
998                       }
999               }
```

979–981 The `mip6_attach_haddrs()` has one parameter, `sc`, which represents the home network whose home addresses will be configured.

987–999 All home addresses related to the home network specified by the `sc` parameter are removed from all the physical interfaces. The `mip6_remove_haddrs()` function removes all home addresses related to the home virtual interface specified as its first parameter from the physical interface specified as the second parameter.

Listing 5-241

```
1001              /* add home addresses for sc to hif(itself) */
1002              error = mip6_add_haddrs(sc, (struct ifnet *)sc);
1003              if (error) {
....
1008                      return (error);
1009              }
1010
1011              return (0);
1012      }
```

1002–1009 The `mip6_add_haddrs()` function is called to assign home addresses. The `mip6_add_haddrs()` function configures all home addresses related to the home virtual interface specified as the first parameter at the physical interface specified as the second parameter.

Listing 5-242

```
                                                                        mip6_mncore.c
1017    int
1018    mip6_detach_haddrs(sc)
1019            struct hif_softc *sc;
1020    {
1021            struct ifnet *hif_ifp = (struct ifnet *)sc;
1022            struct ifaddr *ia, *ia_next;
1023            struct in6_ifaddr *ia6;
1024            int error = 0;
                                                                        mip6_mncore.c
```

1017–1019 The `mip6_detach_haddrs()` function removes all home addresses assigned to the specified virtual home interface as its parameter. Unlike the `mip6_attach_haddrs()` function, `mip6_detach_haddrs()` only removes the home addresses and does not assign home addresses to physical interfaces. Assigning addresses to physical interfaces is done by the Stateless Address Autoconfiguration mechanism (see Chapter 5 of *IPv6 Core Protocols Implementation*).

Listing 5-243

```
                                                                        mip6_mncore.c
1027            for (ia = TAILQ_FIRST(&hif_ifp->if_addrhead);
1028                    ia;
1029                    ia = ia_next)
....
1035            {
....
1037                    ia_next = TAILQ_NEXT(ia, ifa_link);
....
1041
1042                    if (ia->ifa_addr->sa_family != AF_INET6)
1043                            continue;
1044                    ia6 = (struct in6_ifaddr *)ia;
1045                    if (IN6_IS_ADDR_LINKLOCAL(&ia6->ia_addr.sin6_addr))
1046                            continue;
1047
1048                    error = mip6_remove_addr(hif_ifp, ia6);
1049                    if (error) {
....
1054                            return (error);
1055                    }
1056            }
....
1073            return (error);
1074    }
                                                                        mip6_mncore.c
```

1027–1056 The addresses assigned to a particular interface are held in the `if_addrhead` member variable of the `ifnet{}` structure. In the loop defined on line 1027, all addresses whose address family is IPv6 and whose type is not link-local are removed by calling the `mip6_remove_addr()` function.

Listing 5-244

```
                                                        _____mip6_mncore.c
1079    static int
1080    mip6_add_haddrs(sc, ifp)
1081            struct hif_softc *sc;
1082            struct ifnet *ifp;
1083    {
1084            struct mip6_prefix *mpfx;
1085            struct in6_aliasreq ifra;
1086            struct in6_ifaddr *ia6;
1087            int error = 0;
....
1089            struct timeval mono_time;
....
1093            microtime(&mono_time);
                                                        _____mip6_mncore.c
```

1079–1082 The `mip6_add_haddrs()` function has two parameters: The `sc` parameter is a pointer to the virtual home interface which has information of home addresses to be assigned and the `ifp` parameter is a pointer to the network interface to which the home addresses will be assigned.

Listing 5-245

```
                                                        _____mip6_mncore.c
1096            if ((sc == NULL) || (ifp == NULL)) {
1097                    return (EINVAL);
1098            }
1099
1100            for (mpfx = LIST_FIRST(&mip6_prefix_list); mpfx;
1101                mpfx = LIST_NEXT(mpfx, mpfx_entry)) {
1102                    if (hif_prefix_list_find_withmpfx(&sc->hif_prefix_list_home,
1103                        mpfx) == NULL)
1104                            continue;
                                                        _____mip6_mncore.c
```

1099–1104 The home address configuration will be done on every home prefix information entry kept in the virtual home network interface specified as the `sc` variable. The `hif_prefix_list_find_withmpfx()` function checks to see if the prefix information specified by the second parameter is included in the list specified by the first parameter. Since the `sc->hif_prefix_list_home` member variable keeps home prefixes of the virtual home network specified as `sc`, we can use the `hif_prefix_list_find_withmpfx()` function to verify whether the prefix information is a home prefix.

Listing 5-246

```
                                                        _____mip6_mncore.c
1106                    /*
1107                     * assign home address to mip6_prefix if not
```

```
1108                    * assigned yet.
1109                    */
1110                   if (IN6_IS_ADDR_UNSPECIFIED(&mpfx->mpfx_haddr)) {
1111                           error = mip6_prefix_haddr_assign(mpfx, sc);
1112                           if (error) {
....
1117                                   return (error);
1118                           }
1119                   }
1120
1121                   /* skip a prefix that has 0 lifetime. */
1122                   if (mpfx->mpfx_vltime == 0)
1123                           continue;
```
                                                                    ————mip6_mncore.c

1110–1119 The prefix structure (the `mip6_prefix{}` structure) keeps not only prefix information but also a home address which is generated from the prefix information. The home address is kept in the `mpfx_haddr` member variable. If the address has not been generated, the `mip6_prefix_haddr_assign()` function is called to generate a home address.

1122–1123 If the valid lifetime of the prefix is 0, the home address is not assigned because it has expired.

Listing 5-247
                                                                    ————mip6_mncore.c
```
1125                   /* construct in6_aliasreq. */
1126                   bzero(&ifra, sizeof(ifra));
1127                   bcopy(if_name(ifp), ifra.ifra_name, sizeof(ifra.ifra_name));
1128                   ifra.ifra_addr.sin6_len = sizeof(struct sockaddr_in6);
1129                   ifra.ifra_addr.sin6_family = AF_INET6;
1130                   ifra.ifra_addr.sin6_addr = mpfx->mpfx_haddr;
1131                   ifra.ifra_prefixmask.sin6_len = sizeof(struct sockaddr_in6);
1132                   ifra.ifra_prefixmask.sin6_family = AF_INET6;
1133                   ifra.ifra_flags = IN6_IFF_HOME | IN6_IFF_AUTOCONF;
1134                   if (ifp->if_type == IFT_HIF) {
1135                           in6_prefixlen2mask(&ifra.ifra_prefixmask.sin6_addr,
1136                               128);
1137                   } else {
1138                           in6_prefixlen2mask(&ifra.ifra_prefixmask.sin6_addr,
1139                               mpfx->mpfx_prefixlen);
1140                   }
1141                   ifra.ifra_lifetime.ia6t_vltime = mpfx->mpfx_vltime;
1142                   ifra.ifra_lifetime.ia6t_pltime = mpfx->mpfx_pltime;
1143                   if (ifra.ifra_lifetime.ia6t_vltime == ND6_INFINITE_LIFETIME)
1144                           ifra.ifra_lifetime.ia6t_expire = 0;
1145                   else
1146                           ifra.ifra_lifetime.ia6t_expire = mono_time.tv_sec
1147                               + ifra.ifra_lifetime.ia6t_vltime;
1148                   if (ifra.ifra_lifetime.ia6t_pltime == ND6_INFINITE_LIFETIME)
1149                           ifra.ifra_lifetime.ia6t_preferred = 0;
1150                   else
1151                           ifra.ifra_lifetime.ia6t_preferred = mono_time.tv_sec
1152                               + ifra.ifra_lifetime.ia6t_pltime;
```
                                                                    ————mip6_mncore.c

1126–1152 The `in6_aliasreq{}` structure is a common structure used to manipulate address assignment. When configuring a home address, the `IN6_IFF_HOME` flag, which indicates that the address is a home address, must be set. The `IN6_IFF_AUTOCONF` flag (which means the address is configured automatically) must be set, since the KAME

Mobile IPv6 implementation generates home addresses based on the stateless address autoconfiguration algorithm. The prefix length is set to 128 when assigning a home address to home virtual interfaces; otherwise, it is set to the length specified by the prefix information. The lifetimes (the preferred lifetime and the valid lifetime) of the home address are copied from the lifetime information of the prefix information entry.

Listing 5-248

mip6_mncore.c

```
1153                    ia6 = in6ifa_ifpwithaddr(ifp, &ifra.ifra_addr.sin6_addr);
1154                    error = in6_update_ifa(ifp, &ifra, ia6, 0);
1155                    if (error) {
....
1161                            return (error);
1162                    }
1163            }
1164
1165            return (0);
1166    }
```

mip6_mncore.c

1153–1163 The `ia6` variable will point to the home address information which matches the information of the home address we are going to assign. If there is no such address, `ia6` will be a NULL pointer. If such a home address has already been assigned, then `ia6` is passed to the `in6_update_ifa()` function so that the function can update the existing entry; otherwise, a new address will be assigned to the specified network interface as a new home address.

Listing 5-249

mip6_prefix.c

```
183    int
184    mip6_prefix_haddr_assign(mpfx, sc)
185            struct mip6_prefix *mpfx;
186            struct hif_softc *sc;
187    {
188            struct in6_addr ifid;
189            int error = 0;
190
191            if ((mpfx == NULL) || (sc == NULL)) {
192                    return (EINVAL);
193            }
....
200            {
201                    error = get_ifid((struct ifnet *)sc, NULL, &ifid);
202                    if (error)
203                            return (error);
204            }
205
206            /* XXX */
207            mpfx->mpfx_haddr = mpfx->mpfx_prefix;
208            mpfx->mpfx_haddr.s6_addr32[2] = ifid.s6_addr32[2];
209            mpfx->mpfx_haddr.s6_addr32[3] = ifid.s6_addr32[3];
210
211            return (0);
212    }
```

mip6_prefix.c

183–212 The `mip6_prefix_haddr_assign()` function assigns a home address to the
`mip6_prefix{}` instance based on the prefix information stored in the prefix structure. The home address is copied into the `mpfx_haddr` field of the `mip6_prefix{}`
structure. The prefix part is copied from the `mpfx_prefix` variable which stores prefix
information. The interface identifier part is copied from the result of the `get_ifid()`
function, which returns the interface identifier of a specified network interface.

Listing 5-250

_____mip6_mncore.c
```
1171    static int
1172    mip6_remove_haddrs(sc, ifp)
1173            struct hif_softc *sc;
1174            struct ifnet *ifp;
1175    {
1176            struct ifaddr *ia, *ia_next;
1177            struct in6_ifaddr *ia6;
1178            struct mip6_prefix *mpfx;
1179            int error = 0;
```
_____mip6_mncore.c

1171–1174 The `mip6_remove_haddrs()` function has two parameters. The `sc` parameter
is a pointer to the `hif_softc{}` instance which holds home prefix information, and
the `ifp` parameter is a pointer to the network interface from which the home addresses
related to the `hif_softc{}` instance specified as the first parameter are removed.

Listing 5-251

_____mip6_mncore.c
```
1182            for (ia = TAILQ_FIRST(&ifp->if_addrhead);
1183                 ia;
1184                 ia = ia_next)
....
1190            {
....
1192                    ia_next = TAILQ_NEXT(ia, ifa_link);
....
1196
1197                    if (ia->ifa_addr->sa_family != AF_INET6)
1198                            continue;
1199                    ia6 = (struct in6_ifaddr *)ia;
```
_____mip6_mncore.c

1182–1199 All IPv6 addresses assigned to the network interface specified by `ifp` will be
checked.

Listing 5-252

_____mip6_mncore.c
```
1201            for (mpfx = LIST_FIRST(&mip6_prefix_list); mpfx;
1202                 mpfx = LIST_NEXT(mpfx, mpfx_entry)) {
1203                    if (hif_prefix_list_find_withmpfx(
1204                        &sc->hif_prefix_list_home, mpfx) == NULL)
1205                            continue;
1206
```

```
1207                             if (!in6_are_prefix_equal(&ia6->ia_addr.sin6_addr,
1208                                     &mpfx->mpfx_prefix, mpfx->mpfx_prefixlen)) {
1209                                     continue;
1210                             }
1211                             error = mip6_remove_addr(ifp, ia6);
1212                             if (error) {
....
1216                                     continue;
1217                             }
1218                     }
1219             }
1220
1221             return (error);
1222     }
```
——mip6_mncore.c

1201–1205 All home prefixes which belong to the home network specified as sc will be checked.

1207–1217 The home prefix and the prefix part of each address assigned to the network interface specified by ifp are compared. If these prefixes are equal, the mip6_remove_addr() function is called to remove the address which is assigned on the home network.

Listing 5-253

——mip6_mncore.c
```
1227     static int
1228     mip6_remove_addr(ifp, ia6)
1229             struct ifnet *ifp;
1230             struct in6_ifaddr *ia6;
1231     {
1232             struct in6_aliasreq ifra;
1233             int i = 0, purgeprefix = 0;
1234             struct nd_prefixctl pr0;
1235             struct nd_prefix *pr = NULL;
1236
1237             bcopy(if_name(ifp), ifra.ifra_name, sizeof(ifra.ifra_name));
1238             bcopy(&ia6->ia_addr, &ifra.ifra_addr, sizeof(struct sockaddr_in6));
1239             bcopy(&ia6->ia_prefixmask, &ifra.ifra_prefixmask,
1240                     sizeof(struct sockaddr_in6));
```
——mip6_mncore.c

1227–1230 The mip6_remove_addr() function has two parameters. The ifp parameter is a pointer to the network interface and the ia6 parameter is a pointer to the address information which is to be removed.

1237–1240 An in6_aliasreq{} instance, which keeps the information of the address to be removed, is created.

Listing 5-254

——mip6_mncore.c
```
1242             /* address purging code is copied from in6_control(). */
1243
1244             /*
1245              * If the address being deleted is the only one that owns
1246              * the corresponding prefix, expire the prefix as well.
1247              * XXX: theoretically, we don't have to worry about such
1248              * relationship, since we separate the address management
1249              * and the prefix management.  We do this, however, to provide
```

```
1250                * as much backward compatibility as possible in terms of
1251                * the ioctl operation.
1252                */
1253               bzero(&pr0, sizeof(pr0));
1254               pr0.ndpr_ifp = ifp;
1255               pr0.ndpr_plen = in6_mask2len(&ia6->ia_prefixmask.sin6_addr, NULL);
1256               if (pr0.ndpr_plen == 128)
1257                       goto purgeaddr;
1258               pr0.ndpr_prefix = ia6->ia_addr;
1259               for (i = 0; i < 4; i++) {
1260                       pr0.ndpr_prefix.sin6_addr.s6_addr32[i] &=
1261                               ia6->ia_prefixmask.sin6_addr.s6_addr32[i];
1262               }
1263               /*
1264                * The logic of the following condition is a bit complicated.
1265                * We expire the prefix when
1266                * 1. the address obeys autoconfiguration and it is the
1267                *    only owner of the associated prefix, or
1268                * 2. the address does not obey autoconf and there is no
1269                *    other owner of the prefix.
1270                */
1271               if ((pr = nd6_prefix_lookup(&pr0)) != NULL &&
1272                   (((ia6->ia6_flags & IN6_IFF_AUTOCONF) != 0 &&
1273                   pr->ndpr_refcnt == 1) ||
1274                   ((ia6->ia6_flags & IN6_IFF_AUTOCONF) == 0 &&
1275                   pr->ndpr_refcnt == 0)))
1276                       purgeprefix = 1;
```
── *mip6_mncore.c*

1242 As the comment says, the code is based on the address removal code in the
`in6_control()` function.

1253–1262 An instance of the `nd_prefixctl{}` structure, which includes the prefix information of the address to be removed, is prepared.

1271–1276 In the KAME IPv6 implementation, an address information structure and prefix
information structure are linked together. Every IPv6 address whose prefix length is less
than 128 has a corresponding prefix information entry. When an address is removed, the
corresponding prefix information has to be removed properly. The removal algorithm
differs depending on whether the prefix has an autoconfigured address. If an autoconfigured address is removed and the reference count of related prefix information is 1, then
the prefix information related to the address is removed as well. If the address is not an
auto-configured address, then only the related prefix is removed if the reference count of
the prefix is 0.

Listing 5-255

── *mip6_mncore.c*
```
1278     purgeaddr:
1279               in6_purgeaddr(&ia6->ia_ifa);
1280               if (pr && purgeprefix)
1281                       prelist_remove(pr);
1282
1283               return (0);
1284       }
```
── *mip6_mncore.c*

1278–1281 The `in6_purgeaddr()` function is called to remove the specified address.
The `prelist_remove()` function is called if the address has corresponding prefix
information and it needs to be removed.

5.17.5 Sending a Binding Update Message

When a mobile node detects its movement, it needs to send a Binding Update message to update the current care-of address which is registered to its home agent. There are two kinds of Binding Update messages. One type is used for home registration, and the other is sent to correspondent nodes. The `mip6_home_registration()`, the `mip6_home_registration2()` and the `mip6_bu_send_bu()` functions are used for the former purpose, while the `mip6_bu_send_cbu()` function is used for the latter. The overview of the registration procedure is described in Section 5.4.2 and the return routability procedure is described in Section 5.5.1.

Sending a Home Registration Message

Figure 5-58 shows the function call flow when a home registration message is sent.

Listing 5-256

```
                                                              mip6_mncore.c
1671    int
1672    mip6_home_registration(sc)
1673            struct hif_softc *sc;
1674    {
1675            struct in6_addr hif_coa;
1676            struct mip6_prefix *mpfx;
1677            struct mip6_bu *mbu;
1678            const struct in6_addr *haaddr;
1679            struct mip6_ha *mha;
                                                              mip6_mncore.c
```

FIGURE 5-58

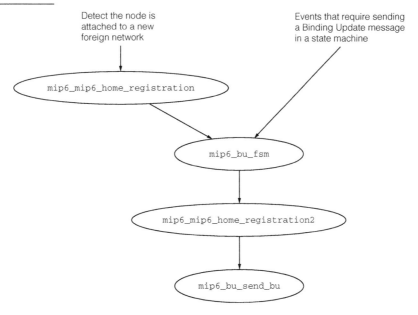

Call flow when sending a home registration message.

1671–1673 The `mip6_home_registration()` function is called from the `mip6_register_current_location()` function to initiate the home registration or home de-registration procedure. The parameter `sc` is a pointer to the `hif_softc{}` instance which indicates the home network of a mobile node performing registration.

Listing 5-257
——mip6_mncore.c

```
1681            /* get current CoA and recover its scope information. */
1682            if (sc->hif_coa_ifa == NULL) {
....
1686                    return (0);
1687            }
1688            hif_coa = sc->hif_coa_ifa->ia_addr.sin6_addr;
```
——mip6_mncore.c

1682–1688 If the current care-of address of the specified home network has not been set yet, there is nothing to do. If there is a valid care-of address, the care-of address stored in the `hif_coa_ifa` variable is copied to the `hif_coa` variable.

Listing 5-258
——mip6_mncore.c

```
1690            for (mpfx = LIST_FIRST(&mip6_prefix_list); mpfx;
1691                mpfx = LIST_NEXT(mpfx, mpfx_entry)) {
1692                if (hif_prefix_list_find_withmpfx(&sc->hif_prefix_list_home,
1693                    mpfx) == NULL)
1694                    continue;
1695
1696                for (mbu = LIST_FIRST(&sc->hif_bu_list); mbu;
1697                    mbu = LIST_NEXT(mbu, mbu_entry)) {
1698                    if ((mbu->mbu_flags & IP6MU_HOME) == 0)
1699                        continue;
1700                    if (IN6_ARE_ADDR_EQUAL(&mbu->mbu_haddr,
1701                        &mpfx->mpfx_haddr))
1702                        break;
1703                }
```
——mip6_mncore.c

1690–1703 The loop searches for home registration entries of home addresses of the mobile node. The home addresses are stored in `mip6_prefix{}` structures. The outer loop finds the home address by checking the `hif_prefix_list_home` field of the `sc` parameter that contains all home prefixes for the virtual home interface. The inner loop looks for home registration entries of the home addresses.

Listing 5-259
——mip6_mncore.c

```
1704                if (mbu == NULL) {
1705                    /* not exist */
1706                    if (sc->hif_location == HIF_LOCATION_HOME) {
1707                        /*
1708                         * we are home and we have no binding
1709                         * update entry for home registration.
1710                         * this will happen when either of the
1711                         * following two cases happens.
```

```
1712                                    *
1713                                    * 1. enabling MN function at home
1714                                    * subnet.
1715                                    *
1716                                    * 2. returning home with expired home
1717                                    * registration.
1718                                    *
1719                                    * in either case, we should do
1720                                    * nothing.
1721                                    */
1722                                    continue;
1723                               }
```
————————————————————————————————————mip6_mncore.c

1704–1723 If there is no existing binding update list entry and the mobile node is at home, there is nothing to do.

Listing 5-260
————————————————————————————————————mip6_mncore.c
```
1725                     /*
1726                      * no home registration found.  create a new
1727                      * binding update entry.
1728                      */
1729
1730                     /* pick the preferable HA from the list. */
1731                     mha = hif_find_preferable_ha(sc);
1732
1733                     if (mha == NULL) {
1734                             /*
1735                              * if no home agent is found, set an
1736                              * unspecified address for now.  DHAAD
1737                              * is triggered when sending a binging
1738                              * update message.
1739                              */
1740                             haddr = &in6addr_any;
1741                     } else {
1742                             haddr = &mha->mha_addr;
1743                     }
1744
1745                     mbu = mip6_bu_create(haddr, mpfx, &hif_coa,
1746                         IP6MU_ACK|IP6MU_HOME
....
1748                         |IP6MU_LINK
....
1750                         , sc);
1751                     if (mbu == NULL)
1752                             return (ENOMEM);
1753                     /*
1754                      * for the first registration to the home
1755                      * agent, the ack timeout value should be
1756                      * (retrans * dadtransmits) * 1.5.
1757                      */
1758                     /*
1759                      * XXX: TODO: KAME has different dad retrans
1760                      * values for each interfaces.  which retrans
1761                      * value should be selected ?
1762                      */
1763
1764                     mip6_bu_list_insert(&sc->hif_bu_list, mbu);
1765
1766                     /* XXX */
1767                     if (sc->hif_location != HIF_LOCATION_HOME)
```

```
1768                                     mip6_bu_fsm(mbu,
1769                                         MIP6_BU_PRI_FSM_EVENT_MOVEMENT, NULL);
1770                         else
1771                                     mip6_bu_fsm(mbu,
1772                                         MIP6_BU_PRI_FSM_EVENT_RETURNING_HOME,
1773                                         NULL);
```
─── mip6_mncore.c

1731–1752 If there is no existing binding update list entry and the mobile node is in a foreign
network, a new binding update list entry is created to register the current location of
the mobile node. The `hif_find_preferable_ha()` function returns the home agent
which has the highest priority from the home agent list maintained in the mobile node. If
the mobile node has not learned any information about its home agents, the unspecified
address is temporarily set as a home agent address. The address will be determined by
the Dynamic Home Agent Address Discovery procedure launched later. When creating
a binding update list entry for home registration, the `IP6MU_ACK`, `IP6MU_HOME` and
`IP6MU_LINK` flags are specified. The `IP6MU_ACK` and `IP6MU_HOME` flags are necessary
for home registration. The `IP6MU_LINK` flag must be set when the interface identifier
part of the home address is the same as the interface identifier of the link-local address of
the mobile node. The flag is always set in the KAME implementation, since it always uses
the interface identifier of the link-local address of the virtual interface when generating a
home address.

1764–1773 The newly created binding update list entry is inserted to the binding update list
and the state machine of the entry is triggered based on the current location. If the mobile
node is at home, the `RETURNING_HOME` event is sent; otherwise, the `MOVEMENT` event is
sent. State machines will be discussed in Section 5.17.19.

Listing 5-261
─── mip6_mncore.c
```
1774                         } else {
1775                                 if (sc->hif_location != HIF_LOCATION_HOME)
1776                                         mip6_bu_fsm(mbu,
1777                                             MIP6_BU_PRI_FSM_EVENT_MOVEMENT, NULL);
1778                                 else
1779                                         mip6_bu_fsm(mbu,
1780                                             MIP6_BU_PRI_FSM_EVENT_RETURNING_HOME,
1781                                             NULL);
1782                         }
1783                 }
1784
1785                 return (0);
1786     }
```
─── mip6_mncore.c

1774–1782 If a binding update list entry already exists, the `mip6_bu_fsm()` function is called
to trigger an event of the state machine based on the current location.

Listing 5-262
─── mip6_mncore.c
```
1788     int
1789     mip6_home_registration2(mbu)
1790             struct mip6_bu *mbu;
```

```
1791     {
1792             struct in6_addr hif_coa;
1793             struct mip6_prefix *mpfx;
1794             int32_t coa_lifetime, prefix_lifetime;
1795             int error;
....
1797             struct timeval mono_time;
```
———mip6_mncore.c

1788–1790 The `mip6_home_registration2()` function is called from the state machine of a binding update list entry as a result of state transition. The `mbu` parameter is a pointer to the binding update list entry which needs to be registered.

Listing 5-263
———mip6_mncore.c

```
1800             /* sanity check. */
1801             if (mbu == NULL)
1802                     return (EINVAL);
....
1808             /* get current CoA and recover its scope information. */
1809             if (mbu->mbu_hif->hif_coa_ifa == NULL) {
....
1813                     return (0);
1814             }
1815             hif_coa = mbu->mbu_hif->hif_coa_ifa->ia_addr.sin6_addr;
```
———mip6_mncore.c

1809–1815 The `hif_coa_ifa` variable points to the current care-of address. If there is no available care-of address, the home registration procedure is aborted.

Listing 5-264
———mip6_mncore.c

```
1817             /*
1818              * a binding update entry exists. update information.
1819              */
1820
1821             /* update CoA. */
1822             if (mbu->mbu_hif->hif_location == HIF_LOCATION_HOME) {
1823                     /* home de-registration. */
1824                     mbu->mbu_coa = mbu->mbu_haddr;
1825             } else {
1826                     /* home registration. */
1827                     mbu->mbu_coa = hif_coa;
1828             }
1829
1830             /* update lifetime. */
1831             coa_lifetime = mip6_coa_get_lifetime(&mbu->mbu_coa);
1832             prefix_lifetime = 0x7fffffff;
1833             for (mpfx = LIST_FIRST(&mip6_prefix_list); mpfx;
1834                 mpfx = LIST_NEXT(mpfx, mpfx_entry)) {
1835                     if (hif_prefix_list_find_withmpfx(
1836                         &mbu->mbu_hif->hif_prefix_list_home, mpfx) == NULL)
1837                             continue;
1838                     if (mpfx->mpfx_vltime < prefix_lifetime)
1839                             prefix_lifetime = mpfx->mpfx_vltime;
1840             }
```

```
1841              if (coa_lifetime < prefix_lifetime) {
1842                      mbu->mbu_lifetime = coa_lifetime;
1843              } else {
1844                      mbu->mbu_lifetime = prefix_lifetime;
1845              }
```
_____mip6_mncore.c

1822–1845 The member variables of the existing binding update list entry are updated. The
care-of address is set to the home address of the mobile node if the current location is
home; otherwise, the care-of address is copied from the care-of address stored in the
hif_softc{} instance. The lifetime of the entry is calculated from the lifetimes of the
care-of and home addresses. The shorter lifetime of the two addresses will be chosen as
the lifetime of the binding update list entry.

Listing 5-265
_____mip6_mncore.c

```
1846              mbu->mbu_expire = mono_time.tv_sec + mbu->mbu_lifetime;
1847              /* sanity check for overflow */
1848              if (mbu->mbu_expire < mono_time.tv_sec)
1849                      mbu->mbu_expire = 0x7fffffff;
1850              mbu->mbu_refresh = mbu->mbu_lifetime;
1851              /* mbu->mbu_flags |= IP6MU_DAD ;*/
1852
1853              /* send a binding update. */
1854              error = mip6_bu_send_bu(mbu);
1855
1856              return (error);
1857      }
```
_____mip6_mncore.c

1846–1854 The expiration time of the entry is set based on the current time and the lifetime
calculated above. The refresh interval is set to the same value with the lifetime for now.
The value will be updated when a Binding Acknowledgment is received and processed
(see Section 5.17.6).

Sending a Binding Update Message

The mip6_bu_send_bu() creates a Binding Update message based on the information passed
as its parameter and sends the message to the home agent of a mobile node.

Listing 5-266
_____mip6_mncore.c

```
2163      int
2164      mip6_bu_send_bu(mbu)
2165              struct mip6_bu *mbu;
2166      {
2167              struct mbuf *m;
2168              struct ip6_pktopts opt;
2169              int error = 0;
....
2171              /* sanity check. */
2172              if (mbu == NULL)
2173                      return (EINVAL);
2174
2175              if (IN6_IS_ADDR_UNSPECIFIED(&mbu->mbu_paddr)) {
2176                      /* we do not know where to send a binding update. */
```

```
2177                          if ((mbu->mbu_flags & IP6MU_HOME) != 0) {
2178                                  error = mip6_icmp6_dhaad_req_output(mbu->mbu_hif);
2179                                  if (error) {
....
2184                                          /* continue, anyway. */
2185                                  }
2186                                  /*
2187                                   * a binding update will be sent
2188                                   * immediately after receiving DHAAD
2189                                   * reply.
2190                                   */
2191                                  goto bu_send_bu_end;
2192                          }
2193                          panic("a peer address must be known when sending a binding
      update.");
2194                  }
```
—— mip6_mncore.c

— *Line 2193 is broken here for layout reasons. However, it is a single line of code.*

2175–2192 If the destination address, mbu_paddr, of the Binding Update message to be sent is unspecified and the binding update list entry is for home registration, a DHAAD request message is sent by the mip6_icmp6_dhaad_req_output() function. This occurs when a mobile node is turned on at a foreign network and does not know anything about its home agents.

Listing 5-267

—— mip6_mncore.c
```
2196                  /* create an ipv6 header to send a binding update. */
2197                  m = mip6_create_ip6hdr(&mbu->mbu_haddr, &mbu->mbu_paddr,
2198                      IPPROTO_NONE, 0);
2199                  if (m == NULL) {
....
2202                          error = ENOBUFS;
2203                          goto bu_send_bu_end;
2204                  }
```
—— mip6_mncore.c

2197–2204 An IPv6 header is prepared based on the source and destination address information stored in the binding update list entry. If the preparation fails, the Binding Update message will not be sent. The code will try to send the message at the next timeout of the retransmission timer of the entry.

Listing 5-268

—— mip6_mncore.c
```
2206                  /* initialize packet options structure. */
2207                  ip6_initpktopts(&opt);
2208
2209                  /* create a binding update mobility header. */
2210                  error = mip6_ip6mu_create(&opt.ip6po_mh, &mbu->mbu_haddr,
2211                      &mbu->mbu_paddr, mbu->mbu_hif);
2212                  if (error) {
....
2216                          m_freem(m);
2217                          goto free_ip6pktopts;
2218                  }
```

```
2219
2220                /* send a binding update. */
 ....
2222                error = ip6_output(m, &opt, NULL, 0, NULL, NULL
 ....
2224                  , NULL
 ....
2226                            );
2227                if (error) {
 ....
2231                    goto free_ip6pktopts;
2232                }
2233
2234      free_ip6pktopts:
2235            if (opt.ip6po_mh)
2236                FREE(opt.ip6po_mh, M_IP6OPT);
2237
2238      bu_send_bu_end:
2239            return (error);
2240      }
```
                                                              _____mip6_mncore.c

2207 A Binding Update message is passed to the output routine as a packet option. The
`ip6_pktopts{}` structure, which keeps the message, is initialized.

2210–2232 A Binding Update message is created by the `mip6_ip6mu_create()` function.
The created message, based on the information stored in the binding update list entry, is
sent by the `ip6_output()` function.

2234–2236 Memory that is allocated to keep the packet option is released before the function
finishes.

Sending a Binding Update Message to a Correspondent Node

The `mip6_bu_send_cbu()` function is used when a mobile node sends a Binding Update
message to a correspondent node. The Binding Authorization Data option must be used when
a mobile node sends a Binding Update message to correspondent nodes. The value that the
option contains will be computed by the return routability procedure which is discussed in
Section 5.17.23.

Listing 5-269
                                                              _____mip6_mncore.c
```
2242      int
2243      mip6_bu_send_cbu(mbu)
2244            struct mip6_bu *mbu;
2245      {
2246            struct mbuf *m;
2247            struct ip6_pktopts opt;
2248            int error = 0;
2249
2250            /* sanity check. */
2251            if (mbu == NULL)
2252                return (EINVAL);
2253
2254            ip6_initpktopts(&opt);
2255
```

```
2256            m = mip6_create_ip6hdr(&mbu->mbu_haddr, &mbu->mbu_paddr,
      IPPROTO_NONE, 0);
2257            if (m == NULL) {
....
2260                    return (ENOMEM);
2261            }
2262
2263            error = mip6_ip6mu_create(&opt.ip6po_mh, &mbu->mbu_haddr,
2264                &mbu->mbu_paddr, mbu->mbu_hif);
2265            if (error) {
....
2270                    m_freem(m);
2271                    goto free_ip6pktopts;
2272            }
2273
2274            mip6stat.mip6s_obu++;
2275            error = ip6_output(m, &opt, NULL, 0, NULL, NULL
....
2277                                    , NULL
....
2279                                    );
2280            if (error) {
2281                    mip6log((LOG_ERR,
2282                        "%s:%d: sending a binding update falied. (%d)\n",
2283                        __FILE__, __LINE__, error));
2284                    goto free_ip6pktopts;
2285            }
2286
2287    free_ip6pktopts:
2288            if (opt.ip6po_mh)
2289                    FREE(opt.ip6po_mh, M_IP6OPT);
2290
2291            return (error);
2292    }
```
———mip6_mncore.c

— *Line 2256 is broken here for layout reasons. However, it is a single line of code.*

2254–2289 The procedure is almost the same as the `mip6_bu_send_bu()` function. The only difference between these two functions is that the `mip6_bu_send_bu()` function may send a DHAAD request message if a mobile node does not know the address of its home agent. This never happens when sending a Binding Update message to correspondent nodes because the address of the peer node must be known before the message is sent.

Create a Binding Update Message

The `mip6_ip6mu_create()` function prepares a Binding Update message.

Listing 5-270
———mip6_mncore.c
```
3584    int
3585    mip6_ip6mu_create(pktopt_mobility, src, dst, sc)
3586            struct ip6_mh **pktopt_mobility;
3587            struct in6_addr *src, *dst;
3588            struct hif_softc *sc;
3589    {
3590            struct ip6_mh_binding_update *ip6mu;
3591            struct ip6_mh_opt_nonce_index *mopt_nonce = NULL;
3592            struct ip6_mh_opt_auth_data *mopt_auth = NULL;
3593            struct ip6_mh_opt_altcoa *mopt_altcoa = NULL;
3594            struct in6_addr altcoa;
```

```
3595        int ip6mu_size, pad;
3596        int bu_size = 0, nonce_size = 0, auth_size = 0, altcoa_size = 0;
3597        struct mip6_bu *mbu, *hrmbu;
3598        struct mip6_prefix *mpfx;
3599        int need_rr = 0, ignore_co_nonce = 0;
3600        u_int8_t key_bm[MIP6_KBM_LEN]; /* Stated as 'Kbm' in the spec */
```
_____ mip6_mncore.c

3584–3588 This function can handle both a home registration message and a correspondent
registration message. The `pktopt_mobility` parameter is a pointer to the memory in
which the created message is stored. The `src` parameter is the home address of the mobile
node, the `dst` parameter is the address of the home agent or the correspondent node, and
the `sc` parameter is a pointer to the `hif_softc{}` instance which indicates the home
network of the mobile node.

Listing 5-271
_____ mip6_mncore.c

```
3604            *pktopt_mobility = NULL;
3605
3606            mbu = mip6_bu_list_find_withpaddr(&sc->hif_bu_list, dst, src);
3607            hrmbu = mip6_bu_list_find_home_registration(&sc->hif_bu_list, src);
3608            if ((mbu == NULL) &&
3609                (hrmbu != NULL) &&
3610                (MIP6_IS_BU_BOUND_STATE(hrmbu))) {
3611                    /* XXX */
3612                    /* create a binding update entry and send CoTI/HoTI. */
3613                    return (0);
3614            }
3615            if (mbu == NULL) {
3616                    /*
3617                     * this is the case that the home registration is on
3618                     * going.  that is, (mbu == NULL) && (hrmbu != NULL)
3619                     * but hrmbu->mbu_fsm_state != STATE_REG.
3620                     */
3621                    return (0);
3622            }
3623            if ((mbu->mbu_state & MIP6_BU_STATE_NEEDTUNNEL) != 0) {
3624                    return (0);
3625            }
```
_____ mip6_mncore.c

3606–3607 The binding update list entry for the destination address and the entry of the home
address of the mobile node are identified. The `mbu` variable will point to the binding
update list entry which contains the information between the mobile node and the node
to which the message is sent, if it already exists. The `hrmbu` variable will point to the
binding update list entry for home registration between the home address of the mobile
node and its home agent, if it exists.

3608–3614 If the mobile node has already registered to its home agent, but it does not have
a binding update list entry for the correspondent node specified by the `dst` parameter,
then nothing will be done. Before sending a Binding Update message to the correspondent
node, the return routability procedure has to be performed to secure the message. The
return routability code will send the message when it completes the procedure.

3615–3622 If the mobile node has not finished home registration, a Binding Update message
cannot be sent to the correspondent node.

3623–3625 If the correspondent node is marked as a node that does not support Mobile IPv6 (that is, the `MIP6_BU_STATE_NEEDTUNNEL` flag is set), a Binding Update message will not be sent. The node will not understand the message and will just reply with an ICMPv6 error.

Listing 5-272

```
                                                                 mip6_mncore.c
3626              if (IN6_IS_ADDR_UNSPECIFIED(&mbu->mbu_paddr)) {
3627                      /*
3628                       * the peer addr is unspecified.  this happens when
3629                       * home registration occurs but no home agent address
3630                       * is known.
3631                       */
....
3635                      mip6_icmp6_dhaad_req_output(sc);
3636                      return (0);
3637              }
                                                                 mip6_mncore.c
```

3626–3637 If the destination address of the binding update list entry for home registration is an unspecified address, the DHAAD procedure is initiated. This only happens when the entry is for home registration.

Listing 5-273

```
                                                                 mip6_mncore.c
3639              if (!(mbu->mbu_flags & IP6MU_HOME)) {
3640                      need_rr = 1;
3641              }
3642
3643              /* check if we have a valid prefix information. */
3644              mpfx = mip6_prefix_list_find_withhaddr(&mip6_prefix_list, src);
3645              if (mpfx == NULL)
3646                      return(EINVAL);
                                                                 mip6_mncore.c
```

3639–3641 If the binding update list entry is for a correspondent node, a Binding Authorization data option has to be included in the Binding Update message. The `need_rr` variable activates the code of the option processing.

3644–3646 The mobile node must have the prefix information related to the source address. The lifetime information of the prefix will be used to calculate the lifetime of binding information later.

Listing 5-274

```
                                                                 mip6_mncore.c
3648              bu_size = sizeof(struct ip6_mh_binding_update);
3649              if (need_rr) {
3650                      /*
3651                       |<- bu_size -> <- nonce_size -> <- auth_size ->
3652                       +-------------+----------------+---------------+
3653                       | bind. up.   |   nonce opt.   |   auth. opt.  |
3654                       +-------------+----------------+---------------+
3655                        <------->
3656                        sizeof(struct ip6_mh_binding_update)
3657                                        <-->
```

```
3658                                    Padding for nonce opt. alignment
3659                            */
3660                           bu_size += MIP6_PADLEN(bu_size, 2, 0);
3661                           nonce_size = sizeof(struct ip6_mh_opt_nonce_index);
3662                           nonce_size += MIP6_PADLEN(bu_size + nonce_size, 8, 2);
3663                           /* (6.2.7)
3664                              The Binding Authorization Data option does not
3665                              have alignment requirements as such.  However,
3666                              since this option must be the last mobility option,
3667                              an implicit alignment requirement is 8n + 2.
3668                           */
3669                           auth_size = IP6MOPT_AUTHDATA_SIZE;
3670                           auth_size += MIP6_PADLEN(bu_size + nonce_size
       + auth_size, 8, 0);
....
3674                           altcoa_size = 0;
3675                   } else {
3676                           bu_size += MIP6_PADLEN(bu_size, 8, 6);
3677                           altcoa_size = sizeof(struct ip6_mh_opt_altcoa);
3678                           nonce_size = auth_size = 0;
3679                   }
3680                   ip6mu_size = bu_size + nonce_size + auth_size + altcoa_size;
```
                                                                    ————————mip6_mncore.c
— *Line 3670 is broken here for layout reasons. However, it is a single line of code.*

3648–3680 The size of the Binding Update message is calculated. The size of the message varies based on the node type of the destination. If the destination is the home agent and the message is for home registration, the message will include the Alternate Care-of Address option, otherwise, the message will include the Nonce Index option and the Binding Authorization Data option.

The alignment requirement of the Nonce Index option is $2n + 0$ and the size of the option is represented by the size of the `ip6_mh_opt_nonce_index{}` structure. The size of the Binding Authorization Data option is defined as the `IP6MOPT_AUTHDATA_SIZE` macro and its implicit alignment requirement is $8n + 2$. If the Binding Update message is for a correspondent node, then these lengths are added to the size of the Binding Update message.

The alignment requirement of the Alternate Care-of Address option is $8n + 2$. The size of the option is the size of the `ip6_mh_opt_altcoa{}` structure. If the Binding Update message is for home registration, the size is added to the size of the Binding Update message.

Listing 5-275
                                                                    ————————mip6_mncore.c

```
3682               MALLOC(ip6mu, struct ip6_mh_binding_update *,
3683                       ip6mu_size, M_IP6OPT, M_NOWAIT);
3684               if (ip6mu == NULL)
3685                       return (ENOMEM);
3686
3687               if (need_rr) {
3688                       mopt_nonce = (struct ip6_mh_opt_nonce_index *)((u_int8_t *)
       ip6mu + bu_size);
3689                       mopt_auth = (struct ip6_mh_opt_auth_data *)((u_int8_t *)
       mopt_nonce + nonce_size);
3690               } else {
3691                       mopt_altcoa = (struct ip6_mh_opt_altcoa *)((u_int8_t *)ip6mu
       + bu_size);
3692               }
```
                                                                    ————————mip6_mncore.c
— *Lines 3688, 3689, and 3691 are broken here for layout reasons. However, they are a single line of code.*

3682–3692 The required memory for the Binding Update message is allocated and all pointers (`mopt_once`, `mopt_auth` and `mopt_altcoa`) point to the proper addresses at which the options are located.

Listing 5-276

```
                                                                _mip6_mncore.c
3694            /* update sequence number of this binding update entry. */
3695            mbu->mbu_seqno++;
3696
3697            bzero(ip6mu, ip6mu_size);
3698
3699            ip6mu->ip6mhbu_proto = IPPROTO_NONE;
3700            ip6mu->ip6mhbu_len = (ip6mu_size >> 3) - 1;
3701            ip6mu->ip6mhbu_type = IP6_MH_TYPE_BU;
3702            ip6mu->ip6mhbu_flags = mbu->mbu_flags;
3703            ip6mu->ip6mhbu_seqno = htons(mbu->mbu_seqno);
3704            if (IN6_ARE_ADDR_EQUAL(&mbu->mbu_haddr, &mbu->mbu_coa)) {
3705                    /* this binding update is for home un-registration. */
3706                    ip6mu->ip6mhbu_lifetime = 0;
3707                    if (need_rr) {
3708                            ignore_co_nonce = 1;
3709                    }
3710            } else {
3711                    u_int32_t haddr_lifetime, coa_lifetime, lifetime;
3712
3713                    haddr_lifetime = mpfx->mpfx_vltime;
3714                    coa_lifetime = mip6_coa_get_lifetime(&mbu->mbu_coa);
3715                    lifetime = haddr_lifetime < coa_lifetime ?
3716                            haddr_lifetime : coa_lifetime;
3717                    if ((mbu->mbu_flags & IP6MU_HOME) == 0) {
3718                            if (mip6ctl_bu_maxlifetime > 0 &&
3719                                lifetime > mip6ctl_bu_maxlifetime)
3720                                    lifetime = mip6ctl_bu_maxlifetime;
3721                    } else {
3722                            if (mip6ctl_hrbu_maxlifetime > 0 &&
3723                                lifetime > mip6ctl_hrbu_maxlifetime)
3724                                    lifetime = mip6ctl_hrbu_maxlifetime;
3725                    }
3726                    mbu->mbu_lifetime = lifetime;
3727                    mbu->mbu_expire = time_second + mbu->mbu_lifetime;
3728                    mbu->mbu_refresh = mbu->mbu_lifetime;
3729                    ip6mu->ip6mhbu_lifetime =
3730                        htons((u_int16_t)(mbu->mbu_lifetime >> 2));
     /* units 4 secs */
3731            }
                                                                _mip6_mncore.c
```

— *Line 3730 is broken here for layout reasons. However, it is a single line of code.*

3695 The sequence number kept in the binding update list entry is incremented to prevent a replay attack.

3699–3730 The packet information is filled based on the binding update list entry. The lifetime is set to 0 when the mobile node is at home. In addition, the `ignore_co_nonce` variable is set to true, since there is no need to differentiate between the home address and the care-of address of the mobile node when it is at home. When the mobile node is in a foreign link, the lifetime is set to the shorter lifetime of the home address or the care-of address of the mobile node. In the KAME implementation, it is possible to limit the maximum lifetime of binding update list entries to prevent a mobile node from creating an entry which has a very long lifetime. For correspondent nodes, the global variable `mip6ctl_bu_maxlifetime` indicates the limit and for home registration, `mip6ctl_hrbu_maxlifetime` limits the lifetime. The value has to be shifted 2 bits when setting it to the lifetime field in the message since the lifetime field is represented in units of 4 seconds.

Listing 5-277

———mip6_mncore.c
```
3733                 if ((pad = bu_size - sizeof(struct ip6_mh_binding_update)) >= 2) {
3734                     u_char *p =
3735                         (u_int8_t *)ip6mu + sizeof
(struct ip6_mh_binding_update);
3736                     *p = IP6_MHOPT_PADN;
3737                     *(p + 1) = pad - 2;
3738                 }
```
———mip6_mncore.c
— Line 3735 is broken here for layout reasons. However, it is a single line of code.

3733–3738 The PadN option between the Binding Update message and the inserted options is filled, if necessary.

Listing 5-278

———mip6_mncore.c
```
3740        if (need_rr) {
3741            /* nonce indices and authdata insertion. */
3742            if (nonce_size) {
3743                if ((pad = nonce_size - sizeof
(struct ip6_mh_opt_nonce_index))
3744                    >= 2) {
3745                    u_char *p = (u_int8_t *)ip6mu + bu_size
3746                        + sizeof(struct ip6_mh_opt_nonce_index);
3747                    *p = IP6_MHOPT_PADN;
3748                    *(p + 1) = pad - 2;
3749                }
3750            }
3751            if (auth_size) {
3752                if ((pad = auth_size - IP6MOPT_AUTHDATA_SIZE) >= 2) {
3753                    u_char *p = (u_int8_t *)ip6mu
3754                        + bu_size + nonce_size
 + IP6MOPT_AUTHDATA_SIZE;
3755                    *p = IP6_MHOPT_PADN;
3756                    *(p + 1) = pad - 2;
3757                }
3758            }
```
———mip6_mncore.c
— Lines 3743 and 3754 are broken here for layout reasons. However, they are a single line of code.

3740–3758 The code from lines 3740–3805 is for Binding Update messages for correspondent nodes. The PanN option is inserted after the Nonce Index option and the Binding Authorization Data option, if these options exist. In this case the padding option is necessary.

Listing 5-279

———mip6_mncore.c
```
3760            /* Nonce Indicies */
3761            mopt_nonce->ip6moni_type = IP6_MHOPT_NONCEID;
3762            mopt_nonce->ip6moni_len = sizeof
(struct ip6_mh_opt_nonce_index) - 2;
3763            SET_NETVAL_S(&mopt_nonce->ip6moni_home_nonce8,
3764                mbu->mbu_home_nonce_index);
```

```
3765                    if (!ignore_co_nonce) {
3766                            SET_NETVAL_S(&mopt_nonce->ip6moni_coa_nonce8,
3767                            mbu->mbu_careof_nonce_index);
3768                    }
```
——mip6_mncore.c
— Line 3762 is broken here for layout reasons. However, it is a single line of code.

3760–3768 A Nonce Index option is created. The option type is `IP6_MHOPT_NONCEID` and the size is that of the `ip6_mh_opt_nonce_index{}` structure. The nonce index values are kept in the binding update list entry. These values are copied to the option fields and sent to the correspondent node. The care-of nonce is only used when the `ignore_co_nonce` variable is set to false, which means the mobile node is in a foreign network.

Listing 5-280
——mip6_mncore.c

```
3770                    /* Auth. data */
3771                    mopt_auth->ip6moad_type = IP6_MHOPT_BAUTH;
3772                    mopt_auth->ip6moad_len = IP6MOPT_AUTHDATA_SIZE - 2;
3773
3774                    if (auth_size > IP6MOPT_AUTHDATA_SIZE) {
3775                            *((u_int8_t *)ip6mu + bu_size + nonce_size
     + IP6MOPT_AUTHDATA_SIZE)
3776                                    = IP6_MHOPT_PADN;
3777                            *((u_int8_t *)ip6mu + bu_size + nonce_size
     + IP6MOPT_AUTHDATA_SIZE + 1)
3778                                    = auth_size - IP6MOPT_AUTHDATA_SIZE - 2;
3779                    }
3780
....
3785                    /* Calculate Kbm */
3786                    mip6_calculate_kbm(&mbu->mbu_home_token,
3787                                    ignore_co_nonce ? NULL :
     &mbu->mbu_careof_token,
3788                                    key_bm);
....
3792
3793                    /* Calculate authenticator (5.2.6) */
3794                    /* First(96, HMAC_SHA1(Kbm, (coa, | cn | BU))) */
3795                    if (mip6_calculate_authenticator(key_bm,
3796                        (u_int8_t *)(mopt_auth + 1), &mbu->mbu_coa,
3797                        dst, (caddr_t)ip6mu,
3798                        bu_size + nonce_size + auth_size,
3799                        bu_size + nonce_size + sizeof(struct ip6_mh_opt_auth_data),
3800                        MIP6_AUTHENTICATOR_LEN)) {
....
3804                            return (EINVAL);
3805                    }
```
——mip6_mncore.c
— Lines 3775, 3777 and 3787 are broken here for layout reasons. However, they are a single line of code.

3771–3780 A Binding Authorization Data option is created. The option type is `IP6_MHOPT_BAUTH` and the size is defined as the `IP6MOPT_AUTHDATA_SIZE` macro. The insertion code of the padding option on lines 3774–3779 is a duplicated code. The same process has already been done on lines 3751–3758.

3786–3805 The key value used to compute the hash value of the Binding Update message is prepared by the `mip6_calculate_kbm()` function. The key is used by the `mip6_calculate_authenticator()` function called on line 3795 to get the hash value of the message. The first 96 bits are used as the authenticator value which will be included in the Binding Authorization Data option.

Listing 5-281

———————————————————————————————————mip6_mncore.c

```
3809                  } else {
3810                          if (altcoa_size) {
3811                                  if ((pad = altcoa_size
3812                                      - sizeof(struct ip6_mh_opt_altcoa)) >= 2) {
3813                                          u_char *p = (u_int8_t *)ip6mu + bu_size
3814                                              + sizeof(struct ip6_mh_opt_nonce_index);
3815                                          *p = IP6_MHOPT_PADN;
3816                                          *(p + 1) = pad - 2;
3817                                  }
3818                          }
3819                          mopt_altcoa->ip6moa_type = IP6_MHOPT_ALTCOA;
3820                          mopt_altcoa->ip6moa_len = sizeof(struct ip6_mh_opt_altcoa) - 2;
3821                          altcoa = mbu->mbu_coa;
3822                          in6_clearscope(&altcoa);
3823                          bcopy(&altcoa, mopt_altcoa->ip6moa_addr,
3824                              sizeof(struct in6_addr));
3825                  }
```

———————————————————————————————————mip6_mncore.c

3810–3825 This part of the code is for home registration. The code from lines 3810–3813 aims to put a PadN option after the Alternate Care-of Address option; however, the code is wrong. Line 3814 should add the size of the `ip6_mh_opt_altcoa{}` structure instead of the `ip6_mh_opt_nonce_index{}` structure. Fortunately, the bug does not cause a problem since the PadN option created here is overwritten by the Alternate Care-of Address option value filled on lines 3823–3824.

The type of the Alternate Care-of Address option is `IP6_MHOPT_ALTCOA` and the size is that of the `ip6_mh_opt_altcoa{}` structure. The care-of address of the mobile node is kept in the binding update list entry. The address is copied to the option data field to complete the option.

Listing 5-282

———————————————————————————————————mip6_mncore.c

```
3827                  /* calculate checksum. */
3828                  ip6mu->ip6mhbu_cksum = mip6_cksum(&mbu->mbu_haddr, dst, ip6mu_size,
3829                      IPPROTO_MH, (char *)ip6mu);
3830
3831                  *pktopt_mobility = (struct ip6_mh *)ip6mu;
3832
3833                  return (0);
3834          }
```

———————————————————————————————————mip6_mncore.c

3828–3833 Finally, the checksum value of the Binding Update message is computed by the `mip6_cksum()` function and the pointer to the created message is returned.

5.17.6 Receiving a Binding Acknowledgment Message

A mobile node will receive a Binding Acknowledgment message in response to a Binding Update message. The processing of the received Binding Acknowledgment message is implemented as the `mip6_ip6ma_input()` function.

Listing 5-283

```
                                                                    mip6_mncore.c
2863    int
2864    mip6_ip6ma_input(m, ip6ma, ip6malen)
2865            struct mbuf *m;
2866            struct ip6_mh_binding_ack *ip6ma;
2867            int ip6malen;
2868    {
2869            struct ip6_hdr *ip6;
2870            struct hif_softc *sc;
2871            struct mip6_bu *mbu;
2872            u_int16_t seqno;
2873            u_int32_t lifetime, refresh;
....
2877            int error = 0;
2878            struct mip6_mobility_options mopt;
2879            u_int8_t ba_safe = 0;
                                                                    mip6_mncore.c
```

2863–2867 The `mip6_ip6ma_input()` function has three parameters: The `m` parameter is a pointer to the mbuf that contains the received Binding Acknowledgment message; the `ip6ma` parameter is a pointer to the address of the message; and the `ip6malen` parameter is the length of the message.

Listing 5-284

```
                                                                    mip6_mncore.c
2894            ip6 = mtod(m, struct ip6_hdr *);
2895
2896            /* packet length check. */
2897            if (ip6malen < sizeof(struct ip6_mh_binding_ack)) {
....
2905                    /* send ICMP parameter problem. */
2906                    icmp6_error(m, ICMP6_PARAM_PROB, ICMP6_PARAMPROB_HEADER,
2907                        (caddr_t)&ip6ma->ip6mhba_len - (caddr_t)ip6);
2908                    return (EINVAL);
2909            }
                                                                    mip6_mncore.c
```

2897–2909 If the received size of the message is smaller than the size of the `ip6_mh_binding_ack{}` structure, an ICMPv6 Parameter Problem message is sent to indicate that the length field of the Binding Acknowledgment message is incorrect. The code value of the ICMPv6 message is set to `ICMP6_PARAMPROB_HEADER` which means there is an error in the header part and the problem pointer is set to the length field of the Binding Acknowledgment message.

Listing 5-285

```
                                                                    mip6_mncore.c
2911    #ifdef M_DECRYPTED      /* not openbsd */
2912            if (((m->m_flags & M_DECRYPTED) != 0)
2913                || ((m->m_flags & M_AUTHIPHDR) != 0)) {
```

```
2914                        ba_safe = 1;
2915                }
2916     #endif
   ....
2923                if ((error = mip6_get_mobility_options((struct ip6_mh *)ip6ma,
2924                    sizeof(*ip6ma), ip6malen, &mopt))) {
2925                        m_freem(m);
   ....
2927                        return (error);
2928                }
```
                                                                _____mip6_mncore.c

2912–2915 The M_DECRYPTED flag of an mbuf means that the packet is protected by ESP.
The M_AUTHIPHDR flag is set if the packet is protected by AH or ESP. If the input packet
has the M_DECRYPTED or M_AUTHIPHDR flag, then the ba_safe variable is set to true
to indicate that the packet is protected by IPsec.

2923–2928 The mip6_get_mobility_options() function parses the options contained
in the received Mobility Header message and stores the option information in the instance
of the mip6_options{} structure specified as the mopt variable.

Listing 5-286
                                                                _____mip6_mncore.c

```
2949                sc = hif_list_find_withhaddr(&ip6->ip6_dst);
2950                if (sc == NULL) {
2951                        /*
2952                         * if we receive a binding ack before sending binding
2953                         * updates(!), sc will be NULL.
2954                         */
   ....
2958                        /* silently ignore. */
2959                        m_freem(m);
2960                        return (EINVAL);
2961                }
```
                                                                _____mip6_mncore.c

2949–2961 The hif_list_find_withhaddr() function returns a pointer to the virtual
home network interface related to the home address specified by the function parameter.
If there is no related virtual home network interface that relates to the destination address
(that is, the home address of the mobile node) of the Binding Acknowledgment message,
the packet is dropped.

Listing 5-287
                                                                _____mip6_mncore.c

```
2962                mbu = mip6_bu_list_find_withpaddr(&sc->hif_bu_list, &ip6->ip6_src,
2963                    &ip6->ip6_dst);
2964                if (mbu == NULL) {
   ....
2968                        /* silently ignore */
2969                        m_freem(m);
   ....
2971                        return (EINVAL);
2972                }
```
                                                                _____mip6_mncore.c

2962–2972 The `mip6_bu_list_find_withpaddr()` function returns a pointer to the binding update list entry identified by its function parameters. If there is no binding update list entry related to the received Binding Acknowledgment message, the packet is dropped.

Listing 5-288

```
                                                            ─mip6_mncore.c
2974              if (mopt.valid_options & MOPT_AUTHDATA) {
2975                      /* Check Autheticator */
2976                      u_int8_t key_bm[MIP6_KBM_LEN];
2977                      u_int8_t authdata[MIP6_AUTHENTICATOR_LEN];
2978                      u_int16_t cksum_backup;
2979                      int ignore_co_nonce;
2980                      ignore_co_nonce = IN6_ARE_ADDR_EQUAL(&mbu->mbu_haddr,
2981                          &mbu->mbu_coa);
                                                            ─mip6_mncore.c
```

2974–2979 A Binding Acknowledgment message from a correspondent node must have the Binding Authorization Data option. If the received Binding Acknowledgment message has the option, the message must be verified using the option value.

2980–2981 The care-of nonce value is not used if the mobile node is at home. The `ignore_co_nonce` variable is set to true if the home address and the care-of address of the mobile node are the same, which means it is at home.

Listing 5-289

```
                                                            ─mip6_mncore.c
2983                      cksum_backup = ip6ma->ip6mhba_cksum;
2984                      ip6ma->ip6mhba_cksum = 0;
2985                      /* Calculate Kbm */
2986                      mip6_calculate_kbm(&mbu->mbu_home_token,
2987                          ignore_co_nonce ? NULL : &mbu->mbu_careof_token, key_bm);
2988                      /* Calculate Authenticator */
2989                      if (mip6_calculate_authenticator(key_bm, authdata,
2990                          &mbu->mbu_coa, &ip6->ip6_dst,
2991                          (caddr_t)ip6ma, ip6malen,
2992                          (caddr_t)mopt.mopt_auth + 2 - (caddr_t)ip6ma,
2993                          min(MOPT_AUTH_LEN(&mopt) + 2,
   MIP6_AUTHENTICATOR_LEN)) == 0) {
2994                              ip6ma->ip6mhba_cksum = cksum_backup;
2995                              if (bcmp(authdata, mopt.mopt_auth + 2,
2996                                      min(MOPT_AUTH_LEN(&mopt) + 2,
   MIP6_AUTHENTICATOR_LEN))
2997                                      == 0)
2998                                  goto accept_binding_ack;
2999                      }
3000              }
                                                            ─mip6_mncore.c
```
— *Lines 2993 and 2996 are broken here for layout reasons. However, they are a single line of code.*

2983–2984 The checksum value of the Mobility Header must be cleared before verifying the header with the Binding Authorization Data option, since the field is assumed to be 0 when computing the checksum on the sender side.

2986–2987 The `mip6_calculate_kbm()` function computes the shared key between the correspondent node and the mobile node using the token values exchanged by the return routability procedure.

2989–2999 The `mip6_calculate_authenticator()` function computes the value of the Binding Authorization Data option using the key computed by the `mip6_calculate_kbm()` function. The result is stored to the `authdata` variable. If the computed value and the value stored in the received Binding Authorization Data option are the same, the message is accepted as a valid message.

Listing 5-290

```
                                                            mip6_mncore.c
3002            if (!mip6ctl_use_ipsec && (mbu->mbu_flags & IP6MU_HOME)) {
3003                    ba_safe = 1;
3004                    goto accept_binding_ack;
3005            }
3006
3007            if (mip6ctl_use_ipsec
3008                && (mbu->mbu_flags & IP6MU_HOME) != 0
3009                && ba_safe == 1)
3010                    goto accept_binding_ack;
3011
3012            if ((mbu->mbu_flags & IP6MU_HOME) == 0) {
3013                    goto accept_binding_ack;
3014            }
3015
3016            /* otherwise, discard this packet. */
3017            m_freem(m);
3018            mip6stat.mip6s_haopolicy++; /* XXX */
3019            return (EINVAL);
                                                            mip6_mncore.c
```

3002–3004 The `mip6ctl_use_ipsec` variable is a tunable variable. If the variable is set to false, Binding Acknowledgment messages for home registration will be accepted even if they are not protected by IPsec.

3007–3010 If the `mip6ctl_use_ipsec` variable is set to true and the packet is protected by IPsec (that is, the `ba_safe` variable is set to true), the Binding Acknowledgment message for home registration is accepted.

3012–3014 There is a bug in this part of the code. If there is no Binding Authorization Data option in the incoming Binding Acknowledgment message from the correspondent node, then the message will be incorrectly accepted. However, as discussed, Binding Acknowledgment messages from correspondent nodes must have the Binding Authorization Data option and must be processed on lines 2974–3000. All messages reached at this point must be dropped.

 Fortunately, the bug usually does not cause any serious problems since Binding Acknowledgment messages from correspondent nodes have the option as long as the implementation of the peer node follows the specification.

Listing 5-291

```
                                                            mip6_mncore.c
3021    accept_binding_ack:
3022
3023            seqno = htons(ip6ma->ip6mhba_seqno);
3024            if (ip6ma->ip6mhba_status == IP6_MH_BAS_SEQNO_BAD) {
3025                    /*
3026                     * our home agent has a greater sequence number in its
3027                     * binging cache entriy of mine.  we should resent
3028                     * binding update with greater than the sequence
3029                     * number of the binding cache already exists in our
```

```
3030                         * home agent.  this binding ack is valid though the
3031                         * sequence number doesn't match.
3032                         */
3033                        goto check_mobility_options;
3034                }
3035
3036                if (seqno != mbu->mbu_seqno) {
....
3044                        /* silently ignore. */
3045                        /* discard */
3046                        m_freem(m);
....
3048                        return (EINVAL);
3049                }
```
——mip6_mncore.c

3023–3034 If the sequence number sent from the mobile node was out of date, the peer node will reply with a Binding Acknowledgment message with the IP6_MH_BAS_SEQNO_BAD status code. In this case, the mobile node re-sends a Binding Update message later.

3036–3049 If the received sequence number does not match the sequence number sent before, the Binding Acknowledgment message is dropped.

Listing 5-292
——mip6_mncore.c
```
3051    check_mobility_options:
....
3060            if (ip6ma->ip6mhba_status >= IP6_MH_BAS_ERRORBASE) {
....
3065                    if (ip6ma->ip6mhba_status == IP6_MH_BAS_NOT_HA &&
3066                        mbu->mbu_flags & IP6MU_HOME &&
3067                        mbu->mbu_pri_fsm_state == MIP6_BU_PRI_FSM_STATE_WAITA) {
3068                            /* XXX no registration? */
3069                            goto success;
3070                    }
```
——mip6_mncore.c

3065–3070 When the home agent of the mobile node does not have a binding cache entry for the mobile node and receives a Binding Update message for de-registration, the home agent will reply with a Binding Acknowledgment message with status IP6_MH_BAS_NOT_HA. This case looks like an error case, however, it occurs even in normal cases when a Binding Acknowledgment message from the home agent to the mobile node is lost. The home agent removes the related binding cache entry of the mobile node after sending the Binding Acknowledgment message. If the mobile node does not receive the message because the message is lost, it will re-send a Binding Update message. The KAME implementation treats the Binding Acknowledgment message with the IP6_MH_BAS_NOT_HA status as successful when it is at home.

Listing 5-293
——mip6_mncore.c
```
3071                if (ip6ma->ip6mhba_status == IP6_MH_BAS_SEQNO_BAD) {
3072                        /* seqno is too small.  adjust it and resend. */
3073                        mbu->mbu_seqno = ntohs(ip6ma->ip6mhba_seqno) + 1;
```

```
3074                          /* XXX */
3075                          mip6_bu_send_bu(mbu);
3076                          return (0);
3077                  }
3078
3079                  /* sending binding update failed. */
3080                  error = mip6_bu_list_remove(&sc->hif_bu_list, mbu);
3081                  if (error) {
....
3085                          m_freem(m);
3086                          return (error);
3087                  }
3088                  /* XXX some error recovery process needed. */
3089                  return (0);
3090          }
```
── mip6_mncore.c

3071–3077 If the recorded sequence number in the binding cache entry of the peer node
is larger than that of the Binding Update message, the peer node will send a Binding
Acknowledgment message with the IP6_MH_BAS_SEQNO_BAD status code. In this case,
the mobile node re-sends a Binding Update message with the latest sequence number
returned with the Binding Acknowledgment message.

3080–3089 If re-sending a Binding Update message fails, then the binding update list entry
related to the message is removed.

Listing 5-294
── mip6_mncore.c

```
3092     success:
3093          /*
3094           * the binding update has been accepted.
3095           */
3096
3097          /* update lifetime and refresh time. */
3098          lifetime = htons(ip6ma->ip6mhba_lifetime) << 2; /* units of 4 secs */
3099          if (lifetime < mbu->mbu_lifetime) {
3100                  mbu->mbu_expire -= (mbu->mbu_lifetime - lifetime);
3101                  if (mbu->mbu_expire < time_second)
3102                          mbu->mbu_expire = time_second;
3103          }
```
── mip6_mncore.c

3098–3103 Lifetime information is extracted from the received message. If the received lifetime
is smaller than that of the related binding update list entry, the expiration time is reduced
based on the new lifetime. If the expiration time is past, the expiration time is set to the
current time. The entry will be removed in the timer function at the next timeout.

Listing 5-295
── mip6_mncore.c

```
3104          /* binding refresh advice option */
3105          if (mbu->mbu_flags & IP6MU_HOME) {
3106                  if (mopt.valid_options & MOPT_REFRESH) {
3107                          refresh = mopt.mopt_refresh << 2;
3108                          if (refresh > lifetime || refresh == 0) {
3109                                  /*
3110                                   * use default refresh interval for an
3111                                   * invalid binding refresh interval
3112                                   * option.
```

```
3113                                         */
3114                                refresh =
3115                                    MIP6_BU_DEFAULT_REFRESH_INTERVAL(lifetime);
3116                        }
3117                } else {
3118                        /*
3119                         * set refresh interval even when a home agent
3120                         * doesn't specify refresh interval, so that a
3121                         * mobile node can re-register its binding
3122                         * before the binding update entry expires.
3123                         */
3124                        /*
3125                         * XXX: the calculation algorithm of a default
3126                         * value must be discussed.
3127                         */
3128                        refresh = MIP6_BU_DEFAULT_REFRESH_INTERVAL(lifetime);
3129                }
3130        } else
3131                refresh = lifetime;
3132        mbu->mbu_refresh = refresh;
```
——mip6_mncore.c

3105–3116 If the binding update list entry is for home registration and the received Binding Acknowledgment message includes a Binding Refresh Advice option, the suggested refresh time is extracted from the option. If the refresh time is greater than the lifetime of the entry or the refresh time is set to 0, the value is ignored. In this case, the refresh interval is calculated based on the lifetime using the `MIP6_BU_DEFAULT_REFRESH_INTERVAL()` macro.

3131 If the binding update list entry is for a correspondent node, the refresh interval is set to the same value as the lifetime, which means the entry is not refreshed for correspondent nodes. The entry will be removed when the lifetime expires.

Listing 5-296

——mip6_mncore.c
```
3134            if (mbu->mbu_refresh > mbu->mbu_expire)
3135                    mbu->mbu_refresh = mbu->mbu_expire;
3136
3137            if (ip6ma->ip6mhba_status == IP6_MH_BAS_PRFX_DISCOV) {
3138                    if (mip6_icmp6_mp_sol_output(&mbu->mbu_haddr,
3139                        &mbu->mbu_paddr)) {
....
3144                            /* proceed anyway... */
3145                    }
3146            }
```
——mip6_mncore.c

3134–3135 The code is intended to make sure that the refresh time is set to the time before the entry expires; however, there is a bug in the code. The `mbu_refresh` variable indicates the number of seconds but it does not indicate the time. The `mbu_refresh` variable must be `mbu_retrans` in this case.

3137–3146 If the home prefix information has changed, the home agent replies with a Binding Acknowledgment message with the status code `IP6_MH_BAS_PRFX_DISCOV`, which indicates that the mobile node needs to perform the prefix discovery procedure. In this case, the mobile node sends a Mobile Prefix Solicitation message by calling the `mip6_icmp6_mp_sol_output()` function.

Listing 5-297

```
3148                     if (mbu->mbu_flags & IP6MU_HOME) {
3149                             /* this is from our home agent. */
3150                             if (mbu->mbu_pri_fsm_state == MIP6_BU_PRI_FSM_STATE_WAITD) {
3151                                     struct sockaddr_in6 coa_sa;
3152                                     struct sockaddr_in6 daddr; /* XXX */
3153                                     struct sockaddr_in6 lladdr;
3154                                     struct ifaddr *ifa;
```

3148–3150 The mobile node will proceed to the home de-registration procedure if the binding update list entry is in the `MIP6_BU_PRI_FSM_STATE_WAITD` state. The state indicates that the mobile node is waiting for a Binding Acknowledgment message in response to the home de-registration message it sent.

Listing 5-298

```
3156                     /*
3157                      * home unregsitration has completed.
3158                      * send an unsolicited neighbor advertisement.
3159                      */
3160                     bzero(&coa_sa, sizeof(coa_sa));
3161                     coa_sa.sin6_len = sizeof(coa_sa);
3162                     coa_sa.sin6_family = AF_INET6;
3163                     coa_sa.sin6_addr = mbu->mbu_coa;
3164                     /* XXX scope? how? */
3165                     if ((ifa = ifa_ifwithaddr((struct sockaddr *)&coa_sa))
3166                         == NULL) {
....
3170                             m_freem(m);
3171                             return (EINVAL);           /* XXX */
3172                     }
```

3160–3172 The mobile node sends an unsolicited Neighbor Advertisement message to update neighbor cache entries of the nodes on the home network. An instance of the `sockaddr_in6{}` structure is created which contains the care-of address of the mobile node. The `ifa_ifwithaddr()` function will return a pointer to the instance of the `in6_ifaddr{}` structure which is assigned to the node. If the care-of address is not assigned to the mobile node, the procedure is aborted. The pointer is used to recover the scope identifier of the all nodes link-local multicast address in the following procedure.

Listing 5-299

```
3174                     bzero(&daddr, sizeof(daddr));
3175                     daddr.sin6_family = AF_INET6;
3176                     daddr.sin6_len = sizeof(daddr);
3177                     daddr.sin6_addr = in6addr_linklocal_allnodes;
3178                     if (in6_addr2zoneid(ifa->ifa_ifp, &daddr.sin6_addr,
3179                         &daddr.sin6_scope_id)) {
3180                             /* XXX: should not happen */
....
```

```
3184                                          m_freem(m);
3185                                          return (EIO);
3186                                  }
3187                          if ((error = in6_embedscope(&daddr.sin6_addr,
3188                                  &daddr))) {
3189                                  /* XXX: should not happen */
....
3193                                  m_freem(m);
3194                                  return (error);
3195                          }
3196
3197                          nd6_na_output(ifa->ifa_ifp, &daddr.sin6_addr,
3198                              &mbu->mbu_haddr, ND_NA_FLAG_OVERRIDE, 1, NULL);
```
——mip6_mncore.c

3174–3195 The sockaddr_in6{} instance daddr which contains the all nodes link-local multicast address is prepared. The scope identifier is recovered from the interface to which the care-of address of the mobile node is assigned.

3197–3198 A Neighbor Advertisement message is sent to the home network. This message overrides all neighbor cache entries stored on the nodes on the home network. While the mobile node is away from home, the neighbor cache entry points to the home agent of the mobile node, since the home agent needs to receive all packets sent to the mobile node to intercept packets. When the mobile node returns home, it needs to update the cache information on all the nodes of the home network.

Listing 5-300

——mip6_mncore.c
```
3204                          /*
3205                           * if the binding update entry has the L flag on,
3206                           * send unsolicited neighbor advertisement to my
3207                           * link-local address.
3208                           */
3209                          if (mbu->mbu_flags & IP6MU_LINK) {
3210                                  bzero(&lladdr, sizeof(lladdr));
3211                                  lladdr.sin6_len = sizeof(lladdr);
3212                                  lladdr.sin6_family = AF_INET6;
3213                                  lladdr.sin6_addr.s6_addr16[0]
3214                                      = IPV6_ADDR_INT16_ULL;
3215                                  lladdr.sin6_addr.s6_addr32[2]
3216                                      = mbu->mbu_haddr.s6_addr32[2];
3217                                  lladdr.sin6_addr.s6_addr32[3]
3218                                      = mbu->mbu_haddr.s6_addr32[3];
3219
3220                                  if (in6_addr2zoneid(ifa->ifa_ifp,
3221                                      &lladdr.sin6_addr,
3222                                      &lladdr.sin6_scope_id)) {
3223                                          /* XXX: should not happen */
....
3227                                          m_freem(m);
3228                                          return (EIO);
3229                                  }
3230                                  if ((error = in6_embedscope(&lladdr.sin6_addr,
3231                                      &lladdr))) {
3232                                          /* XXX: should not happen */
....
3236                                          m_freem(m);
3237                                          return (error);
3238                                  }
3239
```

```
3240                                        nd6_na_output(ifa->ifa_ifp, &daddr.sin6_addr,
3241                                           &lladdr.sin6_addr, ND_NA_FLAG_OVERRIDE, 1,
3242                                           NULL);
....
3248                          }
```
——mip6_mncore.c

3209–3242 If the binding update list entry has the the L flag (the `IP6MU_LINK` flag) set, the
home agent of the mobile node will also receive all packets destined to the link-local
address of the mobile node. Sending the Neighbor Advertisement message for the link-
local address of the mobile node will update all the link-local neighbor cache entries
stored in the nodes on the home network.

Listing 5-301
——mip6_mncore.c
```
3250                          /* notify all the CNs that we are home. */
3251                          error = mip6_bu_list_notify_binding_change(sc, 1);
3252                          if (error) {
....
3256                                  m_freem(m);
3257                                  return (error);
3258                          }
```
——mip6_mncore.c

3251–3258 The `mip6_bu_list_notify_binding_change()` function notifies all the
binding update list entries kept in the virtual home network specified as the first parameter to send Binding Update messages to the peer nodes of each of the entries. The
`ip6_bu_list_notify_binding_change()` function is detailed in Listing 5-306.

Listing 5-302
——mip6_mncore.c
```
3260                          /* remove a tunnel to our homeagent. */
3261                          error = mip6_tunnel_control(MIP6_TUNNEL_DELETE,
3262                                                      mbu,
3263                                                      mip6_bu_encapcheck,
3264                                                      &mbu->mbu_encap);
3265                          if (error) {
....
3269                                  m_freem(m);
3270                                  return (error);
3271                          }
```
——mip6_mncore.c

3260–3271 The bi-directional tunnel between the mobile node and the home agent is
shutdown by the `mip6_tunnel_control()` function.

Listing 5-303
——mip6_mncore.c
```
3272                          error = mip6_bu_list_remove_all(&sc->hif_bu_list, 0);
3273                          if (error) {
....
```

```
3277                              m_freem(m);
3278                              return (error);
3279                      }
3280                      mbu = NULL; /* free in mip6_bu_list_remove_all() */
```

3272–3280 All the binding update list entries managed by the mobile node are removed after the home de-registration procedure has completed.

Listing 5-304

```
3282                  } else if ((mbu->mbu_pri_fsm_state
3283                          == MIP6_BU_PRI_FSM_STATE_WAITA)
3284                          || (mbu->mbu_pri_fsm_state
3285                          == MIP6_BU_PRI_FSM_STATE_WAITAR)) {
....
3292                          /* home registration completed */
3293                          error = mip6_bu_fsm
(mbu, MIP6_BU_PRI_FSM_EVENT_BA, NULL);
3294                          /* create tunnel to HA */
3295                          error = mip6_tunnel_control(MIP6_TUNNEL_CHANGE,
3296                                          mbu,
3297                                          mip6_bu_encapcheck,
3298                                          &mbu->mbu_encap);
3299                          if (error) {
....
3303                                  m_freem(m);
3304                                  return (error);
3305                          }
3306
3307                          /* notify all the CNs that we have a new coa. */
3308                          error = mip6_bu_list_notify_binding_change(sc, 0);
3309                          if (error) {
....
3313                                  m_freem(m);
3314                                  return (error);
3315                          }
```

– Line 3293 is broken here for layout reasons. However, it is a single line of code.

3282–3285 If the state of the binding update list entry is either the `MIP6_BU_PRI_FSM_STATE_WAITA` or the `MIP6_BU_PRI_FSM_STATE_WAITAR`, the mobile node is waiting for a Binding Acknowledgment message for home registration.

3293 The rest of the Binding Acknowledgment message processing is implemented in the state machine. The event `MIP6_BU_PRI_FSM_EVENT_BA`, which indicates that the mobile node receives a Binding Acknowledgment message, is sent to the state machine. The state machine is discussed in Section 5.17.19.

3295–3305 The `mip6_tunnel_control()` function is called to create a bi-directional tunnel between the mobile node and its home agent.

3308–3315 After the successful home registration procedure, the mobile node sends Binding Update messages to all correspondent nodes for which it has binding information by calling `mip6_bu_list_notify_binding_change()` function.

Listing 5-305

_____mip6_mncore.c

```
3316                    } else if (MIP6_IS_BU_BOUND_STATE(mbu)) {
3317                            /* nothing to do. */
3318                    } else {
....
3322                    }
3323            }
3324
3325            return (0);
3326    }
```
_____mip6_mncore.c

3316–3322 The mobile node does not need to do anything if the state of the binding update list entry is in other states. There is no processing code for a Binding Acknowledgment message from a correspondent node since the KAME implementation never sends a Binding Update message to correspondent nodes with the A (IP6MU_ACK) flag set.

Listing 5-306

_____mip6_mncore.c

```
1918    static int
1919    mip6_bu_list_notify_binding_change(sc, home)
1920            struct hif_softc *sc;
1921            int home;
1922    {
1923            struct in6_addr hif_coa;
1924            struct mip6_prefix *mpfx;
1925            struct mip6_bu *mbu, *mbu_next;
1926            int32_t coa_lifetime;
```
_____mip6_mncore.c

1918–1921 The mip6_bu_list_notify_binding_change() function has two parameters. The sc parameter is a pointer to the virtual home network interface on which the registration procedure has been done and the home parameter is set to true when a mobile node returns to home, otherwise it is set to false.

Listing 5-307

_____mip6_mncore.c

```
1931            /* get current CoA and recover its scope information. */
1932            if (sc->hif_coa_ifa == NULL) {
....
1936                    return (0);
1937            }
1938            hif_coa = sc->hif_coa_ifa->ia_addr.sin6_addr;
```
_____mip6_mncore.c

1931–1938 If the mobile node does not have a valid care-of address, the function returns immediately. If there is a care-of address, the address is written to the hif_coa variable.

Listing 5-308

_____mip6_mncore.c

```
1940            /* for each BU entry, update COA and make them about to send. */
1941            for (mbu = LIST_FIRST(&sc->hif_bu_list);
1942                 mbu;
1943                 mbu = mbu_next) {
1944                    mbu_next = LIST_NEXT(mbu, mbu_entry);
```

```
1945
1946                          if (mbu->mbu_flags & IP6MU_HOME) {
1947                                  /* this is a BU for our home agent */
....
1952                                  continue;
1953                          }
```
──mip6_mncore.c

1941–1953 All binding update list entries except home registration entries will be processed
in this loop.

Listing 5-309

──mip6_mncore.c
```
1954                          if (IN6_ARE_ADDR_EQUAL(&mbu->mbu_coa, &hif_coa)) {
1955                                  /* XXX no need */
1956                                  continue;
1957                          }
```
──mip6_mncore.c

1954–1957 If the care-of address of the binding update list entry for a correspondent node is
already updated to the latest care-of address, the entry is skipped.

Listing 5-310

──mip6_mncore.c
```
1958                          mbu->mbu_coa = hif_coa;
1959                          coa_lifetime = mip6_coa_get_lifetime(&mbu->mbu_coa);
1960                          mpfx = mip6_prefix_list_find_withhaddr(&mip6_prefix_list,
1961                              &mbu->mbu_haddr);
1962                          if (mpfx == NULL) {
....
1967                                  mip6_bu_list_remove(&sc->hif_bu_list, mbu);
1968                                  continue;
1969                          }
1970                          if (coa_lifetime < mpfx->mpfx_vltime) {
1971                                  mbu->mbu_lifetime = coa_lifetime;
1972                          } else {
1973                                  mbu->mbu_lifetime = mpfx->mpfx_vltime;
1974                          }
1975                          if (mip6ctl_bu_maxlifetime > 0 &&
1976                              mbu->mbu_lifetime > mip6ctl_bu_maxlifetime)
1977                                  mbu->mbu_lifetime = mip6ctl_bu_maxlifetime;
1978                          mbu->mbu_expire = time_second + mbu->mbu_lifetime;
1979                          /* sanity check for overflow */
1980                          if (mbu->mbu_expire < time_second)
1981                                  mbu->mbu_expire = 0x7fffffff;
1982                          mbu->mbu_refresh = mbu->mbu_lifetime;
```
──mip6_mncore.c

1958–1982 The care-of address and the lifetime of the binding update list entry are updated.
The lifetime of the entry is determined based on the prefix information. The lifetime of the
entry must be set to the smaller of either the care-of address or the home address lifetimes.
The lifetime is limited to the upper limit defined as the `mip6ctl_bu_maxlifetime`
variable, which indicates the maximum lifetime for entries for correspondent nodes. Note
that the limit based on the `mip6ctl_bu_maxlifetime` variable is a local policy of the
KAME implementation.

The expiration time and refresh time are also updated based on the lifetime.
If there is no related prefix information, the binding update list entry is removed.

Listing 5-311

```
                                                          mip6_mncore.c
1983                        if (mip6_bu_fsm(mbu,
1984                             (home ?
1985                                 MIP6_BU_PRI_FSM_EVENT_RETURNING_HOME :
1986                                 MIP6_BU_PRI_FSM_EVENT_MOVEMENT), NULL) != 0) {
....
1991                             }
1992                     }
1993
1994             return (0);
1995     }
                                                          mip6_mncore.c
```

1983–1995 The rest of the procedure is done in the state machine. If the mobile node is at
home, the MIP6_BU_PRI_EVENT_RETURNING_HOME event is sent to the state machine.
If the mobile node is away from home, the MIP6_BU_PRI_FSM_EVENT_MOVEMENT
event is sent. A more detailed discussion appears in Section 5.17.19.

5.17.7   Receiving a Type 2 Routing Header

A mobile node receives a Type 2 Routing Header when it is communicating using route
optimization. The Type 2 Routing Header is processed in the ip6_rthdr2() function.

Listing 5-312

```
                                                          route6.c
309     static int
310     ip6_rthdr2(m, ip6, rh2)
311             struct mbuf *m;
312             struct ip6_hdr *ip6;
313             struct ip6_rthdr2 *rh2;
314     {
315             int rh2_has_hoa;
316             struct sockaddr_in6 next_sa;
317             struct hif_softc *sc;
318             struct mip6_bu *mbu;
319             struct in6_addr *nextaddr, tmpaddr;
320             struct in6_ifaddr *ifa;
                                                          route6.c
```

309–313 The ip6_rthdr2() is called from the route6_input() function when the type
value is 2. The m parameter is a pointer to the mbuf which contains the incoming packet.
The ip6 and rh2 parameters are pointers to the IPv6 header and the Type 2 Routing
Header of the incoming packet respectively.

Listing 5-313

```
                                                          route6.c
322             rh2_has_hoa = 0;
323
324             /*
325              * determine the scope zone of the next hop, based on the interface
326              * of the current hop.
```

```
327                 * [draft-ietf-ipngwg-scoping-arch, Section 9]
328                 */
329                if ((ifa = ip6_getdstifaddr(m)) == NULL)
330                        goto bad;
331                bzero(&next_sa, sizeof(next_sa));
332                next_sa.sin6_len = sizeof(next_sa);
333                next_sa.sin6_family = AF_INET6;
334                bcopy((const void *)(rh2 + 1), &next_sa.sin6_addr,
335                        sizeof(struct in6_addr));
336                nextaddr = (struct in6_addr *)(rh2 + 1);
337                if (in6_addr2zoneid(ifa->ia_ifp,
338                                        &next_sa.sin6_addr,
339                                        &next_sa.sin6_scope_id)) {
340                        /* should not happen. */
....
342                        goto bad;
343                }
344                if (in6_embedscope(&next_sa.sin6_addr, &next_sa)) {
345                        /* XXX: should not happen */
....
347                        goto bad;
348                }
```
── route6.c

331–348 The address which is listed in a Routing Header does not have a scope identifier. The mobile node has to recover the information based on the interface on which the packet arrived. The `ip6_getdstifaddr()` function returns a pointer to the `in6_ifaddr{}` instance which indicates the address of the interface from which the packet specified as the parameter was received.

Listing 5-314
── route6.c
```
350                /* check addresses in ip6_dst and rh2. */
351                for (sc = LIST_FIRST(&hif_softc_list); sc;
352                     sc = LIST_NEXT(sc, hif_entry)) {
353                        for (mbu = LIST_FIRST(&sc->hif_bu_list); mbu;
354                             mbu = LIST_NEXT(mbu, mbu_entry)) {
355                                if ((mbu->mbu_flags & IP6MU_HOME) == 0)
356                                        continue;
```
── route6.c

351–356 The address in the Type 2 Routing Header must be a home address or a care-of address of a mobile node. To validate this condition, all binding update list entries kept as home registration entries will be checked to find all the registered home and care-of addresses.

Listing 5-315
── route6.c
```
360                        if (rh2->ip6r2_segleft == 0) {
361                                struct m_tag *mtag;
362                                struct ip6aux *ip6a;
363
364                                /*
365                                 * if segleft == 0, ip6_dst must be
366                                 * one of our home addresses.
367                                 */
```

```
368                           if (!IN6_ARE_ADDR_EQUAL(&ip6->ip6_dst,
369                                   &mbu->mbu_haddr))
370                                   continue;
....
374                           /*
375                            * if the previous hop is the coa that
376                            * is corresponding to the hoa in
377                            * ip6_dst, the route is optimized
378                            * already.
379                            */
380                           if (!IN6_ARE_ADDR_EQUAL(&next_sa.sin6_addr,
381                                   &mbu->mbu_coa)) {
382                                   /* coa mismatch.  discard this. */
383                                   goto bad;
384                           }
```
                                                                    ————— route6.c

360–384 If the segment left field, `ip6r2_segleft`, is 0, that means the header has already been processed. In this case, the destination address of the IPv6 header must be the home address and the address inside the Routing Header must be the care-of address of the mobile node. If the incoming packet does not satisfy these conditions, the packet is dropped.

Listing 5-316
                                                                    ————— route6.c
```
386                           /*
387                            * the route is already optimized.
388                            * set optimized flag in m_aux.
389                            */
390                           mtag = ip6_findaux(m);
391                           if (mtag) {
392                                   ip6a = (struct ip6aux *)(mtag + 1);
393                                   ip6a->ip6a_flags
394                                           |= IP6A_ROUTEOPTIMIZED;
395                                   return (0);
396                           }
397                           /* if n == 0 return error. */
398                           goto bad;
```
                                                                    ————— route6.c

390–395 At this point, it is confirmed that the incoming packet is a valid route optimized packet. The `IP6A_ROUTEOPTIMIZED` flag is added to the auxiliary mbuf to indicate the packet is route optimized.

Listing 5-317
                                                                    ————— route6.c
```
399                   } else {
400                           /*
401                            * if segleft == 1, the specified
402                            * intermediate node must be one of
403                            * our home addresses.
404                            */
405                           if (!IN6_ARE_ADDR_EQUAL(&next_sa.sin6_addr,
406                                   &mbu->mbu_haddr))
407                                   continue;
408                           rh2_has_hoa++;
409                   }
```

```
410                          }
411                  }
412                  if (rh2_has_hoa == 0) {
413                          /*
414                           * this rh2 includes an address that is not one of our
415                           * home addresses.
416                           */
417                          goto bad;
418                  }
```
—— route6.c

399–408 If the segment left field is 1, the header has not been processed yet. In this case the address in the Routing Header must be the home address of the mobile node.

412–417 If the address in the Routing Header is not the home address, the incoming packet is dropped.

Listing 5-318
—— route6.c
```
420                  rh2->ip6r2_segleft--;
421
422                  /*
423                   * reject invalid addresses.  be proactive about malicious use of
424                   * IPv4 mapped/compat address.
425                   * XXX need more checks?
426                   */
427                  if (IN6_IS_ADDR_MULTICAST(&ip6->ip6_dst) ||
428                      IN6_IS_ADDR_UNSPECIFIED(&ip6->ip6_dst) ||
429                      IN6_IS_ADDR_V4MAPPED(&ip6->ip6_dst) ||
430                      IN6_IS_ADDR_V4COMPAT(&ip6->ip6_dst) ||
431                      IN6_IS_ADDR_LOOPBACK(&ip6->ip6_dst)) {
....
433                          goto bad;
434                  }
435
436                  /*
437                   * Swap the IPv6 destination address and nextaddr. Forward the packet.
438                   */
439                  tmpaddr = *nextaddr;
440                  *nextaddr = ip6->ip6_dst;
441                  in6_clearscope(nextaddr);
442                  ip6->ip6_dst = tmpaddr;
443                  ip6_forward(m, 1);
444
445                  return (-1);                    /* m would be freed in ip6_forward() */
446
447          bad:
448                  m_freem(m);
449                  return (-1);
450          }
```
—— route6.c

427–434 The destination address of the incoming IPv6 packet should be the care-of address of the mobile node. A multicast address, the unspecified address, an IPv4-mapped IPv6 address, an IPv4-compatible IPv6 address and the loopback address cannot be a care-of address.

439–443 The address in the Type 2 Routing Header and the destination address of the IPv6 header are swapped. The packet will be processed as a forwarded packet and is passed to the `ip6_forward()` function.

5.17.8   Receiving a Binding Refresh Request Message

A mobile node may receive a Binding Refresh Request message from a correspondent node
when the lifetime of the binding between the mobile node and the correspondent node becomes
small.

Listing 5-319

```
                                                            _____mip6_mncore.c
3328     int
3329     mip6_ip6mr_input(m, ip6mr, ip6mrlen)
3330             struct mbuf *m;
3331             struct ip6_mh_binding_request *ip6mr;
3332             int ip6mrlen;
3333     {
3334             struct ip6_hdr *ip6;
3335             struct hif_softc *sc;
3336             struct mip6_bu *mbu;
3337             int error;
                                                            _____mip6_mncore.c
```

3328–3332 The `mip6_ip6mr_input()` function is called from the `mobility6_input()`
function when a mobile node receives a Binding Refresh Request message. The m parameter is a pointer to the mbuf which contains the incoming packet and the `ip6mr` and
`ip6mrlen` parameters are a pointer to the head of the Binding Refresh Request message
and its length.

Listing 5-320

```
                                                            _____mip6_mncore.c
3341             ip6 = mtod(m, struct ip6_hdr *);
3342
3343             /* packet length check. */
3344             if (ip6mrlen < sizeof (struct ip6_mh_binding_request)) {
 ....
3351                     /* send ICMP parameter problem. */
3352                     icmp6_error(m, ICMP6_PARAM_PROB, ICMP6_PARAMPROB_HEADER,
3353                         (caddr_t)&ip6mr->ip6mhbr_len - (caddr_t)ip6);
3354                     return(EINVAL);
3355             }
                                                            _____mip6_mncore.c
```

3343–3355 If the length of the incoming Binding Refresh Request message is smaller than the
size of the `ip6_mh_binding_request{}` structure, the mobile node replies with an
ICMPv6 Parameter Problem message. The problem pointer is set to point to the length
field of the received Binding Refresh Request message.

Listing 5-321

```
                                                            _____mip6_mncore.c
3357             /* find hif corresponding to the home address. */
3358             sc = hif_list_find_withhaddr(&ip6->ip6_dst);
3359             if (sc == NULL) {
3360                     /* we have no such home address. */
 ....
```

```
3362                     goto bad;
3363            }
3364
3365            /* find a corresponding binding update entry. */
3366            mbu = mip6_bu_list_find_withpaddr(&sc->hif_bu_list, &ip6->ip6_src,
3367                &ip6->ip6_dst);
3368            if (mbu == NULL) {
3369                    /* we have no binding update entry for dst_sa. */
3370                    return (0);
3371            }
```
———mip6_mncore.c

3358–3371 When a mobile node receives a Binding Refresh Request message, it needs to send
a Binding Update message to extend the lifetime of the binding information. If the mobile
node does not have a binding update list entry related to the incoming Binding Refresh
Request message, no action is required.

Listing 5-322
———mip6_mncore.c
```
3373            error = mip6_bu_fsm(mbu, MIP6_BU_PRI_FSM_EVENT_BRR, ip6mr);
3374            if (error) {
....
3378                    goto bad;
3379            }
3380
3381            return (0);
3382      bad:
3383            m_freem(m);
3384            return (EINVAL);
3385      }
```
———mip6_mncore.c

3373–3379 If the mobile node has a binding update list entry related to the incoming Binding
Refresh Request message, it sends the `MIP6_BU_PRI_FSM_EVENT_BRR` event to its state
machine, which will eventually call the sending function for a Binding Update message.

5.17.9 Receiving a Binding Error Message

A mobile node receives a Binding Error message in the following cases:

- When a mobile node sends a packet when there is no binding information between the
  mobile node and its peer node.

- When a mobile node sends a new (unknown) Mobility Header type to its peer.

The former case occurs when a Binding Update message from the mobile node to a
correspondent node is lost, but the mobile node sends route optimized packets. Since the KAME
implementation does not require a Binding Acknowledgment message from a correspondent
node, the mobile node may send packets with the Home Address option even if there is no
binding cache on the peer node. A packet which contains the Home Address option without
existing binding information is treated as an error.

The latter case does not occur in the current basic specification since there are no unknown
Mobility Header types defined. This error message will be used to detect the future extension
of Mobility Header types.

Listing 5-323

_____mip6_mncore.c

```
3387    int
3388    mip6_ip6me_input(m, ip6me, ip6melen)
3389            struct mbuf *m;
3390            struct ip6_mh_binding_error *ip6me;
3391            int ip6melen;
3392    {
3393            struct ip6_hdr *ip6;
3394            struct sockaddr_in6 hoa;
3395            struct hif_softc *sc;
3396            struct mip6_bu *mbu;
3397            int error = 0;
```

_____mip6_mncore.c

3387–3391 The `mip6_ip6me_input()` function is called from the `mobility6_input()` function when a mobile node receives a Binding Error message. The `m` parameter is a pointer to the mbuf which contains the incoming packet and the `ip6me` and `ip6melen` parameters are a pointer to the head of the Binding Error message and its length.

Listing 5-324

_____mip6_mncore.c

```
3401            ip6 = mtod(m, struct ip6_hdr *);
3402
3403            /* packet length check. */
3404            if (ip6melen < sizeof (struct ip6_mh_binding_error)) {
....
3411                    /* send ICMP parameter problem. */
3412                    icmp6_error(m, ICMP6_PARAM_PROB, ICMP6_PARAMPROB_HEADER,
3413                        (caddr_t)&ip6me->ip6mhbe_len - (caddr_t)ip6);
3414                    return(EINVAL);
3415            }
```

_____mip6_mncore.c

3404–3415 If the length of the incoming Binding Error message is smaller than the size of the `ip6_mh_binding_error{}` structure, the mobile node replies with an ICMPv6 Parameter Problem message. The problem pointer is set to point to the length field of the incoming Binding Error message.

Listing 5-325

_____mip6_mncore.c

```
3417            /* extract the home address of the sending node. */
3418            bzero (&hoa, sizeof (hoa));
3419            hoa.sin6_len = sizeof (hoa);
3420            hoa.sin6_family = AF_INET6;
3421            bcopy(&ip6me->ip6mhbe_homeaddr, &hoa.sin6_addr,
3422                sizeof(struct in6_addr));
3423            if (in6_addr2zoneid(m->m_pkthdr.rcvif, &hoa.sin6_addr,
3424                &hoa.sin6_scope_id)) {
....
3426                    goto bad;
3427            }
3428            if (in6_embedscope(&hoa.sin6_addr, &hoa)) {
....
3430                    goto bad;
3431            }
```

_____mip6_mncore.c

3418–3431 The home address of the mobile node may be stored in the Binding Error message
if the original packet which caused the error used the home address. The home address
is copied to the `hoa` variable. The scope identifier of the home address is recovered from
the interface on which the Binding Error message arrived.

Listing 5-326

_____mip6_mncore.c

```
3433            /* find hif corresponding to the home address. */
3434            sc = hif_list_find_withhaddr(&hoa.sin6_addr);
3435            if (sc == NULL) {
3436                    /* we have no such home address. */
....
3438                    goto bad;
3439            }
```
_____mip6_mncore.c

3434–3439 If the mobile node does not have a virtual home interface related to the home
address indicated in the incoming Binding Error message, it ignores the error message.

Listing 5-327

_____mip6_mncore.c

```
3443            switch (ip6me->ip6mhbe_status) {
3444            case IP6_MH_BES_UNKNOWN_HAO:
3445            case IP6_MH_BES_UNKNOWN_MH:
3446                    mbu = mip6_bu_list_find_withpaddr(&sc->hif_bu_list,
3447                        &ip6->ip6_src, &hoa.sin6_addr);
3448                    if (mbu == NULL) {
3449                            /* we have no binding update entry for the CN. */
3450                            goto bad;
3451                    }
3452                    break;
3453
3454            default:
....
3460                    goto bad;
3461                    break;
3462            }
```
_____mip6_mncore.c

3443–3462 If the error status is either the `IP6_MH_BES_UNKNOWN_HAO` or the
`IP6_MH_BES_UNKNOWN_MH`, the mobile node calls the
`mip6_bu_list_find_withpaddr()` function to find the binding update list entry
related to the Binding Error message. If the mobile node does not have a related
entry, the error message is ignored. Currently, no other error statuses are defined.
A message with an unknown error status code is ignored.

Listing 5-328

_____mip6_mncore.c

```
3464            switch (ip6me->ip6mhbe_status) {
3465            case IP6_MH_BES_UNKNOWN_HAO:
3466                    /* the CN doesn't have a binding cache entry.  start RR. */
3467                    error = mip6_bu_fsm(mbu,
3468                        MIP6_BU_PRI_FSM_EVENT_UNVERIFIED_HAO, ip6me);
3469                    if (error) {
....
```

```
3473                              goto bad;
3474                    }
3475
3476              break;
3477
3478        case IP6_MH_BES_UNKNOWN_MH:
3479              /* XXX future extension? */
3480              error = mip6_bu_fsm(mbu,
3481                 MIP6_BU_PRI_FSM_EVENT_UNKNOWN_MH_TYPE, ip6me);
3482              if (error) {
....
3486                              goto bad;
3487                    }
3488
3489              break;
3490
3491        default:
....
3499              }
3500
3501        return (0);
3502
3503    bad:
3504        m_freem(m);
3505        return (EINVAL);
3506    }
```
———mip6_mncore.c

3464–3489 Based on the error status of the Binding Error message, an event is sent to
the state machine of the related binding update list entry. If the error status is the
IP6_MH_BES_UNKNOWN_HAO, the MIP6_BU_PRI_FSM_EVENT_UNVERIFIED_HAO
is sent. If the error status is the IP6_MH_BES_UNKNOWN_MH, the
MIP6_BU_PRI_FSM_EVENT_UNKNOWN_MH_TYPE is sent. The error processing and
recovery will be done in the state machine. State machines will be discussed in
Section 5.17.19.

5.17.10   Source Address Selection

A mobile node should prefer to use its home address when sending packets. The source address
selection mechanism is modified to meet this recommendation. Source address selection is done
in the in6_selectsrc() function. The following code fragments used in this section are
quoted from the in6_selectsrc() function. The function is discussed in Section 3.13.1 of
IPv6 Core Protocols Implementation.

Listing 5-329
———in6_src.c

```
288              /*
289               * a caller can specify IP6PO_USECOA to not to use a home
290               * address.  for example, the case that the neighbour
291               * unreachability detection to the global address.
292               */
293        if (opts != NULL &&
294             (opts->ip6po_flags & IP6PO_USECOA) != 0) {
295                  usecoa = 1;
296        }
297              /*
298               * a user can specify destination addresses or detination
```

```
299                           * ports for which he don't want to use a home address when
300                           * sending packets.
301                           */
302                          for (uh = LIST_FIRST(&mip6_unuse_hoa);
303                               uh;
304                               uh = LIST_NEXT(uh, unuse_entry)) {
305                              if ((IN6_IS_ADDR_UNSPECIFIED(&uh->unuse_addr) ||
306                                  IN6_ARE_ADDR_EQUAL(dst, &uh->unuse_addr)) &&
307                                  (!uh->unuse_port || dstsock->sin6_port == uh->
     unuse_port)) {
308                                  usecoa = 1;
309                                  break;
310                              }
311                          }
```
—— in6_src.c

– Line 307 is broken here for layout reasons. However, it is a single line of code.

293–311 In some cases, a mobile node may prefer using the care-of address instead of the home address of the node. For example, there is no need to use a home address for very short-lived communications such as DNS queries. The Care-of Test Init message and the Neighbor Solicitation message for the Neighbor Unreachability Detection on a foreign network are other cases that must not use a home address as a source address.

The KAME implementation provides two ways to select a care-of address in the `in6_selectsrc()` function. One is the `IP6PO_USECOA` flag. If the packet being sent has the flag in its auxiliary mbuf, the home address will not be chosen as a source address. The other method is using the address and port filter. The global variable `mip6_unuse_hoa` contains a list of destination addresses and/or port numbers. Packets sent to these addresses or ports should not use a home address.

If the outgoing packet has the `IP6PO_USECOA` flag, or the destination address or the port number is listed in the `mip6_unuse_hoa` list, the `usecoa` variable is set to true.

[RFC3484] defines rule 4 which specifies how a mobile node chooses the source address of packets it sends. Assuming there are two candidates of a source address, SA and SB, the basic rules are as follows:

- If SA is a home address and a care-of address at the same time (that means, the node is at home), and SB is not, prefer SA.
- If SB is a home address and a care-of address at the same time (that means, the node is at home), and SA is not, prefer SB.
- If SA is just a home address and SB is just a care-of address, prefer SA.
- If SB is just a home address and SA is just a care-of address, prefer SB.

Lines 384–525 implement the rules.

Listing 5-330

—— in6_src.c
```
     ....
384                          /* Rule 4: Prefer home addresses */
     ....
390                          {
391                                  struct mip6_bu *mbu_ia_best = NULL, *mbu_ia = NULL;
392                                  struct sockaddr_in6 ia_addr;
393
394                                  /*
395                                   * If SA is simultaneously a home address and
396                                   * care-of address and SB is not, then prefer
```

```
397                              * SA. Similarly, if SB is simultaneously a
398                              * home address and care-of address and SA is
399                              * not, then prefer SB.
400                              */
401                             if (ia_best->ia6_flags & IN6_IFF_HOME) {
402                                     /*
403                                      * find a binding update entry for ia_best.
404                                      */
405                                     ia_addr = ia_best->ia_addr;
406                                     if(in6_addr2zoneid(ia_best->ia_ifp,
407                                                         &ia_addr.sin6_addr,
408                                                         &ia_addr.sin6_scope_id)) {
409                                             *errorp = EINVAL; /* XXX */
410                                             return (NULL);
411                                     }
412                                     for (sc = LIST_FIRST(&hif_softc_list); sc;
413                                         sc = LIST_NEXT(sc, hif_entry)) {
414                                             mbu_ia_best =
       mip6_bu_list_find_home_registration(
415                                                     &sc->hif_bu_list,
416                                                     &ia_addr.sin6_addr);
417                                             if (mbu_ia_best)
418                                                     break;
419                                     }
420                             }
```
——— in6_src.c

— *Line 414 is broken here for layout reasons. However, it is a single line of code.*

401–420 In the `in6_selectsrc()` function, the `ia_best` and the `ia` variables point to candidate source addresses. The `ia_best` variable is the first candidate and the `ia` variable is the second candidate address. The address structure pointed to by each of these variables has the `IN6_IFF_HOME` flag set, if the address is a home address.

If the first candidate address has the flag set and the mobile node has a corresponding home registration entry, the `mbu_ia_best` variable is set to point to the binding update list entry.

Listing 5-331
——— in6_src.c
```
421                             if (ia->ia6_flags & IN6_IFF_HOME) {
422                                     /*
423                                      * find a binding update entry for ia.
424                                      */
425                                     ia_addr = ia->ia_addr;
426                                     if(in6_addr2zoneid(ia->ia_ifp,
427                                                         &ia_addr.sin6_addr,
428                                                         &ia_addr.sin6_scope_id)) {
429                                             *errorp = EINVAL; /* XXX */
430                                             return (NULL);
431                                     }
432                                     for (sc = LIST_FIRST(&hif_softc_list); sc;
433                                         sc = LIST_NEXT(sc, hif_entry)) {
434                                             mbu_ia =
       mip6_bu_list_find_home_registration(
435                                                     &sc->hif_bu_list,
436                                                     &ia_addr.sin6_addr);
437                                             if (mbu_ia)
438                                                     break;
439                                     }
440                             }
```
——— in6_src.c

— *Line 434 is broken here for layout reasons. However, it is a single line of code.*

421–440 If another candidate address is a home address and has a corresponding home registration entry, the `mbu_ia` variable points to the entry.

Listing 5-332

in6_src.c

```
442                              /*
443                               * even if the address is a home address, we
444                               * do not use them if they are not registered
445                               * (or re-registered) yet.  this condition is
446                               * not explicitly stated in the address
447                               * selection draft.
448                               */
449                              if ((mbu_ia_best &&
450                                  (mbu_ia_best->mbu_pri_fsm_state
451                                  != MIP6_BU_PRI_FSM_STATE_BOUND))) {
452                                      /* XXX will break stat! */
453                                      REPLACE(0);
454                              }
455                              if ((mbu_ia &&
456                                  (mbu_ia->mbu_pri_fsm_state
457                                  != MIP6_BU_PRI_FSM_STATE_BOUND))) {
458                                      /* XXX will break stat! */
459                                      NEXT(0);
460                              }
```

in6_src.c

449–460 Even if the candidate address is a home address and has the home registration entry related to the home address, the address is not chosen as a source address if the address has not been registered successfully with its home agent. The home address is valid only when it is successfully registered (that is, the state of the entry must be the MIP6_BU_PRI_FSM_STATE_BOUND state). The REPLACE() macro sets the second candidate as the first candidate. The NEXT() macro discards the second candidate and keeps the first candidate. The comparison will continue until all candidate addresses have been checked.

Listing 5-333

in6_src.c

```
462                              /*
463                               * if the binding update entry for a certain
464                               * address exists and its registration status
465                               * is MIP6_BU_FSM_STATE_IDLE, the address is a
466                               * home address and a care of addres
467                               * simultaneously.
468                               */
469                              if ((mbu_ia_best &&
470                                  (mbu_ia_best->mbu_pri_fsm_state
471                                  == MIP6_BU_PRI_FSM_STATE_IDLE))
472                                  &&
473                                  !(mbu_ia &&
474                                  (mbu_ia->mbu_pri_fsm_state
475                                  == MIP6_BU_PRI_FSM_STATE_IDLE))) {
476                                      NEXT(4);
477                              }
478                              if ((!(mbu_ia_best &&
479                                  (mbu_ia_best->mbu_pri_fsm_state
480                                  == MIP6_BU_PRI_FSM_STATE_IDLE))
481                                  &&
482                                  (mbu_ia &&
483                                  (mbu_ia->mbu_pri_fsm_state
484                                  == MIP6_BU_PRI_FSM_STATE_IDLE)))) {
485                                      REPLACE(4);
486                              }
```

in6_src.c

469–486 This part is actually never executed. The intention of this code is to prefer the address which is a home address and a care-of address simultaneously. The code assumes that the status of the home registration entry becomes the idle state (MIP6_BU_PRI_FSM_STATE_IDLE) when a mobile node is at home; however, since the KAME implementation removes a home registration entry when a mobile node returns to home, such a condition never occurs.

Listing 5-334

```
                                                                _____ in6_src.c
487                     if (usecoa != 0) {
488                             /*
489                              * a sender don't want to use a home
490                              * address because:
491                              *
492                              * 1) we cannot use.  (ex. NS or NA to
493                              * global addresses.)
494                              *
495                              * 2) a user specified not to use.
496                              * (ex. mip6control -u)
497                              */
498                             if ((ia_best->ia6_flags & IN6_IFF_HOME) == 0 &&
499                                 (ia->ia6_flags & IN6_IFF_HOME) != 0) {
500                                     /* XXX will break stat! */
501                                     NEXT(0);
502                             }
503                             if ((ia_best->ia6_flags & IN6_IFF_HOME) != 0 &&
504                                 (ia->ia6_flags & IN6_IFF_HOME) == 0) {
505                                     /* XXX will break stat! */
506                                     REPLACE(0);
507                             }
                                                                _____ in6_src.c
```

498–507 If the usecoa variable is set to true, a care-of address is preferred. The address which does not have the IN6_IFF_HOME flag is chosen as a first candidate. If both addresses do not have the flag, the function will check other conditions to determine a more preferable address.

Listing 5-335

```
                                                                _____ in6_src.c
508                     } else {
509                             /*
510                              * If SA is just a home address and SB
511                              * is just a care-of address, then
512                              * prefer SA. Similarly, if SB is just
513                              * a home address and SA is just a
514                              * care-of address, then prefer SB.
515                              */
516                             if ((ia_best->ia6_flags & IN6_IFF_HOME) != 0 &&
517                                 (ia->ia6_flags & IN6_IFF_HOME) == 0) {
518                                     NEXT(4);
519                             }
520                             if ((ia_best->ia6_flags & IN6_IFF_HOME) == 0 &&
521                                 (ia->ia6_flags & IN6_IFF_HOME) != 0) {
522                                     REPLACE(4);
523                             }
524                     }
525             }
                                                                _____ in6_src.c
```

508–524 Otherwise, a home address is preferred as a source address. The address which has the `IN6_IFF_HOME` flag is chosen as a first priority candidate. If both addresses have the flag, the function will check other conditions to determine a more preferable address.

5.17.11 Home Agent List Management

A mobile node needs to keep the list of its home agents to determine the address to which to send binding information when the node moves to a foreign network.

In the KAME implementation, a mobile node collects the information by two methods. One is listening to Router Advertisement messages while the mobile node is at home before moving to other networks. Since a home agent is an IPv6 router by definition (it forwards packets from/to mobile nodes), it sends Router Advertisement messages periodically as an IPv6 router. The Router Advertisement messages sent from home agents are slightly modified as described in Section 5.3.6. The mobile node can easily distinguish messages of home agents from messages sent from other normal routers.

The other method is using the Dynamic Home Agent Address Discovery mechanism. The Dynamic Home Agent Address Discovery mechanism is used when a mobile node needs to learn the home agent information while in a foreign network. As discussed in Section 5.16.19 the home agent list management is done by a user space program, **had**, on the home agent side; however, on the mobile node side, the home agent list management is done in the kernel.

Home agent information is represented as the `mip6_ha{}` structure. To manage the list of home agents, the KAME implementation provides the following support functions:

- `mip6_ha_create()`
  Create an instance of the `mip6_ha{}` structure.

- `mip6_ha_update_lifetime()`
  Update the lifetime information of the specified `mip6_ha{}` instance.

- `mip6_ha_list_insert()`
  Insert the specified `mip6_ha{}` instance to the list.

- `mip6_ha_list_reinsert()`
  Relocate the specified `mip6_ha{}` instance based on the preference in the list.

- `mip6_ha_list_remove()`
  Remove the specified `mip6_ha{}` instance from the list.

- `mip6_ha_list_update_hainfo()`
  Update the preference and lifetime of the specified `mip6_ha{}` instance in the list.

- `mip6_ha_list_find_withaddr()`
  Find an instance of the `mip6_ha{}` structure which has the specified address.

- `mip6_ha_settimer()`
  Set the next timeout of the `mip6_ha{}` instance.

- `mip6_ha_timer()`
  Called periodically for each `mip6_ha{}` instance.

Create a Home Agent Entry

The `mip6_ha_create()` function creates an instance of the `mip6_ha{}` structure which represents a home agent in a mobile node.

Listing 5-336

```
94      struct mip6_ha *
95      mip6_ha_create(addr, flags, pref, lifetime)
96              struct in6_addr *addr;
97              u_int8_t flags;
98              u_int16_t pref;
99              int32_t lifetime;
100     {
101             struct mip6_ha *mha = NULL;
....
103             struct timeval mono_time;
....
107             microtime(&mono_time);
```

94–99 The `addr` parameter is the address of the home agent and the `flag` parameter is a copy of the flag value of the Router Advertisement message received by the mobile node. The `pref` and `lifetime` parameters are a preference value and a lifetime value of the home agent.

Listing 5-337

```
110             if (IN6_IS_ADDR_UNSPECIFIED(addr)
111                     || IN6_IS_ADDR_LOOPBACK(addr)
112                     || IN6_IS_ADDR_MULTICAST(addr)) {
....
116                     return (NULL);
117             }
118
119             if (!IN6_IS_ADDR_LINKLOCAL(addr)
120                     && ((flags & ND_RA_FLAG_HOME_AGENT) == 0)) {
....
125                     return (NULL);
126             }
```

110–117 The address of the home agent must not be an unspecified address, the loopback address or a multicast address.

119–126 The `mip6_ha{}` structure keeps all router information received by the mobile node. If the router is a home agent, the `flags` variable will include the `ND_RA_FLAG_HOME_AGENT` flag. The address of the home agent must be a global address. If the router is just a router and not a home agent, then the address can be a link-local address. This information is used when the mobile node performs movement detection (see Section 5.17.3).

Listing 5-338

———mip6_halist.c
```
128             MALLOC(mha, struct mip6_ha *, sizeof(struct mip6_ha), M_TEMP,
129                 M_NOWAIT);
130             if (mha == NULL) {
....
134                     return (NULL);
135             }
136             bzero(mha, sizeof(*mha));
137             mha->mha_addr = *addr;
138             mha->mha_flags = flags;
139             mha->mha_pref = pref;
....
143             callout_init(&mha->mha_timer_ch);
....
147             if (IN6_IS_ADDR_LINKLOCAL(&mha->mha_addr)) {
148                     mha->mha_lifetime = lifetime;
149             } else {
150                     mha->mha_lifetime = 0; /* infinite. */
151             }
152             mip6_ha_update_lifetime(mha, lifetime);
153
154             return (mha);
155     }
```
———mip6_halist.c

128–152 Memory for the `mip6_ha{}` instance is allocated and its member variables are set. The `mha_timer_ch` field is a handle to the timer function of this instance. The lifetime initialization code on lines 147–151 is actually meaningless. The lifetime information is updated by the `mip6_ha_update_lifetime()` function called on line 152.

Update the Home Agent Entry

The `mip6_ha_update_lifetime()` function updates the lifetime information of the specified home agent entry.

Listing 5-339

———mip6_halist.c
```
157     void
158     mip6_ha_update_lifetime(mha, lifetime)
159             struct mip6_ha *mha;
160             u_int16_t lifetime;
161     {
....
163             struct timeval mono_time;
....
167             microtime(&mono_time);
```
———mip6_halist.c

157–160 The `mip6_ha_update_lifetime()` function has two parameters. The `mha` parameter is a pointer to the `mip6_ha{}` instance whose lifetime is being updated and the `lifetime` parameter is the new lifetime value.

Listing 5-340

_____mip6_halist.c
```
170              mip6_ha_settimer(mha, -1);
171              mha->mha_lifetime = lifetime;
172              if (mha->mha_lifetime != 0) {
173                      mha->mha_expire = mono_time.tv_sec + mha->mha_lifetime;
174                      mip6_ha_settimer(mha, mha->mha_lifetime * hz);
175              } else {
176                      mha->mha_expire = 0;
177              }
178      }
```
_____mip6_halist.c

170–177 The callback timer is reset on line 170 and the new lifetime of the mip6_ha{}
instance is set. If the lifetime is specified as 0, the entry is treated as an infinite entry.
Otherwise, the timer function is set to be called when the lifetime expires.

Insert a Home Agent Entry

The mip6_ha_list_insert() function inserts a home agent entry into the proper position
of the home agent list based on its preference value.

Listing 5-341

_____mip6_halist.c
```
282      void
283      mip6_ha_list_insert(mha_list, mha)
284              struct mip6_ha_list *mha_list;
285              struct mip6_ha *mha;
286      {
287              struct mip6_ha *tgtmha;
288
289              if ((mha_list == NULL) || (mha == NULL)) {
290                      panic("mip6_ha_list_insert: NULL pointer.");
291              }
292
293              /*
294               * insert a new entry in a proper place orderd by prefernce
295               * value.  if prefernce value is same, the new entry is placed
296               * at the end of the group which has a same prefernce value.
297               */
298              for (tgtmha = TAILQ_FIRST(mha_list); tgtmha;
299                   tgtmha = TAILQ_NEXT(tgtmha, mha_entry)) {
300                      if (tgtmha->mha_pref >= mha->mha_pref)
301                              continue;
302                      TAILQ_INSERT_BEFORE(tgtmha, mha, mha_entry);
303                      return;
304              }
305              TAILQ_INSERT_TAIL(mha_list, mha, mha_entry);
306
307              return;
308      }
```
_____mip6_halist.c

282–285 The mip6_ha_list_insert() function has two parameters. The mha_list
parameter is a pointer to the list of mip6_ha{} instances and the mha parameter is a
pointer to the mip6_ha{} instance to be inserted.

298–307 The list of the mip6_ha{} instances is ordered by the value of the preference field of
each mip6_ha{} instance. The preference value of each entry which is already inserted
in the list is checked and the new entry is inserted at the proper position.

Reinsert the Home Agent Entry

Listing 5-342

———mip6_halist.c
```
310     void
311     mip6_ha_list_reinsert(mha_list, mha)
312             struct mip6_ha_list *mha_list;
313             struct mip6_ha *mha;
314     {
315             struct mip6_ha *tgtmha;
316
317             if ((mha_list == NULL) || (mha == NULL)) {
318                     panic("mip6_ha_list_insert: NULL pointer.");
319             }
320
321             for (tgtmha = TAILQ_FIRST(mha_list); tgtmha;
322                 tgtmha = TAILQ_NEXT(tgtmha, mha_entry)) {
323                     if (tgtmha == mha)
324                             break;
325             }
326
327             /* insert or move the entry to the proper place of the queue. */
328             if (tgtmha != NULL)
329                     TAILQ_REMOVE(mha_list, tgtmha, mha_entry);
330             mip6_ha_list_insert(mha_list, mha);
331
332             return;
333     }
```
———mip6_halist.c

310–333 The `mip6_ha_list_reinsert()` function does almost the same things as the
`mip6_ha_list_insert()` does. The difference between these two functions is
`mip6_ha_list_reinsert()` removes the entry specified by the second parameter,
if the entry already exists in the list, and reinserts it at the proper position. This function
is used to reorder the list of entries when the preference value of the entry is changed.

Listing 5-343

———mip6_halist.c
```
336     int
337     mip6_ha_list_remove(mha_list, mha)
338             struct mip6_ha_list *mha_list;
339             struct mip6_ha *mha;
340     {
341             struct mip6_prefix *mpfx;
342             struct mip6_prefix_ha *mpfxha, *mpfxha_next;
343
344             if ((mha_list == NULL) || (mha == NULL)) {
345                     return (EINVAL);
346             }
347
348             /* remove all refernces from mip6_prefix entries. */
349             for (mpfx = LIST_FIRST(&mip6_prefix_list); mpfx;
350                 mpfx = LIST_NEXT(mpfx, mpfx_entry)) {
351                     for (mpfxha = LIST_FIRST(&mpfx->mpfx_ha_list); mpfxha;
352                         mpfxha = mpfxha_next) {
353                             mpfxha_next = LIST_NEXT(mpfxha, mpfxha_entry);
354                             if (mpfxha->mpfxha_mha == mha)
355                                     mip6_prefix_ha_list_remove(&mpfx->mpfx_ha_list,
356                                         mpfxha);
357                     }
358             }
359
```

```
360                 TAILQ_REMOVE(mha_list, mha, mha_entry);
361                 mip6_ha_settimer(mha, -1);
362                 FREE(mha, M_TEMP);
363
364                 return (0);
365         }
```

337–339 The `mip6_ha_list_remove()` function has two parameters. The `mha_list` parameter is a pointer to the list of the `mip6_ha{}` instances and the `mha` parameter is a pointer to the `mip6_ha{}` instance to be removed.

349–358 When removing an instance of the `mip6_ha{}` structure, the `mip6_prefix{}` instance related to the entry has to be removed. The `mip6_prefix{}` structure has a pointer to the `mip6_ha{}` instance which advertises the prefix information. Before the entry of the `mip6_ha{}` instance is removed, the structure which keeps the pointer has to be removed. The relationship between these structures is illustrated in Figure 5-45 (on page 564).

360–362 The entry is removed from the list and the memory block used for the entry is freed.

Update Home Agent Information

The `mip6_ha_list_update_hainfo()` function updates the information of an instance of the `mip6_ha{}` structure based on the information received with Router Advertisement messages.

Listing 5-344

```
367     int
368     mip6_ha_list_update_hainfo(mha_list, dr, hai)
369             struct mip6_ha_list *mha_list;
370             struct nd_defrouter *dr;
371             struct nd_opt_homeagent_info *hai;
372     {
373             int16_t pref = 0;
374             u_int16_t lifetime;
375             struct mip6_ha *mha;
```

367–371 The `mip6_ha_list_update_hainfo()` function has three parameters: the `mha_list` parameter is a pointer to the list of `mip6_ha{}` instances; the `dr` parameter is a pointer to information about the router which sent the Router Advertisement message; and the `hai` parameter is a pointer to the Home Agent Information option which is included in Router Advertisement messages sent from home agents.

Listing 5-345

```
377             if ((mha_list == NULL) ||
378                 (dr == NULL) ||
379                 !IN6_IS_ADDR_LINKLOCAL(&dr->rtaddr)) {
380                 return (EINVAL);
381             }
382
383             lifetime = dr->rtlifetime;
```

```
384                 if (hai) {
385                         pref = ntohs(hai->nd_opt_hai_preference);
386                         lifetime = ntohs(hai->nd_opt_hai_lifetime);
387                 }
```
                                                                    ──────mip6_halist.c

379 The source address of the Router Advertisement message must be a link-local address according to the specification of Neighbor Discovery.

383–386 The lifetime of the home agent is specified in the Home Agent Information option. If the option does not exist, then the router lifetime specified in the Router Advertisement message is used as the lifetime of the home agent.

Listing 5-346

                                                                    ──────mip6_halist.c
```
389                 /* find an exising entry. */
390                 mha = mip6_ha_list_find_withaddr(mha_list, &dr->rtaddr);
391                 if (mha == NULL) {
392                         /* an entry must exist at this point. */
393                         return (EINVAL);
394                 }
395
396                 /*
397                  * if received lifetime is 0, delete the entry.
398                  * otherwise, update an entry.
399                  */
400                 if (lifetime == 0) {
401                         mip6_ha_list_remove(mha_list, mha);
402                 } else {
403                         /* reset lifetime */
404                         mip6_ha_update_lifetime(mha, lifetime);
405                 }
406
407                 return (0);
408         }
```
                                                                    ──────mip6_halist.c

389–405 The `mip6_ha_list_find_withaddr()` function returns an existing entry of the `mip6_ha{}` structure. If there is an existing entry, its lifetime information is updated. The lifetime value 0 means that the router is going to stop functioning as a home agent. In that case, the entry will be removed. In this function, the preference value is not processed at all. This is a bug and the function should consider updating the preference value and reordering the list.

Find the Home Agent Entry

The `mip6_ha_list_find_withaddr()` function returns a pointer to the home agent entry that has the specified address as its function parameter.

Listing 5-347

                                                                    ──────mip6_halist.c
```
410     struct mip6_ha *
411     mip6_ha_list_find_withaddr(mha_list, addr)
412             struct mip6_ha_list *mha_list;
413             struct in6_addr *addr;
```

```
414      {
415              struct mip6_ha *mha;
416
417              for (mha = TAILQ_FIRST(mha_list); mha;
418                  mha = TAILQ_NEXT(mha, mha_entry)) {
419                      if (IN6_ARE_ADDR_EQUAL(&mha->mha_addr, addr))
420                              return (mha);
421              }
422              /* not found. */
423              return (NULL);
424      }
```
                                                                  ————————mip6_halist.c

410–413 The `mip6_ha_list_find_withaddr()` function has two parameters. The `mha_list` parameter is a pointer to the list of the `mip6_ha{}` instances to be searched and the `addr` parameter is the address of the `mip6_ha{}` instances being searched.

417–423 All entries stored in the list are checked in the `for` loop and the pointer to the entry whose address is the same as that specified as the `addr` parameter is returned, if it exists.

Set Next Timeout of the Home Agent Entry

The `mip6_ha_settimer()` function sets the next timeout.

Listing 5-348
                                                                  ————————mip6_halist.c
```
180      static void
181      mip6_ha_settimer(mha, tick)
182              struct mip6_ha *mha;
183              long tick;
184      {
....
186              struct timeval mono_time;
....
188              int s;
```
                                                                  ————————mip6_halist.c

180–183 The mha parameter is a pointer to the `mip6_ha{}` instance, and the `tick` parameter is the time until the callback function is called next.

Listing 5-349
                                                                  ————————mip6_halist.c
```
191              microtime(&mono_time);
....
197              s = splnet();
....
200              if (tick < 0) {
201                      mha->mha_timeout = 0;
202                      mha->mha_ntick = 0;
....
204                      callout_stop(&mha->mha_timer_ch);
....
210              } else {
211                      mha->mha_timeout = mono_time.tv_sec + tick / hz;
212                      if (tick > INT_MAX) {
```

```
213                                    mha->mha_ntick = tick - INT_MAX;
....
215                                    callout_reset(&mha->mha_timer_ch, INT_MAX,
216                                        mip6_ha_timer, mha);
....
222                            } else {
223                                    mha->mha_ntick = 0;
....
225                                    callout_reset(&mha->mha_timer_ch, tick,
226                                        mip6_ha_timer, mha);
....
232                            }
233                    }
234
235            splx(s);
236    }
```
――― mip6_halist.c

200–204 If the specified time is a minus value, the timer is stopped.

211–232 The next timeout is set. The timer handle `mha_timer_ch` cannot count periods longer than the maximum integer value can represent. If we need to set a longer timeout, the `mha_ntick` variable is used to divide the timeout period into several pieces. If the specified time (`tick`), is longer than the limit of the maximum integer value (`INT_MAX`), the next timeout is set to the maximum time which an integer variable can represent and `mha_ntick` is set to the rest of the time. Otherwise, set the next timeout to the specified time as `tick`.

Periodical Tasks of the Home Agent Entry

The `mip6_ha_timer()` function is called when the lifetime of the entry has expired.

Listing 5-350
――― mip6_halist.c

```
238    static void
239    mip6_ha_timer(arg)
240            void *arg;
241    {
242            int s;
243            struct mip6_ha *mha;
....
245            struct timeval mono_time;
....
249            microtime(&mono_time);
....
255            s = splnet();
....
258            mha = (struct mip6_ha *)arg;
```
――― mip6_halist.c

238–240 The `arg` parameter is a pointer to the `mip6_ha{}` instance to which the timer function is called.

Listing 5-351

————————————————————————————————————mip6_halist.c
```
260                 if (mha->mha_ntick > 0) {
261                         if (mha->mha_ntick > INT_MAX) {
262                                 mha->mha_ntick -= INT_MAX;
263                                 mip6_ha_settimer(mha, INT_MAX);
264                         } else {
265                                 mha->mha_ntick = 0;
266                                 mip6_ha_settimer(mha, mha->mha_ntick);
267                         }
268                         splx(s);
269                         return;
270                 }
271
272                 /*
273                  * XXX reset all home agent addresses in the binding update
274                  * entries.
275                  */
276
277                 mip6_ha_list_remove(&mip6_ha_list, mha);
278
279                 splx(s);
280         }
```
————————————————————————————————————mip6_halist.c

260–277 If the mha_ntick variable has a positive value and it is greater than the maximum integer value (INT_MAX), then the value is reduced by INT_MAX and the next callback time is set after INT_MAX time; otherwise, the next timeout is set after mha_ntick time. In these cases, the entry will not be removed, since the expiration time has not come yet.

If the mha_ntick variable is set to 0 and the timer function is called, the mip6_ha{} instance is removed from the list. In this case, all home agent addresses currently used in the list of binding update list entries of the mobile node have to be updated. However, the function is not implemented.

This will not cause any serious problems because when the mobile node tries to use the binding update list entry for which the home agent address is no longer valid, the mobile node will perform the Dynamic Home Agent Address Discovery mechanism.

5.17.12 Prefix Information Management

A mobile node maintains a prefix list as a clue to check its location. Each prefix information entry is bound to the router information entry which advertised the prefix. The virtual home network structure (the hif_softc{} structure) has two lists of the prefix information entry. One is used to keep all prefix information entries which are announced at home. The other is used to keep all foreign prefix information entries. The lists do not keep the actual values of the prefixes; they keep pointers to the entries in the global prefix list explained below.

The KAME Mobile IPv6 implementation has one global prefix list. Every structure which requires prefix information keeps pointers to the entries in the list. The following functions are provided to manage the prefix information.

- mip6_prefix_create()
  Creates an instance of a prefix information structure (the mip6_prefix{} structure).

- mip6_prefix_update_lifetime()
  Updates the lifetime information of the mip6_prefix{} instance.

- `mip6_prefix_settimer()`
  Sets the next timeout of the prefix information.

- `mip6_prefix_timer()`
  The function that is called when the timer set by the `mip6_prefix_settimer()` function expires.

- `mip6_prefix_send_mps()`
  Sends a Mobile Prefix Solicitation message.

- `mip6_prefix_list_insert()`
  Inserts the specified instance of the `mip6_prefix{}` structure into the list.

- `mip6_prefix_list_remove()`
  Removes the specified instance of the `mip6_prefix{}` structure from the list.

- `mip6_prefix_list_find_withprefix()`
  Searches for an `mip6_prefix{}` instance with prefix information.

- `mip6_prefix_list_find_withhaddr()`
  Searches for an `mip6_prefix{}` instance with home address information derived from the prefix.

- `mip6_prefix_ha_list_insert()`
  Inserts the pointer structure which points to the `mip6_ha{}` instance that includes a router or home agent information.

- `mip6_prefix_ha_list_remove()`
  Removes the pointer structure of the `mip6_ha{}` instance.

- `mip6_prefix_ha_list_find_withaddr()`
  Searches for a pointer structure with a router or a home agent address.

- `mip6_prefix_ha_list_find_withmha()`
  Searches for a pointer structure with the value of the pointer to the `mip6_ha{}` instance.

Create a Prefix Entry

The `mip6_prefix_create()` function creates a new prefix information entry for the Mobile IPv6 stack.

Listing 5-352

```
                                                              mip6_prefix.c
95      struct mip6_prefix *
96      mip6_prefix_create(prefix, prefixlen, vltime, pltime)
97              struct in6_addr *prefix;
98              u_int8_t prefixlen;
99              u_int32_t vltime;
100             u_int32_t pltime;
101     {
102             struct in6_addr mask;
103             struct mip6_prefix *mpfx;
104
105             MALLOC(mpfx, struct mip6_prefix *, sizeof(struct mip6_prefix),
106                     M_TEMP, M_NOWAIT);
```

```
107                 if (mpfx == NULL) {
 ....
111                         return (NULL);
112                 }
113                 bzero(mpfx, sizeof(*mpfx));
114                 in6_prefixlen2mask(&mask, prefixlen);
115                 mpfx->mpfx_prefix = *prefix;
116                 mpfx->mpfx_prefix.s6_addr32[0] &= mask.s6_addr32[0];
117                 mpfx->mpfx_prefix.s6_addr32[1] &= mask.s6_addr32[1];
118                 mpfx->mpfx_prefix.s6_addr32[2] &= mask.s6_addr32[2];
119                 mpfx->mpfx_prefix.s6_addr32[3] &= mask.s6_addr32[3];
120                 mpfx->mpfx_prefixlen = prefixlen;
121                 /* XXX mpfx->mpfx_haddr; */
122                 LIST_INIT(&mpfx->mpfx_ha_list);
 ....
126                 callout_init(&mpfx->mpfx_timer_ch);
 ....
130
131                 /* set initial timeout. */
132                 mip6_prefix_update_lifetime(mpfx, vltime, pltime);
133
134                 return (mpfx);
135         }
```
_____ mip6_prefix.c

95–100 The mip6_prefix_create() function has four parameters: The prefix parameter
is a pointer to the instance of the in6_addr{} structure which holds prefix information;
the prefixlen, vltime and pltime parameters are the prefix length, the valid lifetime
and the preferred lifetime of the new prefix information, respectively.

105–122 Memory space is allocated for the new mip6_prefix{} instance and each member
variable is filled. The mpfx_prefix{} structure keeps only the prefix information. The
interface identifier part will be filled with 0 using the mask value created from the prefix
length information. The mpfx_ha_list field is a list on which pointer structures are
kept. It points to the mip6_ha{} instances advertising the prefix. If multiple routers are
advertising the same prefix, the list will include all of them.

126–132 The timer handle (mpfx_timer_ch) is initialized and the lifetime is updated based
on the parameters passed to the function.

Update Lifetime of a Prefix Entry

The mip6_prefix_update_lifetime() function updates the information of an existing
prefix entry.

Listing 5-353
_____ mip6_prefix.c

```
138     #define MIP6_PREFIX_EXPIRE_TIME(ltime) ((ltime) / 4 * 3) /* XXX */
139     void
140     mip6_prefix_update_lifetime(mpfx, vltime, pltime)
141             struct mip6_prefix *mpfx;
142             u_int32_t vltime;
143             u_int32_t pltime;
144     {
```

```
      ....
146                struct timeval mono_time;
      ....
150                microtime(&mono_time);
      ....
153                if (mpfx == NULL)
154                        panic("mip6_prefix_update_lifetime: mpfx == NULL");
155
156                mip6_prefix_settimer(mpfx, -1);
157
158                mpfx->mpfx_vltime = vltime;
159                mpfx->mpfx_pltime = pltime;
160
161                if (mpfx->mpfx_vltime == ND6_INFINITE_LIFETIME) {
162                        mpfx->mpfx_vlexpire = 0;
163                } else {
164                        mpfx->mpfx_vlexpire = mono_time.tv_sec + mpfx->mpfx_vltime;
165                }
166                if (mpfx->mpfx_pltime == ND6_INFINITE_LIFETIME) {
167                        mpfx->mpfx_plexpire = 0;
168                } else {
169                        mpfx->mpfx_plexpire = mono_time.tv_sec + mpfx->mpfx_pltime;
170                }
171
172                if (mpfx->mpfx_pltime != ND6_INFINITE_LIFETIME) {
173                        mip6_prefix_settimer(mpfx,
174                            MIP6_PREFIX_EXPIRE_TIME(mpfx->mpfx_pltime) * hz);
175                        mpfx->mpfx_state = MIP6_PREFIX_STATE_PREFERRED;
176                } else if (mpfx->mpfx_vltime != ND6_INFINITE_LIFETIME) {
177                        mip6_prefix_settimer(mpfx,
178                            MIP6_PREFIX_EXPIRE_TIME(mpfx->mpfx_vltime) * hz);
179                        mpfx->mpfx_state = MIP6_PREFIX_STATE_PREFERRED;
180                }
181        }
```
——mip6_prefix.c

139–143 The `mip6_prefix_update_lifetime()` function has three parameters. The `mpfx` parameter is a pointer to the instance of the `mip6_prefix{}` structure and the `vltime` and `pltime` parameter are a valid lifetime and a preferred lifetime, respectively.

161–164 If the specified valid lifetime indicates the infinite lifetime, the `mpfx_vlexpire` variable is set to 0 which represents infinity; otherwise, the expiration time is set to `vltime` seconds after the current time.

166–170 The same procedure is performed on the preferred lifetime.

172–179 The next timeout is set to call the timer function. If the preferred lifetime is not set to infinity, the timeout is set based on the preferred lifetime. If the preferred lifetime is set to infinity and the valid lifetime is not infinity, the timeout is set based on the valid lifetime. If both lifetime values are set to infinity, the prefix never expires. The `MIP6_PREFIX_EXPIRE_TIME()` macro returns a value that is three-fourths of the parameter passed to it. The timeout value is set to three-fourths of the lifetime so that the timer function is called before the lifetime of the prefix expires.

Set Next Timeout of the Prefix Entry

The `mip6_prefix_settimer()` function sets the next timeout of the specified prefix entry.

Listing 5-354

─── mip6_prefix.c

```
237     void
238     mip6_prefix_settimer(mpfx, tick)
239             struct mip6_prefix *mpfx;
240             long tick;
241     {
....
243             struct timeval mono_time;
....
245             int s;
....
248             microtime(&mono_time);
....
254             s = splnet();
```

─── mip6_prefix.c

237–240 The `mip6_prefix_settimer()` function has two parameters. The `mpfx` parameter is a pointer to the `mip6_prefix{}` instance for which a timer is being set and the `tick` parameter indicates the timeout value.

Listing 5-355

─── mip6_prefix.c

```
257             if (tick < 0) {
258                     mpfx->mpfx_timeout = 0;
259                     mpfx->mpfx_ntick = 0;
....
261                     callout_stop(&mpfx->mpfx_timer_ch);
....
267             } else {
268                     mpfx->mpfx_timeout = mono_time.tv_sec + tick / hz;
269                     if (tick > INT_MAX) {
270                             mpfx->mpfx_ntick = tick - INT_MAX;
....
272                             callout_reset(&mpfx->mpfx_timer_ch, INT_MAX,
273                                 mip6_prefix_timer, mpfx);
....
279                     } else {
280                             mpfx->mpfx_ntick = 0;
....
282                             callout_reset(&mpfx->mpfx_timer_ch, tick,
283                                 mip6_prefix_timer, mpfx);
....
289                     }
290             }
291
292             splx(s);
293     }
```

─── mip6_prefix.c

257–261 If `tick` is set to a negative value, the timer is stopped.

268–289 If `tick` is set to a positive value and it is greater than the maximum value of an integer variable (INT_MAX), INT_MAX is set as a timeout value and the rest of the time is set in the `mpfx_ntick` variable. If `tick` is smaller than INT_MAX, the `tick` value is set as a timeout value.

Periodic Tasks of a Prefix Entry

The `mip6_prefix_timer()` function is called when the timer set by the `mip6_prefix_settimer()` function expires.

Listing 5-356

```
295     #define MIP6_MOBILE_PREFIX_SOL_INTERVAL 10 /* XXX */
296     static void
297     mip6_prefix_timer(arg)
298             void *arg;
299     {
300             int s;
301             struct mip6_prefix *mpfx;
....
303             struct timeval mono_time;
....
307             microtime(&mono_time);
....
313             s = splnet();
```

296–297 The timer is maintained separately by each `mip6_prefix{}` instance. The parameter is a pointer to the instance of the `mip6_prefix{}` structure whose timer has expired.

Listing 5-357

```
316             mpfx = (struct mip6_prefix *)arg;
317
318             if (mpfx->mpfx_ntick > 0) {
319                     if (mpfx->mpfx_ntick > INT_MAX) {
320                             mpfx->mpfx_ntick -= INT_MAX;
321                             mip6_prefix_settimer(mpfx, INT_MAX);
322                     } else {
323                             mpfx->mpfx_ntick = 0;
324                             mip6_prefix_settimer(mpfx, mpfx->mpfx_ntick);
325                     }
326                     splx(s);
327                     return;
328             }
```

318–328 `mpfx_ntick` is set if the period to the next timeout is greater than the maximum size of an integer value (INT_MAX). In this case, if `mpfx_ntick` is still greater than INT_MAX, the next timeout is set to INT_MAX; otherwise, the next timeout is set to `mpfx_ntick`.

Listing 5-358

```
330             switch (mpfx->mpfx_state) {
331             case MIP6_PREFIX_STATE_PREFERRED:
332                     if (mip6_prefix_send_mps(mpfx)) {
....
```

```
337                        }
338
339                        if (mpfx->mpfx_vlexpire >
340                            mono_time.tv_sec + MIP6_MOBILE_PREFIX_SOL_INTERVAL) {
341                                mip6_prefix_settimer(mpfx,
342                                    MIP6_MOBILE_PREFIX_SOL_INTERVAL * hz);
343                        } else {
344                                mip6_prefix_settimer(mpfx,
345                                    (mpfx->mpfx_vlexpire - mono_time.tv_sec) * hz);
346                        }
347                        mpfx->mpfx_state = MIP6_PREFIX_STATE_EXPIRING;
348                        break;
```
                                                                ─────────── mip6_prefix.c

330–348 Each prefix information has a state field. The field can have either of two states (as
described in Table 5-25 on page 563). If the state is MIP6_PREFIX_STATE_PREFERRED,
a Mobile Prefix Solicitation message is sent by calling the mip6_prefix_send_mps()
function to extend the lifetime of the prefix. The next timeout is set to the time
after MIP6_MOBILE_PREFIX_SOL_INTERVAL seconds for retransmission. The state is
changed to the MIP6_PREFIX_STATE_EXPIRING state.

Listing 5-359

                                                                ─────────── mip6_prefix.c
```
350                case MIP6_PREFIX_STATE_EXPIRING:
351                        if (mpfx->mpfx_vlexpire < mono_time.tv_sec) {
352                                mip6_prefix_list_remove(&mip6_prefix_list, mpfx);
353                                break;
354                        }
355
356                        if (mip6_prefix_send_mps(mpfx)) {
....
361                        }
362
363                        if (mpfx->mpfx_vlexpire >
364                            mono_time.tv_sec + MIP6_MOBILE_PREFIX_SOL_INTERVAL) {
365                                mip6_prefix_settimer(mpfx,
366                                    MIP6_MOBILE_PREFIX_SOL_INTERVAL * hz);
367                        } else {
368                                mip6_prefix_settimer(mpfx,
369                                    (mpfx->mpfx_vlexpire - mono_time.tv_sec) * hz);
370                        }
371                        mpfx->mpfx_state = MIP6_PREFIX_STATE_EXPIRING;
372                        break;
373                }
374
375        splx(s);
376    }
```
                                                                ─────────── mip6_prefix.c

350–354 If the state is MIP6_PREFIX_STATE_EXPIRING and the valid lifetime is expired,
the prefix information is removed.

356–372 A Mobile Prefix Solicitation message is sent by the mip6_prefix_send_mps()
function. The message is resent every MIP6_MOBILE_PREFIX_SOL_INTERVAL seconds
(10 seconds) until the lifetime of the prefix is expired. If a corresponding advertisement message is received, the retransmission is stopped. The state remains in the
MIP6_PREFIX_STATE_EXPIRING state.

Requesting Updated Prefix Information

When a mobile node needs to retrieve the latest prefix information of its home network, the `mip6_prefix_send_mps()` function is called to send a Mobile Prefix Solicitation message.

Listing 5-360

── mip6_prefix.c

```
214    static int
215    mip6_prefix_send_mps(mpfx)
216            struct mip6_prefix *mpfx;
217    {
218            struct hif_softc *hif;
219            struct mip6_bu *mbu;
220            int error = 0;
221
222            for (hif = LIST_FIRST(&hif_softc_list); hif;
223                hif = LIST_NEXT(hif, hif_entry)) {
224                    if (!IN6_IS_ADDR_UNSPECIFIED(&mpfx->mpfx_haddr)) {
225                            mbu = mip6_bu_list_find_home_registration(
226                                    &hif->hif_bu_list, &mpfx->mpfx_haddr);
227                            if (mbu != NULL) {
228                                    error = mip6_icmp6_mp_sol_output(
229                                            &mbu->mbu_haddr, &mbu->mbu_paddr);
230                                    break;
231                            }
232                    }
233            }
234            return (error);
235    }
```

── mip6_prefix.c

215–216 The `mip6_prefix_send_mps()` function takes a pointer to the instance of the `mip6_prefix{}` structure.

222–233 A mobile node needs to update the information about a prefix when the lifetime of the prefix is about to expire. The information can be retrieved by exchanging the Mobile Prefix Solicitation and Advertisement messages. The solicitation message must be sent from the home address of the mobile node to the address of its home agent. In this loop, we check to see if the specified `mip6_prefix{}` instance has a valid home address and find the home agent address to which the home address is registered. The `mip6_icmp6_mp_sol_output()` function sends a Mobile Prefix Solicitation message.

Insert Prefix Entry

The `mip6_prefix_list_insert()` function inserts the specified prefix entry into the prefix list.

Listing 5-361

── mip6_prefix.c

```
378    int
379    mip6_prefix_list_insert(mpfx_list, mpfx)
380            struct mip6_prefix_list *mpfx_list;
381            struct mip6_prefix *mpfx;
382    {
383            if ((mpfx_list == NULL) || (mpfx == NULL)) {
384                    return (EINVAL);
385            }
386
387            LIST_INSERT_HEAD(mpfx_list, mpfx, mpfx_entry);
```

```
388
389            return (0);
390      }
```

378–381 The `mip6_prefix_list_insert()` function has two parameters. The `mpfx_list` is a pointer to the list of instances of the `mip6_prefix{}` structure and the `mpfx` parameter is a pointer to the instance of the `mip6_prefix{}` structure to be inserted.

387 The function just calls a macro function which manipulates a list structure.

Remove Prefix Entry

The `mip6_prefix_list_remove()` function removes the specified prefix entry from the prefix list.

Listing 5-362

```
392      int
393      mip6_prefix_list_remove(mpfx_list, mpfx)
394            struct mip6_prefix_list *mpfx_list;
395            struct mip6_prefix *mpfx;
396      {
397            struct hif_softc *hif;
398            struct mip6_prefix_ha *mpfxha;
399
400            if ((mpfx_list == NULL) || (mpfx == NULL)) {
401                  return (EINVAL);
402            }
403
404            /* remove all references from hif interfaces. */
405            for (hif = LIST_FIRST(&hif_softc_list); hif;
406                  hif = LIST_NEXT(hif, hif_entry)) {
407                  hif_prefix_list_remove(&hif->hif_prefix_list_home,
408                        hif_prefix_list_find_withmpfx(&hif->hif_prefix_list_home,
409                              mpfx));
410                  hif_prefix_list_remove(&hif->hif_prefix_list_foreign,
411                        hif_prefix_list_find_withmpfx
    (&hif->hif_prefix_list_foreign,
412                              mpfx));
413            }
414
415            /* remove all refernces to advertising routers. */
416            while (!LIST_EMPTY(&mpfx->mpfx_ha_list)) {
417                  mpfxha = LIST_FIRST(&mpfx->mpfx_ha_list);
418                  mip6_prefix_ha_list_remove(&mpfx->mpfx_ha_list, mpfxha);
419            }
420
421            LIST_REMOVE(mpfx, mpfx_entry);
422            mip6_prefix_settimer(mpfx, -1);
423            FREE(mpfx, M_TEMP);
424
425            return (0);
426      }
```

— *Line 411 is broken here for layout reasons. However, it is a single line of code.*

392–395 The `mip6_prefix_list_remove()` function has two parameters. The `mpfx_list` parameter is a pointer to the list of instances of the `mip6_prefix{}` structure and the `mpfx` parameter is a pointer to one of the elements in the list to be removed.

405–413 All references from the virtual home interface (the `hif_softc{}` structure) to the `mip6_prefix{}` instance specified as a parameter are removed. As described in Figure 5-46 (page 566), the `hif_softc{}` structure may have references to the prefix information.

415–419 All references to the router information (the `mip6_ha{}` structure) are removed. Each prefix information entry has at least one reference to the instance of the `mip6_ha{}` structure as described in Figure 5-45 (page 564).

421–423 The specified entry is removed from the prefix list. The timer handler is reset and the memory space used by the `mip6_prefix{}` instance is released.

Find the Prefix Entry with Prefix Information

The `mip6_prefix_list_find_withprefix()` function returns the prefix entry that has the prefix information specified by its function parameters.

Listing 5-363
```
                                                              ─mip6_prefix.c
428     struct mip6_prefix *
429     mip6_prefix_list_find_withprefix(prefix, prefixlen)
430             struct in6_addr *prefix;
431             int prefixlen;
432     {
433             struct mip6_prefix *mpfx;
434
435             for (mpfx = LIST_FIRST(&mip6_prefix_list); mpfx;
436                 mpfx = LIST_NEXT(mpfx, mpfx_entry)) {
437                     if (in6_are_prefix_equal(prefix, &mpfx->mpfx_prefix, prefixlen)
438                         && (prefixlen == mpfx->mpfx_prefixlen)) {
439                             /* found. */
440                             return (mpfx);
441                     }
442             }
443
444             /* not found. */
445             return (NULL);
446     }
                                                              ─mip6_prefix.c
```

428–431 The `mip6_prefix_list_find_withprefix()` function has two parameters. The `prefix` parameter is a pointer to the `in6_addr{}` structure which holds the key information used as an index and the `prefixlen` parameter is the length of the prefix specified as the first parameter.

435–442 All prefix information is stored in the list called `mip6_prefix_list`. The prefix information (the `mpfx_prefix` member variable of the `mip6_prefix{}` structure) and the information passed as parameters are compared and the pointer to the entry which has the same information is returned.

Find the Prefix Entry with Home Address

The `mip6_prefix_list_find_withhaddr()` function returns the prefix entry whose home address is the same address as the second parameter of the function.

Listing 5-364

———————————————————————————————————mip6_prefix.c
```
448     struct mip6_prefix *
449     mip6_prefix_list_find_withhaddr(mpfx_list, haddr)
450           struct mip6_prefix_list *mpfx_list;
451           struct in6_addr *haddr;
452     {
453           struct mip6_prefix *mpfx;
454
455           for (mpfx = LIST_FIRST(mpfx_list); mpfx;
456               mpfx = LIST_NEXT(mpfx, mpfx_entry)) {
457               if (IN6_ARE_ADDR_EQUAL(haddr, &mpfx->mpfx_haddr)) {
458                       /* found. */
459                       return (mpfx);
460               }
461           }
462
463           /* not found. */
464           return (NULL);
465     }
```
———————————————————————————————————mip6_prefix.c

448–451 The `mip6_prefix_list_find_withhaddr()` function has two parameters. The `mpfx_list` parameter is a pointer to the list of `mip6_prefix{}` instances and the `haddr` parameter is a home address which is used as a key when searching for an `mip6_prefix{}` instance.

455–461 Each `mip6_prefix{}` instance has a home address which is generated from its prefix information. In this loop, we compare the home address of the `mip6_prefix{}` instance (the `mpfx_haddr` member variable) and the specified parameter. If we find an entry which has the same home address as the `haddr` parameter, a pointer to it is returned.

Insert Home Agent Information to the Prefix Entry

The `mip6_prefix_ha_list_insert()` function inserts the pointer structure which points to the `mip6_ha{}` instance that includes router or home agent information.

Listing 5-365

———————————————————————————————————mip6_prefix.c
```
467     struct mip6_prefix_ha *
468     mip6_prefix_ha_list_insert(mpfxha_list, mha)
469           struct mip6_prefix_ha_list *mpfxha_list;
470           struct mip6_ha *mha;
471     {
472           struct mip6_prefix_ha *mpfxha;
473
474           if ((mpfxha_list == NULL) || (mha == NULL))
475               return (NULL);
476
477           mpfxha = mip6_prefix_ha_list_find_withmha(mpfxha_list, mha);
478           if (mpfxha != NULL)
479               return (mpfxha);
480
481           MALLOC(mpfxha, struct mip6_prefix_ha *, sizeof(struct mip6_prefix_ha),
482               M_TEMP, M_NOWAIT);
483           if (mpfxha == NULL) {
....
486               return (NULL);
```

```
487              }
488              mpfxha->mpfxha_mha = mha;
489              LIST_INSERT_HEAD(mpfxha_list, mpfxha, mpfxha_entry);
490              return (mpfxha);
491      }
```
――mip6_prefix.c

467–470 The `mip6_prefix_ha_list_insert()` function has two parameters. The `mpfxha_list` parameter is a pointer to the list of instances of the `mip6_prefix_ha{}` structure. The list is one of the member variables of the `mip6_prefix{}` structure. The `mha` parameter is a pointer to an instance of the `mip6_ha{}` structure. The function inserts the structure with a pointer to the `mip6_prefix{}` instance whose prefix information is advertised by the router (or the home agent) specified by the `mha` parameter.

477–479 The `mip6_prefix_ha_list_find_withmha()` function is called to find an existing entry of the `mip6_prefix_ha{}` instance which has the specified prefix information. If the entry exists, the pointer is returned to the caller.

481–490 If there is no existing `mip6_prefix_ha{}` instance advertising the prefix information, memory for the new `mip6_prefix_ha{}` structure is allocated and inserted into the list.

Listing 5-366
――mip6_prefix.c
```
493      void
494      mip6_prefix_ha_list_remove(mpfxha_list, mpfxha)
495              struct mip6_prefix_ha_list *mpfxha_list;
496              struct mip6_prefix_ha *mpfxha;
497      {
498              LIST_REMOVE(mpfxha, mpfxha_entry);
499              FREE(mpfxha, M_TEMP);
500      }
```
――mip6_prefix.c

493–500 The `mip6_prefix_ha_list_remove()` function has two parameters. The `mpfxha_list` parameter is a pointer to the list of instances of the `mip6_prefix_ha{}` structure which is kept in the `mip6_prefix{}` structure. The `mpfxha` parameter is a pointer to the instance of the `mip6_prefix_ha{}` structure to be removed. The function removes the specified entry from the list and releases the memory space used by the entry.

Find the Prefix Entry with Home Agent Address

The `mip6_prefix_ha_list_find_withaddr()` function returns the pointer to the instance of the `mip6_prefix_ha{}` structure whose router address is the same as the specified address.

Listing 5-367
――mip6_prefix.c
```
502      struct mip6_prefix_ha *
503      mip6_prefix_ha_list_find_withaddr(mpfxha_list, addr)
504              struct mip6_prefix_ha_list *mpfxha_list;
505              struct in6_addr *addr;
506      {
```

```
507            struct mip6_prefix_ha *mpfxha;
508
509            for (mpfxha = LIST_FIRST(mpfxha_list); mpfxha;
510                mpfxha = LIST_NEXT(mpfxha, mpfxha_entry)) {
511                if (mpfxha->mpfxha_mha == NULL)
512                    continue;
513
514                if (IN6_ARE_ADDR_EQUAL(&mpfxha->mpfxha_mha->mha_addr, addr))
515                    return (mpfxha);
516            }
517            return (NULL);
518    }
```
_____mip6_prefix.c

502–505 The mip6_prefix_ha_list_find_withaddr() function has two parameters.
The mpfxha_list parameter is a pointer to the list of instances of the
mip6_prefix_ha{} structure and the addr parameter is a pointer to the address
information of the router or the home agent being searched for.

509–517 Each mip6_prefix_ha{} instance in the list is compared to the address of the
mip6_ha{} instance to which the mip6_prefix_ha{} instance points. If there is an
entry which has the same address information as the address specified as the second
parameter of this function, the pointer to that mip6_prefix_ha{} instance is returned.

Find the Prefix Entry with Home Agent Information

The mip6_prefix_ha_list_find_withmha() function returns the pointer to the instance
of the mip6_prefix_ha{} structure that has the specified home agent entry information.

Listing 5-368
_____mip6_prefix.c

```
520    struct mip6_prefix_ha *
521    mip6_prefix_ha_list_find_withmha(mpfxha_list, mha)
522            struct mip6_prefix_ha_list *mpfxha_list;
523            struct mip6_ha *mha;
524    {
525            struct mip6_prefix_ha *mpfxha;
526
527            for (mpfxha = LIST_FIRST(mpfxha_list); mpfxha;
528                mpfxha = LIST_NEXT(mpfxha, mpfxha_entry)) {
529                if (mpfxha->mpfxha_mha && (mpfxha->mpfxha_mha == mha))
530                    return (mpfxha);
531            }
532            return (NULL);
533    }
```
_____mip6_prefix.c

520–532 The mip6_prefix_ha_list_find_withmha() function finds an
mip6_prefix_ha{} entry by using the pointer to an mip6_ha{} instance
as a key.

5.17.13   Receiving Prefix Information by Router Advertisement Messages

A mobile node will receive prefix information by two methods: listening to Router Advertisement
messages at home and using Mobile Prefix Solicitation and Advertisement messages in foreign
networks.

Listing 5-369

```
                                                       ————————————mip6_mncore.c
241     int
242     mip6_prelist_update(saddr, ndopts, dr, m)
243            struct in6_addr *saddr; /* the addr that sent this RA. */
244            union nd_opts *ndopts;
245            struct nd_defrouter *dr; /* NULL in case of a router shutdown. */
246            struct mbuf *m; /* the received router adv. packet. */
247     {
248            struct mip6_ha *mha;
249            struct hif_softc *sc;
250            int error = 0;
                                                       ————————————mip6_mncore.c
```

241–246 The `mip6_prelist_update()` function updates the prefix information which is kept in a mobile node based on the Router Advertisement message that the mobile node receives. This function has four parameters: The `saddr` parameter is an address of the node which sent the Router Advertisement message; the `ndopts` parameter is a pointer to the `nd_opts{}` structure which keeps option values included in the incoming message; the `dr` parameter is a pointer to the `nd_defrouter{}` structure which represents an entry of the default router list in the mobile node; and the `m` parameter is a pointer to the mbuf which contains the incoming packet.

Listing 5-370

```
                                                       ————————————mip6_mncore.c
252            /* sanity check. */
253            if (saddr == NULL)
254                    return (EINVAL);
255
256            /* advertizing router is shutting down. */
257            if (dr == NULL) {
258                    mha = mip6_ha_list_find_withaddr(&mip6_ha_list, saddr);
259                    if (mha) {
260                            error = mip6_ha_list_remove(&mip6_ha_list, mha);
261                    }
262                    return (error);
263            }
264
265            /* if no prefix information is included, we have nothing to do. */
266            if ((ndopts == NULL) || (ndopts->nd_opts_pi == NULL)) {
267                    return (0);
268            }
                                                       ————————————mip6_mncore.c
```

253–254 The address of the router which sent the Advertisement message must not be NULL.

257–263 When the router is going to shut down, it sends a Router Advertisement message with its lifetime set to 0. In this case, the pointer to the router information becomes NULL. If the router is in the home agent list, the entry is removed from the home agent list (the `mip6_ha_list` global variable) by calling the `mip6_ha_list_remove()` function.

266–268 If the incoming message does not contain any prefix options, there is nothing to do.

Listing 5-371

```
                                                       ————————————mip6_mncore.c
270            for (sc = LIST_FIRST(&hif_softc_list); sc;
271                 sc = LIST_NEXT(sc, hif_entry)) {
272                    /* reorganize subnet groups. */
```

```
273                        error = mip6_prelist_update_sub(sc, saddr, ndopts, dr, m);
274                        if (error) {
 ....
278                                return (error);
279                        }
280                }
281
282                return (0);
283        }
```
_____mip6_mncore.c

270–280 All the prefix information enclosed in the incoming Router Advertisement message is
passed to each virtual home network interface to update the prefix information of each
home interface.

Listing 5-372
_____mip6_mncore.c

```
285     static int
286     mip6_prelist_update_sub(sc, rtaddr, ndopts, dr, m)
287             struct hif_softc *sc;
288             struct in6_addr *rtaddr;
289             union nd_opts *ndopts;
290             struct nd_defrouter *dr;
291             struct mbuf *m;
292     {
293             int location;
294             struct nd_opt_hdr *ndopt;
295             struct nd_opt_prefix_info *ndopt_pi;
296             struct sockaddr_in6 prefix_sa;
297             int is_home;
298             struct mip6_ha *mha;
299             struct mip6_prefix *mpfx;
300             struct mip6_prefix *prefix_list[IPV6_MMTU/sizeof
   (struct nd_opt_prefix_info)];
301             int nprefix = 0;
302             struct hif_prefix *hpfx;
303             struct sockaddr_in6 haaddr;
304             int i;
305             int error = 0;
```
_____mip6_mncore.c

– *Line 300 is broken here for layout reasons. However, it is a single line of code.*

285–291 The `mip6_prelist_update_sub()` function updates the prefix information and
the router information of each home virtual interface. The function has five parameters.
The `sc` parameter is a pointer to the `hif_softc{}` instance which indicates one home
network. The `rtaddr, ndopts, dr` and `m` parameters are the same as the parameters
passed to the `mip6_prelist_update()` function described previously.

Listing 5-373
_____mip6_mncore.c

```
307             /* sanity check. */
308             if ((sc == NULL) || (rtaddr == NULL) || (dr == NULL)
309                 || (ndopts == NULL) || (ndopts->nd_opts_pi == NULL))
310                     return (EINVAL);
311
312             /* a router advertisement must be sent from a link-local address. */
313             if (!IN6_IS_ADDR_LINKLOCAL(rtaddr)) {
 ....
```

```
318                        /* ignore. */
319                        return (0);
320              }
```
——mip6_mncore.c

308–310 An error is returned if any of the required parameters is NULL.

313–320 The source address of the Router Advertisement message must be a link-local address as specified in the Neighbor Discovery specification.

Listing 5-374
——mip6_mncore.c
```
322              location = HIF_LOCATION_UNKNOWN;
323              is_home = 0;
324
325              for (ndopt = (struct nd_opt_hdr *)ndopts->nd_opts_pi;
326                   ndopt <= (struct nd_opt_hdr *)ndopts->nd_opts_pi_end;
327                   ndopt = (struct nd_opt_hdr *)((caddr_t)ndopt
328                       + (ndopt->nd_opt_len << 3))) {
329                      if (ndopt->nd_opt_type != ND_OPT_PREFIX_INFORMATION)
330                              continue;
331                      ndopt_pi = (struct nd_opt_prefix_info *)ndopt;
332
333                      /* sanity check of prefix information. */
334                      if (ndopt_pi->nd_opt_pi_len != 4) {
```
.... (output warning logs)
```
339                      }
340                      if (128 < ndopt_pi->nd_opt_pi_prefix_len) {
....
345                              continue;
346                      }
347                      if (IN6_IS_ADDR_MULTICAST(&ndopt_pi->nd_opt_pi_prefix)
348                          || IN6_IS_ADDR_LINKLOCAL(&ndopt_pi->nd_opt_pi_prefix)) {
....
353                              continue;
354                      }
355                      /* aggregatable unicast address, rfc2374 */
356                      if ((ndopt_pi->nd_opt_pi_prefix.s6_addr8[0] & 0xe0) == 0x20
357                          && ndopt_pi->nd_opt_pi_prefix_len != 64) {
....
363                              continue;
364                      }
```
——mip6_mncore.c

325–328 The prefix information is stored between the address space pointed to by the `nd_opts_pi` and the `nd_opts_pi_end` pointers of the `nd_opts{}` structure as a Neighbor Discovery option. In this loop, the prefix information included in the incoming Advertisement message is checked to determine whether it is valid.

329–330 Options other than the prefix information option may exist in the space. If the option is not a prefix information option (the option type is not `ND_OPT_PREFIX_INFORMATION`), the option is skipped.

334–339 The length of the prefix information option must be 4. If the length is invalid, the error is logged. The procedure continues.

340–346 If the prefix whose prefix length is greater than 128 cannot be processed, the option is ignored.

347–354 If the prefix is a multicast or a link-local prefix, the option is skipped.

356–364 If the prefix information delivered by the Router Advertisement message is not a prefix of an IPv6 global unicast address, the prefix is not processed. In the KAME Mobile IPv6, only IPv6 global unicast addresses are used.

Listing 5-375

```
                                                                  _____mip6_mncore.c
366                     bzero(&prefix_sa, sizeof(prefix_sa));
367                     prefix_sa.sin6_family = AF_INET6;
368                     prefix_sa.sin6_len = sizeof(prefix_sa);
369                     prefix_sa.sin6_addr = ndopt_pi->nd_opt_pi_prefix;
370                     if (in6_addr2zoneid(m->m_pkthdr.rcvif, &prefix_sa.sin6_addr,
371                         &prefix_sa.sin6_scope_id))
372                             continue;
373                     if (in6_embedscope(&prefix_sa.sin6_addr, &prefix_sa))
374                             continue;
375                     hpfx = hif_prefix_list_find_withprefix(
376                         &sc->hif_prefix_list_home, &prefix_sa.sin6_addr,
377                         ndopt_pi->nd_opt_pi_prefix_len);
378                     if (hpfx != NULL)
379                             is_home++;
                                                                  _____mip6_mncore.c
```

366–373 The prefix information delivered by the Router Advertisement message is restored as a `sockaddr_in6{}` instance. The scope identifier of the prefix is restored from the interface on which the Advertisement message has arrived.

375–379 The `hif_prefix_list_find_withprefix()` is called to see if the received prefix information is registered as one of the home prefixes of the virtual home interface we are now processing. If the prefix is a home prefix, the `is_home` variable is set to true. The `is_home` variable indicates the current location of the mobile node.

Listing 5-376

```
                                                                  _____mip6_mncore.c
381                     /*
382                      * since the global address of a home agent is stored
383                      * in a prefix information option, we can reuse
384                      * prefix_sa as a key to search a mip6_ha entry.
385                      */
386                     if (ndopt_pi->nd_opt_pi_flags_reserved
387                         & ND_OPT_PI_FLAG_ROUTER) {
388                             hpfx = hif_prefix_list_find_withhaaddr(
389                                 &sc->hif_prefix_list_home, &prefix_sa.sin6_addr);
390                             if (hpfx != NULL)
391                                     is_home++;
392                     }
393             }
                                                                  _____mip6_mncore.c
```

386–392 A prefix information option may contain an address of a home agent. If the flag field in the prefix information option has the `ND_OPT_PI_FLAG_ROUTER` flag set, the contents of the option includes not only prefix information but also address information. If the mobile node receives address information, it checks to see whether the received address is registered as a home agent of its home network. If the mobile node has a home agent entry whose address is the same as the address contained in the prefix information, the is_home variable is set to true.

Listing 5-377

```
395                 /* check if the router's lladdr is on our home agent list. */
396                 if (hif_prefix_list_find_withhaaddr(&sc->hif_prefix_list_home, rtaddr))
397                         is_home++;
398
399                 if (is_home != 0) {
400                         /* we are home. */
401                         location = HIF_LOCATION_HOME;
402                 } else {
403                         /* we are foreign. */
404                         location = HIF_LOCATION_FOREIGN;
405                 }
```

396–397 The hif_prefix_list_find_withhaaddr() function is called to check whether the link-local address of the router which sent this Router Advertisement message is registered as a router of the home network of the mobile node. If the router is registered, the is_home variable is set to true.

399–405 The location variable is set based on the value of the is_home variable.

Listing 5-378

```
407             for (ndopt = (struct nd_opt_hdr *)ndopts->nd_opts_pi;
408                     ndopt <= (struct nd_opt_hdr *)ndopts->nd_opts_pi_end;
409                     ndopt = (struct nd_opt_hdr *)((caddr_t)ndopt
410                             + (ndopt->nd_opt_len << 3))) {
411                     if (ndopt->nd_opt_type != ND_OPT_PREFIX_INFORMATION)
412                             continue;
413                     ndopt_pi = (struct nd_opt_prefix_info *)ndopt;
....
450                     bzero(&prefix_sa, sizeof(prefix_sa));
451                     prefix_sa.sin6_family = AF_INET6;
452                     prefix_sa.sin6_len = sizeof(prefix_sa);
453                     prefix_sa.sin6_addr = ndopt_pi->nd_opt_pi_prefix;
454                     if (in6_addr2zoneid(m->m_pkthdr.rcvif, &prefix_sa.sin6_addr,
455                         &prefix_sa.sin6_scope_id))
456                             continue;
457                     if (in6_embedscope(&prefix_sa.sin6_addr, &prefix_sa))
458                             continue;
```

407–413 All prefix information options are checked again to update the prefix and router (or home agent) information stored in the virtual home network structure.

450–458 An instance of the sockaddr_in6{} structure which contains the prefix information is constructed.

Listing 5-379

```
460                 /* update mip6_prefix_list. */
461                 mpfx = mip6_prefix_list_find_withprefix(&prefix_sa.sin6_addr,
462                     ndopt_pi->nd_opt_pi_prefix_len);
```

```
463                 if (mpfx) {
464                         /* found an existing entry.  just update it. */
465                         mip6_prefix_update_lifetime(mpfx,
466                             ntohl(ndopt_pi->nd_opt_pi_valid_time),
467                             ntohl(ndopt_pi->nd_opt_pi_preferred_time));
468                         /* XXX mpfx->mpfx_haddr; */
469                 } else {
470                         /* this is a new prefix. */
471                         mpfx = mip6_prefix_create(&prefix_sa.sin6_addr,
472                             ndopt_pi->nd_opt_pi_prefix_len,
473                             ntohl(ndopt_pi->nd_opt_pi_valid_time),
474                             ntohl(ndopt_pi->nd_opt_pi_preferred_time));
475                         if (mpfx == NULL) {
....
480                                 goto skip_prefix_update;
481                         }
482                         error = mip6_prefix_list_insert(&mip6_prefix_list,
483                             mpfx);
484                         if (error) {
....
489                                 goto skip_prefix_update;
490                         }
....
496                 }
```

———mip6_mncore.c

461 The `mip6_prefix_list_find_withprefix()` function is called to look up an existing prefix information entry (the `mip6_prefix{}` structure) which has the same information as the received prefix information.

463–496 If the mobile node has the prefix information already, it does not need to create a new entry. The mobile node just updates the preferred lifetime and the valid lifetime of the prefix information to the latest value. If the mobile node does not have a prefix information entry which matches the received prefix information, a new `mip6_prefix{}` instance is created and inserted into the list by calling the `mip6_prefix_list_insert()` function.

Listing 5-380

———mip6_mncore.c

```
498                 /*
499                  *  insert this prefix information to hif structure
500                  *  based on the current location.
501                  */
502                 if (location == HIF_LOCATION_HOME) {
503                         hpfx = hif_prefix_list_find_withmpfx(
504                             &sc->hif_prefix_list_foreign, mpfx);
505                         if (hpfx != NULL)
506                                 hif_prefix_list_remove(
507                                     &sc->hif_prefix_list_foreign, hpfx);
508                         if (hif_prefix_list_find_withmpfx(
509                             &sc->hif_prefix_list_home, mpfx) == NULL)
510                                 hif_prefix_list_insert_withmpfx(
511                                     &sc->hif_prefix_list_home, mpfx);
512                 } else {
513                         hpfx = hif_prefix_list_find_withmpfx(
514                             &sc->hif_prefix_list_home, mpfx);
515                         if (hpfx != NULL)
516                                 hif_prefix_list_remove(
517                                     &sc->hif_prefix_list_home, hpfx);
518                         if (hif_prefix_list_find_withmpfx(
519                             &sc->hif_prefix_list_foreign, mpfx) == NULL)
```

```
520                                     hif_prefix_list_insert_withmpfx(
521                                         &sc->hif_prefix_list_foreign, mpfx);
522                     }
523
524                     /* remember prefixes advertised with this ND message. */
525                     prefix_list[nprefix] = mpfx;
526                     nprefix++;
527             skip_prefix_update:
528             }
```
——mip6_mncore.c

502–511 Based on the current location of the mobile node, the prefix information stored in the virtual home network structure is updated. If the mobile node is at home, the prefix should be added/updated as a home prefix. The hif_prefix_list_find_withmpfx() function finds a specified prefix from the list kept in the virtual home network. If the prefix is stored as a foreign prefix, it is removed from the list of foreign prefixes and added to the list of home prefixes.

513–522 If the mobile node is in a foreign network, the received prefix will be added/updated as a foreign prefix. If the received prefix is stored in the list of home prefixes, it is removed and added to the list of foreign prefixes.

525–526 Each pointer to the prefix information structure is recorded in the prefix_list[] array. These pointers are needed when we update the advertising router information of each prefix later.

Listing 5-381

——mip6_mncore.c
```
530             /* update/create mip6_ha entry with an lladdr. */
531             mha = mip6_ha_list_find_withaddr(&mip6_ha_list, rtaddr);
532             if (mha) {
533                     /* the entry for rtaddr exists.  update information. */
534                     if (mha->mha_pref == 0 /* XXX */) {
535                             /* XXX reorder by pref. */
536                     }
537                     mha->mha_flags = dr->flags;
538                     mip6_ha_update_lifetime(mha, dr->rtlifetime);
539             } else {
540                     /* this is a lladdr mip6_ha entry. */
541                     mha = mip6_ha_create(rtaddr, dr->flags, 0, dr->rtlifetime);
542                     if (mha == NULL) {
....
546                             goto haaddr_update;
547                     }
548                     mip6_ha_list_insert(&mip6_ha_list, mha);
549             }
550             for (i = 0; i < nprefix; i++) {
551                     mip6_prefix_ha_list_insert(&prefix_list[i]->mpfx_ha_list, mha);
552             }
```
——mip6_mncore.c

531–549 The mip6_ha_list_find_withaddr() function returns a pointer to the existing entry of the mip6_ha{} instance which has the specified address. If the entry exists, its flag and router lifetime information is updated. As the comment on line 535 says, the mobile node needs to reorder the list when preference information is specified in the Router Advertisement message. However, the current KAME implementation does not implement this feature at this time. If the router which sent the Router Advertisement we are processing is a new router, a new instance of the `mip6_ha{}` structure is created and inserted into the router list.

550–552 Each prefix information entry has a pointer to the router or the home agent which advertises that prefix information. In this loop, the mobile node updates the pointer information of each prefix information entry. The pointer information contains the pointer to the entry of the `mip6_ha{}` instance which is created or updated in lines 532–549.

Listing 5-382
```
                                                                    mip6_mncore.c
554     haaddr_update:
555             /* update/create mip6_ha entry with a global addr. */
556             for (ndopt = (struct nd_opt_hdr *)ndopts->nd_opts_pi;
557                  ndopt <= (struct nd_opt_hdr *)ndopts->nd_opts_pi_end;
558                  ndopt = (struct nd_opt_hdr *)((caddr_t)ndopt
559                      + (ndopt->nd_opt_len << 3))) {
560                     if (ndopt->nd_opt_type != ND_OPT_PREFIX_INFORMATION)
561                             continue;
562                     ndopt_pi = (struct nd_opt_prefix_info *)ndopt;
563
564                     if ((ndopt_pi->nd_opt_pi_flags_reserved
565                         & ND_OPT_PI_FLAG_ROUTER) == 0)
566                             continue;
                                                                    mip6_mncore.c
```

556–566 In this loop, the mobile node creates or updates the `mip6_ha{}` instance that has a global address of the home agent of the mobile node. The global address of the home agent is stored in a prefix information option with the `ND_OPT_PI_FLAG_ROUTER` flag set. Any prefix information option which does not have the flag set is skipped.

Listing 5-383
```
                                                                    mip6_mncore.c
568             bzero(&haaddr, sizeof(haaddr));
569             haaddr.sin6_len = sizeof(haaddr);
570             haaddr.sin6_family = AF_INET6;
571             haaddr.sin6_addr = ndopt_pi->nd_opt_pi_prefix;
572             if (in6_addr2zoneid(m->m_pkthdr.rcvif, &haaddr.sin6_addr,
573                 &haaddr.sin6_scope_id))
574                     continue;
575             if (in6_embedscope(&haaddr.sin6_addr, &haaddr))
576                     continue;
                                                                    mip6_mncore.c
```

568–576 An instance of the `sockaddr_in6{}` structure which contains the global address of the home agent is created. The scope identifier is recovered from the interface on which the incoming Router Advertisement message has been received.

Listing 5-384
```
                                                                    mip6_mncore.c
577             mha = mip6_ha_list_find_withaddr(&mip6_ha_list,
578                 &haaddr.sin6_addr);
579             if (mha) {
580                     if (mha->mha_pref == 0 /* XXX */) {
581                             /* XXX reorder by pref. */
```

```
582                                    }
583                                    mha->mha_flags = dr->flags;
584                                    mip6_ha_update_lifetime(mha, 0);
585                            } else {
586                                    /* this is a new home agent . */
587                                    mha = mip6_ha_create(&haddr.sin6_addr, dr->flags, 0,
588                                        0);
589                                    if (mha == NULL) {
....
593                                            goto skip_ha_update;
594                                    }
595                                    mip6_ha_list_insert(&mip6_ha_list, mha);
....
602                            }
603                            for (i = 0; i < nprefix; i++) {
604                                    mip6_prefix_ha_list_insert(
605                                        &prefix_list[i]->mpfx_ha_list, mha);
606                            }
607                    skip_ha_update:
608                    }
609                    return (0);
610            }
```
——mip6_mncore.c

577–606 The existing or a newly created `mip6_ha{}` instance is updated in the same manner as done on lines 531–549.

5.17.14 Sending a Mobile Prefix Solicitation Message

A mobile node manages prefix information of its home network to keep its home address up to date. A mobile node can receive prefix information by listening to Router Advertisement messages when it is at home. However, when it is away from home, it needs other mechanisms. Sending a Mobile Prefix Solicitation is implemented as the `mip6_icmp6_mp_sol_output()` function.

Listing 5-385
——mip6_icmp6.c
```
693     int
694     mip6_icmp6_mp_sol_output(haddr, haaddr)
695            struct in6_addr *haddr, *haaddr;
696     {
697            struct hif_softc *sc;
698            struct mbuf *m;
699            struct ip6_hdr *ip6;
700            struct mip6_prefix_solicit *mp_sol;
701            int icmp6len;
702            int maxlen;
703            int error;
....
705            struct timeval mono_time;
....
709            microtime(&mono_time);
```
——mip6_icmp6.c

694–695 The `mip6_icmp6_mp_sol_output()` function has two parameters. The `haddr` parameter is a pointer to the home address of a mobile node and the `haaddr` parameter is a pointer to the address of the home agent of the mobile node.

Listing 5-386

```
712                sc = hif_list_find_withhaddr(haddr);
713                if (sc == NULL) {
....
719                        return (0);
720                }
721
722                /* rate limitation. */
723                if (sc->hif_mps_lastsent + 1 > mono_time.tv_sec) {
724                        return (0);
725                }
```

712–720 If we do not have a virtual home network interface which is related to the home address of the mobile node, there is nothing to do.

723–725 To avoid flooding with solicitation messages, the mobile node must limit the number of messages sent to one per second. The `hif_mps_lastsent` variable holds the time when the mobile node sent the last solicitation message.

Listing 5-387

```
727                /* estimate the size of message. */
728                maxlen = sizeof(*ip6) + sizeof(*mp_sol);
729                /* XXX we must determine the link type of our home address
730                    instead using hardcoded '6' */
731                maxlen += (sizeof(struct nd_opt_hdr) + 6 + 7) & ~7;
732                if (max_linkhdr + maxlen >= MCLBYTES) {
....
736                        return (EINVAL);
737                }
738
739                /* get packet header. */
740                MGETHDR(m, M_DONTWAIT, MT_HEADER);
741                if (m && max_linkhdr + maxlen >= MHLEN) {
742                    MCLGET(m, M_DONTWAIT);
743                    if ((m->m_flags & M_EXT) == 0) {
744                        m_free(m);
745                        m = NULL;
746                    }
747                }
748                if (m == NULL)
749                        return (ENOBUFS);
750                m->m_pkthdr.rcvif = NULL;
```

728–737 The packet size which is needed to create a Mobile Prefix Solicitation is calculated. `maxlen` will include the size of an IPv6 header and the Mobile Prefix Solicitation message and the length of a link-layer header. Including the length of a link-layer header will avoid an additional mbuf allocation when the node prepends a link-layer header when sending the packet to a physical link.

740–750 An mbuf to store the solicitation message is allocated. If the requested length cannot be allocated with a single mbuf, the mobile node will try to allocate the same size with a cluster mbuf. If it fails to allocate an mbuf, an error is returned.

Listing 5-388

——————————————————————————————mip6_icmp6.c

```
752                 icmp6len = sizeof(*mp_sol);
753                 m->m_pkthdr.len = m->m_len = sizeof(*ip6) + icmp6len;
754                 m->m_data += max_linkhdr;
755
756                 sc->hif_mps_id = mip6_mps_id++;
```

——————————————————————————————mip6_icmp6.c

752–754 The total size of the allocated mbuf is set to the size of the IPv6 header and the ICMPv6 length which is the length of the Mobile Prefix Solicitation to be sent. The data pointer is set to `max_linkhdr` to reserve a space to prepare a link-layer header.

756 The `hif_mps_id` variable keeps a unique identifier of the solicitation message. When the mobile node receives a Mobile Prefix Advertisement message, it compares the identifier of the received advertisement message to the recorded identifier to check whether the received advertisement message is addressed to the mobile node.

Listing 5-389

——————————————————————————————mip6_icmp6.c

```
759                 /* fill the mobile prefix solicitation. */
760                 ip6 = mtod(m, struct ip6_hdr *);
761                 ip6->ip6_flow = 0;
762                 ip6->ip6_vfc &= ~IPV6_VERSION_MASK;
763                 ip6->ip6_vfc |= IPV6_VERSION;
764                 /* ip6->ip6_plen will be set later */
765                 ip6->ip6_nxt = IPPROTO_ICMPV6;
766                 ip6->ip6_hlim = ip6_defhlim;
767                 ip6->ip6_src = *haddr;
768                 ip6->ip6_dst = *haaddr;
769                 mp_sol = (struct mip6_prefix_solicit *)(ip6 + 1);
770                 mp_sol->mip6_ps_type = MIP6_PREFIX_SOLICIT;
771                 mp_sol->mip6_ps_code = 0;
772                 mp_sol->mip6_ps_id = htons(sc->hif_mps_id);
773                 mp_sol->mip6_ps_reserved = 0;
774
775                 /* calculate checksum. */
776                 ip6->ip6_plen = htons((u_int16_t)icmp6len);
777                 mp_sol->mip6_ps_cksum = 0;
778                 mp_sol->mip6_ps_cksum = in6_cksum(m, IPPROTO_ICMPV6, sizeof(*ip6),
779                     icmp6len);
780
781                 error = ip6_output(m, 0, 0, 0, 0 ,NULL
....
783                     , NULL
....
785                     );
786                 if (error) {
....
790                 }
791
792                 /* update rate limitation factor. */
793                 sc->hif_mps_lastsent = mono_time.tv_sec;
794
795                 return (error);
796         }
```

——————————————————————————————mip6_icmp6.c

760–773 All fields of the IPv6 header and the Mobile Prefix Solicitation message are filled. The message type of the ICMPv6 header is set to `MIP6_PREFIX_SOLICIT` and the code field is set to 0.

776–793 After the checksum value for this ICMPv6 message is computed by the `in6_cksum()` function, the packet is sent by the `ip6_output()` function. After sending the packet, the mobile node updates `hif_mps_lastsent`, which indicates the time when the last message was sent.

5.17.15   Receiving a Mobile Prefix Advertisement Message

A mobile node will receive a Mobile Prefix Advertisement message in response to the Mobile Prefix Solicitation message sent from the mobile node. In addition to the solicited messages, the mobile node may receive an unsolicited Mobile Prefix Advertisement message from its home agent. An unsolicited message is sent when the condition of home prefixes changes. A home agent needs to notify the mobile nodes it is serving of such changes. However, the current KAME implementation does not support unsolicited advertisement messages at this moment; it only processes solicited messages. Receiving a Mobile Prefix Advertisement is implemented as the `mip6_icmp6_mp_adv_input()` function. The function is called from the `icmp6_input()` function.

Listing 5-390
                                                                            ___mip6_icmp6.c

```
798     static int
799     mip6_icmp6_mp_adv_input(m, off, icmp6len)
800             struct mbuf *m;
801             int off;
802             int icmp6len;
803     {
804             struct ip6_hdr *ip6;
805             struct m_tag *mtag;
806             struct ip6aux *ip6a;
807             struct mip6_prefix_advert *mp_adv;
808             union nd_opts ndopts;
809             struct nd_opt_hdr *ndopt;
810             struct nd_opt_prefix_info *ndopt_pi;
811             struct sockaddr_in6 prefix_sa;
812             struct in6_aliasreq ifra;
813             struct in6_ifaddr *ia6;
814             struct mip6_prefix *mpfx;
815             struct mip6_ha *mha;
816             struct hif_softc *hif, *tmphif;
817             struct mip6_bu *mbu;
818             struct ifaddr *ifa;
819             struct hif_prefix *hpfx;
820             int error = 0;
....
822             struct timeval mono_time;
....
826             microtime(&mono_time);
```
                                                                            ___mip6_icmp6.c

798–802 The `mip6_icmp6_mp_adv_input()` function has three parameters: The `m` parameter is a pointer to the mbuf which contains the advertisement message; the `off` parameter is an offset from the head of the IPv6 packet to the head of the advertisement message; and the `icmp6len` parameter is the length of the Mobile Prefix Advertisement message.

Listing 5-391

```
                                                                     mip6_icmp6.c
833             ip6 = mtod(m, struct ip6_hdr *);
  ....
835             IP6_EXTHDR_CHECK(m, off, icmp6len, EINVAL);
836             mp_adv = (struct mip6_prefix_advert *)((caddr_t)ip6 + off);
                                                                     mip6_icmp6.c
```

833–836 The contents of the packet must be located in a contiguous memory space so that we can access each field of the message using offsets from the head of the message.

Listing 5-392

```
                                                                     mip6_icmp6.c
848             /* find mip6_ha instance. */
849             mha = mip6_ha_list_find_withaddr(&mip6_ha_list, &ip6->ip6_src);
850             if (mha == NULL) {
851                     error = EINVAL;
852                     goto freeit;
853             }
854
855             /* find relevant hif interface. */
856             hif = hif_list_find_withhaddr(&ip6->ip6_dst);
857             if (hif == NULL) {
858                     error = EINVAL;
859                     goto freeit;
860             }
861
862             /* sanity check. */
863             if (hif->hif_location != HIF_LOCATION_FOREIGN) {
864                     /* MPA is processed only we are foreign. */
865                     error = EINVAL;
866                     goto freeit;
867             }
                                                                     mip6_icmp6.c
```

849–853 If the mobile node does not have a home agent information entry (the `mip6_ha{}` instance) which is related to the source address of the incoming advertisement message, the mobile node drops the packet. The message must be sent from the home agent of the mobile node.

856–860 If the mobile node does not have a virtual home network interface (the `hif_softc{}` instance) which is related to the destination address of the received message, the node drops the packet. The advertisement message must be sent to the home address of the mobile node.

863–867 If the mobile node is at home, it drops the incoming advertisement message. This behavior is not specified in the Mobile IPv6 specification and some implementation may accept the message. The KAME implementation uses only the Router Advertisement message to get prefix information when a mobile node is home.

Listing 5-393

```
                                                            mip6_icmp6.c
869          mbu = mip6_bu_list_find_home_registration(&hif->hif_bu_list,
870              &ip6->ip6_dst);
871          if (mbu == NULL) {
872                  error = EINVAL;
873                  goto freeit;
874          }
875          if (!IN6_ARE_ADDR_EQUAL(&mbu->mbu_paddr, &ip6->ip6_src)) {
 ....
883                  error = EINVAL;
884                  goto freeit;
885          }
                                                            mip6_icmp6.c
```

869–885 The `mip6_bu_list_find_home_registration()` function will return a home registration entry for the home address specified as its second parameter. The advertisement message must be sent from the address of the home agent which is serving the home address. If the home agent address in the binding update list entry (`mbu_paddr`) is different from the source address of the advertisement message, the mobile node drops the packet.

Listing 5-394

```
                                                            mip6_icmp6.c
887          /* check type2 routing header. */
888          mtag = ip6_findaux(m);
889          if (mtag == NULL) {
890                  /* this packet doesn't have a type 2 RTHDR. */
891                  error = EINVAL;
892                  goto freeit;
893          } else {
894                  ip6a = (struct ip6aux *)(mtag + 1);
895                  if ((ip6a->ip6a_flags & IP6A_ROUTEOPTIMIZED) == 0) {
896                          /* this packet doesn't have a type 2 RTHDR. */
897                          error = EINVAL;
898                          goto freeit;
899                  }
900          }
                                                            mip6_icmp6.c
```

888–900 The Mobile Prefix Advertisement message must have the Type 2 Routing Header since the Mobile Prefix Advertisement message is sent to the home address of the mobile node from its home agent. A message which does not have the Routing Header will be dropped.

Listing 5-395

```
                                                            mip6_icmp6.c
903          /* check id.  if it doesn't match, send mps. */
904          if (hif->hif_mps_id != ntohs(mp_adv->mip6_pa_id)) {
905                  mip6_icmp6_mp_sol_output(&mbu->mbu_haddr, &mbu->mbu_paddr);
906                  error = EINVAL;
907                  goto freeit;
908          }
                                                            mip6_icmp6.c
```

904–908 The identifier stored in the advertisement message (`mip6_pa_id`) must be the same as the identifier which the mobile node specified in the solicitation message. If the identifier is different from the identifier stored in a virtual home network interface which was recorded when the solicitation message was sent, the advertisement message is dropped.

Listing 5-396

```
910             icmp6len -= sizeof(*mp_adv);
911             nd6_option_init(mp_adv + 1, icmp6len, &ndopts);
912             if (nd6_options(&ndopts) < 0) {
....
916                     /* nd6_options have incremented stats */
917                     error = EINVAL;
918                     goto freeit;
919             }
```

911–919 The contents of the Mobile Prefix Solicitation is prefix information, whose format is the same as the Router Advertisement message. The nd6_option_init() function is called to parse the options included in the incoming advertisement message.

Listing 5-397

```
921             for (ndopt = (struct nd_opt_hdr *)ndopts.nd_opts_pi;
922                     ndopt <= (struct nd_opt_hdr *)ndopts.nd_opts_pi_end;
923                     ndopt = (struct nd_opt_hdr *)((caddr_t)ndopt
924                         + (ndopt->nd_opt_len << 3))) {
925                     if (ndopt->nd_opt_type != ND_OPT_PREFIX_INFORMATION)
926                             continue;
927                     ndopt_pi = (struct nd_opt_prefix_info *)ndopt;
928
929                     /* sanity check of prefix information. */
930                     if (ndopt_pi->nd_opt_pi_len != 4) {
....
936                     }
937                     if (128 < ndopt_pi->nd_opt_pi_prefix_len) {
....
943                             continue;
944                     }
945                     if (IN6_IS_ADDR_MULTICAST(&ndopt_pi->nd_opt_pi_prefix)
946                         || IN6_IS_ADDR_LINKLOCAL(&ndopt_pi->nd_opt_pi_prefix)) {
....
952                             continue;
953                     }
954                     /* aggregatable unicast address, rfc2374 */
955                     if ((ndopt_pi->nd_opt_pi_prefix.s6_addr8[0] & 0xe0) == 0x20
956                         && ndopt_pi->nd_opt_pi_prefix_len != 64) {
....
963                             continue;
964                     }
```

921–924 All prefix information options included in the advertisement message will be processed.

930–964 The same sanity checks are done as when the mobile node does the sanity checks against an incoming Router Advertisement message in the mip6_prelist_update_sub() function as discussed in Section 5.16.19.

Listing 5-398
```
                                                              mip6_icmp6.c
966                    bzero(&prefix_sa, sizeof(prefix_sa));
967                    prefix_sa.sin6_family = AF_INET6;
968                    prefix_sa.sin6_len = sizeof(prefix_sa);
969                    prefix_sa.sin6_addr = ndopt_pi->nd_opt_pi_prefix;
970                    /* XXX scope? */
971                    mpfx = mip6_prefix_list_find_withprefix(&prefix_sa.sin6_addr,
972                        ndopt_pi->nd_opt_pi_prefix_len);
                                                              mip6_icmp6.c
```

966–972 An instance of the `sockaddr_in6{}` structure which contains the received prefix information is constructed. The `mip6_prefix_list_find_withprefix()` function will return the pointer to the instance of the `mip6_prefix{}` structure which contains the received prefix if it already exists.

Listing 5-399
```
                                                              mip6_icmp6.c
973                if (mpfx == NULL) {
974                    mpfx = mip6_prefix_create(&prefix_sa.sin6_addr,
975                        ndopt_pi->nd_opt_pi_prefix_len,
976                        ntohl(ndopt_pi->nd_opt_pi_valid_time),
977                        ntohl(ndopt_pi->nd_opt_pi_preferred_time));
978                    if (mpfx == NULL) {
979                            error = EINVAL;
980                            goto freeit;
981                    }
982                    mip6_prefix_ha_list_insert(&mpfx->mpfx_ha_list, mha);
983                    mip6_prefix_list_insert(&mip6_prefix_list, mpfx);
984                    for (tmphif = LIST_FIRST(&hif_softc_list); tmphif;
985                        tmphif = LIST_NEXT(tmphif, hif_entry)) {
986                            if (hif == tmphif)
987                                    hif_prefix_list_insert_withmpfx(
988                                        &tmphif->hif_prefix_list_home,
989                                        mpfx);
990                            else
991                                    hif_prefix_list_insert_withmpfx(
992                                        &tmphif->hif_prefix_list_foreign,
993                                        mpfx);
994                    }
                                                              mip6_icmp6.c
```

973–981 If the mobile node does not have the prefix information received by the advertisement message, a new prefix information entry is created.

982–983 The prefix information is associated with the home agent information which sent the advertisement message and is inserted into the list of `mip6_prefix{}` instances.

984–994 The received prefix is a home prefix of the virtual home network which is represented by the `hif` variable. At the same time, the prefix is foreign prefix information of other virtual home networks other than the `hif_softc{}` instances. The newly created prefix information is inserted into all `hif_softc{}` instances.

Listing 5-400
```
                                                              mip6_icmp6.c
996                    mip6_prefix_haddr_assign(mpfx, hif); /* XXX */
997
998                    /* construct in6_aliasreq. */
999                    bzero(&ifra, sizeof(ifra));
```

```
1000                               bcopy(if_name((struct ifnet *)hif), ifra.ifra_name,
1001                                   sizeof(ifra.ifra_name));
1002                               ifra.ifra_addr.sin6_len = sizeof(struct sockaddr_in6);
1003                               ifra.ifra_addr.sin6_family = AF_INET6;
1004                               ifra.ifra_addr.sin6_addr = mpfx->mpfx_haddr;
1005                               ifra.ifra_prefixmask.sin6_len
1006                                   = sizeof(struct sockaddr_in6);
1007                               ifra.ifra_prefixmask.sin6_family = AF_INET6;
1008                               ifra.ifra_flags = IN6_IFF_HOME | IN6_IFF_AUTOCONF;
1009                               in6_prefixlen2mask(&ifra.ifra_prefixmask.sin6_addr,
1010                                   128);
1011                               ifra.ifra_lifetime.ia6t_vltime = mpfx->mpfx_vltime;
1012                               ifra.ifra_lifetime.ia6t_pltime = mpfx->mpfx_pltime;
1013                               if (ifra.ifra_lifetime.ia6t_vltime
1014                                   == ND6_INFINITE_LIFETIME)
1015                                       ifra.ifra_lifetime.ia6t_expire = 0;
1016                               else
1017                                       ifra.ifra_lifetime.ia6t_expire
1018                                           = mono_time.tv_sec
1019                                           + ifra.ifra_lifetime.ia6t_vltime;
1020                               if (ifra.ifra_lifetime.ia6t_pltime
1021                                   == ND6_INFINITE_LIFETIME)
1022                                       ifra.ifra_lifetime.ia6t_preferred = 0;
1023                               else
1024                                       ifra.ifra_lifetime.ia6t_preferred
1025                                           = mono_time.tv_sec
1026                                           + ifra.ifra_lifetime.ia6t_pltime;
1027                               ia6 = in6ifa_ifpwithaddr((struct ifnet *)hif,
1028                                   &ifra.ifra_addr.sin6_addr);
```
———mip6_icmp6.c

996 A new home address is generated from the prefix information.

999–1028 The mobile node needs to configure a new home address since it has received a
new home prefix. An `in6_aliasreq{}` instance which contains information of the new
home address is constructed.

    The new home address created while the mobile node is away from home is assigned
to the virtual home network. The `IN6_IFF_HOME` and the `IN6_IFF_AUTOCONF` flags
are set to the new address which indicates that the address is a home address and it is
configured using the stateless autoconfiguration mechanism. The prefix length of a home
address is always 128 when a mobile node is away from home. The preferred lifetime and
the valid lifetime are set based on the lifetime information of the prefix information. If the
lifetime is infinite, the address will not expire.

Listing 5-401
———mip6_icmp6.c

```
1030                               /* assign a new home address. */
1031                               error = in6_update_ifa((struct ifnet *)hif, &ifra,
1032                                   ia6, 0);
1033                               if (error) {
    ....
1039                                       goto freeit;
1040                               }
1041
1042                               mip6_home_registration(hif); /* XXX */
```
———mip6_icmp6.c

1031–1042 The new home address is assigned by the `in6_update_ifa()` function and
the home registration procedure is triggered for the newly created home address by the
`mip6_home_registration()` function.

Listing 5-402

_____mip6_icmp6.c
```
1043                         } else {
1044                                 mip6_prefix_update_lifetime(mpfx,
1045                                         ntohl(ndopt_pi->nd_opt_pi_valid_time),
1046                                         ntohl(ndopt_pi->nd_opt_pi_preferred_time));
1047
```
_____mip6_icmp6.c

1043–1047 If the received prefix information already exists, the lifetime is updated based on the received information.

Listing 5-403

_____mip6_icmp6.c
```
1049                         TAILQ_FOREACH(ifa, &((struct ifnet *)hif)->if_addrlist,
1050                                 ifa_list)
....
1055                         {
1056                                 struct in6_ifaddr *ifa6;
1057
1058                                 if (ifa->ifa_addr->sa_family != AF_INET6)
1059                                         continue;
1060
1061                                 ifa6 = (struct in6_ifaddr *)ifa;
1062
1063                                 if ((ifa6->ia6_flags & IN6_IFF_HOME) == 0)
1064                                         continue;
1065
1066                                 if ((ifa6->ia6_flags & IN6_IFF_AUTOCONF) == 0)
1067                                         continue;
1068
1069                                 if (!IN6_ARE_ADDR_EQUAL(&mpfx->mpfx_haddr,
1070                                         &ifa6->ia_addr.sin6_addr))
1071                                         continue;
1072
1073                                 ifa6->ia6_lifetime.ia6t_vltime
1074                                         = mpfx->mpfx_vltime;
1075                                 ifa6->ia6_lifetime.ia6t_pltime
1076                                         = mpfx->mpfx_pltime;
1077                                 if (ifa6->ia6_lifetime.ia6t_vltime ==
1078                                         ND6_INFINITE_LIFETIME)
1079                                         ifa6->ia6_lifetime.ia6t_expire = 0;
1080                                 else
1081                                         ifa6->ia6_lifetime.ia6t_expire =
1082                                                 mono_time.tv_sec
1083                                                 + mpfx->mpfx_vltime;
1084                                 if (ifa6->ia6_lifetime.ia6t_pltime ==
1085                                         ND6_INFINITE_LIFETIME)
1086                                         ifa6->ia6_lifetime.ia6t_preferred = 0;
1087                                 else
1088                                         ifa6->ia6_lifetime.ia6t_preferred =
1089                                                 mono_time.tv_sec
1090                                                 + mpfx->mpfx_pltime;
1091                                 ifa6->ia6_updatetime = mono_time.tv_sec;
1092                         }
1093                 }
1094         }
```
_____mip6_icmp6.c

1049–1050 The lifetime of a prefix affects the lifetime of the home address derived from that prefix. Each home address generated from the prefix is checked and its lifetime is updated.

1058–1071 The mobile node only checks addresses whose address family is IPv6 (AF_INET6) and which have the IN6_IFF_HOME and the IN6_IFF_AUTOCONF flags. The home address generated from the prefix information is stored in the mpfx_haddr member variable of the mip6_prefix{} structure. The mobile node checks to see if it has the home address in its virtual home network interfaces. If it has, the lifetime of the home address is updated.

1073–1091 The lifetime of an address is stored in the ia6_lifetime member variable of the in6_ifaddr{} structure. The preferred and the valid lifetimes of the received prefix information are copied to the ia6_lifetime{} structure. If the preferred or valid lifetimes are infinite, the ia6t_preferred or the ia6t_expire variables of the ia6_lifetime{} structure are set to 0 indicating an infinite lifetime. The ia6t_preferred and the ia6t_valid variables indicate the time that the preferred/valid lifetime will expire.

Finally, the ia6_updatetime variable, which indicates the time that the address is modified, is updated.

Listing 5-404

```
                                                                        mip6_icmp6.c
1096        for (ndopt = (struct nd_opt_hdr *)ndopts.nd_opts_pi;
1097            ndopt <= (struct nd_opt_hdr *)ndopts.nd_opts_pi_end;
1098            ndopt = (struct nd_opt_hdr *)((caddr_t)ndopt
1099                + (ndopt->nd_opt_len << 3))) {
1100            if (ndopt->nd_opt_type != ND_OPT_PREFIX_INFORMATION)
1101                continue;
1102            ndopt_pi = (struct nd_opt_prefix_info *)ndopt;
1103
1104            if ((ndopt_pi->nd_opt_pi_flags_reserved
1105                & ND_OPT_PI_FLAG_ROUTER) == 0)
1106                continue;
                                                                        mip6_icmp6.c
```

1096–1099 The prefix options are processed again to update home agent addresses which may be embedded in the prefix information options.

1104–1106 When the ND_OPT_PI_FLAG_ROUTER flag is set in the prefix information option, the home agent address is embedded in the prefix value.

Listing 5-405

```
                                                                        mip6_icmp6.c
1108        bzero(&prefix_sa, sizeof(prefix_sa));
1109        prefix_sa.sin6_family = AF_INET6;
1110        prefix_sa.sin6_len = sizeof(prefix_sa);
1111        prefix_sa.sin6_addr = ndopt_pi->nd_opt_pi_prefix;
1112        /* XXX scope. */
1113        mha = mip6_ha_list_find_withaddr(&mip6_ha_list,
1114            &prefix_sa.sin6_addr);
1115        if (mha == NULL) {
1116            mha = mip6_ha_create(&prefix_sa.sin6_addr,
1117                ND_RA_FLAG_HOME_AGENT, 0, 0);
1118            mip6_ha_list_insert(&mip6_ha_list, mha);
1119        } else {
1120            if (mha->mha_pref != 0) {
1121                /*
1122                 * we have no method to know the
1123                 * preference of this home agent.
1124                 * assume pref = 0.
```

```
1125                                      */
1126                                      mha->mha_pref = 0;
1127                                      mip6_ha_list_reinsert(&mip6_ha_list, mha);
1128                          }
1129                          mip6_ha_update_lifetime(mha, 0);
1130                  }
```
——mip6_icmp6.c

1108–1111 An instance of the `sockaddr_in6{}` structure, which contains the home agent address delivered with the prefix information option, is constructed.

1113–1118 If the mobile node does not have information about the home agent, then the `mip6_ha_create()` function is called to create an instance of an `mip6_ha{}` structure which keeps the new home agent information.

1120–1129 If the mobile node already has information about the home agent, its lifetime is updated. However, the mobile node cannot know the lifetime of the home agent since the Mobile Prefix Advertisement message does not include any lifetime information of home agents. The mobile node assumes that the home agent has an infinite lifetime. Also, if the existing home agent has a preference value other than 0, the mobile node resets the preference value to 0 because the Mobile Prefix Solicitation message does not include preference information either.

Listing 5-406
——mip6_icmp6.c

```
1131                  for (hpfx = LIST_FIRST(&hif->hif_prefix_list_home); hpfx;
1132                      hpfx = LIST_NEXT(hpfx, hpfx_entry)) {
1133                          mip6_prefix_ha_list_insert(
1134                              &hpfx->hpfx_mpfx->mpfx_ha_list, mha);
1135                  }
1136          }
1137
1138          return (0);
1139
1140    freeit:
1141          m_freem(m);
1142          return (error);
1143  }
```
——mip6_icmp6.c

1131–1135 Finally, the list of pointers to the home agent information of each home prefix stored in the virtual home network interface is updated.

5.17.16 Sending a Dynamic Home Agent Address Discovery Request Message

A mobile node sends a Dynamic Home Agent Address Discovery (DHAAD) message when the node needs to know the address of its home agent. Usually, the mobile node sends the message when it is turned on in a foreign network. Sending a DHAAD request message is implemented as the `mip6_icmp6_dhaad_req_output()` function.

Listing 5-407
——mip6_icmp6.c

```
563    int
564    mip6_icmp6_dhaad_req_output(sc)
565          struct hif_softc *sc;
```

```
566     {
567             struct in6_addr hif_coa;
568             struct in6_addr haanyaddr;
569             struct mip6_prefix *mpfx;
570             struct mbuf *m;
571             struct ip6_hdr *ip6;
572             struct mip6_dhaad_req *hdreq;
573             u_int32_t icmp6len, off;
574             int error;
```
_____mip6_icmp6.c

563–565 The `mip6_icmp6_dhaad_req_output()` function takes one parameter which points to the virtual home network interface to which a mobile node sends a DHAAD request message.

Listing 5-408
_____mip6_icmp6.c

```
583             /* rate limitation. */
584             if (sc->hif_dhaad_count != 0) {
585                     if (sc->hif_dhaad_lastsent + (1 << sc->hif_dhaad_count)
586                         > time_second)
587                             return (0);
588             }
```
_____mip6_icmp6.c

583–588 The number of DHAAD request messages sent to the home network of a mobile node is limited to avoid flooding the network. The KAME implementation performs exponential backoff when resending a message. The initial timeout is set to 1 second. Strictly speaking, the behavior does not satisfy the specification. The specification says the initial timeout is 3 seconds.

Listing 5-409
_____mip6_icmp6.c

```
590             /* get current CoA and recover its scope information. */
591             if (sc->hif_coa_ifa == NULL) {
....
595                     return (0);
596             }
597             hif_coa = sc->hif_coa_ifa->ia_addr.sin6_addr;
```
_____mip6_icmp6.c

591–597 If the mobile node does not have a valid care-of address, the node cannot send a DHAAD request message since the message must be sent from the care-of address of the mobile node.

Listing 5-410
_____mip6_icmp6.c

```
599             /*
600              * we must determine the home agent subnet anycast address.
601              * to do this, we pick up one home prefix from the prefix
602              * list.
603              */
604             for (mpfx = LIST_FIRST(&mip6_prefix_list); mpfx;
```

```
605                    mpfx = LIST_NEXT(mpfx, mpfx_entry)) {
606                        if (hif_prefix_list_find_withmpfx(&sc->hif_prefix_list_home,
607                            mpfx))
608                                break;
609                }
610            if (mpfx == NULL) {
611                    /* we must have at least one home subnet. */
612                    return (EINVAL);
613            }
614            if (mip6_icmp6_create_haanyaddr(&haanyaddr, mpfx))
615                    return (EINVAL);
```
———mip6_icmp6.c

604–614 The destination address of a DHAAD request message is the Home Agent Anycast Address of its home network. The address can be computed from the home prefix of the mobile node. The `hif_prefix_list_find_withmpfx()` function will check to see if the prefix information passed as the second parameter belongs to the list specified as the first parameter. The mobile node searches for at least one prefix information entry that belongs to the `hif_prefix_list_home` variable, which contains all home prefix information of a virtual home network. The `mip6_icmp6_create_haanyaddr()` function creates the Home Agent Anycast Address from the prefix information passed as the second parameter of the function.

Listing 5-411
———mip6_icmp6.c

```
617            /* allocate the buffer for the ip packet and DHAAD request. */
618            icmp6len = sizeof(struct mip6_dhaad_req);
619            m = mip6_create_ip6hdr(&hif_coa, &haanyaddr,
620                        IPPROTO_ICMPV6, icmp6len);
621            if (m == NULL) {
....
627                    return (ENOBUFS);
628            }
629
630            sc->hif_dhaad_id = mip6_dhaad_id++;
631
632            ip6 = mtod(m, struct ip6_hdr *);
633            hdreq = (struct mip6_dhaad_req *)(ip6 + 1);
634            bzero((caddr_t)hdreq, sizeof(struct mip6_dhaad_req));
635            hdreq->mip6_dhreq_type = MIP6_HA_DISCOVERY_REQUEST;
636            hdreq->mip6_dhreq_code = 0;
637            hdreq->mip6_dhreq_id = htons(sc->hif_dhaad_id);
638
639            /* calculate checksum for this DHAAD request packet. */
640            off = sizeof(struct ip6_hdr);
641            hdreq->mip6_dhreq_cksum = in6_cksum(m, IPPROTO_ICMPV6, off, icmp6len);
```
———mip6_icmp6.c

618–641 A DHAAD request message is constructed. An mbuf for the packet is prepared by the `mip6_create_ip6hdr()` function with source and destination addresses. The protocol number of the IPv6 packet is ICMPv6. The `hif_dhaad_id` variable is a unique identifier that distinguishes the reply message to be received. The mobile node drops any DHAAD reply message which does not match the identifier sent with the DHAAD request message. The ICMPv6 type number is set to `MIP6_HA_DISCOVERY_REQUEST` and the code value is set to 0. The checksum is computed by the `in6_cksum()` function in the same manner as other ICMPv6 packets.

Listing 5-412

```
──────────────────────────────────────────────────────mip6_icmp6.c
643                  /* send the DHAAD request packet to the home agent anycast address. */
644                  error = ip6_output(m, NULL, NULL, 0, NULL, NULL
    ....
646                                     , NULL
    ....
648                                         );
649                  if (error) {
    ....
654                          return (error);
655                  }
656
657                  /* update rate limitation factor. */
658                  sc->hif_dhaad_lastsent = time_second;
659                  if (sc->hif_dhaad_count++ > MIP6_DHAAD_RETRIES) {
660                          /*
661                           * XXX the spec says that the number of retires for
662                           * DHAAD request is restricted to DHAAD_RETRIES(=3).
663                           * But, we continue retrying until we receive a reply.
664                           */
665                          sc->hif_dhaad_count = MIP6_DHAAD_RETRIES;
666                  }
667
668                  return (0);
669          }
──────────────────────────────────────────────────────mip6_icmp6.c
```

644–655 The created message is sent by the `ip6_output()` function.

658–666 The Mobile IPv6 specification says that a mobile node must not send a DHAAD request message over 3 times. However, the KAME implementation ignores this rule. When a mobile node is disconnected from the Internet, it soon reaches the maximum transmission limit. Continuing to send DHAAD messages may recover the registration status when the mobile node acquires an Internet connection again.

Create a Home Agent Anycast Address

The `mip6_icmp6_create_haanyaddr()` function creates a home agent anycast address from the specified prefix information.

Listing 5-413

```
──────────────────────────────────────────────────────mip6_icmp6.c
109     static const struct in6_addr haanyaddr_ifid64 = {
110             {{ 0x00, 0x00, 0x00, 0x00, 0x00, 0x00, 0x00, 0x00,
111                0xfd, 0xff, 0xff, 0xff, 0xff, 0xff, 0xff, 0xfe }}
112     };
113     static const struct in6_addr haanyaddr_ifidnn = {
114             {{ 0xff, 0xff, 0xff, 0xff, 0xff, 0xff, 0xff, 0xff,
115                0xff, 0xff, 0xff, 0xff, 0xff, 0xff, 0xff, 0xfe }}
116     };
    ....
671     static int
672     mip6_icmp6_create_haanyaddr(haanyaddr, mpfx)
673             struct in6_addr *haanyaddr;
674             struct mip6_prefix *mpfx;
675     {
```

```
676              struct nd_prefix ndpr;
677
678              if (mpfx == NULL)
679                      return (EINVAL);
680
681              bzero(&ndpr, sizeof(ndpr));
682              ndpr.ndpr_prefix.sin6_addr = mpfx->mpfx_prefix;
683              ndpr.ndpr_plen = mpfx->mpfx_prefixlen;
684
685              if (mpfx->mpfx_prefixlen == 64)
686                      mip6_create_addr(haanyaddr, &haanyaddr_ifid64, &ndpr);
687              else
688                      mip6_create_addr(haanyaddr, &haanyaddr_ifidnn, &ndpr);
689
690              return (0);
691      }
```
_____mip6_icmp6.c

671–674 The `mip6_icmp6_create_haanyaddr()` function has two parameters. The `haanyaddr` parameter is a pointer to store the computed Home Agent Anycast Address and the `mpfx` parameter is a pointer to the home prefix information.

681–688 There are two computation rules for the Home Agent Anycast Address. One is for the address whose prefix length is 64. The other is for the address whose prefix length is not 64. Figure 5-28 (on page 510) shows the algorithm. The `mip6_create_addr()` function creates an IPv6 address using the second parameter as an interface identifier part and the third parameter as a prefix part.

5.17.17 Receiving a Dynamic Home Agent Address Discovery Reply Message

A mobile node receives a Dynamic Home Agent Address Discovery reply message from its home agent in response to a Dynamic Home Agent Address Discovery request message. Receiving the message is implemented as the `mip6_icmp6_dhaad_rep_input()` function. The function is called from the `icmp6_input()` function.

Listing 5-414
_____mip6_icmp6.c

```
382      static int
383      mip6_icmp6_dhaad_rep_input(m, off, icmp6len)
384              struct mbuf *m;
385              int off;
386              int icmp6len;
387      {
388              struct ip6_hdr *ip6;
389              struct mip6_dhaad_rep *hdrep;
390              u_int16_t hdrep_id;
391              struct mip6_ha *mha, *mha_prefered = NULL;
392              struct in6_addr *haaddrs, *haaddrptr;
393              struct sockaddr_in6 haaddr_sa;
394              int i, hacount = 0;
395              struct hif_softc *sc;
396              struct mip6_bu *mbu;
....
398              struct timeval mono_time;
....
402              microtime(&mono_time);
```
_____mip6_icmp6.c

382–386 The `mip6_icmp6_dhaad_rep_input()` function is called from the `icmp6_input()` function and it has three parameters. The `m` parameter is a pointer to the mbuf which contains a DHAAD reply message, the `off` parameter is an offset from the head of the packet to the address of the DHAAD message part, and the `icmp6len` parameter is the length of the ICMPv6 part.

Listing 5-415

── `mip6_icmp6.c`

```
405             ip6 = mtod(m, struct ip6_hdr *);
....
407             IP6_EXTHDR_CHECK(m, off, icmp6len, EINVAL);
408             hdrep = (struct mip6_dhaad_rep *)((caddr_t)ip6 + off);
....
418             haaddrs = (struct in6_addr *)(hdrep + 1);
```
── `mip6_icmp6.c`

405–418 The packet must be located in a contiguous memory space so that we can access the contents by casting the address to each structure. If the packet is not located properly, we drop the packet. Otherwise, `haaddrs` is set to the end of the DHAAD reply message structure to point to the head of the list of home agent addresses. The list of addresses of home agents immediately follows the message part.

Listing 5-416

── `mip6_icmp6.c`

```
420             /* sainty check. */
421             if (hdrep->mip6_dhrep_code != 0) {
422                     m_freem(m);
423                     return (EINVAL);
424             }
425
426             /* check the number of home agents listed in the message. */
427             hacount = (icmp6len - sizeof(struct mip6_dhaad_rep))
428                     / sizeof(struct in6_addr);
429             if (hacount == 0) {
....
434                     m_freem(m);
435                     return (EINVAL);
436             }
```
── `mip6_icmp6.c`

421–424 The ICMPv6 code field of the reply message must be 0. The mobile node drops any packet which does not have the correct code value.

427–436 The number of addresses stored at the end of the reply message can be calculated from the length of the reply message and the size of an IPv6 address, which is 128 bytes. If there is no address information, the packet is dropped.

Listing 5-417

── `mip6_icmp6.c`

```
438             /* find hif that matches this receiving hadiscovid of DHAAD reply. */
439             hdrep_id = hdrep->mip6_dhrep_id;
440             hdrep_id = ntohs(hdrep_id);
```

```
441          for (sc = LIST_FIRST(&hif_softc_list); sc;
442              sc = LIST_NEXT(sc, hif_entry)) {
443                  if (sc->hif_dhaad_id == hdrep_id)
444                          break;
445          }
446          if (sc == NULL) {
447                  /*
448                   * no matching hif.  maybe this DHAAD reply is too late.
449                   */
450                  return (0);
451          }
452
453          /* reset rate limitation factor. */
454          sc->hif_dhaad_count = 0;
```
─── mip6_icmp6.c

439–451 The identifier value (`hdrep_id`) of the reply message is copied from the request message. The mobile node searches for the virtual home network interface relevant to the identifier. If there is no matching interface, the mobile node ignores the reply message.

454 The `hif_dhaad_count` variable is used when a mobile node decides the sending rate of DHAAD messages. After receiving a correct reply message, `hif_dhaad_count` is reset to 0, which means the rate limitation state is in its initial state.

Listing 5-418
─── mip6_icmp6.c

```
456          /* install addresses of a home agent specified in the message */
457          haaddrptr = haaddrs;
458          for (i = 0; i < hacount; i++) {
459                  bzero(&haaddr_sa, sizeof(haaddr_sa));
460                  haaddr_sa.sin6_len = sizeof(haaddr_sa);
461                  haaddr_sa.sin6_family = AF_INET6;
462                  haaddr_sa.sin6_addr = *haaddrptr++;
463                  /*
464                   * XXX we cannot get a correct zone id by looking only
465                   * in6_addr structure.
466                   */
467                  if (in6_addr2zoneid(m->m_pkthdr.rcvif, &haaddr_sa.sin6_addr,
468                      &haaddr_sa.sin6_scope_id))
469                          continue;
470                  if (in6_embedscope(&haaddr_sa.sin6_addr, &haaddr_sa))
471                          continue;
```
─── mip6_icmp6.c

457–471 All home agent addresses contained in the reply message are installed. The scope identifier can be recovered from the interface on which the reply message is received. However, we need not worry about the scope identifier much, since the address of a home agent is usually a global address.

Listing 5-419
─── mip6_icmp6.c

```
472          mha = mip6_ha_list_find_withaddr(&mip6_ha_list,
473              &haaddr_sa.sin6_addr);
474          if (mha) {
475                  /*
476                   * if this home agent already exists in the list,
477                   * update its lifetime.
478                   */
```

```
479                              if (mha->mha_pref == 0) {
480                                      /*
481                                       * we have no method to know the
482                                       * preference of this home agent.
483                                       * assume pref = 0.
484                                       */
485                                      mha->mha_pref = 0;
486                                      mip6_ha_list_reinsert(&mip6_ha_list, mha);
487                              }
488                              mip6_ha_update_lifetime(mha, 0);
```
—— mip6_icmp6.c

472–488 If the received address is already registered as a home agent of this mobile node, the mobile node updates the home agent information. If the existing entry has a preference value other than 0, the mobile node resets the value to 0 since the DHAAD reply message does not have any information about preference. The lifetime is assumed to be infinite for the same reason.

Listing 5-420
—— mip6_icmp6.c

```
489                      } else {
490                              /*
491                               * create a new home agent entry and insert it
492                               * to the internal home agent list
493                               * (mip6_ha_list).
494                               */
495                              mha = mip6_ha_create(&haddr_sa.sin6_addr,
496                                  ND_RA_FLAG_HOME_AGENT, 0, 0);
497                              if (mha == NULL) {
....
501                                      m_freem(m);
502                                      return (ENOMEM);
503                              }
504                              mip6_ha_list_insert(&mip6_ha_list, mha);
505                              mip6_dhaad_ha_list_insert(sc, mha);
506                      }
```
—— mip6_icmp6.c

495–505 If the mobile node does not have a home agent entry for the received home agent address, a new `mip6_ha{}` instance is created by the `mip6_ha_create()` function and inserted into the list of home agents. The preference is assumed to be 0 and the lifetime is assumed to be infinite. The `mip6_dhaad_ha_list_insert()` function updates the home agent information of the virtual home network interface specified as its first parameter.

Listing 5-421
—— mip6_icmp6.c

```
507                      if (mha_prefered == NULL) {
508                              /*
509                               * the home agent listed at the top of the
510                               * DHAAD reply packet is the most preferable
511                               * one.
512                               */
513                              mha_prefered = mha;
514                      }
515              }
```
—— mip6_icmp6.c

507–514 The specification says that the address which is located at the head of the address list of the DHAAD reply message is the most preferred. The `mha_preferred` pointer is set to the `mip6_ha{}` instance processed first, which is the head of the list.

Listing 5-422

```
517                 /*
518                  * search bu_list and do home registration pending.  each
519                  * binding update entry which can't proceed because of no home
520                  * agent has an field of a home agent address equals to an
521                  * unspecified address.
522                  */
523                 for (mbu = LIST_FIRST(&sc->hif_bu_list); mbu;
524                     mbu = LIST_NEXT(mbu, mbu_entry)) {
525                         if ((mbu->mbu_flags & IP6MU_HOME)
526                             && IN6_IS_ADDR_UNSPECIFIED(&mbu->mbu_paddr)) {
527                                 /* home registration. */
528                                 mbu->mbu_paddr = mha_prefered->mha_addr;
529                                 if (!MIP6_IS_BU_BOUND_STATE(mbu)) {
530                                         if (mip6_bu_send_bu(mbu)) {
....
539                                         }
540                                 }
541                         }
542                 }
543
544                 return (0);
545         }
```

523–542 The `mip6_bu_send_bu()` function is called to send a Binding Update message with the home agent address received by the incoming DHAAD reply message for each waiting entry, if the mobile node has binding update list entries which are waiting for the DHAAD reply message to determine the correct home agent address.

Update Prefix Information Entries

The `mip6_dhaad_ha_list_insert()` function inserts a home agent entry received via the Dynamic Home Agent Address Discovery mechanism into the home agent list.

Listing 5-423

```
547     static int
548     mip6_dhaad_ha_list_insert(hif, mha)
549             struct hif_softc *hif;
550             struct mip6_ha *mha;
551     {
552             struct hif_prefix *hpfx;
553
554             for (hpfx = LIST_FIRST(&hif->hif_prefix_list_home); hpfx;
555                 hpfx = LIST_NEXT(hpfx, hpfx_entry)) {
556                     mip6_prefix_ha_list_insert(&hpfx->hpfx_mpfx->mpfx_ha_list,
557                         mha);
558             }
559
560             return (0);
561     }
```

548–550 The `mip6_dhaad_ha_list_insert()` function has two parameters. The `hif` parameter is a pointer to the virtual home network interface whose home agent information is going to be updated. The `mha` parameter is a pointer to the newly created instance of the `mip6_ha{}` structure which is inserted into the virtual home interface.

554–558 The home agent information is referenced from each prefix information entry. In a virtual home network, the `hif_prefix_list_home` variable keeps all home prefix information entries. The `mip6_prefix_ha_list_insert()` function is called for all prefix information entries stored in the variable with the newly created home agent information. The home agent information is added to each prefix information entry.

5.17.18 Receiving ICMPv6 Error Messages

A mobile node sometimes receives an ICMPv6 error message from nodes with which the mobile node is communicating or from routers between the mobile node and communicating nodes. Some of these error messages need to be processed by the Mobile IPv6 stack.

Listing 5-424

———————————————————————————————————————mip6_icmp6.c
```
129     int
130     mip6_icmp6_input(m, off, icmp6len)
131             struct mbuf *m;
132             int off;
133             int icmp6len;
134     {
  ....
195             case ICMP6_PARAM_PROB:
196                     if (!MIP6_IS_MN)
197                             break;
```
———————————————————————————————————————mip6_icmp6.c

195–197 If a mobile node receives an ICMPv6 Parameter Problem message, the mobile node needs to see whether the message is related to Mobile IPv6 mobile node function. The error message is processed only in a mobile node.

Listing 5-425

———————————————————————————————————————mip6_icmp6.c
```
199             pptr = ntohl(icmp6->icmp6_pptr);
200             if ((sizeof(*icmp6) + pptr + 1) > icmp6len) {
201                     /*
202                      * we can't get the detail of the
203                      * packet, ignore this...
204                      */
205                     break;
206             }
```
———————————————————————————————————————mip6_icmp6.c

199–205 The problem pointer (`icmp6_pptr`) points to the address where the error occurred. The pointer may point to an address which is larger than the end of the incoming ICMPv6 message. An ICMPv6 error message may not be able to contain all of the original packet because of the limitation on the packet size. In this case, the packet is ignored since it is impossible to know what the problem was.

Listing 5-426

_____mip6_icmp6.c

```
208                      switch (icmp6->icmp6_code) {
209                      case ICMP6_PARAMPROB_OPTION:
210                              /*
211                               * XXX: TODO
212                               *
213                               * should we mcopydata??
214                               */
215                              origip6 = (caddr_t)(icmp6 + 1);
216                              switch (*(u_int8_t *)(origip6 + pptr)) {
217                              case IP6OPT_HOME_ADDRESS:
218                                      /*
219                                       * the peer doesn't recognize HAO.
220                                       */
....
223                                      IP6_EXTHDR_CHECK(m, off, icmp6len, EINVAL);
224                                      mip6_icmp6_find_addr(m, off, icmp6len,
225                                                      &laddr, &paddr);
....
229                                      /*
230                                       * if the peer doesn't support HAO, we
231                                       * must use bi-directional tunneling
232                                       * to contiue communication.
233                                       */
234                                      for (sc = LIST_FIRST(&hif_softc_list); sc;
235                                          sc = LIST_NEXT(sc, hif_entry)) {
236                                              mbu = mip6_bu_list_find_withpaddr
        (&sc->hif_bu_list, &paddr, &laddr);
237                                              mip6_bu_fsm
        (mbu, MIP6_BU_PRI_FSM_EVENT_ICMP_PARAMPROB, NULL);
238                                      }
239                                      break;
240                              }
241                              break;
```
_____mip6_icmp6.c

— *Lines 236 and 237 are broken here for layout reasons. However, they are a single line of code.*

208–217 A mobile node may receive an ICMPv6 Parameter Problem message against the Home Address option if the node with which the mobile node is communicating does not support the Home Address option.

224–241 The `mip6_icmp6_find_addr()` function is called to get the source and destination addresses of the original packet. With these addresses, the corresponding binding update list entry is found by the `mip6_bu_list_find_withpaddr()` function. If the problem pointer points to one of the destination options and the option type is the Home Address option, the mobile node sends an `MIP6_BU_PRI_FSM_EVENT_ICMP_PARAMPROB` event to the state machine of the binding update list entry of the remote node. The event will mark the entry that the node does not support Mobile IPv6.

Listing 5-427

_____mip6_icmp6.c

```
243                      case ICMP6_PARAMPROB_NEXTHEADER:
244                              origip6 = (caddr_t)(icmp6 + 1);
245                              switch (*(u_int8_t *)(origip6 + pptr)) {
246                              case IPPROTO_MH:
247                                      /*
```

```
248                                        * the peer doesn't recognize mobility header.
249                                        */
250                                       mip6stat.mip6s_paramprobmh++;
251
252                                       IP6_EXTHDR_CHECK(m, off, icmp6len, EINVAL);
253                                       mip6_icmp6_find_addr(m, off, icmp6len,
254                                                            &laddr, &paddr);
....
258                                       for (sc = LIST_FIRST(&hif_softc_list); sc;
259                                            sc = LIST_NEXT(sc, hif_entry)) {
260                                               mbu = mip6_bu_list_find_withpaddr
     (&sc->hif_bu_list, &paddr, &laddr);
261                                                     mip6_bu_fsm
     (mbu, MIP6_BU_PRI_FSM_EVENT_ICMP_PARAMPROB, NULL);
262                                               }
263                                               break;
264                                       }
265                                       break;
266                               }
267                               break;
....
269                       }
270
271               return (0);
272       }
```

<hr>
――mip6_icmp6.c

— Lines 260 and 261 are broken here for layout reasons. However, they are a single line of code.

243–267 A mobile node may receive an ICMPv6 Parameter Problem message against the next
header value of the Mobility Header sent before if the peer node with which the mobile
node is communicating does not recognize the extension header. In this case, the mobile
node will send an MIP6_BU_PRI_FSM_EVENT_ICMP_PARAMPROB event to the state
machine as well.

5.17.19 State Machine

Each binding update list entry has a state machine to hold the registration state and react to
incoming events properly. Table 5-22 (on page 560) shows the list of the states of a state
machine. Table 5-40 shows the list of the events which are sent to the state machine. Table 5-41
shows macros to judge that the specified event is for the primary state machine or the secondary
state machine.

TABLE 5-40

Events (for primary state)	Description
MIP6_BU_PRI_FSM_EVENT_MOVEMENT	Moved from one foreign network to another foreign network
MIP6_BU_PRI_FSM_EVENT_RETURNING_HOME	Returned home
MIP6_BU_PRI_FSM_EVENT_REVERSE_PACKET	Received a bi-directional packet
MIP6_BU_PRI_FSM_EVENT_RR_DONE	Return routability procedure has been completed

(Continued)

TABLE 5-40 (*Continued*)

Events (for primary state)	Description
MIP6_BU_PRI_FSM_EVENT_RR_DONE	Return routability procedure has been completed
MIP6_BU_PRI_FSM_EVENT_RR_FAILED	Return routability procedure failed
MIP6_BU_PRI_FSM_EVENT_BRR	Received a Binding Refresh Request message
MIP6_BU_PRI_FSM_EVENT_BA	Received a Binding Acknowledgment message
MIP6_BU_PRI_FSM_EVENT_NO_BINDING	(not used)
MIP6_BU_PRI_FSM_EVENT_UNVERIFIED_HAO	Received a Binding Error with UNKNOWN_HAO status
MIP6_BU_PRI_FSM_EVENT_UNKNOWN_MH_TYPE	Received a Binding Error with UNKNOWN_MH status
MIP6_BU_PRI_FSM_EVENT_ICMP_PARAMPROB	Received an ICMPv6 Parameter Problem message
MIP6_BU_PRI_FSM_EVENT_RETRANS_TIMER	Retransmission timer expired
MIP6_BU_PRI_FSM_EVENT_REFRESH_TIMER	Refresh timer expired
MIP6_BU_PRI_FSM_EVENT_FAILURE_TIMER	(not used)

Events (for secondary state)	Description
MIP6_BU_SEC_FSM_EVENT_START_RR	Return routability procedure is initiated
MIP6_BU_SEC_FSM_EVENT_START_HOME_RR	Return routability procedure for returning home is initiated
MIP6_BU_SEC_FSM_EVENT_STOP_RR	Return routability procedure needs to be stopped
MIP6_BU_SEC_FSM_EVENT_HOT	Received a Home Test message
MIP6_BU_SEC_FSM_EVENT_COT	Received a Care-of Test message
MIP6_BU_SEC_FSM_EVENT_RETRANS_TIMER	Retransmission timer expired

Events for the state machine.

TABLE 5-41

Name	Description
MIP6_BU_IS_PRI_FSM_EVENT(ev)	True if ev is an event for the primary state machine
MIP6_BU_IS_SEC_FSM_EVENT(ev)	True if ev is an event for the secondary state machine

Macros to determine if the specified event is for the primary state machine or secondary state machine.

Figures 5-59 and 5-60 (on pages 817–818) show the basic state transition graph of both the primary and secondary state machines, respectively. The figures do not describe any error conditions. The error handling is discussed in Sections 5.17.20 and 5.17.21.

FIGURE 5-59

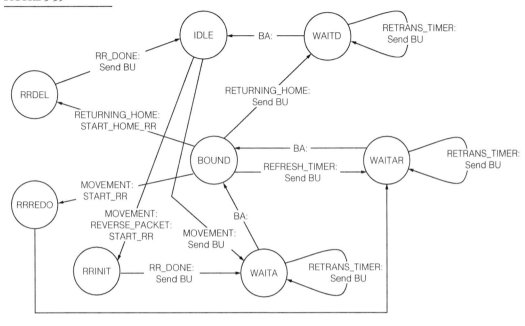

The state transition graph of the primary state machine.

5.17.20 Primary State Machine

The mip6_bu_fsm() function is an entry point to the state machine.

Listing 5-428

_____mip6_fsm.c

```
74      int
75      mip6_bu_fsm(mbu, event, data)
76              struct mip6_bu *mbu;
77              int event;
78              void *data;
79      {
80              /* sanity check. */
81              if (mbu == NULL)
82                      return (EINVAL);
83
84              if (MIP6_BU_IS_PRI_FSM_EVENT(event))
85                      return (mip6_bu_pri_fsm(mbu, event, data));
86              if (MIP6_BU_IS_SEC_FSM_EVENT(event))
87                      return (mip6_bu_sec_fsm(mbu, event, data));
88
89              /* invalid event. */
90              return (EINVAL);
91      }
```

_____mip6_fsm.c

FIGURE 5-60

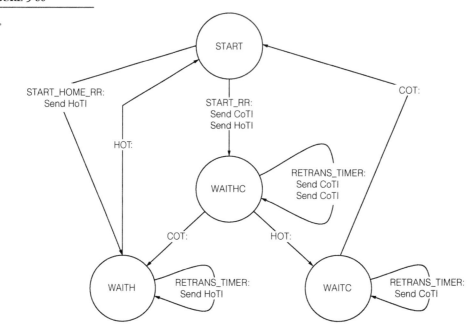

The state transition graph of the secondary state machine.

74–78 The `mip6_bu_fsm()` function has three parameters: The `mbu` parameter is a pointer to the binding update list entry; the `event` parameter is one of the events listed in Table 5-40; and the `data` parameter is a pointer to additional data depending on the event.

84–87 A binding update list entry has two kinds of states. Based on the type of input event, the `mip6_bu_pri_fsm()` function or the `mip6_bu_sec_fsm()` function is called. The former is for the primary state machine which maintains the registration status of the binding update list entry. The latter is for the secondary state machine which maintains the status of the return routability procedure.

Listing 5-429

```
                                                                  mip6_fsm.c
93      int
94      mip6_bu_pri_fsm(mbu, event, data)
95              struct mip6_bu *mbu;
96              int event;
97              void *data;
98      {
99              u_int8_t *mbu_pri_fsm_state;
100             int error;
....
102             struct timeval mono_time;
....
104             struct ip6_mh_binding_request *ip6mr;
105             struct ip6_mh_binding_ack *ip6ma;
```

```
106              struct ip6_mh_binding_error *ip6me;
107              struct icmp6_hdr *icmp6;
108              struct hif_softc *hif;
```
―――mip6_fsm.c

93–97 The `mip6_bu_pri_fsm()` function has three parameters, which are the same as the values passed to the `mip6_bu_fsm()` function.

Listing 5-430

―――mip6_fsm.c
```
118              mbu_pri_fsm_state = &mbu->mbu_pri_fsm_state;
119
120              /* set pointers. */
121              ip6mr = (struct ip6_mh_binding_request *)data;
122              ip6ma = (struct ip6_mh_binding_ack *)data;
123              ip6me = (struct ip6_mh_binding_error *)data;
124              icmp6 = (struct icmp6_hdr *)data;
125              hif = (struct hif_softc *)data;
```
―――mip6_fsm.c

118 The `mbu_pri_fsm_state` pointer points to the address of the `mbu_pri_fsm_state` member variable. This is just for providing an easy way to access the member.

121–125 The `data` parameter points to various structures based on the event input to the function. `ip6mr`, `ip6ma`, `ip6me`, `icmp6` and `hif` point to the same address as the `data` parameter providing access to each structure. Based on the event, zero or one of the variables has the real meaning.

MIP6_BU_PRI_FSM_STATE_IDLE State

Lines 130–214 process events when the primary state machine is in the `MIP6_BU_PRI_FSM_STATE_IDLE` state.

Listing 5-431

―――mip6_fsm.c
```
127              error = 0;
128
129              switch (*mbu_pri_fsm_state) {
130              case MIP6_BU_PRI_FSM_STATE_IDLE:
131                      switch (event) {
132                      case MIP6_BU_PRI_FSM_EVENT_MOVEMENT:
133                              if ((mbu->mbu_flags & IP6MU_HOME) != 0) {
134                                      /*
135                                       * Send BU,
136                                       * Reset retransmission counter,
137                                       * Start retransmission timer,
138                                       * XXX Start failure timer.
139                                       */
140                                      mbu->mbu_retrans_count = 0;
141
142                                      error = mip6_bu_pri_fsm_home_registration(mbu);
143                                      if (error) {
....
149                                              /* continue and try again. */
150                                      }
```

```
151
152                                       *mbu_pri_fsm_state
153                                           = MIP6_BU_PRI_FSM_STATE_WAITA;
```
                                                                    ———————mip6_fsm.c

132–153 If the `MIP6_BU_PRI_FSM_EVENT_MOVEMENT` event is sent to the binding update
list entry for home registration, the `mip6_bu_pri_fsm_home_registration()` function is called to perform the home registration procedure. The state is changed to
`MIP6_BU_PRI_FSM_STATE_WAITA`.

Listing 5-432
                                                                    ———————mip6_fsm.c
```
154                                   } else {
155                                       /*
156                                        * Start RR.
157                                        */
158                                       error = mip6_bu_sec_fsm(mbu,
159                                           MIP6_BU_SEC_FSM_EVENT_START_RR,
160                                           data);
161                                       if (error) {
 ....
167                                           return (error);
168                                       }
169                                       *mbu_pri_fsm_state
170                                           = MIP6_BU_PRI_FSM_STATE_RRINIT;
171                                   }
172                                   break;
```
                                                                    ———————mip6_fsm.c

155–171 If the entry is not for home registration, the `mip6_bu_sec_fsm()` function is called
with the `MIP6_BU_SEC_FSM_EVENT_START_RR` event to initiate the return routability
procedure. The state is changed to `MIP6_BU_PRI_FSM_STATE_RRINIT`.

Listing 5-433
                                                                    ———————mip6_fsm.c
```
174                           case MIP6_BU_PRI_FSM_EVENT_REVERSE_PACKET:
175                                   /*
176                                    * Start RR.
177                                    */
178                                   if ((mbu->mbu_state & MIP6_BU_STATE_NEEDTUNNEL)
179                                       != 0) {
180                                           /*
181                                            * if the peer doesn't support MIP6,
182                                            * keep IDLE state.
183                                            */
184                                           break;
185                                   }
186                                   error = mip6_bu_sec_fsm(mbu,
187                                       MIP6_BU_SEC_FSM_EVENT_START_RR,
188                                       data);
189                                   if (error) {
 ....
194                                           return (error);
195                                   }
196
197                                   *mbu_pri_fsm_state = MIP6_BU_PRI_FSM_STATE_RRINIT;
198
199                                   break;
```
                                                                    ———————mip6_fsm.c

174–199 If the `MIP6_BU_PRI_FSM_EVENT_REVERSE_PACKET` event is input, the `mip6_bu_sec_fsm()` function is called with the `MIP6_BU_PRI_FSM_EVENT_REVERSE_PACKET` event, unless the binding update list entry does not have the `MIP6_BU_STATE_NEEDTUNNEL` flag set. The `MIP6_BU_STATE_NEEDTUNNEL` flag means that the peer node does not support Mobile IPv6 and there is no need to perform the return routability procedure. The state is changed to `MIP6_BU_PRI_FSM_STATE_RRINIT`.

Listing 5-434

```
                                                            mip6_fsm.c
201                    case MIP6_BU_PRI_FSM_EVENT_ICMP_PARAMPROB:
202                        /*
203                         * Stop timers.
204                         */
205                        mip6_bu_stop_timers(mbu);
206
207                        *mbu_pri_fsm_state = MIP6_BU_PRI_FSM_STATE_IDLE;
208
209                        mbu->mbu_state |= MIP6_BU_STATE_DISABLE;
210
211                        break;
212                    }
213                break;
                                                            mip6_fsm.c
```

201–212 If the `MIP6_BU_PRI_FSM_EVENT_ICMP_PARAMPROB` event is input, the `mip6_bu_stop_timers()` function is called to stop all timer functions related to this binding update list entry. The state remains `MIP6_BU_PRI_FSM_STATE_IDLE`. The `MIP6_BU_STATE_DISABLE` flag is set since the input of an ICMPv6 Parameter Problem message indicates that the peer node does not recognize the Home Address option or the Mobility Header.

MIP6_BU_PRI_FSM_STATE_RRINIT State

Lines 215–376 process events when the primary state machine is in the `MIP6_BU_PRI_FSM_STATE_RRINIT` state.

Listing 5-435

```
                                                            mip6_fsm.c
215            case MIP6_BU_PRI_FSM_STATE_RRINIT:
216                switch (event) {
217                case MIP6_BU_PRI_FSM_EVENT_RR_DONE:
218                    if ((mbu->mbu_flags & IP6MU_ACK) != 0) {
219                        /*
220                         * if A flag is set,
221                         *    Send BU,
222                         *    Reset retransmission counter,
223                         *    Start retransmission timer,
224                         *    Start failure timer.
225                         */
226
227                        /* XXX no code yet. */
228
229                        *mbu_pri_fsm_state
230                            = MIP6_BU_PRI_FSM_STATE_WAITA;
                                                            mip6_fsm.c
```

215–230 This part is intended to send a Binding Update message to a correspondent node with the A (Acknowledgment) flag set. However, the current KAME implementation never sets the A flag in the Binding Update message sent to correspondent nodes. This part is not implemented.

Listing 5-436

```
                                                                    _____mip6_fsm.c
231                             } else {
232                                     /*
233                                      * if A flag is not set,
234                                      *    Send BU,
235                                      *    Start refresh timer.
236                                      */
237                                     error = mip6_bu_send_cbu(mbu);
238                                     if (error) {
....
243                                             return (error);
244                                     }
245
246                                     mbu->mbu_retrans
247                                         = mono_time.tv_sec + mbu->mbu_lifetime;
248
249                                     *mbu_pri_fsm_state
250                                         = MIP6_BU_PRI_FSM_STATE_BOUND;
251                             }
252                             break;
                                                                    _____mip6_fsm.c
```

231–251 If the entry does not have the A flag set, the `mip6_bu_send_cbu()` function is called to send a Binding Update message to the correspondent node related to the binding update list entry. The `mbu_retrans` variable is set to the lifetime of the binding update list entry to remove the entry when the lifetime of the entry expires. The state is changed to `MIP6_BU_PRI_FSM_STATE_BOUND`.

Listing 5-437

```
                                                                    _____mip6_fsm.c
254                             case MIP6_BU_PRI_FSM_EVENT_UNKNOWN_MH_TYPE:
255                                     /*
256                                      * Stop timers,
257                                      * Stop RR.
258                                      */
259                                     mip6_bu_stop_timers(mbu);
260
261                                     error = mip6_bu_sec_fsm(mbu,
262                                         MIP6_BU_SEC_FSM_EVENT_STOP_RR,
263                                         data);
264                                     if (error) {
....
269                                             return (error);
270                                     }
271
272                                     *mbu_pri_fsm_state = MIP6_BU_PRI_FSM_STATE_IDLE;
273
274                                     mbu->mbu_state |= MIP6_BU_STATE_DISABLE;
275
276                                     break;
                                                                    _____mip6_fsm.c
```

254–274 If the MIP6_BU_PRI_FSM_EVENT_UNKNOWN_MH_TYPE event is input, the mip6_bu_sec_fsm() function is called with the MIP6_BU_SEC_FSM_EVENT_STOP_RR event to stop the running return routability procedure since the peer node does not recognize the Mobility Header. The timers are stopped by the mip6_bu_stop_timers() function and the state is changed to MIP6_BU_PRI_FSM_STATE_IDLE. Also, the MIP6_BU_STATE_DISABLE flag is set to indicate that the peer node does not support Mobile IPv6.

Listing 5-438

```
                                                                    mip6_fsm.c
278                     case MIP6_BU_PRI_FSM_EVENT_MOVEMENT:
279                             /*
280                              * Stop timers,
281                              * Stop RR,
282                              * Start RR.
283                              */
284                             mip6_bu_stop_timers(mbu);
285
286                             error = mip6_bu_sec_fsm(mbu,
287                                 MIP6_BU_SEC_FSM_EVENT_STOP_RR,
288                                 data);
289
290                             if (error == 0) {
291                                     error = mip6_bu_sec_fsm(mbu,
292                                         MIP6_BU_SEC_FSM_EVENT_START_RR,
293                                         data);
294                             }
295                             if (error) {
....
300                                     return (error);
301                             }
302
303                             *mbu_pri_fsm_state = MIP6_BU_PRI_FSM_STATE_RRINIT;
304
305                             break;
                                                                    mip6_fsm.c
```

278–305 If the MIP6_BU_PRI_FSM_EVENT_MOVEMENT event is input when the current state is MIP6_BU_PRI_FSM_STATE_RRINIT, the mobile node needs to stop the running return routability procedure and needs to start a new return routability procedure using the new care-of address. The mip6_bu_sec_fsm() function is called with the MIP6_BU_SEC_FSM_EVENT_STOP_RR event to stop the current return routability procedure and the same function is called with the MIP6_BU_SEC_FSM_EVENT_START_RR event immediately to start a new procedure. The state remains MIP6_BU_PRI_FSM_STATE_RRINIT.

Listing 5-439

```
                                                                    mip6_fsm.c
307                     case MIP6_BU_PRI_FSM_EVENT_RETURNING_HOME:
308                             /*
309                              * Stop timers,
310                              * Stop RR.
311                              */
312                             mip6_bu_stop_timers(mbu);
313
314                             error = mip6_bu_sec_fsm(mbu,
315                                 MIP6_BU_SEC_FSM_EVENT_STOP_RR,
```

```
316                             data);
317                         if (error) {
....
322                             return (error);
323                         }
324
325                         *mbu_pri_fsm_state = MIP6_BU_PRI_FSM_STATE_IDLE;
326
327                         /* free mbu */
328                         mbu->mbu_lifetime = 0;
329                         mbu->mbu_expire = mono_time.tv_sec + mbu->mbu_lifetime;
330
331                         break;
```
                                                                    mip6_fsm.c

307–329 If the mobile node returns home, the
MIP6_BU_PRI_FSM_EVENT_RETURNING_HOME event is input. In this case, the
mip6_bu_stop_timers() function is called to stop all timer functions related to
this entry and the mip6_bu_sec_fsm() function is called with the
MIP6_BU_SEC_FSM_EVENT_STOP_RR event. The state is changed to
MIP6_BU_PRI_FSM_STATE_IDLE. The lifetime of the binding update list entry is
set to 0 and the mbu_expire variable is set to the current time. The entry will be
removed when the mip6_bu_timer() function is called next time.

Listing 5-440
                                                                    mip6_fsm.c
```
333                     case MIP6_BU_PRI_FSM_EVENT_REVERSE_PACKET:
334                         /*
335                          * Start RR.
336                          */
337                         error = mip6_bu_sec_fsm(mbu,
338                             MIP6_BU_SEC_FSM_EVENT_START_RR,
339                             data);
340                         if (error) {
....
345                             return (error);
346                         }
347
348                         *mbu_pri_fsm_state = MIP6_BU_PRI_FSM_STATE_RRINIT;
349
350                         break;
```
                                                                    mip6_fsm.c

333–350 This code is almost the same as the code for the
MIP6_BU_PRI_FSM_EVENT_REVERSE_PACKET event in the
MIP6_BU_PRI_STATE_IDLE state. The difference is this code does not check
the MIP6_BU_STATE_NEEDTUNNEL flag of the binding update list entry. If the
entry has the MIP6_BU_STATE_NEEDTUNNEL flag set, the return routability procedure has already been previously stopped. The mobile node never enters this part
of the code in that case.

Listing 5-441
                                                                    mip6_fsm.c
```
352                     case MIP6_BU_PRI_FSM_EVENT_ICMP_PARAMPROB:
.... [See lines 255–274]
374                         break;
375                     }
376                     break;
```
                                                                    mip6_fsm.c

352–374 A mobile node receives an ICMPv6 Parameter Problem message if the peer node does not support Mobile IPv6. The procedure when a mobile node receives the ICMPv6 message is the same as with receiving an unknown Mobility Header message described on lines 255–274.

MIP6_BU_PRI_FSM_STATE_RRREDO State

Lines 378–542 process events when the primary state machine is in the MIP6_BU_PRI_FSM_STATE_RRREDO state. Most of the code is the same as for the MIP6_BU_PRI_FSM_STATE_RRREDO state.

Listing 5-442

```
                                                              mip6_fsm.c
378              case MIP6_BU_PRI_FSM_STATE_RRREDO:
379                   switch (event) {
380                   case MIP6_BU_PRI_FSM_EVENT_RR_DONE:
    .... [See lines 218–251]
415                        break;
416
417                   case MIP6_BU_PRI_FSM_EVENT_UNKNOWN_MH_TYPE:
    .... [See lines 256–276]
439                        break;
440
441                   case MIP6_BU_PRI_FSM_EVENT_MOVEMENT:
    .... [See lines 279–304]
468                        break;
469
470                   case MIP6_BU_PRI_FSM_EVENT_RETURNING_HOME:
    .... [See lines 308–330]
497                        break;
    ....
518                   case MIP6_BU_PRI_FSM_EVENT_ICMP_PARAMPROB:
    .... [See lines 255–274]
540                        break;
                                                              mip6_fsm.c
```

380–497, 518–540 The code when a state machine receives
the MIP6_BU_PRI_FSM_EVENT_RR_DONE,
the MIP6_BU_PRI_FSM_EVENT_UNKNOWN_MH_TYPE,
the MIP6_BU_PRI_FSM_EVENT_MOVEMENT,
the MIP6_BU_PRI_FSM_EVENT_RETURNING_HOME,
or the MIP6_BU_PRI_FSM_EVENT_ICMP_PARAMPROB event
is the same as for each event implemented in the MIP6_BU_PRI_FSM_STATE_RRINIT.

Listing 5-443

```
                                                              mip6_fsm.c
499                   case MIP6_BU_PRI_FSM_EVENT_REVERSE_PACKET:
500                        /*
501                         * Start RR.
502                         */
```

```
503                           error = mip6_bu_sec_fsm(mbu,
504                               MIP6_BU_SEC_FSM_EVENT_START_RR,
505                               data);
506                           if (error) {
....
511                                   return (error);
512                           }
513
514                           *mbu_pri_fsm_state = MIP6_BU_PRI_FSM_STATE_RRREDO;
515
516                           break;
....
541                       }
542                   break;
```
——mip6_fsm.c

499–516 The code for the `MIP6_BU_PRI_FSM_EVENT_REVERSE_PACKET` event in the
`MIP6_BU_PRI_FSM_STATE_RRREDO` state is almost the same as the relevant code for
the `MIP6_BU_PRI_FSM_STATE_RRREDO` state. The only difference is that the next state
is set to the `MIP6_BU_PRI_FSM_STATE_RRREDO` state.

MIP6_BU_PRI_FSM_STATE_WAITA State

Lines 544–744 process events when the primary state machine is in the
`MIP6_BU_PRI_FSM_STATE_WAITA` state.

Listing 5-444
——mip6_fsm.c
```
544           case MIP6_BU_PRI_FSM_STATE_WAITA:
545                   switch (event) {
546                   case MIP6_BU_PRI_FSM_EVENT_BA:
547                           /* XXX */
548                           if ((mbu->mbu_flags & IP6MU_HOME) != 0) {
549                                   /*
550                                    * (Process BA,)
551                                    * Stop timer,
552                                    * Reset retransmission counter,
553                                    * Start refresh timer.
554                                    */
555
556                                   /* XXX home registration completed. */
557
558                                   mip6_bu_stop_timers(mbu);
559
560                                   mbu->mbu_retrans_count = 0;
561
562                                   mbu->mbu_retrans
563                                       = mono_time.tv_sec
564                                       + mbu->mbu_refresh;
565
566                                   *mbu_pri_fsm_state
567                                       = MIP6_BU_PRI_FSM_STATE_BOUND;
568                           } else {
569                                   /* XXX no code yet. */
570                           }
571                           break;
```
——mip6_fsm.c

546–567 Receiving the `MIP6_BU_PRI_FSM_EVENT_BA` event means that the registration
message has been successfully accepted by the peer node. If the binding update list entry

related to this event is for home registration, the mobile node sets the `mbu_retrans` variable to indicate the next refresh time so that the mobile node can perform re-registration before the binding update entry expires. The state is changed to `MIP6_BU_PRI_FSM_STATE_BOUND`.

568–570 This code is for a correspondent node. However, as we already discussed, the code is empty since the current KAME implementation does not require correspondent nodes to reply to a Binding Acknowledgment message.

Listing 5-445

```
                                                                    mip6_fsm.c
573                     case MIP6_BU_PRI_FSM_EVENT_RETRANS_TIMER:
574                         /*
575                          * Send BU,
576                          * Start retransmittion timer.
577                          */
578                         if ((mbu->mbu_flags & IP6MU_HOME) != 0) {
579                             /*
580                              * Send BU,
581                              * Start retransmittion timer.
582                              */
583                             error = mip6_bu_pri_fsm_home_registration(mbu);
584                             if (error) {
  ....
590                                 /* continue and try again. */
591                             }
592
593                             *mbu_pri_fsm_state
594                                 = MIP6_BU_PRI_FSM_STATE_WAITA;
595                         } else {
  ....
615                         }
616                         break;
                                                                    mip6_fsm.c
```

573–594 If the `MIP6_BU_PRI_FSM_EVENT_RETRANS_TIMER` event is input while a mobile node is in the `MIP6_BU_PRI_FSM_STATE_WAITA` state, a Binding Update message must be resent. If the binding update list entry related to this event is for home registration, the `mip6_bu_pri_fsm_home_registration()` function is called to send a Binding Update message. The state is not changed.

595–615 This code is for a correspondent node, and is never executed in the KAME implementation.

Listing 5-446

```
                                                                    mip6_fsm.c
618                     case MIP6_BU_PRI_FSM_EVENT_UNKNOWN_MH_TYPE:
619                         if ((mbu->mbu_flags & IP6MU_HOME) != 0) {
620                             /* XXX correct ? */
621                             break;
622                         }
623
624                         /*
625                          * Stop timers.
626                          */
627                         mip6_bu_stop_timers(mbu);
```

```
628
629                                    *mbu_pri_fsm_state = MIP6_BU_PRI_FSM_STATE_IDLE;
630
631                                    mbu->mbu_state |= MIP6_BU_STATE_DISABLE;
632
633                                    break;
```
──mip6_fsm.c

618–633 If a mobile node receives the MIP6_BU_PRI_FSM_EVENT_UNKNOWN_MH_TYPE
event while the node is in the MIP6_BU_PRI_FSM_STATE_WAITA state, the node
stops all timer functions related to the binding update list entry and changes its state
to MIP6_BU_PRI_FSM_STATE_IDLE. The MIP6_BU_STATE_DISABLE flag is also set
in the entry. Note that we do not process this event for a home registration entry in order
to always keep the entry active.

Listing 5-447

──mip6_fsm.c
```
635                        case MIP6_BU_PRI_FSM_EVENT_MOVEMENT:
636                            if ((mbu->mbu_flags & IP6MU_HOME) != 0) {
637                                    /*
638                                     * Send BU,
639                                     * Reset retrans counter,
640                                     * Start retransmittion timer,
641                                     * XXX Start failure timer.
642                                     */
643                                    mbu->mbu_retrans_count = 0;
644
645                                    error = mip6_bu_pri_fsm_home_registration(mbu);
646                                    if (error) {
....
652                                            /* continue and try again. */
653                                    }
654
655                                    *mbu_pri_fsm_state
656                                        = MIP6_BU_PRI_FSM_STATE_WAITA;
657                            } else {
658                                    /*
659                                     * Stop timers,
660                                     * Start RR.
661                                     */
662                                    mip6_bu_stop_timers(mbu);
663
664                                    error = mip6_bu_sec_fsm(mbu,
665                                        MIP6_BU_SEC_FSM_EVENT_START_RR,
666                                        data);
667                                    if (error) {
....
673                                            return (error);
674                                    }
675                                    *mbu_pri_fsm_state
676                                        = MIP6_BU_PRI_FSM_STATE_RRINIT;
677                            }
678                            break;
```
──mip6_fsm.c

635–678 The procedure when a mobile node receives the
MIP6_BU_PRI_FSM_EVENT_MOVEMENT event while it is in the
MIP6_BU_PRI_FSM_STATE_WAITA state is similar to the procedure which
is implemented for the MIP6_BU_PRI_FSM_STATE_IDLE state (on lines 132–172).

The difference is that the `mip6_bu_stop_timer()` function is called before starting the return routability procedure for a correspondent node. In the `MIP6_BU_PRI_FSM_STATE_IDLE` state, there is no active timer. However, in the `MIP6_BU_PRI_FSM_STATE_WAITA` state, a retransmission timer is running which needs to be stopped before doing other state transitions.

Listing 5-448

——`mip6_fsm.c`

```
680                         case MIP6_BU_PRI_FSM_EVENT_RETURNING_HOME:
681                             if ((mbu->mbu_flags & IP6MU_HOME) != 0) {
682                                     /*
683                                      * Send BU,
684                                      * Reset retrans counter,
685                                      * Start retransmittion timer.
686                                      */
687                                 mbu->mbu_retrans_count = 0;
688
689                                 error = mip6_bu_pri_fsm_home_registration(mbu);
690                                 if (error) {
....
696                                         /* continue and try again. */
697                                 }
698
699                                 *mbu_pri_fsm_state
700                                     = MIP6_BU_PRI_FSM_STATE_WAITD;
701                             } else {
702                                     /*
703                                      * Stop timers,
704                                      * Start Home RR.
705                                      */
706                                 mip6_bu_stop_timers(mbu);
707
708                                 error = mip6_bu_sec_fsm(mbu,
709                                     MIP6_BU_SEC_FSM_EVENT_START_HOME_RR,
710                                     data);
711                                 if (error) {
....
717                                         return (error);
718                                 }
719
720                                 *mbu_pri_fsm_state
721                                     = MIP6_BU_PRI_FSM_STATE_RRDEL;
722                             }
723                         break;
```
——`mip6_fsm.c`

681–700 If a mobile node returns home while it is in the `MIP6_BU_PRI_FSM_STATE_WAITA` state, it starts the home de-registration procedure if the binding update list entry is for home registration (the `IP6MU_HOME` flags is set). The `mip6_bu_pri_fsm_home_registration()` function is called to send a Binding Update message for de-registration and the state is changed to `MIP6_BU_PRI_FSM_STATE_WAITD`.

If the entry is for a correspondent node, the `mip6_bu_sec_fsm()` function is called with the `MIP6_BU_SEC_FSM_EVENT_START_HOME_RR` event to perform the return routability procedure for de-registration. The state is changed to the `MIP6_BU_PRI_FSM_STATE_RRDEL` state.

Listing 5-449

```
                                                                    mip6_fsm.c
725                          case MIP6_BU_PRI_FSM_EVENT_REVERSE_PACKET:
```
.... [See lines 334–349]
```
742                                  break;
743                          }
744                  break;
                                                                    mip6_fsm.c
```

725–742 If a mobile node receives the MIP6_BU_PRI_FSM_EVENT_REVERSE_PACKET
event, it starts the return routability procedure. The code is the same as the code implemented for the MIP6_BU_PRI_FSM_STATE_RRINIT state on lines 334–349.

MIP6_BU_PRI_FSM_STATE_WAITAR State

Lines 746–948 process events when the primary state machine is in the
MIP6_BU_PRI_FSM_STATE_WAITAR state. Most parts of the code are similar to the
code for the MIP6_BU_PRI_FSM_STATE_WAITA state.

Listing 5-450

```
                                                                    mip6_fsm.c
746          case MIP6_BU_PRI_FSM_STATE_WAITAR:
747                  switch (event) {
748                  case MIP6_BU_PRI_FSM_EVENT_BA:
```
.... [See lines 547–571]
```
773                          break;
774
775                  case MIP6_BU_PRI_FSM_EVENT_RETRANS_TIMER:
```
.... [See lines 574–592]
```
796                                  *mbu_pri_fsm_state
797                                      = MIP6_BU_PRI_FSM_STATE_WAITAR;
```
.... [See lines 596–615]
```
823                          break;
824
825                  case MIP6_BU_PRI_FSM_EVENT_UNKNOWN_MH_TYPE:
```
.... [See lines 619–632]
```
840                          break;
841
842                  case MIP6_BU_PRI_FSM_EVENT_MOVEMENT:
```
.... [See lines 636–677]
```
882                          break;
883
884                  case MIP6_BU_PRI_FSM_EVENT_RETURNING_HOME:
```
.... [See lines 681–722]
```
927                          break;
928
929                  case MIP6_BU_PRI_FSM_EVENT_REVERSE_PACKET:
```
.... [See lines 334–349]
```
946                          break;
947                  }
948                  break;
                                                                    mip6_fsm.c
```

746–948 The only difference from the code for the MIP6_BU_PRI_FSM_STATE_WAITA
state is the next state for the MIP6_BU_PRI_FSM_EVENT_RETRANS_TIMER event. In
the MIP6_BU_PRI_FSM_STATE_WAITAR state, the next state is kept unchanged when
retransmitting a Binding Update message.

MIP6_BU_PRI_FSM_STATE_WAITD State

Lines 950–1075 process events when the primary state machine is in the
MIP6_BU_PRI_FSM_STATE_WAITD state.

Listing 5-451

```
                                                                    ____mip6_fsm.c
950              case MIP6_BU_PRI_FSM_STATE_WAITD:
951                  switch (event) {
952                  case MIP6_BU_PRI_FSM_EVENT_BA:
953                      /* XXX */
954                      if ((mbu->mbu_flags & IP6MU_HOME) != 0) {
955                          /* XXX home de-registration completed. */
956                      } else {
957                          /* XXX no code yet. */
958                      }
959                      break;
                                                                    ____mip6_fsm.c
```

952–955 There is nothing to do for the MIP6_BU_PRI_FSM_EVENT_BA event while a mobile
node is in the MIP6_BU_PRI_FSM_STATE_WAITD state, since all de-registration processing has already been done in the mip6_process_hurbu() function. The function
has already been called before the state machine is called.

956–958 This part is for processing a Binding Acknowledgment from a correspondent node,
which is not needed in the KAME implementation since KAME never requests a Binding
Acknowledgment message to correspondent nodes.

Listing 5-452

```
                                                                    ____mip6_fsm.c
961              case MIP6_BU_PRI_FSM_EVENT_RETRANS_TIMER:
962                  /* XXX */
963                  /*
964                   * Send BU,
965                   * Start retransmittion timer.
966                   */
967                  if ((mbu->mbu_flags & IP6MU_HOME) != 0) {
968                      /*
969                       * Send BU,
970                       * Start retransmittion timer.
971                       */
972                      error = mip6_bu_pri_fsm_home_registration(mbu);
973                      if (error) {
....
979                          /* continue and try again. */
980                      }
981
982                      *mbu_pri_fsm_state
983                          = MIP6_BU_PRI_FSM_STATE_WAITD;
984                  } else {
....
```

```
1008                            }
1009                            break;
```
——mip6_fsm.c

961–983 If the `MIP6_BU_PRI_FSM_EVENT_RETRANS_TIMER` event occurs while a mobile node is in the `MIP6_BU_PRI_FSM_STATE_WAITD` state, the `mip6_bu_pri_fsm_home_registration()` function is called to resend a Binding Update message for de-registration. The state is kept unchanged.

984–1008 The code for a correspondent node (the `IP6MU_HOME` flag is not set) is never executed since the KAME implementation does not retransmit the de-registration message because it does not set the A (Acknowledgment) flag.

Listing 5-453
——mip6_fsm.c

```
1011                    case MIP6_BU_PRI_FSM_EVENT_UNKNOWN_MH_TYPE:
  .... [See lines 619–632]
1026                            break;
```
——mip6_fsm.c

1011–1026 If a mobile node receives the `MIP6_BU_PRI_FSM_EVENT_UNKNOWN_MH_TYPE` event while it is in the `MIP6_BU_PRI_FSM_STATE_WAITD` state, the binding update list entry is marked to indicate that the peer node does not support Mobile IPv6. The code is the same as the code for the `MIP6_BU_PRI_FSM_STATE_WAITA` state implemented on lines 619–632.

Listing 5-454
——mip6_fsm.c

```
1028                    case MIP6_BU_PRI_FSM_EVENT_MOVEMENT:
  .... [See lines 636–677]
1073                            break;
1074                    }
1075            break;
```
——mip6_fsm.c

1028–1074 If a mobile node moves while it is in the `MIP6_BU_PRI_FSM_STATE_WAITD` state, it starts the registration procedure. The code is the same as the code for the `MIP6_BU_PRI_FSM_STATE_WAITA` state implemented on lines 635–678.

`MIP6_BU_PRI_FSM_STATE_RRDEL` State

Lines 1077–1198 process events when the primary state machine is in the `MIP6_BU_PRI_FSM_STATE_RRDEL` state.

Listing 5-455
——mip6_fsm.c

```
1077            case MIP6_BU_PRI_FSM_STATE_RRDEL:
1078                    switch (event) {
1079                    case MIP6_BU_PRI_FSM_EVENT_RR_DONE:
  .... [See lines 218–251]
```

```
1117                            break;
1118
1119                    case MIP6_BU_PRI_FSM_EVENT_UNKNOWN_MH_TYPE:
```
.... [See lines 256–276]
```
1143                            break;
1144
1145                    case MIP6_BU_PRI_FSM_EVENT_MOVEMENT:
```
.... [See lines 279–304]
```
1172                            break;
1173
1174                    case MIP6_BU_PRI_FSM_EVENT_ICMP_PARAMPROB:
```
.... [See lines 255–274]
```
1196                            break;
1197                    }
1198                    break;
```
──mip6_fsm.c

1078–1198 The code for the MIP6_BU_PRI_FSM_STATE_RRDEL state is almost the same as
the code for the MIP6_BU_PRI_FSM_STATE_RRINIT state. In this state, the
MIP6_BU_PRI_FSM_EVENT_RETURNING_HOME event does not need to be processed
since the mobile node is already at home. For the other events, the mobile node performs
the same procedures as those in the MIP6_BU_PRI_FSM_STATE_RRINIT state.

MIP6_BU_PRI_FSM_STATE_BOUND State

Lines 1201–1453 process events when the primary state machine is in the
MIP6_BU_PRI_FSM_STATE_BOUND state.

Listing 5-456

──mip6_fsm.c
```
1201            case MIP6_BU_PRI_FSM_STATE_BOUND:
1202                    switch (event) {
1203                    case MIP6_BU_PRI_FSM_EVENT_BRR:
1204                            if ((mbu->mbu_flags & IP6MU_HOME) != 0) {
1205                                    /*
1206                                     * Send BU,
1207                                     * Start retransmission timer.
1208                                     */
1209                                    error = mip6_bu_pri_fsm_home_registration(mbu);
1210                                    if (error) {
....
1216                                            /* continue and try again. */
1217                                    }
1218
1219                                    *mbu_pri_fsm_state
1220                                        = MIP6_BU_PRI_FSM_STATE_WAITAR;
1221                            } else {
1222                                    /*
1223                                     * Stop timers,
1224                                     * Start RR.
1225                                     */
1226                                    mip6_bu_stop_timers(mbu);
1227
1228                                    error = mip6_bu_sec_fsm(mbu,
1229                                        MIP6_BU_SEC_FSM_EVENT_START_RR,
1230                                        data);
1231                                    if (error) {
....
```

```
1237                                          return (error);
1238                                      }
1239
1240                                  *mbu_pri_fsm_state
1241                                     = MIP6_BU_PRI_FSM_STATE_RRREDO;
1242                              }
1243                              break;
```
───mip6_fsm.c

1203–1243 If a mobile node receives the MIP6_BU_PRI_FSM_EVENT_BRR event while it is
in the MIP6_BU_PRI_FSM_STATE_BOUND state, the node will resend a Binding Update
message to the requesting peer node.

   If the binding update list entry related to this event is for home registration, the
mip6_bu_pri_fsm_home_registration() is called to perform the home registration procedure. The state is changed to the MIP6_BU_PRI_FSM_STATE_WAITAR state.

   If the entry is for a correspondent node, the return routability procedure is
started   by   calling   the   mip6_bu_sec_fsm()   function   with   the
MIP6_BU_SEC_FSM_EVENT_START_RR   event.   The   state   is   changed   to
the MIP6_BU_PRI_FSM_STATE_RRREDO state.

Listing 5-457
───mip6_fsm.c
```
1245                          case MIP6_BU_PRI_FSM_EVENT_MOVEMENT:
```
  .... [See lines 636–677]
```
1292                              break;
1293
1294                          case MIP6_BU_PRI_FSM_EVENT_RETURNING_HOME:
```
  .... [See lines 681–722]
```
1341                              break;
1342
1343                          case MIP6_BU_PRI_FSM_EVENT_REVERSE_PACKET:
```
  .... [See lines 500–516]
```
1360                              break;
```
───mip6_fsm.c

1245–1341 The   procedure   when   a   mobile   node   receives   the
MIP6_BU_PRI_FSM_EVENT_MOVEMENT   event   or   the
MIP6_BU_PRI_FSM_EVENT_RETURNING_HOME event is same as the code for
the MIP6_BU_PRI_FSM_STATE_WAITA state implemented on lines 636–722.

1343–1360 The procedure for the MIP6_BU_PRI_FSM_EVENT_REVERSE_PACKET event is
the same procedure as for the MIP6_BU_PRI_FSM_STATE_RRREDO state implemented
on lines 500–516.

Listing 5-458
───mip6_fsm.c
```
1362                          case MIP6_BU_PRI_FSM_EVENT_REFRESH_TIMER:
```
  .... [See lines 1204–1242]
```
1402                              break;
```
───mip6_fsm.c

1362–1402 The behavior when a mobile node receives the `MIP6_BU_PRI_FSM_EVENT_REFRESH_TIMER` event is the same as the procedure when the node receives the `MIP6_BU_PRI_FSM_EVENT_BRR` event implemented on lines 1204–1242. The mobile node performs the home registration procedure for the home registration entry, or performs the return routability procedure for the entry of a correspondent node.

Listing 5-459

mip6_fsm.c

```
1404                    case MIP6_BU_PRI_FSM_EVENT_UNVERIFIED_HAO:
 .... [See lines 636–677]
1451                            break;
1452                    }
1453                    break;
1454
1455            default:
1456                    panic("the state of the primary fsm is unknown.");
1457            }
1458
1459            return (0);
1460    }
```

mip6_fsm.c

1404–1451 The `MIP6_BU_PRI_FSM_EVENT_UNVERIFIED_HAO` event indicates that a mobile node sends a packet with a Home Address option although the peer node does not have a binding cache entry for the mobile node. In this case, the mobile node needs to perform the registration procedure to create a proper binding cache entry on the peer node. The procedure is the same as the procedure for the `MIP6_BU_PRI_FSM_STATE_WAITA` state implemented on lines 636–677.

Initiate a Home Registration Procedure

The `mip6_bu_pri_fsm_home_registration()` is called when a mobile node needs to perform the home registration procedure.

Listing 5-460

mip6_fsm.c

```
1462    static int
1463    mip6_bu_pri_fsm_home_registration(mbu)
1464            struct mip6_bu *mbu;
1465    {
1466            struct mip6_ha *mha;
1467            int error;
....
1469            struct timeval mono_time;
....
1471
1472            /* sanity check. */
1473            if (mbu == NULL)
1474                    return (EINVAL);
....
1477            microtime(&mono_time);
```

mip6_fsm.c

1462–1464 This function calls the `mip6_home_registration2()`. The `mbu` parameter is a pointer to the instance of the `mip6_bu{}` structure which needs home registration.

Listing 5-461

```
1480                error = mip6_home_registration2(mbu);
1481                if (error) {
....
1485                        /* continue and try again. */
1486                }
1487
1488                if (mbu->mbu_retrans_count++ > MIP6_BU_MAX_BACKOFF) {
1489                        /*
1490                         * try another home agent.  if we have no alternative,
1491                         * set an unspecified address to trigger DHAAD
1492                         * procedure.
1493                         */
1494                        mha = hif_find_next_preferable_ha(mbu->mbu_hif,
1495                            &mbu->mbu_paddr);
1496                        if (mha != NULL)
1497                                mbu->mbu_paddr = mha->mha_addr;
1498                        else
1499                                mbu->mbu_paddr = in6addr_any;
1500                        mbu->mbu_retrans_count = 1;
1501                }
1502                mbu->mbu_retrans = mono_time.tv_sec + (1 << mbu->mbu_retrans_count);
1503
1504                return (error);
1505    }
```

1480–1486 The `mip6_home_registration2()` function will send a Binding Update message to the home agent of the mobile node of the binding update list entry.

1488–1501 If the mobile node did not receive a Binding Acknowledgment message after `MIP6_BU_MAX_BACKOFF` times retries (currently 7 retries), the node will try another home agent. The `hif_find_next_preferable_ha()` function returns the next candidate of a home agent. If there is no other candidate, the home agent address (`mbu_paddr`) is set to the unspecified address, which indicates the Dynamic Home Agent Address Discovery procedure is required.

1502 `mbu_retrans` is set to the time to send the next Binding Update message. The time is calculated using an exponential backoff algorithm.

Stop Timers of the Binding Update List Entry

The `mip6_bu_stop_timers()` function stops timers of the specified binding update list entry.

Listing 5-462

```
1754    void
1755    mip6_bu_stop_timers(mbu)
1756            struct mip6_bu *mbu;
1757    {
1758            if (mbu == NULL)
1759                    return;
```

```
1760
1761                    mbu->mbu_retrans = 0;
1762                    mbu->mbu_failure = 0;
1763        }
```

1754–1763 The function disables timer functions by setting the `mbu_retrans` and
`mbu_failure` variables to 0. These member variables indicate the time for some tasks
to be processed. These values are checked in the `mip6_bu_timer()` function and the
function does a proper task based on the state of the binding update list entry if these
values are not 0.

5.17.21   Secondary State Machine

The `mip6_bu_sec_fsm()` function is the entry point of the secondary state machine of a
binding update list entry.

Listing 5-463

```
1507    int
1508    mip6_bu_sec_fsm(mbu, event, data)
1509            struct mip6_bu *mbu;
1510            int event;
1511            void *data;
1512    {
1513            u_int8_t *mbu_sec_fsm_state;
1514            int error;
....
1516            struct timeval mono_time;
....
1518            struct ip6_mh_home_test *ip6mh;
1519            struct ip6_mh_careof_test *ip6mc;
```

1507–1511 The `mip6_bu_sec_fsm()` function has three parameters which are as the same
as the parameters for the `mip6_bu_pri_fsm()` function.

Listing 5-464

```
1530            mbu_sec_fsm_state = &mbu->mbu_sec_fsm_state;
1531
1532            /* set pointers. */
1533            ip6mh = (struct ip6_mh_home_test *)data;
1534            ip6mc = (struct ip6_mh_careof_test *)data;
```

1530 The `mbu_sec_fsm_state` pointer points to the `mbu_sec_fsm_state` variable which
indicates the status of the secondary state machine. This variable is used as a shortcut to
the `mbu_sec_fsm_state` variable.

1533–1534 In the secondary state machine, the `data` pointer may point to a Home Test
message or a Care-of Test message. The `ip6mh` and the `ip6mc` variables point to the
`data` parameter.

MIP6_BU_SEC_FSM_STATE_START State

Lines 1539–1576 process events when the secondary state machine is in the
MIP6_BU_SEC_FSM_STATE_START state.

Listing 5-465
```
                                                                    mip6_fsm.c
1536              error = 0;
1537
1538              switch (*mbu_sec_fsm_state) {
1539              case MIP6_BU_SEC_FSM_STATE_START:
1540                      switch (event) {
1541                      case MIP6_BU_SEC_FSM_EVENT_START_RR:
1542                              /*
1543                               * Send HoTI,
1544                               * Send CoTI,
1545                               * Start retransmission timer,
1546                               * Steart failure timer
1547                               */
1548                              if (mip6_bu_send_hoti(mbu) != 0)
1549                                      break;
1550                              if (mip6_bu_send_coti(mbu) != 0)
1551                                      break;
1552                              mbu->mbu_retrans
1553                                  = mono_time.tv_sec + MIP6_HOT_TIMEOUT;
1554                              mbu->mbu_failure
1555                                  = mono_time.tv_sec + MIP6_HOT_TIMEOUT * 5;
       /* XXX */
1556                              *mbu_sec_fsm_state = MIP6_BU_SEC_FSM_STATE_WAITHC;
1557
1558                              break;
                                                                    mip6_fsm.c
```
— Line 1555 is broken here for layout reasons. However, it is a single line of code.

1541–1558 If a mobile node receives the MIP6_BU_SEC_FSM_EVENT_START_RR event
while it is in the MIP6_BU_SEC_FSM_STATE_START state, the node starts the return
routability procedure. The mip6_bu_send_hoti() and the mip6_bu_send_coti()
functions are called to send a Home Test Init message and a Care-of Test Init message.
The mbu_retrans variable is set to MIP6_HOT_TIMEOUT seconds (currently 5 seconds)
to trigger retransmission in case the message is lost. The mbu_failure variable indicates
the failure timeout is set here; however, the variable is not used. The next state is changed
to the MIP6_BU_SEC_FSM_STATE_WAITHC state.

Listing 5-466
```
                                                                    mip6_fsm.c
1560                      case MIP6_BU_SEC_FSM_EVENT_START_HOME_RR:
1561                              /*
1562                               * Send HoTI,
1563                               * Start retransmission timer,
1564                               * Steart failure timer
1565                               */
1566                              if (mip6_bu_send_hoti(mbu) != 0)
1567                                      break;
1568                              mbu->mbu_retrans
1569                                  = mono_time.tv_sec + MIP6_HOT_TIMEOUT;
1570                              mbu->mbu_failure
1571                                  = mono_time.tv_sec + MIP6_HOT_TIMEOUT * 5;
       /* XXX */
1572                              *mbu_sec_fsm_state = MIP6_BU_SEC_FSM_STATE_WAITH;
```

```
1573
1574                                        break;
1575                                }
1576                        break;
```

– Line 1571 is broken here for layout reasons. However, it is a single line of code.

1560–1574 If a mobile node receives the MIP6_BU_SEC_FSM_EVENT_START_HOME_RR event while it is in the MIP6_BU_SEC_FSM_STATE_START state, the node starts the returning home procedure. The node calls the mip6_bu_send_hoti() function to send a Home Test Init message. A Care-of Test Init message does not need to be sent since the home address and the care-of address are the same at home. The mbu_retrans variable is set to 5 seconds after the current time for retransmission. The state is changed to the MIP6_BU_SEC_FSM_STATE_WAITH state.

MIP6_BU_SEC_FSM_STATE_WAITHC State

Lines 1578–1634 process events when the secondary state machine is in the MIP6_BU_SEC_FSM_STATE_WAITHC state.

Listing 5-467

mip6_fsm.c
```
1578                case MIP6_BU_SEC_FSM_STATE_WAITHC:
1579                        switch (event) {
1580                        case MIP6_BU_SEC_FSM_EVENT_HOT:
1581                                /*
1582                                 * Store token, nonce index.
1583                                 */
1584                                /* XXX */
1585                                mbu->mbu_home_nonce_index
1586                                        = htons(ip6mh->ip6mhht_nonce_index);
1587                                bcopy(ip6mh->ip6mhht_keygen8, mbu->mbu_home_token,
1588                                        sizeof(ip6mh->ip6mhht_keygen8));
1589
1590                                *mbu_sec_fsm_state = MIP6_BU_SEC_FSM_STATE_WAITC;
1591
1592                                break;
```
mip6_fsm.c

1578–1592 If a mobile node receives a Home Test message, the MIP6_BU_SEC_FSM_EVENT_HOT event is input. The home nonce index (ip6mhht_nonce_index) and the home keygen token (ip6mhht_keygen8) contained in the received message are stored in the mbu_home_nouce_index and the mbu_home_token variables. The state is changed to the MIP6_BU_SEC_FSM_STATE_WAITC state.

Listing 5-468

mip6_fsm.c
```
1594                        case MIP6_BU_SEC_FSM_EVENT_COT:
1595                                /*
1596                                 * Store token, nonce index.
1597                                 */
1598                                /* XXX */
1599                                mbu->mbu_careof_nonce_index
1600                                        = htons(ip6mc->ip6mhct_nonce_index);
1601                                bcopy(ip6mc->ip6mhct_keygen8, mbu->mbu_careof_token,
1602                                        sizeof(ip6mc->ip6mhct_keygen8));
```

```
1603
1604                          *mbu_sec_fsm_state = MIP6_BU_SEC_FSM_STATE_WAITH;
1605                          break;
```
——mip6_fsm.c

1594–1605 If a mobile node receives a Care-of Test message, the
MIP6_BU_SEC_FSM_EVENT_COT is input. The care-of nonce index
(ip6mhct_nonce_index) and the care-of keygen token (ip6mhct_keygen8) contained in the received message are stored in the mbu_careof_nonce_index
and the mbu_careof_token variables, respectively. The state is changed to the
MIP6_BU_SEC_FSM_STATE_WAITH state.

Listing 5-469
——mip6_fsm.c
```
1607                  case MIP6_BU_SEC_FSM_EVENT_STOP_RR:
1608                          /*
1609                           * Stop timers.
1610                           */
1611                          mip6_bu_stop_timers(mbu);
1612
1613                          *mbu_sec_fsm_state = MIP6_BU_SEC_FSM_STATE_START;
1614
1615                          break;
```
——mip6_fsm.c

1607–1615 If a mobile node cancels the running return routability procedure, the
MIP6_BU_SEC_FSM_EVENT_STOP_RR event is input. The mip6_bu_stop_timers()
function is called to stop all timers related to the binding update list entry and the state is
changed to the MIP6_BU_SEC_FSM_STATE_START state.

Listing 5-470
——mip6_fsm.c
```
1617                  case MIP6_BU_SEC_FSM_EVENT_RETRANS_TIMER:
1618                          /*

1620                           * Send CoTI,
1621                           * Start retransmission timer.
1622                           */
1623                          if (mip6_bu_send_hoti(mbu) != 0)
1624                                  break;
1625                          if (mip6_bu_send_coti(mbu) != 0)
1626                                  break;
1627                          mbu->mbu_retrans
1628                              = mono_time.tv_sec + MIP6_HOT_TIMEOUT;
1629
1630                          *mbu_sec_fsm_state = MIP6_BU_SEC_FSM_STATE_WAITHC;
1631
1632                          break;
1633                  }
1634                  break;
```
——mip6_fsm.c

1617–1630 If a mobile node does not receive either a Home Test message or a Care-
of Test message while it is in the MIP6_BU_SEC_FSM_STATE_WAITHC state, the
MIP6_BU_SEC_FSM_EVENT_RETRANS_TIMER event is input. The mobile node
resends a Home Test message or a Care-of Test message using the
mip6_bu_send_hoti() and the mip6_bu_send_coti() functions. The retransmission timer is set to 5 seconds (MIP6_HOT_TIMEOUT) after the current time. Note that

the retransmission interval is not compliant with the specification. The specification says a mobile node needs to use an exponential backoff when resending these messages.

MIP6_BU_SEC_FSM_STATE_WAITH State

Lines 1636–1690 process events when the secondary state machine is in the MIP6_BU_SEC_FSM_STATE_WAITH state.

Listing 5-471

```
                                                              mip6_fsm.c
1636            case MIP6_BU_SEC_FSM_STATE_WAITH:
1637                switch (event) {
1638                case MIP6_BU_SEC_FSM_EVENT_HOT:
1639                    /*
1640                     * Store token and nonce index,
1641                     * Stop timers,
1642                     * RR done.
1643                     */
1644                    mbu->mbu_home_nonce_index
1645                        = htons(ip6mh->ip6mhht_nonce_index);
1646                    bcopy(ip6mh->ip6mhht_keygen8, mbu->mbu_home_token,
1647                        sizeof(ip6mh->ip6mhht_keygen8));
1648
1649                    mip6_bu_stop_timers(mbu);
1650
1651                    error = mip6_bu_pri_fsm(mbu,
1652                        MIP6_BU_PRI_FSM_EVENT_RR_DONE,
1653                        data);
1654                    if (error) {
....
1659                        return (error);
1660                    }
1661
1662                    *mbu_sec_fsm_state = MIP6_BU_SEC_FSM_STATE_START;
1663
1664                    break;
                                                              mip6_fsm.c
```

1636–1649 When a mobile node receives a Home Test message, the MIP6_BU_SEC_FSM_EVENT_HOT event is input. The mobile node copies the home nonce index (ip6mhht_nonce_index) and the home keygen token (ip6mhht_keygen8) contained in the message to the mbu_home_nonce_index and the mbu_home_token variables of the binding update list entry related to the message. The mobile node stops all the timers and sends the MIP6_BU_PRI_FSM_EVENT_RR_DONE event to the primary state machine of the binding update list entry to notify it of the completion of the return routability procedure, since the node has received both care-of and home tokens from the peer node. The primary state machine will initiate the registration procedure using the tokens.

The state is reset to the MIP6_BU_SEC_FSM_STATE_START state.

Listing 5-472

```
                                                              mip6_fsm.c
1666            case MIP6_BU_SEC_FSM_EVENT_STOP_RR:
1667                /*
1668                 * Stop timers.
```

```
1669                                 */
1670                                 mip6_bu_stop_timers(mbu);
1671
1672                                 *mbu_sec_fsm_state = MIP6_BU_SEC_FSM_STATE_START;
1673
1674                                 break;
                                                                        mip6_fsm.c
```

1666–1674 When a mobile node receives the `MIP6_BU_SEC_FSM_EVENT_STOP_RR` event, the running return routability procedure is stopped. The code is the same code as lines 1607–1615.

Listing 5-473

```
                                                                        mip6_fsm.c
1676                         case MIP6_BU_SEC_FSM_EVENT_RETRANS_TIMER:
1677                             /*
1678                              * Send HoTI,
1679                              * Start retransmission timer.
1680                              */
1681                             if (mip6_bu_send_hoti(mbu) != 0)
1682                                     break;
1683                             mbu->mbu_retrans
1684                                 = mono_time.tv_sec + MIP6_HOT_TIMEOUT;
1685
1686                             *mbu_sec_fsm_state = MIP6_BU_SEC_FSM_STATE_WAITH;
1687
1688                             break;
1689                         }
1690                         break;
                                                                        mip6_fsm.c
```

1676–1690 If a mobile node does not receive a Home Test message in 5 seconds after sending a Home Test Init message, the `MIP6_BU_SEC_FSM_EVENT_RETRANS_TIMER` event is input. The mobile node resends a Home Test message using the `mip6_bu_send_hoti()` function and resets the next retransmission timer. The state is unchanged.

`MIP6_BU_SEC_FSM_STATE_WAITC` State

Lines 1692–1746 process events when the secondary state machine is in the `MIP6_BU_SEC_FSM_STATE_WAITC` state.

Listing 5-474

```
                                                                        mip6_fsm.c
1692             case MIP6_BU_SEC_FSM_STATE_WAITC:
1693                 switch (event) {
1694                 case MIP6_BU_SEC_FSM_EVENT_COT:
1695                     /*
1696                      * Store token and nonce index,
1697                      * Stop timers,
1698                      * RR done.
1699                      */
1700                     mbu->mbu_careof_nonce_index
1701                         = htons(ip6mc->ip6mhct_nonce_index);
1702                     bcopy(ip6mc->ip6mhct_keygen8, mbu->mbu_careof_token,
1703                         sizeof(ip6mc->ip6mhct_keygen8));
1704
1705                     mip6_bu_stop_timers(mbu);
1706
```

```
1707                             error = mip6_bu_pri_fsm(mbu,
1708                                 MIP6_BU_PRI_FSM_EVENT_RR_DONE,
1709                                 data);
1710                             if (error) {
....
1715                                     return (error);
1716                             }
1717
1718                             *mbu_sec_fsm_state = MIP6_BU_SEC_FSM_STATE_START;
1719
1720                             break;
```
──mip6_fsm.c

1692–1720 If a mobile node receives a Care-of Test message, the `MIP6_BU_SEC_FSM_STATE_WAITC` event is input. If the mobile node is in the `MIP6_BU_SEC_FSM_STATE_WAITC` state, the node copies the care-of nonce index (`ip6mhct_nonce_index`) and the care-of keygen token (`ip6mhct_keygen8`) to the `mbu_careof_nonce_index` and the `mbu_careof_token` variables respectively. The node stops the timers related to the binding update list entry and sends the `MIP6_BU_PRI_FSM_EVENT_RR_DONE` event to notify the primary state machine that the return routability procedure has been completed. The state is changed to the `MIP6_BU_SEC_FSM_STATE_START` state.

Listing 5-475
──mip6_fsm.c
```
1722                     case MIP6_BU_SEC_FSM_EVENT_STOP_RR:
1723                             /*
1724                              * Stop timers.
1725                              */
1726                             mip6_bu_stop_timers(mbu);
1727
1728                             *mbu_sec_fsm_state = MIP6_BU_SEC_FSM_STATE_START;
1729
1730                             break;
```
──mip6_fsm.c

1722–1730 If a mobile node cancels the current running return routability procedure, the `MIP6_BU_SEC_FSM_EVENT_STOP_RR` event is input. The code is the same code as in lines 1607–1615.

Listing 5-476
──mip6_fsm.c
```
1732                     case MIP6_BU_SEC_FSM_EVENT_RETRANS_TIMER:
1733                             /*
1734                              * Send CoTI,
1735                              * Start retransmission timer.
1736                              */
1737                             if (mip6_bu_send_coti(mbu) != 0)
1738                                     break;
1739                             mbu->mbu_retrans
1740                                 = mono_time.tv_sec + MIP6_HOT_TIMEOUT;
1741
1742                             *mbu_sec_fsm_state = MIP6_BU_SEC_FSM_STATE_WAITC;
1743
1744                             break;
1745                     }
```

```
1746                    break;
1747
1748            default:
1749                    panic("the state of the secondary fsm is unknown.");
1750            }
1751            return (0);
1752    }
```
——mip6_fsm.c

1732–1744 If a mobile node does not receive a Care-of Test message in 5 seconds after sending a Care-of Test Init message, the node resends a Care-of Test Init message. The code is almost the same as the code in lines 1676–1690.

5.17.22 Virtual Home Interface

A mobile node has a virtual interface which represents its home network. The definition of the virtual interface was discussed in Section 5.11.32. The virtual home interface keeps the current location, the home address of the mobile node and prefix information. The interface is also used as an output routine from the mobile node to correspondent nodes when the node is using the bi-directional tunneling mechanism.

Initialization of the Interface

The hifattach() function is the initialization function of the virtual home interface which is defined as the hif_softc{} structure.

Listing 5-477
——if_hif.c

```
178     void
179     hifattach(dummy)
....
181             void *dummy;
....
185     {
186             struct hif_softc *sc;
187             int i;
188
189             LIST_INIT(&hif_softc_list);
190
191             sc = malloc(NHIF * sizeof(struct hif_softc), M_DEVBUF, M_WAIT);
192             bzero(sc, NHIF * sizeof(struct hif_softc));
193             for (i = 0 ; i < NHIF; sc++, i++) {
....
197                     sc->hif_if.if_name = "hif";
198                     sc->hif_if.if_unit = i;
....
200                     sc->hif_if.if_flags = IFF_MULTICAST | IFF_SIMPLEX;
201                     sc->hif_if.if_mtu = HIF_MTU;
202                     sc->hif_if.if_ioctl = hif_ioctl;
203                     sc->hif_if.if_output = hif_output;
204                     sc->hif_if.if_type = IFT_HIF;
....
209                     IFQ_SET_MAXLEN(&sc->hif_if.if_snd, ifqmaxlen);
210                     IFQ_SET_READY(&sc->hif_if.if_snd);
....
```

```
212                         if_attach(&sc->hif_if);
      ....
218                         bpfattach(&sc->hif_if, DLT_NULL, sizeof(u_int));
```
                                                                    ─── if_hif.c

178–181 The basic procedure is no different from the initialization code of other network
interfaces. We only discuss some specific parameters to the `hif_softc{}` structure here.
The `HIF_MTU` macro is defined as 1280, which is the minimum MTU of IPv6 packets. This
interface is used as an output function for packets which are tunneled from a mobile node
to a home agent. To avoid the Path MTU discovery for this tunnel connection between a
mobile node and a home agent, the implementation limits the MTU to the minimum size.
The `IFT_HIF` macro is a new type number which indicates the virtual home interface. The
virtual home interface sometimes requires special care, since it is not a normal network
interface. Assigning a new type number makes it easy to identify the virtual home interface
when we need to perform specific tasks.

Listing 5-478
                                                                    ─── if_hif.c

```
224                         sc->hif_location = HIF_LOCATION_UNKNOWN;
225                         sc->hif_coa_ifa = NULL;
      ....
230                         /* binding update list and home agent list. */
231                         LIST_INIT(&sc->hif_bu_list);
232                         LIST_INIT(&sc->hif_prefix_list_home);
233                         LIST_INIT(&sc->hif_prefix_list_foreign);
234
235                         /* DHAAD related. */
236                         sc->hif_dhaad_id = mip6_dhaad_id++;
237                         sc->hif_dhaad_lastsent = 0;
238                         sc->hif_dhaad_count = 0;
239
240                         /* Mobile Prefix Solicitation. */
241                         sc->hif_mps_id = mip6_mps_id++;
242                         sc->hif_mps_lastsent = 0;
243
244                         sc->hif_ifid = in6addr_any;
245
246                         /* create hif_softc list */
247                         LIST_INSERT_HEAD(&hif_softc_list, sc, hif_entry);
248             }
249     }
```
                                                                    ─── if_hif.c

224–225 The initial location is set to `HIF_LOCATION_UNKNOWN`. The location is determined
when a mobile node receives the first Router Advertisement message. The care-of address
is also undefined until the mobile node configures least one address.

231–233 The list of binding update list entries (`hif_bu_list`) related to this home network,
the list of home prefixes (`hif_prefix_list_home`) and the list of foreign prefixes
(`hif_prefix_list_foreign`) are initialized.

236–242 The `mip6_dhaad_id` and the `mip6_mps_id` are unique identifiers which are used
when sending a Dynamic Home Agent Address Discovery request message and a Mobile
Prefix Solicitation message, respectively. These variables are managed as global variables
and are incremented by 1 every time they are used to avoid duplication of identifiers.

TABLE 5-42

Name	Description
SIOCAHOMEPREFIX_HIF	Adds one home prefix information entry.
SIOCAHOMEAGENT_HIF	Adds one home agent information entry.

I/O control commands for `hif_softc{}`.

244 The `hif_ifid` variable is used as the interface identifier part of home addresses of this virtual home network. The value is determined when it is first used.

I/O Control of the Virtual Home Interface

The `hif_ioctl()` function manages commands sent by the `ioctl()` system call.

Listing 5-479

```
                                                                        if_hif.c
251     int
252     hif_ioctl(ifp, cmd, data)
253             struct ifnet *ifp;
254             u_long cmd;
255             caddr_t data;
256     {
257             int s;
258             struct hif_softc *sc = (struct hif_softc *)ifp;
259             struct hif_ifreq *hifr = (struct hif_ifreq *)data;
260             struct ifreq *ifr = (struct ifreq *)data;
261             int error = 0;
                                                                        if_hif.c
```

251–255 The `hif_ioctl()` function has three parameters. The `ifp` parameter is a pointer to the virtual home interface to be controlled. The `cmd` and `data` parameters are the command number and pointer to the instance of the `hif_ifreq{}` structure which keeps related data to the command.

There are two commands currently used for I/O control of the `hif_softc{}` structure. The list of commands are shown in Table 5-42.

Listing 5-480

```
                                                                        if_hif.c
269             switch(cmd) {
    ....
294             case SIOCAHOMEPREFIX_HIF:
295                     error = hif_prefix_list_update_withprefix(sc, data);
296                     break;
    ....
337             case SIOCAHOMEAGENT_HIF:
338                     error = hif_prefix_list_update_withhaaddr(sc, data);
339                     break;
    ....
404
405             default:
406                     error = EINVAL;
407                     break;
408             }
```

```
409
410    hif_ioctl_done:
411
412           splx(s);
413
414           return (error);
415    }
```

294–339 The `hif_prefix_list_update_withprefix()` function adds the home prefix information passed from the user space. The `hif_prefix_list_update_withhaaddr()` function adds the home agent information passed from the user space.

Add Home Prefix Information

The `hif_prefix_list_update_withprefix()` function adds home prefix information to a virtual home network.

Listing 5-481

if_hif.c

```
513    static int
514    hif_prefix_list_update_withprefix(sc, data)
515           struct hif_softc *sc;
516           caddr_t data;
517    {
518           struct hif_ifreq *hifr = (struct hif_ifreq *)data;
519           struct mip6_prefix *nmpfx, *mpfx;
520           struct hif_softc *hif;
521           int error = 0;
```
if_hif.c

513–516 The function adds home prefix information to the virtual home network specified as the `sc` parameter with the prefix information passed as the `data` parameter.

Listing 5-482

if_hif.c

```
526           nmpfx = &hifr->ifr_ifru.ifr_mpfx;
527
528           mpfx = mip6_prefix_list_find_withprefix(&nmpfx->mpfx_prefix,
529               nmpfx->mpfx_prefixlen);
530           if (mpfx == NULL) {
531                  mpfx = mip6_prefix_create(&nmpfx->mpfx_prefix,
532                      nmpfx->mpfx_prefixlen, nmpfx->mpfx_vltime,
533                      nmpfx->mpfx_pltime);
534                  if (mpfx == NULL) {
....
538                         return (ENOMEM);
539                  }
540                  error = mip6_prefix_list_insert(&mip6_prefix_list, mpfx);
541                  if (error) {
542                         return (error);
543                  }
```
if_hif.c

526–529 The prefix information is stored in the `ifr_mpfx` variable of the `hif_ifreq{}` structure. If a mobile node does not have the home prefix, it creates a new `mip6_prefix{}` instance using the `mip6_prefix_create()` function and inserts the new entry in the global prefix list by the `mip6_prefix_list_insert()` function.

Listing 5-483

——`if_hif.c`

```
545                        for (hif = LIST_FIRST(&hif_softc_list); hif;
546                             hif = LIST_NEXT(hif, hif_entry)) {
547                            if (hif == sc)
548                                hif_prefix_list_insert_withmpfx(
549                                    &hif->hif_prefix_list_home, mpfx);
550                            else
551                                hif_prefix_list_insert_withmpfx(
552                                    &hif->hif_prefix_list_foreign, mpfx);
553                        }
554                    }
555
556                    mip6_prefix_update_lifetime(mpfx, nmpfx->mpfx_vltime,
557                        nmpfx->mpfx_pltime);
558
559                    return (0);
560                }
```

——`if_hif.c`

545–553 The newly created prefix is a home prefix of the virtual home interface specified as the `sc` parameter. If a mobile node has more than two virtual home networks, the new prefix information can be considered foreign prefix information for the home interface not specified as the `sc` parameter. The new prefix is added to `hif_prefix_list_home`, which keeps all home prefix information of the specified virtual home interface by the `hif_prefix_list_insert_withmpfx()` function. For the rest of virtual home interfaces, the new prefix is added to `hif_prefix_list_foreign`, which is a list of foreign prefix information entries.

556–557 If the mobile node already has the same prefix information, the node updates the lifetime using the `mip6_prefix_update_lifetime()` function.

Add Home Agent Information

The `hif_prefix_list_update_withhaaddr()` function adds home agent information to a virtual home network.

Listing 5-484

——`if_hif.c`

```
562    static int
563    hif_prefix_list_update_withhaaddr(sc, data)
564        struct hif_softc *sc;
565        caddr_t data;
566    {
567            struct hif_ifreq *hifr = (struct hif_ifreq *)data;
568            struct mip6_ha *nmha = (struct mip6_ha *)data;
569            struct mip6_ha *mha;
570            struct in6_addr prefix;
571            struct mip6_prefix *mpfx;
572            struct hif_softc *hif;
573            int error = 0;
....
575            struct timeval mono_time;
```

——`if_hif.c`

562–565 The function adds the home agent information specified by the `data` parameter to the virtual home interface specified as the `sc` parameter. Apparently, the initialization on line 568 is wrong. `nmha` will be overwritten properly later.

Listing 5-485

_____if_hif.c

```
585                nmha = &hifr->ifr_ifru.ifr_mha;
586                if (IN6_IS_ADDR_UNSPECIFIED(&nmha->mha_addr)
587                    ||IN6_IS_ADDR_LOOPBACK(&nmha->mha_addr)
588                    ||IN6_IS_ADDR_LINKLOCAL(&nmha->mha_addr)
589                    || IN6_IS_ADDR_SITELOCAL(&nmha->mha_addr))
590                        return (EINVAL);
591
592                mha = mip6_ha_list_find_withaddr(&mip6_ha_list, &nmha->mha_addr);
593                if (mha == NULL) {
594                        mha = mip6_ha_create(&nmha->mha_addr, nmha->mha_flags,
595                            nmha->mha_pref, 0);
596                        if (mha == NULL) {
....
600                                return (ENOMEM);
601                        }
602                        mip6_ha_list_insert(&mip6_ha_list, mha);
603                }
604
605                mha->mha_addr = nmha->mha_addr;
606                mha->mha_flags = nmha->mha_flags;
607                mip6_ha_update_lifetime(mha, 0);
```

_____if_hif.c

585–590 The home agent information is stored in the `ifr_mha` variable of the `hif_ifreq{}` structure. If the specified address of the home agent is not suitable, the processing is aborted.

592–603 If a mobile node does not have the same home agent information as that passed from the user space, it creates a new `mip6_ha{}` instance using the `mip6_ha_create()` function and inserts the newly created entry in the global home agent information list.

604–607 If the mobile node already has the same home agent information, its flags and lifetime are updated. The lifetime is set to infinite when both creating a new entry or updating an existing entry. The actual lifetime is set when the mobile node receives a Router Advertisement message from the home agent. Until then, the mobile node assumes that the entry has an infinite lifetime.

Listing 5-486

_____if_hif.c

```
609                /* add mip6_prefix, if needed. */
610                mpfx = mip6_prefix_list_find_withprefix(&mha->mha_addr, 64 /* XXX */);
611                if (mpfx == NULL) {
612                        bzero(&prefix, sizeof(prefix));
613                        prefix.s6_addr32[0] = mha->mha_addr.s6_addr32[0];
614                        prefix.s6_addr32[1] = mha->mha_addr.s6_addr32[1];
615                        mpfx = mip6_prefix_create(&prefix, 64 /* XXX */,
616                            65535 /* XXX */, 0);
617                        if (mpfx == NULL)
618                                return (ENOMEM);
```

```
619                          error = mip6_prefix_list_insert(&mip6_prefix_list, mpfx);
620                          if (error)
621                                  return (error);
622                          for (hif = LIST_FIRST(&hif_softc_list); hif;
623                              hif = LIST_NEXT(hif, hif_entry)) {
624                                  if (sc == hif)
625                                          hif_prefix_list_insert_withmpfx(
626                                                  &sc->hif_prefix_list_home, mpfx);
627                                  else
628                                          hif_prefix_list_insert_withmpfx(
629                                                  &sc->hif_prefix_list_foreign, mpfx);
630                          }
631                  }
632                  mip6_prefix_ha_list_insert(&mpfx->mpfx_ha_list, mha);
633
634                  return (0);
635          }
```
─── if_hif.c

610–631 The prefix part of the home agent address means a home prefix. If the mobile node does not have the home prefix, it creates a new `mip6_prefix{}` instance based on the address of the home agent.

632 The home agent entry is considered an advertising router of the home prefix. The `mip6_prefix_ha_list_insert()` function adds a pointer to the home agent information from the home prefix information.

Create the `hif_prefix{}` Structure with the `mip6_prefix{}` Structure

The `hif_prefix_list_insert_withmpfx()` function inserts the specified prefix entry into the prefix list kept in a virtual home network structure.

Listing 5-487
─── if_hif.c
```
637      struct hif_prefix *
638      hif_prefix_list_insert_withmpfx(hif_prefix_list, mpfx)
639              struct hif_prefix_list *hif_prefix_list;
640              struct mip6_prefix *mpfx;
641      {
642              struct hif_prefix *hpfx;
643
644              if ((hif_prefix_list == NULL) || (mpfx == NULL))
645                      return (NULL);
646
647              hpfx = hif_prefix_list_find_withmpfx(hif_prefix_list, mpfx);
648              if (hpfx != NULL)
649                      return (hpfx);
650
651              MALLOC(hpfx, struct hif_prefix *, sizeof(struct hif_prefix), M_TEMP,
652                  M_NOWAIT);
653              if (hpfx == NULL) {
....
656                      return (NULL);
657              }
658              hpfx->hpfx_mpfx = mpfx;
659              LIST_INSERT_HEAD(hif_prefix_list, hpfx, hpfx_entry);
660
661              return (hpfx);
662      }
```
─── if_hif.c

637–640 The `hif_prefix_list_insert_withmpfx()` function creates a new `hif_prefix{}` instance which points to the `mip6_prefix{}` instance specified by the `mpfx` parameter and inserts the newly created entry into the prefix list specified by the `hif_prefix_list` parameter.

647–659 If `hif_prefix_list`, which is a list of the `hif_prefix{}` instances, does not contain the prefix information specified by the `mpfx` parameter, a mobile node allocates memory space for the new `hif_prefix{}` instance. If the allocation succeeds, the prefix information specified as the `mpfx` parameter is copied to the `hpfx_mpfx` variable. The new entry is inserted into the `hif_prefix_list` list.

Listing 5-488

```
                                                            ─if_hif.c
664     void
665     hif_prefix_list_remove(hpfx_list, hpfx)
666             struct hif_prefix_list *hpfx_list;
667             struct hif_prefix *hpfx;
668     {
669             if ((hpfx_list == NULL) || (hpfx == NULL))
670                     return;
671
672             LIST_REMOVE(hpfx, hpfx_entry);
673             FREE(hpfx, M_TEMP);
674     }
                                                            ─if_hif.c
```

664–674 The `hif_prefix_list_remove()` function removes the pointer to the `hif_prefix{}` instance from the list specified by the first parameter and releases the memory space allocated for the `hif_prefix{}` instance.

Listing 5-489

```
                                                            ─if_hif.c
676     struct hif_prefix *
677     hif_prefix_list_find_withprefix(hif_prefix_list, prefix, prefixlen)
678             struct hif_prefix_list *hif_prefix_list;
679             struct in6_addr *prefix;
680             int prefixlen;
681     {
682             struct hif_prefix *hpfx;
683             struct mip6_prefix *mpfx;
684
685             for (hpfx = LIST_FIRST(hif_prefix_list); hpfx;
686                 hpfx = LIST_NEXT(hpfx, hpfx_entry)) {
687                     mpfx = hpfx->hpfx_mpfx;
688                     if (in6_are_prefix_equal(prefix, &mpfx->mpfx_prefix,
689                             prefixlen)
690                         && (prefixlen == mpfx->mpfx_prefixlen)) {
691                             /* found. */
692                             return (hpfx);
693                     }
694             }
695             /* not found. */
696             return (NULL);
697     }
                                                            ─if_hif.c
```

676–696 The `hif_prefix_list_find_withprefix()` function searches for a `hif_prefix{}` instance which has the prefix information specified by the second and third parameters from the list specified by the first parameter. Note that the `hif_prefix{}` structure itself does not include prefix information. It has a pointer to the related `mip6_prefix{}` instance as described in Figure 5-45 (on page 564). If the list specified as the first parameter contains the `hif_prefix{}` instance whose `mip6_prefix{}` instance has the same prefix information specified by the second and third parameters, the function returns the pointer to the `hif_prefix{}` instance.

Listing 5-490

if_hif.c

```
699     struct hif_prefix *
700     hif_prefix_list_find_withhaaddr(hif_prefix_list, haaddr)
701             struct hif_prefix_list *hif_prefix_list;
702             struct in6_addr *haaddr;
703     {
704             struct hif_prefix *hpfx;
705             struct mip6_prefix *mpfx;
706             struct mip6_prefix_ha *mpfxha;
707             struct mip6_ha *mha;
708
709             for (hpfx = LIST_FIRST(hif_prefix_list); hpfx;
710                 hpfx = LIST_NEXT(hpfx, hpfx_entry)) {
711                     mpfx = hpfx->hpfx_mpfx;
712                     for (mpfxha = LIST_FIRST(&mpfx->mpfx_ha_list); mpfxha;
713                         mpfxha = LIST_NEXT(mpfxha, mpfxha_entry)) {
714                             mha = mpfxha->mpfxha_mha;
715                             if (IN6_ARE_ADDR_EQUAL(&mha->mha_addr, haaddr))
716                                     return (hpfx);
717                     }
718             }
719             /* not found. */
720             return (NULL);
721     }
```

if_hif.c

699–720 The `hif_prefix_list_find_withhaaddr()` function performs tasks similar to the `hif_prefix_list_find_withprefix()` function. This function finds a `hif_prefix{}` instance which has the home agent address specified by the second parameter. Each `mip6_prefix{}` structure points to the home agent information as described in Figure 5-45. The function checks all `mip6_prefix{}` instances to which instances from `hif_prefix{}` point and compares the related home agent information to the address specified by the second parameter.

Listing 5-491

if_hif.c

```
723     struct hif_prefix *
724     hif_prefix_list_find_withmpfx(hif_prefix_list, mpfx)
725             struct hif_prefix_list *hif_prefix_list;
726             struct mip6_prefix *mpfx;
727     {
728             struct hif_prefix *hpfx;
729
730             for (hpfx = LIST_FIRST(hif_prefix_list); hpfx;
731                 hpfx = LIST_NEXT(hpfx, hpfx_entry)) {
```

```
732                      if (hpfx->hpfx_mpfx == mpfx)
733                              return (hpfx);
734              }
735              /* not found. */
736              return (NULL);
737      }
```
——if_hif.c

723–737 The `hif_prefix_list_find_withmpfx()` function searches for an `hif_prefix{}` structure which has the `mip6_prefix{}` instance specified by the `mpfx` pointer.

Listing 5-492
——if_hif.c

```
739     static struct hif_prefix *
740     hif_prefix_list_find_withmha(hpfx_list, mha)
741             struct hif_prefix_list *hpfx_list;
742             struct mip6_ha *mha;
743     {
744             struct hif_prefix *hpfx;
745             struct mip6_prefix *mpfx;
746             struct mip6_prefix_ha *mpfxha;
747
748             for (hpfx = LIST_FIRST(hpfx_list); hpfx;
749                 hpfx = LIST_NEXT(hpfx, hpfx_entry)) {
750                     mpfx = hpfx->hpfx_mpfx;
751                     for (mpfxha = LIST_FIRST(&mpfx->mpfx_ha_list); mpfxha;
752                         mpfxha = LIST_NEXT(mpfxha, mpfxha_entry)) {
753                             if (mpfxha->mpfxha_mha == mha)
754                                     return (hpfx);
755                     }
756             }
757             /* not found. */
758             return (NULL);
759     }
```
——if_hif.c

739–759 The `hif_prefix_list_find_withmha()` function searches for an `hif_prefix{}` instance for which the `mip6_prefix{}` instance has a pointer to the home agent information which is the same as that specified by the `mha` pointer.

Find the Preferred Home Agent Information

The `hif_find_preferable_ha()` function returns a pointer to the `mip6_ha{}` instance whose preference is highest.

Listing 5-493
——if_hif.c

```
435     struct mip6_ha *
436     hif_find_preferable_ha(hif)
437             struct hif_softc *hif;
438     {
439             struct mip6_ha *mha;
440
441             /*
442              * we assume mip6_ha_list is ordered by a preference value.
443              */
444             for (mha = TAILQ_FIRST(&mip6_ha_list); mha;
```

```
445                mha = TAILQ_NEXT(mha, mha_entry)) {
446                    if (!hif_prefix_list_find_withmha(&hif->hif_prefix_list_home,
447                        mha))
448                            continue;
449                    if (IN6_IS_ADDR_LINKLOCAL(&mha->mha_addr))
450                            continue;
451                    /* return the entry we have found first. */
452                    return (mha);
453                }
454            /* not found. */
455            return (NULL);
456    }
```
—— if_hif.c

435–437 The `hif` parameter is a pointer to the virtual home interface to which the home agent belongs.

444–453 The global list (`mip6_ha_list`) of `mip6_ha{}` instances is ordered by the preference value of each entry. This function checks each `mip6_ha{}` instance listed in the `mip6_ha_list` from the head of the list. If an `mip6_ha{}` instance is a home agent of a certain virtual home network, one of the home prefixes must have a pointer to the `mip6_ha{}` instance. The `hif_prefix_list_find_withmha()` function will return an `hif_prefix{}` instance if the `mip6_ha{}` instance specified by the second parameter is in the home prefix list specified by the first parameter.

Listing 5-494
—— if_hif.c
```
462    struct mip6_ha *
463    hif_find_next_preferable_ha(hif, haaddr)
464            struct hif_softc *hif;
465            struct in6_addr *haaddr;
466    {
467            struct mip6_ha *curmha, *mha;
468
469            curmha = mip6_ha_list_find_withaddr(&mip6_ha_list, haaddr);
470            if (curmha == NULL)
471                    return (hif_find_preferable_ha(hif));
472
473            /*
474             * we assume mip6_ha_list is ordered by a preference value.
475             */
476            for (mha = TAILQ_NEXT(curmha, mha_entry); mha;
477                mha = TAILQ_NEXT(mha, mha_entry)) {
478                    if (!hif_prefix_list_find_withmha(&hif->hif_prefix_list_home,
479                        mha))
480                            continue;
481                    /* return the entry we have found first. */
482                    return (mha);
483                }
484            /* not found. */
485            return (NULL);
486    }
```
—— if_hif.c

462–465 The `hif_find_next_preferable_ha()` function returns a pointer to the `mip6_ha{}` instance which is the next candidate for the home agent of the virtual home interface specified as the `hif` parameter. The `haaddr` parameter is the address of the current candidate home agent.

469–482 curmha is a pointer to the mip6_ha{} instance of the current candidate home agent searched by the mip6_ha_list_find_withaddr() function. In the loop from lines 476 to 483, all mip6_ha{} entries after the curmha pointer are checked. The first entry found by the hif_prefix_list_find_withmha() function is returned.

Find the Virtual Home Interface

The hif_list_find_withhaddr() function returns the virtual home network related to the specified home address.

Listing 5-495

```
                                                                        if_hif.c
492     struct hif_softc *
493     hif_list_find_withhaddr(haddr)
494         struct in6_addr *haddr;
495     {
496             struct hif_softc *hif;
497             struct hif_prefix *hpfx;
498             struct mip6_prefix *mpfx;
499
500             for (hif = LIST_FIRST(&hif_softc_list); hif;
501                 hif = LIST_NEXT(hif, hif_entry)) {
502                     for (hpfx = LIST_FIRST(&hif->hif_prefix_list_home); hpfx;
503                         hpfx = LIST_NEXT(hpfx, hpfx_entry)) {
504                             mpfx = hpfx->hpfx_mpfx;
505                             if (IN6_ARE_ADDR_EQUAL(&mpfx->mpfx_haddr, haddr))
506                                     return (hif);
507                     }
508             }
509             /* not found. */
510             return (NULL);
511     }
                                                                        if_hif.c
```

492–510 The hif_list_find_withhaddr() function returns a pointer to the hif_softc{} instance which has a home address specified by the haddr parameter. A home address is stored in each mip6_prefix{} structure. This function checks all the home prefix information of all virtual home interfaces. The home prefix information is stored in the hif_prefix_list_home member variable. The pointer to the hif_softc{} instance is returned if its home prefix information includes the home address specified by the haddr parameter.

Send a Packet in IPv6 in IPv6 Format

The hif_output() function sends an IPv6 packet to the destination node using IPv6 in IPv6 tunneling between a mobile node and its home agent.

Listing 5-496

```
                                                                        if_hif.c
811     int
812     hif_output(ifp, m, dst, rt)
813         struct ifnet *ifp;
814         struct mbuf *m;
815         struct sockaddr *dst;
816         struct rtentry *rt;
817     {
818             struct mip6_bu *mbu;
```

```
819                 struct hif_softc *hif = (struct hif_softc *)ifp;
820                 struct ip6_hdr *ip6;
```
                                                                        ___if_hif.c

811–816 The hif_output() function has four parameters: The ifp parameter is a pointer
to the virtual home interface; the m parameter is a pointer to the mbuf which contains the
IPv6 packet; and the dst and rt parameters are the destination address of the packet in
the sockaddr_in6{} format and a pointer to the routing entry, respectively.

Listing 5-497
                                                                        ___if_hif.c

```
822                 /* This function is copied from looutput */
```
.... [copied from looutput() function in if_loop.c]
```
883
884                 switch (dst->sa_family) {
885                 case AF_INET6:
886                         break;
887                 default:
888                         printf("hif_output: af=%d unexpected\n", dst->sa_family);
889                         m_freem(m);
890                         return (EAFNOSUPPORT);
891                 }
```
                                                                        ___if_hif.c

884–891 The hif_output() function only supports IPv6. If the address family of the destination address is not IPv6, the packet is dropped.

Listing 5-498
                                                                        ___if_hif.c

```
897                 ip6 = mtod(m, struct ip6_hdr *);
898                 if (IN6_IS_ADDR_LINKLOCAL(&ip6->ip6_src)
899                     || IN6_IS_ADDR_LINKLOCAL(&ip6->ip6_dst)
900                     || IN6_IS_ADDR_SITELOCAL(&ip6->ip6_src)
901                     || IN6_IS_ADDR_SITELOCAL(&ip6->ip6_dst))
902                         goto done;
903
904                 mbu = mip6_bu_list_find_home_registration(&hif->hif_bu_list,
905                     &ip6->ip6_src);
906                 if (!mbu)
907                         goto done;
908
909                 if (IN6_IS_ADDR_UNSPECIFIED(&mbu->mbu_paddr))
910                         goto done;
```
                                                                        ___if_hif.c

898–902 Addresses of the packet tunneled to the home agent must be global addresses.

904–907 The source address of the outer header is the care-of address of the mobile node.
The mip6_bu_list_find_home_registration() function will return a home registration entry for the source address which is the home address of the mobile node. The
care-of address information is stored in the home registration entry.

909 If the mobile node has not gotten its home agent information, the peer address (mbu_peer)
is the unspecified address. No packet can be sent in this case.

Listing 5-499
_____if_hif.c
```
912                M_PREPEND(m, sizeof(struct ip6_hdr), M_DONTWAIT);
913                if (m && m->m_len < sizeof(struct ip6_hdr))
914                      m = m_pullup(m, sizeof(struct ip6_hdr));
915                if (m == NULL)
916                      return (0);
917
918                ip6 = mtod(m, struct ip6_hdr *);
919                ip6->ip6_flow = 0;
920                ip6->ip6_vfc &= ~IPV6_VERSION_MASK;
921                ip6->ip6_vfc |= IPV6_VERSION;
922                ip6->ip6_plen = htons((u_short)m->m_pkthdr.len - sizeof(*ip6));
923                ip6->ip6_nxt = IPPROTO_IPV6;
924                ip6->ip6_hlim = ip6_deflim;
925                ip6->ip6_src = mbu->mbu_coa;
926                ip6->ip6_dst = mbu->mbu_paddr;
....
929                /* XXX */
930                return (ip6_output(m, 0, 0, IPV6_MINMTU, 0, &ifp
....
932                                         , NULL
....
934                                         ));
....
942        done:
943                m_freem(m);
944                return (0);
945        }
```
_____if_hif.c

912–926 An extra mbuf is prepended to the mbuf which contains the original packet to create a space for the outer IPv6 header. The care-of address of the mobile node (`mbu_coa`) is copied to the source address field of the outer header, and the home agent address (`mbu_paddr`) is copied to the destination address.

930–934 The `ip6_output()` is called with the `IPV6_MINMTU` flag, which indicates the `ip6_output()` function is to send a packet with the minimum MTU size. This flag avoids the Path MTU Discovery procedure between the mobile node and its home agent.

5.17.23 Return Routability and Route Optimization

In this section, we discuss the detailed process of the return routability procedure.

Trigger Return Routability Procedure

A mobile node initiates the return routability procedure, described in Section 5.5.1, when the node receives a tunneled packet.

Listing 5-500
_____ip6_input.c
```
377        void
378        ip6_input(m)
379                struct mbuf *m;
380        {
....
```

```
1092              while (nxt != IPPROTO_DONE) {
1146                      if ((nxt != IPPROTO_HOPOPTS) && (nxt != IPPROTO_DSTOPTS) &&
1147                          (nxt != IPPROTO_ROUTING) && (nxt != IPPROTO_FRAGMENT) &&
1148                          (nxt != IPPROTO_ESP) && (nxt != IPPROTO_AH) &&
1149                          (nxt != IPPROTO_MH) && (nxt != IPPROTO_NONE)) {
1150                              if (mip6_route_optimize(m))
1151                                      goto bad;
1152                      }
       ....
1156              }
```
                                                                                    ─────── ip6_input.c

1092–1152 This while loop processes all the extension headers contained in an incoming
IPv6 packet. The mip6_route_optimize() function is called during the process just
before processing the upper layer protocol headers (e.g., TCP or UDP).

Listing 5-501
                                                                                    ─────── mip6_mncore.c

```
1341      int
1342      mip6_route_optimize(m)
1343              struct mbuf *m;
1344      {
1345              struct m_tag *mtag;
1346              struct in6_ifaddr *ia;
1347              struct ip6aux *ip6a;
1348              struct ip6_hdr *ip6;
1349              struct mip6_prefix *mpfx;
1350              struct mip6_bu *mbu;
1351              struct hif_softc *sc;
1352              struct in6_addr hif_coa;
1353              int error = 0;
```
                                                                                    ─────── mip6_mncore.c

1341–1343 The mip6_route_optimize() function takes a pointer to the mbuf which contains the incoming packet. This function checks to see if the packet was route optimized
and sends a Binding Update message if the packet was not route optimized.

A packet that is not route optimized is delivered as a tunnel packet to a mobile
node. In the BSD network code, we cannot know if the packet being processed in the
ip6_input() function is a tunneled packet or not, because the outer header of a tunnel
packet is removed when it is processed and the inner packet does not have any clue
about its outer header. This function checks to see if the packet includes a Type 2 Routing
Header. If the header exists, that means the packet was sent with route optimization.

Listing 5-502
                                                                                    ─────── mip6_mncore.c

```
1355              if (!MIP6_IS_MN) {
1356                      /* only MN does the route optimization. */
1357                      return (0);
1358              }
1359
1360              ip6 = mtod(m, struct ip6_hdr *);
1361
1362              if (IN6_IS_ADDR_LINKLOCAL(&ip6->ip6_src) ||
1363                  IN6_IS_ADDR_SITELOCAL(&ip6->ip6_src)) {      /* XXX */
1364                      return (0);
1365              }
```

```
1366                    /* Quick check */
1367                    if (IN6_IS_ADDR_LINKLOCAL(&ip6->ip6_dst) ||
1368                        IN6_IS_ADDR_SITELOCAL(&ip6->ip6_dst) ||    /* XXX */
1369                        IN6_IS_ADDR_MULTICAST(&ip6->ip6_dst)) {
1370                            return (0);
1371                    }
1372
1373                    for (ia = in6_ifaddr; ia; ia = ia->ia_next) {
1374                            if (IN6_ARE_ADDR_EQUAL(&ia->ia_addr.sin6_addr,
1375                                &ip6->ip6_src)) {
1376                                    return (0);
1377                            }
1378                    }
```
——— mip6_mncore.c

1362–1371 A simple sanity check is done. A packet whose source address is not a global address will not be optimized. Also, a packet whose destination address is not a global address or whose address is a multicast address will not be optimized.

1373–1378 If the source address of the incoming packet is one of the addresses assigned to a mobile node, then there is no need to optimize the route.

Listing 5-503
——— mip6_mncore.c
```
1380                    mtag = ip6_findaux(m);
1381                    if (mtag) {
1382                            ip6a = (struct ip6aux *) (mtag + 1);
1383                            if (ip6a->ip6a_flags & IP6A_ROUTEOPTIMIZED) {
1384                                    /* no need to optimize route. */
1385                                    return (0);
1386                            }
1387                    }
1388                    /*
1389                     * this packet has no rthdr or has a rthdr not related mip6
1390                     * route optimization.
1391                     */
```
——— mip6_mncore.c

1380–1391 The KAME Mobile IPv6 implementation sets the `IP6A_ROUTEOPTIMIZED` flag in an auxiliary mbuf when processing the Type 2 Routing Header. If the packet has the flag set, it is understood that the packet has been delivered with a Type 2 Routing Header, which means it is route optimized.

Listing 5-504
——— mip6_mncore.c
```
1394                    sc = hif_list_find_withhaddr(&ip6->ip6_dst);
1395                    if (sc == NULL) {
1396                            /* this dst addr is not one of our home addresses. */
1397                            return (0);
1398                    }
1399                    if (sc->hif_location == HIF_LOCATION_HOME) {
1400                            /* we are home.  no route optimization is required. */
1401                            return (0);
1402                    }
```
——— mip6_mncore.c

1394–1402 The `hif_list_find_withhaddr()` function returns a pointer to the `hif_softc{}` instance which has the home address specified by the parameter. If the destination address of the packet is not the home address of the mobile node, the mobile node does not do anything. Also, if the mobile node is at home, no route optimization is needed.

Listing 5-505

```
                                                                    mip6_mncore.c
1404            /* get current CoA and recover its scope information. */
1405            if (sc->hif_coa_ifa == NULL) {
....
1409                    return (0);
1410            }
1411            hif_coa = sc->hif_coa_ifa->ia_addr.sin6_addr;
1412
1413            /*
1414             * find a mip6_prefix which has a home address of received
1415             * packet.
1416             */
1417            mpfx = mip6_prefix_list_find_withhaddr(&mip6_prefix_list,
1418                &ip6->ip6_dst);
1419            if (mpfx == NULL) {
1420                    /*
1421                     * no related prefix found.  this packet is
1422                     * destined to another address of this node
1423                     * that is not a home address.
1424                     */
1425                    return (0);
1426            }
                                                                    mip6_mncore.c
```

1404–1411 If the mobile node does not have a valid care-of address, the node cannot send a Binding Update message. If there is a valid care-of address, the address is set to the hif_coa variable.

1417–1426 Creating a new binding update list entry requires the prefix information of the home address of the mobile node. The mip6_prefix_list_find_withhaddr() function is called to search the prefix information related to the destination address of the incoming packet, which is the home address of the mobile node. If the mobile node does not have the prefix information, it cannot send a Binding Update message.

Listing 5-506

```
                                                                    mip6_mncore.c
1428            /*
1429             * search all binding update entries with the address of the
1430             * peer sending this un-optimized packet.
1431             */
1432            mbu = mip6_bu_list_find_withpaddr(&sc->hif_bu_list, &ip6->ip6_src,
1433                &ip6->ip6_dst);
1434            if (mbu == NULL) {
1435                    /*
1436                     * if no binding update entry is found, this is a
1437                     * first packet from the peer.  create a new binding
1438                     * update entry for this peer.
1439                     */
1440                    mbu = mip6_bu_create(&ip6->ip6_src, mpfx, &hif_coa, 0, sc);
1441                    if (mbu == NULL) {
1442                            error = ENOMEM;
1443                            goto bad;
```

```
1444                          }
1445                          mip6_bu_list_insert(&sc->hif_bu_list, mbu);
1446                  } else {
....
1473                  }
1474                  mip6_bu_fsm(mbu, MIP6_BU_PRI_FSM_EVENT_REVERSE_PACKET, NULL);
1475
1476                  return (0);
1477          bad:
1478                  m_freem(m);
1479                  return (error);
1480          }
```
── mip6_mncore.c

1432–1473 If the mobile node does not have a binding update list entry between its home
address (the destination address of the incoming packet) and the peer address (the
source address of the incoming packet), a new binding update list entry is created by
the mip6_bu_create() function. The new entry is inserted into the list of binding
update list entries of the virtual home interface to which the home address is assigned.

1446–1476 The MIP6_BU_PRI_FSM_EVENT_REVERSE_PACKET event is sent to the state
machine of the newly created binding update list entry, or to the existing entry if the
mobile node already has one. The event will initiate the return routability procedure.

Sending Home Test Init/Care-of Test Init Messages

A mobile node sends a Home Test Init and a Care-of Test Init message to initiate the
return routability procedure. The sending of these messages is implemented by the
mip6_bu_send_hoti() function and the mip6_bu_send_coti() functions respectively.

Listing 5-507
── mip6_mncore.c
```
2061    int
2062    mip6_bu_send_hoti(mbu)
2063            struct mip6_bu *mbu;
2064    {
2065            struct mbuf *m;
2066            struct ip6_pktopts opt;
2067            int error = 0;
```
── mip6_mncore.c

2061–2063 The mip6_bu_send_hoti() function sends a Home Test Init message to the
correspondent node specified in the binding update list entry specified in the parameter.

Listing 5-508
── mip6_mncore.c
```
2069            ip6_initpktopts(&opt);
2070
2071            m = mip6_create_ip6hdr(&mbu->mbu_haddr, &mbu->mbu_paddr,
2072                IPPROTO_NONE, 0);
2073            if (m == NULL) {
....
2077                    return (ENOMEM);
2078            }
```

```
2079
2080              error = mip6_ip6mhi_create(&opt.ip6po_mh, mbu);
2081              if (error) {
    ....
2085                      m_freem(m);
2086                      goto free_ip6pktopts;
2087              }
2088
    ....
2090              error = ip6_output(m, &opt, NULL, 0, NULL, NULL
    ....
2092                                      , NULL
    ....
2094                                      );
2095              if (error) {
    ....
2099                      goto free_ip6pktopts;
2100              }
2101
2102      free_ip6pktopts:
2103              if (opt.ip6po_mh)
2104                      FREE(opt.ip6po_mh, M_IP6OPT);
2105
2106              return (0);
2107      }
```
_____mip6_mncore.c

2069–2087 A Home Test Init message is passed to the `ip6_output()` function in the form of a packet option. The `ip6_initpacketopts()` function initializes the `ip6_pktopts` variable which will contain the created message. An IPv6 header is prepared by the `mip6_create_ip6hdr()` function and a Home Test Init message is created by the `mip6_ip6hi_create()` function, which is discussed later.

2090–2104 The created message is sent by the `ip6_outout()` function. The memory space allocated for the message is released before returning.

Listing 5-509

_____mip6_mncore.c

```
2109      int
2110      mip6_bu_send_coti(mbu)
2111              struct mip6_bu *mbu;
2112      {
2113              struct mbuf *m;
2114              struct ip6_pktopts opt;
2115              int error = 0;
2116
2117              ip6_initpktopts(&opt);
2118              opt.ip6po_flags |= IP6PO_USECOA;
2119
2120              m = mip6_create_ip6hdr(&mbu->mbu_coa, &mbu->mbu_paddr,
2121                  IPPROTO_NONE, 0);
2122              if (m == NULL) {
    ....
2126                      return (ENOMEM);
2127              }
2128
2129              error = mip6_ip6mci_create(&opt.ip6po_mh, mbu);
2130              if (error) {
    ....
```

```
2134                       m_freem(m);
2135                       goto free_ip6pktopts;
2136             }
....
2139             error = ip6_output(m, &opt, NULL, 0, NULL, NULL
....
2141                             , NULL
....
2143                             );
2144             if (error) {
....
2148                       goto free_ip6pktopts;
2149             }
2150
2151     free_ip6pktopts:
2152             if (opt.ip6po_mh)
2153                     FREE(opt.ip6po_mh, M_IP6OPT);
2154
2155             return (0);
2156     }
```
                                                                    ──────mip6_mncore.c

2109–2156 The `mip6_bu_send_coti()` function sends a Care-of Test Init message. This is
almost the same code as the `mip6_bu_send_hoti()` function. There are two differences. One is that the function sets the `IP6PO_USECOA` flag in the packet option to cause
the use of the care-of address of a mobile node when sending the message. If the mobile
node does not specify the flag, then the packet will be sent with a Home Address option
if there is a valid binding update list entry for the correspondent node. The Home Address
option must not be used with the Care-of Test Init message. The other difference is that the
`mip6_ip6mci_create()` function is called instead of the `mip6_ip6mhi_create()`
function to create a Care-of Test Init message.

Listing 5-510
                                                                    ──────mip6_mncore.c
```
3508     int
3509     mip6_ip6mhi_create(pktopt_mobility, mbu)
3510             struct ip6_mh **pktopt_mobility;
3511             struct mip6_bu *mbu;
3512     {
3513             struct ip6_mh_home_test_init *ip6mhi;
3514             int ip6mhi_size;
```
                                                                    ──────mip6_mncore.c

3508–3511 The `mip6_ip6mhi_create()` function has two parameters. The
`pktopt_mobility` parameter is a pointer to the memory space of the `ip6_mh{}`
instance, which will be allocated in this function to hold a Home Test Init message. The
`mbu` parameter is a pointer to the binding update list entry related to the Home Test
Init message.

Listing 5-511
                                                                    ──────mip6_mncore.c
```
3520             *pktopt_mobility = NULL;
3521
```

```
3522            ip6mhi_size =
3523                ((sizeof(struct ip6_mh_home_test_init) +7) >> 3) * 8;
3524
3525            MALLOC(ip6mhi, struct ip6_mh_home_test_init *,
3526                ip6mhi_size, M_IP6OPT, M_NOWAIT);
3527            if (ip6mhi == NULL)
3528                    return (ENOMEM);
3529
3530            bzero(ip6mhi, ip6mhi_size);
3531            ip6mhi->ip6mhhti_proto = IPPROTO_NONE;
3532            ip6mhi->ip6mhhti_len = (ip6mhi_size >> 3) - 1;
3533            ip6mhi->ip6mhhti_type = IP6_MH_TYPE_HOTI;
3534            bcopy(mbu->mbu_mobile_cookie, ip6mhi->ip6mhhti_cookie8,
3535                sizeof(ip6mhi->ip6mhhti_cookie8));
3536
3537            /* calculate checksum. */
3538            ip6mhi->ip6mhhti_cksum = mip6_cksum(&mbu->mbu_haddr, &mbu->mbu_paddr,
3539                ip6mhi_size, IPPROTO_MH, (char *)ip6mhi);
3540
3541            *pktopt_mobility = (struct ip6_mh *)ip6mhi;
3542
3543            return (0);
3544    }
```
                                                              ———mip6_mncore.c

3520–3534 A memory space to hold the Home Test Init message is allocated and each header
value is filled. The size of the message is calculated in the same manner as other extension
headers. The size is in units of 8 bytes excluding the first 8 bytes. The type is set to
IP6_MH_TYPE_HOTI. A cookie value, which is kept in the binding update list entry, is
copied to the ip6mhhti_cookie8 field.

ip6mhhti_cksum is filled with the checksum value of the message by the
mip6_cksum() function.

Listing 5-512
                                                              ———mip6_mncore.c

```
3546    int
3547    mip6_ip6mci_create(pktopt_mobility, mbu)
3548            struct ip6_mh **pktopt_mobility;
3549            struct mip6_bu *mbu;
3550    {
3551            struct ip6_mh_careof_test_init *ip6mci;
3552            int ip6mci_size;
....
3558            *pktopt_mobility = NULL;
3559
3560            ip6mci_size =
3561                ((sizeof(struct ip6_mh_careof_test_init) + 7) >> 3) * 8;
3562
3563            MALLOC(ip6mci, struct ip6_mh_careof_test_init *,
3564                ip6mci_size, M_IP6OPT, M_NOWAIT);
3565            if (ip6mci == NULL)
3566                    return (ENOMEM);
3567
3568            bzero(ip6mci, ip6mci_size);
3569            ip6mci->ip6mhcti_proto = IPPROTO_NONE;
3570            ip6mci->ip6mhcti_len = (ip6mci_size >> 3) - 1;
3571            ip6mci->ip6mhcti_type = IP6_MH_TYPE_COTI;
3572            bcopy(mbu->mbu_mobile_cookie, ip6mci->ip6mhcti_cookie8,
3573                sizeof(ip6mci->ip6mhcti_cookie8));
3574
3575            /* calculate checksum. */
```

```
3576              ip6mci->ip6mhcti_cksum = mip6_cksum(&mbu->mbu_coa, &mbu->mbu_paddr,
3577                  ip6mci_size, IPPROTO_MH, (char *)ip6mci);
3578
3579              *pktopt_mobility = (struct ip6_mh *)ip6mci;
3580
3581              return (0);
3582      }
```
───*mip6_mncore.c*

3546–3582 The `mip6_ip6mci_create()` function does almost the same thing as the
`mip6_ip6mhi_create()` function to create a Care-of Test Init message. We skip the
discussion.

Receiving Home Test Init/Care-of Test Init Messages and Replying
Home Test/Care-of Test Messages

A correspondent node will reply with a Home Test message and a Care-of Test message in
response to a Home Test Init message and a Care-of Test Init message respectively, if the node
supports route optimization.

Listing 5-513
───*mip6_cncore.c*
```
1826    int
1827    mip6_ip6mhi_input(m0, ip6mhi, ip6mhilen)
1828            struct mbuf *m0;
1829            struct ip6_mh_home_test_init *ip6mhi;
1830            int ip6mhilen;
1831    {
1832            struct ip6_hdr *ip6;
1833            struct mbuf *m;
1834            struct m_tag *mtag;
1835            struct ip6aux *ip6a;
1836            struct ip6_pktopts opt;
1837            int error = 0;
```
───*mip6_cncore.c*

1826-1830 The `mip6_ip6mhi_input()` function is called from the `mobility6_input()`
function when a correspondent node receives a Home Test Init message. m0 is a pointer
to the mbuf which contains the packet. The `ip6mhi` and the `ip6mhilen` variables are
pointers to the received Home Test Init message and the size of the message, respectively.

Listing 5-514
───*mip6_mncore.c*
```
1841            ip6 = mtod(m0, struct ip6_hdr *);
1842
1843            /* packet length check. */
1844            if (ip6mhilen < sizeof(struct ip6_mh_home_test_init)) {
....
1850                    /* send an ICMP parameter problem. */
1851                    icmp6_error(m0, ICMP6_PARAM_PROB, ICMP6_PARAMPROB_HEADER,
1852                        (caddr_t)&ip6mhi->ip6mhhti_len - (caddr_t)ip6);
1853                    return (EINVAL);
1854            }
```
───*mip6_mncore.c*

1841–1854 If the length of the packet is smaller than the size of the
`ip6_mh_home_test_init{}` structure, then the correspondent node replies with

an ICMPv6 Parameter Problem message to the mobile node which sent the input
message. The problem pointer of the ICMPv6 message is set to the length field of
the incoming Home Test Init message.

Listing 5-515

```
1856              /* a home address destination option must not exist. */
1857              mtag = ip6_findaux(m0);
1858              if (mtag) {
1859                      ip6a = (struct ip6aux *) (mtag + 1);
1860                      if ((ip6a->ip6a_flags & IP6A_HASEEN) != 0) {
....
1866                              m_freem(m0);
1867                              /* stat? */
1868                              return (EINVAL);
1869                      }
1870              }
```

1856–1870 The Home Test Init message must not have the Home Address option. If the packet
contains a Home Address option, that is, the auxiliary mbuf has the IP6A_HASEEN flag
set, the packet is dropped.

Listing 5-516

```
1872              m = mip6_create_ip6hdr(&ip6->ip6_dst, &ip6->ip6_src, IPPROTO_NONE, 0);
1873              if (m == NULL) {
....
1877                      goto free_ip6pktopts;
1878              }
1879
1880              ip6_initpktopts(&opt);
1881              error = mip6_ip6mh_create(&opt.ip6po_mh, &ip6->ip6_dst, &ip6->ip6_src,
1882                      ip6mhi->ip6mhhti_cookie8);
1883              if (error) {
....
1887                      m_freem(m);
1888                      goto free_ip6pktopts;
1889              }
```

1872–1889 An IPv6 packet is prepared by the mip6_create_ip6hdr() function and a
Home Test message, which is a reply message to the incoming Home Test Init message,
is created by the mip6_ip6mh_create() function. As with other Mobility Headers,
the Home Test message is prepared as an ip6_pktopts{} instance and passed to the
ip6_output() function.

Listing 5-517

```
1892              error = ip6_output(m, &opt, NULL, 0, NULL, NULL
....
1894                              , NULL
```

```
         ....
1896                                    );
1897              if (error) {
         ....
1901                      goto free_ip6pktopts;
1902              }
1903
1904     free_ip6pktopts:
1905              if (opt.ip6po_mh != NULL)
1906                      FREE(opt.ip6po_mh, M_IP6OPT);
1907
1908              return (0);
1909     }
```
                                                            _____mip6_mncore.c

1892–1906 The created Home Test message is sent by the `ip6_output()` function. The memory space allocated for the message is released before finishing this function.

Listing 5-518
                                                            _____mip6_cncore.c

```
1911     int
1912     mip6_ip6mci_input(m0, ip6mci, ip6mcilen)
1913              struct mbuf *m0;
1914              struct ip6_mh_careof_test_init *ip6mci;
1915              int ip6mcilen;
1916     {
1917              struct ip6_hdr *ip6;
1918              struct mbuf *m;
1919              struct m_tag *mtag;
1920              struct ip6aux *ip6a;
1921              struct ip6_pktopts opt;
1922              int error = 0;
```
                                                            _____mip6_cncore.c

1911–1915 The `mip6_ip6mci_input()` function does tasks similar to the `mip6_ip6mhi_input()` function for a Care-of Test Init message. `m0` is a pointer to the mbuf which contains the Care-of Test Init message. The `ip6mci` and the `ip6mclen` variables are the address of the head of the message and the size of the message, respectively. The difference from the `mip6_ip6mhi_input()` function is that this function has a validation code of the source address of the incoming Care-of Test Init message.

Listing 5-519
                                                            _____mip6_mncore.c

```
1926              ip6 = mtod(m0, struct ip6_hdr *);
1927
1928              if (IN6_IS_ADDR_UNSPECIFIED(&ip6->ip6_src) ||
1929                  IN6_IS_ADDR_LOOPBACK(&ip6->ip6_src)) {
1930                      m_freem(m0);
1931                      return (EINVAL);
1932              }
```
                                                            _____mip6_mncore.c

Listing 5-520

_____mip6_mncore.c

```
1934                 /* packet length check. */
1935                 if (ip6mcilen < sizeof(struct ip6_mh_careof_test_init)) {
....
1941                     /* send ICMP parameter problem. */
1942                     icmp6_error(m0, ICMP6_PARAM_PROB, ICMP6_PARAMPROB_HEADER,
1943                         (caddr_t)&ip6mci->ip6mhcti_len - (caddr_t)ip6);
1944                     return (EINVAL);
1945                 }
....
1947                 /* a home address destination option must not exist. */
1948                 mtag = ip6_findaux(m0);
1949                 if (mtag) {
1950                     ip6a = (struct ip6aux *) (mtag + 1);
1951                     if ((ip6a->ip6a_flags & IP6A_HASEEN) != 0) {
....
1957                         m_freem(m0);
1958                         /* stat? */
1959                         return (EINVAL);
1960                     }
1961                 }
....
1963                 m = mip6_create_ip6hdr(&ip6->ip6_dst, &ip6->ip6_src, IPPROTO_NONE, 0);
1964                 if (m == NULL) {
....
1968                     goto free_ip6pktopts;
1969                 }
1970
1971                 ip6_initpktopts(&opt);
1972                 error = mip6_ip6mc_create(&opt.ip6po_mh, &ip6->ip6_dst, &ip6->ip6_src,
1973                     ip6mci->ip6mhcti_cookie8);
1974                 if (error) {
....
1978                     m_freem(m);
1979                     goto free_ip6pktopts;
1980                 }
....
1983                 error = ip6_output(m, &opt, NULL, 0, NULL, NULL
....
1985                             , NULL
....
1987                                 );
1988                 if (error) {
....
1992                     goto free_ip6pktopts;
1993                 }
1994
1995           free_ip6pktopts:
1996                 if (opt.ip6po_mh != NULL)
1997                     FREE(opt.ip6po_mh, M_IP6OPT);
1998
1999                 return (0);
2000         }
```

_____mip6_mncore.c

1926–1932 An inappropriate source address is rejected. The source address of the Care-of Test Init message must be the care-of address of a mobile node. The unspecified address and the loopback address cannot be care-of addresses.

1934–1999 The rest of the function performs the same tasks as the `mip6_ip6mhi_input()` function. We skip the discussion.

Listing 5-521

———————————————————————————————————mip6_cncore.c

```
2314    static int
2315    mip6_ip6mh_create(pktopt_mobility, src, dst, cookie)
2316            struct ip6_mh **pktopt_mobility;
2317            struct in6_addr *src, *dst;
2318            u_int8_t *cookie;                /* home init cookie */
2319    {
2320            struct ip6_mh_home_test *ip6mh;
2321            int ip6mh_size;
2322            mip6_nodekey_t home_nodekey;
2323            mip6_nonce_t home_nonce;
```
———————————————————————————————————mip6_cncore.c

2314–2318 The `mip6_ip6mh_create()` function creates a Home Test message. `pktopt_mobility` is a pointer to the memory space for the message to be created. `src` and `dst` are the source and destination addresses of the message, respectively. These addresses are used to compute a checksum value of the message. `cookie` is a pointer to the home cookie value.

Listing 5-522

———————————————————————————————————mip6_mncore.c

```
2325            *pktopt_mobility = NULL;
2326
2327            ip6mh_size = sizeof(struct ip6_mh_home_test);
2328
2329            if ((mip6_get_nonce(nonce_index, &home_nonce) != 0) ||
2330                (mip6_get_nodekey(nonce_index, &home_nodekey) != 0))
2331                    return (EINVAL);
2332
2333            MALLOC(ip6mh, struct ip6_mh_home_test *, ip6mh_size,
2334                M_IP6OPT, M_NOWAIT);
2335            if (ip6mh == NULL)
2336                    return (ENOMEM);
```
———————————————————————————————————mip6_mncore.c

2325–2330 The current nonce value and nodekey value, pointed to by the global variable `nonce_index`, are retrieved by the `mip6_get_nonce()` and the `mip6_get_nodekey()` functions, respectively.

2333–2336 A memory space to hold the created Home Test message is allocated.

Listing 5-523

———————————————————————————————————mip6_mncore.c

```
2338            bzero(ip6mh, ip6mh_size);
2339            ip6mh->ip6mhht_proto = IPPROTO_NONE;
2340            ip6mh->ip6mhht_len = (ip6mh_size >> 3) - 1;
2341            ip6mh->ip6mhht_type = IP6_MH_TYPE_HOT;
2342            ip6mh->ip6mhht_nonce_index = htons(nonce_index);
2343            bcopy(cookie, ip6mh->ip6mhht_cookie8, sizeof(ip6mh->ip6mhht_cookie8));
2344            if (mip6_create_keygen_token(dst, &home_nodekey,
2345                &home_nonce, 0, ip6mh->ip6mhht_keygen8)) {
....
2349                    return (EINVAL);
2350            }
2351
2352            /* calculate checksum. */
```

```
2353            ip6mh->ip6mhht_cksum = mip6_cksum(src, dst, ip6mh_size, IPPROTO_MH,
2354                (char *)ip6mh);
2355
2356            *pktopt_mobility = (struct ip6_mh *)ip6mh;
2357
2358            return (0);
2359    }
```
──mip6_mncore.c

2338–2354 The size of the message is calculated in the same manner as other extension
headers. The size is in units of 8 bytes excluding the first 8 bytes. The type is set to
IP6_MH_TYPE_HOT. The value of the nonce index field (ip6mhht_nonce_index) is
copied from the global variable nonce_index. The cookie value sent from the mobile
node is copied to the cookie field (ip6mhht_cookie8). The keygen token is computed
by the mip6_create_keygen_token() function and is copied to the keygen field
(ip6mhht_keygen8). Finally, the checksum value is computed by the mip6_cksum()
function.

Listing 5-524
──mip6_cncore.c
```
2361    static int
2362    mip6_ip6mc_create(pktopt_mobility, src, dst, cookie)
2363            struct ip6_mh **pktopt_mobility;
2364            struct in6_addr *src, *dst;
2365            u_int8_t *cookie;                      /* careof init cookie */
2366    {
2367            struct ip6_mh_careof_test *ip6mc;
2368            int ip6mc_size;
2369            mip6_nodekey_t careof_nodekey;
2370            mip6_nonce_t careof_nonce;
2371
2372            *pktopt_mobility = NULL;
2373
2374            ip6mc_size = sizeof(struct ip6_mh_careof_test);
2375
2376            if ((mip6_get_nonce(nonce_index, &careof_nonce) != 0) ||
2377                (mip6_get_nodekey(nonce_index, &careof_nodekey) != 0))
2378                    return (EINVAL);
2379
2380            MALLOC(ip6mc, struct ip6_mh_careof_test *, ip6mc_size,
2381                M_IP6OPT, M_NOWAIT);
2382            if (ip6mc == NULL)
2383                    return (ENOMEM);
2384
2385            bzero(ip6mc, ip6mc_size);
2386            ip6mc->ip6mhct_proto = IPPROTO_NONE;
2387            ip6mc->ip6mhct_len = (ip6mc_size >> 3) - 1;
2388            ip6mc->ip6mhct_type = IP6_MH_TYPE_COT;
2389            ip6mc->ip6mhct_nonce_index = htons(nonce_index);
2390            bcopy(cookie, ip6mc->ip6mhct_cookie8, sizeof(ip6mc->ip6mhct_cookie8));
2391            if (mip6_create_keygen_token(dst, &careof_nodekey, &careof_nonce, 1,
2392                    ip6mc->ip6mhct_keygen8)) {
....
2397                    return (EINVAL);
2398            }
2399
2400            /* calculate checksum. */
2401            ip6mc->ip6mhct_cksum = mip6_cksum(src, dst, ip6mc_size, IPPROTO_MH,
2402                (char *)ip6mc);
2403
2404            *pktopt_mobility = (struct ip6_mh *)ip6mc;
```

```
2405
2406            return (0);
2407      }
```
——— mip6_cncore.c

2361–2407 The `mip6_ip6mc_create()` function performs almost the same task to create the Care-of Test message as the `mip6_ip6mh_create()` does for a Home Test message.

Receiving Home Test/Care-of Test Messages

When a mobile node receives a Home Test message or a Care-of Test message, it sends a related event to its state machine.

Listing 5-525
——— mip6_mncore.c
```
2697    int
2698    mip6_ip6mh_input(m, ip6mh, ip6mhlen)
2699            struct mbuf *m;
2700            struct ip6_mh_home_test *ip6mh;
2701            int ip6mhlen;
2702    {
2703            struct ip6_hdr *ip6;
2704            struct hif_softc *sc;
2705            struct mip6_bu *mbu;
2706            int error = 0;
```
——— mip6_mncore.c

2697–2701 The `mip6_ip6mh_input()` function is called from the `mobility6_input()` function when a mobile node receives a Home Test message. m is a pointer to the mbuf which contains the received packet. The `ip6mh` and the `ip6mhlen` variables are pointers to the head of the Home Test message and its length, respectively.

Listing 5-526
——— mip6_mncore.c
```
2710            ip6 = mtod(m, struct ip6_hdr *);
2711
2712            /* packet length check. */
2713            if (ip6mhlen < sizeof(struct ip6_mh_home_test)) {
....
2721                    /* send ICMP parameter problem. */
2722                    icmp6_error(m, ICMP6_PARAM_PROB, ICMP6_PARAMPROB_HEADER,
2723                        (caddr_t)&ip6mh->ip6mhht_len - (caddr_t)ip6);
2724                    return (EINVAL);
2725            }
```
——— mip6_mncore.c

2713–2725 If the length of the received Home Test message is smaller than the size of the `ip6_mh_home_test{}` structure, the mobile node sends an ICMPv6 Parameter Problem message. The problem pointer points to the length field of the incoming message.

Listing 5-527
——— mip6_mncore.c
```
2727            sc = hif_list_find_withhaddr(&ip6->ip6_dst);
2728            if (sc == NULL) {
```

```
....
2733                    m_freem(m);
....
2735                    return (EINVAL);
2736              }
2737              mbu = mip6_bu_list_find_withpaddr(&sc->hif_bu_list, &ip6->ip6_src,
2738                  &ip6->ip6_dst);
2739              if (mbu == NULL) {
....
2744                    m_freem(m);
....
2746                    return (EINVAL);
2747              }
```
_____mip6_mncore.c

2727–2736 The destination address of the incoming packet must be the home address of the mobile node. If there is not a virtual home interface which has the home address, the mobile node drops the packet.

2737–2747 The status of the return routability procedure is kept in a binding update list entry. If the mobile node does not have a binding update list entry related to the incoming packet, the packet is dropped.

Listing 5-528
_____mip6_mncore.c

```
2749             /* check mobile cookie. */
2750             if (bcmp(&mbu->mbu_mobile_cookie, ip6mh->ip6mhht_cookie8,
2751                 sizeof(ip6mh->ip6mhht_cookie8)) != 0) {
....
2755                   m_freem(m);
....
2757                   return (EINVAL);
2758             }
2759
2760             error = mip6_bu_fsm(mbu, MIP6_BU_SEC_FSM_EVENT_HOT, ip6mh);
2761             if (error) {
....
2765                   m_freem(m);
2766                   return (error);
2767             }
2768
2769             mbu->mbu_home_nonce_index = ntohs(ip6mh->ip6mhht_nonce_index);
....
2774             return (0);
2775      }
```
_____mip6_mncore.c

2750–2758 If the incoming Home Test message is not a response to the Home Test Init message sent from this mobile node, the packet is dropped. A Home Test message must include the same cookie value which is copied from the Home Test Init message sent previously.

2760–2769 The mobile node sends the `MIP6_BU_SEC_FSM_EVENT_HOT` event to its state machine to inform that a Home Test message is received. Line 2769 is redundant because the home nonce index is copied in the state machine as well.

Listing 5-529

———mip6_mncore.c

```
2777    int
2778    mip6_ip6mc_input(m, ip6mc, ip6mclen)
2779            struct mbuf *m;
2780            struct ip6_mh_careof_test *ip6mc;
2781            int ip6mclen;
2782    {
2783            struct ip6_hdr *ip6;
2784            struct hif_softc *sc;
2785            struct mip6_bu *mbu = NULL;
2786            int error = 0;
....
2790            ip6 = mtod(m, struct ip6_hdr *);
2791
2792            if (IN6_IS_ADDR_UNSPECIFIED(&ip6->ip6_src) ||
2793                IN6_IS_ADDR_LOOPBACK(&ip6->ip6_src)) {
2794                    m_freem(m);
2795                    return (EINVAL);
2796            }
2797
2798            /* packet length check. */
2799            if (ip6mclen < sizeof(struct ip6_mh_careof_test)) {
....
2807                    /* send ICMP parameter problem. */
2808                    icmp6_error(m, ICMP6_PARAM_PROB, ICMP6_PARAMPROB_HEADER,
2809                        (caddr_t)&ip6mc->ip6mhct_len - (caddr_t)ip6);
2810                    return (EINVAL);
2811            }
```

———mip6_mncore.c

2777–2781 The `mip6_ip6mc_input()` function performs almost the same tasks for the
Care-of Test message as the `mip6_ip6mh_input()` function does for the Home Test
message.

2792–2796 The intention of this part is to validate the care-of address of the received message.
Apparently, the code is wrong. It should check the destination address instead of the
source address. The destination address must be the care-of address of the mobile node.
A care-of address cannot be the loopback address or the unspecified address.

Listing 5-530

———mip6_mncore.c

```
2813            /* too ugly... */
2814            for (sc = LIST_FIRST(&hif_softc_list); sc;
2815                sc = LIST_NEXT(sc, hif_entry)) {
2816                    for (mbu = LIST_FIRST(&sc->hif_bu_list); mbu;
2817                        mbu = LIST_NEXT(mbu, mbu_entry)) {
2818                            if (IN6_ARE_ADDR_EQUAL(&ip6->ip6_dst, &mbu->mbu_coa) &&
2819                                IN6_ARE_ADDR_EQUAL(&ip6->ip6_src, &mbu->mbu_paddr))
2820                                    break;
2821                    }
2822                    if (mbu != NULL)
2823                            break;
2824            }
2825            if (mbu == NULL) {
....
2830                    m_freem(m);
....
2832                    return (EINVAL);
2833            }
```

———mip6_mncore.c

2813–2833 To get a binding update list entry related to the incoming Care-of Test message, the mobile node checks all the binding update list entries it has. If there is no binding update list entry whose care-of address is the same as the destination address of the incoming packet and whose peer address is the same as the source address of the incoming packet, the packet is dropped.

Listing 5-531

———mip6_mncore.c
```
2835            /* check mobile cookie. */
2836            if (bcmp(&mbu->mbu_mobile_cookie, ip6mc->ip6mhct_cookie8,
2837                sizeof(ip6mc->ip6mhct_cookie8)) != 0) {
....
2841                    m_freem(m);
....
2843                    return (EINVAL);
2844            }
2845
2846            error = mip6_bu_fsm(mbu, MIP6_BU_SEC_FSM_EVENT_COT, ip6mc);
2847            if (error) {
....
2851                    m_freem(m);
2852                    return (error);
2853            }
2854
2855            mbu->mbu_careof_nonce_index = ntohs(ip6mc->ip6mhct_nonce_index);
....
2860            return (0);
2861    }
```
———mip6_mncore.c

2835–2855 After checking the cookie value, the mobile node sends the `MIP6_BU_SEC_FSM_EVENT_COT` event to its state machine.

Sending a Binding Update Message to Correspondent Node

As we have already discussed in Section 5.17.19, a mobile node will call the `mip6_bu_send_cbu()` function to send a Binding Update message after receiving a Home Test and a Care-of Test message from a correspondent node. The route optimization preparation has been completed at this point. The KAME implementation does not require a Binding Acknowledgment message from a correspondent node.

5.17.24 Route Optimized Communication

If both a mobile node and a correspondent node support route optimization, those nodes can communicate with each other directly using extension headers as described in Section 5.5.

Sending a Route Optimized Packet

The extension headers used by the route optimization procedure are inserted during the output processing of a packet.

Listing 5-532

———ip6_output.c
```
372            if (opt) {
373                    /* Hop-by-Hop options header */
```

```
374                         MAKE_EXTHDR(opt->ip6po_hbh, &exthdrs.ip6e_hbh);
375                         /* Destination options header(1st part) */
376                         if (opt->ip6po_rthdr
....
378                             || opt->ip6po_rthdr2
....
380                             ) {
381                             /*
382                              * Destination options header(1st part)
383                              * This only makes sence with a routing header.
384                              * See Section 9.2 of RFC 3542.
385                              * Disabling this part just for MIP6 convenience is
386                              * a bad idea.  We need to think carefully about a
387                              * way to make the advanced API coexist with MIP6
388                              * options, which might automatically be inserted in
389                              * the kernel.
390                              */
391                             MAKE_EXTHDR(opt->ip6po_dest1, &exthdrs.ip6e_dest1);
392                         }
393                         /* Routing header */
394                         MAKE_EXTHDR(opt->ip6po_rthdr, &exthdrs.ip6e_rthdr);
....
396                         /* Type 2 Routing header for MIP6 route optimization */
397                         MAKE_EXTHDR(opt->ip6po_rthdr2, &exthdrs.ip6e_rthdr2);
....
399                         /* Destination options header(2nd part) */
400                         MAKE_EXTHDR(opt->ip6po_dest2, &exthdrs.ip6e_dest2);
....
402                         MAKE_EXTHDR(opt->ip6po_mh, &exthdrs.ip6e_mh);
....
404                 }
```
—— ip6_output.c

372–404 The code is a part of the `ip6_output()` function. We can specify extension headers when calling the `ip6_output()` function using the `ip6_pktopts{}` structure. With regard to Mobile IPv6, the Type 2 Routing Header (line 397) and the Mobility Header (line 402) may be specified. A Home Address option is not usually specified by the `ip6_pktopts{}` structure at this point. The option is usually inserted automatically in the `mip6_exthdr_create()` function, discussed later.

Listing 5-533
—— ip6_output.c

```
406             bzero((caddr_t)&mip6opt, sizeof(mip6opt));
407             if ((flags & IPV6_FORWARDING) == 0) {
408                     struct m_tag *n;
409                     struct ip6aux *ip6a = NULL;
410                     /*
411                      * XXX: reconsider the following routine.
412                      */
413                     /*
414                      * MIP6 extention headers handling.
415                      * insert HA, BU, BA, BR options if necessary.
416                      */
417                     n = ip6_findaux(m);
418                     if (n)
419                             ip6a = (struct ip6aux *) (n + 1);
420                     if (!(ip6a && (ip6a->ip6a_flags & IP6A_NOTUSEBC)))
421                             if (mip6_exthdr_create(m, opt, &mip6opt))
422                                     goto freehdrs;
```

```
423
424                          if ((exthdrs.ip6e_rthdr2 == NULL)
425                              && (mip6opt.mip6po_rthdr2 != NULL)) {
426                                  /*
427                                   * if a type 2 routing header is not specified
428                                   * when ip6_output() is called and
429                                   * mip6_exthdr_create() creates a type 2
430                                   * routing header for route optimization,
431                                   * insert it.
432                                   */
433                                  MAKE_EXTHDR(mip6opt.mip6po_rthdr2,
    &exthdrs.ip6e_rthdr2);
434                                  /*
435                                   * if a routing header exists dest1 must be
436                                   * inserted if it exists.
437                                   */
438                                  if ((opt != NULL) && (opt->ip6po_dest1) &&
439                                      (exthdrs.ip6e_dest1 == NULL)) {
440                                          m_freem(exthdrs.ip6e_dest1);
441                                          MAKE_EXTHDR(opt->ip6po_dest1,
442                                              &exthdrs.ip6e_dest1);
443                                  }
444                          }
445                          /* Home Address Destinatio Option. */
446                          if (mip6opt.mip6po_haddr != NULL)
447                                  have_hao = 1;
448                          MAKE_EXTHDR(mip6opt.mip6po_haddr, &exthdrs.ip6e_haddr);
449                  } else {
450                          /*
451                           * this is a forwarded packet.  do not modify any
452                           * extension headers.
453                           */
454                  }
455
456                  if (exthdrs.ip6e_mh) {
....
458                          if (ip6->ip6_nxt != IPPROTO_NONE || m->m_next != NULL)
459                                  panic("not supported piggyback");
460                          exthdrs.ip6e_mh->m_next = m->m_next;
461                          m->m_next = exthdrs.ip6e_mh;
462                          *mtod(exthdrs.ip6e_mh, u_char *) = ip6->ip6_nxt;
463                          ip6->ip6_nxt = IPPROTO_MH;
464                          m->m_pkthdr.len += exthdrs.ip6e_mh->m_len;
465                          exthdrs.ip6e_mh = NULL;
466                  }
```

—— ip6_output.c

— *Line 433 is broken here for layout reasons. However, it is a single line of code.*

406–422 If the packet being sent requires any extension headers for route optimization, the node will insert those necessary headers by calling the mip6_exthdr_create() function. The IP6A_NOTUSEBC flag is used when a home agent needs to ignore a binding cache entry when sending a Binding Acknowledgment message since the Type 2 Routing Header is already inserted, if needed, when sending a Binding Acknowledgment message, as discussed in Section 5.16.13.

424–444 The mip6_exthdr_create() function creates a Destination Options Header which includes a Home Address option and a Type 2 Routing Header. The created headers will be stored in the mip6_pktopts{} structure specified as the mip6opt variable. If a Type 2 Routing Header is not specified in the ip6_pktopts{} instance and the mip6_exthdr_create() function generates a Type 2 Routing Header, the node will insert the header using the MAKE_EXTHDR() macro. If there is a first Destination Options

Header specified as `ip6po_dest1`, the node needs to insert it since the node has a Routing Header at this point.

445–448 If the `mip6_exthdr_create()` function generates a Destination Options Header which includes a Home Address option, the node inserts the header.

456–466 When a caller of the `ip6_output()` function specifies a Mobility Header as the `ip6_pktopts{}` structure, the node rearranges the packet. Lines 458–459 is a simple validation of the mbuf which contains the outgoing packet. The Mobility Header must not have any following headers. That is, the next header field (`ip6_nxt`) must be `IPPROTO_NONE` and the IPv6 packet must not have a following mbuf.

The mbuf which contains the Mobility Header is rearranged as the next mbuf of the IPv6 header and the next header value is set to `IPPROTO_MH`.

Listing 5-534
```
                                                                    ip6_output.c
824             if ((flags & IPV6_FORWARDING) == 0) {
825                     /*
826                      * after the IPsec processing, the IPv6 header source
827                      * address (this is the homeaddress of this node) and
828                      * the address currently stored in the Home Address
829                      * destination option (this is the coa of this node)
830                      * must be swapped.
831                      */
832                     if ((error = mip6_addr_exchange(m, exthdrs.ip6e_haddr)) != 0) {
....
836                             goto bad;
837                     }
838             } else {
839                     /*
840                      * this is a forwarded packet.  The typical (and
841                      * only ?) case is multicast packet forwarding.  The
842                      * swapping has been already done before (if
843                      * necessary).  we must not touch any extension
844                      * headers at all.
845                      */
846             }
                                                                    ip6_output.c
```

832–837 If the node is acting as a mobile node and the outgoing packet has a Home Address option, the node needs to exchange the source address (which at this point is the care-of address of the mobile node) and the home address stored in the Home Address option before routing the packet.

Listing 5-535
```
                                                                    ip6_output.c
857             if (exthdrs.ip6e_rthdr)
858                     rh = (struct ip6_rthdr *)(mtod(exthdrs.ip6e_rthdr,
859                         struct ip6_rthdr *));
....
861             else if (exthdrs.ip6e_rthdr2)
862                     rh = (struct ip6_rthdr *)(mtod(exthdrs.ip6e_rthdr2,
863                         struct ip6_rthdr *));
....
```

```
865                     if (rh) {
866                             struct ip6_rthdr0 *rh0;
867                             struct in6_addr *addr;
868                             struct sockaddr_in6 sa;
869
870                             finaldst = ip6->ip6_dst;
871                             switch (rh->ip6r_type) {
  ....
873                             case IPV6_RTHDR_TYPE_2:
  ....
875                             case IPV6_RTHDR_TYPE_0:
876                                     rh0 = (struct ip6_rthdr0 *)rh;
877                                     addr = (struct in6_addr *)(rh0 + 1);
```
 .... [Address swapping procedure for a Routing Header]
```
909                             }
910                     }
```
_____ip6_output.c

857–910 If a correspondent node has a Type 2 Routing Header, the destination address and the address included in the Routing Header needs to be exchanged, as well as the Home Address option. The exchange procedure is almost the same as that of the Type 1 Routing Header.

Receiving a Route Optimized Packet

A route optimized packet sent from a mobile node has a Home Address option. The option processing is done while the receiving node is processing the Destination Options header. This procedure was discussed in Section 5.16.15. A route optimized packet sent from a correspondent node has a Type 2 Routing Header. This processing code was discussed in Section 5.17.7.

Creating Extension Headers

Extension headers for route optimized packets are created by the `mip6_exthdr_create()` function.

Listing 5-536
_____mip6_cncore.c
```
513     int
514     mip6_exthdr_create(m, opt, mip6opt)
515             struct mbuf *m;                 /* ip datagram */
516             struct ip6_pktopts *opt;        /* pktopt passed to ip6_output */
517             struct mip6_pktopts *mip6opt;
518     {
519             struct ip6_hdr *ip6;
520             int s, error = 0;
  ....
522             struct hif_softc *sc;
523             struct mip6_bu *mbu;
524             int need_hao = 0;
```
_____mip6_cncore.c

513–516 The `mip6_exthdr_create()` function has three parameters: The m parameter is a pointer to the mbuf which contains a packet to be sent; the `opt` parameter is a pointer to the `ip6_pktopts{}` instance which has been passed to the `ip6_output()` function;

and the `mip6opt` parameter is a pointer to the `mip6_pktopts{}` instance. The function
will create all necessary header information and store it in the `mip6opt` variable.

Listing 5-537

──mip6_cncore.c

```
538             /*
539              * From section 6.1: "Mobility Header messages MUST NOT be
540              * sent with a type 2 routing header, except as described in
541              * Section 9.5.4 for Binding Acknowledgment".
542              */
543             if ((opt != NULL)
544                 && (opt->ip6po_mh != NULL)
545                 && (opt->ip6po_mh->ip6mh_type != IP6_MH_TYPE_BACK)) {
546                     goto skip_rthdr2;
547             }
```

──mip6_cncore.c

543–547 A Mobility Header cannot have a Type 2 Routing Header except for the Binding
Acknowledgment message. If `ip6po_mh`, which contains a Mobility Header, is specified
and the type is not a Binding Acknowledgment, the function skips the creation code of a
Type 2 Routing Header.

Listing 5-538

──mip6_cncore.c

```
549             /*
550              * create rthdr2 only if the caller of ip6_output() doesn't
551              * specify rthdr2 adready.
552              */
553             if ((opt != NULL) &&
554                 (opt->ip6po_rthdr2 != NULL))
555                     goto skip_rthdr2;
556
557             /*
558              * add the routing header for the route optimization if there
559              * exists a valid binding cache entry for this destination
560              * node.
561              */
562             error = mip6_rthdr_create_withdst(&mip6opt->mip6po_rthdr2,
563                 &ip6->ip6_dst, opt);
564             if (error) {
....
568                     goto bad;
569             }
570     skip_rthdr2:
```

──mip6_cncore.c

553–555 If the caller of the `ip6_output()` function explicitly specifies a Type 2 Routing
Header (that is, `ip6po_rthdr2` is specified), the function respects the intention of the
caller.

562–569 A Type 2 Routing Header is created by the `mip6_rthdr_create_withdst()`
function and stored in the `mip6po_rthdr2` pointer.

Listing 5-539

──mip6_cncore.c

```
573             /* the following stuff is applied only for a mobile node. */
574             if (!MIP6_IS_MN) {
```

```
575                     goto skip_hao;
576             }
577
578             /*
579              * find hif that has a home address that is the same
580              * to the source address of this sending ip packet
581              */
582             sc = hif_list_find_withhaddr(&ip6->ip6_src);
583             if (sc == NULL) {
584                     /*
585                      * this source addrss is not one of our home addresses.
586                      * we don't need any special care about this packet.
587                      */
588                     goto skip_hao;
589             }
```
_____mip6_cncore.c

574–576 A Home Address option is inserted only if the node is acting as a mobile node.

582–589 If the source address of the outgoing packet is one of the home addresses of the
mobile node, a pointer to the virtual home interface related to the home address is searched
for. If the source address is not a home address, then no related virtual home interface
will be found. In this case, there is no need to insert a Home Address option.

Listing 5-540
_____mip6_cncore.c

```
591             /*
592              * check home registration status for this destination
593              * address.
594              */
595             mbu = mip6_bu_list_find_withpaddr(&sc->hif_bu_list, &ip6->ip6_dst,
596                 &ip6->ip6_src);
597             if (mbu == NULL) {
598                     /* no registration action has been started yet. */
599                     goto skip_hao;
600             }
```
_____mip6_cncore.c

595–600 If a mobile node does not have a binding update list entry to the peer node, the node
cannot perform a route optimized communication.

Listing 5-541
_____mip6_cncore.c

```
602             if ((opt != NULL) && (opt->ip6po_mh != NULL)) {
603                     if (opt->ip6po_mh->ip6mh_type == IP6_MH_TYPE_BU)
604                             need_hao = 1;
605                     else {
606                             /*
607                              * From 6.1 Mobility Header: "Mobility Header
608                              * messages also MUST NOT be used with a Home
609                              * Address destination option, except as
610                              * described in Section 11.7.1 and Section
611                              * 11.7.2 for Binding Update."
612                              */
613                             goto skip_hao;
614                     }
615             }
```
_____mip6_cncore.c   ·

602–615 A Home Address option must not be used with the Mobility Header except with
a Binding Update message. If the packet has a Mobility Header (that is, `ip6po_mh` is

specified) and the type is not Binding Update, the creation of a Home Address option is
skipped.

Listing 5-542

```
616                 if ((mbu->mbu_flags & IP6MU_HOME) != 0) {
617                         /* to my home agent. */
618                         if (!need_hao &&
619                             (mbu->mbu_pri_fsm_state == MIP6_BU_PRI_FSM_STATE_IDLE ||
620                              mbu->mbu_pri_fsm_state == MIP6_BU_PRI_FSM_STATE_WAITD))
621                                 goto skip_hao;
622                 } else {
623                         /* to any of correspondent nodes. */
624                         if (!need_hao && !MIP6_IS_BU_BOUND_STATE(mbu))
625                                 goto skip_hao;
626                 }
```

616–621 The outgoing packet is destined for the home agent of the mobile node. A Home
Address option must be used only when the mobile node is registered. If the registration
state is MIP6_BU_PRI_FSM_STATE_IDLE or MIP6_BU_PRI_FSM_STATE_WAITD, the
packet must not have a Home Address option.

622–626 The same conditions are checked for a correspondent node.

Listing 5-543

```
627                 /* create a home address destination option. */
628                 error = mip6_haddr_destopt_create(&mip6opt->mip6po_haddr,
629                     &ip6->ip6_src, &ip6->ip6_dst, sc);
630                 if (error) {
....
634                         goto bad;
635                 }
636        skip_hao:
637                 error = 0; /* normal exit. */
....
639
640        bad:
641                 splx(s);
642                 return (error);
643         }
```

628–629 The mip6_haddr_destopt_create() function is called and a Destination
Options Header which contains the Home Address option is created.

Creating a Type 2 Routing Header with a Destination Address

The mip6_rthdr_create_withdst() function creates a Type 2 Routing Header for a
mobile node with the specified home address of the mobile node.

Listing 5-544

```
681        static int
682        mip6_rthdr_create_withdst(pktopt_rthdr, dst, opt)
683                 struct ip6_rthdr **pktopt_rthdr;
684                 struct in6_addr *dst;
```

```
685                 struct ip6_pktopts *opt;
686      {
687                 struct mip6_bc *mbc;
688                 int error = 0;
689
690                 mbc = mip6_bc_list_find_withphaddr(&mip6_bc_list, dst);
691                 if (mbc == NULL) {
692                         /* no binding cache entry for this dst is found. */
693                         return (0);
694                 }
695
696                 error = mip6_rthdr_create(pktopt_rthdr, &mbc->mbc_pcoa, opt);
697                 if (error) {
698                         return (error);
699                 }
700
701                 return (0);
702      }
```
——mip6_cncore.c

681–685 The `dst` parameter is the home address of a mobile node.

690–699 The `mip6_bc_list_find_withphaddr()` function is called to find a binding cache entry for the mobile node whose home address is `dst`. If a correspondent node has such a binding cache entry, the `mip6_rthdr_create()` function is called with the care-of address of the mobile node to create a Type 2 Routing Header which contains the care-of address of the mobile node. The address in the Routing Header will be exchanged with the destination address of an IPv6 header in the `ip6_output()` function later.

Creating a Home Address Option

The `mip6_haddr_destopt_create()` function creates a Destination Options Header which contains a Home Address option.

Listing 5-545
——mip6_mncore.c
```
2420     int
2421     mip6_haddr_destopt_create(pktopt_haddr, src, dst, sc)
2422            struct ip6_dest **pktopt_haddr;
2423            struct in6_addr *src;
2424            struct in6_addr *dst;
2425            struct hif_softc *sc;
2426     {
2427            struct in6_addr hif_coa;
2428            struct ip6_opt_home_address haddr_opt;
2429            struct mip6_buffer optbuf;
2430            struct mip6_bu *mbu;
2431            struct in6_addr *coa;
```
——mip6_mncore.c

2420–2425 The `pktopt_haddr` parameter is a pointer where the created header is placed. The `src` and `dst` parameters are the source address and the destination address of a mobile node, respectively. The `sc` parameter is a pointer to the virtual home interface of the mobile node.

Listing 5-546
——mip6_mncore.c
```
2433            if (*pktopt_haddr) {
2434                    /* already allocated ? */
```

```
2435                     return (0);
2436             }
2437
2438             /* get current CoA and recover its scope information. */
2439             if (sc->hif_coa_ifa == NULL) {
....
2443                     return (0);
2444             }
2445             hif_coa = sc->hif_coa_ifa->ia_addr.sin6_addr;
```
——mip6_mncore.c

2433–2435 If the caller of the `ip6_output()` function has already specified a Home Address option, the caller's intention is respected.

2439–2445 The care-of address of the mobile node is taken from the virtual home interface. If the mobile node does not have a valid care-of address, a Home Address option cannot be created.

Listing 5-547

——mip6_mncore.c
```
2447             bzero(&haddr_opt, sizeof(struct ip6_opt_home_address));
2448             haddr_opt.ip6oh_type = IP6OPT_HOME_ADDRESS;
2449             haddr_opt.ip6oh_len = IP6OPT_HALEN;
2450
2451             mbu = mip6_bu_list_find_withpaddr(&sc->hif_bu_list, dst, src);
2452             if (mbu && ((mbu->mbu_state & MIP6_BU_STATE_NEEDTUNNEL) != 0)) {
2453                     return (0);
2454             }
2455             if (mbu)
2456                     coa = &mbu->mbu_coa;
2457             else
2458                     coa = &hif_coa;
2459             bcopy((caddr_t)coa, haddr_opt.ip6oh_addr, sizeof(struct in6_addr));
```
——mip6_mncore.c

2451–2454 If the destination node does not support Mobile IPv6 (the `MIP6_BU_STATE_NEEDTUNNEL` flag is set), a Home Address option will not be created.

2452–2459 The care-of address of the mobile node is copied to the option. The address will be swapped with the source address of the IPv6 packet later in the `ip6_output()` function.

Note that the variable `mbu` will never be a NULL pointer. The code from lines 2457 to 2458 is old and was never executed. The code was used in the older Mobile IPv6 specification, which allowed using a Home Address option without a correct binding between a mobile node and a correspondent node.

Listing 5-548

——mip6_mncore.c
```
2461             MALLOC(optbuf.buf, u_int8_t *, MIP6_BUFFER_SIZE, M_IP6OPT, M_NOWAIT);
2462             if (optbuf.buf == NULL) {
2463                     return (ENOMEM);
2464             }
2465             bzero((caddr_t)optbuf.buf, MIP6_BUFFER_SIZE);
```

```
2466              optbuf.off = 2;
2467
2468              /* Add Home Address option */
2469              mip6_add_opt2dh((u_int8_t *)&haddr_opt, &optbuf);
2470              mip6_align_destopt(&optbuf);
2471
2472              *pktopt_haddr = (struct ip6_dest *)optbuf.buf;
....
2476              return (0);
2477      }
```
_____ mip6_mncore.c

2461–2472 Memory space to hold a Destination Options Header is allocated and the Home
Address option created just before is inserted on line 2469.

5.17.25   Tunnel Control

Adding/Removing a Tunnel

A mobile node and a home agent create a tunnel interface between them to send/receive
packets between the mobile node and correspondent nodes. The tunnel is created/destroyed
by the generic tunnel mechanism provided by the `mip6_tunnel_control()` function.

Listing 5-549

_____ mip6_cncore.c
```
2869      int
2870      mip6_tunnel_control(action, entry, func, ep)
2871              int action;
2872              void *entry;
2873              int (*func)(const struct mbuf *, int, int, void *);
2874              const struct encaptab **ep;
2875      {
....
2877      #ifdef MIP6_MOBILE_NODE
2878              struct mip6_bu *mbu;
2879              struct sockaddr_in6 haddr_sa, coa_sa, paddr_sa;
2880      #endif
2881      #ifdef MIP6_HOME_AGENT
2882              struct mip6_bc *mbc;
2883              struct sockaddr_in6 phaddr_sa, pcoa_sa, addr_sa;
2884      #endif
```
_____ mip6_cncore.c

2869–2874 The `mip6_tunnel_control()` function has four parameters. The `action`
parameter is the type of operation. The `MIP6_TUNNEL_ADD`, `MIP6_TUNNEL_CHANGE` or
`MIP6_TUNNEL_DELETE` command can be specified. The `entry` parameter is a pointer
to a binding update list entry or a binding cache entry based on the type of the node.
The `func` parameter is a pointer to the function which decides whether the node should
receive a tunneled packet. `ep` is a pointer to the tunnel information provided by the
generic tunnel mechanism.

Listing 5-550

_____ mip6_cncore.c
```
2886              if ((entry == NULL) && (ep == NULL)) {
2887                      return (EINVAL);
2888              }
```

```
.... [IPsec processing]
2959                /* before doing anything, remove an existing encap entry. */
2960                switch (action) {
2961                case MIP6_TUNNEL_ADD:
2962                case MIP6_TUNNEL_CHANGE:
2963                case MIP6_TUNNEL_DELETE:
2964                        if (*ep != NULL) {
2965                                encap_detach(*ep);
2966                                *ep = NULL;
2967                        }
2968                }
                                                                        ___mip6_cncore.c
```

2960–2968 Existing tunnel information is removed by the `encap_detach()` function, which removes the tunnel interface entry from the kernel, before adding/changing the information.

Listing 5-551
                                                                        ___mip6_cncore.c

```
2970                switch (action) {
2971                case MIP6_TUNNEL_ADD:
2972                case MIP6_TUNNEL_CHANGE:
2973                        *ep = encap_attach_func(AF_INET6, IPPROTO_IPV6,
2974                                                func,
2975                                                (struct protosw *)&mip6_tunnel_protosw,
2976                                                (void *)entry);
2977                        if (*ep == NULL) {
....
2982                                return (EINVAL);
2983                        }
2984                        break;
2985                }
2986
2987                return (0);
2988        }
                                                                        ___mip6_cncore.c
```

2970–2984 If the operation is removing, the process has been done already. If the operation is adding or changing, a new tunnel information entry is created by the `encap_attach_func()` function, which inserts the tunnel information into the kernel.

Validation of Packets Received from a Tunnel

The `mip6_bu_encapcheck()` function is called when a mobile node receives an IPv6 in IPv6 packet.

Listing 5-552
                                                                        ___mip6_mncore.c

```
1859    int
1860    mip6_bu_encapcheck(m, off, proto, arg)
1861            const struct mbuf *m;
1862            int off;
1863            int proto;
1864            void *arg;
1865    {
1866            struct ip6_hdr *ip6;
1867            struct mip6_bu *mbu = (struct mip6_bu *)arg;
```

```
1868            struct hif_softc *sc;
1869            struct mip6_prefix *mpfx;
1870            struct in6_addr *haaddr, *myaddr, *mycoa;
```
──mip6_mncore.c

1859–1864 The function must return a positive value (from 1 to 128) if the packet is acceptable and must return 0 if it is not acceptable. m is a pointer to the incoming packet. off and proto are the offset to the inner packet header and a protocol number of the inner packet, respectively. These two parameters are not used in this function. arg is a pointer which is the pointer passed when the tunnel information is registered by the encap_attach_func() function on line 2973 of mip6_cncore.c (Listing 5–551). In a mobile node case, a pointer to a binding update entry is set.

Listing 5-553
──mip6_mncore.c
```
1879            ip6 = mtod(m, struct ip6_hdr*);
1880
1881            haaddr = &mbu->mbu_paddr;
1882            myaddr = &mbu->mbu_haddr;
1883            mycoa = &mbu->mbu_coa;
1884
1885            /*
1886             * check whether this packet is from the correct sender (that
1887             * is, our home agent) to the CoA or the HoA the mobile node
1888             * has registered before.
1889             */
1890            if (!IN6_ARE_ADDR_EQUAL(&ip6->ip6_src, haaddr) ||
1891                !(IN6_ARE_ADDR_EQUAL(&ip6->ip6_dst, mycoa) ||
1892                  IN6_ARE_ADDR_EQUAL(&ip6->ip6_dst, myaddr))) {
1893                    return (0);
1894            }
```
──mip6_mncore.c

1881–1894 The source address of the tunnel packet must be the address of the home agent of the mobile node. The destination address of the tunnel packet must be either the home address or the care-of address of the mobile node. Otherwise, the packet is dropped.

Listing 5-554
──mip6_mncore.c
```
1896            /*
1897             * XXX: should we compare the ifid of the inner dstaddr of the
1898             * incoming packet and the ifid of the mobile node's?  these
1899             * check will be done in the ip6_input and later.
1900             */
1901
1902            /* check mn prefix */
1903            for (mpfx = LIST_FIRST(&mip6_prefix_list); mpfx;
1904                mpfx = LIST_NEXT(mpfx, mpfx_entry)) {
1905                    if (!in6_are_prefix_equal(myaddr, &mpfx->mpfx_prefix,
1906                        mpfx->mpfx_prefixlen)) {
1907                            /* this prefix doesn't match my prefix.
1908                                check next. */
1909                            continue;
1910                    }
1911                    goto match;
1912            }
1913            return (0);
```

```
1914    match:
1915            return (128);
1916    }
```
                                                                        ___mip6_mncore.c

1903–1912 If the prefix part of the home address is not one of the prefixes that the mobile
node is managing, the packet is dropped. This code is redundant and can be removed,
since in the KAME implementation the prefix of a home address is always one of the
prefixes which a mobile node is managing.

Listing 5-555
                                                                        ___mip6_hacore.c

```
662    int
663    mip6_bc_encapcheck(m, off, proto, arg)
664            const struct mbuf *m;
665            int off;
666            int proto;
667            void *arg;
668    {
669            struct ip6_hdr *ip6;
670            struct mip6_bc *mbc = (struct mip6_bc *)arg;
671            struct in6_addr *mnaddr;
672
673            if (mbc == NULL) {
674                    return (0);
675            }
676
677            ip6 = mtod(m, struct ip6_hdr*);
678
679            mnaddr = &mbc->mbc_pcoa;
680
681            /* check mn addr */
682            if (!IN6_ARE_ADDR_EQUAL(&ip6->ip6_src, mnaddr)) {
683                    return (0);
684            }
685
686            /* check my addr */
687            /* XXX */
688
689            return (128);
690    }
```
                                                                        ___mip6_hacore.c

662–667 The mip6_bc_encapcheck() does the validation check for the incoming tunnel
packets on a home agent. The meaning of the m, off and proto parameters are the
same as the parameters of the mip6_bu_encapcheck() function. arg is a pointer to
a binding cache entry, which is registered by the encap_attach_func() function on
line 2973 in Listing 5-551 of mip6_cncore.c.

679–684 The function returns 128 if the source address of the incoming tunnel packet is the
care-of address of a mobile node. The destination address of the tunnel packet is not
checked at this moment, but in theory it should also be checked.

5.17.26 Receiving Packets from a Tunnel

If a mobile node or a home agent accepts a tunnel packet, the packet is input to the
mip6_tunnel_input() function through the protocol switch mechanism.

Listing 5-556

―――in6_proto.c

```
229     struct ip6protosw inet6sw[] = {
....
530     struct ip6protosw mip6_tunnel_protosw =
531     { SOCK_RAW,      &inet6domain,      IPPROTO_IPV6,      PR_ATOMIC|PR_ADDR,
532       mip6_tunnel_input, rip6_output,        0,         rip6_ctloutput,
....
534       0,
....
538       0,                0,                0,                0,
....
540       &rip6_usrreqs
....
542     };
```

―――in6_proto.c

530–542 The inet6sw[] array specifies an input function based on the protocol number. The mip6_tunnel_protosw variable declares the mip6_tunnel_input() function as the IPv6 in IPv6 protocol handing function. The information is passed when the encap_attach_func() function is called on line 2973 in Listing 5-551 of mip6_cncore.c.

Listing 5-557

―――mip6_cncore.c

```
2803    int
2804    mip6_tunnel_input(mp, offp, proto)
2805            struct mbuf **mp;
2806            int *offp, proto;
2807    {
2808            struct mbuf *m = *mp;
2809            struct ip6_hdr *ip6;
....
2811            int s;
```

―――mip6_cncore.c

2803–2806 The mip6_tunnel_input() function is called when a mobile node or a home agent receives an IPv6 in IPv6 packet from its home agent or mobile nodes, respectively.

Listing 5-558

―――mip6_cncore.c

```
2814            m_adj(m, *offp);
2815
2816            switch (proto) {
2817            case IPPROTO_IPV6:
2818                    if (m->m_len < sizeof(*ip6)) {
2819                            m = m_pullup(m, sizeof(*ip6));
2820                            if (!m)
2821                                    return (IPPROTO_DONE);
2822                    }
2823
2824                    ip6 = mtod(m, struct ip6_hdr *);
....
2831                    s = splimp();
....
2838                    if (IF_QFULL(&ip6intrq)) {
2839                            IF_DROP(&ip6intrq);     /* update statistics */
2840                            splx(s);
```

```
2841                          goto bad;
2842                     }
2843                     IF_ENQUEUE(&ip6intrq, m);
  ....
2851                     splx(s);
  ....
2853                     break;
2854            default:
  ....
2859                     goto bad;
2860               }
2861
2862          return (IPPROTO_DONE);
2863
2864    bad:
2865          m_freem(m);
2866          return (IPPROTO_DONE);
2867     }
```
                                                                         ————mip6_cncore.c

2814 The outer header is stripped.

2816–2867 The `mip6_tunnel_input()` function accepts only an IPv6 packet as an inner
packet. If the inner packet is an IPv6 packet, the packet is enqueued to the IPv6 input
packet queue by the `IF_ENQUEUE()` macro, as long as the queue is not full. If the queue
is full, then the packet is dropped. All other packets whose protocol is not IPv6 are also
dropped.

5.17.27 I/O Control

An I/O control interface is provided to manage the Mobile IPv6 features from a user space
program. The I/O control is implemented as the `mip6_ioctl()` function. Table 5-43 shows
the list of I/O control commands.

TABLE 5-43

Name	Description
SIOCSMIP6CFG	Configure features. The following subcommands are required.
SIOCSMIP6CFG_ENABLEMN	Enable a mobile node feature.
SIOCSMIP6CFG_DISABLEMN	Disable a mobile node feature.
SIOCSMIP6CFG_ENABLEHA	Enable a home agent feature.
SIOCSMIP6CFG_ENABLEIPSEC	Enable IPsec signal packets protection.
SIOCSMIP6CFG_DISABLEIPSEC	Disable IPsec signal packets protection.
SIOCSMIP6CFG_ENABLEDEBUG	Enable debug messages.
SIOCSMIP6CFG_DISABLEDEBUG	Disable debug message.
SIOCDBC	Remove binding cache entries.
SIOCSPREFERREDIFNAMES	Set preferences of interface names when a care-of address is chosen.

IO control commands for Mobile IPv6.

Listing 5-559

_____mip6_cncore.c

```
264    int
265    mip6_ioctl(cmd, data)
266            u_long cmd;
267            caddr_t data;
268    {
269            int subcmd;
270            struct mip6_req *mr = (struct mip6_req *)data;
271            int s;
```
_____mip6_cncore.c

264–267 The `mip6_ioctl()` function has two parameters. The `cmd` parameter is one of the control commands listed in Table 5-43 and the `data` parameter is a pointer to the `mip6_req{}` structure which contains data related to the command.

Listing 5-560

_____mip6_cncore.c

```
279            switch (cmd) {
280            case SIOCSMIP6CFG:
281                    subcmd = *(int *)data;
282                    switch (subcmd) {
```
_____mip6_cncore.c

280–282 The `SIOCSMIP6CFG` command configures various Mobile IPv6 features, and it has several subcommands.

Listing 5-561

_____mip6_cncore.c

```
284                    case SIOCSMIP6CFG_ENABLEMN:
285                    {
286                            int error;
287                            error = mip6_mobile_node_start();
288                            if (error) {
289                                    splx(s);
290                                    return (error);
291                            }
292                    }
293                            break;
294
295                    case SIOCSMIP6CFG_DISABLEMN:
296                            mip6_mobile_node_stop();
297                            break;
....
301                    case SIOCSMIP6CFG_ENABLEHA:
....
305                            mip6ctl_nodetype = MIP6_NODETYPE_HOME_AGENT;
306                            break;
```
_____mip6_cncore.c

284–306 The `SIOCSMIP6CFG_ENABLEMN` subcommand activates the mobile node feature. The activation code is implemented in the `mip6_mobile_node_start()` function. The `SIOCSMIP6CFG_DISABLEMN` subcommand stops the mobile node function. The `mip6_mobile_node_stop()` function does the actual work. `SIOCSMIP6CFG_ENABLEHA` activates the home agent function. Currently, no deactivation mechanism is provided to stop the home agent function.

Listing 5-562

───mip6_cncore.c
```
309                     case SIOCSMIP6CFG_ENABLEIPSEC:
....
313                             mip6ctl_use_ipsec = 1;
314                             break;
315
316                     case SIOCSMIP6CFG_DISABLEIPSEC:
....
320                             mip6ctl_use_ipsec = 0;
321                             break;
322
323                     case SIOCSMIP6CFG_ENABLEDEBUG:
....
327                             mip6ctl_debug = 1;
328                             break;
329
330                     case SIOCSMIP6CFG_DISABLEDEBUG:
....
334                             mip6ctl_debug = 0;
335                             break;
336
337                     default:
338                             splx(s);
339                             return (EINVAL);
340                     }
341                     break;
```
───mip6_cncore.c

309–341 The SIOCSMIP6CFG_ENABLEIPSEC, the SIOCSMIP6CFG_DISABLEIPSEC, the
SIOCSMIP6CFG_ENABLEDEBUG and the SIOCSMIP6CFG_DISABLEDEBUG set Mobile
IPv6-related global variables. These global variables can be modified via the sysctl mechanism in addition to the I/O control mechanism.

Listing 5-563

───mip6_cncore.c
```
363             case SIOCDBC:
364                     if (IN6_IS_ADDR_UNSPECIFIED(&mr->mip6r_ru.mip6r_in6)) {
365                             struct mip6_bc *mbc;
366
367                             /* remove all binding cache entries. */
368                             while ((mbc = LIST_FIRST(&mip6_bc_list)) != NULL) {
369                                     (void)mip6_bc_list_remove(&mip6_bc_list, mbc);
370                             }
371                     } else {
372                             struct mip6_bc *mbc;
373
374                             /* remove a specified binding cache entry. */
375                             mbc = mip6_bc_list_find_withphaddr(&mip6_bc_list,
376                                 &mr->mip6r_ru.mip6r_in6);
377                             if (mbc != NULL) {
378                                     (void)mip6_bc_list_remove(&mip6_bc_list, mbc);
379                             }
380                     }
381                     break;
```
───mip6_cncore.c

363 The SIOCDBC command removes a specified binding cache entry if the IPv6 address
to be removed is specified. Otherwise, it removes all binding cache entries kept in a
node.

364–370 If the specified IPv6 address is the unspecified address, the `mip6_bc_list_remove()` function is called for all binding cache entries listed in the global variable `mip6_bc_list`. All cache entries are removed.

371–380 If an IPv6 address is specified, the related binding cache entry found by the `mip6_bc_list_find_withphaddr()` function is removed from the cache list.

Listing 5-564

_____mip6_cncore.c

```
439              case SIOCSPREFERREDIFNAMES:
440              {
441                  /*
442                   * set preferrable ifps for selecting CoA.  we must
443                   * keep the name as a string because other information
444                   * (such as a pointer, interface index) may be changed
445                   * when removing the devices.
446                   */
447                  bcopy(&mr->mip6r_ru.mip6r_ifnames, &mip6_preferred_ifnames,
448                      sizeof(mr->mip6r_ru.mip6r_ifnames));
449                  mip6_process_movement();
450              }
451
452              break;
....
454              }
455
456          splx(s);
457
458          return (0);
459      }
```

_____mip6_cncore.c

439–450 The `SIOCSPREFERREDIFNAMES` command specifies the order in which network interface names are referenced when a mobile node chooses a care-of address from multiple network interfaces. The array of the interface names is copied to the `mip6_preferred_ifnames` variable. The `mip6_process_movement()` function is called to choose the most preferable network interface.

5.18   Mobile IPv6 Operation

In this section, we discuss the configuration of the Mobile IPv6 function using the KAME implementation. We assume the readers know the basic installation of the KAME protocol stack. If you are not familiar with the KAME kit, please read the instruction document which is placed in the top of the KAME distribution directory.

5.18.1   Rebuilding a Kernel with Mobile IPv6 Extension

The Mobile IPv6 features are not enabled by default. You must prepare a new kernel configuration file and rebuild your kernel to be able to support the Mobile IPv6 protocol. Some user-space programs also need to be rebuilt.

Kernel Options for Mobile Node

To enable mobile node features, the following kernel options need to be added to your kernel configuration file.

```
options MIP6
options MIP6_MOBILE_NODE
pseudo-device hif 1
```

`hif` indicates a virtual home interface. If you have more than one home network, you need to specify the number of home networks you use.

Kernel Options for Home Agent

To enable home agent features, the following kernel options need to be added to your kernel configuration file.

```
options MIP6
options MIP6_HOME_AGENT
```

Kernel Options for Correspondent Node

To enable correspondent node features, the following option needs to be added to your kernel configuration file.

```
options MIP6
```

5.18.2 Rebuilding User Space Programs

There are four user space programs related to Mobile IPv6.

1. **rtadvd**
   The router advertisement daemon.

2. **had**
   The daemon program that provides the Dynamic Home Agent Address Discovery and Mobile Prefix Solicitation/Advertisement mechanisms.

3. **mip6control**
   The control program of the KAME Mobile IPv6 functions.

4. **mip6stat**
   The program that displays statistics of packets related to Mobile IPv6.

Rebuilding rtadvd

You need to add a compiler option to the Makefile of the `rtadvd` daemon. You will find the Makefile for `rtadvd` in `${KAME}/freebsd4/sbin/rtadvd/` directory. The following line needs to be added to the Makefile.

```
CFLAGS+=-DMIP6
```

The **rtadvd** daemon compiled with the above option will include a Home Agent Information option in Router Advertisement messages when the daemon is launched with the −m switch. Also, the option will relax the restriction of the advertisement interval. In the basic IPv6 specification, a router must wait a minimum of 3 seconds when sending Router Advertisement messages periodically. With the option, a router can send Router Advertisement messages every 50 milliseconds at minimum.

Building Other Programs

Other user space programs (**had**, **mip6control**, **mip6stat**) require no additional configuration. These commands will be installed to the /usr/local/v6/sbin/ directory with other KAME programs.

5.18.3 IPsec Signal Protection

The Mobile IPv6 specification requires that the signaling packets be protected by the IPsec mechanism. KAME Mobile IPv6 users must set up by themselves properly, IPsec configuration between mobile nodes and its home agent; however, it would be tough work especially for those who are not familiar with IPsec and Mobile IPv6. The KAME implementation provides scripts to generate configuration files to set up IPsec configuration between a mobile node and a home agent.

- **mip6makeconfig.sh**
  Generate necessary configuration files.

- **mip6seccontrol.sh**
  Install IPsec configuration using configuration files generated by the **mip6makeconfig.sh** script.

These scripts are located in ${KAME}/kame/kame/mip6control/ directory.

Configuration Directory

The default configuration directory is /usr/local/v6/etc/mobileip6/. The configuration files for each node are created in a separate directory under this directory. In this example, we use the directory named mobile_node_0 as an example. The names of the directories which contain configuration files are arbitrary.

```
# mkdir /usr/local/v6/etc/mobileip6
# mkdir /usr/local/v6/etc/mobileip6/mobile_node_0
```

Preparing a Base Configuration File

The next step is to create a base configuration file for a mobile node. The name of the configuration file must be config. The file is placed under the configuration directory for each node. In this case, the file should be in the /usr/local/v6/etc/mobileip6/mobile_node_0/ directory.

The configuration file provides the following parameters.

- mobile_node
  The address of a mobile node.

- home_agent
  The address of a home agent.

- transport_spi_mn_to_ha
  The SPI value for the transport mode IPsec packets from a mobile node to a home agent.

- `transport_spi_mn_to_ha`
  The SPI value for the transport mode IPsec packets from a home agent to a mobile node.

- `transport_protocol`
  The name of IPsec transport mode protocol. `esp` or `ah` can be specified.

- `transport_esp_algorithm`
  The name of the encryption algorithm used by IPsec transport mode.

- `transport_esp_secret`
  The secret value for the encryption algorithm.

- `transport_auth_algorithm`
  The name of the authentication algorithm used by IPsec transport mode.

- `transport_auth_secret`
  The secret value for the authentication algorithm.

- `tunnel_spi_mn_to_ha`
  The SPI value for the tunnel mode IPsec packets from a mobile node to a home agent.

- `tunnel_spi_ha_to_mn`
  The SPI value for the tunnel mode IPsec packets from a home agent to a mobile node.

- `tunnel_uid_mn_to_ha`
  The identifier to bind a Security Association and Security Policy for the tunnel mode connection from a mobile node to a home agent.

- `tunnel_uid_ha_to_mn`
  The identifier to bind a Security Association and Security Policy for the tunnel mode connection from a home agent to a mobile node.

- `tunnel_esp_algorithm`
  The name of the encryption algorithm used by IPsec tunnel mode.

- `tunnel_esp_secret`
  The secret value for the encryption algorithm.

- `tunnel_auth_algorithm`
  The name of the authentication algorithm used by IPsec tunnel mode.

- `tunnel_auth_secret`
  The secret value for the authentication algorithm.

When `esp` is set to `transport_protocol` parameter, both the encryption algorithm/secret and the authentication algorithm/secret have to be set to `transport_esp_algorithm`, `transport_esp_secret` and `transport_auth_algorithm`, `transport_auth_ secret` parameters.

When `ah` is set to `transport_protocol` parameter, `transport_esp_algorithm` and `transport_esp_secret` parameters can be omitted.

Figure 5-61 is a sample configuration file.

The algorithms can be selected from all algorithms which are supported by the **setkey** command.

FIGURE 5-61

```
mobile_node=2001:db8:0:0:201:11ff:fe54:4fde
home_agent=2001:db8:0:0:201:11ff:fe54:5ffc
transport_spi_mn_to_ha=2000
transport_spi_ha_to_mn=2001
transport_protocol=esp
transport_esp_algorithm=blowfish-cbc
transport_esp_secret='"THIS_IS_ESP_SECRET!!"'
transport_auth_algorithm=hmac-sha1
transport_auth_secret='"THIS_IS_AUTH_SECRET"'
tunnel_spi_mn_to_ha=2002
tunnel_spi_ha_to_mn=2003
tunnel_uid_mn_to_ha=2002
tunnel_uid_ha_to_mn=2003
tunnel_esp_algorithm=blowfish-cbc
tunnel_esp_secret='"THIS_IS_ESP_SECRET!!"'
tunnel_auth_algorithm=hmac-sha1
tunnel_auth_secret='"THIS_IS_AUTH_SECRET"'
```

A sample configuration file for IPsec.

Generating Configuration Files

The **mip6makeconfig.sh** script generates several configuration files from the base configuration file. Launching the script with the name of the configuration directory will generate these files.

```
# mip6makeconfig.sh mobile_node_0
```

The above command will generate the following files under the configuration directory.

- `add`
  Add Security Associations.

- `delete`
  Delete Security Associations.

- `spdadd_mobile_node`
  Add Security Policies for a mobile node.

- `spddelete_mobile_node`
  Delete Security Policies for a mobile node.

- `spdadd_home_agent`
  Add Security Policies for a home agent.

- `spddelete_home_agent`
  Delete Security Policies for a home agent.

The contents of the above files are actually a command list for the **setkey** command.

FIGURE 5-62

```
mip6seccontrol.sh [-m|-g] [installall|install|deinstallall|deinstall]
[config_directory]
```

mip6seccontrol.sh *format.*

Installing IPsec Configuration

Basically, you do not need to install the configuration by hand. The startup script discussed in the next section will handle installation of the configuration file at boot time. If you need to manage the configuration, you can use the **mip6seccontrol.sh** script.

The **mip6seccontrol.sh** script installs/uninstalls IPsec configuration based on the files generated by the **mip6makeconfig.sh** script. The usage format of the script is shown in Figure 5-62.

On a mobile node, the `-m` switch must be specified, and on a home agent, `-g` must be specified. `installall` and `deinstallall` operations install or deinstall all configuration parameters placed in the configuration directory. If you want to manipulate configuration parameters for a single node, you need to use `install` and `deinstall` operations specifying the directory name of the node as the last argument.

5.18.4 Configuring Node

To provide an easy way to configure a Mobile IPv6 node, the KAME implementation provides a startup script. You will find the `rc` and `rc.mobileip6` scripts in the `${KAME}/freebsd4/etc/` directory. The scripts should be copied to the `/etc/` directory.

The script provides the following configuration parameters.

- `ipv6_mobile_enable`
  Set to `YES` if you use Mobile IPv6.

- `ipv6_mobile_config_dir`
  Set the directory which contains configuration files for IPsec between a home agent and a mobile node.

- `ipv6_mobile_nodetype`
  Define a type of node. Either `mobile_node` or `home_agent` can be set.

- `ipv6_mobile_home_prefixes`
  Set the home prefixes in a form of *prefix/prefixlen*. Multiple prefixes can be defined by separating them with a space character.

- `ipv6_mobile_home_link` [Home agent only]
  Set the physical interface name of a home network.

- `ipv6_mobile_debug_enable`
  Setting to `YES` will print debug messages to console.

- `ipv6_mobile_security_enable`
  Setting to `NO` will disable IPsec check against the signaling messages used by Mobile IPv6.

FIGURE 5-63

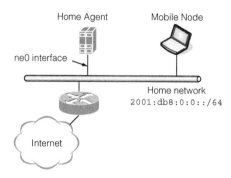

The sample operation network.

Configuring Mobile Node

Figure 5-63 shows the sample network used in this configuration example. In this example the home network is `2001:db8:0:0::/64`. The `rc.conf` file will include the following lines:

```
ipv6_mobile_enable="YES"
ipv6_mobile_config_dir="/usr/local/v6/etc/mobileip6"
ipv6_mobile_nodetype="mobile_node"
ipv6_mobile_home_prefixes="2001:db8:0:0::/64"
```

You need to generate all the necessary configuration files for IPsec signal protection by the **mip6makeconfig.sh** script, and put them in the directory specified by the `ip6_mobile_config_dir` parameter.

If you do not want to use IPsec signal protection, you need to remove all configuration files from the `/usr/local/v6/etc/mobileip6/` directory and add the following line to your `rc.conf` file.

```
ipv6_mobile_security_enable="NO"
```

> Note that the specification says the signaling message must be protected by the IPsec mechanism. Turning the protection off must be used only for testing purposes.

After restarting, your node will start acting as a mobile node.

Configuring a Home Agent

As illustrated in Figure 5-63, the home network is `2001:db8:0:0::/64` and the name of the network interface with which it is used as a home network is `ne0`.

```
ipv6_mobile_enable="YES"
ipv6_mobile_config_dir="/usr/local/v6/etc/mobileip6"
ipv6_mobile_nodetype="home_agent"
ipv6_mobile_home_prefixes="2001:db8:0:0::/64"
ipv6_mobile_home_link="ne0"
```

The configuration files for IPsec signal protection, generated by the **mip6makeconfig.sh** script in the same manner as you did for the mobile node, are stored in `/usr/local/v6/etc/mobileip6/`. You can use the same set of files generated for the mobile node, since the **mip6makeconfig.sh** script generates files for both a home agent and a mobile node.

Similar to the configuration procedure for a mobile node, if you want to dis-able IPsec signal protection, you need to remove all configuration files in the `/usr/local/v6/etc/mobileip6/` directory and add the following line in your `rc.conf` file.

```
ipv6_mobile_security_enable="NO"
```

Configuring Correspondent Node

There is no special procedure to enable correspondent node features. A node which has a kernel with the `MIP6` option acts as a correspondent node by default.

5.18.5 Viewing Status Information

The `mip6control` command provides a way to get the current binding information on a node. To get the current binding update list entries, the `-bl` switch is used. The `-b` switch indicates getting the information about binding update list entries, and the `-l` switch prints the address of nodes in a long format. You can use the `-c` switch to get the binding cache entries instead of the binding update list entries.

The following is the sample output of `mip6control -bl`.

```
$ mip6control -bl
paddr        haddr       coa         lifetim ltexp refresh retexp seqno flags pfsm  sfsm state
ha.kame.net  mn.kame.net 2001:200:11 420     312   210     102    54345 AHL   BOUND INIT
www.kame.net mn.kame.net 2001:200:11 420     130   420     130    34122       IDLE  INIT D
cn.kame.net  mn.kame.net 2001:200:11 420     229   420     229    3423        BOUND INIT
```

In the example, there are three binding update list entries. The first entry is a home registration entry. The other two entries are to IPv6 nodes. The node shown in the middle entry (`www.kame.net`) does not support Mobile IPv6. The state field will show a `D` flag when the node does not support Mobile IPv6. The last entry is performing route optimized communication with the mobile node.

The following is the sample output of `mip6control -cl`.

```
$ mip6control -cl
phaddr        pcoa addr   flags  seqno lifetim ltexp state refcnt
mn.kame.net   2001:200:11 AHL    54345 420     312   BOUND 0
fe80::203:2   2001:200:11 AHL    23414 420     312   BOUND 1
mn.wide.ad.jp 2001:280:45        8473  420     123   BOUND 0
```

The above node has three entries. The first two are home registration entries for mn.kame.net. The upper entry is for the global address of the mobile node, and the lower entry is for the link-local address of the mobile node. Since the mobile node has sent a Binding Update message with the `L` flag, the home agent also needs to protect its link-local address. The last entry is for another mobile node which has registered to another home agent. This node and the last node (`mn.wide.ad.jp`) are performing route-optimized communication.

The complete usage of the mip6control command can be found in manual page.

5.18.6 Viewing Statistics

The `mip6stat` command shows the statistics collected in a kernel. Figure 5-64 shows the sample output of the command. Each entry is related to the each member variable of the `mip6stat{}` structure described in Figure 5-64.

FIGURE 5-64

```
Input:
        82977 Mobility Headers
        1245 HoTI messages
        1245 CoTI messages
        0 HoT messages
        0 CoT messages
        82977 BU messages
        0 BA messages
        0 BR messages
        0 BE messages
        83439 Home Address Option
        12 unverified Home Address Option
        0 Routing Header type 2
        920861 reverse tunneled input
        0 bad MH checksum
        0 bad payload protocol
        0 unknown MH type
        0 not my home address
        0 no related binding update entry
        0 home init cookie mismatch
        0 careof init cookie mismatch
        29 unprotected binding signaling packets
        146 BUs discarded due to bad HAO
        0 RR authentication failed
        4 seqno mismatch
        0 parameter problem for HAO
        0 parameter problem for MH
        0 Invalid Care-of address
        0 Invalid mobility options
Output:
        82774 Mobility Headers
        1245 HoTI messages
        1245 CoTI messages
        0 HoT messages
        0 CoT messages
        0 BU messages
        82774 BA messages
        82774 binding update accepted
        0 BR messages
        12 BE messages
        0 Home Address Option
        83175 Routing Header type 2
        1223198 reverse tunneled output
```

A sample output of the mip6stat command.

5.19 Appendix

5.19.1 The Manual Page of mip6control

NAME

mip6control – control KAME/MIP6 features

SYNOPSIS

mip6control [-**i** *ifname*][-**abcghlmMnNw**][-**H** *home_prefix*][-**P** *prefixlen*]

[-**A** *home_agent_global_addr*][-**L** *home_agent_linklocal_addr*]

[-**C** *addr*][-**u** *address#port*][-**v** *address#port*]

[-**F** *ifp1[:ifp2[:ifp3]]*][-**S** *0|1*][-**D** *0|1*]

DESCRIPTION

mip6control sets/gets KAME/MIP6 related information. If no argument is specified,
   mip6control shows the current status of the node.

-**i**   *ifname*
   Specify home interface of the mobile node. The default value is hif().

-**H**   *home_prefix*
   Set *home_prefix* as a home prefix of the mobile node. You must specify the prefix
   length of *home_prefix* with -**P** option.

-**P**   *prefixlen*
   Specify the length of the prefix to be assigned to the mobile node. Use with -**H** option.

-**A**   *home_agent_global_address*
   Specify the global address of the home agent of this mobile node. If your home agent sup-
   ports DHAAD (Dynamic Home Agent Address Discovery), you need not use this switch.
   Use with -**L** option.

-**L**   *home_agent_linklocal_address*
   Specify the linklocal address of the home agent of this mobile node. If your home agent
   supports DHAAD (Dynamic Home Agent Address Discovery), you need not use this
   switch. Use with -**A** option.

-**m**   Start acting as a mobile node.

-**M**   Stop acting as a mobile node.

-**n**   Show network addresses as numbers.

-**h**   Show the home prefixes currently set to this mobile node.

-**a**   Show the home agents list.

-**b**   Show the binding update list.

-**g**   Start acting as a home agent.

-**c**   Show the binding cache entries.

−C   *addr*

Remove the binding cache entry specified by `addr`. `addr` is a home address of the binding cache entry. If::is specified, **mip6control** removes all binding cache entries.

−l   Show information in a long format.

−u   *Address#Port*

Add a rule that MN doesn't add a Home Address option to the outgoing packet.

−v   *Address#Port*

Delete the rule which specified one.

−w   Show the rule.

−F   *ifp1[:ifp2[:ifp3]]*

Set preferable network interfaces for CoA selection. Specify nothing to remove the preferences.

−S   *0|1*

When set to 0, the IPsec protection check of the incoming binding updates and binding acks will not be performed (always pass the check).

−D   *0|1*

When set to 0, no debug messages are printed.

−N   Show the list of nonces that this host maintains as a correspondent node. The first column is the number of nonce index and the second is a nonce value.

EXAMPLES

To make a node act as a mobile node, issue the following commands as a root.

```
root# mip6control -i hif0 -H 2001:200:1:1:: -P 64
root# mip6control -m
```

Replace 2001:200:1:1:: with your home network prefix.

To make a node act as a home agent, issue the following commands as a root.

```
root\# mip6control -g
```

To set a rule to avoid adding home address option when quering DNS, issue the following commands as a root.

```
root\# mip6control -u ::\#53
```

HISTORY

The `mip6control` command first appeared in WIDE/KAME IPv6 protocol stack kit.

BUGS

Many :).

6

IPv6 and IP Security

6.1 Introduction

The Internet started as a small research network in which all users were assumed innocent participants of open communications of that network. With that assumption, the Internet Protocol (IP) did not have any built-in security features as part of the protocol design initially. A few decades later, however, IP has been deployed worldwide and the Internet has become one of the most important communication media. As IP is becoming the main information exchange protocol, the demand to make the IP communication secure arises. IP Security (IPsec) is designed to protect the IP communication from entities with malicious intents.

IPsec was defined as an extension to the IPv4 specification, but IPsec was designed such that it is independent of the IP protocol versions. Currently, IPsec is widely deployed in IPv4 as a method to connect multiple remote sites for creating a single Virtual Private Network (VPN) over the Internet. In IPv6, supporting IPsec-related protocols is a mandatory requirement for any IPv6 node, which means all IPv6 nodes have IPsec enabled by default. This requirement will accelerate the deployment of IPsec not only for creating VPNs but also to encourage secure communications among IPv6 nodes.

IPsec is a set of mechanisms that adds authentication and encryption to the IP layer. IPv6 nodes must support the following specifications:

- Security Architecture for the Internet Protocol as defined in [RFC2401]

- IP Authentication Header (AH) as defined in [RFC2402]

- IP Encapsulating Security Payload (ESP) as defined in [RFC2406]

903

[RFC2401] describes the general architecture to implement and deploy IPsec in the IP networks. [RFC2402] defines an authentication mechanism that offers packet integrity protection. Authentication is a way to ensure that a packet was really constructed by the peer and has not been injected by a third party or altered along the way. It is similar to the signature written on a contract: Authentication does not provide secrecy. That is why [RFC2406] defines an encryption mechanism that offers packet content confidentiality protection. Encryption makes it impossible for a third party with access to the encrypted packets to read their contents. We refer to IPsec as an integral part of all three specifications in the discussions to follow. The AH is designed as an IPv6 Extension Header (IPv6 Extension Header is discussed in Section 3.3 of *IPv6 Core Protocols Implementation*). The ESP is treated as a special upper layer protocol. The AH is used for communication requiring authentication, while the ESP header is used for communication requiring confidentiality.

In this chapter we will discuss the impact of IPv6 on IPsec at the protocol level, and in the process, uncover some of the myths about what IPv6 brings to security in general. We will discuss the deployment of IPsec and IPv6 in practice through the **racoon** utility.

6.2 Authentication Header

AH offers connectionless data integrity and data origin authentication for IP packets with optional protection against packet replays. The authentication covers the IPv6 header, the extension headers and upper layer protocol data. [RFC2402] defines the AH packet format and is shown in Figure 6-1.

The Next Header field identifies the type of header that immediately follows this AH header.

The Payload Length field gives the length of the AH in 4-byte units minus 2. The AH unit of payload length differs from most of the length encoding done in the other extension headers. The base IPv6 protocol specification ([RFC2460]) states that the extension header length is encoded in 8-byte units minus 1. The "minus 2" part comes from the fact the AH length field encodes the packet length in 32-bit units. The Reserved field is reserved for future use. This field must be set to 0 by the sender and is ignored by the receiver.

FIGURE 6-1

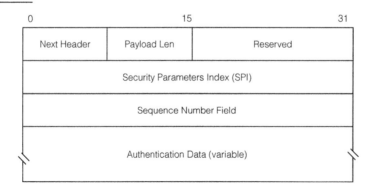

The format of the Authentication Header.

The Security Parameters Index field is a 32-bit value, together with the destination IP address, identifies the Security Association (SA) established between the sender and the receiver. The SA defines the type of authentication methods to apply to the packets exchanged between the communicating peers. We will cover this in Section 6.5. The Internet Assigned Numbers Authority (IANA) reserves the range between 1 and 255 for future use. The value 0 is reserved for local implementation defined usage and must not be sent on the physical link.

The Sequence Number Field is a 32-bit value for preventing packet replay attacks. A sender must increase the sequence number monotonically using the established SA. A sequence number that is part of a previous transmission must never be used in subsequent packets (i.e., every packet sent should have a unique sequence number with a particular SA when the anti-replay is enabled in the SA). For an anti-replay enabled SA the maximum number of packets transmitted is 2^{32}. The communicating peers must establish a new SA once packet transmission reaches this limit.

The Authentication Data field contains the Integrity Check Vector (ICV) for the packet. The ICV is the calculation result of the authentication algorithm employed by the SA. The length of the ICV is variable and depends on the algorithm employed, but the length must be a multiple of 32 bits, so padding may be necessary for alignment purposes.

The AH offers packet integrity by performing authentication computation that covers all of the fields of the packet that do not change during transit (called immutable fields). Mutable fields are the fields that may be modified in transit and are treated as zero-valued fields when performing the computation. Table 6-1 lists both the mutable and immutable fields of the IPv6 and extension headers. Some mutable fields are addressed as predictable in the table. The mutable but predictable fields are modified during packet transmission, but the modification is deterministic and the receiver can recover the original value used for the AH calculation. These fields are taken into account in the AH calculation.

Packet fragmentation occurs after the AH processing of the packet, so Fragment Header is not included in the AH computation.

TABLE 6-1

IPv6 Header	
Immutable fields	Version, Payload length, Next Header, Source Address, Destination Address (without Routing Header)
Mutable but predictable	Destination Address (with Routing Header)
Mutable (zero cleared when calculating authentication data)	DSCP (6 bits, see [RFC2474]), ECN (2 bits, see [RFC3168]), Flow Label, Hop Limit

Routing Header Type 0	
Mutable but predictable	Segments Left, Intermediate Addresses

Hop-by-Hop Options Header/Destination Options Header	
The third highest bit of each option type indicates the mutability. 0 means immutable and 1 means mutable. (See Section 3.3.6 of *IPv6 Core Protocols Implementation*.)	

Mutable/Immutable fields of IPv6/Extension headers.

FIGURE 6-2

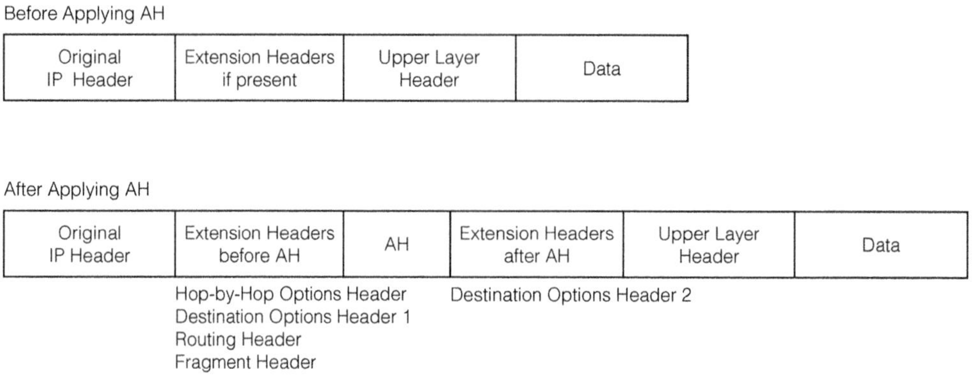

Before Applying AH

Original IP Header	Extension Headers if present	Upper Layer Header	Data

After Applying AH

Original IP Header	Extension Headers before AH	AH	Extension Headers after AH	Upper Layer Header	Data

Hop-by-Hop Options Header   Destination Options Header 2
Destination Options Header 1
Routing Header
Fragment Header

Insertion of Authentication Header.

The AH is inserted after the Hop-by-Hop Options Header, the Routing Header, and the Fragment Header but before the ESP and upper layer protocol headers. The Destination Options Header may appear before or after the AH. Figure 6-2 shows the order of extension headers before and after AH processing.

6.3 Encapsulating Security Payload

ESP provides all of the security services offered by AH. In addition, ESP offers data confidentiality by means of encryption and limited traffic flow confidentiality. The header coverage is the primary difference between the authentication service provided by AH and that provided by ESP. ESP does not cover the IPv6 header and the extension headers unless these are encapsulated in the tunnel.

[RFC2406] defines the ESP packet format and is shown in Figure 6-3.

ESP is a kind of upper layer protocol of IPv6. There is no header length field in the ESP header. The Next Header field that indicates the protocol number of the original packet (that is the packet before being encrypted) is placed at the end of the padding block for including this field in the encryption computation. The size of the ESP header is derived from the total packet length.

The Next Header, SPI and the Sequence Number fields have the same definitions as those identical fields in AH.

The Payload Data field is a variable length field containing the encrypted data described by the Next Header field. The Padding field follows the Payload Data. The two main reasons for including the padding data are for concealing the length of the original payload and for aligning either the plain text or the cipher text. Usually the length is the same for both the plain text and the encrypted data. An attacker may derive the type of communication in progress by monitoring the packet length and traffic pattern. Concealing the length of the original payload can increase the level of traffic flow confidentiality. Padding for the purpose of alignment may be independent of the encryption algorithm in use. In the case of IPv6

FIGURE 6-3

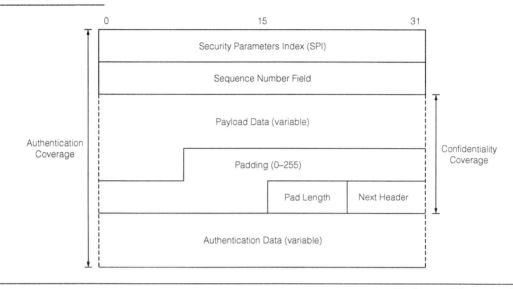

The format of the ESP header.

FIGURE 6-4

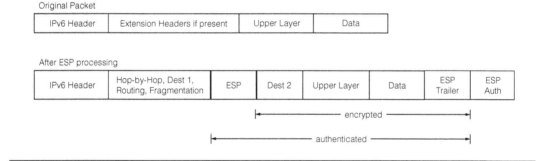

Insertion of the ESP header.

alignment, it may be necessary to align the ESP header to the 8-byte boundary as required by the specification.

The Authentication Data portion of the ESP packet is optional and is included when the SA has selected the authentication service. The length of the Authentication Data depends on the chosen authentication function. The authentication algorithm performs the computation covering the entire ESP header as shown in Figure 6-2. Since data integrity protection is provided only for the ESP header, we must use AH in addition to ESP if the IPv6 header and the extension headers placed before ESP also require integrity protection.

ESP is placed after the IPv6 header but before the second Destination Options header, and before any upper layer protocol headers. ESP is placed just after AH if AH is applied in addition to ESP. Figure 6-4 shows the placement of ESP without the presence of AH.

FIGURE 6-5

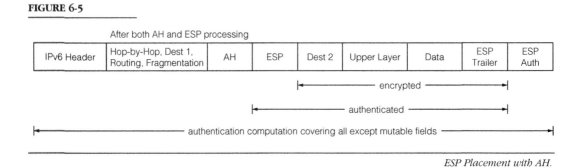

ESP Placement with AH.

The term ESP Trailer refers to the inclusion of the Padding data, Pad Length field and the Next Header field. The term ESP Auth refers to the Authentication Data portion of the ESP frame.

Figure 6-5 shows the placement of ESP when AH is present.

6.4   Transport Mode and Tunnel Mode

There are two modes in which IPsec can be used: *transport mode* and *tunnel mode*. AH and ESP can be applied in either transport mode or tunnel mode. In transport mode, a secure path is established between the communicating end nodes. In tunnel mode, a secure channel is established between two security gateways (SG), which are usually placed at the site borders.

Transport mode is more flexible than tunnel mode operation. However, transport mode is more complex in terms of secure channel setup procedure and administration that results in its limited deployment. In transport mode, IPsec must be properly configured in every node that is on the network and wanting to communicate securely. In comparison, tunnel mode is simpler and is usually accomplished by means of a Virtual Private Network (VPN). Tunnel mode setup procedure reduces the complexity to the setup of security gateways only, and the establishment of secure channels between them.

Figure 6-6 illustrates the concept of transport mode operation. The number of lines between end nodes is equivalent to the number of SAs to be configured. If creating a VPN is the final goal, using tunnel mode is better. Transport mode requires more complex configuration; however, it can be configured on a per node or per service basis and is much more flexible than tunnel mode.

In tunnel mode, the original packet is encapsulated in another IP frame when forwarded by the SG. The SG on the receiving end decapsulates the packet and forwards the original packet toward the destination. Figure 6-7 illustrates the packet structure after the SG completes packet encapsulation for forwarding.

Authentication computation covers the original packet in its entirety. The mutable fields of the encapsulating headers are excluded from the computation.

FIGURE 6-6

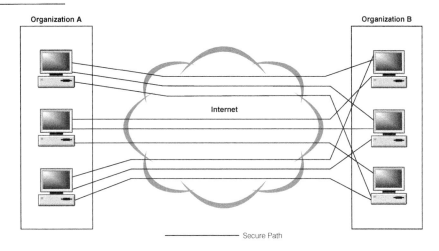

IPsec transport mode.

FIGURE 6-7

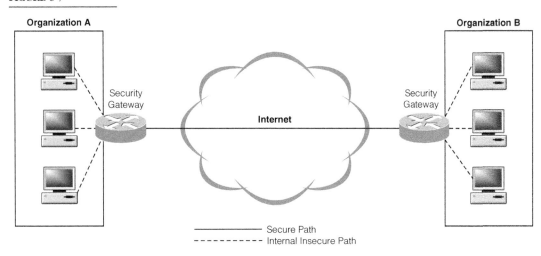

IPsec tunnel mode.

6.5 Security Association Database

A Security Association (SA) represents a specification of the security services offered to traffic carried through a unidirectional channel from one node to another. A separate SA is necessary to offer secure traffic in the reverse direction between the same pair of nodes. In other words, there are two SAs associated with bi-directional traffic between a pair of communicating peers.

FIGURE 6-8

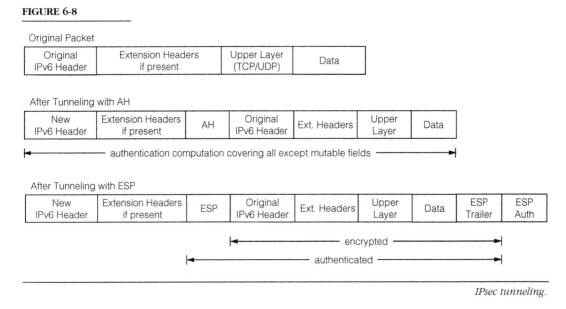

IPsec tunneling.

An SA can offer either the AH or the ESP service, but not both. Two security associations are necessary to provide both types of services simultaneously. A total of four SAs are required for bi-directional traffic using both AH and ESP.

6.5.1 Security Policy Database

The Security Policy Database (SPD) contains a set of rules that determines whether a packet is subject to IPsec processing and governs the processing details. Each entry in the SPD represents a policy that defines how the set of traffic covered under the policy will be processed. Any inbound or outbound packet is processed in one of three ways: discard, perform IPsec processing, or bypass IPsec processing. The SPD policy entry includes an SA or an *SA bundle* specification for traffic that is subject to IPsec processing. An SA bundle refers to a set of SAs that should be applied in order while applicable traffic is processed.

The matching of a packet to a policy entry is by means of a selector that functions as a search key. A selector is a set of IP and upper layer protocol fields which map traffic flow to a security policy in the SPD. The possible fields for constructing the selector can be:

- Source address
- Destination address
- Transport Layer Protocol
- Source and Destination Protocol Ports
- User ID or System name represented by either X.500 name or FQDN.

In general each policy entry in the SPD maintains the following information:

Source address range Source address of the packet.

Destination address range Destination address of the packet. Destination address refers to the destination address of the inner packet after the tunnel end processing in the case of tunnel mode.

Transport layer protocol The protocol number to be protected (e.g., TCP, UDP).

Source and destination ports Transport layer protocol port number to be protected.

Traffic direction Traffic flow. Either one of Inbound or Outbound is specified.

Authentication method AH or ESP.

Confidentiality method Encryption algorithm, initialization vector (IV), keys, etc.

IPsec protocol mode of operation Tunnel mode or Transport mode.

Protection level Require (always) or Use (as much as possible).

If the transmitted packets must be always protected, the Require level has to be specified. If one wants to protect the packet as much as possible, the Use level can be used. When the Use level is specified, packets can be transmitted without any IPsec protection even if there are no matching SAs. With the Require level, packets will be dropped if no matching entry exists.

6.5.2   Security Association Database

Security Association Database (SAD) is a central repository containing all of the active SAs for both inbound and outbound traffic, with each entry defining the parameters for a specific SA. Typically an SA entry maintains the following information:

Security parameter index A unique identifier generated by the creator of the SA, used to distinguish among the SAs of the IPsec protocol terminating at the same destination node.

Destination address The address of the destination node to which this SA entry is applied.

Sequence number counter For generating sequence numbers.

Anti-Replay window A counter and mapping information to determine whether a packet is being replayed.

IP security protocol The type of the IP security protocol which is used to process packets. Either Authentication Header or Encapsulating Security Payload can be specified.

Algorithm The algorithm which is used by the IP security protocol specified by the IP security protocol parameter.

Key The key which is used by the algorithm specified by the Algorighm parameter.

SA lifetime Expressed in either time or byte count. At the expiration of the lifetime the SA must be replaced with a new SA and a new SPI, or the SA is terminated.

IPsec protocol mode of operation Tunnel mode or Transport mode.

For outbound traffic processing, for a matching entry in the SPD, if there is no SA or matching SA entry found in the SAD, then the *key management entity* will create a new SA into the SAD (the concept of key management is discussed in Sections 6.7 and 6.9). The SP entry defines how to create a new SA and what values of the SP will be used in the SA creation.

The SP entry may be thought of as a template for SA creation, and a new SA entry may be thought of as a specific instance of the SP entry. The packet is dropped in the absence of both an SA and the key management entity.

Since an SA applies to a specific direction of traffic flow, each security policy in the SPD has a direction attribute indicating whether the policy applies to inbound or outbound traffic.

6.5.3   SAD and SPD Example

Consider this example: We want to protect the Post Office Protocol v3 (POP3) traffic between a mail client node A and a mail server node B. Since emails contain private exchanges between end users, we want to encrypt the content (i.e., we want to encrypt the traffic exchanged between node A and node B). In order to apply IPsec to the traffic between the nodes, we need to set up the SPD and the SAD on both node A and node B.

We need two SP entries for the bi-directional exchange between A and B. The SP entries on node A are described by the pseudo entries listed in Table 6-2.

Similarly there are two SP entries created at node B as described in Table 6-3. The associated SA entries at node A are shown in Table 6-4. Similarly the SA entries at node B are shown in Table 6-5.

TABLE 6-2

Direction	*Outbound*	*Inbound*
Source Address	Node A	POP Server B
Destination Address	POP server B	Node A
Upper Layer Protocol	TCP	TCP
Upper Layer Source Port	Any	POP3
Upper Layer Destination Port	POP3	Any
IPsec Protocol	ESP	ESP
Mode	Transport	Transport

SP entries on node A.

TABLE 6-3

Direction	*Outbound*	*Inbound*
Source Address	POP Server B	Node A
Destination Address	Node A	POP server B
Upper Layer Protocol	TCP	TCP
Upper Layer Source Port	POP3	Any
Upper Layer Destination Port	Any	POP3
IPsec Protocol	ESP	ESP
Mode	Transport	Transport

SP entries on node B.

TABLE 6-4

Direction	Outbound	Inbound
SPI	1000	1001
Destination Address	POP Server B	Node A
IPsec Protocol	ESP	ESP
Algorithm	3DES-CBC	3DES-CBC
Key	The secret key from A to B	The secret key from B to A
Mode	Transport	Transport

SA entries on node A.

TABLE 6-5

Direction	Outbound	Inbound
SPI	1001	1000
Destination Address	Node A	POP Server B
IPsec Protocol	ESP	ESP
Algorithm	3DES-CBC	3DES-CBC
Key	The secret key from B to A	The secret key from A to B
Mode	Transport	Transport

SA entries on node B.

In this example, we define the parameters of ESP packets to use 3DES-CBC as an encryption algorithm and related keys.

6.6   IPsec Traffic Processing

Both inbound and outbound traffic passes through the IPsec module when IPsec is enabled in the system. The SPD controls how packets are processed.

For each outgoing packet, the packet fields chosen as the selector are matched against outbound security policy entries. For a matching SP entry that calls for security processing, the search for the corresponding SA or SA bundle in the SAD follows. A new SA or SA bundle is created in the SAD if no matching entries are found. Finally the packets are processed according to the security specification given by the SA.

For each incoming packet, the presence of either the AH or the ESP header implies that the packet requires IPsec processing. The packet destination address and the SPI in the security protocol header identify the SA entry in the SAD. A matching SA entry must have the same source address selector as the source address of the packet. The packet is discarded if the SPI does not map to an existing SA in the SAD. IPsec processing is performed on the packet according to the specification given in the matching SA. For tunneled packets, the same process

FIGURE 6-9

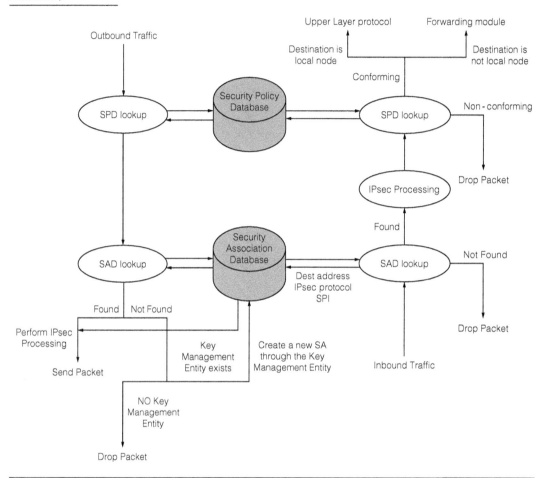

IPsec processing flow.

continues for each IPsec header carried in the packet until encountering an upper layer protocol, or until reaching an IP header with a destination address not of the local node. The matching SAs and the order of applying the SA to each encountered IPsec header is recorded by the processing module. Figure 6-9 illustrates the general packet processing flow through the IPsec module.

6.7   SPD and SAD Management

In the previous section, we mentioned that once a matching SP entry is found, and if a corresponding SA is not available in the SAD, then the key management entity creates a new SA for the new traffic flow. The main functions performed by the key management entity are the establishment of the SA, the establishment of the cryptographic keys for the algorithm deployed by the SA, and the subsequent management of both the SA and the keys for the duration of the communication. The term *keying* refers to the establishment and the management process as a whole. There are two approaches to keying: *manual* keying and *automatic* keying.

6.7.1 Manual Keying and Automatic Keying

Each SA entry consists of a small number of parameters. We can easily define and enter the SA entries by hand (referred to as manual keying) if the number of communicating nodes and the total number of entries required are small. However, we will face a daunting configuration task if there are many nodes requiring IPsec-protected communications among the nodes. For example, in a 10-node system, the configuration requirement is 90 SA entries at a minimum because each node requires 9 SA entries to communicate securely with its nine peers. We will come back to this example in a later section to explain the calculation. A secret piece of information, such as a secret key that is used for encryption and decryption, is maintained in the SA when that SA offers the data confidentiality service. In general, each such SA has a unique secret not shared with other SAs. The secret should be updated periodically to reduce the impact of a compromised secret, and to increase the difficulty for an attacker to deduce the secret. Manual keying is not a scalable operation for large networks to archive these requirements. In the context of this chapter, we will use the term secret key, or simply key, interchangeably to refer to the secret information shared between a pair of communicating nodes protected by IPsec.

One difficult problem facing a pair of nodes requiring secure communication is how to distribute the key information secretly over an insecure network. Since communication takes place over an insecure network, one way to enhance the secrecy level is to frequently change the encryption key or the authentication key. This method can confine the exposure of private information to the attacker to a limited period if a key is compromised. Another method to enhance the secrecy level is to delete an existing SA and establish a new SA when the sequence number field in the security header reaches its maximum value. In other words, the sequence numbers are not recycled in an SA to prevent replay attacks. Obviously manual keying is not suitable in meeting these security requirements; the solution is automatic keying.

In general, automatic keying is accomplished through a well-defined protocol which negotiates and exchanges parameters necessary for securing information exchange. The protocol is responsible for the establishment and the maintenance of both SA and security keys for a communication channel. A minimum set of configurations for the security module is necessary to facilitate automatic keying. This part of manual configuration requirement for automatic keying is far less than the procedures carried out in manual keying. The security module usually executes as a daemon process, which retrieves the static configuration information as the basis for the dynamic keying process.

There are some basic steps involved in establishing secure communication between two entities through an automatic process. First, the two entities must authenticate each other. In other words, each entity must verify the other peer. Once the authentication process completes, the two entities must agree on a basic set of security attributes to protect further communication. Essentially the two entities must establish a special SA for securing traffic involving the establishment of an SA or SAs on behalf of the security protocols such as AH or ESP.

6.8 Manual Configuration

The SA entries should be configured and managed by an automatic key mechanism for enhanced security. The SP entries, however, must be managed through manual configuration. A network administrator defines the security policies for an entire network. The administrator then inserts a subset of the policies at each IP node that has the IPsec capability to enforce the overall network security policies. The **setkey** command is a tool that allows an administrator to perform manual configuration of both SP and SA entries in the two security databases. In this section we will present the details on manual installation of SP and SA entries using the **setkey** command. The next section presents details on automatic configuration of SA entries through the **racoon** command.

The **setkey** command has the following syntax:

```
setkey [-v] -c
setkey [-v] -f filename
setkey [-aPlv] -D
setkey [-Pv] -F
setkey [-h] -x
```

KAME (and most of BSD operating systems) provides the **setkey** command which is used to install SA entries and SP entries. Each option and its description are listed in Table 6-6.

TABLE 6-6

Option	Description
-v	Verbose mode.
-c	Read configuration parameters from standard input.
-f *filename*	Read configuration parameters from the file specified by *filename*.
-D	Display installed SA entries. A combination with the following switches changes -D switch behavior:
	-P Display SP entries instead of SA entries.
	-a Display SA entries which lifetime is already expired, in addition to active SA entries. -a switch has no effect with -P switch because an SP entry does not have lifetime.
	-l Continuously display SA entries (or SP entries with -P switch).
-F	Flush all SA entries. A combination with -P switch will flush all SP entries.
-x	Display kernel messages which manage SA/SP entries in a kernel continuously. Multiple -x switch will display timestamp on each message.

setkey options.

6.8.1 Configuration File Format

When adding new SA or SP entries, the **setkey** command can read the operation request and its associated parameters either from the standard input or from a given file, depending on the command option. The input format is the same regardless of the input method.

Creating SP Entries

The operation for creating an SP entry is **spdadd**. The **spdadd** operation has the following syntax:

```
spdadd [-46n] source_range destination_range upperspec policy;
```

The **spdadd** operation has 4 arguments, *source_range*, *destination_range*, *upperspec* and *policy*. In addition to these arguments, **spdadd** may have an option switch with regard to the address resolution policy. -4 and -6 specify that the node names specified in arguments result in an IPv4 address and an IPv6 address respectively. That means if -4 is specified, then the node name will be replaced to its IPv4 address even if the node has both IPv4 and IPv6 addresses. -n means that no name resolution is performed. If -n is explicitly specified, addresses should be written in the numeric form. In addition, -n affects both service name resolution and protocol name resolution.

If *source_range* or *destination_range* is specified in the string form, name resolution may result in multiple numeric addresses. In this case, the **setkey** command installs all possible combinations of SP entries. For example, if *source_range* has two numeric addresses and *destination_range* has two numeric addresses, then four SPD entries are installed. Note that the address family of the source and the destination address must be the same. There is no policy in which source address is an IPv4 address and the destination address is an IPv6 address. The detailed syntax of each parameter follows.

source_range *source_range* specifies the source address range of this policy. The formats are any one of:

- *address*
- *address*/*prefixlen*
- *address*[*port*]
- *address*/*prefixlen*[*port*]

For example,

- `2001:db8:100::1` matches packets in which the source address is `2001:db8:100::1`.
- `2001:db8:100::/56[110]` matches packets in which the source address is `2001:db8:100::/56` and its source port number of the transport layer is 110.

destination_range The same format as *source_range*, *destination_range* specifies the destination address range of a policy.

upperspec *upperspec* specifies the upper layer protocol name. For example, `tcp` or `ipv6-icmp`. The protocol name must be defined in /etc/protocols. Also, *upperspec* can be specified directly as a protocol number. For example 6 for TCP and 58 for ICMPv6.

policy *policy* specifies behavior of a policy as one of following forms:

- -P *direction* `discard`
- -P *direction* `none`
- -P *direction* `ipsec` *protocol*/ *mode*/ *[source-destination]*/ *level*

direction specifies the direction of flow of packets. Either `in` for incoming packets or `out` for outgoing packets can be specified as a direction. If the `discard` policy is specified, the packets matched to this policy will be discarded.

If `none` is specified, then the packets matched to this policy will be passed without IP security processing. If `ipsec` is specified, the packets will be processed by the IPsec protocol stack based on the rest of the parameters. *protocol* is either `esp` for encryption or `ah` for authentication.[1] *mode* is either `transport` or `tunnel`. If `tunnel` is specified as a mode, we must specify the addresses of the endpoints of this IP security tunnel in the form of *source-destination*. *source* and *destination* are IP addresses or host names. *level* is either one of `default`, `require`, `use` or `unique`. `default` means obeying the system default. We can specify either `require` or `use` as the system default value, which can be changed by the **sysctl** command. There are four sysctl switches to change the value.

```
net.inet6.ipsec6.esp_trans_deflev
net.inet6.ipsec6.esp_net_deflev
net.inet6.ipsec6.ah_trans_deflev
net.inet6.ipsec6.ah_net_deflev
```

All these values are initialized to 1, which means the `use` level. We can change these values to 2 to change the default level to the `require` level. If the `use` level is specified, the packets are processed by the IPsec protocol stack if there is any corresponding SA entry. If there is no SA entry corresponding to these packets, then packets are sent or received without IP security processing. If the `require` level is specified, packets are sent or received only when there is a corresponding SA entry. The `require` level is used when we do not permit insecure communication at all. The `unique` level is used when we want to bind a specific SA entry to this policy. The usage of the `unique` level is shown in Section 6.8.3.

Displaying SP Entries

The operation for displaying the SP entries is **spddump**. The **spddump** operation has the following syntax:

```
spddump;
```

Deleting SP Entries

The operation for deleting SP entries is **spddelete**. The **spddelete** operation has the following syntax:

```
spddelete [-46n] source_range destination_range upperspec -P direction;
spdflush;
```

The **spddelete** operation removes SP entries specified by its arguments. When we need to remove specific SP entries, we must specify *source_range*, *destination_range*, *upperspec* and *direction* to match the target SP entries.

---

1. `ipcomp` can be specified for compression. We do not discuss IP compression in this book.

To delete all SP entries, the **spdflush** operation can be used instead of the **spddelete** operation for each SP entry. The result is the same as the −FP switch of the **setkey** command.

Creating SA Entries

In general the SA entries are created automatically by the IKE daemon. There are situations, for example, during policy testing and the debugging phase, where manual creation of SA entries may be useful. The **setkey** command allows for the manual creation of SA entries. The operation for creating an SA entry is **add**. The **add** operation has the following syntax:

add [−46n] *source destination protocol spi [extensions] algorithm . . . ;*

The −4, −6, −n switches have the same definitions and effects as those for the **spdadd** operation.

The meanings of other parameters follow.

source *source* specifies the source address of this SA entry.

destination *destination* specifies the destination address of this SA entry.

protocol *protocol* specifies the IP security protocol to be used. Following values can be specified.[2]

- ah
  AH protocol defined in [RFC2402]

- esp
  ESP protocol defined in [RFC2406]

spi *spi* specifies the SPI value for this SA entry. The value is a 32-bit integer. However, 1–255 are reserved by IANA for future use.

algorithm Specifies the algorithm for this SA entry. One of following formats can be specified.

- −E *encryption_algorithm encryption_key*
- −E *encryption_algorithm encryption_key* −A *authentication_algorithm authentication_key*
- −A *authentication_algorithm authentication_key*

    The first format is used for the ESP case without authentication. The second format is used for the ESP case with authentication. The last format is used for the AH case without encryption. *encryption_algorithm* is one of the algorithms listed in Table 6-7. *authentication_algorithm* is one of the algorithms listed in Table 6-8. For each algorithm, the table lists the key length, and the RFC that defines the algorithm. *encryption_key* and *authentication_key* are keys for the corresponding algorithms. These keys must satisfy the required bit length defined in each algorithm. Keys can be specified in either a hexadecimal form or a string.

extension *extension* specifies some optional property for this SA entry.

- −m *mode*
  The −m switch specifies the IP security mode. one of tunnel, transport or any can be specified as *mode*. If we want to restrict this SA entry to be used only for tunnel or

---

2. There are other old protocols which are defined as [RFC1826] and [RFC1827]. However, those protocols are obsolete and should not be used.

TABLE 6-7

Name	Key length (in bits)	Reference
des-cbc	64	[RFC1829]/[RFC2405]
3des-cbc	192	[RFC2451]
null	0 to 2048	[RFC2410]
blowfish-cbc	40 to 448	[RFC2451]
cast128-cbc	40 to 128	[RFC2451]
des-deriv	64	[DES-DERIVED]
3des-deriv	192	no document
rijndael-cvc	128, 192, 256	[RFC3602]
twofish-cbc	0 to 256	[RFC3602]
aes-ctr	160, 224, 288	[RFC3686]

The list of encryption algorithms.

TABLE 6-8

Name	Key length (in bits)	Reference
hmac-md5	128	[RFC2403]
hmac-sha1	160	[RFC2404]
keyed-md5	128	no document
keyed-sha1	160	no document
null	0 to 2048	no document
hmac-sha2-256	256	[SHA-256]
hmac-sha2-512	384	no document
hmac-sha2-512	512	no document
hmac-ripemd160	160	no document
aes-xcbc-mac	128	no document

The list of authentication algorithms.

transport mode, we must explicitly specify the mode. The default value is any, which means this SA entry can be used for both modes.

- **-r** *size*
  The -r switch specifies the window size of reply protection as a 32-bit integer. If 0 is specified, no replay protection is performed.

- **-u** *identifier*
  The -u switch specifies a unique identifier for this SA entry. The identifier is used when we want to bind a specific SA entry to a specific SP entry by the unique protection level discussed in Section 6.8.1.

- -f *padoption*
  The -f switch specifies the content of padding area in an ESP trailer. One of following values can be specified.

  — zero-pad fills with 0.
  — random-pad fills with random numbers.
  — seq-pad fills with sequential increasing numbers.

- -f nocyclic-seq
  The -f nocyclic-seq switch specifies not to use a cyclic sequence number.

- -lh *time*

- -ls *time*
  The -lh and -ls switches specify a hard lifetime and a soft lifetime, respectively, in a unit of 1 second. These values are usually inapplicable in manual keying. In dynamic keying, when the soft lifetime expires, renegotiation of the corresponding SA entries will occur. When the hard lifetime expires, the SA entry is deleted from the SA database.

Displaying SA Entries

There are two methods of displaying SA entries: One is the **get** operation and the other is the **dump** operation. The **get** operation can only retrieve one SA entry from the SAD, while the **dump** operation shows all the entries installed. The **get** and **dump** operations have the following syntax:

```
get [-46n] source destination protocol spi ;
dump [ protocol] ;
```

source and *destination* are the source address and the destination address of the SA entry to be displayed. *protocol* is either esp or ah. *spi* is the SPI value of the SA entry in question.

The **dump** operation displays all SA entries which are installed in the database. The same result can be achieved with the -D switch when executing the **setkey** command. If *protocol* is specified with the **dump** operation, then only SA entries which are defined for the specified protocol are displayed.

Deleting SA Entries

There are three operations to delete SA entries, **delete**, **deleteall** and **flush**. Following are the syntax of these oparations:

```
delete [-46n] source destination protocol spi ;
deleteall [-46n] source destination protocol ;
flush [ protocol] ;
```

The **delete** directive deletes one SA entry specified by its 4 arguments. The arguments are the same as those of the **get** directive. The **deleteall** directive deletes all SA entries which have same *source*, *destination* and *protocol* values regardless of its SPI value.

The **flush** directive deletes all SA entries currently installed. We can get the same result with the -F switch when executing the **setkey** command. If an optional *protocol* argument is specified, then only SA entries related to the specified protocol are deleted.

6.8.2   Examples of Manipulating SP Entries

Figure 6-10 is an example configuration of adding SP entries. The corresponding network topology is shown in Figure 6-11.

This example defines a secure POP3 connection from node A to POP3 server B. On node A, all outgoing packets from node A to server B's POP3 port must be encrypted using the ESP header. At the same time, incoming packets from server B's POP3 port to node A must be encrypted using the ESP header. We can see that the source address and the destination address of SP entries of server B are opposite those of node A.

Figure 6-12 is another example of adding SP entries. Figure 6-12 defines tunnel mode SP entries between two security gateways (SG A and SG B). Figure 6-13 shows the corresponding network configuration.

FIGURE 6-10

Node A (2001:db8:100::100):

```
# setkey -c
spdadd 2001:db8:100::100[any] 2001:db8:100::200[pop3] tcp
        -P out ipsec esp/transport//require;
spdadd 2001:db8:100::200[pop3] 2001:db8:100::100[any] tcp
        -P in ipsec esp/transport//require;
^D
```

POP3 server B (2001:db8:100::200):

```
# setkey -c
spdadd 2001:db8:100::200[pop3] 2001:db8:100::100[any] tcp
        -P out ipsec esp/transport//require;
spdadd 2001:db8:100::100[any] 2001:db8:100::200[pop3] tcp
        -P in ipsec esp/transport//require;
^D
```

Adding transport mode SP entries.

FIGURE 6-11

The sample network using secure POP traffic.

FIGURE 6-12

SG A (2001:db8:100::1):

```
# setkey -c
spdadd 2001:db8:100::/48[any] 2001:db8:200::/48[any] any
        -P out ipsec esp/tunnel/2001:db8:100::1-2001:db8:200::1/require;
spdadd 2001:db8:200::/48[any] 2001:db8:100::/48[any] any
        -P in ipsec esp/tunnel/2001:db8:200::1-2001:db8:100::1/require;
^D
```

SG B (2001:db8:200::1):

```
# setkey -c
spdadd 2001:db8:200::/48[any] 2001:db8:100::/48[any] any
        -P out esp/tunnel/2001:db8:200::1-2001:db8:100::1/require;
spdadd 2001:db8:100::/48[any] 2001:db8:200::/48[any] any
        -P in esp/tunnel/2001:db8:100::1-2001:db8:200::1/require;
^D
```

Adding tunnel mode SP entries.

FIGURE 6-13

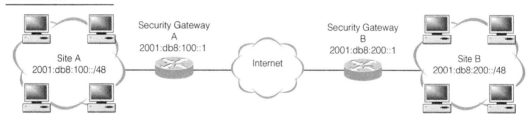

The sample network connected by two security gateways.

Site A has the IPv6 address block 2001:db8:100::/48, and site B has 2001:db8:200::/48. This example defines SP entries for the VPN tunnel between site A and site B. All outgoing packets from site A (to which the source address belongs to site A and the destination address belongs to site B) are tunneled from SG A (2001:db8:100::1) to SG B (2001:db8:200::1) by using the ESP header. Also, all incoming packets from site B to site A must be tunneled from SG B (2001:db8:200::1) to SG A (2001:db8:100::1). Otherwise, packets will be dropped. The opposite SPD configuration is done on SG B.

Figure 6-14 is the sample result of the **spddump** directive on node A described in Figure 6-11 after installing Security Policy Database entries described in Figure 6-10.

We can get the same result by specifying the -DP switch when executing the **setkey** command.

FIGURE 6-14

```
# setkey -c
spddump;
2001:db8:100::200[110] 2001:db8:100::100[any] tcp
        in ipsec
        esp/transport//require
        lifetime:0 validtime:0
        spid=16403 seq=1 pid=7181
        refcnt=1
2001:db8:100::100[any] 2001:db8:100::200[110] tcp
        out ipsec
        esp/transport//require
        lifetime:0 validtime:0
        spid=16402 seq=0 pid=7181
        refcnt=1
```

A sample result of dumping SP entries.

FIGURE 6-15

Node A (2001:db8:100::100):

```
spddelete 2001:db8:100::100[any] 2001:db8:100::200[pop3] tcp -P out;
spddelete 2001:db8:100::200[pop3] 2001:db8:100::100[any] tcp -P in;
```

POP3 server (2001:db8:100::200):

```
spddelete 2001:db8:100::200[pop3] 2001:db8:100::100[any] tcp -P out;
spddelete 2001:db8:100::100[any] 2001:db8:100::200[pop3] tcp -P in;
```

Deleting SP entries.

Figure 6-15 is an example of removing SP entries which are added in the procedure described in Figure 6-10.

6.8.3   Examples of Manipulating SA Entries

Figure 6-16 installs SA entries which can be applied to the network described in Figure 6-11.

Figure 6-16 installs two SA entries. One is from node A to POP server B with the 3des-cbc encryption algorithm and the hmac-md5 hash algorithm. The other is for the reverse direction. Since an SA entry describes a path between two nodes, the same SA entries must be installed on both nodes, in this case, both node A and POP server B must have the same SA entries described in Figure 6-16.

Figure 6-17 is an example of using unique identifiers. We can specify a unique identifier per SA entry. Such SA entries can be bound by a `unique` keyword specified in an SP entry.

With the configuration described in Figure 6-17, node A always uses the SA entry which has a unique identifier of 2000 when node A sends packets to the POP3 port (110) of server B.

FIGURE 6-16

```
# setkey -c
add 2001:db8:100::100 2001:db8:100::200 esp 1000
    -E 3des-cbc "-THE-SECRET-FROM-A-TO-B-"
    -A hmac-md5 "AUTH-FROM-A-TO-B";
add 2001:db8:100::200 2001:db8:100::100 esp 1001
    -E 3des-cbc "-THE-SECRET-FROM-B-TO-A-"
    -A hmac-md5 "AUTH-FROM-B-TO-A";
^D
```

Adding SA entries.

FIGURE 6-17

```
Node A (2001:db8:100::100):
# setkey -c
spdadd 2001:db8:100::100[any] 2001:db8:100::200[110] tcp
      -P out ipsec esp/transport//unique:2000;
spdadd 2001:db8:100::200[110] 2001:db8:100::100[any] tcp
      -P in ipsec esp/transport//unique:2001;
add 2001:db8:100::100 2001:db8:100::200 esp 1000
    -u 2000
    -E 3des-cbc "-THE-SECRET-FROM-A-TO-B-"
    -A hmac-md5 "AUTH-FROM-A-TO-B";
add 2001:db8:100::200 2001:db8:100::100 esp 1001
    -u 2001
    -E 3des-cbc "-THE-SECRET-FROM-B-TO-A-"
    -A hmac-md5 "AUTH-FROM-B-TO-A";
^D
```

Adding SA entries with unique identifiers.

Figure 6-18 is an example of displaying installed SA entries. If we just want to dump all SA entries, we can use the **dump** directive or the −D switch when executing the **setkey** command. Figure 6-19 shows an example of deleting an SA entry.

As mentioned previously, if we want to remove all SA entries between two nodes of a specified protocol (such as esp, ah), we can use the **deleteall** directive. We can also use the **flush** directive or the −F switch if we want to delete all installed SA entries.

6.9 Internet Security Association and Key Management Protocol (ISAKMP) Overview

In a nutshell, ISAKMP defines a generic high-level framework with abstract syntax and semantics for automatic keying. The framework defines the parameters and payload formats for negotiating an SA, establishing the SA, modifying the SA and removing the SA at the conclusion of the secure communication.

FIGURE 6-18

```
# setkey -c
get 2001:db8:100::100 2001:db8:100::200 esp 1000;
2001:db8:100::100 2001:db8:100::200
        esp mode=any spi=1000(0x000003e8) reqid=0(0x00000000)
        E: 3des-cbc 2d544845 2d534543 5245542d 46524f4d 2d412d54 4f2d422d
        A: hmac-sha1 41555448 2d46524f 4d2d412d 544f2d42
        seq=0x00000000 replay=0 flags=0x00000040 state=mature
        created: Oct 29 16:47:27 2003 current: Oct 29 16:47:40 2003
        diff: 13(s)     hard: 0(s)     soft: 0(s)
        last:           hard: 0(s)     soft: 0(s)
        current: 0(bytes) hard: 0(bytes) soft: 0(bytes)
        allocated: 0 hard: 0 soft: 0
        sadb_seq=0 pid=8037 refcnt=1
```

Dumping an SA entry.

FIGURE 6-19

```
# setkey -c
delete 2001:db8:100::100 2001:db8:100::200 esp 1000;
```

(will delete one SA entry)

```
# setkey -c
delete 2001:db8:100::100 2001:db8:100::200 esp;
```

(will delete all esp SA entries between 2001:db8:100::100 and
2001:db8:100::200 regardless of SPI value)

```
# setkey -c
flush;
```

(will delete all SA entries)

Deleting SA entries.

Through the ISAKMP framework, two nodes can agree on the type of security services, also known as a protection suite, to be afforded to the communication about to take place: for example, the security services that use IPsec in tunnel-mode with ESP having 3-DES as the encryption algorithm, and with AH having the HMAC-MD5 as the authentication method.

The two nodes must exchange information to authenticate each other and then generate a set of secret keys to be shared exclusively between them. The generated keys must have the *perfect forward secrecy* property (i.e., the set of keys generated in one session is independent of the set of keys generated in another session). The establishment and the management of the secret keys are integral parts of the overall management of the security associations to which the secret keys apply.

The protection suite specifies the properties of the secret key such as key size, lifetime, and its refreshment policy. The protection suite also specifies information such as the cryptographic algorithms that will be using the keys, and the parameters of the cryptographic algorithms such as what the initialization vectors are.

In the ISAKMP framework, one node is the *initiator* of the secure communication and the other node is the *responder*. The initiator sends the responder a proposal containing a list of protection suites in decreasing order of preference. The responder then selects one of the protection suites from the proposal and indicates its selection back to the initiator. The next step is the generation of the shared key once the two nodes agree on a protection suite. As discussed in Section 6.5.2, the SA is composed of the protection suite, the shared keys, and the identities of the two parties. This process is known as negotiation.

More precisely speaking, an ISAKMP proposal is encoded and carried in both a *Proposal payload* and one or more *Transform payloads*. The Proposal payload specifies the security protocol, which can be ISAKMP, IPsec ESP, IPsec AH, etc. The Transform payload lists the exact algorithm of the security protocol. For example, if the Proposal payload specifies the IPsec ESP as the security protocol, then the Transform payload may list 3-DES as the algorithm. Each Transform payload also carries the SA attributes such as the SA lifetime or the key size for the cryptographic algorithm.

6.9.1 ISAKMP Exchanges

The ISAKMP terminology, *exchange*, refers to an ISAKMP predefined template that specifies the number of messages sent by each party, the types of payloads included in each message, and how to process the payloads of each message.

The ISAKMP framework uses a two-phase negotiation. The Phase-I negotiation establishes an ISAKMP SA, also known as Phase-I SA that protects the Phase-II negotiation. The Phase-II negotiation establishes SAs on behalf of other security protocols to protect data traffic. In the IPsec Domain of Interpretation (DOI) these Phase-II SAs are called IPsec SAs. DOI is discussed in Section 6.9.2. Figure 6-20 illustrates the ISAKMP two-phase negotiation.

All of the Phase-II exchanges carried out for the establishment of the Phase-II SAs are protected under Phase-I SA. Phase-II exchanges can be optimized to reduce both the number of messages exchanged and the amount of information carried in the messages by using the already protected communication path. The key generation algorithms and exchange

FIGURE 6-20

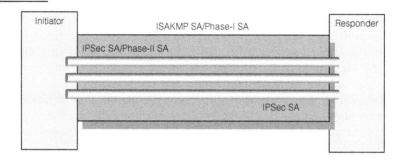

ISAKMP phases.

FIGURE 6-21

(1) Initiator
HDR; SA proposal; Noncei
Responder
(2)
HDR; SA choice; Noncer
(3)
HDR; KEi; IDi; Authi
(4)
HDR; KEr; IDr; Authr

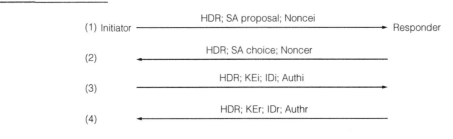

ISAKMP base exchange.

FIGURE 6-22

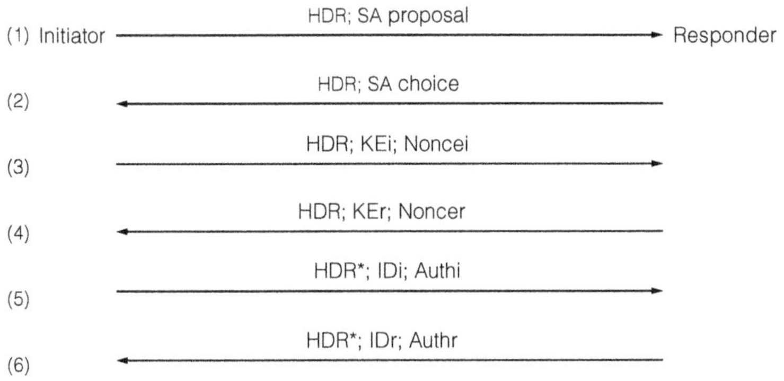

(1) Initiator
HDR; SA proposal
Responder
(2)
HDR; SA choice
(3)
HDR; KEi; Noncei
(4)
HDR; KEr; Noncer
(5)
HDR*; IDi; Authi
(6)
HDR*; IDr; Authr

ISAKMP identity protection exchange.

protocols deployed in Phase-II should be more efficient because there are a large number of SAs established in Phase-II.

The ISAKMP exchanges are: *Base Exchange*, *Identity Protection Exchange*, *Authentication Only Exchange*, *Aggressive Exchange*, and *Informational Exchange*.

Figure 6-21 illustrates the Base Exchange. The numeric values in brackets are the message numbers. The Base Exchange has four messages in total. HDR is the message header. Nonce is a large random number. The initiator sends the SA proposal and the responder replies with its choice of the protection suite. KE is the key exchange payload defined by the ISAKMP framework, which is used to generate the shared secret for the SA. IDi contains the identity information of the initiator, and IDr contains the identity information of the responder. The Base Exchange combines the keying information and the authentication information in one message as shown in messages (3) and (4). The agreed authentication function protects both the keying material and the identities of the two parties during the exchange, but the identity information is not encrypted because the shared key has not been established until the initiator processes the message (4).

Figure 6-22 illustrates the ISAKMP Identity Protection Exchange. The identities of the two parties are protected at the expense of two additional messages in the Identity Protection

FIGURE 6-23

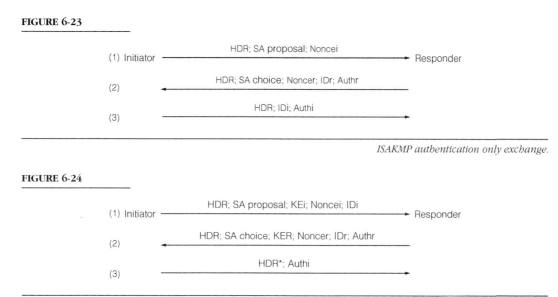

ISAKMP authentication only exchange.

FIGURE 6-24

ISAKMP aggressive mode exchange.

Exchange. The identity information is encrypted because the keying information is exchanged in messages (3) and (4) followed by the exchange of identities in messages (5) and (6). The symbol HDR* means all of the payloads are encrypted. In Figure 6-22, the payloads are the ID and the Auth data.

Figure 6-23 illustrates the ISAKMP Authentication Only Exchange. With the Authentication Only Exchange, the responder replies with its choice of the protection suite. In addition, the responder identity information is transmitted in message (2) under the protection of the agreed authentication function. The initiator transmits its identity information under the protection of the agreed authentication function.

Figure 6-24 illustrates the ISAKMP Aggressive Exchange. The Aggressive Mode Exchange combines the SA proposal, key exchange and identity information into one message. The SA proposal limits the protection suite to a single Proposal payload and a single Transform payload. The responder will reply if it accepts the protection suite. The reply message is protected under the proposed authentication function, which includes the key exchange payload and the identity information of the initiator. As Figure 6-24 shows, the identity information is not encrypted.

The reason that we refer to ISAKMP as a framework instead of as a protocol is because ISAKMP defines high-level payload formats but does not provide sufficient detail necessary for actual implementation. A *Domain of Interpretation* and a particular key exchange protocol defines a specific context in which ISAKMP operates. This context specifies the necessary and detailed information for implementing ISAKMP in that context.

6.9.2   Domain of Interpretation

A Domain of Interpretation (DOI) defines various *situations*, with each situation describing the characteristics of a particular type of communication requiring security protection. A situation maps to a set of security services to be provided by both the initiator and the responder in order for the communication to take place. For each situation, the DOI provides the details on the format of the various payload contents, the exchange types, and the conventions for the naming (or the encoding) of security-relevant information. The ISAKMP exchange types are described in Section 6.9.1.

For example, the Internet IP Security Domain of Interpretation for ISAKMP [RFC2407] defines the context in which to interpret the ISAKMP payloads when ISAKMP is used with IP and IP security protocols. The [RFC2407] also defines the attribute types for the Internet Key Exchange Protocol Phase II SA negotiation, and how to encode each attribute type.

6.9.3   Internet Key Exchange Protocol

The Internet Key Exchange (IKE) protocol is a hybrid protocol of the Oakley and Skeme key exchanges, which is designed according to the ISAKMP framework. IKE is a protocol that negotiates and establishes both the ISAKMP SA and the IPsec SAs. IKE manages the SA and re-establishes the SA if its lifetime expires. Such SA lifetime management prevents sequence number wrapping and minimizes the risk of replay attacks. IKE facilitates the easy and secure management of SA entries.

IKE Phase I negotiation establishes an ISAKMP SA through either the Identity Protection exchange or the Aggressive Mode Exchange. In the context of the IKE, the Identity Protection exchange is termed the *Main Mode*, and the Aggressive Mode exchange is termed the *Aggressive Mode*. The ISAKMP SA is a bi-directional SA in that each part can initiate the Phase II negotiation. Three shared keys are established between the initiator and the responder at the conclusion of IKE Phase I negotiation. One of the keys is used for authentication. Another key is used for encryption of the fifth and sixth message of the IKE Main mode exchange as shown in Figure 6-22. This key is also used for encryption of all Phase II traffic. The third shared key is used for deriving keys for non-ISAKMP security associations.

IKE Phase II negotiation establishes IPsec SAs through a newly defined exchange termed the *Quick Mode*. The Quick Mode exchange is more efficient because the exchange assumes protection from the ISAKMP SA. IKE Phase II negotiation establishes two uni-directional SAs, one for inbound traffic and one for outbound traffic.

FIGURE 6-25

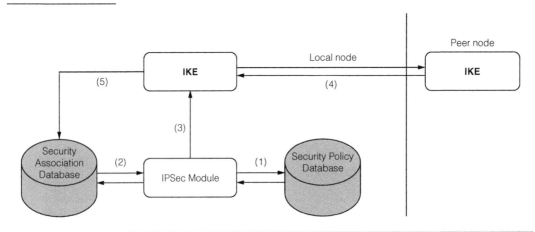

The relationship between IP security-related modules.

IKE can create all necessary SAs automatically. The only requirement for this mechanism to work is that the two end nodes must have a shared secret to create ISAKMP session between them as discussed in Section 6.9.1. The way to install such a secret is outside of the IKE mechanism, for example, install a shared key on both nodes or retrieve the peer's identifier by using the Public Key Infrastructure (PKI) mechanism.

Figure 6-25 provides a simplified view of the relationships among IP security protocol stack, IP security databases (SAD and SPD) and IKE.

As Figure 6-25 illustrates, as a first step the IPsec module examines the SPD to determine if IPsec processing is enabled on the outgoing traffic. For IPsec processing enabled traffic that does not have a corresponding entry in the SAD, the IPsec module requests the IKE module to establish the necessary SA. The IKE module negotiates and performs the necessary exchange with the peer IKE module to establish the SA. Then the IKE module inserts this new SA into the SAD.

6.10 Racoon Operation

Racoon is an implementation of the IKE protocol specification. It establishes SA entries between two nodes based on the SP entries configured in the kernel in advance. The parameters of the SA entries are automatically negotiated by Racoon and the IKE process running on the other end node. All we have to do is to specify the SP entries we require. When the kernel processes the outgoing packets or incoming packets, it searches the Security Policy database to see if there is any policy definition for that packet. If the kernel finds a matching SP entry, it searches for an appropriate SA entry from the SAD. If no SA entry is found, the kernel informs Racoon of the lack of required SA entry. After receiving the notification, Racoon starts the IKE negotiation procedure to establish requested SA entries.

6.10.1 Configuring Racoon

The command name of Racoon is **racoon**. **racoon** is a user space application. Figure 6-26 describes the synopsis of the **racoon** command.

In most cases, we need to create a suitable configuration file for **racoon** and pass the configuration file to **racoon**. The following describes the option switches of **racoon** briefly.

−B Install SA entries from the file specified by the `path backupsa` directive in a configuration file. **racoon** can back up SA entries which are negotiated in the file. The directives will be discussed in Section 6.10.2.

−d Increase log level. Multiple −d will increase log level.

−F Run **racoon** as a foreground process.

FIGURE 6-26

---

racoon [-BdF46] [-f *configfile*] [-l *logfile*] [-p *isakmp-port*]

---

*The synopsis of **racoon**.*

-f **configfile** Specify a configuration file. The default location of the configuration file depends on the build environment of **racoon**. `/usr/local/v6/etc/racoon.conf` is the default location if you are using the KAME distribution.

-l **logfile** Use *logfile* as an output file of log messages. **racoon** usually writes its log messages using the syslog mechanism with the LOG_DAEMON facility.

-p **isakmp-port** Specify the port number which is used for ISAKMP. The default port number is 500.

6.10.2   Configuration File Format

In this section, we explain the directives used in the **racoon** configuration file. To make it easy to understand the configuration format, we divide the directives into six categories.

Path specification part   Specify path names which are included by a configuration file.

Timer specification part   Specify several timeout/counter values.

Listening address specification part   Specify the address and port number used by **racoon**.

Remote node specification part   Specify Phase-I parameters and behavior per remote node.

SAinfo specification part   Specify negotiation parameters of SAD entries.

Other part   Other miscellaneous parameters.

Path Specification

Path specification is used to define the directory in which other configuration files are located.

- `path include` *path*;
  Specify the path in which other configuration files are located. Other configuration files may be specified by the `include` directive.

- `path pre_shared_key` *file*;
  Specify the filename which contains a pre-shared secret which is used to create the ISAKMP SA entry.

- `path certificate` *path*;
  Specify the path which stores X.509 certificate files.

- `path backupsa` *file*;
  Specify the filename to which **racoon** backs up the SA entries negotiated. If the −B switch is used when executing **racoon**, **racoon** reads the contents of the specified file and recovers SA entries negotiated before.

- `include` *file*;
  Include another file. We can divide the configuration file, for example, per remote node.

Timer Specification

Timer specification defines the retry counter and interval. All definitions are quoted by the `timer` block. For example,

```
timer {
     # definition of timer block statements
}
```

There are four directives.

- `counter` *number*;
  Specify the retry count of IKE messages to *number*. The default value is 5. **racoon** resends a message if there is no reply where the specified timeout period is elapsed. The timeout period can be specified by the `interval` directive.

- `interval` *number timeunit*;
  Specify the interval to resend a message. *timeunit* is one of `sec`, `min`, `hour`. The default value is 10 seconds.

- `persend` *number*;
  Specify the number of packets per one message. Since ISAKMP messages are sent as UDP packets, **racoon** can be configured to sent multiple same messages at one time. The default value is 1.

- `phase1` *number timeunit*;
  Specify the maximum time to wait to complete an ISAKMP SA creation. *timeunit* is one of `sec`, `min`, `hour`. The default value is 15 seconds.

- `phase2` *number timeunit*;
  Specify the maximum time to wait to the complete the IPsec SA creation. *timeunit* is one of `sec`, `min`, `hour`. The default value is 10 seconds.

Listening Address Specification

Listening address specification defines addresses and port numbers which **racoon** uses. All definitions are quoted by listen block as follows:

```
listen {
      # definitions of listen block statements
}
```

There are two directives.

- `isakmp` *address* [[*port*]];
  Specify the address and port number to use for ISAKMP communication. If we do not specify any address in the `listen` directive, **racoon** will use all available addresses for ISAKMP communication. The port number is 500, if it is not specified explicitly. The port number must be quoted by brackets (`[` and `]`) if specified.

- `strict_address`;
  If `strict_address` is specified, **racoon** will exit when binding addresses by the `isakmp` directive fails. This statement does not have any effect if `isakmp` is not specified.

Remote Node Specification

Remote node specification defines parameters used in Phase-I per remote node or a set of remote nodes. The statements are quoted by the `remote` block.

```
remote address|anonymous [[ port]] {
      # definition of remote statements
}
```

The `remote` directive has up to two arguments. The first argument which is used to specify the address of a remote node is mandatory. We can specify the exact address of the remote node or `anonymous`. When `anonymous` is specified, all communications for Phase-I use the same parameters defined in this remote block, unless there are other specific remote blocks for a particular node.

If we want to use a port number other than the default ISAKMP port number (500), *port* can be specified.

- `exchange_mode main|aggressive|base;`
  Specify the exchange mode that **racoon** uses to establish ISAKMP SA. Possible options are `main`, `aggressive` and `base`, which means the main mode, the aggressive mode, and the base mode, respectively.

- `doi ipsec_doi;`
  Declare that **racoon** uses key exchange parameters defined in [RFC2407]. Since **racoon** does not support other domains of interpretation, this statement can be omitted.

- `situation identity_only;`
  Declare that racoon uses SIT_IDENTITY_ONLY as a situation definition. Other types of definitions defined in [RFC2407] are not supported. This statement can be omitted.

- `my_identifier` *type;*
  Specify the type of identifier of this node. The remote IKE process distinguishes the local node by this identifier. The following five types are defined.

  — `address` [*address*]
  The identifier is an IP address. If we do not specify the type of identifier by the `my_identifier` directive, `address` is the default type.

  — `user_fqdn` *string*
  The identifier is a fully qualified domain name with user name. For example, `user@kame.net`.

  — `fqdn` *string*
  The identifier is a fully qualified domain name. For example, `mobilenode1.kame.net`.

  — `keyid` *file*
  Specify the identifier as the ID_KEY_ID type defined in [RFC2407]. The identifier should be stored in *file. file* is just a byte stream of arbitrary length.

  — `asn1dn` [*string*]
  Specify the identifier as an ASN.1 distinguished name specified by *string. string* must be the same as specified in the subject field in the certificate file of this node. If *string* is omitted, **racoon** automatically extracts a distinguished name from the subject field of the X.509 certificate.

- `peers_identifier` *type;*
  Specify the identifier of a peer node. *type* has the same format as that used in the `my_identifier` directive. Note that **racoon** verifies the peer's identifier only if the peer's identifier is defined by this parameter and the verification is enabled by the `verify_identifier` directive.

- `verify_identifier on|off;`
  If set to `on`, **racoon** verifies the identifier passed by the communicating node. If the identifier does not match the identifier defined by the `peers_identifier` directive, **racoon** aborts the Phase-I negotiation. The default value is `off`.

- `certificate_type` x509 *certfile privatekeyfile;*
  Specify the X.509 certificate file of the local node. *certfile* is the file name of the certificate file and *privatekeyfile* is the file name of the private key.

- `peer_certfile dnssec|`*certfile;*
  Specify the certificate file of a peer node. If `dnssec` is specified, **racoon** tries to retrieve the peer's certificate using DNS. Otherwise, *certfile* should be specified as the file name of the certificate file of the peer node.

- `send_cert on|off;`
  Specify whether **racoon** sends the certification of the local node. The default is `on`.

- `send_cr on|off;`
  Specify whether **racoon** requests the certification of a peer node. The default is `on`.

- `verify_cert on|off;`
  Specify whether **racoon** verifies the certificate file sent from a peer. The default is `on`.

- `lifetime time` *number timeunit;*
  Specify the lifetime of ISAKMP SA entries. The lifetime can be specified separately for each proposal by the `proposal` block if the `exchange_mode` is set to `main`.

- `initial_contact on|off;`
  Specify if **racoon** sends INITIAL-CONTACT messages when it communicates with peer nodes the first time. This is useful when a node is unintentionally rebooted or has crashed. The remote node may still have the state of the local node, which is already outdated. Since the INITIAL-CONTACT message suggests removing all existing state information corresponding to the local node, the IKE procedure can be started cleanly. The default is `on`.

- `passive on|off;`
  If set to `on`, **racoon** will act as only a responder. That is, **racoon** never initiates IKE negotiation. The default is `off`.

- `proposal_check` *level;*
  Specify the proposal check level. **racoon** compares the length of lifetime and PFS (Perfect Forward Secrecy) group of the Phase-II proposal sent from the initiator when it is acting as a responder. If those values are different from the local proposal, then **racoon** acts based on the following specified level.

  — `obey`
  Always obey the proposal of an initiator.

  — `strict`
  If the lifetime of the responder is longer than the proposal of an initiator, the lifetime of the initiator is used. Otherwise, the proposal is rejected.

If PFS is not required by the responder, the responder will accept one of proposals based on the lifetime validation above.

If PFS is required by both nodes and the group specified as a PSF group is different, the responder rejects the proposal.

— claim

If the lifetime of the responder is longer than the proposal of that of the initiator, the lifetime of the responder is used. With regard to PFS, the same rules are applied with the case of strict.

— exact

Accepts a proposal only when the lifetime of the responder is equal to the lifetime of the initiator. With regard to PFS, the same rules are applied with the case of strict.

- generate_policy on|off;
  In some cases, an administrator may want to accept a node which has a dynamically assigned IP address. Since the IP security processing requires pre-configured SP entries, such a node cannot use IP security. If the generate_policy directive is set to on, **racoon** will install an SP entry based on the contents of the proposal for Phase-II. This directive has an effect only when **racoon** is acting as a responder. The default value is off.

- nonce_size *number*;
  Specify the length of nonce in a unit of a byte which is exchanged in Phase-I. Usually, *number* is 8 to 256 as specified in [RFC2409].

- proposal
  The proposal block defines parameters for Phase-I negotiation. The following directives can be specified.

  — encryption_algorithm *algorithm*;
  Specify the encryption algorithm used for Phase-I. Any one of des, 3des, blowfish or cast128 can be specified.

  — hash_algorithm *algorithm*;
  Specify the hash algorithm used for Phase-I. Either md5 or sha1 can be specified.

  — authentication_method *type*;
  Specify the type of authentication method for Phase-I. Either pre_shared_key, rsasig or gssapi_krb can be specified.

  — dh_group *group*;
  Specify the group of Diffie-Hellman exponentiations. Either modp768, mpdp1024 or modp1536 can be specified. Or, just specify the number of DH group as 1, 2 or 5 respectively.

  — lifetime time *number timeunit*;
  Specify the lifetime of ISAKMP SA entries for each proposal. This can be specified when **racoon** uses the main mode in the exchange_mode directive.

  —gssapi_id *string*;
  Specify the GSS-API endpoint name.

SAinfo Specification

The SAinfo specification defines parameters for IPsec SA entries which are negotiated in Phase-II. All parameters must be specified in the `sainfo` block.

```
sainfo source_id [fig destination_id|anonymous {
        # definition of sainfo statements
}
```

source_id and *destination_id* are either of the following formats.

- `address` *address*{*/prefixlen*}{ [*port*] } *ul_proto*
  ul_proto is a transport protocol name.

- *idtype string*
  idtype is either `user_fqdn` or `fqdn`.

The `sainfo` block has the following directives.

- `pfs_group` *group*;
  Specify the group of Diffie-Hellman exponentiations. This directive is required when we need PFS for Phase-II negotiation.

- `lifetime time` *number timeunit*;
  Specify the lifetime for IPsec SA entries.

- `encryption_algorithm` *algorithm*{, *algorithm* ...};

- `authentication_algorithm` *algorithm*{, *algorithm* ...};
  Specify available algorithms for IPsec SA entries.
      Algorithms for encryption can be chosen from `des`, `3des`, `des_iv64`, `des_iv32`, `rc5`, `rc4`, `idea`, `3idea`, `cast128`, `blowfish`, `null_enc`, `twofish`, or `rijndael`. Algorithms for authentication can be chosen from `des`, `3des`, `des_iv64`, `des_iv32`, `hmac_md5`, or `hmac_sha1`.
      If the specified algorithm has a variable key length, the bit length can be specified immediately after the name of the algorithm. For example, `blowfish 448` for using the blowfish algorithm with a 448-bit key.
      racoon automatically expands the possible combinations based on the specified algorithms above, and includes all of them in the proposal.

Other Specifications

We can specify the logging level by the `log` directive.

- `log` *level*;
  level is either `notify`, `debug` or `debug2`. `notify` is the default level.

6.11   Scenarios

In this section, we describe some practical scenarios and configuration examples using **racoon**. As we have seen, **racoon** has many configuration knobs. However, in most cases, using the default values suffices.

6.11.1   Creating a VPN between 3 Networks

It is very common to create a VPN using IPsec. Figure 6-27 shows the network described in this example. There are three organizations. Organization A has `2001:db8:100::/48` as its IPv6 address block and the security gateway SG A. Organization B has `2001:db8:200::/48` and the security gateway SG B. Organization C has `2001:db8:300::/48` and the security gateway SG C.

Setting Up Security Policies

To connect the three organizations described in Figure 6-27 using IP security, we need the following policies.

- All traffic from organization A to organization B must be tunneled from SG A to SG B.
- All traffic from organization A to organization C must be tunneled from SG A to SG C.
- All traffic from organization B to organization A must be tunneled from SG B to SG A.
- All traffic from organization B to organization C must be tunneled from SG B to SG C.
- All traffic from organization C to organization A must be tunneled from SG C to SG A.
- All traffic from organization C to organization B must be tunneled from SG C to SG B.

These policies can be written in a setkey form as in Figure 6-28.

Setting Up racoon

SA entries are configured by **racoon**. We use the following configuration.

FIGURE 6-27

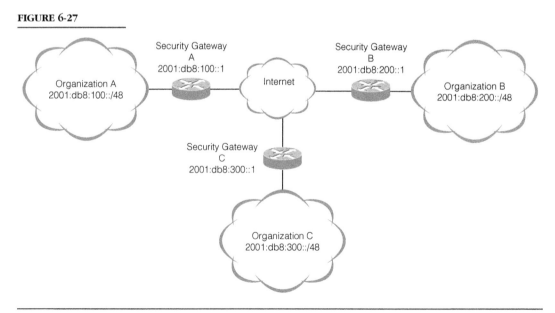

Creating a VPN between 3 networks.

FIGURE 6-28

For SG A:

```
spdadd 2001:db8:100::/48[any] 2001:db8:200::/48[any]
        any -P out ipsec
        esp/tunnel/2001:db8:100::1-2001:db8:200::1/require;
spdadd 2001:db8:200::/48[any] 2001:db8:100::/48[any]
        any -P in ipsec
        esp/tunnel/2001:db8:200::1-2001:db8:100::1/require;
spdadd 2001:db8:100::/48[any] 2001:db8:300::/48[any]
        any -P out ipsec
        esp/tunnel/2001:db8:100::1-2001:db8:300::1/require;
spdadd 2001:db8:300::/48[any] 2001:db8:100::/48[any]
        any -P in ipsec
        esp/tunnel/2001:db8:300::1-2001:db8:100::1/require;
```

For SG B:

```
spdadd 2001:db8:200::/48[any] 2001:db8:100::/48[any]
        any -P out ipsec
        esp/tunnel/2001:db8:200::1-2001:db8:100::1/require;
spdadd 2001:db8:100::/48[any] 2001:db8:200::/48[any]
        any -P in ipsec
        esp/tunnel/2001:db8:100::1-2001:db8:200::1/require;
spdadd 2001:db8:200::/48[any] 2001:db8:300::/48[any]
        any -P out ipsec
        esp/tunnel/2001:db8:200::1-2001:db8:300::1/require;
spdadd 2001:db8:300::/48[any] 2001:db8:200::/48[any]
        any -P in ipsec
        esp/tunnel/2001:db8:300::1-2001:db8:200::1/require;
```

For SG C:

```
spdadd 2001:db8:300::/48[any] 2001:db8:100::/48[any]
        any -P out ipsec
        esp/tunnel/2001:db8:300::1-2001:db8:100::1/require;
spdadd 2001:db8:100::/48[any] 2001:db8:300::/48[any]
        any -P in ipsec
        esp/tunnel/2001:db8:100::1-2001:db8:300::1/require;
spdadd 2001:db8:300::/48[any] 2001:db8:200::/48[any]
        any -P out ipsec
        esp/tunnel/2001:db8:300::1-2001:db8:200::1/require;
spdadd 2001:db8:200::/48[any] 2001:db8:300::/48[any]
        any -P in ipsec
        esp/tunnel/2001:db8:200::1-2001:db8:300::1/require;
```

Security policy setup for the network described in Figure 6-27.

- Phase-I parameters

  — lifetime of ISAKMP SA entries is 24 hours

  — pre-shared key for authentication

  — 3des algorithm for encryption

  — sha1 algorithm for integrity

  — mpdp1024 group for Diffie-Hellman exponentiation

  — always obey an initiator

- Phase-II parameters

    — lifetime of IPsec SA entries is 12 hours
    — possible encryption algorithms are: 3des, cast128, blowfish with a 448-bit key, des, rijndael
    — possible authentication algorithms are: hmac_sha1, hmac_md5
    — mpdp1024 group for Diffie-Hellman exponentiation

Figure 6-29 shows the actual configuration file of **racoon** in this scenario.

We need a file which contains pre-shared keys of each security gateway. Figure 6-30 shows the content of the file which should be placed as `/usr/local/etc/psk.txt` on each security gateway.

FIGURE 6-29

```
For SG A:

# path for the file which includes pre-shared keys
path pre_shared_key "/usr/local/etc/psk.txt" ;

# phase 1 parameters for 2001:db8:200::1
remote 2001:db8:200::1
{
    exchange_mode main,base;

    # define identifiers as an address
    my_identifier address "2001:db8:100::1";
    peers_identifier address "2001:db8:200::1";

    # lifetime of ISAKMP SAD entries is 24 hours
    lifetime time 24 hour;

    proposal {
        # authentication method is pre-shared key
        authentication_method pre_shared_key;

        # define encryption and hash algorithm for this proposal
        encryption_algorithm 3des;
        hash_algorithm sha1;

        # use mpdp1024 Diffie-Hellman group
        dh_group 2;
    }

    # always obey the initiator's proposal
    proposal_check obey;
}

remote 2001:db8:300::1
{
    exchange_mode main,base;

    my_identifier address "2001:db8:100::1";
    peers_identifier address "2001:db8:300::1";

    lifetime time 24 hour;

    proposal {
        authentication_method pre_shared_key;
```

```
            encryption_algorithm 3des;
            hash_algorithm sha1;
            dh_group 2;
      }

      proposal_check obey;
}

# phase 2 parameters
sainfo anonymous
{
      # use mpdp1024 Diffie-Hellman group
      pfs_group 2;

      # lifetime of IPsec SAD entries is 12 hours
      lifetime time 12 hour;

      # define possible encryption and authentication algorithms
      encryption_algorithm 3des, cast128, blowfish 448, des, rijndael;
      authentication_algorithm hmac_sha1, hmac_md5;

      # following line is needed even if we don't need compression
      compression_algorithm deflate;
}
```

For SG B:

```
path pre_shared_key "/usr/local/etc/psk.txt" ;

remote 2001:db8:100::1
{
      exchange_mode main,base;

      my_identifier address "2001:db8:200::1";
      peers_identifier address "2001:db8:100::1";

      lifetime time 24 hour;
        proposal {
          encryption_algorithm 3des;
          hash_algorithm sha1;
          authentication_method pre_shared_key;
          dh_group 2;
        }

      proposal_check obey;
}

remote 2001:db8:300::1
{
      exchange_mode main,base;

      my_identifier address "2001:db8:200::1";
      peers_identifier address "2001:db8:300::1";

      lifetime time 24 hour;

      proposal {
          encryption_algorithm 3des;
          hash_algorithm sha1;
          authentication_method pre_shared_key;
          dh_group 2;
      }

      proposal_check obey;
}
```

Continued

```
sainfo anonymous
{
      pfs_group 2;
      lifetime time 12 hour;
      encryption_algorithm 3des, cast128, blowfish 448, des, rijndael;
      authentication_algorithm hmac_sha1, hmac_md5;
      compression_algorithm deflate;
}
```

For SG C:

```
path pre_shared_key "/usr/local/etc/psk.txt" ;

remote 2001:db8:100::1
{
      exchange_mode main,base;

      my_identifier address "2001:db8:300::1";
      peers_identifier address "2001:db8:100::1";

      lifetime time 24 hour;

      proposal {
          encryption_algorithm 3des;
          hash_algorithm sha1;
          authentication_method pre_shared_key;
          dh_group 2;
      }

      proposal_check obey;
}

remote 2001:db8:200::1
{
      exchange_mode main,base;

      my_identifier address "2001:db8:300::1";
      peers_identifier address "2001:db8:200::1";

      lifetime time 24 hour;

      proposal {
          encryption_algorithm 3des;
          hash_algorithm sha1;
          authentication_method pre_shared_key;
          dh_group 2;
      }

      proposal_check obey;
}
  sainfo anonymous
{
      pfs_group 2;
      lifetime time 12 hour;
      encryption_algorithm 3des, cast128, blowfish 448, des, rijndael;
      authentication_algorithm hmac_sha1, hmac_md5;
      compression_algorithm deflate;
}
```

The configuration file for the network described in Figure 6-27.

6.11.2 Creating Star Topology VPN

The example described in the previous subsection can be extended to an arbitrary number of networks. However, it is not scalable, apparently. One solution for creating a VPN network with

FIGURE 6-30

For SG A:

```
2001:db8:200::1        SGAandSGB
2001:db8:300::1        SGAandSGC
```

For SG B:

```
2001:db8:100::1        SGAandSGB
2001:db8:300::1        SGBandSGC
```

For SG C:

```
2001:db8:100::1        SGAandSGC
2001:db8:200::1        SGBandSGC
```

Pre-shared key file for the network described in Figure 6-27.

a number of networks is to design the network as a star topology. Figure 6-31 is an example of a VPN with a star topology. This figure represents the internal topology of the organization in which the IPv6 block is `2001:db8:100::/48`. This organization has 4 sites, A to D. Site A connects to all other sites. Sites B to D are not connected directly to each other.

Setting Up Security Policies

In this example, the following policies are needed.

- All traffic from site A to site B must be tunneled from SG A to SG B.
- All traffic from site A to site C must be tunneled from SG A to SG C.
- All traffic from site A to site D must be tunneled from SG A to SG D.
- All traffic from site B to other sites must be tunneled from SG B to SG A.
- All traffic from site C to other sites must be tunneled from SG C to SG A.
- All traffic from site D to other sites must be tunneled from SG C to SG A.

These policies can be written in a setkey form as Figure 6-32.

If we design the network as a full mesh network as the previous example, we must have 6 policies for each site. This results in 24 policies in total. Using a star topology reduces the number of security policies. In addition, adding a new site is easier than a full mesh topology. In a star topology, we only need to add two policies to add a new site. One policy is from SG A to a new SG, another is from the new SG to SG A. Other SGs need not be modified, while a full mesh topology requires modification on all SGs to add security policies to the newly added SG.

Setting Up racoon

We apply the same parameters used in the previous example.

FIGURE 6-31

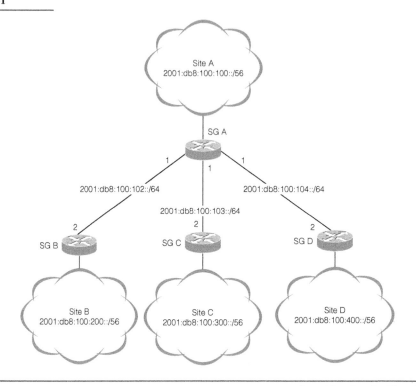

A sample network with a star topology.

- Phase-I parameters

  — lifetime of ISAKMP SA entries is 24 hours
  — pre-shared key for authentication
  — 3des algorithm for encryption
  — sha1 algorithm for integrity
  — mpdp1024 group for Diffie-Hellman exponentiation
  — always obey an initiator

- Phase-II parameters

  — lifetime of IPsec SA entries is 12 hours
  — possible encryption algorithms are: 3des, cast128, blowfish with a 448-bit key, des, rijndael
  — possible authentication algorithms are: hmac_sha1, hmac_md5
  — mpdp1024 group for Diffie-Hellman exponentiation

The configuration file used for this example is not very different from the previous one. Figure 6-33 shows the configuration files for SG A and SG B.

FIGURE 6-32

For SG A:

```
spdadd 2001:db8:100::/48[any] 2001:db8:100:200::/56[any]
      any -P out ipsec
      esp/tunnel/2001:db8:100:102::1-2001:db8:100:102::2/require;
spdadd 2001:db8:100:200::/56[any] 2001:db8:100::/48[any]
      any -P in ipsec
      esp/tunnel/2001:db8:100:102::2-2001:db8:100:102::1/require;
spdadd 2001:db8:100::/48[any] 2001:db8:100:300::/56[any]
      any -P out ipsec
      esp/tunnel/2001:db8:100:103::1-2001:db8:100:103::2/require;
spdadd 2001:db8:100:300::/56[any] 2001:db8:100::/48[any]
      any -P in ipsec
      esp/tunnel/2001:db8:100:103::2-2001:db8:100:103::1/require;
spdadd 2001:db8:100::/48[any] 2001:db8:100:400::/56[any]
      any -P out ipsec
      esp/tunnel/2001:db8:100:104::1-2001:db8:100:104::2/require;
spdadd 2001:db8:100:400::/56[any] 2001:db8:100::/48[any]
      any -P in ipsec
      esp/tunnel/2001:db8:100:104::2-2001:db8:100:104::1/require;
```

For SG B:

```
spdadd 2001:db8:100:200::/56[any] 2001:db8:100::/48[any]
      any -P out ipsec
      esp/tunnel/2001:db8:100:102::2-2001:db8:100:102::1/require;
spdadd 2001:db8:100::/48[any] 2001:db8:100:200::/56[any]
      any -P in ipsec
      esp/tunnel/2001:db8:100:102::1-2001:db8:100:102::2/require;
```

For SG C:

```
spdadd 2001:db8:100:300::/56[any] 2001:db8:100::/48[any]
      any -P out ipsec
      esp/tunnel/2001:db8:100:103::2-2001:db8:100:103::1/require;
spdadd 2001:db8:100::/48[any] 2001:db8:100:300::/56[any]
      any -P in ipsec
      esp/tunnel/2001:db8:100:103::1-2001:db8:100:103::2/require;
```

For SG D:

```
spdadd 2001:db8:100:400::/56[any] 2001:db8:100::/48[any]
      any -P out ipsec
      esp/tunnel/2001:db8:100:104::2-2001:db8:100:104::1/require;
spdadd 2001:db8:100::/48[any] 2001:db8:100:400::/56[any]
      any -P in ipsec
      esp/tunnel/2001:db8:100:104::1-2001:db8:100:104::2/require;
```

Security policy setup for the network described in Figure 6-31.

6.11.3   Using Transport Mode IP Security

IPsec can be used to enhance end-to-end security by using the transport mode IPsec. In this subsection, we use Figure 6-11 as a reference network and provide configuration files for **racoon** to create SA entries dynamically.

FIGURE 6-33

For SG A:

```
# path for the file which includes pre-shared keys
path pre_shared_key "/usr/local/etc/psk.txt" ;

# phase 1 parameters for 2001:db8:100:102::2
remote 2001:db8:100:102::2
{
     exchange_mode main,base;

     # define identifiers as an address
     my_identifier address "2001:db8:100:102::1";
     peers_identifier address "2001:db8:100:102::2";

     # lifetime of ISAKMP SAD entries is 24 hours
     lifetime time 24 hour;

     proposal {
         # authentication method is pre-shared key
         authentication_method pre_shared_key;

         # define encryption and hash algorithm for this proposal
         encryption_algorithm 3des;
         hash_algorithm sha1;

         # use mpdp1024 Diffie-Hellman group
         dh_group 2;
     }

     # always obey the initiator's proposal
     proposal_check obey;
}

remote 2001:db8:100:103::2
{
     exchange_mode main,base;

     my_identifier address "2001:db8:100:103::1";
     peers_identifier address "2001:db8:100:103::2";

     lifetime time 24 hour;

     proposal {
     authentication_method pre_shared_key;
     encryption_algorithm 3des;
     hash_algorithm sha1;
     dh_group 2;
     }

     proposal_check obey;
}

remote 2001:db8:100:104::2
{
     exchange_mode main,base;

     my_identifier address "2001:db8:100:104::1";
     peers_identifier address "2001:db8:100:104::2";
     lifetime time 24 hour;

     proposal {
```

```
            authentication_method pre_shared_key;
            encryption_algorithm 3des;
            hash_algorithm sha1;
            dh_group 2;
        }

        proposal_check obey;
}

# phase 2 parameters
sainfo anonymous
{
        # use mpdp1024 Diffie-Hellman group
        pfs_group 2;

        # lifetime of IPsec SAD entries is 12 hours
        lifetime time 12 hour;

        # define possible encryption and authentication algorithms
        encryption_algorithm 3des, cast128, blowfish 448, des, rijndael;
        authentication_algorithm hmac_sha1, hmac_md5;

        # following line is needed even if we don't need compression
        compression_algorithm deflate;
}
```

For SG B:

```
path pre_shared_key "/usr/local/etc/psk.txt" ;

remote 2001:db8:100:102::1
{
        exchange_mode main,base;

        my_identifier address "2001:db8:100:102::2";
        peers_identifier address "2001:db8:100:102::1";

        lifetime time 24 hour;

        proposal {
            authentication_method pre_shared_key;
            encryption_algorithm 3des;
            hash_algorithm sha1;
            dh_group 2;
        }

        proposal_check obey;
}

sainfo anonymous
{
        pfs_group 2;
        lifetime time 12 hour;
        encryption_algorithm 3des, cast128, blowfish 448, des, rijndael;
        authentication_algorithm hmac_sha1, hmac_md5;
        compression_algorithm deflate;
}
```

The configuration file for the network described in Figure 6-31.

In Figure 6-11, there are two nodes. One is node A and the other is POP server B. In this configuration, we consider protecting all POP3 traffic by using transport mode IP security. The configuration of security policies is the same as that described in Figure 6-10. Corresponding **racoon** configuration files are described in Figure 6-34. We use the same parameters in the previous examples.

FIGURE 6-34

For node A:

```
# path for the file which includes pre-shared keys
path pre_shared_key "/usr/local/etc/psk.txt" ;

# phase 1 parameters for 2001:db8:200::1
remote 2001:db8:100::200
{
exchange_mode main,base;

# define identifiers as an address
my_identifier address "2001:db8:100::100";
peers_identifier address "2001:db8:100::200";

# lifetime of ISAKMP SAD entries is 24 hours
lifetime time 24 hour;

proposal {
# authentication method is pre-shared key
authentication_method pre_shared_key;

# define encryption and hash algorithm for this proposal
encryption_algorithm 3des;
hash_algorithm sha1;

# use mpdp1024 Diffie-Hellman group
dh_group 2;
}

# always obey the initiator's proposal
proposal_check obey;
}

# phase 2 parameters
sainfo anonymous
{
```

For POP server B:

```
path pre_shared_key "/usr/local/etc/psk.txt" ;

remote 2001:db8:100::100
# use mpdp1024 Diffie-Hellman group
pfs_group 2;

# lifetime of IPsec SAD entries is 12 hours
lifetime time 12 hour;

# define possible encryption and authentication algorithms
encryption_algorithm 3des, cast128, blowfish 448, des, rijndael;
authentication_algorithm hmac_sha1, hmac_md5;
```

```
# following line is needed even if we don't need compression
compression_algorithm deflate;
}
{
exchange_mode main,base;

my_identifier address "2001:db8:100::200";
peers_identifier address "2001:db8:100::100";

lifetime time 24 hour;

proposal {
encryption_algorithm 3des;
hash_algorithm sha1;
authentication_method pre_shared_key;
dh_group 2;
}

proposal_check obey;
}

sainfo anonymous
{
pfs_group 2;
lifetime time 12 hour;
encryption_algorithm 3des, cast128, blowfish 448, des, rijndael;
authentication_algorithm hmac_sha1, hmac_md5;
compression_algorithm deflate;
}
```

The configuration file for the network described in Figure 6-11.

- Phase-I parameters

    — lifetime of ISAKMP SA entries is 24 hours
    — pre-shared key for authentication
    — 3des algorithm for encryption
    — sha1 algorithm for integrity
    — mpdp1024 group for Diffie-Hellman exponentiation
    — always obey an initiator

- Phase-II parameters

    — lifetime of IPsec SA entries is 12 hours
    — possible encryption algorithms are: 3des, cast128, blowfish with a 448-bit key, des, rijndael
    — possible authentication algorithms are: hmac_sha1, hmac_md5
    — mpdp1024 group for Diffie-Hellman exponentiation

As we can see, there is no difference between the configuration files for tunnel mode.

6.11.4 Connecting to the Server from Public Access Points

Recently, many Internet Service Providers are offering many access points in various locations. It is natural that we see the demand to use these access points to connect to the VPN server of our office. In this case, the IP address we will have at the access point is not fixed as shown in Figure 6-35. Unlike the previous configurations described before, we cannot specify the exact

FIGURE 6-35

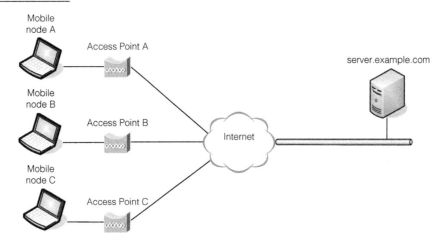

Using public access points.

FIGURE 6-36

```
remote anonymous
{
        exchange_mode main,base;

        # define identifiers as an fqdn
        my_identifier fqdn "server.example.com";

        # enable passive mode
        passive on;

        # lifetime of ISAKMP SA entries is 24 hours
        lifetime time 24 hour;

        proposal {
                # authentication method is pre-shared key
                authentication_method pre_shared_key;

                # define encryption and hash algorithm for this proposal
                encryption_algorithm 3des;
                hash_algorithm sha1;

                # use mpdp1024 Diffie-Hellman group
                dh_group 2;
        }
```

```
        # always obey the initiator's proposal
        proposal_check obey;
}
```

Server side Phase-I configuration.

FIGURE 6-37

```
remote anonymous
{
        exchange_mode main,base;

        # define identifiers as an fqdn
        my_identifier fqdn "mobilenode1.example.org";
        peers_identifier fqdn "server.example.org";

        # lifetime of ISAKMP SA entries is 24 hours
        lifetime time 24 hour;

        proposal {
                # authentication method is pre-shared key
                authentication_method pre_shared_key;

                # define encryption and hash algorithm for this proposal
                encryption_algorithm 3des;
                hash_algorithm sha1;

                # use mpdp1024 Diffie-Hellman group
                dh_group 2;
        }

        # always obey the initiator's proposal
        proposal_check obey;
}
```

Mobile node side Phase-I configuration.

addresses in the Phase-I setting. Figure 6-36 shows a part of the Phase-I configuration file of the server side.

The important points of server-side configuration are the following:

- Do not specify peer's identifier to accept multiple mobile nodes.

- Enable passive mode so that the server never initiates the IKE negotiation.

Figure 6-37 shows a part of the Phase-I configuration of the mobile node side.

FIGURE 6-38

For server.example.com:

```
mobilenode1.example.com        SERVERandMN1
mobilenode2.example.com        SERVERandMN2
mobilenode3.example.com        SERVERandMN3
```

For mobilenode1.example.com:

```
server.foo.com                 SERVERandMN1
```

For mobilenode2.example.com:

```
server.foo.com                 SERVERandMN2
```

For mobilenode3.example.com:

```
server.foo.com                 SERVERandMN3
```

Pre-shared secret for public access.

The point of the mobile node side is to specify the identifier as FQDN, not as an IP address. The address may differ depending on the access point that the mobile node attached to. Note that the identifier is used only locally. The value of FQDN need not match the actual domain name of the dynamically assigned address.

Since we use FQDN as their identifiers, the pre-shared secret file must be written based on them. Figure 6-38 shows the pre-shared secret file used in this example.

References

Most of the references for this book are RFCs. Some specifications are in the process of standardization or revision, for which Internet Drafts are referred to. Both types of documents are freely available from the IETF web page: http://www.ietf.org. Note, however, that an Internet Draft is a work-in-progress material, which may expire or may have become an RFC by the time this book is published. There are WWW or FTP sites on the Internet that provide a copy of old versions of Internet Drafts when necessary. At the time of this writing, the KAME project's FTP server provides this service, which is located at ftp://ftp.kame.net/pub/internet-drafts/.

The following list of references are categorized into three parts: The first part consists of non-IETF references; the second part is a list of RFC referred to or mentioned in this book; the last part is a reference list of Internet Drafts.

[Abl03]   J. Abley, "Hierarchical Anycast for Global Service Distribution," ISC Technical Note, 2003 (available at http://www.isc.org/index.pl?/pubs/tn/index.pl?tn=isc-tn-2003-1.html).

[Abl04]   J. Abley, "A Software Approach to Distributing Requests for DNS Service Using GNU Zebra, ISC BIND 9 and FreeBSD," ISC Technical Note, March 2004 (available at http://www.isc.org/index.pl?/pubs/tn/index.pl?tn=isc-tn-2004-1.html).

[Baa88]   Sara Baase, "Computer Algorithms—Introduction to Design and Analysis Second Edition," Addison Wesley, 1988.

[ISO 10589]   "Intermediate System to Intermediate System Intra-Domain Routeing Exchange Protocol for Use in Conjunction with the Protocol for Providing the Connectionless-mode Network Service (ISO 8473)," ISO 10589, 1992.

[Liu02]   C. Liu, "DNS & BIND Cookbook," O'Reilly, 2002.

[Liu06]   C. Liu and P. Albitz, "DNS and BIND, 5th Edition," O'Reilly, 2006.

[Som03]   R. Somegawa et al., "The Effects of Server Placement and Server Selection
                 for Internet Services," IEICE Trans. on Communication, Vol. E86-B No. 2.
                 February 2003, pp. 542–551.

[Suz06]   S. Suzuki et al., "Fixing DNS Misbehavior Hindering IPv6 Deployment,"
                 SAINT 2006 IPv6 Workshop, January 2006.

[Wil00]   B. Williamson, "Developing IP Multicast Networks," Cisco Press, 2000.

[RFC791]   J. Postel, "Internet Protocol," RFC791, September 1981.

[RFC905]   ISO, "ISO Transport Protocol Specification ISO DP 8073," RFC905, April
                 1984.

[RFC1034]   P. Mockapetris, "Domain Names—Concepts and Facilities," RFC1034,
                 November 1987.

[RFC1035]   P. Mockapetris, "Domain Names—Implementation and Specification,"
                 RFC1035, November 1987.

[RFC1075]   D. Waitzman et al., "Distance Vector Multicast Routing Protocol,"
                 RFC1075, November 1988.

[RFC1123]   R. Braden, "Requirements for Internet Hosts—Application and Support,"
                 RFC1123, October 1989.

[RFC1195]   R. Callon, "Use of OSI IS-IS for Routing in TCP/IP and Dual Environ-
                 ments," RFC1195, December 1990.

[RFC1826]   R. Atkinson, "IP Authentication Header," RFC1826, August 1995.

[RFC1827]   R. Atkinson, "IP Encapsulating Security Payload (ESP)," RFC1827, August
                 1995.

[RFC1829]   P. Karn et al., "The ESP DES-CBC Transform," RFC1829, August 1995.

[RFC1930]   J. Hawkinson and T. Bates, "Guidelines for Creation, Selection, and Reg-
                 istration of an Autonomous System (AS)," RFC1930, March 1996.

[RFC2080]   G. Malkin and R. Minnear, "RIPng for IPv6," RFC2080, January 1997.

[RFC2104]   H. Krawczyk et al., "HMAC: Keyed-Hashing for Message Authentication,"
                 RFC2104, February 1997.

[RFC2328]   J. Moy, "OSPF version 2," RFC2328, April 1998.

[RFC2362]   D. Estrin et al., "Protocol Independent Multicast-Sparse Mode (PIM-SM):
                 Protocol Specification," RFC2362, June 1998.

[RFC2373]   R. Hinden and S. Deering, "IP version 6 Addressing Architecture,"
                 RFC2373, July 1998.

[RFC2401]   S. Kent and R. Atkinson, "Security Architecture for the Internet Protocol,"
                 RFC2401, November 1998.

[RFC2402]   S. Kent and R. Atkinson, "IP Authentication Header," RFC2402, November 1998.

[RFC2403]   C. Madson and R. Glenn, "The Use of HMAC-MD5-96 within ESP and AH," RFC2403, November 1998.

[RFC2404]   C. Madson and R. Glenn, "The Use of HMAC-SHA-1-96 within ESP and AH," RFC2404, November 1998.

[RFC2405]   C. Madson and N. Doraswamy, "The ESP DES-CBC Cipher Algorithm With Explicit IV," RFC2405, November 1998.

[RFC2406]   S. Kent and R. Atkinson, "IP Encapsulating Security Payload (ESP)," RFC2406, November 1998.

[RFC2407]   D. Piper, "The Internet IP Security Domain of Interpretation for ISAKMP," RFC2407, November 1998.

[RFC2409]   D. Harkins and D. Carrel, "The Internet Key Exchange (IKE)," RFC2409, November 1998.

[RFC2410]   R. Glenn and S. Kent, "The NULL Encryption Algorithm and Its Use with IPsec," RFC2410, November 1998.

[RFC2451]   R. Pereira and R. Adams, "The ESP CBC-Mode Cipher Algorithms," RFC2451, November 1998.

[RFC2453]   G. Malkin, "RIP version 2," RFC2453, November 1998.

[RFC2460]   S. Deering and R. Hinden, "Internet Protocol, version 6 (IPv6) Specification," RFC2460, December 1998.

[RFC2461]   T. Narten et al., "Neighbor Discovery for IP version 6 (IPv6)," RFC2461, December 1998.

[RFC2462]   S. Thomson and T. Narten, "IPv6 Stateless Address Autoconfiguration," RFC2462, December 1998.

[RFC2463]   A. Conta and S. Deering "Internet Control Message Protocol (ICMPv6) for the Internet Protocol version 6 (IPv6) Specification," RFC2463, December 1998.

[RFC2466]   D. Haskin and S. Onishi, "Management Information Base for IP version 6: ICMPv6 Group," RFC2466, December 1998.

[RFC2474]   K. Nichols et al., "Definition of the Differentiated Services Field (DS Field) in the IPv4 and IPv6 Headers," RFC2474, December 1998.

[RFC2526]   D. Johnson and S. Deering, "Reserved IPv6 Subnet Anycast Addresses," RFC2526, March 1999.

[RFC2535]   D. Eastlake, "Domain Name System Security Extensions," RFC2535, March 1999.

[RFC2545]   P. Marques and F. Dupont, "Use of BGP-4 Multiprotocol Extensions for IPv6 Inter-Domain Routing," RFC2545, March 1999.

[RFC2671]   P. Vixie, "Extension Mechanisms for DNS (EDNS0)," RFC2671, August 1999.

[RFC2672]   M. Crawford, "Non-Terminal DNS Name Redirection," RFC2672, August 1999.

[RFC2673]   M. Crawford, "Binary Labels in the Domain Name System," RFC2673, August 1999.

[RFC2710]   S. Deering et al., "Multicast Listener Discovery (MLD) for IPv6," RFC2710, October 1999.

[RFC2711]   C. Partridge and A. Jackson, "IPv6 Router Alert Option," RFC2711, October 1999.

[RFC2740]   R. Coltun et al., "OSPF for IPv6," RFC2740, December 1999.

[RFC2796]   T. Bates et al., "BGP Route Reflection—An Alternative to Full Mesh IBGP," RFC2796, April 2000.

[RFC2858]   T. Bates et al., "Multiprotocol Extensions for BGP-4," RFC2858, June 2000.

[RFC2874]   M. Crawford and C. Huitema, "DNS Extensions to Support IPv6 Address Aggregation and Renumbering," RFC2874, July 2000.

[RFC2918]   E. Chen, "Route Refresh Capability for BGP-4," RFC2918, September 2000.

[RFC3019]   B. Haberman and R. Worzella, "IP version 6 Management Information Base for the Multicast Listener Discovery Protocol," RFC3019, January 2001.

[RFC3041]   T. Narten and R. Draves, "Privacy Extensions for Stateless Address Auto-configuration in IPv6," RFC3041, January 2001.

[RFC3107]   Y. Rekhter and E. Rosen, "Carrying Label Information in BGP-4," RFC3107, May 2001.

[RFC3152]   R. Bush, "Delegation of IP6.ARPA," RFC3152, August 2001.

[RFC3168]   K. Ramakrishnan et al., "The Addition of Explicit Congestion Notification (ECN) to IP," RFC3168, September 2001.

[RFC3315]   R. Droms et al., "Dynamic Host Configuration Protocol for IPv6 (DHCPv6)," RFC3315, July 2003.

[RFC3363]   R. Bush et al., "Representing Internet Protocol version 6 (IPv6) Addresses in the Domain Name System (DNS)," RFC3363, August 2002.

[RFC3392]   R. Chandra and J. Scudder, "Capabilities Advertisement with BGP-4," RFC3392, November 2002.

[RFC3446]   D. Kim et al., "Anycast Rendevous Point (RP) Mechanism Using Protocol Independent Multicast (PIM) and Multicast Source Discovery Protocol (MSDP)," RFC3446, January 2003.

[RFC3484]   R. Draves, "Default Address Selection for Internet Protocol version 6 (IPv6)," RFC3484, February 2003.

[RFC3493]   R. Gilligan et al., "Basic Socket Interface Extensions for IPv6," RFC3493, February 2003.

[RFC3513]   R. Hinden and S. Deering, "Internet Protocol version 6 (IPv6) Addressing Architecture," RFC3513, April 2003.

[RFC3542]   W. Stevens et al., "Advanced Sockets Application Program Interface (API) for IPv6," RFC3542, May 2003.

[RFC3590]   B. Haberman, "Source Address Selection for the Multicast Listener Discovery (MLD) Protocol," RFC3590, September 2003.

[RFC3602]   S. Frankel et al., "The AES-CBC Cipher Algorithm and Its Use with IPsec," RFC3602, September 2003.

[RFC3686]   R. Housley, "Using Advanced Encryption Standard (AES) Counter Mode with IPsec Encapsulating Security Payload (ESP)," RFC3686, January 2004.

[RFC3775]   D. Johnson et al., "Mobility Support in IPv6," RFC3775, June 2004.

[RFC3776]   J. Arkko et al., "Using IPsec to Protect Mobile IPv6 Signaling Between Mobile Nodes and Home Agents," RFC3776, June 2004.

[RFC3633]   O. Troan and R. Droms, "IPv6 Prefix Options for Dynamic Host Configuration Protocol (DHCP) version 6," RFC3633, December 2003.

[RFC3646]   R. Droms, "DNS Configuration Options for Dynamic Host Configuration Protocol for IPv6 (DHCPv6)," RFC3646, December 2003.

[RFC3736]   R. Droms, "Stateless Dynamic Host Configuration Protocol (DHCP) Service for IPv6," RFC3736, April 2004.

[RFC3879]   C. Huitema and B. Carpenter, "Deprecating Site Local Addresses," RFC3879, September 2004.

[RFC3810]   R. Vida and L. Costa, "Multicast Listener Discovery version 2 (MLDv2) for IPv6," RFC3810, June 2004.

[RFC3956]   P. Savola and B. Haberman, "Embedding the Rendezvous Point (RP) Address in an IPv6 Multicast Address," RFC3956, November 2004.

[RFC3973]   A. Adams et al., "Protocol Independent Multicast—Dense Mode (PIM-DM): Protocol Specification (Revised)," RFC3973, January 2005.

[RFC4007]   S. Deering et al., "IPv6 Scoped Address Architecture," RFC4007, March 2005.

[RFC4074]   Y. Morishita and T. Jinmei, "Common Misbehavior Against DNS Queries for IPv6 Addresses," RFC4074, May 2005.

[RFC4075]   V. Kalusivalingam, "Simple Network Time Protocol (SNTP) Configuration Option for DHCPv6," RFC4075, May 2005.

[RFC4242]   S. Venaas et al., "Information Refresh Time Option for Dynamic Host Configuration Protocol for IPv6 (DHCPv6)," RFC4242, November 2005.

[RFC4271]   Y. Rekhter et al., "A Border Gateway Protocol 4 (BGP-4)," RFC4271, January 2006.

[RFC4291]   R. Hinden and S. Deering, "IP version 6 Addressing Architecture," RFC4291, February 2006.

[RFC4294]   J. Loughney, "IPv6 Node Requirements," RFC4294, April 2006.

[RFC4443]   A. Conta et al., "Internet Control Message Protocol (ICMPv6) for the Internet Protocol version 6 (IPv6) Specification," RFC4443, March 2006.

[RFC4584]   S. Chakrabarti and E. Nordmark, "Extension to Sockets API for Mobile IPv6," RFC4584, July 2006.

[RFC4601]   B. Fenner et al., "Protocol Independent Multicast—Sparse Mode (PIM-SM): Protocol Specification (Revised)," RFC4601, August 2006.

[RFC4607]   H. Holbrook and B. Cain, "Source-Specific Multicast for IP," RFC4607, August 2006.

[RFC4610]   D. Farinacci and Y. Cai, "Anycast-RP Using Protocol Independent Multicast (PIM)," RFC4610, August 2006.

[RFC4640]   A. Patel and G. Giaretta, "Problem Statement for Bootstrapping Mobile IPv6 (MIPv6)," RFC4640, September 2006.

[AS4BYTES]   Q. Vohra and E. Chen, "BGP Support for Four-Octet AS Number Space," Internet Draft: draft-ietf-idr-as4bytes-10.txt, July 2005.

[BGP4-MPEXT]   T. Bates et al, "Multiprotocol Extensions for BGP-4," Internet Draft: draft-ietf-idr-rfc2858bis-10.txt, March 2006.

[CN-IPSEC]   F. Dupont and J.M. Combes, "Using IPsec between Mobile and Correspondent IPv6 Nodes," draft-ietf-mip6-cn-ipsec-03.txt, August 2006.

[DES-DERIVED]   P. Metzger and W. Simpson, "The ESP DES-CBC Transform," Internet Draft: draft-ietf-ipsec-ciph-des-derived-00.txt, July 1997.

[DHCP6AUTH]   T. Jinmei, "Clarifications on DHCPv6 Authentication," Internet Draft: draft-ietf-dhc-dhcpv6-clarify-auth-01.txt, June 2006.

[EDNS1]   P. Vixie, "Extensions to DNS (EDNS1)," Internet Draft: draft-ietf-dnsext-edns1-03.txt, August 2002.

[IDR-RESTART]   S. Sangli et al., "Graceful Restart Mechanism for BGP," Internet Draft: draft-ietf-idr-restart-08.txt, September 2003.

[ISIS-IPV6]   C. Hopps, "Routing IPv6 with IS-IS," Internet Draft: draft-ietf-isis-ipv6-06.txt, October 2005.

[MIP6-NEMO-V4TRAVERSAL] H. Soliman et al., "Mobile IPv6 Support for Dual Stack Hosts and Routers (DSMIPv6)," Internet Draft: draft-ietf-mip6-nemo-v4traversal-02.txt, June 2006.

[PIMSM-BSR] N. Bhaskar et al., "Bootstrap Router (BSR) Mechanism for PIM," Internet Draft: draft-ietf-pim-sm-bsr-09.txt, June 2006.

[RA-DNSDISC] J. Jeong et al., "IPv6 Router Advertisement Option for DNS Configuration," draft-jeong-dnsop-ipv6-dns-discovery-09.txt, August 2006.

[ROUTE-FILTER] E. Chen and Y. Rekhter, "Cooperative Route Filtering Capability for BGP-4," Internet Draft: draft-ietf-idr-route-filter-02.txt, November 2000.

[SHA-256] S. Frankel and S. Kelly, "The HMAC-SHA-256-128 Algorithm and Its Use with IPsec," Internet Draft: draft-ietf-ipsec-ciph-sha-256-01.txt, June 2002.

Index

Printed and bound by CPI Group (UK) Ltd, Croydon, CR0 4YY

03/10/2024

01040320-0006